Foreign Relations of the
United States, 1964–1968

Volume XXI

Near East Region
Arabian Peninsula

Editor   Nina Davis Howland

General Editor David S. Patterson

United States Government Printing Office
Washington
2000

DEPARTMENT OF STATE PUBLICATION 10691

OFFICE OF THE HISTORIAN

BUREAU OF PUBLIC AFFAIRS

For sale by the U.S. Government Printing Office
Superintendent of Documents, Mail Stop: SSOP, Washington, DC 20402-9328

ISBN 0-16-049828-7

Preface

The *Foreign Relations of the United States* series presents the official documentary historical record of major foreign policy decisions and significant diplomatic activity of the United States Government. The series documents the facts and events that contributed to the formulation of policies and includes evidence of supporting and alternative views to the policy positions ultimately adopted.

The Historian of the Department of State is charged with the responsibility for the preparation of the *Foreign Relations* series. The staff of the Office of the Historian, Bureau of Public Affairs, plans, researches, compiles, and edits the volumes in the series. This documentary editing proceeds in full accord with the generally accepted standards of historical scholarship. Official regulations codifying specific standards for the selection and editing of documents for the series were first promulgated by Secretary of State Frank B. Kellogg on March 26, 1925. These regulations, with minor modifications, guided the series through 1991.

A new statutory charter for the preparation of the series was established by Public Law 102–138, the Foreign Relations Authorization Act, Fiscal Years 1992 and 1993, which was signed by President George Bush on October 28, 1991. Section 198 of P.L. 102–138 added a new Title IV to the Department of State's Basic Authorities Act of 1956 (22 USC 4351, *et seq.*).

The statute requires that the *Foreign Relations* series be a thorough, accurate, and reliable record of major United States foreign policy decisions and significant United States diplomatic activity. The volumes of the series should include all records needed to provide comprehensive documentation of major foreign policy decisions and actions of the United States Government. The statute also confirms the editing principles established by Secretary Kellogg: the *Foreign Relations* series is guided by the principles of historical objectivity and accuracy; records should not be altered or deletions made without indicating in the published text that a deletion has been made; the published record should omit no facts that were of major importance in reaching a decision; and nothing should be omitted for the purposes of concealing a defect in policy. The statute also requires that the *Foreign Relations* series be published not more than 30 years after the events recorded. The editor is convinced that this volume, which was compiled in 1994–1997, meets all regulatory, statutory, and scholarly standards of selection and editing.

Structure and Scope of the Foreign Relations Series

This volume is part of a subseries of volumes of the *Foreign Relations* series that documents the most important issues in the foreign policy

III

of the 5 years (1964–1968) of the administration of Lyndon B. Johnson. The subseries presents in 34 volumes a documentary record of major foreign policy decisions and actions of President Johnson's administration. This volume documents U.S. policy toward the Near East region and the Arabian Peninsula.

Principles of Document Selection for the Foreign Relations Series

In preparing each volume of the *Foreign Relations* series, the editors are guided by some general principles for the selection of documents. Each editor, in consultation with the General Editor and other senior editors, determines the particular issues and topics to be documented either in detail, in brief, or in summary.

The following general selection criteria are used in preparing volumes in the *Foreign Relations* series. Individual compiler-editors vary these criteria in accordance with the particular issues and the available documentation. The editors also apply these selection criteria in accordance with their own interpretation of the generally accepted standards of scholarship. In selecting documentation for publication, the editors gave priority to unpublished classified records, rather than previously published records (which are accounted for in appropriate bibliographical notes).

Selection Criteria (in general order of priority):

1. Major foreign affairs commitments made on behalf of the United States to other governments, including those that define or identify the principal foreign affairs interests of the United States;

2. Major foreign affairs issues and activities, including dissenting or alternative opinions to the process ultimately adopted, undertaken on behalf of the United States by government officials and representatives in all agencies in the foreign affairs community;

3. The decisions, discussions, actions, and considerations of the President, as the official constitutionally responsible for the direction of foreign policy, including important information that attended Presidential decisions;

4. The discussions and actions of the National Security Council, the Cabinet, and special Presidential policy groups, including the policy options brought before these bodies or their individual members;

5. The policy options adopted by or considered by the Secretary of State and the most important actions taken to implement Presidential decisions or policies;

6. Diplomatic negotiations and conferences, official correspondence, and other exchanges between U.S. representatives and those of other governments that demonstrate the main lines of policy implementation on major issues;

7. The main policy lines of intelligence activities if they constituted major aspects of U.S. foreign policy toward a nation or region or if they provided key information in the formulation of major U.S. policies;

8. The role of the Congress in the preparation and execution of particular foreign policies or foreign affairs actions;

9. Economic aspects of foreign policy;

10. The main policy lines of U.S. military and economic assistance as well as other types of assistance;

11. The political-military recommendations, decisions, and activities of the military establishment and major regional military commands as they bear upon the formulation or execution of major U.S. foreign policies;

12. Diplomatic appointments that reflect major policies or affect policy changes.

Sources for the Foreign Relations Series

The *Foreign Relations* statute requires that the published record in the *Foreign Relations* series include all records needed to provide comprehensive documentation on major U.S. foreign policy decisions and significant U.S. diplomatic activity. It further requires that government agencies, departments, and other entities of the U.S. Government engaged in foreign policy formulation, execution, or support cooperate with the Department of State Historian by providing full and complete access to records pertinent to foreign policy decisions and actions and by providing copies of selected records. Many of the sources consulted in the preparation of this volume have been declassified and are available for review at the National Archives and Records Administration. The declassification review and opening for public review of all Department of State records no later than 30 years after the events is mandated by the *Foreign Relations* statute. The Department of State and other record sources used in the volume are described in detail in the section on Sources below.

Focus of Research and Principles of Selection for Foreign Relations, 1964–1968, Volume XXI

The editor of the volume sought to include documentation illuminating the foreign policymaking process of the U.S. Government, with emphasis on the highest level at which policy on a particular subject was determined. The documents include memoranda and records of discussions that set forth policy issues and options and show decisions or actions taken. The emphasis is on the development of U.S. policy and on major aspects and repercussions of its execution rather than on the details of policy execution.

President Johnson made foreign policy decisions himself with the advice of top administration officials. The editor sought to document, as far as possible, the President's decision-making. Although the foreign policy record of the Johnson administration is voluminous, many internal discussions between Johnson and his advisers were not recorded. The record of Johnson's involvement as well as that of Secretary of State Rusk in the policy process often had to be pieced together from a variety of sources.

The volume focuses on the issues that primarily engaged high-level policymakers. Major topics include: 1) U.S. efforts to prevent the Soviet Union from gaining influence in the strategically located and oil-rich Near East region; 2) the attempts of U.S. policymakers to promote peace and stability in the region and to avoid being drawn into either inter-Arab or Arab-Israeli disputes; 3) U.S. efforts to preserve access to the region's oil supplies by maintaining and strengthening its position in the moderate Arab states, especially Kuwait and Saudi Arabia; 4) reiteration of the long-standing U.S. commitment to Saudi Arabia's territorial integrity in the event of unprovoked aggression, while warning that such support would be difficult if Saudi involvement in Yemen provoked military confrontation with the United Arab Republic; 5) U.S. military assistance to the Saudi armed forces combined with support for a Saudi program of political, social, and economic progress; 6) the attempts of U.S. policymakers to prevent the escalation and spread of the civil war in Yemen by encouraging a negotiated settlement; 7) the attempts of U.S. policymakers to delay British withdrawal from South Arabia and the Persian Gulf; 8) U.S. support for British efforts to negotiate an orderly and peaceful transition to independence for Aden and the British Protectorates in South Arabia; 9) U.S. efforts to maintain access to and influence in the Arabian Peninsula and Persian Gulf as British forces prepared to withdraw; 10) the 1968 decision to establish a U.S. military facility on Diego Garcia, with British support, as a means of improving the overall Western military posture in the Indian Ocean; 11) the desire of the United States to preserve Iraq's political and social stability, thereby ensuring the continued flow of oil and lessening the danger of inroads by Communists or radical Arab nationalists; and 12) U.S. efforts to rebuild relations with the Arab states after the Six-Day War.

Editorial Methodology

The documents are presented chronologically according to Washington time or, in the case of conferences, in the order of individual meetings. Memoranda of conversation are placed according to the time and date of the conversation, rather than the date the memorandum was drafted.

Editorial treatment of the documents published in the *Foreign Relations* series follows Office style guidelines, supplemented by guidance from the General Editor and the chief technical editor. The source text is reproduced as exactly as possible, including marginalia or other notations, which are described in the footnotes. Texts are transcribed and printed according to accepted conventions for the publication of historical documents in the limitations of modern typography. A heading has been supplied by the editors for each document included in the volume. Spelling, capitalization, and punctuation are retained as found in the source text, except that obvious typographical errors are silently corrected. Other mistakes and omissions in the source text are corrected by bracketed insertions: a correction is set in italic type; an addition in roman type. Words or phrases underlined in the source text are printed in italics. Abbreviations and contractions are preserved as found in the source text, and a list of abbreviations is included in the front matter of each volume.

Bracketed insertions are also used to indicate omitted text that deals with an unrelated subject (in roman type) or that remains classified after declassification review (in italic type). The amount of material not declassified has been noted by indicating the number of lines or pages of source text that were omitted. Entire documents withheld for declassification purposes have been accounted for and are listed by headings, source notes, and number of pages not declassified in their chronological place. The amount of material omitted from selected documents because it was unrelated to the subject of the volume, however, has not been delineated. All brackets that appear in the source text are so identified by footnotes.

The first footnote to each document indicates the document's source, original classification, distribution, and drafting information. This note also provides the background of important documents and policies and indicates whether the President or his major policy advisers read the document. Every effort has been made to determine if a document has been previously published, and, if so, this information has been included in the source footnote.

Editorial notes and additional annotation summarize pertinent material not printed in the volume, indicate the location of additional documentary sources, provide references to important related documents printed in other volumes, describe key events, and provide summaries of and citations to public statements that supplement and elucidate the printed documents. Information derived from memoirs and other first-hand accounts has been used when appropriate to supplement or explicate the official record.

Advisory Committee on Historical Diplomatic Documentation

The Advisory Committee on Historical Diplomatic Documentation, established under the *Foreign Relations* statute, reviews records, advises, and makes recommendations concerning the *Foreign Relations* series. The Advisory Committee monitors the overall compilation and editorial process of the series and advises on all aspects of the preparation and declassification of the series. Although the Advisory Committee does not attempt to review the contents of individual volumes in the series, it does monitor the overall process and makes recommendations on particular problems that come to its attention.

The Advisory Committee has not reviewed this volume.

Declassification Review

The Information Response Branch of the Office of IRM Programs and Services, Bureau of Administration, Department of State, conducted the declassification review of the documents published in this volume. The review was conducted in accordance with the standards set forth in Executive Order 12958 on Classified National Security Information and applicable laws.

Under Executive Order 12958, specific information may be exempt from automatic declassification after 25 years if its release could be expected to:

1) reveal the identity of a confidential human source, or reveal information about the application of an intelligence source or method, or reveal the identity of a human intelligence source when the unauthorized disclosure of that source would clearly and demonstrably damage the national security interests of the United States;

2) reveal information that would assist in the development or use of weapons of mass destruction;

3) reveal information that would impair U.S. cryptologic systems or activities;

4) reveal information that would impair the application of state of the art technology within the U.S. weapon system;

5) reveal actual U.S. military war plans that remain in effect;

6) reveal information that would seriously and demonstrably impair relations between the United States and a foreign government, or seriously and demonstrably undermine ongoing diplomatic activities of the United States;

7) reveal information that would clearly and demonstrably impair the current ability of U.S. Government officials to protect the President, Vice President, and other officials for whom protection services, in the interest of national security, are authorized;

8) reveal information that would seriously and demonstrably impair current national security emergency preparedness plans; or

9) violate a statute, treaty, or international agreement.

The principle guiding declassification review is to release all information, subject only to the current requirements of national security as embodied in law and regulation. Declassification decisions entailed concurrence of the appropriate geographic and functional bureaus in the Department of State, other concerned agencies of the U.S. Government, and the appropriate foreign governments regarding specific documents of those governments.

The final declassification review of this volume, which began in 1996 and was completed in 1999, resulted in the decision to withhold about .3 percent of the documentation proposed for publication; 1 document was withheld in full.

The Office of the Historian is confident, on the basis of the research conducted in preparing this volume and as a result of the declassification review process described above, that the documentation and editorial notes presented here provide an accurate account of U.S. policy toward the Near East region and Arabian peninsula during the 1964–1968 period.

Acknowledgments

The editor wishes to acknowledge the assistance of officials at the Lyndon B. Johnson Library of the National Archives and Records Administration, especially Regina Greenwell and Charlaine Burgess, who provided key research assistance. The editor also wishes to acknowledge the assistance of historians at the Central Intelligence Agency, particularly Scott Koch.

Nina Davis Howland did the research, compiled, selected, and annotated this volume, under the general supervision of Harriet Dashiell Schwar and General Editor of the *Foreign Relations* series David S. Patterson. Gabrielle Mallon prepared the lists of names, sources, and abbreviations. Vicki E. Futscher and Rita M. Baker did the copy and technical editing, and Susan C. Weetman coordinated the final declassification review. Breffni Whelan prepared the index.

William Slany
The Historian
Bureau of Public Affairs

August 2000

Johnson Administration Volumes

Following is a list of the volumes in the *Foreign Relations* series for the administration of President Lyndon B. Johnson. The titles of individual volumes may change. The year of publication is in parentheses after the title.

Contents

Sources

The editors of the *Foreign Relations* series have complete access to all the retired records and papers of the Department of State: the central files of the Department; the special decentralized files ("lot files") of the Department at the bureau, office, and division levels; the files of the Department's Executive Secretariat, which contain the record of international conferences and high-level official visits, correspondence with foreign leaders by the President and Secretary of State, and memoranda of conversations between the President and Secretary of State and foreign officials; and the files of overseas diplomatic posts. All the Department's indexed central files for these years have been permanently transferred to the National Archives and Records Administration (Archives II) at College Park, Maryland. Many of the Department's decentralized office (or lot) files covering this period, which the National Archives deems worthy of permanent retention, have been transferred or are in the process of being transferred from the Department's custody to Archives II.

The editors of the *Foreign Relations* series also have full access to the papers of President Johnson and other White House foreign policy records. Presidential papers maintained and preserved at the Presidential libraries include some of the most significant foreign affairs-related documentation from the Department of State and other Federal agencies including the National Security Council, the Central Intelligence Agency, the Department of Defense, and the Joint Chiefs of Staff.

Department of State historians also have access to records of the Department of Defense, particularly the records of the Joint Chiefs of Staff and the Secretaries of Defense and their major assistants.

In preparing this volume, the editor made extensive use of Presidential papers and other White House records at the Lyndon B. Johnson Library, which proved the richest source of documentation on President Johnson's role in the Near East region and the Arabian Peninsula. Within the National Security File, the Country Files, the Special Head of State Correspondence File, the Meetings with the President file, the Memos to the President file, and the files of Harold Saunders, McGeorge Bundy, and Robert Komer were particularly valuable. The Papers of George Ball within the White House Central File were also useful.

Thanks to the leadership of the Johnson Library, the Department of State historians had full access to the audiotapes of President Johnson's telephone conversations. These audiotapes include substantial numbers of telephone conversations between President Johnson and Secretary of State Rusk, Secretary of Defense McNamara, the President's Special Assistant for National Security Affairs McGeorge Bundy, and key members of Congress. The editor of this volume selected for publication one audiotape of a President Johnson telephone conversation with Secretary Rusk dealing with Yemen and prepared a transcript of the conversation specifically for this volume. Although the transcripts give the substance of the conversations, readers are urged to consult the recordings for a full appreciation of those dimensions that cannot be captured fully in a transcription, such as the speakers' inflections and emphases that may convey nuances of meaning.

Second in importance to the records at the Johnson Library were the records of the Department of State. The central files of the Department of State provide rich detail on U.S. policy toward the Near East region and the Arabian Peninsula. They are augmented in this regard by the lot files of the Department and by the files of the Secretary of Defense and the Assistant Secretary of Defense for International Security Affairs. The Papers of General Maxwell D. Taylor at the National Defense University, Washington, D.C., were also useful.

The Central Intelligence Agency provides the Department of State historians access to intelligence documents from records in its custody and at the Presidential libraries. This access is arranged and facilitated by the CIA's History Staff, part of the Center for the Study of Intelligence, pursuant to a May 1992 memorandum of understanding.

The editor included a selection of intelligence estimates and analyses seen by high-level policymakers, especially those that were made available to President Johnson. Among the intelligence records reviewed for the volume were those in country and intelligence files at the Johnson Library, the files of the Directors of Central Intelligence, especially John McCone, CIA intelligence reports and summaries, retired files of the Department of State's Bureau of Intelligence and Research containing National Intelligence Estimates, and the INR Historical Files.

Almost all of this documentation has been made available for use in the *Foreign Relations* series thanks to the consent of the agencies mentioned, the assistance of their staffs, and especially the cooperation and support of the National Archives and Records Administration.

The following list identifies the particular files and collections used in the preparation of this volume. Although much of the research in Department of State records for this volume occurred while they were still in the custody of the Department, the declassification and transfer to the National Archives of Department of State records, including the central files through mid-1973 and increasing numbers of lot files, as well as the records of other agencies is in process. Many of those records are already available for public review at the National Archives and Records Administration (Archives II) at College Park, Maryland. The declassification review of these records is going forward in accordance with the provisions of Executive Order 12958, under which all records over 25 years old, except file series exemptions requested by agencies and approved by the President, should be reviewed for declassification by 2002.

Unpublished Sources

Department of State

Central Files. See National Archives and Records Administration below.

Lot Files. These files may be transferred to Archives II at College Park, Maryland, Record Group 59. See also National Archives and Records Administration below.

INR/IL Historical Files

> Files of the Office of Intelligence Coordination, containing records from the 1940s through the 1970s, as maintained by the Office of Intelligence Liaison, Bureau of Intelligence and Research, Department of State.

NEA Files: Lot 71 D 287

> Miscellaneous files relating to the Middle East crisis of 1967.

NEA/ARP Files: Lot 67 D 619

> Arabian Peninsula subject files for 1965, as maintained by the Bureau of Near Eastern and South Asian Affairs, Department of State.

NEA/ARP Files: Lot 69 D 350

> Arabian Peninsula subject files for 1967, as maintained by the Bureau of Near Eastern and South Asian Affairs, Department of State.

NEA/ARP Files: Lot 69 D 523

> Arabian Peninsula subject files for 1968, as maintained by the Bureau of Near Eastern and South Asian Affairs, Department of State.

NEA/ARP Files: Lot 69 D 547

> Arabian Peninsula subject files for 1956, 1961–1962, 1964–1966, and 1968, as maintained by the Bureau of Near Eastern and South Asian Affairs, Department of State.

NEA/IRA Files: Lot 70 D 503

> NEA/IRG files 67–1 through 68–42, as maintained by the Bureau of Near Eastern and South Asian Affairs, Department of State.

NEA/RA Files: Lot 71 D 218

> NEA Regional Affairs subject files for 1962–1968, as maintained by the Bureau of Near Eastern and South Asian Affairs, Department of State.

Central Intelligence Agency

> Job 79–R01012A, ODDI Registry of NIE and SNIE Files
> Job 80–00105A, DDO/NE (Critchfield) Files
> Job 80–B01285A, DCI (McCone) Files, DCI Memos for the Record
> Job 80–R01580R, DCI Executive Registry Files

National Archives and Records Administration, College Park, Maryland

Record Group 59, Records of the Department of State

Central Files. During the 1964–1968 period, the Department's central files were filed according to a subject-numeric system. The records were divided into broad categories: Administration, Consular, Culture and Information, Economic, Political and Defense, Science, and Social. Within each of these divisions were subcategories. For example, Political and Defense contained four subtopics: POL (politics), DEF (defense), CSM (Communism), and INT (intelligence). The subcategories were divided into numerical subdivisions or, in some cases, country files with numerical subdivisions. The POL series began with files with numerical subdivisions on international issues, such as issues relating to international rivers, and continued with country files. The list below is arranged in the order of the Department's filing system.

ORG 7 NEA: organization and administration, Bureau of Near Eastern and South Asian
    Affairs, Department of State
AID (US) YEMEN: general policy, U.S. aid to Yemen
AID (US) 8 YEMEN: U.S. grants and technical assistance to Yemen
PET 10–3 SAUD: concessions, leases of resources and oil fields, Saudi Arabia
DEF 4: collective defense pacts and alliances
DEF 1 IND: defense policy, Indian Ocean
DEF 15 IND–US: bases and installations, Indian Ocean–U.S.
DEF 19 IRAQ: military assistance, Iraq
DEF 1 IRAQ–US: defense policy, Iraq–U.S.
DEF 1 KUW: defense policy, Kuwait
DEF 12–5 KUW: procurement and sale of armaments, Kuwait
DEF 12–5 KUW–US: procurement and sale of armaments, Kuwait–U.S.
DEF 1–4 SAUD: air defense, Saudi Arabia
DEF 6–2 SAUD: naval forces, Saudi Arabia
DEF 12–5 SAUD: procurement and sale of armaments, Saudi Arabia
DEF 12–5 SAUD–UK: procurement and sale of armaments, Saudi Arabia–U.K.
DEF 7 SAUD–US: visits and missions, Saudi Arabia–U.S.
DEF 1 UK: defense policy, United Kingdom
DEF 19–8 US–SAUD: defense equipment and supplies, U.S. –Saudi Arabia
POL 7 ADEN: visits and meetings with Aden officials
POL 13 ADEN: non-party blocs, Aden
POL 19 ADEN: government of dependencies, Aden
POL 23–9 ADEN: rebellions and coups, Aden
POL ADEN–UAR: political affairs and relations, Aden–United Arab Republic
POL 19 ADEN/UN: government of dependencies, Aden–UN
POL ADEN–US: political affairs and relations, Aden–U.S.
POL 1 ADEN–US: general policy and background, Aden–U.S.
POL 31–1 ADEN–YEMEN: air disputes and violations, Aden–Yemen
POL 32–1 ADEN–YEMEN: Aden–Yemen boundary disputes
POL 27 ARAB–ISR: military operations, Arabs–Israel
POL BAHRAIN IS: political affairs and relations, Bahrain
POL 19 BAHRAIN IS: government of dependencies, Bahrain
POL BAHRAIN IS–US: political affairs and relations, Bahrain–U.S.
POL 7 IRAN: visits and meetings with Iranian leaders
POL IRAN–IRAQ: political affairs and relations, Iran–Iraq
POL 32–1 IRAN–IRAQ: Iran–Iraq boundary disputes
POL IRAQ: political affairs and relations, Iraq
POL 7 IRAQ: visits and meetings with Iraqi leaders

POL 13–3 IRAQ: ethnic and national minorities, Iraq
POL 15–1 IRAQ: head of state, executive branch, Iraq
POL 23–9 IRAQ: rebellions and coups, Iraq
POL IRAQ–KUW: political affairs and relations, Iraq–Kuwait
POL 32–1 IRAQ–KUW: Iraqi-Kuwaiti boundary disputes
POL IRAQ–UAR: political affairs and relations, Iraq–United Arab Republic
POL IRAQ–US: political affairs and relations, Iraq–U.S.
POL 1 IRAQ–US: general policy, Iraq–U.S.
POL 17 IRAQ–US: diplomatic and consular representation, Iraq–U.S.
POL 3 ISLAMIC: Islamic organizations and alignments
POL 6 KUW: people, biographic data, Kuwait
POL 7 KUW: visits and meetings with Kuwaiti leaders
POL 23 KUW: internal security and counter-insurgency, Kuwait
POL 1 KUW–US: general policy, Kuwait–U.S.
POL MUSCAT & OMAN: political affairs and relations, Muscat and Oman
POL 19 MUSCAT & OMAN: government of dependencies, Muscat and Oman
POL 33 PERSIAN GULF: waters and boundaries, Persian Gulf
POL SAUD: political affairs and relations, Saudi Arabia
POL 7 SAUD: visits and meetings with Saudi Arabian leaders
POL 15–1 SAUD: Saudi Arabian head of state
POL SAUD–UAR: political affairs and relations, Saudi Arabia–United Arab Republic
POL 1 SAUD–UAR: general policy, Saudi Arabia–United Arab Republic
POL 17 SAUD–UAR: diplomatic and consular representation, Saudi Arabia–U.A.R.
POL 27 SAUD–UAR: military operations, Saudi Arabia–U.A.R.
POL 31–1 SAUD–UAR: air disputes and violations, Saudi Arabia–U.A.R.
POL SAUD–US: political affairs and relations, Saudi Arabia–U.S.
POL 1 SAUD–US: general policy, Saudi Arabia–U.S.
POL 32–1 SAUD–YEMEN: territory and boundary disputes, Saudi Arabia–Yemen
POL 15 S YEMEN: South Yemen Government
POL 16 S YEMEN: independence and recognition, South Yemen
POL 23–9 S YEMEN: rebellions and coups, South Yemen
POL S YEMEN–US: political affairs and relations, South Yemen–U.S.
POL 3 TRUCIAL ST: organizations and alignments, Trucial States
POL 19 TRUCIAL ST: government of dependencies, Trucial States
POL 7 UAR: visits and meetings with United Arab Republic leaders
POL 1 UAR–UK: general policy, United Arab Republic–United Kingdom
POL 27 UAR–YEMEN: military operations, United Arab Republic–Yemen
POL UK–YEMEN: political affairs and relations, United Kingdom–Yemen
POL 31–1 UK–YEMEN: air disputes and violations, United Kingdom–Yemen
POL 31–1 UK–YEMEN/UN: air disputes and violations, U.K.–Yemen and the UN
POL 15–1 US/JOHNSON: head of state, executive branch, President Lyndon B. Johnson
POL US–YEMEN: political affairs and relations, U.S. –Yemen
POL 17 US–YEMEN: diplomatic and consular representation, U.S. –Yemen
POL 15–1 YEMEN: Yemeni head of state
POL 16 YEMEN: independence and recognition, Yemen
POL 23–9 YEMEN: rebellions and coups, Yemen
POL 27 YEMEN: military operations, Yemen
POL 27–10 YEMEN: chemical and germ warfare, Yemen
POL 27–14 YEMEN: truce, cease-fire, armistice, Yemen
POL 27–14 YEMEN/UN: truce, cease-fire, armistice, Yemen–U.N.
POL 17 YEMEN–US: diplomatic and consular representation, Yemen–U.S.

Lot Files

NEA/ARP Files: Lot 69 D 257

Arabian Peninsula subject files for 1954–1966, as maintained by the Bureau of Near Eastern and South Asian Affairs, Department of State.

Rusk Files: Lot 72 D 192

Files of Secretary of State Dean Rusk, 1961–1969, including texts of speeches and public statements, miscellaneous correspondence files, White House correspondence, chronological files, and memoranda of telephone conversations.

S/S Files: Lot 68 D 451

Minutes of meetings and memoranda of the Special Group, Counterinsurgency, for July–December 1964, as maintained by the Executive Secretariat of the Department of State.

S/S Conference Files: Lot 69 D 182

Collection of documentation on visits to the United States by ranking foreign officials and on major conferences attended by the Secretary of State January–November 1968, as maintained by the Executive Secretariat of the Department of State.

Washington National Records Center, Suitland, Maryland

Record Group 330, Records of the Office of the Secretary of Defense

OASD/ISA Files: FRC 68 A 306

Secret and lower-classified general files of the Assistant Secretary of Defense for International Security Affairs, 1964.

OASD/ISA Files: FRC 70 A 3717

Secret files of the Assistant Secretary of Defense for International Security Affairs, 1965.

OASD/ISA Files: FRC 70 A 5127

Top Secret files of the Assistant Secretary of Defense for International Security Affairs, 1965.

OASD/ISA Files: FRC 70 A 6648

Secret files of the Assistant Secretary of Defense for International Security Affairs, 1966.

OASD/ISA Files: FRC 72 A 1498

Secret files of the Assistant Secretary of Defense for International Security Affairs, 1968.

OSD Files: FRC 69 A 7425

Top Secret files of the Secretary of Defense, Deputy Secretary of Defense, and Special Assistants, 1964.

OSD Files: FRC 70 A 1265

Top Secret files of the Secretary of Defense, Deputy Secretary of Defense, and Special Assistants, 1965.

OSD Files: FRC 70 A 1266

Secret files of the Secretary of Defense, Deputy Secretary of Defense and Special Assistants, 1965.

OSD Files: FRC 72 A 2468

Files of the Secretary of Defense, Deputy Secretary of Defense, and Special Assistants, 1967.

OSD Files: FRC 73 A 1250

Files of the Secretary of Defense, Deputy Secretary of Defense, and Special Assistants, 1968.

National Defense University, Washington, D.C.

Taylor Papers

Papers of Maxwell D. Taylor, Military Adviser to the President, 1961–1962, and Chairman of the Joint Chiefs of Staff, 1962–1964.

Lyndon B. Johnson Library, Austin, Texas

Papers of President Lyndon B. Johnson

National Security File

Country File: India, Iraq, Kuwait, Middle East, Saudi Arabia, United Arab Republic, United Kingdom, Yemen
Special Head of State Correspondence File
Meetings with the President
Memos to the President, McGeorge Bundy
National Intelligence Estimates
National Security Action Memorandums
Files of Robert W. Komer
Name File: Komer Memos, Saunders Memos
President's Appointment File
Files of Harold Saunders

Special Files
President's Daily Diary
Recordings and Transcripts of Telephone Conversations and Meetings

White House Central Files
Subject File

Other Personal Papers
Papers of George Ball

Abbreviations

ACSI, Assistant Chief of Staff, Intelligence (Department of Defense)
AID, Agency for International Development
Amb, Ambassador
AMINOIL, American Independent Oil Company
ANM, Arab Nationalist Movement
ARAMCO, Arabian-American Oil Company
ATUC, Aden Trade Union Congress

BAC, British Aircraft Corporation
BAPCO, Bahrain Petroleum Company
BBC, British Broadcasting Corporation
BIOT, British Indian Ocean Territory

CARE, Cooperatives for American Relief Everywhere, Inc.
CAS, controlled American source
CCPC, Civil Communications Planning Committee (NATO)
CENTO, Central Treaty Organization
CHICOM(S), Chinese Communist(s)
CHUSMTM, Chief, United States Military Training Mission in Saudi Arabia
CIA, Central Intelligence Agency
CINCLANT, Commander in Chief, Armed Forces, Atlantic
CINCMEAFSA, Commander in Chief, Middle East/South Asia and Africa South of the Sahara
CINCPAC, Commander in Chief, Pacific
CINCSTRIKE, Commander in Chief, Strike Command
CINCUSNAVEUR, Commancer in Chief, U.S. Naval Forces, Europe
CIRTEL, circular telegram
CLA, Cooperative Logistics Agreement
CNO, Chief of Naval Operations
COMIDEASTFOR, Commander, Middle East Forces
CONUS, continental United States
CP, Crown Prince
CSAF, Chief of Staff, Air Force

DAF, Dhahran Air Field
DATT, Defense Attaché
DCI, Director of Central Intelligence
DD/I, Deputy Director of Intelligence; Directorate of Intelligence (CIA)
DDP, Directorate for Plans (CIA)
Dept, Department of State
Deptel, outgoing Department of State telegram
DeptOff, Department of State officer
DIA, Defense Intelligence Agency
DMZ, demilitarized zone
DOD, Department of Defense
DOD/ISA, Department of Defense, International Security Affairs

EIS, Egyptian Intelligence Service
EmbOff, Embassy Officer

Embtel, Embassy telegram
EP, estimated period
Exdis, Exclusive Distribution (extremely Limited Distribution)
EXIM, Export-Import Bank

FAA, Federation of Arab Amirates
FLOSY, Front for the Liberation of Occupied South Yemen
FonMin, Foreign Minister
FonOff, Foreign Office
FRA, Federal Regular Army (South Arabia)
FSA, Federation of South Arabia
FY, fiscal year
FYI, for your information

GOI, Government of Iran; Government of Iraq; Government of Italy
GOK, Government of Kuwait
G/PM, Deputy Assistant Secretary of State for Politico-Military Affairs
GUAR, Government of the United Arab Republic

HICOM, High Commissioner
HMG, Her Majesty's Government

IBRD, International Bank for Reconstruction and Development (World Bank)
ICJ, International Court of Justice
ICRC, International Committee of the Red Cross
IGA, Investment Guarantee Agreement
ILS, instrument landing system
IMF, International Monetary Fund
INR, Bureau of Intelligence and Research, Department of State
IOTF, Indian Ocean Task Force
IPC, Iraq Petroleum Company
IRG, Interdepartmental Regional Group

JCS, Joint Chiefs of Staff
JCSM, Joint Chiefs of Staff Memorandum

KDP, Kurdistan Democratic Party
K/FAED, Kuwait Fund for Arab Economic Development

LBJ, Lyndon B. Johnson
Limdis, Limited Distribution

MAP, Military Assistance Program
MATS, Military Air Transport Service
MIDEASTFOR, Middle East Forces
MIG, Soviet fighter aircraft named for designers Mikoyan and Gurevich
MinFin, Minister of Finance
MinPet, Minister of Petroleum
MisOff, Mission Officer
MOD, Minister of Defense
MODA, Minister of Defense and Aviation
MTT, Mobile Training Team

NAC, North Atlantic Council
NATO, North Atlantic Treaty Organization
NEA/ARN, Office of Lebanon, Jordan, Syrian Arab Republic, and Iraq Affairs, Bureau of Near Eastern and South Asian Affairs, Department of State
NEA/ARP, Office of Saudi Arabia, Kuwait, Yemen, and Aden Affairs, Bureau of Near Eastern and South Asian Affairs, Department of State
NEA/NE, Office of Near Eastern Affairs, Bureau of Near Eastern and South Asian Affairs, Department of State
NEA/NR, Office of Near Eastern and South Asian Regional Affairs, Bureau of Near Eastern and South Asian Affairs, Department of State
NESA, Near East and South Asia
NIE, National Intelligence Estimate
NIOC, National Iranian Oil Company
NLF, National Liberation Front
Noforn, no foreign dissemination
NOTAL, not received by all addressees
NSC, National Security Council
NYT, *New York Times*

OAU, Organization of African Unity
OCI, Office of Current Intelligence (CIA)
ODM, Ministry of Overseas Development (South Arabia)
ONE, Office of National Estimates (CIA)
OSD, Office of the Secretary of Defense

PM, Prime Minister
POL, petroleum, oil, lubricants
POLAD, Political Adviser
PRC, People's Republic of China
PRSY, People's Republic of South Yemen
PSP, People's Socialist Party (Aden)

RAF, Royal Air Force (UK)
RAMP, weapons repair and maintenance program
RCD, Regional Cooperation for Development
reftel, reference telegram
reps, representatives
res, resolution
RSAF, Royal Saudi Air Force

SAA, South Arabian Army
SAF, South Arabian Federation
SAFG, South Arabian Federation Government
SAG, Saudi Arabian Government
SAL, South Arabian League
SAM, surface to air missile
SAMP, Saudi Arabian Mobility Program
SC, Security Council (United Nations)
septel, separate telegram
SYG, Secretary-General (United Nations)

TACAN, Tactical Air Navigation
TIAS, Treaties and International Acts Series
TOS, Trucial Oman Scouts
TR, terms of reference

UAC, United Arab Command
UAR, United Arab Republic
UARG, United Arab Republic Government
UDI, unilateral declaration of independence
UK, United Kingdom
UKG, United Kingdom Government
UKUN, United Kingdom Mission at the United Nations
UNEF, United Nations Emergency Forces
UNESCO, United Nations Educational, Scientific and Cultural Organization
UNGA, United Nations General Assembly
UNRWA, United Nations Relief and Works Agency for Palestine Refugees in the Near East
UNSYG, United Nations Secretary-General
UNYOM, United Nations Yemen Observation Mission
UPI, United Press International
USAF, United States Air Force
USG, United States Government
USMTM, United States Military Training Mission
USSR, Union of Soviet Socialist Republics
UST, *United States Treaties and Other International Agreements*
USUN, United States Mission at the United Nations

YAR, Yemen Arab Republic
YARG, Yemen Arab Republic Government
YRF, Yemen Revolutionary Front

Persons

Adams, General Paul D., USA, Commander in Chief, Strike Command (CINCSTRIKE) until November 1966; concurrently Commander in Chief, Middle East/South Asia and Africa South of the Sahara (CINCMEAFSA)

Aini, Muhsin al-, Foreign Minister of Yemen April–July 1965; Ambassador to the United States August 1965–October 1966; Prime Minister, November–December 1967

Amer, Field Marshal Abdel Hakim, First Vice President of the United Arab Republic and Deputy Supreme Commander of the Armed Forces from 1964 until June 1967

Amri, General Hassan al-, Prime Minister of Yemen February–April 1964, January–April 1965, July 1965–September 1966, and from December 1967; also Minister of Defense from December 1967

Ansary, Hushang, Iranian Ambassador to the United States from 1967

Aram, Abbas, Foreign Minister of Iran, January 1965–February 1967

Aref, Lieutenant General Abdul Rahman Muhammad, President of Iraq April 1966–July 1968

Aref, Field Marshal Abdul Salam Muhammad, President of Iraq until April 1966

Atherton, Alfred L., Deputy Director, Office of Near East Affairs, Bureau of Near Eastern and South Asian Affairs, Department of State, November 1965–June 1966; Country Director for Lebanon, Jordan, Syrian Arab Republic, and Iraq July–December 1966; thereafter, Country Director for Israel and Arab-Israel Affairs

Badeau, John S., Ambassador to the United Arab Republic until June 1964

Bakr, General Ahmed Hassan al-, President of Iraq from July 1968

Ball, George W., Under Secretary of State until September 1966; Representative to the United Nations, June 1968–September 1968

Barzani, Mustafa, leader of Iraqi Kurds, and President of the Command Council of the Kurdish Revolution in Iraq

Battle, Lucius D., Ambassador to the United Arab Republic September 1964–March 1967; Assistant Secretary of State for Near Eastern and South Asian Affairs April 1967–September 1968

Bazzaz, Abdul Rahman al-, Prime Minister of Iraq and Minister of Foreign Affairs September 1965–August 1966

Bergus, Donald C., Country Director for United Arab Republic Affairs, Bureau of Near Eastern and South Asian Affairs, Department of State, July 1966–July 1977; thereafter, Principal Officer of the U.S. Interests Section in the United Arab Republic

Bohlen, Charles E., Ambassador to France until February 1968; thereafter, Deputy Under Secretary of State for Political Affairs

Brewer, William D., member of the Policy Planning Council, Department of State, September 1965–November 1966; thereafter, Country Director for Saudi Arabia, Kuwait, Aden, and Yemen, Bureau of Near Eastern and South Asian Affairs, Department of State

Brown, George, British Secretary of State for Foreign Affairs August 1966–March 1968

Buffum, William B., Director, Office of United Nations Political and Security Affairs, Bureau of International Organization Affairs, Department of State, until August 1965; Deputy Assistant Secretary of State for International Organization Affairs September 1965–December 1966; thereafter, Deputy Representative to the United Nations

Bundy, McGeorge, Special Assistant to the President for National Security Affairs until February 1966

Butler, Richard Austen, British Secretary of State for Foreign Affairs until October 1964

Campbell, Stephen J., Officer-in-Charge, UN Political Affairs in Middle East, Bureau of International Organization Affairs, Department of State, until November 1966; Deputy Director, Office of UN Political Affairs, November 1966–August 1967; thereafter, Consul General in Jerusalem

Carter, Lieutenant General Marshall S., USA, Deputy Director of Central Intelligence until April 1965; thereafter Director, National Security Agency

Cleveland, J. Harlan, Assistant Secretary of State for International Organization Affairs until September 1965

Cottam, Howard R., Ambassador to Kuwait

Davies, Rodger P., Director, Office of Near Eastern Affairs, Bureau of Near Eastern and South Asian Affairs, Department of State, until October, 1965; thereafter, Deputy Assistant Secretary of State for Near Eastern and South Asian Affairs

Dean, Sir Patrick, British Permanent Representative to the United Nations until March 1965; thereafter, British Ambassador to the United States

Dhalai, Sayf Ahmad, Foreign Minister of Southern Yemen

Dinsmore, Lee F., Officer-in-Charge of Iraq–Jordan Affairs, Office of Near East Affairs, Bureau of Near Eastern and South Asian Affairs, Department of State, May 1965–January 1966; political officer, then Chargé d'Affaires in Sanaa January 1966–July 1967; Office of Saudi Arabia, Kuwait Yemen, Aden Affairs, Department of State, August 1967–July 1968; Principal Officer in Dhahran from September 1968

Eilts, Hermann F., Ambassador to Saudi Arabia from January 1966

Eliot, Theodore L., Jr., Country Director for Iran, Bureau of Near Eastern and South Asian Affairs, Department of State, from July 1966

Fahd bin Abdul Aziz (Prince), Second Deputy Prime Minister of Saudi Arabia and Minister of the Interior

Faisal ibn Abdul-Aziz Al Saud, Crown Prince of Saudi Arabia until November 1964; thereafter, King

Farid Al Awlaqi, Mohammed, Foreign Minister of Aden until November 1967

Fawzi, Mahmoud, United Arab Republic Foreign Minister until March 1964; Deputy Prime Minister for Foreign Affairs March 1964–March 1968

Foster, John W., member of the National Security Council staff

Ghoussein, Talat al-, Kuwaiti Ambassador to the United States

Goldberg, Arthur J., Representative to the United Nations July 1965–June 1968

Grant, James P., Deputy Assistant Secretary of State for Near Eastern and South Asian Affairs until September 1964

Hamid, Subhi Abd al-, Iraqi Foreign Minister until November 1964; thereafter, Minister of the Interior

Handley, William J., Deputy Assistant Secretary of State for Near Eastern and South Asian Affairs from September 1964

Hani, Nasir, Iraqi Ambassador to the United States April 1964–June 1967; Foreign Minister from July 1968

Hare, Raymond A., Ambassador to Turkey until August 1965; Assistant Secretary of State for Near Eastern and South Asian Affairs September 1965–November 1966; thereafter, President of the Middle East Institute

Harlech, Lord (Sir David Ormsby Gore), British Ambassador to the United States until March 1965

Harriman, W. Averell, Under Secretary of State for Political Affairs until March 1965; thereafter, Ambassador at Large

Hart, Parker T., Ambassador to Saudi Arabia until May 1965; Ambassador to Turkey October 1965–October 1968; thereafter, Assistant Secretary of State for Near Eastern and South Asian Affairs

Helms, Richard M., Deputy Director of Central Intelligence April 1965–June 1966; thereafter, Director of Central Intelligence

Houghton, Robert B., Country Director for Lebanon, Jordan, Syrian Arab Republic and Iraq, Bureau of Near Eastern and South Asian Affairs, Department of State, January 1967–August 1968

Hughes, Thomas L., Director, Bureau of Intelligence and Research, Department of State

Hussein I, ibn Talal, King of Jordan

Ignatius, Paul R., Secretary of the Navy from September 1967

Iryani, Qadi Abd al-Rahman al-, Member of the Presidency Council of Yemen from April 1965; President of the Presidency Council from November 1967

Jarring, Gunnar, Swedish Ambassador to the Soviet Union, detailed to the United Nations to serve as Special Representative, United Nations Middle East Mission

Jernegan, John D., Deputy Assistant Secretary of State for Near Eastern and South Asian Affairs until July 1965

Johnson, Lyndon B., President of the United States

Johnson, U. Alexis, Deputy Under Secretary of State for Political Affairs until July 1964; Deputy Ambassador to Vietnam July 1964–September 1965; Deputy Under Secretary of State for Political Affairs November 1965–October 1966

Jones, Curtis F., Officer-in-Charge of United Arab Republic Affairs, Bureau of Near Eastern and South Asian Affairs, Department of State, until June 1965; Principal Officer at Aden July 1965–April 1967

Kamel, Mostafa, United Arab Republic Ambassador to the United States until June 1967

Katzenbach, Nicholas deB., Deputy Attorney General until February 1965, Attorney General February 1965–October 1966; thereafter, Under Secretary of State

Khalid ibn Abdul-Aziz (Prince), Saudi Arabian Deputy Prime Minister

Khouli, Hassan Sabri al-, top adviser to President Nasser

Kitchen Jeffrey C., Deputy Assistant Secretary of State for Politico-Military Affairs until February 1967

Kohler, Foy D., Deputy Under Secretary of State for Political Affairs November 1966–December 1967

Komer, Robert W., member of the National Security Council Staff until September 1965; Deputy Special Assistant to the President for National Security Affairs October 1965–March 1966; Special Assistant to the President March 1966–May 1967

Lang, William E., Deputy Assistant Secretary of Defense for International Security Affairs

Lee, Guy A., Director, Office of Near East and South Asia Regional Affairs, Bureau of Near Eastern and South Asian Affairs, Department of State, until September 1966

McNamara, Robert S., Secretary of Defense until February 29, 1968

McNaughton, John T., General Counsel, Department of Defense, until July 1964; Assistant Secretary of Defense for International Security Affairs July 1964–July 1967

Makkawi, Abdel Kawi Hassan, Prime Minister of Aden until September 1965; General Secretary of the Front for the Liberation of South Yemen (FLOSY)

Makki, Hassan, Yemeni Minister of Economy until February 1964; Foreign Minister from February–May 1964; and November 1967–September 1968

Moore, George C., Officer-in-Charge of Arabian Peninsula Affairs, Bureau of Near Eastern and South Asian Affairs, Department of State, August 1964–July 1966; thereafter, Acting Country Director for Arabian Peninsula Affairs

Naaman, Ahmed Mohammed, Vice President of the Yemen Executive Council February–December 1964; Chairman of the Consultative Council April–December 1964, concurrently member of the Security Council; Prime Minister March–July 1965; member of the Presidency Council from November 1967

Nasser, Gamel Abdel, President of the United Arab Republic

Nitze, Paul H., Secretary of the Navy until June 1967; thereafter, Deputy Secretary of Defense

Pachachi, Adnan M., Iraqi Foreign Minister April 1966–July 1967

Pahlavi, Mohammed Reza, Shah of Iran

Pharaon, Rashad, Special Counselor of King Faisal of Saudi Arabia

Riad, Mahmoud, Foreign Minister of the United Arab Republic from March 1964

Rockwell, Stuart W., Deputy Assistant Secretary of State for Near Eastern and South Asian Affairs from September 1966

Rostow, Eugene V., Under Secretary of State for Political Affairs from October 1966

Rostow, Walt W., Counselor of the Department of State and Chairman of the Policy Planning Council until March 1966; thereafter, Special Assistant to the President

Rusk, Dean, Secretary of State

Russell, H. Earle, Jr., Officer-in-Charge of Lebanon–Israel Affairs, Bureau of Near Eastern and South Asian Affairs, Department of State, until July 1965; Officer in Charge of United Arab Republic and Syrian Arab Republic Affairs July 1965–July 1966

Sabah, Sheikh Sabah al-Ahmed al Jabir al-, Foreign Minister of Kuwait

Sabah, Sheikh Sabah al-Salim al-, Amir of Kuwait

Sabri, Ali, President of the Executive Council of the United Arab Republic until September 1965; Vice President October 1965–June 1967; Deputy Prime Minister June 1967–April 1968

Sadat, Anwar el-, Vice President of the United Arab Republic and Speaker of the National Assembly from March 1964

Sallal, Field Marshal Abdullah al-, Prime Minister of Yemen and Minister of Foreign Affairs until February 1964; and September 1966–November 1967

Saqqaf, Sayyid Omar, Deputy Foreign Minister of Saudi Arabia; Personal Representative of King Faisal on diplomatic missions

Saunders, Harold H., member of the National Security Council staff

Seelye, Talcott W., Officer-in-Charge of Arabian Peninsula Affairs until August 1964; Deputy Chief of Mission and Counselor at the Embassy in Jidda from June 1965 until July 1968; thereafter, Country Director for Lebanon, Jordan, Syrian Arab Republic, and Iraqi Affairs

Shaabi, Qahtan Muhammed El-, President of the People's Republic of South Yemen from November 1967; also Prime Minister and Commander of the Armed Forces

Sirri, Mohsin al-, Yemeni Foreign Minister May 1964–January 1965

Sisco, Joseph J., Assistant Secretary of State for International Organization Affairs from September 1965

Sowayel, Ibrahim Al-, Saudi Arabian Ambassador to the United States from September 1964

Spinelli, Pier P., Special Representative of the UN Secretary-General, and head of the United Nations Yemen Observation Mission

Stewart, (Robert) Michael Maitland, British Secretary of State for Foreign Affairs January 1965–August 1966, and from March 1968

Stoddart, Jonathan D., Deputy Director, Near East and South Asia Region, Office of the Assistant Secretary of Defense for International Security Affairs

Stoltzfus, William A., Jr., Deputy Chief of Mission in Saudi Arabia from July 1968

Strong, Robert C., Ambassador to Iraq until April 1967

Sultan ibn Abdul-Aziz (Prince), Saudi Arabian Defense Minister

Symmes, Harrison M., Deputy Director, Office of Near Eastern Affairs, Bureau of Near Eastern and South Asian Affairs, Department of State, until October 1965; Director, then Country Director, Office of Israel and Arab-Israel Affairs October 1965–July 1966; Ambassador to Jordan from November 1967

Talbot, Phillips, Assistant Secretary of State for Near Eastern and South Asian Affairs until September 1965

Talib, Naji, Iraqi Foreign Minister November 1964–September 1965; Prime Minister August 1966–July 1967

Thant, U, Secretary-General of the United Nations

Walsh, John P., Deputy Director, Office of Near Eastern and South Asian Regional Affairs, Bureau of Near Eastern and South Asian Affairs, Department of State, until May 1965; Deputy Executive Secretary May 1965–September 1967; thereafter, Acting Executive Secretary

Warnke, Paul C., Assistant Secretary of Defense for International Security Affairs from August 1967

Wheeler, General Earle G., USA, Chief of Staff, U.S. Army, until July 1964; thereafter Chairman of the Joint Chiefs of Staff

Wilson, Harold, British Prime Minister from October 1964

Wolle, William D., Officer in Charge of Arab-Israel Affairs, Bureau of Near Eastern and South Asian Affairs, Department of State, August 1965–August 1967

Wriggins, W. Howard, member of the National Security Council staff

Yahia, Lt. Gen. Tahir, Prime Minister of Iraq until September 1965, and July 1967–July 1968

Zahedi, Ardeshir, Iranian Foreign Minister from March 1967

Zuckert, Eugene M., Secretary of the Air Force until October 1965

b producers in cutting off oil to West over what is in
srael issue.) End FYI. Suggest you develop presentation
ng lines. Aside from disruptions in economies of Near
ng countries as result oil cut off there would be serious
insurmountable problems facing countries of Western
of course has sufficient capacity meet own needs and
her countries outside NE would be in position provide
tern Europe in emergency. However, ultimate result cut
d be force major consuming countries band together for
tection against NE producing countries and greatly stimulate
ment alternative energy sources i.e. atomic power, European
al, tar sands, shale; all of which have promising future
ding upon economics of situation. Should Near East come to
nsidered unstable source of petroleum supply with perennial
t of cut off for political reasons, West would develop alternative
ces irrespective of cost.

Rusk

---

2. **Memorandum From Robert W. Komer of the National
Security Council Staff to the President's Special Assistant for
National Security Affairs (Bundy)**[1]

Washington, February 14, 1964.

Mac,

Attached fascinating report (from a source reliable in the past) is
one indication among many that Arabs sense a change in our ME
policy.[2] Though largely the product of circumstance (JFK's assassination, Jordan Waters crisis), it comes out as LBJ being pro-Israeli and
reversing the three years of skillful Kennedy handling of the Arabs.
It's around here too; Joe Kraft and Rollie Evans both mentioned it to
me—and I most stoutly denied.

---

[1] Source: Johnson Library, National Security File, Name File, Komer Memos,
Vol. I. Secret.
[2] Reference is to TDCS 3/572, 910, February 12, from Cairo; not attached.

Near East Rec~

**1.   Telegram From the
    Lebanon**[1]

616. Embtel 611.[2] Cairo Sumn,

In your discussion with Preside.

re effect on West of cutting off of Arak

held in Washington last June[5] concludeɩ

involving the denial of the Suez Canal a,

bringing into service available surplus of

ment of new pattern of supply it should b

Europe's full normal demand by end of three ɪ

period of supply readjustment, in first 90 dayı

shortfall of about $7^{1}/2$ percent of normal supply ɩ

Europe which probably could be accommodated

of about seven days. Supply to all other Free Worlɑ

tinue to be fully maintained.

(2) In event total denial of Middle East oil (definitiɩ

includes Iran but excludes Libya) and no increases in prɔ

OPEC countries outside Middle East, the Eastern hemisphei

could be satisfied only to the extent of approximately one-halɪ

demand. Further alleviation of Eastern hemisphere shortfall ɩ

accomplished by rationing of supply in Western hemisphere coɩ

(In point of fact we think it highly unlikely that Iran and Venɛ

---

[1] Source: National Archives and Records Administration, RG 59, Central Files 1964–66, POL 7 UAR. Limited Official Use. Drafted by Slator C. Blackiston, Jr., (NEA/NE); cleared by Director of the Office of Near Eastern Affairs Rodger P. Davies, in substance by Chief of the Fuels and Energy Division Andrew F. Ensor of the Office of International Resources, and Officer in Charge of Lebanon–Israel Affairs H. Earle Russell, Jr.; and approved by Jernegan. Repeated to Cairo.

[2] In telegram 611 from Beirut, January 6, Ambassador Meyer stated that in his talk with President Chebab regarding the forthcoming Cairo summit conference, he would like to be able to say that while cutting off Arab oil would create problems for the West, it would by no means be fatal. (Ibid.)

[3] The heads of state of 13 Arab nations met in Cairo, January 13–17. The conference reached agreement on a three-part program of action: 1) a joint Arab project to divert large quantities of water from the headwaters of the Jordan River; 2) establishment of a unified Arab Military Command under Egyptian leadership; and 3) creation of a "Palestine entity" that would represent Palestinians in the Arab League.

[4] For documents relating to U.S. international oil policy, see *Foreign Relations, 1964–1968*, vol. XXXIV, Documents 175ff.

[5] For the conclusions of the U.S.–U.K. oil talks in Washington, June 10–14, 1963, see ibid., 1961–1963, vol. XVIII, Document 291.

Somehow LBJ has gotten wind of this. He was strong against saying too much in Weizmann speech;[3] more recently he chided Harriman for getting him in trouble with the Arabs.

But more is needed. I'm putting together with State a program of steps needed to protect our Arab policy through 1964, and to balance the things we'll do for Israel: (1) a loan to the UAR under certain conditions, (2) reassurance we're not helping Israel go nuclear; (3) LBJ letter to Nasser, etc. (4) Hussein visit; (5) another quiet try at arms control with Gamal. We've worked hard under JFK to come up with a promising NE policy; it worked—in Yemen, Iraq, Syria, and at Cairo Conference. We can't let it slide away by inaction—and I don't think LBJ would want this, because among other things it would create painful problems for us in the area (which with luck and suppleness we can avoid).[4]

Bob K.

---

[3] Regarding the President's speech at the Weizmann Institute of Science on February 20, see footnote 3, Document 13 in *Foreign Relations, 1964–1968,* vol. XVIII.

[4] A notation in Bundy's handwriting reads: "*Good, Do it*—and let's get LBJ Nasser letter ready to go with Eshkol answer." For documentation regarding the actions Komer proposed, see ibid.

3.   Background Paper Prepared in the Department of State[1]

CWM–B/10   Washington, April 6, 1964.

TWELFTH CENTO MINISTERIAL COUNCIL SESSION[2]
Washington, April 28–29, 1964

Background Paper

The Situation in the Middle East

General Developments

After a year of readjustment and realignment among the Arab
States a "Summit" meeting in Cairo in January 1964 called by President
Nasser created a stronger sense of unity among the Arabs than had
earlier and more formal attempts to attach and join states in legal
but unhappy union. In Iraq a Ba'th dominated government came in
February and went in November of the same year. The Ba'th Party
(pan Arab socialists) has held on in Syria only by packing the Syrian
army with its adherents. Yemen is still a sensitive problem, with the
strength of UAR troops in the country apparently about the same as
a year ago. However, the Arab Summit sparked a series of contacts
between the Governments of the UAR and Saudi Arabia, and there
now seems to be a disposition on the part of the states concerned to
settle the dispute over Yemen. Yemen itself will have to endure a drawn
out period of organization, consolidation and adjustment. Meanwhile,
Israel's forthcoming off-take of Jordan River waters from Lake Tiberias
looms as possibly the most acute source of tension in the area.

United States Policy in the Near East

Political instability has been endemic in the Near East for the past
several decades. Despite this, there has been considerable economic

---

[1] Source: Johnson Library, National Security File, Komer Files, 12th CENTO Ministerial Council Session, April 28–29, 1964. Confidential. Drafted by Lee F. Dinsmore of the
Office of Near Eastern Affairs; cleared by Davies, Jernegan, Deputy Director of the Office
of Near Eastern and South Asian Regional Affairs John P. Walsh, and NEA/NR Officer
in Charge of CENTO Affairs Matthew D. Smith, Jr.

[2] The Twelfth Session of the Ministerial Council of the Central Treaty Organization
(CENTO) was held in Washington April 28–29. The session was attended by Foreign
Minister Abbas Aram of Iran, Foreign Minister Zulfikar Ali Bhutto of Pakistan, Foreign
Minister Feridum Camal Erkin of Turkey, Foreign Secretary R.A. Butler of the United
Kingdom, and Secretary of State Rusk. For text of the communiqué, see *American Foreign
Policy: Current Documents, 1964*, pp. 683–685. For documentation relating to the session,
see Johnson Library, National Security File, Komer Files, 12th CENTO Ministerial Council
Session, April 28–29, 1964, and Department of State, NEA/RA Files: Lot 75 D 312, CENTO
Ministerial Files, 1962–1968, 12th CENTO Ministerial Council Session, Washington, D.C.,
April 28–29, 1964.

and social development which gives promise of providing a basis for greater political stability. The United States attempts to conduct its relations with states of the area on a strictly bilateral basis and to avoid being drawn into disputes either in an inter-Arab or an Arab state-Israeli context, except where vital United States interests are affected. The United States is equally interested in the integrity and well-being of all states of the area. It has no "chosen instrument" in its dealings with Near Eastern states; its aid programs, if examined on a per capita basis, have been remarkably evenhanded. The United States economic assistance and other programs are motivated by the belief that Free World interests will be served by economic, social, and political development of the peoples of the area. The United States believes that problems arising among the Arab states should be solved by those states without outside interference.

Arab Unity and the CENTO Countries

Just as the urge to unity is inherent in the Arab Islamic culture, so is the tradition and habit of strong individuality. Inevitably, the two drives clash. The ambitious plans of April 1963 for uniting the UAR, Syria, and Iraq were discarded as unworkable before September. Nevertheless, the January 1964 Arab Summit meeting brought Arab leaders back together long enough for them to remember their common heritage and to take new steps toward increased military, economic, and cultural consultation. Unity, in the strict sense of a single state made up of federated components, is unlikely in the foreseeable future. However the sense of unity, essentially a psychological phenomenon, was never stronger and cannot be ignored. Nevertheless, the United States believes that Arab unity does not pose a threat against CENTO states. It believes that the Arab states in considering the form of association they believe best for their interests should not be subjected to outside influences or pressures. The United States does not take a position for or against unity but would not favor any association brought about against the will of the majority of the peoples involved, brought about by force, or clearly directed against other states. The United States does not believe that, given geographic, organizational, and logistical considerations, a joint military command or other form of association of Arab military forces would appreciably affect the capabilities of these forces.

Saudi Arabia and Jordan

The United States has made clear its interests in the integrity of the kingdoms of Jordan and Saudi Arabia and has encouraged and contributed to the economic and social development of both countries. Jordan has made most satisfactory progress in the economic and social fields over the past several years and the United States believes that prospects for continued development and stability in this country are good. Jordan has recognized the USSR and the two countries are exchanging Embassies. The United States does not believe that this step will have any significant effect on its relations with Jordan nor that the present Government of Jordan intends to shift its international posture basically. In Saudi Arabia, Crown Prince Faysal has initiated a program of modernization, reform, and economic development which should in time serve to meet the aspiration of the Saudi people. The United States considers these programs to be the real first line of defense of these countries against subversive influence. A recent confrontation between Crown Prince Faysal, the effective ruler, and King Saud has resulted in Faysal's convincing the ailing and feeble King to relinquish all active leadership of government to Faysal.

Kuwait

In the past year Kuwait has consolidated its independence and has become a significant source of funds for Arab world economic developments. This use of its financial strength gives tiny Kuwait an opportunity to buy "integrity insurance." The comparatively vast resources of Kuwait as compared with its own needs also offer an Arab alternative to external sources of funding to support economic development. The extent to which Kuwait will be prepared to fund military equipment purchases by Arab states is not yet clear, but this eventuality cannot be overlooked.

Yemen

Despite agreement on July 4, 1963 between the UAR and Saudi Arabia to disengage from involvement in Yemen, UAR troops remain in large numbers (around 30,000), and Saudi Arabia, while stopping material aid to the royalists, is still giving moral encouragement and probably financial assistance. Nevertheless, the disengagement agreement has confined the conflict to within the borders of Yemen, has served to preserve and even strengthen the Saud regime, and has protected Free World interests in the Arabian Peninsula. Precipitate withdrawal of all Egyptian troops at this time would result in chaos in the country, and some form of outside security force will no doubt be required to keep peace in Yemen for years to come. Meanwhile the UAR-Saudi resumption of diplomatic relations on March 3, 1964 and a mutual announcement that neither had designs in Yemen are positive steps in the direction of some kind of a modus vivendi over Yemen. Yemen's economy is not in dire straits at the moment, but a certain amount of outside foreign assistance will be needed for any real economic development. Before this can be effective, however, Yemen needs a governmental mechanism which can make use of outside help.

The Kurdish Situation (Noforn)

After two and a half years of fighting, during which time the Kurds at their peak were able to engage regular units of the Iraq Army and defeat them and at their weakest were able to hold only the more inaccessible high country, the Government of Iraq and Iraqi Kurdish representatives agreed on February 10, 1964 to a cease fire. Unfortunately, a misunderstanding of the terms of that agreement seems already to have arisen, the government taking the position that it has complied with conditions agreed upon and the Kurds asserting bad faith on the government's part for not carrying out its bargain (the Kurds claim more concessions were made than the government is now ready to honor). Nevertheless, the government has been withdrawing Army units and equipment from the north, giving every indication it is not planning to make war any longer. There are reports of dissidence within Kurdish circles in Iraq, of a lack of cohesion between the tribal fighters and the Kurdish party's educated and more sophisticated cadre. The party militants are said to be threatening to resume the violence if the "autonomy" they fought for is not granted in sufficiently clear detail by the government. A final settlement is not yet clear nor is it in sight.

Meanwhile, there are reports of arrests in Iranian Kurdish areas of persons believed to entertain similar Kurdish aspirations in Iran. These developments will bear close watching. The Kurdish nationalist fever is not new to Iran. The United States would regard Kurdish unrest in Iran, as it has in Iraq, as an internal problem.

4.   National Intelligence Estimate[1]

NIE 36–64   Washington, April 8, 1964.

MAIN TRENDS IN THE ARAB WORLD[2]

The Problem

To estimate general trends in the Arab world over the next several years.

Conclusions

A. Political turmoil in the Arab world appears likely to continue for many years to come. The military have come to play an increasing role, but—except in Egypt—they have not proved to be a stabilizing factor. Iraq and Syria in particular are likely to remain highly unstable. The monarchies in Jordan, Saudi Arabia, and Libya will come under increasing revolutionary nationalist pressure, and one or more of them may be extinguished in the next several years. Nasser appears likely to remain the single most influential Arab leader. The noteworthy economic and social progress of the past ten years will continue, although, as in the past, it will be uneven and varied. (Paras. 3, 5, 8–10, 16–19)

B. The emotional appeal of Arab unity will remain very strong, but in general the pan-Arab movement is likely to be confined to the kind of cooperation among independent countries that occurred at the Cairo summit meeting in January 1964. (Paras. 20–22)

C. Arab attitudes toward Israel remain basically hostile, but a fair proportion of Arabs have gradually come privately and reluctantly to accept the fact that Israel will exist for many years to come. The Arab-Israeli arms race will cause tensions and could lead to limited or selective hostile action. Other danger points are the Jordan waters problem and the possibility of Israeli military action in the event of a radical political change in Jordan. Nevertheless, the general inhibitions on open warfare would be strong, and a serious rise in tensions could probably be contained by great power pressures. (Para. 23–26, 29, 30)

---

[1] Source: Central Intelligence Agency, Job 79–R01012A, ODDI Registry of NIE and SNIE Files. Secret; Controlled Dissem. According to a note on the cover sheet, the estimate was submitted by the Director of Central Intelligence, and concurred in by the U.S. Intelligence Board on April 8. The Central Intelligence Agency and the intelligence organizations of the Departments of State, Defense, AEC, and NSA participated in its preparation. The State, Defense, AEC, and NSA representatives concurred; the FBI representative abstained, the subject being outside his jurisdiction. Paragraph references are to the Discussion portion of the estimate, not printed.

[2] This estimate does not cover Sudan and the Maghreb. [Footnote in the source text.]

D. Arab relations with the West remain heavily influenced by hatred of "imperialism" and by Western support of Israel. The possibility of a sudden deterioration of Western relations with the Arabs over Israel is always present. The Arab nationalists generally will press for termination of Western base rights in the area. While they will also press for a greater share of oil revenues and a greater degree of participation in production, nationalization appears unlikely. (Paras. 31–33, 35)

E. The Soviets probably believe that the tide is running against the West in the Arab world and that they can capitalize on the unsettled political situation and upon various tensions between the Arabs and West. If US-Arab relations should deteriorate sharply, there would probably be a noticeable strengthening of Soviet influence. We do not believe, however, that this would result in one-sided reliance on the Soviets or a more accommodating attitude toward local Communist parties. (Paras. 36–38)

[Here follows the Discussion section of the estimate.]

5.   Memorandum of Conversation[1]

Washington, September 10, 1964.

SUBJECT

U.S./U.K. Policies in Middle East—Working Level Discussions, First Round

PARTICIPANTS

Mr. John E. Killick, Counselor, British Embassy
Mr. Patrick R. H. Wright, First Secretary, British Embassy

NE—Rodger P. Davies
NE—Curtis F. Jones
NE—George C. Moore

Mr. Davies opened the discussion by noting that our aim was to compare mutual assessments of the situation and to summarize the approaches of our two countries in order to lay the groundwork for

---

[1] Source: National Archives and Records Administration, RG 59, Central Files 1964–66, POL 1 NEAR E. Secret; Limit Distribution. Drafted by Officer in Charge of Arabian Peninsula Affairs George C. Moore.

subsequent higher level discussions. He stressed that both the U.S. and the U.K. had the same overall objectives in the Near East: we wished to prevent the U.A.R. from imposing itself on the area or from imposing a U.A.R.-dominated Arab solidarity. Where we differed was really only in methods of attaining these objectives. He would be less than frank if he did not admit that some courses of action proposed by London caused concern since they could only lead to a confrontation with the U.A.R. and Arab nationalism in situations where it is doubtful that the West had the capabilities to come out on top.

Mr. Davies then spoke from the attached paper[2] (a copy of which was subsequently given to the British participants) which gave working level views point-by-point on the British paper concerning the Middle East which had previously been provided. During this presentation the following additional comments were made.

Concerning Libya, Mr. Killick summed up HMG's view that while the British might preserve certain overflight and landing rights in Libya as a result of the present discussions, they were under no illusion that these would last; realistically, they expected that Nasser would ultimately force them completely out. He agreed that, in the event of a republican coup in Libya, Libyan sentiment would be opposed to a U.A.R. takeover; it was questionable, however, if the Libyans would be sufficiently strong to prevent such a takeover.

The British were in general agreement concerning our views on Jordan and noted that talks on Jordan's economy were again due in the coming few months.

On Iraq, Mr. Killick commented that HMG feared Iraqi instability would be enhanced because the GOI lacked the governmental machinery to be able successfully to operate the socialized state which it appeared to be developing. He made no particular comments concerning the Gulf, Iran or the Omani rebels.

On Yemen, Mr. Killick noted that, from the U.A.R. standpoint, this was a special operation, pre-dating the First Arab Summit; it did not fit the pattern with which Nasser was working elsewhere to advance Arab Socialism. Mr. Davies asked if much of the reported U.A.R. activity in the south (which was not yet as strong as it might be considering the resources available to the U.A.R.) should not be considered as a reaction to covert Saudi and U.K. aid to the royalists. He noted that success of his military in intervention in the form of continued existence of the YAR was vital for Nasser if he were to continue to have the support of his military commanders. On the other hand, the situation in that country was important for the British and only of peripheral

---

[2] Neither of the papers was attached.

concern for us. Thus, a determined effort to promote a viable YARG might be the best way to get U.A.R. troops moving out of Yemen. Mr. Davies also noted that return of one-third of Nasser's fighting forces from an area where they could easily be isolated increased his capabilities for action in other areas.

On the question of oil in the Middle East, Mr. Killick emphasized that Nasser's activities were only a potential, not an actual, danger at the present time. He commented that London was perhaps more sensitive to the problems of Western Europe's need for oil than was the United States; that London's concern over the balance of payments and the necessity for relying on U.S.-dollar sources of oil supply was much greater than the United States perhaps realized. Mr. Davies said that the situation throughout the oil industry would change over time. There was a mutuality of interest between the Arabs and the West and the main Western needs would in effect be met as long as there was free access to the oil on reasonable price terms.

Mr. Davies referred to a recent informal U.S. intelligence estimate that the U.S.S.R. was prepared to give massive political and economic support to the U.A.R. in the belief that the parallels between their system and the Arab Socialist Union gave them an opening for increasing their influence in the area. The U.A.R. was aware of Soviet motivations but was confident Arab nationalism and Islam were strong enough to prevent any Soviet breakthrough; in the interim, the U.A.R. could profit by continuing its contacts with the U.S.S.R. The estimate concluded that U.S. policy was based on an assessment that in the Arab world Cairo would always have more influence than Moscow, that any losses to our position throughout the area occasioned by Nasser's Arab nationalist drive would be essentially peripheral ("special positions," e.g., loss of Wheelus Air Base) and that our basic interests in the Near East would be maintained. We believed that forcing a major confrontation between the U.A.R. and the West would threaten our basic interests, rather than our peripheral ones, and could well lead to establishment of a true Communist puppet state in the area which would present problems of a much greater magnitude for us all. Mr. Davies suggested that, on this basis, we (the U.S. and the U.K.) and, later, our Western allies should work to improve our capability to influence trends in the U.A.R. particularly by increasing our aid to that country. The aim would be to make the U.A.R. economic structure more compatible with that of the West and to woo the U.A.R. into closer ties with the Western world.

As a general final comment, Mr. Killick said that he agreed with much of the U.S. presentation. Noting that his remarks were personal, informal and unofficial, he said that there was a great deal of emotionalism in the U.K. in this pre-election time concerning issues in the Middle East. He agreed with Mr. Davies that the interests of both our governments would be served by delaying a confrontation between us concerning our policies in the Middle East until after our mutual election periods. Specifically, he said that London would not want us to change our policies except perhaps to give more importance to the threat of Nasser. In Yemen, HMG believed Nasser was after total victory and was himself forcing a confrontation.

Mr. Davies responded that we did not disagree that Nasser should be prevented from establishing hegemony over Yemen, but we felt strongly that encouraging Saudi aid to the royalists—with almost inevitable U.A.R.-Saudi hostilities—was not the way to achieve this. We agree that Nasser aspires to dominate the Arab world, but we do not believe he has the capability. In the long run, the Arabs themselves, not we, will be the ones able to give check to Nasser if we do not unnecessarily interpose ourselves between them in their disputes and give free rein to the divergent and divisive forces among them. Western intervention could only consolidate the Arabs.

---

6.   Memorandum of Conversation[1]

Washington, January 13, 1965.

SUBJECT

    Discussion of Near East Developments

PARTICIPANTS

    Oil Executives

    Arabian American Oil Company
    Thomas C. Barger, President
    Garry Owen, Vice President and Head of Washington Office
    J. J. Johnston, Secretary and General Manager of New York Operations

    Gulf Oil Company
    Elston Law, Associate General Counsel for Foreign Operations
    Stuart Nelson, Gulf's Washington Office

    Socony Mobil Oil Company
    William P. Tavoulareas, Senior Vice President

---

[1] Source: National Archives and Records Administration, RG 59, Central Files 1964–66, POL 2 NEAR E. Confidential. Drafted by Wolle.

Standard Oil Company of California
George Parkhurst, Vice President

Standard Oil Company of New Jersey
Howard Page, Vice President

Department Officers
M—Governor Harriman

NEA—Assistant Secretary Phillips Talbot
E/OR/FSE—Andrew F. Ensor
AFN—Grant McClanahan
NE/E—George M. Bennsky
NE/E—William D. Wolle

Governor Harriman after welcoming the visitors said the Department believed that USG Near Eastern policy had achieved a reasonable degree of success since the Suez crisis of 1956. The Arab-Israel problem and the question of Communist penetration continued to occupy much time and effort. He thought the Soviets had had very little reason to be happy over Near Eastern developments in the same period, though perhaps they were somewhat more happy recently due to Nasser's cooperation with the Congo rebels. The arms race in the area had been held fairly well under control. There were constant threats from Arab nationalism in the area. Recent actions by Nasser brought us face to face with a major policy question: how far does the USG want to push Nasser? The Governor said he thought nothing would please the Russians more than for the US to break with Nasser. Anyone advocating such action on our part would do well to give the question the most serious consideration. The Department views as dangerous the present trend in Congress toward taking legislative action which would end American aid to the UAR. Governor Harriman asked Mr. Talbot to extend these remarks.

Oil Information Activity

Mr. Talbot began by discussing the dissemination in the Middle East of information on petroleum and energy matters. He said British government officials had discussed with the Department recently the possible intensification of oil information efforts. What was contemplated was a program aimed at attacking the notion that the Near Eastern oil producing countries can dominate and thereby control the international energy market both now and in the future. The Department's basic feeling was that this task is and should remain the main responsibility of the oil companies, but wondered if the government could play an expanded role to supplement company efforts. Mr. Page confirmed that the companies had been doing a good deal along this line although relatively little through the press. He referred to various speeches given at regional professional and technical conferences and to frequent private discussions with government policymakers during the companies' frequent OPEC negotiations in the past two years. He felt it was a question of deciding whether to put on a campaign or simply keep at the present efforts. Mr. Barger thought the government could assist in this effort in some respects. He said Near Eastern oil leaders were often highly impressed by this type of information and gave as an example the deep impression made on the two Saudi members of the ARAMCO Board at a recent meeting by a Pacific Gas and Electric Company presentation on its activities in the nuclear energy field. Mr. Parkhurst thought that to be more effective the proper information should flow more to Arab politicians in addition to oil ministers and technicians as at present.

Mr. Law warned of a possible adverse effect from putting too much stress on potential energy resources outside the Near East, in that it might make the Arabs want to get still greater benefits now from their oil to build up a reserve against the day 10 to 15 years from now when their oil earnings potential might be reduced. Mr. Tavoulareas added another word of caution, noting that Middle East oil production was bound to keep rising and that this fact might belie our admonitions about the energy potential of other areas. Mr. Barger reiterated he felt there was an appropriate US Government role aimed at preventing unthinking use of oil as a political weapon by radical Arabs. He thought the Bureau of Mines could increase its publicity on its research activities in western oil shales. Mr. Talbot summarized, stating that this discussion led him to believe the word is getting through now to the people who really count in oil decision-making in the area. The government's role was perhaps one of waiting for targets of opportunity rather than mounting a major information campaign. Governor Harriman added that the government might, however, do well to increase its dissemination of pertinent portions of scientific publications on oil.

Review of 1964

Mr. Talbot recalled the Department's belief a year ago that 1964 would be an extremely rough year politically in the Near East. Fortunately there had been no real blowups, either over the Jordan Waters issue or others, and the year had been completed with far less damage than we had dared hope. There had been real problems, however, in several fields. Arab summitry had brought renewed threats to the status quo along the Israel-Arab borders. The UAR seemed to be soberly cognizant of the possible dangers of stirring things up, but the Syrians were plainly less averse to gambling with this potentially explosive situation. There had fortunately been no revival of fedayeen units. We remain concerned lest the Lebanese permit foreign (Arab) troops on their soil under the UAC banner. Jordan's United Arab Command-inspired military buildup plans also remain a large problem.

In the boycott field the proposed Arab action against the Chase Manhattan Bank almost became a runaway. The Department interpreted the recent six-month postponement announced by the Arabs at Bahrain as a face-saving device, and we believe that barring unexpected developments Chase is now in the clear. The UAR action with its sister Arab states had been crucial on this issue and was a good example of the way the UAR could help us if the overall US-UAR relationship was satisfactory.

Kuwait and Saudi Arabia had agreed during the year to bank the UAC. Whether they would keep this up was an important question. There were indications the Kuwaitis were beginning to get tired of being the financial "fall guy" all the time. Yet their keen hunger to be accepted as a full-fledged member of the Arab club might keep them on this tack.

Mr. Talbot congratulated the oil companies on the success with OPEC issues which their painstaking negotiations seemed to have won.

Current Situation

Mr. Talbot said the principal focus of attention is now on our UAR policy. He reviewed in some detail recent events which had received much press attention, such as the library burning, the Mecom plane incident and Nasser's speech at Port Said. The library destruction clearly had been the work of African students who got out of hand in their demonstration over our Congo rescue operation due in part to laxity of the UAR policy. After much initial hesitation the UAR expressed regret and followed up by offering a building to house our library temporarily. The matter is now "on the tracks." Regarding the plane incident there are still many unanswered questions, yet it is not as fundamental an issue in our UAR relations as several others. Nasser's Port Said speech had been irresponsible, unnecessary and uncalled-for. We would probably never know just what kind of report was given Nasser of Ambassador Battle's conversation with Deputy Supply Minister Stino, which had prompted Nasser to lash out at us in his speech. Yet it is obvious that had not basic differences in UAR-US relations been nagging at him Nasser would not have waxed so suddenly and bitterly emotional over the Battle–Stino meeting.

Yemen remains a matter on which the US and UAR do not see eye-to-eye, yet vital US interests are no longer seriously threatened by the Yemeni turmoil as had been the case in 1963, when the situation appeared to have within it the seeds of destruction for Saudi Arabia and perhaps a much wider area. The Yemen issue was now one among the Arabs. It is Nasser's problem, not ours, how to get his troops out, and the situation does not require US intervention.

Mr. Talbot said the most serious current clash of US and UAR policies is in the Congo. Curiously, several Arab states, notably Algeria, Sudan and the UAR, have been more active in supporting the rebels in the Congo than have the great majority of black African states. Our present objective is to find a way to remove these three Arab countries from their active support to Congolese rebels. Governor Harriman pointed out that the Congo question is not solely an African matter but is tied in somehow to Russian policy, though the precise Russian role is not easily defined. He said the Department found it hard to tell whether the Soviets had stimulated the rebellion or were aiding and abetting it. He said that some thought the Russian participation in Congo troublemaking represented a Russian desire to offset the Chinese Communist penetration of Africa, which in recent years had been much more successful than Russian efforts in Africa. He noted the difficulty of defining just what the new Sudanese Government is doing and intending to do vis-à-vis the Congo.

Mr. Talbot spoke of the great strains on the UAR economy. What is happening is precisely what Harvard economist Edward Mason had foreseen two or three years ago: UAR economists had planned a workable economic development program, but UAR politicians had forced its pace, desiring to double national income in ten years rather than twenty. Serious economic difficulty has resulted. The magnitude of Soviet and Chicom economic aid, and promises of future aid, dwarfs the scale of US economic assistance, and Nasser's present economic plight makes it natural for him to swing more and more toward reliance on his Communist supporters rather than on the West. Kuwait weighed in with massive financial support in 1964 when the UAR economic crisis became clearly recognized. For our part, we have not made any kind of development loan to the UAR since 1963. There is an Egyptian tendency to relate this fact to President Kennedy's assassination inferring that somehow the present administration has not the will or the skill for understanding and cooperation with the Arabs. We have not been able completely to disabuse them of this fallacy. Mr. Talbot recounted the history of the proposed $20 million commodity loan to the UAR, noting that in the end we had not proceeded with it.

Mr. Talbot pointed out that our three-year PL 480 agreement with the UAR ends in July. This is our one instrument of policy with Cairo. Our present intention is to live up to this existing commitment by issuing purchase authorizations for the remaining commodities, provided there is UAR compliance with the normal terms of such PL 480 agreements. We are faced with deciding soon on a PL 480 agreement for the future. Was this the time to squeeze the UAR, or was it the time to give additional assistance to increase our leverage on her? There was the possibility that Congress in its present anti-UAR mood might legislate a decision.

Mr. Talbot noted that our national interests in the area have not yet been put in jeopardy by the UAR. We still enjoy MATS rights, our warships can still proceed through the Suez Canal without inspection for nuclear weapons, our civil air rights remain untouched, the flow of oil to Western markets continues uninterrupted, and there had been no major outbreak on the Arab-Israel border. While the UAR had sided increasingly with the Soviets we have had a surprising number of comments in the last month from sources close to the UAR pulse that the UAR really thinks it has swung too far to the Soviet side this time and wants to move the pendulum back. Governor Harriman mentioned Nasser's potential influence for bad with respect to US base rights in Libya as well as US oil interests.

Regarding the area arms buildup, Mr. Talbot noted that any Arab efforts which may be undertaken, either through the UAC or other means, are self-defeating due to Israel's refusal to be left behind at any level of armaments.

Mr. Talbot said the US is going to push hard to attain rectification of the UNRWA ration rolls and expected considerable agitation by Palestinian refugees.

Discussion

Leading off for the companies Mr. Parkhurst said that what stood foremost in his mind was the depth of feeling in the Iranian, Saudi and perhaps Libyan attitude toward our UAR policy. The Iranians and the Saudis could not understand why we aided Nasser, and Mr. Parkhurst believed their doubts were justified. He believed personally that we should live up to our existing commitments, however.

Mr. Page said it should be realized that a policy of continued aid to Egypt causes losses in the area as well as gains. During the recent OPEC negotiations the Shah had complained long and bitterly against US policy toward Nasser and had given the impression that Iran was moving closer to the Soviet camp. Governor Harriman interjected that he challenged this. He felt he knew the Shah extremely well, and over a long period of time, and he believed the Shah simply wanted more and better jet aircraft from the US. He did not believe the US would lose Iran over what the US did toward Nasser. He repeated an earlier observation that he was convinced the Russians would pay a tremendous price for the US to break with Nasser.

Mr. Barger suggested the essentiality of forming a judgement as to what Nasser's real personal objectives are before one can properly decide how to deal with him. He went on to recommend that the US use USIS for some attacks on Nasser just as Nasser continually attacks us with propaganda. Governor Harriman stressed again that one should weigh very carefully the idea of breaking relations with the UAR. He found it extremely difficult to believe we could break with Nasser and still hope that Nasser would retain his freedom and not become a tool of the Soviet bloc. The Governor drew a parallel with the

Yugoslavian situation, pointing out that our long and patient support of Tito against Moscow since 1948 was paying great dividends today, since Tito's staunch stand against the dictates of Moscow had made possible the growing independent spirit of other East European states. Concluding, the Governor admitted a good case could be made that both the US and USSR had been played for suckers by Nasser. He submitted that while this was not to our liking it left us in a much better position than if we pulled out of the UAR completely and left the field to the Russians. Governor Harriman left the meeting at this point.

Mr. Barger felt that his remarks had been misapprehended. He was not advocating a complete break with the UAR but only a much stricter policy toward aiding Cairo. Mr. Talbot, addressing himself to Mr. Barger's earlier comment about Nasser's objectives, said there was no question but that Nasser had ambitions to be "Mr. Big" in the area. He believed that Nasser realized, however, that he had been blocked whenever and wherever he tried to achieve his ambitions by outright domination and that Nasser therefore was switching tactics in favor of a more congenial, cooperative effort characterized by Arab summitry. He remarked that it was surprising how many had expressed concern to us since the Nasser speech at Port Said lest the US actually break with Nasser. King Hussein did not see such a break as being in his interest, nor did the Lebanese.

Mr. Law asked what the Department foresaw for Egypt after Nasser. Mr. Talbot responded that while it was always extremely hard to predict this kind of thing his best guess would be a closing of ranks around Ali Sabri and others distinctly more leftist leaning than today's UAR regime.

Mr. Owen referred to the "story" around Washington that the oil companies were out to get Nasser and were lobbying in Congress for legislative action in this regard. Mr. Talbot said the version reaching him had it that the oil companies and the Zionists were cooperating under the inspiration of Bushrod Howard to achieve this. Mr. Owen wanted to make it clear the companies were taking no such action. Mr. Barger emphasized that he believed it entirely improper and unwise for the legislative branch of government to interfere with the responsibility of the President and executive branch to determine foreign policy.

Mr. Law, referring to an earlier statement by Governor Harriman critical of Kuwait for indiscriminately showering financial support among her neighbors, stated that the Kuwaitis are realists and have but one interest in life: survival. They are spending their only asset—money—to buy friends and are likely to continue to do so. They are scared to death of the UAR.

Mr. Tavoulareas called attention to the importance of understanding the way the Iranians and Saudis, and perhaps others, view the fact of extensive US aid to the UAR. They felt the US was showing neglect to its real friends while aiding a country that was playing ball with the Soviets and often intriguing against its Middle Eastern neighbors. Mr. Talbot remarked that the US and British Governments had made repeated assessments of Iranian allegations that Nasser was stirring up the Arab minority in Iranian Khuzistan. We had developed nothing indicating the Shah should be fearful of this, and had said as much to him, but there apparently continued to be a feeding of incorrect intelligence tales to the Shah which kept him stirred up on this subject.

Mr. Parkhurst said the Department might be interested to know that the Shah, speaking to him privately a few days before, said he was favorably disposed to a Russian proposal that Iran pipe gas to the Soviet border for sale in Azerbaijan.

Mr. Talbot concluded by stating that the protection of our interests in the area requires continual reassessment. Mr. Parkhurst readily agreed and on behalf of the visitors thanked the Department for this opportunity to be briefed and exchange views.

As the meeting concluded Mr. Page came to Mr. Talbot and said he understood the Department had suggested having the Jersey Standard and Socony Mobil representatives brief it concerning the status of IPC negotiations with Iraq. He said Socony's Henry Moses, one of the IPC negotiators, was expected back from Baghdad the same day and would be in touch with the Department. He said if the Department wished he would send down a copy of memorandum containing some of Wattari's more extreme remarks on OPEC and IPC views on them. Mr. Talbot accepted the offer. Mr. Talbot said the Department was continuing to hold the line on third-party activity, but the clock was continuing to run and there was a limit to our ability to hold the line in this situation.

---

7.   **Editorial Note**

The Thirteenth Session of the Ministerial Council of the Central Treaty Organization (CENTO) was held in Tehran, April 7–8, 1965. The session was attended by Foreign Minister Abbas Aram of Iran, Finance Minister M. Shoaib of Pakistan, Foreign Minister Hasan Esat Isik of Turkey, Foreign Secretary Michael Stewart of the United Kingdom, and Secretary of State Rusk. For text of the communiqué, see *American Foreign Policy: Current Documents, 1965*, pp. 585–587. For documentation relating to the session, see Johnson Library, National Security File,

Komer Files, CENTO—13th Ministerial Council, Tehran, April 7–8, 1965; Department of State, NEA/RA Files: Lot 75 D 312, CENTO Files, 1965–1968 and CENTO Ministerial Files, 1962–1968; and National Archives and Records Administration, RG 59, S/S Con-ference Files: Lot 66 D 347, CF 2468, CENTO Meeting, Tehran, April 7–8.

---

8.   Special National Intelligence Estimate[1]

SNIE 10–2–65   Washington, July 15, 1965.

SOVIET AND CHINESE COMMUNIST STRATEGY AND TACTICS IN NORTH AFRICA, THE MIDDLE EAST, AND SOUTH ASIA

The Problem

To assess the nature, extent, and present effectiveness of Soviet and Chinese Communist overt and covert efforts in North Africa, the Middle East, and South Asia,[2] and to estimate the outlook for such efforts over the next several years.

Conclusions

A. Most of the countries in this area have been opened up to Soviet and other Communist penetration by the liquidation of European colonial empires and by the widespread emergence of movements of protest against the concentration of political and economic power in the hands of a small ruling class. Over the past decade or so, the USSR has injected itself dynamically into the whole area. China plays a significant role mainly in South Asia. With the exception of Yugoslavia,

---

[1] Source: Central Intelligence Agency, Job 79–R01012A, ODDI Registry of NIE and SNIE Files. Secret; Controlled Dissem. According to a note on the cover sheet, the estimate was submitted by the Director of Central Intelligence, and concurred in by the U.S. Intelligence Board on July 15. The Central Intelligence Agency and the intelligence agencies of the Departments of State, Defense, and NSA participated in its preparation. The State, Defense, and NSA representatives concurred; the AEC and FBI representatives abstained, the subject being outside their jurisdiction. Paragraph references are to the Discussion portion of the estimate, not printed.

[2] The following countries are included in this estimate: all the Arab states (including those in northern Africa, i.e., UAR, Libya, Sudan, Tunisia, Algeria, and Morocco), Israel, Greece, Turkey, Cyprus, Iran, Afghanistan, Pakistan, India, Nepal, and Ceylon. [Footnote in the source text.]

whose progress while maintaining a balance between the USSR and the West has greatly impressed certain leaders in the area, the East European countries have ridden into the area on Soviet coattails. (Paras. 1–4)

B. Soviet influence in the area has been achieved principally through the customary instruments of contemporary statecraft. With a considerable degree of success, Moscow has exploited nationalist and anti-colonial resentments, encouraged neutralist sentiment, and taken sides in local disputes. The USSR, and to a lesser extent China, have mounted cultural and student exchange programs and expanded their trade relationships. The Soviets have extended economic aid to 16 of the 23 countries in the area, and six of them have armies that are largely equipped with Soviet arms and trained in Soviet methods. The economic and military aid programs have not only contributed to the Soviet image in the area, but also provide Moscow with some potential for leverage by slowing down projects, failing to deliver spares, and the like, though this leverage could not be exerted without some political cost. (Paras. 9–20, 33)

C. The overt Soviet presence—for example, diplomatic, trade, military missions—provides cover for an extensive clandestine apparatus. The Committee for State Security (KGB) and the Chief Intelligence Directorate (GRU) play a wide role in carrying out foreign policy. Aside from the classic intelligence collection functions, these services conduct operations to denigrate the US and other Western powers, to capture and exploit press and other propaganda outlets, and to place individuals in positions in local governments, political parties, etc., where they can influence policy in Moscow's favor. The Soviets have recruited local officials at various levels, including some holding senior government positions. In general, the Soviet covert operations have been fairly successful. (Paras. 26–32)

D. The Communist nations also strive to develop and use local Communist movements and international front organizations. The former include a few sizable legal or quasi-legal organizations, as in India, Greece, and Cyprus, and a dozen or so small, mostly illegal, but fairly well organized parties. Their organizational strength has enabled them to survive repression and, on occasion, to make significant but temporary gains in the wake of political upheaval. On the whole, the Communist parties have made little progress as mass movements; they have done best in attracting discontented intellectuals, while making little headway among the peasants who comprise the bulk of the population, and only somewhat more among workers. This has led the Soviets, in some countries at least, to slacken their efforts to develop a mass organization and turn instead to a tactic of infiltrating ongoing nationalist or revolutionary movements. (Paras. 21–25)

E. In both overt and covert operations, the Soviets probably consider that they have met with a fair degree of success in establishing
their presence and influence in the area. They have, broadly speaking,
been most successful in the Arab world and least successful where fear
of Slavic domination remains strong—in Greece, Turkey, and Iran. They
will probably continue their efforts to establish an identity of feeling
and interest with the modernizing forces in the "Third World," though
tailoring their approach for individual countries. Some of the countries
we are dealing with have adequately functioning political systems,
sufficiently coherent societies, or strong enough leadership to be relatively impervious to Communist efforts to make them into Marxist
socialist societies, barring a major upheaval. A number of others lack
most or all of these qualities, and upsets in their fragile political situations could present Communists with good opportunities to gain a
position of power. (Paras. 33, 34, 64–66)

F. The prospects for the Communist powers in the Middle East,
North Africa, and South Asia over the next several years might best
be characterized as "more of the same." The generally low state of the
local Communist parties is likely to persist, although the presence and
influence of the Communist countries will expand. The influence of
Marxism is likely to increase, particularly in those states following a
socialist path. The Chinese will also be more active, although much of
their effort will be directed against the Soviets, thus inhibiting Communist progress. We recognize that in some places situations could develop
so as to provide promising opportunities for the Communists to come to
power; nevertheless, we cannot specifically identify any such situation
and—all things considered—doubt that any country of the area will
come under Communist control. We believe that the forces of nationalism in the area will remain strong, and that nationalist leaders will
continue, by and large successfully, to play off East against West. (Paras.
56, 57, 67, 69)

G. Two sorts of development could give the Communists a considerable victory. The first, essentially unpredictable, is the emergence of
a leader who decided to take his country into the Communist world,
either rapidly like Castro, or by stages. Another would arise from a
successful Soviet or Chinese effort to achieve a complete and continuing
identity of interests with the nationalist forces of the "Third World."
As long as this identity remains negative, devoted to eliminating special
Western positions and the like, it will be troublesome, sometimes serious, but not fatal. But if these nationalist forces came to believe that the
Western powers, and especially the US, were fundamentally opposed
to their desire for national independence and domestic progress, the
opportunities for the Communist powers to achieve a fundamental
gain in the "Third World" would go up sharply. Countries which felt

they had no other way to turn would be under very strong pressures to enter upon still closer collaboration with the Communist world. (Paras. 67–68)

[Here follow the Discussion section of the estimate and an annex.]

9.   **Memorandum From Robert W. Komer of the National Security Council Staff to President Johnson**[1]

Washington, September 23, 1965, 4:15 p.m.

SUBJECT

Week's Developments in the Near East

While we came out of the Arab Summit[2] unusually well, we don't want to crow about it. You've already asked the new Moroccan Ambassador to tell King Hassan you're pleased at his role in keeping the lid on. Feisal also deserves credit. But this kind of statement is best kept confidential, since we get farther in this part of the world by quiet diplomacy.

Arab Summit. As far as we can tell from preliminary reports, the Arab Summit *did little* more than maintain a semblance of momentum toward Arab unity. If the communiqué is a measure, the moderates prevented any tough positions against our role in Vietnam or the Congo, our support of Israel or our base in Libya. However, anti-Israeli plans were given another small push forward.

Jordan. One troublesome result was that Hussein had a rough time explaining why he hasn't contracted for supersonics yet. His brethren gave him 60 days to sign up. According to one clandestine report, *he agreed in effect to take MIGs then if he fails to get Western planes.* We're working hard to persuade the French or British to sell planes, but the big problem is competing with the cut-rate MIG price. Hussein did resist stationing other Arab troops in Jordan, but reported offers to send an "interim" air squadron will be harder to resist.

---

[1] Source: Johnson Library, National Security File, Memos to the President, McGeorge Bundy, Vol. 15. Secret. The initial "L" on the memorandum indicates that the President saw it.

[2] Leaders of 12 Arab states held a summit meeting in Casablanca September 13–17.

Nasser. We reserve judgment on how Nasser came out until more of the clandestine reports are in, but so far it looks as if he made no effort to dominate and was relatively restrained. He stuck to the position that no military action against Israel is possible in the near future. So we continue to get a picture of a somewhat subdued Nasser, although he *may have adopted a wait-and-see attitude toward us until he finds out how we answer his food requests.* We have indications, too, that government censors have been weeding anti-US noises out of the Cairo press recently.

Water diversion and United Arab Command. The Arabs paid lip service to pushing ahead with diversion projects, but concentrated on building up their military ability to protect them. This will increase the pressure on Lebanon and Jordan to station other Arab troops on their soil, but may take a little of the heat off the diversion works. The Lebanese will still have a problem, however. They stopped work in July, under US and Israeli pressure, on the Arab plan to divert water into Syria. But they'd now like to divert enough water within Johnston Plan limits to irrigate their own arid south. They're sure the Israelis will retaliate, even if they only divert for their own needs.

Iraq. An abortive coup against President Aref by so-called "pro-Nasser" elements apparently took even Nasser by surprise. As far as we can tell, there wasn't any Egyptian collaboration, even though the Egyptians are pretty well wired into those groups. The whole thing quieted down quickly without any significant change in the balance of political forces.

Israel. The election (2 November) campaign is getting more tense. Eshkol's forces came close to losing a majority in elections in Histadrut, the big labor confederation (which may be a weathervane since it reaches most Israeli workers). This doesn't mean they'll lose control in the election, but it does underscore the vote-getting power of the Ben-Gurion name, especially among the less literate voters who have trouble understanding that Ben-Gurion is wrong this time. Since it increases the possibility that BG might win enough seats to be included in a governing coalition, Eshkol will probably run a little more scared; he'll increase the pressure on us to say something about our secret arms help or on desalting.

[Here follows discussion of Greece and Turkey.]

R. W. Komer[3]

---

[3] McGeorge Bundy initialed below Komer's signature.

10.   **Editorial Note**

On January 27, 1966, a U.K. delegation headed by Foreign Secretary Stewart and Defence Secretary Healey, in Washington to discuss problems relating to the current U.K. Defense Review, met with a U.S. delegation headed by Secretary Rusk and Secretary McNamara. Stewart stated that his government was extremely anxious that the United Kingdom not run away from its proper responsibilities, but pointed out that it had been overstretched in trying to maintain a wide range of commitments and was facing a serious foreign exchange drain. In discussing Middle East defense problems, Stewart argued that arrangements for defense of Libya could be more efficient and economical if the United States undertook a bigger share of its defense.

Regarding the Arabian Sea–Persian Gulf area, he said it had been proposed that Aden become independent by 1968 and that the United Kingdom then withdraw from the base there. This would be compensated for by an increase in British forces in the Persian Gulf area, which they hoped would reassure the Shah. The U.K. Government hoped that Nasser would not represent the withdrawal as a triumph for himself, and that the U.S. Government would use its influence with Nasser to encourage him to refrain from making difficulties for them in connection with the withdrawal. The United Kingdom also planned to modify its commitment to Kuwait somewhat by not providing land forces hereafter except in case of a coup.

Rusk said that the United States understood the British problem of being overstretched; it had a comparable problem with its Great Society programs being set back by the costs of Vietnam. He emphasized that the United States attached the greatest importance to Britain's retaining a world power role, and noted that it would be disastrous if the American people were to get the impression that the United States was entirely alone. On Aden and the Persian Gulf, he thought they could reach a common understanding, and he said that the United States would see what it could do to influence Nasser. (Memorandum of Conversation, January 27, Washington National Records Center, RG 330, OSD Files: FRC 77–0075, Memo of Conversation Between Secretary McNamara and the United Kingdom)

For documentation on the U.K.-U.S. discussions relating to the U.K. Defense Review, see *Foreign Relations, 1964–1968*, volume XII, Documents 252–257. On February 22 the U.K. Government issued a Defence White Paper announcing that British forces overseas would be reduced by one-third over the next 4 years, and that the British base at Aden would be evacuated in 1968.

11.   National Intelligence Estimate[1]

NIE 36–66   Washington, February 17, 1966.

THE EASTERN ARAB WORLD

The Problem

To assess the present situation and the outlook for the eastern Arab world over the next two or three years.[2]

Conclusions

A. For the last year or so, the Arab states have generally been more concerned with domestic problems than with such inter-Arab matters as the conflict between conservative and radical governments or rivalries among the radical leaders. However, the odds are against a long continuation of this inter-Arab détente. The Arab states are generally susceptible to sudden political turmoil. An upheaval in any one of them, or the death of a ruler, could easily precipitate a collision of forces not only within that state but among others. Much still depends on Nasser who, though unlikely to regain the paramount influence he once had, remains the most important Arab leader. (Paras. 1–12)

B. In the Arab-Israeli dispute, neither side is likely to initiate major hostilities, but neither will move toward a basic settlement. Border tensions will occasionally flare up, and the arms race will lead to increasing pressures on the US to supply expensive modern weapons. (Paras. 27–32)

C. The socialist programs of the UAR, Syria, and Iraq are beset by economic difficulties, stemming from more ambitious development efforts than resources justify. The conservative governments, most of them blessed with oil revenues, are better off. In virtually all cases, government, rather than private enterprise, will be the directing force

---

[1] Source: Department of State, NEA/IAI Files: Lot 70 D 304, POL 1 Israel, 1966, General Policy Background. Secret; Controlled Dissem. According to a note on the cover sheet, the estimate was submitted by Acting Director of Central Intelligence Helms, and concurred in by the U.S. Intelligence Board on February 17. The Central Intelligence Agency and the intelligence organizations of the Departments of State, Defense, and NSA participated in its preparation. The State, Defense, and NSA representatives concurred; the AEC and FBI representatives abstained because the subject was outside their jurisdiction. Paragraph references are to the Discussion portion of the estimate, not printed.

[2] This estimate deals principally with the Arab states from Libya eastward; the three Maghreb countries of Tunisia, Algeria, and Morocco are considered only insofar as they are involved in eastern Arab affairs. [Footnote in the source text.]

in the economies. Inter-Arab economic cooperation is likely to be limited, although oil-rich states are beginning to finance Arab economic and military schemes. (Paras. 13–19)

D. Arab oil production will grow, and so will pressures on the oil companies for more revenue and greater control over production. Strong competition in the world oil market, however, sets limits on how far either side can go in this respect, and outright nationalization is unlikely. (Paras. 20–26)

E. Britain's position will dwindle further. The UK will probably be able to maintain control in its protected states of the Persian Gulf over the next few years; its tenure in Aden, however, is considerably less certain. (Paras. 36–38)

F. Tendencies toward Arab détente have helped the US position in the area. However, US relations with the Arab world will remain troubled by the general Arab conviction that the US is basically pro-Israel, by the Arab radicals' belief that the US favors the conservatives, and by the conservatives' feeling that the US should support them more than it does. (Paras. 39–40)

[Here follows the Discussion section of the estimate.]

12.   Editorial Note

The Fourteenth Session of the Ministerial Council of the Central Treaty Organization (CENTO) was held in Ankara, April 20–21, 1966. The session was attended by Foreign Minister Abbas Aram of Iran, Foreign Minister Zulfikar Ali Bhutto of Pakistan, Foreign Minister Ihsan Sabri Caglayangil of Turkey, Foreign Secretary Michael Stewart of the United Kingdom, and Secretary of State Rusk. For text of the communiqué, see *American Foreign Policy: Current Documents, 1966,* pp. 515–516. Documentation on the session is in the Department of State, NEA/RA Files: Lot 75 D 312, CENTO Files, 1965–1968 and CENTO Ministerial Files, 1962–1968.

13.   Circular Telegram From the Department of State to Certain Posts[1]

Washington, May 20, 1966, 7:15 p.m.

2285. 1. Department concerned about increasing charges US sponsoring Islamic Alliance.[2] Following is contingency guidance for background use with friendly diplomats, host government officials and others where appropriate on target of opportunity basis:

a. US has neither supported nor opposed formation Islamic Alliance and sees no advantage in doing so. US aware published reports consultations among Islamic countries, but has played no role in them and, as non-Muslim country, has no position concerning them.

b. Present indications are that no organized grouping such as Baghdad or Saadabad Pacts intended. Both Faisal and Hussein have stressed what they have in mind is not formal pact but greater Islamic solidarity designed to expand traditional Islamic conferences held annually Mecca following Haj. As for Shah of Iran, we see no evidence he has unrealistic expectations that Islamic solidarity could become important anti-Nasser device and doubt that he intends invest either prestige or resources in effort promote it.

c. While we recognize significant common cultural element provided by Islamic heritage, we see little likelihood effective Islamic Alliance taking shape, given lack genuine community political interests Arab states and other Muslim nations. Notable recent examples Muslim failure agree on Islamic policy are Cyprus and Kashmir. In fact, renewed India–Pakistan hostilities in 1965 proved to be divisive issue among Arabs. Reaction of UAR and Syria to proposed Islamic Alliance raises doubt whether Islam still serves as force for unity of political action even among Arab states.

d. We wonder whether any action, either Islamic Pact or Nasserist socialist crusade, serving to polarize Arab world into camps having

---

[1] Source: National Archives and Records Administration, RG 59, Central Files 1964–66, POL 3 ISLAMIC. Secret. Drafted by H. Eugene Bovis (NEA/UAR); cleared by Country Director for Israel and Arab-Israel Affairs Harrison M. Symmes, Director of the INR Office of Research and Analysis for Near East and South Asia James W. Spain, Bruce Buttles (NEA/P), Country Director for Ethiopia, Somalia, and Sudan Matthew J. Looram, Country Director for Turkey John M. Howison, and Staff Assistant Morris J. Amitay in the Office of the Assistant Secretary of State for European Affairs; and approved by Davies. Sent to Rabat, Algiers, Tunis Tripoli, Khartoum, Mogadiscio, Cairo, Amman, Beirut, Damascus, Baghdad, Jidda, Taiz, Kuwait, Tel Aviv, Tehran, Ankara, Karachi, London, Paris, Rome, and Moscow.

[2] Since December 1965, Saudi King Faisal had been calling for stronger ties among Islamic states, i.e., including non-Arab but Islamic states such as Iran, as a counter to Nasser's Arab Socialist movement.

image of "reactionary monarchs" versus "extremist" Arab states, might not be detrimental in long run to interests of all concerned. Polarization could lead to renewed propaganda campaigns, public attacks against one another and subversion in both camps.

Rusk

---

14.   **Memorandum From Harold H. Saunders of the National Security Council Staff to the President's Special Assistant (Rostow)**[1]

Washington, June 24, 1966.

WWR:

It is not too hard to build a list of undramatic but *constructive developments in the Middle East 1964–66.* That may be all you can use in public. However, for in-house purposes, a much more sophisticated argument clinches your line.

The big question is whether our basic position in the Middle East is stronger or being eroded. The long-run answer is that, while the Soviets continue to inch their way in, this is inevitable and the important thing is that we keep a base from which to protect our interests and to build the kind of Middle East that will stop the USSR short of eventual predominant influence a la Eastern Europe or Cuba. We are doing pretty well.

We have succeeded in maintaining satisfactory working relationships on all sides of a series of local disputes that have threatened to drive us and the USSR into opposing camps. We have long believed that splitting the Middle East is a major Soviet objective. Our interests in the area are wide and varied enough that we judge it essential to avoid that kind of split. Carrying water on both shoulders sometimes seems immoral and is always difficult. But for power like the U.S. with its far flung conflicting interests there seems no other choice. The alternative is being driven to choose half our interests, sacrifice half and let the USSR pick up our losses.

In *early 1964* shortly after President Johnson took office, we were writing that:

---

[1] Source: Johnson Library, National Security File, Name File, Saunders Memos. Secret.

—1964 would be the year of the Jordan Waters crisis, forcing us to choose between Arabs and Israelis. The Arabs were strengthening their United Command and threatening to dry up the Israeli share of the Jordan.

—Cyprus would become the center of a minor war, forcing us to choose between two NATO allies with the USSR gaining from the split.

—Yemen would flare up again and force us to choose between defaulting on commitments to Saudi Arabia and opposing Nasser.

None of these problems is solved. But none has erupted into the kind of showdown that would force us to take sides and effectively remove ourselves from the race in half of the Middle East.

Shortly thereafter we began worrying with the Israelis that a serious arms imbalance was developing against them with Soviet help. With a series of arms sales to both Arabs and Israelis in 1965 and 1966, we have temporarily succeeded in restoring a deterrent balance. While we have made modest moves toward dampening the arms race, they have not been ripe enough to avoid establishing a new balance of forces.

The USSR is making a new push in the Middle East, taking advantage of the new rift that seems to be opening between moderates and radicals and of neutralist pressures in Turkey and Iran. Recent modest successes in Damascus and Baghdad belong with the older Soviet position in Cairo and suggest that they are gaining ground. CIA argues that Soviet covert assets are building a formidable position. This argument demands consideration, but the fragile nature of Arab politics assures that the situation may change again and that the competition is still very much open. Soviet gains have been far less impressive than we feared in 1956. As long as we can avoid a complete split, we can compete.

The key question in assessing these developments is, who profits from Arab unity? The new unity of early 1964—via summits and United Arab Command—seemed a growing threat to Israel then. Now it is disintegrating again. Presumably we should rest easier. Our strategists have debated for years whether we gain more from Arab unity or from Arab fragmentation.

One side of the argument is that an efficient, united Arab movement backed by an integrated military could do a great deal of harm, although any such unity may be a pipe dream. One can also argue that, while we have nothing to lose from cooperation of like-minded Arabs or from Islamic friendship, our interests are better served by evolution of effective national centers than by a Nasser-dominated Arab union of some sort.

But it is discomfiting that Moscow is pleased with the breakdown of Arab unity. The disadvantages of this spring's new fragmentation are that:

—It sharpens the Cold War confrontation in the Middle East and gives the USSR new encouragement to fashion a pro-Soviet camp.

—Nasser is pretty rational in calculating Arab chances in a fight with Israel, and he actually dampened down the more radical talk of driving Israel into the sea. Now the restraining influence of mild-tongued Arab unity is lifted. While Nasser may not feel any readier to drive Israel into the sea, he may feel forced to talk a more radical game in order to stay in line with his radical company. This talk encourages groups like the Fatah and PLO.

—When Arabs are squabbling, both Israel and the US are convenient scapegoats, so tension and chances of a flareup increase.

While on balance, the widening Arab split may seem a modest setback for us, Israel is a success and clearly here to stay—partly because of our help, largely because of Israeli's own efforts. Whether our support for Israel in 1948 was right or wrong, this has been a main tenet of our Middle East policy. Our purpose now is to buy time for an Arab-Israeli accommodation. While Arab-Israeli animosity is as great as ever, winds of change have begun to blow in the past year. The New Israeli government (particularly Eban) is seriously looking for bridges to build to the Arabs. Bourguiba on the Arab side has broken the solid Arab line that Arabs and Jews can never coexist. Resolution is far off, but the seeds of détente may be in the ground.

On balance, then, the real answer to your question is that, since 1964, we have surmounted a steady stream of problems that could have undermined our stance in the Middle East. Since our main purpose is to stay there and plug away at basic development, we can argue that we have bought time for the undramatic achievements which are going our way.

HS

15.   Position Paper Prepared in the Department of State[1]

21GA/GP–16   Washington, September 12, 1966.

TWENTY-FIRST GENERAL ASSEMBLY
New York—September–October, 1966

Position Paper

SOVIET ROLE IN THE NEAR EAST (ARAB STATES)

The Soviet Union regards the Near East as a highly significant strategic area, and as a key element in the struggle between the USSR and the Western Powers for world domination. Soviet aims are to disrupt the West's defensive alliances in the area, deny the West the use of strategic bases, achieve predominance in the supply of military weapons, and establish economic and cultural ties which will in time supplant Western economic and political influence. At the same time, however, the USSR has been careful not to provoke a crisis in the area (as, for example, in the Arab-Israeli dispute) which might involve the Soviets in a confrontation with the Western powers.

In its relations with the Arab States in the Near East, the Soviet Union has readily subordinated the interests of the local Communist parties to the larger purpose of establishing "correct" state to state relations. The Soviets have aimed at creating the image of the USSR as a respectable great power unselfishly assisting those states desiring its aid.

The Soviet Union has had its most dramatic success in Nasir's United Arab Republic, which today depends upon bloc assistance for its military strength and much of its economic development. Internally, Nasir's revolution has adopted forms of state socialism and one party control which conform, superficially at least, with the Communist prescription for a "national democracy." Soviet influence has had some success in limiting Nasir's formerly severe repression of Egypt's Communists. At the same time Nasir continues to maintain contacts with some Western Powers. Aid from the United States, especially in the

---

[1] Source: Department of State, NEA/RA Files: Lot 71 D 218, Papers re Communist Presence in the Middle East, 1966. Confidential. Drafted by Robert H. Flenner (EUR/SOV); cleared by Country Director for Soviet Union Affairs Malcolm Toon, Igor N. Belousovitch (INR/RSB), George C. Moore (NEA/ARP), Symmes, Country Director for United Arab Republic Affairs Donald C. Bergus, Country Director for Lebanon, Jordan, Syria, and Iraq Alfred L. Atherton, and NEA Director of Regional Affairs Sidney Sober.

area of food grains, has relieved the Soviet Union from the unwanted burden of total support for the Nasir regime.

Significant Soviet influence is also present in the Yemen, Syria and Iraq, all of which are largely dependent on bloc supplied arms for their military establishments, and have significant economic aid projects furnished from Soviet or other Communist sources. In none of these states, has Soviet influence succeeded in completely eradicating the Western presence. Only in Saudi Arabia and the British supported South Arabian Federation and the Sheikdoms of the Trucial Coast is there no Soviet diplomatic representation.

Of the current problems in the area, from the Soviet policy point of view, the following are considered the most significant:

1. Breakdown of Arab Summitry

The relapse suffered by the concept of Arab unity and the present disarray of the Arab world following the breakdown of Arab summit conferences signifies a return to the patterns of intra-Arab rivalry which the Soviets have exploited before. With the ranging of the self-styled "progressive" states receiving Soviet military and economic aid in contrast to more traditional regimes of Jordan and Saudi Arabia receiving assistance from the US and UK, great power rivalry becomes an integral aspect of the local confrontation. Support by the Western Powers for Israel gives the Soviets further opportunities to extend this influence with the "progressive" Arab regimes.

2. Instability in Syria

Although the Soviets have been cautious in committing themselves to support the present highly unstable regime in Syria, they have already registered some important gains in the local political context. They wish to bolster the left wing Ba'th regime which offers them prospects of increased influence in Syria but apparently do not wish to weaken their influence in the UAR in the process and thus at the same time are working for a détente in Syrian-UAR relations. However, the Soviets, mindful of the potential impermanence of any Arab regime, seek to establish in Syria a possible alternative to their existing power base in the UAR.

3. Arab–Israel Dispute

The current shrillness and bellicosity of Syria's stand against Israel is in part a function of the regime's internal weakness, although Syria has historicially taken an extreme position on Israel. The Soviet Union's support for the Arab position in this dispute does not appear to have changed significantly. Soviet propaganda is still generally directed against Israel's alleged role as an agent of Western imperialism rather than at its existence as a state. The Soviet Union will probably continue to support the Arabs with anti-Israel propaganda but will continue to attempt to limit Arab military action. At the same time, they will maintain correct, although not friendly, relations with Israel.

4. Arms Aid

There does not appear to be any likelihood that the Soviet Union would agree in the near future to any arms limitation schemes in the Near East. Major shipments of arms continue to arrive in the UAR. A new multi-million dollar contract has just been signed with Iraq covering the period up to 1970 which will include modern supersonic planes and rockets. This deal is expected to stir demands of the neighboring states for increased aid from Western sources. Although the Soviet Union has supported the idea of a nuclear free zone in the Middle East, their interpretation of such a zone would presumably cover all US and other Western forces and bases in the Eastern Mediterranean.

5. Yemen and the Arab South

Soviet arms aid to the UAR has contributed greatly to Nasir's ability to continue his intervention in the Yemen. The USSR has a sizeable investment in economic aid in the Yemen and can be expected to continue to support Nasirist influence as the best means to protect its own position there. At the same time, Soviet interests will be served by the British withdrawal from Aden and the possible supplanting of British by Egyptian influence in the area of the Red Sea. The Soviets will therefore probably attempt to prevent UAR supported attacks against Saudi Arabia or Aden, which might delay British withdrawal or, worse still, invite US involvement.

---

16.   Circular Telegram From the Department of State to Certain Posts[1]

Washington, October 28, 1966, 3:48 p.m.

74768. US-Arab Relations in the Near East.

1. As is generally case of any major development in Near East, collapse of phase of "Arab unity" built around summitry has not proven unmixed blessing to U.S. interests or position in area.

---

[1] Source: National Archives and Records Adminstration, RG 59, Central Files 1964–66, POL NEAR E–US. Secret; Limdis. Drafted by Bergus on October 26; cleared by Davies, and Country Director for Algeria, Libya, Morocco, Spanish Sahara, and Tunisia John F. Root; and approved by Hare. Sent to Cairo, Baghdad, Amman, Tel Aviv, Tripoli, Beyda, Jidda, Kuwait, Beirut, Algiers, Tunis, Damascus, Taiz, and Rabat.

2. Some of after-effects, e.g. reduction in Israel apprehensions, diminution of pressure on Jordan and Lebanon acquire Soviet arms, have been clearly advantageous. Prospect of united and effectively integrated Arab military confrontation with Israel has receded much further into future.

3. But in resulting disarray of Arab world and open resumption previous rivalries and intrigues there has arisen a welter of suspicion and unfounded charges against the United States. Moreover, some Arab states have taken actions against others which run counter to overall long-term U.S. (and Arab) interest in stability and peaceful development of area. Resulting increased intra-Arab tension has not yet threatened any U.S. vital interest in area. It has, however, produced less promising atmosphere for progress towards U.S. objectives.

4. Most difficult present case is that of U.S.-UAR relationship. For reasons primarily of UAR's making, status of U.S.-UAR relations at beginning of summer was such that we were unable continue food assistance. We have discussed situation frankly with UAR and expressed continuing readiness work for improvement relations to point whereby USG could resume some participation in UAR economic development. We think we have got this message across but at same time Cairo seems plagued by atmosphere of doubt and suspicion U.S. motives. Chorus we have heard from many UAR quarters recently generally consists of following elements:

a. Most explicit acknowledgement we have yet had that UAR regime, under pressures worsening economic situation and continued Yemen impasse, is in difficulties and concerned about its future. In this context there have been indications of concern at appeals of Islamic traditionalism to large numbers of Egyptians.

b. That Hussein and Faisal sensing possibility of overthrow Nasser regime are "up to something" in the Arab world. As examples Egyptians use alleged machinations in Yemen, "plot" against Syrian regime, Jordanian-Saudi support of Moslem Brotherhood elements within and outside of UAR, and of course, Faisal's efforts through Islamic solidarity movement "isolate and constrict" Egypt.

c. Some elements in Egypt seem to believe USG, particularly "CIA," actively engaged in joint planning and operations against UAR regime with Saudis and Jordanians. Other Egyptians, while professing believe our assurances of innocence, take line that USG with its vast resources knows all that is going on in Arab world. Thus USG, although it preaches its desire for stability and development in Arab world, is not using its very considerable influence with Hussein and Faisal to forestall their actions.

5. Simplest and most effective means dispelling UAR suspicions would probably be indication to GUAR that USG prepared give generous consideration its food needs. But USG not yet in position make decision one way or other on this point. Our present concern is that UAR in present atmosphere of doubt and suspicion will take actions

whose effect on public and legislative opinion in U.S. would be such as to reduce our options in U.S.–UAR relations for protracted period. This in turn could diminish what capabilities we have to exercise restraining influence on UAR and other "revolutionary" Arab states.

6. There are events in other parts of Arab world growing out of current intra-Arab tension which also trouble us. While current Syrian instability probably organic and generally unavoidable, strident statements of some Jordanians, including present PriMin, have seemed provocative. Indications that Saudis played role in precipitating current Leb bank crisis, for reasons of spite and against their own best interest in promoting free enterprise system in Arab world are measure of damage which can arise from current intra-Arab rifts.

7. Nor do we take particular comfort from prospect of increasing effort to rally area countries around Islamic banner. Long term implications for such non-Moslem groups in area as Israelis, Lebanese, Christian minorities, among others, are not pleasant. While there something to be said for Islam as bar to communism, there other good arguments to contrary. Certainly during pre-revolutionary period in Egypt when Moslem Brotherhood at peak its powers, this movement was implacably anti-Western and gave no impression that it understood or could cope with problems of economic and social development. Most of all, however, we think there has been trend towards secularization of Arab life, "separation of church and state" over last two or three decades. While it would be inappropriate for USG to praise or condemn efforts of individual Arab leaders to revivify political Islam, we believe it very much to our interest stay distinctly aloof from these efforts.

8. All of foregoing highlights present dilemma: How can USG, while retaining credible stance of neutrality in intra-Arab disputes, do what it can to prevent present quarrels from developing to point where there would be definite risks to our interests? How can we demonstrate that we play no favorites in Arab world and wish good relations with all against background of developing situation where it inevitable that at diverse times and in sundry places (currently Jordan and Saudi Arabia) there highly visible collaboration on programs in such important areas as budgetary support and military assistance, and where, as in Saudi Arabia, there natural close economic ties?

9. We have, of course, done what we could by way of high level conversations with UAR officials make clear our total lack of interest in UAR's internal affairs. We have supported Kuwait efforts for Yemen mediation and have urged all parties to Yemen dispute exercise restraint. We have pointed out to Arab leaders, both "traditional" and "revolutionary," unfortunate effect of inflammatory statements. We have deplored trends towards "polarization" in Near East.

10. What more can we usefully do? We would appreciate suggestions by addressees. Would authoritative public statement by high USG officials be of assistance? Statement could cite past public declarations of all Arab states of desire "practice tolerance and live together in peace with one another as good neighbors" and undertakings stabilize intra-Arab relations "on basis of respect for the independence and sovereignty of these States and to direct their efforts toward the common good of all the Arab countries. . . ." This language might be appropriate in that it taken from UNGA resolution 1237 (ES–III) of August 7, 1958.[2] Resolution was introduced by all Arab states, was drafted by them, and was passed without a dissenting vote.

11. Purpose of foregoing exercise would be lay appropriate foundation for appropriate diplomatic follow-up to effect that U.S. has broken free from mold that plagued Arab-West relations between two World Wars. U.S. shares aspirations of Near East peoples themselves for peace, independence, and economic development. We seek neither protectorates nor proteges in areas.

Katzenbach

---

[2] For text, see *American Foreign Policy: Current Documents, 1958*, pp. 1047–1048. The resolution was actually adopted unanimously by the UN General Assembly on August 21, 1958.

17. Information Memorandum From the Assistant Secretary of State for Near Eastern and South Asian Affairs (Hare) to Secretary of State Rusk[1]

Washington, November 15, 1966.

SUBJECT

US-Arab Relations in the Near East

[Here follows a summary of circular telegram 74768, Document 16.]

Twelve replies to our telegram have now been received. Several of them were too diffuse to be of much value. There were two posts in the area, Tripoli and Tunis, who seemed basically content with the situation as it now is. It would be difficult to say that any kind of consensus was reached by the other posts, but some of their findings are of interest.

1. It was generally felt that a mere public statement by a high U.S. official would not in itself be of much use.

2. There was considerable support for the idea of a visit to Near East and North African capitals by a high-ranking U.S. official. The Vice President, the Secretary, and the Under Secretary were put forward in this connection.

3. Four posts (Cairo, Baghdad, Beirut, and Amman) urged that PL 480 assistance to the UAR be resumed. Jidda said that it should not be resumed unless there were a quid pro quo (unspecified) from the UAR. Rabat spoke of the resumption of PL 480 assistance in terms of maintaining ties with the people (as opposed to the regime) of Egypt.

4. Three posts urged the halting or stringent restriction of future arms sales to the Near East.

5. There were also expressions of concern lest diminution of U.S. support for UNRWA rekindle Arab resentment at U.S. efforts to "liquidate" the Palestine problem.

In conclusion, it is interesting that a general feeling of malaise about the situation in the Near East was signalled by ten of our posts in Arab capital. This was before the Israeli attack on Jordan of November 13, 1966.

---

[1] Source: National Archives and Records Administration, RG 59, Central Files 1964–66, POL UAR–US. Secret. Drafted by Bergus. The initials "DR" on the memorandum indicate that Rusk saw it.

18.   **Paper Prepared in the Department of State**[1]

Washington, February 8, 1967.

UNITED STATES GOVERNMENT COMMITMENTS
IN THE NEAR EAST

Present Status

The U.S. Government is committed extensively to countries in the Near East, although not in formal treaty relationship with Israel or any Arab state. The principal landmark or reference point in this regard is President Kennedy's May 8, 1963 statement that "we support the security of both Israel and her neighbors. . . . We strongly oppose the use of force or the threat of force in the Near East. . . . In the event of aggression or preparation for aggression, whether direct or indirect, we would support appropriate measures in the United Nations, adopt other courses of action on our own to prevent or put a stop to such aggression . . . "[2] Subsequent reaffirmations have been made by President Johnson and[3] as recently as December 1966 by Vice President Humphrey.

It is clear from the background and circumstances of these affirmations that our commitment to the security of Israel, in particular, is unequivocal. We believe the intention of the U.S. Government to uphold Israel's continued existence is clearly known and respected by the governments and peoples of the Near East, no matter how much some of them may argue that it is unjust.

Vis-à-vis the Arab countries, the U.S. Government's security involvement is deepest in two instances: Saudi Arabia and Jordan. In Saudi Arabia a closeness of relations arising from a wholly American-owned oil industry has led us to give a special guarantee of territorial integrity. In essence, this commits us to come to Saudi assistance in event of what we regard as unprovoked attack.[4]

---

[1] Source: Department of State, NEA/ARP Files: Lot 69 D 350, POL 2a, Briefing Book Materials, Middle East, 1967, Meeting of NEA Advisers. Confidential. Prepared in the Office of Israel and Arab-Israel Affairs, Bureau of Near Eastern and South Asian Affairs. No date appears on the memorandum; the date used was the drafting date. This paper was one of ten staff studies prepared for a panel of outside academic advisers scheduled to meet with NEA officers for a Near East Policy Review, February 10–11.

[2] For Kennedy's statement, see *Public Papers of the Presidents of the United States: John F. Kennedy, 1963*, p. 373.

[3] See ibid.: *Lyndon B. Johnson, 1963–1964*, Book I, pp. 740–741 and ibid., *1966*, Book II, pp. 796–797.

[4] For a discussion of the nature of U.S. assurances to Saudi Arabia, see Document 287.

In Jordan, because it controls a piece of geography we have consistently considered of great importance to area stability, we have over the last decade committed one-half billion dollars of aid as a sort of insurance premium against an explosion. The apparent result of this vast sum of material and moral support we have given King Hussein's regime is that we find ourselves increasingly seeing the preservation of this regime as an end in itself, so much so that our commitment to keep it afloat is fast becoming regarded in the area as nearly comparable to our guarantee to Saudi Arabia.

Problem Area

The constantly threatening lack of Near East stability causes us to wonder if the United States is in fact over-committed, or wrongly committed, there. From the point of view of resources for the task, it is realistic to expect that a declining quantity of USG money and material resources will be made available by the Congress for this area over the next few years. Perhaps we should apply the scarce available resources more selectively than at present. From another point of view, we might question whether existing USG undertakings in the area have materially contributed to the little stability the region has witnessed in recent years. One might argue that the region would have been more stable without our involvement, since area states might have been more concerned at the possible consequences to themselves of their own acts. From yet another angle, it has become very difficult to say with any precision whether in a given set of circumstances affecting Israel, Saudi Arabia or Jordan one of these clients is provoking a third party into the very action from which it wants our protection. This grey area may become even harder to interpret as time goes on. Should we therefore recede from our present commitments?

Some Alternatives

We could recede on all fronts from our 1948–66 historical record of promises of support for the security of Near Eastern states. This might, at the outset, take the form of placing new stress on a pledge of support for the United Nations' peacekeeping efforts—both the existing mechanisms and any future UN involvement triggered by complaints of aggression.

Alternatively, we might simply drop, either in outright fashion or by gradually watering-down, our policy of support for one or more of the states with which we have special relations. This would of course raise a great hue and cry, and with respect to Israel would be virtually impossible. The logical outcome of this course would be for the USG to become the formal guarantor of Israeli security alone—a position favored by some elements of U.S. public opinion.

Another possibility would be to change the nature of our commitments from virtual guarantees of territorial integrity against *any* aggression to guarantees only against threats from *outside* the area.

Or we could consciously pick out one or more pieces of geography in the region and pledge our prestige to preserving the government(s) in control there. Such choice(s) would presumably be determined by a careful assessment of just where we should make a stand to retain the most important combination of United States interests.

Finally, we can continue along present policy lines, determining as best we can, case by case, what actions are needed either to shore up our prime clients or to prevent major adverse affects on our own national interests.

---

19.   Paper Prepared in the Department of State[1]

Washington, February 8, 1967.

NEAR EAST OIL: HOW IMPORTANT IS IT?

Current Assessment

The demand for Middle East petroleum will continue to increase for the next several years. The annual percentage rate of growth will gradually decline by 1970, however. *The essential aspect seems to be that we and our allies must continue to have reasonable access to area oil supplies at reasonable cost in the decade ahead.*

Simple statistics on Middle Eastern oil can only be defined as staggering. Some of them:

—The area contains $^2/_3$ of the Free World's oil reserves, and provides over $^1/_3$ of its current production.
—Production costs are roughly $^1/_{10}$ those in the U.S.
—The area supplies over half of Western Europe's oil.
—Over 85% of Japan's oil comes from the Persian Gulf.

---

[1] Source: Department of State, NEA/ARP Files: Lot 69 D 350, POL 2a, Briefing Book Materials, Middle East, 1967, Meeting of NEA Advisers. Confidential. Prepared in the Office of Saudi Arabia, Kuwait, Yemen, and Aden Affairs, Bureau of Near Eastern and South Asian Affairs. No date appears on the memorandum; the date used is the drafting date. This paper was one of ten staff studies prepared for a panel of outside academic advisers scheduled to meet with NEA officers for a Near East Policy Review, February 10–11.

—Area oil production has increased from 1.3 million barrels per day in 1948 to over 9.5 million b/d at present, for an annual growth rate of 12%.

The significance of the Middle East as a petroleum supplier was comprehended relatively slowly, since world demand for petroleum has increased more rapidly and to a higher level than was predicted. The area's productivity was also underestimated. Development of sources of energy other than petroleum—such as atomic energy—has proceeded more slowly than was expected, and development of sources of petroleum other than the Middle East has so far failed to diminish significantly the Middle East's primacy.

Nevertheless, the absolute dominance of the pattern of supply by the Middle East to Western Europe is decreasing, as newer oil sources are factored into markets by the producing companies. This is a trend favorable to European security, since the lessons of 1956 disruptions were not lost on Western Europe. Production in Libya, for example, in late 1966 reached the level of a major Persian Gulf producer and actually surpassed Iraq's output, owing to the cut-back in Iraqi production because of Syrian blocking of the pipelines. Algeria and Nigeria have also become major suppliers to Europe, and Nigeria has the potential to become a Middle East scale producer. Intensive exploration of the Northwest European–North Sea gas fields is being pressed forward. Soviet oil is being bought in increasing quantities by several European countries. On the other hand, the Middle East producing countries are exhibiting signs of becoming more responsible and even more conservative in their relations with petroleum operators so as not to interrupt the flow of royalties and taxes from their oil production. The blow of the Mossadegh Madness to the Iranian treasury in 1951–54 was not lost on the other producing states, nor is Iraq's current loss of $630,000 per day because of Syria's closing of IPC pipelines unnoticed by other area oil suppliers.

The USG's world-wide military commitments—including those in NATO, Viet-Nam, and general patrol operations by the Sixth and Seventh Fleets—require heavy reliance on Mid-East petroleum for both ourselves and our allies. No amount of effort could replace Arab-Persian oil in the Western European market within a reasonable length of time and for a reasonable cost. More than 60 per cent of our POL requirements in Viet-Nam are being met from the Persian Gulf. More than half of the Sixth and Seventh Fleet fuel supplies come from the area. Without Persian Gulf oil, production facilities of the US would be strained to the utmost to supply our military forces, and the cost would be upped about 150 per cent. (US oil reserves are being consumed rapidly. About one-fifth of our consumption is being imported now, and the percentage is increasing. Recovery of oil from shale and tar sands is technically feasible, but costs will be high and large investments will be required at a time when cheap petroleum could be brought from the Middle East in great quantities. Thus, the Persian Gulf area is a prolific potential future reserve for the US itself.)

Strategic significance of Mid-East oil aside, the financial aspects are of prime importance. US companies have invested $2.75 billion in the area, and from this investment $750 million in profits flows back to the US annually. About 93 per cent of the US investment in the Middle East is in the oil industry. In addition, US companies have enormous investments in downstream operations—tankers, terminals, refineries, bulk plants—that would have to be re-programmed, modified, or abandoned if access to Gulf oil were denied.

The Soviet view of Mid-East oil is difficult to assess as a whole. However, the commercial sales of Soviet oil, at costs in the West well below those charged East European states, suggest that the USSR expects to be competitive in the oil market place. It has been presumed that the Soviets would exploit difficulties that companies and host countries might encounter in mutual negotiations and operations, yet the evidence of significant Soviet activity in this connection is limited. The long-feared drive of the Russians for Mid-East oil is a restrained one if it is, indeed, an actual, sustained one. On balance, it appears that the oil producing states will continue for the foreseeable future to be greatly dependent on the West for marketing their oil. Nevertheless, we have attempted to inhibit the significant political penetration of the USSR into the Persian Gulf area.

Some Alternatives

1. Our continuing and mounting problems in the area may be leading us into situations that can be so costly in money and strategic risks that the USG and its allies should embark on virtually a *crash program to obtain fuel energy from other petroleum areas and from other sources of energy* (atomic power, coal, oil shale, tar sands). We could then loosen political relations with the Mid-East producers and permit US companies to coast along for the life of their concessions, meanwhile expanding their production elsewhere.

2. Perhaps a more feasible course would be to *strengthen our political ties with Iran and the Arab Middle East countries, play down our relations with Israel, and protect our fortunate access to the prolific oil resources of the area.* We would hope that the countries themselves would continue to grow more responsible, interdependent among themselves, and interdependent with the West—which is, after all, the market for Mid-East oil.

3. We could *focus on two or three of the most prolific producers and more friendly states—perhaps Saudi Arabia, Kuwait, and Iran*—and maintain minimum contacts with the other producers. Studies have shown that the West can stand loss of output from one or two major Mid-East producers but not three or four.

20.   Memorandum From Harold H. Saunders of the National Security Council Staff to the President's Special Assistant (Rostow)[1]

Washington, May 16, 1967.

SUBJECT

The President's Stake in the Middle East

I. I went to the Middle East[2] with this question: Why should the President care about the Middle East? I've been up and down US interests in the Middle East many times. But this time I set out to decide what President Johnson's interests are, given the goals that are closest to his heart. I came back with these thoughts:

A. He has *more than the usual stake in peace* for two quite personal reasons:

—Especially while we are engaged in Vietnam, we want to spare him the political—and the human—burden of having to commit American forces in the Middle East too.

—The "war of national liberation" as a technique has come to the Middle East—on Israel's borders and now in South Arabia. President Johnson in Vietnam has invested much of himself in demonstrating that we will not tolerate this brand of aggression. His friends in the Middle East are asking how he can stand against terrorist attackers in Vietnam and not in Israel or South Arabia? We must find a way to contain them or risk losing the respect the President has won for his courage in Vietnam.

B. He has a political need as well as a personal desire to maintain a *warm relationship with Israel.* His friends in Israel see Arab terrorism as the greatest threat to their security today.

C. In his effort to keep the dollar sound, he has a substantial *balance of payments interest in the Arab states.* The Middle East is the one part of Afro-Asia where we're solidly in the black. Our economists' estimate that the balance in our favor runs $400–500 million yearly. Against a worldwide deficit of $1.4 billion, that's significant.

D. He has a stake in *arms limitation.* Israel must maintain qualitative superiority. But beyond that, the President is deeply committed to *nuclear non-proliferation.* The main hurdle in the Middle East is Israel. Before signing an NPT, Israel may want assurance from the US and

---

[1] Source: Johnson Library, National Security File, Name File, Saunders Memos. Secret.

[2] On his trip to the Middle East, February 26–March 15, Saunders visited the United Arab Republic, Saudi Arabia, Bahrain, Aden, Jordan, and Israel. For his report on U.S.–UAR relations following his visit to Cairo, see Document 394 in *Foreign Relations, 1964–1968,* vol. XVIII.

USSR that major arms suppliers will keep the lid on the Arab arms inventory while the conventional balance is still in Israel's favor. In addition to his stake in the NPT, he is under increasing pressure on the Hill not to feed arms races and to reach an understanding with Moscow.

E. He has a stake in *economic development and social justice*. This will influence fewer US voters than the other issues, but it will influence how the world judges his Presidency. He has said that the Great Society is his foreign policy. We know how earnestly he means that. Many people around the world judge him a great President because he shows America's concern for them as individuals. In the Middle East, he can be proud of our role in the many constructive things going on there. But on the political front we are cast only on the side of the remaining monarchies—the side of "Zionism, imperialism and reaction." One issue in particular overrides all others—the failure of over a million Palestine refugees to win "recognition of their rights." In their eyes, the President has compromised his own creed of justice by bowing to "Zionist pressure" and failing to force Israel to meet its obligations.

II. Some of these interests are contradictory. The only way we have managed to protect them all at the same time is via a policy of friendship for all and refusing to choose sides. That policy has been remarkably successful when we consider the sharp animosities we've had to work around. But that *policy will be severely tested in 1967–68*. It is no longer certain that it—at least as we have balanced it in the recent past—is feasible or can serve the President's interests.

What hits the visitor to the Middle East hardest today are the deepening political cleavages. First, there is the widening gulf among the Arabs themselves, between the moderate (Saudi Arabia, Jordan, Lebanon) and the pro-Nasser states. Second, the Arab-Israeli issue is heating up again. Third, there are the states who are making a good job of development and those whose political systems still seem unable to cope. This year, the *pressures forcing us to choose sides*—to abandon our past policy—are greater than at any time in this decade. How the Johnson Administration responds will affect each of the President's interests.

Each Middle Eastern leadership group states the problem differently, but it all adds up to mounting pressure on us to choose sides:

A. In *Egypt*, Foreign Minister Riad told me bluntly, "You are working against us everywhere in the Middle East. You have chosen sides." No amount of logic or argument will break this strong web of suspicion among the political leaders. One is almost forced to agree with many of our Israeli and Arab friends that the only language Nasser understands is firmness backed by unmistakable military power and the willingness to apply it. Nowhere in the Arab world is there cooler calculation that now is not the time to take on Israel. But Nasser sees clearer sailing in South Arabia and may stop there only if met by force.

While this Egyptian suspicion makes Nasser all but impossible to work with, the visitor comes away convinced that nowhere else in the Middle East—save Israel—is there such a potential modern power to reckon with. If Egypt ever gets over revolutionary phobias and inferiority complexes, its 30 million people, its economic inheritance, its drive to lead, its pride of achievement and its military power make it unquestionably *the* Arab power. One could even go so far as to say that the UAR and Israel together or separately hold the key to the future of the Middle East. This is why I cannot believe it would serve the President's interests to break with Nasser.

B. In *Saudi Arabia*, King Faisal's main concerns are Nasser's foothold in Yemen and fear that he will expand this by moving into South Arabia when the British pull out. For Faisal, Nasser is the agent of Communism and is out to topple moderate regimes throughout the area. Our failure to oppose a Nasserist takeover in Aden would be in Faisal's eyes our failure to oppose the advance of Communism in the Middle East and would cast doubt on the reliability of our commitment to preserve Saudi integrity. Faisal backs our stand in Vietnam and could not understand our hesitation to oppose openly the beginnings of terrorism in Saudi Arabia. He feels no one can trust Nasser and that our policy of trying to build a bridge to him has completely failed.

C. In *Jordan*, King Hussein told me that the breach between Arab moderates and Nasser is complete. Hussein says this more in sorrow than in anger because he admits there was a time when he himself believed Jordan must back Nasser to the hilt. But Nasser has failed to live up to his responsibilities. Wasfi Tell, former PM and still a power behind the throne, told me bluntly, "It's time for you to choose sides." He believes that radicalism is on the wane and that Nasser will have to adopt more moderate policies or be replaced. In their eyes, Nasser's brand of revolution and "progressivism" is a dead wave of the past—not the wave of the future. These Jordanian leaders believe that our interests lie with the moderates. They feel we're wrong if we think we can still build a bridge to Nasser. Only by taking a firm stand against him can we halt the spread of subversion, buy time for the Arabs to learn to accept Israel (they were remarkably frank about this) and create an atmosphere conducive to development.

D. Among the *Palestinians* on Jordan's West Bank, there is no sign of resignation to loss of their homes in Israel. "Don't make the mistake of thinking that time will solve the refugee problem," I was told over and over. "We have been wronged. America must acknowledge that our rights have been violated. President Johnson is a just man; he will help." From among the bitterest of these refugees the Palestine Liberation Army recruits its ranks and the Fatah terrorist group sends its saboteurs into Israel. But even the prosperous ones who have jobs in the fast-growing Jordanian economy say they will never forget and will look to the President for justice.

E. *Syrian* officials are quite frank to say privately that their strategy is to make life in Israel so dangerous by their terrorism that new immigration will cease and people will even begin to leave Israel. At the same time, officially they disclaim responsibility for the terrorists. They hold us responsible for Israel's every move and believe— somewhat inconsistently—that the "Zionists exercise a veto over the President's policy."

F. In *Israel*, Prime Minister Eshkol told me of the agony he suffers— not to mention the political pressures—when terrorists' mines take Israeli lives. They believe that limited use of force may be the only way to stop terrorism. They can't see why we should disagree. Chief of Staff Rabin as well as top officials in the Foreign Office argue that the US and the USSR have drawn the de facto limits of Communist expansion in Europe, Northeast Asia, Latin America and now in Southeast Asia. The time has come, they say, to draw the line in the Middle East. The Soviets are mounting a new offensive and must be stopped in their tracks. They see South Arabia as the potential turning point.

Curiously, while they believe Nasser and the Soviets are working hand in hand in South Arabia, they admit that he has been the most restrained of the Arab leaders against them. They doubt we could buy him off from his main objectives today—which are largely directed against other Arabs—but no one took issue with our trying to maintain some kind of foot in the Cairo door.

III. *What this adds up to* is great pressure on us to join a confrontation with Nasser and prediction that the US will lose its stature in the area if we refuse and fail to stop him, the USSR and the liberation armies. Against this is the almost unanimous feeling of our people in the area that, prickly as Nasser is, we're better off talking than fighting and we're better off working in Cairo than slamming the door.

The problem, then, is to call a halt to aggression without open confrontation or appeasement. Our success—and our success in protecting all of the President's contradictory interest—will depend on *two separate sets of decisions* through the rest of this year: (1) How we deal with Nasser. (2) What we do in Aden.

The great temptation—greater even now than when I was in Cairo before the current mess in Yemen—is to conclude without our friends that Nasser is a lost cause and throw in the sponge on trying to deal with him. But the question to answer is whether the President's interests will be better served by an open showdown or by trying to find some basis for cooperation. We will be looking at this in greater detail in the next few weeks, decision-by-decision, but my own conclusion—even after extensive talks in Cairo, Saudi Arabia, Aden, Jordan, Israel, and London—is that we can't afford to give up on the UAR.

So in my book, *working out a scenario for putting our relations with Nasser back in perspective is the first item on our agenda.* Wheat is a dead issue for the moment now that Nasser has withdrawn his request, and we couldn't do much anyway in the wake of his recent speeches and humiliation of our people in Yemen. But there are other less conspicuous ways for us to be economically helpful. The main problem, however, is to break down the web of suspicion in Cairo that we are actively working to unseat Nasser's regime. In the end, this can only be done at the top political levels—and even then success isn't assured.

The *second problem is whether we stand by and allow a pro-Nasser element to take over in South Arabia and Aden as the British pull out.* Even the British in Aden and London, I found, are not optimistic about their ability to avoid chaos. This is one of the most emotion-charged issues in the Labour Party and Parliament, and the Wilson government is determined to pull out on schedule. However, it has shown new flexibility in the last few weeks, and the President may want to press Wilson to stick with it during their talk next month. Our NSC meeting on 24 May will deal with this problem in more detail.

Hal

21.   Editorial Note

Following the outbreak of the Six-Day War on June 5, 1967, all Arab states officially embargoed oil shipments bound for the United States, the United Kingdom, and West Germany. For documentation on the embargo, see *Foreign Relations, 1964–1968,* volume XXXIV, Documents 228ff. For documentation relating to the Six-Day War, see *Foreign Relations, 1964-1968,* volume XIX.

22.   Report Prepared by the Special State–Defense Study Group[1]

Washington, undated.

NEAR EAST, NORTH AFRICA AND THE HORN OF AFRICA:
A RECOMMENDED AMERICAN STRATEGY

Introduction

In late March 1967, the Special State–Defense Study Group under-took a study to develop perspectives on how best the United States could promote its long term national interests in the region encompassing the Near East, North Africa and the Horn of Africa.[2] The study group operated under the auspices of a Senior Policy Group consisting of the Deputy Secretary of Defense; the Director of Central Intelligence; the Chairman, Joint Chiefs of Staff and the Deputy Under Secretary of State for Political Affairs. The content of this report represents the views of the study group and not necessarily those of the Senior Policy Group. Participating members of the study group were:

> Ambassador Julius C. Holmes, Study Director
> Brigadier General Stephen W. Henry, USAF, Deputy Study Director
> Raymond W. Alexander, Captain, USN, Chief of Staff
> [name not declassified] Central Intelligence Agency
> Robert J. Davenport, Colonel, USA
> William H. Fielder, Major, USA
> Frank A. Kierman, Central Intelligence Agency
> Raymond A. Komorowski, Captain, USN
> Dr. William H. Lewis, Department of State
> Edward F. Miller, Department of Interior
> George C. Moore, Department of State
> Willard A. Nichols, Colonel USAF
> Frank G. Siscoe, Department of State

---

[1] Source: Washington National Records Center, RG 330, OSD Files: FRC 72 A 2468, Middle East 319.2, 17 July 67. Secret. A stamped notation on the report indicates it was received in the Office of the Secretary of Defense on July 17 at 12:49 p.m. Attached to the memorandum is a July 17 transmittal memorandum from Ambassador Holmes to the Deputy Secretary of Defense, the Director of Central Intelligence, the Chairman of the Joint Chiefs of Staff, and the Deputy Under Secretary of State for Political Affairs explaining that the report consists of an examination of U.S. national interests and develops a series of interlocking strategies and recommended policy initiatives which, if undertaken, should help to relieve many of the existing U.S. difficulties in the Middle East. Holmes noted that, taken together, these strategies and policy initiatives could serve as a sound doctrinal foundation for U.S. actions.

[2] For purposes of this study regional groupings are defined as: *Near East*—United Arab Republic, Syria, Lebanon, Israel, Jordan, Iraq, Iran, Kuwait, Saudi Arabia, Yemen, the Persian Gulf States, Muscat and Oman, and the South Arabian States. *North Africa*—Morocco, Algeria, Tunisia and Libya. *Horn of Africa*—Sudan, Ethiopia, French Somaliland, and Somalia. *Middle East*—The area encompassing all of the above. (See Map, p. iv) [Footnote in the source text; the map is not reproduced.]

Joseph J. Wagner, Department of State
William B. Westfall, Colonel, USAF

As originally conceived, the study was to consist of an analysis in depth of U.S. interests and policy objectives as they interact with the interests of other powers and with the evolution of forces and trends within the area. The purpose was to provide policy makers with doctrinal guidance that would be relevant to U.S. policy toward the area for the period 1967–1972.

The Middle East crisis of May 1967, culminating in Arab-Israeli hostilities on 5 June, so profoundly affected the regional situation as to cause a reconsideration of the continuing validity of the original study concept. It was determined that certain primal elements within the study area would continue to dictate the broad pattern of events and that a regional study covering the longer term would still be of value. On that basis, the study group was directed to continue, integrating into its efforts as much of the post-hostilities situation as could be discerned. The scope of the study effort was foreshortened and the focus shifted toward the development of a U.S. strategy for the five year period. The immediate problems of a post-war settlement are not addressed except as necessary to develop a longer range perspective.

It is recognized that resumption of large-scale Arab vs. Israeli hostilities would once again change drastically the factors on which this study is based, although as previously suggested, the significance of the residual factors is apt to remain high. The study group has proceeded on the assumption that such a war will not again occur within the five year period. Evidence is far from conclusive at this early stage and the possibility of Soviet cooperation in achieving a basic settlement of area problems appears remote, but there are elements in the situation which support this assumption. The study group believes that the general policy and specific initiatives recommended in the study would remain valid even in the event of renewed hostilities. Furthermore, they should help to delay or possibly prevent large-scale fighting.

Within this framework, the study offers an appraisal of the basic forces and problems of the Near East, North Africa and Horn of Africa and their impact on U.S. national interests. It proposes long term U.S. policy objectives, outlines a strategy for the U.S. over the next five years and recommends a series of policy initiatives to promote attainment of the objectives.

Abstract

At mid-summer 1967 the Arab-Israel problem is at center stage in the triangle of counties covered by this study. However, narrow attention to the recent war and its aftermath can cloud evaluation of how forces in the area interact with U.S. and USSR global interests. It is abundantly clear that the USSR has a firm policy to achieve dominant influence in the eastern and southern Mediterranean basin. It is equally clear that the Arabs are as emotionally committed to destruction of Israel as were their ancestors to elimination of the Christian Kingdom of Jerusalem. The Soviets use Arab hatred of Israel to advance their interests and the Arabs use the Soviet presence and assistance to further their objective. The result is a situation which is damaging and dangerous for United States interests. These interests relate to the security and orientation of Western Europe which are of primary importance for the United States. In recent years the USSR has masked its direct threat to Europe by proclaiming a desire for détente but has continued that threat indirectly by its thrust into the Mediterranean. The Soviet Union has turned the area into a field of competition beyond which lie the ultimate targets of Europe and the worldwide position of the United States.

U.S. National Interests

U.S. interests in the study area are:

—to prevent the Soviet Union or other hostile states from securing a predominant position.

—to establish a basic compatibility between the West and the forces of political, social and economic modernization in the region and to prevent their falling under Soviet control.

—to maintain the means of strategic access, particularly through the Mediterranean, that are required if Western strength is to be brought to bear in the Northern Tier of Greece, Turkey and Iran; and to hinder Soviet access to the region by strengthening the Northern Tier countries themselves.

—to continue the use of U.S. military operational and strategic intelligence facilities insofar as they are needed to fulfill area and global needs. However, conditions could occur in which the presence of these facilities might imperil the political existence of host governments. In such cases, our use of the facilities will become less important than continuation of moderate Western-oriented regimes.

—to preserve free world access to area oil supplies on acceptable terms. Although the U.S. is not itself dependent on this oil for its economic viability, Western Europe and Japan would face sharp economic dislocation, at least in the near term, if Middle Eastern oil were cut off.

—to protect U.S. private investments and insure reasonable access to markets for U.S. commerce, both of which equate primarily to oil activities. In combination, net return from oil in the Arab countries and other trade with them contributes about one billion dollars annually toward the U.S. balance of payments. Additionally, U.S. interests are involved in the critical dependence of the U.K.'s world financial position on oil revenues and Britain's ability to purchase its petroleum needs for sterling.

—to preserve the independence of Israel, as dictated by the broad sentiments of the American people.

Soviet Activities

In the study area, the Soviet Union pursues its indirect attack on Europe by using all means to eliminate Western, mainly U.S., influence; to disrupt NATO, CENTO and bilateral Western security ties in the area; and to obtain comparable positions of political, military and economic influence for itself. Its few direct material interests in the region are subordinate to these broad strategic goals. It is principally limited by the concern that local conflicts do not lead to direct U.S.-USSR hostilities and that Communist China does not gain from these situations. It profits from and fosters friction between Western-oriented and other states. It desires the continuation of Arab hostility to Israel since, by siding with the Arabs, it can count on long-term gains. It supports the radical Arab states, primarily the UAR, Algeria and Syria. At the same time it is opportunistic, ready to develop closer relations with any area state regardless of its political orientation and willing to take advantage of Western failures to give requested assistance. This is particularly true in the supply of arms, which the USSR does liberally, with great flexibility and success. It shows no concern for the destabilizing effects of weapons shipments and no interest in formal arms control arrangements. A change in this pattern of Soviet activity is not to be expected during the five-year period of this study.

Certain trends in the area favor these Soviet tactics. The USSR is a relative newcomer to the region, not hampered by previous ties. It benefits from popular opposition to real or fancied Western "imperialism." It is favored by the continued domestic political flux in much of the study area and the anti-Westernism of increasingly more vocal and dissatisfied social elements.

Favorable Factors

There are also many factors which work in favor of the U.S. As the USSR becomes more firmly tied to certain policies, regimes and leaders, it will lose flexibility of response. It will face growing problems of conflicting interests among countries which it supports. Most importantly, its attempts to dominate the region will conflict increasingly with popular aspirations of independence, nationalism and Arabism. The U.S. and the West have solidly based ties of friendship and mutual interest with many of the area countries, particularly the Northern Tier. There is a reservoir of strength in the large numbers of persons throughout the area who have been trained in Western concepts. There are ties with the West of mutual economic interest, embodied in private commercial and oil enterprises and in the availability of vast amounts of capital and expertise for development.

Strategy for the United States

The following strategy for the U.S. is designed to blunt the Soviet drive and to capitalize on those forces which favor our interests. Central to this strategy is the conviction that any diminution of Soviet influence, even if initially favorable only to Western European nations, will ultimately benefit the U.S. The interlocking principles of this strategy are:

—*Safeguard the southern flank of Europe through diversification of Western involvement.* Since World War II, the U.S. has often had to deal with problems in the study area virtually unaided and at considerable cost. There are major Western European interests remaining in the region; but our European allies have been unwilling fully to recognize this and to assume their share of the burden. Europe is a natural source of influence in the region. Consequently, the U.S. should press for greater unilateral and multilateral involvement of Western Europe, commensurate with its interests. France should play a stronger role, particularly in North Africa. DeGaulle's present position is not promising for the type of coordinated activity foreseen. However, the study group believes that French national interests will increasingly impel it in this direction, even though it may only be after DeGaulle that France again fully recognizes the extent to which its own interests and those of the U.S. are commingled both in Europe and the study area. The greater involvement of other powers in the region will also lessen the present tendency toward unstable bipolarization and a direct U.S.-USSR confrontation.

—*Strengthen the blocking power of the Northern Tier of Greece, Turkey and Iran.* These states are of priority interest to the Soviets because of their Western security orientation and their geographic position. A secure Mediterranean remains the vital link between these countries and the Western alliance. There are serious doubts in the minds of Turkish, Iranian and Greek leaders concerning the likely responsiveness of the U.S. and most of the NATO community to Soviet challenges. Therefore the highest importance must be placed on strengthening U.S. and European ties with the Northern Tier. U.S. support for Turkey and Iran should emphasize more competitive U.S. terms for both economic and military assistance to counter Soviet efforts. Turkey and Iran also should be encouraged to play more influential roles in neighboring Arab states.

—*Lessen the public U.S. role in Arab-Israeli relations.* U.S. interest in the security of Israel is at variance with other U.S. interests in the Near

East, where the drawbacks of our association with Israel outweigh any advantages it could bring us. Nonetheless, the sentiment of the American people and government is such that in time of crisis the U.S. will support Israel. The U.S. should adopt a less obvious and direct role in Arab-Israel affairs to ease the impact on daily U.S.-Arab relations and reduce the extent to which the USSR profits. To avoid untenable positions, we should not in the future give broad assurances of concern for the territorial integrity and political independence of all area states.

—*Seek to rebuild U.S. relations with the Arab states, concentrating on the moderates.* Reality compels us to build on those positions of strength we now have in states which are in various degrees fearful of and opposed to Egyptian imperialism. We will have to be more forthcoming materially and politically than in the past, but should avoid additional security assurances which harness us to particular leaders. Although we will be accused of siding with conservative monarchs, the distinction between so-called "revolutionary" and "evolutionary" routes to modernization is largely theoretical and need not disturb us. We must, however, press our friends toward modernization and political reform as being in their own interest. Prospects for the early establishment of harmonious U.S.-UAR relations are exceedingly slim. The U.S. cannot accept Egyptian efforts to resolve the Palestine question through force, eliminate Western presence or influence in the Middle East, or topple moderate Arab leaders. The foundations for long term U.S.-UAR cooperation can be laid only when Cairo signifies its willingness to develop communities of interest based on mutual trust and respect. Meanwhile, Western European nations should be encouraged to exercise whatever means they can to maintain the Western position in the UAR, and the U.S. should endeavor to keep the door open for development of mutual interests whenever this can be done with dignity. Comparable difficulties exist with Algeria. For the next few years, the principal expression of U.S. concern for Egypt and Algeria may have to emanate from private institutions.

—*Center primary U.S. interest in the Horn of Africa on Ethiopia.* Our overriding concern has been the retention of the Kagnew Station facility. We have, however, developed more lasting assets among the modern element—particularly the military—which will constitute the important power center in the post-Selassie period. We should anticipate future developments by the gradual removal from Kagnew of activities that can be carried on elsewhere and plan for eventual total relocation when possible or necessary. Although withdrawal from Kagnew will reduce Ethiopian leverage for obtaining arms from us, we should continue to meet reasonable requests for military assistance. We should couple this assistance with pressure for Ethiopian armed forces reorganization as well as social and economic reforms. Somalia and the Sudan are of secondary importance. We should try to maintain some position of influence in both countries to protect our regional interest in Ethiopia. For the same reason, we should encourage the French to remain in French Somaliland or, upon decolonization, to maintain a significant base and provide a territorial guarantee.

—*Seek an improved U.S. military ability to operate in the area, consistent with political realities.* The ability of the U.S. to support its interest or commitments in the area with military power involves complex political problems ranging from overflight and access rights to over-identification of U.S. power with specific nations in the region. Consideration of the possible employment of U.S. military forces has been conditioned by so many interacting and conflicting political factors that the credibility of U.S. commitments and extent of U.S. will to use military means are suspect by both friends and potential foes. To meet these difficulties in the Red Sea–Indian Ocean–Persian Gulf region, we should establish an "on call" military capability and regularly exercise it into the area. Politically secure bases in the British Indian Ocean Territories and alternate air access routes should be sought. To avoid U.S. over-commitment, planning for protection of U.S. and Western European interests should be multinational. In those area countries where we have a permanent military presence, we should strive for a low visibility to minimize problems for host governments.

—*Supply conventional arms pragmatically and flexibly to promote U.S. national interests, tempered by certain restraining guidelines.* The supply and acquisition of arms are functions of the political context in which they occur. They are reflections of political events rather than primary causes of tension. Limitation efforts have little chance of success unless potential suppliers believe they would enhance their interests. Furthermore, states tend to measure the degree of their supporters' concern by their willingness to fulfill requests for arms. The USSR has continuously used the provision of weapons as the chief tool for promoting its political advantage in the area and is expected to continue to do so. It has no desire to enter limitation agreements. Since this is the case, we cannot unilaterally renounce the supply of arms as a tool for promotion of our interests. We desire certain states to be able to defend themselves. Additionally, furnishing weapons is a partial quid pro quo for our use of needed special facilities. For these additional reasons we should continue to supply arms on a pragmatic and flexible basis. Gradual increases in arms levels are to be expected until the evolution of events shows the USSR that its gains through an open arms policy are ephemeral. Although this is not apt to occur in the next five years, we should be alert for this eventuality and seize appropriate opportunities to probe Soviet receptivity to limitation agreements; should generally not supply any party to a dispute with a more sophisticated capability than is available to the other side; should where possible divert arms requests to other Western suppliers; and should seek a coordinated position among all Western suppliers.

—*Dissuade Israel and the Arabs from acquisition of nuclear weapons and strategic missiles and press for acceptance of international safeguards.* The Arabs have no discernible prospects for developing nuclear weapons. They are not likely to receive meaningful assistance in this field from the USSR nor to jeopardize the further receipt of Soviet economic aid by accepting such help from Communist China so long as Israel does not have a nuclear capability. Israel, on the other hand, has the ability on its own to develop nuclear weapons in the relatively near future. Similarly, while the Arabs are not apt soon to obtain operational strategic missiles, Israel may receive such missiles under a contract with the French in the next two years. Forestalling Israeli acquisition of either nuclear weapons or missiles is of critical importance for area stability. Since Israel may develop the nuclear option for fear that its qualitative superiority in conventional arms will ultimately vanish, U.S. strategy should be composed ideally of two interlocking elements: the use of all possible means of pressure to induce Israel to accept suitable international safeguards on its nuclear activities and to delay indefinitely receipt of missiles; and, if needed as a bargaining tactic, the formal but secret guarantee by the U.S. to maintain Israel's qualitative superiority in conventional arms, from western European sources if possible, otherwise from the U.S.

—*Apply new techniques in the technical assistance field and encourage regional economic development.* The drive for modernization is a fundamental phenomenon in the region. However, most study area states have expanding economic development needs which severely tax their modest capabilities in the public service, planning, financial and marketing fields. Their problems are compounded by multiplying populations and, for most, insufficient capital. It is important to the U.S. that the Soviet Union not be the uncontested supplier of these needs. The declining level of U.S. funds available for foreign development assistance limits the financial burden we can assume. However, there are specific inexpensive techniques which should be adopted for providing U.S. technical assistance and for assuring for the U.S. a role in modernization efforts. Although local political considerations frequently outweigh rational economic arguments for regional cooperative efforts, we should also seek to develop plans and projects that promise benefits on a regional basis, particularly those that spring from application of modern technological concepts.

Policy Initiatives

This study recommends thirty-seven specific policy initiatives for implementation of the proposed strategy. They vary in difficulty of application. However, it is envisaged that the full gamut of resources available to the United States would be used as appropriate to develop these initiatives, including bilateral and multilateral governmental discussions; political action programs; USIA activities; facilities of the U.N., IMF, IBRD and other public international agencies; and encouragement of the efforts of private organizations. These policy initiatives are, in summary:

—*Mediterranean Region:* initiate discussions to focus the attention of Western European nations, particularly France, on their own security interests and the need to take greater responsibility; urge them to strengthen ties with radical states where the U.S. has little influence; promote combined NATO military planning for contingencies in the study area; create a small permanent NATO Mediterranean naval force.

—*Northern Tier:* designate Turkey and Iran as countries for concentrated U.S. military and economic support; provide comparable aid to Greece; provide additional incentives for U.S. private investment and trade in Turkey and Iran; press the NATO countries to share in providing military assistance to Turkey; conduct low-level NATO naval exercises off the Turkish Black Sea littoral; preempt further Soviet arms sales to Iran; encourage greater Turkish and Iranian roles in neighboring Arab states.

—*North Africa:* urge greater Western European, particularly French, involvement in economic development; press France to give greater military assistance to Algeria, reinstitute its military aid programs in Morocco and Tunisia, and play an active role in settling border disputes between Algeria and its neighbors.

—*Eastern Arab states and Israel:* reduce U.S. prominence in Arab-Israel affairs, avoiding public unilateral initiatives while striving to perform an indirect conciliatory role; concentrate on support for multilateral solutions to the refugee problem; avoid any further broad assurances for the territorial integrity and political independence of all area states; insure that Israeli qualitative conventional arms superiority over potential Arab opponents is maintained; seek Israeli acceptance of international supervision of its nuclear activities, secretly guaranteeing its conventional arms superiority as a bargaining tactic if all other pressure fails; strengthen U.S. support of the conservative states; maintain a reserved official posture toward radical states, working through private U.S. institutions to cultivate mutual interests in non-controversial fields; assist the British to remain in the Persian Gulf and encourage Saudi Arabia to assume greater responsibility there; seek normal diplomatic relations with whatever regime arises in South Arabia and take no initiatives with respect to Yemen.

—*Horn of Africa:* begin gradual reduction of U.S. presence at Kagnew Station; promise needed military assistance to Ethiopia, while pressing for the reorganization of the armed forces and social and economic reforms; in Somalia, continue a low level of development activities and police training; encourage France to remain in French Somaliland and to link ultimate departure to retention of a French base and security guarantee for the new state.

—*General Military Actions:* create a modest multinational Indian Ocean naval force; establish an "on call" military capability, with forces ranging from the U.S. component of the multinational naval force to elements of the strategic reserve, supported by the C5A aircraft/Fast Deployment Logistic ship mix; regularly exercise "on call" forces into the Red Sea–Indian Ocean–Persian Gulf region; establish U.S.-U.K. facilities at Aldabra and Diego Garcia at an early date; plan alternate air access routes to the Near East; develop contingency alternatives for Kagnew Station and Wheelus AFB.

—*Technical Assistance:* supply some AID financing for broadened activities of U.S. management firms; assign *Technology Advisers* to U.S. Embassies where we no longer have AID programs; subsidize salaries to facilitate employment by area governments of U.S. technicians and advisers; detail U.S. government experts to governments in the study area; encourage regional cooperation for application of new technological concepts for development.

[Here follows the body of the report in 5 chapters constituting the remainder of Volume I and Volume II, consisting of 6 annexes.]

---

23. Memorandum From Harold H. Saunders of the National Security Council Staff to the President's Special Assistant (Rostow)[1]

Washington, August 9, 1967.

SUBJECT

The World Bank's Middle East Planning

To supplement my earlier memo on USG water planning,[2] here is a clearer picture of what the World Bank is doing as a result of Mac Bundy's request.

---

[1] Source: Johnson Library, National Security File, Saunders Files, Middle East Water. Confidential.
[2] Not printed.

As background, it's useful to know that the Bank decided back in February to create a new Middle East and North Africa Department. Heretofore, the Middle East had been tacked on either to South Asia or to Europe. The Bank decided that if it were to give full attention to the Middle East's own regional prospects, it would have to get the area off by itself. Fortuitously, this department began operation on June 1st. Mac's approach came just at a time when they were beginning basic studies for their own purposes. To insure the most comprehensive planning possible, they've set up a special task force within the new department to concentrate on planning in the area from the Suez Canal through Iraq.

They have made water their first priority with primary concentration on the Jordan Valley and secondary focus on the Sinai and Mesopotamia. They also hope to have preliminary views by mid-September on the role which desalting might play. Beyond their work on water, they will also be looking at prospects for industrialization, tourism, and natural resource exploitation.

We've made our data available to the Bank, and it will probably turn to other governments later for similar support.

Comment: While these studies will proceed at the usual measured Bank pace, Michael Lejeune, who heads this department, does appreciate their potential relationship to political settlement. My own feeling on this count is that what we really need, if politics requires, is enough staff work so that we could mention some of these plans in a speech and be certain that we were not completely off base. I don't feel that completed staff work is essential for this purpose. In any case, we probably can't expect the staffers to come up with finished plans in the political vacuum that exists today.

On a related front, Dave Bell is in touch with the Bank to avoid overlap, and Ford is just getting its thoughts in order for a couple of projects to be done by Brookings and by Rand. I do not have the details on these yet.[3]

Hal

---

[3] A handwritten notation on the memorandum reads: "HS—You are correct. Concentrate on that. WR"

24.   Memorandum for the Record[1]

Washington, August 16, 1967.

SUBJECT

    Near East-South Asia IRG Meeting
    Wednesday, 16 August 1967
    Discussion of the Holmes Study

1. There was really no discussion of the Holmes Study[2] as such; several central related issues were raised and debated for almost two hours.

2. Stuart Rockwell, the action officer on the IRG/NEA effort which parallels the Holmes Study, reported that a group centered in EUR and INR (Tom Hughes) thought the Soviet threat was overdrawn and the need for action less urgent than described in the Study.

3. Harold Saunders (White House) observed that the policy initiatives are the same tired old programs with which Congress is disenchanted. Additionally, he posed the following questions:

a. Is the Middle East–North Africa an area of real significance to the United States?

b. Even if the Soviet threat to the Middle East–North Africa is as described, would Soviet domination of this area really threaten our interests in Europe?

c. Is it useful to consider policy initiatives that obviously are unsupported by Congress and are outside of our available resources and capabilities?

4. Assistant Secretary Battle held firmly to the view that the Holmes Study Group properly did not include the U.S. domestic political climate and the availability of resources in their consideration. At the same time, he said, it would be unrealistic to proceed very far with the Holmes proposals without obtaining broad policy guidance from the President on the proposed strategy. The alternative to the Holmes proposal, he thought, was a policy of disengagement and isolationism.

5. I briefly traced the history of the debate over the past decade on Soviet intentions and capabilities in the Middle East and noted the relevance of NIE 10–2/65 and more recent estimates on the Mediterranean, the Horn of Africa and the Near East.

---

[1] Source: Central Intelligence Agency, DDO/NE (Critchfield) Files: Job 80–00205A, Box 5, IRG/NEA Working File, Near East, North Africa & Horn of Africa. Secret.

[2] Document 22.

6. Saunders' persistent effort to dismiss the Holmes policy initiatives as "old, tired and ineffectual measures" was vigorously met by State and Defense with the assertion that a thorough and responsible review had simply reaffirmed the efficacy of some of the old and tested instruments. Saunders was supported by Battle on the point that our existing arms sales and military aid policies were in serious trouble; that here a new approach was needed. Battle proposed that the IRG/NEA place this problem on its agenda for an early meeting.

7. Finally, there was much discussion of Western European interests in the Mediterranean and the Middle East. Saunders argued that if the Soviet activities in the area were, as alleged, a threat to Europe, the Europeans had demonstrated remarkably little interest; thus, either the Europeans or the Study Group members were wrong. The dominant view expressed was that the U.S. relationship with most Western European nations in Africa and the Middle East had been partly competitive and that the role of the UK and U.S. as police of the Middle East and defenders of Western interests against Soviet aggression had long been taken for granted by Western Europe. I argued that the U.S. had hardly paid lip service to any policy of encouraging the Western Europeans to play a greater role in the area; in isolated instances when the United States Government had gotten into trouble, it had shown an interest, ad hoc, in increasing the consultation and cooperation with specific European countries on the problem at hand. There was full agreement that, regardless of the cause, Europe appears reluctant to play a military-political role in the Middle East.

James H. Critchfield[3]
Chief, Near East and
South Asia Division

---

[3] Printed from a copy that indicates Critchfield signed the original.

25.   Record of Meeting[1]

Washington, September 14, 1967.

SENIOR INTERDEPARTMENTAL GROUP

Record of Discussion and Agreement of 21st Meeting
of September 14, 1967

PRESENT

Under Secretary of State, Chairman
Deputy Secretary of Defense
Gen. Brown, for the Chairman, JCS
The Director of Central Intelligence
Director, United States Information Agency
Administrator, Agency for International Development
Under Secretary of the Treasury
Counselor of the Department of State
Staff Director

Mr. Battle—NEA
Ambassador Holmes
Gen. McDonald
Gen. Orwat, JCS
Mr. Hoopes, ISA

[Here follows discussion of administrative matters.]

C. Holmes' Study

Chairman thanked Ambassador Holmes and his group for work they have done in preparing this useful input into general USG consideration of policies and actions in Middle East over coming years. He asked that this discussion concentrate on Soviet threat aspect and Ambassador Holmes' projected consultation in NAC. Chairman mentioned that instructions to Ambassador Holmes for his NAC consultation were circulated to SIG members for information and that State would clear these in normal course. IRG/EUR will undertake to coordinate the "sanitized" version of Holmes' Report which would be authorized for circulation to other NATO partners.

Ambassador Holmes presented his report and rather than repeating contents of report, concentrated on answering comments and criticisms he had received. He emphasized that the report had started out in March to estimate the situation in the area and particularly Soviet

---

[1] Source: Central Intelligence Agency, DDO/NE (Critchfield) Files: Job 80–00205A, Box 6, Soviet Presence in ME; Events Surrounding 1967 ME War. Secret. Drafted by Staff Director Arthur A. Hartman on September 18.

activity but that the emphasis of the report had changed after the outbreak of hostilities in June. He wanted to stress that the report had not intended to conclude that the sole or main aim of Soviet policy was to out-flank NATO. Rather, it was the intention of the drafters to indicate that Soviet activity in the Middle East was an expression of historic Soviet policy—an attempt to break out to warm water ports. He recalled that this had been Soviet aim at Potsdam and in later confrontations. He said that there had been Soviet gains since 1955 when the first Czech arms deal was announced, mentioning latest evidence in shipment of 400 tanks and 120 aircraft to Algeria. The report, he said, makes no claim to correlate the decline in Western influence with the increase in Soviet activity. They see no Soviet blue-print for what has happened in the area, but rather the Soviet Union has set out to move in where it could, and it has had some successes. He said that while the study may have over-emphasized Soviet ability to achieve dominance, they had pointed out certain blocks to Soviet activity in the form of radical nationalism and moderate leadership. He felt that they could not deal with all aspects of the problem and suggested that more work could usefully be done on trends in the area.

He ended his presentation by saying he felt it was important for US to take whatever actions necessary to blunt Soviet penetration and that it is prudent to regard the threat as of maximum potential in deciding what actions might be taken. He hoped that out of consideration of this report and further activity would come agreement on a set of objectives—a strategy (quite separate from any initiatives) that would be a guide and doctrine, particularly for our overseas posts.

Various members of the SIG made the following suggestions and comments, as of use to Ambassador Holmes in his consultations in NATO and as guidelines for future study within the Government:

1. Without appearing to over-emphasize likelihood US might in calm way suggest that NATO military authorities take a look at the implication for NATO of possibility Soviets might at some future date put forces in study area. Thought was expressed that Soviets might have come close to this in Syria in June.

2. In attempting to convince Europeans of importance Soviet activity, analysis should be more along lines Ambassador Holmes' oral presentation to SIG, in sense that it recognizes this is not just Soviet-Western clash in area, but that indigenous political forces play major role. In fact, these forces call in Soviets and encourage East-West competition as way of establishing their own independence. Our emphasis should be more on supporting the moderate, independent forces, rather than just obtaining influence.

3. We should examine the role of propaganda in recent Middle East Crisis and consider further what we and NATO countries can do in

future to improve and coordinate our propaganda. (USIA has recently prepared a report on this which might be useful to Ambassador Holmes and Ambassador Cleveland.)

4. Although Holmes' Report indicates it unlikely Soviets will want bases in area, fact is Soviets have had operational access to facilities in area and intelligence community might wish to evaluate this access as a factual input into NATO study. Also use of Soviet instructors.

5. We also might prepare as much information as possible on the Soviet role in triggering recent events for discussion with our NATO allies.

In addition, SIG members agreed study should continue on various gaps noted in the report and on the initiatives suggested. The Chairman directed the IRG/NEA in coordination with IRG/AF, to prepare an analysis on the trends in the area which would give a better view of what obstacles there might be to Soviet action in terms of indigenous activity by radical nationalists or moderates. (This report should be completed by November 1 and a SIG meeting scheduled to discuss it.) He also directed the IRG/NEA and IRG/AF to canvass immediate actions which we might be able to initiate in the study area even with present limited resources. (This should be completed by November 1.)

Three other actions were requested:

1. A policy should be developed by IRG/NEA in cooperation with IRG/AF which provides guidance for our future arms transfers to the area and puts in some framework the recent requests for arms shipments and our proposed responses. (This should be completed by October 15.)

2. We should have a better assessment of our oil interests by the IRG/NEA in cooperation with the IRG/AF and whether or not the threat to these interests can be minimized. (This should be completed by November 15.)

3. We ought to have a better study of Soviet capabilities (political, military and economic) by the intelligence community—including the amount of resources the Soviet Union might be likely to devote to the area. This should be compared with the on-going costs in external resources needed by such major countries in the area as the UAR and Algeria. (This should be done by October 1.)

It was agreed that there should be further discussions in the SIG on these subjects and that sometime in the near future it might be useful to schedule an NSC meeting or meetings for the purpose of airing these issues.

I will send separate individual action memos based on the above.

AA Hartman
Staff Director

26.   Paper Prepared in the Department of State[1]

Washington, December 27, 1967.

WESTERN INTERESTS IN ARAB OIL

Summary

During the June 1967 Middle East crisis certain Arab countries attempted to use their oil to retaliate against the U.S., U.K., and West Germany, which were believed to be unfriendly to Arab aspirations and partial to Israel. As a result, partial and total embargoes on oil exports were imposed with the objective of exerting political and economic pressures on the Western countries. These actions, which initially caused a dislocation in sources of oil supply and a sharp rise in prices, were regarded with concern by Western governments. Although the Arab governments later decided to reinstitute exports to Western consumer countries, the danger of recurrence of these embargoes and the continued closure of the Suez Canal require careful appraisal of the role of Arab oil.

Libya's geographical position and high production make it uniquely important for Europe today, but neither Libya nor any combination of two major Arab producers will be irreplaceable when the large number of mammoth tankers comes into use next year. The significance of Arab oil and its inherent danger to Western interests lies in the fact that Arab oil, as a whole, cannot be replaced now or at any time in the next ten or fifteen years.

The Arab oil producers supply ten million barrels of oil per day, that is, one-third of non-Communist world production. The United States consumes a negligible amount of this Arab oil and has the capacity in the United States and the rest of the Western hemisphere to meet its present and anticipated requirements up to 1980, the final date of the time period projected in this study. Although certain military supplies have come from Arab sources, these would be replaceable at higher cost from Western hemisphere sources. In a physical sense, therefore, the United States does not now or in the foreseeable future require Arab oil. However, about 65% of the oil produced in Arab

---

[1] Source: National Archives and Records Administration, RG 59, SIG Files: Lot 70 D 263, SIG/MEMO: #52, 2/9/68, IRG/NEA, IRG/AF Study on "Western Interests in Arab Oil." Secret. No drafting information appears on the memorandum. An attached memorandum from Battle to Katzenbach, January 18, 1968, states that the study was prepared by an interagency group in response to Katzenbach's request at the time of the Senior Interdepartmental Group's consideration of the Holmes report, and was approved by IRG/NEA and IRG/AF. It was forwarded to SIG members by Staff Director Hartman on February 8, 1968.

countries is from United States investments there. According to company sources these investments return an annual profit of about $1.5 billion to the American oil industry and make a net contribution of over $1 billion per annum to the balance of payments of the United States.[2] While these are considerable sums and have great importance to the United States economy, it is believed that the loss of profits would not have more than a temporary depressive consequence. On the other hand, the loss of $1 billion annual credits to the U.S. balance of payments would be a matter of very great concern to the U.S. Government.

The oil consuming countries of Western Europe and Japan would be very adversely affected should they lose their supplies of Arab-produced oil. These countries now consume about 11.3 million barrels a day of which 8.3 million barrels come from the Arab world. While about 35% of total Arab country output is produced by Western European-owned capital, the loss of all income generated from this production by the Western European countries would be an excessive burden only for the U.K. and the Netherlands. However, if Western Europe and Japan were deprived of all of the oil, undoubtedly a very critical situation would ensue. This heavy dependence on Arab oil can only be partially compensated by additional production, at most 1.6 million barrels per day in the short-run,[3] leaving a gap of 8.4 million barrels a day which would have to be absorbed largely by Western Europe and Japan. By 1980, these two areas are expected to be even more dependent on Arab oil, requiring 18 million barrels per day of Arab oil of a total consumption of 28 million barrels. Under the most favorable assumption, other free world conventional sources might supply 5 million barrels per day by 1980 while non-conventional sources such as tar sands, shale, and coal might under a crash development program at huge economic cost—mainly to the United States—raise another seven million barrels per day. The shortfall for Western Europe and Japan by 1980 would still be six million barrels per day. Even then, these new supplies would cost at least double the current price. Under these circumstances, Western Europe and Japan are likely to be vulnerable to Arab threats of an embargo of exports.

While a total embargo may not be regarded as likely, since 90% of the foreign exchange income earned by Arab oil exporting countries[4] comes from the sale of crude oil, the potential Arab capacity severely

---

[2] This does not include investment in downstream facilities outside the Arab world. [Footnote in the source text.]

[3] Within six months, given a crash program, a total of an additional four million barrels per day might be produced in the non-Communist, non-Arab world, leaving a deficit of about six million barrels per day. [Footnote in the source text.]

[4] For Algeria, the amount is 50 percent. [Footnote in the source text.]

to disrupt supplies to Western Europe and Japan cannot be discounted. Such extreme action might possibly occur as a result of renewal of Arab–Israel hostilities, nationalizations, a unified anti-Western policy by the Arab countries themselves and/or Communist domination of the area. (At present, however, Soviet activities do not constitute a major threat.)

The danger exists that Western Europe and Japan would be willing to pay heavy political and economic prices to avert the loss of Arab oil. We have, therefore, a prime interest in improving the bargaining power which Western Europe and Japan would have in face of a possible oil export embargo by the Arab countries.

Some Arab nationalists are discussing the possibility of the nationalization of Western oil interests and an offer to sell the oil to politically acceptable buyers. This is by no means out of the question. While it would mean the loss of the substantial investment in the area and the loss of a valuable addition to the balance of payments especially for the U.S. and the U.K., at least part of the Free World would continue to receive its energy supplies as the Arab states which might have nationalized would wish to continue to sell their oil and even increase their profits.

Given the inherent instability in the Arab world, it is important to seek and develop alternatives to Arab oil while recognizing that complete independence thereof is not likely to be achieved in the foreseeable future. As a tactical matter, to reduce Arab confidence that oil can be used as a political weapon, we should give maximum publicity to new developments. We should do this in a manner, however, which does not give unnecessary offense to the Arabs to whom we should stress that we welcome access to Arab oil so long as it is offered on reasonable terms.

The following are specific recommendations:

(1) Importing countries should increase their storage capacity to reduce the immediate adverse impact on their economies and to give additional time for economic pressures to attenuate any future Arab embargoes.

(2) The search for and development of non-Arab sources of oil should be accelerated to the extent possible.

(3) U.S. imports should be kept as at present to a small proportion of consumption and further consideration should be given to imports from the Western hemisphere.

(4) Projects to expand production of oil from shale and tar sands should be accelerated.

(5) Our NATO allies and Japan should be permitted and encouraged to participate in the development of our shale and tar sand resources. This should take the form of capital investments and sales contracts both of which would help the U.S. balance of payments.

Our political strategy should aim at encouraging Western European countries, whose stake in Arab oil is greater than ours, to take greater responsibilities in the Arab world.

The Suez Canal remains important economically if not strategically. The closing of the Canal appears also a situation in which the stake of Western Europe and other maritime nations is greater than ours and one on which they might well take the lead. We should give such support as is feasible in terms of our efforts to achieve an overall settlement of the Arab–Israel problem.

Without prejudice to the principles governing our attitude on the Arab–Israel problem, it remains important, in light of continued Western dependence on Arab oil, that we maintain and strengthen our position in the moderate Arab states.

[Here follows the body of the paper.]

---

27.   Memorandum for the Record[1]

Washington, January 8, 1968.

SUBJECT

> Near East-South Asia IRG Meeting
> Friday, 5 January 1968
> NSC Draft on U.S. Policy Objectives
> Near East-South Asia 1968

1. Assistant Secretary Battle dispensed with further review of the draft NSC Middle East paper, accepting as essentially accurate the assertion that we do not have a comprehensive Middle East policy and that U.S. Middle East policy during the past year had been a patchwork of reactions to crises—Yemen and South Arabia in early 1967, the Athens Coup in April 1967, the Gulf of Aqaba in May followed by the Six-Day June War, Cyprus and the Vance Mission, King Constantine's abortive 13 December coup and, completing the circle, a year-end focus on the Yemen. Although the IRG/NEA had concluded in late 1966 that an updated Middle East policy was an urgent requirement, 1967 had

---

[1] Source: Central Intelligence Agency, Job 80 R–01580R, DCI Ex. Reg. Files, IRG. Secret. Copies of this document with its attachment were distributed to the DCI and seven other offices in the CIA.

slipped by without real accomplishment. A single IRG/NEA meeting on the Holmes Study[2] had been inconclusive. The IRG had never met to consider the IRG paper on NEA policy prepared by a small group chaired by Stuart Rockwell.

2. Reaction to the paper I had drafted and tabled on 4 January 1968[3] was that it represented a balanced and streamlined statement of policy but probably exceeded our capabilities. Also, it did not highlight the problems the NSC would have to deal with in 1968. Assistant Secretary Battle said that he had no problem with the substance of the paper; he thought the policy proposed probably came close to the minimum U.S. action required to preserve U.S. interests but that it almost certainly exceeded the means which would be available.

3. There was a lengthy discussion of the consideration the IRG should give to anticipated Congressional and public attitudes, domestic politics and limitations on resources in formulating foreign policy for consideration by the SIG, the NSC and the President. Throughout the meetings on 4 and 5 January 1968, the State NEA officers tended to be excessively negative and defeatist in this respect. Several of us, including Mr. John Campbell of State (who is updating a State position on the Holmes Study), argued that the IRG should, within reasonable limits, present the senior policy-makers with a realistic description of the minimum U.S. effort required to protect U.S. interests without attempting to pre-judge what was specifically feasible in terms of politics and resources.

4. Assistant Secretary Battle expressed particular interest in the concept of regional cooperation and solidarity and growing European and Japanese involvement in fields that had been dominated in past years by the U.S. and the U.K.

5. It was agreed that Mr. Campbell would develop an inventory of U.S. assets and liabilities opposite each of the proposed policy measures. Where major shortfalls in our ability to carry out the policy proposed were revealed, the policy-makers would have clearly and separately identified (a) the specific policy proposal, (b) the assumptions concerning political and material resources required to carry out the policy and (c) the assumptions concerning political and material resources available.

---

[2] Document 22.

[3] Attached but not printed. Critchfield stated that the major U.S. policy objective in the Near East and South Asia in the next year was to preserve the peace while supporting the development of regional solidarity, stability, and independence free from any dominant great power influence. The problem was how to limit the spread of Soviet and Chinese influence while simultaneously keeping the intra-regional conflicts below the threshold of conventional warfare.

6. At the conclusion of the meeting, Assistant Secretary Battle (a) instructed the IRG Secretary, Sidney Sober, to draft a new version of the NSC paper drawing on comments made during the 4 and 5 January 1968 IRG meetings; (b) instructed Mr. Campbell to combine the paper I had submitted with his own efforts to distill something from the Holmes Study and to adopt the formula that the IRG had evolved for dealing with the growing problem of dwindling American resources for conducting foreign policy in the Middle East.

7. The IRG/NEA meeting on 8 January 1968—the third in the current series—will deal mainly with financial and technical problems related to longer-term aid to India and Pakistan.

8. A copy of the initial draft I had circulated on 4 January 1968 which was discussed in the IRG on 5 January 1968 is attached. It has no status as either an Agency or an IRG/NEA document. While it provoked a scattering of nitpicks and a few substantive disagreements on isolated elements, I think it probably represents a solid consensus of what the principals of the IRG/NEA feel should, in 1968, be U.S. Middle East policy. There is a majority view, however, that the means to carry out this policy will not be available.

James H. Critchfield[4]
Chief, Near East and
South Asia Division

---

[4] Printed from a copy that indicates Critchfield signed the original.

28.   Paper Prepared in the Department of State[1]

CENTO/G–2   Washington, April 18, 1968.

FIFTEENTH CENTO MINISTERIAL COUNCIL SESSION
London, April 23–24, 1968

Scope Paper

I. U.S. Policy Interests

CENTO continues to have a positive, if limited, value to the U.S. This value is mainly political. The effectiveness of CENTO as a military alliance is marginal, and its military activities proceed at a low level, but it does continue to have a certain military usefulness. CENTO has provided a security umbrella for the region against Communist aggression, and its existence is a key element in signaling the posture of intent of the U.S. and U.K. to defend the integrity of the region from Communist attack, and of acceptance by the regional members of such support.

CENTO increases the U.S. (and U.K.) channels of communication with the regional members and the number of ways we can cooperate with them. It provides our only security tie with Iran. We have a leading role in CENTO economic development activities, the alliance's most active program. Iran and Turkey continue to see moderate advantages in cooperating with us in CENTO, and even Pakistan—which believes that changing circumstances have left CENTO with little current relevance—has been reluctant to cut this tie with the West.

Our best course at present is to maintain without significant change our current sympathetic but relaxed policy toward, limited commitment to, and moderately active participation in CENTO. The utility of CENTO to us and our policy of continuing support depend on the regional countries' continuing desire to maintain the alliance.

---

[1] Source: National Archives and Records Administration, RG 59, Conference Files: Lot 69 D 182, CF 293, 15th CENTO Ministerial Meeting, London, April 23–24, 1968, Vol. VII. Confidential. Drafted by NEA/NR Multilateral Organizations Adviser Robert A. Stein; cleared by Thomas Ball of the AID/NESA Office of South Asia Affairs, Irving Cheslaw (EUR/BMI), Colonel March (OJCS), Reed (DOD/ISA), Sober, Battle, and Katzenbach. This session of the council was attended by Foreign Minister Ardeshir Zahedi of Iran, Foreign Minister S.K. Dehlavi of Pakistan, Foreign Minister Ihsan Sabri Caglayangil of Turkey, Foreign Secretary Michael Stewart of the United Kingdom, and Under Secretary of State Katzenbach. For text of the communiqué, see Department of State *Bulletin*, May 13, 1968, p. 613. For documentation relating to the session, see the National Archives and Records Administration, RG 59, Conference Files: Lot 69 D 182, CF 293, 15th CENTO Ministerial Meeting, London, April 23–24, 1968, Vol. VII, and Department of State, NEA/RA Files: Lot 75 D 312, CENTO Files, 1965–1968 and CENTO Ministerial Files, 1962–1968.

II. Current Situation in CENTO

CENTO is in a quiet phase, one of marking time. There is tacit agreement among the partners not to stir up controversial issues or to take initiatives which upset normal cooperation.

The active new Secretary General, Turgut Menemencioglu, is fully alert to the special problem of Pakistan's attitude and hopes that new economic initiatives can be found which would be attractive to the Pakistanis. He is looking for ways to make CENTO more meaningful within its limitations, and would like to improve the image of CENTO among the peoples of the regional countries as being relevant and responsive to their own needs. The Secretary General is also seeking to modify some of the formalities and rigidities which have character-ized the functioning of CENTO and generally to speed up the comple-tion of business.

We are pleased that both Turkey and Iran appear to be increasingly realistic with regard to the limitations on U.S. and British economic aid funds under CENTO. A new disturbing factor is the strain which has recently developed in Iran's relations with the U.K. over the future of the Persian Gulf area, and to a lesser extent in Iran's relations with Pakistan over the latter's increasingly close ties with the Arabs. If these strains are not eased, the alliance stands to suffer generally.

III. Scope of U.S. Participation in CENTO

There is special importance to our economic support of CENTO which, though limited in volume, is the most "visible" operational effort in which we are engaged under the alliance. The U.S. supports a continuing AID technical assistance program now in the $400,000 range (after a recent $100,000 cut due to the general reduction in AID funds) that is a primary source of substance for the current CENTO economic program. Some other AID funds also get a CENTO label. The U.S. continues to expend substantial funds previously com-mitted to such capital projects as the CENTO railroad between Iran and Turkey.

We continue high level participation in meetings of the Military Committee and take an active part in CENTO military exercises, plan-ning, and development programs. We contribute U.S. personnel to the permanent military staff in Ankara, as well as to the civilian Secretariat. We also participate in the activities of the alliance in the field of counter-subversion.

IV. U.S. Posture and Aims in this Meeting

There are no items on the agenda that should cause real difficulty. The outlook of the British is similar to ours, and we should coordinate generally with them—using care that there is no appearance of our ganging up on the regionals. We and our British hosts for the meeting will: a) expect a wide-ranging discussion of international affairs; b) avoid controversy on the basic military points of difference, while reassuring the regionals of our continuing political and economic support for CENTO; c) support efforts for expeditious conduct of CENTO business.

During its thirteen years of existence, CENTO has been helping to stimulate regional economic cooperation and planning among Iran, Pakistan and Turkey. In the past few years the regional members have shown increased interest in such collaboration, as evidenced in their creation of the Regional Cooperation for Development (RCD) among themselves. (The RCD Foreign Ministers are scheduled to meet in Tehran April 14–15.) This is a promising trend which we encourage. We are willing to respond to the regional countries' desires to highlight CENTO's economic development aspect. We are adapting our regular contribution to the economic program to concentrate efforts, as the regionals wish, on the fields of agriculture, industrial development and health.

At the same time we expect that more should be done by the regional members themselves to exploit the potential of regional cooperation. The availability of U.S. resources to underwrite CENTO activities is more limited than previously; our CENTO partners are all aware of our balance of payment difficulties. The regional members know too that the great bulk of our aid to them has been under bilateral programs rather than under a CENTO label. The fact that all our assistance, "bilateral" or "regional," has come from the same source should be clearly recognized.

29.   Memorandum From the Assistant Secretary of State for Near Eastern and South Asian Affairs and Member of the Senior Interdepartmental Group (Battle) to the Under Secretary of State and Chairman of the Senior Interdepartmental Group (Katzenbach)[1]

IRG/NEA 68–29   Washington, July 19, 1968.

SUBJECT

> Paper on "U.S. Policy in the Middle East"[2]

As requested by you at the 26th SIG meeting, IRG/NEA has prepared a new paper on U.S. Policy in the Middle East. This paper, which I attach for your consideration, takes off from last year's Holmes Study[3] and, taking into account subsequent analyses of indigenous trends and certain other factors as well as developments during the past year, lays out a comprehensive U.S. strategy for the next five years or so.

You will note differences between the attached paper and the Holmes Study in geographic scope and in format. After careful consideration, it was decided to concentrate in the revised paper on the Middle East and to touch on North Africa and the Horn of Africa only marginally insofar as they affect our consideration of Middle East policy. Conceptual advantages in a comprehensive treatment including the latter two regions were recognized, but in practice we found it confusing and unhelpful to deal in any detail in one paper with all of the Middle East, North Africa, and the Horn. Therefore we concentrated on the Middle East. (AF concurs in this method of treatment.)

In approaching the problem, the attached paper undertakes to set out broad policy considerations and principles to guide us in dealing with the Middle East over the next several years. It does not try to spell out in detail the specific operational means by which those policy principles can or should be executed. This approach makes for a less forceful impression than that conveyed by the Holmes Study, which dealt much more directly in the *how* of achieving our objectives by offering a large number of current action recommendations. Recognizing that the policy principles remain to be fleshed out, I consider the approach in the attached paper preferable as a basic guide to U.S. policymakers for a five-year period.

---

[1] Source: Department of State, NEA/IRG Files, 68–29: Lot 70 D 503, U.S. Policy in the Middle East, Final Draft. Secret. Drafted by Staff Director for the Interdepartmental Regional Group Sidney Sober and cleared by Director of the Office of Inter-African Affairs Fred L. Hadsel.

[2] Document 30.

[3] Document 22.

The essence of the policy set forth in the attached paper is that the United States will continue to be active in the Middle East because our interests require it. We recognize the critical importance of the Middle East especially to Western Europe and hence to our global position. We recognize that we will have a continuing competition with the Soviet Union for influence in the area. In these respects the attached paper and the Holmes Study are in substantial agreement.

The principal substantive differences between the two papers revolve around the treatment of the indigenous climate for Soviet penetration and the estimate of Soviet capabilities in the Middle East. The Holmes Study saw the issue basically as a cold-war clash and was more activist in approach, focusing on a direct US/NATO response. The attached paper gives greater weight to factors which temper the prospects for an aggressive policy by the Soviets including (a) other demands on their resources, (b) their own dilemmas in policy choices, and (c) the indigenous forces of nationalism and modernization, which act as barriers to Soviet dominance in the area. Although in its principal policy guidelines the attached paper is basically similar to the Holmes Study, it is less urgent in tone and less demanding in this call for U.S. involvement. It would concentrate on the political aspects of our competition with the Soviets, and build on strengthening the local forces of independence while maintaining the overall U.S.-USSR military balance. I believe the flexible approach advocated in the attached paper is the more realistic.

In considering the attached paper we are painfully aware of the problems we face in protecting and promoting our interests in the Middle East. I have been most concerned that our overall policy approach be designed to meet the threat, the need and the realities of the situation in the area. I have been insistent that we not back away from advocating a policy that will certainly lay important claims on our resources, merely out of some pessimistic forecast as to the availability of such resources in the years immediately ahead. We do live in, and must plan for, a real world. But if the issues are important to us, as we are convinced they are, we should not avoid facing up to the priorities in allocating resources that they may entail.

We have also been struck, in considering this paper, by the need for further, more detailed planning in anticipation of certain contingencies foreseen in it. These include possible changes in the regimes in the UAR and Jordan, as well as the possibility of a resumption of Arab-Israel hostilities and the related possibility of some type of U.S.-USSR military confrontation. The IRG plans to pursue its study of these contingencies in the near future.

Finally, I must express our debt to Ambassador Julius Holmes in formulating a policy for the Middle East. The importance of his personal leadership in the policy study done last year is reflected in the fact that his name was, by common understanding, given to that study. We have been stimulated by the clear statement of issues and have benefited greatly from both the analysis and strategy offered in the Holmes Study. I deeply regret that Ambassador Holmes will not be on hand to help us further in regard to the attached paper, which already owes so much to him.

30.   Paper Prepared in the Department of State[1]

Washington, July 19, 1968.

U.S. POLICY IN THE MIDDLE EAST

Introduction

American policy in the Middle East in the early 1950's was shaped in the cold war context with the objective of containing the expansion of Soviet power, largely by constructing a barrier of regional military pacts buttressed by military and economic aid. NATO, the Baghdad Pact, and SEATO all overlapped in the Middle East, broadly defined. The Soviet threat was envisioned largely in Korea-style military terms.

Our policy in that period also assumed that decolonization would proceed but that outside powers, principally the U.K and the U.S., could continue to play an effective role in shaping developments there, including organization for defense in which the states of the region would cooperate. The Soviet Union was not admitted to the circle of Middle East powers.

By the late 1950's we had to recognize that the Soviet Union had leapfrogged the northern-tier barrier, using basically political and economic methods, and had become a Middle East power in fact. At the same time we saw that local forces, of which the strongest was militant Arab nationalism, threatened the ability of the Western powers to control developments. The Western attempt to organize strength in the area against both Soviet influence and radical nationalism led and

---

[1] Source: Department of State, NEA/IRG Files 68–29: Lot 70 D 503, U.S. Policy in the Middle East, Final Draft. Secret. No drafting information appears on the memorandum. The paper was prepared by the Interdepartmental Regional Group for Near East and South Asia in the Bureau of Near Eastern and South Asian Affairs.

personified by Nasser came to grief in the crisis of 1958, which brought an end to the pro-Western regime in Iraq and weakened Western influence in Lebanon. We then began to question the usefulness of heavy involvement in local rivalries.

Adopting a more relaxed posture at the end of the 1950's, we had the pleasure of seeing the Soviets feuding with Arab nationalist leaders and the latter with each other. We gradually reestablished a tolerable relationship with the radical nationalist governments while keeping our ties with the moderate Arabs and continuing to rely on our security arrangements with the non-Arab states of the northern tier. Even the Arab-Israel dispute was relatively quiet, an unexpected benefit for the U.S.

In the early 1960's, while maintaining this line of policy, we turned to the general theme that economic development, whether the recipients were our military allies or not, provided the best means of stabilizing the area and the best defense, south of the northern tier, against the Soviet threat. That threat was now seen largely in terms of subversion and "wars of national liberation." We hoped that by playing a major role, largely in economic aid, we could counteract Soviet influence and keep the Middle East countries friendly toward the United States or at least neutral. The program of heavy food assistance to the U.A.R., at the same time that it was getting military and economic aid from Russia, was a symbol of this policy.

The policy faltered, however, when Nasser did not turn inward but revived his attempts to spread his influence throughout the Arab world (notably in Yemen). At the same time he moved closer to the Soviet Union and was increasingly abusive of the United States. U.S.-Egyptian relations came to a low point even before the Arab-Israel war of June 1967, when they were broken. It was the war, too, and not U.S. persuasion or intervention, which shattered Nasser's ambitions and brought an end to his adventure in Yemen.

These recent events have caused us to question further our ability to control local forces in the area or to attain our objectives through some broad and consistent policy applied to the area as a whole. Neither containment nor development provides the key. We continue to recognize the critical importance of the Middle East to Western Europe and hence to our global position. We continue to have commitments and important interests there. Development remains our concern, as it is the concern of the peoples of the region. But we recognize the need for a redefinition of policy reflecting the manifold realities as we now see them.

The essence of the policy set forth in this paper is that the United States will continue to be active in the Middle East because our interests require it. Our relationship with the USSR in this sensitive area has yet to reach the kind of balance it has achieved in Europe. Local forces, especially in the Arab-Israel zone of conflict, are not wholly within the control of either power. The area is in a period of transition in which local violence and crises will be endemic.

It is recognized that some trends in the past few years have been adverse to the U.S. position, and that we should attempt to check and reverse them. Other trends have been adverse to the Soviet position. The paper that follows outlines a policy of competing with the USSR for influence in the Middle East, recognizing that this contest is taking place primarily on the political level and that the governments and peoples of the region will have much to say about their own future. Thus, the main obstacle to Soviet domination will lie in strengthened local forces of independence, provided the overall U.S.-USSR military balance is maintained.

For American policy the need is for flexibility: to oppose the Soviets while trying over time to convince them of the need for cooperation in order to avert dangers to both; to hold to necessary commitments and interests while taking account of local aspirations; to avoid over-involvement in local politics and disputes peripheral to our main interests while seeking to control those conflicts which could bring on wider war; and to find a sound policy for the Arab-Israel impasse where we labor under the handicap of our own conflicting interests.

It is a policy which calls for political skill and the development of long-term relationships more than for heavy outlays of material resources. We should recognize, however, that certain critical objectives may not be achievable without some provision for expenditure of U.S. resources at relatively high levels either for continuing programs (such as aid to Turkey) or for emergencies.

[Here follows the body of the paper.]

31.   **Memorandum From the Principal Deputy Assistant Secretary of Defense for International Security Affairs (Earle) and the Deputy Director of Plans and Policy for the Joint Chiefs of Staff (Orwat) to the Deputy Secretary of Defense (Nitze) and the Chairman of the Joint Chiefs of Staff (Wheeler)[1]**

I–26041/68   Washington, November 22, 1968.

SUBJECT

   IRG/NEA Paper on United States Policy in the Middle East

The Staff Director of SIG has circulated a paper prepared by IRG/NEA (Tab B).[2] He proposes that this be approved "as policy guidance" by the SIG members without a SIG meeting. The paper would then be sent to Secretary Rusk for his approval, and finally forwarded to the President for his information.

The paper proposes the following guidelines: (1) the U.S. should meet the threat of expanded Soviet influence primarily by helping to support the forces of independence and modernization in the area, (2) American policy should pay particular attention to our relationship with certain key countries (Turkey, Iran, Israel, and Saudi Arabia), (3) the U.S. should keep to a low level of involvement in local politics, (4) in dealing with the Arab/Israeli conflict, the U.S. should seek a modus vivendi between them which takes into account Israel's need for security and also U.S. interests in the Arab world; the U.S. should avoid identification with the aims or policies of one side alone and should be prepared to bring pressure to bear on either or both parties as a means of moving the dispute towards a settlement, (5) the U.S. should promote a larger role in the area for Western European states, (6) oil is an important interest but it doesn't require special commitments or the use of military power for its protection, (7) military aid should be related to political objectives in each country, (8) the U.S. should support economic development, and (9) the U.S. should giver greater attention to cultural and information programs.

It was our understanding that the IRG paper would go forward to the SIG for information, not for action. Frankly, we do not believe that the paper is of adequate quality to publish as policy guidance. It neither analyzes fully those issues and problems raised in the paper,

---

[1] Source: Washington National Records Center, RG 330, OSD Files: FRC 73 A 1250, Middle East, 092. Secret. Drafted by Murray (DOD/NESA) on November 20.

[2] Document 30.

nor does it consider other important policy questions which we will face in the coming year.

For example, the paper states that the Soviets appear to be aiming at becoming the dominant external power in the Middle East and the Soviet objectives include the building-up of a system of pro-Soviet states, neutralization of U.S. power, and the reduction of Western influence in the area. To meet this threat the paper proposes that we support local forces of independence and modernization. The paper doesn't make clear who these forces are, how we support them, or what impact this will have on Soviet activities. It poses, however, two unreal alternatives to this strategy: on the one hand, a substantial build-up in U.S. and Western armed forces in the area and large increases in U.S. military aid; or, on the other hand, withdrawal from the area.

Another example, the paper proposes we concentrate on certain key countries, but goes on to say that we should also pay particular attention to Egypt and to do what we can everywhere else. It makes, in effect, a strong argument for selectivity, but holds out the opposite prospect.

The paper fails to treat certain important policy questions, such as: whether or not we should deal directly with the Soviet Union on certain problems in the Middle East (e.g., the Arab/Israeli conflict); the implications of the continuing arms race, and the increasing sophistication of weapons coming into the area; the impact of the growing instability in Jordan and Lebanon on the Arab/Israeli and conservative-radical Arab conflicts; and the role of military forces in the area generally and the Sixth Fleet in particular.

Finally, we do not believe it would be helpful to publish a policy paper in the last weeks of the Administration; even if it would be helpful, we believe this paper is inadequate policy guidance.

We recommend that Mr. Nitze sign the letter at Tab A to Mr. Katzenbach[3] suggesting that the paper be published for background use rather than policy guidance.

---

[3] Nitze's November 26 letter to Katzenbach is attached but not printed. On December 5 Katzenbach responded to Nitze, noting that he had some difficulty with Nitze's proposal that they deal with the paper as simply a background-information document rather than as useful general policy guidance. The Under Secretary pointed out that the paper was the product of a 2-year dialogue in the IRG and the SIG, drawing on the Holmes report and on subsequent work by all of the agencies under IRG/NEA auspices. He noted that no basic disagreements had been raised by OSD or JCS representatives or by other agencies when the paper was approved by the IRG. Katzenbach said he did not agree with withholding approval merely because the IRG paper did not cover every issue in full detail nor prescribe specific courses of action dealing with those issues. He proposed that they approve the document as general policy guidance while explicitly recognizing that certain aspects of the Middle East situation needed further study. (Washington National Records Center, RG 330, OSD Files: FRC 73 A 1250, Middle East, 092)

Genl Wheeler concurs in attached letter.[4]

Ralph Earle
JS Orwat

---

[4] This sentence is handwritten.

---

32.   National Intelligence Estimate[1]

NIE 30–2–68   Washington, December 19, 1968.

THE EASTERN ARAB WORLD IN THE AFTERMATH OF DEFEAT

Conclusions

A. Of the issues that previously occupied the attention of the eastern Arab states, that of Israel has dominated the scene since the June 1967 war. Nasser and the Arab unity drive that he symbolized have been weakened, and the wealthy conservative states have acquired some leverage over him. This has brought some moderation of traditional inter-Arab rivalries, but antagonisms and suspicions between individual Arab states remain and will manifest themselves again.

B. The war has further slowed the already glacial movement toward economic and social modernization in the Arab world, and has increased political instability in Jordan, Egypt, Syria, and Iraq. The many factors which make the Arabs technologically and militarily inferior to the Israelis will continue to be operative for a long time.

---

[1] Source: Central Intelligence Agency, Job 79–R01012A, ODDI Registry of NIE and SNIE Files. Secret; Controlled Dissem. According to a note on the cover sheet, the estimate was submitted by Deputy Director of Central Intelligence Rufus Taylor, and concurred in by the U.S. Intelligence Board on December 19. The Central Intelligence Agency and the intelligence organizations of the Departments of State, Defense, and NSA participated in its preparation. The State, Defense, and NSA representatives concurred; the AEC and FBI representatives abstained because the subject was outside their jurisdiction.

A note on the first page of the estimate reads: "A detailed presentation of the postwar posture of the eastern Arab states is contained in the *Arab-Israeli Handbook* (revised 15 February 1968, with most recent information to be included in a new edition to be published in January 1969)."

C. The chances of any genuine movement toward a modus vivendi between the Arabs and Israel are slim indeed, except possibly in response to strong pressure by the US on Israel and by the USSR on the radical Arabs. Meanwhile, the war has given new stature to the fedayeen, and the present pattern of raids by these free-wheeling commando organizations and Israeli reprisals seems likely to perpetuate a situation of chronic violence between the two sides. This could develop—by accident or design—into broader hostilities which could in turn lead to a direct confrontation between the US and the USSR.

D. The war and its aftermath have greatly reduced US influence in the Arab world and increased that of the USSR. So long as Arab-Israeli tensions remain high, Soviet influence is likely to remain strong, particularly among the radical Arabs. It will be limited by Arab resistance to external dominance and by the likelihood that the USSR will continue to support the existence of the Israeli state. But the ability and will of the radical Arabs to resist Soviet pressures are less than they were two years ago.

[Here follows the 8-page Discussion section of the estimate.]

Indian Ocean

33. Airgram From the Department of State to the Embassy in the United Kingdom[1]

CA–7176   Washington, January 21, 1964, 10:47 a.m.

SUBJECT

    Indian Ocean Talks with British

REF

    Embtels 3248,[2] 2379[3] and previous messages.

State–Defense message. Attached is the preliminary talking paper on Indian Ocean islands which the British requested from us before beginning discussions in London on this subject. The Embassy is requested to review this paper and make any modifications deemed advisable. Substantive changes should, of course, be referred to Washington for State–Defense approval before submission to the British. Otherwise, you should present this paper to the Foreign Office, stating that we are ready to begin discussions in London on February 25 or 26.

There have been several developments concerning the Indian Ocean since these talks were first proposed, including the proposed visits to the area by a carrier task force, and the transfer of theater responsibilities to CINCSTRIKE/CINCMEAFSA. Any discussions with the British on the Indian Ocean will logically relate these various elements in an integrated approach to overall US–UK future intentions in the area. Therefore, while we have kept the attached talking paper focused on the original subject of possible small island bases, we have also inserted some language at the end of it which would permit us to expand the scope of the talks to the extent that we and the British are prepared to do at the time.

Rusk

---

[1] Source: National Archives and Records Administration, RG 59, Central Files 1964–66, DEF 1 IND. Secret. Drafted by C. Arnold Freshman and Winston Lord (G/PM) on January 20; cleared by Gatch (DOD/ISA), Officer in Charge of UK Affairs Thomas M. Judd, FE Office of Regional Affairs Politico-Military Affairs Adviser Captain Robert B. Wood, AF Office of Inter-African Affairs Politico-Military Adviser Eric E. Oulashin, NEA Office of Near Eastern and South Asian Regional Affairs Officer in Charge of Politico-Military Affairs Colonel Donald W. Bunte, and Office of UN Political Affairs Officer in Charge of Dependent Area Affairs Richard V. Hennes; and approved by Office of Politico-Military Affairs Director for Operations Howard Meyers. Repeated to New Delhi, Karachi, CINCSTRIKE for POLAD, CINCPAC for POLAD, and CINCLANT for POLAD.

[2] Dated January 15. (Ibid., POL AFR)

[3] Dated November 15, 1963. (Ibid., DEF 15 UK–US)

Attachment

DEFENSE PROBLEMS IN THE INDIAN OCEAN AREA

The United States interest in exploring certain aspects of the US/ UK military posture in the Indian Ocean area arises from an essentially simple proposition. On the one hand, we note a variety of threats to the political stability and security of the area. Among these factors we would include the existence of massive communist military power north of the Indian Ocean periphery with the added prospect of Communist China attaining a nuclear capability in the foreseeable future.

We are also concerned that dissidence among and within the nations of the periphery could produce local disorders, offering the communists attractive opportunities for various forms of influence and intervention. In the Arabian Peninsula, the United States has important interests in Saudi Arabia and has pledged its support to the reformist-minded Faisal regime. Arab nationalism in the Persian Gulf Shaykhdoms, which are under varying degrees of British protection, is becoming a threat to Western interests, particularly the British. This, coupled with the fact that the Persian Gulf area is the largest source of petroleum available to the West on financially acceptable terms, makes the Peninsula a key area which warrants our joint attention. There is also the problem of Malaysia.

We assess these threats against the acknowledged interest of the West in maintaining the general stability of the area and the independence of its governments from Communist Chinese and/or Soviet domination. Since the end of World War II the UK has provided the predominant Western military forces in the area, and it is expected that this will continue. The US, however, believes it is desirable to examine ways and means of improving, even on an austere basis, the overall Western military posture in the Indian Ocean.

On the other hand, we are conscious of serious potential difficulties in the application of US military influence in the area, should this ever become necessary. The circumstances in which such a decision might be taken, and the level of force required under any set of conditions, are, of course, not fully predictable. Such factors as the nature of the particular threat, the practicability of seeking concerted action under UN auspices, and the requirement for reserve capability to meet simultaneous contingencies elsewhere would all demand consideration at the time. It is clear, however, that once a decision was made to bring military force to bear, its application should be swift and decisive.

The area itself does not possess, for example, indigenous forces or support systems capable of protracted defense against a determined external challenge. This would increase the urgency of any response we decided to make, and in this respect difficult problems can be foreseen. The difficulties lie largely in the great distances over which operational units and their follow-on support would have to travel. Even more important would be the possibility that even these long routings could not be politically assured, but might be beset by possible complications such as refusal of overflight rights, terminal air facilities, or the denial of passage through Suez.

We are currently studying various ways in which these potential difficulties might be alleviated. For a variety of reasons, we are not now considering the continuous deployment of forces or the establishment of extensive facilities within the area. We feel that such an approach is outside the scope of our present defense resources, considering the demands of other theatres. We are, therefore, focusing on less conspicuous ways of supplementing and facilitating the employment of the highly mobile air, land, and naval forces on which we would expect to rely. In this regard, studies are in progress on the possible use of vessels as floating depots in forward areas, and on the possible prestockage of equipment at key locations for subsequent marrying with mobile combat units which might be deployed into the area under various contingencies.

In this context, we are particularly interested in the potential usefulness of a number of strategically situated Indian Ocean islands under British control. It is not possible to predict, apart from the specific circumstances of a case, how various governments on the Indian Ocean periphery would react to US or UK military operations in the area. However, it is evident that strategic locations on the continental mainlands might be controlled preponderantly by regimes which were not, or could not appear to be, sympathetic to any active Western military presence. Thus, we cannot assume that in any military operation we might undertake in the area we would have adequate access to staging or support sites on the periphery. This makes it important, in our view, to keep available wherever possible those island locations which could be put to the military service of the West in an emergency without delay, negotiation, or political restraint. Such locations might then be used on an "as is" basis during a spontaneous contingency, or for the development of austere staging or other facilities in a pre-emergency period. It is believed that certain of the Indian Ocean islands under British control might lend themselves to such planned or pre-arranged use. They do not appear to us to be capable of supporting serious independence movements and probably are too remote and culturally isolated to figure plausibly in the plans of any mainland government.

Examples of the island locations we have in mind are those in the Chagos Archipelago and those administered as part of the Seychelles Colony, but lying outside the main Seychelles group (Coetivy, Ile des

Roches, Aldabra). Our concern with the future availability of such islands for possible contingency use is, of course, distinct from our more immediate and concrete interests in the satellite tracking station now operational in the Seychelles and an Indian Ocean communications station (in which regard we have requested authorization to conduct a survey of the Chagos Archipelago).

We believe that the exploration of this total problem could usefully proceed in both military and political discussions. We envisage the military talks as encompassing a joint assessment of (a) the potential military threats confronting us in the area, (b) general plans for the use of forces and facilities existing in the area, and for bringing additional force to bear as necessary, and (c) the potential military value in a contingency situation of the various Indian Ocean islands. In connection with (c), a joint UK-US military survey of promising island locations may be desirable.

At the political level we would anticipate discussing (a) the prospects for long-term retention of various of the Indian Ocean islands for use in various forms by our military establishments; (b) arrangements which it might be suitable and feasible to make now for this purpose, including arrangements to minimize exposure of these islands to decolonization pressures being exerted in and through the UN; and (c) the local political and economic impacts of any military utilization of such islands. On the latter point, we would wish initially to have the British participants, given the more extensive British experience in the area, identify the specific problems which might emerge, and suggest for consideration ways in which these problems might be handled.

We envisage that the talks will focus primarily on these islands. In addition, we would be prepared to discuss generally the related aspects of such[4] developments as the forthcoming deployment of U.S. Naval units into the Indian Ocean and the new responsibilities of the U.S. unified command CINCSTRIKE/CINCMEAFSA.

In view of the current indigenous reaction to recent unfortunate public revelations of US intent to periodically deploy an attack carrier task force into the area as well as of our interest in exploring the possibilities of providing for support facilities there, it would be hoped that the substance of the talks can be closely held.

---

[4] Note: "such" includes East Africa if necessary. [Footnote in the source text.]

34.   **Memorandum From the Deputy Assistant Secretary of State for Politico-Military Affairs (Kitchen) to Secretary of State Rusk[1]**

Washington, March 3, 1964.

SUBJECT

Discussions with the British on Indian Ocean Island Facilities

1. You approved on February 14 a memorandum outlining the area of discussions which Frank Sloan (DOD) and I expected to cover with British officials in London (Tab B).[2] The talks were held February 25–27 and centered on long range U.S. defense interests in the Indian Ocean area and on U.K. support for this American presence as complementary to their own.

2. Before departing London, we prepared a report which transmits an agreed U.S.-U.K. statement of the results of the discussions, a joint analysis of the political effect of such increased U.S. defense presence in the area, a British military appreciation of the potential for strategic development of Indian Ocean Islands under British sovereignty, and a summary of essential data on the islands. Pending arrival of the report, I summarize here the major impressions received and attach for your perusal the agreed statement of recommendations for future action (Tab A).[2]

a. It was clear that the Foreign Office and Ministry of Defence were pleased at the U.S. initiative and that they wished to be as cooperative as feasible, having in mind their own interests. They noted they intend to remain in the area in force, and that our presence would complement theirs, rather than substitute for it.

b. British strategic concepts are similar to our own, in that they envisage development of islands as supplementing existing bases or

---

[1] Source: Washington National Records Center, RG 330, OASD/ISA Files: FRC 68 A 306, 381 UK, 6 March 1964. Secret. Drafted by Meyers and Kitchen. Copies were sent to Assistant Secretary of State for African Affairs G. Mennen Williams, Assistant Secretary of State for European Affairs William R. Tyler, Deputy Assistant Secretary of State for Far Eastern Affairs Marshall Green, and Talbot. Sent through U. Alexis Johnson. Attached to a March 6 memorandum from Kitchen to Deputy Assistant Secretary of Defense for Regional Affairs Frank K. Sloan stating that the Secretary had approved the statement and recommendations that they and the British had developed jointly in London, which meant that the Department was prepared to move forward as rapidly as State and Defense jointly deemed it desirable to put into effect the recommendations that called for U.S. action. Kitchen said he hoped for a similarly affirmative reaction from Defense and the Joint Chiefs of Staff.

[2] Not attached to source text.

staging facilities on the Indian Ocean littoral, and as reinforcement in depth for mainland commitments. For example, they favor U.S. development of the Chagos Archipelago for a central ocean communications station and austere supporting facilities. The U.K. would like to share use of an oil storage depot and might share airfield facilities if their position in Gan became untenable.

The U.K. strongly favors development of an airfield on Aldabra (an uninhabited Crown island 500 miles off Tanganyika), which we would share, in order to anticipate inability to overfly Africa from Ascension Island, and to provide a staging area for actions in East Africa. (Similarly Aldabra would be useful to the USAF and CINC-STRIKE for operations either from Ascension or through Turkey and Iran.)

They, as we, could usefully employ facilities in the Cocos/Keeling Islands in conjunction with the Australians thus, with Diego Garcia and Aldabra, creating a strategic triangle.

They understand we envisage development of austere air and harbor facilities over a long term, and that except for a communications station on Diego Garcia, firm decisions as to the future have yet to be made in the USG.

c. Colonial Office representatives, while sympathetic to U.S. interests tried unsuccessfully to obtain some indications the U.S. could help with aid programs or by large employment operations to benefit local economies. We made clear we preferred exclusive control, preferably without employing local inhabitants, in islands where we might install facilities, while of course being willing to share these facilities with the U.K. As you will note in the summary of agreed recommendations at Tab A, the U.K. delegation agreed that the U.K. should be responsible for acquiring land, resettling the population and compensating them therefor, at HMG's expense, while the U.S. would be responsible for construction and maintenance costs.

d. With regard to our present and funded requirement for a communication station, it was agreed a joint survey of Diego Garcia should take place quickly, the timing being dependent on British decisions when and how to transfer the administration of Diego Garcia from Mauritius. Here, despite Colonial Office reservations and desire to consult local authorities, the Foreign Office clearly indicated that control over the Chagos Archipelago (including Diego Garcia) should be transferred in such way as to minimize substantially or remove the possibility that use of the islands could be hampered by external pressures for self-determination.

e. Incident to the central negotiation, the British accepted the U.S. draft on terms of operation for the U.S. satellite tracking station in the Seychelles.

3. If you approve the statement and recommendations regarding U.S. actions contained at Tab A, I will take the necessary steps to proceed with DOD to move forward as recommended, in concert with all concerned agencies and departments.[3]

---

[3] Approved by Rusk on March 5.

---

35. Memorandum From Robert W. Komer of the National Security Council Staff to President Johnson[1]

Washington, March 16, 1964.

Bundy and I heartily endorse the concept of intermittent (and perhaps later permanent) deployment of a small carrier task force in the Indian Ocean.

Suez to Singapore is the only area where, despite some major commitments and responsibilities, we have as yet no deployed quick-reaction combat power. So as the area farthest removed from the US, it is ideally suited for the unobtrusive use of carrier-based air power (which minimizes the need for politically sensitive onshore bases).

The pending initial deployment has caused some reactions, especially from Indonesia, which sees it as a possible attempt to deter moves against Malaysia. But there is merit in letting Sukarno think so. To minimize the risk of more Indo noisemaking, we hope to slip the squadron quietly past Sumatra, and to emphasize that it is going to cruise in the *other* end of the area (East Africa–Persian Gulf). In any case, the longer term plusses from quietly showing US power in the Indian Ocean seems to justify braving any initial reactions, which will probably soon die down.[2]

R.W. Komer

---

[1] Source: Johnson Library, National Security File, NSAMs, NSAM 289, Indian Ocean Naval Deployment. Secret. Attached was a March 15 memorandum from Rusk to Johnson recommending that the President approve the cruise in the Indian Ocean area of a U.S. Navy carrier with three destroyer escorts and an oiler, to be known as "the Concord Squadron," as the first phase of the introduction into that area of U.S. military force on an intermittent but regular basis.

[2] A notation in Bundy's handwriting reads: "RWK: This needs a strong memo for my sig.: President has approved & why." The President initialed a handwritten approval line.

36.   National Security Action Memorandum No. 289[1]

Washington, March 19, 1964.

MEMORANDUM FOR

The Secretary of State
The Secretary of Defense

SUBJECT

Indian Ocean Naval Deployment

The President approves both the concept of periodic naval task force cruises in the Indian Ocean and the initial deployment recommended in the Secretary of State's March 15 memorandum to him on "Cruise of 'Concord Squadron' in Indian Ocean."[2] He regards this as a most appropriate use of mobile air/sea power in an area of considerable strategic importance to the United States.

In the light of this decision, it is requested that plans for regular intermittent deployments be developed and submitted.[3]

McGeorge Bundy

---

[1] Source: Johnson Library, National Security File, NSAMs, NSAM 289, Indian Ocean Naval Deployment. Secret.

[2] See footnote 1, Document 35.

[3] On March 21 circular telegram 1747 was sent to various posts stating that the President had approved an aircraft carrier cruise in the Indian Ocean area as the first phase of introduction of U.S. military power into this region on an intermittent but regular basis. The carrier, escorted by three destroyers and supported by a fleet oiler, would be referred to as the "Concord Squadron" with no reference to the Seventh Fleet or the "Indian Ocean Task Force." (Johnson Library, National Security File; Country File, India, Vol. I, Indian Ocean Task Force)

37.   Memorandum From Secretary of State Rusk to President Johnson[1]

Washington, July 15, 1964.

SUBJECT

Indian Ocean Island Facilities

Action Recommendations

1. *The weekend press may have stories saying that the US and UK are jointly engaged in developing new bases in the Indian Ocean.* If you are asked about it, *you may wish to follow the same general line as the press guidance sent key posts (Tab B).*[2] I would hope you could *limit comments to the first two paragraphs in quotes* in the attachment.

2. *If, however, you are pressed hard* regarding our intentions to develop military facilities in the area, I think the *suggested line in the last paragraph in quotes at Tab B should be adequate.*

Discussion

1. *In February,* we initiated *discussions with the British* in London about possible future requirements for military resources in the Indian Ocean. Our *objectives* were *to encourage the UK to remain in strength in this area,* and to plan *to develop with the UK island airstrips and anchorages* to supplement existing bases and staging facilities on the Indian Ocean littoral. The *joint US/UK recommendations* were approved by me March 5 and by DOD April 21. They *involve developing a "strategic triangle" of virtually uninhabited British or Australian islands* 500 miles off Tanganyika and the southernmost parts of India and Indonesia. We plan *initially* to develop *in the Chagos Archipelago (south of India) a central ocean communications station (already funded)* and *austere supporting facilities.*

2. *The British Cabinet agreed to these concepts May 6.* While we have settled tentatively on the British islands involved, as indicated, *final determination will be based upon a joint US/UK survey commencing July 17.*

3. The *Washington Post* has somehow *acquired all details of this story.* At State Department urging, Alfred *Friendly has deferred publishing* the story *since June 15,* on *condition that he would publish if it looked as though the story would leak elsewhere.* Latest conversations with Friendly indicate that the *Post is apt to print the story this coming weekend.* We are very grateful that he has withheld publication this long.

---

[1] Source: Johnson Library, National Security File, Komer Files, Indian Ocean (incl. IOTF), December 1963–March 1966. Secret; Limit Distribution.

[2] Attached but not printed.

4. Bob Komer and McGeorge Bundy have been kept advised of developments. Attached (Tab A) is a more detailed explanation, which you may wish to read.

DR

Tab A

SUBJECT

Indian Ocean Island Facilities

1. Following discussions in London February 25–27, I approved on March 5, and the Department of Defense and Joint Chiefs approved on April 21, a joint US/UK agreed statement and recommendations, involving the development over the long-term of a strategic triangle of austere air and harbor facilities on Indian Ocean islands. These would supplement existing bases and staging facilities on the Indian Ocean littoral, and would reinforce in depth mainland commitments. We initiated the discussions. We thought that, by drawing the British into forward thinking about possible future requirements for military resources in the area from the Gulf of Oman eastward, the UK would be encouraged to remain East of Suez in strength. Also, we could plan for mutually advantageous island airstrips and/or anchorages to support our intermittent naval presence in the area and to facilitate necessary CINCSTRIKE/MEAFSA operations under its responsibilities in Africa and the Asian subcontinent.

(a) Initially, the U.S. would develop on the Chagos Archipelago (roughly 500 miles below the southern tip of India) a central ocean communications station and austere supporting facilities (already funded). Here, the U.K. would like to share use of an oil storage depot and might share airfield facilities, if their presence in Gan becomes untenable.

(b) The U.K. plans to develop an airfield on Aldabra (an uninhabited Crown island 500 miles off Tanganyika), which we would share, in order to anticipate U.K. inability to overfly Africa from Ascension Island and to provide a staging area for actions in East Africa. Aldabra would be useful to the USAF and CINCSTRIKE for operations either from Ascension or through Turkey and Iran.

(c) The U.K. and the U.S. could usefully employ facilities in the Cocos/Keeling Islands in conjunction with the Australians, thus completing the strategic triangle.

2. Apart from the communications station in the Chagos, what we have in mind are prestockage, anchorages and logistic air strips. It was agreed that the U.K. would be responsible for acquiring land,

resettling population and compensating them therefor, at HMG's expense, while the U.S. would be responsible for construction and maintenance costs. We have carefully chosen areas where there is a limited number of transients or inhabitants (e.g. 100–200 people).

3. Except for Cocos, the islands in which we are interested are administered from Mauritius or the Seychelles. The British have already obtained an initially favorable reaction to our joint concepts from the Mauritian Prime Minister, and expect to sound out other key members of the local administrations on July 14. The British Cabinet decided May 6 that they would transfer, to direct administration from London, those islands on which facilities would be constructed. Although we are reasonably certain which islands would be chosen, the actual choice will depend on a joint US/UK survey, to commence July 17. The question of transferring administration is a somewhat delicate one, on which the Mauritian Prime Minister reserved his view, and the British consequently are not now raising this issue with the other members of the local administrations.

4. The London correspondent of the *Washington Post*, during a recent trip to the Middle East, somehow acquired nearly all details of this story. At State Department request, the Managing Editor of the *Post*, Alfred Friendly, has agreed to defer publication unless it seems likely the story would leak elsewhere. The *Post* has held this story since June 15 but has become increasingly apprehensive. On July 11, Friendly insisted that the London *Economist* had all the details, the *Daily Express* had part of the story, and that the *Post* had succeeded in keeping the Washington correspondent of the London *Observer* from publishing the story. Friendly reluctantly agreed that he would withhold the story at least until July 17 or 18, when the island survey would begin, or until it looked as if the story was about to break.

5. In the judgment of my staff, with which I agree, it is unlikely that the *Post* will continue to hold off publishing a story of this magnitude longer than Friday, July 17. We are very grateful that Friendly has deferred publication over a month and, in so doing, rendered considerable service to the USG. We have an agreed press-line with the British (Tab B) and have alerted concerned posts in the Indian Ocean littoral to this effect. We are trying to persuade the British to approach key governments in the area and explain to them, before the story breaks, what our objectives are, generally along the line of the press guidance. The British are resisting informing third countries, until the story breaks. If the matter becomes public and you are asked about it, you may wish to follow the same general line as the attached guidance.

38.   Letter From the Assistant Secretary of Defense for International Security Affairs (McNaughton) to Secretary of Defense McNamara[1]

I–23,914/65   Washington, June 12, 1965.

SUBJECT

    Indian Ocean Islands

I. Problem

Whether to contribute towards the price the British feel they must pay to detach certain islands now part of the British dependencies that might become independent, and thus assure the availability of these islands for military purposes over the long term.

II. Background and Discussion

Concept. In early 1962, the JCS expressed their concern about the political uncertainty of US and UK overflight and staging facilities in Africa, and the Near and Middle East. They recommended making arrangements with the British that would assure the availability of selected islands in the Indian Ocean area which could be used, should the need arise, to develop alternate staging and support facilities.

Talks with the British. In early 1964, discussions were held by Jeff Kitchen (State) and Frank Sloan (ISA) with the British who agreed on the importance of setting aside a reserve of strategic islands that could be used, if needed, by both parties. At that time, it was agreed that the UK would bear the costs of detachment and that the US would bear the costs of developing those facilities needed to meet its requirements. Once developed, the facilities would be available for joint use by the UK. There was no discussion on the joint use of facilities that might be developed by the British. As a result of joint surveys last summer, the British are willing to detach the *Chagos Archipelago* from Mauritius (far to the southwest) and *Aldabra, Farquhar* and *des Roches* from the Seychelles. (See Map at Tab A.)[2] On the grounds that "the ante has gone up," they now ask that we contribute one-half of the anticipated detachment costs (estimated up to £10 million; US share about $14 million).

US and UK Plans. At present, we have firm plans only to develop a Navy–DCS relay communications station and austere support facilities,

---

[1] Source: Washington National Records Center, RG 330, OASD/ISA Files: FRC 70 A 3717, 680.1. Indian Ocean Islands. Secret.

[2] None of the tabs is printed.

including a landing strip, at Diego Garcia (Chagos Archipelago). This station would strengthen the weak link in the DCS between Europe and the Far East, would afford a partial alternative in the event the communications facilities at Asmara were lost, and would fill a current void in ship-shore communications in the area. Funds were sought in FY 1964, but were not approved by the Congress because firm rights to the site were not available. The Navy intends to put this item in its FY 1967 budget. The British have expressed an interest in developing Aldabra as an alternative against the possible loss of their present facilities in Aden, East Africa, and the Maldives. Both the JCS and the Secretary of the Air Force have advocated the funding in FY 1967 of austere staging facilities at Aldabra in support of potential US contingency operations (Tabs B and C). There are no other facilities in the East Africa area that the US could rely on using in the event of a need to deploy US forces to this area. Further, facilities at Diego Garcia and Aldabra plus the existing facilities at Cocos Island, an Australian dependency in the Eastern Indian Ocean, would provide access to any area in the Indian Ocean periphery via the Pacific or the Atlantic (from Ascension Island without overflights over Africa when longer range transports come into the inventory). Farquhar and des Roches have a potential use for the prestockage of material and POL, but neither we nor the British plan their development in the near future.

Implications for British presence in the Indian Ocean Area. When we raised the matter with the British last year, they sought an explicit assurance that we had no intention of replacing them in the Indian Ocean area. We gave that assurance. They made clear that they saw the project as offering alternate British routings into the area should they be forced out of East Africa, Aden or the Maldives. They spoke of joint construction at Aldabra and have set aside half of Diego Garcia for their own future use. Our proposal to the British calls only for the development of facilities by the US when needed to meet our requirements. It does not commit us to any Indian Ocean force posture, or to any construction except to meet our own needs. We have no development plans extensive enough to give the British justification for withdrawal from the area. The detachment of the islands, in my judgment—particularly if they build at Aldabra, would tend to link the British more securely to the area, since they would be assuming direct political responsibility for the islands and would have alternatives available if East Africa, Aden, and the Maldives were lost. The State Department concurs in this assessment and, for this reason, urges some form of US assistance with respect to the detachment proceedings.

Detachment Proceedings. The British are anxious to complete the detachment proceedings before the following events later this summer:

(1) the constitutional conference on the future of Mauritius (sometime between August–October); (2) renewed hostile debates in the UNGA on colonial administration; and (3) the UK Defense Policy Review which could expose the project to attack by the "west of Suez" group. To accomplish speedy detachment, the British feel they must provide various forms of compensation that could amount to £10 million (Mauritius £5.5 million; Seychelles £3.0 million; private property owners £1.5 million). The British now state that the full detachment costs would be a burden on their defense budget and have asked for a US contribution of approximately half.

III. Recommendations

(1) That you approve a US contribution of one-half of the British detachment costs (estimated up to £10 million; US share about $14 million). This contribution would be premised on the explicit understanding that the British would continue their responsibilities east of Suez.

(2) That the contribution in (1) above be arranged as a set-off against R&D surcharges owed by the UK to the US. The arrangement would make clear that this set-off would in no way derogate from the principle of R&D surcharges, and that the set-off reflects a US payment towards the costs of detaching the Indian Ocean islands.

(3) That you not approve the Air Force proposal to construct a US base at Aldabra, but that you authorize working out an arrangement that would keep the British in the lead in building a British facility at Aldabra. The latter step may require a USAF contribution towards the British costs of constructing facilities at Aldabra, for which we should receive the return consideration of US use of the facilities should the need arise.

If you approve of the foregoing, I recommend that you sign the attached memoranda to the Secretary of the Air Force[3] and the Chairman of the Joint Chiefs of Staff. We will work out with the State Department appropriate guidance for further discussions with the British on a contribution towards their detachment costs and on the possibility of a US contribution towards the cost of British construction at Aldabra.[4]

John T. McNaughton

---

[3] Document 39.
[4] McNamara initialed the approval line on June 14.

39.   Memorandum From Secretary of Defense McNamara to the Secretary of the Air Force (Zuckert)[1]

I–23,914/65   Washington, June 14, 1965.

SUBJECT

Request for Approval of Facilities to Support Contingency Planning

I have this date authorized an offset arrangement against R&D surcharges owed by the United Kingdom, under which the United States would contribute one-half of the British costs of detaching certain islands in the Indian Ocean from their present administering authorities. I am not prepared, however, to approve the recommendation in your memorandum of May 14, 1965,[2] that we indicate to the British our intention to proceed with the development of staging facilities at Aldabra. I consider it of cardinal importance that the British continue to shoulder their responsibilities east of Suez and, consequently, do not favor any US action that would suggest the possibility that we are willing to replace them in this area. I am prepared to assist the British, if they need our help, in the establishment of British staging facilities at Aldabra. In return, I would expect that the facilities would be available for our use should the need arise. I am authorizing the Assistant Secretary of Defense (ISA) to work with the State Department on discussions with the British towards this end. Should these discussions lead to a requirement for USAF construction funds, I will ask that you prepare an appropriate Program Change Proposal. To avoid a premature indication to the British of our willingness to assist them in meeting the costs of construction to Aldabra, there should be no release of this information without the prior coordination by the Assistant Secretary of Defense (ISA).

Robert McNamara[3]

---

[1] Source: Washington National Records Center, RG 330, OASD/ISA Files: FRC 70 A 3717, 680.1, Indian Ocean Islands. Secret. Drafted by Lang. Copies were sent to the Secretary of Defense and the Deputy Secretary of Defense.

[2] Not printed. (Ibid.)

[3] Printed from a copy that indicates McNamara signed the original.

40.   Memorandum From Robert W. Komer of the National
Security Council Staff to the President's Special Assistant for
National Security Affairs (Bundy)[1]

Washington, October 15, 1965.

Mac—

FYI, on *Indian Ocean bases* I find that all seems to be under control.
Kitchen in London a few weeks ago managed to settle matters with
the UK. They have since told Mauritius it could have its independence but that the Chagos Archipelago (Diego Garcia) would be
detached.

Kitchen suspects that the Brits may have over-read a new development—we now wonder whether a commo relay station in Diego Garcia
would be as useful as a communications satellite. This is simply technological progress, not a loss of interest. At any rate, the Navy is simply
holding up budgeting till this matter is sorted out.

You probably know better than I that the Brits are probing for US
subsidies on various specifics East of Suez. I gather our position is that
these matters can only be discussed as part of a much larger issue,
including our support of sterling.

RWK

---

[1] Source: Johnson Library, National Security File, Name File, Komer Memos, Vol.
II. Secret.

41. **Memorandum From the President's Deputy Special Assistant for National Security Affairs (Komer) to the President's Special Assistant for National Security Affairs (Bundy) and Francis Bator of the National Security Council Staff[1]**

Washington, January 26, 1966.

The big remaining issue on the UK defense review seems to be the extent of future British presence in the Suez–Singapore area. I won't argue the minor aspects (e.g. evacuation of Aden, Africa, etc.). But it seems to me that our larger response must be based on the fact that, viewed globally, the new area where the US itself is militarily weakest is the Indian Ocean area. An even greater vacuum here 1968–75, because of gradual drawdown of the modest UK presence, is worrisome.

Despite our natural current focus on Southeast Asia and Indonesia, it's essential to look ahead and anticipate many new problems over the next decade in Burma, South Asia, Iran, Arabian Peninsula, and East Africa. Though we are increasingly able to deploy US forces there quickly, the Indian Ocean is the area farthest from the US. Moreover, we have to worry not only about the actual threats in this vast area but a likely decline of confidence in western support on the part of Indians, Paks, Burmese, Persians, etc., if the UK withdraws further.

So I see real advantage in attempting to keep a mobile UK carrier force in the Indian Ocean, whether based in Singapore or Australia. Even one carrier would have real flexibility to meet situations throughout the area (conventional even more than nuclear). If the UK doesn't maintain at least a carrier on station, I predict that the pressures on us to set up an Indian Ocean squadron will increase. No matter how we slice the pie, it would be far more expensive if we had to fill the power vacuum in the Indian Ocean area than to keep the UK there.

This leads to the question of what we could offer in order to encourage HMG to maintain such a force. For example, need we charge such a high price for selling secondhand carriers? Even giving them to the British under ship loan or some such device would be cheaper than maintaining US carrier task force in the Indian Ocean. A US contribution to Indian Ocean island bases or to the Australia base project might also seem sensible in this connection.

---

[1] Source: Johnson Library, National Security File, Name File, Komer Memos, Vol. II. Secret.

In sum, my basic point is that looking ahead for the ten years 1966–75 someone (either the US or UK) is likely to have to maintain some flexible sea/air power in the Indian Ocean. It would be far cheaper to subsidize HMG than to wake up a few years from now to find that we must substitute for the power vacuum its drawdown of forces creates.

RWK

---

42.   Position Paper Prepared in the Department of State[1]

UKR/P–3   Washington, January 27, 1966.

UK DEFENSE REVIEW

Indian Ocean Island Base Plans

Recommended US Position:

It is in the US interest for the UK to maintain a credible presence "East of Suez" with the British Indian Ocean Territory (BIOT) playing an important role in a *support* capacity.

Although the US has no immediate construction plans, we should welcome any indications of a British intention to establish such facilities as a fuel depot in Diego Garcia and an air staging base on Aldabra, with priority on the latter.

With regard to the latter, the Defense Department would be willing to contribute to construction costs of an RAF station in return for joint usage rights.

Anticipated UK Position:

The British are caught between a need to reduce Defense expenditures as well as the atrophy of political acceptancy of so-called foreign bases on the one hand, and the necessity to protect their own interests in the area (as well as those of the West) on the other.

---

[1] Source: Johnson Library, National Security File, Country File, United Kingdom, UK Defense Review, 1/27/66. Secret. Drafted by Captain Asbury Coward (G/PM) and cleared by AFI Politico-Military Adviser W. Paul O'Neill, Jr., Kitchen, and Assistant Secretary for European Affairs John M. Leddy.

They may be expected, therefore, to seek the general US attitude regarding the development of these islands for defense purposes, and more immediately and precisely, if we are interested in joining them in any projects such as the air staging facility on Aldabra.

Background:

There are no known immediate firm construction or usage plans on the part of either the US or UK for the BIOT.

At one time the US was considering construction of an austere communications station and supporting facilities on Diego Garcia; however, this is not the case at this time. (HMG has been so notified.)

The UK has recently alluded to an interest in developing a POL depot on Diego Garcia.

Within the respective Defense Establishments of both governments there have been indications of an awareness of the potential value of an air staging facility on Aldabra.

The future utility of the BIOT may well be surfaced in the context of British plans "East of Suez", i.e., withdrawal from Aden, consolidation in the Persian Gulf, reductions in Southeast Africa, and even as a specific alternative to Singapore.

---

43.   Memorandum From the Assistant Secretary of Defense for International Security Affairs (McNaughton) to Secretary of Defense McNamara[1]

I–25133/66   Washington, August 2, 1966.

SUBJECT

    Indian Ocean Islands

Issue:

The British Embassy informed us officially on 14 July (Tab A)[2] that HMG has decided in principle to build an air staging facility on Aldabra

---

[1] Source: Washington National Records Center, RG 330, Records of the Office of the Secretary of Defense, OASD/ISA Files: FRC 70 A 6648, 680.1, Indian Ocean Islands. Secret.

[2] Neither tab is printed.

Island. They estimate the cost at 18 million pounds ($50 million). They ask:

(a) Whether we wish to send a small group to participate in engineering surveys in September, and

(b) *Whether we are willing to fund one-half of the cost ($25 million) in return for equal use of the facility.*

Discussion:

(a) The British have recently made counter-proposals on our draft agreement concerning future defense use of the "detached" islands, including Aldabra and Diego Garcia, which now constitute the British Indian Ocean Territory. Some differences remain for negotiation, but we do not anticipate that these differences will seriously delay conclusion of the agreement. One theme of the agreement is that the islands are available for defense use over a long period by both Governments and that to assure coordination there should be consultation on plans. The agreement also recognizes the possibility of joint financing for facilities in which both Governments may be interested.

(b) Last year the Air Force proposed a facility on Aldabra similar to that now planned by the British. You did not approve funding for a USAF installation per se, but indicated willingness to help fund a British installation if we had assured use. The Air Force continues to have a strong interest in such a facility (see Tab B), and is supported by the Joint Chiefs. The current Air Force cost estimate for the facility is considerably lower than the British figure.

(c) Last February you authorized Navy to make in-house studies toward development of engineering plans for construction of logistic support facilities on Diego Garcia, preparatory to programming action. A Navy PCP detailing this plan is in the final stages of preparation. The fact of this planning has been closely held.

(d) A British installation on Aldabra would promote their continued military presence in the western Indian Ocean. Further, if we should fail to contribute toward its development, it is doubtful that the British would build it alone. Our contribution would thus advance the case of those within the HMG who have supported a British presence East of Suez. We would also have the physical facilities available for our own use whenever necessary.

(e) A contribution toward the British facility on Aldabra would give us an excellent opportunity to stimulate British interest in participating in the construction and operation of facilities we may decide to build on Diego Garcia. By letting it be known in this context that we are examining the feasibility and utility of naval support facilities on Diego Garcia, we may be able to promote British participation and their continued presence in the central Indian Ocean area.

Recommendations:[3]

(a) That we accept in principle the British proposal for a jointly financed facility on Aldabra, and authorize the Air Force to participate in detailed planning with the British authorities, join in the September surveys, and include funding of the U.S. share in its FY 68 program.

(b) That we inform the British that we are examining the feasibility and utility of austere naval support facilities including an air strip on Diego Garcia, and seek early arrangements with the British for a joint engineering survey. We would make clear to the British that we have made no final decision to build, and would seek to stimulate some degree of British participation in the project should it materialize.

John T. McNaughton

---

[3] McNamara approved both recommendations on August 4.

---

44.   Memorandum From the Secretary of the Navy (Nitze) to Secretary of Defense McNamara[1]

Ser 001653   Washington, February 24, 1967.

SUBJECT

Proposed Limited Support Facility on Diego Garcia (S)

1. I believe we should reconsider the decision made last fall that approval for the proposed limited support facility at Diego Garcia would depend on substantial British participation and financing. The two recent episodes involving U.S. ships and South African ports have dramatically underscored the lack of any politically neutral and usable facility for the Navy in the entire Western Indian Ocean.[2]

2. This situation is not likely to improve with time nor is the use of the Indian Ocean by U.S. ships likely to diminish. In these

---

[1] Source: Washington National Records Center, RG 330, OSD Files: FRC 72 A 2468, Indian Ocean 323.3, 24 Feb. 67. Secret. A copy was sent to the Under Secretary of the Navy.

[2] For documentation on the controversies surrounding scheduled visits of the USS *Independence* and the USS *Roosevelt* to South African ports, see *Foreign Relations, 1964–1968*, volume XXIV, Documents 602, 605, 620, and 630.

circumstances the logic of making early use of Diego seems to me to be impressive. We have just concluded a base rights agreement with the British providing for the use of Diego and other islands of the British Indian Ocean Territory. The location is ideal for use by our ships transiting the Indian Ocean to and from Viet Nam (Tab A)[3] and its political visibility is very low.

3. More specifically, with a facility at Diego, a carrier transiting from the South China Sea to the east coast of the United States could refuel at Diego, then transit to Rio de Janeiro, thence homeward—all without oiler support and independent of Cape Town or any other politically vulnerable port. The extra distance would be only some 1200 miles. A tabulation of transit times and the money advantages of Diego as against present refueling arrangements not using Cape Town is at Tab B.

4. Developing Diego would not involve protracted new negotiations, nor would it foreclose any other option—such as renewing use of South African ports at a later time or of using fleet oiler support—but it would give us a valuable option for operations in the Indian Ocean which we now lack.

5. By no means am I suggesting that we abandon the effort to attract British participation. I share fully your views on the importance of their continued presence in that area. In accordance with Mr. Vance's decision, we have discussed with the Royal Navy the possibility of their participation. These talks have been encouraging and, although there has been no commitment, we anticipate a British response sometime in the spring. We are also going forward with plans for a joint UK–US survey of Diego which is now scheduled for 25 June–5 August 1967. It has been clear in our discussions with them thus far that, based on their earlier experience with our communications requirement on Diego, they have some reservation as to the firmness of present U.S. requirements to support this project. A decision by the U.S. to construct the facility would resolve British doubts and give support to those in the Government who favor continued UK presence East of Suez.

6. However, I am convinced that whether the British ultimately participate or not, we should make the decision now to build the kind of limited facility on Diego Garcia that you and I have discussed over the past year. In brief, that proposal was for a 26 million dollar austere facility, funded in two increments, which would meet existing require-

---

[3] The tabs are attached to the source text but not printed. On December 30, 1966, the U.S. and U.K. Governments signed a base rights agreement on the availability of certain Indian Ocean islands, including Diego Garcia, to meet the defense needs of both Governments. (TIAS 6196; 18 UST 28) For text, see *American Foreign Policy: Current Documents, 1966,* pp. 640-642.

ments for transiting units and provide a nucleus that could be expanded if need arose. That proposal to my mind, remains feasible. A summary of it is at Tab C.

7. I therefore request your approval in principle to include in the Defense FY 69 Military Construction budget the first increment—$13 million—for a U.S. Naval facility at Diego with the understanding that we will continue our efforts to obtain British participation.

Paul H. Nitze

---

45.   Memorandum From the Joint Chiefs of Staff to Secretary of Defense McNamara[1]

JCSM–420–67   Washington, July 25, 1967.

SUBJECT

    Proposed Naval Facility on Diego Garcia (S)

1. (S) Reference is made to:

a. A memorandum by the Assistant Secretary of Defense (ISA), I–23377/67, dated 2 June 1967,[2] subject as above, requesting the views of the Joint Chiefs of Staff on the desirability of proceeding now with construction of such a facility, its value in various contingencies, and an evaluation as to whether the United States should proceed with construction in the absence of UK agreement to share costs.

b. JCSM–392–65, dated 20 May 1965,[3] subject: "Indian Ocean Islands (U)," which reaffirmed the views of the Joint Chiefs of Staff that there were military requirements for the Chagos Archipelago and Aldabra and stated that funds should be programmed to assist the United Kingdom in reserving these and other Indian Ocean islands for future joint defense use.

2. (S) The Joint Chiefs of Staff have examined the proposal for a Navy facility at Diego Garcia. An analysis of the requirement for a

---

[1] Source: Washington National Records Center, RG 330, OSD Files: FRC 72 A 2468, Indian Ocean 323.3, 25 Jul. 67. Secret.

[2] Not printed. (Ibid.)

[3] Not printed. (Ibid.: FRC 69 A 7425, India 381, 10 Jul. 64)

military facility on Diego Garcia and additional supporting data are contained in Appendices A through D hereto.[4] The following conclusions are derived from this examination:

a. Construction of the facility would carry out, partially, the strategic island concept previously recommended by the Joint Chiefs of Staff as a guide for US policy in the Southern Hemisphere.

b. Construction of the facility now is fully warranted. US strategic interests in the area are important and will increase in importance in the future. Political instability of states along the Indian Ocean littoral is likely to continue for many years. Soviet Union infiltration of and pressure on those states are likely to increase, and it can be expected that Communist China as well will increase its efforts to exert influence upon them. An assured base, strategically located in the Indian Ocean, is, therefore, required. Increased base flexibility in the Middle East and east African areas would be realized by the unhampered use (as opposed to restricted use, that could be imposed politically) of an austere staging base for contingency operations; provision of a capability to meet multiple routing requirements of the Services; establishment of communications facilities to improve command and control of ships and aircraft in transit and operating in the area; and the availability of an alternate base to facilitate aircraft/ship operations where weather and range considerations are influencing factors. These conditions emphasize US interests and requirements in the Indian Ocean area.

c. Because of the present lack of assured facilities in the Indian Ocean, the United States is limited in the range of options it can employ in deciding the level of response to a particular threat and, therefore, limited in the effectiveness with which it can protect US interests. The proposed facility would provide the means to support the options for a graduated and flexible response but would not, in itself, increase US commitments in the area.

d. At the same time, a facility on Diego Garcia would be unlikely to embroil the United States in exclusively local problems, because of its isolated geographic location and the political arrangements which the British have made for the islands of the British Indian Ocean Territories.

e. The facility would support the existing and projected Service requirements listed in Appendix A in an effective manner and with minimum investment. Although the initial project would be primarily a naval facility, the bulk of investment would provide improvements

---

[4] Attached but not printed.

of a general purpose nature which could be developed further to meet additional future requirements.

f. The facility would not, in itself, ensure a satisfactory UK presence east of Suez but could be a step in retaining a UK military capability, if it were to participate in the operation and manning of the facility. Though it would be desirable to obtain UK participation, the US requirement for Diego Garcia is such that the project should be undertaken unilaterally, if necessary.

3. (S) Accordingly, the Joint Chiefs of Staff recommend that:

a. Since initial conversations have indicated that the United Kingdom is interested in the facility but is unable to contribute to the cost of construction, an approach be made to the Government of the United Kingdom to ascertain its interest in the following proposals:

(1) The United States to build the facility ($26 million).

(2) The United States and the United Kingdom to share equally the operating and maintenance costs, estimated at $1.47 million annually.

(3) The United Kingdom to provide the commanding officer, man the facility, and pay manning costs.

(4) The United Kingdom to pay for construction to meet any requirements beyond the US proposal.

(5) Each country to have equal user rights.

b. A decision be made to fund the first increment of construction ($13 million) in the FY 1969 defense military construction budget, regardless of the British decision.

For the Joint Chiefs of Staff:
J.O. Cobb
Rear Admiral, USN
Deputy Director, Joint Staff

46.   Memorandum From Secretary of Defense McNamara to the Secretary of the Navy (Ignatius)[1]

Washington, October 27, 1967.

SUBJECT

Austere Support Facility on Diego Garcia (S)

Last February the Navy sent forward a proposal to construct a $26 million "austere" support facility on Diego Garcia, whether or not the British participate in its funding and use, because there would be money advantages to refueling carriers transiting the Indian Ocean at Diego Garcia as compared with current refueling arrangements. In April information on what other uses a Diego Garcia base might serve was furnished by the Navy in a separate study. I have reviewed the reasons for the facility that were set forth in these papers and have decided not to approve investment in Diego Garcia at this time. If in the future, investment in such a project can be arranged with the United Kingdom and will assure a significant British presence in the Indian Ocean, such a base proposal may be reconsidered.

The money advantages the February 24, 1967, Navy memorandum[2] showed for refueling carriers transiting the Indian Ocean are now open to question. If the cost tabulations include (1) the cost of carrier days lost by diverting to Diego Garcia from the quickest transit, (2) the cost of transporting oil by MSTS to Diego Garcia, (3) a reduction in oiler requirements that occur as a result of the base, and (4) the cost of the base, it is clear that using Diego Garcia for carrier refueling is more expensive than current arrangements. Moreover since the value of the carrier days lost by diverting to Diego Garcia is so much greater than the value of the oiler days saved by using the base, we probably would not use the island for refueling if its cost and use were free.

Though I accept the principal cost conclusions of the April 15, 1967, Navy study, "Cost-Effectiveness Analysis of Diego Garcia in Meeting Indian Ocean Contingencies,"[3] I still do not see a clear requirement for the base. As that study indicated, the base starts paying for itself only after a carrier task group is deployed continuously for more than 15 weeks. Current intelligence suggests no requirement for such an extended and uninterrupted show of force.

---

[1] Source: Washington National Records Center, RG 330, OSD Files: FRC 72 A 2468, Indian Ocean 323.3, 27 Oct. 67. Secret.

[2] Document 44.

[3] Not printed.

My interest in encouraging a British military presence in the Indian Ocean area continues to be high. It is possible that the United Kingdom might be interested in a joint naval facility on Diego Garcia in the future, perhaps after a decision is reached on the Aldabra base. I would be prepared to reconsider the Diego Garcia proposal after we have reached a firm understanding with the British on Aldabra.

Robert S. McNamara[4]

---

[4] Printed from a copy that indicates McNamara signed the original.

---

47.   Memorandum From the Joint Chiefs of Staff to Secretary of Defense McNamara[1]

JCSM–226–68   Washington, April 10, 1968.

SUBJECT

Proposal for a Joint US Military Facility on Diego Garcia (U)

1. (S) Reference is made to:

a. JCSM–420–67, dated 25 July 1967, subject: "Proposed Naval Facility on Diego Garcia (S),"[2] which recommended funding the first increment of construction ($13 million) in the FY 1969 Defense Military Construction Budget.

b. A memorandum by the Secretary of Defense, dated 27 October 1967, subject: "Austere Support Facility on Diego Garcia (S),"[3] which deferred approval of a recommendation by the Joint Chiefs of Staff to construct a naval facility on Diego Garcia. The memorandum, however, did contain a provision for reconsideration of the proposal after a firm understanding had been reached with the British on Aldabra.

---

[1] Source: Washington National Records Center, RG 330, OSD Files: FRC 73 A 1250, Indian Ocean 323.3, 10 Apr. 68. Secret. The memorandum indicates that McNamara saw it.

[2] Document 45.

[3] Document 46.

c. American Embassy, London, message 3989, dated 18 November 1967 (JCS IN 24820),[4] which advised that: (1) the present state of Britain's financial condition had made it clear that the United Kingdom would be unable to go ahead with the Aldabra project; and (2) the British intend to remain in the Far East and the Persian Gulf, though there might be adjustments in the phasing of the UK force reequipment.

d. American Embassy, London, message 5577, dated 16 January 1968 (JCS IN 40259),[5] which reported Prime Minister Wilson's announcement to withdraw UK forces from the Far East and Persian Gulf by the end of 1971.

e. A memorandum by the Deputy Secretary of Defense, dated 15 February 1968, subject: "Determination of U.S. Overseas Military Base Requirements,"[6] which directed that a special State–Defense study on overseas military base requirements for the period of the next decade be conducted for completion by 15 December 1968.

2. (S) The Joint Chiefs of Staff have reexamined the political situation and strategic requirements in the Indian Ocean area against the background of events evolving from the Arab/Israeli war and the UK decision to accelerate withdrawal from east of Suez. At the time of the decision made in reference 1a, the prospects for a limited but effective British presence in the Indian Ocean appeared excellent. Now, however, the British financial condition and the attendant retrenchment offer little probability of future UK participation in the development or manning of any joint US/UK Indian Ocean facility. The combination of circumstances emphasizes the necessity for reappraisal of US opportunities, responsibilities, and interests in the Indian Ocean area.

3. (S) The UK presence in the Indian Ocean area throughout the years has tended to stabilize the region and constrain internal strife. The accelerated British withdrawal east of Suez will create a power vacuum which has the potential to generate situations inimical to US national interests and long-range security. The Soviet Union and the Chinese People's Republic (CPR) can be expected to capitalize on the opportunities made available through the British withdrawal. The large number of newly independent nations of Africa and Asia, many with unstable governments and underdeveloped economies, generates political and economic tensions which facilitate Soviet/CPR penetration.

4. (S) The Soviets historically have sought to extend their domination over the neighboring nations to the south and long have coveted

---

[4] Telegram 3989 from London, November 18, 1967. (National Archives and Records Administration, RG 59, Central Files 1967–69, DEF 1 UK)

[5] Telegram 5577 from London, January 16. (Ibid.)

[6] Not printed.

the natural resources of the Persian Gulf and Indian Ocean littoral. Through military assistance, various forms of political, cultural, and economic contact, visits of high officials and military units, and the provision of military hardware, the USSR has recently undertaken a more active and direct presence in the Indian Ocean area. Predominance over the natural resources of the Indian Ocean area or dominating influence over the governments of the surrounding land areas by the USSR could have a serious impact on the economic and strategic positions of the United States and its allies.

5. (S) The Chinese have traditionally exerted strong influence in Southeast Asia, and Peiping now appears bent on restoring such a position. In Africa, the Chinese communists will probably continue to concentrate on establishing closer contact with governments such as Tanzania, at the same time supporting certain national liberation movements and engaging in subversive activities against other governments.

6. (S) Expanding Soviet and/or CPR presence in the Indian Ocean area could lead to serious situations in which the interests of the United States and/or its allies would be threatened. In such cases, the United States would probably be required to deploy forces to the area for sustained operations. The ability to support operations which may be required in this area will necessitate more timely, more effective, and, politically, more acceptable measures than currently are feasible.

7. (S) The United States contributes to the security of many nations throughout the area in various ways, including the Southeast Asia Collective Defense Treaty, participation in CENTO, and announced policy. In Africa, US objectives include safeguarding of strategic interests and promoting the development of independent nations free of external interference. It is anticipated that the use of regional facilities will be necessary to meet these commitments, yet there is no assurance that former UK military facilities or resources will be available following completion of UK retrenchment or that the use of local national resources will be politically or militarily feasible.

8. (S) A joint US military facility on Diego Garcia would provide the United States with a strategically located and politically insulated logistic support and staging base in the Indian Ocean in consonance with the Strategic Island Concept, previously recommended by the Joint Chiefs of Staff, and would serve as a link in an air line of communication in the Southern Hemisphere. The base on Diego Garcia should be an austere military facility capable of supporting limited forces deployed in response to contingency situations and occasional transitors. The central location makes it suitable for support of important functions, such as scientific research, intelligence collection, strategic communications, and strategic ICBM detection and warning. Appendices A and B hereto contain specific data and rationale.

9. (S) The Indian Ocean is a critical, strategic area from which large portions of both the USSR and CPR can be targeted from a submarine. Indian Ocean-based ballistic missile systems could expose targets within a 2,100-nautical mile window along the Soviet southern border to an additional threat. This threat would compound Soviet antiballistic missile defenses and further dilute the Soviet antisubmarine warfare effort.

10. (S) Immediate development of a joint US military facility on Diego Garcia will not in itself prevent the establishment of a Soviet or CPR presence; however, continued delay in construction of the facility, until circumstances demand counteraction, will permit the USSR/CPR to seize the initiative in the area without significant opposition. While the Special State–Defense Study Group is beginning a study of overseas base requirements, which would include consideration of Indian Ocean requirements in a worldwide context, the results and decisions thereon will probably not be available for at least one year. A decision on Diego Garcia should not be deferred awaiting completion of that study.

11. (S) The Joint Chiefs of Staff conclude that the early establishment of a joint US military facility on Diego Garcia is a valid military requirement. Accordingly, they recommend the approval of immediate establishment of a joint US military facility on Diego Garcia. They also recommend that you hold early discussions with the Secretary of State to examine and develop US political and military policy in the Indian Ocean area, with particular reference to the immediate establishment of a joint US military facility on Diego Garcia.

For the Joint Chiefs of Staff:
John B. McPherson
Major General, USAF
Vice Director, Joint Staff

48.   Memorandum From the Deputy Secretary of Defense (Nitze)[1]

Washington, June 15, 1968.

MEMORANDUM FOR

Chairman, Joint Chiefs of Staff
Secretary of the Navy
Assistant Secretary of Defense (ISA)

SUBJECT

Proposal for a Joint US Military Facility on Diego Garcia (U)

A JCS memorandum dated 10 April 1968[2] proposed the establishment of a $44 million joint military facility on Diego Garcia to enable the US to respond militarily to contingencies in the Indian Ocean area. I have reviewed the reasons presented by the JCS and have concluded that no justification exists at present for the establishment of a major support facility. We can reasonably anticipate that logistic requirements for the introduction of American forces into South Asia or the Middle East will be met by local governments in the event of serious crises in these areas.

I do believe, however, that adequate justification exists for the construction of a modest facility at Diego Garcia. This facility—including ship-to-shore communications, telemetry, scientific, and intelligence monitoring capabilities, and attendant support installations—would provide us increased future flexibility at moderate cost. It could provide a potential backup site in the event that MIDEASTFOR cannot be based at Bahrein after the UK withdraws. In addition, some of our activities at Kagnew Station, Ethiopia, could be transferred to Diego Garcia should the security situation in Ethiopia warrant a reduction in our military presence there. The establishment of the facility would also demonstrate to concerned leaders that we are not totally uninterested in the area.

Should further study reveal that Polaris submarine operations in the Indian Ocean are both feasible and desirable, Diego Garcia could serve as a useful site for replenishment and support. No additional construction or maintenance costs would be incurred in providing such support since the necessary anchorage work would have been accomplished. Moreover, we could in the future move quickly to Indian Ocean basing for Polaris should the Soviet ABM capability or ASW threat change suddenly.

---

[1] Source: Washington National Records Center, RG 330, OSD Files: FRC 73 A 1250, Indian Ocean 323.3, 15 Jun. 68. Secret. A copy was sent to the Assistant Secretary of Defense (SA).

[2] Document 47.

Consequently, I approve in principle the concept of a modest facility, and the development of a plan for its construction to include austere communications, POL storage, an 8000 foot runway and anchorage dredging, at a cost of approximately $26 million. This plan, including engineering specifications and Program Change Requests, should be submitted for my review by the Secretary of the Navy, in coordination with the Joint Chiefs of Staff. Submission should be made in time for development of the FY 1970 budget.

The Assistant Secretary of Defense for International Security Affairs should coordinate with the Department of State to make an early approach to the British to obtain agreement to fly a British flag over the facility and to obtain whatever financial and manning participation may be possible. These negotiations should be undertaken with the clear understanding that implementation of any agreement is subject to final approval and release of funds by the US Government.

Paul H. Nitze

---

49.   Telegram From the Department of State to the Embassy in the United Kingdom[1]

Washington, July 3, 1968, 1912Z.

195858. Subj: US Military Facility on Diego Garcia. Ref: London 8538.[2] State/Defense message.

1. Following lengthy consideration here, decision has been reached in principle to establish modest US military facility at Diego

---

[1] Source: National Archives and Records Administration, RG 59, Central Files 1967–69, DEF 15 IND US. Secret. Jointly drafted in G/PM, and by DOD/ISA Director of the Office of Foreign Military Rights Affairs Philip E. Barringer on June 28; cleared by Irving Cheslaw of the Office of UK Affairs, Deputy Assistant Secretary of State for African Affairs Thomas H.E. Quimby, Carleton S. Coon, Jr., of the NEA Office of India, Ceylon & Nepal Affairs, Admiral James W. O'Grady of OPNAV, Thomas T. Huang of the Office of the Assistant Legal Adviser for Military and Regional Affairs, Deputy Assistant Secretary of Defense for Plans and Arms Control Morton H. Halperin, Bader (DOD/ISA), Kerr (DOD/ISA Office of International Logistics Negotiations), Major General Orwat (J–5), Deputy Assistant Secretary of Defense for International Security Affairs Ralph Earle, Deputy Assistant Secretary of State for European Affairs Winthrop G. Brown, and Deputy Assistant Secretary of State for Politico-Military Affairs Philip J. Farley; and approved by Deputy Under Secretary of State for Political Affairs Charles E. Bohlen. Repeated to CINCUSNAVEUR, CNO, CSAF, and Nairobi.

[2] Telegram 8538 from London, April 30, reported that in principle the British Government would have no serious problem with the United States undertaking development of military facilities on Diego Garcia under terms of the December 1966 agreement. (Ibid.)

Garcia, British Indian Ocean Territory. DOD plans for this facility as presently approved, subject to modification based on detailed engineering study, envisage construction of following:

—Austere communications
—POL storage
—8000 ft runway
—Anchorage dredging

2. Cost is estimated at $26 million, to be funded over two fiscal years. 36 months would be needed to make these facilities operational, and 48 months to complete them. Detailed construction plans will be based upon report of joint US/UK survey conducted in June 1967, and on "Project Rest Stop," prepared by Wall-Grad as joint venture for Naval Facilities Engineering Command. 1967 joint survey report is presumably available to interested UK Ministries, and latter document has been furnished to CINCUSNAVEUR and DAO London.

3. We recognize from reftel that possibility of UK participation is slim indeed. As bare minimum, however, we consider that British flag should fly over facility and that UK liaison officer would need to be appointed in order to establish necessary relations with other HMG officials and local inhabitants. Although facility would be available for UK use under 1966 BIOT Agreement and other applicable service-level arrangements, British financial participation would permit greater adaptation of Diego Garcia facility for line of communications support to UK forces in Hong Kong, thus assuming to some extent former role of Aden in this connection.

4. Majority of work to establish Diego Garcia facility would be undertaken either by Navy construction battalions or by use of US civilian contractors. We recognize US obligation under 1966 BIOT Agreement to utilize Mauritian labor to maximum practicable extent, but trust that under that same agreement UK will also take into consideration our own balance of payments situation and consequent need to undertake project with minimum adverse B/P impact. Migrant Mauritian laborers could be utilized for some aspects of construction, but for most part would not be likely to possess requisite skills.

5. Congressional funding for Diego facility has not been secured, but is contemplated for FY 70 budget. Previous experience on such matters indicates that prior UK consent is needed before individual line items will be considered by Congressional committees concerned. Accordingly, we would hope to obtain UK agreement in principle before September 1.

6. Embassy London should outline foregoing proposals and seek HMG approval in principle for construction and installation of proposed facilities pursuant to para 2(b) of BIOT Agreement. (Authority to use the facilities is provided by BIOT Agreement and no further UK

approval is required.) London should particularly emphasize that (a) we plan no facilities at this time beyond $26 million package listed above; (b) we attach great importance to UK participation, and hope HMG will view matter in same light; and (c) implementation of any agreement is subject to final approval and release of funds by USG.

Rusk

---

50.   **Telegram From the Embassy in the United Kingdom to the Department of State**[1]

London, September 4, 1968, 1037Z.

12335. Subj: Diego Garcia. Ref: State 195858 (Notal).[2]

1. FonOff has finally ejected its long-awaited reply to our démarche of July 5 on US-proposed project for Diego Garcia. Text FonOff's letter being pouched Department by airgram.[3] Substance of British reply as follows:

2. HMG prepared to agree to proposed USG development of a facility on Diego Garcia, on understanding that

A) Normal British participation will be provision of one or more liaison officers, and UK flag flying over facility;

B) British naval ships and military aircraft shall have full rights of access to facility at all times under arrangements to be mutually agreed;

C) Administrative details of project will need to be subject of detailed negotiations before construction is due to begin. These negotiations will encompass use of Mauritian and Seychellois labor, and question of resettlement of migrant population. Brooke Turner suggests two possibilities might be considered: Removal of population alto-

---

[1] Source: National Archives and Records Administration, RG 59, Central Files 1967–69, DEF 15 IND–US. Secret. Repeated to CNO, CSAF, Nairobi, Port Louis, CINCUS-NAVEUR, CINCSTRIKE, and DOD for OSD/ISA.

[2] Document 49.

[3] Airgram A–4507, September 5. (National Archives and Records Administration, RG 59, Central Files 1967–69, DEF 15 IND–US)

gether to some locale outside territory, or onto other islands in Chagos group. In order approach this question, FonOff wishes to know US views on whether all should move, or whether some of them will be offered employment, during and after construction phase. FonOff also wishes further info about eventual size of facility, and which, if any, of other islands in Chagos group might be required for further development.

D) Most difficult question likely to be how and when to make project public knowledge: It will clearly be necessary for both govts to concert closely over this. It is essential to preclude unfavorable reactions by Govts of India and Mauritius by taking them into our confidence before there is any possibility of project becoming publicly known or rumored. UKUN would prefer no public announcement before end of coming session of General Assembly.

3. Brooke Turner, presumably in prudence as well as courtesy, has appended copy of draft report by Dr. Stoddart on conservation at Diego Garcia. Essences synopsized in earlier Embassy reporting, but briefly recapitulated, recommend that before development of DG Atoll proceeds, further study take place by qualified entomologist, and that access to three small islets at mouth of lagoon be limited and that these be considered nature preserves.

4. We hope to be able to pass Department's thinking re points 2(C) and 2(D) in due course.

Bruce

Arabian Peninsula

51. Memorandum of Conversation[1]

Washington, January 30, 1964, 10 a.m.

US–UK TALKS

SUBJECT

Persian Gulf and Arabian Peninsula

PARTICIPANTS

Sir Geoffrey Harrison, Deputy Under Secretary of State, British Foreign Office
Mr. T. Frank Brenchley, Head of Arabian Department, British Foreign Office
Mr. Anthony Ackland, UKUN
Mr. John E. Killick, Counselor, British Embassy
Mr. Patrick R. H. Wright, First Secretary, British Embassy

NEA—John D. Jernegan
DOD/ISA—Frank K. Sloan
NE—Rodger P. Davies
NE—Talcott W. Seelye

1. Saudi Arabia

Mr. Jernegan said that despite the Saudi family squabble and the unpopularity of the Saud regime in certain circles in Saudi Arabia, Crown Prince Faisal's position remains quite strong. While there is the ever-present possibility that a cabal of princes could cause trouble, Faisal has emerged successfully from his power struggle with King Saud. Sir Geoffrey Harrison agreed with this assessment. Mr. Jernegan expressed the view that Faisal might be even better off now had he attended the Cairo Summit Conference. It appeared that the King's prestige may have risen a bit as a result of his attendance.

Sir Geoffrey inquired whether the Department had any information indicating that the King had "given anything away" at Cairo. Mr. Jernegan said the King had been effusive in his response to Nasser's cordial reception but that he had not been in a position to commit himself to anything. At least Nasser is now disposed to improve his relations with Saudi Arabia.

Sir Geoffrey thought Faisal had lost nothing tactically by not going to Cairo. The British had heard from Saqqaf that there was a possibility of a continuation of the Saudi–UAR dialogue. Mr. Jernegan said that

---

[1] Source: National Archives and Records Administration, RG 59, NEA/ARP Files: Lot 69 D 257, POL—Political Affairs & Rel., 1964, Middle East General, POL 3–a, US–UK Talks, January Position Papers, January 29–30, 1964. Secret. Drafted by Seelye on February 3.

Saqqaf had indicated to our Ambassador at Jidda a Saudi desire that UAR representatives visit Saudi Arabia. However, the Department has the impression from reports emanating from Cairo that the UAR will probably not agree to send anyone to Saudi Arabia. Mr. Jernegan hoped that Mr. Spinelli, who has proceeded to Jidda from Cairo, might lay the groundwork for further talks.

Mr. Jernegan said we are pleased with the cessation of UAR propaganda. Sir Geoffrey expressed the view that it would take some months to overcome the unsettling effects in Saudi Arabia of past UAR propaganda attacks. Mr. Jernegan thought that Faisal personally appeared to be more affected by these attacks than the Saudi public. Mr. Seelye said the Department has received reports in the last year that UAR propaganda has been considered somewhat of a joke in some Saudi circles. Sir Geoffrey cautioned against underestimating the effects of Nasser's propaganda.

Mr. Jernegan commented that the Department is encouraged by recent signs of more rational economic development in Saudi Arabia. He thought that there had been an important "take-off". Sir Geoffrey said he was struck by the incredible incompetence of the Saudi Government machinery. Mr. Davies said that the situation in the Government has improved compared to what it was some ten to fifteen years ago. There is now a semblance of modern government. Sir Geoffrey acknowledged that there had been some progress in this regard. If the Saudis can agree increasingly to accept foreign advice, they can make more rapid progress. Mr. Davies said the Ford Foundation is under contract to modernize the administrative apparatus of the Government. Sir Geoffrey commented that the greater the natural resources of a country such as Saudi Arabia, the more waste there is likely to be.

Mr. Jernegan inquired as to the latest British information regarding the size of the White Army. Mr. Brenchley said that the figure being "used in the planning stage" is 10,000 or ten units composed of 1,000 men each. Mr. Davies said that our figures indicate that the present size of the White Army is between 16,000 and 20,000. Mr. Jernegan recalled a recent report suggesting that the White Army is three times this size. Mr. Seelye said that the report to which Mr. Jernegan referred emanated from the chief British advisor to the White Army; the figure of 50,000 which he is quoted as citing, however, may have been garbled in transmission. Mr. Brenchley said that the British advisors favor decreasing rather than increasing the size of the White Army to make it more mobile. The Foreign Office has no recent report on its current size. Mr. Davies expressed the hope that our two military advisory missions can keep in close contact and follow "parallel lines".

Mr. Brenchley noted that the British do not have representation in the Eastern Province, as does the United States, and therefore information available to the Department on Saudi Arabia is likely to be more complete. Mr. Davies said that the size of Saudi Arabia and the dispersion of the populace makes it difficult always to feel the pulse of public opinion. In reference to earlier discussion, he wished to call attention to a message which had just come in from the field reporting that the UAR has been dropping leaflets over Yemeni royalist territory showing pictures of King Saud meeting with Sallal, Nasser and Hussein in Cairo.

2. *Aden and the Persian Gulf*

Switching to Aden and the Persian Gulf, Mr. Jernegan commented that it is the Department's understanding that HMG considers Aden as the key to its commitment in the Persian Gulf. He said that the Department has followed recent developments in Aden with interest and anxiety. Sir Geoffrey said, "So have we." He said that since he had to leave the meeting briefly in a few minutes he would at this point prefer to talk about the Persian Gulf and return to Aden later.

Sir Geoffrey recalled the Persian Gulf US–UK talks held in London in April 1963[2] and said that the British have little to add at this time. The UK political and military presence in the Gulf accomplishes the twin objectives of fulfilling the British obligations to the Persian Gulf states and to Kuwait. Aden is the base which gives the British commitment in the Gulf political and military "substance". If the British political and military influence were removed, anarchy would result. This would have two dangerous implications: (1) it would open the Gulf to the influence of other powers, such as the USSR (Mr. Brenchley interjected to include Saudi Arabia in this connection, noting that the Saudis have still not cut their links to the Omani rebels) and (2) it would threaten the flow of oil to the West. Disruption of the oil could be "inconvenient". If all the Gulf oil resources fell under one state, it would be difficult to keep the price of oil within reasonable limits. Sir Geoffrey said that while the form of the British relationship with the Gulf states appears anachronistic, it is important to remember that the rulers are backward and conservative and it is difficult to get them to move forward as fast and as far as one would like. Nevertheless, HMG is conscious of the need to do so.

Sir Geoffrey said that the basic British philosophy is to preserve order and stability in the Gulf while at the same time encouraging progress at a rate circumstances will allow. It is not in HMG's interest to encourage developments which threaten the traditional society. HMG recognizes that the pace of change in the Gulf will not satisfy the Afro-

---

[2] For documentation on the April 1964 talks, see *Foreign Relations, 1961–1963*, vol. XVIII, pp. 559–561.

Asian powers and that the issue may be raised in the UN. He said the Labor Party thinks HMG should move faster.

Mr. Jernegan inquired whether the British have an overall plan for dealing with the Gulf states. He recalled mention a few years ago of a federation. Mr. Brenchley replied that HMG is thinking of a federation of Trucial States (excluding Bahrein, Kuwait and Qatar) but this would be difficult to achieve. Sir Geoffrey said that to produce coherence in an area which is so fragmented is an intractable problem.

3. Kuwait

With regard to Kuwait, Mr. Brenchley said HMG is encouraged by the recent rapprochement with Iraq. Kuwait's admission to the United Nations, Iraq's recognition of Kuwait and agreement on the Kuwait-Iraqi border are good signs which remove the immediacy of the Iraqi threat. There had been no change in Iraq's policy toward Kuwait following the recent change in the Iraqi Government. The British know from talking with the Emir of Kuwait that he is extremely cautious in dealing with Iraq. He considers the 1961 agreement with the UK[3] as the key to safeguarding Kuwait's integrity.

Mr. Brenchley said that HMG is determined to maintain its capability to come to Kuwait's defense. In order to be able to do so, British forces must be kept on the alert and be available on short notice. The commitment of British troops to East Africa complicates the picture somewhat. In addition, Iraq, for internal reasons, recently moved a tank regiment to the Basra area. This regiment could conceivably capitalize on any internal coup effort in Kuwait and move in a matter of hours.

Mr. Brenchley said that the available British military force has two functions: (1) its very existence encourages Kuwait to undertake an independent policy, and (2) it serves as a deterrent to Iraq. The critical military element consists of one battalion of troops and Hawker Hunter aircraft located in Bahrein. The British do not know to what extent the Iraqis are aware of the need for backing up the Bahrein military contingent with troops from Aden.

Mr. Brenchley asserted that the UAR political support for Kuwait's independence is of considerable importance. Obviously, the UAR would not wish Iraq to swallow up Kuwait. While UAR teachers exercise influence in Kuwait, it is the British view that Nasser has no

---

[3] On June 19, 1961, the United Kingdom signed a new treaty with Kuwait recognizing its independence and providing for U.K. military assistance if Kuwait were threatened and the Amir asked for protection. Following a June 26 Iraqi claim that Kuwait was "an indivisible part of Iraq" and what seemed to be an imminent Iraqi invasion, the Amir asked the United Kingdom for military assistance and U.K. military forces were sent back to Kuwait.

intention of subverting the Kuwait Government. If Nasser so desired, he could "do a lot" in Kuwait. His influence there is much stronger than Baathist influence.

Mr. Sloan noted that this seemed to indicate that the UAR was using "more subtlety" in its dealings in Kuwait than elsewhere. Mr. Brenchley agreed. Kuwaitis are satisfied that the UAR is not using its assets against the Kuwait Subah family. Meanwhile, the Kuwait Government undertakes to maintain good relations with the UAR by doing such things as financing UAR-approved projects and by hard currency deposits in the UAR.

Mr. Jernegan asked to what extent HMG tries to influence Kuwaiti policy. Mr. Brenchley replied that since the treaty of 1961 the British have been careful not to seem to be endeavoring to exert influence on Kuwait policy. HMG proffers advice only in response to Kuwaiti initiative. The British have the potential to influence Kuwait more and would do so if the stakes were high enough. The British are confident that any lingering Kuwaiti suspicions of the UK will subside and that the "pendulum will swing back" in the direction of increasing Kuwaiti solicitation of British advice. "A known devil is preferable to the unknown."

4. Southern Gulf

With regard to the southern Gulf, Mr. Brenchley said the British have been devoting attention to getting rid of "the anachronisms". This flows from a desire to bring about modernization and because of the prospect that the UN will give increasing attention to the Persian Gulf. He noted that the British are responsible for the defense and external affairs of these states. In certain respects HMG is involved in internal affairs—for example, in exercising legal jurisdiction over foreigners. Since 1960 the British have been pressing the rulers to set up the necessary machinery for dealing with non-Muslim foreigners. This policy of "retrocession" has progressed furthest in Bahrein.

Mr. Jernegan inquired how the British exercised legal jurisdiction in these states. Mr. Brenchley replied that jurisdiction is exercised by British Political Agents and special British judges. British courts apply Indian law. In addition to Bahrein and Qatar, the policy of retrocession is now being applied in Abu Dhabi in the form of turning over traffic matters to the local administration. In all cases the British make the appointment of a qualified judge as a sine qua non for the turnover.

Mr. Brenchley said that a council of Trucial States exists which meets under the chairmanship of the Dubai Political Agent. The British have suggested to the Trucial State rulers that an executive committee be formed composed of their deputies which would meet regularly and concern itself essentially with economic development. As an inducement, the British have doubled the previous amount of British funds earmarked for economic projects in the Trucial States. The momentum toward federation is difficult to generate since each ruler tends to hate his immediate neighbor.

Mr. Brenchley said that some progress had been made in resolving frontier problems. Negotiations are taking place with regard to the "one remaining undemarcated border" between Abu Dhabi and Muscat.

5. Buraimi

Mr. Jernegan asked whether the Buraimi question were quiescent. Mr. Brenchley said that this was not entirely the case. He recapitulated the UN step-by-step approach to the problem envisaging the return of the refugees. By October 1962 Mr. de Ribbing's work was virtually completed. However, the Saudis "went back on their promise" to allow the refugees to return, setting a condition that there be a modus vivendi. By this they meant the establishment of an international body to oversee Buraimi. This was not acceptable to the Sultan of Muscat since it threatened his sovereignty. The Saudi representative, Azzam Pasha, keeps reminding the Secretary General that the next move is up to the British. HMG has frankly dragged its feet since it wishes to keep up UN interest in the matter while at the same time recognizing that in view of the Sultan's adamant position the British reply must be negative. Mr. Brenchley thought that the reason the Saudis had recently become more interested in the problem was because the British oil company in Abu Dhabi recently drilled a well close to the modified Riyadh line. The location is in the so-called "standstill" area, which the British do not consider applicable.

Mr. Jernegan wondered what Aramco's response to this development had been. Mr. Seelye said that Aramco has reflected Saudi concern with the British company's drilling of a well in the "standstill" area but is not itself operating in this area. Mr. Brenchley preferred the term "ex-standstill" area and stated that in any case this area is not in the Aramco concession.

6. Muscat and Oman

With regard to Muscat and Oman, Sir Geoffrey said that the British have acquainted the Committee of Five in detail with the history and nature of British relations with the Sultan of Muscat and Oman. He expressed the hope that the US would also provide the Committee with the details of its treaty relationship. Mr. Jernegan said he was under the impression we already had. Mr. Seelye said that we had earlier made a statement before the Committee of Twenty-four and that we would be happy to explain our treaty relationship with the Sultanate before the newly-formed Committee of Five.

Sir Geoffrey said that HMG will decline to act as a channel of communication between the Sultan and the UN. The British have found the Secretary General to be understanding of British difficulties with the Sultan. The SYG saw an analogy between the situation of the Omani rebels and internal chieftains in Nigeria. Mr. Jernegan wondered why the General Assembly had shown so much voting enthusiasm on the subject. Sir Geoffrey said there has been a great deal of "mystification" over the UK–Sultan relationship. It is the British view that if the Sultan would be more forthcoming, he might be able to make a good case before the Afro-Asian Bloc. HMG regrets that the Sultan cares so little about the UN.

Mr. Jernegan inquired whether the Sultan is an Arab. Sir Geoffrey responded in the affirmative. Mr. Seelye said it was his understanding that the Sultan is half Indian. He said the problem is that the Arabs do not regard him as an Arab. Sir Geoffrey acknowledged that this was why the British hoped that no Arab would be appointed to the Committee of Five. Mr. Brenchley noted that the question is sometimes asked why the British bother with the Sultan. They do so for the following three reasons: (1) the desire for stability in the area; (2) the fact that if the British rupture relations with the Sultan, the confidence of the other rulers of the Persian Gulf in the British would be undermined; and (3) the British have important staging rights at Salalah and Masira, essential links in their Persian Gulf defense chain.

Sir Geoffrey noted that the American Consul in Aden has responsibility over Muscat and Oman and wondered whether the Department has any plans to establish a resident Vice Consul in Muscat. Mr. Seelye recalled that six or seven years ago the Department had seriously considered appointing a resident Consul in Muscat. However, because he would have little to do and in view of the difficulties of living in Muscat, the Department had decided against doing so. Mr. Davies said that the Department has been considering the possibility of assigning two Arab specialists to Dhahran who would develop special expertise in the Persian Gulf area. Sir Geoffrey hoped the Department would bear in mind the need to build up the image of the sovereignty of the Sultanate.

7. Aden

Mr. Brenchley, while noting that Aden comes under the jurisdiction of the Colonial Office, said that Aden as a colony presents the UK with difficulties. A large portion of the population is Yemeni. The internal situation is complex. The Yemen revolution has "complicated things". Recently, there has been a certain "swinging back" as the Adenis have recognized the ineffectiveness of the YARG and the fact that Yemen is "no bed of roses". The resolution of the moderates has been weakened.

One of the problems being tackled is that of the franchise. Britain's principal interest continues to be the free use of the military base.

Mr. Brenchley identified three sources of trouble for Aden: the nationalists, Yemeni threats from across the border, and the UAR. Pressure from the direction of the UAR has increased in recent months, including propaganda and incitement. He referred to a report just received concerning the ambush of a Federal Regular Army patrol by Yemeni dissidents masquerading in Yemeni Republican National Guard uniforms. He said that the Army had been attempting to intercept a camel convoy headed into Radfan from Yemen. The Yemeni dissidents had apparently been trained in Yemen. Mr. Seelye noted that those troubles in the Aden–Yemen border areas which appear to have been stirred up from outside have occurred only in recent months. He suggested the possibility that they had been inspired by reports, some accurate and some inaccurate, of arms shipments from Aden to the royalists. It seemed unfortunate that the Federal Regular Army, while tracking an incoming caravan, failed to intercept caravans headed outward into Yemen. Mr. Davies commented that reports of shipments of arms from the Sharif of Beihan to the Yemeni royalists were first received last October, before the border troubles began to mount.

Mr. Brenchley thought that the stepping up of outside-inspired incidents may have been connected with forthcoming elections in Aden. In any case, these developments complicate steps which might be taken in the direction of independence. HMG has not yet reached a decision on this matter and the matter of franchise is now being considered. Mr. Davies commented that the organization of the SAF appeared to have progressed fairly well. He noted the complex problem of endeavoring to meld the less advanced protectorate shaikhs with the more advanced Aden Colony residents. The security measures taken in Aden following the deplorable grenade-throwing incident appeared to have been dictated by the shaikhs, who oppose the forces of change. Mr. Brenchley noted that the SAF Council decided on these measures and Aden State has a representative in this Council who voted in favor of the strict measures taken. Aden must accept the consequences of the federal government being responsible for the state of emergency.

52.   Telegram From the Department of State to the Embassy in the United Arab Republic[1]

Washington, February 7, 1964, 8:01 p.m.

3631. During recent US–UK talks HMG requested USG use its influence with Nasser to desist from campaign of propaganda and subversion directed against Aden. We were non-committal at time, noting that this campaign appears to have occurred in last 2–3 months since circulation of reports that Aden (Sharif of Beihan) source of arms shipments to royalists.

We have decided to respond positively to HMG request. In so informing British Embassy here February 7, we have expressed strong hope that HMG will redouble its efforts to prevent Aden territory from being used for activities in support of Yemeni dissident elements. Accordingly, Cairo should at appropriate UARG level (1) express USG hope that, in consonance with spirit of Summit Conference and in interest of easing Yemen–Aden tensions, Cairo will desist from further propaganda and other types of inflammatory attacks against Aden; and (2) indicate that although USG has already been assured by UK that latter doing utmost restrain Adeni rulers from aiding Yemeni royalists, we have requested HMG to make further special effort frustrate any such activities which may be occurring.[2]

For London: You should inform Foreign Office of foregoing.

Rusk

---

[1] Source: National Archives and Records Administration, RG 59, Central Files 1964–66, POL ADEN–UAR. Secret. Drafted by Seelye on February 6; cleared by Davies and Officer in Charge of U.K. Affairs Thomas M. Judd; and approved by Jernegan. Repeated to London, Jidda, Taiz, Dhahran, and Aden.

[2] Telegram 1816 from Cairo, February 12, reported that an Embassy officer had met with Presidency Director Hassan Sabri al Khouli to discuss the question of UAR propaganda attacks on Aden. Al Khouli responded that such attacks had been purely defensive but that in view of the recent British release of political detainees in Aden, UAR propaganda attacks on Aden had ceased. (Ibid.)

53. Research Memorandum From the Director of the Bureau of Intelligence and Research (Hughes) to Acting Secretary of State Ball[1]

RSB–40   Washington, April 13, 1964.

SUBJECT

   Indications of Soviet–Arab Pressures Against Aden

The way in which the Soviet Union has been handling three events—the Cyprus crisis, Yemeni President Sallal's visit to the Soviet Union, and Khrushchev's scheduled visit in May to the UAR—provides evidence of renewed initiatives by Moscow in the Arab world. This paper assesses the pattern, probable direction, and scope of the Soviet moves.

Abstract

   The British position in the Near and Middle East, specifically the base at Aden and the South Arabian Federation, appears to have become the principal target of Soviet policy in the region. Moscow has followed two paths to this end. The first has been direct, consisting of increased propaganda against British interests and based in "unliberated" areas of the Arab world, support of Arab charges of British "aggression" against the Yemeni Arab Republic, consolidation of direct influence in Yemen as a result of YAR President Sallal's visit to Moscow, and the use of the Cyprus crisis to undercut the British position in the area. The second has been indirect, designed, by removing distractions, to concentrate Arab attention on the British. The Soviets have advised the Arabs against violence towards Israel and have muted previous stimulation of inter-Arab rivalries between "progressive" and "reactionary" regimes.

   Apparently, Moscow believes that the British position in southern Arabia is vulnerable to a combination of border harassment, internal subversion, and pressure in the UN. Khrushchev, we believe, will try to exploit these weaknesses during his visit to Cairo in May, by encouraging Nasser to use the UAR presence in Yemen to support a "national liberation" struggle. He will take care not to involve the Soviet Union directly and will advise Nasser not to make any reckless moves.

   [Here follows the body of the memorandum.]

---

[1] Source: Johnson Library, National Security File, Komer Files, Aden, 1964–1966. Secret; No Foreign Dissem.

54.   Circular Telegram From the Department of State to the Embassy in the United Arab Republic[1]

Washington, April 25, 1964, 4:33 p.m.

1990. 1. Important you bring to attention UARG authorities concern with which USG views Nasser's speech April 23 in Yemen violently attacking UK position in Aden.[2] You should point out not only fact that such public statements by UAR President serve exacerbate tense situation already existing between Yemen and Aden but, insofar as they relate to important Western interests, threaten to place strain on UAR–US relations. You should recall that on several occasions in past 18 months USG has made clear to highest UARG levels that USG considers Aden, no less than Saudi Arabia, an important Western interest (see Presidential correspondence; also Cairo tels 655, 671, and 726 Oct–Nov 1962).[3] At same time on at least two occasions UARG gave us assurances that it had no intention subvert territory surrounding Yemen (Cairo tels 655, 671) and at other times has acknowleged our interests in Peninsula. While USG favors progress and eventual independence for Aden (SAF), it would deplore any radical action which seeks to force peremptory and premature UK withdrawal from Aden base. This the UARG should clearly understand in following any future course of action re Aden.

2. Also you should note that speech appears to contradict public official UARG statement of December 18, 1962.[4] Latter commenced, "UAR confirms and supports the full contents of the communiqué released by the Government of the YAR". YARG communiqué stated inter alia "We hope to live in peace and harmony with our neighbors to the extent that they share our hope". While UARG might argue that Yemen's southern neighbor has not manifested desire live at peace with YARG, you should take stand this is not in fact the case. While

---

[1] Source: National Archives and Records Administration, RG 59, Central Files 1964–66, POL 19 ADEN. Secret. Drafted by Seelye on April 24, cleared by Davies and Judd, and approved by Jernegan. Repeated to Jidda, Taiz, Aden, London, Dhahran, and USUN.

[2] On a surprise visit to Yemen, Nasser made a speech on April 23 stating that the people in Aden and the neighboring British protectorates were suffering from the "harshest form of tyranny, oppression, and torture at the hands of British colonialism" and vowing to expel Britain from all parts of the Arab world. (*The United States in World Affairs 1964*; Harper and Row, New York, 1965)

[3] Telegram 655 from Cairo, October 18, 1962, is printed in *Foreign Relations, 1961–1963*, vol. XIII, pp. 184–186. Telegram 671 from Cairo, October 22, 1962 is not printed. (National Archives and Records Administration, RG 59, Central Files 1961–1963, 786H.02/10–2262) Telegram 726 from Cairo, November 9, 1962 (786H.00/11–962), is Document 289 in the microfiche supplement for *Foreign Relations, 1961–1963: Near East; Africa*.

[4] See the editorial note in *Foreign Relations, 1961–1963*, vol. XVIII, pp. 268–269.

HMG has failed to recognize YARG, nevertheless we convinced HMG wishes "live at peace" and avoid tensions with YARG as reflected, for example, in HMG desire work out satisfactory pull-back arrangements along Yemen–Aden frontier.[5]

3. We intend to call in UAR Ambassador early next week and make similar approach.[6]

Rusk

---

[5] In telegram 2660 from Cairo, May 10, Ambassador Badeau reported that he had met with Foreign Minister Mahmoud Riad that day to discuss the Yemen–Aden situation. Badeau said he had emphasized that he was speaking on behalf of the U.S. Government's independent interest in the tranquility and orderly progress of the Arabian peninsula and Aden area and not on behalf of the British position. The Ambassador said that he had argued that the British presence in the Persian Gulf had been a stabilizing factor and that rapid British withdrawal could only result in chaos, of which the situation in Yemen was a disturbing current example. (National Archives and Records Administration, RG 59, Central Files 1964–66, POL 19 ADEN)

[6] Circular telegram 2022 to Cairo, April 29, reported that Jernegan met with Ambassador Kamel on April 27 to discuss prospects for defusing the Aden–Yemen dispute. Jernegan said that Nasser's call for expulsion of the British from the "Arab South" sounded like political war against a Free World base. Kamel responded that Nasser's speech did not reflect a calculated campaign to oust the United Kingdom from the Arabian peninsula, but a heated reaction to U.K. non-recognition of Yemen, infiltration, and the Harib attack. Jernegan emphasized the need to take steps to avoid confrontation, such as resumption of efforts to separate SAF and YAR forces and initiation of UK–UAR talks. (Ibid., POL 32–1 ADEN–YEMEN) For Ambassador Hart's discussion of Yemen with Nasser on May 7, see Document 336.

55.   Memorandum of Conversation[1]

Washington, April 27, 1964.

SUBJECT

Countering UAR Pressure against the British Position in Aden

PARTICIPANTS

British Side	United States Side
R. A. Butler, British Secretary of State for Foreign Affairs	The Secretary
	NEA—Mr. Phillips Talbot
The Lord Harlech, British Ambassador	IO—Mr. Harlan Cleveland
Sir Harold Caccia, Permanent Undersecretary of Foreign Affairs	EUR—Mr. William Burdett
	EUR—Mr. Thomas Judd
Mr. John Henderson, Private Secretary to the Foreign Minister	S/S—Mr. Benjamin Read
	NE—Mr. Rodger Davies
Mr. R. S. Crawford, Assistant Undersecretary of Foreign Affairs	
Mr. Denis Greenhill, Minister, British Embassy	
Mr. Patrick Wright, First Secretary, British Embassy	

Mr. Butler noted Nasser's recent attacks in his Yemen speeches against Britain and Israel and said there was no doubt now that he is a major enemy of Great Britain and, he believed, of the United States. He recalled that a previous speech had created problems for the United States and Great Britain in Libya. In addition, he has ambitions against the British in Arabia and is guilty of resuscitating the Israel problem. Clearly he is our enemy. Therefore, we must frame a joint Anglo-American policy to cope with him. The British Cabinet doubts that continuing Western aid to Nasser is in our interests. It also doubts that any attitude of friendliness toward Nasser is appropriate in present circumstances.

Mr. Butler noted that an intelligence paper on subversion had been provided the Department. This paper was well documented. It was quite clear that UAR subversive activities against the South Arabian Federation (SAF) will have to be fought by countersubversive measures.

In Yemen itself, instead of a reduction of UAR military strength as agreed by Nasser, there are now more than 40,000 UAR troops in the country. The position seems to be in stalemate. It is true that the Royalists cannot take the country but they can harass the YAR suffi-

---

[1] Source: National Archives and Records Administration, RG 59, Central Files 1964–66, POL 19 ADEN. Secret; Limit Distribution. Drafted by Davies. The text was coordinated with Patrick Wright of the British Embassy.

ciently (e.g., by cutting roads) to tie down 40,000 UAR troops. Mr. Butler noted that Hafiz Wahba in London had said there was increasing collusion between the UAR troops and the Royalists in that, hungry for food, the soldiers were trading arms for supplies. Efforts to establish an "intermediate, moderate, government" have failed and it is obvious that we cannot deal with Sallal.

The British Cabinet is determined to maintain the Aden base since it is vital for Britain's position in the Near East and the Gulf. The British economy is dependent on Gulf oil. If the supply were disrupted, there are alternate sources but not at reasonable rates.[2] Therefore, the Aden base and the hinterland constitute a vital interest to the British Government which must be preserved at all costs. Nasser's power to undermine this base must be stopped. A variety of steps can be taken. We should, at the outset, recognize the link of the UAR, the YAR and the USSR. With agreements reached during Sallal's recent visit to Moscow, the Russians are in a better position to set up a pincer movement based on states they are helping: Yemen, Somalia and the UAR. It was clear that this movement created a situation of utmost delicacy and danger for us.

Mr. Butler said the British would like to concert action with the U.S. in using the United Nations to bring about a demarcation and demilitarization of the Aden frontier and a dispatch of observers to the area. Sir Patrick Dean considered a major move in the United Nations with U.S. support could bring this about. Without U.S. support, little could be done. Ambassador Beeley in Cairo thought a British approach to Nasser was no longer necessary before making a move in the Security Council.

Mr. Butler said that it must be made clear that HMG is not willing to let the YAR get away with what it is doing. The British will not see the Royalists go down. The government intends to see that the Royalists are provided money covertly to supply their needs. This would preferably be channeled through Saudi Arabia.

In summary, the British felt they must take action in the United Nations and mount countersubversive activities against hostile YAR actions.

The Secretary said he would ask Assistant Secretary Talbot to comment on UAR-Saudi Arabian relations, particularly insofar as Saudi Arabia might not be sufficiently resilient to withstand pressures that might arise from reactivation of the Yemen problem. The USG had no illusion about the disengagement agreement insofar as the reduction

---

[2] For documents relating to U.S. international oil policy, see *Foreign Relations, 1964–1968*, vol. XXXIV, Documents 175ff.

of UAR troops is concerned but quite clearly it had contributed in large degree to Saudi Arabia's present stability. We are concerned at Nasser's activities which are certainly not helpful to our area interests. However, insofar as the threat to Israel is concerned, at this point this is mostly talk. This is a gambit to mobilize Arab opinion, Israel being the only subject on which Arabs can agree. Insofar as Libya is concerned, Nasser's February 22 speech inflamed the issue, but we think the situation is manageable. There are strong indications that the King and the Prime Minister are seeking a solution. Our ability to restrain Nasser's propaganda will be helpful in bringing this about. The problem in the area basically comes down to Aden and South Arabia. The Secretary asked Mr. Cleveland to give his estimate of the possibility of gaining Security Council endorsement along the lines proposed.

Mr. Cleveland replied that we might get a general "standdown" on threats. In the last go-around on Yemen, the atmosphere had been inflamed by Britain's Harib raid, and there was a reluctance on both sides to involve the UAR. On another round, now that the issue of the raid is out of the Security Council's system, it might be possible to get some kind of machinery on the ground in South Yemen.

The Secretary asked about the problem of delimiting the Federation–Yemen boundary.

Mr. Crawford replied that in the West the border is marked, but that the greater part of it in the East is not. Since 1934, Britain has attempted to gain Yemen's cooperation in demarcating the Eastern section but Yemen has consistently dragged its feet. The line agreed on in 1934 sets the status quo line in the area and is regarded by Britain as the frontier. Mr. Cleveland noted that Yemenis oppose demilitarization efforts since this connotes acceptance of some frontier line.

Mr. Talbot said that last fall some progress had been made on a drawback agreement. It is worthwhile pressing to see if this affords a possible means for progress now.

In response to the Secretary's query as to the ability of Aden Federation spokesmen, Mr. Crawford replied that the Minister of External Affairs had made an exceedingly good impression in corridor conversations in the UN. It was difficult for him to speak in open forum, however, because the UK is responsible for the Federation's foreign relations. Nevertheless, the UK were trying to arrange for him to tour various Arab capitals.

Mr. Talbot said the situation in Saudi Arabia had improved greatly over last year. Faysal's personal position was better and the position of his Government within the country was stronger. There was a semi-rapprochement with the UAR. Faysal had said he would go to Cairo although since Nasser's Yemen speeches this may now be less likely.

If the Yemen conflict is reactivated and Faysal is reinvolved in support of the Royalists, his position might well be impaired.

Mr. Butler said that he was not suggesting overt British aid to the Royalists. The Saudis themselves had been giving a lot of covert assistance. The Secretary responded that in the Near East, covert activities seem rapidly to become overt.

The Secretary then asked why the British felt Nasser had gone to Yemen. Mr. Butler said he thought with 40,000 troops tied down, he needed to bolster morale. He noted that Ambassador Spinelli had said there was trouble among the troops in Yemen and also among their families in Egypt.

The Secretary said we thought Nasser would have a problem with his troops and that his speeches were designed to bolster morale among them. He asked whether there were any indication that he was contemplating more than just propaganda attacks at this juncture.

Mr. Butler replied that the bulk of UAR troops are still in the north of Yemen. What concerns the British is subversion in the Arabian Federation. Recent indications were that the UAR would increase its subversive activities, and assassination of British officials in Aden has even been mentioned. There are, however, no indicators of contemplated UAR military action against Aden but rather active UAR encouragement in centers of dissidence within the Federation. A new turn has been the introduction of more sophisticated weapons.

In response to Lord Harlech's question as to what Saudi Arabian reaction would be to the collapse of the disengagement formula, Mr. Talbot said that it had been our presumption that the UAR would move to renew UNYOM's mandate. In view of Nasser's recent speeches, Faysal might well not agree to continuation. The Secretary inquired as to Saudi Arabia's attitude toward Aden and the Federation. Sir Harold Caccia noted Hafiz Wahba had said that Faysal seeks to restore the same relations that his father, Abdul Aziz, had maintained with the British. Faysal saw clearly that his support to Nasser in 1956 had been a serious mistake. He had also said that he saw no prospect of the UAR withdrawing its troops from Yemen or agreeing to a real coalition government. He seems content with the British position in Aden and the Gulf.

In response to the Secretary's questions as to whether the Royalists had access to seaports and what value money would be to them, Mr. Crawford said the tribes were very venal and money would buy support as well as arms which could be brought over borders.

The Secretary asked Mr. Butler whether he had the actual figures on U.S. aid and thought that the British should know actually what is involved. The USG was concerned over its relations with the UAR: If we start actions which will annoy and antagonize Nasser, we have not helped our situation but have hindered it by closing a channel of communication to him and losing what little influence we have in Cairo.

Mr. Butler said that the question of aid is less essential than that Nasser understand clearly that the U.S. is displeased with his performance.

The Secretary said that, in brief, he understood the British were suggesting that we support British initiative in the UN to bring about disengagement and demilitarization on the Aden–Yemen frontier, and desired our comments on possible British extension of covert aid to the Royalists, and aid to the UAR.

Mr. Butler said the UK would not mind taking the initiative itself in the Security Council although it wanted U.S. support. Sir Patrick Dean thought that the non-permanent members of the Security Council, particularly Brazil, Morocco, and Norway would support any moderate move to improve the situation in Yemen and it was important to gain their support. Mr. Talbot said that insofar as the UNYOM was being financed by Saudi Arabia and the UAR, he assumed that any extension to the South would be financed by the UK.

Mr. Butler thought this would probably be the case. He noted that if he were "in the hands of the extremists in the Cabinet", the position he expounded would be much more radical. At present, the Cabinet had decided to give aid covertly to the Royalists although some members favored more direct action. He did not wish to put too much emphasis on the question of covert support for the Royalists, but he considered it vital that the U.S. know what is in HMG's mind. He wished to make clear that what he had presented reflected Sir Alec Home's view.

The Secretary said that we have told Nasser more than once of our interest in both Saudi Arabia and Aden. If augmented support to the Royalists generates pressure against Saudi Arabia, a major problem would be created for us since Saudi Arabia is not the best place to confront Arab nationalism. Quite clearly, the British suggestions would have to be discussed with the President; he would also raise the question of aid to the UAR. He inquired whether the British were in contact with Nasser. Mr. Butler replied that Ambassador Beeley had planned a meeting with Nasser, but had suggested, after Nasser's latest speech, that an approach through the Security Council would be more effective. If the USG were interested, however, HMG would consider an approach in Cairo first. For the record, Mr. Butler wanted to note that the British have in mind improvement schemes for the Federation initially involving around three million pounds. Similarly, it is ready to examine the question of independence. He wanted to make clear also that the British would have to take military action to put down insurrection within the Federation. The first instance was likely to be action against the Dhala tribe. The Secretary asked whether Adenese constituted the bulk of the Federal Army and police and, if so, whether they were loyal. Mr. Crawford replied that they were, in principle. However, if worked upon they would be unreliable. The allegiance of tribal leaders was important, but all tribes were venal.

56.   Telegram From the Department of State to the Embassy in the United Arab Republic[1]

Washington, May 5, 1964, 6:25 p.m.

5164. Ref: Cairo's 2536;[2] USUN's 3689 rptd info Cairo 221.[3] Subject: Committee of 24—Aden.

US voted against Aden res in Comite of 24 as it not conducive settlement difficult Aden problem and contrary our general position of support UK this issue. However, we did not make statement during Comite debate in effort avoid overexposure our differences with Afro-Asians. Embassy will recall US voted no on similar Comite of 24 and General Assembly resolutions in 1963.

We particularly opposed to para in recent res calling for removal UK Aden military base because of importance we attach maintenance base as protection for special UK position in Persian Gulf. We also

---

[1] Source: National Archives and Records Administration, RG 59, Central Files 1964–66, POL 19 ADEN/UN. Confidential. Drafted by Briggs; cleared by Seelye, EUR United Nations Adviser Richard Friedman, Francois M. Dickman (NEA), Colonel Robinson (G/PM), and Buffum; and approved by Sisco. Repeated to USUN.

[2] Telegram 2536 from Cairo, April 29, asked for information regarding the U.S. position on the resolution on Aden adopted by the UN Committee of 24 (the Special Committee on the Situation With Regard to the Implementation of the Declaration on the Granting of Independence to Colonial Countries and Peoples) on April 9. (Ibid.) The resolution, which urged early removal of the U.K. base at Aden, was adopted by a vote of 19 to 3 (Australia, United Kingdom, United States) with 2 abstentions (Denmark, Italy). For text, see *American Foreign Policy: Current Documents, 1964*, pp. 716–717. For information on the U.S. position on the UN Security Council resolution of April 9 condemning U.K. reprisals for Yemeni attacks on the South Arabian Federation, see Documents 325–330. The text of the resolution is printed in *American Foreign Policy: Current Documents, 1964*, pp. 715–716.

[3] Dated April 24. (National Archives and Records Administration, RG 59, Central Files 1964–66, UN 10–4)

highly doubtful that Comite subcommittee visits to Aden called for by res would be desirable in present circumstances.[4]

Believe your discussions with UARG re Aden will be more productive in general context than in specific terms Comite res. UAR, which not member Comite of 24, has not raised question our Comite vote with Dept.

Re discussion with UAR on over-all Aden issue see cable to follow.[5]

Rusk

---

[4] Following a number of incidents along the Aden–Yemen border, the Committee of 24 passed a resolution on May 11 stating that recent British military actions in the region endangered international peace and security and urging the United Kingdom to cease all military measures against the people of the territory. The resolution was adopted by a vote of 18 to 3 (Australia, United Kingdom, United States) with 2 abstentions (Denmark, Italy). For text, see *American Foreign Policy: Current Documents, 1964*, pp. 718–719.

[5] See Document 57.

---

57.   Circular Telegram From the Department of State to Certain Posts[1]

Washington, May 5, 1964, 7:59 p.m.

2064. Depcirtel 1990;[2] Cairo's 2572,[3] 2585[4] and 2586[5] to Department.

Concur in your assessment re Nasser's motives for unleashing attack on British position in Aden. Agree also he has been operating on basis tactical rather than strategic considerations. For this reason

---

[1] Source: National Archives and Records Administration, RG 59, Central Files 1964–66, POL 19 ADEN. Secret; Priority. Drafted by Seelye; cleared by Davies, Curtis F. Jones, Judd, Buffum, Colonel Robinson (G/PM), and in substance by Quinn (DOD/ISA), and Colonel McKinnon (NAVY/OPS–611); and approved by Jernegan. Sent to Cairo and London and repeated to Jidda, Taiz, Aden, USUN, Amman, Baghdad, Beirut, Damascus, Kuwait, Tehran, Tel Aviv, Tripoli, and Dhahran.

[2] Document 54.

[3] Telegram 2572 from Cairo, May 2; not printed. (National Archives and Records Administration, RG 59, Central Files 1964–66, POL 19 ADEN)

[4] Telegram 2585 from Cairo, May 3, reported the Embassy's view that Nasser's frustration at his inability to resolve the Yemen imbroglio lay at the heart of his motives for unleashing violent attacks on the United Kingdom's position in Aden. (Ibid., POL 1 UAR–UK)

[5] Telegram 2586 from Cairo, May 4; not printed. (Ibid., POL 7 UAR)

we suggest in your forthcoming call on Nasser[6] you have confidential and forthright discussion re Aden making points along following lines in manner you deem most likely to have impact (assume in addition you will draw on ref Depcirtel):

1. As long as British maintain dominant influence in Persian Gulf, considered necessary for British have military base at Aden. In short run and at this stage of primitive political development of most Persian Gulf principalities problem is who is to replace British in Gulf and occupy vacuum created by abrupt withdrawal? UAR certainly does not have this capability and US has enough other worries. Nasser must realize that if British pulled out precipitously, neighboring states, each of whom harbors separate designs, would try step into breach. Result would be build-up of tensions, chaos and perhaps local war. Only USSR would ultimately benefit therefrom.

2. At same time not in Nasser's or our interests that chaos and instability prevail in South Arabia. If British left Aden suddenly, what would result? Neither YARG nor presumably UARG has capability to control for long large assortment of primitive, unruly and venal tribes stretching from Gulf of Aden to Yemen-Saudi border. UAR's current problems in Yemen in obtaining and keeping loyalties of tribes would only be multiplied. Without arguing pros and cons of nature of political entity British endeavoring to create and sustain in South Arabia (i.e., South Arabian Federation), must be admitted British administrative and security umbrella there tends to keep lid on. We would submit to Nasser that reasonably orderly change in South Arabia, rather than uncontrollable chaos which would ensue in wake of sudden British withdrawal, in our mutual interests.

3. If Nasser examines history of British program for "constitutional advance" in South Arabia, he will note that British have promised independence and that in their own way British endeavoring train Adenis take over government. Therefore, while case could perhaps be made that path toward self-government too slow, no denying that British on right track. Recognition that British military base at Aden important link in UK commitment to Persian Gulf does not preclude possibility of negotiation of satisfactory base terms with emerging South Arabian Federation government.

4. Best way now to move toward desirable objective of independence, progress and stability of Aden area is to give British chance to sit back and take fresh look at situation. Unquestionably recent developments have pricked HMG to an increasing awareness of necessity to be more accommodating to forces of change. However, in these

---

[6] See Document 336.

circumstances HMG, like any other country, can hardly be placed in position of seeming to succumb to outside pressures. Accordingly, further UARG drum-beating on subject should be avoided. At same time Nasser can be assured that USG will continue its efforts at persuading British to acknowledge existence of YARG and to curtail any unorthodox operations from SAF territory. UN offers current best prospect for damping down Yemen–Aden border tensions.

FYI. You may also, if you feel useful, continue to plug theme of US subsidiary naval interest in Aden base. US naval visits to Aden occur on average of one per week. US Naval Liaison Officer to Aden Consulate being assigned. However, you should keep in mind that US naval consideration secondary. Beyond this, fact that our allies place such stress on importance their position is something we cannot ignore, as Nasser must appreciate. End FYI.

For London: You may inform Foreign Office that we are making another démarche to Nasser re importance of Aden to our interests and urging an end to UAR drum-beating re British position there. Also, drawing on appropriate material contained in Cairo reftels 2585 and 2586 to Department, rptd 154 and 155 to London, request you stress importance HMG avoid overreacting to Nasser's speeches, etc. "Cool and measured" response by British best likely to de-fuse situation. We would urge British take up matter directly with highest UAR authorities. Certainly there is no harm in direct UK–UAR dialogue and probably something to be gained.

FYI. Our hope that combination of United Kingdom restraint and acceleration of process of Adeni "constitutional conference" (which British officials here last week hinted at) will check current trend toward erosion of British position. End FYI.[7]

Rusk

---

[7] Telegram 5522 from London, May 6, reported that an Embassy officer had discussed the points in circular telegram 2064 with Brenchley of the Foreign Office, who replied that his government was not overreacting to Nasser's speeches but that its actions were the direct result of the magnitude of the UAR/YAR-inspired subversive threat in the South Arabian Federation. (National Archives and Records Administration, RG 59, Central Files 1964–66, POL 32–1 ADEN–YEMEN)

58. **Memorandum From the Executive Secretary of the Department of State (Read) to the President's Special Assistant for National Security Affairs (Bundy)**[1]

Washington, May 8, 1964.

SUBJECT

Rising Tensions Among Officials in Aden and Latest Report on European Mercenaries Fighting with Yemeni "Royalists"

Our Consul at Aden reports that local conservative Arab leaders, as well as British colonial officials, have been rudely awakened by the revelation that they stand isolated and insulated from the currents of world opinion. The recent Security Council vote following the British attack on Harib and the recent resolution of the anti-colonialist Committee of 24 have been contributing factors. This, added to an almost pathological fear of infiltration from Yemen, has brought on what our Consul characterizes as "local jitters". The trouble is that rather than inducing the British officials to accommodate themselves increasingly to the forces of change at work in South Arabia, there has been an intensification of their garrison mentality. A demand for immediate independence by two of the leading Shaikhs, whose territory borders Yemen, derives purely from a desire for more drastic retaliatory action across the border. Since it is not clear how the removal of the British colonial umbrella would enable them to perform such action with impunity, it is probable that their demand for independence is designed as a stratagem to get the British to take more drastic retaliatory action.

Our Consul believes that U.K. policy in South Arabia has been one of "temporizing and muddling through". He notes that nothing has been done to seek to reconcile opposing factions inside the South Arabian Federation and that former plans for "constitutional advance" for Aden have been shelved. In our Consul's view the best way for the British to preserve their base in Aden is to accelerate the process of "constitutional advance" leading to self-government.

Meanwhile, a principal reason for the intensification of pressures on the British position in Aden is illustrated by a report just received from Cairo. It states that U.A.R. intelligence has documentary evidence that the number of European mercenaries recruited and organized by

---

[1] Source: Johnson Library, National Security File, Country File, Yemen, Cables, Vol. I, 11/63–6/64. Secret.

a British reserve officer for service with the Yemeni "royalists" is now forty-two.

Benjamin H. Read[2]

---

[2] Signed for Read in an unidentified hand.

---

59.   Special Report Prepared in the Central Intelligence Agency[1]

OCI No. 0333/64B   Washington, May 28, 1964.

THE CONFLICT IN SOUTH ARABIA

The recent British campaign to put down the Egyptian-aided tribal rebellion in the Radfan area of the South Arabian Federation has focused attention on a border that has never been wholly defined and on problems of dissidence and sovereignty which for centuries have plagued whoever has held Aden and its surrounding hinterland. The largest natural port between Suez and the Persian Gulf, Aden has always played a major role in the trade of the southwest corner of the Arabian Peninsula, and its history has been intimately bound up with that of Yemen proper. Indeed, in traditional Arab usage, the term "al-Yemen" has been understood to include the area that now comprises the South Arabian Federation, and Yemenis and Arab nationalists often refer to this territory as the "occupied Yemeni south." Cairo, despite only lukewarm support from the Yemeni republican regime, now appears determined to end that "occupation." London seems equally determined to hang on because Aden's strategic importance—both militarily and economically—is all the more pronounced in view of the loss of British influence elsewhere in the Middle East.

[Here follows the body of the special report.]

---

[1] Source: Johnson Library, National Security File, Komer Files, Saudi Arabia, 12/1/63–12/31/64. Secret; No Foreign Dissem. Prepared in the Office of Current Intelligence.

60.   National Intelligence Estimate[1]

NIE 30–64   Washington, June 24, 1964.

THE OUTLOOK FOR THE ARABIAN PENINSULA

The Problem

To estimate probable developments in the Arabian Peninsula over the next few years, and to discuss the interaction of these developments and of such external forces as the UAR, the UK, the US, the oil interests, and the Communist countries.

Conclusions

A. The modernizing, nationalist movement which has profoundly changed the rest of the Middle East in the past two decades has only recently started in the Arabian Peninsula. The great wealth which oil has brought in recent years, improved communications, and education are stimulating modernization and the intrusion of external forces. The conflict of these forces with traditional society and government and with one another will increasingly set the tone for the years ahead. (Paras. 1–4)

B. The principal current problem is the confrontation between Nasser and the British, between Arab nationalism and Western strategic and commercial interests. The British feel that they need a special political and military position in the Peninsula in order to maintain their access to oil at an acceptable price. Nasser opposes the British presence and probably hopes eventually to replace British influence with his own. The most significant current manifestation of this controversy is the tension between the UK and the UAR over Aden and Yemen. (Paras. 10, 19–20, 39, 42)

C. In Yemen, sentiment against the massive UAR presence is growing among republicans and royalists alike. The republicans are attempting to reach an accommodation with important northern tribes and certain royalist leaders, and thus effect a decrease in that presence. Nasser's fear of losing a predominant influence will make resolution of Yemen's internal problems long and difficult. (Paras. 7–9, 39, 43)

D. British difficulties in building a stable Federation of South Arabia, by combining the relatively advanced Aden Colony with the back-

---

[1] Source: Johnson Library, National Security File, NIEs, 30, Middle East. Secret; Controlled Dissem. According to a note on the cover sheet, the estimate was submitted by the Director of Central Intelligence, and concurred in by the U.S. Intelligence Board on June 24.

ward sheikhdoms, are increased by UAR support for dissidents in both places. Nasser is likely to continue this support, and the British are likely to retaliate against rebels supported by him, possibly with attacks on Yemeni territory. Nasser almost certainly will not deliberately commit Egyptian troops to major action against the British, but hostility between Nasser and the UK is so strong that either side might take risks leading to an unintended military confrontation. (Paras. 23, 25, 43)

E. Saudi Arabia's recent modest social and economic progress will probably continue at least as long as Faysal rules. Faysal will find it difficult to win positive support from the small but growing educated class and from urban labor, especially if the country fails to make political progress. However, we do not believe that critical pressures against the monarchy are likely to develop in the short term. Kuwait is taking its place among the modernizing Arab states, and, although free of direct British control, remains on good political and commercial terms with the UK. In the other sheikhdoms of the Persian Gulf, Britain, recognizing that political changes are inevitable, will probably be able to cope with such pressures for change as arise over the next few years. (Paras. 12–15, 46, 47)

F. The Soviets projected themselves into the Middle East with the 1955 arms deal with Egypt, but their only access to the Peninsula until recently has been Yemen. They would like to eliminate the Western position and influence, hence they are willing to assist Nasser's efforts to achieve the same ends. In Yemen, the Soviet presence and influence are considerable and may increase; they are not likely to match those of the UAR or to overcome traditional Yemeni xenophobia. Elsewhere there probably will not be any great increase in Soviet fortunes. We believe that Communist China will not achieve a significant position in the area within the period of this estimate. (Paras. 49–55)

[Here follow the Discussion section of the estimate and an annex.]

61.   Intelligence Memorandum[1]

OCI No. 1812/65   Washington, June 9, 1965.

THE SECURITY SITUATION IN ADEN[2]

Summary

For the past nine months, the British authorities in Aden have been confronted with a terrorist campaign mounted from Yemen but directed by Egyptian intelligence. The British believe that this campaign is coming to have serious political impact, but they are reluctant to enforce rigorous new security measures for fear of blighting the development of an independent, relatively friendly government in southern Arabia.

1. Last November, an "Arab nationalist" campaign of terrorism began to attack the British position in Aden. This campaign is the work of a relatively small group of trained men, who are directed by Egyptian intelligence experts and who use Yemen as a safe-haven. So far, the attacks have been aimed mainly at British forces and Aden government officials, especially the Special Branch of the Aden Police, which is concerned with subversive activities.

2. The scale of the terrorism is not yet large. During the first five months of this year there was a total of 75 incidents, in which 8 persons (3 British) were killed and 69 (40 British) wounded. Together with other developments in Aden, however, the terrorism has had a significant depressing effect on local morale. Moreover, the campaign has succeeded to the point that local Special Branch officers must be replaced by expatriates, [2 *lines of source text not declassified*].

3. The forces available to maintain internal security in Aden are considerable. There are 1,050 civil police, who may be assisted by 13,500 British troops in the Aden garrison. There are also nearly 5,000 British-led troops in the army of the South Arabian Federation, but most of these are already committed to security duties in the hinterland behind Aden which constitutes the Federation's territories.

4. These forces cannot function effectively, however, unless the authorities receive either substantial cooperation from the local population or backing from London for the enforcement of considerably more

---

[1] Source: Johnson Library, National Security File, Country File, Saudi Arabia, Memos, Vol. I, 12/63–4/67. Secret; No Foreign Dissem/Background Use Only. Prepared in the Office of Current Intelligence, Directorate of Intelligence, Central Intelligence Agency.

[2] This memorandum has been coordinated with the Office of National Estimates and NE Division/DDP. [Footnote in the source text.]

rigorous security measures. At present, neither of these conditions is being fulfilled.

5. The majority of Aden's 250,000 inhabitants are apathetic rather than positively anti-British; they tend to stand aside from a struggle which they feel is simply between the British and the Egyptian-backed terrorists. This attitude is very largely a reflection of the population mix—only a fifth to a quarter of the people are Aden Arabs, while some 80,000 (mostly laborers) are from Yemen, 40,000 are hillmen from the hinterland who themselves dislike the Adenis, and another 80,000 are orientals, mostly of Indian origin, who stand aloof from Arab politics.

6. The British are reluctant to introduce more rigorous security measures, which under the circumstances almost certainly would require using British troops, because they are in the process of trying to link the backward territories of the Federation with heterogeneous Aden to form what they hope will be a viable state functioning under their general guidance. This process began with the founding of the Federation in 1963 and looks toward completion—in the form of independence—possibly by 1968. Such an evolution would be difficult to guide under the best of circumstances. Faced with the pressures of Arab nationalism from at least a vocal minority inside Aden and from Cairo radio outside, the British are understandably chary of suspending the embryonic local government and using strong measures to suppress a terrorist campaign of which only they and the police have been the principal victims.

7. Thus the local government has been allowed to retain responsibility for antiterrorist action, although it has actually impeded security efforts. Curfews are applied only occasionally and in limited districts, to avoid offending any major part of the population, and the enforcement of special emergency decrees is lax. Moreover, travelers still pass freely to Egyptian-occupied Yemen. The situation is not helped by pay disputes between the government and the police and fire brigades, nor by a slowdown among the workers at the oil refinery, Aden's only large industrial installation.

8. The effect of British restraint is to put at risk one of Britain's most valuable military assets. Aden is a base for the protection of Persian Gulf oil; a garrison area for the defense of British interests in the Arabian Peninsula and in the Indian Ocean area generally; and a major British contribution to the world-wide Western defense system. As currently operated, it is the largest and busiest RAF station in the world and, after Singapore, the largest British base complex outside the UK itself. In terms of commercial strategy, Aden is the largest bunkering port in the world and the third largest port of any kind in the Commonwealth. It is not surprising, therefore, that the British high

commissioner stresses the psychological importance of not giving the impression that this prize will shortly fall to Nasir.

9. [*11 lines of source text not declassified*] At some point in the not too distant future the British will have to decide whether the threat from terrorism is sufficiently dangerous that they must put the political development of Aden in jeopardy and use their own forces. (Map)[3]

---

[3] Not reproduced.

---

62.   Telegram From the Department of State to the Embassy in the United Kingdom[1]

Washington, June 10, 1965, 7:21 p.m.

7810. Ex-Aden Prime Minister Zein Baharoon, at start Leader Grant tour US, made following points in call on Assistant Secretary Talbot June 8:

1. Baharoon pessimistic about British efforts bring SAF to independence by 1968, anticipated HICOM would merely change his title to Ambassador at that time but would continue dictate to SAF government made up of feudal shaikhs and sultans. General form of government, unitary or otherwise, was of little importance, primary requirement being British goodwill to bring area to actual independence. Ridiculed proposed Constitutional Commission as having no authority and being of little use in determining desires population if British not aware of latter after 130 years in area.

2. Current terrorism clearly fostered by Cairo and connected to events in Yemen; would stop once Britain straightened up its relations with YAR.

3. Yemen–South Arabia union will not take place; Yemenis in Aden not in favor of such a union.

4. Faisal in fact seems desirous see Nasser remain in Yemen where he bogged down and being bled white. Nasser, for his part, clearly desires withdraw if possible without humiliation.

---

[1] Source: National Archives and Records Administration, RG 59, Central Files 1964–66, POL 7 ADEN. Secret. Drafted by Moore, cleared by Davies and Judd, and approved by Talbot. Repeated to Cairo, Jidda, Taiz, and Aden.

5. Concerning future of British military base, Baharoon said he and British had reached substantial agreement on its continuation. Additionally, alleged Zakaria Muhi-al-Din had specifically told him UAR not opposed to continuation of base provided it not used against Arab countries.

6. In summary, Baharoon predicted Aden could become "second Congo" in 1968 if more realistic and practical steps not taken by British to prepare for independence and if British did not rectify their relations with YAR. Without latter, successful independent life for SAF impossible.

7. Throughout conversation, Baharoon requested "greater activity" by US in Aden, London and Riyadh to bring about climate for successful Federation independence.

On June 10 Department conveyed gist of above (except last point) to British Embassy (Everett). Latter correctly commented that Baharoon devoid of specific recommendations for steps British should take prepare people for independence. British, Baharoon and others obviously continuing struggle with problem of lack of framework for administration of area aside from that provided by present feudal rulers. Everett also mentioned recent meeting Minister State Tomson with UAR Ambassador in which Egyptian unyielding on practically all points connected with southern Arabia. Ambassador stated categorically at that time that UAR not ready withdraw troops from Yemen until favorable situation developed that country.

London may also wish discuss Baharoon's views with Foreign Office.

Rusk

---

63.   Paper Prepared in the Department of State[1]

Washington, September 2, 1965.

SUBJECT

British Position in Aden and the Persian Gulf

The British, because of the importance of Persian Gulf oil, have been particularly concerned with maintaining their primacy in the Gulf, espe-

---

[1] Source: National Archives and Records Administration, RG 59, NEA/ARP Files: Lot 67 D 619, Political Affairs & Rel.—POL 2–a, Middle East General, 1965, Talbot–Mansfield Briefing Book. Secret. Drafted by Moore and cleared by Davies.

cially Kuwait. Their military deployment along the rim of the Arabian Peninsula has been geared speedily to implement the Anglo-Kuwaiti defense agreement of 1961. Aden, with a military base of some 14,000 British and Colonial troops, is the major logistic and command post for this deployment. However, because of growing local nationalist opposition, it is also the weak link in the Peninsular defense chain. To meet nationalist sentiment, HMG is attempting to groom for ultimate independence the South Arabian Federation, a loose grouping of semifeudal shaikhdoms comprising much, but not all, of the Protectorate, to which the more modern, prosperous, developing city of Aden has been joined. Within Aden, nationalist activity is centered in the combined People's Socialist Party and Aden Trade Union Congress (PSP–ATUC) and in the UAR-inspired National Liberation Front. The PSP–ATUC has publicly dissociated itself from the wave of terrorist activities in recent months in Aden and the Protectorate for which the National Front has claimed responsibility.

In a Constitutional Conference in London in June 1964, HMG and the Federation leaders agreed that SAF independence would take place no later than 1968, that a new constitution would be drawn up providing for a bicameral legislature elected by direct means where practicable, and that the UK would surrender its sovereignty over Aden State as soon as possible. UK interest in retaining the military base was recognized. Subsequently the Federation rulers, with HMG approval, announced their intent to establish a unitary state. The PSP–ATUC rejected the results of this conference and demanded more rapid independence with a broader democratic base. British attempts to hold a further constitutional conference in March 1965 and, subsequently, to bring a fact-finding commission to Aden were thwarted by radical nationalist opposition. A July 1965 meeting in London of representatives of all Adeni and Federation political elements also foundered over Adeni insistence that HMG agree to evacuation of the military base and to immediate lifting of emergency security measures. The British insisted that the former was a subject for negotiation with the future independent Federation government and that the latter was impossible in the face of increasing terrorist acts. (In the last days of August and first of September the terrorists moved into a new phase of activity with the assassination of two ranking British civil officials in Aden.) There are no current indications of how the British now propose to move forward toward establishment of a constitution.

HMG's attitude concerning the Yemen Arab Republic is dictated by its concern for the future of the SAF and the threat to the Federation which it feels is posed by a UAR-dominated Yemen. It views with particular concern support stemming from Cairo, as well as Yemen, for subversion activities by the National Front, whose members have frequently publicly espoused a *Yemeni irredenta* movement.

Under the spur of economic necessity, HMG is currently undergoing an intensive review of its world-wide defense commitments. Consideration is being given in some quarters to cutting British troop strength in the Aden–Gulf area. The decisions taken as the result of this review will have a direct bearing on the course of British policies in Aden.

---

64.   Circular Telegram From the Department of State to Certain Posts[1]

Washington, September 28, 1965, 7:10 p.m.

509. Following is background, FYI, to British September 25 announcement suspension operation Aden Constitution. Over one year ago British promised independence to South Arabia, including Aden, not later than 1968. They have since been endeavoring work out with elements in area a constitutional framework for future state. Their efforts have been aborted by nationalist elements supported from Cairo who insisted on immediate implementation 1963 UN resolutions which inter alia called for national referendum, evacuation of British military base in Aden prior to independence, and immediate lifting emergency security measures. These latter measures have been instituted to preserve modicum of law and order in face growing terrorist campaign carried out by nationalists to enforce their demands. British have indicated their acceptance in principle of 1963 resolutions except for 1) evacuation of base, which they insist is matter for discussion between them and future independent South Arabian Government, and 2) lifting of security measures, which cannot be done in the face of terrorist attacks without plunging area into further chaos. In face deteriorating security situation and refusal of Aden State Ministers to condemn

---

[1] Source: National Archives and Records Administration, RG 59, Central Files 1964–66, POL 19 ADEN. Confidential. Drafted by Moore on September 27; cleared by Symmes, Judd, Deputy Director of the Office of Northern African Affairs James J. Blake, Campbell, Ollie B. Ellison (NEA/P), and in substance by Director of the Office of News Robert J. McCloskey; and approved by Davies. Sent to Aden, Aleppo, Alexandria, Algiers, Amman, Baghdad, Baida, Basra, Beirut, Cairo, Casablanca, Damascus, Dhahran, Jerusalem, Jidda, Kuwait, Port Said, Rabat, Taiz, Tel Aviv, Tripoli, Tunis, London, and USUN.

terrorism or cooperate in maintenance of law and order, British have suspended operation Aden constitution. They emphasize that this does not affect continued operation constitution other states in SAF, nor does it indicate any weakening their resolve grant independence not later than 1968. End FYI.

If queried, Department press spokesman intends reply as follows. Addressees authorized draw on this in discussions with host government, press and diplomatic colleagues.

We recognize that people of Aden and Saudi [*South*] Arabia have increasingly made manifest their legitimate desires for independence. The British Government has for some time been trying to bring together the various political groupings in Aden and Saudi [*South*] Arabia to work out a constitutional transition to independence, the date for which is set for not later than 1968. We note that, even though the Aden Constitution has been suspended in connection with acts of terrorism, the British Government has reaffirmed its intention to abide by that timing. We support an orderly evolution to independence in South Arabia and believe the ending of terrorism is a necessary step toward this end.

Ball

---

65. Circular Airgram From the Department of State to Certain Posts[1]

CA–4185 Washington, October 15, 1965, 10:19 a.m.

SUBJECT

Aden Debate in UNGA

---

[1] Source: National Archives and Records Administration, RG 59, Central Files 1964–66, POL 19 ADEN. Confidential. Drafted by David A. Korn (NEA/NE) on October 14; cleared by Campbell, Grant V. McClanahan (AF/AFN), Officer in Charge of Dependent Area Affairs Patricia Byrne, and Director of the Office of UN Political Affairs Elizabeth Ann Brown; and approved by Symmes. Sent to Aleppo, Amman, Asmara, Baghdad, Beirut, Cairo, Dhahran, Damascus, Jidda, Kuwait, Taiz, Algiers, Rabat, Tripoli, Tunis, Addis Ababa, Mogadiscio, Nouakchott, Paris, Basra, Tel Aviv, and Khartoum and repeated to USUN, Aden, and London.

REF

Depcirtel 509, Sept. 28, 1965[2]

A particularly strong Arab campaign against the British on Aden now appears to be in the offing in the current UNGA. The UK's suspension of the Aden constitution on September 25 (Department circular telegram 509) has been followed by demonstrations and strikes in Aden. On October 5 Arab representatives at the UN sent a letter to the Security Council protesting the British action. The Adeni oppositionists, meeting in Cairo, have formed a joint delegation (including two representatives each from the former Aden Government, the *Organization for the Liberation of the Occupied South, and the National Liberation Front*) to the UNGA to press their attack on British policy in South Arabia.

The Aden question is scheduled for debate by the GA's Fourth Committee from October 14 to 25. The Arabs and the "anti-colonialist" bloc are expected to base their attack on the British on two previous UN resolutions: General Assembly resolution 1949 (XVIII) of December 11, 1963[3] and a Committee of 24 resolution of May 17, 1965.[4] General Assembly resolution 1949 calls inter alia for self determination through universal suffrage, the "early removal" of the British military base, the freeing of political detainees and an end to "repressive actions", the formation of a provisional government, and the establishment of a UN presence in Aden. The Committee of 24 resolution reiterates these points, though in somewhat stronger language. It is anticipated that Arab UN representatives will introduce in the October 14–25 Fourth Committee debate a resolution similar to that voted by the Committee of 24, with added passages condemning the UK's recent suspension of the Aden constitution and requesting *immediate* liquidation of the base.

Background

In January 1963 the Crown Colony of Aden became the State of Aden and joined with a number of the Shaikhdoms and Sultanates of the former East and West Aden Protectorates to form the South Arabian Federation (SAF). A conflict immediately emerged between the Protectorate leaders and the Adenis. The latter, more advanced and better educated than the inhabitants of the Protectorates, feared that they would have little weight in a federation of states which were essentially

[2] Document 64.

[3] For text, see *American Foreign Policy: Current Documents, 1963*, pp. 593–594.

[4] The Committee of 24 (Special Committee on the Situation with Regard to Implementation of the Declaration on the Granting of Independence to Colonial Countries) adopted the resolution by a vote of 19 to 3 (including the United States) with 2 abstentions.

tribal monarchies. The Adeni politicians demanded a unitary state, believing that this type of arrangement would give them a much better chance of dominating and directing the new entity. After the Labor victory in 1964, the UK agreed to consider a unitary state concept and SAF leaders also announced their willingness to support a unitary state. However, disagreement persisted between the British, the Adeni politicians and the leaders of the former Protectorate states regarding the timetable for independence and the definition of the new state.

During the 1964 London Conference on Aden the British Government announced its intention of granting independence to Aden and the SAF not later than 1968. British efforts to follow up this announcement by the holding of a constitutional conference to create a framework for an independent state have been blocked largely by nationalist elements supported by the UAR who insisted on immediate implementation of the 1963 UN resolution. With funds and arms supplied by the UAR from its base in Yemen, the nationalists instituted an increasingly active terrorist campaign. This UAR support increased markedly following British retaliatory bombing of the Yemeni town of Harib in the spring of 1964, and the UN's subsequent "deploring" of the UK's action. Deterioration of the security situation and refusal of the Aden State Ministers to condemn terrorism and cooperate in the maintenance of law and order led the UK to suspend operation of the Aden constitution on September 25, 1965.

The Base

The UK insists that the future of its strategic base in Aden be determined by negotiation with whatever government emerges following independence. While most of the inhabitants of Aden State benefit either directly or indirectly from the base, there is strong nationalist sentiment against it, encouraged by the UAR. The UK apparently anticipates that the leaders of an independent government, faced with the full weight of their responsibilities and cognizant of the economic impact of a sudden British military withdrawal, would be more inclined to agree to the maintenance of the base for at least a limited period.

British Position in UN

The British position regarding the 1963 UNGA resolution is outlined in the attached Foreign Office guidance paper, recently given the Department by the British Embassy.[5] As indicated therein the British declare their general agreement with the resolution except for 1) evacua-

---

[5] Attached but not printed.

tion of the base, which they insist is a matter for discussion with the future independent South Arabian Government; and 2) the lifting of security measures, which cannot be done in the face of terrorist attacks without plunging the area into further chaos. British reservations regarding a popular vote and the formation of a provisional government under present conditions are also set forth.

British officials admit that, for the present at least, they have no specific plans for solving the Aden crisis beyond the hope that suspension of the constitution will enable them to restore order and regain control of the situation in South Arabia. The Foreign Office is understood to be considering inviting the UN to send some type of representation to Aden to study the situation.

US Position

Any precipitate British withdrawal from the Aden area at this time would result in a chaotic situation in South Arabia harmful to general Western interests. Recognizing that the growth of nationalist pressures requires the granting of independence in the next few years, the British have been exerting efforts to establish the framework of a potentially viable government and to promote an orderly evolution to independence. Although we do not necessarily endorse all the moves which the British have taken, we support their goal of an orderly evolution to independence in South Arabia and believe that the ending of terrorism is a necessary step in this process. As in the past, we expect to continue to express this support in the United Nations.

Our position in the forthcoming Fourth Committee debate on Aden will be along the following lines.

1. We favor the principle of self determination for the people of South Arabia and believe that the UK is endeavoring to work out acceptable constitutional arrangements toward that end. In this regard we note that despite its suspension of the Aden constitution the UK has reaffirmed its intention of abiding by its earlier promise to grant independence no later than 1968.

2. The ending of terrorism is a necessary step in an orderly evolution toward independence.

3. We opposed the May 17 resolution of the Committee of 24 on grounds that the resolution failed to take account of the progress toward independence already made in Aden and British proposals for further action in this direction. We will continue to oppose similar resolutions if presented to the Fourth Committee. (Our final decision can of course be made only after examination of the resolutions put forward in the Committee.)

4. We will be prepared to support the above points in a statement to the Committee.

Posts may draw on the foregoing as appropriate in discussion of the Aden question with host Government representatives and diplomatic colleagues.[6]

Rusk

---

[6] On November 3, by a vote of 83 to 11 (including the United States) with 8 abstentions, the Fourth Committee adopted a resolution deploring the attempts of the administering power to set up an unrepresentative regime in the territory, calling on all states not to recognize any independence not based on the wishes of the people of the territory freely expressed through elections held under universal adult suffrage, and calling the complete and immediate removal of the British base at Aden essential. Resolution 2023 (XX) was adopted by the UN General Assembly on November 5 by a vote of 90 to 11 (including the United States) with 10 abstentions. The text is printed in *American Foreign Policy: Current Documents, 1965*, pp. 615–616.

---

66.   Memorandum of Conversation[1]

Washington, October 19, 1965.

SUBJECT

  South Arabia

PARTICIPANTS

  British Colonial Secretary Anthony Greenwood
  British Colonial Under Secretary Eastwood
  Mr. Noakes, Chief Information Officer, British Colonial Office
  Minister Michael Stewart, British Embassy
  Mr. Christopher Everett, British Embassy
  Ambassador Hare, Assistant Secretary, NEA
  Mr. Kitchen, G/PM
  Mr. George C. Moore, NEA/NE

Mr. Greenwood opened the conversation with the statement that while Britain would study UN developments concerning Aden, it did not expect that they would contribute towards progress in the area. He then briefly described political developments concerning Aden subsequent to the Labor Government's assuming power, including the

---

[1] Source: National Archives and Records Administration, RG 59, Central Files 1964–66, POL 19 ADEN. Secret. Drafted by Moore.

UK–Federation agreement to establish a unitary state, the breakdown of plans to hold a constitutional conference in March 1965, and his subsequent trip to Aden in August when he persuaded Adeni leaders to talk in London on the basis of the UN principle of self-determination. He credited al Asnag with being of considerable help in bringing this conference about. Subsequently, however, al Asnag, Makkawi and other Adeni leaders brought a breakdown of the conference by their rigid insistence on full acceptance of the UN 1963 resolutions, particularly including lifting of the state of emergency. The subsequent deterioration in the security situation in Aden required the British to suspend operation of the constitution last month.

Mr. Greenwood said that he honestly did not know what the next British step should be. He hoped to restore stability in the country and then perhaps build further on the moderate progressive forces there. He felt that all efforts should be exerted to persuade Nasser that the British were firm in their commitment to grant independence by 1968 and in their belief that no military base was defensible, either politically or morally, if its presence was not in accord with the wishes of the people concerned. He said that the future of the British military base in Aden, within the framework of the worldwide UK defense review, was still completely undecided. It was possible that the base might be given up or might be maintained on a reduced status. In response to Mr. Hare's question, he said that a reduction in the forces there might indeed abate Arab pressure since the fear existed that, with a larger number of troops, military pressure might at any time be exerted against Arab countries. He believed Nasser opposed the base partly because it was an insult to Arab nationalism, partly because it impeded his own aims at influencing the Gulf, and partly because he feared the growth of Saudi influence in the area which it fostered.

Mr. Hare asked, aside from Nasser, what were the elements of difficulty in Southern Arabia. Mr. Greenwood said the basic problem was one of conflict between the more advanced Aden group and the Federation and Eastern Aden Protectorate leaders. The Adenis had great fear of domination by the Federal Army. Britain, for its part, could not impose actions on the Federation states since it maintained only advisory treaties with them.

Responding to Mr. Hare's question about relations with Yemen, Mr. Greenwood said the Federation rulers were essentially closer to the royalists, while the Adenis favored the republicans. He did not expect that Yemen would in the foreseeable future be interested in the take-over of South Arabia since the Yemenis would have more than enough of their own troubles to think about.

Mr. Hare asked if terrorism was continuing. Mr. Greenwood said there now appeared to be little terrorism in the Protectorate and that it had been greatly abated in Aden itself, with the exception of special snipers trained in Yemen. The biggest problem on the horizon was potential industrial unrest promoted by the NLF. While the ATUC was sympathetic to the British view, there was little they could do. The economy of Aden had already been greatly affected since many ships were now bypassing the port. (The port's continued importance for bunkering is indicated by the fact that four million of the six million tons of fuel oil annually produced at the refinery are dispensed to ships in Aden.) It was feared that if a tough line were adopted toward labor unrest, the result would be a general strike which would seriously hinder operation of the military base.

Concerning the base, Mr. Greenwood said that the British did not want to vitiate its capabilities until we (the Anglo-Americans) had developed suitable alternatives, e.g., Indian Ocean facilities. In response to Mr. Stewart's query, Mr. Kitchen said that we indeed considered British military presence in Aden as important since, for instance, it gave the British the possibility of moving forces quickly to various areas of potential trouble. Mr. Kitchen continued that the British, because they are already in situ, have the potential to take many military actions which we do not have. Mr. Stewart responded that he did not see why the British should be "mercenaries" for the Free World if any particular action involved was not also specifically helpful to UK interests.

In further discussion of the base, Mr. Greenwood noted that its usefulness for support of activities in the Far East was rapidly becoming impaired as "the various doors" for reaching it from the UK were being closed. Mr. Kitchen emphasized that the Shah of Iran was also concerned with the relaxation of Britain's hold in Aden. Mr. Stewart said that, nonetheless, the Shah had not raised the subject with the UK.

67.   Special Memorandum Prepared in the Central Intelligence Agency[1]

No. 26–65   Washington, November 5, 1965.

OUTLOOK FOR ADEN AND THE FEDERATION
OF SOUTH ARABIA

Summary

British efforts to forge a viable Federation of South Arabia out of Aden Colony and the former Protectorate sultanates, and to work out some arrangement for the future of the military base in Aden, are in trouble. The main internal problems are traditional antipathy between town and tribe, Egyptian-sponsored terrorism in Aden and the sultanates and Adeni fear that the sheikhs would suppress political liberties through arbitrary police power. The UK has promised independence to the Federation in 1968, but British refusal to discuss the future of the military base with the Adenis have raised doubts among them about Britain's intentions.

In the wake of deteriorating security situations, the UK has suspended local government in Aden proper. The British probably will make no significant political moves in the near term, but will concentrate on keeping terrorism under control which they can probably do. Over the longer term, the British will probably have to come to terms with those elements now in opposition if they are to have any chance of both creating a viable Federation and keeping the base on acceptable terms.

1. The status of Aden and the neighboring British-protected states in South Arabia is confronting the UK with a troublesome problem. It is the familiar but difficult one of granting independence to a colonial possession without abandoning local friends and interests deemed to be important. Among these latter, Britain's military base in Aden has loomed large, and this issue is a part of the broader question of the whole British military posture east of Suez and indeed of Britain's role in the Western alliance itself.

---

[1] Source: Johnson Library, National Security File, Country File, Saudi Arabia, Memos, Vol. I, 12/63–4/67. Secret. Prepared in the Office of National Estimates, Central Intelligence Agency.

2. The UK's proposed solution was to establish the Federation of South Arabia,[2] now composed of 16 sultanates and sheikhdoms on the southern Peninsula, together with Aden itself. Although the British retain overriding powers in respect of foreign affairs, defense, and internal security, the Federation is slowly assuming more authority in internal administration, education, and finance. The Federation's governing body is a Council, three-fourths of whose members are from ruling families from the Protectorate states and the remainder from Aden. Mutual suspicion between progressive Aden and the backward sheikhdoms is greatly hampering Britain's efforts to grant independence by 1968.

Aden

3. In British hands since 1839, Aden has been a major bunkering port on the imperial lifeline to India, since the opening of the Suez Canal in 1869. It has grown from a tiny village to a city of some quarter million people of diverse backgrounds, chiefly Arabs but with many Indians and Somalis. About a third of the population is temporary migrant labor from Yemen. Thanks to a very large bunkering trade (Aden has a large refinery), its free port status, and its role as entrepot for Yemen, Aden enjoys a moderately high standard of living. There is a fair degree of education, and a vigorous labor organization of about 10,000 members, the Aden Trades Union Congress (ATUC), has grown up.

4. The British permitted limited political activity in the 1950s, and in 1959 12 members of the 23-man Legislative Council were elected under a restricted franchise. By the early 1960s there had arisen a sizeable political force, the People's Socialist Party (PSP), based on the ATUC. Both were headed by Abdallah al-Asnag, a middle class Adeni whose family has close ties with Yemen. The PSP has fought to broaden the franchise to include Arabs not born in Aden, which would give political control to the laboring class. As a long term goal it also advocates union of South Arabia and Yemen. No other party has much popular support.

The Protectorate

5. In sharp contrast to Aden itself, the Protectorate states are economically backward and politically primitive. British control has been

---

[2] The Federation of South Arabia consists of the former Aden Colony (75 square miles and an estimated population of 220,000), and the Protectorate area. The Protectorate was for administrative purposes divided into the Eastern Protectorate (the Hadramaut) with four states, 90,000 square miles in area, and with an estimated population of 320,000, and the Western Protectorate with 16 states, comprising 22,000 square miles and a population of about 550,000. The Federation includes 15 of the Western Protectorate sultanates, but only one—the smallest—of the Eastern sultanates. [Footnote in the source text.]

exercised indirectly through long-standing treaties of protection with some twenty sheikhdoms and sultanates. The British paid subsidies to the rulers and for years intervened only when tribal warfare threatened trade routes or general security. Beginning in the 1930s the UK largely pacified both Eastern and Western Protectorates. More recently, London has begun to stimulate education and some economic development. But the region's size, backwardness, and lack of resources— notably water—have impeded progress. The Protectorate states are still ruled in traditional fashion by leading families, although their participation in Federation ministries has given them some political experience.

The Federation

6. The British were aware that this congeries of petty states had little chance to survive in the long run. In 1958, they dragooned six sultanates in the Western Protectorate into forming a Federation. The rulers were hesitant, but they were persuaded that federation would increase their ability to resist absorption by Yemen, and their heavy dependence on British subsidies made them amenable to British desires. All but one of the 16 Western Protectorate states have now become members; a Federation capital has been established near Aden; and the Protectorate Levies have become the nucleus of an army. The Federation government is beginning to function, but it remains dependent on UK subsidies for nearly two-thirds of its revenue. The three principal Eastern Protectorate sultanates, more educated and aware of the outside world through long-standing connections with Indonesia, East Africa, and Saudi Arabia, have remained aloof from the Federation. They are unwilling to join a state with so many problems, and at least for the present prefer their own semi-independent status.

7. Adenis generally are dubious about the benefits of the Federation, and their participation has been half-hearted at best. Aden joined in 1963 only after the governor exerted strong pressure on the Legislative Council, and half of the Council's Adeni members walked out before the vote was taken. Most Adenis fear that their money may be drained off to support the Protectorate areas. They demand representation in the Federation government out of proportion to the size of their population lest Aden be outvoted by the Protectorate representatives. Most important, and related to the representation issue, Adenis of all political shadings worry that the unreconstructed sheikhs and sultans will not only refuse to extend the electoral process in the Federation, but will also be able to suppress Adeni political freedom by control of the police and security forces. The British have responded to those fears by arranging that Federation police power be "delegated" to the High Commissioner.

8. Relations between the British and the responsible Adeni opposition deteriorated as a result of difficulties over elections for the Legislative Council in October 1964. [4 lines of source text not declassified] Asnag has been helped by Cairo, but he is probably a Baathist rather than a Nasserist. He has pushed for a government in South Arabia run by its people, not by hereditary chiefs or foreigners.

9. In response to the British move, Asnag boycotted the elections, though he probably could have won a third or more of the elected seats on the Council. Others in the PSP leadership wanted to contest the elections; some did, and the dispute between them and Asnag weakened both the PSP and Asnag's control over it. As a move to bolster his own position, and as a counter to more radical elements, Asnag has joined with other Adeni and Federation opposition elements in the Organization for Liberation of Occupied South (OLOS), which is based in Yemen. This group is pressing for a drastically reduced measure of British influence now and for its own dominance when independence is granted. In particular, it wants the status of the base settled before independence. Asnag's own current views on the future of the base are not clear, but 5,000 of his ATUC members are employed there, and as of 1964, he stopped short of demanding British withdrawal from it.

The Military Base

10. The British have not made up their minds about the need for the Aden base over the long term. On the one hand, the base represents a political vulnerability for the UK, not only on the Peninsula, but in the area as a whole. It is a target of nationalist criticism and a rallying-cry for anti-British propaganda by Nasser and others. It is also an expensive proposition. On the other hand, a number of factors have combined to increase the military value of the base since 1950. Suez is gone. Growing nationalist movements in the area have increased the chances of military or terrorist activities against British oil interests. Troops formerly stationed in Kenya have had to be relocated. Since 1962, the UK military garrison has grown from 7,000 to some 22,000 personnel—5,000 RAF, 14,000 army, and 3,000 navy—and there has been a vast amount of military associated construction—barracks, warehouses, dependent quarters, etc. [3 lines of source text not declassified]

11. The future of the base is now under debate in London, and there are divided counsels, not only on its military worth, but also on the political measures necessary to keep it. We believe it highly unlikely that Britain will decide to abandon the base completely, and the real question is how and on what terms it can be kept. Senior British officials in Aden and in the Colonial Office in London have believed that a substantial measure of control over the political institutions of the Federation and of Aden state was needed to assure the UK's tenure at

the base. Moreover, many of these officials—including the last governor, who developed and pushed the Federation scheme—felt more at home with traditionalist sheikhs than with modernizing nationalists. [3 *lines of source text not declassified*] Another school of thought in London prefers to work for a deal with an independent federation which would allow Britain to keep the base.

Yemeni and Egyptian Involvement

12. A further complication is the long-standing Yemeni claim to all of South Arabia. For years, border troubles between Yemeni and the Protectorate were endemic. The Yemeni revolution of 1962 made no substantial change in this situation until the appearance of Egyptian forces and the rise of Egyptian influence in republican Yemen led to strong British fears of UAR meddling in Aden and the Protectorate. [2 *lines of source text not declassified*] the Yemeni Republicans and particularly the Egyptians began in 1963 to increase their efforts to cause trouble in South Arabia. Dissident tribesmen, armed and trained by the UAR, and sometimes including important exiled members of South Arabian ruling families, have tied down a substantial proportion of the Federation's 5,000-man army and some British forces as well.

13. British and Federal forces, however, have been able to control the dissidents in the Protectorate. Therefore, in late 1964, the Egyptians turned to Aden itself. Their puppet National Liberation Front (NLF) began to attack Arab police and British soldiers, as well as civilians. This campaign has seriously damaged the morale of the Adeni police officers, and the British have been forced to rely more and more on their own personnel to maintain security. Strikes and slowdowns have caused considerable economic loss. In particular, during a two-month labor slowdown in the port, more than half the bunkering trade was diverted elsewhere.

14. Though the Aden government was by no means a group of radicals, it tended to side with the NLF against the British, and blamed the terrorism on lack of progress toward independence. [2½ *lines of source text not declassified*] In September, however, the killing of two senior British officials goaded London into suspending the local government and imposing direct rule by the High Commissioner. The security situation is now fairly well under control.

Outlook

15. The British have enough force in Aden to maintain security for the foreseeable future, but they will continue to be vulnerable to terrorist attacks and will probably continue to be harassed by labor troubles in the port, refinery, and base areas. British ability to control terrorism would be improved if the projected settlement in Yemen

actually does lead to withdrawal of Egyptian forces there. They can continue to help the Federation leaders to organize ministries, get them functioning, and in general lay down the necessary foundation of an administrative system for the Federation. But this does not get at the basic problems: the restoration of local government in Aden and the forging of a working relationship between Aden and the sheikhs.

16. Beyond this kind of temporizing, the longer term choices open to the British are not particularly attractive. On the one hand, they can press ahead with the Federation plans, make whatever arrangements with the Federation sultans they feel they need for continued tenure at the base hoping that the sultans will prove able to make these arrangements stick. This would bring on an increase in violence, political disturbance, not only among the political articulate forces in Aden, but also to some extent in the more troublesome states of the hinterland. In such circumstances, Aden might try to withdraw from the Federation. In the Arab world generally, the issue would continue to constitute a liability for the UK. This course would probably prove too costly in terms of property damage, lives lost, and economic decline to endure for long.

17. On the other hand, the UK could move to permit the nationalist elements to take political power in Aden. This would probably require new elections under a broadened franchise, and the consequent installation of a nationalist government, probably radical, and certainly hard to deal with. Establishment of confidence between the British and the Adeni politicians will be at best a long and difficult task. Given recent terrorist activity, it is doubtful that British authorities could bring themselves to let even a few terrorists or terrorist supporters into the government. Moreover, the authorities would have to put heavy pressure on the sultans, who applaud vigorous British actions in Aden, to conform, and this would cause other problems in the Federation. Particularly in view of the economic importance to Aden of the base, however, we believe that the British could probably work out with the nationalists a reasonably satisfactory arrangement.

18. For the next several months at least, the UK is most likely to avoid a clear-cut decision and will concentrate on providing greater assurance of security in Aden. However, unless the independence promised for 1968 is to be postponed, London will have to begin soon to get a government in Aden which represents local opinion and which can participate in the Federation. The longer the period of drift persists, the more the nationalist forces will grow in size and strength and the harder the British task will be. In the end, the UK will probably be forced, in order to avoid chaos, to deal with the very people they have sought to exclude.

For the Board of National Estimates:
Sherman Kent
Chairman

68.   Memorandum of Conversation[1]

Washington, February 4, 1966.

SUBJECT

British Talks: Nasser–Faisal Relations; Yemen; South Arabia; Persian Gulf
(afternoon session)

PRINCIPAL PARTICIPANTS

United Kingdom
Sir Roger Allen, Deputy Undersecretary, Foreign Office
Frank Brenchley, Head, Arabian Department
Denis Speares, Head, North and East Africa Department
Christopher Everett, First Secretary, UK Embassy

United States
Ambassador Hare
Rodger P. Davies, Deputy Director, NEA
Harrison M. Symmes, Director, NE
John M. Howison, GTI
Guy Lee, NR
George C. Moore, OIC, Arabian Peninsula Affairs

Observers

United Kingdom
David Crawford, First Secretary, UK Mission, New York
Francis Brown, Minister, UK Mission, New York
Nigel Trench, Counselor, UK Embassy
Noel Martin, Petroleum Attaché, UK Embassy

United States
William Brewer, S/P
James Spain, INR/RNA
Jonathan Stoddart, DOD/ISA
Howard Meyers, G/PM

[Here follows section I: Nasser–Faisal Relations and Yemen.]

II. Aden and South Arabia

Sir Roger stated that the British decision to withdraw from the
Aden military base would be officially announced in the Defense Review White Paper February 23.[2] While at present uncertain of the form
of the announcement, he thought it might be phrased very simply

---

[1] Source: National Archives and Records Administration, RG 59, Central Files 1964–
66, POL 3 ISLAMIC. Secret. Drafted by Moore on February 9.
[2] The U.K. Government, faced with a serious balance-of-payments problem, was
undergoing a defense review. It had previously informed the U.S. Government that the
British base at Aden would be evacuated in 1968 and that British forces overseas would
be reduced by one-third over the next 4 years. On February 22, it issued a Defense White
Paper formally announcing these decisions.

along the lines of, "We do not intend to seek base facilities after the independence of South Arabia." It might contain some reference to British intention to continue economic aid to South Arabia after independence. At present, HMG contributes £12 to 15 million annually. The High Commissioner is insistent that this be continued since, if the SAF leaders thought they were being abandoned, it would be difficult to obtain their agreement to any constitutional progress. Defense Minister Healey believes it necessary to continue paying for the South Arabian Federal Army. Additionally, HMG might keep a military mission under the aegis of its Embassy. It is expected that the British will simply move out of their present facilities in Aden at the appropriate time although they might try to retain limited staging and communications facilities. This has not yet been finally decided. Responding to Ambassador Hare's question, Mr. Brenchley said that the British would try to keep the refinery operating since this was the main British asset in the area.

The current British timetable calls for first obtaining the approval of the Rulers of Bahrain and Sharjah to expand base facilities in that area. (This has just been obtained, although the Rulers have not been informed about Aden withdrawal.) The Hone–Bell draft constitution will be taken to Aden on February 10 and formally presented to the Rulers on February 12; Lord Beswick will travel to Aden on the 15th and inform the Federal Supreme Council on the 16th of the decision to withdraw militarily from Aden; Faisal will be informed on the 16th.

Sir Roger said that Nasser's continued presence in Yemen presented a grave problem with respect to military withdrawal from Aden. Nasser continues strongly to support terrorist activities and HMG has evidence that he is currently training some 300 terrorists in Taiz. With announcement of British military withdrawal it is expected Nasser will increase these activities in order to hasten the departure and multiply its disorder. The announcement may well encourage him to stay in Yemen.

The announcement, said Sir Roger, is certain to have a bad effect on the situation in South Arabia. Some of the Federal leaders will no doubt consider switching their full support to Nasser; others may more strongly push their demands for immediate control of Aden town. The Adenis, in turn, will stiffen their opposition to greater Federal control. If Nasser were to withdraw from Yemen it is very possible that the Federal Army would move into Aden and liquidate the Nationalist leaders. In contrast, so long as Nasser's troops are present in Yemen they could move into Aden under the pretext of protecting the Nationalists against Federal Army incursions.

In response to Ambassador Hare's question, Sir Roger said that once the British had departed it was doubtful if Nasser would have any continuing interest in the Federation. He might maintain some concern for Aden town, probably in the form of indirect support to Nationalist politicians. However, the area would not in general be of much value to Nasser.

Ambassador Hare posed the theoretical question of what would occur if the British made no proposal for a constitution but merely departed. Sir Roger predicted increased disorder and, on the completion of the British withdrawal, the full control of Aden town by Federal troops. He said, leaving Nasser aside, there was little affinity between Yemenis and South Arabians/Adenis.

In response to a question from Mr. Symmes, Sir Roger said categorically that, even if asked, the British would not give any security guarantee to the SAF after independence.

Responding to a further query by Ambassador Hare, Sir Roger said that some consideration had been given to bringing in the UN. However, this was ruled out so long as Great Britain continued to be responsible for law and order. The UN, judging by its past attitude toward Aden, basically reflected only an extension of Egyptian policy. At present, the UN could be expected to be only trouble makers rather than contribute to a solution. Nonetheless HMG did not rule out UN intervention at some stage. ("Matters could get so bad we might throw the subject into the UN.") Mr. Brenchley indicated he would spend the next two days in New York studying the feasible role of the UN but did not consider UN participation to be possible at present.

Sir Roger said that prospects generally were exceedingly gloomy in Aden and that it was difficult to foresee the necessary progress to enable the British peacefully to hand over the reins of power in 1968.

Sir Roger admitted that it was conceivable the Russians and Chinese Communists might take interest in Aden if a vacuum developed but doubted that this was an actual danger. Ambassador Hare suggested that Nasser would not react favorably to the Communists' getting a firm foothold there. Mr. Brenchley said there were only a few Leftists in Aden and the Hadramaut at the present time; while their proportionate size would probably increase in the future as the overall population of Aden shrank due to emigration because of worsening economic problems, it was doubtful that the Leftists in the area would offer a conceivable base to facilitate Soviet encroachment.

III. Persian Gulf

Forces Buildup in the Gulf

Sir Roger stated that, as a result of the withdrawal from Aden, HMG was now seeking added facilities in the Gulf in order to maintain in some fashion its commitments to Kuwait and to the Rulers of the Gulf Shaikhdoms. If HMG were to maintain its present level of commitment to Kuwait it would need an added 11,000 troops in the Gulf—

impossible on both political and financial grounds. Therefore it now must modify its Kuwait commitment to offer only air assistance unless given sufficient warning for it to be able to bring in additional troops prior to any attack. This change must now be discussed with the Kuwaitis; it is not unexpected that the Kuwaitis may use this shift as the basis for letting lapse their arrangement with the British.

It is currently contemplated to add 600 troops in Bahrain and 2000 in Sharjah. No buildup is planned at Masirah and it is quite possible that the current strength at Salalah will be decreased. The new troops can be accommodated in Bahrain with no new land acquisitions above the 3000 acres presently held. It will be necessary to construct a new battalion camp outside of the airfield at Sharjah and add a few new hangars. The Sharjah airfield will not need to be enlarged. At present it can take Canberras and similar aircraft. Bahrain would continue to be the main staging point for troop movement further east and would form the link between Kuwait and Sharjah. (A detailed British list of proposed troops in the Gulf is attached.)

The British hope that their troop increases in the Gulf will mitigate in the Arab World the impression of weakness which may be implied in their withdrawal from Aden and will underline their determination not to relinquish their position in the Gulf. They have informed the Shah of their contemplated moves in Aden and the Gulf and have assured him of their intention to maintain their Canberra bomber force in Cyprus. The Shah accepted the changes cheerfully and seemed to have no doubts about their future determination to remain in the Gulf. They doubt however that Faisal will react in the same accommodating fashion.

[Here follows discussion of Kuwait, Iran, and Dubai.]

---

69.   Telegram From the Department of State to the Embassy in the United Arab Republic[1]

Washington, February 19, 1966, 5:36 p.m.

4691. 1. On Feb 18 British Ambassador Dean delivered to Under-Secretary Ball message to Secretary from FonMin Stewart requesting

---

[1] Source: National Archives and Records Administration, RG 59, Central Files 1964–66, POL 19 ADEN. Secret. Drafted by Moore on February 18; cleared by Hare, Symmes, Russell, and Judd; and approved by Ball. Repeated to London, Aden, and Jidda.

USG use publication of British Defense White Paper on 22 Feb as opportunity urge Nasser adopt more constructive policy toward South Arabia. Message made following supporting points:

a. UK troop withdrawal from Aden will add to tremendous difficulties foreseen in bringing area to independence by 1968. Extent of difficulties will depend on attitude of UAR.

b. In past UAR has made clear its intention frustrate any constitutional advance except on terms of "unrealistic" UN resolutions and has used terrorism and intimidation to support this goal.

c. Hope US Ambassador in Cairo can make strong approach to Nasser as soon as possible after Feb 22 making plain that South Arabia is common US–UK concern and that he speaking for USG not HMG (since Canada is protecting power for latter).

d. Believe announcement UK decision withdraw from Aden gives perhaps last opportunity influence Nasser. Suggest that, in view absence incidents since January 18, stress not be placed on terrorist aspect, but rather on positive approach that announcement base withdrawal has removed Nasser's main objection UK policies in Aden and should enable him adopt more constructive attitude. It in Nasser's interest that South Arabia enjoy stable independence rather than become another Yemen.

e. Anticipate Nasser's reaction will be he does not control attitudes South Arabians; any UAR support given is justified by alleged British support royalists in Yemen; UN resolutions provide ready-made solution. HMG willing supply additional detailed factual material counter these arguments if desired.

2. UnderSec pointed out we had made similar approaches in past to UAR and would be most happy repeat them directly to Nasser unless our Ambassador has strongly overriding reasons for making presentation at lower level UARG.

3. Request you take action in accordance with foregoing unless strong objections perceived.

Rusk

70.   Telegram From the Embassy in the United Arab Republic to
the Department of State[1]

Cairo, March 8, 1966, 0810Z.

2268. My conversation with Foreign Minister Riad last evening,
his Chef de Cabinet and my DCM being present, covered Yemen,
Aden, Ghana and US assistance to UAR. Latter two subjects will be
reported separately.

1. I opened by commenting favorably on Sadat visit saying all
reports and press comments seemed to indicate it had been highly
successful. Riad agreed and confirmed GUAR very gratified by manner
and level his reception.

2. Turning to Yemen I said had just come from call on Hassan
Sabry al-Khouly who had informed me of new GUAR initiative (Embtel
2267).[2] As result, this subject could be taken off agenda. Expressing
great relief and pleasure at UAR effort break impasse through new
constructive proposals I said this act of real statesmanship.

Foreign Minister stated that Yemen frankly very serious question
for UAR and new proposals should make it clear President Nasser
sincerely desired its resolution. Key was improved UAR-Saudi relations and were progress achieved here Yemen settlement would no
longer pose problem. In effect it was not really a question of Jidda
agreement or its implementation but what King Faisal wants. Latter
has been acting on false assumption that UAR beset with serious
internal problems and so can be pushed around. Unless this attitude
changes Yemen problem would not be solved regardless of what
UAR offered.

3. I then raised Aden in context situation created by British Defense
White Paper and made following points:

A. South Arabia is a common US–UK concern. We have no military
or economic interest in area but believe that instability there contributes
to instability throughout the Middle East.

B. British are irrevocably committed evacuate their military base
at Aden by 1968. They have no plans to leave any troops whatsoever behind.

C. Constitutional proposals which British have put forward for
South Arabia are basis for discussion and not final proposal which
must be either accepted completely or else rejected. British are sincerely

---

[1] Source: National Archives and Records Administration, RG 59, Central Files 1964–
66, POL UAR–US. Secret; Limdis. Repeated to London, Jidda, Aden, and Taiz.
[2] See footnote 2, Document 392.

interested in leaving behind stable and independent South Arabia and believe this can best be done by working out in advance constitutional arrangement acceptable to majority of people involved. They welcome participation of all political elements of South Arabia in reaching this agreement.

D. We believe announcement of British plans withdraw from Aden removes UAR's main objection UK policies in South Arabia. UAR, because of its connection with nationalist groups there, now has responsible role play in helping assure that transition from colonial government to independent state is performed peacefully. Alternative is likely be political chaos and economic stagnation. We assume UAR wishes avoid another situation like Yemen and hope we can count on UAR use its considerable influence toward rational and peaceful transition.

Riad reviewed again Thompson talks and said British base was not main question but genuine independence. UK must negotiate with key nationalist leaders on basis UN resolution and self determination. I suggested provisions UN resolution already being complied with or shortly would be as result British actions on ground. We wanted stable, viable, representative government in area. This is all British wanted and we assumed it UAR objective also. Riad agreed but reiterated situation would be greatly eased were UK formally to accept UN resolution and begin talking directly to FLOSY. He recognized that forthcoming British elections made any progress virtually impossible at present.

Comment:

On Yemen Foreign Minister clearly feels his govt has now made optimum gesture and future is up to Faisal.

With Aden he got the point namely that we are interested in peace and stability in area and UAR activities which are not conducive to this objective will inevitably adversely affect US–UAR relations.

Battle

71.   **Telegram From the Department of State to the Embassy in the United Kingdom[1]**

Washington, March 18, 1966, 6:49 p.m.

5494. Embtel 4367, Aden.[2]

1. In any forthcoming conversations following points might be used with Brenchley and other FonOff officials:

2. USG in full agreement on importance strong U.S. démarche Cairo that UAR pursue moderate course in Aden–South Arabia. Ambassador Battle has already made extensive presentation UAR FonMin Riad (Cairo tel 215 to London)[3] whom we consider increasingly effective channel, and is currently seeking appointment Nasser to discuss this and other items of concern.

3. As British aware (e.g., Hare–Allen talks February), US–UAR relations complex matter; actions in South Arabia are but one of variety indices we use to judge Nasser's over-all performance. However, South Arabia of sufficient concern that we singling it out (together with Yemen) for specific mention to Nasser as among factors to be weighed in considering any future PL–480 program.

4. While UAR doubtless playing major role instigating disturbances South Arabia, it would scarcely have been so successful without extensive indigenous support. Latter appears increasing as reported Aden tel 117 (67 to London).[4]

5. We continue fully willing do all possible bring UAR to moderate its activities. However, cannot hope for success without concurrent and continued British willingness use appropriate opportunities continue discuss constructive settlement with South Arabian nationalists. (Per-

---

[1] Source: National Archives and Records Administration, RG 59, Central Files 1964–66, POL 23–9 ADEN. Secret. Drafted by Moore; cleared by Judd, Russell, and Symmes; and approved by Davies. Repeated to Aden, Cairo, Jidda, Taiz, and CINCSTRIKE.

[2] In telegram 4367 from London, March 16, Ambassador Bruce reported that in reply to his direct question as to what could be done to combat erosion of the security situation in Aden, Brenchley had responded that in spite of the evidence that the Front for the Liberation of Occupied South Yemen (FLOSY) had considerable indigenous support, the terrorist campaign itself could be called off immediately from Cairo. Thus, his government had placed its greatest hope in the possibility that the United States might be able to influence Nasser toward moderation following the British announcement regarding the Aden base. (Ibid.)

[3] Document 70.

[4] Dated March 16. (National Archives and Records Administration, RG 59, Central Files 1964–66, POL 23–ADEN)

haps further opening given in Chargé Clark's talk with Makkawi and Asnag, Taiz tel 141 to London.)[5]

Rusk

---

[5] Telegram 348 from Taiz, March 16 repeated to London as telegram 141. (Ibid., POL 13 ADEN)

---

72.   Telegram From the Consulate in Aden to the Department of State[1]

Aden, May 18, 1966, 0345Z.

147. Contel 145.[2] South Arabian Search for a Security Guaranty.

1. Foreign Minister Farid told me May 17 his government has not yet given up hope of securing post-independence defense agreement with UK. He leaves May 20 to join South Arabian delegation which will argue this point as well as negotiate for military assistance.

2. Farid criticized Wilson and Beswick for playing politics in Commons—twisting words of South Arabian ministers in their efforts to get off the hook on which Sandys has impaled them.

3. Farid asked my personal reaction to suggestion that, if UKG adheres to its decision to terminate defense agreement with independence, SAFG ask it to intercede in interest of defense agreement from US.[3]

---

[1] Source: National Archives and Records Administration, RG 59, Central Files 1964–66, POL 19 ADEN. Secret; Limdis. Repeated to Cairo, Jidda, London, Taiz, and CINC-STRIKE.

[2] Dated May 18. (Ibid.)

[3] Circular telegram 2452, June 13, transmitted press guidance for embassies to use in response to questions regarding a newspaper report that the South Arabian Federation was planning to ask the U.S. Government for a security guarantee. The guidance stated that no such request had been received, quoted President Kennedy's May 8, 1963, statement that the United States was "strongly opposed to the use of force or threat of force in the Near East," and expressed the hope that the people of South Arabia would be successful in setting up a government with the broadest possible base when becoming independent in 1968. (Ibid.)

4. I expressed personal view that USG, unlike UKG, has endeavored to maintain constructive relations with both extremist and moderate states in Near East and to this end sought to minimize special ties with any one faction. USG had not signed defense agreement with Saudi Arabia, and would be unlikely to do so with any other Near Eastern state.

5. However, repeated statements on UAR intentions toward Saudi Arabia showed US refusal to tolerate aggression from any quarter.

6. Farid observed that it would be very helpful if US could make similar statements with specific reference to South Arabia.

7. I expressed view that USG is further inhibited from categorical statements of this nature by difficulty in distinguishing between aggression and intervention in civil war—as UAR has done in Yemen. (Later in conversation, in a different context, Farid said Aden would undoubtedly fall under UAR influence if Egyptian troops remained in Yemen after South Arabian independence.)

8. Farid inquired about US attitude toward latest Egyptian wheat request. I said as far as I knew no decision had been taken. USG recognized that continued wheat shipments could be construed as encouragement to UAR to stay in Yemen, from which it could threaten SAF. Whereas cutting off wheat sales might bring UAR to terms, it might also force UARG into taking desperate actions detrimental to interests of more than one country.

9. Farid said he felt UARG would have to give in to US pressure unless Soviet Union bailed them out—an unlikely prospect. I suggested that much depended on what Soviets stood to gain; Aden Radio had repeated rumors of Soviet request for naval base in Egypt. Farid said he hoped UARG would grant Soviets a base and thus expose the hollowness of their claim to being neutral.

10. In any event, Farid concluded, he was not personally disturbed. If the Egyptian troops stay in Yemen, he could easily take refuge in his home state. What he regretted was that continued Egyptian presence in Yemen would undoubtedly destroy the South Arabian Federation.

Jones

73.   Telegram From the Department of State to the Embassy in the United Kingdom[1]

Washington, June 29, 1966, 7:39 p.m.

7856. Ref: Embtel 6243.[2]

1. We would feel better about FonOff recommendations on Aden if we could discern any alternative to UN role in solution of Aden problem. Unless UN steps in in some acceptable manner, it seems to us, British have no alternative to continuing unpromising policy of trying to turn over power to Federation Government whose access to power as independent state may well be signal for civil strife involving not only Aden, but UK, Yemen, UAR, and Saudi Arabia.

2. We understand British difficulties with Committee of Twenty-four resolution and HMG's commitments to SAF rulers. We do not, therefore, wish to press HMG too closely on Aden problem.

3. However, if occasion presents itself Embassy might try out one additional suggestion for UK consideration: Would it be possible for UKUN to inform the Secretary-General that the UK would be willing to receive a Special Mission, provided that composition of that Mission was acceptable to HMG, and provided further that it was understood in advance that while HMG would be prepared to consider recommendations of Mission, it would be in no way bound, in advance, to implement all of its recommendations, particularly those involving the safety and security of populations in South Arabia for which HMG would continue to feel responsible until independence (this refers to paragraphs 7 and 8 of June 23 resolution).

4. Problem of paragraph 2 (relative to "unrepresentative regime") remains, but conceivably this problem would diminish if acceptable

---

[1] Source: National Archives and Records Administration, RG 59, Central Files 1964–66, POL 19 ADEN/UN. Confidential. Drafted by Campbell; cleared by Moore, Brown, and Judd; and approved by Sisco. Also sent to USUN and repeated to Cairo, Taiz, and Aden.

[2] Telegram 6243 from London, June 28, reported a discussion between an Embassy officer and Foreign Office officials regarding the most recent UN resolution on Aden. On June 15 the Committee of 24, meeting in Cairo, had adopted a resolution calling on the Secretary-General to appoint immediately a special mission to Aden for the purpose of recommending practical steps necessary for full implementation of previous UN resolutions on Aden. It also deplored any defense arrangement the United Kingdom might enter into with "the unrepresentative regime" in Aden. (UN doc. A/6300/Rev. 1, ch. VI, par. 382) The Embassy officer urged the British to try to work out a formula that would provide for a mission led by Omar A.H. Adeel, appointed on June 9 by the UN Secretary-General as his Special Representative for the question of Aden. The Foreign Office response was that the real sticking point was the direct tying of the mission to the Cairo resolution, which was less acceptable than previous UN resolutions on South Arabia. (Ibid.)

role for UN supervision of elections could be worked out. Ultimately, it seems to us, this matter depends on whether Federation rulers can indeed control the hinterland vote (note Aden Consulate telegram 174 to Department on this subject).[3] If Federal rulers cannot control tribes, their government is doomed to failure in any case.

5. It seems to us, line suggested in para 3 puts British in more favorable position than out-and-out rejection of Special Mission "so long as its terms of reference are those of Committee of Twenty-four resolution" (Embtel 6192).[4] *For USUN*—You may also offer UKUN the above as informal suggestion if appropriate occasion arises.

Ball

---

[3] Dated June 15. (Ibid.)
[4] Dated June 24. (Ibid.)

---

74. Telegram From the Department of State to the Consulate in Aden[1]

Washington, August 5, 1966, 3:48 p.m.

22442. Ref: Aden's 128.[2]

1. FYI. While Dept naturally prepared see Farid if he insists on visiting US, talks at this time would be of limited usefulness. As you told Farid Aug 3, there is at present little possibility of even token US aid to SAF. Re SAF security we unable go beyond June 13 press guidance (Deptel 2452,[3] para la) reiterating Kennedy May 8, 1963, statement opposing use or threat of force in the Near East.

---

[1] Source: National Archives and Records Administration, RG 59, Central Files 1964–66, POL ADEN–US. Secret. Drafted by Korn; cleared by Held (NEA/ARP), Judd, NEA Director of Regional Affairs Sidney Sober, and Director of the AID Office of Near Eastern Affairs James C. Flint; and approved by Davies. Repeated to London, Cairo, Jidda, Taiz, and CINCSTRIKE.

[2] In telegram 128 from Aden, August 4, U.S. Consul Curtis F. Jones reported that Foreign Minister Muhammad Farid called on him August 3 to discuss ways the United States might help meet some of South Arabia's needs and suggested his traveling to the United States to meet with U.S. officials. Farid said that it would not be necessary for him to go as a guest, formal or informal, of the U.S. Government. Jones noted he reiterated to Farid and other South Arabian officials that there seemed little possibility of even token U.S. aid to the South Arabian Federation, particularly in light of increased British contributions. (Ibid.)

[3] See footnote 3, Document 72.

2. Dept will be undertaking in coming months extensive review South Arabian question in framework IRG. Would hope be better able discuss SAFG problems early 1967. End FYI.

3. You should inform Farid we sympathize with SAFG efforts in face many problems posed by forthcoming independence. We would of course be happy to receive him and exchange views if he desires visit Washington but feel talks at this time would have little to offer either as regards SAFG aid needs or security concerns. Assume SAFG will continue to look to HMG, as South Arabia's long-time friend, for primary assistance in both fields. USG would hope possibly be in better position discuss South Arabian situation in coming year.

4. Dept informing British Emb Farid proposal visit US and substance para 3 above. Emb London should convey same to FonOff.

Rusk

---

75.   **Memorandum From Harold H. Saunders of the National Security Council Staff to the President's Special Assistant (Rostow)**[1]

Washington, August 8, 1966.

WWR:

Since it might cause a little noise, you ought to have the background on the *latest UAR–UK clash in South Arabia*. The UN Security Council is meeting on it this afternoon.

The British claim that two Egyptian MIGs last week bombed a town (Nuqub) well within South Arabian borders. They have Soviet-made shell casings to show as evidence but nothing else except eye-witness reports. Our intelligence indicates that two planes were in a position to make this raid but can't produce tracking. Cairo denies that any of its planes were in the area. New Zealand may try to break the deadlock by proposing a UN investigation, but the UAR opposes.

Motives are hard to assess. The UAR may be trying to intimidate some of the local tribal leaders to swing to their side by demonstrating British inability to protect them. To prove their mettle, both to the locals and to their own Parliament, the British had to do something. They

---

[1] Source: Johnson Library, National Security File, Name File, Saunders Memos. Secret.

went to the UN in hopes they could avoid retaliating. However, if they don't get results there, they may still feel compelled to strike back.

There is no planned relationship between this incident and the longer range British problem of getting the UN to lay down satisfactory terms for a UN group to monitor the process of setting South Arabia free. However, they are coincidentally negotiating with U Thant to put together a responsible observer team. So their resorting to the UN is partly to establish good faith there.[2]

Hal

---

[2] The UN Security Council met August 4–16 to consider the British complaint concerning an "unprovoked and indefensible attack" on the town of Nuqub in the South Arabian Federation. The United Kingdom stated the evidence showed the attack was carried out by two MIG aircraft belonging to the United Arab Republic and operating out of an airfield in Yemen. UAR and Yemeni representatives categorically denied the charges. On August 16 the President of the Security Council read a consensus statement noting that the Council had not been able to produce a constructive solution and asking the parties concerned to contribute to lessening the tension in the region and to invite the Secretary-General to continue his good offices. For text, see *American Foreign Policy: Current Documents, 1966*, pp. 543–544.

---

76.   Paper Prepared by the Joint Chiefs of Staff[1]

Washington, August 9, 1966.

US MILITARY INTERESTS IN SOUTH ARABIA AND ADEN

US security interests in the area are:

a. Access to Aden facilities.
b. An adequate flow of Persian Gulf oil to Europe.
c. Denial of the area of the Soviets and the ChiComs.
d. Availability of British forces for operations with the area.
e. Prevention of a UAR–Saudi Arabia confrontation.

Periodic bunkering for COMIDEASTFOR ships (there are three), periodic fueling and logistic support of trans-Indian Ocean ships and

---

[1] Source: National Archives and Records Administration, RG 59, Central Files 1964–66, POL MUSCAT & OMAN. Secret. Attached to a note from Sober to Ambassador Hare, Deputy Assistant Secretary Davies, and NEA/ARP that reads: "The attached assessment by the JCS of *US Military Interests in South Arabia and Aden* has been forwarded to me by Brig. Gen. Sibley, JCS member of the IRG/NEA, at my request in anticipation of IRG consideration of the South Arabian situation."

aircraft and a few other flights constitute the US cold war needs. In limited war and area evacuation plans, Aden is an area of primary importance, although there are alternates which are somewhat less acceptable. The Gemini/Apollo plan for forcible recovery of astronauts and capsules designates Aden as a primary staging area for MEAFSA.

The loss of the availability of Aden for US military operations will:

a. Require revision of current plans.
b. Hamper but not prevent attainment of objectives envisioned in present plans by means of alternate and, in some cases, not quite as convenient routes and facilities.
c. Lend emphasis to expeditious construction of alternative US/UK military facilities in the Indian Ocean area.

The appendix to this paper sets forth a discussion of the more important US military interests in Aden, oil for Europe, communist penetration, the availability of British forces and the position of the Joint Chiefs of Staff concerning Aden and support of US military operations in the area.

It is concluded that Aden serves as a useful US military enroute and staging area but US military interests can be met by other alternatives.

[Apparent omission] British to remain as long as possible. From an operational point of view, the loss of the availability of Aden for US operations will:

a. Require revision to current plans.
b. Hamper but not prevent attainment of objectives envisioned in present plans by means of alternate and, in some cases, not quite as convenient routes and facilities.
c. Lend emphasis to expeditious construction of alternative US/UK military facilities in the Indian Ocean area.

The Joint Chiefs of Staff have addressed the problem of US security interests in the midst of continuing instability in the Near East and Africa in connection with contingency planning in the area. They conclude that the instability will continue notwithstanding all the efforts to prevent it and that rights of any sort will probably be more difficult to obtain and, if obtained, of uncertain tenure over the coming years because of this instability. Instability would be present with or without Soviet influence, but is often aggravated by Soviet support. Thus, the US ability to project forces into the area should focus on more reliable alternatives than "rights" which one day may be granted and the next denied. The Joint Chiefs of Staff have provided guidance to CINC-STRIKE/USCINCMEAFSA in this regard concerning the development of contingency plans which involve operations through or in the area.

Over the years Aden has lost much of its strategic iimportance except in case of general war. Ships rely less upon enroute support facilities. Development of the French port of Djibouti, but a few hours from Aden, has further reduced Aden's importance to shipping. The increasing number of ships which cannot be accommodated by the Suez Canal (the largest US carriers and the newer super tankers of 79 feet draft) reduces further Aden's importance.

From the standpoint of air traffic, longer range, faster and larger aircraft have lessened Aden's importance. US access to air facilities in Ethiopia, Dhahran, Bahrein, and Sharjah, Masirah as well as planned facilities in the British Indian Ocean Territory when developed will lessen still further the impact of the British withdrawal from Aden upon US military interests.

[Here follows the body of the paper.]

---

77. National Intelligence Estimate[1]

NIE 30–1–66   Washington, September 8, 1966.

THE OUTLOOK FOR SOUTH ARABIA

Conclusions

A. The British-sponsored Federation of South Arabia, comprising the prosperous port of Aden and the backward states of the Protectorate, is opposed by many Adeni politicians and by many sheikhs of the hinterland. Nonetheless, the UK has stated publicly that it will grant South Arabia its independence by the end of 1968, at the same time closing its base in Aden and ending its obligation to defend the area. London will almost certainly pull out by the appointed date, and may even do so earlier.

B. The British withdrawal will end the ten-year boom in Aden that has greatly increased the economic activity of that port and swollen its population by 50 percent. Closing the British base will cause a decrease of at least 25 percent in Aden's income. Political unrest could further reduce the use of Aden's port, leading to the loss of another quarter of Aden's income. There is likely to be little change in economic conditions in the hinterland of South Arabia.

C. Local political forces are now jockeying for power and seeking the backing of other Arab states. Saudi Arabia is giving some help to

---

[1] Source: Johnson Library, National Security File, NIEs, 30, Middle East. Secret; Controlled Dissem. According to a note on the cover sheet, the estimate was submitted by Helms and concurred in by the U.S. Intelligence Board on September 8.

conservative elements, especially in the eastern part of the Protectorate. More importantly, the UAR and Yemeni republicans are supporting dissident elements, especially in Aden, and are sponsoring subversive and terrorist campaigns there which make continued turbulence likely. In the circumstances we believe it unlikely that the Federation will long survive the British withdrawal.

D. Even in the period before independence, the chances of an accommodation between the Protectorate rulers and Aden are not good. There is little likelihood that the British could bring to power an Aden government sufficiently conservative to be acceptable to the Protectorate rulers without its being unacceptable in Aden. If the British permit the tribal leaders to control Aden, nationalist violence would be likely; and if they permit the nationalists to regain a voice in the government, the sheikhs would be disturbed. The nationalists themselves might even refuse to participate. In any event, the issue could probably not be solved without violence. In either case, the Adenis would need, and probably get, outside support for their cause.

[Here follow the Discussion section of the estimate and an annex.]

---

78.   Memorandum Prepared in the Central Intelligence Agency[1]

Washington, October 12, 1966.

SOVIET ACTIONS IN RESPECT OF POSSIBLE SUCCESSOR REGIMES IN SOUTH ARABIA[2]

1. Soviet actions in the southern part of the Arabian Peninsula will be governed in large measure by the nature of the successor regime that the British are able to leave in South Arabia, although the Soviets will have little to do with shaping that regime. The USSR's activity will also be influenced, though to a lesser degree, by such external factors as the outcome of the Saudi Arabian-UAR dispute and the consequences of Egyptian efforts to run Yemen as a colony, which could serve either to increase or decrease the options available. The course

---

[1] Source: Johnson Library, National Security File, Saunders Files, Aden & South Arabia, 4/1/66–1/20/60. Secret.

[2] This memorandum was prepared by the Near East Staff of the Office of National Estimates and coordinated with the Office of Current Intelligence for presentation to the IRG/NEA. It is to be read in conjunction with NIE 30–1–66, "The Outlook for South Arabia," 8 September 1966. [Footnote in the source text. NIE 30–1–66 is Document 77.]

of Soviet rivalry with the Chinese Communists may also have some effect on Soviet activity in South Arabia.

2. There are three broad categories of successor arrangements which might emerge in South Arabia, each embracing a number of possible variants. In the first instance, the South Arabian Federation or some similar entity may survive, perhaps ruled by a tribal or military strong man. As NIE 30–1–66 states, the chances of survival of such a state are not bright, but neither are they nonexistent. Any such regime would probably retain an essentially conservative outlook, friendly to the West—at least as long as the latter provides assistance (as Britain has promised to do until 1971). Saudi Arabia would probably have considerable influence over this sort of state, which would in any event almost certainly be antagonistic to any radical Yemeni state. In this situation, Moscow would probably not find a receptive field for its activity in South Arabia and extensive relations are unlikely to develop.

3. The second—and somewhat more likely—general category of possible developments in South Arabia is for the Federation to fragment. While this could mean splitting into as many parts as there are states in the Federation, the small size and lack of resources of many of them would argue against such a development. It seems more likely that two broad groupings might appear—one conservative and one progressive or radical. In such an eventuality, Aden might become an independent entity, or it might join in a greater Yemen along with some of the westerly sheikhdoms of the Federation which are contiguous to Yemen. (This greater Yemen might be a truncated version of the present state, involving only the southern Shafa'i part.) The willingness of such a "nationalist" Aden to join Yemen or to seek UAR support would depend in large measure on developments in Egyptian handling of Yemeni affairs. The Adeni "nationalist" leaders are in many cases close and long time associates of the Yemenis who have been ousted from government and jailed by the UAR, and they are not, on the whole, working to hand Aden over to Egypt but to free it from foreign domination. Thus the radicals may even be wary of receiving Soviet military equipment from the UAR if this entails a substantial Egyptian military presence in Aden.

4. The third possibility is that virtually all of South Arabia would fall under the domination of a radical nationalist regime. In view of the scarcity of radical talent in the sheikhdoms and the fact that the more conservative elements have most of the military power while the town radicals have virtually none, the prospects for this are not likely. Such a government probably would not have a very firm grip on internal security and would probably want external assistance, and the USSR would be an obvious source of aid. However, the same constraints in respect of association with Yemen and of assistance from the UAR would apply here as in category two.

5. In virtually all of the imaginable cases in which South Arabia might develop, the USSR and other Communist countries will have an official, diplomatic presence, providing them cover for clandestine activities. (A possible exception would be a conservative Federation, heavily influenced by the Saudis, but even this is quite remote.) In the event of some version of categories two or three evolving, a radical or a progressive regime would probably seek assistance from the USSR— and from anyone else willing to contribute. The Soviets would probably be willing to expend what for this area would be significant amounts of money, say some tens of millions of dollars annually, but they might have some difficulty in finding a government sufficiently effective to be worth aiding. Aden without its hinterland is tiny, vulnerable to harassment, and of itself of very little value. A "Greater Yemen" state would be more attractive, but would be under siege from north and east and might be an expensive proposition to support. Military aid might be part of a Soviet assistance package, and this would probably involve a Soviet training mission.

6. In general, the Soviets are considerably limited in the range of options open to them in South Arabia, and, at least initially, would probably work with the UAR if the latter was still maintaining a significant presence in Yemen and was on good terms with the South Arabian radicals. Likewise an effort by the USSR to take precedence over the UAR in the area would risk such a disruption of UAR-Soviet relations that Moscow is unlikely to try it. Over the years, the USSR has invested so much energy and effort into castigating the West for its "imperialist" presence in under-developed countries that the option of replacing Western with Soviet bases is almost certainly foreclosed. Further, the Soviets are constrained by their distaste for any conflict between Middle Eastern powers which might lead to direct US intervention. For Moscow does not want to be faced with the necessity for any direct confrontation with the US.

79.   Record of Meetings[1]

IRG/NEA 66–35   Washington, October 14, 1966.

INTERDEPARTMENTAL REGIONAL GROUP FOR NEAR EAST AND SOUTH ASIA

Record of IRG/NEA Meetings—October 5 and October 12, 1966

In considering the prospects for, and our interests in, *South Arabia*, the Group:

Noted the general assessment contained in National Intelligence Estimate 30–1–66,[2] and the Joint Staff evaluation of our military interests in the area[3] circulated with IRG/NEA 66–34.

Expressed its general agreement, subject to certain modifications, with the analysis contained in the State (Country Director) paper on the "Future of South Arabia" circulated with IRG/NEA 66–34, a revised copy of which is attached.[4]

Reviewed the potential threat to US interests as the UK prepares to withdraw from South Arabia in 1968, as the UAR seeks the establishment of a local government responsive to its wishes and as the USSR—working to a large degree through the Egyptians—aims at achieving significant influence (although probably not military bases) in the area.

Noted the statement by the UK Foreign Minister at the UNGA on October 11, 1966 reiterating British intent to withdraw and further welcoming UN participation in effecting the transition to an independent South Arabia.

Agreed that it is in the US interest that the West retain a significant influence in South Arabia; also that dominant Communist influence in the area be prevented, and that major regional disputes (such as a Saudi-UAR confrontation) over the area be avoided.

Recognized, however, that any attempt to pre-empt the area for the West and to ensure its political and economic stability would require a major commitment of resources, the justification for which has not been established.

---

[1] Source: Johnson Library, National Security File, Saunders Files, Saudi Arabia, 4/1/66–2/31/67. Secret.

[2] Document 77.

[3] Document 76.

[4] Not attached.

Agreed that we should support British efforts to bring the conflicting local factions to an agreement on the future government of South Arabia; and that particularly the conditions for establishing an expanded—and perhaps continuing—UN presence in the area should be explored.

Agreed that we should encourage continued British support of the South Arabian security forces; in this connection, we should consider the advantages and disadvantages of extending explicitly to South Arabia our general security assurances against the use of force or the threat of force in the Near East.

Agreed that we should, in early discussions with the UK, seek to obtain a detailed British assessment of the future viability of South Arabia, determine current British intentions concerning economic aid to the area, and explore the conditions under which the British might increase their security and economic commitments to South Arabia.

Agreed that we should keep under review and consult from time to time with the Saudis and the Iranians, as well as other nations friendly to us, on the extended security threat which they claim to see in UAR/USSR encroachment into South Arabia.

Agreed that it would also be desirable to consult with the UAR, on appropriate occasions, on the desirability of a peaceful transition in South Arabia; and to explore the scope for useful exchanges on this subject with the USSR, perhaps in the context of our other security concerns in the Near East.

Agreed that we should be prepared to elevate our present Consulate General in Aden to an Embassy, when South Arabia becomes independent.

Agreed that AID should make an assessment of the potential requirements of an independent South Arabia for external economic assistance, and of the conditions under which such assistance might be obtained and administered. While the study should not preclude an official US aid effort, it should also examine the feasibility of developing an assistance effort limited to non-USG sources such as the UN or other international agencies, oil-producing countries of the Middle East, and private Foundations, as well as the UK and other third countries.

Agreed that potential requirements for expanded US cultural exchange and information programs in South Arabia should also be explored.

Noted, finally, the desirability of proceeding with such steps as are now appropriate, but that our general course of action can be only tentative at this stage and must be kept under review in the light of future developments as South Arabia moves toward independence.

MEMBERS PRESENT

Executive Chairman: Ambassador Hare
AID: Mr. Farr (10/5); Mr. Macomber (10/12)
CIA: Mr. Critchfield
DOD: Col. Jordan
JCS: Brig. Gen. Sibley
NSC: Mr. Wriggins, Mr. Saunders
USIA: Mr. Austin

State (NEA): Mr. Davies; Mr. Moore; (S/P): Mr. Brewer
JCS: Capt. Zimmerman (10/5)
Staff Director: Mr. Sober

S.S.

80.   Memorandum of Conversation[1]

Washington, October 19, 1966.

SUBJECT

South Arabia

PARTICIPANTS

Mr. Christopher Everett, First Secretary, British Embassy
Mr. Rodger P. Davies, Deputy Assistant Secretary, NEA
Mr. George C. Moore, Acting Director, NEA/ARP

1. *British Departure Plans.* Mr. Everett referred to the Secretary's conversation with U.K. Foreign Secretary Brown on October 15 in which the Secretary expressed concern that British withdrawal from South Arabia might be too rapid. He asked for an elaboration of the extent of this "concern." Mr. Davies said that various foreign governments had raised with us the possibility of the British conditioning their withdrawal from Aden on UAR withdrawal from Yemen. We, among ourselves, recognized the political problems—both domestic and foreign—which this would pose for the U.K. and thus had not suggested this item in our briefing paper for the Secretary's conversation. At the same time, some of us would like to see all pressure possible put on Nasser to withdraw from Yemen. The Secretary was doubtless con-

---

[1] Source: National Archives and Records Administration, RG 59, Central Files 1964–66, POL 23–9 ADEN. Secret. Drafted by Moore on October 21 and initialed by Davies. The memorandum is Part I of II.

cerned with the chaotic situation which he could see developing in South Arabia and the general impact which this would have on affairs in the Horn of Africa.

Mr. Everett emphasized that HMG had firmly stressed its withdrawal decision in Parliament and the U.N. and that it would be extremely difficult for it to shift its position even if it had decided to do so. He continued that Mr. Brown, personally, had for many years held the firm belief that the only way for ultimate solution in South Arabia was via early British withdrawal. This belief had been stressed to the South Arabians. He noted that many in the U.K. had in any event never expected Nasser to get out of Yemen so that the latter's statement that he would stay, made following announcement of British intent to withdraw, came as no surprise to them.

2. *U.N. Involvement.* Mr. Everett said the process of establishing a U.N. Commission for Aden had been slowed by the departure from New York of Pachachi[2] who had been most helpful, and by the continued intransigeance of Committee of 24 Chairman Collyer.[3] However, the UNSYG is continuing to press for setting up the Committee. He has a 50% chance of being successful in getting the Commission to Aden after the end of Ramadan (mid-January) and with terms of reference which will keep it involved on a continuing basis in the birth of the new state. With SAL and Federation leaders now getting together and the expectation of U.N. involvement, HMG now feels that prospects for establishment of an independent South Arabia are somewhat more encouraging. It is hoped that the U.S., in addition to its moral support, will join the U.K. in some tangible aid to the new state for political and psychological reasons. Mr. Davies said that the Secretary's remarks could be interpreted as an indication of our concern. He also expressed the hope that other powers in the Peninsula—especially Saudi Arabia and Kuwait—would be willing to aid South Arabia.

3. *U.K. Military Withdrawal.* Responding to a query, Mr. Everett said that the British military timetable called for beginning of ground force withdrawals in June 1967, with some units being shifted to the Gulf. The intent was to lower the number of troops to a minimum level consistent with maintaining security so as to be in a position to pull out completely at any time on or after January 1, 1968. The troop numbers would be held at that minimum level until the political decision on the timing of final withdrawal had been made.

4. *Nasser's Intentions.* In response to a question, Mr. Davies said he thought we could not take at face value Nasser's statement of intent

---

[2] Former Iraqi Representative to the United Nations and current Iraqi Foreign Minister Adnan M. Pachachi.

[3] Sierre Leone's Representative to the United Nations Gershon B.O. Collyer.

to stay in Yemen; that he would withdraw if he found a convenient way out. If he stays indefinitely in Yemen he will find increasing problems with terrorism directed at the Egyptian presence there.

5. *Soviet Intentions.* Mr. Everett asked for our assessment. Mr. Davies noted that the USSR has established an expanded position in Yemen which it will be able to maintain irrespective of UAR withdrawal and of whether a republican or Imamate regime takes over. The Soviets have a better chance of staying in Yemen than do the Egyptians. We feel that Aden, while not of major world strategic significance, is of importance, particularly in the event of hostilities when access to the facilities there might be required. While we would anticipate a South Arabian receptiveness to Soviet aid offers, we would hope that a significant Western presence could also be maintained.

---

81.   Record of Meeting[1]

IRG/NEA 66–38   Washington, November 2, 1966.

INTERDEPARTMENTAL REGIONAL GROUP FOR NEAR EAST AND SOUTH ASIA

Record of IRG/NEA Meeting—November 2, 1966

In continuing its consideration of the *Communist presence in the Near East,* the Group reviewed the situation in those parts of the Arabian Peninsula not previously covered, the Persian Gulf, and Jordan. In doing so, the Group took note of the assessments of Communist activity provided by our field posts (circulated with IRG/NEA 66–36).[2]

Arabian Peninsula (except Yemen and South Arabia) and Persian Gulf

The Group: *Noted* evidence of the beginning of a pattern of subversive pressure applied from sources principally in the UAR against *Saudi Arabia* and *Kuwait,* and principally from sources in Iraq against the *Shaikhdoms.* The sources of pressure emanate from a mixture of both Arab nationalism and pro-Soviet Communism. The Communists find

---

[1] Source: Central Intelligence Agency, DDO/NE (Critchfield) Files: Job 80–00105A, Box 2, IRG/NEA Working File, Communist Presence—Arabian Peninsula, Persian Gulf. Secret. Drafted by Sober on November 4.

[2] Not printed.

it expedient to identify themselves with, and attempt to infiltrate and control, various nationalist elements seeking radical change.

Noted that there is no overt indigenous Communist Party activity in the area; and that the only official Communist outposts in the area are the Soviet and Czech and Polish embassies in Kuwait.

Noting the increasing strategic importance of Near Eastern oil for Western Europe, *agreed* that CIA should prepare a comprehensive study on the current and prospective availability of oil in the area. The study should serve to identify likely future points of subversive pressure.

On *Saudi Arabia, agreed* that despite certain signs of potential trouble, particularly among the labor force in the ARAMCO oil-producing area, the present nature and magnitude of subversive activity do not provide cause for serious concern. The Saudi Government is determined to avoid the establishment of any Communist presence. Nevertheless, the situation bears watching because oil-rich Saudi Arabia is a natural target for subversion.

On *Muscat and Oman, noted* the propaganda support given from abroad by the Soviets and Chinese Communists to local revolutionary movements.

Agreed that we should keep under consideration the desirability of opening a Foreign Service post at Muscat in the next few years.

Noted that there is virtually no known direct Communist penetration of the *Trucial Shaikhdoms.*

Noted that *Bahrain* is the major center of organized subversive activity in the Persian Gulf—a fact related to the relatively high levels of education and the inadequacy of job opportunities.

Noted the evidence of some direct Communist inspiration and infiltration of the active and well organized Bahrain National Liberation Front.

Agreed that the situation in Bahrain should be kept under close review. [*1 line of source text not declassified*] In addition, our own civil (Consulate General, Dhahran) and military (Commander, Mid-East Force) representatives in the area should be alerted to the continuing need for pertinent information.

Agreed on the central importance of the British military establishment in Bahrain and British security commitments for the protection of vital British and other Western interests in the Persian Gulf area; but *recognized* that the continuance of a strong British presence will hinge on the fiscal health as well as the political determination of the United Kingdom Government.

On *Kuwait, noted* the fair, but limited, degree of success in establishing a legitimate presence, achieved by overt Communist diplomatic, commercial and cultural activities.

[*1 paragraph (3 lines of source text) not declassified*]
[Here follows discussion of Jordan.]

MEMBERS PRESENT

Executive Chairman—Ambassador Hare
AID—Mr. Macomber
CIA—Mr. Critchfield
DOD—Col. Jordan
JCS—Brig. Gen. Sibley
NSC—Mr. Wriggins
USIA—Mr. Carter

State (NEA)—Mr. Davies, Mr. Moore, Mr. Atherton
NSC—Mr. Saunders
Staff Director—Mr. Sober

S.S.

82.   Circular Telegram From the Department of State to Certain Posts[1]

Washington, November 17, 1966, 5:05 p.m.

86582. Amman 1045 (Notal), South Arabia.[2]

1. Deptel 85204[3] outlines some current Department views on South Arabia.

2. We continue keep in close touch with British re developments there and re extent their planned military and economic assistance to independent South Arabia. Seems abundantly clear, however, judging

---

[1] Source: National Archives and Records Administration, RG 59, Central Files 1964–66, POL 19 ADEN. Secret. Drafted by Moore; cleared by Mary J. Sommer (EUR/BMI), Frederick H. Sacksteder, Jr. (AF/AFN), Gabriel J. Paolozzi (IO/UNP), and Atherton; and approved by Davies. Sent to Cairo, London, Jidda, Kuwait, Taiz, Amman, Baghdad, Beirut, Aden, Dhahran, USUN, CINCSTRIKE, and Tunis.

[2] Telegram 1045 from Amman, November 7, reported that Prime Minister Tell informed the Ambassador that, during their recent visit to Amman, the SAF Foreign and Information Ministers asked that he and King Hussein urge the United States and the United Kingdom to enter into a security defense pact with the South Arabian Federation. The ministers argued that, unless such a pact was created, the United Arab Republic would easily succeed in subverting Aden after the British withdrawal in 1968 leading to "another Yemen" in South Arabia. (Ibid.)

[3] Dated November 15. (Ibid.)

both from Fon Sec Brown's categoric statement to UNGA Oct 11 and private discussion with Secretary at that time, that British firm in their decision evacuate South Arabia both politically and militarily by 1968. At same time their promise of military aid at least through 1970 and their apparent expectation to provide economic assistance indicate fairly substantial UK interest in new state will continue.

3. Despite agitation in various quarters (e.g., London, Amman, Tunis, Jidda) by SAF and SAL leaders for UK (and US) security guarantee, British (and we) are not disposed to comply. Regardless of whether some security arrangement might ultimately be useful, its absence at this stage provides major pressure for conflicting South Arabian factions to coalesce in support a single state in face of need to be responsible for their own security. Contrary to SAFG argument reported reftel, a security guarantee at this juncture would probably reduce pressure for cohesion.

4. Major immediate hope for bringing progress in South Arabian situation is early establishment of active and continuing UN presence. We intend continue support British efforts bring this about and believe area states interested in future South Arabia would be well advised to give similar support.[4]

Rusk

---

[4] On December 12, by a vote of 96 (including the United States) to 0 with 3 abstentions, the UN General Assembly adopted Resolution 2183 (XXI) requesting the Secretary-General, in consultation with the Committee of 24 and the administering Power (the United Kingdom), to appoint immediately a special mission to be sent to Aden for the purpose of recommending practical steps for the full implementation of previous UN resolutions, in particular for UN participation in the preparation and supervision of elections. For text, see *American Foreign Policy: Current Documents, 1966,* pp. 544–545. The United States announced that it supported the resolution because of its firm belief that a special UN mission should go to Aden.

83.   Airgram From the Department of State to the Consulate
General in Saudi Arabia[1]

CA–3933   Washington, November 22, 1966, 4:37 p.m.

SUBJECT

Bahraini Views on Gulf Security and Request for Help from U.S.

1. Shaikh Khalifah ibn Salman al-Khalifah, Director of Finance for
the Bahraini Government and brother of the Ruler, made a private
visit to the United States in mid-November under the sponsorship of
CALTEX Oil Company. On November 17, accompanied by Deputy
Finance Director Mahmud Allawi, he called on NEA Assistant Secretary
Hare and left the enclosed paper[2] as a statement of Bahrain's concerns
and desires.

2. The bulk of Shaikh Khalifah's oral remarks was devoted to
emphasizing and reiterating the following points:

a. Bahrain and all the other Gulf states are most worried over
anticipated developments in South Arabia following the 1968 British
departure. They fear the U.A.R. will take over in that region and ultimately threaten seizure of the Gulf. The U.A.R.'s current activities in
Yemen foreshadow the nature of its possible future activities elsewhere
in the Peninsula.

b. Bahrain is most desirous that the British remain as protectors
in the Gulf and has received strong assurances from HMG that they
intend to do so. However, Bahrain feels that the same type of internal
British financial and political pressures which led HMG to evacuate
Aden may similarly lead it suddenly to leave the Gulf. In this contingency Bahrain most strongly hopes that the U.S. will be willing to
assume some responsibility for Gulf security.

c. Bahrain has close ties with Saudi Arabia, but the Saudis are,
understandably, deeply involved in building up their own defensive
capability and thus could not be fully counted on to assist others.

d. Bahrain hopes that the U.S. will be in close touch with the
British concerning developments in the Gulf and that we will begin to

---

[1] Source: National Archives and Records Administration, RG 59, Central Files
1964–66, POL BAHRAIN IS. Secret. Drafted by Moore; cleared by Eliot, Sommer, and
Director of the AID Office of Near Eastern Affairs James C. Flint, Churchill (PC), UN
Economic Affairs Division Chief Leighton van Nort, CU Near Eastern Programs Chief
David Scott, and William C. Salmon (SCI); and approved by Hare. Repeated to Jidda,
London, Kuwait, and Tehran.

[2] Attached but not printed.

show a greater interest in the welfare and stability of the Gulf region. (Some possibilities for this are outlined in the paper left by the Shaikh.)

3. In responding to Shaikh Khalifah, Assistant Secretary Hare summarized the U.S. attitude toward various Peninsula states as follows:

a. *Saudi Arabia*. We have had a long relationship with the Saudis which, despite some ups and downs, has been fruitful and cordial. As a logical outgrowth of our general policy of opposition to the use of force or threat of force in the Near East, expressed in the 1950 Tripartite Declaration and on various subsequent occasions, we have made clear our interest in preservation of the territorial integrity of Saudi Arabia.

b. *Yemen*. Our goals, enunciated repeatedly both in public and in private, are to see an end to foreign interference and development of a situation where all Yemenis are free to decide their own future. This is the extent of our desires in Yemen.

c. *South Arabia*. Except for maintaining our Consular post in Aden, we have not in the past been directly involved with this area in view of the dominant British position there. Since the British have decided to relinquish this position, we have had frequent and close consultations with them regarding the area's future. The British recognize the need to leave a capable security force there and to provide for economic assistance. They are taking steps in this direction. We follow their efforts with great interest and are concerned about the future of South Arabia.

d. *Gulf*. We are now taking a new look at this region. We hope and expect that the British will remain there as long as needed. We have no direct military interest in the area although the presence of the headquarters of our Naval Middle East Force in Bahrain is a token of our general concern. We are most appreciative of Shaikh Khalifah's comments, which fall on open ears at a time when we are giving extensive consideration to what our future activities in the Gulf area should be. The time available, while not limitless, is sufficient to allow us further to ponder this subject before reaching final decisions. In general, we hope all states with a common interest in the Gulf (including Iran) will work for its stability.

4. Mr. Allawi commented that currently the American Protestant Mission in Bahrain, which has been in existence since the 1890's, is in serious financial straits and might be forced to close either or both of the men's or women's hospitals it operates there. This would be taken by the populace as an unfortunate sign of waning U.S. interest. While understanding the problems which aid to a religious sponsored group might pose, he hoped the U.S.G. could be of some assistance. (The Department is not aware of any problem in the Mission's operations, Dhahran's report on this subject would be appreciated.)

5. The enclosed paper from Shaikh Khalifah proposes some rather practical ways in which the U.S. might become more active in Bahrain. We have given a copy of it to the British Embassy in Washington and indicated that we wished to reply to Shaikh Khalifah. In view of British responsibility for the foreign affairs of Bahrain, we asked for HMG's recommendation as to the most suitable channel for such a reply and said we would welcome British views on the paper itself.

6. The addressees' comments on the Khalifah paper would be appreciated.[3]

Rusk

---

[3] Circular airgram CA–6646 to Dhahran, March 3, 1967, transmitted an informal response to Shaikh Khalifah's paper. The Consulate was instructed to make clear continued U.S. support for the British position in the Gulf as providing the best framework for peaceful progress in the region and to stress the importance for security and stability of Bahrain's cooperation with its Gulf neighbors. (Ibid.)

---

84.   Telegram From the Embassy in the United Kingdom to the Department of State[1]

London, January 27, 1967, 1231Z.

5986. Subject: South Arabia.

1. Future South Arabian developments reviewed in detail at two-hour session FonOff Jan 26 attended by Brewer (Dept NEA/ARP), Palmer (Embassy) and reps FonOff MOD, and Ministry of Overseas Development (ODM). Discussions were frank and specific, providing greater clarity on how both governments see situation developing and what can be done about it. Detailed airgram under preparation, but following gives highlights:

2. British side led by Marnham (superintending Under-Secy) and his replacement, Brenchley, made following points:

A. Though HMG still interested in helping provide stable future after independence, primary British goal remains "withdrawal in good order."

---

[1] Source: National Archives and Records Administration, RG 59, Central Files 1967–69, POL 19 ADEN. Secret; Noforn. Repeated to Aden.

B. British believe security situation will continue get worse and increasingly dubious independent local government derived from present SAFG can maintain itself thereafter. While independent South Arabia authorities will be able exercise "greater persuasion" vis-à-vis suspected terrorists without inhibition Western methods, this may be offset by disappearance British technical proficiency in security field. Planned expansion Federal Regular Army (FRA) is based on blanketing into army portions police. Additional police recruitment will thus be necessary. UK plans provide police superintendent shortly (two candidates under consideration) but outlook in police field particularly discouraging.

3. Regarding expansion FRA, three-year British subsidiary expected cover: (a) build up from five battalions to nine, including armored cars but no tanks; (b) addition reasonable air components of eight subsonics for internal security uses; (c) three small naval vessels. MOD reps could not immediately provide details re breakdown subsidy but promised do so.

On civil side ODM reps stated two economists (Selwyn and Holland) now in final stages preparation report on future economic prospects for SAFG. ODM promised provide Embassy copy when available. British could not meet all prospective needs, but 40 percent of total UK civil aid (other than to Commonwealth and colonies) next fiscal year would be designated for South Arabia. Specific figures now before cabinet for approval. "Substantial" budgetary support envisioned at outset, but on "sharply declining scale." Long term, interest-free loans will also be offered, as well as topping-up salaries expatriate officials now employed by SAFG (of whom now some 50 British). Immediate problem will be covering SAFG April–December operating deficit. British will provide continuing assistance, but will cease covering whatever deficit may arise at end current UK fiscal year (March). SAFG will shortly be informed this unhappy prospect.

5. Re possibilities creating diplomatic enclave out of portion British base, Steamer Point already being discussed as possibility, though uncertain whether Aden local authorities or SAFG will take this over.

6. British agree accession Hadhramaut would be most helpful in strengthening new state but increasingly doubtful this will occur. Likeliest prospect may be some sort weak confederation between Saft and newly federated Hadhramaut states under Sultan Ghalib at Mukalla.

7. Brewer stressed continued USG recognition primary British responsibilities this region. Outlined Dept intentions give what support we could to SAFG in terms early establishment effective diplomatic presence and develop modest cultural and information programs. ODM reps expressed disappointment no direct USAID activity in prospect. Brewer responded by outlining Congressional and other limita-

tions in this field and offered no hope direct aid help might be forthcoming.

Comment

8. Large British participation from three ministries indicates importance British attach to future US–UK cooperation on South Arabia problem. They seemed reassured at indications Dept intention work with SAFG after independence, but would of course have welcomed more in economic field.

9. Since some points foregoing particularly sensitive, believe should not be discussed even with British reps.

Kaiser

---

85.   Memorandum From W. Howard Wriggins of the National Security Council Staff to the President's Special Assistant (Rostow)[1]

Washington, March 6, 1967.

SUBJECT

Arabian Peninsula

1. Saturday, March 4, I had lunch with Bill Brewer, who has just returned from a tour of the Arabian Peninsula. He found:

(a) The Sheikdom of Abu Dabi is as reactionary as ever, though senior members of the British Foreign Office have a romantic notion that he is likely to change his spots.

(b) The situation in Aden is a mess, and substantial disorders are in the wind.

(c) There is no doubt in Bill's mind that Nasser is warming up to play a preponderant role in Aden. As you know, over a thousand members of a "liberation" army have returned from training in Cairo and Yemen. All they need is for arms to be given to them and for the British to withdraw. Presumably more trainees will be coming from Cairo.

---

[1] Source: Johnson Library, National Security File, Name File, Wriggins Memos, 1967. No classification marking.

(d) Bill found the Saudis deeply concerned by our seeming passivity in the face of Britain's withdrawal and UAR ambitions. Bill feels we have a serious credibility problem with Faisal.

(e) Bill does not think we would all take with equanimity an Egyptian move into Aden with the increased Soviet influence in this area such a move would imply. Bill is exploring in State the political implications to us of uncontested UAR control of Aden. He wonders whether it might not be possible to beef up our small naval forces off of Aden to demonstrate to the UAR that we do not favor a movement of UAR or "liberation" forces into Aden. His argument is that if we do not do something like this, Faisal, the Shah, and all the other oil rulers will feel we have abandoned them to the "revolutionary forces".

(f) Combining this view with Hal's report[2] leads me to the following tentative propositions:

(i) we must find ways of asserting more unambiguous U.S. interest in the area promptly;

(ii) we should proceed with some food to the UAR as a partial way of demonstrating we are not attempting to bring Nasser down; a new Ambassador may help;

(iii) at the same time, we should increase our naval presence in the Aden area to demonstrate to both Faisal and Nasser that we do not expect an Egyptian take-over in Aden.

Such a two-pronged policy should not be beyond our ability to define and to get accepted. We can explore this and other variations when Hal returns.

2. *In the meantime*, Rodger Davies is sorting out the "Food for the UAR" issue between Brewer (representing the Saudis) and Don Bergus (representing Cairo). I'll keep you informed of their recommendations to Nick.

---

[2] For Saunders' report on U.S.-U.A.R. relations, see *Foreign Relations, 1964–1968*, vol. XVIII, Document 394.

86.   Intelligence Memorandum[1]

No. 0797/67   Washington, March 9, 1967.

SOUTH ARABIAN DISSIDENT AND FEDERAL ARMED FORCES

Summary

In anticipation of the independence of South Arabia in 1968, the Adeni dissidents in Yemen are preparing a "Liberation Army" of South Arabian tribesmen. This army is being trained at Egyptian army camps in conventional and guerrilla warfare for use as a disciplined commando-type unit against the Federal Army. The Federal Army, which consists of 5,000 British-trained tribesmen, will become the security force of South Arabia after the British evacuation.

The new "Liberation Army" is intended to secure South Arabia for the dissidents, who will probably form a government-in-exile, but the army's ultimate effectiveness will depend upon whether it remains loyal to the political group which formed it or whether it ultimately aligns itself with its military opponent, the Federal Army. Both forces, composed of the same type of hill tribesmen, share a contempt for the urban politicians who will dominate any independent government.

[Here follows the body of the paper.]

[1] Source: Johnson Library, National Security File, Country File, Saudi Arabia, Memos, Vol. I, 12/63–4/67. Secret; No Foreign Dissem; No Dissem Abroad; Controlled Dissem. Prepared in the CIA's Directorate of Intelligence. A note on the memorandum indicates it was produced solely in the CIA by the Office of Current Intelligence and coordinated with the Clandestine Services.

87.   Telegram From the Department of State to the Embassy Office in Yemen[1]

Washington, March 9, 1967, 4:27 p.m.

151922. Taiz 1231.[2] Appreciate info reftel and approve your attempt establish personal acquaintance al-Asnag. Should meeting occur, you should stress you are commenting on personal basis but may make following points: (a) with crucial phase South Arabia nation-building now taking place, those with most influence will be ones working inside rather than those who choose to opt out; (b) FLOSY's decision boycott UN Special Mission will deny it constructive role in establishing stable South Arabian state and at same time run counter UN Resolution establishing UN Mission for which almost entire UN membership, including UAR, voted; (c) terror will solve no problems in South Arabia but merely create new ones; and (d) since British definitely and finally are leaving, shrewder course for all Arab patriots would be cooperate with UN Mission and their fellow citizens in effort establish an orderly independent administration in which all Arabs could take pride. You might also discreetly suggest to al-Asnag that UAR aims and South Arabian nationalist aims may now increasingly diverge.[3]

Rusk

---

[1] Source: National Archives and Records Administration, RG 59, Central Files 1967–69, POL 19 ADEN. Confidential. Drafted and approved by Brewer and cleared by Bergus. Repeated to Sanaa, London, Cairo, Jidda, and Aden.

[2] In telegram 1231 from Taiz, March 9, Chargé d'Affaires Dinsmore reported that during a discussion of South Arabian problems with UAR Consul al-Masri, the latter insisted that FLOSY was the sole representative of the people of South Arabia, to which Dinsmore responded with skepticism based on his own recent observations of conflict in Aden among FLOSY, NLF, SAL, and other organizations. Dinsmore emphasized U.S. Government interest in the peaceful settlement of differences among nationalist groups, which is why it fully supported the UN Special Mission. Al-Masri encouraged Dinsmore to establish a personal acquaintance with FLOSY representative al-Asnag, who was in Taiz—an effort which Dinsmore said he had initiated. (Ibid.)

[3] In telegram 1236 from Taiz, March 11, Dinsmore reported that he met with al-Asnag, who expressed FLOSY's hopes for direct discussions with the U.K. Government. Dinsmore pointed out that FLOSY threats to the UN Mission were not reassuring, to which al-Asnag responded that its policy toward the UN Mission visit was one of "non-cooperation" rather than open hostility. (Ibid.)

88.   Telegram From the Department of State to the Consulate in Aden[1]

Washington, March 15, 1967, 12:14 p.m.

155272. Aden 1168.[2]

1. Dept appreciates detailed analysis reftel. There is no question USG providing security commitment to new South Arabian state. As reftel indicates, protection South Arabia is matter for SAFG with such military and financial help as British may choose to provide. USG role must perforce be secondary, though we planning do what we can encourage forces moderation and stability.

2. Re paras 6 and 17 of reftel, Secretary's letter to Javits included no "warning" to UAR nor was it basis NYT item which prompted Farid's elation (London 7228).[3] Guidance re latter article was contained State Circular 149571,[4] while info re letter to Javits included in State 141188,[5] both of which repeated Aden.[6]

---

[1] Source: National Archives and Records Administration, RG 59, Central Files 1967–69, POL 19 ADEN. Secret; Noforn. Drafted and approved by Brewer; cleared by Judd, Bergus, Wolle, and by Davies in substance. Repeated to London, Cairo, Sanaa, USUN, Amman, Athens, Baghdad, Beirut, Damascus, Jidda, Kuwait, Moscow, Dhahran, CINCMEAFSA, and Tel Aviv.

[2] In telegram 1168 from Aden, March 14, Jones reported that as the evacuation deadline approached, pressure was building for U.S. involvement in the defense of an independent South Arabian state. He argued that U.S. national interest dictated the avoidance of any security commitment or even the semblance thereof. (Ibid.)

[3] Telegram 7228 from London, March 8, reported that Farid was elated that The New York Times had interpreted the Secretary's letter to Senator Javits as a "warning" to the UAR. (Ibid.)

[4] Circular telegram 149571, March 6, discussed the March 4 New York Times story that reported the U.S. Government had "issued what appeared to be a warning to UAR and other outside powers not to attempt armed intervention in troubled South Arabian Federation" and that the State Department had made a "brief public statement" linking President Kennedy's May 8, 1963, press conference remarks opposing the use or threat of force in the Near East to the current situation in South Arabia. The telegram noted that the Department spokesman declined to speculate whether his remarks should be interpreted as an extension of Kennedy's statement to South Arabia. If queried, posts were to state that the Department had merely restated the general principle of U.S. Government opposition to use or threat of force in the area and there was no reason to characterize this response as a "warning" to any party or in any sense a new policy statement. (Ibid.)

[5] Telegram 141188 to London, February 21, stated that Rusk's letter to Javits did not contain a warning to the UAR regarding Aden. (Ibid.)

[6] Printed from an unsigned copy. In telegram 1207 from Aden, March 23, Jones reported that he had told Farid The New York Times had misconstrued remarks by a Department official and guidance from Washington made it clear that the U.S. Government had issued no warnings and that its Near East policy was unchanged. (Ibid.)

89.   Telegram From the Embassy in the United Arab Republic to the Department of State[1]

Cairo, March 16, 1967, 1150Z.

5379. Ref: Aden 1168[2] and State 155272.[3]

1. As seen from here there is little possibility that SAFG with limited British support now planned will either be able maintain order after independence and withdrawal British forces or become viable government.

2. It seems increasingly clear that UAR is committed to establishment of progressive revolutionary regime in South Arabia and is prepared use force to this end. This intent was most recently confirmed by President Nasser during his final conversation with Ambassador Battle on March 4 and is evident in UARG public statements, reports of creation nationalist "liberation army" and rising pace of terrorism and extremism in Aden.

3. We believe our ability thwart UARG designs in South Arabia is extremely limited and virtual chaos which likely result from actively pursued insurgency against regime created and supported by British can only be avoided by adequate UN military and political presence during several year interim period. We do not see direct British–FLOSY talks as having much chance producing anything unless British willing sacrifice SAFG and begin working with nationalists in effort find combination acceptable to FLOSY and NLF leadership and to UAR.

4. Alternatively, all concerned including British and ourselves can let nature take its course, which we see as messy rearguard British withdrawal, period of civil war perhaps followed by de facto split of South Arabia with revolutionary pro-UAR Aden either independent or absorbed by Yemen on one hand and fragmented tribes of protectorate falling under whatever protection Saudi Arabia can afford them on the other.

5. Question we cannot answer here is whether such a situation would in truth be harmful to US political and stategic interests in area. We seem to have been able to live quite happily with UAR control of Suez Canal and Red Sea as exercised during past decade and may be able tolerate UAR presence in South Arabia without damage our position in area. In any event believe it essential we determine now what our interests are and what we are prepared to live with.

---

[1] Source: National Archives and Records Administration, RG 59, Central Files, 1967–69, POL 19 ADEN. Secret; Limdis. Repeated to London, Taiz, Aden, and USUN.

[2] See footnote 2, Document 88.

[3] Document 88.

6. Also we must not forget that South Arabia is essentially an Arab problem. The conflicts in both areas result largely from Arab quarrels and except for our security guarantee and military support for Saudi Arabia and Britain's colonial role, foreign influences have thus far been minimal. Must be recognized however, that present trends if continued will probably lead to far more active Soviet involvement on side revolutionary progressive forces and Vietnam type situation could result.

Nes

90.   Circular Telegram From the Department of State to Certain Posts[1]

Washington, March 22, 1967, 1:32 p.m.

160010. Subj: South Arabia. Re Aden 1198,[2] 1200.[3]

1. As result SAFG revelations to journalists (Aden 1198), Dept again pressed British Embassy here for authority inform posts on limited background basis of revised British withdrawal plans South Arabia communicated to us initially in London on most secret basis March 10.[4] EmbOff conveyed FonOff agreement March 21. Following summary accordingly provided for background only.

2. Revised UK plans conceived February–March to meet need give SAFG as much assurance for the future as possible, provide some reassurance against aggression thereafter and meet SAFG demand for control internal security Aden before state entirely on its own.

---

[1] Source: National Archives and Records Administration, RG 59, Central Files 1967–69, POL 19 ADEN. Secret; Limdis; Noforn. Drafted by Brewer on March 21, cleared by Davies and Judd, and approved by Katzenbach. Sent to Aden, Cairo, London, Jidda, Sanaa, USUN, and CINCSTRIKE.

[2] Telegram 1198 from Aden, March 20, reported that the SAF Government had revealed to journalists on March 19 that talks with U.K. Minister of State for Foreign Affairs George Thomson had centered on Thomson's effort to win SAF approval of November 1 as independence day, which had been rejected as premature. (Ibid.)

[3] Dated March 20. (Ibid.)

[4] On March 16 U.K. Chargé Sir Michael Stewart called at his request to hand the Under Secretary a copy of a British paper setting forth revised British plans for withdrawal from Aden and South Arabia, and for subsequent "offshore" British military protection of the new state for a period of up to 6 months after the date of independence, November 1, 1967. (Memorandum of Conversation, March 16, 1967; ibid.)

3. Specifics included proposal advance date of independence to November 1, 1967, at which time Federal security forces would assume responsibility for Aden security. British base would be closed same day but some military strength would be kept off-shore in region for limited period thereafter for sole purpose of providing some assurance against outside aggression. HMG favored SAFG application UN membership soon after independence date while UNGA in session.

4. MinState Thomson presented foregoing to SAFG in Aden March 18. HMG hoped for prompt Federal acceptance to permit announcement by FonSec in Commons March 20 but Federals balked, giving reasons Farid has furnished ConGen Jones (Aden 1200). SAFG assured Thomson they did not wish close door but hoped they could defer reply to proposals for month to permit full consideration. Thomson said he was not in position give assurance UK offer would remain open indefinitely.

5. In the event, FonSec's detailed announcement was cancelled. FonSec instead limited remarks to short general statement reported London 7591.[5]

6. Foregoing remains highly classified British proposal, and addressees cautioned fully observe Noforn designation. Uncertain whether even British Embassies in field have been informed and earlier plans give advance word friendly rulers such as King Faisal have been dropped. Appropriate guidance will be provided when and if HMG makes public announcement.

7. At lunch with Ambassador Battle in Washington, March 21, Thomson reported on his Aden talks along lines foregoing and reftels. He said HMG had agreed to Federal request that modified British proposal could be kept under consideration for about a month. Thomson added somewhat surprising footnote that one factor in SAFG position had been telegram they had received from Sharif Beihan counselling against acceptance UK proposal.

Rusk

---

[5] Dated March 20. (Ibid.)

91.   Telegram From the Department of State to the Embassy in the United Kingdom[1]

Washington, April 20, 1967, 2:51 p.m.

178848. South Arabia. Re State 177971.[2]

1. FonSec Brown had brief corridor exchange re South Arabia with Under Secretary Rostow and Assistant Secretary Battle during SEATO meeting early April 20. Brown said British now hoped to establish broadly based coalition government, though he admitted chances somewhat slim. Battle responded we thought this was right tack to take and that British should continue efforts have contacts with all South Arabian political groups. Brown said he had seen British message indicating Dept might be reluctant continue pass messages on HMG behalf to FLOSY officials. Battle assured him this not the case and said we continued willing help British on this in any way we can.

2. Brown asked whether we had info indicating FLOSY government-in-exile was about to be set up. Battle replied indications FLOSY considering this were coming in but no irretrievable step had apparently yet been taken. Brown commented establishment such government would make things far more difficult for British but then said he supposed HMG could still talk with FLOSY as political party.

3. *Comment:* Exchange took place just prior receipt Taiz 1376.[3] Brown's reference to Dept reluctance pass messages apparently stems from lack full information surrounding despatch State 177971. In initial discussions reported therein, Dept had taken position USG official could hardly be instructed see Makkawi without taking account latter's tendentious April 18 public anti-US reference and statement that a FLOSY government would close Straits to Israeli shipping.[4] On insist-

---

[1] Source: National Archives and Records Administration, RG 59, Central Files 1967–69, POL 19 ADEN. Secret; Noforn. Drafted by Brewer, cleared by Mary Sommer Seasword (EUR/BMI), and approved by Battle. Repeated to Sanaa, Taiz, Cairo, USUN, and Aden.

[2] Telegram 177971 to Taiz, April 19, instructed the Embassy to pass to FLOSY leaders Asnaj and Makkawi separate oral messages that Lord Shackleton, U.K. Minister without Portfolio in Aden, wished to confirm that he would be glad to meet with them soon at a place to be determined. (Ibid.)

[3] In telegram 1376 from Taiz, April 20, Dinsmore reported that he had conveyed the British message to both men in separate private meetings at FLOSY headquarters that morning. Makkawi responded that on April 18 the FLOSY Command Council passed a formal resolution stating that FLOSY was unwilling to talk to any British minister unless the United Kingdom agreed to recognize FLOSY as the sole representative of the people of South Arabia. (Ibid.)

[4] Circular telegram 178435, April 19, quoted press reports that Makkawi had stated that a future South Arabian Government under FLOSY would be anti-United Kingdom, anti-United States, and anti-Israel, and would close Bab al-Mandeb to Israeli shipping. (Ibid., POL 13 ADEN)

ence British no such instructions included State 177971 in order maximize favorable atmosphere for passing British message to Makkawi. British Minister phoned Davies late April 19 express appreciation prompt transmission UK message but FonSec apparently not yet briefed. Brown expressed appreciation for Battle's assurance we continued ready be of whatever assistance we could to UK in seeking bring all South Arabian parties together.

Rusk

---

92. Information Memorandum From the Assistant Secretary of State for Near Eastern and South Asian Affairs (Battle) to Secretary of State Rusk[1]

Washington, May 9, 1967.

SUBJECT

Revised UK Timetable for Leaving South Arabia

1. Under cover of an Exdis letter, Embassy London has reported to us the following revised details regarding the British plan for withdrawal from South Arabia:

—Independence on January 1, 1968.
—A British carrier task force to remain off-shore for six months thereafter (2 of 3 British carriers are already in South Arabian waters).
—No defense treaty.
—Thought of South Arabia's achieving early UN membership has been abandoned.

2. In addition to the foregoing, Lord Shackleton wants an RAF squadron kept in Aden for three months after independence. The Foreign Secretary disagrees but is willing to have Shackleton state his case to the Cabinet Defense Committee. This Committee, followed by the full Cabinet, is expected to complete its deliberations on the revised plan by May 16 at the latest. The Foreign Secretary hopes for the first

---

[1] Source: National Archives and Records Administration, RG 59, Central Files 1967–69, POL 19 ADEN. Secret; Exclusive Distribution. Drafted by Brewer and cleared by Davies.

reading in Commons of an Enabling Act empowering HMG unilaterally to legislate South Arabian independence. (This would not require divulging details.) How much the British reveal in the subsequent Commons debate about the independence plan and the carrier task force will depend on the then existing circumstances.

93.   Memorandum From the Joint Chiefs of Staff to Secretary of Defense McNamara[1]

JCSM–281–67   Washington, May 18, 1967.

SUBJECT

  Military Importance of South Arabia (C)

  1. (C) Reference is made to a memorandum by the Acting Assistant Secretary of Defense (ISA), I–22913/67, dated 10 May 1967,[2] subject as above, which requested that the Joint Chiefs of Staff provide an analysis of the military importance of South Arabia.

  2. (S) The Joint Chiefs of Staff consider that:

  a. The anticipated UK withdrawal from Aden in early 1968 could make Khormaksar Airfield and Aden port facilities unavailable for US contingency operations. Execution of CINCSTRIKE/USCINCMEAFSA's contingency plans for Ethiopia, Somalia, Kenya, Sudan, and French Somaliland will be hampered by the loss of this staging base. Execution of these contingency plans would be simplified if en route staging bases and overflight rights were granted and if alternate staging facilities such as Dhahran, Addis Ababa, and Aldabra Island were available. A long-term implication of UK withdrawal from Aden could be the creation of a power vacuum which, if filled by forces hostile to the West, would increase the threat to nations oriented toward the West.

  b. Aden, if available, would be valuable, but not essential, for various contingency operations. Its military value to the United States

---

  [1] Source: Washington National Records Center, RG 330, Records of the Office of the Secretary of Defense, OSD Files: FRC 72 A 2468, Saudi Arabia 1967, South Arabia 092, 9 May 67. Secret.
  [2] Not printed. (Ibid.)

stems from its port, airbase, and troop facilities which provide a staging base for US contingency operations in northeast Africa, the Arabian Peninsula, and the Persian Gulf. Aden also provides an en route and refueling base for contingency operations in South Asia. Elimination of UK bases in the Persian Gulf would not alter the value of Aden as a potential base for US operations. The military significance of the elimination of British bases in the Persian Gulf is that British forces would not be readily available for contingency operations and, therefore, instability would be aggravated. A US/UK base on Aldabra Island would assist in the conduct of contingency operations into Kenya or east Africa but could require en route stops and/or overflight of various countries. Development of a base complex at Diego Garcia could also support contingency operations by providing facilities in the Indian Ocean.

c. The availability of bases in Aden to the United Arab Republic (UAR) or the USSR would provide additional means for projecting UAR/USSR-sponsored subversion or military assistance into Africa and the remainder of the Arabian Peninsula. The use of Aden would also provide opportunities for extension of Soviet electronic intelligence and electronic warfare capabilities, support for Soviet ships, a means of establishing greater influence through an increased Soviet presence, and a contingency staging and logistics base.

d. It is not likely that the Soviets would make an effort to establish a direct military presence in the Arabian Peninsula or the Horn of Africa through the establishment of overt Soviet bases or the development of Soviet military forces. However, the long-term Soviet goal in this area is to supplant Western influence with communist influence, leading in time to a Moscow-oriented communist political, economic, and social system. However, for the near term, provision of military advisors, as in Somalia, or economic advisors, as in Yemen, will remain the probable Soviet tactic.

e. UAR or Soviet control of the southern entrance to the Red Sea would have an important military significance if the UAR or USSR attempted to exercise this control to prevent passage by tankers or other ships in conjunction with closure of the Suez Canal. If this action were taken, it would have a serious impact on shipping to the Red Sea ports of Saudi Arabia, Ethiopia, Israel, and Jordan. Such an eventuality is unlikely in view of the resultant adverse international reactions and the effect on UAR finances through loss of Suez tolls. While control of Aden might make a blockade easier, a more feasible method would be to close the Suez Canal.

f. The military implications of US military assistance or security assurances to South Arabia are:

(1) Drain on already taxed US military capabilities and the possible generation of additional US force requirements.

(2) Possible commitment of sizable US forces in order to preserve an unstable government of questionable alignment.

(3) Involvement of US military forces (possibly with the UAR/USSR) in an area of limited strategic interest.

(4) Potential requirement for semipermanent US military presence.

(5) Further reductions in current military assistance programs in other countries where the United States has interests.

(6) Acceleration of British troop withdrawal from the Persian Gulf.

(7) Reliance by the United Kingdom on US military involvement rather than on the use of British forces.

g. Saudi Arabia, Jordan, Iran, and Ethiopia would view additional UAR or USSR military influence in South Arabia as an increased threat. These countries probably would request increased US or other Western military aid or security commitments. Failing to receive US assistance, they would probably then turn to neutral or communist nations not involved. Iran and Saudi Arabia may provide support to opposing factions in an attempt to contain further UAR/USSR expansion.

h. It is considered unlikely that UAR/USSR control of Aden's airfield or port facilities would cause a peacetime stoppage or reduction of Persian Gulf oil to Europe. Currently, very few oil-carrying tankers stop at Aden. In any case, Free World tankerage could transport, though at a greater cost, oil to Western Europe via the Cape of Good Hope or, when completed, through an Israeli-owned pipeline.

3. (S) From the above and the additional rationale in the Appendix[3] hereto, the Joint Chiefs of Staff conclude that:

a. UK withdrawal from Aden could hamper but not prevent execution of certain CINCSTRIKE/USCINCMEAFSA contingency plans. UK follow-on withdrawal from the Persian Gulf would not alter this assessment.

b. Use of Aden air base and port facilities by UAR and USSR military units would improve UAR/USSR abilities to project forces into South Arabia and the Indian Ocean area and provide facilities for other military or subversive activities.

c. Soviet effort to establish a direct military presence in the area of the Arabian Peninsula or the Horn of Africa is unlikely.

d. The military significance of UAR or Soviet control of the Southern entrance to the Red Sea lies in their capability to attempt a physical blockade; however, this eventuality is considered unlikely.

e. Considering the worldwide military assistance commitments of the United States, a program which would involve additional commitments of US resources to South Arabia is not recommended at this time. Continuous efforts should be exerted to enlist the United King-

---

[3] Attached but not printed.

dom, United Nations, or other Western-oriented governments in preserving the internal and external security of South Arabia. It is not advisable to offer assurances of US military support to any government of South Arabia.

4. (S) In summary, the further extension of UAR/USSR influence in the Near East area would be contrary to US interests. In this connection, while South Arabia (particularly Aden) is of some military significance, it is not critical to the security interests of the United States.

For the Joint Chiefs of Staff:
Earle G. Wheeler
Chairman
Joint Chiefs of Staff

---

94.   National Intelligence Estimate[1]

NIE 30–1–67   Washington, May 18, 1967.

THE PERSIAN GULF STATES

The Problem

To estimate probable developments and trends over the next several years in the Persian Gulf.

Note

Though our basic concern in this estimate is with the prospects for Kuwait and the British-protected states—Bahrain, Qatar, the Trucial States[2] and Muscat/Oman—we will also consider the ambitions and capabilities of the larger states bordering the Gulf—Iran, Iraq, and Saudi Arabia—to control or influence developments, as well as the role of countries outside the area, particularly the UAR and the USSR. In addition, we will examine the likelihood of a British withdrawal and its consequences for the Gulf.

---

[1] Source: Central Intelligence Agency: Job 79–R01012A, ODDI Registry of NIE and SNIE Files. Secret; Controlled Dissem. According to a note on the cover sheet, the estimate was submitted by Director of Central Intelligence Helms, and concurred in by the U.S. Intelligence Board on May 18.

[2] The seven Trucial States are Abu Dhabi, Dubai, Sharjah, Ajman, Umm al Qaiwain, Ras al Khaimah, and Fujairah. [Footnote in the source text.]

Conclusions

A. Massive oil revenues and the accompanying influx of people and ideas are bringing change and ferment to the Gulf. At the same time, the UK, as part of its retrenchment from east-of-Suez commitments, is reassessing its role there. It seems likely that it will be at least three to five years before the UK abandons its special military and political position in the Gulf. But increased trouble in the Gulf or economic problems at home might hasten British departure.

B. The UAR is the most influential of the regional forces working against the British position and other Western interests. Nasser enjoys some support in the area among reformist and dissident elements, and Cairo Radio has a wide audience. Nasser will continue to aid local forces of discontent, though this will not be as easy as in South Arabia. Nasser will receive little support from other radical Arab states. The USSR, while supporting Nasser and generally encouraging movements directed against Western interests, will be wary of direct or open involvement in Gulf maneuvering.

C. Nasser will be strongly opposed by both King Faisal and the Shah, and less openly by the Kuwaitis. They all fear that UAR influence in the Gulf would be a threat not only to their interests but also to the stability of their own governments.

D. So long as the British remain, we would expect general political stability in the Gulf. Kuwait is likely to preserve its security and independence by a policy of neutrality in Arab affairs and of financial handouts to potentially predatory Arab states. Qatar and some of the Trucial States that enjoy large oil revenues may successfully follow Kuwait's example after the British leave; the others will probably look to Saudi Arabia for protection.

E. In Bahrain, the situation is more volatile, and instability and occasional violence are likely. Terrorism is likely to mark at least the final stages of a British withdrawal, and some form of radical regime will probably emerge in Bahrain after the British depart.

F. The oil-producing states in the Gulf will continue to press the Western oil companies for a greater share of the profits, and recurrent crises in country-company relations are probable. Although these efforts will reduce the share of profits to the companies, they will not materially affect the flow of oil to the West.

G. A British withdrawal from the Persian Gulf would provide the USSR with some opportunities to expand its influence there. However, the USSR's course would be complicated, requiring a careful balancing of regional forces. On the whole, we do not think it likely that the Soviets will make dramatic advances.

H. The US will be urged to take over some of the British responsibilities in the Gulf. If it did so, it would become the principal target of Arab revolutionary propaganda and subversion and would become involved in a variety of dynastic rivalries and troublesome political disputes.

[Here follow the Discussion section and an annex.]

---

95.   Record of Meetings[1]

IRG/NEA 67–18   Washington, May 24, 1967.

INTERDEPARTMENTAL REGIONAL GROUP
FOR NEAR EAST AND SOUTH ASIA

Record of IRG/NEA Meetings—May 13, 16 and 20, 1967

The series of three meetings was devoted to a further consideration of our *policy towards South Arabia*, in the light of developments since the IRG/NEA meetings of October 1966 (IRG/NEA 66–35, 10/14/66).[2] The Group:

Reviewed relevant information on (a) the present situation in South Arabia itself, (b) current British planning concerning the timing and conditions of South Arabian independence, (c) the attitudes and possible future actions of other area states, especially the United Arab Republic, and (d) the current and prospective United Nations role in the matter.

Reviewed the military aspects of the South Arabian problem. In this respect, the Group *noted* the JCS assessment of May 18, 1967 that while South Arabia (particularly Aden) is of some military significance, it is not critical to United States security interests.

Agreed, however, that apart from the military aspects, the outcome of the struggle for control of South Arabia following the imminent withdrawal of the United Kingdom is of considerable importance for United States interests. Seizure of control by elements hostile to the West would be at least a serious psychological setback to moderate

---

[1] Source: Johnson Library, National Security File, Saunders Files, Saudi Arabia, 4/1/66–12/31/67. Secret.

[2] Document 79.

states in the area (e.g., Saudi Arabia, Iran, and Ethiopia) with which we maintain friendly relations. United States acquiescence in UAR domination of South Arabia would be interpreted as a decision on our part to play a diminishing role in the Near East generally. It is in our interest to see a peaceful transition of power through the creation of a broadly based government in South Arabia.

Noted, however, that current prospects are not substantially in favor of the establishment of such a broadly based government, but point rather to the creation in the first instance of a post-independence government either fairly subservient to Cairo, or else subject to very severe pressures (including terrorism and subversion) from elements supported by the UAR and probably the USSR.

Agreed that continued consideration will have to be given to possible courses of action to protect and promote our interests in South Arabia as the date for independence approaches. In this regard the Group *agreed* to the submission of a paper, "Future of South Arabia," as a basis for a discussion scheduled by the National Security Council for May 24, 1967. The paper, a copy of which is attached,[3] identifies the key issues facing us, suggests possible courses of action, and raises some principal questions which still need to be answered. It was expected that guidance would emanate from the NSC discussion for further IRG consideration of our policy on South Arabia. (Subsequent to the IRG meeting, the NSC discussion of South Arabia scheduled for May 24 was postponed.)

MEMBERS PRESENT

    Executive Chairman—Mr. Battle
    AID: Mr. Williams (5/16, 5/20), Mr. Funari (5/13)
    CIA: Mr. Critchfield
    DOD: Mr. Hoopes
    JCS: Brig. Gen. Sibley
    NSC: Mr. Saunders
    USIA: Mr. Austin

    State (NEA): Messrs. Davies, Brewer, Bergus; (IO): Mr. Campbell; (M): Mr. Enders
    DOD: Col. Jordan
    SSDSG: Ambassador Holmes (5/16), Mr. Moore
    Staff Director: Mr. Sober (5/20), Mr. Ernst

S.S.
Staff Director

---

[3] Document 97.

96.   Memorandum From the President's Special Assistant (Rostow) to President Johnson[1]

Washington, May 23, 1967.

SUBJECT

NSC Discussion—South Arabia

The main issue in the Middle East today is whether Nasser, the radical states and their Soviet backers are going to dominate the area. A related issue is whether the US is going to stand up for its friends, the moderates, or back down as a major power in the Near East.

Two weeks ago, we expected South Arabia to provide the test. The gulf between moderates and radicals has been getting wider for over a year. But with the British pulling out of South Arabia next January, Faisal, Hussein, Haile Selassie, the Shah and Eshkol were watching closely to see whether we and the British would stand for a Nasser takeover there. The current Arab-Israeli crisis has brought the test sooner than we expected, but the South Arabian problem will still provide the follow-up to the current showdown.

The policy question in South Arabia as on Israel's borders is how far we can and should commit ourselves to block Nasser and his Soviet supporters. Our dilemma is that we have no stake in South Arabia itself—no immediate reason for involving ourselves in the uncertain political process there. However, the effect of the outcome on the broader confrontation makes it impossible to ignore what happens.

An active attempt to stave off a Nasser takeover would amount to a sharp shift in our Middle East policy. Since 1961, we have tried to avoid splitting the area into two camps. Given all of our conflicting interests, it has seemed wiser to build a good working relationship in all capitals. Now Nasser has all but forced us to choose sides. As your message to him[2] said, we don't want to give up entirely our effort to build some kind of relationship with him. But the time may already have come when we must make him respect us first.

I believe our first step must be to keep the British on the ground. They're intimately involved in working out a political solution, and

---

[1] Source: Johnson Library, Meeting Notes File, Briefing Papers for NSC Meeting, May 24, 1967. Secret. Attached to a May 23, 7 p.m., memorandum from Rostow to the President noting that although the regular May 24 NSC meeting was scheduled to discuss problems the United States faced in South Arabia, Rostow recommended that following Nasser's move against Israel the President use the NSC meeting to discuss the Middle East crisis instead. A record of the May 24 NSC meeting is scheduled for publication in *Foreign Relations, 1964–1968*, volume XIX.

[2] President Johnson's May 22 message to Nasser is scheduled for publication ibid.

we can't afford to see them walk out in despair. I originally scheduled this discussion (a) to give you a sense of the problem before you see PM Wilson and the Shah and (b) to give our planners a sense of your desires.

The underlined portions of the attached State paper,[3] detail the problem.

Walt

---

[3] Document 97.

---

97.   **Paper Prepared in the Department of State**[1]

Washington, undated.

FUTURE OF SOUTH ARABIA

(For NSC Meeting of May 24, 1967)

(*Note:* The following paragraphs were prepared independent of the current Arab-Israel crisis, resolution of which will no doubt shed considerable light on, among other things, Egyptian and Soviet intentions.)

I. Background

The current contest for South Arabia has meaning far beyond its size or importance. For 20 years the US has managed to maintain in the Near East its major interests of access to oil, freedom of air and sea transit and prevention of the dominance of the area by any one power. However, our significant political influence in the Arab Near East is now confined to the Arabian Peninsula and Jordan. There it already is undermined by the running sore of the Egyptian presence in Yemen. US acquiescence in UAR domination of South Arabia would

---

[1] Source: Johnson Library, Meeting Notes File, Briefing Papers for NSC Meeting, May 24, 1967. Secret. Prepared in the Office of Saudi Arabia, Kuwait, Yemen, and Aden Affairs of the Bureau of Near Eastern and South Asian Affairs for a May 24 meeting of the National Security Council. Attached to Rostow's May 23 memorandum to the President (Document 96).

be interpreted in the Peninsula, and elsewhere, as a decision by Washington to play a diminishing role in the Near East.

II. Summary Outlook

The British will grant independence to South Arabia in the first half of January 1968. They are willing to leave a military presence in the area for six months thereafter as an assurance against external aggression.

The complexion of the successor government is unclear. We share the British hope that the United Nations Special Mission will be instrumental in setting up a broadly-based regime. If this happens, the South Arabian problem will be much reduced. At present, there is no confidence between conservative and radical elements in South Arabia and the two radical groups, FLOSY and the NLF, have been at each other's throats. FLOSY operates from a headquarters in Yemen and may set up a government-in-exile. It is backed by the Egyptians and includes some Soviet-oriented communists. The NLF has a trade union base in Aden, suspected ties with the British and represents the leftist, Marxist wing of the Arab National Movement.

The UAR has put its money on FLOSY. Cairo is helping to train a FLOSY "Liberation Army" and will probably do everything it can, short of military invasion by Egyptian units from Yemen, to assure FLOSY domination of the newly independent state.

III. The Alternatives

The evolution to independence in South Arabia will probably develop along one of the following lines:

—A broadly-based coalition worked out under UN aegis which might be quite radical (even with substantial initial FLOSY participation) but would not be under the Egyptian, or any other, thumb.

—A British-sponsored coalition which might, or might not, include FLOSY. More likely it will not. In that case, the government might have to fight for survival against a FLOSY government-in-exile backed by UAR and probably the USSR. Its military strength, coupled with UK military support, might be successful in preventing a major invasion, but terrorism and subversion would be difficult problems.

—A FLOSY-dominated radical government which had fought its way to power with major Egyptian support, thus making its leaders more beholden to Cairo than otherwise.

IV. The Oil Problem

Domination of South Arabia by unfriendly powers would not cut off oil movements from the Persian Gulf to Western Europe. It would nevertheless represent a threat to the more economic oil lifelines and would have implications for the longterm future of the Western (predominantly British) position in the Persian Gulf. That area contains more than 60 percent of the free world's petroleum reserves. It currently supplies 55 percent of Western Europe's oil needs. This percentage will decline slightly in the next five years, but the absolute amount supplied will increase by $1/3$ to 330 million metric tons a year, by 1972. According to a 1967 OECD study, Western Europe could withstand loss of up to 60 percent of oil "East of Suez" in a peacetime situation and by drawing on other world sources. A period of up to six months of dislocation would be undergone, and some oil from the Near East would still be required. The extreme situation of a cut-off of all Persian Gulf oil would clearly be more damaging but is also a much remoter contingency.

V. US Interests

Our most important concern is not with respect to South Arabia itself but with the implications of the transition for neighboring regimes friendly to us, notably Saudi Arabia, Iran and Ethiopia. These implications will be less disturbing if the transition is relatively peaceful and takes place with a minimum of outside intervention, since the resultant South Arabian regime is more likely to be able to reflect the strong impulses of independence and nationalism which exist. Our primary interest is how the transfer of power occurs rather than to whom among internal elements the transfer is made.

We do not want to become involved in internal squabbles in South Arabia but we do want to discourage adventures by external powers, notably the UAR and the USSR. We do not want to get overly involved but we must make clear that we have a legitimate and continuing interest in South Arabia if we are to have any influence in what happens there.

VI. US Military Considerations

The JCS have concluded that South Arabia (particularly Aden) is of some military significance to us but is not critical to US security. Its port and airfield, if available to us, would be valuable for various contingency operations but they are not essential.

VII. The British Role

The British are willing to provide insurance against a UAR attack for six months after South Arabian independence. They should be urged to extend this period if this seems necessary. It is in our view essential for the British to give enough support to the new South Arabian government to get it on its feet, as well as to remain in the Persian Gulf. We believe the British can remain in the Persian Gulf for an indefinite period provided the government at home does not yield to domestic pressure. We are for our part continuing our strong support to Saudi Arabia and would want to take other steps to oppose further extension of UAR influence by subversive or other military means.

VIII. The Iranian Position

The Shah regards Aden as the backdoor to the Gulf. He exaggerates but is quite right in regarding South Arabia as a major test of strength between Arab radicals and Arab moderates. Because the Iranians are not Arabs and come from a different Moslem sect from most South Arabian Moslems, it would be counterproductive for Tehran to seek to exert certain types of influence on the situation. Iranian clandestine involvement with particular groups should be avoided, since this would prompt a higher level of activity by the UAR, and the UAR has more going for it to win such a contest. Iranian support, including economic assistance, should be actively solicited for any independent South Arabian government that seems likely to be able to maintain itself.

IX. The Israeli Position

Israel is concerned at FLOSY assertions that it would close the southern straits of the Red Sea to Israeli shipping if it came to power in South Arabia. This is largely a propaganda ploy designed to help FLOSY in its bid for power. The South Arabian government will have no significant military capability in that region, and the straits are clearly international waters. Israel should encourage its Ethiopian and Iranian friends to give strong support to the new South Arabian government regardless of its coloration. In this way they will have influence on that regime which otherwise will be abdicated to radical powers, notably the UAR.

X. US Action Considerations

Efforts to achieve a peaceful transition through creation of a broadly-based government are in our interest. We should do what we can to foster these efforts, making clear to South Arabian radicals, and to the UAR, the risks of opting out, proclaiming a government-in-exile, and seeking to take over the area by force. The following moves illustrate what might be done to encourage our friends and increase our own influence:

—A greater US military presence in the Red Sea–Arabian Sea area, particularly in support of our existing assurances to Saudi Arabia.

—USG willingness to undertake a full range of normal USG contacts with the new South Arabian state provided it is able to maintain itself (any economic aid would require a high-level political determination).

—Adoption of a blunter line in Cairo, and development of international support for the position, to emphasize concern that any new South Arabian regime not be threatened with aggression from outside its frontiers and that the internal political situation be permitted to evolve without outside interference.

—Consideration of the utility of discussing South Arabia with the USSR to signal our concern lest outside forces seek to exploit internal stresses there that seem inevitable.

—Continued efforts with the British to assure: (a) that everything feasible be done to create a broadly-based coalition, including UK willingness to extend its six-month security assurance as may be necessary; and (b) that the current British military build-up in the Persian Gulf is sustained.

—Discussion with the Saudis to focus their attention on this problem and develop additional tangible Saudi support for a moderate solution, if possible, or for more conservative elements if a civil war-type situation occurs.

—Continued support for a UN role in the situation, including specifically encouragement to the UN Special Mission to hold a round-table conference and develop a coalition of all major South Arabian political elements.

XI. Some Key Questions

—Is US military strength sufficient to assume additional tasks in the Red Sea–Arabian Sea region?

—Is it realistic to contemplate constructive discussions with the Russians on South Arabia?

—How far should Prime Minister Wilson be pushed to maintain a British military commitment to South Arabia?—in the Persian Gulf?

—How much pressure should be exerted on the Shah to discourage him from counterproductive efforts to oppose radical Arab nationalism in South Arabia? What positive lines of action should he be encouraged to follow?

---

98.   Information Memorandum From the Assistant Secretary of State for Near Eastern and South Asian Affairs (Battle) to Acting Secretary of State Katzenbach[1]

Washington, June 19, 1967.

SUBJECT

Independence Arrangements for South Arabia

1. Foreign Secretary Brown announced the following British decisions for South Arabia in the House of Commons on June 19:

—Independence for "all South Arabia" early in January 1968.

—Early application to Aden of an independence-type constitution which would replace the current Federal constitution for the whole country as soon as possible.

—Additional British financial help to the SAFG military establishment, continuing support for the Hadhrami Bedouin Legion in the

---

[1] Source: National Archives and Records Administration, RG 59, Central Files 1967–69, POL 19 ADEN. Secret. Drafted by Brewer. A copy was sent to Director of the INR Office of Research and Analysis for Near East and South Asia Granville S. Austin.

Eastern Protectorate for two years after independence and establishment of a British military aid mission to assist the organization and training of the SAFG forces.

—Measures to tighten up against terrorism (e.g., suspension of trial by jury) combined with measures designed to facilitate political reconciliation (e.g., lifting the ban on the NLF).

2. The foregoing announcement confirms that HMG has decided to give full support to the SAFG as the only means at hand of assuring any kind of logical and, hopefully, orderly transfer of power. Several points in the British proposals are of interest:

a. *Constitutional:* The British have decided to adopt the constitutional proposals contained in the Hone–Bell report of February 1966. Various changes are designed to bring the draft nearer the desiderata of the UN resolutions. The constitution is to provide for country-wide elections on the basis of universal adult franchise, which in turn will be based on liberal nationality legislation giving the vote to genuine "belongers" of various races. This provision would appear not to cover the very substantial population in Aden of Yemeni origin and, accordingly, will not be acceptable to FLOSY and other opposition groups.

b. *Aden:* A "capital territory" is being established which will include Aden and its environs, including the present Federal capital. It is indicated that this arrangement will be made prior to independence. It might thus be possible to deal with the vexing issue of giving the SAFG some responsibility for security before 1968. However, the UK plans to take care of the constitutional problem (Aden will remain a Colony until independence) by "reservations" with respect to certain fields of continuing responsibility. One of these may well prove to be security.

c. *Defense:* The UK will reportedly increase by ten million sterling the amount previously committed to the SAFG military for the first three years of independence. The funds will be devoted to additional arms and equipment for the Federal Army, as well as the establishment of a British military aid mission to help organize and train the Federal forces and to supply key personnel for those forces' base and medical service. No line officers are apparently to be seconded. A number of Hunter aircraft will be supplied to give the SAFG a small operational air force. An additional squadron of eight armored cars will also be provided, as well as eight additional 25-pounders. These will be in addition to the off-shore British naval force which will be in the area for six months after independence. To this force, a unit of V bombers has been added which will be stationed at Masirah Island for at least six months and longer if the UK so decides. These forces are to deter and, if necessary, repel external military aggression.

d. *Hadhramaut:* The British proposals seem to accept that this area will not join the SAFG prior to independence. To assist in maintaining stability, the UK has now decided to finance the Hadhrami Bedouin

Legion until 1970. The hope is that this will provide sufficient calm for the SAFG to work out terms for the Hadhramaut's eventual accession to the new Republic of South Arabia.

3. These unilateral British proposals are likely to be seized upon by the moribund UN Special Mission for South Arabia as the excuse to terminate its activities. While it is true that the British proposals preempt the constitutional processes envisaged by the UN Resolutions, the Special Mission's inability to obtain the cooperation of all South Arabian groups has made it difficult for London to envisage any other course. The British hope to meet the expected criticism from South Arabian radicals on this point by including in the new constitution a special provision calling for the formation of a "central caretaker government" if and when this becomes possible. This is unlikely to mollify the radicals who will contend that they are not in a position to join a regime whose constitution they had no hand in forming.

4. The outlook is thus for continued polarization in South Arabia, with the British giving greater military and political support to the conservatives. They clearly hope that, by so doing, the terrorist threat from elements in Yemen can be contained until the new government finds its feet. They recognize, however, that this is a gamble, and it seems virtually certain that the political scene in South Arabia will become even more tense as these arrangements are now put in train on the ground.

---

99. Intelligence Memorandum[1]

No. 1368/67   Washington, July 24, 1967.

SOUTH ARABIA

Summary

Britain has taken the first step toward forming a representative government to succeed the South Arabian Federation government.

---

[1] Source: Johnson Library, National Security File, Country File, South Arabia, Vol. I, 7/67–11/67. Secret; No Foreign Dissem; No Dissem Abroad/Controlled Dissem. Prepared in the Central Intelligence Agency's Directorate of Intelligence. A note on the memorandum indicates it was produced solely in the CIA for the use of the CIA representative on the Interdepartmental Regional Group, Middle East. It was prepared by the Office of Current Intelligence and coordinated with the Office of National Estimates and the Clandestine Services.

On 5 July the Supreme Federal Council, the governing body of the federation, appointed an Adeni moderate, Husayn Bayumi, as prime minister-designate to form a caretaker government until independence, now scheduled for 9 January 1968. According to present plans, elections will then be held and a permanent government established. British carriers will be stationed offshore for six months to ensure that the fledgling state is not overthrown by the Egyptians in Yemen.

Despite the anarchy of recent months, the British hope not to leave behind "another Congo." The vital question, however, is whether it is not already too late to achieve any kind of order out of the present chaos of tribal feuds, ethnic prejudices, social backwardness, and political machinations by other Arab states such as Egypt.

1. Aden is today an armed camp, with assassination and terrorism commonplace. In June there were 445 incidents in Aden alone, compared with 376 in April and a peak figure of 80 per month last fall. Known casualties due to incidents in Aden for the first half of 1967 are 116 killed and 527 wounded.

Egyptian Involvement

2. The force behind this terrorism is the Egyptian intelligence organization in Yemen. Egypt's proclaimed purpose was to eject the British from Aden, but Cairo has continued its operations even though London has long since announced its intention to grant independence by 1968. Although Egypt has asserted that the terrorism is punishment of the British for their tyranny, the great majority of casualties have been Arab. Egypt has also boasted that Britain will no longer grow wealthy on Aden's trade. Terror and destruction have almost reached the point where Aden will soon have no trade, nor will it have the bankers or traders needed to revive commerce after peace is restored.

The Terrorist Groups

3. Now even the Egyptians appear to have lost control of the situation. Cairo deserted its original terrorist group, the National Liberation Front (NLF)—which it had used earlier in back-country dissidence—for a more broadly based group backed chiefly by the Aden labor movement, the Front for the Liberation of Occupied South Yemen (FLOSY), when the target of terrorism was switched to the city of Aden in 1965. The NLF, however, continued to be strong in the 16 other states of the federation, as well as in the federation army, the federal guards, the police, and many workers of back-country origin employed in Aden. Despite the lack of Egyptian support, the NLF fought a bloody back-alley war with FLOSY, and at present seems to hold a slight edge in Aden and a definite advantage in the hill states.

4. Not much is known about the amazingly successful leadership of the NLF, even by British intelligence in Aden. It is known, however, to

have ties with the Arab National Movement (ANM), another successful terrorist movement with branches in many Arab countries. The ANM is supposedly supported by the Egyptian Intelligence Service (EIS), but on several occasions has bucked the EIS with impunity. Occasional reports link leading AMM members with Arab Communist movements.

5. Both FLOSY and the NLF have refused to talk with the British, or even with the UN Mission to Aden, about taking part in any independent government which Britain might be able to establish. Furthermore, FLOSY has taken the extreme view that it alone speaks for the people of South Arabia. Consequently London has been left to deal with the existing federation government—made up primarily of hill-country sultans despised by most liberal Adenis.

Efforts to Resolve Differences

6. When conditions in South Arabia began to deteriorate swiftly, all parties involved began to search for some compromise solution. Several states tried to intervene and the UN sent missions to assess the situation, all to no avail. With the onset of the Arab-Israeli war, the situation became even more murky. Many South Arabians, believing that Britain and the US were behind Israel's success, were even more antagonistic about negotiating with Britain.

7. On 19 June the British Foreign Secretary announced that independence, long scheduled for the end of 1968, would take place on 9 January 1968. He said that London would increase its commitments of military aid to about $168 million over a three-year period and would station a naval force for six months and a bomber force for perhaps longer to protect South Arabia against "open external aggression." London said it fully supported the present government and welcomed its intention to form a caretaker government "if and when cooperation with others makes this possible." On 5 July Bayumi, an Adeni moderate with shadowy connections with the NLF, was appointed prime minister-designate. He announced on 18 July the formation of an eight-man interim administration—five Adenis and three from other states, whose ability and affiliations are not impressive.

8. These actions are remarkable especially because they were carried out during open mutiny by the South Arabian security forces and during the Arab-Israeli war. The real time of testing for the administration is yet to come, however, and numerous problems remain.

Attitudes

9. The blood feuds engendered by the terrorism have built up a residue of bitterness, and there are many scores to settle. With arms readily available, public security will be exceedingly difficult to restore,

particularly the stable type which had made Aden almost unique in the Middle East. Nasir, moreover, has not yet given any solid evidence that he is prepared to cooperate in building a viable state in South Arabia, and the EIS may be capable of subverting any new state, with or without the assistance of the present nationalist groups. Finally, disillusionment and apathy have set in, and those who could once have ensured South Arabia's future viability are giving up. The Somalis, Hindus, Jews, and British who built and carried on Aden's trade are leaving, and the present situation does not encourage new investment.

10. Britain's role is a critical factor. London has been trying to encourage those Adenis who might be able to salvage something. The continued recalcitrance of all parties, however, has hampered British efforts to establish a successor government. At the time of the uprising in the Crater district, there was strong sentiment in Britain for pulling out early. Even if London hangs on until 9 January, as now seems likely, the successor government may well take on an increasingly pro-Nasir tinge. Britain might in that case reconsider contributing $168 million to arm a pro-Nasir army in South Arabia, whatever commitments may have been made.

11. The lack of British assistance and trade would sharply limit the future of South Arabia. Egypt does not possess the economic strength to fill the vacuum, however easily it may fund and supply the large-scale terrorist campaign. To date no other state has shown any interest in bailing South Arabia out of its political and economic mire, and the UN is unlikely to accept large-scale responsibility there.

---

100. Record of Meeting[1]

IRG/NEA 67–24   Washington, July 26, 1967.

INTERDEPARTMENTAL REGIONAL GROUP FOR NEAR EAST AND SOUTH ASIA

Record of IRG/NEA Meeting—July 26, 1967

The meeting was devoted to a further consideration of our *policy towards South Arabia,* in the light of the developments since the IRG/

---

[1] Source: Johnson Library, National Security File, Saunders Files, Saudi Arabia, 4/1/66–12/31/67. Secret. Drafted by Sober on July 27.

NEA meetings of May 1967 (see IRG/NEA 67–18, 5/24/67, for a record of agreements reached at that time).[2] The Group:

Reviewed recent significant developments, including the announcement by the United Kingdom that it would give independence to South Arabia on January 9, 1968, as noted in the paper prepared by the Country Director (State) for the meeting (see IRG/NEA 67–23, 7/21/67)[3] and as elaborated by the CIA member.

Agreed that, although our previous tentative planning with respect to an independent South Arabia remains basically valid, the recent Middle East hostilities and the break in our diplomatic relations with various Arab countries, especially the UAR, were important new elements to be taken into account as we formulate our policy. The UAR's continued military presence in the Yemen, although below the pre-hostilities level, and its activities in Aden, remain critical. The success of efforts by the British to extricate themselves gracefully from South Arabia, and to leave behind a reasonably independent and viable regime, also remain critical. The Group *agreed* that our planning must continue to be tentative for the time being, and that our policy and specific actions will have to depend on developments and on circumstances as the new South Arabian state comes into being. It *recognized* that our actions would necessarily be influenced not only by our own assessment of our interests but also by the willingness of the new South Arabian government to work with us.

Agreed that, meanwhile, our tentative planning should include:

1) Recognition of the new South Arabian state and elevation of our Consulate General at Aden to Embassy status, with assignment of a resident Ambassador.

2) Assignment of Defense Attaché staff and opening a one-man USIS operation as the Embassy is established.

3) Consideration of possible limited programs including, for example, Peace Corps volunteers, MAP training in the US, and cultural exchanges, should local conditions justify and the new government voice an interest.

[1 *paragraph (2 lines of source text) not declassified*]

Agreed that we should maintain our close contacts with the British on developments in South Arabia, endeavoring to influence their moves in the direction of greater post-independence stability in the region. We should also continue to consult with Saudi Arabia and other friendly states to foster greater interest in South Arabian stability. During the Shah's visit to the United States in August 1967, we should solicit his views on developments and prospects in Yemen and Aden;

---

[2] Document 95.
[3] Not found.

we should take sympathetic note of his concern over the area and encourage him to play a responsible role in promoting stability in South Arabia.

Agreed, finally, that the situation in South Arabia and the formulation of our policy with respect to it need to be kept under close review, although it would not be desirable to reach decisions until much closer to the time of independence.

MEMBERS PRESENT

    Executive Chairman—Mr. Battle
    AID: Mr. Funari
    CIA: Mr. Critchfield
    DOD: Mr. Barringer
    DOD: Col. Alba
    USIA: Mr. Saunders
    USIA: Mr. Austin

    State: (NEA) Ambassador Strong, Mr. Brewer; (IO) Mr. Campbell
    Staff Director: Mr. Sober, Mr. Buckle

Sidney Sober[4]
Staff Director

---

[4] Printed from a copy that bears this typed signature.

101. Memorandum of Conversation[1]

Washington, August 9, 1967.

US–UK TALKS ON UN AFFAIRS
Washington, August 9–10, 1967

ADEN–YEMEN GAS

PARTICIPANTS

United Kingdom	United States
Ambassador Dean, UK Embassy Washington	Ambassador Goldberg
	IO Assistant Secretary Sisco
Minister Tomkins, UK Embassy Washington	NEA Assistant Secretary Battle
Sir Leslie Glass, UKUN	USUN Ambassador Buffum
Sir Richard Beaumont, Foreign Office	USUN Ambassador Pedersen
David Hildyard, Foreign Office	NEA Deputy Assistant Secretary
Anne Warburton, Foreign Office	Davies
Stephen Egerton, UKUN	Helmut Sonnenfeldt, INR/RSB
Alan Urwick, UK Embassy Washington	

Aden

Ambassador Beaumont offered to give a briefing on the latest situation in Aden. He said British objectives were (1) to extricate British forces from Aden in good order, and (2) to leave behind a viable and unified independent state. The first objective he described as "imperative"; the second, although less imperative, was one that the British were trying very hard and sincerely to achieve. The HMG offer to provide a deterrent naval force after independence (the date for which, Beaumont said, was still January 9, 1968) was designed to give confidence to the new state. The British would also keep a bomber force on Masira Island and continue to support the Bedouin Legion in the East Aden Protectorate.

The British remained faced with a political deadlock in Aden resulting from the intensification of extremism in Adeni political groupings brought about by outside pressures and the intimidation of the population caused by terrorism. Today it was hard to say who controls Aden. The British believed, however, that the Federal Government, with its backwoods tribal support, represented a genuine political force which would have to be recognized in any post-independence government. The British were having a hard time convincing the UN Special Mission of this. The British felt strongly that the rural component of the population must have appropriate representation in the new

---

[1] Source: National Archives and Records Administration, RG 59, Central Files 1967–69, POL UK–US. Secret. Drafted by Michael Sterner (NEA/IAI).

government if the new state were not to disintegrate. The danger of giving the urban elements an overwhelming voice was borne out by recent defections from the Federal Army. There was a real danger that if the post-independence government was of an extremist nationalist complexion the Shaikhs would withdraw their forces from the army and civil war would ensue.

The British believed that FLOSY had lost ground to some extent to the NLF in recent months and that the NLF, although still primarily a terrorist organization, was nevertheless developing some political leadership capability. The trade unions, which used to be the most important force in Aden politics, were now split between FLOSY and the NLF. The South Arabian League contained able men but the organization seemed to fall between two stools—not radical enough for the urban nationalists and too radical for the up-country rulers. Also, most of the SAL leaders were in exile.

Beaumont wished to put two requests to the USG in the interest of facilitating the transition to a viable independent South Arabian state. First, it would be helpful if the US could make some kind of statement in support of the territorial integrity of the new state. Secondly, it would also help if the US could in the near future make a decision to offer some kind of economic assistance to the new state. The British appreciated the problems that the US would have in extending economic aid of any magnitude. However, even a token gesture along these lines would help to steer the situation in a constructive direction. The aid offer would not have to be specific, and it could be directed to the newly-created state rather than to the present government. HMG itself was planning to extend economic assistance to the new state in the amount of $140 million spread over three years.

Beaumont emphasized that the British adhered to their timetable for withdrawal from Aden. In fact the withdrawal of military forces was slightly ahead of schedule.

Ambassador Glass said that so far as the UN Mission was concerned HMG's objectives were to achieve a caretaker government which would provide for a cooling off period and a coalescing of political forces. The original effort of the Mission had been a great disappointment to the HMG. Now British efforts were concentrated on keeping the Mission from "becoming a nuisance." In recent days the Mission had become somewhat more constructive. HMG had hoped that the nationalist political groups would agree to meet with it in Geneva but FLOSY had now said it would not, and the NLF had done likewise. High Commissioner Trevelyan had urged that the Federal Government send representatives to meet with the Mission.

Responding to the two British requests of the USG, Ambassador Battle said that both would pose difficult problems. This would be particularly true in terms of Congress, which recently had expressed criticism of our extending our commitments to additional territories. We would look into the question of whether our existing statements concerning support for the territorial integrity of the states of the area could somehow be defined to include South Arabia. On aid, he did not wish to leave the British with unjustified expectations. Given existing pressures on foreign aid generally, it would be difficult for the US to do anything substantial in South Arabia. Perhaps some technical assistance would be feasible. Ambassador Battle assured the British officials that their requests would receive careful consideration.

Use of Poison Gas in Yemen

Ambassador Beaumont said there were two aspects to this issue. First, the UAR's use of poison gas, now pretty well established, had shocked people on humanitarian grounds in Britain. Secondly, it seemed to offer an opportunity to attack the double standard that prevailed in the Afro-Asian world whereby the "imperialist" powers came under constant criticism for "atrocities" but apparently the Afro-Asian states could never commit any sins. Ambassador Beaumont saw an advantage in raising the issue in various forums so as to bring some pressure to bear on the UAR to stop this practice and also to adopt moderate policies generally in Yemen.

Ambassador Glass said unfortunately the Arab-Israel conflict had made it more difficult to condemn the UAR for its use of gas. Such a move could now be labelled by the Arab extremists as an anti-Arab tactic. The most feasible tack might be to get the GA's third Committee to consider a general resolution condemning the use of gas (without specifying the UAR). The trouble was the Third Committee tended to be erratic. The General Assembly had adopted a resolution in 1966 condemning the use of gas in wartime, and it might be possible to introduce another resolution extending this condemnation to use under any circumstances. This resolution had been dealt with in the First Committee with disarmament questions.

Ambassador Battle said it was difficult for us to do anything in the UN when the parties most directly concerned were unwilling to push a charge against the UAR. Of late the Saudis had not been willing to break Arab solidarity by pushing this issue. At present we didn't see any other group that would be willing to take the lead on it. Sir Patrick Dean wondered whether the Scandinavians might not play this role. He pointed out that the Scandinavian Foreign Ministers would be meeting in a week or so and that perhaps the UK and US might wish to stimulate them to take the lead on this issue. Mr. Sisco said he was doubtful that they would, adding that one problem with bringing up the gas issue in the GA was that it might tend to unify Arabs on the broader Arab-Israel question.

Ambassador Goldberg said that personally he had been shocked at the use of gas, and that American public opinion was outraged. It was becoming increasingly difficult for the US because of Congressional and private pressures, not to make some move. However, he saw that the US could not bring the issue up formally but he thought we should actively stimulate either the Scandinavians or the Latin Americans to raise it. Mr. Sisco said that as a fallback position we might want to organize certain states to take the lead in preparing documentation on the case. It was left that the US and UK delegations in New York would consult on the matter inter alia to consider means of moving ahead if Saudi Arabia remained reluctant to give active support. It would be necessary to be in touch with the Scandinavians and the Saudis.

---

102. Telegram From the Department of State to the Consulate in Aden[1]

Washington, September 22, 1967, 2057Z.

42401. Aden 344.[2] View uncertainties South Arabian situation, Dept does not believe action should be taken which might convey impression either USG special interest in particular South Arabian group or certainty early recognition any government which may emerge (re final para reftel). With these caveats, however, we perceive no objection your letting it be known on appropriate occasions to representatives various South Arabian groups that USG hopes circumstances will permit establishment friendly relations with whatever government emerges in

---

[1] Source: National Archives and Records Administration, RG 59, Central Files 1967–69, POL 13 ADEN. Confidential. Drafted by Brewer and approved by Davies. Repeated to Jidda and London.

[2] In telegram 344 from Aden, September 21, U.S. Consul William Eagleton described a meeting with NLF representative Ali Nasser in Aden and stated that an NLF-dominated South Arabian Government would probably find its place in the radical Arab nationalist camp, although opportunism might keep it on reasonably good terms with the British as long as the United Kingdom was a major source of aid. Eagleton concluded that as long as the NLF political orientation was fluid, it would be in the U.S. interest to make it known that the establishment of friendly relations with whatever government emerged in South Arabia would depend on that government's attitude toward the United States. (Ibid.)

South Arabia, but that this will of course depend on attitude such government toward USG.

Rusk

---

103. **Telegram From the Department of State to the Embassy in the United Kingdom**[1]

Washington, October 2, 1967, 2150Z.

47358. London 2384.[2]

1. US continues attach great importance to UK presence in Gulf. We support current British position and will encourage HMG to continue maintain military forces in Gulf equal to task of providing security for Shaikhdoms.

2. We also concur in UK estimate which sounds experienced note of caution against too facile comparison between situations in South Arabia and Gulf States. Radical Arab organizations will without doubt increasingly direct attention to Gulf states and attempt erode hold of traditionalists over their populations. But we believe there smaller base on which build organized revolutionary activity in Gulf States than there was earlier in such cities as Aden, Taiz, Hodeida, while rapidly rising oil income in some states may reduce dissident pressures.

3. Addressees may accordingly, as circumstances warrant, make clear to appropriate British contacts that we continue believe UK can play major stabilizing role in Gulf area for indefinite period without encountering irresistable pressures from radical groups.

Katzenbach

---

[1] Source: National Archives and Records Administration, RG 59, Central Files 1967–69, POL 19 ADEN. Confidential; Limdis. Drafted by Brewer and Dinsmore on September 29; cleared by Irving Cheslaw (EUR/BMI), David W. McClintock (INR/RNA), Edward A. Padelford (NEA/RA), Brewer, and Davies; and approved by Battle. Repeated to Aden, Dhahran, Jidda, Kuwait, Tehran, and CINCSTRIKE/MEAFSA.

[2] Telegram 2384 from London, September 27, described a recent Foreign Office circular instruction contrasting the situation in South Arabia with that of the Gulf states and emphasizing the advantages of the latter. The circular pointed out that the Gulf rulers were recently assured by public statements of U.K. ministers, that the United Kingdom intended to stand by its commitments in the Gulf while there was a need for them. (Ibid.)

104. Memorandum From the Country Director for Saudi Arabia, Kuwait, Yemen, and Aden (Brewer) to the Director of the Office of Regional Affairs, Bureau of Near Eastern and South Asian Affairs (Sober)[1]

Washington, October 13, 1967.

SUBJECT

Immediate Actions Consistent with Holmes Study[2]

REFERENCE

Your Memo, September 22, 1967[3]

The Holmes Study made no suggestions for any major courses of action to be taken in the region of the Arabian Peninsula at this time. Nevertheless, as your memorandum recalls, even with our present limited resources there are certain actions already underway and others whose relevance to the Study deserve mention.

In *Kuwait,* for instance, a $50 million loan has been approved by the Export-Import Bank to the Kuwait National Petroleum Company for partial financing of a refinery. The loan is a further evidence of United States support for this important small Persian Gulf State whose continued development is a key factor in the maintenance of stability in the area.

The United States Government is following through with planning to elevate its Consulate General in Aden to an Embassy when *South Arabian* independence follows British withdrawal (possibly before the end of 1967). This, of course, assumes that a viable government will be established which we will find it in our interest to recognize.

With reference to the Study's repeated mention of the desirability of our contributing to a *multinational naval task force* for the area, NEA/ARP suggests that improvement of US Naval capacity for the region might be more realistic. There are increasing numbers of isolated groups of US citizens in the Peninsula for whose welfare and protection we have some responsibility. The region's vast oil reserves remain important to us. NEA/ARP therefore urges that further study now be

---

[1] Source: National Archives and Records Administration, RG 59, NEA/RA Files: Lot 71 D 218, Holmes Study, 1967. Confidential. No drafting information appears on the memorandum.

[2] See Document 22.

[3] Sober's September 22 memorandum to IRG/NEA members reported that the Chairman of the SIG had asked IRG/NEA and IRG/AF to propose actions that might be initiated immediately in the Holmes Study area, even with present limited resources. (Department of State, NEA/RA Files: Lot 71 D 218, Holmes Study, 1967)

given to this question. The particular thrust of this effort should be to flesh out what is meant by the need to develop an "on call" military capability, including naval forces operating in waters contiguous to the area as is suggested in Annex B, Section V.C and D of the Holmes Study. As a basis for discussion, we would favor the immediate examination of the possibility of increasing the strength of our Middle Eastern naval forces from two destroyers to four. This would appear particularly useful right now, due to the much longer time required to support and reinforce COMIDEASTFOR due to the closure of the Suez Canal.

---

105.   Telegram From the Embassy in Iran to the Department of State[1]

Tehran, October 25, 1967, 0830Z.

1835. Security of Persian Gulf.

1. Shah evening 24th indicated he intends speak in strong terms re British Mideast policies when British Minister of State Roberts (successor to Thompson) visits Tehran in November.

2. Noting he had that day received telegram from Iran Amb Aram in London to effect there is likelihood British will recognize Sallal regime, Shah said he will ask Roberts what is motivating incomprehensible UK policy. Shah's remarks were extension GOI's expression of concern re what it considers unseemly British efforts to woo Nasser (Tehran 1711).[2]

3. Shah said he has received another report re move to merge Yemen and Aden. This in his view opens prospect of either Nasserist or, even worse, Communist-dominated country at mouth of Red Sea. He noted Russians increasingly active in Yemen.

4. Shah said he cannot understand Britain's so cavalierly letting down so many friends, i.e. Arabian Peninsula sheikhs, who had placed their faith in British. Each sheikhdom, he said, seems to have some London School of Economics leftist leaders ready to manipulate the destinies of these desert principalities.

---

[1] Source: National Archives and Records Administration, RG 59, Central Files 1967–69, POL 33 PERSIAN GULF. Secret. Repeated to Jidda, London, Kuwait, Dhahran, and CINCSTRIKE/USCINCMEAFSA.

[2] Dated October 17. (Ibid., POL 27 YEMEN)

5. Obviously concerned by what he considers vacuum in sheikh-doms as British influence diminishes in area, Shah said Iran not interested in additional land. In fact, it clear Iranian attempts to exercise domination over Arab areas would be failure. Obviously one solution would be Saudi hegemony over anachronistic sheikhdoms. However, Saudis in Shah's view are having enough trouble controlling their own partiarchal society.

6. I took occasion to mention that in informal discussion some of us held some months ago, my distinguished colleague in Kuwait Ambassador Cottam voiced suggestion there might be established some sort of economic consortium of all riparian countries on Gulf. This idea seemed to intrigue Shah. He thought perhaps some sort of Persian Gulf development bank might be practical vehicle for developing regional cooperation in Gulf Area. He likened such project to RCD.

7. From British Ambassador I had already heard that British are sending State Minister Roberts to Tehran. In response to HMG inquiries, Iranians made clear they would like formal discussions and came up with agenda of four points, three of which are Mideast, Persian Gulf security and Iran oil production.

Meyer

---

106.   Telegram From the Embassy in Saudi Arabia to the Department of State[1]

Jidda, October 28, 1967, 1130Z.

1647. Subj: Apprehension of Persian Gulf Rulers. Ref (Notal).[2] From Seelye.

1. King told UK Ambassador Man in connection King's criticism UK policy in South Arabia (Jidda's 1646)[3] that Persian Gulf rulers have

---

[1] Source: National Archives and Records Administration, RG 59, Central Files 1967–69, POL 19 ADEN. Confidential. Repeated to London, Kuwait, Aden, Dhahran, and Tehran.

[2] Not further identified.

[3] Dated October 28. (National Archives and Records Administration, RG 59, Central Files 1967–69, POL 19 ADEN)

expressed considerable concern to him re prospect UK will disengage from Persian Gulf as peremptorily as they have from South Arabia. King told Man that he shared this concern and that he was worried also that UK would undercut existing regimes by handing over authority to nationalists prematurely.

2. Man states he endeavored to disabuse King of this belief, assuring King that any UK withdrawal from Gulf would not occur for sometime (Ustaqbal ba'eed). King probed Man as to precisely what this meant. Would it mean next year? Man affirmed that it assuredly did not, but, he confides, he was not authorized to tell King that British have in mind staying at least until 1970. Man endeavored to persuade King that he must have faith in British and expressed hope that King would pass his reassurances along to Gulf rulers. (Man states that political resident Stewart Crawford reports from Bahrein aroused their apprehensions by warning that British will pull out of Gulf sooner rather than later.)

3. [3^1/2 *lines of source text not declassified*] King acknowledged he had exchanged letters with Zaid re Buraimi but noted that a misunderstanding had developed. He had expected Zaid in initiating correspondence to make specific proposals re settlement Buraimi dispute but, instead, Zaid had asked King to initiate proposals. King had thereupon tossed ball back at Zaid by asking Zaid to make first move.

4. *Comments:* Ambassador Man expressed belief that he had succeeded somewhat in reassuring King that UK planned no peremptory disengagement from Gulf but he expressed personal reservations re determination of present UK Government remain in Gulf through 1970. Should nationalist uprising occur in Bahrain before then, for example, he doubts whether UK would intervene militarily to support regime.[4]

Eilts

---

[4] Telegram 61726 to London, October 30, expressed the Department's puzzlement over the reference to British plans to remain in the Gulf "at least until 1970," noting that a British decision might have been taken that the U.K. Ambassador was not yet authorized to communicate. The telegram noted that the U.S. Government believed that the United Kingdom intended to remain in the Gulf to protect its interests there for the foreseeable future, i.e., well beyond 1970. (Ibid.)

107. Memorandum of Conversation[1]

Washington, November 1, 1967, 10 a.m.

SUBJECT

UK Withdrawal from South Arabia

PARTICIPANTS

The Secretary
Sir Patrick Dean, British Ambassador
Mr. Allen Urwick, First Secretary, British Embassy
Mr. William D. Brewer, Country Director, Arabian Peninsula States

Sir Patrick called at 10:00 a.m. on November 1 to inform the Secretary in advance of the November 2 British announcement on withdrawal from South Arabia. Sir Patrick said that withdrawal would be completed "within the second half of November" but that the exact date still remained open. In announcing this in Commons on November 2, the Foreign Secretary would also make clear that the previously scheduled naval and air deterrent forces for South Arabia were being cancelled due to the changed situation in both Yemen and South Arabia. The Foreign Secretary would also announce that decisions on post-independence British military and economic support to South Arabia would have to be taken at a later date. London simply had to suspend judgment until the future could be seen more clearly and an opportunity provided for discussions with a new government. Mr. Brown would also underline the continued readiness of the High Commissioner in Aden to negotiate if the nationalists wished to do so. However, British withdrawal would go forward whether or not such negotiations took place.

Sir Patrick added that it had also been decided that Perim and Kamaran Islands would go to South Arabia, subject to any UN action on internationalization of Perim. The Kuria Murias would be ceded to Muscat. No announcement on these points would be made on November 2.

The Secretary asked what would happen following the British withdrawal. Sir Patrick replied that the UK simply did not know. The NLF/FLOSY talks in Cairo were apparently not going well. No government might be formed. However, if serious trouble broke out, it now looked as if it might be contained within South Arabia. The Secretary

---

[1] Source: National Archives and Records Administration, RG 59, Central Files 1967–69, POL 16 ADEN. Confidential. Drafted by Brewer on November 3 and approved in the Office of the Secretary of State on November 7.

wondered whether the nationalists might ask, and receive, Egyptian troops. Sir Patrick replied that he thought not, noting that the UAR withdrawal from Yemen was proceeding.

The Secretary asked about post-independence naval dispositions by HMG. Sir Patrick said that naval forces now in Aden waters (two carriers) would cover the final withdrawal phase. He had no information regarding subsequent dispositions but undertook to inquire of London. The Ambassador stressed that these British actions in no way reflected on HMG's determination to remain in the Persian Gulf.

The Secretary observed that, even though the Egyptians were leaving Yemen, this did not mean that their forces could not turn up in South Arabia, or that other foreign elements might not intrude. We would very much hope that the UK would continue to support the South Arabian Army, one of the few elements of stability in the current situation, until the local situation became firmer. Sir Patrick said that a Military Advising and Training Mission would be standing by to take up its duties with the South Arabian Army on fourteen days' notice, but that it would not be sent without a further decision.

For Sir Patrick's information, the Secretary went over brief Department press guidance designed to meet expected questions on November 2, following the British announcement. The Ambassador indicated that he thought the comments would be helpful.

On leaving, the Ambassador said that the British were similarly informing King Faisal, the Shah and the Amir of Kuwait in advance. He was uncertain whether the UN Mission on Aden was also being informed. In response to the Secretary's question, the Ambassador said that King Faisal did not seem to have much influence in South Arabia but was most concerned about the current British policy.

After leaving the Secretary, an opportunity was provided to go over the British guidance in detail. Mr. Urwick made clear that the British would decide on November 13 the exact date on which withdrawal would be completed and said that it would fall in the period November 22 to 30. He said that the removal of the air deterrent referred specifically to the proposed stationing of V bombers on Masirah Island. In the event that no government was formed prior to the British departure, Mr. Urwick opined that the British position of suspending judgment on future financial aid to the new state would continue to obtain. Negotiations on the subject could be initiated by the future British diplomatic mission in Aden whenever an acceptable government was established.

108. Telegram From the Department of State to the Mission to the North Atlantic Treaty Organization and Regional Organizations[1]

Washington, November 1, 1967, 1444Z.

62888. NATUS. Deliver Wilson 0900, Thursday, November 2. Subject: Recognition of New Government in Aden. Re USNATO 164.[2]

1. Dept agrees in principle re desirability early recognition South Arabia by number Western countries, including USG. For present, however, absence of any government in the state and uncertainty as to whether one, and if so what type, will be in charge on independence makes it difficult speak today in concrete terms.

2. Furthermore, international acceptability new state would, in our view, be enhanced if several regional governments were to recognize it ahead of most Western powers. This does not, of course, apply to UK which we would think should recognize at once assuming successor government in place.

3. You should take line at POLAD meeting that prompt recognition by Western countries is desirable, depending on local circumstances at time and assuming earlier comparable action by several area states. Should Communist countries themselves extend immediate recognition without, as seems more likely, waiting for area states, fact British had already recognized would reduce impact. View fluidity situation and to coordinate actions as closely as possible, would appreciate British keeping POLAD currently informed re attitude London as independence date approaches.

Rusk

---

[1] Source: National Archives and Records Administration, RG 59, Central Files 1967–69, POL 16 ADEN. Secret; Priority. Drafted by Brewer on October 31; cleared by Davies, William Dixon Boggs (EUR/RPM), and Seasword; and approved by John I. Getz (EUR/RPM). Repeated to London, Aden, Jidda, and Tehran.

[2] Dated October 31. (Ibid.)

109. Memorandum From John W. Foster and Harold H. Saunders of the National Security Council Staff to the President's Special Assistant (Rostow)[1]

Washington, November 7, 1967.

SUBJECT

South Arabia Moves Toward Independence

The British Cabinet decided last week that, come what may, British forces will pull out of South Arabia sometime November 22–30. No one—least of all the Brits—pretends to know what will follow. But this will at least describe the *main elements in the situation.*

The *intelligence community's guess today is that the National Liberation Front (NLF) has the best chance of taking over.* This is the most home-grown of the nationalist groups, having opposed both the UAR-backed FLOSY and the Saudi-backed South Arabian League. The NLF has already taken over fairly easily in most of South Arabia, and in the past week's fighting continues to appear stronger than FLOSY in Aden. Nasser's pullout in Yemen apparently weakened FLOSY's base.

This would mean a *short-term victory for one nationalist group rather than establishment of the broader coalition which Nasser and Faisal envisioned at Khartoum.* South Arabian nationalist leaders have been in Cairo trying to negotiate the composition of a post-independence government. But the NLF in Aden seems to have pre-empted. Renewed fighting between the NLF and FLOSY and the army's announcement yesterday that it will back the NLF in forming a government probably make any Cairo agreement meaningless.

The *army remains the big question mark.* Until now it has played a mediating role, trying to enforce a cease-fire on all contending groups. As long as it kept on that tack, its leaders were able to keep its own contending factions together. The next couple of days will tell *whether the army is mainly pro-NLF or whether it will split* into substantial factions that will end up on opposite sides in a civil war. If the army stands firm, then we may have seen the worst of the bloodshed. If it splits, the fighting in Aden could be severe, and even the up-country sultans might be tempted to reclaim the domains which the NLF has recently taken over from them.

No one—including the British—is sure that the NLF can form a viable government, or how such a government will act. Having fought rather than

---

[1] Source: Johnson Library, National Security File, Country File, South Arabia, Vol. I, 7/67–11/67. Secret.

negotiated its way to near-power, it will be vulnerable to continued opposition. The survival of any government will depend for a time on outside aid, and the British have suspended any decision on continuing aid until after they see what government they're dealing with.

Others appear to be waiting too. Saudi Arabia, Yemen, Iran and probably the USSR all appear to be waiting for the dust to settle before doing anything. Faisal, despite his feeling that the British have dumped his up-country conservative friends, will probably stand aside for fear of creating any excuse for Nasser to delay his withdrawal from Yemen. Faisal's final position will depend on which faction of the NLF appears to have come out on top—the radicals or a relatively moderate group.

We and the British had hoped to line up an impressive string of early friendly recognitions for the new state, but we're temporarily stymied by the absence of any government to recognize. State has contingency plans for recognizing and getting an ambassador out, but they're holding back too. They may have to evacuate our people instead.

Despite the potential disruption and danger to our people, we shouldn't ignore the *positive elements* in this situation. Much as we may hate to admit it, the June war has probably made the South Arabian transition easier for us and our friends. Nasser's role there is diminished, and we long ago decided—as we thought Faisal would, too—that we could live with any regime that did not have his hand in it. The new government may well be hostile to us, but unless there is an unexpected amount of Communist activity we can probably ride it out.

John
Hal

110.   Paper Prepared in the Department of State[1]

Washington, November 8, 1967.

SOUTH ARABIAN PROSPECTS

(Paper prepared by State—NEA/ARP)

Introduction

Almost everything that could have happened in South Arabia to impede its orderly transmutation to independence has already occurred. By early November, 1967, the conservative regime on which Britain had earlier built its hopes had collapsed, feudal rulers in the Adeni hinterland had taken refuge in Saudi Arabia, a low-key civil war between local radicals (FLOSY and NLF) had put the NLF in control of most provincial centers, the collapse of sultanic rule in the Hadhramaut had made it likely that this vast area would join with the rest of South Arabia on independence, and "agreement on all issues so far discussed" was announced by NLF and FLOSY delegations in Cairo while their supporters were engaged in an armed struggle for the control of populous sections of Aden proper. Meanwhile, the UAR withdrawal from Yemen had reduced the external threat and the British had announced plans for an accelerated withdrawal, to be completed by December 1. London is holding in suspense plans to finance and train the South Arabian Army (SAA) and otherwise assist the new state pending the formation of a viable central government.

Periodic Department Assessments

IRG/NEA from time to time has reviewed developments in South Arabia. The Holmes Study[2] included the area in its purview. A year ago, October 1966, IRG/NEA reviewed the potential threat to US interests as the UK prepared to withdraw from South Arabia and agreed, among other things, at the time that it was in the US interest that the West retain a significant influence in South Arabia and that dominant communist influence in the area could be prevented.[3]

---

[1] Source: Johnson Library, National Security File, Saunders Files, Aden & South Arabia, 4/1/66–1/20/69. Confidential. Drafted by Brewer. Prepared for a meeting of the Interdepartmental Regional Group for Near East and South Asia on November 16 at 3 p.m. Attached to a November 9 memorandum from Sober to IRG/NEA members (IRG/NEA 67–43) noting that the forthcoming meeting on November 16 would be devoted to a review of developments since the last meeting on the subject and further consideration of U.S. policy toward the emerging new state of South Arabia. He suggested that the attached paper might serve to focus the discussion.

[2] See Document 22.

[3] See Document 79.

AID/NESA was asked by IRG/NEA to make an assessment of the potential requirements of an independent South Arabia for external assistance. This paper[4] concluded that if the UK continues after independence to provide financial support to the South Arabian military and if Saudi Arabia performs on an earlier offer of economic assistance, the shortfall in a restricted South Arabian budget would be small. Prior to informal discussions with the British Foreign Office by the ARP Country Director in January, 1967, an inter-agency paper[4] was prepared which assumed that an effective independent government in Aden would succeed the British in a year's time. On that assumption, the paper concluded that: (a) prompt USG recognition should be forthcoming; (b) our Consulate General should be raised to Embassy status with an Ambassador, Defense Attaché and small staff; (c) a one-man USIA operation should be set up; and (d) normal cultural and similar programs instituted. The paper pointed out that, since no AID or MAP help could be assumed, it would be important for us to establish a normal presence early as a means of maximizing our influence with the new state at an early stage.

In May 1967 IRG/NEA again reviewed the situation and agreed that "the outcome of the struggle for control of South Arabia following imminent withdrawal of the UK is of considerable importance for US interests."[5] A paper prepared by the Department for a scheduled NSC meeting of May 24, 1967[6] conveyed the foregoing case and suggested several moves the US might make in consideration of the future of South Arabia. Among them were: a greater military presence in the Red Sea–Arabian Sea area and a willingness to undertake a full range of normal USG contacts with the new state.

A Joint Chiefs of Staff study prepared for the Secretary of Defense in May 1967[7] regarded that if Aden were available to us it would be valuable, but not essential; that it was unlikely the Soviets would try to establish a military presence in the Arabian Peninsula or on the Horn of Africa; that the implications of US military or security assistance would be largely unfavorable to US interests. While a combination of UAR/USSR influence in the area would be contrary to US interests, South Arabia was adjudged not a critical area for our security interests.

On July 26, 1967 IRG/NEA agreed that policy and specific actions must depend on circumstances, that tentative planning should go forward for recognizing the new government, elevating the Consulate

---

[4] Not found.
[5] See Document 95.
[6] Document 97.
[7] Document 93.

General to Embassy status, and appointing a resident Ambassador.[8] Preliminary steps have been taken in implementation of these proposals. Further consideration was recommended for possible limited programs including Peace Corps volunteers, several MAP training spaces, and cultural exchanges should a new government voice an interest.

Following the November 2 UK announcement that withdrawal would be completed by the end of the month, the Department's spokesman told the press:

"The British announcement that their withdrawal from South Arabia will be completed relatively soon is not unexpected, although the timing for independence is somewhat earlier than originally planned. With the day of independence approaching for South Arabia, we desire to extend the hand of friendship to all that country's people, with every good wish for their future prosperity, stability and orderly development."

On the recognition question, the spokesman noted that local groups had not yet agreed on a successor government and questions of the USG attitude towards it were premature. Congen Aden reports that the USG announcement received wide and favorable coverage in South Arabia.

Outlook

What is going from South Arabia is much clearer than what is coming. Both the Egyptians and the British are withdrawing militarily from the region. Far from driving the disparate nationalist groups in South Arabia together in some viable coalition, recent developments have only prompted further splits in their serried ranks. The key element is the unity of the SAA, which so far has fortunately withstood serious tendencies to split along tribal and faction lines. It is by no means certain that a coalition can be put together by November's end to take over from the British. If no such government is formed, the SAA will be the only representative South Arabian body to which responsibility can be transferred. In talking with the British Ambassador on November 1, the Secretary said that we hoped HMG would continue to support the army until some local stability could be established.

What the independent regime may look like is still an enigma. NLF leader Qahtan al-Shaabi has stated that its orientation will be "progressive," i.e. that the regime would take a radical view of regional and world events. On broad outlines, this may be true. But, in the inevitable sorting out process, much will depend on who actually emerges as head of NLF and whether the UK decides to continue

---

[8] See Document 100.

subsidizing the SAA, since such help would make the army both a more united and a more moderate element of influence.

Saudi Arabia watches developments closely. King Faisal would prefer to see a conservative regime take over, preferably one headed by tribal leaders, whose desire to preserve their own status would provide some sort of guarantee to him that radically inclined groups would not be allowed to influence affairs. Faisal already recognizes, however, that NLF and FLOSY possess power which cannot be overlooked, and Saudi sources suggest that an army take-over by the SAA is the most acceptable, realistic alternative. If this does not happen, SAG may seek to undermine a government of "progressive" Adenese by assisting South Arabian tribal leaders.

The degree of interest the Soviets have in an independent South Arabia cannot be gauged, but they have been and continue to be active in Yemen, providing substantial economic and some military aid. It would appear reasonable for the USSR to extend its contact and influence in the Peninsula by recognizing the new South Arabian state and offering it assistance. Communist China probably has similar plans (there has been one report of Chicom arms arriving in the Hadhramaut, allegedly for the NLF).

There is no reason to think that the South Arabians would refuse communist offers. The British have asked NATO states to consider prompt Western recognition of the new state to get in ahead of communist countries. Influence of the latter is more likely to be curtailed, however, by a British decision to support the new state financially.

Pacification and consolidation of the country's hinterland will be a long drawn out process. Indeed, the formula for the amalgamation of Aden city with its primitive neighbors was never found by the British, nor do their successors have any easier time ahead of them in their search for a mutually satisfactory arrangement. Whether or not the Saudis offer encouragement to unruly tribes, there is likely to be trouble upcountry for a government in Aden made up largely of non-tribal, or detribalized young men. Conversely, any attempt to establish a government solely made up of these provincials would be opposed by the Aden city-based organizations.

South Arabia, particularly in Aden, has the ingredients for a capable, if modest, government bureaucracy. The British have been there since 1839 and have created systems and routines as well as an experienced cadre of civil servants. There is a small army and a central police force, both of which, although made up of diverse city and tribal elements, have so far maintained their unity. South Arabia is better equipped now with trained human resources than is Yemen, a much older, independent state. Once the state is launched there is reason to believe that South Arabian nationalism may develop its own character, and its own loyalties, some of which may be uniquely local. Adenese and their back country cousins may well join wider Arab ranks, but perhaps on their own terms. With the UAR for the present curtailing its activities in the Peninsula, South Arabia will be spared at least some of the pressure, guidance, and manipulation associated with UAR interventionist tactics. It remains to be seen whether the Saudis will resist their own inclination to arrange matters as they would like them to be.

While the new state can be expected to find its place within the Arab world, joining its causes, Arabism may be less a concern than the immediate problem of the creation of a unified nation.

Assuming a viable government is formed, the USG ought not delay recognition for long lest we create an appearance of reluctance and indecision to do so because of the complexion of whatever government is established. Moreover, our failure to act would no doubt cause the regime to expel our consular staff, thus closing our remaining post in Southwest Arabia. Since the Soviets, Eastern Europeans and the Chinese will be in a position to be forthcoming with economic and military assistance, our prompt recognition could be a positive act of friendly intentions which might help offset our inability to do likewise.

If no government appears, but local security is adequately maintained by the SAA and police, both we and the British would expect to keep our diplomatic staffs in place. Should security break down, British warships will be available offshore for the prompt evacuation of our staffs.

---

111.   Record of Meeting[1]

IRG/NEA 67–47   Washington, November 16, 1967.

INTERDEPARTMENTAL REGIONAL GROUP
FOR NEAR EAST AND SOUTH ASIA

Record of IRG/NEA Meeting—November 16, 1967

The meeting was devoted to a further consideration of *our policy towards South Arabia,* in the light of the developments since the

---

[1] Source: Johnson Library, National Security File, Saunders Files, Aden & South Arabia, 4/1/66–1/20/69. Secret. Drafted by Acting Staff Director John F. Buckle on November 17.

IRG/NEA meeting of July 26, 1967 (see IRG/NEA 67–24, 7/26/67, for a record of agreements reached at that time).[2] The Group:

Reviewed recent significant developments in the rapidly moving situation as noted in the paper prepared for the meeting by the Country Director (IRG/NEA 67–43)[3] and as elaborated by him.

Agreed that, although our previous tentative planning with respect to an independent South Arabia might prove to be basically valid, there was now more reason to be concerned regarding the viability of the emerging government than anticipated last July and we should be convinced that the government in power was going to be able to govern successfully and intended to honor its international obligations before we extended our recognition. Should we decide to do so, we might prefer initially to establish our mission at the Chargé level. In this connection, the Group *agreed* that we should keep in close consultation with the British and the Saudi Arabians both regarding their assessments of the new government as it emerges and their intentions towards it.

Agreed that we should certainly not be ahead of the British in the matter of recognition and would also look for prior action by some of South Arabia's regional neighbors. The Saudi attitude would be important but her decision not to recognize would not necessarily cause us to withhold recognition.

MEMBERS PRESENT

> Executive Chairman—Mr. Battle
> AID—Mr. Wheeler
> CIA—[*name not declassified*]
> DOD—Mr. Schwartz
> JCS—Brig. Gen. Sibley
> USIA—Mr. Carter
> NSC—Mr. Saunders
> STATE: (ARP) Mr. Brewer
> Acting Staff Director—Mr. Buckle

JFB
Acting Staff Director

---

[2] Document 100.
[3] Document 110.

112. Telegram From the Department of State to the Embassy in the United Kingdom[1]

Washington, November 17, 1967, 1556Z.

70917. Subject: Recognition of South Arabia.

1. Dept aware British in throes preparations for Geneva UK/NLF talks and no doubt still uncertain what their final attitude will be toward regime likely arise Aden. Questions British attitude towards NLF government and extent to which HMG may be willing extend it tangible support are nevertheless important keys to basic question of South Arabian regime's survivability and international recognition. We accordingly hope Embassy will remain in closest touch with British in effort provide as timely readings as possible of evolving British policy.

2. Will also be desirable seek assure that Saudi attitude as understanding as possible re Western position, in event UK and others decide have dealings with NLF regime. We assume HMG intends keep Saudis, and no doubt Iranians, abreast of British intentions, particularly with reference financial support to South Arabian Army (SAA).

3. *For Rome and Addis:* State 62888[2] being repeated you separately gives our tentative attitude on recognition question. While we do not think it necessary at this stage to initiate contacts with host governments on this subject, it will be appreciated if Embassies can be alert to any signs host government attitudes on South Arabian recognition issue.

Rusk

---

[1] Source: National Archives and Records Administration, RG 59, Central Files 1967–69, POL 19 ADEN. Secret; Priority. Drafted by Brewer on November 16; cleared by Deputy Assistant Secretary of State for European Affairs Walter J. Stoessel and Looram; and approved by Brewer. Repeated to Beirut, Amman, Tehran, Kuwait, Jidda, Aden, USUN, Rome, and Addis Ababa.

[2] Document 108.

113.   Information Memorandum From the Assistant Secretary of State for Near Eastern and South Asian Affairs (Battle) to Secretary of State Rusk[1]

Washington, November 20, 1967.

SUBJECT

    British Presence in Persian Gulf

You will recall that Sir Patrick Dean, in his meeting with you on November 1, made it clear that British withdrawal from South Arabia would not affect HMG's determination to remain in the Persian Gulf. This is further encouraging evidence that this remains the British view, in fact stemming from the trip to the Gulf this month of the new UK Minister of State at the Foreign Office, Goronwy Roberts (vice George Thompson).

Roberts' trip was primarily for purposes of area familiarization but HMG is using the occasion to seek to counter speculation on the part of Gulf states that the ouster of the Sultans in South Arabia is a harbinger of things to come in the Gulf. These local leaders have felt that the British were willing passively to allow this to happen, and that they were in fact prepared to abandon traditional friends in order to make a deal with the activist insurgents. The Saudis have been particularly bitter in their criticism of what they regard as British policy, i.e. that the UK is turning its back on conservative, traditional elements in the peninsula.

In response to our London Embassy's queries on the subject, Foreign Office representatives have also recently confirmed that the UK intends to maintain a military presence in the Gulf at least until the mid-1970's. One qualified spokesman assured us that HMG intends to remain in the Gulf as long as needed, i.e., until adequate local security arrangements are devised.

Roberts has been renewing expressions of British support in order to preserve the Gulf States relations with, and dependence upon, Britain in the years immediately ahead. In the British view (with which we concur), should the Gulf States lose the incentive to cooperate with the UK (for fear of losing control), the Rulers would take whatever courses seemed most likely to preserve their position. Their moves might well obstruct modernization and initiate restrictive practices which would stimulate growth of the very opposition they fear.

---

[1] Source: National Archives and Records Administration, RG 59, Central Files 1967–69, POL 33 PERSIAN GULF. Secret. Drafted by Dinsmore and Brewer on November 17 and cleared by Davies and Cheslaw.

Meanwhile, the Saudis, who want the British to remain engaged for sometime longer, view themselves as their logical successors in the role of the major stabilizing factor in the area. However, the Saudis do not want to deal with the multitude of petty shaikhdoms which now exist. They are already thinking in terms of one or more federations of peninsula states with which they could more easily deal. SAG is talking with the British about a possible £100 million program to build up the Saudi navy, primarily in the Gulf. Such action is presumably directed to improving the Saudi bargaining position vis-à-vis Iran.

The evident British intention to soldier on in the Gulf is reassuring. We believe every opportunity should be taken to encourage them in this direction, since no power on the horizon is likely to replace the security and stability the British now provide. We should also take advantage of opportunities as they arise quietly to encourage: (a) greater Saudi/Iranian understanding on Gulf problems, and (b) more cooperation among Gulf mini-states to improve changes for regional stability after the British go.

---

114. Circular Telegram From the Department of State to Certain Posts[1]

Washington, November 22, 1967, 0021Z.

72852. 1. Report of UN Special Mission on Aden was circulated at UN November 20.[2] Conclusions were summarized USUN 2306,[3] which being repeated Tel Aviv, Beirut, Amman, Kuwait and Tehran. They are strongly biased against British. Committee of 24 decided Nov 21 to pass Mission report on to UNGA without comment. Following

---

[1] Source: National Archives and Records Administration, RG 59, Central Files 1967–69, POL 16 ADEN. Confidential. Drafted by Brewer and Dinsmore on November 21, cleared by Brown, and approved by Brewer. Sent to Aden, Amman, Beirut, Jidda, Kuwait, London, Tehran, Tel Aviv, and USUN.

[2] The Special Mission reported on November 10 that it was not able to meet with representatives of all political groups in the territory because conditions were not conducive, for which it blamed the United Kingdom. The Mission reported it made clear to the United Kingdom that negotiations for forming a caretaker government should include representatives from both FLOSY and NLF, but that the army, which was under British control, had announced on November 6 that it recognized only the NLF. (UN doc. A/6700/Rev. 1, Ch. VI, Annex III)

[3] Dated November 16. (National Archives and Records Administration, RG 59, Central Files 1967–69, POL 19 ADEN/UN)

line may be used by addressees in event subject raised by others during normal contacts.

2. UN Mission's claim that its efforts make contact with South Arabian political groups were obstructed by British overlooks fact that both NLF and FLOSY refused for long period to cooperate with Mission. When FLOSY finally did offer talk with Mission, events had overtaken their efforts. When NLF asserted its supremacy over FLOSY through para-military struggle, British had no choice except to deal with changing situation on the ground. Until recently FLOSY/NLF agreement seemed likely but this no longer the case due further fighting for which both radical groups to blame. Idea that NLF victory in South Arabia was made possible through British-South Arabian Army collusion overlooks both indigenous strength and dynamism of NLF and fact NLF responsible for more terror killings of British than any other group. Furthermore it is our impression South Arabian Army is political power on its own and British Commander has only tenuous control, particularly over political activities of Arab officers, as UK prepares to depart.

3. In making foregoing points, addressees should make clear we hold no particular brief for either NLF or FLOSY and particularly deplore impact on innocent South Arabians, as well as foreigners, which terror tactics both organizations have caused. There is enough blame in South Arabian situation for all. UN Mission made extended effort to bring parties together; it is to be regretted that Mission in its report seems to have preferred dwelling on past rather than focussing pragmatically on situation as it exists in South Arabia today.

Rusk

115. Telegram From the Department of State to the Consulate in Aden[1]

Washington, November 27, 1967, 2247Z.

75257. Aden 640.[2]

1. Congen quite right (para 4 reftel) no action should be taken which might imply official recognition. At same time, there no objection personal or unofficial evidences of cordiality which could assist in developing contacts with new regime. Because of fast pace of developments, we leave to your judgment those circumstances when such personal acts would be appropriate without implying recognition. As example, we see no objection to your greeting Qahtan at airport should you believe this desirable and other members Consular Corps in attendance.

2. Welcome your efforts establish channel to NLF command for use during period before recognition of new government (para 5 reftel). In course such contacts, you may assure local representatives that Americans friendly and well disposed newly independent state but that your official position must accord with international practice as long as formal recognition not yet established. In particular, formal written communications on government-to-government basis must be avoided.

Rusk

---

[1] Source: National Archives and Records Administration, RG 59, Central Files 1967–69, POL 16 ADEN. Secret. Drafted by Brewer, cleared by Robert H. Newman (L/NEA), and approved by Battle. Repeated to Addis Ababa, Beirut, Jidda, London, Asmara, COMIDEASTFOR, and CINCSTRIKE/CINCMEAFSA.

[2] In telegram 640 from Aden, November 27, Eagleton reported that in a discussion with U.K. officials as to whether it was appropriate to meet NLF Leader Qahtan al-Shaabi at the airport when he returned from the Geneva negotiations, he stated that the position of the United States was different since it did not want to take any action that might imply official recognition. Eagleton informed the Department that he had made plans to meet informally with NLF Command Council member Abdullah al-Khameri, a former U.S. consulate employee, that evening, with the purpose of establishing a channel to the NLF command to use prior to official recognition of the new government. (Ibid.)

116.   Information Memorandum From the President's Special Assistant (Rostow) to President Johnson[1]

Washington, November 29, 1967.

SUBJECT

South Arabia Independent Today

Just a word on what we're doing about the independence of South Arabia—the new People's Republic of South Yemen. British negotiations with the National Liberation Front concluded in Geneva yesterday, and for the first time we have a fairly clear picture of the post-independence government.

We are not recognizing immediately. Today and tomorrow we'll respond to press queries by welcoming South Yemen to the family of nations. Then if the NLF continues in firm control for a week or two and acknowledges its international obligations, Secretary Rusk will recommend to you that we recognize. We want to be more sure first of Saudi views and of the ability of the NLF to act like a government.

The new government will take the usual anti-imperialist, anti-colonialist, suspicious-of-the-West line. We expect it will proclaim a Nasser-style or Algerian-style "socialism," but so far don't have any evidence of extensive Communist ties. The NLF itself probably doesn't know yet what its policies will be. Its only policy so far has been to get the British out and win power.

The government will face two main problems—staying in power and keeping afloat economically. South Arabia is still a collection of tribes—not a nation—and is vulnerable to a number of disruptive influences. The Saudis may exploit tribal opposition. The pro-Egyptian nationalists, who lost to the NLF in the final drive to power, may fight on. The South Arabian Army has backed the NLF so far, but it could turn to opposition. We still don't know what kind of continuing aid the British have agreed to, but that will be crucial in determining whether the new government has to look to Cairo or Moscow.

The situation is still uncertain—and a good target for Moscow—but Nasser's pullout in Yemen has made the transition to independence easier than we thought it could be earlier this year. We don't look to the new government for much, but this is probably as good an outcome as we could have hoped for.

Walt

---

[1] Source: Johnson Library, National Security File, Country File, South Arabia, Vol. I, 7/67–11/67. Secret.

117. Memorandum From Secretary of State Rusk to President Johnson[1]

Washington, December 4, 1967.

SUBJECT

Recognition of Newly Independent State in South Arabia

Recommendation:

That you approve in principle USG recognition of the People's Republic of Southern Yemen which became independent on November 30. Southern Yemen's application for membership in the UN could come before the Security Council as early as December 4. We would not want its admission to the UN and our own recognition to become too widely separated in time, lest we appear reluctant or indifferent. Accordingly, if you approve in principle, I will be glad to authorize an implementing telegram to Aden, instructing our principal officer to communicate the fact of recognition to the Foreign Minister of the new state.[2]

Discussion:

British colonial rule in South Arabia formally ended on November 29, and independence took place the following day. The new state, called the People's Republic of Southern Yemen, has an area of some 112,000 square miles and a population of about one million. Its government is expected to be radical Arab nationalist in character and will follow socialist policies internally and non-alignment internationally. The new state is also expected to make clear that it will pay due regard to existing international obligations and will seek prompt admission to the UN.

The regime in charge (the National Liberation Front or NLF) has fought its way to power during the last six months against both conservative and other radical groups. It seems to have established itself securely, notably by personnel transfers which assure the loyalty of the 9,000 man army. Border tension and threats to stability may be expected after independence, but we believe the new state will survive.

HMG has recognized the new state. The Southern Yemenis would like more aid over a longer term than the British are prepared to commit. The regime would also like a compromise over several islands which

---

[1] Source: National Archives and Records Administration, RG 59, Central Files 1967–69, POL 16 S YEMEN. Secret.

[2] The approval line is checked and handwritten notations indicate that on December 7 instructions were sent to Aden in telegram 81196. (Ibid.)

have been retroceded by the British to neighboring Muscat and Oman but which were administratively a part of the new state's territory. It appears that British military and economic aid will be provided for at least the first six months of independence, at about the level of $29 million. This should stabilize the situation and encourage the local armed forces to use their influence in the direction of stability and moderation.

One NLF official recently raised in Beirut the question of closing the southern end of the Red Sea to Israeli shipping. This has not, however, been enunciated as the regime's official policy nor has it been suggested by NLF officials in Aden. Meanwhile, Foreign Secretary Brown stated in Commons on November 29 that the NLF in Geneva had agreed to accept the international obligations the British had extended to Aden. One of these was the Geneva Convention which applied to Bab al-Mandab. Should the new government on assuming power nevertheless espouse closure of the Straits as a matter of policy—which we doubt—we would then of course have to review our whole attitude.

USG recognition will help balance expected early recognition by the USSR and other Communist countries. It will thus aid in maintaining the Western position in an area of considerable importance to the Arabian Peninsula as a whole. We have ourselves been represented in Aden since 1880. Were we to fail to establish relations with the new state, or to be seen to defer our decision for a protracted period, the NLF itself might well close our Consulate General. We would thus lose our single remaining listening post in the southern half of Arabia, now that relations with Yemen have been broken off.

Dean Rusk

118. Airgram From the Embassy in the United Kingdom to the Department of State[1]

A–1898   London, December 9, 1967.

SUBJECT

Bleak Prospects for Southern Yemen?

1. It is the personal view of the Foreign Office officials who deal on a day-to-day basis with PROSY affairs that the new republic's chances for holding together long under the present NLF (or for that matter, any foreseeable) regime are slight. They do not regard FLOSY as a serious threat. Nor do they think the Sharif of Beihan, even with Saudi backing, can traverse the comeback trail.

2. Rather, our sources' pessimistic estimate is based on the assumption that PROSY's cash income will prove inadequate to meet Adeni post-independence expectations and to buy continued tribal loyalties. They point out that even when the Suez Canal is open and Aden Port bustling, the country requires an annual input of sixteen to twenty million pounds merely to stand still.

3. Our contacts wonder where this money, and the additional funds the Southern Yemen authorities want in order to demonstrate they are doing something for the people, will be found. Many Labor and Conservative voters are writing to 10 Downing Street and the Foreign Office to protest HMG's twelve million pound aid to PROSY over the period ending June 1. There appears to be no public support for this assistance program. As of now, it appears unlikely to be renewed on the same scale.

4. The USG is not disposed to fill the gap. The FRG probably will not be willing to shoulder virtually the entire burden. Assuming the Saudis decide next year to seek an accommodation with PROSY, they are likely to attach unacceptable conditions to offers of assistance. Kuwait probably will hang back unless both Saudi Arabia and the UAR are favorably disposed to the Southern Yemen regime. Whether the Soviets or Chicoms can and want to subsidize PROSY indefinitely with large amounts of hard cash is problematical.

5. But if a major benefactor is not found by mid-1968, this line of reasoning goes, Southern Yemen will be subjected to serious internal stresses. Old rivalries will reassert themselves, tribal leaders will turn

---

[1] Source: National Archives and Records Administration, RG 59, Central Files 1967–69, POL 15 S YEMEN. Secret; Limdis. Drafted by Political Officer Stephen J. Palmer, Jr., and approved by Political Officer William J. Galloway. Repeated to Aden, Beirut, Bonn, Dhahran, Jidda, Kuwait, Tehran, Tel Aviv, and USUN.

to outside sources of gold and rifles, and the volatile Adeni proletariat will become disenchanted with the NLF.

Comment: It should be noted that the officials who privately express the line summarized above were quite attached to the Federalis, on whom so much effort and money had been expended. One Britisher who participated in the Geneva negotiations with the NLF confided that he hoped those talks would fail. We very much doubt that George Brown shares the sentiments of these officials. But the combination of their personal dispositions and the British public's distaste for aiding "those terrorists who killed our boys" augurs ill for major, long-term UK assistance to PROSY.

Bruce

---

119.   Telegram From the Department of State to the Embassy in Iran[1]

Washington, December 13, 1967, 1709Z.

83752. For the Ambassador. Developments of past weeks indicate the Soviets may have moved in a phase of heightened direct involvement and greater risks to establish a dominant position in the Southwest Arabian Peninsula.[2] In fact the character and scope of their activities suggest an intent to carry out an armed intrusion that would exacerbate the inherently unstable conditions in this troubled area.

Although the South Yemen People's Republic has achieved a degree of control and stability in the few days that it has existed, Soviet and Chicom governments have at a minimum an influential fraction in the controlling elements. In the event the civil war in the Yemen itself produces a partition between North and South Yemen, the latter seems likely to merge with the SYPR under a growing Soviet influence. The emergence of a radical South Yemen government with control of port,

---

[1] Source: National Archives and Records Administration, RG 59, Central Files 1967–69, POL 27 YEMEN. Secret; Immediate; Exdis. Drafted by Walsh; cleared by Battle, Eugene Rostow, and Helms; and approved by Acting Secretary Katzenbach. Also sent to Ankara, Tel Aviv, Amman, and Jidda and repeated to London, USUN, US MISSION NATO TOSEC, Moscow, Tunis, Morocco, Beirut, Addis Ababa, New Delhi, and Rawalpindi.

[2] Regarding current Soviet activities in Yemen, telegram 86028 to Ankara, December 18, reported the Department spokesman's statement that reports of the delivery of Soviet planes to Yemen and the arrival there of Soviet technicians appeared to be substantially accurate. (Ibid., POL 16 S YEMEN)

communications and air bases in Aden–Taiz–Bodeida triangle is an eventuality that must be realistically considered. The implications of such a development for the already strained situation in the Near East resulting from the June war is apparent.

It is requested that action addressees approach host governments and express USG interest and concern in the situation and a desire for a close and continuing exchange of information on developments in the Arabian Peninsula in [*less than 1 line of source text not declassified*] diplomatic [*less than 1 line of source text not declassified*] channels.

Katzenbach

---

120. Telegram From the Embassy in Southern Yemen to the Department of State[1]

Aden, December 15, 1967, 1000Z.

719. Ref: State 83660.[2] Southern Yemen.

1. Accompanied by Davis, Commander Perry and Niner I met for one hour with President Qahtan al Shaabi at presidential residence (ex-government house) after Ramadhan breakfast evening December 14. Qahtan's manner was quiet, friendly and relaxed. His approach was direct but not forward. (Illustrative of his style was recent request by Catholic Bishop in Aden for an appointment to see him to which Qahtan replied "No, I will call on you.")

2. During early part of conversation I was able to make points suggested in Department's reftel except for question of Jarring mission which we will discuss along with general Arab problems before Qahtan goes to Arab summit meeting in Rabat. In addition to polite response to USG's congratulations Qahtan seemed impressed by our stand against interference in internal affairs of other countries and he stressed that this was his

---

[1] Source: National Archives and Records Administration, RG 59, Central Files 1967–69, POL S YEMEN–US. Confidential. Repeated to Jidda and London. The Embassy in Aden was established on December 7, 1967.

[2] Telegram 83660 to Aden, December 13, instructed the Chargé to congratulate President Shaabi upon creation of the People's Republic of Southern Yemen and to extend the best wishes of the United States to the new state and its people. He was to assure the President that the U.S. Government considered the internal political, economic, and social system of each country to be its own people's affair, noting that the United States had consistently sought not to become involved in intra-Arab disputes. (Ibid., POL 16 S YEMEN)

govt's policy also. He also acknowledged as true my observation that USG had remained strictly outside NLF/FLOSY dispute, and he seemed aware that republican Yemen's accusations against US were false.

3. Without forcing issue Qahtan brought conversation around to Southern Yemen economic problems and hope for aid from advanced countries. In reply I outlined budgetary difficulties that made consideration of economic aid impossible at this time. On other hand Embassy and USG would hope to establish very close relations with Southern Yemen govt at all levels and would be on lookout for ways in which we might be helpful. Meanwhile we considered development aid primarily responsibility of former colonial power and oil producing states in area.

4. In response to my question re PRSYG's attitude toward neighboring states Qahtan strongly reaffirmed policy of non-intervention. He reviewed at some length his discussions with Kamal al Adham in Geneva from which he said he had received impression there would be no problem in developing good ties between his govt and "brothers" of Saudi Arabia. He could not understand why Saudi recognition was still being delayed. He smiled when I replied that we were less surprised by Saudi delay in view of statements that had been made by NLF during revolutionary pre-independence period. Although USG had found that PRSYG met criteria for recognition Saudis perhaps had reason to be more cautious and wait until all aspects of PRSY policy were defined. Furthermore we understood Kamal Adham had delayed his return to Saudi Arabia. Qahtan again affirmed brotherly feeling towards Saudis and referred to presence 250,000 Southern Yemenis in Saudi Arabia. He said he hoped that both FonMin Saif al Dhalai in New York and Labor Minister, Abdul Malik Ismail in Cairo had been able to contact Saudi representatives to reassure them re Southern Yemen's good intentions.

5. Qahtan several times referred to poverty and backwardness up-country. He asked whether we had been able to travel there to see for ourselves. When we replied that conditions have not permitted travel he said he would see to it that arrangements were made.

6. In low key Qahtan asked whether US could be of any assistance in giving special medical treatment to several NLF veterans who had lost limbs during recent fighting. I replied that treatment in US would involve long travel and considerable expense but that we would discuss matter with American doctor who is now in Aden at Queen Elizabeth hospital on temporary duty under International Committee Red Cross.

7. Qahtan mentioned hope that oil could be found in eastern regions and mentioned forthcoming visit Atlantic Richfield representative to Aden. He indicated he would welcome interest by US companies in oil exploration.

8. Qahtan said he anticipated that his govt would open an Embassy in Washington but he was awaiting return of FonMin before

making definite plans. He also said it would be decided later whether an independence ceremony to which special foreign representatives would be invited, would be held after Ramadhan.

9. Before leaving I asked Qahtan whether there was any specific message he wished me to pass to USG. He replied that he could not give up hope that US as well as other advanced countries would be able to help Southern Yemen rise from its backwardness. He said he would also appreciate anything USG could do to convince Saudi Govt of his government's good intentions toward them.

Eagleton

121. Telegram From the Department of State to the Embassy in the United Kingdom[1]

Washington, December 19, 1967, 2326Z.

86853. 1. British EmbOff December 18 asked DeptOff for his views re likelihood USG assistance to PRSY. Wondered whether USG might be considering something like "one or two well chosen impact projects."

2. DeptOff replied recent foreign aid cuts such that funds simply not available for kind of programs EmbOff had in mind. Our Chargé had been careful not to arouse hopes of members new government PRSY and we had similarly made our limitations in this regard clear to FonMin Dhalai in New York. DeptOff added we well aware opportunity which impoverished PRSY presents for Soviets and Chicoms should they offer attractive aid programs to new state. They might consider such aid cheap price for influence in what for them might be strategic location in Near East. Nevertheless, we not now in position compete in this field.

3. View foregoing, DeptOff stressed desirability British continuing make every effort sustain an effective level assistance to new state after present six-month stop-gap help completed in order obviate full PRSY

[1] Source: National Archives and Records Administration, RG 59, Central Files 1967–69, POL 16 S YEMEN. Confidential; Noforn. Drafted by Dinsmore, cleared by Deputy Director of AID's Office of Near Eastern Affairs Ruth Fitzmaurice and Cheslaw, and approved by Brewer. Repeated to Aden and Jidda.

dependence on Communists for essential needs. DeptOff noted PRSY reluctance accept British military mission but speculated new regime perfectly willing rely on HMG for financial help which could well give them fewer problems than major Communist support.

4. EmbOff reminded us of tight British financial position and said that he surmised in six weeks to two months Treasury would be taking close look at future aid for PRSY in light world-wide expenditures.

5. *Comment:* Our impression that EmbOff's approach was prompted by Foreign Office desire elicit indications US support for continued UK aid in order strengthen its hand in later jousting with British Treasury.

Rusk

---

122. Briefing Memorandum From the Assistant Secretary of State for Near Eastern and South Asian Affairs (Battle) to Secretary of State Rusk[1]

Washington, January 9, 1968.

SUBJECT

> British Plans to Accelerate Withdrawal of Military Presence from Persian Gulf: Your Meeting with Foreign Secretary Brown, January 11

Background

Present intense pressures on HMG to reduce government expenditures are leading the British to an imminent decision to accelerate removal of their military presence from the Persian Gulf, perhaps by 1970 if not sooner. In an effort to head off a precipitate decision of this nature, you sent last week a personal message to Foreign Secretary Brown (attached)[2] expressing our concern and asking that a final decision be deferred until you see him this week. His reply,[3] relayed by Sir Patrick Dean, makes no commitments. In transmitting it, however, Sir Patrick made clear the Foreign Secretary wished you to know that our

---

[1] Source: Department of State, NEA/ARP Files: Lot 69 D 523, Persian Gulf, POL—General, January 1968. Secret. Drafted by Sterner; and cleared by Brewer and Davies, and in draft by Cheslaw and Eliot. A copy was sent to G/PM Director of Operations for Politico-Military Affairs Joseph J. Wolf.

[2] Not attached; for text of Rusk's message to Brown, see *Foreign Relations, 1964–1968,* vol. XII, Document 61.

[3] Not found.

views, as expressed in your coming meeting with Brown, would be taken into careful consideration.

While I appreciate that you will be discussing the effect of the British cuts in terms of its global implications, I believe we are justified in making a particularly strong point of our concern for British actions in the Persian Gulf. In our judgment, a total withdrawal of British military forces in the next few years would seriously undermine the Western position in the Gulf. It will take another five years at least before the economic and political development of the Gulf states has progressed sufficiently to create an indigenous base for political stability. In the interim, at least a small British military presence will be an essential stabilizing force. While a British military withdrawal from the Gulf would not necessarily mean the end of British influence, their political presence would be far less effective if it did not have behind it the implied commitment and visible capability for military intervention. Except for Kuwait, the regimes of the Gulf states rest on shaky political foundations. It would not take much to undermine their confidence to resist the encroachment of Arab radicalism.

Moreover, the Western position in the Persian Gulf is almost entirely dependent on the British presence. There is no politically feasible way for the US or other Western power to step in with an equally effective presence once the British are gone.

Talking Points

We recommend that you make the following points to Foreign Secretary Brown when you see him later this week.

—British influence in the Persian Gulf has been the principal stabilizing force securing Western interests in that area. The US has always attached a very high importance to the maintenance of that influence. In our judgment, any sudden or drastic weakening of the British position will seriously undermine the existing regimes and render the entire area far more vulnerable to pressures from the radical Arabs.

—A key element of the British position is a military presence which can be deployed rapidly to support British political commitments. In our view it does not have to be large, but it would be dangerous to try to dispense with it entirely. Western "support" of a more general nature is not likely to be effective unless the Rulers have the confidence, and their radical Arab opponents the fear, that an effective military force can and will be employed.

—Early British announcement of a specific date for leaving the Gulf could have particularly unsettling effects at the present time. We are witnessing a concerted Soviet attempt to make further inroads in the area. Their recent heightened support for the Yemeni republican government, the prospect that they may achieve a position in Southern

Yemen (Aden), and the inviting target presented by the weak but oil-rich Gulf shaikhdoms, all combine to give us a good deal of concern. There is not quite a "momentum" behind these developments yet, but public knowledge of an early British move out of the Gulf could well create one.

—We are fully sympathetic with the pressing needs of HMG to reduce government expenditures. But we wonder if, short of total withdrawal, quite substantial savings could not be effected through a reduction in the strength of the British force. In our view, maintenance of a continuing military presence will be far more important than its actual size.

—We all hope the present period of international financial difficulties will be temporary. While some programs can be cut back now and started up again later without serious problems, the elimination of the UK military position in the Gulf would be an irreversible decision. The USG feels strongly that such an irrevocable act is warranted neither by present circumstances nor future prospects. Moreover, economies effected now could be penny-wise, pound-foolish if political changes in the Gulf were to bring about revisions in the terms by which the UK gets its oil.

—Our own resources have been sharply curtailed by Congress. Nevertheless, we would wish to examine carefully any proposals for creating greater indigenous cohesion in the Gulf, including regional self-help measures, as a means of fostering the orderly economic and political development of the area.[4]

---

[4] When the Secretary discussed British budget and defense cuts with the Foreign Secretary on January 11, Brown said that the post-devaluation financial crisis had forced the U.K. Government to look at cutting defense expenditures overseas. The decision to leave the Persian Gulf was dictated primarily by the fact that there would be no carriers or bases available to support or relieve the Persian Gulf after March 1971 when British forces would have been withdrawn from the Far East. Rusk responded that he was profoundly distressed by the proposed withdrawals from Southeast Asia and the Persian Gulf, particularly by the intention to announce these decisions. (Memorandum of conversation, January 11; Johnson Library, National Security File, Country File, United Kingdom, Memos, Vol. XIII, 1/68–7/68) The memorandum of conversation is printed in *Foreign Relations, 1964–1968*, vol. XII, Document 64.

123. Telegram From the Department of State to the Embassy in Iran[1]

Washington, January 12, 1968, 8:53 p.m.

98266. Subject: Iran, Persian Gulf and Middle East Situation.

1. Iranian Ambassador Ansary in call January 12 on Under Secretary Rostow raised Shah's proposal for joint Iranian-Saudi-Kuwaiti oil activities in Persian Gulf. Rostow said it useful idea but tied up with problem of median line.[2] Assuming progress on median line problem, Rostow indicated we would be willing support Iranian efforts for regional cooperation. Both efforts can proceed at same time but it important Iran take initiative on median line question.

2. Rostow stressed importance regional cooperation has increased in light of probable UK decision about its future presence in Gulf. He said Secretary had spoken strongly to Foreign Secretary Brown concerning importance of UK decision to security of Free World but we do not know what effect our representations will have in London or for how long. Our impression is that decision on 1971 withdrawal "not quite" final. We hope it can be changed but in meantime we all have to plan. The risk of radical Arab movements into the area and the problem of security for the Gulf will not go away. Ansary said British had indicated they were thinking of granting complete independence to some of Sheikhdoms and federating others. In this connection, Bahrein is problem for Iran.

3. Concerning future arrangements for Gulf, Ansary said GOI believes joint air and naval policing of area with participation of Sheikhdoms might be desirable. Defense pact of some kind might also be possible. He asked for Rostow's views. Rostow replied we wish encourage cooperation in area, including Pakistan, Turkey, Iran and Saudi Arabia, for both development and security. We are well disposed encourage sympathetically efforts in these directions including policing which are politically feasible. He said it important also in order to bring about change in Iraq's orientation in the longer run. In response Ansary's comment all this costs money Rostow said our estimate of annual local costs of British effort in Gulf is about 14 million pounds.

---

[1] Source: National Archives and Records Administration, RG 59, Central Files 1967–69, POL 19 TRUCIAL ST. Secret. Drafted by Eliot; cleared by Dinsmore and Staff Assistant Robert G. Grey, Jr. in the Office of the Under Secretary for Political Affairs; and approved by Rockwell. Repeated to London, Jidda, Dhahran, Kuwait, and CINCSTRIKE.

[2] Discovery of large deposits of oil under the waters of the Persian Gulf sharpened differences between the Iranian and Saudi Governments over the location of a median line to delineate oil exploration and exploitation rights between them.

New arrangements in Gulf need not duplicate what British have been doing, and burden would not fall entirely on Iran.

4. On other aspects Mideast situation, Rostow mentioned he will wish get Shah's reading on his visit with Feisal when Rostow is in Tehran February 7–9. We regard Feisal as key, constructive figure in our efforts strengthen King Hussein. On Jarring mission, Rostow said neither Jarring nor we are discouraged although nothing decisive has yet happened.

Katzenbach

---

124. Telegram From the Department of State to the Embassy in Saudi Arabia[1]

Washington, January 24, 1968, 0114Z.

103449. Jidda 2485[2] and 2526.[3]

1. In addition to good line reported reftels, Ambassador may draw on following in discussions with Saudi officials and diplomatic colleagues on question of readjustments in Persian Gulf following British withdrawal.

2. USG naturally concerned re implications British troop withdrawal from Gulf by end 1971. Nevertheless, while we will be studying question in detail in coming months, we have no plan, general or specific, as to future.

---

[1] Source: National Archives and Records Administration, RG 59, Central Files 1967–69, POL 19 TRUCIAL ST. Confidential. Drafted by Brewer and Dinsmore on January 23; cleared by Eliot, Cheslaw, and Country Director for Turkey John M. Howison; and approved by Brewer. Repeated to Ankara, Dhahran, London, Kuwait, Rawalpindi, Tehran, and CINCSTRIKE.

[2] In telegram 2485 from Jidda, January 21, Ambassador Eilts reported that he had discussed Under Secretary Rostow's recent comments in a BBC interview on new security arrangements in the Persian Gulf separately with Saudi Foreign Ministry Official Mohammad Mas'ud, and the Turkish and Iranian Ambassadors, each of whom had expressed surprise that Rostow had included Turkey and Pakistan among countries having security interests in the Gulf. (Ibid.)

[3] In telegram 2526 from Jidda, January 23, Eilts reported that he had discussed the U.S. assessment of the current Yemen situation with Mas'ud and urged the Saudi Government to do its utmost to encourage the Yemeni royalists to cooperate with the tripartite committee's efforts to find a peaceful political solution acceptable to all. (Ibid., POL 27 YEMEN)

3. In our view, evolving situation in Gulf is one to which states of area should address themselves. It will require patience and statesmanship to develop improved relations and take other measures which may seem necessary to states themselves in order safeguard area stability. We remain sympathetic and desire be helpful where practicable in this evolutionary process, but USG is not contemplating direct role.

4. We do feel strongly that there are elements in British presence, unconnected with military position, which littoral states may find beneficial retain. Those states themselves will know best what these elements are, but in our view it is premature to suggest that the UK will have no interest or influence in the Persian Gulf after 1971. We ourselves believe there will be continuing need for constructive and mutually helpful association smaller Arab littoral states with UK and are appropriately encouraging British authorities to continue do what they can play meaningful role in Gulf. British troop withdrawal is only one step in long process of gradual emergence Gulf area in modern world and we do not believe this can take place either dramatically or overnight.

Rusk

---

125. Research Memorandum From the Director of the Bureau of Intelligence and Research (Hughes) to Secretary of State Rusk[1]

RNA–3   Washington, January 25, 1968.

SUBJECT

The Sultanate of Muscat and Oman Enters the Twentieth Century

A newcomer among the petroleum-exporting nations, the Sultanate of Muscat and Oman may become a problem area if its anachronistic ruler fails to meet the challenges of his political rivals. With important economic interests in neighboring Saudi Arabia and the Persian Gulf,

---

[1] Source: National Archives and Records Administration, RG 59, Central Files, 1967–69, POL 19 MUSCAT & OMAN. Secret; No Foreign Dissem; Controlled Dissem. No drafting information appears on the memorandum. A note on the memorandum reads: "This report was produced by the Bureau of Intelligence and Research. Aside from normal substantive exchange with other agencies at the working level, it has not been coordinated elsewhere."

the US thus could become increasingly involved in the affairs of this obscure country. We examine here the Sultanate's potential problems and future role in Arabian Peninsula developments.

Abstract

The remote Sultanate of Muscat and Oman is about to move from obscurity into the modern world as the result of its new-found petroleum wealth. Oil income is expected to reach about $30 million per year within the near future and will alter significantly the economic circumstances of the country's 600,000–800,000 inhabitants. The ruling Sultan, Sa'id bin Taymur al Bu Sa'id, who is preoccupied with protecting his regime against his rivals, including the Imam of Oman and several members of his own family, heretofore has actively resisted modernization and reform. Armed dissidence has occurred sporadically since 1955, supported mainly by outside Arab states such as the UAR, Syria, and Iraq. The Sultan's Armed Forces (SAF), whose officer corps of 100 includes 30 seconded and 40 contract British officers, thus far has been able to contain this dissidence, both in the Dhofar and Oman regions.

A recent intelligence report indicates that the Sultan's son Qabus and his half-brother Tariq may be plotting his overthrow. At a meeting in September 1967, Tariq and Qabus agreed to join forces in such an attempt; the plot's timing and bona fides are unknown, but the report alleges that Qabus intends to become Sultan and Tariq the prime minister and regent for a period of five years. Other plots involving the Imam may be in the blueprint stage, but disorganization within the Imam's camp and the temporary preoccupation of potential backers such as the UAR, Syria, Iraq and Saudi Arabia with the Arab–Israel issue make it unlikely that serious coup attempts will be made from this quarter within the near future.

Although it has at present minimal political importance, the Sultanate may play a growing role in future Persian Gulf developments. The Sultanate already has certain strategic importance by virtue of its location adjacent to the Straits of Hormuz at the entrance to the Gulf. With the takeover of South Arabia (the People's Republic of South Yemen) by the National Liberation Front (NLF) and the increasing Soviet involvement in Yemen, the Saudis, Iranians, and the lesser rulers of the Persian Gulf are worried that an NLF-style revolution will spread from southern Arabia to the Gulf. Having acquired a petroleum industry and the accompanying influx of foreign workers, Muscat and Oman is now a more inviting target for such Gulf-directed activities. Anti-Sultan and anti-British propaganda attacks have long been pursued by communications media in the Arab nationalist states; recently, the USSR has turned its propaganda in this direction. The political fortunes of the Sultanate will directly influence the future of the Trucial States,

Qatar, and Bahrain, as well as the policies of Saudi Arabia and Kuwait. If a moderately progressive regime were to emerge, whether under the Sultan, Qabus, or some as yet unknown successor, Muscat and Oman could contribute to political stability in the Gulf; conversely, a radical Arab nationalist takeover would lead to increased agitation and instability in the states to the north.

Having no diplomatic representation and virtually no political or economic influence, the US can do little to affect the course of events in Muscat and Oman. However, a treaty between the US and the Sultanate[2] provides a basis for establishment of a diplomatic mission and possibly a small aid or Peace Corps program. The US already has expressed its willingness to provide a Peace Corps program, and is awaiting the Sultan's decision.

Whether dissidence in Muscat and Oman will remain at the present controllable level or increase with growing public awareness is open to speculation. We expect, however, that the Arab revolutionary countries may increase their subversive efforts in this area, particularly if there is renewed infighting between the moderate and radical camps. While it is possible that the Sultan could remain in power without adapting to his new economic conditions, or that he or a successor might institute reforms sufficient to contain popular disaffection, it is more likely that outside Arab interference and the influx of foreign elements into the Oman oilfields will lay the groundwork for increased dissidence and perhaps eventually the Sultan's overthrow.

[Here follows the body of the memorandum.]

---

[2] The United States and the Sultanate of Muscat and Oman signed a Treaty of Amity, Economic Relations, and Consular Rights at Salalah on December 20, 1958. The Treaty entered into force June 11, 1960. (11 UST 1835; TIAS 4530; 380 UNTS 181)

126.   Memorandum of Conversation[1]

Washington, January 25, 1968.

SUBJECT

Bahrain Situation; US-Bahrain Relations

PARTICIPANTS

Mr. Ray Lay, Chairman, Bahrain Petroleum Company (BAPCO)
Mr. Walter Stolz, Director, BAPCO
Mr. H. G. Story, BAPCO
Mr. William D. Brewer, Country Director, NEA/ARP
Mr. John Oliver, E/FSE
Mr. James E. Akins, E/FSE
Mr. David Newton, NEA/ARP

Mr. Lay said he had recently returned from Bahrain. He had seen the Ruler just after Goronwy Roberts had told the Ruler of the British intention to withdraw by 1971 and had never seen the Ruler so upset. The Ruler has concluded that he can no longer count on the British and he is now trying to ally himself with King Faisal.

Mr. Lay pointed out that the Bahrainis are good friends of the United States and he hoped that we could support them within reason. Right now they are looking for some small gesture of US interest. Perhaps it would be possible to open a "sub-office" of the Consulate General in Dhahran. In reply Mr. Brewer pointed out that at present we are under instructions to cut the number of our personnel overseas by 10 percent and have no resources available for any establishment in Bahrain. We feel that the Shah has no intention of pushing Iran's claim to Bahrain but he will not publicly retract it. It is important for the parties to keep cool and let the problem disappear by itself over time. Mr. Stolz noted that elimination of the "dual passport" problem would be a help and stressed that the Iranians should show good faith to the Bahrainis.

Mr. Brewer pointed out that the British had acted as a de facto buffer for conflicting interests in the Persian Gulf. Now that they are leaving militarily, the Gulf countries will need to do more themselves to develop a cooperative atmosphere. Stolz observed that the area will face a much greater threat from leftists and perhaps the USG should consider giving some assurances. Mr. Brewer noted this is no time for the USG to assume new commitments. Our position is that the littoral

---

[1] Source: National Archives and Records Administration, RG 59, Central Files 1967–69, POL BAHRAIN IS–US. Confidential. Drafted by David G. Newton on February 5.

states, not the USG, must replace the British presence by establishing new bases for cooperation.

Mr. Brewer asked Mr. Stolz how he viewed Bahrain's future. Mr. Stolz thought that the country would remain independent but seek close ties with Saudi Arabia. At present Saudi-Bahraini relations were very good. Mr. Brewer observed that British withdrawal presented us with major problems, but we are still optimistic that some local stability can be developed. The recent *New York Times* article on the willingness of local rulers to pay for the upkeep of British troops was apparently true. However, the reason for withdrawal was not just financial; internal politics of the Labour Party were involved. Nevertheless we hope that the British will still play a role in the Gulf and that the results there will not be like those in Aden. Mr. Stolz repeated his suggestion about American assurances but Mr. Brewer reiterated that this was not a good time to suggest further American commitments. Mr. Lay suggested again that the Ruler would like something more than monthly visits by Amcongen Dhahran, but any indication of further American interest would be appreciated.

---

127. Telegram From the Consulate General in Saudi Arabia to the Department of State[1]

Dhahran, January 28, 1968, 1450Z.

505. Subj: Persian Gulf. Following is from Ambassador in Riyadh:

1. When meeting with Rashad Pharaon last night, he spoke of Saudi concern re future of Gulf in view Brit withdrawal, growing Soviet activity in ME area and generally unsatisfactory Yemeni and South Arabian situations (septels—Notal).[2] He wanted to know if HMG had talked to USG before taking withdrawal decision? I told him that to best my knowledge, Brits had done so at about same time Roberts Mission sent to brief King Faisal and other interested states, but not before. As I had told King, USG not happy about Brit decision and has urged HMG take no irrevocable steps. USG has also pointed out to

---

[1] Source: National Archives and Records Administration, RG 59, Central Files 1967–69, DEF 1 UK. Secret. Repeated to Jidda, Tehran, Kuwait, and London.
[2] Reference is to telegrams 503 and 504 from Dhahran, January 28. (Ibid., POL 27 YEMEN)

Brits that, apart from military position, elements exist in Brit presence which littoral states may feel can continue to be of benefit and which we hope Brits will be willing discuss with littoral states. I suggested that Saudis should consider this same matter and talk to Brits about it (SecState's 103449).[3] Idea seemed new one to Rashad, but he undertook give it some study. He also wondered why HMG had not accepted offer of various Trucial States to finance continuation Brit troop commitment.

2. In answer my question if King had raised confederation idea with Ruler of Bahrain, Rashad said Ruler deeply disturbed by continuing Iranian claim and had asked Faisal for Saudi security guarantee. According Rashad, Faisal agreed give such security assurance if Ruler of Bahrain able get together with other Trucial rulers in some form of confederation. (Note: If Rashad's version correct, Saudi security assurance to Bahrain not as categoric as some other sources have suggested.)

3. Rashad continued that status of Bahrain is major obstacle to cooperation among principal Gulf riparian states, especially with Iran. While SAG wants to cooperate with Iran, it can do so only if Shah will publicly renounce claim to Bahrain and Iranian Majlis approves such declaration. Unless this takes place any effort on part of SAG to cooperate with Iran will incur ire of other Arabs. In past few days UAR public media have already begun to attack Iranian role in Gulf. SAG has asked its Ambassador in Tehran to sound out Iranians on possibility such public declaration. Rashad asked for my thoughts on this.

4. I said would want to query Ambassador Meyer re his views, but meanwhile wished make few personal observations. It my understanding, and King Faisal had confirmed it also his, that Shah of Iran is not actively seeking to incorporate Bahrain, but that for domestic reasons he cannot publicly say so. If this true, idea of making public renunciation approved by Majlis a condition for any Saudi-Iranian cooperation in Gulf struck me as asking too much. It would not surprise me if Iranians rejected any such suggestion and if it leaves sour taste.

5. I suggested that in exploring among themselves future of Gulf, littoral states ought to get away from such terms as "ambitions" and "designs" which connote nasty, selfish competition. Instead, littoral states should begin think in terms of legitimate "interests" in Gulf on latter there understandably considerable overlap and mutuality which should constitute basis for needed cooperation in various spheres. Instead of demanding public self-denying declaration, why not work

---

[3] Document 124.

with Iran and Kuwait in developing multilateral regional institutions in fields of economic, security, etc? Such institutions would demonstrate by practical means that each littoral state is renouncing any individual ambitions in terms of the common interest. Rashad insisted such cooperation feasible only if there is self-denying declaration by Iran since otherwise Shah's successor might jettision any arrangements now made and reassert claim to Bahrain.

6. I emphasized all littoral states are going to have to take a few "risks" in attempting develop climate of confidence which meaningful cooperation requires. Shah still young and vigorous and it seemed to me practical cooperative arrangements worked out with him now offer reasonable promise being able continue for considerable period of time. After all Shah could raise same question re King Faisal's eventual successor. A bit of good faith is essential if anything is to be worked out.

7. Although Rashad accepted point, he remained worried that in absence some public Iranian renunciation of Bahrain, broader Arab pressures would preclude SAG from cooperating with Iran. He again alluded to UAR public media attacks. I reminded him that King has succeeded in handling Nasser during five years of intensive UAR villification for doing what Faisal considered right in Yemen. Even now UAR heavily dependent on Saudi subsidy. Seemed to me that if King persuaded cooperation with Iran and other Gulf states is right way to proceed, he able do so with minimal regard for UAR or other radical Arab states' views and indeed has few screws of his own that he can use if necessary. King has private assurances from Shah that he not seeking incorporate Bahrain. Cooperation among Gulf riparians should be possible in knowledge of this fact. Surely need for public declaration simply to satisfy radical Arab peripheral states hardly necessary. Those Arab states that want to attack Faisal will do so anyway irrespective whether Iranian public renunciation of Bahrain exists or not. While Rashad agreed in principle, he remained worried that so long as Iran maintains constitutional claim to Bahrain as one of its provinces, Saudis and other Arabs will find it difficult cooperate.

8. When asked what is alternative to cooperation, Rashad argued SAG can deal with each of Trucial States separately. All but Abu Dhabi now look to SAG and SAG in position "surround" Abu Dhabi. I suggested this scarcely statemanslike approach. If Saudis go it alone, so will everyone else. Each of lower Gulf rulers will play off one principal riparian against others for own advantage. Gulf will become cockpit of heightened differences of kind of which Commies and other subversives thrive. I urged SAG not attempt make price of cooperation with Iran for Gulf cooperation so high that Iranians cannot reasonably pay. I reminded him SAG always sensitive any suggestion of "conditions" and others might be expected be equally so. Shah's forthcoming visit

offers timely opportunity explore fully and frankly all ideas re future of Gulf and I hoped that on its part SAG will take advantage of visit for constructive talks.

9. *For Tehran:* Would appreciate your views re likelihood Iranians agreeing such Majlis approved self-denying declaration re Bahrain. Will be in Riyadh next week or so and any message best to me via Dhahran, rptd info Jidda.[4]

Allen

---

[4] Telegram 10787 to Dhahran, January 30, "heartily" endorsed Allen's comments to Rashad Pharaon (senior adviser to King Faisal) as reported in telegram 505 and noted that, at the Ambassador's discretion, the same points might usefully be made directly to the King prior to the Shah's arrival. (National Archives and Records Administration, RG 59, Central Files 1967–69, DEF 1 UK)

---

128.   Action Memorandum From the President's Special Assistant (Rostow) to President Johnson[1]

Washington, January 31, 1968.

SUBJECT

    Message to the Shah on the Persian Gulf

We have an opportunity this afternoon—much sooner than we expected—to strike a blow for regional cooperation in the Persian Gulf following Britain's withdrawal.

State proposes you send the attached message[2] to the Shah tonight trying to head off trouble between him and King Faisal. The Shah's actions in the next few days could seriously damage Iran's relations with the Saudis at a time when we want the two countries to work together at filling the vacuum the British will leave behind.

The Shah planned a visit to Faisal beginning 3 February, but has decided to cancel the trip because he thinks the Saudis are trying to undermine the Iranian claim to Bahrain Island which is now a British protectorate between Iran and Saudi Arabia. If the Shah stays home,

---

[1] Source: Johnson Library, National Security File, Special Head of State Correspondence File, Iran, 1/1/68–6/30/68. Secret.
[2] See Document 129.

the Saudis will take it as a deliberate insult. Armin Meyer has seen the Shah several times about this, but the best he has been able to get is a delay in announcing the "postponement" of the visit.

The attached message is skillfully drafted to make clear that you expect the Shah to go, but it is not so specific as to be offensive or useless if he decides not to—the only risk is a negative reaction, but this draft stops at praising his foresight and saying you are counting on his leadership.

Our main concern anyway is not the immediate issue of the visit but the future of the Persian Gulf. Good relations between Saudi Arabia and Iran will be necessary to keep things under control when the British leave. The alternatives are instability with a strong chance of an increased Soviet presence. We don't want to have to replace the British, and we don't want the Russians there. So we must count on the Shah and Faisal. The proposed message concentrates on these broader issues and would be worth sending even if the visit were not an issue. Since it is, it's worth trying to get this out tonight if possible to do double duty.

Walt

Approve[3]

Disapprove

Call me

---

[3] This option is checked.

---

129. Telegram From the Department of State to the Embassy in Iran[1]

Washington, February 1, 1968, 0138Z.

108214. Please deliver following message to Shah: "Your Imperial Majesty:

---

[1] Source: National Archives and Records Administration, RG 59, Central Files, 1967–69, POL 33 PERSIAN GULF. Secret; Immediate; Exdis. Drafted by Eliot on January 31; cleared by Brewer and Saunders, and in draft by Battle and Katzenbach; and approved by Rockwell. Repeated to Dhahran for Ambassador Eilts, and to Jidda, Kuwait, and New Delhi for Rostow.

Now that the British have reached their decision on the future of their military presence in the Persian Gulf, I would like to share some preliminary thoughts with you on the situation there.

In the first place, let me stress, as I have said before, that the United States attaches importance to the future security of the Gulf. We would not wish to see outside powers, bent on promoting their interests by creating trouble, intrude into the area. I believe you share these views.

The United States interest in the security of the area does not, however, envisage that we would wish either to replace the British military presence or participate in any new regional security arrangement. The United States looks to the countries of the area to ensure the area's security.

The United States is also, as you know, deeply interested in the economic and social progress of the Persian Gulf area. Here again, it is our hope that the countries of the area will take the lead in cooperating with each other to forward this progress.

I am aware that there are a number of specific problems at issue between the states bordering on the Gulf. It is of the utmost importance that these problems be solved so that all concerned may proceed to work on fundamental matters looking to the future stability and prosperity of the area. Their solution will require patience, understanding and a high degree of statesmanship. In this connection, I was delighted to learn of your recent talks with the Ruler of Kuwait. Since so much will depend on the maintenance of the cordial ties and mutual understanding between Iran and Saudi Arabia which you have done so much to develop, we have welcomed plans for an early meeting between you and King Feisal.

I am encouraged and comforted, Your Majesty, about the future of the Persian Gulf area because you and our Saudi friends are there. Your Majesty's leadership will, I know, continue to be directed at realizing our shared desire for peace, stabilility and progress. Ambassador Meyer has informed me of his conversations with you on these matters, and I look forward to hearing from Under Secretary Rostow of his talk with you next week. I hope we can continue to stay in touch as the situation unfolds.

With my warmest personal regards.

Sincerely,

Lyndon B. Johnson"

Rusk

130.   Message From the Shah of Iran to President Johnson[1]

Tehran, February 1, 1968.

Dear Mr. President,

Thank you for your letter which I have received today[2] and have perused with great care, and I am happy to observe that your views correspond exactly with mine.

We have done everything to secure the stability of the Persian Gulf area in cooperation with the relevant countries of the region. We have gone very far in that direction, and as far as any one can go, but our efforts so far have, unfortunately, been answered by precisely the opposite reaction to that expected. But we will continue to show patience until the parties concerned come to their senses.

The Persian Gulf is vital for Iran and is a matter of life and death to us. So long as our heart beats and there is any strength left in us, we shall do our utmost to keep it a free zone and a stable one.

I am sure that your Ambassador, Mr. Meyer, has reported to you on the conversation I had with him on the thirtieth of January. It is most heartening to witness the interest that you, Mr. President, and your government evince in the safeguarding of the stability and security of the Persian Gulf and its immunity from outside intrusion, now that the British have decided to withdraw.

It is also my firm conviction that no foreign power outside the relevant countries of the Persian Gulf should get involved in the maintenance of the peace of the area.

I look forward to receiving Under Secretary Rostow and to having discussions with him.

With my kindest regards and warmest good wishes,

Sincerely,

Mohammad Reza Pahlavi[3]

---

[1] Source: Johnson Library, National Security File, Special Head of State Correspondence File, Iran, 1/1/68–6/30/68. No classification marking. Telegram 108773, February 2, which transmitted the text of the message, states that it was delivered at 3 p.m. on February 1.

[2] See Document 129.

[3] Printed from a copy that bears this typed signature.

131.   Record of Meeting[1]

IRG/NEA 68–8   Washington, February 1, 1968.

INTERDEPARTMENTAL REGIONAL GROUP
FOR NEAR EAST AND SOUTH ASIA

Record of IRG Meeting—February 1, 1968

The major part of the meeting was devoted to a consideration of *our interests in and policy vis-à-vis the Persian Gulf*, with particular regard to the forthcoming British withdrawal. (The first part of the meeting, regarding the forthcoming overseas personnel reduction, is recorded in IRG/NEA 68–7.[2])

The CIA member gave an intelligence briefing on the current status and prospects of subversive forces in the Gulf area, as well as of the elements of stability in the region. He said that the Arab Nationalist Movement (ANM) has emerged as the dominant subversive organization in the Gulf area, and that Bahrain is probably the Gulf state most vulnerable to subversion. The CIA member concluded, however, that on balance the chances are reasonably good that general stability will be maintained in the Gulf region for the next several years, largely because of the limited capabilities of those who would foment unrest. Contingencies which he felt could change this picture include the death of King Faisal of Saudi Arabia and the entry into the Gulf area of a sizable quantity of Soviet weapons, possibly through an increase of UAR activity. The CIA member provided copies of a report just prepared by the Office of National Estimates on the new situation in the Gulf (copy attached).[3]

Reviewing the Country Directors' paper on the "Effect of British Withdrawal from the Persian Gulf and Recommended US Action" (circulated with IRG/NEA 68–6),[2] the Group *agreed* that it provided a sound assessment of the problems and identification of US interests in the area. Although there were differences on some of the specific recommendations, the low-key policy approach recommended by the paper was generally endorsed.

The Group *agreed* that although the Soviets will try to increase their presence and influence in the Gulf area, the key to the future of

---

[1] Source: Central Intelligence Agency, DDO/NE (Critchfield) Files: Job 80–00105A, Box 2, IRG/NEA Working File, Communist Presence—Arabian Peninsula, Persian Gulf. Secret. Drafted by Sober on February 3.
[2] Not printed.
[3] Not attached.

the region in the next few years will be developments within and among the various Gulf states themselves. It is neither politically feasible nor desirable for the US to "replace" the British presence in the Persian Gulf. Our policy should be directed along the lines of (a) encouraging the British to maintain as much of their present special role in the Gulf as they can, as long as possible (including their role as principal arms supplier to various Gulf states); (b) encouraging the Saudis and Iranians to settle their outstanding differences regarding the median line and other issues; (c) encouraging greater political and economic cooperation generally among the Gulf states; and (d) avoiding an undue military buildup by Gulf littoral states.

Our very important oil and strategic interests in Iran and Saudi Arabia will require us to continue to play a leading role in those countries. It was *agreed,* however, that in other respects the most suitable direct US involvement, under the above policy guidelines, would be generally in low key and peripheral to the activities of the British and the indigenous Gulf states. Among other things, it would be useful to increase the American commercial presence in the region. It was agreed that the American oil companies operating in the Gulf area should be sounded out on the possibility of expanding their activities among the Gulf populations and take a more enlightened view of their role in that part of the world.

The Chairman noted that a study had been undertaken within State aiming at a preliminary Department view on the security aspects of the British withdrawal and on possible alternative military arrangements. It was agreed that results of this study should be fully coordinated with Defense and the Joint Staff prior to possible preparation of a recommendation for IRG consideration.

MEMBERS PRESENT

    Executive Chairman: Mr. Battle
    AID: Mr. Williams
    CIA: Mr. Critchfield
    DOD: Mr. Schwartz
    JCS: Captain Murphy
    NSC: Mr. Saunders
    USIA: Mr. Carter
    Commerce: Mr. Kearns-Preston

    State (NEA): Messrs. Davies, Rockwell, Brewer, Eliot
    DOD: Mr. Reed
    Staff Director: Mr. Sober

S.S.
Staff Director

132.   Background Paper Prepared in the Department of State[1]

Washington, February 2, 1968.

VISIT OF BRITISH PRIME MINISTER WILSON
February 1968

PERSIAN GULF

Prime Minister Wilson announced in the House of Commons on January 16 that British military forces would be withdrawn from the Persian Gulf by the end of 1971. The forces involved, consisting of air and naval units as well as ground troops, at present number 6,000–7,000 men. Some 1,500 men associated with the limited British security commitment for Kuwait may be withdrawn sooner, but the remaining force will probably be lifted out in one operation about three months before UK troops leave the Far East at the end of 1971.

The Persian Gulf littoral comprises both independent nations and dependencies greatly varying in size, economic resources, and power. Two states—Iran and Saudi Arabia—dominate the scene. Only these two, and to some extent Iraq, have any real capability to extend political influence beyond their present borders. One small state—Kuwait—is reasonably stable and secure. The other ten entities—Bahrain, Qatar, the seven Trucial States, and the independent Sultanate of Muscat and Oman—are politically weaker with regimes dependent in one degree or another on British protection.

While the British announcement will give radical political movements in the Gulf a psychological shot in the arm, we do not expect it to lead to any dramatic political changes in the immediate future. Internal security is reasonably sound in most of the Gulf dependencies. Much will depend on the vigor with which the British now move to reassure the local rulers and give credible evidence of their intention to continue political and other forms of support.

In the longer run, stability will depend on whether more viable indigenous political and economic mechanisms can be created, and this will probably only be possible if a greater measure of regional cooperation can be established among the weaker Gulf states. There will be an increasing need for regional mechanisms to allow the have-nots to benefit to some extent from the area's wealth. Long-range stability will also depend on whether (a) the Iranians and Saudis can be

---

[1] Source: Johnson Library, National Security File, Country File, United Kingdom, Visit of PM Harold Wilson Briefing Book, 2/7–9/68. Secret. Drafted by Sterner and cleared by Brewer.

persuaded to restrain their competition for influence in the weaker Gulf states so that orderly political and economic development can take place, (b) the Iraqis can limit their support for radical splinter groups down the Gulf, and (c) the Persian Gulf does not become the scene of proxy activities in larger disputes (e.g., between the US and USSR or between Iran and the UAR).

In broadest terms, the US objective is to prevent the Soviets or Chinese from gaining positions which might help them undermine our strategic interests in the Middle East, and to maintain unimpeded access to Gulf oil on commercial terms. This can best be accomplished by: (a) encouraging the British to maintain as much of their present special role in the Gulf as long as possible; (b) encouraging the Saudis and Iranians, in particular, to settle outstanding differences (sure to be an uphill struggle); (c) encouraging greater regional economic and, as feasible, political cooperation among the Gulf states; and (d) avoiding any undue military build-up by Gulf littoral states while recognizing that some increase in indigenous forces is no doubt inevitable.

While the basic British decision to withdraw UK forces by 1971 probably cannot be reversed, we think we should urge the British to maintain certain elements of their position beyond 1971—particularly in providing leadership and technical assistance for indigenous security forces.

---

133. Memorandum From Harold H. Saunders of the National Security Council Staff to the President's Special Assistant (Rostow) and Edward Fried of the National Security Council Staff[1]

Washington, February 2, 1968.

SUBJECT

Prime Minister Wilson and the Persian Gulf

I have refrained during previous Wilson visits from pressing any of my concerns because I realize that higher priority items are on the agenda for these talks. However, this time I would like to make a plea for one sentence in your Memorandum for the President on the Persian

---

[1] Source: Johnson Library, National Security File, Country File, United Kingdom, Visit of PM Wilson, 2/7–9/68. Secret.

Gulf. I should imagine this would not distort the agenda you are planning since it is part of the larger subject of British retrenchment.

The point I would like to see the President make is: We hope the British will retain a substantial political position in the Persian Gulf and not dismantle its present network of political posts and treaties.

Our reasoning is that the British, even if they may have to pull their troops out, can still do a lot to encourage new political and economic relationships in the Gulf. They have the influence and the experience where we do not.

I also want to strike one note of caution. I understand that the following sentence now appears in the Secretary's Memo to the President: "The President may want to urge the Prime Minister to insure that the UK Government does everything possible to promote regional security arrangements in Southeast Asia *and the Persian Gulf.*"[2] If you haven't seen the reaction to Gene Rostow's offhand comment in a BBC interview about new security arrangements in the Persian Gulf, you ought to know that this got every major country in the region up in arms against us. The fact is that we have no intention of participating and want to make this clear. Any equation of Persian Gulf and security arrangements in Southeast Asia will do more harm than good, although we obviously want the nations of the Persian Gulf to unite on their own initiative in a variety of ways to ward off Soviet penetration.

Hal

---

[2] The language in the Secretary's February 3 memorandum to the President reads: "In the case of Southeast Asia, urge that the UK concert with the countries of the area to promote regional security arrangements prior to the British departure. In the case of the Persian Gulf, stress importance of maintaining other elements of British position thereafter." (Ibid., Visit of PM Wilson Briefing Book, 2/7–9/68)

134.   Telegram From the Department of State to the Embassy in Southern Yemen[1]

Washington, February 3, 1968, 0055Z.

109563. Aden 924.[2]

1. Concur would be useful again seek meeting with President al Shaabi. Believe preferable you not request appointment "on instructions," however, but rather state you interested maintaining close contact and assuring highest level PRSY fully informed USG views on number subjects on which you have current guidance.

2. Concerning Yemen you should take following line: USG disappointed over lack success to date of Arab Tripartite Committee to bring conflicting sides together. USG continues hold view that settlement Yemen's problems should be arrived at peacefully by Yemenis themselves. Despite allegations in some quarters, USG is not involved. There no Americans on either side current conflict and USG not extending support to either. We have clearly stated our opposition foreign intervention, position which NLF should understand and appreciate. USG has no chosen instrument in Arab world nor is type of government in Yemen our concern. We hope President Shaabi and his government who are in position establish truly independent and non-aligned state themselves will not be misled by unsubstantiated allegations re US policy.

3. Line you have taken in previous meetings with President and with cabinet Ministers in response request for assistance has been correct. We have little to add. You may wish again refer to Peace Corps but should not push view apparent PRSY lack of interest. You should avoid discussing question military training spaces since no decision yet taken and favorable action cannot be assumed. You may of course reiterate offers (as per 1968 allocation sheets sent to Embassy) of cultural exchange scholarships and leader grant.

4. With respect Persian Gulf, you should make clear USG has no intention replacing British. We hope littoral states themselves will seize

---

[1] Source: National Archives and Records Administration, RG 59, Central Files 1967–69, POL S YEMEN–US. Secret. Drafted by Dinsmore and Brewer on February 2; cleared by CU Near Eastern Programs Chief David Scott, McCloskey, and Quinn (DOD/ISA); and approved by Brewer. Repeated to Jidda.

[2] In telegram 924 from Aden, January 31, Eagleton reported that he thought it was time to see al-Shaabi again, since much had happened since his courtesy call on the President on December 14 (see Document 120), and suggested that it would be useful if he could ask to see him "under instructions from the Department." (National Archives and Records Administration, RG 59, Central Files 1967–69, POL S YEMEN–US)

opportunity to resolve differences and to establish relationships mutually acceptable to them which will contribute peace and orderly development of Gulf region.[3]

Rusk

---

[3] In telegram 1010 from Aden, February 20, Eagleton reported that on February 19
he met alone with President al-Shaabi, who was friendly and whose delivery was calm
and moderate in contrast to his fiery stance on public occasions. Eagleton noted that
the main purpose of the meeting had been to clarify U.S. policy in the area, particularly
U.S. nonintervention in the internal affairs of North and South Yemen. (Ibid.)

**135.   Memorandum From the President's Special Assistant
(Rostow) to President Johnson[1]**

Washington, February 6, 1968.

SUBJECT

Shah's Reply on the Persian Gulf—and Your Talk with Wilson

The Shah replied immediately to your message on the Persian Gulf
(attached).[2] He had already made his final decision to postpone his
visit to Saudi Arabia, but your letter let him know you expect him to
act the statesman in developing local cooperation in the Gulf.

The Shah says he agrees with your view of the Gulf, and, although
he tries to throw the blame for recent disagreements with Faisal on the
Saudis, Armin Meyer thinks the Iranians are feeling guilty and will be
especially good for a while. The quickness of the Shah's reply is one
indication of how he takes your views.

This doesn't mean clear sailing ahead in the Gulf. The Shah may
be feeling a bit overconfident, and his muscle-flexing may be part of
the Gulf scene for some time. Also, local feuds and suspicions have
long histories. But we have injected a sobering perspective at a heated
moment. Fortunately, King Faisal—although deeply hurt by the Shah's
actions and more distrustful than ever—is being much more patient
than anyone expected.

---

[1] Source: Johnson Library, National Security File, Special Head of State Correspondence File, Iran, 1/1/68–6/30/68. Secret.

[2] Document 130.

The next step we will propose in your efforts to foster an orderly evolution in the Gulf is a word to Prime Minister Wilson.[3] The main point is: Don't rock the boat any more than you already have; help us buy time for the locals to work out their own arrangements for the future.

First, we want the British to leave their treaties and political relationships intact to help calm local rulers' feelings of being deserted. Second, we want to keep the British from rushing around trying to arrange security pacts and other deals that won't work because they'll have an obvious "made in the UK" label. We think the best tack is for them to sit tight with their present relationships and let the locals come up with their own scheme for the future.

Walt

---

[3] For a record of the President's meeting with Wilson February 8–9, see *Foreign Relations, 1964–1968*, vol. XII, Document 69.

---

136.   Circular Telegram From the Department of State to Certain Posts[1]

Washington, February 12, 1968, 1649Z.

113711. Subject: Discussions with British re Persian Gulf.

1. Assistant Secretaries Battle and Sisco, in course discussions with Greenhill (UK Fonoff) and British Embassy officers had brief exchange on Britain's future role in Gulf.

2. Battle noted that although British military presence being phased out, USG hoped British political presence and ties with Gulf states will remain. To this end, and in view of our major interests in Arabian Peninsula, USG hopes that it can participate in British planning for future.

3. Greenhill said that British economic interests in Gulf were "profound and enduring." HMG would use time to 1971 to seek to leave an orderly political situation behind and is keen to get moving in this direction. As thinking evolves British will want to discuss planning with USG and to enlist US help as possible.

Rusk

---

[1] Source: National Archives and Records Administration, RG 59, Central Files 1967–69, DEF 1 UK. Secret. Drafted by Davies, cleared by Sisco, and approved by Battle. Sent to London, Jidda, Tehran, Aden, Kuwait, and Dhahran.

137.   Circular Telegram From the Department of State to Certain Posts[1]

Washington, February 21, 1968, 2104Z.

118823. State 116285 (Notal).[2]

1. Reftel dealt with USG position regarding status Bahrain. In light evolving situation in Gulf generally, notably reported announcement "federation" Abu Dhabi and Dubai (Jidda 2921, Notal),[3] addressees may find following guidance helpful with respect USG attitude toward Gulf problems generally. We would not wish publicize our position at this time but following paragraphs may be drawn on in response queries.

2. With respect various small Arab states in Persian Gulf, US has considered them independent states in special treaty relationship with UK. We cannot at this time comment on the situation as it may evolve in the future. For example, it would be premature for US to take position regarding UN membership for any of these states at this time.

3. Re arms supplies, we believe these states should continue to fill their legitimate arms requirements from their traditional British supplier. The UK has long provided these items for the Persian Gulf states and British officers have been closely associated with many of them, both in operational and training capacities. Continued reliance on British procurement will therefore, among other things, serve to reduce maintenance and spare parts problems.

4. With respect political evolution among these Arab states, we believe strongly this is matter for states themselves to determine without outside interference as part evolution their previous special relationship with British. We have noted with interest communiqué re possible federation of lower Gulf states, notably Abu Dhabi and Dubai,

---

[1] Source: National Archives and Records Administration, RG 59, Central Files 1967–69, POL 19 BAHRAIN IS. Confidential. Drafted by Brewer on February 20; cleared by Rockwell, Davies, Hartley, Eliot, Assistant Legal Adviser for Near Eastern and South Asian Affairs Donald A. Wehmeyer, Cheslaw, Murray (DOD/ISA), and Colonel Herbert J. McChrystal (G/PM); and approved by Battle. Sent to Beirut, Amman, Jidda, Aden, Dhahran, Kuwait, Tehran, London, CINCSTRIKE/CINCMEAFSA, and COMIDEASTFOR.

[2] Telegram 116285 to Dhahran, February 16, noted that in responding to queries about the U.S. position toward the future status of Bahrain, the Department believed it important to continue to avoid any possible erroneous impression that the United States was planning to "replace" the British in the Gulf or that it favored certain specific solutions to Gulf problems. The response to any such questions should be that the U.S. Government had considered Bahrain an independent state in a special treaty relationship with the United Kingdom, and that it could not comment on the situation as it might evolve in the future. (Ibid.)

[3] Dated February 20. (Ibid., POL 7 TRUCIAL ST)

and would wish any such arrangement well. We have, however, no plan regarding developments in this region and do not expect to be consulted by the states concerned as to any political arrangements which they may find useful or desirable for themselves. We are maintaining our interest in this region and hope developments will provide for maintenance of stability and orderly progress there.

5. *For Beirut:* Do not believe you should make any direct response to Kazzan (Beirut A–704, Notal).[4] Should he again raise question assistance to Qatar, you may comment along foregoing general lines.

Rusk

---

[4] Dated February 16. (Ibid., DEF 12 QATAR)

---

138.   Information Memorandum From the Assistant Secretary of State for Near Eastern and South Asian Affairs (Battle) to Secretary of State Rusk[1]

Washington, February 22, 1968.

SUBJECT

    Outlook in the Persian Gulf States

Background

By the end of 1971, British troops totalling some 6,000 ground units and small air and naval components will have been withdrawn from the Persian Gulf. Existing special UK treaty relationships may have then been renegotiated to remove any implication of British "protection." Decisions have not yet been taken re post-1971 UK subsidies to local security forces in the area, nor policies with respect to secondment of British officers to such forces. With luck the British may be willing to carry on this type of role for a limited additional period.

---

[1] Source: National Archives and Records Administration, RG 59, Central Files 1967–69, POL 33 PERSIAN GULF. Secret. Drafted by Brewer on February 9 and cleared by Davies and Eliot. Copies were sent to Country Director for Soviet Union Affairs Malcolm Toon, Country Director for United Kingdom, Ireland, and Malta Affairs J. Harold Shullaw, Sober, and Director of the INR Office of Research and Analysis for Near East and South Asia Granville S. Austin. Secretary Rusk's initials on the memorandum indicate he read it.

Several states—Bahrain, Qatar and Abu Dhabi—are expected to opt for full independence. The smaller Trucial Shaikhdoms may evolve into one or more federations. Irrespective of the precise course of developments, the opportunity for direct contacts around the Gulf by major foreign powers will vastly increase.

Strategic Significance

The Gulf's importance in the world oil picture often obscures its fundamental strategic significance. Together with the Iranian plateau, the region forms the keystone in an arch of non-Communist countries stretching from Africa to South Asia. Here Russia is closest to access to the wide seas. Russian agents and emissaries were active in Kuwait and down the Gulf in the 1890's. The Molotov/Ribbentrop correspondence of 1939 makes clear that the Persian Gulf has remained a center of Russian aspirations. With the British hold in the Gulf loosening, a new opportunity will arise for the USSR to "leapfrog" over Iran and establish positions for the first time in the Gulf itself.

Attitudes of Smaller Gulf States Towards USG

The concern of Gulf littoral states at the British announcement has already prompted significant gestures in our direction. Kuwait has suddenly become receptive to renewed visits by the US Navy (COMID-EASTFOR) and is urgently seeking to buy naval craft from us. Bahrain has inquired as to our attitude towards the island's independence and has asked hopefully for information on COMIDEASTFOR's dispositions beyond 1971. Even Muscat, still slumbering in primordial isolation, has addressed a congratulatory message to Ambassador Bohlen on his new appointment. In their search for powerful protectors, it seems clear that the Gulf states would prefer a greater role on the part of the US, but they will trim their sails in any direction that future circumstances may dictate.

USG Role

The NEA IRG examined implications of the foregoing on February 3 [1].[2] The IRG agreed that the key to the future of the region in the next few years will be developments within and among the various Gulf states themselves. Our policy should be directed to: (a) encouraging the British to maintain as much of their present special role as they can, (b) fostering greater political and economic cooperation generally among the Gulf states, and (c) seeking to avoid an undue military buildup there.

Some strengthening of the USG presence was discussed. There are now no USG officials posted anywhere in the Horn of Arabia, from

---

[2] See Document 131.

Dhahran around to Aden. We have in the past considered opening posts in the Trucial States, in Muscat (where our former Consulate was closed in about 1912)[3] and on Bahrain, but budgetary limitations presently preclude action.

The IRG agreed that it would be useful if the American commercial presence in the region could be increased. We will be sounding out the oil companies on the possibility of expanding their activities among the Gulf populations. There are suggestions that the IBRD might consider helping the littoral states establish a regional economic development institution, using funds from the oil rich among them. An informal proposal to this effect emanating from the Chase Bank is already before the IBRD. We will do what we can quietly to encourage such initiatives, bearing in mind both the severe limitations on our own capabilities and the fact that undue support from major non-Gulf powers could well reduce indigenous enthusiasm for any particular scheme.

With due regard for our important interests in Iran and Saudi Arabia, we will continue to examine what we can do ourselves with respect to the Gulf states, now that this region is rapidly becoming both more active politically and attractive economically.

_____

[3] The Consulate was closed in 1915.

_____

139. Intelligence Report[1]

No. 0582/68   Washington, March 1, 1968.

SECURITY AND SUBVERSION IN THE PERSIAN GULF

Summary

The Persian Gulf is one of the least known corners of the globe, parts of it virtually unchanged since the 15th century. Only two or three of the states in the area deserve to be called countries—Iran,

_____

[1] Source: Johnson Library, National Security File, Country File, Middle East, Vol. I, 6/65–3/68. Secret; No Foreign Dissem. Prepared in the Directorate of Intelligence of the Central Intelligence Agency. A note on the first page of the memorandum indicates it was "produced solely by CIA" in the Office of Current Intelligence and coordinated with the Office of Strategic Research and the Clandestine Services.

Saudi Arabia, and possibly Kuwait. Most of the rest are shabby sheik-doms with a few square miles of territory and a few thousand inhabit-ants. But the entire area lies above some 67 percent of the world's known oil reserves, much of it exploited by US companies and vital to Europe's economy and to Western defense.

British troops have been stationed in the gulf area for over a century. Air, naval, and ground contingents in Bahrain and Sharjah were, until last November, backed up by even greater troop strength in Aden. Now, Aden has become the radical independent "People's Republic of Southern Yemen," and the UK has announced its intention to pull its remaining troops—some 9,000 at present—out of the gulf area before the end of 1971. In an attempt to plan for the future, the nine protectorates in the area—Bahrain, Qatar, and the seven Trucial sheikdoms—have agreed to federate this March, although few details have been worked out. The British apparently also plan to sever their semipaternalistic ties with the Sultanate of Muscat and Oman. Whether British political advisers and seconded officers will continue to work with the governments and security forces in the region is still an open question.

Except for Iraq, with its minuscule border on the Persian Gulf, all of the states in the area are conservative—some medievally so—and are vulnerable to agitation for change. Iran can certainly take care of itself, however, and Saudi Arabia may prove able to do so despite a growing threat in its Eastern Province. So far, subversive activity in the Trucial States is minimal. But open revolt has already broken out in Muscat and Oman, and Southern Yemen is making revolutionary noises on its border; Bahrain and Kuwait are sitting on top of highly developed networks of subversion; and the ruling regime in Qatar seems to have thoroughly alienated the population. Whether the indige-nous security forces are capable of coping with such problems—with or without British assistance—is far from certain. What is certain is that they can expect no help from radical regimes in Egypt, Syria, and Iraq, whose agents have been working for years to spread the "Arab revolution" to the gulf.

[Here follows the body of the report.]

140.   Memorandum From John W. Foster of the National
        Security Council Staff to the President's Special
        Assistant (Rostow)[1]

Washington, March 21, 1968.

SUBJECT

The Situation in South Yemen

We still don't have a clear picture of the situation in South Yemen, but there are a few things that can be said.

Prior to yesterday's events,[2] we knew there was a struggle for power within the government and the National Liberation Front, and we felt—on the basis of sketchy evidence—that the moderates supported by the British trained army were winning over the radicals. The two groups have been at odds since the country became independent late last year, and matters came to a head at a party convention earlier this month. Our limited information on the convention suggested that a compromise was worked out which left the moderates in control at the price of adopting radical policies. If this reading is correct, the latest developments could be a moderate attempt to renege on the agreement, possibly because of pressure from the military.

If the moderates win, South Yemen could swing away from its current efforts to develop close relations with the Communist nations. This doesn't mean that the government will be easy to deal with, and the government still has to solve tremendous financial problems. A number of side issues will probably prevent the current troubles from developing strictly on moderate-radical lines, and we will still be dealing with some radicals. More important, the moderates are moderate only in South Yemeni terms. They are Arab nationalists and socialists whose outlook is basically anti-Western.

Yesterday's activities led to some sort of compromise, but we don't even know the specific issues the new agreement is supposed to settle. Guessing is that the NLF has resolved none of its problems, and that South Yemen is in for more trouble.

---

[1] Source: Johnson Library, National Security File, Country File, Yemen, Cables & Memos, Vol. 11, 7/64–12/68. Secret.

[2] On March 20, in response to a series of radical pronouncements by the NLF party congress and a March 18 purge of the civil service, the Southern Yemen army and internal security forces imposed a curfew in Aden and arrested a number of NLF radicals, including the Defense and Information Ministers.

It would be hard to argue that any American initiative would be worth the effort, and even if we wanted to influence events there is little we could do. State isn't planning to do much more than to watch the situation and hope for the best.

John

---

141.   Intelligence Note From the Director of the Bureau of Intelligence and Research (Hughes) to Secretary of State Rusk[1]

No. 214   Washington, March 22, 1968.

SUBJECT

Federation of Arab Amirates to be Born March 30

Gulf Shaikhs Announce Unity Plan for Persian Gulf. The Federation of Arab Amirates (FAA), consisting of Bahrain, Qatar, and the Trucial States (Abu Dhabi, Dubai, Sharjah, 'Ajman, Umm al Qaiwain, Ras al Khaimah, and Fujairah), is scheduled to come into existence on March 30. The union was proposed at a meeting of the ruling shaikhs in Dubai in late February "to promote regional cooperation, coordinate development and welfare plans, and regulate collective defense measures." According to a February 27 communiqué, the FAA will have a Supreme Council consisting of the 9 rulers; this Council will draw up a permanent charter and future legislation as required. Leadership of the Council will rotate annually among its members, any one of whom may veto proposed legislation. A Federal Council will be formed to execute Supreme Council decisions. Persistent rumors suggest that Shaikh 'Isa of Bahrain will be the first to lead the FAA. The next Federation meeting is scheduled to be held in Bahrain in late April, but Qatar has asked for a change of venue because of Iranian sensitivity to the issue of Bahrain sovereignty.

UK Withdrawal Plans Inspire Gulf Unity Efforts. Prime Minister Wilson announced on January 16 that the UK intends to withdraw its military forces and thus terminate its special position in the Persian

---

[1] Source: National Archives and Records Administration, RG 59, Records of the Department of State, Central Files 1967–69, POL 3 TRUCIAL ST. Secret; No Foreign Dissem; Limdis. No drafting information appears on the source text.

Gulf by 1971. Fearful of Arab nationalist agitation and possible Soviet inroads, Iran and the Arab littoral states (except Iraq) have been apprehensive about the effects of the UK decision.[2] Opportunities for cooperation between the Shah and traditionalist Arab leaders, however, were blighted [by] the Shah's irritation over Saudi and Kuwaiti statements concerning the "Arabism" of Bahrain, his subsequent cancellation of a state visit to Saudi Arabia, and concurrent exacerbation of the Saudi-Iranian Gulf median line dispute. Basically, the Shah perceives for Iran a major role in Gulf affairs following Britain's departure, and believes that present Arab attitudes indicate a rejection of Iranian offers of military and economic cooperation. Shortly after the Wilson announcement, the Shaikhs of Abu Dhabi and Qatar offered to finance a continuing British military presence; Shaikh 'Isa of Bahrain quickly joined in the offer. The UK rejected it, indicating that its decision to leave the Gulf was based on more far-reaching policy considerations than troop costs. On February 19, Shaikh Za'id of Abu Dhabi and Shaikh Rashid of Dubai announced the union of their two states. This union probably will continue to exist after inauguration of the FAA. The UK has encouraged continuation of the union because it appears more potentially viable than the loosely knit FAA. Shaikh 'Isa contends that the FAA was proposed by Qatar as a means of scuttling the Abu Dhabi–Dubai Union. Qatar's relations with Dubai are close because of the intermarriage of the ruling clans and their use of a common currency, but Qatar has a long-standing territorial dispute with Abu Dhabi and is its traditional rival for regional influence. The Saudi role in the formation of the FAA remains obscure, but King Faysal allegedly has backed Qatar's efforts to form the FAA to protect Bahrain from Iranian irredentism by having it absorbed in a regional Arab entity. In any case, the ambitious Shaikh 'Isa, who is described as unenthusiastic about the FAA, wishes to obtain full independence for Bahrain with UN and Arab League membership. Kuwait thus far has indicated enthusiasm for the FAA.

FAA Faces An Uncertain Future. According to the Lebanese Foreign Minister, "coordinated Arab action" is under way to recognize the FAA, presumably on its March 30 birth date. On the other hand, the Pan-Arab, socialist-leaning Arab Nationalist Movement (ANM) sharply attacked the nascent Federation in the Beirut newspaper *al Hurriyah* on March 18. The ANM position is a fair example of what can be expected from the Arab socialist states, which view the FAA as an artificial,

---

[2] For more extensive discussion of Gulf unity problems see: RNA–6, "Persian Gulf Leaders Search for Regional Cooperation as Britain's Stabilizing Influence Begins to Wane," February 23, 1968 (Secret/No Foreign Dissem/Controlled Dissem/Limdis). [Footnote in the source text. This document is ibid., DEF 6 UK.]

"imperialist" creation. A UK Foreign Office source has indicated that March 30 would be "without significance" as far as Britain's relations with the Gulf states are concerned; as before, the UK will treat the nine members as separate, British-protected states. The Shah of Iran, however, is angered over the Arab position toward Bahrain and the general attitude toward "Arabism" in the Gulf which the traditionalist Arab regimes have taken. He has indicated that he will react to the Federation with a "formal denunciation of the FAA and British trickery." The Shah's attitude reflects his conviction that the FAA was engineered by the UK to protect Bahrain and disputed mid-Gulf islands against Iranian claims. His stance will make Iranian cooperation with such conservative states as Saudi Arabia and Kuwait much more difficult and may even lead to a considerable cooling of Irano-British relations.

Considering that the traditionally quarrelsome and mutually suspicious member states must approve all FAA legislation unanimously, that the Federation will be opposed by Iran as well as the radical Arab regimes, and that the UK appears indifferent, the FAA is unlikely to be a successful venture in Gulf unity. Nevertheless, it represents a realization by the traditionalist leaders of the Arab littoral that the vacuum created by Britain's withdrawal will attract outside hostile elements that can only be resisted by unified action. Whether the Federation will be a useful stepping stone to more meaningful cooperation or merely another monument to the elusiveness of Arab unity remains to be seen.

142. Paper Prepared in the Department of State[1]

Washington, April 15, 1968.

THE POLITICO-MILITARY PROBLEM FOR THE US IN THE ARABIAN SEA LITTORAL

Summary

Over the next few years the US will face a potentially difficult situation in the Arabian Sea littoral (see map following page 3).[2] This situation is the product of several factors.

First, this is basically an unstable area. The Arab nations generally are underdeveloped; many of the regimes are highly conservative, lacking in modern administrative machinery; and there is wide disparity in the division of wealth. To these problems must be added century old suspicions between states and deep religious and ethnic cleavages. Radical nationalist movements are beginning to make themselves felt; some with outside instigation and support, but others with mainly nationalistic drives.

Second, the radical Arab states, particularly the UAR, and the Soviet Union pose a threat to exploit the latent instability in the area. Nasser will most likely concentrate on using such exploitation to reinforce his position of leadership in the Arab world. The Soviet Union will probably work toward expanding its trade, political presence and general influence in the area with the primary purpose of denying other outside powers the option of securing a preeminent position such as the British have enjoyed. The Soviets might, based on the reaction to their efforts, seek to project a military presence into the area.

Third, the British, whose military presence has acted as a factor for stability and a check on outside exploitation, have announced their intention to complete the withdrawal of their military forces by the end of 1971.

---

[1] Source: Department of State, IRG/NEA 68–24 Files: Lot 70 D 503, U.S. Policy and Future Military Presence in the Arabian Littoral, 7/10/68. Secret. Drafted by Robert H. Neuman (L/NEA). Attached to an April 22 memorandum from Deputy Assistant Secretary of State for Politico-Military Affairs Philip J. Farley to Battle noting that the study was prepared by G/PM with assistance from an Interdepartmental Working Group in response to Battle's memorandum of January 10. In G/PM's opinion, the study in its present form represented the closest point that could be reached in obtaining an "agreed" paper. Farley recommended that Battle place the study before the NEA/IRG so that it might decide whether it was appropriate to forward it to the SIG for consideration.

[2] Not reproduced.

The principal US interest is in maintaining US access to and influence in the area. In short, the US seeks to deny to potentially hostile outside powers, particularly the Soviet Union, a position of dominance in the area. Such a position could be used to put pressure on Western Europe, for which Near East oil is vital, and would complicate our own trade with, peaceful entry into, transit through, or ability to influence the various states concerned. Because of the strategic location of the Arabian Sea littoral as a vital crossroad connecting Europe, Africa, and Asia, denial of US access to this area by a potentially hostile power would constitute a blow to US interests considerably beyond those involved in the immediate area. In addition to this principal interest, the US has the traditional interests in this area of protecting both US citizens and the substantial US oil investment and trade with area states. The US also has a formal bilateral security agreement with Iran, has agreed to cooperate with the signatories of the Baghdad Pact (CENTO), and has given certain assurances to Saudi Arabia.

There are a number of steps in the political, economic, and sociological fields which the US can take to assist in maintaining access to and influence in the area. These are being considered in other studies and may prove to be the most effective steps open to us.[3] The purpose of this study is to analyze certain politico-military approaches which may also be useful in meeting the security aspect of the problem.

In the politico-military field, a spectrum of alternative approaches have been considered, ranging from withdrawal from the area, through maintenance of our current policy, to seeking to assume the full British military role. Of the alternative approaches considered, those which appear to have practical value are limited. In summary, they are:

a. To encourage the British to continue to play as full a role as possible in the Arabian Sea littoral, particularly in the political, economic and military spheres.

b. If and when politically feasible, to consider supporting in a low-key fashion efforts on the part of the local states to form mutual security arrangements which show any promise of reducing the incidence of locally induced instability. We should not encourage any particular arrangement nor should we delude ourselves as to the real security value which such arrangements would represent.

c. To manifest a reassuring military presence in the area, offshore and largely "over the horizon," to strengthen the confidence of the

---

[3] A number of these were considered in the paper, "Effect of British Withdrawal from Persian Gulf and the Recommended US Action," which was considered by the NEA/IRG on February 1, 1968. The NEA/IRG approved the broad policy recommendations contained in the paper. [Footnote in the source text. For a record of the February 1 meeting, see Document 131.]

local moderate states to evolve and progress free of concern that hostile outside powers might exploit local tensions through the use of military force. We should be clear that such a presence is not intended directly to affect the course of political events within or between local states, nor, for that matter, would it prevent efforts by outside powers to enhance their influence through peaceful means. What it can do is provide a signal to hostile outside powers that attempts at exploitation through military means carry risks which may well exceed the benefits likely to accrue. To be reassuring, the presence would have to be somewhat larger and more flexible than that represented by the current MIDEASTFOR. It should either contain or have rapid access to some limited air and ground capability in addition to the naval capability of MIDEASTFOR.

d. As a corollary to manifesting a reassuring military presence in the area, to undertake on an urgent basis a reappraisal of the proposal to use Diego Garcia, or another of the islands previously considered, for an offshore fueling and staging base for possible operations around the Arabian Sea littoral, along the East African coast and in the Indian Ocean in general. With the British no longer willing to maintain a military presence in the region, this reappraisal should be primarily a USG concern.

e. While continuing current "show the flag" visits by MIDEAST-FOR, as possible, arrange for additional "show the flag" visits by US military forces which may be transiting the area.

[Here follow the body of the paper and two annexes.]

143. Memorandum From the Deputy Assistant Secretary of Defense for International Security Affairs (Schwartz) to the Assistant Secretary of Defense for International Security Affairs (Warnke)[1]

I–22215/68   Washington, April 22, 1968.

SUBJECT

    US Arms Sales in the Persian Gulf

When the British announced on 16 January that they would, by the end of 1971, withdraw their forces and commitments in the Persian Gulf, a US spokesman said publicly that we would "not fill the vacuum." It has been ISA's position since that we will indeed not "fill the vacuum." We will, of course, continue our relations with Saudi Arabia and Iran. Relations between those states, and ours with each of them, involve us quite enough without becoming further involved with other riparian states.

When this subject was discussed in February at the IRG/NEA,[2] there were proposals from the State Department that we might consider selling arms to some of the riparian states other than Iran and Saudi Arabia. I objected on the grounds that this is a good way to begin a process contrary to our publicly stated, as well as intended, position. What finally was put in the IRG record was the following paragraph:

"The Group *agreed* that although the Soviets will try to increase their presence and influence in the Gulf area, the key to the future of the region in the next few years will be developments within and among the various Gulf states themselves. It is neither politically feasible nor desirable for the US to 'replace' the British presence in the Persian Gulf. Our policy should be directed along the lines of (a) encouraging the British to maintain as much of their present special role in the Gulf as they can, as long as possible (including their role as principal arms supplier to various Gulf states); (b) encouraging the Saudis and Iranians to settle their outstanding differences regarding the median line and other issues; (c) encouraging greater political and economic cooperation generally among the Gulf states; and (d) avoiding an undue military buildup by Gulf littoral states."

Now we have a request from Kuwait for 60 "open troop carriers." The telegraphic exchange is attached.[3] The working level at State just can't bring themselves to say "no." Regardless of what we say, I believe

---

[1] Source: Washington National Records Center, RG 330, OASD/ISA Files: FRC 72 A 1498, Persian Gulf 000.1—1968. Secret.

[2] See Document 131.

[3] Not found attached.

we should sell no arms to these states. Since I know your views on this subject, this memorandum is largely informational. Given Paul Nitze's work load, I hate to bother him now and suggest we could go to him when and if necessary for support on this policy.

Approve above[4]
Go to Paul Nitze now
See me

Harry H. Schwartz

---

[4] Warnke initialed this option on April 23.

---

144.   Telegram From the Department of State to the Embassy in Southern Yemen[1]

Washington, April 24, 1968, 2358Z.

152721. Aden 1261,[2] 1266,[3] 1272 (Notal).[4] Southern Yemen.

1. Appreciate full reporting reftels indicating new Army/radical NLF confrontation may be impending. You, of course, took right line in telling source USG could in no way become involved in internal political affairs PRSY (para 4 Aden 1261).

2. Re source's curiosity as to reaction USG (para 2 Aden 1272), Embassy should continue policy of refusing be drawn into further elaboration our standard position. Should source again approach you,

---

[1] Source: National Archives and Records Administration, RG 59, Central Files 1967–69, POL 23–9 S YEMEN. Secret. Drafted by Brewer and approved by Davies. Repeated to Beirut, Jidda, London, CINCSTRIKE, and COMIDEASTFOR.

[2] In telegram 1261 from Aden, April 22, Eagleton reported that on April 21 a South Yemeni he did not know had asked to see him, said he represented those in the NLF who could not accept its drift toward extremism and communism, and asked for U.S. assistance. Eagleton responded that the U.S. Government could not in any way become involved in the internal affairs of Southern Yemen. (Ibid.)

[3] Dated April 23. (Ibid.)

[4] In telegram 1272 from Aden, April 24, Eagleton reported that an NLF official had twice interrogated a part-time Embassy translator regarding the U.S. reaction to an anti-NLF document left with the Embassy on April 21. The employee responded that he had not been given the document to translate and was unable to comment. (Ibid.)

you will no doubt wish continue play him for maximum intelligence value while making clear USG deals with duly constituted government authorities PRSYG. As source aware, our contacts with PRSYG continue be correct, despite expulsion DATT in aftermath March 20 events.[5]

Rusk

---

[5] On March 26 the People's Republic of Southern Yemen Government had declared the U.S. Defense Attaché persona non grata after alleging that he was implicated in the army's attempted counter-revolution on March 20. Despite U.S. protests, he was ordered to leave the country by March 28.

---

145.   Memorandum From John W. Foster of the National Security Council Staff to the President's Special Assistant (Rostow)[1]

Washington, May 21, 1968.

SUBJECT

  The Situation in Yemen and Southern Yemen

Yemen and Southern Yemen are so confusing that we thought a word might be in order. We don't foresee any US involvement, but what's going on does affect the general balance of forces in the area.

After a month of confused maneuvering during which the military seemed to be moving closer and closer to a coup, *the situation in Southern Yemen has taken a turn for the better.* The pro-Western army has put down a revolt of the extremist wing of the radical NLF, giving the NLF moderates a firmer hold on the country, and the military a fairly good grip on the government. This shift to the right will make the South Yemenis less eager to rush into the arms of the Soviets, and ought to make the regime somewhat more acceptable to the Saudis—at least, Faisal isn't likely to intervene, and he might even bring himself to recognize the government.

---

[1] Source: Johnson Library, National Security File, Country File, Yemen, Cables and Memos, Vol. II, 7/64–12/68. Secret.

Despite this apparent shift, there are still more than enough personal, ideological, tribal and regional rivalries to upset things easily. The basic cause of many of the problems—the lack of money—is no nearer a solution, and solving it may force the regime into political affiliations it would rather avoid.

Whatever its politics, any Southern Yemeni government will have to get foreign assistance—and from any willing source. The British are out of the picture now that aid negotiations have broken down. (The Southern Yemenis wanted $144 million in the next five years, the UK offered $3 million in the next nine months.) The government thinks the Russians are its best bet, and rumor has it that President Qahtan plans to leave for Moscow shortly. We just don't have the money—or the interest—to buy in, and the Saudis are still too skeptical of even this latest shift to be ready to pick up the burden themselves, though that would be the ideal from our viewpoint.

Farther north *in Yemen*, the civil war drags on. The Republicans are winning this month, but there isn't much chance that they—or the Royalists—will win the war. On the Republican side, the moderates are still in control, but differences with the Soviet-backed leftists could lead to an open break. In the other camp, there is a definite split between the Royalist tribes and the followers of the Royal family. An effort is underway to bring the tribal Royalists and the Republican moderates together, but there is no guarantee that it will be successful. The Egyptians have been out of the picture for six months, and the Saudis have had about all the Royalist feuding they can take. The Russians are still there, but the pace of their activities has slowed sharply since their early December rush to replace the Egyptians.

John

146. Memorandum From the Assistant Secretary of Defense for International Security Affairs (Warnke) to Secretary of Defense McNamara[1]

I–23190/68   Washington, June 12, 1968.

SUBJECT

    The Soviets and the Persian Gulf

1. Long before the October Revolution of 1917, the Russia of the Czars was restlessly seeking warm-water ports in which their shipping would not be bottled by narrow waterways. The last few years have seen a large increase in the Soviet navy and its appearance in the Mediterranean. The last few months have seen expressions of Soviet interest in the Persian Gulf, Indian Ocean, and adjacent seas. These latest expressions of Soviet interest in the Persian Gulf have coincided with the recent announcement of the UK that by 1971 they would withdraw their forces from that area, and their protection from the sheikdoms of the Gulf. To the states bordering the Gulf as well as to the Soviet Union, this British statement is practically tantamount to withdrawal, and there has been among the various states and sheikdoms a great deal of confused activity as they seek, ineffectually so far, to rearrange their lives without Great Britain. The Soviets brought a cruiser, a destroyer, and an oiler all the way from the maritime provinces to this area only two weeks ago, and visited Indian, Pakistani, and Iraqi ports, and one Iranian port (the Shah's invitation reportedly "reluctant"). The Soviet ships are now headed for East Africa. It has been a "Show the Flag" operation highly comparable to the visits paid to ports in the area by our own Mideast Force of three ships, stationed in Bahrein.

2. The significance of threat to the US of these phenomena is being debated throughout the government. Some see these Soviet activities as a large and growing threat to US world-wide interests; others are more inclined to view it only as a natural movement out onto the seas of the world of a large and powerful nation which can now afford that sort of activity. I am more inclined to the latter view, particularly as the Soviet Union whose naval ships are now appearing in these southern waters—although it still does not wish us well—is not the Soviet Union of the 1950s. The Soviet Union of today simply has too many problems

---

[1] Source: Washington National Records Center, RG 330, OSD Files: FRC 73 A 1250, Persian Gulf 800, Persian Gulf 1968. Secret. The memorandum indicates it was seen by the Secretary of Defense on June 15.

at home, with China, with the states of Eastern Europe, and with the communist parties outside the Soviet Union, to be dangerously aggressive in the overt manner of the past.

3. Our view in ISA has been that US policies and actions in the general area of the Persian Gulf should rather precisely correspond to our public statements that we have no intention of "filling the vacuum" left by the British withdrawal. By this, we mean that we should undertake no new programs in the area, nor get involved in the affairs of the small Arabic states that stretch along the southwestern littoral of the Persian Gulf. The reasons are several:

a. We already have a fairly high degree of interest in and close relations with Saudi Arabia (i.e., King Faisal and ARAMCO), and with Iran, whom we have just agreed to sell during the next five years $600 million worth of additional arms.

b. Aside from that, we think that the people of the area can manage their lives better without additional interference from us than they can with it.

c. We anticipate that the small states and sheikdoms of the Gulf will rather naturally look to us to take the place of the British, and that it is easier to avoid this temptation at the outset than it would be later to attempt to extricate ourselves.

d. In effect, we are placing our money on a modern Persian Emperor to keep open the Persian Gulf; and I advocate that we sell arms to no one else on the Gulf except Saudi Arabia.

4. Although it is difficult to make predictions about such matters, my own guess would be that the Soviets have begun a diplomatic game highly reminiscent of the ones played by both the Russians and the Western European powers during the last century. Although we should keep an active eye on our present investments in the area, a fine restraint of exuberant activism would best serve our long-term interests. While it is quite possible that Iran's "peacekeeping" in the Persian Gulf may become from time-to-time a rather messy operation, I doubt that a large role by the United States would be any more effective—or less messy. I think that we are already sufficiently immersed in Arab affairs with respect to those states immediately surrounding Israel.

Any or all of the above thoughts which you adopt as your own can, of course, be declassified for use as background with the *New York Times*.

Paul C. Warnke

147.   Memorandum From the Joint Chiefs of Staff to Secretary of Defense McNamara[1]

JCSM–380–68   Washington, June 19, 1968.

SUBJECT

Persian Gulf Study (U)

1. (C) In view of the announced decision of the United Kingdom to withdraw its military forces from the Persian Gulf in 1971, CINC-STRIKE/USCINCMEAFSA has submitted a study concerning the political and military impact of this withdrawal as it relates to his responsibilities. A copy of this study is attached hereto.[2]

2. (C) The study has been reviewed by the Joint Chiefs of Staff and determined to be a timely and useful document for consideration in future policy actions in connection with the UK decision. Because of the wide range of the recommendations in the study, the contingent nature of some, and the time frame during which actions might become appropriate, it is not considered necessary, at this time, to forward recommendations on all matters addressed by the study. With the exception of those considered to be of a more immediate nature and addressed below, the recommendations will be considered when time and events determine such action to be appropriate. The Joint Chiefs of Staff will forward any resultant recommendations requiring your attention.

3. (S) The recommendations which are considered appropriate for attention in the near future are:

a. Establishment of a US arms policy for the lower Persian Gulf States and Kuwait.

b. Establishment of a Defense Attaché Office in Kuwait.

4. (S) With regard to an arms policy for the area, we should continue to regard the United Kingdom as the primary arms supplier for the lower Gulf States and Kuwait (Iran and Saudi Arabia are not included in this grouping). However, if we were unwilling even to consider requests for purchase of arms to assist in their self-defense, we could soon find those states turning to radical Arab or communist sources to meet requirements not filled by the British. Therefore, it is recommended that, while we should continue to look to the United Kingdom as the principal arms supplier in this area, the United States should be prepared to consider favorably on a case-by-case basis limited

---

[1] Source: Washington National Records Center, RG 330, OSD Files: FRC 73 A 1250, Persian Gulf 092, 19 June 68, 1968. Secret.

[2] Attached but not printed.

sales of arms to Kuwait and the lower Gulf States to meet legitimate defense needs not met by the United Kingdom.

5. (S) With respect to the establishment of a Defense Attaché Office in Kuwait, there will be a definite need for such representation by the time British military forces depart the area. Even now, increasing Soviet and radical Arab activity in the area and the loss of the Attaché Office at Baghdad call for more complete intelligence collection capability. (Three Soviet Navy ships have visited Persian Gulf ports during the past 2 months.) In view of the lead time required and the current need for representation, the Joint Chiefs of Staff recommend that the Department of State be requested to undertake negotiations with the Government of Kuwait for approval of a Defense Attaché Office.

6. (S) For your information, CINCSTRIKE/USCINCMEAFSA has been informed that action by the Joint Chiefs of Staff on his proposal for upgrading the ships assigned to the Middle East Force will be held in abeyance until such time as the threat may warrant and the Middle East Force has a higher relative priority for available resources.

For the Joint Chiefs of Staff:
J. O. Cobb
Rear Admiral, USN
Deputy Director, Joint Staff

---

148. Record of Meeting[1]

IRG/NEA 68–27 Washington, July 10, 1968.

INTERDEPARTMENTAL REGIONAL GROUP FOR NEAR EAST AND SOUTH ASIA

Record of IRG Meeting—July 10, 1968

The IRG met to consider U.S. *policy and future military presence in the Arabian Sea littoral.* The discussion was focused on a paper (see IRG/NEA 68–24)[2] which had analyzed our continued interest in the area and made certain action proposals.

---

[1] Source: Department of State, IRG/NEA 68–27 Files: Lot 70 D 503, U.S. Policy & Future Military Presence in Arabian Sea Littoral. Secret. Drafted by Sober on July 15.

[2] Document 142.

The IRG noted a recent decision by the Department of Defense, approving in principle the concept of constructing a modest military facility at *Diego Garcia*.[3] It would provide certain capabilities for communications and POL storage, and include an 8,000-foot runway. It could provide a potential backup site in the event that MIDEASTFOR cannot be based at Bahrein after the U.K. withdraws. British agreement is to be sought to fly a British flag over the facility and to obtain whatever financial and manning participation may be possible.

The IRG agreed that new problems will arise as the British withdraw militarily east of Suez, including the Persian Gulf, by the end of 1971. The recent Soviet naval calls at ports in India, Pakistan, the Persian Gulf, East Africa, and Aden presumably foreshadow the Soviet Union's intentions to expand its naval presence in the years ahead.

Focusing on the Persian Gulf area, the IRG reaffirmed its view that the key to the future of the region in the next few years would be developments within and among the various Gulf states themselves, and that it is neither politically feasible nor desirable to "replace" the British presence in the Gulf; our policy should be directed along the lines of encouraging greater cooperation among the Gulf states themselves, and particularly between Saudi Arabia and Iran.

The IRG agreed that *MIDEASTFOR* continues to serve a useful purpose in "showing the flag" and in manifesting a continued U.S. military presence and interest in the region. Militarily, MIDEASTFOR has a potential role in evacuating American citizens in an emergency and could perform certain other limited functions. Its main mission, however, will probably continue to be defined very largely in political and psychological terms. The IRG agreed that, in connection with future decisions on MIDEASTFOR, we should keep in mind the importance of avoiding any impression that the United States Government was backing out of the area.

The IRG decided to defer action on a proposal for a modest expansion of MIDEASTFOR (which currently consists of one tactical command vessel and two destroyers) pending a *further study of MIDEASTFOR's mission*. This study, to be undertaken by Defense and Joint Staff representatives with participation by State and by other agencies as may be appropriate, should consider MIDEASTFOR's capabilities and limitations, in both a military and political sense; the future requirement for a U.S. naval presence in the area; and the question of whether a force of the present size is appropriate

---

[3] See Document 48.

to its mission. This study should be submitted to the IRG for its consideration.

S.S.
Staff Director

MEMBERS PRESENT

> Executive Chairman—Mr. Battle
> AID—Mr. Wheeler
> CIA—Mr. Critchfield
> DOD/ISA—Mr. Schwartz
> Treasury—Mr. Cross
> USIA—Mr. Carter
> OJCS—Brig. Gen. Doyle
> State—Messrs. Davies, Brewer, Eliot (NEA); Hadsel, Ruchti (AF); Ausland
> G/PM; Neuman (L)
> DOD—Mr. Murray
> Staff Director—Mr. Sober

---

149. Memorandum From the Country Director for Saudi Arabia, Kuwait, Yemen, and Aden Affairs (Brewer) to the Assistant Secretary of State for Near Eastern and South Asian Affairs (Battle)[1]

Washington, July 30, 1968.

SUBJECT

> Developments in the People's Republic of Southern Yemen

Anti-regime turbulence in the PRSY hinterland commenced about July 23. Since then, clashes with the military, in Aulaqi tribal districts, and in upper Yafai, Dathina, and adjacent Lahej, Radfan and Haushabi areas of Southern Yemen (see attached map)[2] have posed the first substantial threat to the National Liberation Front (NLF) regime in PRSY since its founding November 30, 1967. A serious complication for the government arises from a sizeable element of Aulaqi officers in the Army whose sentiments parallel those of their kinsmen in the hinterland. According to one report, some hundred Aulaqi officers

---

[1] Source: National Archives and Records Administration, RG 59, Central Files 1967–69, POL 15 S YEMEN. Secret. Drafted by Dinsmore and Brewer.
[2] Attached but not printed.

have been suspended as the result of their petition to the Army High Command in favor of "national unity" (see below). Aulaqi officers have long been lukewarm to the NLF, and were known before independence to harbor some sympathy for FLOSY.

Southern Yemenis have plenty of reasons for unhappiness, no doubt including a growing sense of possible economic disaster ahead of them. There is, moreover, growing impatience with single party government as represented by the NLF and an attempt by anti-government groups to broader representation. This reflects the political ambitions of factions in the country which have been excluded from a share in ruling the country.

An interesting aspect of the situation has been the call by various disparate groups for "national unity", presumably envisaging a coalition government. It is not clear to what extent the up-country disturbances are indigenous in origin, or to what extent they may reflect organization from outside, but signs suggest something of the latter. Representatives of FLOSY, the PRSY Army, and the South Arabian League (SAL) have reportedly been meeting in Beirut since July 23. They are said to be seeking an agreeable basis for a coalition government to take the place of the present single party (NLF) regime, with some moderate NLF participation. The PRSY Foreign Minister went to Taiz, Yemen, on July 29 for urgent discussion with the YARG. Both FLOSY and émigré elements recently returned there, and we surmise the PRSY mission is aimed at getting the YARG to neutralize their possible cross-border activities.

Aden radio on July 28 carried a PRSYG communiqué alleging that Saudi Arabia, "international imperialism" and its intelligence service (read CIA), agents of the Sultans, the SAL and the remnant of FLOSY are behind the trouble. More serious, "NLF Commandos" and "People's Guard" members were asked to report to NLF headquarters to pick up weapons, an indication of less than full Army support for the Government and an act implying there is a lack of security resources available to the PRSY and NLF establishment. On July 29, the regime also called for "general mobilization".

While the NLF has not yet shown any readiness to share the seat of power, President al-Shaabi had, since March, moved toward the center politically in response to Army pressures against the extreme leftist tendencies of some NLF leaders. Now that tribal opposition has broken out, the regime may be faced with its most serious crisis yet. Whether the tribes are only responding to the outside stimulation mentioned above, or whether their move is strictly their own response to what they must consider to be an increasingly intolerable situation, is not clear. Unruly as they are, even under normal conditions, it takes leadership to mount sustained and effective tribal actions. It will take money and more leadership to keep them going if their efforts to assert themselves are not successful. On balance, it would appear more than likely that there is an organization with a pointed objective behind the reports of tribal skirmishes, probably including some Saudi encouragement.

There is just a chance, given the relatively demoralized state of affairs in PRSY at the moment, that a move for power by a combination of anti-radical forces could succeed in either forcing President al-Shaabi to accept a moderate coalition of political forces or to step down. If, on the other hand, he and his regime are able to weather this threat, he will be in debt to the radicals for stemming the opposition. He seems already to be turning to the radicals (i.e. People's Guard) for help. The crucial question now seems to be whether the bulk of the Army will remain loyal and thus succeed in continuing the increasingly divisive inter-tribal disturbances.

We have advised the Office of News in case a question is raised to label as sheerest fancy any reference to PRSY claims that the US is involved in these events. Interested posts have been so informed. We are counselling our Embassy to maintain a low profile and have asked London and Jidda for their host government's assessments of the situation.

---

150. Memorandum From the Deputy Secretary of Defense (Nitze) to the Chairman of the Joint Chiefs of Staff (Wheeler)[1]

Washington, August 2, 1968.

SUBJECT

Persian Gulf Study

I refer to your memorandum JCSM 380–68,[2] dated 19 June 1968, forwarding a study on the Persian Gulf by CINCSTRIKE and requesting appropriate action to (a) establish a U.S. arms policy for Kuwait and the lower Persian Gulf states, and (b) establish a Defense Attaché office in Kuwait.

---

[1] Source: Washington National Records Center, RG 330, OSD Files: FRC 73 A 1250, Persian Gulf 092, 2 Aug 68. Secret.

[2] Document 147.

Over the past months U.S. policy and possible action in the Persian Gulf after British withdrawal have been carefully considered in the IRG as well as by the appropriate agencies. As a result, the U.S. Government has publicly announced that we should not "fill the vacuum" caused by the British withdrawal. By this we mean we should undertake no new programs in the area nor become involved in the affairs of the small Arab states on the Persian Gulf. Instead, we should continue to concentrate our principal efforts to support Iran and Saudi Arabia. The reasons are several:

a. We anticipate that the small states and sheikdoms of the Gulf will naturally look to the U.S. to take the place of the British as a thoroughly enmeshed protector, and it is easier to avoid this role at the outset than it would be to extricate ourselves at some later point.

b. We think that the people of the area, particularly those in Iran and Saudi Arabia, can better manage the situation in the Gulf without additional involvement by the U.S.

c. We already have a high degree of interest in and close relations with Saudi Arabia and Iran. We have in fact just agreed to sell the latter $600 million of additional arms.

Therefore, the U.S. should avoid selling arms to the small states in the area and should permit them to rely on the British or other Western European sources for whatever military equipment or other assistance they may require. (In this connection, General Hall of the British MOD recently surveyed Kuwait's defense forces and found that their matériel requirements were of a low order of priority.) However, even in the event that they turn to non-Western sources for arms, it is preferable that we not become involved in an effort to make the sales ourselves.

I have asked the ISA staff to consider with your office, the Defense Intelligence Agency, and the Department of State the need for a Defense Attaché in Kuwait. I will furnish the results of these considerations to you at a later date.

Paul H. Nitze

151. **Telegram From the Department of State to the Embassy in Iran[1]**

Washington, August 2, 1968, 2350Z.

214602. Subject: Bahrein. Ref: Tehran 5903.[2]

1. FYI. We believe it would be preferable have British continue take lead in attempting resolve problem of Iranian claim to Bahrein. As you know, Ambassador Wright has instructions to probe Shah's intentions and desires (CA–9741).[3] We understand he has requested audience with Shah for next few days. We see real risks in our becoming involved in terms of our relations with all parties to dispute. We also do not wish undercut British efforts find solution. We believe preferable for us remain on sidelines urging parties be flexible in interest finding permanent solution.

2. In this context our pursuing idea of ICJ role in solving dispute appears inadvisable. In addition it is highly unlikely using ICJ to promote solution would be feasible. Statute of court provides that only states may be parties in cases before court. Acceptance Bahrein in such role would have direct implication concerning issue to be litigated, i.e., Iran's claim to sovereignty over island. While Iran would thus presumably prefer UK as adversary, believe we must be particularly careful not to stimulate Shah in this direction since question what UK might be willing consider obviously highly sensitive. While UK has accepted compulsory jurisdiction of ICJ (Article 36(2) of Statute of ICJ annexed to UN Charter) Iran has not and (in absence special agreement with UK for reference this case to court) would be required to do so in order to proceed against UK. Should Iran go this route UK could conceivably find itself in court, but UK in all probability would argue it not a party to dispute and Bahrein would insist UK take such a position. Bahrein would in any case not accept a court decision on Bahrein in which Bahrein not consulted. End FYI.

3. In light foregoing you should inform Shah we believe best way to handle Bahrein problem is by continuing discussions with British

---

[1] Source: National Archives and Records Administration, RG 59, Central Files 1967–69, POL 19 BAHRAIN IS. Secret; Exdis. Drafted by Eliot; cleared in draft by Brewer, Wehmeyer, Assistant Legal Adviser for UN Affairs Herbert K. Reis, and Officer in Charge of UN Political Affairs Betty-Jane Jones; and approved by Rockwell.

[2] In telegram 5903 from Tehran, July 30, Ambassador Meyer reported that during a July 29 discussion of Bahrain Island, the Shah suggested taking the issue either to the UN Security Council or to the International Court of Justice. Meyer said he tried to discourage the Security Council action, and secured the Shah's approval of having U.S. legal experts determine the feasibility of seeking an ICJ opinion. (Ibid.)

[3] Dated July 29. (Ibid.)

and that we doubtful that ICJ can play role in dispute. You might wish brief Ambassador Wright on this exchange.

4. Re Security Council consideration, you should continue as appropriate discourage any Iranian ideas that resort SC would be helpful. It our view public debate problem of this nature, in which parties tend state positions in extreme terms, likely make solution more, rather than less, difficult.

5. Ansary has not mentioned ICJ possibility in meetings with Department officials since his return although he had opportunity during brief discussion on FAA and Bahrein with Under Secretary Rostow, July 30.[4]

Rusk

---

[4] In telegram 5967 from Tehran, August 5, Meyer responded that although he shared the Department's view that the U.S. Government should not get involved, he hoped that some face-saving device regarding Bahrain could be provided to the Shah before December. (Ibid.)

---

152.   Telegram From the Department of State to the Embassy in Italy[1]

Washington, August 2, 1968, 2354Z.

214612. State 213375.[2]

1. FYI. As Embassy no doubt aware, PRSY and other Arab media have alleged USG involved in current unrest in PRSY. Embassy Aden's 1544[3] (being repeated Rome) suggests PRSY regime may even see advantage in using USG as scapegoat for its troubles and break diplomatic

---

[1] Source: National Archives and Records Administration, RG 59, Central Files 1967–69, POL 23–9 S YEMEN. Confidential. Drafted by Brewer and Dinsmore, cleared by Rush W. Taylor, Jr., of EUR/AIS, and approved by Rockwell. Repeated to Aden, Jidda, and London.

[2] Telegram 213375 to Aden, August 1, instructed the Embassy to tell Foreign Office Permanent Secretary Rashad that although his private assurances that he recognized that there was no U.S. involvement in the current disturbances in Southern Yemen were welcome, the U.S. Government could not ignore the tendentious radio and press items accusing the United States of complicity in anti-regime activities without expressing its concern. (Ibid., POL S YEMEN–US)

[3] Dated July 30. (Ibid., POL 7 S YEMEN)

relations. Moreover, PRSY FonMin Dhalai has been in Taiz and may well have been filling YARG officials full of lurid and unsupported allegations. End FYI.

2. Since Italians looking after our interests in Yemen, we believe you should inform FonOff of substance para 3 below. You should add that we would have no objection Italian authorities passing this info to YARG Ambassador Rome, and to YARG in Taiz, in event they believe this useful.

3. There has not been, nor is there now, any USG connection with recent turbulence in Southern Yemen. Recent Arab broadcasts, and any other reports YARG may have received to contrary, are inaccurate and should be carefully re-examined. USG, of course, unaware what allegations PRSY representatives may be making in private as to alleged USG involvement but wishes to set the facts straight. Allegations that USG backing or participating PRSY's tribal troubles are sheerest fancy. Current YARG leaders should particularly appreciate this, since they familiar with events in spring 1967 in Yemen when previous Government of YAR leveled similarly baseless charges against USG.

Rusk

---

153. **Information Memorandum From the Assistant Secretary of State for Near Eastern and South Asian Affairs (Battle) to Secretary of State Rusk[1]**

Washington, August 5, 1968.

SUBJECT

Implications for Yemen Problem of Current Dissidence in Southern Yemen

The serious tribal dissidence which broke out in the People's Republic of Southern Yemen (PRSY) on July 25 has introduced considerable fluidity in that quarter of Arabia. It could have important implications for solution of the Yemen problem. Dissident groups in PRSY comprise disparate tribal and political elements with apparently little direct outside support. But the Saudis have no doubt privately been

---

[1] Source: National Archives and Records Administration, RG 59, Central Files 1967–69, POL 23–9 S YEMEN. Secret. Drafted by Brewer on August 2 and cleared by Rockwell. A copy was sent to Austin (INR/RNA). Rusk's initials on the memorandum indicate he read it.

giving mild encouragement to dissident exile groups. In the Yemen Arab Republic (YARG), Prime Minister al-Amri has for more than a month permitted anti-PRSY elements to take up residence in Taiz, knowing full well that they would mount efforts to undermine PRSY.

Parallel to these developments in the PRSY situation have been renewed indications that both the Saudis and the YARG would like to settle the Yemen conflict. The Saudis were notably disheartened by the failure of their efforts last spring to make the Royalist regime more unified and effective. Al-Amri is worried by radicals in his own government and army, as well as by their connections with the NLF regime in Aden.

The resultant situation is both complex and confused. We do not believe that any direct coordination exists between the Saudis and al-Amri nor do we think the Saudis are in any major way responsible for PRSY's current turbulence. But one key factor has emerged: both King Faisal and al-Amri have important reasons for wishing to see the demise of the NLF regime in Aden. Al-Amri may well have calculated that, by permitting PRSY exile groups to operate from Yemeni territory, he would increase his chances of working out some meaningful compromise with Saudi Arabia which would end the longstanding Yemen civil war. It is too early to predict what may come of this, but at least the Saudis and al-Amri have a common interest in hoping that the Government of President Qahtan al-Shaabi in Aden will soon be overthrown. Should events in PRSY not require al-Amri to trim his sails in the Aden regime's direction, the likelihood of some movement on the Yemen issue would seem to be enhanced.

154.   Telegram From the Department of State to the Embassy in Southern Yemen[1]

Washington, August 5, 1968, 2232Z.

215394. State 213375 (Notal).[2]

1. In addition recent anti-US propaganda by PRSY media, Dept has noted with concern August 5 ticker item from Aden, carried on Cairo MENA, to effect FonMin Dhalai at rally August 4 at al-Hawtah in Lahej, directly accused USG of complicity in current troubles. According report, Dhalai stated USG "closely involved in the current events in PRSY" and "certain elements taking part in the mutiny have been in contact with the US Embassies in Beirut and Asmara". Dhalai then apparently referred to fact Ali Gallas and Asnaj had called on US Consul in Asmara and that another individual (he indicated al-Aswadi) maintained contact with US Ambassador in Beirut.

2. Question endemic PRSY suspicion USG has been raised by Dhalai and Qahtan with Chargé periodically during last two months (Aden 1409, 1442 and 1528—Notal).[3] On each occasion Chargé has denied reports of any such improper USG activity. Dhalai told Chargé June 5 that he would let Chargé know "if there were any proofs" that we should discuss but failed to do so other than allege that Asnaj present when Asmara officer saw Gallas (para 5 Aden 1442). Chargé categorically denied these reports to Qahtan July 24 (Aden 1528). In circumstances, we assume PRSY seeking scapegoat for its upcountry problems and may be planning either PNG someone from Aden or possibly breaking diplomatic relations with us.

3. While we have little influence over PRSYG leaders in their current mood, we would prefer remain in Aden if this can be done with dignity. Accordingly, Chargé should request appointment with FonMin to convey orally personal message[4] in para 4 from USG.

---

[1] Source: National Archives and Records Administration, RG 59, Central Files 1967–69, POL S YEMEN–US. Confidential; Immediate. Drafted by Brewer; cleared by Rockwell, Chief of the Office of Operations Evacuation and Relocation Staff James P. McDonnell, and Director of the Office of Special Consular Services Allyn C. Donaldson (paragraph 6); and approved by Battle. Repeated to Jidda, Asmara, London, Addis Ababa, and Beirut.

[2] See footnote 2, Document 152.

[3] Telegram 1409 from Aden, June 5; telegram 1442 from Aden, June 17; telegram 1528 from Aden, July 24. (National Archives and Records Administration, RG 59, Central Files 1967–69, POL S YEMEN–US)

[4] Telegram 219105 to Aden, August 12, instructed the Embassy to change "personal message" to "message from USG." (Ibid.)

4. "Excellency: In context current situation in PRSY, USG has been concerned to note number[5] public references implying some USG role in current situation. We have been particularly disturbed to note one press report to the effect that Your Excellency may now have given public acceptance to such unsubstantiated charges. Your Excellency is reported to have described the USG as being closely involved in these events, and to have said that certain elements unfriendly to your government have been in contact with US Embassies in Beirut and Asmara. The USG wishes categorically to assure Your Excellency that it is in no way involved in the current situation nor have our Embassies engaged in any improper activities. Our Chargé fully explained to you in June the innocuous nature of Consulate Asmara's contact with former local employee of the then Congen in Aden. In the interest of maintaining normal relations between our two countries, we earnestly hope that Your Excellency will accept this assurance that our officials are in no way involved in the current difficult situation. Should you receive allegations to the contrary, we would hope that these might be discussed with the US representative in Aden before there is a public airing of unsubstantiated charges."

5. In the event addressee posts contacted by press, you should limit your response to denying that USG officials in any way involved in current events in PRSY.

6. In view uncertainties re PRSY actions, Embassy Aden may wish take preliminary steps internally which would facilitate closing post and transferring American interests to protecting power. We assume this would be British but would appreciate your recommendation.[6]

Rusk

---

[5] Telegram 219105 instructed the Embassy to change "number" to "continuing."

[6] In telegram 1608 from Aden, August 14, Acting Chargé d'Affaires Thomas W. Davis, Jr., reported that he just met with Foreign Minister Dhalai to deliver the Department's message. Dhalai had expressed no regret for his recent anti-American comments, but discussed the subject in a conciliatory manner and expressed his desire for good relations with the U.S. Government and for U.S. support in regard to the external dangers facing Southern Yemen. (National Archives and Records Administration, RG 59, Central Files 1967–69, POL S YEMEN–US)

155.   Briefing Memorandum From the Acting Country Director for
       Iranian Affairs (McClelland) to the Deputy Assistant
       Secretary of State for Near Eastern and South Asian Affairs
       (Handley)[1]

Washington, August 28, 1968.

SUBJECT

Talking Points for your meeting with CINCSTRIKE survey team making Persian
Gulf defense study, August 29, 10:00 a.m.

During his 11–12 June 1968 visit,[2] the Shah of Iran expressed concern
to the President about the security of the Persian Gulf after the 1971 British withdrawal and asked the President what types of weapons the US
would recommend that he obtain for the most effective defense of the
Straits of Hormuz and the Persian Gulf area. The President agreed to
look into the matter and later decided to offer the Shah a comprehensive
military study of the problem. This offer was conveyed to the Shah by
Ambassador Meyer on July 29 and was promptly accepted.

The Joint Chiefs of Staff have drawn up the Terms of Reference
for a military survey to be carried out by CINCSTRIKE (attached).[3] A
team of seven CINCSTRIKE officers headed by Major General Rich-
mond, USAF, will call at the Department for a briefing a few hours
before departure to Iran for an on-the-spot survey.

You may wish to make the following points for your briefing of
the CINCSTRIKE team:

1. *Background.* This study is extremely sensitive and could have
important implications not only for Iran but also for the other States
of the Gulf area with whom we have good relations.

a) Our close diplomatic relations with Iran are to a large degree
dependent on our military cooperation so that the study must take
into account, in its conclusions, other than strictly military factors. Iran
has reasonable but not unlimited financial resources, and its ability to
absorb and maintain new complex equipment is limited. Our position
continues to be to discourage large military expenditures that would
adversely affect Iran's economic development and not to recommend
equipment that could not be effectively utilized.

---

[1] Source: National Archives and Records Administration, RG 59, Central Files, 1967–
69, POL 33 PERSIAN GULF. Secret. Drafted by Acting Country Director for Iranian
Affairs Walter M. McClelland.

[2] For documentation on the Shah's visit, see *Foreign Relations*, 1964–1968, vol. XXII,
Documents 290–300.

[3] Attached but not printed.

b) Our policy in the Gulf is one of encouraging maximum cooperation among the Persian Gulf riparian States to work out the problems
there. (We have been encouraged by the recently reported Median Line
agreement.) The following factors must therefore be taken into account:

i) Iran's armaments should not be so augmented as to frighten
other riparian states and thus endanger prospects for Arab-Iranian
cooperation. (By 1971, Iran will have 2 squadrons of F–4's, a Radar
Warning net, a destroyer, and several small craft in the area.)

ii) Conclusions should take into consideration the international
character of the Persian Gulf.

c) We do not consider that there is an imminent threat to Iran in
the Gulf (although the situation could deteriorate); nor do we believe
that Iran could successfully meet a real Soviet threat by itself. What
we believe is needed is a reasonable augmentation to the forces the
GOI will have in the Gulf in 1971—if such an augmentation appears
necessary—to improve Iranian defense of its "lifeline" and legitimate
interests there.

2. *Team Activities in Iran.* We would hope that the team would be
very guarded in any discussions with Iranian officials, give them no
papers, and not indicate the directions in which their conclusions and
recommendations tend. The team should take the attitude that it is
going to Iran to learn and listen and will bring data back for technical
evaluation before writing the report. (Para 7 of attachment covers the
points of sensitivity of the study and prohibition of discussion with
the Iranians.) Any problems or questions should be resolved with the
Ambassador in cooperation with the Country Team (Para 6 of attachment).[4]

---

[4] For a record of Deputy Assistant Secretary Handley's briefing of the CINCSTRIKE
Survey Team, see memorandum of conversation, August 29. (National Archives and
Records Administration, RG 59, Central Files 1967–69, POL 33 PERSIAN GULF)

156.   Memorandum of Conversation[1]

Washington, September 13, 1968.

SUBJECT

US/UK Middle East Talks—Washington—September 13, 1968

PARTICIPANTS

UK	US
Sir Denis Allen, Foreign Office	Mr. Battle, Assistant Secretary, NEA
Edward E. Tomkins, Minister, UK Embassy	Mr. Rockwell, Deputy Assistant Secretary, NEA
Michael Wilford, Counselor, UK Embassy	Mr. Brewer, Country Director, NEA/ARP
Alan Urwick, First Secretary, UK Embassy	Mr. Gatch, NEA/ARP

1. Persian Gulf: Saudi/Iranian/Kuwaiti Relations; the Bahrain Question

Sir Denis Allen said the UK aim was to try and steer things towards stability on a local basis in the Persian Gulf while the UK still has a military presence there. Fufilling this aim is difficult because of local Arab rivalries and because of the Iranian objection to the Federation of Arab Amirates (FAA) including Bahrain. Immediately after the UK announced its intentions to withdraw, these rivalries intensified as the parties concerned came to the UK for assistance in getting future arrangements worked out in the Gulf, of course on terms favorable to their particular interests. The UK had worked hard for six months behind the scenes, urging the need for compromise. The UK could not of course please everyone, but there had been some slight success, particularly in recent weeks when hopeful progress had been made. The countries concerned seemed to be trying to get together. Admittedly the Iranians were not giving very much, as reflected in talks UK Ambassador Wright has had with the Shah, but there were encouraging signs. After the initial meeting of the FAA, the Iranians blamed the "imperialists"—i.e. the British, for the formation of the FAA. They got this on record in a more or less pro forma way, and then went to work building bridges with individual Trucial States. They had worked on Rashid of Dubai, had received the Rulers of Ras al-Khaimah and Fujaira in Tehran, the Ruler of Sharja was also going, Zayyid of Abu Dhabi was sending a son to school in Iran, etc. The UK believes Iran is trying to be construc-

---

[1] Source: National Archives and Records Administration, RG 59, Central Files 1967–69, POL 33 PERSIAN GULF. Secret. Drafted by John N. Gatch (NEA/ARP) on September 18.

tive as the dominant power in the area in establishing these direct contacts.

The Iranians have told the British it would be easier if the UK could hold up the formation of the FAA until after some of the area problems are worked out, notably Bahrain. The Saudis, on the other hand, want the UK to press ahead with the formation of the FAA, believing that they would then find it easier to talk to the Iranians. Sir Denis noted, however, that the Saudis have been very helpful lately, for example in the median line negotiations. It appears to the UK that both Saudi Arabia and Iran are being careful not to upset the plans for the Shah's meeting with Faisal in November. He added that the Kuwaitis also have been helpful recently, particularly in connection with the FAA July meeting. Foreign Minister Sabah al-Ahmad had encouraged the participating states to work constructively.

All in all, the British felt there has been a great deal of movement in the right direction since January. We must not forget, however, that the Bahrain issue is still unsolved. The UK thinks the Shah is perplexed and views Bahrain as a public relations problem. He wants to get it out of the way. This was why he suggested the possibility of a plebiscite. The UK is reluctant to get caught in the middle, since the Ruler of Bahrain could not contemplate a plebiscite. Arab rulers traditionally do not lay matters of this nature before their peoples. Further, the Ruler of Bahrain fears that a plebiscite would stir up radical Arab elements and would make the small Iranian minority in Bahrain uneasy. The UK had nonetheless discussed the idea of a plebiscite with the Ruler, but had received the expected negative reaction. Sir Denis said that Iran, Saudi Arabia, Kuwait and Bahrain had all approached the UK unilaterally seeking to find a solution to the Bahrain issue. Kuwait may prove to be helpful. Sir Denis asserted that the Iranians actually have moved a good way, since Tehran had recently muted its public attacks on the FAA and Bahrain.

Mr. Battle said that we and the UK obviously shared the assessment that the countries of the Gulf region must solve their own problems. We also both believed the key to the overall problem is a good relationship between Iran and Saudi Arabia; and, to a lesser extent, between Iran on the one hand and Kuwait and the smaller states on the other. We have been encouraged by the improvement in the situation since the low point of the cancellation of the Shah's visit to Saudi Arabia last February. We see a new sense of common purpose. We think it very important that the Shah's visit to Saudi Arabia be successful.[2] We also

---

[2] The Shah made a state visit to Saudi Arabia in November 1968.

are pleased with the apparent settlement of the median line question.[3] We must all remember however that the situation is fragile, and could easily be upset by a wrong word or a wrong move. Both the US and the UK must continue to work diligently and quietly behind the scene.

Regarding the FAA, Mr. Battle said we have tried to convince the Iranians that it is not a UK plot. We sense that the Iranians are a little more relaxed on this issue.

Mr. Rockwell said he did not see too much comfort in the situation, since the Iranians still want the British to solve all the problems "150%" in Iran's favor. Since this obviously will not suit the Arab side, had the UK any new plans. How did the UK see it all coming out?

Sir Denis said the British really could not foresee the end at this stage. They are encouraging contacts among all the parties concerned and are trying to make them think about the problems facing them. Mr. Battle said we find it encouraging that all of the parties are talking to the UK.

Sir Denis said for the moment the UK is sitting back until after the Shah's visit with Faisal. He agreed that the situation is delicate and easy to upset. Mr. Rockwell wondered whether the Iranians weren't having direct contacts with the Trucial rulers for the purpose of upsetting the FAA. Allen said this was a possibility, but the UK had no indication they are working on the rulers this way. The UK had argued with Iran that the FAA would provide a way to close out the Bahrain claim gracefully, since Bahrain would be submerged in the greater whole. The Iranians had countered by saying because of Bahrain's possible inclusion in the FAA, Iran came into conflict with the other eight states with whom they want good relations and whom they would like to see united. Sir Denis said the UK had no evidence one way or another whether the Iranians were sincere when they said this.

Mr. Rockwell said it could be argued that the Iranians were trying to gain control over various of the rulers. Mr. Brewer noted that Iran had moved rapidly after the announcement of the UK withdrawal and had developed much knowledge and many contacts in the Trucial area which they had not had before. They now have a greater capability to exploit differences. Iran seems more relaxed on the surface about the FAA now, perhaps because they believe they can make it not work if they choose. Mr. Brewer also said that if Bahrain were excluded from

---

[3] On August 21 following negotiations in Tehran, National Iranian Oil Company (NIOC) Chairman Manuchehr Eqbal and Saudi Minister of Petroleum Shaykh Ahmad Zaki Yamani initialed an agreement on a new median line for the area in the Persian Gulf disputed between Saudi Arabia and Iran. (Telegram 6139 from Tehran, August 22, 1968, National Archives and Records Administration, RG 59, Central Files 1967–69, POL 33 PERSIAN GULF)

the FAA the present lower Gulf balance would be upset and an 8-member FAA would be less likely to work. The problem is still very much before us. Sir Denis said there is no doubt of the hazards. He recognized that there are small differences that can be exploited by Iran. That is why it is important to bring the area states together on common ground.

Mr. Rockwell asked whether the UK saw any possibility of progress on Bahrain coming out of the Shah–Faisal talks. Sir Denis said that the UK did not expect any dramatic solution. A long process is involved and it is difficult to see too far ahead. Mr. Battle said we had no particular solution to suggest, but believed that if situation deteriorates everyone will look to the UK to save it. We cannot relax and perhaps new ideas should be "pumped in". We will do our best to help but have no plan or certain solutions. We will continue to work behind the scenes but want the UK to retain as much influence as possible for as long as possible.

Mr. Brewer noted that there was a negative aspect in the relations between Saudi Arabia and Iran as far as the FAA is concerned—i.e. when the FAA showed some signs of progress this soured Iranian/Saudi relations. In this connection, keeping the importance of the Shah–Faisal meeting in mind, we had been encouraged by several unconfirmed reports that the FAA meeting scheduled for October might be postponed until after the Shah's visit to Saudi Arabia.

Sir Denis said the UK was conscious of the desirability of postponing the October meeting. The FAA countries themselves are becoming more aware of the need to take Iranian interests into account. While they might decide on their own it would be a good idea to postpone, the UK did not want to press the rulers at this point.

2. FAA

Sir Denis said the obvious question is—will it work? So far it is a paper structure and it might very well be that within the structure each ruler will go his own way. It may also be that all efforts will break down and there will not be any FAA.

Mr. Battle said there will have to be a lot of work done over a long period of time just to set the organization in the right direction—let alone solving the problems of sovereignty, judicial systems etc. for each state.

Sir Denis said the process of delay poses problems for the UK in connection with renegotiating treaties with the individual rulers—it obviously would be better to deal with one nation, but if the formation of the FAA took too long the UK would have to deal unilaterally. The UK has the same problem in the defense field. The British are keen that the Trucial Oman Scouts be maintained. They feel that the TOS is the right organization for the security of the FAA if the FAA is sufficiently well established to direct the TOS. The UK is raising the pay of the TOS and plans to continuing seconding UK officers to it until 1971, and perhaps afterwards. Officers could also be made available by private contract. However the UK is coming up against individual demands from Dubai and Abu Dhabi which are attempting to stake out private ground for themselves by strengthening their own security forces—possibly in the hope of dominating the FAA or possibly foreseeing that the FAA will not work. Zayyid is ahead in this game because he has had more resources. The British are trying to restrain his demands. Rashid wants to expand the Dubai Defense Force. The British are trying to discourage him by suggesting that an additional TOS be stationed in Dubai. This may not satisfy him. Even if the British have to expand the DDF, they hope eventually that it and the TOS would be made available to the FAA. The problem is that the rulers seem to have a split-minded approach—they are working on forming the FAA but at the same time are working individually to strengthen their own particular states.

Sir Denis noted that the UK has done a great deal in the past to improve the security situation in the area by building up police and counter-intelligence forces in the various states. The UK has had to be careful to avoid overdoing this and thus accentuating rivalries.

Mr. Battle said he was glad the UK and not the US had the responsibility, and attendant problems, of military assistance in the area. Sir Denis said it was important that the defense efforts were geared into the FAA.

Meanwhile, progress is being made in turning over local administrative institutions. Retrocession is proceeding well, particularly in Bahrain. This will go on even if the FAA does not succeed. The UK felt it still had a bit of time. Mr. Battle agreed but said if time dragged on until 1971 without an FAA or alternate arrangements for stability, our mutual interests would suffer.

Sir Denis pointed out that the UK intends to maintain a position in the Gulf, except for defense and special treaty arrangements. The UK will be prepared to consider aid, technical assistance or military missions in the same way it is doing with Kuwait. Mr. Battle stressed that the US wanted the UK there in all fields. The UK has a big stake in the Gulf area.

3. Miscellaneous Gulf Matters

a. Kuwait Defense

Sir Denis said the UK was grateful that the US continues to tell Kuwait that the UK should be its principal source of military supplies. He wanted to report the following results of the recent UK Military Team visit to Kuwait. The team had recommended:

(1) An integrated air defense system with two squadron of Lightnings

(2) Expansion to two Hawker Hunter squadrons

(3) Slight expansion of the army, including increased armor

(4) Establishment of a small navy. Its nucleus would be six fast patrol boats with surface-to-surface missiles

(5) Higher priority on training

(6) Establishment of a better administrative system for the Kuwait armed forces.

Sir Denis said all of these recommendations had been accepted by the Kuwaitis, except that the Kuwaitis were still considering the addition of some strike aircraft to the Kuwait Air Force. They had Mirage-5's in mind. The UK was attempting to discourage them but the issue was still unresolved. Mr. Rockwell noted that if Kuwait and Iraq got patrol craft with surface-to-surface missiles this would stir up the Iranians.

(b) Abu Dhabi–Dubai

Mr. Brewer asked whether the initial Abu Dhabi–Dubai federation was legally dead, since its status would have relevance for the two off-shore oil concessions involved. Sir Denis said he believed it was moribund and indicated that any change in oil concession boundaries was most unlikely.

(c) TOS

Mr. Brewer asked whether HMG might be willing to extend financial assistance to the TOS after 1971. Sir Denis did not rule out the possibility, but said the UK hoped the FAA would finance it. He could not give a categorical answer, however. The UK was approaching Bahrain in the same spirit—i.e. assisting Bahrain now with the National Guard and the airport in the expectation that Bahrain would provide the finances after the UK military withdrawal.

(d) Retrocession

Mr. Brewer asked how the UK military forces on Bahrain would be affected by the retrocession process. Sir Denis said they would be the last to be affected and that the UK would really maintain jurisdiction under the current status of forces agreement until the final withdrawal. Mr. Brewer noted that this would be helpful to us in connection with MIDEASTFOR.

4. MIDEASTFOR

Mr. Battle said we have no present plans to augment or decrease MIDEASTFOR. Additionally we have no plans to move MIDEASTFOR from Bahrain after the British military withdrawal, although we would have to examine alternate bases for MIDEASTFOR on a contingency basis.

Sir Denis said he appreciated this information. The UK does have a problem in planning the dismantling of its own facilities. In effect the UK would like to give us first refusal of what is there. The sooner the UK could learn what we needed the more orderly the planning could be. Mr. Rockwell asked whether we might have a list of what was available. Mr. Wilford said he believed "everything was for sale", since the UK will not be retaining any military force on Bahrain.

Mr. Battle said the studies and the decisions regarding MIDEAST-FOR would be made here in Washington and we would need precise information. Sir Denis said it would be appropriate to use the US Embassy–Foreign Office–Ministry of Defense channel in London. Mr. Battle agreed and said that we would respond to the British when we had a clearer idea of what MIDEASTFOR might require.

5. US Diplomatic Representation in the Gulf Area

Mr. Battle said we have no intention at the moment of opening an office in the area pending the inauguration of the FAA and a determination of where its capital will be. We are, however, definitely interested in representation there. The administrative processes for setting up a new office take time and we want to be ready to move when the occasion arises. We would like the UK views on this concept.

Sir Denis said it was an awkward situation. The US was really the victim of the delay surrounding the FAA. The UK was relieved to hear that the US is not immediately planning to open an office, since it would be difficult to decide where to put it. A decision now in favor of Abu Dhabi, Dubai or wherever would inevitably lead to an intensification of local rivalries. It would also probably lead to demands by the UAR to be allowed to open an office. The UK simply believes it would be premature for the US to go ahead now.

Mr. Battle, in accepting this judgment, wanted the British to bear our interest in mind.

Sir Denis then turned to the possibility of the US opening an office in Muscat. The UK would welcome this. Mr. Brewer noted that we had had an office in Muscat for many years, but that at present we were not in a position to reopen the post. This situation would, however, change as oil production and income grows and more Americans go there. It is not unlikely that in the next few years we will want to re-open an office, particularly should the Sultan decide to spend more time at the capital. However, Muscat does not have the same priority with us as has the FAA. In this connection, Mr. Brewer wondered if the UK position now is that the UK has no objection to the US opening an office as soon as it is clear where the capital of the FAA will be.

Sir Denis said this is the UK position in principle, but the British would want to look at the position again when the capital is determined.

For example, if the FAA chose Bahrain, this might pose serious problems. Mr. Battle said we appreciated the delicacy of the situation. We want to coordinate fully with the UK. We find these present discussions on the subject useful and look forward to further discussions as the situation evolves. Sir Denis said the UK reluctance was prompted by expediency rather than principle.

Mr. Brewer recalled the history of Kuwait's entrance into the UN—i.e. the Soviets withdrew their veto on the understanding that they would be permitted to open a mission in Kuwait. Mr. Brewer wondered whether the Soviets might use the same tactics at such time as the FAA might apply for UN membership. Sir Denis said the UK had not done much speculation on this point. His immediate reaction was that in the beginning it might be better for the FAA to join a few specialized UN agencies rather than seek full membership. He had no doubt that if the FAA achieved UN membership status the Soviets would want to establish relations.

Mr. Battle said Soviet interest in the area was clear. Sir Denis agreed, and said the Soviets at the moment appeared to be watching and waiting, in much the same way as the UAR is. The UK had lately noted very little in the way of adverse propaganda or subversive efforts from either the Soviets or the UAR.

6. Iraq

Mr. Battle asked how the UK assessed the situation. Allen said the question in Iraq now, as usual, is the possibility of survival of the present regime. The UK impression is that the regime's base is narrower than previous ones. Takriti and Ammash seem to be the strong men. The UK Embassy has had routine contacts with the new regime. The Embassy judges the regime as trying to establish an image of respectability, but doubts that it has wide popularity. The best that can be said about it is that it is sort of a middle, moderate Ba'ath regime, not as bad as the Syrian one.

According to Sir Denis, the Iraqis are judging all countries by their stand on the Palestine problem. This puts the Soviets, the Communist Chinese and, just barely, the French in the Iraq plus column. The UK of course doesn't pass as a friend, but there has been no extreme denunciation of the UK in Iraq. To the contrary there have been some hopeful signs. The Iraqi boycott on UK goods has been lifted and UK-Iraqi commerce is returning to normal. The British Council probably will reopen on a modest basis before the end of the year. The UK is also exploring the possibility of providing some technical assistance to Iraq.

Sir Denis asked how we saw the situation. Did we see a possibility of an unholy marriage between Iraq and Syria? Mr. Battle said we do not of course have the opportunity of talking to either of them. Our impression was that things in Iraq look a bit better. There is, however, little likelihood of a resumption of US-Iraqi relations soon. This will no doubt depend on what the UAR does. We still consider Iraq as basically unstable, and we are concerned about the formation of the Eastern Arab Command of Iraq, Jordan and Syria. He noted that if King Hussein departs from the scene, all bets are off with Iraq, Syria and Jordan. The situation would then be most unpredictable.

Sir Denis said there have been no recent developments in the Iraq Petroleum Company's relations with Iraq. IPC is quietly hopeful that the situation will not get worse, but has just about written off the likelihood of access to the North Rumaila fields on a regular basis. Mr. Urwick noted the possibility that IPC might exploit the fields on a contract basis for the Iraq National Oil Company.

Sir Denis concluded the discussion on Iraq by noting that the UK has not talked at all to the Iraqis regarding Gulf developments. He supposed that they would at some point express an interest. Mr. Gatch recalled that Iraq had reserved the right to have its interests taken into account in the event of a settlement of the Iran–Kuwait median line question.

7. Yemen–South Yemen

Mr. Brewer characterized the situation in Yemen as a mess. The civil war between the Republicans and the Royalists goes on, and at the same time there has been a mutiny within the Republican army ranks. Armi seems to have survived this, in part by sending off the dissident officers to Algeria for "training". Nonetheless his base of power is narrower. Consequently there is less likelihood of his being able to establish contact with the Saudis in order to work out through them a compromise settlement with the Royalists, who were themselves split into factions.

In South Yemen, Mr. Brewer said, we have noted with concern the agreement on military and technical assistance with the Soviets, and also that the PRSY Foreign Minister was on a mission to Peking. He foresaw the possibility of the Soviets and the Chinese Communists competing for influence in PRSY as they had in Yemen a decade before.

Sir Denis speculated on the possibility of Yemen and South Yemen uniting eventually. Mr. Brewer said this was not likely. What was less unlikely was the possibility that Yemen would split, with perhaps the Imam regaining power in the north. In that event, it was possible that the southern half would join forces with PRSY.

8. Conclusion

At this point Mr. Battle said the items for discussion on the agenda had been covered. He had two further matters he would like to discuss.

a. Nasser's Health

Mr. Battle asked whether the UK had an assessment. Sir Denis said the UK had gone over various medical reports carefully. The consensus seems to be that Nasser's symptoms suggest his diabetes has advanced to a stage where insulin treatment is not effective. When this happens, the diabetic tires easily and is not capable of sustained effort. If this diagnosis is correct, Nasser could not now be treated in a way to prevent further decline. The decline is slow and could go on for a long time, but eventually he probably will reach a stage where he will decide to remove himself from office.

Mr. Battle said this was substantially our understanding. He noted that Nasser's condition had become aggravated by the extreme tension he has been under during the past year and a half. We thought Nasser might be able to function for a year or two or even longer, but the trend is inevitably downward.

b. The Fatah

Mr. Battle asked whether the UK had a current assessment of foreign connection with the Fatah. We had noted intelligence reports indicating the Fatah had been using Chinese Communist equipment, including mines. Sir Denis said the UK did not have much new, and said that a current assessment would be useful. Mr. Battle noted that the activities of the Fatah often seemed directed as much at the host nations, particularly Jordan, as at the Israelis. Sir Denis said he believed the Fatah was bound to grow as long as the Israelis remained in occupation.

157. Memorandum of Conversation[1]

Washington, October 23, 1968.

SUBJECT

Bahrain Situation; US-Bahrain Relations

PARTICIPANTS

Mr. Roy Lay, Chairman, Bahrain Petroleum Company, New York
Mr. J. J. Josephson, General Manager, BAPCO, Bahrain
Mr. Ed Lavery, Caltex Representative, Washington
Mr. Rodger P. Davies, Deputy Assistant Secretary, NEA
Mr. William D. Brewer, Country Director, NEA/ARP
Mr. James E. Akins, Deputy Director, E/FSE
Mr. David G. Newton, Economic Officer, NEA/ARP

Mr. Lay said that Mr. Josephson was completing his home leave and returning to Bahrain shortly. He thought it was a good time to compare notes on the situation.

Mr. Lay explained that the Ruler of Bahrain has a very high regard for Americans. His relationship with BAPCO and Mr. Josephson is much closer than an ordinary business relationship. The Ruler remembers the warm treatment that he was given during his visit to the US two years ago. He hopes one day to see tangible expressions of US interest in Bahrain.

Mr. Davies responded that the USG has a strong interest in the Gulf. We are concerned at what will come after the British withdrawal. We have attempted to smooth dispositions ruffled because of Saudi-Iranian differences over Bahrain. Responding to Mr. Josephson's questions, he opined that Bahrain was a matter of considerable face for the Shah. Faisal has acted with considerable dignity and is looking forward to the Shah's visit on November 9 when we hope some progress on this issue may be feasible.

Mr. Lay said that he felt that Faisal would never stand for Iranian "muscling in" on Bahrain, but he felt the King doubted the Iranians would go so far. He asked why the Shah did not recognize the situation as it is. Mr. Davies responded that what the Iranians needed was a formula to permit them to back away gracefully. The Shah's formula, a plebiscite, is not regarded as compatible with Shaikh Isa's dignity. However, Mr. Davies said that he personally was taken with the idea of some sort of "consensus" involving consultation with local leaders,

---

[1] Source: National Archives and Records Administration, RG 59, Central Files 1967–69, POL 19 BAHRAIN IS. Confidential. Drafted by David G. Newton (NEA/ARP) on October 30.

as the UN did in Libya. If there were a plebiscite, the Iranians as a minority would lose. Mr. Brewer underlined the fact that the plebiscite desired by the Shah would have to be specific. It would ask people whether they wanted to join Iran or not. The Iranian idea of a plebiscite has been put to Shaikh Isa by the British but turned down. Mr. Davies said that he did not think the Shah would take Bahrain by force, but he evidently could not accept a change of status which would impair his claim.

Mr. Lay said that the Ruler was deeply concerned and preoccupied over the impending British withdrawal. Mr. Brewer responded that we were worried that the local rulers might feel that we had no interest in the area because we failed to step in and solve their problems. We would, of course, like to see them solved, but it is very difficult for *us* to do so.

Mr. Josephson said that the Ruler had been approached twice by the Russians from Baghdad to permit a twelve-man team to visit Bahrain. The Ruler is "scared to death" and hasn't even acknowledged their request. Mr. Brewer pointed out that some sort of federation, such as the FAA, would presumably apply for UN membership. The Russians could agree or veto, as in the case of Kuwait in 1961. Their price would no doubt be establishment of a Russian resident mission.

Mr. Lay indicated that the Ruler had his doubts about the success of the FAA. He and the local merchants would like to see it work but are skeptical, in view of inertia and jealousy of some of the local rulers. Mr. Brewer said that it was his hunch that the FAA would be established for lack of an alternative; whether it would work was another matter. Bahrain would not pull out and leave the Federation to its enemies. Mr. Davies pointed out that much depends on the Shah–Faisal meetings in November. If they go well, the shaikdoms will move towards some type of amorphous federation structure. Mr. Josephson added that, if the FAA fails, the Ruler wants some type of Bahraini association with the UN and embassies in the UK and US. He also wants to get some type of US office in Bahrain.

Mr. Brewer emphasized that the foregoing underlined the need for some solution to the current Bahrain issue. Mr. Josephson said that Shaikh Isa was worried to the point of emotionalism. Mr. Brewer said that the problem boiled down to the Iranian claim; the Iranians feel strongly about it. Mr. Josephson added that the Ruler told him that Faisal has assured Shaikh Isa he will provide military assistance if the Iranians land troops.

After Mr. Davies and Mr. Lay departed to attend other meetings, Mr. Josephson pointed out to Mr. Brewer that the Ruler would "pick his brains" when he returned to Bahrain. Shaikh Isa is determined to settle the problem and has written to the Shah that he would meet him at any time, in any place. Mr. Brewer emphasized that developments are taking place on which we are uninformed. The fact that we are not seeking to solve the problem does not mean that we are not doing what we can to encourage its solution.

Mr. Josephson said that the Ruler was delighted with the new American school in Bahrain. It now has forty students and he would like to make it an American International School. The school has received many requests for admission from outsiders, including Bahrainis, and the Ruler is totally cooperative.

Mr. Brewer summed up by saying that, while he could not speak for Iran, it was his impression that the Iranians felt their present policies were simple realism. The recent FAA meeting went well and it is making progress. We are trying to encourage a cooperative atmosphere and look to the coming Shah/Faisal meeting to produce some progress. He said that Mr. Josephson could assure the Ruler that we retain our friendly interest. However, with the UK departing, the local rulers must work out their own problems. Mr. Josephson responded that the Ruler understands this, but is looking for tangible evidence of US interest.

---

158. Telegram From the Department of State to the Embassy in Saudi Arabia[1]

Washington, November 2, 1968, 0004Z.

265734. Armed Opposition to PRSY. Jidda 5799.[2]

1. As result your effective approach to Acting MinState for Foreign Affairs and our comments to Saqqaf in Washington (State 264410)[3] SAG should now have gotten message we have serious reservations re efficacy any military effort against PRSY from Najran. Whether Sau-

---

[1] Source: National Archives and Records Administration, RG 59, Central Files 1967–69, POL 23–9 S YEMEN. Secret; Limdis. Drafted by Brewer on November 1 and approved by Davies. Repeated to Aden, London, and Kuwait.

[2] In telegram 5799 from Jidda, October 31, Eilts reported that he had called on the Acting Foreign Minister and given him in strict confidence the Embassy's assessment of the current strength of the People's Republic of Southern Yemen. He emphasized that the U.S. Government was not speaking in support of the PRSY regime, but believed that the Saudi Government would want to weigh carefully such first-hand information before deciding on any actions in South Arabia that could boomerang and exacerbate the existing instability of the region. (Ibid.)

[3] Dated October 31. (Ibid., POL 7 SAUD)

dis will be importantly influenced by our comments is of course another question but point has been made.

2. Concur your comment reftel that we not seeking tell SAG what to do but rather offering best friendly advice we can on basis our admittedly limited knowledge situation in PRSY hinterland. We do not think it appropriate for us propose what SAG should do. However, in light Mas'ud's comments (para three reftel), we would see no objection in course your continuing contacts with senior Saudi officials on this subject to putting forward counter-thesis to use of force for consideration by SAG. Thought would be that more flies might be caught with honey than vinegar and that instead of wasting time, effort and money in probable vain attempt get rid PRSY regime, SAG might seek develop position from which it could influence PRSYG toward more reasonable course. Thus, SAG willingness continue curb exile cross-border military activity and seek ways establish some quiet contact with NLF regime, perhaps ultimately leading to financial assistance along lines which Kuwaitis have in past contemplated, would seem to us approach best calculated strengthen hand "moderate" NLF wing. We have no illusions that results such approach would be attainable overnight, but gradual improvement SAG/PRSY ties leading hopefully to some degree financial reliance on SAG would seem best calculated contribute regional stability and limit opportunities for development major Communist positions of influence in fledgling South Arabian state.[4]

Rusk

---

[4] In telegram 5874 from Jidda, November 6, Eilts reported that Saudi Foreign Minister Sayyid Omar Saqqaf had told him that King Faisal was displeased at U.S. "advice" against a Saudi military venture in Southern Yemen and had asked if the U.S. Government was now supporting Communist regimes in the Arabian peninsula. Eilts responded that he had conveyed the Embassy's assessment of Southern Yemen's current strength in an informative rather than advisory context and that the U.S. action was not intended to endorse the PRSY Government, its policies or objectives. (Ibid., POL 23–9 S YEMEN)

159. Telegram From the Department of State to the Embassy in Southern Yemen[1]

Washington, November 5, 1968, 2355Z.

267326. Subject: Southern Yemen/US Relations. Ref: Aden 1796,[2] 1797.[3]

1. Department believes protracted delay in responding to PRSYG October 20 note could only provide further opportunity misunderstanding, perhaps leading hostile elements in PRSY to conclude USG embarrassed by unfounded accusations. On basis conversation reported Aden 1795,[3] it appears that PRSYG "proof" of US involvement likely to be no more than possession some American-made arms and ammunition and cases with USG handclasp insignia. Whether or not pictures of such items forthcoming, we believe formal and forthright rejection charges of USG involvement would emphasize our position that discovery of such weapons in hands anti-PRSYG elements would in no way denote USG involvement or hostile intent toward PRSYG. Believe you should therefore seek early appointment with Foreign Minister Dhalai or his deputy to transmit formal USG response, substantive portion of which contained in following paras. (unessential words omitted):

2. "USG firmly and categorically denies that the USG is in any way engaged in hostile activities against the government and people of PRSY. Assertions to that effect by the PRSY authorities are unfounded and have been repeatedly refuted by the US Chargé d'Affaires in Aden.

3. "The USG has no knowledge of the provenance of the arms, ammunition, or foodstuffs which are said to have been captured by elements of the PRSY armed forces on the Beihan border on October

---

[1] Source: National Archives and Records Administration, RG 59, Central Files 1967–69, POL 23–9 S YEMEN. Confidential. Drafted by Brewer and Brooks Wrampelmeier (NEA/ARP) on November 4, cleared by Davies and Katzenbach, and approved by Assistant Secretary of State for Near Eastern and South Asian Affairs Parker T. Hart. Repeated to Jidda, London, and USUN.

[2] Telegram 1796 from Aden, October 30, transmitted an unofficial translation of a Southern Yemen Government note dated October 20 to the U.S. Government stating that the "forces of mercenaries and traitors" who had battled PRSY forces on October 14–15 had been armed with American-made weapons that had been captured by government forces. The note alleged that the presence of American arms, ammunition, and foodstuffs with the mercenaries directed by Saudi "reactionaries" could only be interpreted as U.S. cooperation and approval of the attack, and asked that the U.S. Government submit a clear explanation of how such materials were in the possession of mercenary elements. (Ibid.)

[3] Dated October 30. (Ibid.)

14–15, 1968. The USG would of course be willing to examine any documentary evidence which might be presented to it by PRSYG in support of its charges and, if the evidence warrants, to conduct an investigation to determine whether any violation of USG laws or regulations might have occurred. In the meantime, however, the USG must point out that the presence, even if confirmed, of arms of American manufacture or of shipping cases bearing USG insignia could not be construed as evidence of USG 'cooperation with and approval for' an attack on the sovereignty, security, independence, or stability of PRSY as asserted in the PRSYG note of October 20. Many billions of dollars worth of arms have been manufactured in the United States during and after World War II. Some of these arms are now distributed widely throughout the world by private dealers having no connection with the United States Government. PRSY itself could prove the validity of this point by making such purchases itself. That some American-made arms may have found their way into the hands of elements unfriendly to PRSYG can thus in no way be construed as evidence of the intentions or actions of the USG.

4. "USG policy, which has been conveyed to PRSYG on numerous occasions by our Chargé d'Affaires in Aden, is to seek to maintain friendly relations with government and people of Southern Yemen. USG is deeply disturbed that responsible PRSYG officials have chosen to make public and unfounded charges against USG. These charges have been aired over government-controlled radio and in the PRSY press before USG has been given any opportunity to comment upon their accuracy or any evidence on which such allegations might be based. USG has noted with regret that PRSY press and radio have been conducting violent anti-American campaign alleging existence of 'proof' of USG involvement in PRSY internal affairs. USG takes this opportunity to point out that not one shred of evidence has yet been presented to document these charges.

5. "The USG believes that reiteration of such charges by responsible PRSGY officials and by the PRSY press and radio can only serve to increase misunderstandings between our two governments and peoples. The result will be to undermine the basic goodwill which the American people and their official representatives have always exhibited toward the people of Southern Yemen and their government and render more difficult the establishment of mutually beneficial relations between our two countries. USG representatives, whether in Aden or in Washington, stand ready at any time to discuss frankly and in a friendly fashion any concerns which PRSYG may have which could unfavorably affect the relations between PRSYG and the USG.

6. "USG takes this opportunity to reaffirm to PRSYG that USG policy has always been, and continues to be, support for the mainte-

nance of peace and stability in the Arabian Peninsula and opposition to the use of force or threat of force in settlement of disputes in the area."

7. In presenting foregoing, Chargé may, if he deems useful, make following oral comments: (a) despite prompt USG recognition of PRSYG and establishment Embassy Aden to seek develop friendly relations, we note PRSYG has yet to make any move to open normal relations with USG here, either by establishment Embassy in Washington or development bilateral contacts on part PRSYG UN representative; (b) unsupported allegations such as those refuted in our note are of the "have you stopped beating your wife" character which cannot satisfactorily be countered and thus raise basic question as to why they are being made; and (c) we would accordingly be interested in Foreign Ministry comments as to PRSYG policy towards USG.[4]

Rusk

---

[4] In telegram 1818 from Aden, November 7, Eagleton reported that he met for half an hour with the Foreign Ministry's Acting Permanent Secretary, Abdul Qawi Rashad, to deliver the U.S. response and discuss the deterioration of U.S.–PRSY relations. After ascertaining that Rashad did not intend to publicize the U.S. denial, Eagleton told him that the United States would be issuing a brief press statement. (Ibid.)

160. Telegram From the Department of State to the Embassy in Southern Yemen[1]

Washington, November 19, 1968, 0040Z.

273624. Subject: PRSY–US Relations. Ref: Aden 1833,[2] 1847.[3]

1. Department concurs with general line Embassy's proposed response to Faisal al-Shaabi contained para 6 reftel. Visit by Shaabi or other PRSYG leaders to Washington at this time in quest of USG aid should be discouraged. While we would of course welcome suspension PRSY anti-US campaign, budgetary stringencies such that any grant aid program for PRSY not now in cards. Moreover, advent of new US Administration and inevitable settling-in problem make it unlikely any PRSYG delegation coming here at this time could receive high-level USG attention it would expect.

2. Should Shaabi or Abdul Muhsin Luqman raise matter, you authorized say we would of course be willing to give sympathetic consideration to PRSY requests of an emergency or humanitarian nature, should general atmosphere in our relations make this feasible. Despite the fact that budgetary stringencies have precluded a grant aid program, we have endeavored, for example, help PRSY re emergency drug supplies (see para 3).

3. In this regard, you should note that US private organizations have, with considerable trouble in case of some scarce items, assembled in New York medicines requested by PRSY on an emergency basis. Air India agreement to transport medicines to Aden free of charge remains firm. AMER now believes that it can obtain within next few days from private sources additional funds required for packaging and local transportation of medicines to airport. While early delivery this shipment thus likely, you might note to Shaabi that continued willingness

---

[1] Source: National Archives and Records Administration, RG 59, Central Files 1967–69, POL S YEMEN–US. Confidential. Drafted by Wrampelmeier on November 18; cleared by Brewer and AID/NESA Officer in Charge of CENTO, UAR & Limited Programs Thomas Ball; and approved by Davies. Repeated to Jidda and London.

[2] In telegram 1833 from Aden, November 10, Eagleton reported that PRSY official Faisal al-Shaabi had expressed interest in improving relations with the United States, and asked a mutual friend to determine whether a mission led by Faisal would be well-received in the United States and whether it would be possible to obtain a substantial amount of foreign aid. Eagleton noted that if Faisal wanted to discuss this matter directly, the Embassy could brief him on the present state of U.S.–PRSY relations, although it would want to show sympathy for Faisal and others who would like to bring PRSY policy into better balance, and would point out that the unfounded charges against the United States and the PRSY attitude on other issues did not make it easy to discuss U.S. aid seriously. (Ibid.)

[3] Dated November 16. (Ibid.)

US private agencies participate in activities of this sort hardly to be expected as long as strident PRSY anti-American campaign continues. FYI. AMER Executive Secretary Collins has informed us some members his Executive Board already uneasy over AMER's involvement in shipment of medicines to PRSY at time when latter co-sponsoring resolution at UNGA to seat Chicoms, flaunting its relations with Chicoms and North Koreans and continuing bitter and occasionally personal attacks against USG and its President. End FYI.

Katzenbach

---

161. Memorandum of Conversation[1]

Washington, December 12, 1968, 10 a.m.

SUBJECT

Bahrain Problem

PARTICIPANTS

His Highness Sabah al-Salim al-Sabah, Amir of Kuwait
His Excellency Shaikh Sabah al-Ahmad al-Jabir al-Sabah, Minister of Foreign Affairs
His Excellency Abdul Rahman Ateeqi, Minister of Finance and Oil
His Excellency Talat al-Ghoussein, Kuwait Ambassador to the US
The Secretary
Ambassador Howard R. Cottam, US Ambassador to Kuwait
Mr. Parker T. Hart, Assistant Secretary for NEA
Mr. William D. Brewer, Country Director, NEA/ARP
Mr. Camille Nowfel, Interpreter

The Amir asked the Secretary's view regarding the Iranian claim to Bahrain. The Secretary said he did not wish to get into the technical aspects but there was one basic idea which helped predict the attitude of the American people on such disputes, i.e., what did the people concerned (in this case Bahrain) think about it. We did not seek to judge the 30–40 territorial disputes around the world. We did believe

---

[1] Source: Johnson Library, National Security File, Saunders Files, Visit of Amir of Kuwait, Dec. 11–12, 1968. Secret; Exclusive Distribution. Drafted by Brewer on December 13 and approved in the office of the Secretary of State on December 30. The memorandum is Part II of III. The meeting was held at Blair House. The time and place of the meeting are from Rusk's Diary. (Ibid.)

these issues should be solved peacefully and in accordance with the interests and wishes of the people concerned. The Secretary said it was not his impression that Iran sought a solution by force.

Iran had taken a responsible attitude but there was an historical claim and some way should be found to work out a solution in accordance with views of the people concerned. These ancient lands, which had exchanged Ambassadors long before the US existed, should be able to find a way to settle this problem.

The Amir said that the Shah had made clear when in Kuwait in mid-November that Iran had no intention to resort to force on this problem. The Shah was seeking a way out with dignity. The question was what way. The Amir felt USG help was needed, noting that Kuwait was doing its part. Two months ago Kuwait had been instrumental in arranging an Iran/Bahrain meeting at Geneva and the two sides would meet again.

The Secretary said he would consult his colleagues as to whether we might have any ideas to help produce a settlement. The Amir said he would appreciate it if the USG could keep in touch with the GOK on this matter. The Secretary congratulated the Amir for arranging the first Geneva meeting and said he hoped good would come out of this process.

Assistant Secretary Hart asked whether the Amir had close personal contact with the Ruler of Bahrain and requested the Amir's estimate as to the loyalty of Bahrainis to their Ruler. The Amir replied that his information was that the people fully support the Ruler. Mr. Hart asked whether, should a mechanism be found to manifest Bahraini public opinion on this issue, would there be any side effects likely to undermine the island's security. The Amir felt anything like a plebiscite unacceptable. Perhaps some effort to gather the facts regarding the wishes of the people, perhaps through the UN, might be acceptable. Ambassador Ghoussein noted that the Bahrain position did not reflect fear of the outcome but rather concern at the establishment of a principle. Minister Ateeqi said a plebiscite would represent a "shaking of confidence and a submission to a claim".

Iraq

162. Airgram From the Embassy in Iraq to the Department of State[1]

A–786   Baghdad, March 24, 1964.

SUBJECT

Visit of Assistant Secretary Talbot to Baghdad.

Mr. Talbot's truncated and brief visit (9:15 a.m. March 21 to 2:30 p.m. March 22)[2] was politically successful despite its brevity, despite the fact that the bulk of it fell on a Moslem "Sunday," despite the necessity for making arrangements on short notice, despite the twelve-hour delay in reaching here from Ankara, and despite the fact that his arrival coincided with an airport ceremony marking the departure of President Aref and Foreign Minister Abd al-Hamid for Pakistan and India.

Apart from briefings and discussions within the Embassy, and mixed business-culture visits to Babylon and Iraqi museums, Mr. Talbot was able to meet several ministers and other leading military and civilian personalities at social gatherings (including the moderate Kurdish leader, Baba Ali), talk privately with the British Ambassador and Foreign Office Under Secretary Ali Haidar Suleiman, and meet with the Prime Minister and Acting Foreign Minister separately.

The atmosphere, which on Friday could have been interpreted as correct but cool, warmed up considerably on Saturday in the various calls and at the Ambassador's luncheon. At this final event, which just preceded air departure, the several Iraqi ministers present spent a good deal of time arguing US policy on Israel. While more constructive conversation would have been useful, Mr. Talbot was very effective in his responses.

The main event, from which several conclusions can be drawn, was the fifty-minute talk with the Prime Minister, who was pleasant and restrained in his handling of controversial subjects.

Several memoranda of conversations are enclosed.[3] No effort has been made to cover all talks.

---

[1] Source: National Archives and Records Administration, RG 59, Central Files 1964–66, ORG 7 NEA. Confidential. Drafted by Strong. Repeated to Amman, Beirut, Cairo, Damascus, Jidda, Kuwait, Taiz, Tel Aviv, Tehran, London, Paris, Moscow, Ankara, Basra, Aleppo, Dhahran, and Jerusalem. Sent by air pouch.

[2] Assistant Secretary Talbot visited a number of Near East countries on this trip.

[3] Attached but not printed.

Conclusions:

1. Ranking officials from Washington are welcome and will be treated with courtesy (in contrast to past years).

2. The GOI is a moderate regime and does not wish to let the Palestine issue destroy mutually advantageous relations with the US, but we shall hear a good deal from the GOI about our policy in this area.

3. The GOI is expecting continuing and increasing economic and technical benefits from the US, and the field for cultural and educational cooperation is a wide one.

4. The GOI genuinely wants to handle the Kurdish problem[4] in a fashion which will reasonably satisfy the bulk of the Kurds and isolate the extremists. The GOI is likely to want Title II surplus food.

5. The current political situation is the most hopeful in years, and there is good prospect for its continuation. The Prime Minister and President are cooperating.

Robert C. Strong

---

[4] A cease-fire between the Iraqi Government and the Kurdish insurgents was announced in early February.

---

163.   Memorandum of Conversation[1]

Washington, April 20, 1964, noon.

SUBJECT

Iraq, Internal and External Affairs

PARTICIPANTS

Dr. Nasir al-Hani, Ambassador of Iraq

G—U. Alexis Johnson
NEA/NE—Lee F. Dinsmore

Deputy Under Secretary Johnson opened the conversation with a reference to his speech before the Citizens Committee for American Policy in the Near East,[2] and said he had been amazed at the reaction

---

[1] Source: National Archives and Records Administration, RG 59, Central Files 1964–66, POL IRAQ. Confidential. Drafted by Dinsmore.

[2] For text of Johnson's speech on January 20, see Department of State *Bulletin*, February 10, 1964, pp. 208–211.

to a statement he had thought was unexceptionable. The Ambassador said that after he had read the text he had been one of the persons in the Ministry of Foreign Affairs who had tried to temper the interpretations put on it, but the damage had been done. Mr. Johnson thought reaction may have mistakenly been based on the press treatment given the speech in the United States.[3]

Mr. Johnson asked Ambassador al-Hani about Iraq's relations with Jordan. The Ambassador thought relations were quite good, and that they have improved since the Arab Summit meeting in January 1964. The Jordanians had done a "spectacular job" of improving the country's economy, he added. When Mr. Johnson commented that both King Hussein and the Shah of Iran were changing their countries by an evolutionary rather than a revolutionary process, the Ambassador merely commented that Iran still had a "long way to go", and that the Shah's "white revolution" was "a bit late."

In answer to a question regarding the stability of Iraq, Dr. al-Hani replied, "We have entered a new era of moderation." He said the previous government (Ba'ath Party dominated) was almost as extreme as the communists (referring possibly to the heavy handed communist influence during the Qasim regime). Now the main task is to "put our home in order", he said. Iraq must "restore" itself economically. Once it is clear that Iraq can maintain its stability, other countries will step forward voluntarily to invest in and to assist Iraq. The country needs all kinds of investments, for large housing schemes and for industrialization.

The agrarian reform program had been something of a failure, the Ambassador stated. Mr. Johnson asked about relations with the oil company (Iraq Petroleum Company). Dr. al-Hani said there is as yet no settlement of outstanding differences, but he thought the government was now ready for discussions.[4]

The Ambassador answered Mr. Johnson's question about the Kurds positively, saying the problem was "settled, finished", he hoped, for good, but added that the job of reconstruction would take a long time.

---

[3] Following Johnson's speech, which was described in U.S. press reports as a warning to Arabs against taking any actions hostile to Israel, the Department received many informal protests from Arab embassies.

[4] For documents relating to U.S. international oil policy, see *Foreign Relations, 1964–1968*, vol. XXXIV, Document 175ff.

164. Letter From Secretary of State Rusk to Minister of Foreign Affairs al-Hamid[1]

Washington, May 7, 1964.

Dear Mr. Minister:

Following the return of Assistant Secretary Talbot from his visit to your country,[2] I wish to thank you for the cordial reception he received. He found his talks with Acting Foreign Minister Farhan most rewarding, as well as those he had with several other of your Cabinet colleagues and leading Iraqi citizens.

Mr. Talbot has informed me of the Iraqi point of view on the issue which acts as an irritant in our relations. You may be sure that United States policy in the Near East has not changed since the tragic death of President Kennedy. President Johnson is aware of Iraqi concerns and, I can assure you, will continue to conduct the even-handed, impartial policy pursued by President Kennedy.

The United States maintains a keen interest in the stability and progress of Iraq and in its tranquil exsistence within an area of peace.

Mr. Talbot's report to me has confirmed accounts received from Ambassador Strong with regard to the improvement of relations between our two countries. I welcome these reports. We want to continue and to expand the areas of cooperation between our two countries. While we seldom are able to do all we should like to do, we will constantly be on the alert for feasible measures, including the services of private institutions, by means of which Iraq–United States cooperation may prosper. I am particularly hopeful that our two governments will keep in close touch, and that we will not allow a misunderstanding or an occasional disagreement to stand in the way of communication with each other.

I wish you and your colleagues all success in your constructive efforts on behalf of the Iraqi people.

Sincerely,

Dean Rusk[3]

---

[1] Source: National Archives and Records Administration, RG 59, Central Files 1964–66, POL 17 IRAQ–US. No classification marking. Drafted by Strong and Dinsmore on May 5 and cleared by Davies and Jernegan.

[2] Talbot visited Iraq March 21–22; see Document 162.

[3] Printed from a copy that indicates Rusk signed the original.

165. Telegram From the Department of State to the Embassy in Iraq[1]

Washington, June 5, 1964, 6:01 p.m.

569. Cairo's 2924.[2] Neither Shawqat Aqrawi nor Luqman al-Barzani could advance Kurdish interests in Washington. On the contrary, delicate Kurdish–GOI situation might be irritated unnecessarily by conversations here with avowed Kurdish nationalists. Embassy Baghdad capable of serving as channel for conveying to USG subjects of concern to Iraqi Kurds and of making clear US positions. Department believes Kurdish representatives, while not unwelcome visit US, would experience only frustration to find reaction USG circles parallel to Embassy Baghdad's replies and counsel.

In response numbered questions reftel: (1) United States surplus commodities are made available only after agreement with the government concerned on means to assure that the donated food will reach the intended recipients. (2) There is no truth to story reported by Kurds to Embassy Cairo officer that US has promised assistance to Kurds through third country in event fighting renewed in Iraq.

Department interested in learning more about identity "new channel" mentioned reftel.

Rusk

---

[1] Source: National Archives and Records Administration, RG 59, Central Files 1964–66, POL 23–9 IRAQ. Secret. Drafted by Dinsmore; cleared by Officer-in-Charge of United Arab Republic Affairs and Syrian Arab Republic Affairs Curtis F. Jones, Davies, William D. Wolle (NEA/NE), Hallpress (AID/MR/ARD), and AID Director of the Office of Near Eastern Affairs James C. Flint; and approved by Jernegan. Also sent to Cairo and repeated to Beirut.

[2] Telegram 2924 from Cairo, June 2, reported that Kurdish representative Aqrawi and Luzman Barzani, son of Kurdish leader Mulla Mustafa Barzani, met with an Embassy officer in Cairo and told him that Mustafa Barzani wanted them to go to the United States to present the Kurdish case to officers in the Department. They also asked how they could be sure that U.S. rehabilitation aid given through the Iraqi Government would reach the Kurds and if it were true that the United States had promised assistance through a third country if the Kurds were driven to renewed fighting. (Ibid.)

166.   Telegram From the Department of State to the Embassy in Iran[1]

Washington, September 3, 1964, 2:49 p.m.

198. Begin FYI. In its assessment of UAR–Iraq unity declaration May 26, 1964[2] Department was persuaded that President Arif, rather than President Nasser, took initiative for the move. Arif, it was felt, needed added prestige of UAR support for what he realized was not popular government. Subsequent Iraqi steps such as nationalization of number private enterprises and establishment of Arab Socialist Union were indicative of Iraqi regime's intentions make changes in traditional character Iraqi political and commercial life that would have favorable reception in Cairo. However, basic sociological and political facts of Iraq have not changed. President Arif's government must come to terms with Iraqi reality soon, or face pressures from diverse ethnic, commercial and political factions that are increasingly inimical and even hostile to his regime. Some of hostility is related directly to Arif's moves toward coordination of Iraqi with UAR institutions and concepts.

Government of Iran is intimately aware of dissident elements of Iraqi society. Iranian liaison and continuous contact with anti-government Iraqi Kurds and the anti-Arif Shi'a (who comprise an estimated 55% population of Iraq) not only give Iran a very instructive (even if one sided) view of the inherent weakness of Iraq as a political unit, but, unfortunately, have tempted Iranians to consider action tantamount to subversion of Arif government. Department is aware it also increases Shah's concern that Arif cannot cope with his flirtation with Nasser. Whatever Iran may deem to be provocations for its practice of intrigue in Iraq, it should not be surprised if a weak and suspicious President Arif seeks bolster himself by alliance and ties unity with another Arab state. Further, Iraqis (as well as UAR and other Arabs) are aware of Iranian friendship with Israel. With that knowledge as take-off point, Iraqis are capable of exaggerated assumptions of content and product of that friendship. Any undue notice by foreign states of military cooperation between UAR and Iraq could help that cooperation to coalesce.

---

[1] Source: National Archives and Records Administration, RG 59, Central Files 1964–66, POL IRAQ–UAR. Secret; Immediate. Drafted by Dinsmore; cleared by Jones, Davies, Director of the Office of Greek, Turkish, and Iranian Affairs Katherine W. Bracken, Spain, and Officer-in-Charge of United Kingdom Affairs Thomas M. Judd (info); approved by Deputy Assistant Secretary of State for Near Eastern and South Asian Affairs James P. Grant. Repeated to Baghdad, Cairo, and London.

[2] On May 26 President Arif and President Nasser signed an agreement in Cairo to set up a joint military command in war time and for exploratory talks on unifying the two governments. The accord was described as "the first step toward full Arab unity."

According to British Embassy Washington, Foreign Office proposes British Ambassador take following line with Shah: U.K. intends leave the Shah in no doubt that UAR military presence in Iraq would be most unwelcome development.

UK would expect that UAR military presence in Iraq over extended period might arouse hostile Iraqi reactions.

UK would make point that outside attempts to influence situation in Iraq would only strengthen UAR–Iraqi unity.

UK would point out that UAR is already heavily committed in Yemen and vis-à-vis Israel. It is not in position to send large numbers troops to Iraq to remain for long. End FYI.

Department concurs generally in British line and suggests you pass to Shah the following as our assessment Iraqi situation in light reports to date.

To date, limited UAR–Iraq unit has been imposed on Iraq by President Arif who estimates he needs UAR support in order maintain himself at home. The initiative appears to have been Arif's.

Steps toward implementation of unity declaration (nationalization of businesses, creation of Arab Socialist Union) are unpopular in many Iraqi circles and have contributed to already widespread lack confidence in or respect for Arif.

Divisive factors of Iraqi society (Shi'a-Sunni, Kurds, suppressed political parties) will weaken and erode Arif's ability impose preponderant UAR influence in Iraq.

Introduction of significant numbers of UAR troops in Iraq would be an unwelcome development for us. We have no firm reports numbers UAR troops that might maneuver nor information length of time they might stay in Iraq. We have only Chief of Staff's announcement of intention hold joint maneuvers.

However, we do not believe that Iraqis would permit large contingent UAR troops to remain in Iraq indefinitely. Any attempt by UAR to control Government of Iraq from position of military strength in Iraq would be resisted and rejected. Such an attempt could very well cost Arif his position of leadership. Logistical demands on UAR to maintain unwelcome military presence in Iraq would be almost insurmountable.

Even in unlikely event that some UAR troops were stationed for extended period in Iraq, this would pose no threat to Iran.

Any public evidence undue foreign concern over presence UAR troops in Iraq would have effect of strengthening rather than disturbing UAR–Iraq unity.

British Embassy apprised of foregoing.

Rusk

167. Telegram From the Embassy in Iraq to the Department of State[1]

Baghdad, October 26, 1964, 0845Z.

362. On October 23 Masud Muhammad, Minister of State for Northern Affairs, informed me he planned leave same day for north carrying tentative procedural agreement resulting from several meetings between himself, Interior Minister, Army division heads, Army Intelligence Chief and Northern Mutasarrifs. GOI now prepared make first move involving following steps: (1) release of all Kurdish prisoners including those convicted of military crimes; (2) return of government employees of Kurdish origin to former positions, especially in north; (3) removal of Salahaddin cavalry from north; (4) removal of Arab tribes from Kurdish areas and return of Kurds forced from their villages; (5) compensation to those who suffered during recent troubles.

Following these GOI actions, Kurds to (1) withdraw Pesh Merga from major roads and stop harassment; (2) return weapons captured from Iraqi Army (Masud said token amount would satisfy GOI's honor); and (3) permit establishment local administration, made up mainly of Kurds but under GOI supervision. Once these moves completed, GOI and Kurds to sit down and tackle political settlement. Masud expects to return from north in week with Kurdish acceptance since agreement offers sound opportunity test good faith of GOI. Masud emphasized Mulla Mustafa regards USG as key to settlement of Kurdish problem and USG can get what it wants. He had told Iraqi colleagues he lunching with me to discuss tentative agreement.

Comment: Although first steps by GOI do not incorporate acceptance Kurdish political demands, they do include what Kurds have always requested as proof GOI's good faith. Kurds, therefore, should find it easy accept offer provided that only nominal return of weapons will, indeed, be acceptable to GOI. If GOI and Kurds carry out their parts of bargain, political talks likely follow.

Masud identified himself as prime mover in creation new situation but agreed Egypt is big factor as result of delay in unity until internal Iraqi problems met. He gives us large share of credit. In any event, that GOI willing make first move is significant, indicating tacit recognition of strong Kurdish position and effectiveness of Egyptian pressure. Given Embassy's assessment that neither GOI or Mulla Mustafa wish resume hostilities, present GOI offer may mark turning point. In essence

---

[1] Source: National Archives and Records Administration, RG 59, Central Files 1964–66, POL 23–9 IRAQ. Confidential. Repeated to Ankara, Tehran, Aleppo, Basra, Beirut, Cairo, Damascus, London, and Tabriz.

I told Minister, who several times during conversation indicated Mulla Mustafa would heed US advice, that (1) US hopes for peaceful negotiated settlement within framework Iraq without foreign interference, (2) Kurds should cooperate, having nothing to lose, and (3) Kurds must be prepared be patient in long drawn-out negotiations over internal political settlement and must be prepared compromise their extreme demands. Also stated Kurdish cause best served by avoiding appearance of acting as agents; they should avoid entangling themselves in interests of others.

At end of conversation Masud asked in all seriousness whether in event of trouble he could seek political asylum in American Embassy. I told him case would have to be judged on its merits at the time but US did not encourage such action. While he may have been trying create impression he laboring under great pressure, it is possible he believes there is chance Kurdish extremists in Baghdad may start a racial conflict which would be bloody and would endanger his life.

Addendum. At end of my conversation with FonMin October 24 I said that to counteract any rumors he might hear about my luncheon with Masud. I wanted to tell him that I had told Masud (a) USG continues to advocate a peaceful, negotiated settlement of the Kurdish problem; (b) that use of force could not settle it; (c) that it was evident GOI wished avoid further military action; (d) that Kurds would be well advised concur in procedural agreement reached by Masud with GOI; (e) that it would be possible to observe whether GOI acting in good faith; (f) that if GOI acts in good faith then Kurds obligated do so; (g) that when time for political negotiations came Kurds should recognize these are complicated and must be prepared be patient; (h) and that USG intends continue avoid getting into specifics of problem. Minister commented he understood our position and he appreciated learning what I had said. He gave no sign of objecting to our role and his manner was as friendly and relaxed when I left as it had been throughout.

Comment: Transfer of Iraqi 3rd division to H–3 further strengthens Kurdish position and increases pressure on GOI reach settlement. Was this one of UAR purposes in request by UAC that Iraq move 3rd division?[2]

Strong

---

[2] Circular telegram 765, October 28, stated that the developments reported in telegram 362 were encouraging and that the Department concurred in the line taken by the Ambassador. It commented that Masud's call on the Ambassador pointed up a situation where the United States, without seeking the role, had in effect become a psychological support in Kurdish minds. (Ibid.)

168. Telegram From the Department of State to the Embassy in Iraq[1]

Washington, December 4, 1964, 7:14 p.m.

325. Baghdad's 439.[2] Department (Jernegan) called in Iraq Ambassador Nasir al-Hani December 3 to raise subject recent harassment Embassy local employees.

Jernegan said interrogations and arrests reminiscent Qasim period. Pointed out that Embassy given no explanations for arrests and detentions nor are persons brought to trial. We concerned since (1) as employer we interested humanely and because of adverse effects on other employees and (2) we disturbed because actions appear indicate renewed suspicion of USG and our policies toward Iraq. Jernegan recalled during period he was Ambassador Iraq devoting much time attempting assure Qasim and other officials there was no substance behind then-existing suspicion.[3] Neither then nor now did USG have any desire overthrow GOI. We had expended great effort attempting get on good terms with government and had thought since 1963 relations were gradually improving. Jernegan pointed to EXIM loans, credit on sales military equipment, encouragement American businessmen participate in Iraqi development, provision of professors for university.

Recent unjustified suspicion adds up to unhappy picture. Jernegan personally disturbed and said if substituting Americans for all Iraqi-held jobs would improve relations he would recommend it. This he realized impractical. Asked Ambassador al-Hani explain Department's unhappiness and to convey to his government our absolute assurances USG in no way opposed present Iraq government or wants see it changed.

Ambassador indicated he sorry hear foregoing and said he had heard Khan had been arrested. Added he assumed Khan by now had been released. Asked Department not take arrest one Embassy local as evidence change GOI's attitude towards US. "Isolated case" should

---

[1] Source: National Archives and Records Administration, RG 59, Central Files 1964–66, POL IRAQ–US. Confidential. Drafted by Dinsmore, cleared by Davies, and approved by Jernegan. Repeated to USUN for Deputy Director of the Office of Near Eastern and South Asian Regional Affairs John P. Walsh.

[2] In telegram 439 from Baghdad, November 30, Strong recommended that the imprisonment of Yacub Khan, one of the Embassy's Iraqi employees, be taken up with the Iraqi Embassy in Washington and perhaps when the Secretary met with the new Iraqi Foreign Minister. He noted other recent incidents during which U.S. local employees had been interrogated, detained, or otherwise harassed by Iraqi authorities. (Ibid.)

[3] Jernegan served as U.S. Ambassador to Iraq January 12, 1959–June 2, 1962, when he was recalled at the request of the Iraqi Government. General Abdul Karim Qassim was Prime Minister of Iraq July 1958–February 8, 1963.

not be reason for Department see change in GOI policy. "Behavior of police" towards local employee should not be taken as against USG.

Jernegan said accumulation of cases begins look like 1959. Said Embassy Baghdad should be informed if there is real evidence against employees, in which case we will consider discharging them.

Al-Hani said personally he hoped Khan will be released. Promised bring matter to attention his government immediately. Said he had raised question Khan this week with FonMin Naji Talib in New York. Latter had indicated his awareness Khan's arrest. Al-Hani gave no indication Talib's attitude.

Jernegan said he thought Secretary might raise subject with Talib during December 9 meeting.

Ball

169. Memorandum of Conversation[1]

Sec Del/MC/28   New York, December 10, 1964, 4:30 p.m.

SECRETARY'S DELEGATION TO THE NINETEENTH SESSION OF
THE UNITED NATIONS GENERAL ASSEMBLY
New York, November 1964

SUBJECT

The Kurdish Problem

PARTICIPANTS

U.S.	Iraq
The Secretary	Foreign Minister Naji Talib
NEA—Mr. Walsh	Under Secretary for Foreign Affairs Kadhim Khalaf

The Minister said that he had one problem which he wished to bring to the attention of the Secretary, namely, the Kurdish situation.

The Minister said that the Kurdish problem fundamentally dominated the Iraqi scene. The Iraqi Government is preoccupied with this

[1] Source: National Archives and Records Administration, RG 59, Central Files 1964–66, POL 23–9 IRAQ. Confidential. Drafted by Walsh on December 11. Approved in the Office of the Secretary of State on December 17. The memorandum is Part I of III.

issue and has little time or energy to turn to other pressing economic and social issues. He was not sure that they were any closer to a solution now than they were before the fighting started several years ago.

The Minister went on to say that he could not understand certain elements of the Kurdish problem. Manifestly there are unidentified forces supporting the Kurds. The Kurds are poor people and their land has been damaged by war. Where are they getting money from to buy staple foods, arms, and equipment? Who are these mysterious forces? What do they want?

The Minister stated that his Government might be able to deal with Mullah Mostafa Barzani but the Communists and the Democratic Party were much more difficult. In his opinion, the Kurds were controlled by the Communists. If a Kurdish state were established, it would be a Communist enclave which would split the Arab world, pierce the protective CENTO belt, and shatter the stability of Turkey and Iran. He had seen Kurdish maps indicating a Kurdish state stretching from Iskendrun in Turkey to Basra in Iraq.

He said that the Turks had sealed their Kurdish frontier. On the other hand, some support was drifting into Kurdish hands across the long Iranian frontier. This did not appear to be the result of deliberate Iranian Government intent but rather reflects the inability of a weak government to patrol its frontiers.

He asserted that he did not wish to suggest that the U.S. was supporting the Kurds but he did wish to emphasize that his Government is sore-perplexed by the machinations of some mysterious force which is supporting the Kurds.

In reply, the Secretary categorically assured the Minister that the United States was not directly or indirectly supporting the Kurdish movement. The U.S. supported the independence, integrity, and prosperity of Iraq. It had no other interest in Iraq affairs. Furthermore, he shared the Minister's concern about the dangers of Communist penetration of the Near East by means of a Kurdish independence movement.

The Minister said that he was very pleased to have had this exchange of views and to receive this reassurance in respect to what he had known was American policy. He said that the U.S. could help Iraq by determining who is the financing and supplying source for the Kurds and what the motivation of this source is.

170. **Telegram From the Department of State to the Embassy in Iraq**[1]

Washington, December 14, 1964, 7:44 p.m.

343. Ref. NIT–6583/Noforn.[2] Department is persuaded that Kurdish participation in any scheme to overthrow Iraq government would not guarantee establishment regime more sympathetic to Kurdish aspirations. Nasser could hardly be expected continue his current role in favor peaceful solution and agreement between GOI and Kurds, particularly in event plot involved Iran. Furthermore even with new government Kurds would still be faced with problem obtaining agreed settlement.

Kurds would have exposed themselves as willing collaborators with Iranian intrigue against government Iraq thus earning deepened Arab suspicion and resentment of Kurdish ambitions. Until now many Arabs have some sympathy for Kurds. No successor Iraqi government could be expected either deal magnanimously or leniently with Kurds or excuse Iranians. Iranian connection with plot bound be uncovered sooner or later, and in view reports recent close GOI monitoring of communist and Baathi attempts overthrow GOI (various CAS reports) there is good reason believe GOI already privy to Iranian subversive activity.

Embassy's view solicited re whether it could or should find way, without revealing knowledge, let appropriate Kurds know how we would view any plans participate in coup d'état. Attempt seems to us bound backfire and to worsen Kurdish position vis-à-vis GOI.

Ball

---

[1] Source: National Archives and Records Administration, RG 59, Central Files 1964–66, POL 23–9 IRAQ. Secret; Noforn. Drafted by Dinsmore on December 11; cleared in draft by Deputy Director of the Office of Greek, Turkish, and Iranian Affairs John M. Howison and by Davies; and approved by Talbot. Repeated to Tehran.

[2] Not found.

171.   Telegram From the Embassy in Iraq to the Department of State[1]

Baghdad, December 16, 1964, 3 p.m.

486. Ref: Deptel 343.[2] Kurds have told us Iranians urging them resume fighting (Embtel 458)[3] but they understand Iranian motives. We have already told Kurds they should avoid appearing act as agents of others or entangling themselves in interests of others (Embtel 362),[4] and would be unwise listen to those who want resumption hostilities (Akins' memcon with Aqrawi, Dec. 8).[5] Masud Mohammad and Aqrawi understood what we meant. Should note that in my October 24 talk with ForMin (addendum to Embtel 362) this was the one point made to Masud Mohammad which I did not reveal to Subhi Abd al-Hamid.

Emb officer plans see representative Ibrahim Ahmad faction December 17 and representatives Mulla Mustafa and new political bureau December 19. Without mentioning any specific plot he will refer to their earlier statements that Iranians trying stir up Kurds; he will tell them we think Kurds have wisely resisted Persian blandishments and we hope they will continue remain calm and try work out solution with GOI—many of whose members favorably disposed toward Kurds; we think Kurds cause will be severely damaged in Iraq if Kurds appear to act as agents for interests of others.

Must bear in mind that Kurds need supply line through Iran and can only be attracted by Iranian offers of material assistance, which they also need. These factors will decline in importance only if GOI shows good faith and proves willing enter into genuine negotiations.

If GOI so acts, Kurds likely eschew participation in Iranian-managed plot although some city-based Kurdish nationalists might act independently. Aqrawi believes (and says Mulla Mustafa shares his belief) that Nasser wants peaceful settlement and that almost any conceivable successor regime—particularly military dictatorship—would be less conciliatory than present one. But if GOI does not soon indicate willingness open negotiations Mulla will conclude, as most Kurds have already, that GOI has been acting in bad faith since last February. He will not then need foreign encouragement to resume revolt. While

---

[1] Source: National Archives and Records Administration, RG 59, Central Files 1964–66, POL 23–9 IRAQ. Secret. Repeated to Tehran and Ankara.

[2] Document 170.

[3] Dated December 8. (National Archives and Records Administration, RG 59, Central Files 1964–66, POL 2–2 IRAQ)

[4] Document 167.

[5] Not found.

impossible estimate when this conjuncture will arrive, Kurds will not stand still forever.

If war starts would be too much to expect Kurds could be dissuaded accepting Iranian supplies and money including variety of strings Iranians might choose attach. Annoying Nasser or alienating Arabs—many of whom have lack sympathy for Kurds would be least of Kurdish worries. Once war recommences, current limitations on Kurdish objectives might well disappear, in which case would become international with serious implications.[6]

Strong

---

[6] Telegram 350 to Baghdad, December 16, agreed that the Embassy should continue to urge restraint on all Kurdish factions and warned it to avoid appearing to give credence to Kurdish claims that Iran was urging them to resume fighting. (Ibid.)

---

172. Telegram From the Embassy in Iran to the Department of State[1]

Tehran, April 12, 1965, 1500Z.

1128. Man who identified himself as Shamsuddin Mofti and his colleague as Masoud Barzani appeared at Emb today with letter of introduction from Mollah Mustafa Barzani and oral message from him. It was essentially a strong plea for direct US assistance. He said Iraqi Kurds need financial and military assistance, especially heavy weapons, and would be willing receive American officials in their area and wanted be regarded as "another state of the union." He also said Barzani considers oil resources should be handled by an American firm in direct arrangement with the Iraqi Kurds.

We of course gave him no encouragement whatsoever. Mofti stated Barzani asked that his message be sent to Washington and that USG henceforth use Tehran as point of contact with Barzani. Baghdad, he said, had become too difficult for Barzani to use because of recent Iraqi Army movements. He also said Barzani would like to have direct

---

[1] Source: National Archives and Records Administration, RG 59, Central Files 1964–66, POL 23–9 IRAQ. Confidential. Repeated to Baghdad, Ankara, and Cairo.

channel of communication with US rather than through Iranians whom he did not trust to report his views accurately.

EmbOff pointed out steadfast US policy toward Iraqi-Kurdish dispute along lines CA–9411 of March 2, 1963.[2] Said message would be transmitted to Washington, but said could give no commitment regarding a response nor place any response might be given. Nevertheless, Mofti said he would wait in Tehran. Mofti and Barzani said Iranian authorities are unaware of their presence here.[3]

Herz

---

[2] CA–9411 stated that the United States should continue to regard the Kurdish revolt as strictly an internal Iraqi matter in which there was no role for the United States either directly or indirectly. (*Foreign Relations*, 1961–1963, vol. XVIII, Document 174)

[3] Telegram 938 to Tehran, April 14, instructed the Embassy to continue courteously to refuse to enter into a dialogue with "self-styled Barzani representatives," emphasizing that the U.S. policy of non-involvement in the Iraq–Kurdish dispute was unchanged. It added that through appropriate channels, SAVAK should be informed promptly of the visit and of the reply given. (National Archives and Records Administration, RG 59, Central Files 1964–66, POL 23–9 IRAQ)

---

173.   Telegram From the Embassy in Iraq to the Department of State[1]

Baghdad, April 30, 1965, 1115Z.

937. Embtels 804,[2] 929.[3] Kurds and Iran.

FonMin Talib had at me again last night at Japanese reception. Obviously he has not wanted to stay "set straight" very long. In presence of Education Minister Zaki he repeated old theme that Iranian policy is in fact CENTO policy, said it was vital to GOI to know what was discussed in CENTO meetings[4] or in private talks. For first time

---

[1] Source: National Archives and Records Administration, RG 59, Central Files 1964–66, POL 23–9 IRAQ. Confidential. Repeated to London, Tehran, Kuwait, Jidda, Dhahran, Taiz, Cairo, Ankara, and Karachi.

[2] Dated March 25. (Ibid., POL 15–1 TUN)

[3] Dated April 29. (Ibid., POL 23–9 IRAQ)

[4] The Thirteenth Session of the Ministerial Council of the Central Treaty Organization (CENTO) was held in Tehran, April 7–8; see Document 7.

accused Iran of giving material assistance to Kurds, and declared Shah's policy on Kurds would lead to situation which would be dangerous to Iran itself and to CENTO. He pointed out that Iran had had no issues with Iraq when both were members of Baghdad Pact and seemed to imply that an Iranian objective was to create a situation in Iraq through the Kurdish problem which would lead to government willing take Iraq into CENTO. He objected strenuously to Shah's basing of his policy toward Iraq on his allergy to Nasser.

I repeated that Kurdish problem not discussed in CENTO and I unaware of any private conversations. Reminded him Pakistan member of CENTO, yet Pakistan had been doing utmost through good offices role to try bring Iran and Iraq into some degree of harmony. Pakistanis could tell GOI whether Kurds discussed in CENTO and whether Shah amenable to US advice on this matter.

At my request, Talib identified Iranian material assistance to Kurds as comprising several loads of unidentified equipment transported onto Iraqi soil in jeeps without license plates. (Zaki chimed in that Shah was also sending aid to Yemeni royalists, but this was not pursued.)

I then gently chided Talib for backsliding after my previous talks with him. Said would report conversation, including information about material assistance; was gratified at obvious respect Talib showed for power and influence of USG but wished assure him there were great many things US could not control or even influence. Talib said GOI felt USG could get Shah change policy if wished. As we parted, to cheer him up I told Talib our latest report was that armored personnel carriers would be delivered in May, June and July, but since this report conflicted with other information, I was seeking authoritative statement. He was pleased.

Comment: Talib himself probably is pursuing CENTO scent as tactic, but some of his colleagues surely believe it. They all believe US can make Shah change policy on Kurds.

Turkish Ambassador in call April 5 (reported by memcon Dept and Ankara)[5] expressed idea that out of Iraqi Army failure defeat Kurds could come govt willing take Iraq into area pact with Turkey and Iran. In our opinion this is nonsense. If Shah thinks pro-Iranian government can be brought about by helping Kurds, believe he is as wrong as he proved to be in past on imminence of UAR–Iraqi union.

Action request. I still hope to see Talib in his office before long to discuss some other matters. Have about run out of arguments on Kurds–Iran–Iraq triangle except possibly pointing out Arab interference in Khuzistan cannot be ignored by Shah. Would appreciate any

---

[5] Not found.

thoughts Department may think useful with Talib. Also would be helpful have instructions responsive to his insistent references to Secretary's
private talk in Tehran. Seems useless any longer try pretend Iran not
helping Kurds.[6]

Strong

_____

[6] Telegram 655 to Baghdad, May 4, stated that the Department believed the Ambassador had given the Iraqis all the arguments available to convince the Iraqi Government
that the U.S. Government was not involved in Kurdish dissidence. It was unlikely that
further arguments could erase the Foreign Minister's suspicions, but U.S. officials should
continue to reiterate the U.S. policy line. Strong could also tell Talib that Secretary
Rusk had not brought any new element into his discussion of Iranian security with the
Shah. (Ibid.)

_____

**174.   Telegram From the Department of State to the Embassy in
Iraq[1]**

Washington, May 6, 1965, 4:51 p.m.

661. Your 956.[2] Assume Deptel 655[3] received too late for use May
5 conversation with Fon Min.

Additionally, you may tell GOI (1) Iranians are and have been
kept fully aware of US view that Iranian and US interests dictate making
every effort improve Iran–Iraq relations and avoid disruptive steps.
However, as we have often said to Iraqis, we do not control Iranian
foreign policy, just as we do not control foreign policies Turkey, Paki-

_____

[1] Source: National Archives and Records Administration, RG 59, Central Files 1964–
66, POL 23–9 IRAQ. Confidential. Drafted by Dinsmore and Howison on May 5, cleared
by Davies, and approved by Jernegan. Repeated to Ankara, London, Tehran, and Tel Aviv.
[2] In telegram 956, May 5, Strong reported another meeting with Talib during which
the Foreign Minister again raised the question of U.S. policy on the Kurds. Talib also
expressed doubt that Kurdish representative Vanli, who was attempting to establish a
permanent headquarters in the United States for Kurdish rebels, could be operating
there against the will of the U.S. Government. He requested that the United States
preclude Vanli from engaging in political activity and expel him from the United States,
and persuade Iran to cease encouraging and aiding Iraqi Kurds. Strong commented that
it appeared that the Iraqi Government was reaching the point of desperation. He suggested that Vanli's visa be canceled and deportation proceedings started and that he be
authorized to pass to Mulla Mustafa Barzani a U.S request that Vanli be instructed to
leave the United States. (Ibid.)
[3] See footnote 6, Document 173.

stan, Greece, India, others. We cannot recall any instance where country in free world agreed relinquish control over any element its national policy as result its relations with another nation.

(2) Department recommends Embassy go ahead with procedure suggested reftel concerning recall Vanli from US by Kurds in Iraq. FYI: Meanwhile we checking regulations and implications involved possible deportation including possible bearing registration as foreign agent on deportation proceedings. End FYI.

Jernegan in meeting with Ambassador al-Hani on other matter (reported separately) May 5 conveyed points in 1 and 2 above except for first sentence under 1. He reiterated that our reply to Kurdish petitions is always the same, we regard their problem an internal affair of Iraq. Jernegan said he thought Fon Min over-concerned about Vanli who has been singularly unsuccessful in US. (Ambassador al-Hani volunteered he had reported in same vein to Foreign Office.)

Rusk

---

175.   **Telegram From the Department of State to the Embassy in Iran**[1]

Washington, August 11, 1965, 7:15 p.m.

138. Baghdad's 74 to Department.[2]

Iraqi request for support efforts halt flow of arms from Iran to dissident Iraqi Kurds cannot reasonably be refused. Our consistent policy has been Kurdish insurrection matter concerning only Iraq and flow of arms and men across border to bring pressure to bear against Iraqi government incompatible our goal area stability. Kurdish victory in Iraq in pragmatic terms could have only most ominous import for

---

[1] Source: National Archives and Records Administration, RG 59, Central Files 1964–66, POL 23–9 IRAQ. Confidential. Drafted by Davies and Dinsmore; cleared in draft by Bracken and by Judd; and approved by Deputy Assistant Secretary of State for Near Eastern and South Asian Affairs William J. Handley. Repeated to Ankara, Baghdad, Karachi, and London.

[2] In telegram 74 from Baghdad, August 11, Chargé d'Affaires J. Wesley Adams reported that Iraqi Under Secretary for Foreign Affairs Kadhim Khalaf had called him to the Foreign Office to request "in the strongest terms" that the United States intervene with the Iranians to obtain cessation of the flow of arms from Iran to the Kurds. Adams noted that he made the usual disclaimer regarding the U.S. ability to influence Iran but agreed to forward the request. (Ibid.)

stability if not integrity Iran and Turkey. Indications Iraq now has fairly accurate information nature and extent Iranian assistance insurrectionists makes it probable continuance support will lead to rapid deterioration relations.

At level GOIran you deem appropriate you should note Iraqi démarche and express US concern over pressures by Iraqis arising out of Iranian assistance to Kurds. US desires maintain good relations with Iraq and Department views it also to Iran's advantage that US limited potential for influence in Iraq not be weakened.[3]

For Baghdad. Embassy may inform Foreign Office Embassy Tehran instructed raise matter with GOI.

For London. You may apprise Foreign Office of foregoing.

Rusk

---

[3] In telegram 153 from Tehran, August 13, Chargé d'Affaires Martin F. Herz reported that on August 12 he had conveyed the Iraqi demand to the Foreign Office with comments as instructed in telegram 138. The next day he was summoned by Iranian Foreign Minister Abbas Aram to his residence to discuss Iran–Iraq relations. Aram had insisted that Iran was not aiding the Kurds, and complained that Iraq seemed to be following a studied policy of annoying Iran. Herz commented that Aram seemed distressed that the United States had become involved in the matter. (Ibid.)

---

176.   Telegram From the Department of State to the Embassy in Iraq[1]

Washington, October 26, 1965, 2:01 p.m.

193. Embtel 255.[2] Following summary of conversations FYI and Noforn. It is uncleared and subject to amendment upon review.

1–a. During October 8 conversation with Secretary,[3] Prime Minister raised Kurdish question. While recognizing matter basically internal

---

[1] Source: National Archives and Records Administration, RG 59, Central Files 1964–66, POL 7 IRAQ, Confidential. Drafted by Dinsmore; cleared by Staff Assistant Howard V. Funk of M, in substance by John E. Rielly in the Vice President's Office, and Deputy Director of the Office of Near Eastern Affairs Harrison M. Symmes; and approved by Davies. Repeated to Cairo and Tehran.

[2] Dated October 25. (Ibid.)

[3] The Secretary's conversation with Prime Minister Abd al-Rahman Bazzaz took place at the United Nations. Memoranda of conversation recording their meeting are ibid., Conference Files: Lot 66 D 347, CF 2547. Bazzaz became Prime Minister of Iraq on September 21, 1965.

problem, noted there were also external aspects to it. Said GOI willing look at Kurdish peoples as nation, however he predicted there would never be Kurdish state including all Kurds. PM suggested progress might be made on problem if US and UK would advise Shah unwisdom his policy.

b. Secretary reiterated US supports territorial integrity Iraq and asked PM try understand limited influence US has in such matters. He cited India–Pakistan as example.

c. In response Secretary's question whether he might consider making discreet probes to learn whether there is mutual desire friendship between Tehran and Cairo, PM claimed Shah has exaggerated fear President Nasser. Nasser would like cooperate with Iran. Iran's provocations cause him react. PM contrasted Shah's professed fear Nasser's ambitions with Shah's ambitions among Arab territories in Persian Gulf. Secretary suggested Iranian Foreign Minister Aram might be engaged in dialogue but PM responded it unrealistic think anyone but Shah could change official attitude toward Egypt and Arab world. He thought only advice from friendly powerful governments could persuade Shah.

d. As first civilian PM Iraq in many years, he felt atmosphere of stability. Secretary said US has elementary interest in welfare and territorial integrity Iraq adding we have no national ambitions in Iraq and that we ready explore ways assist Iraq on road to development.

e. PM raised particular program in which he personally interested, namely building University Baghdad into great institution. Secretary said Department would be glad review possibility US assistance on some aspect of University scheme.

f. PM agreed worthwhile examine possibilities investment guarantee agreement.

2–a. In talk with Vice President October 15,[4] Bazzaz conveyed President Arif's highest regards to President and wished speedy recovery from operation. Stated Iraq after series revolutions is developing and in evolutionary stage as member Free World. Present government is non-aligned. Past governments had interpreted non-alignment badly. Present GOI socialistic but not Marxist or Communist. Recognizes role private enterprise.

b. Bazzaz stated Nasser only Arab world leader who effectively combatting communism and Marxism. Key to good relations with Arabs is good relations with Nasser.

---

[4] The Prime Minister's October 15 conversation with Vice President Humphrey is recorded in a memorandum of conversation ibid., Central Files 1964–66, POL 7 IRAQ.

c. PM alleged Iran encouraging disturbances northern Iraq for purely destructive reasons. Shah's problem is his attitude towards Nasser. US should use good offices convince Iran stop aiding Kurds.

d. Finally PM urged US persuade British adopt better attitude toward South Arabia.

e. VP stated PM was speaking to sympathetic mind. Social reform in US occurs within structure mixed economy. VP emphasized distinction between communism and socialism. Real secret of freedom is right express and exchange opinions.

f. VP noted he had visited UAR and had talked with Nasser as well as having brought message from President Kennedy.[5] We have differences but it is US policy try find ways agree. Recently in response strong feeling on part American people Congress reacted against Nasser. President, Vice President and Secretary had to work hard to reverse Congressional decision in order keep flow food continuing to Egypt. We appreciate frank words such as PM's, however Nasser also needs frank talk.

g. VP did not comment on Kurdish situation, saying he was uninformed details. Finally Vice President referred question British and South Arabia to Assistant Secretary Hare.

3–a. In call on Under Secretary Mann October 15,[6] PM contrasted his own modern liberal interpretation of socialism with rigid views his predecessors. He eschews slogans and doctrinaire theories. Under Secretary said he could agree with PM comments, adding economic doctrines devised hundred years or more ago not applicable today without modification.

b. In response Under Secretary's question re US-Iraqi economic relations, PM said Iraq's policy is true non-alignment, that GOI would examine every case on own merits and according Iraq interests but there would be good opportunities for US cooperation and assistance.

c. Under Secretary raised claims US firms pending in Iraq. Bazzaz' response provided Deptel 168 (to Baghdad).[7]

d. PM reiterated idea re US assistance in building new university. It would cost $30–35 million. Iraq able repay in 7–8 years. Mann said he would look into matter.

---

[5] For information on Humphrey's meeting with Nasser on October 22, 1961, see *Foreign Relations, 1961–1963*, vol. XVII, Document 131.

[6] The Prime Minister's October 15 conversation with Under Secretary of State for Economic Affairs Thomas C. Mann is recorded in a memorandum of conversation. (National Archives and Records Administration, RG 59, Central Files 1964–66, POL 7 IRAQ)

[7] Dated October 18. (Ibid., E 7 IRAQ)

e. Bazzaz raised Kurdish problem in economic sense as drain on Iraq's finances. He mentioned building loan program and said existing Iraqi institution needs capital. GOI might request $7–8 million loan from US. Mann said he would also look into this.

Rusk

177. Airgram From the Embassy in Iraq to the Department of State[1]

A–424   Baghdad, October 30, 1965.

SUBJECT

Analysis of the Kurdish Problem

Enclosed is an analysis in outline form of the Iraqi Kurdish problem prepared by Ambassador Strong.[2] The analysis sets forth the many and varied competing interests and motivations involved and should be helpful to all concerned with United States policy on this problem.

The central conclusion from the standpoint of the United States is that a high degree of autonomy or independence for the Iraqi Kurds would be disruptive of area stability and inimical to our interests in the long run. Neither is the continuation of the fighting in United States interests, although the consequences do not, at least for the time being, warrant a major initiative by the United States. That the communists and Soviets will gain control of a large-scale insurrection seems unlikely, as is Kurdish ability to establish an autonomous or separatist regime.

The analysis brings out that while the United States, Soviet and UAR postures advocating a peaceful, negotiated settlement are superficially parallel, the positions are differently motivated and, especially in the United States and Soviet cases, based on different assumptions as to probable results.

Similarly, the Iranians and Israelis—and perhaps the British—appear for varying motivations to favor continuation of the conflict for its debilitating effect on Iraq.

---

[1] Source: National Archives and Records Administration, RG 59, Central Files 1964–66, POL 13–3 IRAQ. Confidential. Drafted by Strong and Duncan on October 29, and approved by Duncan. Repeated to Adana, Aleppo, Ankara, Basra, Beirut, Cairo, Damascus, London, Tabriz, and Tehran.

[2] Attached but not printed.

Continued Iranian/Israeli intervention is a threat to the United States position in Iraq but, unfortunately, neither country is likely to be heedful of United States interests in the matter.

For the immediate future, neither the Kurds or the GOI appear able to force a military solution. Similarly even a negotiated solution is not likely to be permanent. The Kurdish problem is long-term.

The current United States policy stance seems the most suitable— that the problem is an internal Iraqi one for which a negotiated political solution is desirable.

For the Ambassador:
Enoch S. Duncan
Counselor for Political Affairs

---

178.   **Telegram From the Department of State to the Embassy in Iraq**[1]

Washington, January 6, 1966, 6:22 p.m.

330. Iraqi Ambassador Hani called on Assistant Secretary Hare 6th to register Iraq's complaint against Iran re recent border incidents. In restrained vein Hani covered main points of public Iraqi note of 4th. Stated alleged Iranian action not only harming Iraq–Iran relations but endangering peace in entire area. Therefore Iraqis are also raising issue with other states in area such as Saudi Arabia. Turks cooperative on issue in interests their own security. Iraqi rep at UN will inform UNSYG of situation. Iraq exercising restraint, but "there is a limit." Iraq hopes USG, in view of mutual concern and friendly relationship with both sides, can do something helpful. During presentation, Hani repeatedly went out of his way to stress Iraq's desire for good relations with Iran, comparing their situation with US and Canada.

Hare replied he gratified by Hani's statement Iraqi Government trying to keep situation under control and prevent it from reaching explosion point. Hoped Iraq would continue to maintain this policy,

---

[1] Source: National Archives and Records Administration, RG 59, Central Files 1964–66, POL 32–1 IRAN–IRAQ. Confidential. Drafted by Officer in Charge of Iraq–Jordan Affairs Lucien L. Kinsolving, cleared in draft by Symmes and Howison, and approved by Hare. Also sent to Tehran and repeated to London.

since problem cannot be solved by force. We would take similar attitude towards Iran, which also close friend of US. Nature of question such that we have not drawn up "balance sheet." We not sure we should attempt to be judge of rights and wrongs in matter. Would hope Iraq and Iran could resolve difficulties by own means without allowing issue to become further overheated.

Rusk

---

179.   **Telegram From the Embassy in Iran to the Department of State**[1]

Tehran, January 20, 1966, 1440Z.

1044. Iran–Iraq Relations.

1. Shah Relaxed. When I suggested 20th that he must be confident Iran–Iraq situation under control or he would not be making his planned trip to Europe, Shah answered affirmative. He said he felt Iran's main aim been accomplished, i.e. to let Iraqis know that any military action across Iran border would meet with vigorous response and that Iran meant it when it said it would "silence" sources of any such activity.

2. Long Range Aims. Shah said at no time has Iran objective been acquisition any Iraqi territory, two countries have everything to gain by neighborly relations. He mentioned they both oil producers. They have common water resources which should be utilized equitably. Shia community in Iraq inevitably has close affinity for Iranian Shias, etc.

3. Kurdish Problem. Shah indicated he has no intention antagonizing his Kurds by actions against Iraq's Kurds. He described Kurds as "purest Aryan" segment of Persian race. Shah's point was that problem of Kurds in Iraq is an internal Iraqi problem, not solvable by "butchering" Kurds and not exportable to Iran.

4. Shatt in Perspective. While this might be moment, Shah said, to exploit tension with Iraq to force solution of Shatt issue, clearly this not Iran's intention. This question has history of many decades, he said, and Iran can afford to wait few more years. In fact, in few years with development Iran's Persian Gulf ports, Iran will be virtually independent of Shatt. At that time, when few ships come to Iranian ports,

---

[1] Source: National Archives and Records Administration, RG 59, Central Files 1964–66, POL IRAN–IRAQ. Secret. Repeated to Ankara, Baghdad, Jidda, and London.

Iraqis will have increasing difficulty with financial burden of keeping Shatt navigable. Shah predicted at that time, Iraqis will come to Iran in hope of sharing this burden, and dividing Shatt between them. Shah noted, however, that without some discussion Shatt differences issue likely be source of unending trouble between two countries.

5. Recent Progress. Referring to my lengthy chat (Embtel 1034)[2] with Hassan Dujaili, new Iraqi Ambassador to Iran, I told Shah that although I had not seen this friend for eighteen years I quickly had recalled what a sincere and constructive fellow he is. I told Shah Dujaili made sense to me when he said no Iraqi Govt. could discuss question like Shatt under duress. Dujaili seemed completely earnest in wanting reduce tensions and develop neighborly ties.

6. Give Bazzaz a Chance. Noting that evidence seems to be coming in almost every day that while Iraq Govt. still has long way to go to attain competence and constructive purpose of pre-1958 days, I gave as my impression that Bazzaz, now that he is in chair of responsibility, is acquitting himself relatively well and that Iranians ought to give him fair chance. Shah appeared to agree and noted that since Labor government took over in England it has behaved much more responsibly than what one would have expected from its declarations when it was out of power. Shah seemed also to have better realization than previously that Bazzaz and IRWP are not necessarily subservient to Cairo. He characterized Aref as pro-Nasser and "crazy." He referred this time merely to Iraq's Egyptian "friends." He also agreed that even Nasser must realize that Iraq could prove more indigestible than Syria.

7. Three-point Program. Shah said Iran had tried to move half way by accepting Bazzaz's three-point proposal but he said three points must be reciprocal. Be third point, he said Iran did not wish Iraqis to be left with impression that payment of compensation which joint investigating commission might determine would resolve all outstanding Iraq–Iran differences. Door must be left open for discussion other problems such as Shatt and also distribution of water resources, 65 per cent of which rise in Persian highlands.

8. Comment. My impression is that Shah is leaving here with instructions to his govt. that Iran not take any initiatives to cause resurgence in Iraq–Iran tensions. Re long-range issues, he considers both question of Iran aid to Kurds and Shatt-al-Arab question unresolved, but resolution not imperative now. Purpose of my remarks was to encourage Shah to leave his Ministers in no uncertainty as to his wish that situation remain calm during his absence.

Meyer

---

[2] Dated January 19. (Ibid.)

180.   Telegram From the Embassy in Iraq to the Department of State[1]

Baghdad, May 17, 1966, 1240Z.

688. Subject: Call on President Aref.[2] Ref: Embtel 677,[3] Deptel 538.[4]

1. Had 35 minute talk with President Aref noon May 17. After my delivery of President Johnson's personal best wishes to Aref and for well being of Iraq, Aref expressed sincere appreciation and asked that his personal best regards and best wishes be transmitted to President Johnson. He then recalled our frequent friendly contacts before he became President and said he wished our relationship to continue on same basis.

2. Briefly described main feature of my mission as further development of US–Iraqi relations and US cooperation in promoting stability and political, economic and social development of Iraq to extent desired by Iraq and within means available. Aref expressed understanding and appreciation and turned conversation to Iranian aid to Kurds.

3. I explained in detail USG position on Kurdish problem, outlined Iranian concerns, recounted our efforts to encourage Iran and Iraq to find way to settle differences peacefully and said I thought only Iran and Iraq could settle their mutual problems. Aref said Iran had nothing to fear from Iraq or from UAR–Iraqi relations, but if Shah, who alone responsible for Iranian hostility to Iraq, for whatever reason persists in helping Kurds, then Iraq will be obliged make as much trouble for Iran as possible (airgram being submitted with more detailed account).[5]

Aref expressed gratitude for frank discussion which he said he would hold in confidence. Said he wished our talks to be as friend to friend rather than President to Ambassador. I said I looked forward to quiet, friendly talks from time to time.

5. *Comment:* Aref was friendly, relaxed and mild throughout. He showed good sense of humor several times. In no way did he place blame on US for Iranian actions and he acknowledged USG not helping

---

[1] Source: National Archives and Records Administration, RG 59, Central Files 1964–66, POL 15–1 IRAQ. Confidential.

[2] President Abdul Salam Aref was killed in a plane crash on April 13 and succeeded on April 16 by his brother, Major General Abdul Rahman Aref.

[3] Dated May 16. (National Archives and Records Administration, RG 59, Central Files 1964–66, POL 15–1 IRAQ)

[4] Telegram 538 to Baghdad, May 14, instructed Strong to reiterate the President's congratulations on Aref's assumption of office and noted that the initial call should be primarily a courtesy call, although the Ambassador could discuss specific subjects at issue between the two governments if he felt it appropriate. (Ibid.)

[5] Airgram A–959 from Baghdad, May 18. (Ibid., POL 2 IRAQ)

Kurds. When I referred to great principles for which US fighting in Vietnam he expressed understanding and agreement. Interpreter was used throughout except for several brief exchanges of personal nature at beginning and end of talk. His English is adequate for ordinary conversation.

6. Consider talk to have confirmed earlier belief that Aref well disposed toward US, although we cannot expect him to take cordial public posture and there inevitably will be events which will embarrass our relations somewhat.

Strong

---

181. Circular Airgram From the Department of State to the Embassy in Iraq[1]

CA–39   Washington, July 1, 1966, 7:42 p.m.

SUBJECT

    U.S. Arms Policy for Iraq

REF

    CA 11684, Apr 18, 1963[2]

The instruction contained in the airgram under reference continues to constitute the basic U.S. policy guidance on the sale of arms to the Government of Iraq. However, recent developments in the arms build-up in the Near East warrant certain minor revisions of that instruction. Accordingly, the specific provisos on page 3 of the instruction are modified and restated herewith as follows:

The U.S. should:

1. Avoid sale to Iraq of any heavy military equipment or sophisticated weapons, including napalm and other chemicals, tanks, military aircraft (except unarmed helicopters), and naval vessels classified as anything higher than a "craft".

---

[1] Source: National Archives and Records Administration, RG 59, Central Files 1964–66, DEF 1 IRAQ–US. Confidential. Drafted by Kinsolving; cleared in draft by Stoddart (DOD/ISA), G/PM Director of Operations Howard Meyers, Colonel Billy W. Byrd (NEA/NR), and Symmes; and approved by Hare. Repeated to Amman, Ankara, Beirut, Cairo, Damascus, Jidda, Kuwait, London, Tehran, and CINCSTRIKE/CINCMEAFSA.
[2] See *Foreign Relations*, 1961–1963, vol. XVIII, Document 216.

2. Agree to requests for reasonable quantities of small arms up to and including machine guns, but not preclude consideration on a case by case basis of requests for small numbers of light and medium artillery guns provided the latter are no heavier than 105 MM.

3. Be willing to sell quantities of transport vehicles, communications equipment, engineering equipment, and other "non-shooting" material.

4. Continue the present program of grant aid non-combat training, consider requests for additional training on a reimbursable basis, but not preclude additional grant aid training if U.S. interests would be served.

5. Interpose no objection if the British sell Iraq military equipment of a type which does not violate USG arms policy, though we would also bid on these items ourselves if asked to do so by the Iraqis. If the Iraqis should seek to negotiate a military sales package with the British, the U.S. would be willing to cooperate with the British and furnish those items of military hardware not precluded by our arms policy.

6. Agree to continue to sell Iraq spare parts and ammunition for equipment of U.S. origin still employed by the Iraqi Army.

7. Given Iraq's relatively favorable foreign exchange position, undertake only cash sales to Iraq.

8. Sell nothing classified to Iraq.

9. Consult with the Iranian and Turkish Governments before concluding agreements for major arms purchases by Iraq.

10. After informing the UK and French Governments of the foregoing, acquaint the Iraqi Government informally in the near future of the essentials of this policy as restated above.

Ball

182. Telegram From the Embassy in Iraq to the Department of State[1]

Baghdad, July 2, 1966, 1300Z.

12. State 396.[2]

1. Rather than delivering congratulatory message from USG on thwarting of coup, propose use suitable occasions to express orally to Iraqi leaders USG (a) regret that Iraq has had to suffer another outbreak of violence, (b) hope that GOI efforts maintain stability and proceed with development will be successful, (c) congratulations on GOI political program for Kurds and on gaining Kurdish acceptance, and (d) hope that settlement will be implemented promptly, consistently and in good faith by both GOI and Kurds. Believe foregoing will be appreciated and avoid possibility of embarrassment.[3]

2. Timing of coup attempt could possibly in part have related to Bazzaz June 29 announcement of Kurdish settlement. Coup leaders perhaps hoped other elements such as military officers originating Mosul, many of whom anti-Kurd, would join movement to overthrow regime which "betrayed Iraq by capitulating to Kurds." Participation of Moslawi commander of fourth division Attarbashi perhaps secured this basis (but GOI apparently already aware his unreliability since Brigadier Adnan Abd al-Jalil several days ago said to have been named to replace him). On other hand coup leaders' first radio announcement accepted Kurdish settlement. Fact settlement being reached and general outline of terms widely known more than week before coup attempt. These points lead to belief that other factors more important in selection of time. For example, Bazzaz due leave for Turkey July 1. Also, afternoon June 30 was eve of two-day holiday, government establishments close 1:30 p.m. and by 3:10 p.m. when ruckus started siesta is general rule, and large numbers of officers and troops normally given weekend and holiday leave.

3. From speed and smoothness of reaction by loyal forces seems evident GOI aware of coup plans and preferred catch leaders redhanded

---

[1] Source: National Archives and Records Administration, RG 59, Central Files 1964–66, POL 23–9 IRAQ. Secret. Repeated to Cairo.

[2] Telegram 396 to Baghdad, July 1, noted that the Department was considering whether it might be useful for the Embassy to convey U.S. congratulations quietly to President Aref or Prime Minister Bazzaz on successful thwarting of the recent coup attempt. It also asked for the Embassy's analysis of the degree to which that attempt had been triggered by announcement of the Kurdish settlement. (Ibid.)

[3] Telegram 1207 to Baghdad, July 3, stated that the Department concurred in the Ambassador's proposed course of action. (Ibid.)

rather than try to round them up ahead of time and have them on GOI hands without proven case. This quite in keeping with way Iraqis look at things, particularly when they confident of winning.

Strong

---

183. **Telegram From the Embassy in Iraq to the Department of State**[1]

Baghdad, August 19, 1966, 1015Z.

241. Subject: Talk with New Prime Minister.[2]

1. I saw Talib for 50 minutes August 18. Much of time spent on Kurdish question and Iran at his initiative. I told him USG prepared work with present GOI as with previous Iraqi Governments in pursuit of fundamental goal of stable prosperous Iraq; explained in detail our concern over lack of progress on claims of contractors; and explained basic facts of Vietnam situation, its meaning to free world, and firmness of US purpose; expressed deep disappointment at Bazzaz's alignment of Iraq with Soviet position. Talib made a note to look into handling of claims. He avoided further discussion of Vietnam by saying cabinet absorbed in domestic affairs and had no time, as had Bazzaz in Moscow, to concern itself with world issues such as Vietnam and German question.

2. Talib declared GOI would implement Kurdish program fully, but he dwelt extensively on difficulties and gave no hint how GOI to proceed. Most serious problem he identified is three-way split among Kurds, with Barzani insisting GOI deal only with him; GOI cannot ignore Kurds who sided with GOI or those of old KDP. Talib said Barzani wants to be "King of Kurdistan," but apart from that nobody knows what he really wants.

3. Talib asked my views, whether Kurds serious, what GOI should do. I said GOI had real opportunity settle problem. Kurds not likely start conflict unless GOI failed act. I urged GOI take very generous attitude over extended period of time in order create confidence in

---

[1] Source: National Archives and Records Administration, RG 59, Central Files 1964–66, POL 15–1 IRAQ. Confidential. Repeated to Tehran, Algiers, Amman, Ankara, Basra, Beirut, Cairo, Damascus, Dhaharan, Jerusalem, Jidda, Khartoum, Kuwait, London, Moscow, Rabat, Tel Aviv, Tripoli, Tunis, and CINCSTRIKE/CINCMEAFSA.

[2] Bazzaz resigned as Prime Minister on August 6 and was succeeded by Naji Talib.

good faith of GOI. As Kurds see GOI serious, support for armed rebellion likely decline. Talib listened, but he again stressed difficulies and need for Kurdish cooperation.

4. Talib expressed conviction Iran still supplying arms to Kurds. He did not ask that USG take action with Iran nor did he imply USG helped Kurds. I said I thought arms supply from Iran cut off sometime after June 29; possibly other types supplies moving in but if so this would stop if GOI would drop economic blockade of north as it promised. Talib took very hard line, asked what Iran wants of Iraq and compared Iranian attitude with that of Turkey. He said GOI wants good relations with Iran; Bazzaz and Taher Yahya had not wanted bad relations but Iran had created them. Now Iran tries to impose impossible conditions; no GOI can even discuss Shatt al-Arab. I explained Iranian concerns and then noted that in past few weeks opportunity has arisen for Iraq to move toward better relations with Iran. I urged Talib to try to capitalize on it. Talib responded neither aye nor nay but listened carefully.

5. I pointed out that Iran gave limited help to Kurds for limited objective, whereas USSR keeps stirring up Kurdish aspirations and so-called clandestine broadcasts hostile to GOI continue from Eastern Europe. These things ultimately more dangerous to Iraq; Soviets have longstanding ambitions in direction Persian Gulf; their agitation of Kurdish question targeted at this objective. Talib admitted this but went on that USSR is friend of Iraq which needs Soviet help.

6. *Comment:*

A. Talib revealed nothing of general lines of policies to be pursued. He said ministerial policy statement will be issued in few days. It is still too early for evaluation of current GOI. Next few weeks should provide clues as to character and direction.

B. As Shi'a, Talib may deem it necessary be extra hardboiled with Iran. He has been antagonised by Iranian Ambassador Pirasteh who has told Talib that as a Shi'a he (Talib) is practically an Iranian and should cooperate closely with Iran. I still hope Iran will patiently keep door open to genuine efforts toward improvement in relations.

C. Talib was physically tired. He was business-like but friendly in attitude. He failed raise question of PL–480 wheat or relief program for north.

Strong

184. **Telegram From the Department of State to the Embassy in Iraq**[1]

Washington, October 8, 1966, 3:56 p.m.

62624. FYI. Following summary of Secretary's meeting with Pachachi October 5[2] is drawn from uncleared memcon and is FYI, Noforn and subject to review.

1. *Kurdish Problem.* Pachachi stated Iraq had been able solve this. Iraq had hoped US could do something about Iranian assistance to Kurds. Pachachi will meet with Aram in New York. Stated, "It would be gesture of great help if US could aid in reconstruction in Northern Iraq."

2. *Economic Affairs.* Pachachi stated GOI hopes ratify Investment Guarantee Agreement. Hopes USG will work with HMG and US companies involved in IPC to press them to seek agreement with GOI.

3. *Arab–Israel Problem.* Pachachi complained US arms sales to Israel made US appear pro-Israeli. Stated his Govt rather unhappy about further US reductions in its contributions to UNRWA. Re refugees themselves, noted no genuine attempt had ever been made to ascertain refugees' own views. Attempt by Joseph Johnson good effort, but weakened by linking consultation with implementation. End FYI.

Rusk

---

[1] Source: National Archives and Records Administration, RG 59, Central Files 1964–66, POL 23–9 IRAQ. Secret. Drafted by Kinsolving, cleared by Atherton, and approved by Handley. Repeated to Beirut and Tehran.

[2] The Secretary's meeting with Foreign Minister Pachachi took place at the United Nations. The memorandum of conversation recording their discussion of the Arab-Israeli problem is in *Foreign Relations, 1964–1968,* vol. XVIII, Document 323. Other memoranda of conversations are at the National Archives and Records Administration, RG 59, Conference Files: Lot 67 D 305, CF 83.

185. Memorandum From the Country Director for Israel and Arab–Israel Affairs (Atherton) to the Assistant Secretary of State for Near Eastern and South Asian Affairs (Hare)[1]

Washington, November 1, 1966.

SUBJECT

IRG Meeting November 2, 1966: Communist Presence in Iraq, Jordan and Lebanon

The following discussion and recommendations provide suggested talking points for your use in tomorrow's IRG meeting.[2] They are focussed on the nature of the Communist presence in Iraq, Jordan and Lebanon and its policy implications for the USG. Although limiting the discussion in this way is admittedly somewhat arbitrary, we have not therefore attempted to cover the entire range of possible U.S. policy initiatives with the countries concerned.

IRAQ

A. Communist Presence in Iraq

The Communist presence in Iraq is large, centering more around Soviet official missions than an indigenous Communist Party. Soviet and Communist assets include 1) the acceptance by the Iraqi Government of a large-scale military and economic aid program that gives the Soviet Union influence with the Iraqi Government and entree for its personnel into Government operations and plans; 2) Dependence of the Iraqi Armed Forces on supplies and replacement parts from Russia for their largely Soviet equipment; 3) The image of the Soviet Union as a counterbalance to the "imperialists" in diplomatic and economic relations; 4) Iraqi resentment and fear of Western support for Israel in particular; 5) The close association of the U.S. and the UK with "reactionary" Arab states and Israel and the belief that the U.S. and the UK are fundamentally hostile to revolutionary Arab regimes.

On the other hand, the weaknesses of the local Communist position are numerous and deep and include: 1) Iraqi hatred of local Communists stemming from the latter's excesses during the Qasim period; 2) Iraqi Government resentment of clandestine Soviet support for Kurds

---

[1] Source: Department of State, NEA/RA Files: Lot 71 D 218, Papers re Communist Presence in the Middle East, 1966. Secret. No drafting information appears on the source text.

[2] For a record of the IRG/NEA meeting on November 2, see Document 81. The Group discussed the Communist presence in the Arabian Peninsula and Persian Gulf (except Yemen and South Arabia) and Jordan. It did not discuss the situation in Iraq.

and local Communists; 3) The failure of some Soviet aid projects; 4) The cultural affinity of educated Iraqis for the West; 5) Iraqi preference for Western goods, travel, contacts and higher education, and the poor calibre of Soviet products and personnel; 6) Iraqi dread of USSR "great power" dominance; and 7) Mutual antipathies (Arabism, Islam vs atheistic communism, etc.)

B. Policy Considerations and Opportunities

Since 1963 there has been a gradual but continuing swing of the pendulum back toward moderation in the policies of successive Iraqi Governments. There is also a broadly based desire in Iraq to preserve and develop Iraqi national identity and to avoid overdependence on the USSR or an overly close tie with the UAR.

The USG should pursue policies designed to strengthen the foregoing tendencies and those elements in the power structure who support them. The problem of limiting the Communist presence in Iraq is long range—there are no gimmicks—and consists essentially of devising policies and actions which will maintain an effective western presence.

C. Recommended IRG Decisions

1. Continue within current availabilities to offer the Government of Iraq relief assistance for the devastated north in the form of surplus food, and otherwise attempt to offset Soviet influence in the Kurdish area by maintaining a friendly though correct relationship with the main body of the Kurds, who constitute a sizeable proportion of the population and hold strategic Iraqi territory.

2. Encourage Iran to pursue a more friendly, flexible policy toward Iraq in Iran's own interest.

3. Maintain the program for military training in the U.S. and offer other courses such as counter-guerrilla training when appropriate.

4. Continue police training.

5. Maintain the educational and cultural exchange program at the highest feasible level.

[Here follows discussion of Lebanon and Jordan.]

186.   Draft Message From President Johnson to President Aref[1]

Washington, undated.

I was delighted to have the opportunity to talk to Ambassador Hani November 17[2] and when I learned of Ambassador Strong's call on you I wanted to use the opportunity to send you my personal greetings. I have been impressed with your efforts to create stability in an atmosphere of moderation and to strengthen national unity by conciliating all elements. Your achievement of peace in the north is a monument to your leadership. I have noted with pleasure the development of Iraqi–United States relations on a sound basis and look to even more mutually beneficial relations in the future. I offer you my best personal wishes for your continued success and the well-being of your country.[3]

---

[1] Source: National Archives and Records Administration, RG 59, Records of the Department of State, Central Files 1964–66, POL 15–1 IRAQ. No classification marking. Sent to the White House with a November 25 memorandum from Read to Rostow stating that the message had been drafted by Ambassador Strong, who recommended that he be authorized to convey a brief oral message from President Johnson to President Aref when he paid an expected formal call on Aref in the near future.

[2] According to the President's Daily Diary, Ambassador Hani and Lebanon Ambassador Ibrahim Hussayn el-Ahdab called on the President, who was recuperating from surgery, at the U.S. Naval Hospital in Bethesda, Maryland, from 12:10 to 12:15 p.m. on November 17. (Johnson Library)

[3] Telegram 91650 to Baghdad, November 25, authorized the Ambassador to convey the oral message to President Aref. (National Archives and Records Administration, RG 59, Central Files 1964–66, POL 15–1 IRAQ)

187.   Telegram From the Embassy in Iraq to the Department of
       State[1]

Baghdad, November 30, 1966, 0830Z.

1022. Call on President Aref. Baghdad 964,[2] State 91650.[3]

1. Called on Aref for 50 minutes November 29. Aref obviously
very pleased at message from President Johnson and at my initiative
make call. Gave him text of oral message on plain paper.

2. Aref asked me transmit to President his appreciation for message, his best wishes for speedy recuperation and good health in future,
his best wishes for President's personal success, his hope that American
people will enjoy increasing prosperity and happiness, and his hope
that US will continue its tradition of helping the weak and will continue
to assist in development of underdeveloped countries; if US does this
without hidden purpose, US will benefit immensely and its position
in world will be enhanced far beyond any costs involved.

3. I gave Aref impressions from trip to north and indicated that
appeared best way USG could help at [apparent omission] obtain USG
approval. Aref expressed satisfaction.[4]

4. Reviewed other ways US cooperating in Iraq development: We
encourage reputable companies seek contracts and others enter joint
ventures such as sulfur, vehicle assembly and tires, but absence investment guarantee agreement is serious barrier. Aref understood but
avoided commitment.

5. Aref proposed US assistance for Euphrates and Eski Mosul
Dams. I explained background of US offer on Eski Mosul and said
USG uninterested in less important Euphrates Dam. At his request
made suggestions for Iraqi first steps toward consortium for Eski Mosul
pointed to necessity for good Iraqi relations with potential contributors,
and discussed claims of contractors. Aref pointed to Iraqi potential to
help meet prospective world food shortage. I indicated USG interest

---

[1] Source: National Archives and Records Administration, RG 59, Central Files 1964–
66, POL 15–1 IRAQ. Confidential; Limdis.

[2] Telegram 964 from Baghdad, November 22, contained Strong's suggested text for
an oral message from the President to President Aref. (Ibid.) See Document 186.

[3] See footnote 3, Document 186.

[4] The detailed account of the meeting in airgram A–383 from Baghdad, December
1, reports the Ambassador's statement to Aref that it seemed to him that the most
promising way the U.S. Government could be of assistance with reconstruction in the
short term would be food-for-work programs, whereby people would return to their
villages and be paid mostly in food to rebuild houses, schools, clinics, etc. and to repair
roads. (National Archives and Records Administration, RG 59, Central Files 1964–66,
POL 1 IRAQ–US)

in Iraqi agricultural development and particular need for training technical-level manpower.

6. I referred to numerous rumors and press comments accusing USG and Embassy of nefarious actions. Said I could assure Aref neither USG nor Embassy working against Iraqi interests and had no intention doing so. US concerned to support Iraqi search for stability and prosperity. Aref said he aware of this but went on that in zeal know what is going on "boys at Embassy" sometimes in contact with "suspicious elements"; Embassy knows whom he means (he said this in all good humor).

7. *Comment:* Meeting was cordial, timely and achieved purpose. Was careful avoid committing USG to anything new. Appreciate having message from President to deliver; it was very valuable.

8. Detailed account of meeting being sent by airgram.[5]

Strong

---

[5] Airgram A–383 from Baghdad, December 1. (Ibid.) See footnote 4 above.

---

188. Memorandum From the President's Special Assistant (Rostow) to President Johnson[1]

Washington, January 21, 1967.

SUBJECT

Gift and Message from Iraq's President

Attached[2] is a special recommendation from Secretary Rusk that you briefly receive the Deputy Chief of the Iraqi Army on January 23, 24 or 25 just long enough for a few words and an exchange of gifts.

This is a rather unusual request but one that warrants serious consideration. General Sabri is here at the Pentagon's invitation for an orientation tour with four other senior officers who have considerable political power in Iraq. But President Aref at the last minute took

---

[1] Source: Johnson Library, National Security File, Country File, Iraq, Cables & Memos, Vol. I, 12/63–7/68. Confidential.

[2] Attached but not printed.

advantage of his trip to have him bring you a personal gift (a carpet) and message.

I wouldn't normally recommend you spend your time this way—nor would Secretary Rusk. However, we both feel strongly this is an opportunity we shouldn't miss.

Iraq is at a crossroads. If its moderates—headed by Aref—can win out, Iraq could break out of Nasser's sphere and become stabilizing influence. In the short run, this is important to our oil companies which are trying to work their way out of the box Syria has them in. A more radical government in Iraq might threaten to nationalize them. In the longer run, our objective in the Middle East is to encourage governments like Aref's to stand on their own—and not to get sucked into the more radical Arab nationalist movements that cause us (and Israel) so much trouble.

We have considered inviting Aref here for a visit but so far have judged that would do him more harm than good in his own sensitive political situation. However, by this gesture he is reaching out to strengthen his relationship with you. This is unexpectedly encouraging. I believe we ought to reciprocate by receiving his emissary.

Secretary Rusk, to save you, has suggested only that you receive General Sabri. It would spread the advantage we gain to receive all five of the generals because the corps commanders in Iraq are often the keys to political stability. I recommend you receive the entire delegation.

Walt

I'll see General Sabri
I'll see all five together if Secretary Rusk would like[3]
Disapprove

---

[3] This option is checked. According to the President's Daily Diary, the President saw the five Iraqi senior officers from noon to 12:09 p.m. on January 25. (Johnson Library)

189.   Memorandum From the Executive Secretary of the Department of State (Read) to the President's Special Assistant (Rostow)[1]

Washington, February 16, 1967.

SUBJECT

Letter from Kurdish Insurgent Leader Barzani to the President[2]

Enclosed is a letter from the leader of the Kurdish insurrection in Iraq, General Barzani, to the President. The letter was brought to the United States by one of General Barzani's chief supporters, Dr. Osman. It was delivered to the Department of State at the desk level, where Kurds and Kurdish emissaries are received.

The letter requests the United States to employ its influence to urge a final and just settlement of the Kurdish question in Iraq, and also requests material help for the destitute Kurds. In fact, our Ambassador in Iraq, Robert Strong, has discreetly but repeatedly urged the Iraqi Government to take more steps to satisfy legitimate Kurdish requests within the framework of Iraqi sovereignty. Since 1964 we have been carrying on a program of supplying surplus US food to Kurdish refugees in Iraq.

Since June 1966 a de facto truce has existed between the Kurdish insurgents and the Iraqi Government pending an over-all settlement. Toward the end of 1966 Barzani sent a memorandum to the President of Iraq, a copy of which he also enclosed in his letter to the President, complaining that the Iraqi regime has not been acting in good faith in implementing the truce arrangements.

In view of the fact that Barzani has technically still not submitted to the Iraqi Government, we recommend that no written reply be sent to Barzani's letter to the President. Instead, we recommend that a Department of State officer at the desk level orally acknowledge receipt of the letter on behalf of the President and reassure the Kurds of United States Government's concern on a humanitarian basis as evidenced by the continuing flow of surplus foods to the destitute Kurds in Iraq. Such a reply would be consistent with our previous handling of messages from Barzani.[3]

BR

---

[1] Source: National Archives and Records Administration, RG 59, Central Files 1967–69, POL 23–9 IRAQ. Secret. Drafted by Kinsolving on February 14 and cleared by Davies and Country Director for Lebanon, Jordan, Syrian Arab Republic, and Iraq Robert B. Houghton.

[2] Attached but not printed.

[3] A notation typed on the memorandum dated May 9 states that the White House determined that no action or reply was necessary.

190.   Telegram From the Department of State to the Embassy in Iraq[1]

Washington, April 5, 1967, 12:32 p.m.

168758. Baghdad 1696 and 1719.[2]

1. Dept concurs subjects you intend discuss in your April 6 meeting with Pres Aref. We have discussed with Mobil your intention raise IPC problem and company concurs in full confidence your judgment. If opportunity arises discuss idea of settlement (para 2 Baghdad 1696) you should not give Aref impression company would accept settlement significantly different from that defined 1965 agreement. Dept believes would be most useful your examining oil problem with President in effort determine his thinking on subject and make sure he understands efforts IPC made accommodate Iraqi requirements.

2. Dept would also be interested any comments President might make concerning his recent Tehran visit. For example, what steps are now being taken or what steps does he think should be taken as result visit to further improve relations between two countries. In this connection you might also mention that we impressed wisdom his efforts build bridges of good will with his neighbors.

3. You should also inform him USG pleased with improvement US/Iraqi relations and would welcome any comments he may have as to future trends these relations.

Rusk

---

[1] Source: National Archives and Records Administration, RG 59, Central Files 1967–69, POL 15–1 IRAQ. Confidential; Immediate. Drafted by Houghton, cleared in substance by Country Director for Iran Theodore L. Eliot, Jr., and James E. Akins (E/OR/FSE), and approved by Davies.

[2] In telegram 1696 from Baghdad, April 3, Strong reported that he would meet with Aref to discuss U.S.–Iraqi relations, Kurdish affairs, and the IPC problem. He hoped to use whatever prestige he had to promote on a personal basis the idea of an Iraqi settlement with the IPC (the Iraq Petroleum Company—a consortium of foreign firms in which British, French, Dutch, and U.S. companies held various shares). The Ambassador asked the Department to advise him of anything it wished him to take up with Aref. (Ibid.) In telegram 1719 from Baghdad, April 5, Strong reported that he was meeting with Aref on April 6 and would appreciate having the authorization he had requested. (Ibid.)

191.   Telegram From the Embassy in Iraq to the Department of State[1]

Baghdad, April 8, 1967, 1000Z.

1744. Call on President Aref. State 169615[2] and 168758.[3]

1. Aref welcomed me in usual friendly fashion. I expressed appreciation for his receiving me and said I wished to present congratulations of diplomatic corps on removal of previous limitation on his term of office; members of corps look forward with pleasure to the continuation of relations with him. I went on that USG was happy to note this development and is looking forward to further development of our relations basis of mutual interests. I added my personal congratulations.

2. Aref said he wanted to thank President Johnson, Secretary of Defense, US Army, USG generally and me for highly successful visit of Iraqi military mission. Visit left deep impression on members of mission and mission was able to create favorable impression of Iraq in US. I concurred, expressed delight, promised to transmit this thanks, and said my government had instructed me to say it is happy with improvement in US-Iraqi relations in recent months and would appreciate any comment Aref wants to make on how he thinks this trend can be further developed.

3. Aref responded at some length, referring to widespread efforts of Communists and Ba'this to subvert Iraq, interference Iraq has suffered from other countries, numerous difficulties Iraq has had to face and price it has had to pay in struggling against them. He said aim of his government is to develop Iraq to point that its people could have dignity, jobs, homes, better things and some money in their pockets. While Iraq cannot rightly think of becoming another US, it must do more for its people. Iraq has proved its anti-communism. He himself has worked hard to promote stability in Iraq and stability in area. He is doing his best to improve relations with Iraq's neighbors so that all can benefit from tranquility to devote themselves to development. He does not want to have to spend tremendous sums on farms but to use money to build his country. Iraq is doing what it can with its own resources.

---

[1] Source: National Archives and Records Administration, RG 59, Central Files 1967–69, POL 15–1 IRAQ. Confidential. Repeated to London, Amman, Ankara, Beirut, Cairo, Damascus, Jidda, Kuwait, Tehran, Tel Aviv, Basra, and Dhahran.

[2] Telegram 169615 to Baghdad, April 6, instructed the Ambassador to convey the President's congratulations to Aref on having had his term of office extended by the cabinet and defense council. (Ibid.)

[3] Document 190.

4. Aref went on that he hoped continued development would lead to greater assistance from the US toward this objective. Iraq particularly needs to draw on the scientific and technical know-how of the US. He hopes US will respond to Iraq's needs and thus help Iraq continue to defeat forces of communism and other extremism which are trying to create anarchy in Iraq.

5. I referred to long list which I provided him some months ago of USG and private activities in Iraq all targeted at this objective. I said the USG's principal interest in Iraq is creation of stability, economic development and social reform, and prosperity. My government had instructed me to state that it has observed with gratification Aref's efforts to improve relations with Iraq's neighbors and to express hope that this process will continue. The means available for direct USG assistance to Iraq are limited; the means of private American companies and foundations are greater and we continue to encourage them to work there. There are many American companies interested in investing capital and know-how in joint ventures in Iraq, but this of course raises the question of investment guarantee agreement which the companies feel must exist to [garble] capital. If IGA can be considered from economic viewpoint, there should be little problem in signing it. It is not political agreement. Aref interjected that IGA is now before the Council of Ministers and added that he understands it is necessary.

6. I went on to explain measures USG is proposing to assist in the reconstruction of the north (food for work, village development expert, and Ex-Im loan of $[2?] million for materials and equipment); these proposals are limited in size and scope. Situation in north continues to develop favorably, if this small program is successful. If there is organization and money devoted to north, and if new arrangement with Italy to use Italian consultant to plan reconstruction and development works then further measures of cooperation will come to light and can be examined sympathetically; agriculture will be extremely important and there are many things that can be done in this field.

7. Aref expressed appreciation. He went on to say there are forces at work harmful to Iraq. Some of these forces he had already explained. Another force is oil companies which prefer to overlook conditions in Iraq, which fail to understand efforts by other baneful forces to destroy country. Oil companies of course are interested in increasing their profits, but he has had to conclude there is something more behind their attitude; there must be a political motive. (From here on for [the better?] part of an hour we discussed oil problem which is dealt with in separate messages.)

8. In conclusion I reported that I would be leaving for US on April 13 for just over two months and would return in mid-June with my wife. Hopefully to remain for another year or two. I said Aref could

count on me constantly to look for feasible ways to improve US–Iraqi relations and to increase US–Iraqi cooperation. It is my fondest hope that before my assignment in Iraq is completed Iraq and IPC will have settled all issues and that Iraq will be well on the road to stability, development and prosperity. Aref responded that he always appreciates my attitude, he shares my hopes and he wishes me a nice vacation.

9. *Comment:*

A. Aref was serious and more preoccupied than usual during our talk. He gave more impression of bearing heavy burdens than in past. However, he responded well to my occasional efforts to lighten atmosphere and showed his usual good humor and friendly personality number of times. He intently followed my words and interpretation of his remarks into English as though working to improve his comprehension of English. A number of times he understood clearly what I said and reacted before interpretation; and occasionally he made brief comments in English. I was unable to find suitable opportunity to work in question about Iraq's future relations with Iran without diverting from main issues undesirably.

B. Interview was valuable both in content and in terms of maintaining periodic contact with Aref.

C. Addendum: State 169615 authorizing delivery of an oral message from President Johnson to Aref did not arrive until the evening of April 6 and therefore was not in hand for my meeting with Aref. An inquiry might be made into reasons for delay in transmission. I am having the message delivered to Aref through master of ceremonies on April 8.

Strong

192.   Memorandum From the President's Special Assistant (Rostow) to President Johnson[1]

Washington, May 31, 1967, 8:45 p.m.

SUBJECT

Appointment With Iraqi Foreign Minister

Attached is Sec. Rusk's recommendation that you see Iraqi Foreign Minister Pachachi.[2] Since he has just been in Cairo and is a responsible man, he could turn out to be one of our better channels to the Arabs. We shall aim to tie him to the same kind of commitment to secrecy we got from Eban.

Sec. Rusk would see him before you, but Pachachi would probably have to be told before he'd come down from New York that he had an appointment with you.

I believe you should give serious consideration to seeing him. In Arab eyes, we are completely committed to Israel. It would be healthy, if we are to salvage any of our Arab interests from this crisis, if a responsible Arab could carry away an impression of both your resolution and your good will for Arabs who are trying to restore peace.

My recommendation is that he carry away a firm sense of how deeply meant were all aspects of your May 23 speech.

Walt

I'll see him[3]
See me

---

[1] Source: Johnson Library, National Security File, Country File, Iraq, Cables & Memos, Vol. I, 12/63–7/68. Secret.

[2] Rusk's May 31 memorandum stated that Pachachi had come to the United States in hope of seeing the President in connection with the Arab–Israel crisis, and argued that Johnson's reception of an Arab statesman of this caliber would help balance any Arab reaction to the visit of Foreign Minister Eban of Israel. (National Archives and Records Administration, RG 59, Central Files 1967–69, POL 7 IRAQ)

[3] Johnson completed the statement by writing: "only if you get same promises of secrecy as we got from Eban & under same conditions." The President's Daily Diary records that Johnson and Rostow met with Pachachi and Ambassador Hani on June 1 at the White House from 7:26 p.m. to 8 p.m. (Johnson Library) No record of their conversation has been found. Telegram 207808 to Baghdad, June 2, stated that the President requested that there be no publicity on his meeting with Pachachi, and Ambassador Hani had agreed, stating that he understood that Pachachi also desired no publicity. (National Archives and Records Administration, RG 59, Central Files 1967–69, POL 7 IRAQ)

193.   Telegram From the Department of State to the Embassy in Iraq[1]

Washington, June 2, 1967, 1:09 a.m.

206672. 1. Foreign Minister Pachachi met separately with Under Secretary Rostow and Secretary afternoon June 1 immediately prior to meeting with President. Following points emerged:

2. The Under Secretary said two fundamental principles not directly related to Israel–Arab dispute were involved in present situation which had been precipitated almost by accident following SYG's sudden withdrawal of UNEF particularly from Sharm el Sheikh. These were (a) freedom of seas which US defended all over world and (b) territorial integrity and political independence of states.

3. Rostow pointed out that US commitment to territorial integrity and political independence of states in Middle East had been clearly demonstrated in 1956 when US action in effect saved Nasser. Pachachi reply that this US action in 1956 was something which Arab States will never forget. Rostow commented that of all States in area, UAR was one which should be most aware of this.

4. Rostow pointed that freedom of passage through Strait of Tiran was affected by arrangements reached in 1957. At that time Israel withdrew from Sinai with the assurance that we and other maritime nations would support the international character of these waters. At the same time, the Ambassador of Israel stated in the United Nations that Israel would regard any violation of this principle by armed force as a hostile act justifying retaliation under Article 51 of the United Nations Charter. Our Ambassador "took note" of this statement. The Government of Israel has recently reaffirmed the view that it regards its rights of passage through the Strait, as they have been exercised for ten years, as a vital national interest. In present situation, USG had successfully exercised maximum diplomatic pressure to restrain Israel from a strike to which GOI felt entitled as a result of Nasser's action in announcing blockade of Strait of Tiran. It had not been easy to achieve as Israelis believe they have strong legal position. As result, time had been bought. During this breathing period peaceful settlement might be arranged. In this context it was encouraging to note that Nasser, while he had announced closing of Strait, had not yet used force to do so.

---

[1] Source: National Archives and Records Administration, RG 59, Central Files 1967–69, POL 27 ARAB–ISR. Secret; Priority; Exdis. Drafted by David L. Gamon (NEA/ARN), Houghton, and Eugene Rostow on June 1; cleared by Davies; and approved by Rostow. Repeated to Cairo, Beirut, Amman, Jidda, Tel Aviv, London, Jerusalem, and USUN.

5. Pachachi said arrangements USG made in 1957 did not bind UAR and that Nasser had simply returned situation to that which had existed before "aggression of 1956." Egypt's move was not an offensive act. He questioned whether desire to secure freedom of passage through Tiran Strait was based on legal principles because maritime nations had been silent on issue prior to 1956. One thing on which all parties agreed was importance of providing for breathing spell during which modus vivendi could be worked out. SYG had informed him that he had proposed and Nasser had agreed that for a two week period the UAR would refrain from search and seizure at Strait, provided no Israeli flag ship and no petroleum tanker bound for Eilat attempted passage. Israel had refused. He thought SYG's proposal offered reasonable formulas for breathing period.

6. Under Secretary said nub of problem was right of freedom of passage through Strait on which US position was firm. Any use of force to interfere with that right could constitute the first shot in a war which would be disastrous to all concerned. US and UK were in agreement that if hostilities occurred Israel would win and win hard. It was this war that USG sought to prevent.

7. The Foreign Minister said that the Arab states had often repeated that they would take no offensive action against Israel. The closing of the Strait was not an offensive act. War would be averted if Israel could be prevailed upon to refrain from using force to open the Strait. Mr. Rostow pointed out that the only way this could be achieved would [be] if everybody agreed not to use force during the breathing spell, and specifically if UAR agreed not to use force to close the Strait. On the basis of some such understanding, which would leave the situation as it was before Nasser's announcement, the problem could be solved by agreement, or the UAR could take the matter to the International Court.

8. The Foreign Minister replied that Mr. Rostow's approach was different from that of Ambassador Goldberg, who talked in terms of belligerent rights. Perhaps a resolution based on the idea that neither side would use force during the breathing spell could work, if supplemented by private understandings about the actual movement of ships during the period.

9. Mr. Rostow said he was not aware of differing from Ambassador Goldberg. The essence of the problem was that we could see grave risks of war, given the GOI position on Article 51, and the support it would attract, unless the UAR agreed not to use force to carry out its threat to close the Strait.

10. The Foreign Minister observed that all agreed that there should be a breathing spell. The question was what conditions would prevail during that interim. Either Egypt could be asked to restore the situation

to what it was before May 22 and thus surrender completely to Israel's demands or the present situation could be frozen and tacit understanding reached on the details of traffic through the Strait while efforts were made to reach a more permanent solution. Mr. Rostow said this led to the key issue on which agreement should be reached. The US position was very clear. He did not suggest the withdrawal of Egyptian troops nor did we wish to humiliate the UAR. At the same time he admitted that there were grounds for discussion on the appropriateness of the Secretary General's action. He was not suggesting any surrender of principle by either side, but the prevention of war.

11. In conclusion Under Secretary said speaking personally that he would go along with any combination of public or private words that accomplished the result and preserved things as they were. The strength of the US position on this point should not be underestimated. We were against aggression, and against the first shot. The US would remain loyal to its commitments. He noted as a matter of fact that no Israeli vessels were scheduled to pass the Strait during next two weeks. If force were not used to curtail freedom of passage, a breathing spell acceptable to all might be worked out.

12. In his conversation with Secretary, Pachachi covered essentially same ground as above. He emphasized again importance of two week breathing period in which to explore possibilities longer term arrangement. He maintained arrangements for two week period must be based on practical considerations with principles held in abeyance without prejudice to position either party at end period. Secretary stressed importance USG attached to maintaining freedom of passage through Strait of Tiran. Our position involved a principle which we defended in similar situations all over world.

13. In this talk, however, he seemed to back away from the hint he gave Under Secretary Rostow that oil shipments might be accepted on the ground they were "economically necessary."

Rusk

194.   Telegram From the Embassy in Iraq to the Department of State[1]

Baghdad, June 6, 1967, 2315Z.

2111. 1. Fon Min Under Sec Nuri Jamil called me in 0120 a.m. local time June 7 inform me Iraq has broken diplomatic relations with United States and Great Britain for alleged air and other aid to Israel. Iraqi memorandum had no further details. I asked for assurance re protection premises and personnel. He suggested I raise any question with protocal. I mentioned damages our installations June 5 and June 6. He suggested claims would be received and indicated paid through protecting power.

2. I probed for any time factor in winding up affairs and he merely replied "reasonable period" in accordance established practice.

3. Please advise intended protecting power and confirm where personnel should be sent. Assume Tehran. While Jamil typically vague about timing, I note other countries gave 48 hours. Our time may get shortened. Request instructions.

4. Dependent convoy departed at 0135 local time June 7. Jamil assured me they would be protected through to border.

Duncan

---

[1] Source: National Archives and Records Administration, RG 59, Central Files 1967–69, POL 17 US–IRAQ. Confidential; Flash. Repeated to London, Tehran, USUN, DIA, CINCEUR, and CINCSTRIKE. Passed to the White House.

---

195.   Telegram From the Embassy in Iraq to the Department of State[1]

Baghdad, June 8, 1967, 1600Z.

2143. Iraqi Situation—Assessment.

1. The Iraqi regime entered present crisis reluctantly. Moderates were in saddle. They were carried deeper and deeper by events. First

---

[1] Source: National Archives and Records Administration, RG 59, Central Files 1967–69, POL 23–9 IRAQ. Confidential; Priority. Repeated to USUN, Beirut, Tel Aviv, Jidda, London, Moscow, Paris, CINCSTRIKE, and DIA.

military demonstrations then commitment to action. Then concessions to some extremists in name national unity such as release notorious plotters. Measures on oil probably taken to safeguard own position but would not be surprised they now consider this essential weapon, et cetera.[2]

2. Iraqi's position hardening, both official and private. Reflects disillusion with US not only on part those who believe story our military involvement (which very credible in Iraqi eyes given way it developed) but also on part great majority who feel our concern for Israel has dominated our statements and actions both inside United Nations and out. References to opposing aggression by either side were early dismissed as barest lip service to impartiality. They now claim our avoidance acknowledgment Israel initiated hostilities and our reference Israeli interests Aqaba Gulf while cease-fire in question are further proof our partisanship.

3. While obviously our information resources have sharply declined, we sense from press and a few other sources that an internal Iraqi political confrontation may be shaping up behind the scenes. Such plotters as Aref Abd al-Razzaq and Subhi Abd al-Hamid were released. The press is beginning to criticize different conservative elements for not contributing to the national cause. The long silent Shia Divine Muhsin Hakim has finally spoken out to support the cause (possibly motivated by fear of consequences if he doesn't). The cautious and deliberate techniques of most of the cabinet members and President Aref probably cannot satisfy these extremists as the military situation becomes more critical. If UN efforts fail to calm situation soon, a major blow-up here is a real prospect.

4. Today is first in some time without reports of significant demonstrations, which government efforts, sometimes frantic, have so far contained. This may be breathing spell based on today's newspaper reports British and American Embassies closed down and personnel departing within five days (we have only newspapers' word on time limit however). All media continue blare reports of "tripartite aggression." American professor checking out Baghdad University today told by girl cashier he lucky be leaving because "we're going to kill all of you." Asked by British Air Attaché about disposition of British pilot instructors, Iraqi Air Force contact said he would prefer see them hanging from lamp posts. These instructors hope go out on British convoy tonight. Two captured Israeli pilots scheduled go on Iraqi television tonight.

---

[2] Following the outbreak of war in the Middle East on June 5, Iraq severed diplomatic relations with the United States, suspended oil shipments, refused to permit U.S. aircraft to overfly Iraq, and announced a boycott of U.S. goods.

5. Foregoing has somewhat grim ring. I think it about right for this traditionally violent and divided country which is only just now beginning to come to grips with the trauma of the outbreak of hostilities and subsequent Israeli gains. We think most Iraqis can still accept the concept of a compromise; but the longer the crisis continues, the worse the Iraqi internal situation is likely to become, both from the standpoint of public security and the survival of the forces of moderation.

6. In the broader area context as viewed from here, it seems to us that the various opportunities to compromise area issues in the broader interest of ourselves and the international community generally have each time been accepted too late or not at all. We think it is becoming critical to catch the next such opportunity and exploit it, or if necessary to generate some compromise proposals. While as noted above we think Iraqis can still think in terms of compromise, they along with several other Arabs are now beginning to make fatalistic sounds of accepting their losses and settling in for a long war. They presumably hope for Soviet resupply and believe they can exploit the obvious Arab strategic advantages of great distances and dispersed population.

Duncan

---

196. Memorandum From the Ambassador to Iraq (Strong)[1]

New York, June 29, 1967.

SUBJECT

Talk with Iraqi Foreign Minister Adnan Pachachi

I ran into Pachachi this noon, telling him of my departure from New York tomorrow, thanking him for his cooperation and assistance during my tour in Baghdad, expressing deep regret at our official differences, and doubting that I would be seeing him again.

Pachachi expressed regret that our mutual efforts in Baghdad seemed in process of being obliterated. Admitting to personal bitterness, Pachachi said that the Arabs had been misled as to what they could expect from the United States, or they had misled themselves.

---

[1] Source: National Archives and Records Administration, RG 59, Central Files 1967–69, POL 7 IRAQ. Confidential. Drafted by Strong. Copies were sent to the Secretariat, Davies, and NEA/ARN.

He noted that in the Suez crisis of 1956 the United States had immediately and forcibly publicly stated that Israel would not be allowed any territorial gains. This time the United States had not done the same thing and had shown an utter lack of concern for the Arabs or consideration for their feelings. In addition the United States had gone right ahead with a food agreement with Israel as though nothing had happened. The United States position is so close to that of Israel that there is no meaningful distinction to make. He can only hope, he said, that in time the United States will realize that its interests require a better balance, and that improvement in relations can then occur.

At this point we were interrupted.

---

197.   Intelligence Note From the Director of the Bureau of Intelligence and Research (Hughes) to Secretary of State Rusk[1]

No. 709   Washington, September 1, 1967.

SUBJECT

New Kurdish Insurgency Threatens

In addition to its many other problems, the Near East may have to face a new round of fighting between the Kurdish guerrillas and the Iraqi army during the next three or four months. Mulla Mustafa's followers are growing restive. Minor clashes are occurring more frequently between the rival Kurdish factions, and between Mustafa's bands and isolated small army units. The Kurds probably would not move in force before late September, when the harvest is in, but action could be triggered earlier by government miscalculation or by outside pressures.

Kurds Feel That They Must Be Militant. Several factors, both local and regional, tempt the Kurds to reopen hostilities at a time of their own choosing. Locally: *The government is defaulting on peace promises.* The financial strain of the oil cutoff, first in November–December and then during the war with Israel, paralyzed the Iraqi government's plans for extensive reconstruction in the Kurdish area, which were part of the

---

[1] Source: National Archives and Records Administration, RG 59, Central Files 1967–69, POL 23–9 IRAQ. Secret; No Foreign Dissem. Prepared in the Bureau of Intelligence and Research.

peace agreement with the Kurds. *The Kurds distrust Tahir Yahya,* the new Prime Minister who took office July 10. The Kurds feel that he played them false in earlier dealings. Yahya further angered Barzani by appointing as Kurdish minister in the present Cabinet one Abd al-Fattah al-Shali, an opportunist who is soft on the rival Kurdish faction of Jalal Talabani. *The Arab defeat encourages Kurdish militants.* Younger Kurdish militants must want to seize the opportunity to pounce on the defeated Arab armies, and Mustafa may be concerned to hold their loyalty. *The government is weak.* The Iraqi Cabinet and regime are very shaky. Mulla Mustafa believes that only by demonstrating his readiness and ability to fight can the Kurds make their weight felt politically now or with a successor government. Also, he must maintain his standing against Talabani.

Kurds May Receive Israeli and Iranian Support. Unsupported, the Kurds would probably not attempt full-scale hostilities, even of the guerrilla type. Mustafa's outside supporters, however, seem now in the mood to sustain some limited Kurdish action. At least, they apparently wish to keep alive Mustafa's capability and will to fight. *An Israeli second front?* Just before the war started an Israeli agent reportedly visited Mulla Mustafa to arrange, if possible, some Kurdish action to tie down the Iraqi army. He did not succeed. However, convoys of matériel to the Kurds resumed around the end of April. For some months before that time, assistance had been limited to relief supplies. Israel may now be urging on the Kurds in order to keep up pressure on the Arabs. In view of Syrian intransigence they might now want to extend the agitation to Syrian Kurds who had begun to take a minor part in the revolt just before the truce. *Iran suspicious.* The Iranian government, once a strong supporter of the Kurdish insurgency, was pursuing a slow and delicate rapprochement with Iraq before the June war. This policy has been shaken by Iraq's extreme pronouncements during the war, and by the appointment of Tahir Yahya, whom Iranians regard as pro-Nasser. Moreover, SAVAK reportedly believes that Nasserite subversive activities have increased since the war. The Iranian government is said to believe that neither Mulla Mustafa nor the Iraqi government has the confidence for a major showdown at this time, but it does not rule out strong harassing action on the part of the Kurds. Iran shares Mulla Mustafa's view that the Iraqi regime is in serious trouble and it may well be tempted to renew its aid to the Kurds in an effort to help topple the present government and get a successor regime more sympathetic towards Iran.

A New Kurdish Rising Potentially Dangerous. Kurdish guerrilla activities against the Iraqi government have occurred periodically for a long time. Just now, however, renewed fighting in the Kurdish area could be a further unsettling factor in an already brittle situation, particularly if unrest were to spill over into Syria. Should any Israeli or Iranian involvement become known, Arab radical propaganda would no doubt claim that this is a new "plot" against the Arabs instigated by the US.

---

198.   Telegram From the Embassy in Belgium to the Department of State[1]

Brussels, June 7, 1968, 1643Z.

7128. Dept pass Cairo.[2] Subject: Replr: Resumption of US-Iraqi relations. Ref: Department's CA–8354.[3]

1. Contents of Refair passed to Belgian Foreign Office (Callebaut) Wednesday, June 5. Foreign Office told us they would pass substance to Ambassador Dupret immediately and that we could expect a reply shortly.

2. Callebaut commented that requirements as listed in Refair would probably be unacceptable to Iraqis. Specifically he believed Iraqis would not be able to rescind entirely general boycott on US goods and services, even though they now recognize they committed mistake in breaking relations and want to restore them.

Knight

---

[1] Source: National Archives and Records Administration, RG 59, Central Files 1967–69, POL 17 IRAQ–US. Confidential. Repeated to Beirut, London, and Tehran.

[2] A note on the telegram indicates it was not passed to Cairo by OC/T.

[3] Circular airgram CA–8354 to Brussels, May 29, stated that if the Iraqi Government raised questions as to the U.S. position on resumption of U.S.-Iraqi diplomatic relations, Ambassador Dupret could indicate that the United States was prepared to resume relations whenever the Iraqi Government signified that it had a genuine interest in so doing. The only U.S. requirements would be that Iraq agree to compensate the U.S. Government for damages to its Consulate in Basra and Embassy in Baghdad, that the United States have unimpeded access to U.S. properties in Iraq, and that the Iraqi boycott of U.S. goods and services and ban on U.S. overflights be rescinded. (National Archives and Records Administration, RG 59, Central Files 1967–69, POL IRAQ–US)

199.   **Memorandum From John W. Foster of the National Security Council Staff to the President's Special Assistant (Rostow)[1]**

Washington, July 17, 1968.

SUBJECT

The Iraqi Coup

Until things sort themselves out, and until we get better information—we have no representation in Baghdad—it's impossible to tell what the effect of last night's coup[2] will be. We can't even be sure that the coup leaders' claim of military support is true. A counter-coup tomorrow is conceivable.

The intelligence community's initial reading is that the new group—apparently Baathists—will be more difficult than their predecessors, but at this point no one knows how radical they will be. So far, their communiqués have taken a fairly moderate line by Iraqi standards, promising economic reforms, honest government, a "wise" solution of the Kurdish problem,[3] and Arab unity against the Zionist and Imperialist threats. On the other hand, if these people are Baathists, their tendencies will be towards moving Iraq even closer to Fatah, the Syrians and the Soviets. From our point of view, the most important question is whether they will continue Iraq's support for King Hussein. Iraq has about 25,000 troops in Jordan and could easily make life difficult for the King.

This is just to give you the best reading we have before you leave.

John

---

[1] Source: Johnson Library, National Security File, Country File, Iraq, Cables & Memos, Vol. I, 12/63–7/68. Secret.

[2] An almost bloodless army coup overthrew the regime of President Aref at dawn on July 17. The new Revolution Command Council assumed absolute powers at 7 a.m. and unanimously elected former Vice President and retired Major General Ahmed Hasan al-Bakr, as President. Baghdad radio subsequently announced that former President Aref had been retired on pension and deported to "join his family" in England. (Intelligence Note 561, July 17; National Archives and Records Administration, RG 59, Central Files 1967–69, POL 23–9 IRAQ)

[3] The Aref government had made little progress on implementation of the June 1966 cease-fire agreement. Barzani had refused to disband his army until the Iraqi Government made good on its promises for limited Kurdish autonomy in the North, Kurdish proportional representation in the still unreconstituted Iraqi Parliament, and disbanding of the government's anti-Barzani Kurdish irregulars. In the meantime, Barzani's forces maintained de facto control of the North and had recently secured renewed military and financial aid commitments from Iran and Israel. (Intelligence Note 488, June 20; ibid.)

200.   Memorandum From John W. Foster of the National Security Council Staff to the President's Special Assistant (Rostow)[1]

Washington, July 22, 1968.

SUBJECT

A Clearer Picture of the Iraqi Coup

While you were gone, the situation in Iraq became much clearer. The new government could still be a little harder for us to deal with than the old—if we ever have a chance to deal with it—but if we had to have a Baathist government there, this is probably the best we could expect.

The Baathists are from the right-wing of the party—the opponents of those in control in Syria—and non-Baathists are playing a major role in the new government. The Syrians had nothing to do with the coup; in fact, one of the most interesting questions raised by the coup is whether the Iraqi example will encourage the moderate Syrian Baathists now in exile to take a crack at the Syrian regime.

The inability of the Aref government to deal with Iraq's domestic problems was the reason—or excuse—for the coup, and the new government is talking mainly about economic reforms, eliminating corruption and solving the Kurdish problem. They have made the usual statements about Zionism, Imperialism and Arab unity, but so far there have been no indications that Iraq's foreign policy will become more radical. It's too early to know whether there will be progress on a Kurdish settlement or more trouble—a key determinant of how free Iraqi troops will be to menace Israel.

Until we see these people in action, we won't know for sure what problems we might face, but there seems to be less cause for concern over anything radically different now than there was last Wednesday.

John

---

[1] Source: Johnson Library, National Security File, Country File, Iraq, Cables & Memos, Vol. I, 12/63–7/68. Secret.

201. Memorandum of Conversation[1]

Washington, October 23, 1968, 12:33–1 p.m.

SUBJECT

Situation in Iraq

PARTICIPANTS

H.E. Ardeshir Zahedi, Foreign Minister of Iran
H.E. Hushang Ansary, Ambassador of Iran
H.E. Manuchehr Fartash, Political Director General, Iranian Ministry of Foreign Affairs
Mr. Hushang Batmanglidj, Supervisor, RCD Affairs, Iranian Ministry of Foreign Affairs

The Hon. Dean Rusk, Secretary of State
Mr. Stuart W. Rockwell, Deputy Assistant Secretary, NEA
Mr. Walter M. McClelland, Office of Iranian Affairs, NEA

In response to a question from Ambassador Hart, Mr. Zahedi said that no one knew the real situation in Iraq since it changes from day to day. The new Iraqi Government has been pleasant toward Iran and has not attacked it with propaganda, but the Iraqis never seem to take any action to carry out their "good words." It appears that there is no strong hand at the top and that the government is trying to keep everyone happy—Nasserites, Baathis, and Mulla Mustafa. This is impossible. Mr. Zahedi said each succeeding government just tries to see how long it can last and can make no progress.

Mr. Zahedi added that Iran has tried to maintain good relations with Iraq. There have been reciprocal visits and talks between Foreign Ministers, etc. Iran is interested in Iraq's remaining independent, but Iran can only hope—it sees no positive signs.

Mr. Zahedi said there were no pilgrims from Iran to Iraq last year, but that this year the situation will be back to normal and Iranian pilgrims will be permitted to go.

---

[1] Source: National Archives and Records Administration, RG 59, Central Files 1967–69, POL IRAN–IRAQ. Confidential. Drafted by McClelland and approved in the Office of the Secretary on October 29. The memorandum is Part VI of VI. The meeting was held at the Department of State and the time is taken from Rusk's Daily Diary. (Johnson Library)

Kuwait

202. Telegram From the Department of State to the Embassy in Kuwait[1]

Washington, January 2, 1964, 4:45 p.m.

169. Embtel 292.[2] You should, as you propose, play customary COMIDEASTFOR visit to Kuwait in low key. Should Amir query re future USG role in support Kuwait integrity, you should state that view UK–Kuwait defense treaty, we consider UK has primary responsibility for military protection Kuwait's integrity (Deptel 21).[3] You may call attention to past USG public statements of support for Kuwait's integrity (made in UN in connection Kuwait's application for UN membership) and record of cordial relations between two countries. In event Amir probes further, you authorized indicate USG always in close consultation with UK and supports UK position in Gulf.

You should not question Amir as proposed numbered paras 1 and 2. We do not consider appropriate for us to question Amir on aspects and implications GOK–UK defense commitment. Re para 3 (Jordan waters), you will receive separate instruction.[4]

Rusk

---

[1] Source: National Archives and Records Administration, RG 59, Central Files 1964–66, POL IRAQ–KUW. Secret; Immediate; Limited Distribution. Repeated to COMIDEASTFOR. Drafted by Seelye; cleared by Davies, NEA/NR Officer in Charge of Politico-Military Affairs Donald W. Bunte, and Judd (BNA); and cleared by Jernegan.

[2] In telegram 292 from Kuwait, January 2, Ambassador Cottam asked for instructions on how to deal with likely query of the Amir on January 6 about U.S. intentions to defend Kuwait in the event that the United Kingdom was unable or unwilling to do so. (Ibid., DEF 1 KUW)

[3] Dated July 31, 1963. (Ibid., Central Files 1961–63, DEF 4 KUW–UK)

[4] See circular telegram 1176, January 2. (Ibid., POL 33–1 JORDAN RIVER)

203. Airgram From the Embassy in Kuwait to the Department of State[1]

A–209   Kuwait, March 26, 1964.

SUBJECT

Secretary Talbot's Visit to Kuwait

In two days, Assistant Secretary Talbot[2] had an intimate and wide exposure to Kuwait, its royal family, its bureaucracy, its business oligarchy, its oil industry, and its modernization. Two main themes of the discussions were: 1) US policy in the Middle East and 2) modernization of Kuwait. Every principal official directly or indirectly queried Mr. Talbot about US views and intentions on the Palestine issue: The Amir, the Foreign Minister, other officials, members of the Foreign Affairs Committee of the National Assembly and 25 prominent businessmen. Mr. Talbot sought to assure them of the evenhandedness, the continuity and the friendly understanding of the United States and the personal ardent desire of the President for peace in the Middle East and elsewhere.

The Amir asked for understanding and flexibility in US policy toward the Palestine question, implying that he expected unreasonable and uncontrollable actions which, if dealt with too abruptly by the US, might have disastrous results. The Foreign Minister and other officials more explicitly stressed that fear and affirmed Kuwait's intention to aid and abet the inevitable unification of the Arab states. What Kuwait expected was a federation which will preserve independence of each (i.e., Kuwait could retain its higher standard of living). The Foreign Minister affirmed that while cooperation in cultural, educational and economic matters would proceed rapidly, political association was even more important. While he was less explicit about how political unification would be achieved, he acknowledged that many present Arab governments would fall as would others after them. In the meantime, the Arab people would accelerate cooperation in every possible way.

The Foreign Minister maintained that many Arab problems such as Yemen could be settled by Arabs themselves if left to their own devices. UAR, Saudi Arabia and Yemen had made considerable progress toward a settlement. US assistance was no longer needed there, the Foreign Minister affirmed.

---

[1] Source: National Archives and Records Administration, RG 59, Central Files 1964–66, ORG 7 NEA. Secret. Drafted by Cottam.

[2] Assistant Secretary Talbot visited a number of other Near East countries on this trip.

While GOK's aid program permitted loans, it did not permit grants to Arab brothers (except for education and health through GUPAC). Kuwait aid and US aid programs to Arabs are not alike. Kuwait must treat brother Arabs as equals; hence, no grants. US should continue its grant aid to Jordan and to Palestine refugees. However, money alone would not be enough for the refugees, UN Resolution 194, Article 11[3] had to be implemented. Mr. Talbot's mention of other aspects of the resolution fell on deaf ears.

The Foreign Minister asked how long US would continue its "foolish" policy toward Peiping, China. Kuwait would be evenhanded and non-aligned. Mr. Talbot gave an effective defense, but Sabah still felt GOK could handle two-China policy up to point of who would get the UN Security Council seat. The Minister implied that the UN General Assembly would have to meet the issue when it arises.

UK Ambassador Jackson told Mr. Talbot that GOK hadn't recently raised question of the UK-GOK treaty. Jackson volunteered information that GOK had been spending too much and drawing down its reserves. With respect to Israel and oil, Jackson felt GOK would not "cut off its nose to spite its face." The Prime Minister had told him recently that Arab world would be better off if it admitted that Israel exists.

Mr. Talbot's visit served US interests effectively by providing an intimate dialogue on emotionally-toned subjects and by demonstrating US interest in Kuwait. He was well received and appreciated by everyone.

Howard R. Cottam
American Ambassador

---

[3] Article 11 of UN General Assembly Resolution 194, December 11, 1948, called for repatriation of Palestinian refugees and compensation for those who did not choose to return.

204.   Telegram From the Department of State to the Embassy in Kuwait[1]

Washington, September 10, 1964, 2:25 p.m.

52. Embtels 76[2] and 88,[3] US Arms Sales Kuwait. Basic guideline concerning US and UK military sales in Kuwait continues to be as stated Deptel 112, November 1, 1963.[4] That is, tacit understanding that we are prime supplier to Saudi Arabia while British have same position in Kuwait. This does not preclude US companies trying sell Kuwait but it does mean we will keep British informed whenever approval is given for such sales attempt. Embassy is of course authorized accord usual commercial assistance to US firms which have received prior Departmental approval required under munitions control regulations.

Douglas (in March 1964) and Northrop (in September 1963) received appropriate authorization to make unclassified sales presentation on A–4E and F–5, respectively. (No authorization given for Sidewinders, Hawks, or other missiles.) Douglas representative Washington confirms present company sales plans as reported Kuwait tel 88.

Kuwait and London should inform British Embassy and FonOff, respectively, of foregoing. We are informing British Embassy Washington.

Rusk

---

[1] Source: National Archives and Records Administration, RG 59, Central Files 1964–66, DEF 12–5 KUW–US. Confidential. Drafted by Moore on September 9; cleared by Bunte, and Colonel Evans (G/PM), and in substance by Steve Koumanelis (G/MC) and Quinn (DOD/ISA); and approved by Davies. Also sent to London and repeated to CINCSTRIKE/CINCMEAFSA for Ramsey.

[2] In telegram 76 from Kuwait, September 2, Cottam asked for guidance on handling the possibility of Kuwaiti arms purchases from the United States in commercial or official discussions, saying that the Embassy had been approached by a Douglas aircraft representative. (Ibid.)

[3] Telegram 88 from Kuwait, September 9, reported that Douglas had made a package offer of six jet planes, including training, which the Government of Kuwait was apparently ready to accept. (Ibid.)

[4] Not printed. (Ibid., Central Files 1961–63, DEF 12–5 KUW)

205. Telegram From the Department of State to the Embassy in Kuwait[1]

Washington, January 14, 1965, 7:24 p.m.

136. Embtel 296.[2] Appreciate your telegraphic summary our recommended response should GOK officially follow up Jabir Ali's remarks concerning Security Guarantee and other arrangement with US. (Department recalls Jabir Ali in past has tended be outspokenly pro-West and speak personally without prior clearance GOK.) We look forward promised Embassy airgram analysis and will no doubt have more detailed comments. Should be noted now, however, that possibility official visit for Ruler is practically nil this year because of tight Presidential schedule. Thus, you should give no encouragement for such trip. If other ranking Kuwait personages wish travel US on own, we would naturally take steps insure they received at as high level and with as much ceremony as possible and appropriate.

Department notes that Embassy already has authority approach GOK concerning Investment Guarantee Agreement (A–18, February 13, 1964).[3] With reference Embtel 277,[4] forthcoming message will also describe situation regarding possible Consular Agreement.

Rusk

---

[1] Source: National Archives and Records Administration, RG 59, Central Files 1964–66, POL 7 KUW. Secret. Drafted by Moore, cleared by NEA/NE Officer in Charge of Economic Affairs George M. Bennsky and Special Assistant to the Deputy Under Secretary for Political Affairs Windsor G. Hackler, and approved by Davies. Repeated to London.

[2] In telegram 296 from Kuwait, January 13, Cottam reported that Acting Prime Minister Jabir Ali had proposed a "red carpet" visit to the United States by the Crown Prince or Finance Minister, to culminate in an agreement affirming U.S.-Kuwaiti amity and cooperation, preferably including a security guarantee. (Ibid.)

[3] Not printed. (Ibid., FN 9–3 KUW–US)

[4] Dated December 31, 1964. (Ibid., POL 17–2 US–KUW)

206. Telegram From the Department of State to the Embassy in Kuwait[1]

Washington, May 3, 1965, 6:31 p.m.

221. Deptel 67 October 16, 1964.[2] Embtels 492,[3] 500.[4] Douglas Washington Rep reported same info Embtel. Department told Douglas Nike-Hercules classified and introduction this missile would entail security survey. We doubt GOK can meet requirement U.S. security standards. Although Douglas authorized talk GOK about aircraft, we did not authorize discussion missiles and related equipment. We did not wish encourage sale Hawks, sidewinders or any other type missile. Informed Douglas that if GOK made Government to Government request we would study problem. You authorized respond along foregoing lines to any further queries Douglas agent Kuwait.

FYI. GOK not eligible purchase mil equipment under Military Assistance Sales Program. In view tacit understanding with UK that we are prime supplier to Saudi Arabia while British have same position Kuwait, we have not asked that GOK be added eligibility list.

We do not intend sell Nike-Hercules to Douglas to make them available GOK. In view (1) necessity security survey and unlikely event GOK can meet US security standards and (2) current problems arms sale this area vis-à-vis Israel, we do not wish sell this type equipment GOK. Rationale Deptel 67 applicable. If approach made by GOK you should endeavor discourage their requesting such equipment. End FYI.

Rusk

---

[1] Source: National Archives and Records Administration, RG 59, Central Files 1964–66, DEF 12–5 KUW. Secret. Drafted by Bunte; cleared by Quinn, Stevens (ILN), Moore, G/PM Office of Politico-Military Affairs Director for Operations Howard Meyers, G/MC Policy and Intelligence Division Chief J. Harold Darby, and NEA/NR Director of the Office of Near Eastern, South Asian Regional Affairs Guy A. Lee; and approved by Jernegan. Repeated to London, CINCSTRIKE/CINCMEAFSA, and CINCSTRIKE POLAD for Ramsey.

[2] Not printed. (Ibid.)

[3] In telegram 492 from Kuwait, April 28, Cottam reported that the Douglas aircraft representative in Kuwait had told the Embassy that Kuwait wanted to purchase U.S. Nike-Hercules or Hawk defensive missiles immediately. (Ibid.)

[4] Dated May 3; not printed. (Ibid.)

207.   Memorandum of Conversation[1]

Washington, February 25, 1966.

SUBJECT

Kuwait Oil Problems

PARTICIPANTS

His Excellency Abdul Rahman al-Ateegi, Kuwaiti Foreign Ministry Under
Secretary
His Excellency Talat al-Ghoussein, Ambassador of Kuwait
Ambassador Raymond A. Hare, Assistant Secretary, NEA
Mr. Harrison M. Symmes, NE
David Korn, NE

Ambassador Hare said he was pleased to note that U.S.-Kuwaiti relations are very good. He hoped that the current conversations between the oil companies and the GOK were working out well.[2]

Mr. Ateegi said the oil question is a very irritating and delicate problem. The companies must make an effort to understand the situation in Kuwait and be prepared to reach a compromise. The companies, Mr. Ateegi stressed, must be very careful. They think the Kuwaiti Minister of Foreign Affairs and Finance is taking an extreme position. This, Mr. Ateegi emphasized, is a dangerously false assumption. Mr. Ateegi complained that, while oil offtake was rising in Saudi Arabia, Iran and other countries, it had increased hardly at all in Kuwait. The companies had furnished no satisfactory explanation for this. Despite these difficulties, Mr. Ateegi felt that there was some hope for an agreement.

Ambassador Hare said experience had taught him that such matters as oil offtake were very complicated. As far as details were concerned he felt that the oil companies were best qualified to speak for themselves. However it might be noted that even the Shah of Iran, despite an increase in Iranian offtake, was dissatisfied with the oil companies on this score. Offtake depends upon an extremely complex set of factors which only an expert can understand. For this reason it is necessary to have thorough talks before reaching any conclusions.

Mr. Ateegi said the oil companies' failure to increase offtake would not really be an issue if conditions between the GOK and the companies were normal. However, under present circumstances people in Kuwait

---

[1] Source: National Archives and Records Administration, RG 59, Central Files 1964–66, POL 6 KUW. Confidential. Drafted by David A. Korn (NEA/NE).

[2] For documentation on U.S. international oil policy, see *Foreign Relations, 1964–1968*, vol. XXXIV, Documents 175ff.

interpret the companies' action as punishment or pressure, thus making it a very sensitive issue.

Ambassador Hare said that while there had always been and will always be differences of views, over the years the company-Government relationship in the oil producing countries had been a very constructive and beneficial one. This is another reason we hope the dialogue can be maintained.

Mr. Ateegi said the GOK wished to maintain the dialogue but felt that the matter would be made much easier if the companies showed greater understanding. The GOK does not want to enact laws or regulations which would "upset" the companies. Mr. Ateegi suspected, however, that the fact that the companies had not sent their highest level representatives to the current talks in Kuwait meant that they are not thinking seriously about solving the problem. While he could not state categorically that this was the case, Mr. Ateegi said that the companies sending their "third ranking" representatives might be interpreted to mean that they are not really ready to come to an agreement. Mr. Ateegi indicated that the Kuwaitis did not regard the company representatives currently in Kuwait as of sufficient rank to negotiate with a Minister. Mr. Symmes remarked that while Gulf Oil's Elston Law may not be the highest level of company representation he is probably more knowledgeable and better able to negotiate on the matters at issue in Kuwait than someone more senior.

208. Telegram From the Department of State to the Embassy in the United Kingdom[1]

Washington, June 7, 1966, 7:14 p.m.

7326. Joint State–Defense message. Ref: Deptels 6906 (Kuwait 191)[2] and 6923 (Kuwait 192).[3]

Begin FYI only.

1. Following are basic aspects of decision not license sale US arms (including combat aircraft and SAMs) to Kuwait:

a. Conclusion recently announced aircraft sale to Israel (and anticipated HAWK sale to Lebanon) marks end of a cycle in arms acquisitions Near East where we trying halt added capital weapons purchases. New US sale to UAC member Kuwait would threaten further escalation, renewed pressure from Israel for purchase US arms, and heightened opposition by Congress (where Jordanian and Israeli deals have already brought expressions of grave concern over recent sale of arms to area of tension).

b. We do not desire introduce US arms into Kuwait in any way which would (1) undermine Britain's ability perform on its defense commitment to Kuwait, (2) encourage British relinquish that commitment, (3) give Kuwaitis renewed idea of turning to US for defense of country, or (4) result in US-UK friction which could limit our efforts work with British for orderly political development in Lower Gulf or lead to UK hindering our commercial activities in that region. (In long run, anticipate Lower Gulf market will be of greater significance for US balance of payments than sale US arms Kuwait.)

c. Kuwait revenues enormous but not unlimited. It is of more importance for US world interests to encourage Kuwaitis increase their assistance programs in other countries (e.g., South Arabia) than purchase sophisticated weapons.

2. At same time, for purpose gaining maximum benefits from UK in connection with collaborative US-UK arm sales Near East under

---

[1] Source: National Archives and Records Administration, RG 59, Central Files 1964–66, DEF 12–5 KUW. Secret. Drafted by Moore; cleared by Deputy Assistant Secretary of Defense Townsend Hoopes, NEA/NR Officer in Charge of Politico-Military Affairs Lieutenant Colonel Billy R. Byrd, Meyers, Officer in Charge of United Kingdom Affairs Thomas M. Judd, and Symmes, and in substance by Deputy Assistant Secretary of Defense for International Logistics Negotiations Henry J. Kuss and Dwight M. Cramer (G/MC); and approved by Davies. Repeated to Kuwait and USCINCMEAFSA and pouched to Jidda and Dhahran.

[2] Telegram 6906 to London, May 18, instructed the Embassy to approach the British Government and request that it give urgent consideration to meeting Kuwait's combat aircraft needs. (Ibid.)

[3] Telegram 6923 to London, sent as telegram 192 to Kuwait, May 19. (Ibid.)

F–111 offset arrangement, or at least some moral credit for an assist in Britain's balance of payments problem as a means of encouraging accelerated UK payments to US on the F–111 sale, we do not wish categorically inform British or Kuwaitis at this time re our negative decision on US arms to Kuwait. End FYI only.

3. Request you approach Ministry of Defense and Ministry of Aviation at appropriate level along following lines:

a. Recently British Ambassador Sir Patrick Dean undertook to inform Secretary McNamara of Iranian overtures to UK arms manufacturers, and to sound out US attitude toward UK participation in military sales to Iran. USG appreciates UK consideration and cooperation in this regard.

b. In similar manner, USG wishes inform HMG that Government of Kuwait has made official requests for purchase of US combat aircraft, and that several US aircraft firms are pressing for approval of export licenses.

c. US has no desire undermine UK defense commitment to Kuwait through introduction of American equipment, and is willing not press sale of US aircraft. However, request from Government of Kuwait and strong interest of US manufacturers may impel USG give practical consideration this matter.

d. In these circumstances, we would welcome expression of view by HMG on this matter.

Ball

209. Telegram From the Department of State to the Embassy in Kuwait[1]

Washington, April 27, 1967, 6:03 p.m.

183614. Ref: Kuwait's 1099.[2]

1. Appreciate your efforts steer Sabah toward UK as supplier Kuwait's air defense needs. It quite correct underscore stringent USG security protection requirements in connection with any Hawk missile sale. While Sabah may choose overlook these now, GOK might well have serious second thoughts when time came sign agreements and carry out investigations.

2. Dept/DOD see no basis for Sabah statement para 6 reftel that UK unable supply stationary defensive rockets. UK Thunderbird as fixed-installation surface-to-air missile (of type emplaced around US cities) might be even more appropriate to Kuwait's needs than Hawk, which is mobile field system. Since Kuwaitis have already contracted for UK Lightning fighter aircraft, British Thunderbirds would appear be natural complement to their air defense system.

3. You should inform Sabah we sympathetic Kuwaiti concern re air defense but believe Kuwait's best defense assurance lies in continued close military supply arrangement with UK. Believe GOK should fully explore possibility of obtaining Thunderbirds from UK before proceeding any further to discuss possible availability of Hawks, which in any case may be less appropriate to GOK needs than Thunderbirds.

4. *For London:* Agree Embassy's suggestion (London 8829)[3] we take advantage Sabah approach to build F–111 offset case with British in event successful UK Thunderbird sale to Kuwait. Embassy should inform appropriate HMG officials we have been approached by Kuwaiti Govt with request for sale Hawk missiles. In view UK-Kuwaiti defense tie, we are suggesting to Kuwaitis that they first explore possibility

---

[1] Source: National Archives and Records Administration, RG 59, Central Files 1967–69, POL 32–1 IRAQ–KUW. Secret. Drafted by Korn; cleared by Quinn and Thieberger (DOD/ISA), G/PM Assistant for Special Facilities Joseph J. Wolf, Judd, NEA/RA Political-Military Adviser Colonel Edgar J. Fredericks, and Brewer; and approved by Rockwell. Repeated to London, Baghdad, Tehran, COMIDEASTFOR, and CINCSTRIKE/CINCMEAFSA.

[2] In telegram 1099 from Kuwait, April 25, Cottam reported that he had tried to discourage Foreign Minister Shaikh Sabah al Ahmad from expecting the United States to sell Kuwait sophisticated weapons, and had expressed U.S. support for Kuwait's treaty with the United Kingdom and the primacy of the British-Kuwaiti defense relationship. (Ibid.)

[3] Dated April 26. (Ibid., DEF 12–5 KUW)

acquisition Thunderbird surface-to-air missile system. FYI. For purpose making our case for including an eventual Kuwaiti sale in offset arrangement, Embassy should leave our ultimate intentions re Hawk sale to Kuwait vague and avoid anything indicating USG has reached firm decision refuse Kuwaiti request. End FYI.

Rusk

---

210. Telegram From the Embassy in Kuwait to the Department of State[1]

Kuwait, June 7, 1967, 1130Z.

1275. 1. In frank, friendly talk with Foreign Minister Sabah al Ahmad, he reiterated promise full security for all Americans, including homes of those somewhat isolated. He noted that Kuwaitis have volunteered for national guard and that labor unions have volunteered to help protect oil communities.

2. After reaffirming US not supporting Israel during hostilities, I asked Sabah for his personal view. He asked me to understand the reasons Kuwait had participated in the propaganda war and had cut off oil to US–UK.[2] I told him that I had understood pressures, politics, psychology and tactics, and that I had reported them fully to Washington. What was missing, I said, was first-hand knowledge of GOK's attitude and hence its intentions. I had assumed personally that Kuwait was doing effectively, even cleverly, what it had to, under extremely difficult circumstances. I was faced with an immediate decision. Washington had instructed me to start evacuating official dependents and

---

[1] Source: Johnson Library, National Security File, Country File, Middle East Cables, Vol. IV. Secret; Flash; Exdis. Repeated to London. Another copy of this telegram is filed in the National Archives and Records Administration, RG 59, Central Files 1967–69, POL 27 ARAB–ISR. Handwritten notations on the telegram read: "Mr. President—This is good news! Walt" and "Another place to hold the line."

[2] Telegram 208481 to Kuwait, June 6, reported that the Kuwaiti Ambassador telephoned at 11:30 a.m., saying he had been instructed urgently to convey to the Department that the Government of Kuwait had adopted two resolutions: 1) to stop all oil exports to the United States and the United Kingdom; and 2) to accept Iraq's invitation to hold an urgent meeting of Arab Foreign Ministers. The Ambassador said it was his understanding that the decision to stop oil exports was based on the conviction that Cairo's reports that U.S. carrier-based aircraft were assisting Israel were correct. (Ibid.) For documentation on the Arab oil embargo following the Six-Day War, see *Foreign Relations, 1964–1968*, vol. XXXIV, Documents 228ff.

advising other Americans to leave. I was not asking Sabah for advice, but trying to ascertain Kuwait's intentions. Were I to act from what I saw and heard, we would start evacuations at once.

3. Sabah reiterated Kuwait's problems, the pressures from other Arab states, and its desire for continued good relations with the United States. He hoped that the oil would be flowing again in a few days. Again he promised absolute security for all Americans, and added that the decision on evacuation is, of course, your own. Please tell your government that and ask them to bear with us.

4. I said these assurances were not sufficient. I had to know GOK attitude and intentions, whereupon Sabah confided personally and privately that he did not believe US planes had accelerated the flow of supplies immediately prior to the hostilities. I thanked him for the information, but said I would have to report it, and that I had been instructed to ascertain the views of His Highness the Amir. Sabah said that his views reflect official opinion and that it would be unnecessary for me to see the Amir. He again asked that what he had said be kept confidential. I assured him that it would not be thrown back at him. I also agreed to defer my request for an audience with the Amir until further instructed.

5. Sabah assured me of full GOK cooperation in event we should evacuate dependents and other Americans. He would not object to our chartering planes. At this point he made a grand gesture: "You can use our planes." I told him we may have a thousand people to go, to which he replied "That doesn't matter, we are at your disposal." To my query, Sabah said he disapproved of cease-fire at this time, but noted that the point of cease-fire was up to those most directly involved. He acknowledged disappointment with the military situation. He asked where all the planes Israel had used could possibly have come from. Again I said not from US; perhaps your intelligence estimates were low. I referred to an earlier private conversation with Bishara in which I said "Israel has much more capability than you think." Bishara, who was present, recalled it.

6. Seeking to underscore the importance of maintaining diplomatic relations with us, I mentioned the likelihood of UK and US working together on post-war reconstruction. Sabah said Kuwait would certainly do her duty, but this was no time to talk about it.

7. The idea of an Arab Foreign Ministers meeting in Kuwait beginning June 8 was not his. Baghdad was the sponsor and had made the agenda. Sabah thinks it untimely. However, when I pressed him on his long-standing reliance on summitry, he agreed that the meeting might be useful. Replies have not come in from all of the possible participants.

8. *Comment:* In view of assurances for security and unlikelihood that Kuwait intends to break relations, I will postpone the evacuation of dependents. UK Ambassador taking similar position. Morale of entire staff and dependents high. I reiterate opinion Kuwait may be place we can hold on and look to future.

Cottam

211. Telegram From the Embassy in Kuwait to the Department of State[1]

Kuwait, June 10, 1967, 1020Z.

1299. Ref: State 209821;[2] Kuwait 1290.[3]

1. Amir received me in cordial and relaxed manner, reflecting his belief, which emerged during conversation, that for Kuwait worst of crisis has passed. He insisted I finish my tea before talking business, and we chatted about how we both had had postpone vacation plans. I reminded him that this was my first call since becoming Dean in Kuwait.

2. When we turned to business, there was immediate and full acceptance of my affirmation that US had not participated in the hostilities. He had had no doubts and never any intentions of breaking relations. He was surprised to learn that Americans had doubted Kuwait's intentions or capabilities to protect them. He gave a long explanation of his objectives and tactics, including declaration of war, martial law, cutting oil, and participation in the Arab propaganda war. He hoped we would understand. I told him that we had understood the psychology, the politics and the tactics, including the cutting off of oil, but that

---

[1] Source: National Archives and Records Administration, RG 59, Central Files 1967–69, POL 27 ARAB–ISR. Secret; Immediate. Repeated to Algiers, Amman, Beirut, Jidda, Rabat, Tel Aviv, Tripoli, Tunis, London, USUN, Paris, Moscow, Dhahran, COMAC POLAD, and COMIDEASTFOR. Passed to S/S–O, the White House, and USIA.

[2] Telegram 209821 to Kuwait, June 9, instructed the Ambassador that his approach when meeting with the Amir should be to emphasize: 1) the U.S. Government's military non-involvement in recent hostilities, which it had striven to prevent; and 2) the urgent attention that now had to be given to the many post-hostilities problems, which would require major efforts from all interested countries. (Ibid.)

[3] In telegram 1290 from Kuwait, June 9, Cottam reported he had asked to see the Amir that day or in any event before the Kuwaiti cabinet meeting the next day. He added that the Acting Under Secretary had assured him that Kuwait certainly would not break relations with the United States. (Ibid.)

we had hoped for some secret assurances of Kuwait's intentions. It was for that reason that I had gone to the Foreign Minister on June 7.

3. I thanked the Amir for the clarity with which he now assured me of a desire to maintain, and even to improve relations with US. He returned several times to the sequence of events, repeating his reasons and his tactics. He wanted more approbation than I proffered. I congratulated and thanked him for the effective security and hoped that he could soon turn off the propaganda and turn on the oil. He had already started on the radio programs, he said. He also assured me that Kuwait does not want to lose any more income than necessary by its oil restrictions. (I will report more after I discuss with UK Ambassador what Amir told me at end of my interview.)

4. The Amir asked what I thought of the situation; what would happen. I said it depended upon, first, implementation of the cease-fire, second, upon the attitude of the belligerents, and upon the actions of the United Nations, particularly the Security Council. I hoped that GOK would support forcefully strengthening of the peacekeeping machinery. I then explained the US and Soviet draft resolutions which had not yet come to his attention. I also offered him detailed US intelligence on the war situation. I passed on some authorized [*less than 1 line of source text not declassified*] information which Amir appreciated and asked for more. I found him surprisingly uninformed about the Kuwaiti troops. He implored me to pass on any new information that we might obtain.

5. Amir thought it unnecessary for Kuwait to say anything about cease-fire. He observed that Saudi Arabia had said nothing.

6. To my query about the Amir's view of the situation, he agreed with the importance of the cease-fire and build-up of peacekeeping. My efforts to interest him in post-war reconstruction were not very productive, but he is aware of Kuwait's responsibilities.

7. Amir dismissed the interpreter. Even with my limited Arabic capability, I understood that he had telephoned President Nasser to reiterate his allegiance and best wishes. I also learned that designee Zakaria Muhyi-al-Din had not made a good impression on His Highness during the recent visit. Unfortunately, I could not get the nuances.

8. I then called on Deputy Grand Chamberlain Ibrahim Shatti, political advisor, to arrange [*less than 1 line of source text not declassified*] for passing [*less than 1 line of source text not declassified*] information and to plant some ideas about settlement. I found him open-minded, but it was evident that he has not yet given consideration to this aspect of the present situation.

9. *Comment:* I am fully convinced the Amir and GOK want an increasingly intimate association with US and that the Amir will move

rapidly to restore the status quo ante in public relations and oil. Strong security will be continued in expectation of backlash demonstrations. As I left palace, a demonstration was forming and my route was prescribed by a chamberlain who later telephoned the Embassy to see if I had arrived safely.

Cottam

212.   Telegram From the Department of State to the Embassy in Kuwait[1]

Washington, June 15, 1967, 4:09 p.m.

211350. Deliver following personal message dated June 15, 1967 from the President to His Highness the Ruler:[2]

"Your Highness:

During these difficult days it is important for us to understand one another's views on the rapidly changing situation in the Middle East.

Above all, I want to be sure that Your Highness has no doubt that the United States continues to value its relations with all Arab countries. I regret very much that our formal ties with some of them have been cut, especially since the charges which prompted that break are totally invented. I can assure Your Highness categorically that no US aircraft have been involved in any way against the interests of the Arab countries.

We particularly value the long and friendly relationship between our governments and peoples. Therefore I respect Your Highness' statesmanship, which has helped maintain this relationship throughout this trying period.

---

[1] Source: National Archives and Records Administration, RG 59, Central Files 1967–69, POL 27 ARAB–ISR. Secret; Immediate; Exdis. Drafted by Brewer on June 9, text revised in the White House; cleared by Davies, Battle, Saunders, and Eugene Rostow; and approved by Herbert B. Thompson (S/S).

[2] A June 14 memorandum from Rostow to the President reads: "We are taking advantage of all quiet opportunities to keep our lines open to those moderate Arab leaders who have resisted Nasser's pressure to break with us. They hope we'll soon be able to make some pro-Arab gesture that will justify their policy. Except for limited humanitarian actions, this will be hard, and any hand-holding we can do is so much to the good." Rostow noted that the attached message to the Amir of Kuwait was a general response to the Ruler's assurances to Ambassador Cottam that Kuwait would not break relations and would protect our people. (Johnson Library, National Security File, Saunders Files, Kuwait, 4/1/66–1/20/69)

We will continue to work for the establishment of peace in the Middle East on the basis of mutual respect and cooperation. I hope the cease-fire can in fact become a first step toward peace and progress for all the peoples of the area and pray that God may grant us all the wisdom and courage to bring this about.[3]

With personal greetings and high regards,

Sincerely,

Lyndon B. Johnson"

Rusk

---

[3] In telegram 1370 from Kuwait, June 17, Cottam reported that he had handed the President's message to Shaikh Khalid al Ahmad, President of Amiri Diwan, early on June 17. The Ambassador warned that every Kuwaiti official had affirmed that Kuwait would follow the will of all Arabs to her last drop of blood and of oil. (National Archives and Records Administration, RG 59, Central Files 1967–69, POL 27 ARAB–ISR)

---

213.   Memorandum From Acting Secretary of State Katzenbach to President Johnson[1]

Washington, June 27, 1967.

SUBJECT

Appointment for the Foreign Minister of Kuwait

Recommendation:

I recommend that you receive the Foreign Minister of Kuwait, Shaikh Sabah al-Ahmad al-Jabir al-Sabah, brother of the Kuwaiti Prime Minister, at a time of your convenience between now and July 2. The Foreign Minister, in New York for the UNGA, has asked to call on you briefly to deliver a reply from his first cousin, the Ruler of Kuwait, to your letter to the Ruler of June 15, a copy of which is enclosed.[2] If you approve, a briefing memorandum with talking points for the meeting will be submitted.[3]

---

[1] Source: National Archives and Records Administration, RG 59, Central Files 1967–69, POL 7 KUW. Secret. Drafted by Korn.

[2] See Document 212.

[3] The approved option is checked.

Discussion:

While hewing to the Arab line on Israel, Kuwait has nevertheless played a fundamentally constructive role during the recent crisis. The Kuwaiti Government assured us privately in the early days of the crisis that it did not believe UAR charges of American and British participation in the fighting and that it had no intention of breaking relations. Oil production was shut down briefly and shipment of oil to the Continental US and UK remain banned, but full protection was given to installations of the Kuwait Oil Company (half-owned by Gulf Oil) and to American citizens residing in Kuwait. At the Arab Foreign Ministers meeting in Kuwait which immediately preceded the UNGA, Shaikh Sabah as host is understood to have played a moderate and constructive role. A brief meeting with the Foreign Minister would give you an opportunity to underscore our hope that Kuwait will continue to play a moderating role in Arab councils during the weeks and months ahead.

Nicholas deB Katzenbach

---

214.   Telegram From the Department of State to the Embassy in Kuwait[1]

Washington, June 30, 1967, 8:48 p.m.

220347. Following summary FYI only and Noforn. It is uncleared and subject to revision upon review.

1. Following FonMin Sabah al-Ahmad's delivery oral message from Ruler (reported separately),[2] President expressed appreciation and said he would give it serious study. He noted problems exist on both sides but said he appreciated the fairness, moderation and judiciousness which has characterized Ruler's approach. Saying there enough blame to go around, President noted that Israelis had not been the ones to close Gulf of Aqaba which immediate cause hostilities, but suggested

---

[1] Source: National Archives and Records Administration, RG 59, Central Files 1967–69, POL 7 KUW. Secret; Exdis. Drafted by Brewer on June 29, cleared by Saunders, and approved by Davies. Repeated to USUN.

[2] Telegram 218799 to Kuwait, June 29, reported that Kuwaiti Foreign Minister's Sabah al-Ahmad had called on the President on the evening of June 28 to deliver the Ruler's oral message, which stated that Israel had initiated aggression and that the community of nations had long accepted the view that acquisition of territory by force should not be recognized. (Ibid., POL 27 ARAB–ISR)

that was a bygone and we should look ahead. President stressed USG had in no way participated with Israel in fighting as UAR alleged.

2. FonMin said he wished speak frankly as representative friendly country. Arabs were human and not infallible. At same time they did not want to see one wrong followed by another. Many responsible Arab officials continued look to USG. Sabah stressed his hope that measures USG might take in present situation would not "force" them away from that position.

3. President reacted to notion that US actions "forced" moderates to take any position. He responded not USG intentions, but Nasser's actions which had led to fighting, should be Arab concern. Sabah cautioned against taking Nasser "as point of reference." Officials would come and go, but attitude Arab common people what counts. President replied USG would do what is right but could do little as long as moderates continue to follow Nasser's misguided leadership. FonMin again asked USG do what it could remove "encroachments on our territory." Sabah indicated our failure would leave moderates open to serious threat on part USSR.

4. President said solution could not be one-way proposition. Sabah replied all problems could be solved after withdrawal, to which President rejoined all problems should be considered together. Sabah said this very difficult and not question of one or two Arab leaders. Arab masses simply would not accept any package deal. President inquired whether masses seriously expected Israel withdraw without achieving right of passage. FonMin suggested authority could be given to UN or SYG to examine specific issues and work out settlement.

5. Noting we would be glad have detailed Kuwaiti views on latter point, President said we respected Kuwait and liked way Kuwaitis had handled their affairs. If FonMin submitted further thoughts, we would carefully consider them. Our rule was never to leave a friend, though regrettably a friend sometimes left us.

6. FonMin expressed warm appreciation President's frankness which bore witness our continuing friendship and mutual respect. These factors explained why GOK had not broken relations with us. Sabah nevertheless pleaded that USG avoid actions which would put Arab moderates in position where they would be vulnerable "outside" pressure. President assured FonMin we would not do so but noted that others might and reminded Sabah that USG lacks power to control events.

7. In subsequent talk with Presidential Assistant Rostow, FonMin again voiced concern lest USG actions force moderates abandon moderation. Rostow noted Soviet policy appears aimed at Israel but in fact is aimed at Arab moderates. Problem was how USG could help moderates while still doing what is just and feasible in situation. Clearly troops

must be withdrawn but Syrian heights, Aqaba and other specific issues would have to be worked out. FonMin said Arabs could not accept conditional Israeli withdrawal but would be willing have SYG given certain powers in wake withdrawal resolution to work out specific issues. Russians for own reasons were already taking advantage situation by warmly espousing Arab cause. Unquestioned Arab support for Nasser modified by recent events but, for this be meaningful, USG must take helpful position. Rostow said Soviets in recent discussions had noted they had ended war with Japanese 10 years before they signed peace treaty. He wondered whether this might be example for Arabs. FonMin rejoined that USG now had opportunity strengthen Arab moderates and encourage realism in Arab councils if we wished. Rostow concluded we would welcome additional suggestions. We had tried hard to prevent war but failed which indicated limits USG influence. Peaceful conditions in Near East depended mainly on peoples of Near East. President's five principles designed be helpful but USG could not alone provide solutions.

8. *Comment:* Exchange with President was warm and friendly despite expression of sometimes opposing views. Kuwaitis subsequently expressed pleasure at meeting, indicating they might have further specific suggestions following FonMin's speech at UNGA afternoon June 29.

Rusk

---

215.   **Telegram From the Department of State to the Embassy in Kuwait**[1]

Washington, November 25, 1967, 1942Z.

74837. 1. Chargé requested deliver to FonMin following personal message from Secretary:

"Excellency:

Thank you for your recent letter which I have just received through Ambassador Cottam.[2] I appreciate your taking the time in these difficult

---

[1] Source: National Archives and Records Administration, RG 59, Central Files 1967–69, POL KUW–US. Confidential. Drafted by Brewer, cleared by UNP Director Elizabeth Ann Brown and Davies, and approved by Rusk.

[2] An unofficial translation of the Foreign Minister's undated message is attached to a November 24 memorandum from Battle transmitting a draft of telegram 74837 to the Secretary for his signature. (Ibid.)

days to bring your views directly to my attention. I fully share your view that relations between Kuwait and the US are based on solid friendship, mutual interest and fruitful cooperation, and share your determination to keep these ties firm and enduring.

The recent debate at the UN on the Near East has been a difficult and trying time for us all. I know that you and we have done everything we can to assure that moderation prevails and a climate is created in which a mutually acceptable settlement can be envisioned. It is a source of great gratification to me that these efforts have now been rewarded. The unanimous action of the Security Council on November 22[3] in approving a resolution on the Near East gives us all a particular opportunity, which may not recur, to try to resolve outstanding problems on a basis acceptable to both sides.

The fact that the Council approved unanimously a set of principles including withdrawal of armed forces from occupied territories, termination of claims or states of belligerence, secure and recognize boundaries, and other points which have been the focus of recent discussion in New York, is a clear manifestation of world opinion. It should materially assist the Secretary General's Special Representative in his efforts to help the parties in the working out of appropriate solutions.

The Council's action, and what we understand to be the willingness of the parties to cooperate with the Special Representative, are encouraging. For its part, I wish to assure Your Excellency that the US Government is prepared to use all its diplomatic and political influence to assist the Special Representative in helping to establish lasting conditions of peace in the region.

It was a pleasure to see Your Excellency in Washington last summer. I would like to thank you again for your recent letter.

With warm regards,

Sincerely, Dean Rusk"

2. Dept planning no publicity here and suggests there be none in Kuwait. Suggest you make this point to FonMin.

Rusk

---

[3] Reference is to Resolution 242; for text, see *American Foreign Policy: Current Documents, 1967*, pp. 616–617. Documentation on the Six-Day War and Resolution 242 is scheduled for publication in *Foreign Relations, 1964–1968*, volume XIX.

216.   Airgram From the Embassy in Kuwait to the Department of State[1]

A–150   Kuwait, February 21, 1968.

SUBJECT

U.S. Policy Assessment

REF

II FAM 212.3–5; Embassy's A–274 of March 21, 1967[2]

SUMMARY

Since the Embassy's last policy assessment three events, the Arab-Israeli war, the devaluation of sterling and the UK announcement of military withdrawal east of Suez, have severely tested the ability of Kuwait's leaders to sustain the country's sovereign independence and to maintain its impressive pace of modernization. These same events had a profound effect on the ability of the U.S. to pursue our objectives in Kuwait, and added a new factor in the equation which suggests that a third, broader objective be included in our basic policy which we now would describe as:

1. To maintain maximum free-world access to Kuwait's resources and to limit access to Communist and other nations who actively espouse systems different from ours.

2. To obtain maximum support from Kuwait for the free world and its basic institutions.

3. To convince Kuwait that its future progress and (even its survival) as an independent nation depend on its willingness and ability to cooperate in regional efforts to maintain area stability.

U.S. capabilities in Kuwait were eroded by the Arab-Israeli war and its aftermath. It is widely believed that Israel owes its military and political successes to U.S. support, and that the U.S. is the main enemy of Kuwait and the rest of the Arab world as far as Israel is concerned. The U.S. is still tacitly regarded in Kuwait, however, as the protector against the spread of communist influence. The U.S. also continues to be the prime market and source of technical skill, equipment and capital. Thus hate and distrust intensified while awareness of the need for

---

[1] Source: National Archives and Records Administration, RG 59, Central Files 1967–69, POL 1 KUW–US. Secret. Drafted by Cottam, Deputy Chief of Mission John N. Gatch, Jr., Political Officer Robert H. Carlson, Public Affairs Officer John W. Vonier, and Economic Officer James A Placke; and approved by Cottam. Pouched to Arab capitals, Ankara, Karachi, London, Moscow, New Delhi, Paris, Tehran, Tel Aviv, Tokyo, CINCSTRIKE/ CINCMEAFSA for POLAD, and USUN.

[2] Not printed. (Ibid.)

the U.S. increased. Kuwait became extremist on the Palestine issue, remained committed but dubious about pan-Arabism and turned towards cautious moderation on matters concerning oil and money.

U.S. tactics must be accommodated to the sharper ambivalence, but we should continue to identify mutual interests and to urge Kuwait to support its national interests in free world institutions and systems, with special emphasis on regional cooperation.

[Here follows the body of the paper.]

217. Record of Meeting[1]

IRG/NEA 68–21   Washington, June 4, 1968.

INTERDEPARTMENTAL REGIONAL GROUP
FOR NEAR EAST AND SOUTH ASIA

Record of IRG Meeting—June 4, 1968

The meeting was devoted to *several current Near East military problems*, as outlined in IRG/NEA 68–19.[2]

Possible Arms Sales and Presidential Determination for Kuwait

The IRG noted recent requests by the Government of Kuwait to purchase military equipment (patrol boats, helicopters, armored personnel carriers and 155mm howitzers) from the USG. The Defense member expressed the view that the Kuwaitis hoped for some kind of USG involvement in their security going beyond the mere supply of arms, in anticipation of the British military withdrawal from the Persian Gulf by the end of 1971 and the prospective termination before that time of the British defense commitment to Kuwait. He thought a decision to sell arms to Kuwait would be followed by requests to us by other small states in the Gulf (e.g., Qatar, Abu Dhabi) for the supply of arms. The Defense member expressed concern over the dangers of our taking steps to "fill the vacuum," by selling arms to states with which we do not now have a military supply relationship, as the British withdraw.

The CIA member remarked that we had to take into account the possibility that Kuwait might seek to buy arms from the Soviets, if it

---

[1] Source: Department of State, NEA/IRG Files: Lot 70 D 503, IRG/NEA 68–21— Record of IRG Mtg June 4 on Current Near East Military Problems. Secret. Drafted by IRG Staff Director Sidney Sober on June 6.

[2] Not found.

could not meet its requests from the British or, failing that, from other Western sources. He recalled that "deal" of 1963 when the USSR succeeded in getting GOK approval for the establishment of a Soviet Embassy in Kuwait in return for Soviet agreement to remove its blackball on Kuwait's entry into the United Nations. The CIA member said the Soviets would almost certainly wish to introduce military personnel into Kuwait in connection with any supply of Soviet arms. The establishment of such a relationship by the USSR and Kuwait would inevitably tend to damage our interests in the area.

The Chairman said he saw the issue in terms of our broad interests in the Persian Gulf area. He recalled that the IRG had recently agreed on the general outlines of our policy vis-à-vis the Gulf, and it was entirely consistent with that policy that we should encourage Kuwait to continue to look to the UK as its source of arms.[3] However, in cases where the United Kingdom could not adequately meet Kuwait's requests, it could be in the U.S. interest to sell certain things to the Kuwaitis. The Chairman said he appreciated the concern expressed on this point, but it was his view that if we should decide that it was in our interest to sell some arms to Kuwait in accordance with our current restrictive policy, we could do so without involving ourselves deeply in the question of maintaining Kuwait's security. In any event, we would have to have more information—including a clear idea of British views—and a specific transaction in mind before proceeding further. If we eventually decide that we should agree to any Kuwaiti request for arms, we should be prepared to seek the President's approval at that time, spelling out the basic policy issues (e.g., close collaboration with the British, the requirements of legitimate defense, avoidance of an unnecessary arms race, the Soviet angle, etc.). The Chairman stated it would be premature at this time to seek a general Presidential Determination under Section 521(c) of the Foreign Assistance Act, which would be required to make Kuwait eligible for purchases through Department of Defense channels.

---

[3] The following is a paragraph from IRG/NEA 68–8, the record of the IRG meeting of February 1, 1968:

"The Group agreed that although the Soviets will try to increase their presence and influence in the Gulf area, the key to the future of the region in the next few years will be developments within and among the various Gulf states themselves. It is neither politically feasible nor desirable for the US to 'replace' the British presence in the Persian Gulf. Our policy should be directed along the lines of (a) encouraging the British to maintain as much of their present special role in the Gulf as they can, as long as possible (including their role as principal arms supplier to various Gulf states); (b) encouraging the Saudis and Iranians to settle their outstanding differences regarding the median line and other issues; (c) encouraging greater political and economic cooperation generally among the Gulf states; and (d) avoiding an undue military buildup by Gulf littoral states." [Footnote in the source text. For a record of the February 1 meeting, see Document 131.]

It was agreed that there should be further staffing of the pending Kuwaiti requests. This should include consultation with the British, seeking the UK's views on the reasonableness of Kuwait's requests and on the UK's ability to meet them; we should also seek a general British view on the future development of the Kuwaiti armed forces.

[Here follows discussion of other subjects.]

MEMBERS PRESENT

Executive Chairman: Mr. Battle
ACDA: Mr. van Doren
AID: Mr. Wheeler
CIA: Mr. Critchfield
DOD: Mr. Schwartz (Mr. Earle)
JCS: Brig. Gen. Doyle
NSC: Mr. Saunders
USIA: Mr. Carter

State (NEA): Messrs. Davies, Dinsmore, Houghton, Atherton
State (G/PM): Mr. Wolf
State (L): Mr. Wehmeyer
Staff Director: Mr. Sober

S.S.
Staff Director

---

218.   **Memorandum From Secretary of State Rusk to President Johnson**[1]

Washington, December 3, 1968.

SUBJECT

Your Meeting with the Amir of Kuwait, Shaikh Sabah al-Salim al-Sabah, 12 noon, Wednesday, December 11

Shaikh Sabah al-Salim al-Sabah

This is Shaikh Sabah's first visit to the United States as Amir of Kuwait. When he was Prime Minister, he visited New York briefly in

---

[1] Source: National Archives and Records Administration, RG 59, Central Files 1967–69, POL 7 KUW. Confidential. Drafted by Brewer; cleared by William H. Hallman (NEA/IRN), Atherton, Hart, Officer in Charge of UN Political Affairs Betty-Jane Jones, Deputy Assistant Secretary of Defense for ISA/NESA Harry H. Schwartz, and Heyward Isham (EA/VN). A typed notation reads: "Signed original to Amir of Kuwait briefing book 12/5/68."

1963 when Kuwait was admitted to the UN. You have not met the Amir, but his cousin, Foreign Minister Sabah al-Ahmad (who will be in the Kuwaiti party), called on you in June, 1967, during the special UNGA session on the Arab/Israel crisis.

Shaikh Sabah succeeded to the Amirate in 1965 on the death of his elder brother. Kuwait has a constitution and a parliament but almost all key positions are still held by members of the ruling Sabah family. At present, the Salim and Ahmad branches of the family govern in tacit alliance. The Amir is head of the Salim branch. The Foreign Minister's elder brother, Crown Prince and Prime Minister Jabir, heads the Ahmad branch.

To Americans who know him, the Amir is something of a bantam— short, cocky, unctuous and protocol-conscious. This attitude seems in part to reflect a basic lack of confidence and, as a result, the Amir responds very warmly to flattery and full recognition of his position.

What Shaikh Sabah Wants

Shaikh Sabah has for years craved an official visit to this country. Now that he is Amir, he no doubt sees it as giving him, and his small nation, additional stature on the world stage.

The Amir was nevertheless ambivalent about coming now because of Arab concern at USG policy on issues growing out of the June war. We think he checked with several other Arab heads of state before accepting, rationalizing to them his desire to come as a way of exerting influence on both the outgoing and incoming US Administrations. He is disappointed that his desire to meet with President-elect Nixon has not been granted (Mr. Nixon has taken the position that it would be inappropriate for him to see any visiting heads of state or similar leaders during the transition period).

In addition to wanting to discuss Arab-Israel issues, Shaikh Sabah will probably inquire as to the USG attitude towards Persian Gulf problems in the light of the scheduled British withdrawal by the end of 1971 and heightened Soviet interest in the region. Kuwait, Saudi Arabia and Iran have recently exchanged Heads of State visits and relations are cordial. There is nevertheless considerable historical and religious suspicion between the Arab Sunni Moslems on the Western side of the Gulf and the Persian Shi'a Moslems across the way. In fact, the Arabs steadfastly refer to the Persian Gulf as "the Arab Gulf". We therefore generally use the simple term "the Gulf" in talks with Arab leaders.

Despite differences over Israel, Kuwait is interested in cultivating USG interest in Gulf affairs as a counterpoint to Soviet interest and as a means of furthering local stability and helping assure Kuwait's continued independence. The Kuwaiti attitude was made particularly clear in January 1968 after the British withdrawal announcement. The Kuwait Government had earlier been dragging its feet on a routine US naval visit request but, immediately on hearing the announcement, asked how soon the visit could take place. Kuwait has since then been concerned at the Soviet naval visit to Iraq in May, 1968, the first Gulf visit by a Russian squadron since 1903.

Subsequent to the British announcement, the Kuwaitis have approached us several times regarding their desire to purchase modern US arms. We took the position that Kuwait should continue to look to the UK as its principal arms supplier but said that we would be prepared to discuss any legitimate requests which the British could not meet. The British have subsequently concluded some arms sales with Kuwait, but the Amir may conceivably raise this subject with you.

What We Want

1. We have not previously had a high-level visit from Kuwait, though it became independent in 1961. This visit will thus be useful in marking the cordiality of USG/Kuwaiti relations which have existed (except for Arab-Israel issues) since the state's independence.

2. No Eastern Arab Head of State has paid an official visit here since the June war. The Amir's trip is thus useful to us in stressing publicly that there are moderate Arab regimes with which we still enjoy close relations. We hope publicity about the visit will have a favorable impact throughout the Arab world, particularly at a time when Arabs accuse us of undue support for Israel.

3. We are concerned regarding stability in the Gulf area after the British go. Kuwait's financial strength and past mediatory role on Gulf problems make it a force for stability in the region which we are hoping to encourage. Additionally, we hope the USSR will not fail to note the visit as an indication that the USG will continue to have an interest in Gulf affairs after 1971.

Assistant Secretary Hart and Country Director Brewer will stand by during your meeting with Shaikh Sabah following the arrival ceremony.

Talking points are at Tab A.[2] We also transmit (Tab B)[3] a draft communiqué which is under discussion with the Government of Kuwait. We will replace it with the final version as soon as possible.

Dean Rusk

---

[2] The tabs are attached but not printed.

[3] For text of the joint communiqué issued on December 11, see *Public Papers of the Presidents of the United States: Lyndon B. Johnson, 1968–69*, Book II, pp. 1182–1183.

219. Memorandum of Conversation[1]

Washington, December 11, 1968, 11:56 a.m.–1 p.m.

SUBJECT

US/Kuwaiti Relations

PARTICIPANTS

His Highness Shaikh Sabah al-Salim al-Sabah, Amir of the State of Kuwait
His Excellency Shaikh Sabah al-Ahmed al-Jabir, Minister of Foreign Affairs of
   the State of Kuwait
His Excellency Abd al-Rahman Salem al-Ateeqi, Minister of Finance and Oil
His Excellency Talat al-Ghoussein, Ambassador of the State of Kuwait to the
   United States

The President
The Honorable Howard R. Cottam, American Ambassador to the State of
Kuwait
Parker T. Hart, Assistant Secretary for Near Eastern and South Asian Affairs,
   Department of State
Harold H. Saunders, White House
Camille Nowfel, Interpreter

The President opened the conversation by expressing pleasure that the Amir was here and had brought some of his beautiful sunshine with him. He hoped the Amir would enjoy his stay. He was honored to have the Amir for his last State visit. As he had said in his arrival statement, the people of America are enthusiastic about Kuwait and its willingness to share its treasure with its fellowmen. He would be pleased to hear the Amir's views on anything of common interest.

The Amir thanked the President for his invitation, for his kind words of welcome and for the warmth of his reception. He trusted that their conversation would be "as clear and cloudless as the weather." He wished the President continued health and prosperity.

As for his views on substantive issues, he said he would like to discuss matters of direct concern to his area.

As for the "Arab Gulf," he said he would like to hear what plans the US might have in view of the British withdrawal from the area.

In response to the President's request for comment, Assistant Secretary Hart said Gulf affairs would continue to be of great interest to the United States. The US has no plan to take the unique place the British once held. The British position developed under circumstances that do

---

[1] Source: Johnson Library, National Security File, Country File, Kuwait, Cables & Memos, Vol. I, 11/63–1/69. Secret; Exdis. Drafted by Saunders on December 17 and approved by the White House on December 31. The meeting was held in the Oval Office. The time of the meeting was taken from the President's Daily Diary. (Ibid.)

not exist today, and it is the people of the Gulf themselves who will determine the future of the Gulf area. The Amir said he realized that the people of the area would have to carry a larger share of the burden, but he would like to reiterate his question about exactly what position the US plans to take. In response to Mr. Hart's question about precisely what the Amir meant by "position", the Amir said that there is no threat to the Gulf from the "Arab area." The danger is from outside the area and the threat may be military or subversive or in unknown forms.

Mr. Hart said that if he had to look into the future, he would say that we will be just as greatly concerned with the independence and integrity of states of the Gulf as we are with the independence and integrity of states all over the world. We have demonstrated this beyond doubt. The Gulf area is no exception. We have strong ties with all the peoples on the Gulf shores.

The Amir said, "Suppose there is an armed attack on any countries of the area, could we expect armed support?"

The President said that that is a matter that would have to be considered through the Constitutional procedures of the US, taking into account the circumstances, the recommendations of the President at the time, the attitudes of the Congress, the existence of treaties, the justice of the causes involved and the American people's views of the situation. He emphasized that one President could not bind another and, therefore, he could not speak for future Presidents.

The President continued, saying that we are very anxious that stability prevail in all parts of the world. We are anxious to make no statement that would encourage aggression. We have not had to deal with aggression by force in that part of the world, but the Amir knows of our friendship for the people of that area. The US will under its Constitutional procedures face whatever situation may develop and act accordingly.

The Amir shared the hope that no such situation would arise. He believed that problems of aggression should be solved "by men's minds rather than by force." However, he could not help but think about the problem and wanted to know what he could count on. The US is a symbol of peace in the world, and he just wanted to know what the attitude of the US would be in such a situation.

When the President asked Mr. Hart whether he wished to raise anything else, the Assistant Secretary asked about the meetings in Kuwait with the Shah of Iran. The Amir called them "100% successful." Disagreement remains as far as Bahrein is concerned. He said that "we" are looking for a solution and doing "our" best to reach a settlement. The Shah "assured us that he has no ambitions," but he has an old claim. The Amir expressed his view that the Shah is "seeking a way out." He said the Shah had asked him to "help him find a way out." The Amir realized the Shah's difficulty.

The Amir said he would like to ask the President's opinion of the Federation of Arab Amirates. The President asked Mr. Hart to comment.

Mr. Hart said we feel this was basically a good idea. It will help the states of the area work together in using their resources to best advantage. The main problem is the Shah's problem with respect to the inclusion of Bahrain in the Federation. The main question is whether a solution can be found for the Shah.

The Amir said that Iran would "undoubtedly oppose" the inclusion of Bahrain. The Government of Iran is seeking a way out of this problem. The Amir felt that the US might possibly use its influence to help and encourage Iran to find a way out with dignity. He hoped the problem could be solved with US help.

Mr. Hart said that we would encourage this in an informal way. We understand the problems of both sides. We are encouraged that there have been recent meetings among the Saudis, Iranians and Kuwaitis and that some of the Shaikhs of the lower Trucial Coast have visited Iran. Considering the fact that there was little communication not too many years ago, we view this as progress.

The Amir said that Kuwait had tried to increase contact between Iran and Bahrain. Representatives of the two sides had met in Geneva two months ago and "we hope there will be another meeting soon."

The Foreign Minister said that as one looks at South Arabia one cannot but fear for the rest of the area. The "Soviets and the Communists" have established footholds in the area. Is the United States happy about this? When Mr. Hart answered quickly that we are "most unhappy", the Foreign Minister said, "Then we find a meeting point." He went on to say that he hopes the US would use its good offices with Iran to help settle the Bahrain issue.

Mr. Hart said he believes the Shah is aware of the problem and has just as much interest as anyone else in defending the area against outside interests, but he has a problem on Bahrain. "We all have to help him find a solution." The Shah is dealing with a tradition of long standing, and it is not easy to bury a tradition. It is in the interests of all of us that he finds a solution.

The Amir said that it would only be through the joint efforts of the US, Iran and Kuwait, that a favorable settlement would be found. Mr. Hart nodded and said, "Quiet diplomacy."

The President said that he had asked Secretary Hart to respond to the Amir's questions because Mr. Hart is a career officer deeply involved in the area. The President felt that Mr. Hart's judgment would be called on "long after I am gone" from office.

Generally speaking, the President felt that his record on aggression was well known. He and his administration have looked with great disfavor on any power that tried to impose its will on others by might. Our position has been made clear all around the world.

On the Federation, we encourage regional cooperation and foster the association of neighbors in efforts to strengthen their economies. We have done this in Latin America, Africa and on continents all over the world.

The President expressed his pleasure that the Amir's meeting with the Shah had gone well. He felt that "whoever sits in this chair" will do everything possible to encourage just solutions to problems of this kind.

The President said that, at the White House dinner in the evening, leading citizens from all over the United States would come to welcome the Amir and to pay their respects. He had had "fewer declines" on this dinner than on any other and he was looking forward to seeing the Amir in the evening.

The Amir said there were other points that could be covered, but he knew the President's time was limited. He would like to mention in parting the Palestine issue.

The President said that we are "alert to it". We believe that the people of the area should work out a solution. We support the UN efforts to help them. We are anxious to do anything we can on our side to help. If the Amir had any specific suggestions on how we might help, he might wish to take them up with Secretary Rusk.

The Amir asked how soon the US might resume relations with the UAR.

The President said that would be a problem that Mr. Nixon would have to act on. He said that we have been "anxious to resume relations right along." We had been concerned that the record of our erroneously alleged involvement in the June 1967 war be corrected. We had let the Egyptians know that, if they would correct that record, we would be glad to resume relations. But that is now an issue which the new Administration will have to take up. The Scranton mission[2] had created some hope in this direction, and he hoped something would come out of it. He would like to see a genuine move toward better relations. "We would be glad to resume tomorrow if they would just state for the record that we did not attack them." The President reiterated that

---

[2] Former Governor of Pennsylvania Scranton visited the United Arab Republic December 6–7 as part of a six-nation fact-finding tour of the Middle East undertaken on behalf of President-elect Nixon. Documentation on the Scranton mission is in the National Archives and Records Administration, RG 59, Central Files 1967–69, POL 7 US/SCRANTON.

he could not bind his successor, but he hoped and believed that relations would be resumed.

The Amir pointed out that the UAR government had made a statement to *Look* magazine for the record. The President, smiling, replied that maybe we have resumed relations with *Look* magazine, but not with each other. He said he had seen and was aware of the *Look* article, but felt that the best way to clear up misunderstandings of this kind is to talk directly to each other.

The President repeated that we would like to see relations resumed, that we regretted their having been broken. He said we had not attacked the UAR and as soon as the UAR had made a statement directly to us, we would be happy to resume relations.

The Amir asked what the US position would be should Cairo request resumption.

The President said that, as he had just stated, "we would be very glad to resume." When the Amir said that there had been an understanding that the *Look* statement was tantamount to an Egyptian admission of the error of its charges, the President said he did not have much to add to what he had already said, except to say that if we can have that statement in *Look*, why not have it in a cable?

The Amir said he had not been asked to pursue this issue. He was just personally interested in it. The President reiterated that we are very much interested in resuming relations. We are sorry they were broken and would be happy to resume under the conditions he had described.

In parting, the President said he looked forward to seeing the Amir in the evening.

Comment: Toward the end of the meeting, there was much conversation among the Kuwaitis in Arabic. Presumably the Foreign Minister and Ambassador Ghoussein were urging the Amir to get to the Palestine issue. At that point, the President was running behind on his schedule and was under some pressure to meet his next appointment.

220. Telegram From the Department of State to the Embassy in Kuwait[1]

Washington, December 13, 1968, 1344Z.

286622. Persian Gulf. Following based on uncleared memcon and subject revision on review. FYI only and Noforn.

1. Summary. Amir of Kuwait took up at length with Secretary GOK concern at security situation in Gulf in wake British withdrawal, as well as problem created by Iranian claim Bahrain. Secretary reaffirmed our interest in region and said we would see whether there anything constructive USG might do to help resolve Bahrain issue. End summary.

2. Secretary met with Amir of Kuwait for two hours December 12. Kuwaiti Foreign Minister, Minister of Finance/Oil Affairs, Kuwaiti Ambassador to US, Ambassador Cottam, Assistant Secretary Hart and Country Director Brewer also present. Amir referred at outset, as he had with President previous day, to uncertainty as to USG position re Gulf affairs following UK withdrawal.

3. Secretary responded this primarily matter for new US Administration. On personal basis, he noted if there were group Gulf states which arranged give each other mutual support in case attack, any USG support would not have divisive effect which unilateral USG assurances to any one area state would have. Secretary stressed our strong interest in security of Kuwait and recalled USG action in moving destroyers towards Kuwait during Iraqi crisis in 1961. Secretary also noted our continuing support for CENTO, importance of close Iran/Kuwait/Saudi Arabia ties and opined some UK role in Middle East perhaps not ended.

4. Amir asked if USG interests or regional stability in Gulf threatened by outside power would USG take some action. Secretary responded answer to this most solemn question could only come from next President under our Constitution. Personally he would like say yes but this would be like giving check without funds in bank. If there were major Soviet threat, this would no doubt be major East/West crisis involving totality our relations to which we could not remain indifferent. If threat came from neighboring state, then solidarity among Kuwait and its neighbors would provide basis on which outside support might be provided.

---

[1] Source: National Archives and Records Administration, RG 59, Central Files 1967–69, POL 7 KUW. Secret; Exdis. Drafted by Brewer on December 12; cleared by Cottam, Eliot, and Davies; and approved by Hart. Repeated to Tehran, Jidda, London, and Dhahran.

5. FonMin explained GOK did not have in mind conclusion mutual defense treaty but rather wished know whether USG interested in regional stability and territorial integrity each state there. Secretary said he could give categorical response. USG was deeply interested both as matter general policy and specific USG interests. Secretary then cited our actions in Middle East since World War II, noting record made clear general policy USG is to support territorial integrity and political independence all states in region. Secretary noted, however, most USG actions to which he referred had reflected general policy considerations rather than specific textual commitments. It one thing to act when situation requires it but, under our system, much more difficult make promises in advance. Thus, though USG has serious interest in independence and security of Kuwait, it constitutionally difficult explain what we might do in specific circumstances.

6. Amir then raised question Iranian claim to Bahrain. Secretary said thing that most concerned American people on such territorial disputes was wishes people concerned in this case on Bahrain. We did not think Iran sought solution by force but there is historical Iranian claim. Secretary hoped "quiet diplomacy" would produce acceptable compromise.

7. Amir said Shah had made clear during November visit Kuwait GOI desire find peaceful solution. Question was how. Amir felt USG help needed. Kuwait doing what it could, such as being instrumental in arranging quiet Iran/Bahrain meeting at Geneva two months ago. Two sides would meet again. Secretary congratulated Amir on this development and said we would be glad examine problem further and see whether we could come up with some constructive suggestions. Amir expressed appreciation and said he hoped we could keep in touch on issue. In response question from Hart, Amir said he believed Bahraini people fully support Ruler. While in principal anything like plebiscite unacceptable, perhaps there could be effort collect info re wishes people, e.g., through some UN mechanism. Minister of Finance noted opposition plebiscite not based on fear outcome but rather that it would be "a form of submission to a claim".

8. *Comment.* Kuwait clearly concerned both at future Gulf stability after British go and apparent intractability Bahrain problem. Dept planning take advantage concurrent presence here Ambassadors Meyer and Cottam for full review subject in effort see whether there anything useful we might propose.

Rusk

Saudi Arabia

221. Telegram From the Embassy in Saudi Arabia to the Department of State[1]

Jidda, January 12, 1964.

729. Faysal–Johnson Correspondence. Following is letter from Crown Prince to President Johnson which was delivered to me January 11 by Saqqaf. Translation moderates where necessary for clarity some of more flowery examples of Arabic style.

"Your Excellency:

I have received with great pleasure Your Excellency's letter dated 19 December 1963.[2] I appreciate the heaviness of Your Excellency's responsibilities at the present time following the tragic death of your great predecessor. I also fully appreciate the pleasant gesture represented by your personal interest in the relations between our two countries and your re-examination of the past and study of the future of these relations. I am firmly convinced that the strengthening of understanding between the Kingdom of Saudi Arabia and the United States of America is imperative and that frank exchanges of views between them is most desirable.

I in turn emphasize my sincere desire that the frank rapport which existed between the late President John F. Kennedy and myself still continue between Your Excellency and me. For such rapport would strengthen the friendly ties between us and be the means raising the relations between our two countries to new heights.

I share with Your Excellency the conviction that the relations between our two countries and peoples have not been confined to the mere utterance of words. These relations have often manifested themselves in deeds, facts and achievements which have filled the long history of relations between our countries—that history whose foundations were laid by his majesty, the late King 'Abd al-Aziz and the late Presidents Franklin Roosevelt and John F. Kennedy; it is a history which continues to the present.

Your Excellency's assurances that your only purpose in regard to Yemen[3] is to protect Saudi Arabia's integrity have given me great

---

[1] Source: National Archives and Records Administration, RG 59, Central Files 1964–66, POL SAUD–US. Secret; Priority; Limdis. No time of transmission is on the telegram. Repeated to Dhahran. Received on January 13 at 5:37 a.m. Passed to the White House at 10:15 a.m.

[2] President Johnson's letter is printed in *Foreign Relations*, 1961–1963, vol. XVIII, Document 389.

[3] See Document 319ff.

satisfaction. For my part I should like to explain very frankly that the guarantee of the safety of the Kingdom of Saudi Arabia is the single matter which dominates our thinking in these difficult circumstances. Without that safety we would not be able to devote all our efforts to attaining happiness for our people and to leading them in the path of progress that they might assume their place in the march of civilization and might attain the stature merited by their country's time-honored significance as the recipient of divine inspiration and the fountain of light.

We fully realize that the present course followed by the UAR is benefiting no-one, and that the UAR is losing much after it caused, by its persistent acts of interference, numerous calamities and mishaps which have resulted in havoc being wrought upon thousands of the Yemeni people and in the devastation of their means of subsistence. It is our conviction that all these calamities have had no justification save the desire to satisfy deeply rooted arrogance and conceit.

I hope that Your Excellency will permit me to explain why I find it difficult to understand the viewpoint which holds that cutting off aid to the UAR would push it more dangerously in the direction of the Soviet Union. I have never been, nor will I at any time be, against the people of sister Egypt receiving aid from any quarter which wishes to offer it. But I am certain that Your Excellency discerns, as I do, the clear distinction between directing those aids towards their intended goal, namely the raising of the standard of living of the Egyptian people and directing it, indeed dedicating it, to the service of aggression and the imposing of calamities on others. As a country which loves peace and justice and always desires to spread them as widely as possible, we have exerted our maximum effort towards support of the United Nations. There is no greater proof of this than our favorable response to the mediation of your late predecessor manifested in our signing of the disengagement agreement. Your Excellency, of course, knows that I acceded to the agreement only after long discussions with your predecessor's representative, Ambassador Bunker, and with your Ambassador, Mr. Hart. Those discussions embodied clear assurances that the United States of America would work for the implementation of this agreement in letter and spirit. It had never occurred to me that six months after the signing of the agreement, and eight months after we cut off aid to the Royalists, the situation in the Yemen would remain without any change worth mentioning. Neither did it occur to me to agree to the renewal of the agreement beyond the fourth of November last without there being conditions therein to terminate the Egyptian presence in the Yemen within a specific period or without its including the necessary guarantees for accomplishing that termination. The greater part of the people of sister Yemen are undergoing ordeals and great suffering while being denied even the means of subsistence. They are appealing to humanity at large to help remove aggression from their home. Indeed, they look up to Your Excellency's efforts filled with prayer and hope that peace and safety will quickly return to their country.

We do not err when we consider that the only solution which is compatible with logic, justice and international law is to leave the Yemenis to decide for themselves the fate of their country in an atmosphere assuring them of all the necessary guarantees of their freedom to do so without external intrusions and in the absence from the country of any foreign forces. Yet, in memory of your great predecessor and confident in Your Excellency's efforts, and in order to prove our good intentions, we have agreed to extend the validity of the disengagement agreement for two months starting from the fifth of January.

I have benefited greatly from the spirit of candor and friendship which Your Excellency has inaugurated. The sure confidence which I have in Your Excellency's good intentions makes it incumbent upon me to cooperate with you truthfully and honorably, deeply believing in your personal friendship and support as well as the support of the friendly American people.

I express to Your Excellency my sincere good wishes and the good wishes of the Saudi people for your happiness and prosperity and that of the American people. I further wish Your Excellency every success.

Sincerely, /s/ Faysal

January 5, 1964"

Comment: Saqqaf stated he drafted this message and that Faysal made no changes whatever in text. (Sabbagh however is convinced this arabic is above Saqqaf's style and probably a staff job under Saqqaf's supervision.) Remarks on significance this letter follow in separate message.[4]

Hart

---

[4] Not further identified.

222. Telegram From the Embassy in Saudi Arabia to the Department of State[1]

Jidda, January 30, 1964, 3 p.m.

791. Department pass DOD for ACSI. Presentation Air Defense Survey. This is Country Team message (coordination delayed by transmission difficulties).

At six hour meeting January 20 at Ministry of Defense Riyadh DOD team composed of Colonels Toliver and Taylor and Mr. Quinn presented Air Defense Survey report[2] to Saudi group headed by Minister Prince Sultan and including Chief of Staff Mutlaq. US group attending included CHUSMTM Colonel Wilson, Richard Murphy, Air Attaché Scott and myself.

Presentation received with keen interest by Saudis who compared operational concept, troop structure and broad equipment requirements with air defense annex of Saudi "Armed Force Defense Plan Number 1." Saudis were obviously pleased to find there was close correlation. Prince Sultan reacted most favorably and wound up by requesting US team confer with Saudi Army/Air Force team to finalize as far as possible detailed equipment list and construction requirements. Stated he would study point committee recommendations and asked for twice daily progress reports while committee in session. Asserted he would present his findings to Supreme Defense Council as soon as definite figures furnished him. Mentioned twice he desired buy best equipment available and wanted to be sure cost considerations had not prevented survey team from recommending latest design in optimum hardware.

Team emphasized repeatedly their recommendations based on best estimate of what SAG able support both financially and with Saudi personnel over next five years. Sultan seemed to accept equipment requirements for communications, radar and aircraft without particular reservation. He was told if he bought F-86 aircraft GAR air to air missiles could be installed immediately. He asked specifically for US recommendations as to whether Northrop F-5A or Lockheed F-104

---

[1] Source: National Archives and Records Administration, RG 59, Central Files 1964-66, DEF 1-4 SAUD. Secret. Repeated to Dhahran, CHUSMTM Dhahran, and CINCSTRIKE/CINCMEAFSA. Passed to DOD for ACSI.

[2] In April 1963 the United States offered Saudi Arabia assistance in expediting the build-up of Saudi air defense capabilities to be financed from Saudi resources, and agreed to conduct an air defense survey. The U.S. Air Defense Survey Team transmitted its report on Saudi air defense requirements to the Joint Chiefs of Staff on October 4, 1963. A summary of the Team's recommendations (undated, ca 1/30/64) is in the Johnson Library, National Security File, Country File, Saudi Arabia, Memos, Vol. 2, 12/63–4/67.

should be selected. Our reply stressed comparative costs and character-istics, avoided plugging either. Sultan accepted generally requirements for modernizing army air defense equipment expressing doubts, how-ever, on need for 54 Twin–40 mm M–42 "Dusters," feeling these would be expensive and apt to have only limited value in future.

Missiles. Sultan seemed to accept justification non-inclusion sur-face-to-air missiles at this time because of great expense higher priority need for other air defense elements and long lead time needed to prepare candidates to even begin training. Nevertheless he and his staff showed persistent interest in same. Sultan specifically asked how many units of Hawk would be needed to protect Saudi Arabia's four main urban areas. (Was told it would require one battalion each area, at estimated cost of 25 million dollars each.)

Maintenance. Sultan evidenced interest in idea of maintenance contract with single company for all communications and radar equip-ment as well as for aircraft. Apparently intends secure such bids from Lockheed and Northrop.

Credit. From several remarks made by Sultan and staff it apparent that credit terms available from US sources will be major consideration. At one point he said he had been offered favorable terms on wide range equipment by several countries, including offer of pilots to fly Saudi aircraft even in combat, until Saudis were ready.

Comment: Sultan and his staff were stimulated to surprising degree by detailed and thoughtful presentation. Sultan said he knew SAG lagging behind other Arab countries in modernizing armed forces but asserted "today we think in terms of seconds not minutes." Hopefully we may have reached turning point in galvanizing Saudi energies for new effort at modernizing armed forces. Atmosphere distinctly en-couraging.

Recommendation: That DOD promptly support CHUSMTM in any requests he may make for technical assistance from Air and Army Air Defense representatives to develop answers to questions arising from joint committee's review of report. Important that momentum gained at this stage not be dissipated.

Hart

223. Telegram From the Department of State to the Embassy in Saudi Arabia[1]

Washington, February 5, 1964, 8:57 p.m.

571. Joint State/Defense Message. In course US–UK talks January 29–30[2] (full memcons being pouched) US again repeated arguments against supplying overly sophisticated weapons to Saudis (waste of Saudi money, strain on scarce personnel resources, lack of capability to maintain and operate). UK spokesmen noted our mutual agreement to principle of opposition to introduction offensive weapons, but indicated FonOff problems in seeking discourage British arms salesmen from supplying these or overly sophisticated items to Saudis. FonOff could not forbid British firms from trying sell when these firms aware that Saudis would turn to Swedes, Swiss or French if UK were banned from competition. Also was not possible to confine sales to White Army only. Thus, in British view, burden is clearly on US, with its Military Training Mission and position of primacy, to dissuade Saudis from purchase unneeded or undesirable items; UK fully expected US to do this.

Concerning British Aircraft Corporation attempts sell Canberras (which BAC proposed to Saudis as part of "package" together with Lightning interceptors and Thunderbird missiles), British said FonOff position against licensing their export would be greatly strengthened if US able state it would refuse export licenses for Douglas A–4E's. Department position was that, while we not able make flat commitment at this time, it probable that USG would refuse license export of A–4E's to Saudis since they do not have characteristics to perform any mission which would be meaningful in terms of Saudi air defense requirement (in contrast to shorter range, supersonic F–5A and F–104H type recommended in Air Defense Survey Report); and since their acquisition, together with other aircraft, would result in further proliferation different types of weapons in Saudi arsenal, additionally complicating the increasingly severe logistics and maintenance problem.

Comment: British, while acknowledging validity of reasons for excluding offensive and overly sophisticated arms, have emphasized that

---

[1] Source: National Archives and Records Administration, RG 59, Central Files 1964–66, DEF 12–5 SAUD. Secret. Drafted by George C. Moore (NEA/NE); cleared by Davies, Bunte, and Deputy Assistant Secretary of Defense for Regional Affairs Frank K. Sloan; and approved by Jernegan. Repeated to London, Dhahran for CHUSMTM, and CINCSTRIKE/CINCMEAFSA.

[2] A memorandum of conversation recording the January 30 U.S.–U.K. talks on arms sales in the Arabian Peninsula is ibid., NEA/ARP Files: Lot 69 D 547, CHRON 1964, Telegrams to Aden.

they see US as having the responsibility for curbing Saudi appetites. Additionally, although Douglas has received license for export technical data on A–4E's, it apparent that SAG decision purchase this aircraft would seriously complicate our arms supply program for Saudi Arabia. Thus Embassy and CHUSMTM should continue efforts wherever possible to dissuade Saudis from endeavoring purchase inappropriate items of whatever national origin. In this context suggest you re-emphasize to Saudis multi-mission capability of F–5A and F–104H as close support aircraft in addition to interceptor role, a fact which would seem to preclude need to purchase other types aircraft such as A–4E or comparable foreign configuration. (In this regard, we pleased to note from USMTM message CH 64[3] that MODA Joint Committee recommends deferring consideration acquisition surface-to-air missiles.)

Rusk

---

[3] Not found.

---

224.   **Telegram From the Department of State to the Embassy in Saudi Arabia**[1]

Washington, April 3, 1964, 6:38 p.m.

641. Joint State/Defense Message. Air Defense Survey. Realize Saudi leaders have had little time available in last two weeks to consider Air Defense Survey package. However, with settlement political crisis, hope Embassy and USMTM will again be able encourage SAG in whatever ways appropriate make early decision accept Air Defense recommendations and request US assistance in their implementation. In view backing initially given last year to F–5 by US authorities (in order assist MAP production program), might now be particularly useful for CHUSMTM to remind Saudis that F–104H as well as F–5 was included in Survey recommendations, that both aircraft meet Air Defense interceptor requirements, and that US would not object to Saudis' purchase

---

[1] Source: National Archives and Records Administration, RG 59, Central Files 1964–66, DEF 1–4 SAUD. Secret. Drafted by Moore; cleared by Quinn (OSD/ISA), Bunte, George L. Warren (G/PM), and Deputy Director of the Office of Munitions Control John W. Sipes; and approved by Davies. Repeated to Paris for DEFREPNAMA, Dhahran for CHUSMTM, and CINCSTRIKE/CINCMEAFSA.

of either. (FYI. Hope that early selection will be made between the two US-produced aircraft rather than continue possible risk that foreign aircraft might be chosen. End FYI.)

With regard selection of aircraft Department has just received formal note from Saudi Embassy[2] indicating that Lockheed has presented proposal to SAG on F–104H; that SAG understands (correctly) F–104H is same as F–104G minus certain electronic packages; that "because F–104G more capable carrying out required mission RSAF", SAG requests approval consider offer F–104G from Lockheed. (Lockheed has submitted application through normal US Government channels for approval export technical data on F–104G.) This request obtain 104G being strongly pushed by SAG Assistant Attaché Washington, but unclear if represents reasoned desire on part MODA or perhaps only request from lower echelon Saudi military. Department strongly doubts advisability selling more advanced model to SAG in view initial price difference (approximately quarter million dollars per plane), heightened maintenance problems and cost (difference between G and H estimated at quarter million dollars per plane per year), and problem for general Middle East arms balance presented by increased limited all-weather attack capability. We are inclined, however, to approve export technical data this model (with caveat that decision reserved on approval export aircraft itself) on basis that this information useful in order dissuade Saudis from increased expenditure for this much more complicated aircraft.

Appreciate Embassy and CHUSMTM comments and, as appropriate, attempts dissuade Saudis from going beyond recommendations Air Defense Survey.

Rusk

---

[2] Not found.

225. Telegram From the Embassy in Saudi Arabia to the Department of State[1]

Jidda, May 11, 1964, 4 p.m.

1050. Saqqaf Visit to US. Deptel 706;[2] Embtel 1030.[3]

One of strongest aspects our position Saudi Arabia has been relationship personal trust and confidence developed between President and Prince Faysal. During Kennedy administration this stemmed from highly satisfactory personal contact of President with Crown Prince in October 1962 which was maintained and strengthened through letters exchanged in ensuing months. Similar Johnson–Faysal relationship commenced by President's cordial letter December 19, though since then we have not had another appropriate occasion for full length exchange views through letter and there has, of course, been no opportunity for face to face meeting.

Saqqaf's visit Washington seems offer chance which should not be missed for further building kind of personal ties and friendship to which Faysal attaches great importance and which could stand us in particularly good stead during weeks ahead. Call on President by Saqqaf, who is probably Faysal's closest and most influential advisor, would provide excellent substitute for President–Crown Prince meeting and would be more effective than Presidential letter for which in fact we see at moment no appropriate peg. Saqqaf would be immensely complimented by being granted brief interview, his confidence and friendship for US would be doubly reinforced, and his influence with Faysal as spokesman for strong ties with US and policy of restraint and cooperation with other Arab countries would be materially strengthened.

Should Department, White House find possible work brief Saqqaf interview into President's schedule suggest President Johnson might wish take opportunity send to Faysal through Saqqaf expression warmest personal regards and admiration for Faysal's leadership and determination carry Saudi Arabia on road social, political, economic progress. Faysal's endeavors adapt hallowed values, traditions and principals of ancient society to evolving needs and challenges modern times attracting increasing public sympathy and interest in US. Presi-

---

[1] Source: National Archives and Records Administration, RG 59, Central Files 1964–66, POL 7 SAUD. Confidential; Priority.

[2] Dated May 7. (Ibid., POL SAUD–UAR)

[3] In telegram 1030 from Jidda, May 6, Ambassador Hart reported that Deputy Foreign Minister Saqqaf would arrive in Washington on May 12 and transmitted his recommendations for the visit. (Ibid., POL 7 SAUD)

dent hopes CP will feel free communicate with him directly on matters mutual interest. In closing President might express to Saqqaf his appreciation Saqqaf's own role in aiding evolution statesmanlike Saudi policy toward Yemen problem. US sincerely believes CP took wisest step in withdrawing from involvement Yemen civil war and in providing active support to UN instrumentalities seeking resolution difficult Yemen problem. We realize from our own experience value of inexhaustible patience and ingenuity in dealing thorny seemingly insoluble situations. We confidently hope Saudi Arabia, which has demonstrated these qualities in such large measure with regard Yemen problem, will not be deflected from present policy of disengagement from Yemen struggle to return to role active support for Royalists. This would distress USG which for its part is loyal to disengagement principle and has recently renewed its representations to UAR on this subject. It is confident that disengagement will eventually be completed.

Hart

226. Memorandum of Conversation[1]

Washington, May 15, 1964, 3:30 p.m.

SUBJECT

Call on Secretary by SAG Deputy Foreign Minister

PARTICIPANTS

The Secretary
NEA—Phillips Talbot
NE—Talcott W. Seelye

His Excellency Omar Saqqaf, Saudi Arabian Deputy Foreign Minister
Mr. Abdullah Hababi, Chargé d'Affaires, Embassy of Saudi Arabia

Mr. Saqqaf mentioned his mission as Arab emissary in connection with the Jordan Waters diversion and stated that he was asking an aide to make a presentation to working officials in the Department. He enumerated three current concerns in the Middle East as Syria, Yemen disengagement and Khrushchev's visit to Cairo. In Syria the conservative wing of the Baath party has taken over and appears to

---

[1] Source: National Archives and Records Administration, RG 59, Central Files 1964–66, POL 7 SAUD. Secret. Drafted by Seelye on May 18 and approved in S on June 2. The time of the meeting is taken from Rusk's Appointment Book. (Johnson Library)

command the support of the majority of Baath party members. In response to the Secretary's question, he said that Iraq, Jordan and the UAR all desire the overthrow of the present Syrian regime. Regarding Yemen disengagement, he expressed an interest in hearing the Department's latest views. He called attention to the danger to our mutual positions of Khrushchev's visit to Cairo.

The Secretary said we are watching Syrian developments closely. He commented that Khrushchev's successful visit to Cairo flows from the Soviet Union's commitment some ten years ago to build the Aswan Dam. We have to admit that the Soviet performance in building the Dam has been good. He saw two reasons behind the Khrushchev visit: (1) an effort to strengthen the Soviet position vis-à-vis the Western world and (2) competition with the ChiComs. He thought it unwise to take too much comfort, however, from the latter. Following Khrushchev's departure we will have a better opportunity to assess accurately the impact of his visit. Mr. Saqqaf expressed the view that Nasser did not fully approve Khrushchev's speeches and noted that Communism is outlawed in the UAR.

The Secretary noted USG interest in maintaining good relations with the Arab world and referred to the strong USG commitment to the independence and territorial integrity of Saudi Arabia. He said that we would disapprove of Arab unity if it comes about as a result of pressures; however, if reached by free choice, we could not disapprove. He asked Mr. Saqqaf for his views as to what posture the USG should take toward those Arab states who wish to remain independent. While the United States would come to Saudi Arabia's assistance if it were attacked, is there not a danger that such Western military moves would be resented in the area? He characterized our objectives in Yemen as (1) to enable the Yemenis to decide their own future and (2) to prevent Yemen from becoming a base for pressures against Saudi Arabia. While our disengagement plan has not produced full disengagement, it has reduced the threat to Saudi Arabia. Mr. Saqqaf agreed. The Secretary noted that Saudi Arabia is stronger than it was two years ago and that Prince Faisal is forging ahead on a constructive program to develop the country.

Mr. Saqqaf commented that every Arab wants Arab unity, but in his own way. He alleged that Nasser could have "had the Arab world" after the Suez crisis of 1956 had he acted in the right manner. He failed because Arabs as a whole, by nature and by religion, are opposed to socialism. While Syria, Iraq and Algeria have socialist tendencies, each system differs from Nasser's. Arab unity requires one belief. Mr. Saqqaf felt that the USG should protect countries who are fighting Communism and backing the West. Saudi Arabia wants "radical progress through evolution". He saw no indications that the UAR would change but, despite the current dangerous situation, he considered the future of Syria as hopeful.

The Secretary inquired after Saudi Arabia's relations with other Arab states. Mr. Saqqaf said that Saudi Arabia enjoys good relations with all Arab states, including the UAR. Saudi Arabia has nothing against the UAR if the latter leaves Yemen and stops attacking Saudi Arabia. In response to the Secretary's query, Mr. Saqqaf said that UAR propaganda attacks against Saudi Arabia had discontinued.

Mr. Saqqaf asserted that Prince Faisal had been too busy to go to Cairo, needing a month or so to clear up internal matters. He noted that President Arif has asked Prince Faisal to be present in Cairo while Arif was there, but that Faisal had declined. He said that the Prince would visit Cairo "if the Egyptians behave".

The Secretary recalled reports received before and during Nasser's recent visit to Yemen indicating that morale among Egyptian troops in Yemen was poor. Did Mr. Saqqaf believe the UAR was determined to stay in Yemen? Mr. Saqqaf said that the UAR wishes to leave but is looking for "a solution". He said that Anwar Sadat and Hakim al-Amer had not hidden from him the fact that the UAR faces a difficult situation in Yemen. When Prince Faisal had asked their views as to a solution, they had turned the question back to the Crown Prince. He said the Egyptian visitors had suggested that an Arab League army be sent to Yemen and that Faisal had countered with the proposal that an Arab "mission" be dispatched to Yemen. Mr. Saqqaf acknowledged that the UAR cannot be expected to withdraw its army from Yemen "at once" because, as admitted by Sadat and Amer, this would "be dangerous for the UAR regime". According to Mr. Saqqaf, Prince Faisal had agreed that it would probably not be in Saudi Arabia's interest for the UAR regime to fall and, therefore, he would not insist on an immediate withdrawal of all UAR forces from Yemen.

The Secretary noted that the USG had worked hard on the UAR to curtail its propaganda attacks and had also helped force the discontinuance of UAR air attacks mounted against Saudi supply depots a year or so ago. He inquired as to the prospect of an agreement between Saudi Arabia and the UAR on modifications to the Yemeni regime. Mr. Saqqaf replied that Saudi Arabia is "ready to help" but cannot do anything which requires "the use of force". He said he had never lost hope concerning reaching a solution with the UAR on the Yemen problem.

The Secretary inquired whether the Western presence in the area—for example, the important USG facility in Libya and the British base in Aden—were helpful to Saudi Arabia or whether this caused Saudi Arabia concern. Mr. Saqqaf replied that while Saudi Arabia "says" it disapproves of the presence of "foreign troops," at the same time it believes that as long as the country in which the bases are located is independent and does not oppose these bases, then the matter is of "no concern" to Saudi Arabia. While Saudi Arabia "says" that the British base in Aden must go, the Government knows that this is impossible. Speaking personally, he felt that the British should remain in Aden unless some alternative stabilizing presence could be arranged. There is the ultimate danger that Communism, which has been effectively prevented from penetrating the Near East from the north, will infiltrate from the south and prosper on the backwardness and weakness of the people of South Arabia. In response to Mr. Rusk's question, Mr. Saqqaf stated that Communism is making headway in Yemen. He said that Communist propaganda is not currently being aimed at Saudi Arabia.

Mr. Saqqaf conveyed to the Secretary Prince Faisal's best regards and said the Prince looked forward to the opportunity of seeing the Secretary some time in the future. The Secretary said that he held Prince Faisal in the highest regard and had long been one of his admirers. He commented that we are strongly encouraged by current developments in Saudi Arabia. Mr. Saqqaf said that the Prince is still not wholly satisfied by the progress that has been achieved so far and hopes to move faster now that the Royal Family problem has been solved.[2]

---

[2] On March 28 Saudi Prime Minister Crown Prince Faisal, with the support of other members of the Royal family and the uluma, assumed the powers of the monarchy and reduced King Saud's role to that of figurehead.

227. **Memorandum From the Assistant Secretary of State for Near Eastern and South Asian Affairs (Talbot) to the Special Group (Counterinsurgency)**[1]

Washington, May 18, 1964.

SUBJECT

    Saudi Arabia Internal Defense Plan

I. General Statement of Threat

The threat to internal stability in Saudi Arabia arises more out of the weakness and exposure of stabilizing forces than out of the presence of easily identified powerful subversive elements. Stability is dependent upon the will and the strength of the Royal Family, or, more precisely, upon Crown Prince Faysal. [*4½ lines of source text not declassified*]

The danger of instability and violent change within Saudi Arabia is heightened by the inherent instability in the region as a whole. The success of any search for internal stability will depend, in unusual degree, upon the achievement of satisfactory external relationships, as well as upon the strengthening of the internal fabric of the country. Hence this paper, while not examining in detail the international situation of Saudi Arabia, does take into account in analyzing the problem and presenting recommendations.

At the height of the Yemen crisis in the months following the revolution of September 1962, there were tensions in Saudi Arabia flowing from Saudi involvement in support of the "Royalists." These tensions placed a strain on the fabric of government [*1 line of source text not declassified*]. There was also much concern that the UAR would capitalize on these weaknesses to unleash its subversive assets. Negotiations of the disengagement agreement removed the immediate UAR threat, alleviated the tensions and strengthened Faysal.

The latter is now in firm control of the governmental machinery in Saudi Arabia, and shows every evidence that he intends to keep this control. The stripping of all effective power from King Saud has eliminated a potential source of conflict, and will enable Faysal to concentrate even more on financial, educational, and social welfare problems. At the same time, Faysal seems to be somewhat more aware of the desirability of developing an esprit de corps in the military.

---

[1] Source: National Archives and Records Administration, RG 59, S/S Files: Lot 68 D 451, Special Group (CI), 5/28/64–7/10/64, May 28, 1964. Secret. Drafted by Edward A. Padelford (NEA/NR). The memorandum was sent through Under Secretary of State for Political Affairs W. Averell Harriman.

Also, particularly since the Arab Chiefs "summit" conference, there has been a lessening of UAR-Saudi tensions. The disruptive Yemen problem remains, but the current focus by the UAR is directed against Great Britain, rather than Saudi Arabia.

Nevertheless, [1 *line of source text not declassified*] the basic UAR threat to Saudi Arabia remains as explained in detail in Section II.

We consider that the removal of Crown Prince Faysal from the scene would probably present the most serious problem for the regime. His driving influence behind present reform and development programs has had a considerable stabilizing influence both on the political situation and on the economy. His successor has not been designated. While there are certain other vigorous and experienced members of the Royal Family who, if selected, could provide needed stability in the country, [4 *lines of source text not declassified*].

[Here follows sections II and III.]

IV. U.S. Policy Objectives and Courses of Action

United States policy aims at strengthening and preserving the Faysal regime. We seek to achieve this objective by urging the regime to proceed in timely fashion on its program of political, social, and economic progress; and by assuring that it eschews involvement in foreign military or semi-military ventures. The United States desires to maintain its present dominant position, particularly in the military sphere (through the United States Military Training Mission) and in the economic sphere (through Aramco). However, we also believe it is desirable for the Saudis to have a good working [relationship] with the United Kingdom Government. The following are some more specific objectives:

A. Minimize UAR Subversive Potential

As much as possible, the United States desires to minimize the subversive potential of the UAR. To achieve this end it is essential to minimize the potential for UAR–Saudi conflict. Disengagement of the Egyptian forces from Yemen, the continuing bar of Saudi support of the Royalists, and the containment of UK–UAR conflict contributes to this objective.

B. Support Saudi Social and Educational Development

The Country Team suggests expanded exchange of persons efforts, including those in law and medicine, to improve Saudi education. The University of Texas English language teachers program is an example of the type project that might be most constructive. Our Country Team also asks that we review thoroughly the possibilities for establishment of an American-sponsored medical or educational institution in Saudi Arabia.

C. Continue to Improve the U.S. Image in Saudi Arabia

Efforts should be made to further contacts with important Saudis, including young people, by all possible means, including the USIS Cultural Center in downtown Jidda. As the Center progresses, plans should be developed for the teaching of English to selected educators and other important individuals. We should increase information among target groups about the U.S., its institutions, and policies through circulation of periodicals and books in both Arabic and English; through lectures and other events; and by placement of selected materials in the Saudi press and on Radio Mecca when possible. The United States should promptly fulfill the commitment made under the recently signed United States-Saudi agreement to supervise installation of two telecasting stations and should provide programming assistance and appropriate television materials to Saudi officials responsible for the stations.

D. Encourage Saudi Efforts to Improve Effectiveness, Morale, Organization, and Equipment of the Armed Forces

With advice from USMTM, the Saudis drafted a plan for the improvement of their defense forces. This plan contains an estimate of the external threat and proposes a five-year program for equipment purchases and training at an estimated cost of two billion riyals (some $450 million). USMTM also prepared a basic document recommending both organizational reforms and changes in basic attitudes in the Saudi Armed Forces. Neither of these documents has yet been adopted. More recently, a special DOD team carried out a detailed survey of the Saudi air defense requirements, which has just been presented to the Saudi Government. The air defense survey recommends improvement in anti-aircraft artillery and purchase of up to 36 United States interceptor aircraft (F–5A or F–104H). Conclusion of a United States-Saudi cooperative logistics supply agreement has also been proposed. The relationship of the Saudi prepared plan and the United States air defense survey remains to be clarified.

With a number of signs of greater Saudi interest in improvement of the military forces, it is particularly important that the U.S. military training and advisory effort in Saudi Arabia be developed to maximum effectiveness. In this connection, it is essential that key USMTM officers serve longer tours. King Saud assured President Kennedy in 1962 that he desired that a U.S. military training mission remain indefinitely in Saudi Arabia. A new mission training agreement is under negotiation.

The Country Team strongly recommends that there be no decrease in the size of the USMTM since a sharp cut would be viewed as an indication of lessening United States interest. It also recommends several other modifications respecting United States officers assigned to the

USMTM, including longer tours for some officers and more advanced Arabic training for United States Air Force officers.

The Country Team recommends additional use of mobile training teams in Saudi Arabia, as well as additional training of Saudis in the United States. The five MTT's which visited Saudi Arabia in 1963 were considered highly successful. A further intensive review is suggested on the possibility of a civic action program for Saudi Arabia. Both MTT's and civic action should be financed by the Saudis.

E. *Support Improvement in Police and Intelligence Field*

The Country Team recommends, if the Saudis request it, United States support aimed at improving the Saudi police, including training in the United States. [11 *lines of source text not declassified*]

F. *Encourage, as Possible, the Pace and Effectiveness of the Saudi Economic Development Effort*

The Country Team recommends that the United States assist the Saudi Government in whatever way we can in improving Saudi Arabia's economic development effort, particularly in meeting requests for technical advisors on a reimbursable basis. If the opportunity is presented, the Country Team believes a follow-up to the 1962 economic development survey conducted by Professor A. J. Meyer of Harvard should be considered.

G. *Have Prepared and Ready for Implementation a U.S. Contingency Plan in Event of Attempts to Overthrow or Actual Overthrow of the Saudi Government*

A U.S. Contingency Plan is now in the final stages of development which sets forth the course of U.S. actions in the event of an attempt to overthrow or actual overthrow of the Saudi Government, either with or without assistance from the United Arab Republic. The plan considers a range of possible U.S. responses to safeguard important western oil and security interests in the Arabian Peninsula. It defines the U.S. intent to prevent military intervention by outside parties either to support any of the conflicting groups in Saudi Arabia or to seize Saudi territory. It also emphasizes the U.S. aim of deterring foreign intervention rather than accepting an open confrontation and foresees no U.S. military force involvement within Saudi Arabia except to prevent the imminent entrance of foreign forces or to safeguard American lives.

V. *Recommendations*

A. The United States should continue to support Prince Faysal, while at the same time encouraging him to promote political and social reforms, as well as economic development. [3 *lines of source text not declassified*]

B. The United States should continue to play a principal military role in Saudi Arabia. Every effort should be made to increase the confidence of the members of the armed forces in the regime, both by utilizing the now planned television network and through other means including civic action. The following specific recommendations in the military sphere are particularly important:

1. Civic Action

The Country Team has suggested that further intensive review be given to the possibility of a civic action program for Saudi Arabia. The Country Team recommends that an expert in civic action programs be sent to Saudi Arabia for temporary assignment to review in detail civic action possibilities. We recommend that this be done.

2. U.S. Military Training Mission (USMTM)

The USMTM, which now numbers 239, should be continued at about the same level. Urgent consideration should be given to extending the tours of selected key officers at the USMTM from one to two years in order to enhance their impact. Also, it is recommended that the Air Force consider providing USAF officers with a level of Arabic training comparable to that of the U.S. Army officers. Consideration should also be given to the movement of USMTM Headquarters from Dhahran to Riyadh.

3. Mobile Training Teams (MTT's)

MTT's have been utilized successfully in Saudi Arabia. The USMTM believes that their use can be expanded. It is recommended that USMTM wishes in this field be implemented to the extent possible.

4. Air Defense Survey

Assuming Saudi acceptance of the Air Defense Survey, the United States should be prepared to expeditiously implement the survey.

5. Credit for Military Sales

The United States should be prepared to provide a limited amount of credit for military sales, both for matériel in the Air Defense Survey, and for other military items. For FY 1965, credit requirements are roughly estimated at $20 million. Such credit should be at a rate of interest competitive with foreign interests.

C. If requested and if a survey reveals a requirement, support should be provided the Saudi police and internal security forces.

D. Various agencies of the United States Government should be prepared to respond promptly to Saudi requests for technical advice and assistance, particularly in the economic, social, labor, and public administration fields. The labor administration field will become increasingly significant, as the organized labor force increases. Periodic visits by our regional Labor Attaché and also U.S. Department of Labor technicians should be considered.

E. Special attention should be directed towards the evolving Saudi youth. USIS activities aimed at influencing youth in Saudi Arabia should be wholeheartedly supported. As feasible, efforts should be made to orient Saudi educational practices towards the United States. The USMTM should within limitations devote special attention towards selecting well-qualified Saudi non-commissioned and junior officers for training in the United States.

F. In so far as possible, any assistance (military, police, technical, labor, etc.) should be on a reimbursable basis in keeping with Saudi Arabia's improving economic status. However, in event of a high priority U.S. objective, the U.S. should be prepared to provide assistance on whatever terms are considered necessary.

G. [7 lines of source text not declassified]

H. The U.S. Contingency Plan should be fully integrated with the Internal Defense Plan and necessary action taken to provide for quick implementation in event of necessity.

VI. *Recommendations for the Special Group (CI)*

A. We recommend that the plan, as submitted and as modified by the recommendations and observations in this memorandum, be approved as a basis for internal defense planning.

B. The Country Team in Saudi Arabia should be commended for the preparation of the plan. The Country Team should be encouraged but not required to submit modifications to the plan, as the Team feels are necessary.

228. Memorandum for the Record[1]

Washington, May 28, 1964, 2:30 p.m.

SUBJECT

> Minutes of the Meeting of the Special Group (CI), 2:30 p.m., Thursday, May 28, 1964

PRESENT

> Governor Harriman, Mr. Bell, Mr. Rowan, Mr. Forrestal, Mr. Solbert vice Mr. Vance, General Anthis vice General Taylor, Mr. Karamessines vice Mr. McCone, Mr. Nolan vice the Attorney General
> Governor Williams was present for Item No. 2
> Mr. Jernegan and Mr. Seelye were present for Item No. 3
> Mr. Adams was present for Item No. 4
> Mr. James was present for Item No. 5
> Mr. Maechling was present for the meeting

[Here follows discussion of other subjects.]

3. Internal Defense Plan for Saudi Arabia

Mr. Jernegan reviewed the salient points of the Internal Defense Plan for Saudi Arabia[2] adding that the US does not consider the situation critical. He said that there is always the danger of the UAR stepping up its activities in Saudi Arabia. He explained that at the beginning of the Yemen crisis, the stability of the present regime had been threatened by the UAR, but that the agreement reached between Saudi Arabia and UAR has eased the situation. He discussed the internal political influences of other Groups noting that there is very little Communist influence, but any internal strife would be an invitation to Nasir to reinstigate his activity. He discussed Faysal's assets and ambitious programs, emphasizing US interest in assisting Faysal in the implementation of these programs. He pointed out that it is in our best interest to maintain the present regime since Faysal is the best leader available.

Mr. Jernegan indicated that it is very important that we continue our military training mission in Saudi Arabia and also our interest in the economic sphere (through Aramco).

He informed the Group that the Country Team will continue to try to find ways to develop youth and labor programs, areas which today are barely existent. He added that USIA recently opened a cultural center and library in Jidda, the first of this kind in Saudi Arabia, which will assist in reaching the youth.

---

[1] Source: National Archives and Records Administration, RG 59, S/S Files: Lot 68 D 451, Special Group (CI) Minutes of Meetings (cont'd), Jan.–June 1964. Secret.

[2] Document 227.

Mr. Bell observed that the US community is split between Jidda and Dhahran, with hardly anyone in the city of Riyadh. Part of the military training mission is being moved to Riyadh, but we are having difficulty in moving part of the mission. He reminded the Group that we have no AID economic program in Saudi Arabia and that in view of the country's sound finances, it would be a departure for us to institute one.

[1 paragraph (3 lines of source text) not declassified]

The Group approved the Plan and suggested that the Country Team be directed to take the required action. The Group also requested that it be kept informed, in the form of a letter from the Ambassador every six months, or earlier, as significant developments arise.

[Here follows discussion of Bolivia and civic action assessment.]

C. G. Moody, Jr.
Executive Secretary
Special Group (CI)

---

229.   Telegram From the Department of State to the Embassy in Saudi Arabia[1]

Washington, June 15, 1964, 2:27 p.m.

759. Embtel 1082[2] and Cirtel 2210.[3] Following is letter from President to Prince Faisal for delivery by Ambassador. Ambassador should draw on appropriate portions of Cirtel 2210 in supplementary oral exposition of USG assessment of Khrushchev's visit to UAR:

"Your Highness:

"Secretary Rusk has spoken to me of his satisfaction at his recent meeting with your Deputy Foreign Minister. He noted that your able emissary expressed your concern over various aspects and implications of Mr. Khrushchev's recent visit to the UAR. We have now had an opportunity to assess the import of this visit, which I wish to share with you in all candor.

"The Soviet Union has achieved a short-run propaganda advantage but I do not for a moment believe that Khrushchev's visit has apprecia-

---

[1] Source: National Archives and Records Administration, RG 59, Central Files 1964–66, POL 7 USSR. Secret. Drafted by Seelye; cleared by Davies, Curtis F. Jones, and Komer; and approved by Jernegan.

[2] Dated May 22. (Ibid.)

[3] Dated May 27. (Ibid.)

bly enhanced—or will enhance—Soviet influence in the area. On the contrary, by his own statements he has spotlighted the fundamental incompatibility between the Communist concept of class unity and the Arab doctrine of national unity. His disparaging remarks on Arab unity have not gone unnoticed by the very Arab nationalists whom he has sought to befriend. He blundered by attacking Kuwait.

"It is true that the UAR has found a temporary coincidence of interest with the Soviet Union. Since the USSR is helping to build the High Dam, the UAR could hardly deny Khrushchev a visit to the celebration. Nevertheless whatever Nasser's own ambitions in the Arab World may be, he hardly desires to share them with Khrushchev. The UAR continues to ban Communism in Egypt and I suspect will continue to recognize the advantages of seeking to maintain good relations with other Arab states. Nasser, still desiring good relations with the United States, has given no indication whatsoever of moving into the Soviet camp. I have asked Ambassador Hart to give you a more detailed account of our assessment of the Soviet threat in the Near East.

"While you and I may not entirely agree on the best way to deal with certain other forces in the area, we stand firmly together in a mutual desire to combat Communism and Soviet penetration, and to live in freedom. As you know, we are dealing with the Soviet problem constantly, intimately and on a worldwide basis; it is currently our primary concern.

"We are resolved as ever to stand solidly and steadfastly beside our valued friends in the area, including Saudi Arabia. I have the highest regard for Your Highness' firm and enlightened leadership and have been impressed by the course of reform you are charting for Saudi Arabia. This is the true road to national unity and strength. As you proceed on this course, you may be assured of full United States support. Progress for the benefit of all the people is the best insurance against the spread of extremist doctrines in Saudi Arabia or elsewhere in the Arab world.

"With regard to events occurring in South Arabia, I am both disturbed and encouraged. I am disturbed at the pressures being placed on the British position in Aden to which we attach considerable importance. Yet I cannot refrain from pointing out that you and we, by a policy rather different from the British, greatly reduced the immediate threat to Saudi Arabia from the same source. I am encouraged at signs that the Yemeni republican leaders are now seeking actively to widen their popular support and are continuing to express a desire for peaceful relations with Saudi Arabia and the United Kingdom. I would urge your Government to take special note of these developments.

"We stand by our commitment to obtain the disengagement of foreign forces from Yemen. We shall continue our efforts. The process has been slow but I remain confident of ultimate success. Meanwhile,

I know I can count on your characteristic patience, forbearance and magnanimity.

"I wish you success and send you my warm personal regards. May God keep you and the Saudi people and grant you peace."

FYI: Re possible discussion of USG confrontation with SovBloc in key world trouble spots (suggested reftel), you might wish draw Faisal's attention to fact that Dept gave Saqqaf two-hour briefing this subject and latter may wish give Faisal report. If you wish have further material, Department happy to provide. End FYI.

Rusk

230.   **Telegram From the Embassy in Saudi Arabia to the Department of State[1]**

Jidda, June 23, 1964, 8 a.m.

1164. Deptel 759;[2] DepCirctel 2210;[3] CA–12519.[4] Presentation President Johnson's letter to Crown Prince Faysal; discussion of Dhahran Airfield, General Adams participating.

Details extensive conversation with Faysal June 17 based on President Johnson's letter are being covered by airgram. Highlights of this and accompanying discussions attendant on General Adam's visit follow:

1. President Johnson's letter was appreciated and I believe served very useful purpose of (a) re-establishing personal contact between President and Faysal; (b) reassuring Faysal of President's continued interest in welfare and advancement Kingdom; and (c) giving strong support to continuance disengagement.

2. At same time Faysal did not agree with all points made in President's letter. In particular he took exception to implication at end paragraph six that he should be responsive to desire YAR leaders to make contact with SAG. Remarking that while Khrushchev did not gain 100 percent success from visit to UAR, impact on Middle East

---

[1] Source: National Archives and Records Administration, RG 59, Central Files 1964–66, POL 15–1 US–Johnson. Secret. Repeated to Lagos for General Adams, Dhahran and CINCSTRIKE/CINCMEAFSA.

[2] Document 229.

[3] Dated May 27. (National Archives and Records Administration, RG 59, Central Files 1964–66, POL 7 USSR)

[4] Dated June 2. (Ibid., DEF 19–4 US–SAUD)

should by no means be discounted, Faysal again insisted at length that source of infection and instability throughout Middle East was Nasir, and again urged us to recognize this fact and at very least stop supporting a malignant influence.

3. General Adams expressed to Faysal appreciation for current US military use (landing and take-offs) of Dhahran International Airfield. He hoped this use would continue. Faysal queried Prince Sultan, who had entered meeting late, and confirmed that US use was permitted and asked if there were any problems. General Adams indicated that perhaps there some facilities and working arrangements could be devised whereby if US had to come to Saudi Arabia's aid at some future date, all would go smoothly. Faysal apparently took this as referring to secret understanding of 1963 constituting US–SAG advance ground-rules for Hard Surface (which at Faysal's request were not to [be] disseminated in either government). He replied that US military should not misunderstand precautions taken by SAG to avert possible criticism; it implied no absence of trust. This particular probe of Faysal's reactions was not pursued further.

4. However, during lengthy discussion which followed my presentation re Soviet threats in Near East, Faysal expressed alarm over Soviet-directed fishing fleet which will operate out of Egyptian base Ra's Banas. He expressed such concern over Saudi exposure to this first Soviet presence in Red Sea that with CA–12519 in mind I used opportunity to make strictly personal observation: In retrospect I entertained divided feelings over American exit from Dhahran Airbase 1962. On one hand base had become irritant between US and embarrassment to SAG; on other hand it had afforded American military presence. Faysal nodded his agreement and made reference to his late 1960 talk with my predecessor, Ambassador Heath. He commented that during conversation he had suggested to Heath that USG take initiative to reduce embarrassing and overt aspects of its position at Dhahran Airfield so as to abate criticism which SAG was incurring from other Arabs.

Since I remembered record this conversation quite differently, i.e. that Faysal had urged that USG take initiative to withdraw completely from Dhahran Airbase before SAG forced into embarrassing position of requesting withdrawal,[5] I felt that Faysal intentionally or unintentionally was changing the record. Again in strictly personal vein I asked Faysal whether he felt in retrospect that it might have been good idea if SAG and USG had agreed that instead of completely withdrawing US forces from Dhahran we had reduced our presence and after handing over DAF to SAG had retained under umbrella of USMTM some

---

[5] For Ambassador Heath's November 28, 1960, conversation with Faisal regarding the Dhahran airbase, see *Foreign Relations, 1958–1960*, vol. XII, pp. 768–769.

arrangement which would have kept a US military cadre on hand. Faysal backwatered gently, saying Nasir could always make mountain out of molehill. I responded Nasir did not need the molehill and he agreed. I was left with feeling that door not entirely shut to CINCSTRIKE needs, although chances not good.

During subsequent session with General Adams I asked latter to outline to me his desiderata which are as follows:

Category 1. Preposition at Dhahran International Airfield under US control:

Starting machines (to be tested periodically and routinely by starting USMTM aircraft).

Tools and equipment.

Repair equipment.

Few vehicles, including perhaps two tank trucks.

Extra wing tanks.

Volume this category: 2 or 3 boxcar loads.

Category 2. Preposition at DIA under US control:

Conventional aircraft ammunition including: 750 and 500 lb. bombs (500 iron bombs) 2000 rockets; 50 caliber ammo. ("For training purposes"; to be expended and replaced in training of RSAF.)

Volume this category: around 10,000 cu. ft.

(Bunkers available at DIA)

Category 3. One USAF fighter-bomber squadron to periodically visit Saudi Arabia from Turkey for training and familiarization. Three or four days each visit.

Cover for operation: "Training of RSAF." Would involve around 70 men in each squadron. This would be a work force.

Category 4. Annual joint Saudi-US air-ground combined exercise, a smaller "exercise Delawar." Combined HQ. Would serve as instrument for training Saudi forces and require full year's preparation. Political timing to be determined by USG and SAG. This would be open demonstration and could be used to make US intentions clear.

While I am by no means sanguine that all or any these items are obtainable from Faysal it is conceivable that in his present mood he might agree to Categories 1, 3 and 4 without as much trouble as to Category 2. If State and DOD wish me to make further sounding I suggest following tactic: I would request private interview and pick up this portion our June 17 conversation on very informal basis. I would say General Adams had expressed to me privately his interest in Categories 1 through 4 but had as yet no instructions; and that if Faysal saw merit in some such arrangement well camouflaged by USMTM I was prepared ask Washington whether highest level US Govt might be interested.

Hart

231.   **Telegram From the Department of State to the Embassy in the United Kingdom**[1]

Washington, September 21, 1964, 5:49 p.m.

2027. Joint State/Defense Message. Embtels 1130,[2] 1208;[3] UK Offer of Thunderbirds to SAG.

At appropriate level you should voice our strong concern at reported renewed offer HMG sell Thunderbird surface-to-air missiles to SAG. As described in Deptel 3760, December 18, 1963 (480 to Jidda)[4] and detailed to Harrison and Brenchley in Washington in January, our view continues to be that Saudis have a low priority requirement for SAMs, that their purchase of such overly-sophisticated weapons would represent foolhardy drain on their financial resources and useless diversion of their scarce personnel and skills from badly needed development program. Both US and UK have basic interest in Saudi stability and orderly development which far exceeds any concern either of us has for selling weapons in that region. Encouraging SAG to put resources into extremely technical and expensive hardware of relatively marginal military value for them, particularly in face of latent internal nationalist discontent, is not the role of a friend nor is it in our mutual enlightened self-interest. As the British know, we removed the recommendation for SAMs from our technicians Air Defense Survey Report for these reasons. We believe they are valid independent of any concern that the SAG should look to us for its equipment desires in view of our training commitment.

FYI. In face FonOff demurral that HMG position different from that stated in January, we see nothing to be gained by pressing for clarification of Harrison statement to Talbot in March (London tel 4270).[5]

We continue deeply concerned over prospects introduction SAMs to Saudi Arabia from any source. Nonetheless, if Saudis become more responsive to British persistence in pressing Thunderbirds it would face us with necessity, albeit reluctantly, of reviewing possible US offer

---

[1] Source: National Archives and Records Administration, RG 59, Central Files 1964–66, DEF 12–5 SAUD–UK. Secret. Drafted by Moore; cleared by Bunte, Colonel Evans (G/PM), Quinn, and Officer in Charge of United Kingdom Affairs Thomas M. Judd; and approved by Davies. Repeated to Jidda, Dhahran, CHUSMTM Dhahran, and CINCSTRIKE/CINCMEAFSA for Ramsey.

[2] Dated September 7. (Ibid.)

[3] In telegram 1208 from London, September 15, Bruce reported his discussion of possibility of a U.K. sale of Thunderbird missiles to Saudi Arabia with Assistant Under Secretary Crawford. (Ibid.)

[4] Dated December 18, 1963. (Ibid., DEF 1–4 SAUD)

[5] Dated March 3. (Ibid., DEF 12–5 SAUD)

of Hawk to Saudis. However, pending further developments, do not wish to suggest to British at this time that we could be forced to make Hawk competitive with Thunderbird. End FYI.[6]

Will forward separate cable re Iranian Hawk question.

For Jidda: On target of opportunity basis, you and CHUSMTM should continue dissuade Saudis from acquisition SAMs, drawing on numbered points Deptel 480.

Ball

---

[6] In telegram 1558 from London, October 2, Bruce reported that he had made the démarche to Crawford as instructed. Crawford responded that the U.K. Government had not offered to sell Thunderbird missiles to the Saudi Arabian Government, but told British manufacturers it had no objections to such a sale, which it was prepared to license. (Ibid., DEF 12–5 SAUD–UK)

---

232.   Telegram From the Department of State to the Embassy in Saudi Arabia[1]

Washington, October 7, 1964, 7:18 p.m.

188. Joint State/Defense Message. Should Saudi arms evaluation team, currently in US, raise question of surface-to-air missiles, DOD and State plan reply as follows. (Similar statement contained Deptel 516 to Jidda of December 31.)[2] If SAG officials broach subject, you should use same approach.

"Surface-to-air (SAM) missiles were seriously considered by Air Defense Survey Team for inclusion in report. Although they have not been recommended for initial stages of development of an air defense capability in Saudi Arabia, SAM's are logical future addition which might be added after the proposed defense system is operational. Complexity and sophistication of SAM acquisition and control systems, dearth of sufficient trainable personnel even for operation of system presently proposed, adverse impact on development program of absorption large number skilled men into static defense set-up, and the

---

[1] Source: National Archives and Records Administration, RG 59, Central Files 1964–66, DEF 1–4 SAUD. Secret. Drafted by Moore; cleared by Stoddart, Padelford, and Warren; and approved by Davies. Also sent to Dhahran and CHUSMTM Dhahran and repeated to London and CINCSTRIKE/CINCMEAFSA for Ramsey.

[2] Not found.

considerable expense of a SAM system are main barriers to recommending such a system for Saudi Arabia. The air defense program presently proposed consists of the basic steps which must be taken towards establishing an adequate air defense. These are the communications nets, the early warning and control radar nets, and the fighter-interceptors required for identification, interception, and destruction, if required.

"In view our continued interest in assisting in developing a viable air defense for SAG, US will of course be willing consider Saudi request for purchase SAM's at appropriate future time."

Rusk

---

233. Memorandum From the Joint Chiefs of Staff to Secretary of Defense McNamara[1]

JCSM–904–64   Washington, October 28, 1964.

SUBJECT

Dhahran Airfield and Broadened Saudi-US Military Cooperation (C)

1. Reference is made to:[2]

a. American Embassy, Jidda, message 133, Control 15663, dated 19 August 1964.
b. American Embassy, Jidda, message 134. Control 15633, DTG 181429Z August 1964.
c. CINCSTRIKE/USCINCMEAFSA message, STRJ–5–E 7717, DTG 251938Z July 1964.
d. CINCSTRIKE/USCINCMEAFSA message, STRJ–5–E 7387, DTG 160040Z July 1964.

2. At a meeting on 17 June 1964, CINCSTRIKE/USCINCMEAFSA and the American Ambassador to Saudi Arabia discussed utilization of Dhahran Airfield with Crown Prince Faysal. The references contain details of that meeting, the political background, and a request that the Joint Chiefs of Staff:

a. Obtain DOD approval in principle for installation of an Instrument Landing System (ILS) and for repair/replacement of the Tactical

---

[1] Source: Washington National Records Center, RG 330, OSD Files: FRC 69 A 7425, Saudi Arabia 686, 28 Oct. 64. Secret.
[2] The references are attached but not printed.

Air Navigation (TACAN) facility at Dhahran Airfield, conditional on substantial Saudi agreement to US approaches for increased military co-operation.

b. Forward such conditional approval, via Department of State channels, to the Ambassador for possible use in his forthcoming approaches to the Saudis toward obtaining increased Saudi-US military cooperation encompassing prestockage of ground handling equipment at Dhahran Airfield, periodic visits by a US fighter squadron, and an annual Saudi-US joint exercise.

c. Furnish preliminary views concerning the appropriate program approval authority and source of funds for purchase, installation, and support costs.

3. The TACAN and ILS are of concern only as bargaining instruments. The basic question is whether or not there is a sufficient need for the increased use of Dhahran Airfield, as expressed by CINCSTRIKE/USCINCMEAFSA, to warrant US provision of an ILS and TACAN.

4. Should the United States be denied Wheelus, the requirement for Dhahran Airfield as a substitute staging base to the East Africa area would be most urgent. There is a current requirement for staging rights into Dhahran Airfield for improved access into Iran and Pakistan. An alternate route into the East Africa area is also required should Wheelus be temporarily denied because of weather or other factors. The possible loss of Wheelus and the peacetime training that would be obtained under this proposal by both the US and Saudi military are factors which make Dhahran Airfield base rights a highly desirable commodity.

5. Current US military operations into Dhahran Airfield consist principally of three scheduled MATS flights a week. Although existing navigational aids are considered adequate to support these flights (weather conditions permit visual flight rules/instrument flight rules approach and landing operations 96.8% of the time), the availability of an ILS and TACAN would contribute to increased operational capability and safety aspects of both MATS and commercial carriers transiting Dhahran Airfield. Additionally, the existence of such fixed aids would reduce planned US Air Force mobile support requirements for this base.

6. From the Saudi Arabian point of view, the modernization of Dhahran Airfield resulting from these two navigational aids would undoubtedly contribute to Saudi prestige by providing an all-weather capability comparable to that of other international airports. Furthermore, the TACAN would be a primary instrument approach aid for any Saudi military aircraft of US origin. Thus, it is hoped that the Saudi Arabian Government will be favorably disposed to the acceptance of improved navigational aids at Dhahran Airfield as at least a partial quid pro quo for expanded Saudi-US military cooperation.

7. The US military services have both ILS and TACAN equipment which could be diverted to Dhahran Airfield. Neither the equipment nor the required installation and maintenance funds for Dhahran Airfield is included in current military programs. All items in current military programs are considered to be of equal or greater military priority than those in the CINCSTRIKE/USCINCMEAFSA proposal; therefore, funds are not available from the military services for this purpose.

8. Nevertheless, it is the opinion of the Joint Chiefs of Staff that the United States should agree, in principle, to the rehabilitation/ replacement of the TACAN and installation of an ILS at Dhahran Airfield and to recurring maintenance of both facilities, subject to Saudi agreement as outlined above. Since funds are not available from the Services and since the political benefits to be gained by increased US presence in Saudi Arabia could equal or exceed the military benefits, consideration should be given to the possibility of accomplishment of this program by the Department of State. Informal working level coordination with the Federal Aviation Agency Office of International Aviation Affairs indicates the possibility that, upon request by the Department of State, the Federal Aviation Agency may provide the required equipment, installation, and maintenance. This approach would have the added benefit of reducing the military connotation which might otherwise be apparent should the ILS and TACAN be installed and maintained by military personnel.

9. Accordingly, it should be determined if the Saudi Arabian Government is favorably disposed toward the acceptance of improved navigational aide at Dhahran Airfield in exchange for expanded Saudi–US military cooperation, generally as outlined in reference 1 d, above.

10. The Joint Chiefs of Staff recommend that:

a. The United States agree, in principle, to the rehabilitation/replacement of the TACAN and installation of an ILS at Dhahran Airfield, subject to Saudi agreement on substantial Saudi–US military cooperation.

b. The Department of State be requested to consider funding arrangements.

c. The Department of State convey the US position to the Saudi Arabian Government.

For the Joint Chiefs of Staff:

J. W. Davis[3]
Rear Admiral, USN
Deputy Director, Joint Staff

---

[3] Printed from a copy that indicates Davis signed the original.

234.   Memorandum for the Record[1]

Washington, December 3, 1964, 2 p.m.

SUBJECT

   Minutes of the Meeting of the Special Group (CI); 2 p.m., Thursday, December 3, 1964

PRESENT

   Governor Harriman, General Wheeler, Mr. McCone, Mr. Rowan, Mr. Solbert vice Mr. Vance, Mr. Gaud vice Mr. Bell, Mr. Brubeck
   Mr. McElhiney was present for Item 1.b
   Ambassador Hart and Mr. Davies were present for Item 2
   Mr. Maechling was present for the meeting

[Here follows discussion of the counterinsurgence intelligence summary.]

2. Saudi Arabia

Ambassador Hart informed the Group that Saudi Arabia/United States relations are good and that the present government is attempting to build for the future from a good base rather than pointing its program towards an immediate threat. He said that the danger comes more from forces within Saudi Arabia, rather than externally. He pointed out that the present plan of the Government of Saudi Arabia is "for the people," and there is no evidence that the people oppose the plan at this time. He said that for all practical purposes Saudi Arabia runs a welfare state, though the government is anti-Socialist, anti-Ba'athist, and certainly anti-Communist; they do not maintain relations with any Communist nation. He reminded the group that Nasser's failure to achieve upheaval in Saudi Arabia in '62 and '63 has given the government renewed confidence in its own ability.

Ambassador Hart continued by saying that Faisal's image abroad has suffered because of his recent deposed brother's reputation, but that his image at home is definitely improving.[2] He suggested that correspondents visiting the country can assist in improving his image by observing and reporting progress and giving credit where it is due. He commented also on the sensitivity of the Saudis to absence of public support by the United States and requested that any visiting US dignitaries to the Near East who go to Cairo not by-pass Saudi Arabia.

---

[1] Source: National Archives and Records Administration, RG 59, S/S Files: Lot 68 D 451, Special Group (CI) Minutes of Meetings, July–Dec. 1964. Secret. Drafted on December 4.

[2] On November 2 King Saud was deposed and Crown Prince Faisal proclaimed King.

Ambassador Hart strongly recommended that a high-ranking labor advisor be assigned to assist in the organization of emerging labor forces. He suggested that we look favorably on such requests for technical assistance as managerial, administrative, and technical advisors. He informed the Group that we have been asked to assist in the English language training program and to provide advisors for the new University of Jidda, which they will finance. He pointed out that the Country Team wishes to expand its cultural center in Jidda in order to provide our own English language training facilities and hoped that the necessary $5,000 can be found for this purpose. He recommended continued US military assistance for the regular armed forces and that the British continue to advise the National Guard (White Army) and provide police training. He suggested that we consider assistance for some proposed engineering projects, which in the long run might stimulate US-Saudi trade.

General Wheeler observed that Saudi Arabia could prove to be the key to the entire peninsula, that this new Arab approach in developing free enterprise will be a good example to the others if it succeeds.

Mr. McCone pointed out that we should consider Saudi Arabia in its true perspective, recognizing that enormous progress has been accomplished in the last 25 years both physically and culturally. Ambassador Hart agreed, but emphasized that progress must proceed slowly because the elder generation is very conservative; the young people are coming along fine and being trained for the future.

The Chairman thanked Ambassador Hart for appearing before the Group, requesting that he leave a list of his requests and stating that they would receive sympathetic consideration.

C. G. Moody, Jr.
Executive Secretary
Special Group (CI)

235.   Telegram From the Embassy in Saudi Arabia to the Department of State[1]

Jidda, December 18, 1964.

458. King's Interest in Visit to US:

In interview with Kermit Roosevelt December 16, King Faysal talked of his interest in visiting US. King said he had thought of possibility of going in spring of 1965 but now felt there were so many pressing matters which would over next few months require him remain Saudi Arabia that he would not be able to go until later. Faysal mentioned also that he had already received several invitations travel to other friendly states and that he had to take into consideration in order in which he made official visits abroad.

It apparent to Roosevelt, however, from King's remarks that he deeply interested in early trip to US and that he desires very much develop warm personal understanding and sense reassurance from contact with President Johnson of kind to which Faysal attached so much importance result his meeting with President Kennedy in Oct. 1962.

In talk later with Faysal's son, Prince Mohamed, and Mohamed's brother-in-law, Omar Azam (who is very much member of family's inner circle), Roosevelt found both affirming Faysal's desire to visit US, although neither seemed to have any idea as how King hoped visit could be arranged (informal, official, or state).

Embassy officer who good friend of Abdulla Thanayyan, young sportsman and pilot who is close to Mohamed Faysal and other members of Royal family, has received broad hints of Faysal's interest in travel to US. Few days ago Thanayyan said he understood Faysal believes he could not, in view his elevation to kingship appropriately travel US again unless officially invited. Apparently topic has been considerably discussed in Royal family recently. Dhahran's 156[2] is evidence of this also.

Faysal's dwelling on possibility of visit to US indicates his continued preoccupation with US-Saudi relations, his sense of dependence on US and his desire strengthen ties on which he places great reliance. Official or state visit would seem logical and mutually beneficial endeavor from several viewpoints:

---

[1] Source: National Archives and Records Administration, RG 59, Central Files 1964–66, POL 15–1 SAUD. Secret; Limdis. Repeated to Dhahran. No time of transmission appears on the telegram.

[2] Not found.

1. Faysal as monarch will be undertaking state visits to various countries using this traditional means reinforce relationships important to success his policies. Appropriate that strength of US-Saudi link should be particularly emphasized by early visit to US.

2. Visit would seem fit well into pattern our present policies toward Near East as whole. Faysal seems uncontroversial figure among US public and has received generally favorable US press. While regarded by radical Arab elements as symbol of "outworn" regimes, yet Faysal presents in reality image of modern Saudi desire for progress and reform as new leader sharply contrasting in outlook and reputation to King Saud. His presence in US would reflect our clear intention encourage sincere endeavors of a tradition-rooted regime meet in orderly, evolutionary fashion inevitable challenges of modern Western civilization.

3. As continuing demonstration US interest and friendship for Arab world, Dept may be considering invitations to one or two Arab leaders for visits in 1965. Since Faysal has never before been official US guest, he would seem highly eligible candidate.

4. Lastly and most fundamentally, USG invitation to Faysal would be worth more than almost any other gesture we could make in terms strengthening US-Saudi relations, establishing favorable atmosphere in which we could move ahead with variety of measures we would like see implemented strengthen prospects of secure and stable future for Faysal regime.

In suggesting Faysal visit to US we are, of course, fully aware many complex policy and programming problems which must be resolved permit it to take place. With, no doubt, many other official visits by heads state and government under consideration question timing may be specially difficult one. Barring any sharp deterioration situation here or in Near East generally, believe Faysal would be inclined go at almost any time convenient for President despite his remarks to Roosevelt. However Faysal would find it difficult be away for period of annual Muslim Haj (pilgrimage) extending this year from about six weeks before to one month after April 12 when Saudi monarch traditionally receives visitors coming for pilgrimage and performs key role in holy rites. Hopefully by end of Haj, Yemen situation, for whose resolution his presence here indispensable, would be nearer solution.

Hope foregoing can be reviewed with Ambassador Hart before his return Jidda.

Thacher

236.   Telegram From the Department of State to the Embassy in Saudi Arabia[1]

Washington, December 23, 1964, 6:52 p.m.

304. Following is oral message from President to be delivered to Faisal by Ambassador Hart following his return to Saudi Arabia December 28.

"Your Majesty:

"Ambassador Hart's return to Saudi Arabia after a series of fruitful discussions here in Washington concerning your country gives me the opportunity again to express, through him, my personal good wishes and respect. Since assuming office over one year ago, it has been my constant aim to further the harmonious relations that continue to exist between our two countries and to strengthen our personal understanding. I consider the historical and current friendship between our countries and ourselves to be a basic foundation on which our policies in the Near East rest. The frank and friendly messages we have exchanged in the past year have amply sustained our relationship. It has thus been with particular pleasure that I learned of the orderly processes by which you ascended to the throne, with the promise that this brings of a continuation of your wise leadership. The many signs of devotion and loyalty that this move elicited amply attest to the high respect accorded you by your people—a respect which I also share.

"Your reaffirmation of policy at the time of assuming the kingship showed that we both feel a strong concern for preserving a peaceful world in which free peoples may follow their own national destinies. It is clear that we share the objective of halting the spread of Communism by providing individuals throughout the world with clearly superior and freely chosen alternatives. This calls for a continued vigilance in the face of threats to our interests and a measured and responsible use of the powerful implements placed in our hands to meet such threats. With the spread of weapons of mass destruction, I shall need your help and that of all the leaders of the Free World to prevent the outbreak of nuclear war while defending our freedom.

"It is of great importance for the whole world that we also strive to halt strife and bloodshed in specific countries so as to preclude dislocation in these areas from becoming the means by which world Communism extends its area of influence. It was thus with great gratifi-

---

[1] Source: National Archives and Records Administration, RG 59, Central Files 1964–66, POL 15–1 SAUD. Secret. Drafted by Moore; cleared by Davies, Komer, Hart, and Harriman; and approved by Jernegan.

cation that I heard of your agreement with President Nasser to mediate between the conflicting groups in Yemen to put an end to the struggle there. I realize, as you do, that a final solution to the Yemen problem must depend on the Yemenis themselves and that with such conflicting interests among them there may arise a series of problems before the end is reached. The great advance in the situation, however, in which your statesmanship has played so great a part, is that a solution now is to be sought by the road of peace, internationally as well as nationally.

"Of equal importance are our efforts to bring the tangible benefits of our national well-being to our individual peoples. Thus it is with great interest that we in this country have been following the progress in your program of economic development and social reform for Saudi Arabia. The efforts to broaden educational opportunities for your people and better enable women to contribute to the general productiveness of the country are ones of which I am especially aware. These problems also occupy much of my time in America. Your success in preserving the fundamental guiding religious principles, while at the same time modernizing social relationships, draws our respect and admiration.

"I have welcomed, Your Majesty, this opportunity again to exchange views with you. I hope you agree that these exchanges are valuable.

"May God keep you and your people and grant you prosperity and peace,

Lyndon B. Johnson"

Rusk

237. Telegram From the Department of State to the Embassy in Saudi Arabia[1]

Washington, January 4, 1965, 6:17 p.m.

319. British Arms Sales Saudi Arabia.

Acting on instructions, British Embassy officer Jan. 4 stated Foreign Office wishes keep us informed its action with respect arms sales policy to Saudi Arabia. HMG continues recognize and support US position of primacy with respect training and maintenance facilities in Saudi Arabia. At same time UK balance of payments problem has become particularly acute, especially with respect to aircraft industry, and HMG is under great pressure assist actively in foreign sales. HMG thus required give British Aircraft Corporation full support throughout world. Acting under this pressure, HMG has recently again reassured Saudis that, if requested by SAG, it would be willing issue licenses for sale Thunderbird missiles, Lightning aircraft and radar facilities. In last few days, Labor Member Parliament Cronin (who formerly in Aviation Ministry but does not now have official position in Government) has gone to Saudi Arabia under BAC auspices in attempt to sell equipment.

Responding informally Department officer noted inherent conflict between British assurances for support U.S. primacy in training and maintenance of Saudis and attempts sell British equipment on which U.S. markedly less able provide such training and maintenance.

Would appreciate reports any indication from Saudi Arabia of renewed British arms sale activities.

Rusk

---

[1] Source: National Archives and Records Administration, RG 59, Central Files 1964–66, DEF 12–5 SAUD–UK. Secret. Drafted by Moore, cleared by Judd and Quinn, and approved by Deputy Director of the Office of Near Eastern Affairs Harrison M. Symmes. Repeated to Dhahran, London, CINCSTRIKE for POLAND, and CHUSMTM Dhahran.

238.   Telegram From the Embassy in Saudi Arabia to the
        Department of State[1]

Jidda, March 2, 1965, 6 p.m.

643. Saudi Air Defense Survey. Deptel 400 to Jidda.[2]

On 28 Feb, I met with Prince Sultan to introduce DEFREPNAMA Hooper. We were accompanied by Adm Sweeney and CHUSMTM Gen. Leahy. Among other subjects we discussed air defense for Saudi Arabia at length.

Our opening remarks were based on Deptel 400 and covered certain desirable features in an aircraft such as twin-engine reliability, maintenance characteristics, accident rate comparison, degree of difficulty in pilot training and performance characteristics. These remarks included advantages of F–5. It was stated USG desired to help Prince Sultan solve his air defense problem.

Sultan indicated information received from various aircraft manufacturers contained proposals beyond recommendations in Air Defense Survey. He stated his air defense evaluation teams report compared Lockheed, Northrop, British Aircraft Corporation (BAC) and French Government proposals and had rated aircraft in the following priority to satisfy Saudi air defense requirement:

1. Lockheed F–104G
2. Lightning Mark II and III
3. Mirage III
4. Northrop 5–A
5. Lockheed F–104H.

Discussion then centered around comparisons of F–104 with Sidewinder and Sparrow weapons, Lightning with Fire Streak and Red Top weapons, Mirage III with Metra IR and radar missiles. Prince Sultan indicated Egyptians had MIG–21 equipped with a weapon equivalent to Sparrow. He asserted Saudi military air needs were purely defensive

---

[1] Source: National Archives and Records Administration, RG 59, Central Files 1964–66, DEF 12–5 SAUD–US. Secret; Priority. Sent also to CINCSTRIKE/CINCMEAFSA and repeated to Dhahran, London, Paris, CHUSMTM Dhahran, DEFREPNAMA Paris, DIA, DOD, and 1127th USAF FAG Fort Belvoir, Virginia

[2] Telegram 400 to Jidda, February 17, instructed the Ambassador to approach Saqqaf and Prince Sultan to discuss Saudi air defense needs, noting that the U.S. Government had attempted to maintain neutrality between the F–5 and the F–104 and was reluctant to favor one U.S. manufacturer over another. Since both aircraft were capable of providing an adequate air defense for Saudi Arabia, it seemed advisable for the Saudis to choose the one with the greatest ease of maintenance and the lowest accident rate. With this approach, it should be possible to make the U.S. position clear without specifically recommending the F–5, but rather by recommending its virtues as those that should be most important to the Saudis. (Ibid.)

in character and noted that threat from neighboring countries consisted of MIG–21 and Mirage III. Therefore he concluded, Saudi Arabia must have the F–104G, preferably with Sparrow. He emphasized Saudi Arabia requests a US weapons system to counter threat of its neighbors and pointed out cost differential not important where safety of country at stake.

In reply Hooper pointed out to Sultan that this was first time USG representatives had received official Saudi request for F–104G model and that this request was beyond aircraft recommended by Air Defense Survey and that request would be passed to Washington immediately for study. (Officers attending meeting however took immediate occasion to indicate F–104G with Sparrow should not be considered further since combination not developed. Radar development could change aircraft characteristics. Sultan was told that several NATO countries found F–104G equipped with Sparrow to be too expensive a weapons system.)

Sultan revealed that complete Lockheed package proposal with ground environmental (GE) radar and communications including 36 F–104G with Sidewinders would cost 180 million dollars. At this point in meeting we were joined by additional US representatives from Embassy, ISA (Feigl), DEFREPNAMA's party and USMTM.

Sultan was then asked if he would be interested in F–104H with latter conversion to G model, after training completed. He made no direct response but stated he wanted to buy one package, under USG supervision or under BAC or French Government. He did not want a mixture of aircraft and GE equipment from differing national design. He then requested that, through USMTM, a reassessment of original SAG Air Defense Survey and of Saudi evaluation team report be arranged. He will provide USMTM with first review these packages to ascertain what qualified personnel would be necessary to conduct assessment.

Subject to STRICOM approval, USMTM will review material made available to it and subsequently request:

1. Qualified personnel beyond its resources to establish necessary review board.
2. Necessary policy guidance to assist review board in drawing up its recommendations.
3. Final approval by DOD and State of Review Board's recommendations prior to submission to SAG.
4. Intercession with US manufacturers by DOD to suspend sales promotion contact with SAG or USMTM during period this review.

Comment: Additional comments by DEFREPNAMA will follow from Paris. Embassy also preparing comments. Meanwhile, Embassy sees no objection to STRICOM authorizing USMTM to review materials which Sultan is going to make available.

Hart

239. Telegram From the Department of State to the Embassy in Saudi Arabia[1]

Washington, March 16, 1965, 7:32 p.m.

458. Embtel 654.[2] We do not think there is any significant lack knowledge on part American petroleum industry concerning fact Saudis in market for offers in available oil concession areas.[3] We believe initiative re bidding for concessions best left to companies. Any indication USG interest likely be misunderstood and taken as official encouragement that they enter the competition.

FYI. Occurs to us relative lack interest by American firms derives from some or all following factors: (1) generally poor results oil exploration efforts Red Sea area to date; (2) focus of interest on proven Persian Gulf area; (3) rumors that Robert Ray geophysical work for Saudis either improperly done or has produced unpromising results, or both; (4) unwillingness attempt match French (RAP) offers at time when French known be seeking new production sources assiduously and therefore probably willing offer extremely generous terms. Informal discussion with Aramco officials here has established their agreement this analysis. End FYI.

Rusk

---

[1] Source: National Archives and Records Administration, RG 59, Central Files 1964–66, PET 10–3 SAUD. Limited Official Use. Drafted by Officer in Charge of Economic Affairs in the Office of Near Eastern Affairs George M. Bennsky; cleared in draft by William D. Wolle (NEA/NE) and Chief of the Fuels and Energy Division in the Bureau of Economic Affairs Office of International Resources Andrew F. Ensor; and approved by Davies. Repeated to Dhahran.

[2] Telegram 654 from Jidda, March 10, reported that Saudi Petroleum Minister Shaykh Ahmad Zaki Yamani had asked an Embassy officer why U.S. oil companies were not showing interest in available Saudi petroleum concession areas. (Ibid.)

[3] For documents relating to U.S. international oil policy, see *Foreign Relations*, 1964–1968, vol. XXXIV, Documents 175ff.

240. Memorandum From the Director of the Office of Near Eastern Affairs (Davies) to the Assistant Secretary of State for Near Eastern and South Asian Affairs (Talbot)[1]

Washington, March 23, 1965.

SUBJECT

Sale of Advanced Aircraft and Hawk Missiles to Saudi Arabia

Problem:

We are faced with some apparent Saudi distrust of the honesty of our recommendations in the Air Defense Survey that they purchase Northrop F–5 or Lockheed F–104H aircraft rather than the electronically more complex F–104G. They also suspect our advice against their purchasing Hawk surface-to-air missiles (SAMs) at this time. The problem is compounded by heavy British and French sales efforts, including offers to supply advanced aircraft, three-dimensional radar, SAMs, and pilots to fly the aircraft even on war-time missions. This is coupled with Saudi uncertainty about our willingness to support US equipment, if they should select it, in view of our position concerning their re-involvement in Yemen. It is thus feared that they will accept the French or British offers. The result would be a significant set-back for our long-term position of primacy in Saudi Arabia and would have adverse repercussions on our gold-flow difficulties. To meet this threat it has been proposed that we alter our offers to the Saudis to indicate willingness to supply more advanced equipment.

Discussion:

The Saudis have still made no decision on purchase of the aircraft and ground environment systems recommended in our 1963 Air Defense Survey. The Saudi Minister of Defense recently informed us that his choices of aircraft were, in order, F–104G, British Lightning, French Mirage, F–5, and F–104H. We had recommended only the latter two, and had advised the Saudis that, in terms of their needs, the F–5 was probably the most suitable. The F–104G is much more expensive to purchase and maintain and would give them an unnecessary low-level attack bombing capability. Similarly, for reasons of economy of money and trained manpower, we have been reluctant to see them purchase SAMs at this stage in their development.

The Minister of Defense also asked us for advanced air-to-air missiles (the Sparrow), which are precluded from sale to the Saudis for

---

[1] Source: Department of State, NEA/NE Files: Lot 69 D 547, Defense Affairs, Saudi Arabia, 1965. Secret. Drafted by Moore and cleared by Bunte.

security reasons, and requested a further US evaluation team to review current US offers, and possibly, at a later date, those of the British and French. We see little point to such an exercise, although would be willing to comply if the Saudis continue to request it.

While we could not meet the reported British and French offers to supply pilots to fly the aircraft in combat, we are able immediately to deliver a squadron of twelve F–5's and train present Saudi jet pilots so that the Saudis themselves could have their own combat group in six months' time.

Another element is the report from a Northrop representative that Faisal would like an aircraft-missile combination, such as the F–5/ Hawk package, for internal political purposes. With the planes in the hands of the Air Force and the missiles under Army control, all of his air defense would not be in the hands of a single service in case of defections. Both services would also be mollified at receiving advanced equipment. Northrop is preparing such a combined proposal for presentation to the Saudis if US Government approval is given.

The economic and technical arguments against advising the Saudis to obtain SAMs or the F–104G still appear valid. However, the US went on public record following announcement of the Hawk sale to Israel that it would also consider selling Hawks to the Arab countries. There is also a very good possibility that if we dispel Saudi suspicions by making a clear statement of our willingness to sell the F–104G, Hawks and three-dimensional radar, and couple it with a specific recommendation from us for less complicated equipment, they will accept our recommendation.

Any offer such as this would have to be accompanied by the clear caveat that much of the equipment (e.g., components of the Hawk, F–104G and the radar) is subject to US security controls. Its sale would be subject to Saudi agreement to a US security survey and compliance with security measures set forth in such a survey. (We should honestly recognize that these requirements might ultimately prevent consummation of sale of much of the equipment.)

In view of the numerous representations we have made to the British against selling SAMs to the Saudis, some difficulty from them might be expected. However, their specific statement to us on January 4 (see Deptel 319, attached)[2] that they had reassured the Saudis of their willingness to license the sale of Thunderbird missiles (SAMs) should relieve us of any obligation to them.

---

[2] Document 237.

Peter Solbert has requested a meeting with you in the next few days to discuss this subject. It is suggested that we and Col. Bunte brief you orally in advance of such a meeting.

Recommendation:

It is recommended:[3]

1. That you approve as the NEA position for discussion with DOD and other interested Department Bureaus our telling the Saudis, preferably at the Faisal level, that (a) to dispel any questions they may have we are willing to sell them the F–104G, three-dimensional radar, Sidewinders and Hawk missiles if they so desire; (b) sales of much of this equipment to any country in the world, including Saudi Arabia, are subject to a US security survey of the country and Saudi compliance with the security measures recommended in that survey; (c) our strong and specific recommendation in view of Saudi capabilities and requirements is that they purchase the Northrop F–5; (d) we will support whatever equipment is purchased with spares, training assistance and other appropriate services; (e) our original Air Defense Survey represents an honest US view of what the Saudis need and are able to maintain and operate, but if the King still desires further evaluation group study we will accede to his wishes.

2. That you approve the attached draft cable for coordination with Defense.

---

[3] Talbot initialed his approval of both recommendations.

---

241.   Letter From Secretary of Defense McNamara to Minister of Defense and Aviation Prince Sultan[1]

Washington, April 5, 1965.

Your Royal Highness:

I should like to express my appreciation to you for your very kind reception of my personal representative, Mr. John Hooper, and

---

[1] Source: Washington National Records Center, RG 330, OSD Files: FRC 70 A 1266, Saudi Arabia, 381, 3 Mar. 65. Secret. The text of the letter was transmitted to Jidda on April 5 in telegram 509. (National Archives and Records Administration, RG 59, Central Files 1964–66, DEF 12–5 SAUD)

members of his staff during their recent visit to Saudi Arabia. Mr. Hooper has informed me of your meeting with him and the discussions regarding your air defense program. Furthermore, I am aware of the recent conversation which you had with our Ambassador about your desire to improve rapidly the defenses of Saudi Arabia along its border with Yemen and that you are concerned with the possibilities of both ground and air attack.

The President has been made fully aware of your deep concerns in this matter and has asked that I give part of the reply to you, offering suggestions and recommendations with regard to the defense of Saudi Arabia. I am addressing myself to the military factors of your air defense and not to any of the political aspects of the problem which only you can evaluate.

The Air Defense survey prepared for your country by the United States last year concluded that either the F–5 or the F–104H equipped with proven air-to-air missiles of the Sidewinder variety is capable of meeting the military threat facing your country. Since either aircraft can perform the air defense mission and additionally can play a tactical or ground support role, all factors, including military capability, maintenance and other technical problems, training problems, economic impact and delivery dates must be considered in selecting one of the two aircraft. After careful review of these, I am strengthened in my belief that the recommendation initially given you in the summer of 1962 was sound and that if I were asked to make a present choice for your country, I would select the F–5 for the following reasons:

The F–5 was specifically designed as a dual purpose supersonic air defense and ground support aircraft offering maximum combat readiness and reliability through its relative design simplicity, ease of maintenance, and flight safety. In your present border situation, ground support capability is particularly important. This gives the F–5 a great advantage over a plane designed solely for interception.[2] Moreover, operational readiness can be obtained much earlier in the F–5 than in the F–104 because it is easier to learn to fly. I doubt the complex electronic equipment of the F–104G which adds greatly to cost and maintenance is necessary for your mission. The lower attrition rate of the F–5 is another important factor.

In addition, the twin engine reliability of the F–5 is, of course, a major consideration when flying over large expanses of desert. When the F–5 was selected as the modern follow-on aircraft for Norway, Greece, Turkey, Spain, Iran, Korea, Thailand, Ethiopia, the Philippines

---

[2] Telegram 514 to Jidda, April 6, instructed the Embassy to delete this sentence from the letter to avoid a possibly misleading implication. (Ibid.)

and the Republic of China, the various factors mentioned above were taken into consideration. For defense against bomb-carrying aircraft attacking your country, either the F–5 or the F–104 will be effective. In the light of your recent expressions of grave concern about the threat facing the kingdom, I will do my utmost to expedite deliveries of either type of aircraft and related equipment such as mobile radars to be stationed on your southern borders. At this time I can state that we believe we can deliver up to twelve F–5 aircraft within three to four months. I expect combat training time for Saudi pilots may require at least this long.

While I am fully aware that in defense of one's country no expense should be spared, it is the belief of myself and my staff that the additional capabilities of the F–104 would not justify the difference of nearly $35,000,000 between the cost of three squadrons of F–5s and a like number of F–104Gs. That difference could, in my judgment, be used more effectively to cover some of your other requirements.

In analyzing your air defense requirements, and in order to provide a greater overall air defense, you might wish to use the difference between the initial cost and the maintenance and operational costs of F–5s and F–104Gs to supplement the F–5 with some HAWK batteries of surface-to-air missiles, which we are still prepared to sell to you for deployment to defend Jidda and possibly other areas in Saudi Arabia. These missiles have an all-weather defense capability.

The F–104 is, of course, also an excellent and fast aircraft. If you consider that you require an F–104 series aircraft, we would gladly supply you with the F–104G or, as previously offered, the F–104H.

I have noted your interest in acquiring the Sparrow missile for the aircraft you select. Neither the F–5, the F–104G nor the F–104H has been designed to carry the Sparrow, the ultimate adaptation to either of these aircraft is questionable. Accordingly, I would recommend for your use the Sidewinder, which is an excellent air defense weapon.

At the time you inform me of your decision on your choice of aircraft we will be prepared to follow up promptly the other recommendations in the air defense survey required to develop an integrated air defense system. These include the communications facilities, ground radar and RSAA air defense weapons recommended in our survey.

With respect to your stated interest in 3–D radar, I understand that various proposals have been made to you. However, I recommend the more reliable and proved FPS 100/FPS 89 combination, which replaces the FPS 20/FPS 6 respectively, recommended in the air defense survey. Most 3–D radar systems are still under development. Our experience has shown that the height or altitude of a target is not generally required on every sweep of the search antenna and reliability and simplicity are more important. In fact, it is the third dimension of height finding which is still unsatisfactory. A radar operational for a maximum part of the time under all conditions is much more valuable in defense than a more complicated system requiring more frequent repair and maintenance.

I hope the foregoing is helpful. I assure you that General Leahy and the staff of the United States Military Training Mission stand ready to advise you not only on training but on the immediate and longer range problems relating to the defense of the integrity and security of Saudi Arabia, for which my government has so often demonstrated its concern. If I can be of further assistance, please do not hesitate to contact me.[3]

Sincerely,

Robert S. McNamara[4]

---

[3] In telegram 771 from Jidda, April 6, Hart reported that he had delivered McNamara's letter to Saqqaf that morning. (Ibid.) Telegram 778 from Jidda, April 7, reported that the Embassy had sent the amended page to Saqqaf, who had not yet delivered the letter to Sultan. (Ibid.)

[4] Printed from a copy that indicates McNamara signed the original.

---

242. Telegram From the Department of State to the Embassy in Saudi Arabia[1]

Washington, April 16, 1965, 8:04 p.m.

541. For Talbot and Hart. Propose following talking points for Assistant Secretary Talbot meeting with Faisal,[2] which we hope could be on most informal level with minimum number of people present. Presidential letter (now in clearance process)[3] and Deptels 439[4] and 489[5] perhaps useful as background.

---

[1] Source: National Archives and Records Administration, RG 59, Central Files 1964–66, ORG 7 NEA. Secret. Drafted by Moore; cleared by Symmes, Frank M. Tucker (EUR/BNA), Officer in Charge of Iranian Affairs M. Gordon Tiger, and Bunte; and approved by Jernegan. Also sent to Cairo.

[2] Assistant Secretary Talbot met with Faisal on April 21 in the course of visiting several countries in the Middle East; see Document 367.

[3] See Document 245; the President's letter was sent subsequent to Talbot's visit.

[4] Dated March 9. (National Archives and Records Administration, RG 59, Central Files 1964–66, POL 27 YEMEN)

[5] Dated March 26. (Ibid., DEF 12–5 SAUD)

Assume you first will deliver Presidential letter with appropriate remarks. Further to set broad framework for talk, suggest you then mention you have just come from NE Mission Chiefs conference where broad aspects Near East situation were discussed. King might be interested in summary of these discussions particularly as they pertain to Saudi Arabia. Such initial presentation could then lead to following specific points:

1. Oft repeated US concern for, and friendship with, Saudi Arabia remains unabated. Thus we disturbed over Saudi fears of UAR aggression from Yemen. Our prime concern Yemen has always related to maintenance security and stability Saudi Arabia. This has dominated our actions there. We aim at peaceful solution area disputes and at same time continue willing assist SAG against unprovoked attack. However, Saudi aid to royalists poses problem. Saudi restraint on border would enable us more easily come to SAG assistance, if need be, without complications posed by Saudi assistance to movement in opposition to government in Yemen which we recognize.

2. Similarly we continuing urge Nasser exercise restraint and resume discussions with Faisal. (Talbot may wish inform Faisal re his recent meeting with Nasser as appropriate.)

3. In addition continued efforts our Military Training Mission, we endeavor remain responsive to Saudi defense requirements and have offered supply aircraft and ground environment systems (including Hawk surface-to-air missiles if Saudis desire). In response urgent request MinDef Sultan, we now doing utmost obtain C–130 transport on urgent basis despite limited world-wide availability in view great demand for this plane to support US commitments Vietnam and elsewhere.

4. We greatly encouraged at positive aspects Saudi international relations as reflected in recent SAG–Iran moves to demarcate median line in Gulf. We currently exploring ways in which USG can be helpful in this effort.

5. Although we not directly involved in problem, we hope similar peaceful solution will be possible to long-standing Saudi border problems with Gulf states and Muscat. (FYI. Suggest Ambassador Hart's advice be followed on whether to make foregoing point.)

6. Saudi development program is particularly bright spot and provides basic strength for long-term maintenance Saudi independence. We pleased to be of assistance through such activities as US Geological Survey project and Corps Engineers television construction work. King's son Prince Muhammad now in Washington discussing with Department of Interior further steps implementation construction plans for desalting plant Jidda. Understand talks are promising. We im-

pressed by planned integration, as described by him, of desalting plant with new Jidda refinery and steel-rolling mill—petroleum fuel to be obtained for former and electricity to be supplied to latter. Hope SAG will be able proceed rapidly with desalting project with our technical assistance.

Rusk

243.   Memorandum From Robert W. Komer of the National Security Council Staff to the President's Special Assistant for National Security Affairs (Bundy)[1]

Washington, April 19, 1965.

McGB:

Talking with Lockheed. You'll recall past annoyance of McNamara, Rusk, and yourself about US aircraft manufacturers causing USG trouble by overselling. Worst offender has been *Lockheed* with F–104, and worst case has been *Saudi Arabia.*

I volunteered some time ago that WH would probably have to talk with Lockheed if it needed turning off. I believe I checked this out with you.

Now the time has come. McNamara has directly advised Saudis that, if it were up to him, he'd buy the Northrop F–5.[2] Regrettably this letter was leaked to Lockheed, so we want to turn off: (a) any Lockheed effort to undermine this deal; (b) any publicity here that we're interfering with free enterprise.

Our pitch ought to be made at the top, to Courtland Gross, and I'd urge by you. Here's a full brief, but the key selling point isn't mentioned. It is that USG does so well by Lockheed (of $1.6 billion in 1964 sales 44.4% was to USG) that it has no need to keep pushing for an extra few bucks by selling F–104s to countries that can't handle 'em. With Polaris, C–130, and all sorts of other big deals on (Lockheed got largest government contracts in whole aerospace industry for last three

---

[1] Source: Johnson Library, National Security File, Komer Files, Saudi Arabia, 1965–March 1966. Secret.

[2] See Document 241.

years' running), it should get off our backs in trying to sell F–104s to peanut countries. In fact, we've done mighty well by Lockheed on F–104 itself (European consortium, Japan). What say?[3]

R. W. Komer[4]

---

[3] An April 26 memorandum from Deputy Director of the Office of Near Eastern Affairs Harrison Symmes to Talbot states that Bundy had telephoned Lockheed Chairman of the Board Courtland Gross requesting that Lockheed cease its sales efforts for the F–104 interceptor aircraft in Saudi Arabia in light of the U.S. political decision to recommend to the Saudis purchase of the competing Northrop F–5. Gross reportedly had agreed, but asked for assistance in consummating a $15 million sale of four C–130 transport planes to the Saudis. (National Archives and Records Administration, RG 59, NEA/ARP Files: Lot 69 D 547, Defense Affairs—Saudi Arabia—1965, DEF 12–5–a–1, Aircraft (January–June))

[4] Printed from a copy that bears this typed signature.

---

244. Memorandum From Robert W. Komer of the National Security Council Staff to President Johnson[1]

Washington, April 23, 1965.

Here is another flowery, but essentially bread and butter letter which we urge you send to King Faisal of Saudi Arabia in lieu of inviting him for an early visit here.[2] Faisal has been angling to come.

Our Saudi friends need recurrent massage of this sort because of their nervousness over attack by the UAR troops in Yemen. We see little evidence that this is likely (and are just as happy to have 50,000 UAR troops in Yemen rather than deployed against Israel), but we see merit in periodically reassuring Faisal. We also want to sell about $200 million in US planes and other hardware to the Saudis instead of letting the UK and France get the sale. Finally, we want to protect our billion dollar oil investment.

I've carefully gone over this non-letter. It says nothing we haven't said before, and will be strictly private. The length arises from custom of the country. We beg your indulgence.

R. W. Komer[3]

---

[1] Source: Johnson Library, National Security File, Special Head of State Correspondence File, Saudi Arabia, King Faisal Correspondence, Vol. I. Secret.

[2] Document 245.

[3] McGeorge Bundy initialed below Komer's signature.

245.   Letter From President Johnson to King Faisal[1]

Washington, April 24, 1965.

Your Majesty:

The recent visit to Saudi Arabia of Assistant Secretary Talbot was a further indication of our continued great interest in you and your country. The long history of our friendly relations bears witness to the ties between our countries. We are further linked by mutual goals of opposing the spread of Communism through encouraging free peoples to develop their own potentials. Your leadership in guiding the people of Saudi Arabia forward on the road to progress and in ensuring the wise use of resources for development is a most hopeful augury for the future.

Defense of one's country is also an absolute requirement. Unfortunately, diversion of national wealth to this essentially unproductive field is one of the inescapable demands which we all must face so long as the state of the world remains as uncertain as it is. We will seek to be helpful in your effort to modernize your military forces. Secretary McNamara has written to your Minister of Defense, Prince Sultan, giving further recommendations and specific suggestions concerning equipment to meet your security needs. I want you to know that we are greatly interested in the safety and security of Saudi Arabia and sincerely desire to assist you in your defense arrangements, as in your development measures.

Ambassador Hart has reported to me your continuing concern over the presence of large numbers of United Arab Republic troops in Yemen and the threat which you believe they present to your country. This is a concern we share. As you are aware, our goal continues to be to bring about a withdrawal of these troops and a cessation of foreign interference in Yemeni affairs. In pursuing this goal, the security of Saudi Arabia has been uppermost in our mind. We have at no time espoused a policy toward the United Arab Republic which we believed was in any way injurious to the interests of your country. On the contrary, our actions throughout the Near East have continued to be aimed only at promoting harmonious dealings and the reduction of frictions among the countries there.

The statesmanship and patience that you have shown during our long search for a solution by peaceful means in Yemen have been most

---

[1] Source: Johnson Library, National Security File, Special Head of State Correspondence File, Saudi Arabia, Presidential Correspondence. Secret. Transmitted to Jidda in telegram 559, April 27. (National Archives and Records Administration, RG 59, Central Files 1964–66, POL 15–1 US/JOHNSON) The signed original was sent by pouch.

gratifying. I realize that in seeking to resolve the Yemen dispute, you, as well as we, have frequently met with an uncompromising rigidity. This indeed makes the path of negotiation difficult. But only by our continued joint efforts to follow this path can we hope to develop peaceful relations among all peoples of the Near East. It is in such peaceful relations that Saudi Arabia will find the most lasting assurances for its safety.

I have found exchanges of messages with Your Majesty most valuable. Believe me, your explanations of your position have not fallen on deaf ears. I have welcomed these contacts and hope for the continuation of the spirit of frankness which has marked them. In this spirit I trust we can continue to explore our mutual concerns in the world and deepen the already strong friendship which exists between our two countries.

May God preserve you in good health and grant peace and prosperity to you and your country.

Sincerely,

Lyndon B. Johnson

---

246. Telegram From the Embassy in Saudi Arabia to the Department of State[1]

Jidda, May 7, 1965, 1205Z.

872. Deptel 558.[2] US–SAG Military Relationship.

Background.

On May 3 I met with Saqqaf and delivered to him for advance study copy of President's message to King.[3] Saqqaf read it carefully and remarked it was "good letter." I then delivered to him summary list of measures we had taken to be helpful to SAG, in particular MODA, which contained Deptel 558. Saqqaf looked it over, commented it was important. I then asked his advice whether I should detail this list orally to King when I saw him. Saqqaf suggested that instead I might wish inform King I had delivered it to Saqqaf.

---

[1] Source: National Archives and Records Administration, RG 59, Central Files 1964–66, DEF 19 US–SAUD. Secret; Priority. Repeated to Dhahran, London, CHUSMTM Dhahran, CINCSTRIKE/CINCMEAFSA, and DEFREPNAMA Paris.

[2] Dated April 27. (Ibid.)

[3] Document 245.

May 5 Meeting with King (Embtel 869).[4]

Upon delivery Presidential letter (signed original and Embassy translation) to Faysal in presence Saqqaf, I noted President had made general reference to US Govt desire be helpful to Saudi effort modernize its military forces. While I had delivered to Saqqaf comprehensive list of what we had done, I wished draw HM's attention to certain specifics:

1. USG was now prepared to transfer to SAG without cost the F–86 aircraft currently on loan to SAG after completion overhaul and repairs at US expense. I would be discussing details of this with Saqqaf in near future. King seemed pleased, commented he was surprised to hear this since had understood these aircraft were to be taken out of Kingdom. I said this would be only for purpose repair, which could not be accomplished in Kingdom.

2. USG now ready sign military construction agreement, as US reply to Sultan's requests for changes in draft text were now in hands Foreign Ministry or MODA itself.

3. Noted CHUSMTM had been informed by Sultan during meeting same day that MODA definitely wanted DOD evaluation team to weigh Lockheed and Northrop package offer re fighter aircraft and related ground equipment. Secretary McNamara had said in earlier letter to Sultan he was prepared send team and I would therefore notify Washington immediately that it was desired.

4. Noted MODA request made to General Adams (CINCSTRIKE) one year ago for survey military vehicle requirements. We had performed survey immediately and delivered final report to MODA followed by letter of offer December 1964.[5] This was under study in MODA.

5. Noted we had presented Air Defense Survey Report in Riyadh January 1964.

I then commented that so far as I could determine US had answered all Prince Sultan's requests. However, I stood ready to check into any matters King might feel were outstanding. King thanked me, saying "We appreciate all your efforts and will try to find the road to cooperation with you in all respects." He had no specific questions but noted there were two considerations he wished mention. First, there was no use buying military equipment which Saudis could not operate. "We are lying to ourselves if we think we are ready to use certain equipment. We need help." Secondly, Faysal noted prices for much of equipment were very high. While SAG was obliged to buy equipment, since it

---

[4] Dated May 6. (National Archives and Records Administration, RG 59, Central Files 1964–66, POL 15 YEMEN)

[5] Not found.

could not just look on when it was being attacked, he wanted expenditures to benefit his people and country as a whole. I assured him we were not interested in urging him to spend heavily on military equipment and that Secretary McNamara's letter drew particular attention to costs. King responded Secretary McNamara had talked only about technical matters. "More important even than price is that we be able to make use of this equipment. McNamara did not touch on this, he turned it over to you, the politicians." As Faysal was being purposely vague at this point, I felt it much the better course not to ask him to be more specific and turned to other matters separately reported.

Comment: I draw two interpretations from Faysal's remarks, which were made in low key. First, he leans toward American equipment and backing, is not yet satisfied with UK or French relationship and hopes USG will assist, directly or indirectly, in operating his air defense equipment, particularly by facilitating or at least not impeding the hiring of pilots and technicians for supersonic aircraft and related ground equipment. Secondly, I believe Faysal has always been more conscious of price tag involved in developing modern military forces than has Sultan and that cumulation of military budgeting at this point has become rather staggering. Recent relaxation in Yemen threat, coupled with his own desire to avoid wasting money, makes him reluctant grant early approval for major air defense expenditures unless package is sound and represents "force in being."

Recommendations:

1. That DOD evaluation team be sent as soon as possible to Riyadh, giving earliest advance notice to CHUSMTM for clearance with Sultan.

2. That Lockheed be informed by Dept now that Lockheed team, which will soon be handling terms C–130 sale at Riyadh (Deptel 574)[6] should stay away from discussion with MODA of terms of defense package fighter aircraft plus ground environment, and if approached by MODA staff on such matters it reply it understands DOD evaluation team at (or about to begin) work and while company stands ready study any Saudi requests discussion thereof would be best postponed until evaluation team has rendered report and latter fully studied by MODA; lastly that Lockheed team leave Saudi Arabia as soon as C–130 sale papers signed, to avoid or cut down overlapping presence at Riyadh with DOD evaluation team and thereby obviate basis legitimate complaint by Northrop.

---

[6] Dated May 6. (National Archives and Records Administration, RG 59, Central Files 1964–66, DEF 12–5 SAUD)

3. That Northrop be informed of foregoing procedure and be asked to stay clear of Saudi Arabia until evaluation report rendered and studied.

4. That thereafter both companies await further indication from MODA or USG before again visiting Saudi Arabia on air defense packages.

5. That foregoing procedure be explained by me to Saqqaf for relay to Sultan, CHUSMTM following up and discussing details with MODA as required.

Hart

---

247.   Airgram From the Embassy in Saudi Arabia to the Department of State[1]

A–332   Jidda, May 15, 1965.

SUBJECT

King Faysal Answers President Johnson's Letter of April 24

REF

Deptel 559;[2] Embtels 869;[3] 911[4]

The Embassy forwards as an enclosure to this airgram the original text of a letter from King Faysal to President Johnson dated May 11 acknowledging the President's letter of April 24.

---

[1] Source: National Archives and Records Administration, RG 59, Central Files 1964–66, POL 15–1 US/JOHNSON. Secret. Drafted by Political Officer Richard W. Murphy, and approved by Deputy Chief of Mission Nicholas G. Thacher. Repeated to Dhahran.

[2] See footnote 1, Document 245.

[3] Dated May 6. (National Archives and Records Administration, RG 59, Central Files 1964–66, POL 15 YEMEN)

[4] In telegram 911 from Jidda, May 15, Hart informed the Department that the Embassy was forwarding by pouch the King's letter in response to the President's letter of April 24, and commented that the Embassy found the message to be a courteous reaffirmation of Faisal's basic policy. He noted that the lack of any implied disagreement with U.S. views might be taken as an indication that the King was in a much more relaxed frame of mind than a few weeks earlier when he was much concerned with the possibility of a UAR attack from the south. (Ibid., POL 15–1 US/JOHNSON)

Following is the Embassy's informal translation of this letter:

"His Excellency President Lyndon B. Johnson

Excellency:

Ambassador Hart conveyed to me, upon his return from Washington, Your Excellency's noble feelings towards this country and its leadership. I thank Your Excellency for your letter expressing your praise for the progress of the Saudi Arabian Kingdom and for its wise exploitation of resources in the service of economic progress which, God willing, will promote the country's welfare and future.

There is no doubt that an exchange of viewpoints is always useful to attain our joint goal of combatting Communism in the world. The contacts and visits undertaken by responsible officials of your government aid in the attainment of this goal. I was pleased with the recent visit to my country of Mr. Talbot, Assistant Secretary of State. It confirmed to me the extent of Your Excellency's concern and that of your government for this country which is bound to the U.S. by friendly and historic ties that become increasingly stronger.

It gives me pleasure to hear from Your Excellency that you are concerned with the security and peace of the Saudi Arabian Kingdom, that these are at the forefront of the problems which preoccupy you, and that you sincerely wish to aid the Kingdom in its defense planning and in its economic development.

We are studying with great care the recommendations and suggestions Secretary McNamara sent to Brother Sultan pertaining to the equipment which we need to protect the integrity and security of our country.

Ambassador Hart informed you of the worries which the current situation in Yemen causes us, and which apart from the direct effect on our country, provides a foothold for the growth of doctrines we are both combatting and which also block achievement of a peaceful and just solution bringing peace and security to beloved Yemen.

I am convinced that the policy which the United States of America is following towards our country is dictated by our historical friendship and by our joint desire to combat the spread of Communism in the world. There has not entered our mind for a single moment that the friendly United States of America might initiate any project harmful to our country's interest.

We also esteem highly the assistance which the USA provides the people of the developing countries if it is spent correctly to raise living standards of peoples inside the frontiers of their countries.

Your Excellency also noted that we have been zealous since armed conflict began in the Yemen to find a solution for this problem in peaceful ways and that we used patience and self control despite the various types of meddling and provocation to which our country has been exposed. We have demonstrated continuously a friendly intent for everyone whose concern was the return of peace and security to Yemen. However, all of these efforts failed to give the desired effect in view of our meeting—as Your Excellency noted—an uncompromising rigidity which kept us from reaching a solution.

It is our firm hope that by continuation of our joint efforts and our continuous contacts, marked by frankness of spirit, we will be able to conquer the difficulties to which the road to a peaceful just solution has been exposed and, by so doing, to strengthen the good relations between our brothers in the region. There would be among its fruitful results the growth of economic development in an atmosphere dominated by peace and stability.

Mr. President, I am happy that this opportunity has been given me to speak with you and to exchange opinions with you in such frankness. This frankness will no doubt have the greatest effect on our joint study of our common aims: resisting Communism and strengthening the historic friendship which binds our two countries.

Wishing health and succor for Your Excellency and progress and prosperity for the people of the United States,

Sincerely,

Faysal

11 Muharram 1385h

11 May 1965"

For the Ambassador:
Richard W. Murphy
Second Secretary of Embassy

248.   Memorandum From Robert W. Komer of the National Security Council Staff to President Johnson[1]

Washington, June 16, 1965, 9 a.m.

Saudi Arms Talks. Given the occasional press flurry,[2] I want to keep you briefed. This is quite unlike the Jordan arms deal: (a) there's no problem of pre-empting the Soviets; (b) there's little real threat to Israel involved—Saudi Arabia is too far away and too incompetent; (c) we're not running after this business—it's the Saudis who are coming to us.

The Saudi desire for modern air defense is aimed at the Nasser threat from Yemen, not at Israel. The issue arose way back to *early 1963*, when as bait for the Bunker mission effort to get a Yemen disengagement, we offered to help the Saudis develop an air defense system. We gave them our views in September 1963, and they've been hemming and hawing in typical Arab style ever since. Meanwhile the British, French, and two US companies have been actively seeking the business, so at Saudi request we're sending yet another survey team to help them make up their minds.

Our goal is to keep our oil-rich Saudi friends happy and to insure that if they finally do buy anything we get the sale. We've recommended against fancy aircraft and Hawk because Saudis couldn't handle them; but we're willing to sell if they insist. The total package could range from $110–210 million over several years, but we think Faisal will end up buying only the lower figure, if that.

We've made other sales to Saudi Arabia. In 1957 we offered a $100 million credit to facilitate extension of our Dhahran air base rights. Since 1961 we've extended two small credits totalling $18 million. The Saudis also bought four C–130s for $15 million cash this spring.

The Israelis have never objected to these sales, since they recognize the Saudis are too far away and too ineffective to be a threat. The one problem in the current deal is that if we sell F–104s, the Jordanians and then the Israelis might press for them. This is one reason (the other

---

[1] Source: Johnson Library, National Security File, Name File, Komer Memos, Vol. I. Secret. A handwritten note on the memorandum indicates it was received at 10 a.m. A notation on the memorandum indicates it was seen by the President on June 22.

[2] On June 2 Komer sent Bundy a draft memorandum for the President commenting on "quite inaccurate" weekend press stories stating that McNamara had sent a letter to the Saudis pushing U.S. arms sales. He pointed out that the Saudis had been interested in air defense for more than a year because of their fears that Nasser would launch air attacks across the border. The United States had not been pressing the Saudis to buy arms, but had simply decided that if they were going to buy it might as well be from the United States. McNamara's letter had not been a sales pitch, but merely an attempt to resolve Saudi doubts about the F–5 versus the F–104. (Ibid., Komer Files, Saudi Arabia, 1965–Mar. 1966) McNamara's letter is Document 241.

is that F–104s are just too complex for Saudis) why McNamara wrote recommending the F–5. I personally doubt the Saudis will make up their minds soon on anything.[3]

R. W. Komer[4]

---

[3] Telegram 102 from Jidda, August 11, reported that the Saudi Government had decided to purchase the F–104G. (National Archives and Records Administration, RG 59, Central Files 1964–66, POL SAUD–UAR)

[4] McGeorge Bundy initialed below Komer's signature.

---

249.   Telegram From the Department of State to the Embassy in Saudi Arabia[1]

Washington, August 1, 1965, 10:48 a.m.

47. Embtel 60.[2] Agree it unlikely UAR plans bomb Saudi territory while al-Khouli in Jidda. However, you should report immediately any added evidence confirming UAR overflights.

UAR aware our continued support Saudi integrity. This point reiterated to UAR Ambassador Washington on three occasions during past week. He claims to have reported this to Cairo in strong terms. Embassy Cairo is also to discuss with UAR FonMinistry.

Concur your recommendation American pilots continue fly SDI flights as usual.

Will comment subsequently on proposed contingency position with SAG.

Rusk

---

[1] Source: National Archives and Records Administration, RG 59, Central Files 1964–66, POL 31–1 SAUD–UAR. Secret; Priority. Drafted by Moore, cleared by Hart in substance, and approved by Davies. Repeated to Cairo, Taiz, London, Dhahran, CHUSMTM Dhahran, CINCSTRIKE/CINCMEAFSA, and COMIDEASTFOR.

[2] In telegram 60 from Jidda, July 31, Seelye wrote that Saudi aviation technicians had reported that UAR aircraft, allegedly MIGs, had been overflying Jizan in recent days. He noted that this was one of several recent indicators that the United Arab Republic was either engaged in a campaign to make Nasser's July 22 threat against Saudi Arabia appear credible or that it in fact was planning an imminent air attack on Saudi supply depots in Jizan and Najran. If the latter, Seelye noted that it was unreasonable to expect that such an attack would be carried out while al-Khouli was negotiating with the Saudi Arabian Government. (Ibid.)

250. Memorandum for the Record[1]

Washington, August 5, 1965.

SUBJECT

> Minutes of the Meeting of the Special Group (CI); 2 p.m., Thursday, August 5, 1965

PRESENT

> Governor Harriman, Admiral Raborn; General Wheeler, Mr. Rowan and Mr. Marks, Mr. Komer, Mr. Gaud vice Mr. Bell
>
> Ambassador Hart, General Anthis, and Messrs Davies and Maechling were present for the meeting

[Here follows discussion of the counterinsurgency intelligence summary and the chairman's trip to Europe.]

3. Report on Security Situation in Arabian Peninsula

Ambassador Hart briefly reviewed the situation in Saudi Arabia and the peninsula, pointing out that there is no serious internal threat as long as King Faysal remains in power. He said that the immediate threat is internal, stemming from the Yemen situation and Nasserist activity in neighboring states, and that the long term threat comes from the possibility that the Government of Saudi Arabia will be unable to modernize fast enough to meet the rising expectations of dissident groups.

Ambassador Hart reviewed US efforts in the youth, labor, military and police fields in Saudi Arabia. He informed the Group of the Minister of Agriculture's request for the assistance of four US agricultural specialists. *The possibility of providing such specialists was discussed and the Chairman requested that the State Department look into this.*

The Group discussed the recommendations contained in the memorandum and suggested that the US Government consider what action it would be prepared to take in the contingency of an eruption in the Yemen situation. *The Group agreed with the desirability of providing a police survey team as recommended, and requested that the feasibility of funding such a team be reconsidered by AID and CIA.*

Mr. Komer suggested that a visible demonstration of US interest in the security and stability of the Arabian peninsula, such as visits by US Navy ships and possible helicopter demonstrations, be made now

---

[1] Source: Department of State, NEA Files: Lot 70 D 503, Internal Defense (inc. Meeting 7/13/66). Secret. Attached to an August 13 transmittal memorandum from Alexander Rattray of S/S–S to various Department of State bureaus.

before Egyptian provocation against Saudi Arabia becomes more flagrant.

[Here follows discussion of a miscellaneous item.]

C. G. Moody, Jr.
Executive Secretary
Special Group (CI)

251. Telegram From the Department of State to the Embassy in Saudi Arabia[1]

Washington, August 19, 1965, 9:06 p.m.

83. Following is based on uncleared memcon and is FYI–Noforn and subject to revision.

Saudi Ambassador Sowayel, acting under instructions, called urgently on Secretary August 18 and expressed appreciation our August 4 press statement reaffirming US support Saudi integrity.[2] He referred to recent Saudi requests for US Navy and Air Force visits and noted Chargé Seelye's response that US destroyer now scheduled call Jidda on 17th and 25th, but that Air Force unit presented problem. Ambassador continued that another idea came up concerning possibility US aircraft visiting Saudi Arabia as part of combined US-Saudi training demonstration, that SAG would very much like such visit and hoped USG would implement it.

Secretary responded that we continued our support for Saudi Arabia, but that we found some problem with visit of US Air Force element, particularly in view Saudi involvement in border area. In any event would have to discuss idea of US training exercise with President before replying Sowayel. Expressed hope reported early Faisal–Nasser meeting would be fruitful. Noted Saudi progress in recent years of relative calm and said deterioration in US–UAR relations during this period to some extent attributable our support of Saudis.

Rusk

---

[1] Source: National Archives and Records Administration, RG 59, Central Files 1964–66, POL SAUD–US. Secret. Drafted by Moore, cleared by Davies, and approved by Hart. Repeated to Cairo, London, Dhahran, CHUSMTM Dhahran, and CINCSTRIKE/CINC-MEAFSA.

[2] Telegram 22 to Taiz, August 4, reported the Department spokesman's statement reiterating U.S. support for the maintenance of Saudi Arabia's integrity. (Ibid., POL 27 YEMEN)

252. Memorandum of Conversation[1]

Washington, October 8, 1965.

SUBJECT

    Sale of British Aircraft to Saudi Arabia and Jordan

PARTICIPANTS

    Mr. Michael N. F. Stewart, Minister, British Embassy
    Mr. Christopher Everett, First Secretary, British Embassy
    NEA—Assistant Secretary Raymond A. Hare
    NE—Mr. Harrison M. Symmes
    NE—David Korn

1. *Saudi Arabia.* Mr. Stewart said that Sir Donald Stokes of Leyland Motors, who is spearheading the effort to promote sales of British arms abroad, had recently approached Secretary McNamara concerning sales of British Lightning aircraft to the Saudi Air Force. Mr. McNamara had told him that the United States would see no objection to such British sales, provided the U.S. had not already entered into a commitment to sell American aircraft. British Ambassador Dean had subsequently (October 6) called on Secretary McNamara at which time the Secretary had confirmed his remarks to Stokes. Mr. Stewart asked if the Department knew whether the Saudis had reached a decision concerning what aircraft they desired to purchase. Mr. Symmes responded that our latest information was that the Saudis were still considering the matter. Mr. Stewart stressed that if the U.K. is to continue to shoulder its share of the Western defense burden it must meet its balance of payments problem. Sales of Lightnings to the Saudis were part of this problem.

[Here follows discussion of aircraft sales to Jordan.]

---

[1] Source: National Archives and Records Administration, RG 59, Central Files 1964–66, DEF 12–5 SAUD. Secret; Exclusive Distribution. Drafted by Moore.

253.   Telegram From the Embassy in Saudi Arabia to the Department of State[1]

Jidda, October 13, 1965, 0700Z.

287. Air Defense Purchases.

On October 12th Acting Deputy Foreign Minister Mas'ud handed me copy of letter dated October 11 and marked "Secret" from MODA Prince Sultan to Secretary of Defense McNamara.[2] Mas'ud explained original of letter (in Arabic) being transmitted to DOD via Saudi Embassy Washington.

In letter Sultan refers to Secretary McNamara's April 6 [5] letter[3] and expresses his appreciation for Secretary's interest in Saudi air defense program and for dispatch of review team to assist Saudi military in choosing best equipment for air defense of Kingdom.

Sultan then refers to joint recommendations submitted by US and Saudi members review team and states that SAG has now decided to implement these. At same time Sultan requests USG obtain ammunition for use with F104G for training, operational, and war reserve purposes. He also asks USG to supply Saudi Arabia with any additional arms now developed or to be developed for F104G such as Sparrow and Falcon missiles.

Sultan, after emphasizing friendly relations and mutual cooperation existing between USG and SAG, asks Secretary McNamara to exert his influence to reduce prices of aircraft and related equipment involved in sale, although neither dollar amount nor percentage of reduction desired specified. Sultan also seeks Secretary's assistance in obtaining credit terms permit SAG pay for package over ten-year period in view of heavy drain on Saudi resources resulting from SAG development and reform programs in all sectors. Specifically, Sultan proposes five percent down payment at time contract signed with remaining ninety-five percent to be paid in twelve installments beginning ten months after arrival aircraft and related basic equipment in Kingdom.

Letter concludes with Sultan's hope to receive positive reply from Secretary McNamara as soon as possible. Embassy preparing translation to be pouched October 16.

---

[1] Source: National Archives and Records Administration, RG 59, Central Files 1964–66, DEF 12–5 SAUD. Secret. Repeated to Dhahran, London, Paris, CINCSTRIKE/CINCMEAFSA, CHUSMTM Dhahran, DIAAQ, CSAF, DA, and DEFREPNAMA Paris.

[2] A copy of Prince Sultan's letter is in the Washington National Records Center, RG 330, OSD Files: FRC 70 A 3717, 381, Jordan, 10 Nov. 65.

[3] Document 241.

Comment: Mas'ud expressed hope USG would move rapidly in servicing order. I assured him that this would be the case.

Seelye

254. **Memorandum of Conversation**[1]

Washington, October 19, 1965, 4:30 p.m.

SUBJECT

Saudi Arms Purchase

PARTICIPANTS

H.E. Omar Saqqaf, Deputy Foreign Minister of Saudi Arabia
H.E. Ibrahim al Sowayel, Ambassador of Saudi Arabia
The Secretary
NE—Harrison M. Symmes
NE—David Korn

The Secretary said he would like to ask a delicate question. Is Saudi Arabia still troubled by agents from abroad?

Mr. Saqqaf replied that foreign agents are no longer a problem and explained that the people are satisfied with King Faisal's policies and give him full support. One of the reasons for this is that the King spends no money on himself and sets aside as much as possible for economic development projects.

Mr. Saqqaf said that in line with this policy the SAG wished to ask the United States for help in the purchase of American supersonic aircraft, Hawk missiles and radar equipment, as proposed in Defense Minister Sultan's letter of October 12 to Secretary McNamara.[2] The Saudis need payment facilities because the King insists on spending every available cent on development.

Mr. Saqqaf said the SAG had gotten offers of good terms from the UK and France. Now that the Council of Ministers had been persuaded to buy the US planes and equipment, he hoped the US would move

---

[1] Source: National Archives and Records Administration, RG 59, Central Files 1964–66, DEF 12–5 SAUD. Secret. Drafted by David Korn (NEA/NE) on October 21 and approved in S on November 12. The memorandum is Part III of IV. Part I is Document 382. The time of the meeting is from Rusk's Appointment Book. (Johnson Library)

[2] See footnote 2, Document 253.

rapidly to help them. Mr. Saqqaf again made a plea for rapid action and said he hoped that for once the Saudis could ask the US for something and have it done rapidly, without getting bogged down in negotiations.

The Secretary remarked that modern aircraft are very expensive but promised to look into the matter and get in touch personally with Secretary McNamara. He said a problem might arise if the Saudi request involved military assistance credits, as these were already overdrawn.

255.   Telegram From the Department of State to the Embassy in Saudi Arabia[1]

Washington, October 29, 1965, 7:18 p.m.

213. Joint State/Defense Message. Ref exchange letters UK Min Aviation Jenkins[2] and McNamara[3] and separate Cirtel[4] (being repeated to addressees).

1. You will note in developing combined package with British we have insisted that we cannot withdraw our own F–104G offer without

---

[1] Source: National Archives and Records Administration, RG 59, Central Files 1964–66, DEF 12–5 SAUD. Secret; Priority; Limdis. Drafted by Moore; cleared by G/PM Director for Operations Howard Meyers, Judd, Officer in Charge of Politico-Military Affairs in the Office of Near Eastern and South Asian Regional Affairs Lieutenant Colonel Billy R. Byrd, Symmes, and Stoddart; and approved by Davies. Repeated to Beirut, Amman, Dhahran, Paris for DAUSRO, CINCSTRIKE/CINCMEAFSA POLAD (by pouch), CHUSMTM Dhahran, and London.

[2] On October 25 Jenkins wrote McNamara concerning their joint problems in meeting the defense requirements of Saudi Arabia, Jordan, and Lebanon. As part of an over-all program, he suggested a joint U.S.–U.K. proposal to Saudi Arabia of a defense package consisting of British Lightning aircraft together with U.S. Hawk missiles and a U.S.–U.K. combination of ground environment equipment, with U.S. concentration on communications and U.K. concentration on radar. (Telegram 1902 from London, October 27, ibid., DEF 12–5 NEAR E)

[3] On October 28 McNamara responded that since he had received a letter from Prince Sultan the previous week indicating his government's decision on an F–104G package if arrangements for financing and missiles could be worked out, it was already late for reconsideration of the Saudi Arabian program. Nevertheless, there was merit in the tri-country program Jenkins had outlined and the United States would be willing to agree to inclusion of U.S. equipment in such a proposal if it was absolutely clear that the United States was also willing to stand by its original offer of F–104G aircraft to Saudi Arabia. (Letter from Secretary McNamara to Minister Jenkins, October 28, 1965; Washington National Records Center, RG 330, OSD Files: FRC 70 A 1266, Saudi Arabia 381, 3 Mar. 65)

[4] Circular telegram 782, October 29. (National Archives and Records Administration, RG 59, Central Files 1964–66, DEF 12–5 NEAR E)

risking serious damage US–SAG relations. We intend proceed with own presentation, as witnessed by McNamara response to Sultan. At same time we willing join with British in making available to Saudis another choice of equipment mix. (Latter may have pricing advantage in comparison with Lockheed offer, although this unclear until precise comparison of components can be made.)

2. We have insisted that new package be presented by British as having been formulated at their initiative; that they had obtained authorization from us for inclusion US equipment in this proposal.

3. After combined proposal presented to SAG by British, you should confirm to Saudis that we in fact have agreed to inclusion US equipment and stand ready supply full logistic, training and other requisite support for this equipment should Saudis choose combined proposal. At same time you should make absolutely clear we remain fully ready and willing supply completely US package, as reiterated in McNamara response to Sultan.[5]

Rusk

---

[5] Telegram 207 to Jidda, October 29, transmitted McNamara's letter to Prince Sultan. (Ibid., DEF 1–4 SAUD) In telegram 342 from Jidda, November 2, Seelye reported that on that day he had informed Acting Deputy Foreign Minister Mas'ud that the U.S. Government had authorized inclusion of U.S. equipment in the latest U.K. proposal, but that the United States remained fully ready and willing to supply a completely U.S. package. He added that if the Saudi Arabian Government decided to opt for the combined package, the U.S. Government was prepared to supply the requisite equipment, training, and support. In response to Mas'ud's query as to why he had not communicated this when he met with Sultan the previous day, Seelye responded that he had not been authorized to do so until after the U.K. presentation. (Ibid., DEF 12–5 SAUD)

---

256.   Telegram From the Embassy in Saudi Arabia to the Department of State[1]

Jidda, November 2, 1965, 0645Z.

338. MODA Prince Sultan summoned me, together with Acting Deputy Foreign Minister Mas'ud, to Ministry of Defense Office in Jidda

---

[1] Source: National Archives and Records Administration, RG 59, Central Files 1964–66, DEF 12–5 SAUD. Secret; Limdis. Repeated to CINCSTRIKE/CINCMEAFSA, London, Paris for DAUSRO, Dhahran, CHUSMTM Dhahran, Amman, and Beirut.

November 1. (HMG Aviation representatives saw Sultan five hours later.) Purpose of meeting was discussion Secretary Defense McNamara's letter to Sultan[2] received Jidda October 29. Sultan said he gratified by letter and welcomed its "spirit." He then asked we go over letter together paragraph by paragraph.

After completing paragraphs one through four, he went into long dissertation re USG–SAG relationship. Recalling his five-hour conversation with Ambassador Hart earlier in year, he emphasized importance SAG regime be enabled demonstrate that SAG's primary reliance on USG sound and productive. He referred to MTM relationship with SAG and noted that other Arab countries had questioned benefits derived from USG–SAG military relationship. He cited fact SAG pays most of costs of MTM, excluding salaries USG advisors. He commented that recent visit to Jordan had impressed him with fact USG financing purchase all Jordanian military equipment which, he contended, Jordanian people fuly recognize and appreciate. Sultan continued that in Saudi Arabia there are elements both in military as well as in Council of Ministers who are unfriendly to U.S. What SAG needs and wants is tangible evidence USG desire be helpful Saudi Arabia in order to help validate in eyes of public SAG determination continue its close relationship with USG. (What Sultan appeared be driving at was that USG should pick up portion of defense package tab.)

Addressing specifics of letter, Sultan said he taken aback by [$]600 million figure cited as maximum possible cost of defense package. He claimed that few months before arrival USG Air Defense Review Team Lockheed had quoted figure of some $200 million as cost of package exclusive Hawk missiles. Adding estimated cost of Hawk missiles as provided by review team plus additional amount for unforeseen items, SAG had come up with total of $330 to 340 million. This had been figure presented to King and on basis of which he had authorized Sultan proceed with negotiation defense package.

I indicated my understanding that cost of labor in U.S. had risen since initial quotations and that considerable portion of 600 million figure included estimate of cost of simultaneous construction of all facilities. If construction phased, costs would be less. Lockheed had also indicated it might be prepared to adjust this figure downward now that it had had an opportunity to undertake further on-site survey. I emphasized fact only way Lockheed could hire and keep top flight technicians on job in Saudi Arabia was by providing them with housing equivalent to US standards as well as accustomed recreational facilities. I said further that once Lockheed had had opportunity cost out each

[2] See footnote 5, Document 255.

item, Sultan would probably find that cost of hardware, including aircraft, not unreasonable. In any case we would urge Lockheed reduce its prices as much as possible.

With regard to Sultan's oblique suggestion that USG finance portion of air defense package, I noted extreme difficulty Executive branch USG having these days in obtaining Congressional support for additional—let alone existing—military and economic aid programs. Re generous credit terms, I expressed view Secretary Defense letter showed that USG making extraordinary effort to satisfy SAG request. I said that while true SAG not receiving USG grant assistance, His Highness might wish to remind "unfriendly elements" in Saudi Arabia of fact USG provides most important assistance of all, namely, clear, public undertaking to support and preserve integrity of Saudi Arabia. Sultan did not pursue point further.

Sultan then asked whether would be useful invite into our meeting Lockheed representatives who waiting outside his office. Since latter had just completed round of discussions with RSAF committee resulting in agreement Lockheed would work up price lists on basis two alternative time-phased programs, I suggested any further discussion of details await Lockheed's completion its financial estimates. Sultan indicated this agreeable and asked that USG official be present during next round of discussions. He said he had spent most of night discussing two alternative Lockheed proposals. He tentatively favored second proposal which would phase in program over 4–5 year period since he said he recognized need first train Saudi personnel adequately. Meanwhile, he asked his military staff to draw up third alternative time-phased program.

I noted Lockheed had indicated would take two weeks complete financial estimates. When Sultan commented this too long, I offered undertake urge Lockheed complete estimates in one week and to assure that USG official either from Washington or from Country Team would be present during next round. Sultan expressed desire that highest priority be attached to installation of Hawk missiles.

Finally, Sultan asked that I convey to Mr. McNamara on King's and his behalf two points: (1) their gratification with SecDefense's latest letter and (2) their desire to continue maintain special relationship with USG and their belief that forthcoming USG response in implementing defense package would reflect reciprocal USG desire.

Meyers of Lockheed briefed re portions of foregoing including 1) request financial estimates be prepared in week instead of two weeks; 2) SAG concern re high prices and our hope Lockheed can reduce; 3) Sultan desire USG official attend next round of discussions.

I have been in close consultation with CHUSMTM, who now in Jidda and endorses foregoing.

Comment: Hope that DOD can persuade Lockheed complete its financial estimates in less than two weeks and arrange have representatives in Saudi Arabia prepared discuss and cost any alternative time-phasing proposed by Saudis. Welcome suggestions as to who from USG side might attend next round Lockheed–MODA–RSAF discussions.

Seelye

---

257. **Telegram From the Department of State to the Embassy in Saudi Arabia**[1]

Washington, November 8, 1965, 7:56 p.m.

239. Embtel 344.[2] Saudi Air Defense.

1. You may assure Sultan that US Hawk missile system is completely autonomous system and can be effectively integrated with British air defense warning radar (e.g., 3–D radar) and Lightning aircraft, provided UK does not attempt substitute UK components for US Hawk system components. If Saudis desire, US prepared to send OSD and/or Raytheon rep to answer technical questions or present price proposal, respectively.

2. We do not believe we would have great difficulty in equalling UK credit terms for our portion of combined package. Suggest you so inform Sultan jointly with UK reps on Wednesday when they expected present their credit offer. (UK MinAv official Christie suggested this.)

---

[1] Source: National Archives and Records Administration, RG 59, Central Files 1964–66, DEF 1–4 SAUD. Secret; Limdis. Drafted by Moore and Quinn; cleared by Warren, Judd, Feigl (DOD/ISA/ILN), Colonel E. Dreiss (DOD/DDRE/OAD/DS), Symmes, Colonel Byrd, and Stoddart; and approved by Davies. Repeated to London, CHUSMTM Dhahran, Paris, CINCSTRIKE, Dhahran, and Paris for DAUSRO.

[2] In telegram 344 from Jidda, November 3, Seelye reported that the King was "somewhat irritated" that, in view of the special U.S.-Saudi relationship, the United States had not revealed in advance of the British the nature of the combined U.S.-U.K. proposal. On November 3 at a meeting with Sultan, U.K. Ambassador Mann, and U.K. Ministry of Aviation officials, Sultan noted that he wanted the United Kingdom to understand that Saudi Arabia relied primarily on U.S. Government military support and on its undertaking to maintain Saudi Arabia's integrity. He said he would be inclined toward the combined package if he could be assured: 1) that the Hawk system could be integrated effectively with British components; 2) that the U.S. Government fully endorsed it as being a viable air defense for Saudi Arabia, and 3) that the United States could provide the same credit terms as the United Kingdom. (Ibid.)

3. Providing Lightning aircraft, ground radars and Hawk system radars use Mark 10 IFF interrogator/transponder equipment and manual command control is used, the proposed joint US–UK air defense package consisting of Lightnings, 3–D radars, Hawks and communication systems does appear to constitute a viable air defense system. Categoric assurance can only be given after US and UK technical experts discuss detailed composition of UK package elements. Discussion expected within next two weeks.

4. Raytheon currently preparing cost estimates on basis Col. Vaughn's survey. Unable at this time to determine when such estimates will be available. However, will attempt have Raytheon ready to submit costing data within ten days. Advise how you think this data best submitted, i.e., through Lockheed, BAC, UK or US Embassy, or directly by Raytheon.

5. Lockheed rep Hansen ETA Jidda Nov. 10.

6. Re your 349,[3] agree that if SAG accepts combined package we and British faced with much sorting out our respective roles Saudi Arabia. While it perhaps not worthwhile delve into details until Saudi decision known, we hope Dep Asst Sec Davies will have opportunity initial discussions with British during London trip toward end this month.

7. *For London:* We have informed Brit Emb. of paras 1–3 above. You may also inform HMG.

Rusk

---

[3] Dated November 4. (Ibid., DEF 12–5 SAUD)

258. Memorandum From the President's Deputy Special Assistant for National Security Affairs (Komer) to President Johnson[1]

Washington, February 16, 1966, 11:30 a.m.

Saudi Visitor. Here is yet another plea that you receive an Arab special emissary.[2] King Faisal wants to send his brother Prince Sultan, we think to talk about Yemen. What probably triggered this is the pending visit of Anwar Sadat, the No. 3 Egyptian, which Faisal fears is a play to get us to back the UAR.

We keep trying to get these clients to realize that a letter will do the trick just as well and no need to send a dignitary to present it. But kings and emperors do these things differently.

So State urgently recommends that you agree to see him. It would only take 15 minutes, and Faisal is a very good friend. However, we'd tell Faisal not to worry about the Egyptian or to embarrass us by sneaking his man in first.

R. W. Komer[3]

Approve

Work out some other way[4]

---

[1] Source: Johnson Library, National Security File, Country File, Saudi Arabia, Memos, Vol. I, 12/63–4/67. Secret.

[2] In telegram 691 from Jidda, February 16, Eilts reported that Deputy Foreign Minister Omar Saqqaf had informed him that the King wanted to send his brother, Prince Sultan, to Washington with a special message from him to President Johnson, and had asked if the President could see Sultan either February 21 or 22. The Ambassador had responded that the President's schedule was always very full, but that he would immediately send the King's request to the Department. Saqqaf said he did not know the nature of the message, but suspected it would have to do with the Yemen situation. (National Archives and Records Administration, RG 59, Central Files 1964–66, POL 7 SAUD)

[3] McGeorge Bundy initialed below Komer's signature.

[4] Johnson added a third option by hand: "I may not be here. Call me—L."

259.   Telegram From the Consulate General in Saudi Arabia to the Department of State[1]

Dhahran, February 20, 1966, 1454Z.

235. From Ambassador Eilts. Contel 234.[2]

1. After trade mission had withdrawn, King and I had lengthy, two-hour private discussion attended only by Saqqaf. I first conveyed substance Deptel 470 to Jidda[3] that President will receive Prince Sultan noon February 21. King expressed real pleasure and outlined background Sultan's mission as follows:

2. As I knew, King had long been worried about growing Communist threat in Middle East area. Admittedly this threat still largely latent, but something should be done nip it in time before situation degenerates into open conflict as it has in Southeast Asia. He had therefore decided send his brother, Sultan, even though he could ill afford to spare him, in order to convey to the President his deep personal concern and his belief that the USG and SAG cooperate to meet the threat.

3. In first instance, the King spoke of the large number of Soviet and ChiCom technicians in the area. He reiterated his often expressed belief that the UAR is providing a protective screen for Soviet influence to gain foothold and spread. He did not think Nasser is a Communist, but he noted Nasser is ambitious and sometimes allows his ambition to further Communist purposes.

4. It not only foreign Communists, the King continued, but also steady growth of "local" Communists that worry him. Such indigenous Communists have already been identified in South Arabia, the Persian Gulf, Iraq, the UAR, Syria, and elsewhere (he did not mention Saudi Arabia). Here again their strength is still limited, but unless they are nipped now, their capability will steadily grow until they are able to subvert Western interests in the Middle East as well as governments friendly to the West. The King said he hoped Sultan would be able to explain his concern to the President and obtain some reading on how the USG views the problem and what might be done about it.

5. I again reminded Faysal that there is no government which has been consistently anti-Communist as the USG. I observed that greater part of his eloquent disquisition could have been made by an American

---

[1] Source: National Archives and Records Administration, RG 59, Central Files 1964–66, POL 15–1 SAUD. Secret; Immediate; Exdis. Repeated to Jidda, London, and Cairo.

[2] Dated February 20. (Ibid., POL 23–7 NEAR E)

[3] Dated February 19. (Ibid., POL 7 SAUD)

official. Said I found this encouraging since it again underscored our community of interest in this as in so many other matters. I had in all frankness to tell him, however, that USG does not at present share his view that the UAR is for all practical purposes Communist. We may be worried about UAR tolerance of Soviet and ChiCom presence in various parts of the Middle East, including Yemen, but have had no real evidence to justify suggestion that the UAR deliberately furthering Commie objectives. I hoped we could agree that this was an area where we might have to continue to disagree, but that it not be allowed obscure our very real identity of interest in guarding against Communist subversion. I also hoped it might be possible explore in the future ways in which our two governments could cooperate in combating the incipient Communist threat.

6. King reiterated his belief that UAR is for all practical purposes Communist. Referring to UAR national charter, he claimed it reads like Marxist Communist Manifesto. Entire UAR economy, education, etc. is socialist which King equated with communism. I suggested that while UAR economy might be operated on socialist basis, this was still a far cry from political communism. As far as I aware, UAR has shown no tendency to be any more subservient to Moscow than to anyone else. King disagreed. Nasser and Moscow, he contended, are working together more and more. He professed be puzzled why USG seemed to ignore fact that Nasser and Egyptians largely responsible for introducing Soviet and ChiCom presences into Middle East.

7. King then assured me Sultan's mission intended present Faysal's anxiety about Communist threat in general terms rather than in specific Yemeni terms. I said I thought Sultan's meeting with President and other top level USG officials in Washington could be helpful to SAG in clarifying USG's assessment of the Communist threat. I reiterated to King that he would never find USG blind to dangers of communism, although USG may differ on some aspects of problem. In this context, I cautioned King not to accept exaggerated estimates of numbers or activities of Soviets or ChiComs in various parts of Middle East without first carefully checking facts. It neither in his nor our interests to try to tackle problem on basis grossly exaggerated figures. Soviet and ChiCom activities in Middle East and particularly Red Sea area may indeed be reaching point where they require closer surveillance, but they have also to be kept in perspective in terms of magnitude and numbers and the intentions of the governments of the area.

8. King reiterated SAG wants USG help to combat Communist threat and expressed strong hope that Sultan's mission will be successful. In answer my query if Sultan carrying any specific ideas or suggestions, King was vague. I rather suspect about best he may come up with will be do something about Yemeni situation. I hope, however,

that we may be able to make some proposal to him calling for joint USG–SAG analysis of Communist threat in Middle East area and ways and means coping with it.

Eilts

---

260.   Memorandum of Conversation[1]

Washington, February 21, 1966, 12:06–12:26 p.m.

SUBJECT

>   Special message from King Faisal concerning Communist activity in the Middle East

PARTICIPANTS

>   The President
>   Mr. Robert Komer, White House
>   Mr. George C. Moore, NEA/NE
>   Mr. Isa Sabbagh, USIA

>   Prince Sultan ibn Abdul Aziz, Saudi Arabian Minister of Defense
>   Ambassador al-Sowayel, Saudi Ambassador to U.S.
>   Ambassador Jamil Baroody, Saudi Ambassador to U.N.

The Prince expressed King Faisal's high respect for the President and said that the King had sent him, on His Majesty's behalf, to express his views on certain problems and to present a sealed letter.

The President opened the letter and Mr. Sabbagh translated it verbally as follows (full translation attached):[2] We appreciate the great efforts you are making for the cause of peace in the world and for opposing the tide of Communism which threatens the future of the entire free world. The United States has shouldered specific responsibilities to stem this tide in Asia and Africa through its economic assistance to raise the standard of living of the various countries concerned. This is done to enable those countries to fight Communism, just as we fight it on the basis of our religion, and you fight against it as a doctrine. Communism in the Middle East aims at setting up bases in that area to advance the aims of a broad plan of world domination. In view of

---

[1] Source: Johnson Library, National Security File, Country File, Saudi Arabia, Memos, Vol. I, 12/63–4/67. Secret. Drafted by Moore. The meeting was held at the White House. The time and place of the meeting are taken from the President's Daily Diary. (Ibid.)

[2] Not attached; see Document 262.

the cordial ties of traditional friendship between our two countries, I would like to exchange views with you concerning our joint efforts to halt the Communist advance. I have sent my brother to convey to you the details of these views. He has my fullest confidence.

The President said he would give the letter careful study.

The Prince said that His Majesty had wanted to come in person but that various circumstances, which he would subsequently explain, had prevented him from having this pleasure, which he would greatly look forward to at a future date. The Prince continued that a great danger was posed in the Middle East by intrigues hatched by the Communists to give them a foothold in the area. The Arabian Peninsula was particularly threatened at this time. Saudi Arabia strongly opposed Communism because of its religious principles. Thus, Faisal had sent him (the Prince) to explain certain concepts.

The Prince continued that the Arabian Peninsula had never felt the closeness of the Communist presence until the outbreak of the Yemen conflict brought it sharply to focus as an immediate danger. In the King's view, the Communists seem to be using Nasser as an implement to carry out their aims in the area.

Last year the Government found several Communist cells in Saudi Arabia and took vigorous steps to eliminate them. However, this has not dispelled Saudi fears, in view of the strong Communist desire to establish bases in the Middle East. The King hoped the U.S. would help Saudi Arabia in its attempts to thwart these efforts.

The President said he would be glad to have the Secretary of State and Mr. Komer review the subject with the Prince and further study what the Saudis had in mind. He understood that the Prince was seeing Secretary Rusk today or tomorrow; the Secretary would be able to discuss the subject in detail.

The Prince responded that he appreciated this reasonable suggestion. He added the assurances that King Faisal continued to adhere to the sensible policies with respect to Yemen which the President had in the past suggested; and that the King would continue to exert his efforts to eradicate the Communist problem in Yemen.

261. Memorandum From the President's Deputy Special Assistant for National Security Affairs (Komer) to President Johnson[1]

Washington, February 21, 1966, 4:30 p.m.

I'll be giving Prince Sultan a sympathetic ear for an hour or so Tuesday. He'll see Rusk, McNamara, and others too.

What the Saudis would really like is US backing if they resume the war in Yemen. We can't go this far—it would put us right back in the middle between the UAR and Saudis. But we'll all give the Saudis a sympathetic hearing—and gently try to dissuade them from doing anything foolish. To this end, I'd like to say the following sympathetic non-things on your behalf.

1. You greatly appreciate Feisal's sending Prince Sultan here to discuss these matters directly.
2. You have ordered a prompt and careful re-examination of risk of Communist takeover in Yemen.
3. You will reply to King Feisal's letter shortly.[2]
4. You want to send your warmest regards to his brother King Feisal and to reassure him of our continuing deep interest in the progress and integrity of Saudi Arabia—you feel as strongly on this as all of your predecessors since FDR met Ibn Saud in 1944 on the destroyer in the Red Sea.[3]

R. W. Komer

Approve[4]

Just Listen

---

[1] Source: Johnson Library, National Security File, Country File, Saudi Arabia, Memos, Vol. I, 12/63–4/67. Secret.

[2] For the text of Faisal's letter and Johnson's response, see Document 262.

[3] President Roosevelt's meeting with King Ibn Saud was in February 1945. A memorandum of conversation recording the meeting is in Foreign Relations, 1945, vol. VIII, The Near East and Africa, pp. 2–3.

[4] This option is checked.

262. Telegram From the Department of State to the Embassy in Saudi Arabia[1]

Washington, February 26, 1966, 2:22 p.m.

484. 1. Following texts letters exchanged President and King. Following FYI only. Noforn.

2. Letter from Faisal dated Feb 16, delivered by Prince Sultan to President Feb 21:

"Your Excellency:

"I have the greatest esteem for the efforts which you have undertaken in order to establish world peace and your firm stand in the face of the Communist current which is affecting the future of the free world and its destiny.

"The United States has borne the responsibility of stopping the Communist advance in the countries of Asia and Africa. It has done this by extending a helpful hand to the various states and by participating in economic development and raising the standard of living in the countries which stand against the Communist current which we combat on religious grounds and which you combat for doctrinaire reasons. Our aims are the same in this matter. It is my belief that the Communist elements in the Middle Eastern area regard it as only a part of the broad scale Communist plan for establishing bases for itself in the various parts of the world in order to spread out therefrom to carry out its aims and to realize its intentions.

"In view of the many ties and the traditional friendship which bind our two countries, I take the liberty of exchanging views with Your Excellency in order to coordinate our joint efforts aiming at putting an end to the spread of Communism in the world as a first step toward eliminating it.

"For this reason I have deemed it useful to send His Highness my brother Amir Sultan ibn Abdul Aziz bearing a special letter from me to Your Excellency. He will also give you a detailed explanation of the situation as I see it. He enjoys my confidence in all matters he will discuss with you.

"I take this opportunity to express to Your Excellency my high esteem and to wish Your Excellency good health and happiness, and for the people of the United States increased prosperity and progress.

---

[1] Source: National Archives and Records Administration, RG 59, Central Files 1964–66, POL 23–7 NEAR E. Secret; Limdis. Drafted by Moore on February 25, cleared by Komer and Symmes, and approved by Davies.

Your friend, Faisal"

3. Letter from President dated Feb 24,[2] given Saudi Emb Feb 25 for Prince Sultan to deliver to King:

"Your Majesty:

"I was glad to receive in Washington your distinguished brother, His Royal Highness Prince Sultan ibn Abdul Aziz. In meetings with me and members of my Cabinet[3] and my personal staff he most ably and eloquently explained your views. I thank you for sending him and for the personal message from you which he delivered.

"I share your concern that international Communism and Soviet and Chinese imperialism not extend their sway over free peoples. An abiding principle of our policy in the Near East, as elsewhere in the world, has been to insure that the peoples and governments have an alternative to Communism in support of their own efforts to develop in freedom. We have had this principle in mind with regard to the situation in Yemen. Accordingly, Your Majesty, we would welcome the opportunity to share our analysis of the present and potential threat of Communism in the Near East. After we have further studied your views, as presented by Prince Sultan, I will request Ambassador Eilts to discuss this subject in detail with you.

"With respect to the other aspects of our talks with Prince Sultan, we feel that the Jidda Agreement negotiated between Your Majesty and President Nasser represented an act of statesmanship which still affords the best approach for peaceful resolution of the Yemen conflict and hope that a way can be found to move toward peace on this basis despite certain difficulties which have arisen. Since we fully share your view that renewal of hostilities in Yemen would be inimical to the best interests of all concerned, would seriously threaten the stability of the area, and provide further opportunity for Communist exploitation, I hope and pray that every effort will be made to avert this dangerous situation.

"His Royal Highness Prince Sultan has kindly offered to deliver this letter to you. With it he also brings my warm personal greetings

---

[2] In a February 24 memorandum to the President, Komer wrote: "State strongly urges that we give Prince Sultan a presidential letter to take back to his brother King Faisal. Since these Saudis are staunch friends, and we can't give them the answer they want—that we'll back them against Nasser in Yemen—a warm non-letter makes sense. State has carefully drafted it to skirt the prickly Yemen issue, but gently plug for a statesmanlike political compromise. Recommend your *signature*, so we can get it to Sultan in New York." (Johnson Library, National Security File, Special Head of State Correspondence File, Saudi Arabia, King Faisal Correspondence, Vol. I)

[3] See Document 389.

and my prayers for your continued good health, and the prosperity and peace of the people of Saudi Arabia.

Your friend, Lyndon B. Johnson."

Rusk

---

263. **Action Memorandum From the Assistant Secretary of State for Near Eastern and South Asian Affairs (Hare) to Secretary of State Rusk**[1]

Washington, March 17, 1966.

SUBJECT

Provision of Fighter Aircraft to Saudi Arabia

Discussion:

1. In my memorandum of March 12 (Tab B)[2] I apprised you of a note received from the British Embassy on that day informing us of the U.K. decision to provide Saudi Arabia with certain fighter aircraft to be manned by British pilots, and of their subsequent readiness, if required, to move in an RAF squadron of Lightning supersonic interceptors for a short period.[3] They noted that the possibility of military operations could not be ruled out and sought our assurance on an urgent basis that the United States would come to the aid of Saudi Arabia if that country were attacked.

2. We understand from Embassy Jidda that the Saudis are apparently satisfied with the offer to supply a limited number of fighter

---

[1] Source: National Archives and Records Administration, RG 59, Central Files 1964–66, DEF 12–5 SAUD. Secret; Limit Distribution. Drafted by Moore and Korn; cleared by Director of the Office of British Commonwealth and Northern European Affairs J. Harold Shullaw, Meyers, Colonel Byrd, and Symmes.

[2] None of the tabs is attached. A copy of Hare's March 12 memorandum to the Secretary is ibid. In it, Hare states that the British offer was in response to a request from Sultan, and that, according to the British, the decision was an effort to ensure successful conclusion of the arrangement to sell Lightning MK IIIs under the US/UK Joint Air Defense Proposal.

[3] Telegram 520 to Jidda, March 12, reported that when in London recently Sultan had requested that the U.K. Government supply an RAF fighter squadron to fly under Saudi colors if fighting resumed in Yemen. In response to a discouraging reply, Sultan asked that the United Kingdom supply Lightning aircraft urgently, even without crews, and strongly hinted that conclusion of the previously negotiated Lightning sale depended on U.K. readiness to comply. (Ibid., DEF 1–4 SAUD)

aircraft and civilian pilots at an early date and that the provision of an RAF squadron no longer seems required.

3. We have also learned from London (telegram at Tab C)[4] that British decisions to assist the Saudis and to query us concerning our intentions of honoring our commitment to the Saudis were made by the Cabinet. Foreign Office experts tend to feel it is unrealistic to expect a clear reply from us regarding our commitment since so many hypothetical factors are involved. We therefore anticipate the British Embassy will not press us on this matter. Nonetheless, the Ministers have not rescinded their request for a response from us, and in the circumstances we believe it desirable to reply to the original letter.

4. There is attached (Tab A) a proposed response to the British[5] expressing our concern over the effects of introducing RAF units into Saudi Arabia at this time or the employment of British subjects to fly Saudi aircraft which might be engaged in combat operations, and stating that our commitment to the Saudis does not extend to protecting them in hostilities arising from their provocatory actions.

Recommendations:

1. That you sign the attached letter to the British Ambassador.

and if:

2. Ambassador Dean raises this subject during his call on you at 3 p.m. March 17 that you respond along the lines of the attached letter.

---

[4] Telegram 4324 from London, March 14, is ibid.
[5] See Document 264.

264. Telegram From the Department of State to the Embassy in Saudi Arabia[1]

Washington, March 22, 1966, 2:14 p.m.

548. Re Deptel 520.[2] Following is summary Secretary's March 17 letter to British Ambassador in reply UK démarche March 12 (text being pouched):

1. USG shares UK desire that UK/US air defense sales Saudi Arabia be carried out without change.

2. However sending squadron RAF aircraft to Saudi Arabia under present circumstances would have seriously disturbing effect on Saudi-UAR negotiations regarding Yemen. Could be disservice to SAG since would invite hostile propaganda attacks by UAR and others. Introduction RAF units or employment British subjects to fly Saudi aircraft in combat operations would not be in US, UK or Saudi interest.

3. US would naturally be most concerned should Saudi integrity be threatened. However, US commitment is of strictly limited nature. Has been made clear to Faisal it does not extend to providing military cover for Saudi operations in support of hostilities in Yemen or to any Saudi actions of provocative nature.

4. We hope report Prince Sultan's apparent satisfaction at UK offer supply limited number Lightning MKI and Hunter MK6 aircraft at early date is indication that Saudis will not press for RAF units or put forward other request which could disturb current delicate balance in Near East.

Rusk

---

[1] Source: National Archives and Records Administration, RG 59, Central Files 1964–66, DEF 12–5 SAUD. Secret; Priority; Limdis. Drafted by Korn; cleared by Symmes, Judd, Colonel Byrd, and Meyers; and approved by Davies. Repeated to London, Cairo, Taiz, and CINCSTRIKE.

[2] See footnote 3, Document 263.

265. Telegram From the Consulate General in Saudi Arabia to the Department of State[1]

Dhahran, April 23, 1966, 1805Z.

297. From Ambassador: Meeting With Sultan re Hawks.

1. Had two and half hour meeting with MODA Prince Sultan today in Riyadh. UK Ambassador Man, with whom I flew to Riyadh, met with Sultan just before me since he required take early afternoon plane back to Jidda be present at Queen's birthday reception. Able have only brief snatch of conversation with Man when he came out looking very distressed. Told me Sultan in bad humor and had insisted he must have operational Thunderbird battery in five weeks and specifically made this a condition for signing of BAC contract.

2. I then saw Sultan who was most affable although at times became quite excited. I first recalled his urgent request of several weeks ago for loan or sale Hawk battery and accelerated naval visits and mentioned in passing USS *Thomas* visits to Yenbo and Jidda had been success. While we had had to tell him no Hawk battery available on off-the-shelf basis due US military's operational requirements elsewhere, we had continued look at how we might help as next best thing. In this context, US had now authorized Raytheon indicate availability one Hawk battery, capable of split deployment, in October, about six months' time. Said we aware his request to Brit's for Thunderbirds and, as I was sure he understood in matter involving joint US–UK air defense package, had been consulted by Brits who had indicated availability two Thunderbird batteries in four to six months' time, i.e. about same time as battery of Hawks now available. Added I wished him clearly understand that October delivery of Hawk battery was USG's response to his request to it and not to Raytheon's request be allowed schedule earlier deliveries. It being made at some sacrifice US military commitment, but we hoped it would satisfy his immediate requirements. In this connection, I noted his frequently expressed desire for standardization in Saudi army and undesirability moving his SAMs systems which will only cause problems in training, logistics maintenance, etc. Stressed Hawk and Thunderbirds not interchangeable. I also reiterated USG estimate UAR will not attack Saudi Arabia unless there provocation and noted that current Kuwaiti mediation effort appeared be of interest to Egyptians as well as Saudis and, hopefully, makes entire problem of early establishment SAMs capability slightly less urgent than it seemed to be several weeks ago. Noted

---

[1] Source: National Archives and Records Administration, RG 59, Central Files 1964–66, DEF 12–5 SAUD. Secret; Immediate. Repeated to Jidda, London, CINCSTRIKE, and CHUSMTM. Passed to White House and USIA.

Hawk battery would have additional advantage of being in context contract SAG presently negotiating with Raytheon and should obviate need spending on SAMs additional monies which might better be used elsewhere.

3. Sultan replied by again relating SAG's concern over UAR intentions. Recalled he had first gone to his "best-friends", USG and only after they unable help had he approached Brits. Some of UAR talk might be mere sabre rattling, but he under pressure from his officers provide early SAMs capability protect coastal region between Jizan and Jidda and also Riyadh. He agreed SAG desire is standardize if at all possible and said he would prefer Hawks if first battery for Jidda be made available in five weeks and second battery for Riyadh by October. Claimed Brits told him Thunderbird battery could be available in seven weeks. When I commented dummy missiles not likely be of much use to him, he said had insisted to Brits they must be operational missiles. I said knew of HMG instruction which expressed hope SAG would find advance delivery schedule for Hawks agreeable. He acknowledged this had been done by Man, but insisted BAC representative (Edwards, who was in outer office) had yesterday assured him operational Thunderbird battery could be available in seven weeks. He had therefore let it be known to Brit Ambassador Man that signing of BAC contact conditioned on early availability operational Thunderbird battery. (He said this with broad smile as if to indicate this likely be helpful spur to get Brits respond positively.) He reiterated that if USG could provide Hawk battery in five weeks, he would much prefer Hawks. He appreciated effort make Hawk battery available in October, but asked if USG could in meantime guarantee safety of Jizan area. He felt there 80 per cent chance Egyptians would not attack Jidda, but Jizan perhaps yes.

4. I said would pass on his remarks, but I wished make few personal observations. Saudi Arabia's friends in USG have worked hard try to be helpful, but it sometimes very hard when SAG seemed to have almost complete disregard for problems confronting its friends. USG involved in shooting war in Vietnam against Commie enemy who as King had told me equally repugnant to SAG. Understandably this conflict had first priority on allocation our resources. Despite this real effort had been made be responsive SAG's concern. USG could obviously not guarantee there would be no attack on Jizan, but in our view best way avoid such contingency is, as I had told him before, if SAG exercise restraint. Sultan surely aware of US security commitment to SAG which qualified only by need avoid provocation. King and Sultan had assured me SAG has not resumed arms aid to Yemeni royalists. So long as this true I would have thought Sultan would have greater confidence in long established friends than his present remarks seemed

to suggest. There ample evidence UAR aware of US security interest in Saudi Arabia, which I personally believe probably main deterrent thus far rash Egyptian actions.

My remarks took Sultan somewhat aback. After some more comments on his possible security problems next few months, he said wanted amend his earlier request on Hawks.

[5.] He would welcome having Hawk battery delivered by Raytheon in October and appreciates USG's help in making this possible. However, he also wished ask USG consider lending him another Hawk battery to be available in late June or July which might be for training purposes. Such battery would in his view, be effective deterrent to UAR attack and would ease pressure of Saudi officers and Saudi public on SAG for adequate defense capability. If this could be provided, and if no attack on Jizan takes place, he ready drop Thunderbird idea. Meanwhile, pending USG's reply, he will put off Brits. He hoped might be possible let him have answer by end coming week. He again remarked with chuckle Brits working under pressure because of his threat not sign BAC contract unless operational Thunderbirds are made available five weeks. When I said hoped he was not also attempting pressure US this way on Raytheon contract, he quickly assured me he was not.

6. Told him I would report his comments and request, but that I could make no commitments. Would let him have answer soon as possible.

7. *Comment:* Sultan obviously in one of his more difficult moods. He seems to have panicked Brits by threatening withhold BAC contract signing, but I cannot be certain Edwards may not have put him up to this tactic as best way get HMG agree to quick BAC sale of two operational Thunderbird batteries. Although my personal comments shook him somewhat, his amended request to me is really no more than what some of his officers have told us he really wants, namely one battery of SAMs available by July from whatever source.

Unless we can stop Brits from running scared on this one, recommend we explore whether there any way getting Hawk battery here by July or shortly thereafter. Perhaps we could airlift to Jidda one or more sections of such a battery which might cut down transport time and make August delivery date feasible. Alternatively, we might review General Leahy's earlier suggestion deploy Hawk battery to Saudi Arabia for EP–90 days' training purposes pending October delivery first battery actually sold to Saudi Arabia. Would appreciate Dept/DOD's preliminary reaction above proposals soon as possible since, if we willing explore these courses, I may be able conduct holding operation. But we should reckon with BAC pressuring HMG very hard be responsive Sultan's latest request

Note: Since today's SDI flight back to Jidda cancelled, I will not be able return until tomorrow night. Hence, am sending this message to Dhahran through General Leahy with request Dhahran forward immediately to Dept. Other subjects discussed with Sultan will be reported from Jidda following my return.

Allen

266.   Circular Telegram From the Department of State to Certain Posts[1]

Washington, May 2, 1966, 6:31 p.m.

2138. 1. *NY Times* reporter (Finney) at Dept noon press briefing May 2 referred to Nasser's May 1 threat attack Saudi Arabia[2] and asked Dept spokesman if there exists valid agreement pursuant to which USG would come to Saudi assistance should UAR threat materialize.

2. Though no formal press statement being made, Dept replying Finney as follows:

Every U.S. Administration since that of President Truman has indicated its concern over the territorial integrity of Saudi Arabia. While we have no mutual defense treaty with Saudi Arabia or any other Near Eastern state, we remain as President Kennedy declared in his May 8, 1963, press statement, "strongly opposed to the use of force or the threat of force in the Near East".

3. If specifically pressed by Finney regarding form US opposition would take in context Saudi–UAR conflict, Dept spokesman would say that decision in this respect would obviously have to be taken in light of circumstances at the time.

---

[1] Source: National Archives and Records Administration, RG 59, Central Files 1964–66, POL SAUD–UAR. Confidential; Priority. Drafted by Korn and Atherton; cleared by Bruce Buttles (NEA/P), Special Assistant in the Bureau of Public Affairs James B. Freeman, and Officer-in-Charge of Aden, Iraq, Jordan, UAR, and Yemen Affairs in the USIA Office of Near Eastern Affairs Robert T. Curran; and approved by Davies. Sent to Jidda and repeated to Cairo, Athens for Ambassador Hare, Taiz, Beirut, Damascus, Baghdad, Amman, Tel Aviv, Dhahran, CHUSTM Dhahran, CINCSTRIKE, London, Paris, and Moscow.

[2] In his May 1 speech Nasser threatened that, in the event of any Saudi infiltration or aggression against Yemen, the United Arab Republic would not only strike Saudi bases of aggression, but would occupy them.

4. Jidda should inform SAG of Finney query and Dept reply soon-est. Other addresses may use foregoing as appropriate.[3]

Rusk

---

[3] In telegram 1048 from Jidda, May 3, Eilts reported that Saqqaf had asked him how the U.S. Government had reacted to Nasser's May 1 speech. The Ambassador replied that he had no official U.S. reaction, but had given Saqqaf the substance of the Department's expected reply as reported in circular telegram 2138. (National Archives and Records Administration, RG 59, Central Files 1964–66, POL SAUD–UAR) Circular telegram 2164, May 4, reported that the question of U.S. assurances to Saudi Arabia had been raised at the Department's press briefing that day and the Department spokesman had replied along the lines of paragraph 2 of circular telegram 2138. When asked whether Kennedy's October 25, 1962, letter to Faisal contained language which could be construed as a guarantee of Saudi territorial integrity, the spokesman had replied affirmatively. (Ibid.) For text of Kennedy's letter, see *Foreign Relations, 1961–1963*, vol. XVIII, Document 88.

---

267. **Telegram From the Embassy in Saudi Arabia to the Department of State**[1]

Jidda, May 4, 1966, 1247Z.

1056. Ref: Embtels 857[2] and 922.[3]

1. Met with Saqqaf today to complete USG analysis Commie threat in Middle East. In country by country review, covered Iraq, Jordan, Lebanon and Syria. On completion, told Saqqaf that if SAG has specific questions over and above info already provided, we would be pleased try be of help. After thanking me Saqqaf told me he will now prepare overall report of USG analysis based on our several meetings and send it to me for factual accuracy. Thereafter, he will transmit it to King

---

[1] Source: National Archives and Records Administration, RG 59, Central Files 1964–66, POL 23–7 NEAR E. Secret; Limdis.

[2] Dated March 24. (Ibid.)

[3] In telegram 922 from Jidda, April 9, Eilts reported that he met with Saqqaf to continue discussing the U.S. Government analysis of the Communist threat in the Middle East. He had stressed that the most important stage lay ahead: development of programs which the U.S. and Saudi Governments might undertake separately and jointly to counter the threat. (Ibid.)

since he believes growing Commie threat in Middle East is one item King will wish discuss while in US.[4]

2. Saqqaf noted our overall estimate of Commie threat much lower than what he has heard in King's Majlis. He called it more in line with his own estimate than with exaggerated ones which King is receiving. In answer my query where King gets his info, Saqqaf replied somewhat laconically "from the Syrians around him". He mentioned no names. I stressed USG's estimate based on extensive world-wide info and we have great confidence in it.

3. Saqqaf pointed out major point of disagreement between us is whether UAR and Syria are Commie or not. King and others around him have persuaded themselves they are. Claimed he shares USG view that while UAR and Syria walk hand in hand with Commies, neither UAR or Syria are Commie governments.

4. We agreed that after King has seen report Saqqaf and I will meet to discuss what USG and SAG might singly and jointly do to counter growing Commie threat.

Eilts

---

[4] Telegram 678 to Jidda, April 29, stated that the President had approved a state visit for King Faisal June 21–23. (Ibid., POL 7 SAUD)

---

268.   Intelligence Memorandum[1]

No. 0827/66   Washington, May 26, 1966.

SAUDI ARABIAN ARMS PURCHASES

1. During the last few months long-standing US–Saudi Arabian military aid discussions have come to a head. The stepped-up pace of the negotiations has reflected King Faysal's rising concern over the Egyptian threat in Yemen. A good part of Faysal's requests now have been met by combined US and UK efforts. However, Faysal may well refer to these matters when he visits the US beginning on 20 June. The following detailed roundup may prove useful for background on where we stand at the present time.

---

[1] Source: Johnson Library, National Security File, Country File, Saudi Arabia, Memos, Vol. I, 12/63–4/67. Secret; No Foreign Dissem; Background Use Only; CIA Internal Use Only. Prepared in the Directorate of Intelligence of the Central Intelligence Agency.

2. From 1957 to 1965 Saudi Arabia obtained $119.3 million in military assistance from the US; in addition, from 1954 to 1965 it obtained $24.1 million from all other sources, but none from the Communist bloc.

3. For at least two years Saudi Arabia has been dickering with several agents for a military aid package. The make-up of this package has varied, as has the nationality of the agents. The US was always predominant, the other bidders being French, British, Swiss, and German. By last fall the US (Lockheed) had won out over all other bidders.

4. At this point the British approached the US and asked if we would agree to offer a joint defense package with them as a means of offsetting British balance-of-payments problems. We agreed, with the condition that the all-US bid also remain in the competition. In the end, the joint UK-US bid was accepted, and the letter of intent was signed in late December. The joint package contracts were signed on 5 May 1966.

5. Under the joint arrangement, the British were to furnish 40 M3 Lightning supersonic jet fighters with Firestreak air-to-air missiles and 25 Provost jet trainers (British Aircraft Corp.) at about $155 million; a radar system, Type 40, with data-handling equipment (Allied Electrical Industries) at about $70 million; and training, technical operations, and maintenance work (Airwork, Ltd.) at about $76 million. Total British sales are thus about $301 million. The US portion of the package consists of ten batteries of Hawk ground-to-air missiles (Raytheon) at about $100 million.

6. After the first of this year, relations between Saudi Arabia and Egypt became tense, and Saudi Arabia sought immediate interim purchases of air defense weapons. King Faysal told the US ambassador on 20 February[2] that he "understood" the US position vis-à-vis Egypt and would not ask the US for such interim assistance.

7. On 28 March the British stated that Saudi Arabia had purchased six subsonic Hawker Hunter jet fighters and two T4 Lightning trainers, and has requested four additional Lightnings. Airwork, Ltd. was to provide maintenance and civilian pilots for "instructional" purposes. The four extra M2 Lightnings were eventually provided. This contract, in excess of $35 million, was also signed on 5 May 1966, and on 7 May two Hunters landed in Saudi Arabia.

8. In early April we learned that Saudi Arabia was negotiating with Britain for the purchase and delivery of two Thunderbird ground-to-air missile batteries by late June or July, at about $42 million. The US,

---

[2] See Document 259.

attempting to avoid undue Saudi expense and multiplicity of weapons, offered to advance delivery of one Hawk battery to October 1966. Saudi Arabia said it had expected partial early delivery and still wanted delivery by July or at least the loan of a training Hawk battery from July to October. The US said it could not do this.

9. Saudi Arabia has continued to negotiate with the British for Thunderbirds. However, as time passes and an Egyptian attack fails to materialize, the Saudis may have second thoughts about Thunderbirds. The most recent report indicates that the Saudis now feel that two batteries are too expensive and have asked if one battery could be had at a reduced price. The British will probably try to oblige.

269. Memorandum From the President's Special Assistant (Rostow) to President Johnson[1]

Washington, May 30, 1966, 10 a.m.

SUBJECT

Raising the Level of State Visits: The Upcoming Case of King Faisal

We have been exploring ways of stepping up the dignity of state visits and will have more to report later.

But Faisal's visit in late June is not a good place to start, as the attached State Department memorandum[2] makes clear.

1. A big show for Faisal might intensify his struggle with Cairo and worsen our own poor relations with Nasser who has already read certain of our moves as an effort to back Faisal in a bloc against him.

2. Faisal has made good progress in developing his country since 1962; but it is still a mighty backward place. Moreover, he has not worked for a Yemen settlement with 100% good faith.

---

[1] Source: Johnson Library, National Security File, Country File, Saudi Arabia, King Faisal Trip to U.S., 6/21/66–7/1/66. Confidential.

[2] Attached is an unsigned, undated memorandum on the subject "Downplaying Faisal's Visit."

I recommend, therefore, that we play this visit correctly, and save any Billy Rose upgrading for a less ambiguous guest.

Walt

Play it correct and low key[3]
Upgrade
See me

_____

[3] None of the options is checked.

_____

270. Background Paper Prepared in the Department of State[1]

KFS/B–2   Washington, June 7, 1966.

VISIT OF KING FAISAL OF SAUDI ARABIA
June 21–23, 1966

U.S. POLICY ASSURANCES ON SAUDI SECURITY

The U.S. interest in the territorial integrity of Saudi Arabia *was first expressed by President Truman and has been reaffirmed in varying terms and intent by each succeeding Administration. Behind these assurances lie our considerable economic and political interests in Saudi Arabia,* which are to a significant degree bound up with the fate of the Saudi dynasty, in the absence of a suitable alternative.

Saudis Fear Israeli Expansion

From 1948 until the late 1950s Saudi Arabia's main security concern was of attack by Israel. The Saudis sought and were given assurances that we would oppose any expansion by Israel at the expense of its neighbors. It was with Israel in mind that *President Truman wrote King Abdul Aziz on October 31, 1950 that aggression or the threat of aggression against Saudi Arabia would be a matter of "immediate concern" to the United States.* These assurances were reiterated by President Eisenhower in letters to King

_____

[1] Source: Johnson Library, National Security File, Country File, Saudi Arabia, Faisal Visit Briefing Book, 6/21–27/66. Secret. Drafted by Korn and cleared by Symmes, Davies, and Hare.

Saud. President Eisenhower again told Crown Prince Faisal, in a meeting at the White House in September 1957, that we would "allow no aggression on the part of Israel against the Arab nations".

U.A.R. Becomes Major Potential Adversary

Saudi concern shifted from Israel to the U.A.R. in the late 1950s and particularly following the Yemeni revolution in September 1962. *We responded to Saudi requests for support in the event of U.A.R. attack with public and secret statements designed:* a) to *encourage the Saudi Government along the path of internal reform and development;* b) to *secure Saudi disengagement from Yemen;* and c) to *deter U.A.R. aggression on Saudi Arabia* and *prevent the Saudis from taking actions which might provoke U.A.R. attack.* In the public domain are:

—President Kennedy's October 25, 1962 letter to Faisal stating that in pursuit of his modernization program the Crown Prince "may be assured of full United States support for Saudi Arabia's integity".

—Secretary Rusk's March 8, 1963 press conference statement that "we are very much interested in the security of our friends in Jordan and Saudi Arabia".

—President Kennedy's May 8, 1963 press conference declaration of U.S. opposition to the threat of force or use of force in the Near East.

—A Department press spokesman statement on August 4, 1965 that "we have clearly indicated our support for the maintenance of Saudi Arabia's integrity".

Almost all the many letters exchanged secretly by Presidents Kennedy and Johnson with Faisal contain some mention of our interest in or concern for Saudi integrity.

What Do U.S. Assurances Mean?

To the Saudis

The Saudis place considerable reliance on our assurances. There may be *some tendency within the Saudi Government to overestimate the extent to which the U.S. is actually committed to defend Saudi Arabia,* and perhaps at times even a temptation to use our assurances to provoke a showdown with the U.A.R. *Faisal however seems to understand the dangers of such a course and appears to realize that he cannot count on an unconditional U.S.G. security commitment.*

To the United States

Our security assurances to the Saudis represent *a continuing expression of U.S. policy designed to protect our interests in the Arabian Peninsula. Our statements have been vaguely worded* and, with the exception of an offer (which was accepted) of the presence in Saudi Arabia for eight months of a squadron of U.S.A.F. interceptors, "Operation Hard Surface", in the framework of the Bunker Yemen disengagement negotiations, have never included specific promises of military action. Our assurances to the Saudis have never been submitted for Congressional consideration. *We have on frequent occasions in past years (most recently in Ambassador Eilts' conversation with the King on March 23)[2] sought to impress upon the Saudis that our assurances cannot be used as a shield behind which they could stimulate hostilities in Yemen or provoke an attack by U.A.R. forces there.*

The intent of our assurances was defined most clearly in an *instruction from President Kennedy to Special Ambassador Bunker* in March 1963 stating that we *"should seek to avoid giving the impression of an open-ended U.S. commitment to defend Saudi Arabia* under all or any circumstances, or for an indefinite long term period. . . . *we want to avoid future misunderstandings and to preserve U.S. freedom of action"*.

---

[2] See footnote 2, Document 396.

---

271.   Memorandum for the Record[1]

Washington, June 8, 1966, 2:30 p.m.

SUBJECT

Near East South Asia IRG Meeting
Wednesday, 8 June 1966 at 2:30 PM

1. There were two items on the agenda for discussion—Policy for Faysal Visit and Soviet-Syrian Relations.

Faysal Visit

2. The policy paper prepared by State[2] called for the USG to use Faysal's visit to emphasize (a) the dangers of polarization in the NE, (b) the importance the USG attaches to maintaining our ties of mutual interest with all the States of the Near East, including Egypt, (c) that Faysal should not contribute to polarization, (d) that we assess the Communist penetration of the NE to be less than Faysal's assessment

---

[1] Source: Central Intelligence Agency, Job 80–R01580R, DCI Executive Registry Files, Box 1, IRG. Secret. Drafted by James H. Critchfield, Chief of the CIA's Near East and South Asia Division on June 9.

[2] "Proposed Strategy for Visit of King Faisal," June 1. (National Archives and Records Administration, RG 59, S/S Visit Files: Lot 67 D 587, Visit of King Faisal of Saudi Arabia, June 21–23, 1966, Vol. II, Memcons, Admin and Sub. Misc.)

(Faysal has declined a State briefing), (e) that he should be flexible on Yemen and avoid provocation and (f) that Saudi assistance to formation of as broadly based a regime as possible in South Arabia is desirable but that such assistance should be through multi-national organization to avoid impression that it is directed against any specific group.

3. Macomber (AID) took general exception to the paper. He urged State not use the term "progressive" in describing the radical Arab regimes, implying a desirable alternative to "conservative" regimes such as Faysal's monarchy. Also, he disagreed with the principle that we should be impartial in our relations with friendly governments and those hostile to us. He thought the paper was negative, could have been written in 1962 and did not provide the basis for a positive approach.

4. Critchfield (CIA) said that in the brief 24 hours available, preliminary staffing of the paper in the Agency had produced a consensus that this approach, used by the President, would "go over like a lead balloon". The implication throughout the paper was that Faysal was somehow a principal contributor to the tension of the area, had an exaggerated view of the Communist threat to the area, was being inflexible and obstructive vis-à-vis the Yemen, would be well advised to concentrate on internal economic and political reforms to keep the Communist wolf away from the door and that Faysal did not understand that polarization in the area, to which he was contributing by his policies, was dangerous. There was no suggestion that there are principles, objectives and interests in the area to which the USG attaches importance which could be identified quite separately from the issue of the radical revolutionary regimes versus the conservative regimes. We could and should identify the dilemma we face in the current polarization of forces in the area and the dangers to world peace and our interests that we could see in a deepening of the division of the two camps. We could acknowledge that there was a Soviet-sponsored threat to the area, and that the USSR was giving support to the revolutionary regimes for its own pragmatic purposes. We could point out that, whatever Faysal's original intent, the Soviet Union had elected to distort the Islamic solidarity issue to suit its own purposes and anxieties and, for better or worse, it had become an element in the growing schism between Cairo and Jidda. Having shared our dilemma with Faysal, we could invite him to give us the benefit of his assessment and guidance. We could state that we had attempted to preserve a relationship with every Arab country—regardless of the character of its regime—as a means of preserving peace in the area. We were reluctant to abandon this policy, regardless of its weaknesses, in the absence of an alternative that accommodated our basic interest of peace and some stability in the Near East.

5. (USIA) said that the visit basically offered USIA problems since the mere fact of Faysal's visit would provide an issue for the hostile

press in foreign areas. USIA found it a difficult subject to deal with in its output. The fact that the President has ordered the full protocol treatment of a State visit made the USIA task even more difficult. Rodger Davies thought the treatment given Faysal would not be obviously that much better. The White House (Saunders) was quite firm that the form of the visit had been decided.

6. Hoopes (Defense/ISA) was interested in how the visit came about. Davies said that the invitation was extended by Ambassador Eilts when he presented his credentials. The idea dated back to the summer of 1965 when the Faysal–Nasser rapprochement and the Jidda Agreement provided the right atmosphere for a Faysal visit. Hoopes' main interest was that the visit not result in any strengthening of our public commitment to "preserve the integrity of Saudi Arabia".

7. Macomber thought that it was counterproductive to argue with Faysal about the character of the Communist threat. Hoopes recalled that Critchfield had indicated at the Iran session that our intelligence on the Communist threat was weak. Critchfield corrected this recollection; the statement was that our information on the threat to the immediate areas of Kuzistan and the areas of the Upper Gulf which the Shah felt were threatened was weak. For the area as a whole, we felt reasonably confident. Hoopes thought it would be good if the IRG were better informed. Symmes said that a statement of the threat had been sent out to Jidda for Faysal which represented the views of the community. Critchfield said that this was not the case; the version sent to Jidda was uncoordinated, incomplete and not entirely accurate. However, Faysal had been exposed to a good deal of briefing over a period of time and probably had a reasonably accurate understanding of the Communist threat. What he lacked was current intelligence on the Soviet presence, leaving him vulnerable to false reports on Soviet military activities in the area. The secretary of the IRG recalled the language of the NSAM setting it up required that the IRG keep the President informed of impending crisis.[3] Critchfield said that it was the Agency's intent to have appropriate intelligence memoranda on potentially critical problems which would be brought to the attention of the IRG— related where possible to items on the agenda. Scheduling of the agenda well in advance would be helpful for this reason.

---

[3] NSAM 341, "Direction, Coordination, and Supervision of Interdepartmental Activities Overseas," March 2, 1966, set up the Senior Interdepartmental Group (SIG) and the Interdepartmental Regional Groups (IRGs). (National Archives and Records Administration, RG 59, NSAM Files: Lot 72 D 316, NSAM 341) NSAM 341 is scheduled to be printed in Foreign Relations, 1964–1968, vol. XXXIII. The first IRG/NEA meeting took place on March 17, 1966.

8. Rodger Davies recalled that Nasser had apparently been pre-pared to leave the Yemen when he went to Jidda. I questioned that there was any real evidence of this. Nasser was pressed at the time, was probably reassessing his chances for ultimate success and might have been simply seeking a break in an increasingly rough game. We had no reliable evidence that he had reached a decision to disengage—all the UAR statements to U.S. officials notwithstanding. Turning back from the Yemen would be a very tough decision for Nasser and not one that he would be likely to come to until convinced that chances of success were nil. Davies also noted that we should keep in mind that the single greatest overseas investment that U.S. business holds anywhere in the world is in Saudi Arabia and that it is an important factor in our gold balance. He thought we should distinguish in our thinking of what we would really do if Saudi Arabia were threatened and what we indicated to Faysal, the Arabs and the world we would do. He personally thought we would end up intervening in a real crunch. This was obviously not something to convey to Faysal in the upcoming visit. Mr. Davies seemed to have unanimous support in the views he expressed on this point.

9. At the end of the discussion on Faysal's visit it was agreed that, with AID and CIA dissenting, the paper would have to be re-drafted. The White House was also associated with this requirement—less on substance than on the point that it contained little usable for the Presi-dent. State invited the CIA representative to provide any comment or ideas in writing.

[Here follows discussion of Syria and the Soviet Union.]

---

272. Memorandum From the President's Special Assistant (Rostow) to President Johnson[1]

Washington, June 18, 1966.

King Faisal's visit will depend—more than usual—as much on the tone you set as on the substance. He is apprehensive—largely because he has been fed a variety of myths about our motives in the Middle East. For example, he has never completely believed that we have not made Nasser our "chosen instrument" there. He is suspicious of Zionist

---

[1] Source: Johnson Library, National Security File, Country File, Saudi Arabia, King Faisal Trip to U.S., 6/21/66–7/1/66. Secret.

influence in Washington. These are not chip-on-the-shoulder views—probably because he knows better. But they are deep-seated enough to make him uneasy about what he will find here.

There is also real substance to talk about. Your first look may make you feel it will be hard to hit it off with this bearded, robed desert king. But Faisal is a lot more modern than he looks. Under those robes, you will find a sharp mind and deep devotion to educational and social progress. I am sure he will warm to your sincerity and frankness. I would be surprised if you do not find him a man you can like and draw out.

It is worth the effort. Our largest single overseas private enterprise is the Arabian-American Oil Company's $1.2 billion investment in Saudi Arabia. In addition, all our other Middle East interests—from blocking Communism to preserving Israel—depend heavily on gradual modernization under moderate leaders like Faisal who oppose the revolutionary methods of Nasser and Communism.

Nasser's propaganda machine will have a field day with this visit. After two years of relative harmony, the Middle East is splitting again into two camps centering around Faisal and Nasser. The Egyptians see moderate leaders like Faisal, the Shah and King Hussein as "imperialist tools" and accuse us of conspiring with them and the Israelis to undercut him.

So State recommends we keep the public part of this visit low-key. While I agree that we do not want to throw our arms around Faisal, I feel the tone of State's briefing papers is too negative. We have invited Faisal for good reason, and we realize that some Arabs will give us a hard time for it. But within reason, we want to treat him like the friend he is.

Faisal comes with two worries. First, he believes the Communists are intensifying their push into the Middle East. Second, he sees evidence of this in his rising tension with Nasser over Yemen. He sees Nasser as Moscow's pawn. He has never understood why we have tried to get close to Nasser and feels we overlook the real menace. He is uncertain that we will stick by him in a showdown.

I will give you a brief talking paper Monday night, but here in outline are the points we want to get across:

1. We share his opposition to Communism.

—We do not define Communism as broadly as he does. We do not see Nasser, for instance, as a Communist. But we know full well how Moscow can exploit Nasser's kind of local nationalism.

—We think the main Soviet objective is to split the Middle East into two camps—the revolutionaries (UAR, Syria, Iraq) and the evolutionaries (Iran, Jordan, Saudi Arabia, Lebanon).

—One way to undercut this Soviet strategy is to keep Moscow from posing as the only champion of modernization by proving that the methods of the moderate regimes offer better hope of effective social and economic development.

—Another way is for Faisal and Nasser to patch up their dispute over Yemen. Although we sympathize with Faisal's grievances about Nasser's behavior there, we think it would be worth considerable effort and maybe even a little loss of face to reach agreement and undercut the Soviet effort to divide the Middle East.

2. We have not made Nasser our chosen instrument.

—You can be quite candid in admitting we are disappointed with our effort to get closer to Nasser. Faisal has always felt we judged Nasser wrong, and he will appreciate your not being defensive.

—However, we still feel our objective is right. We still do not see how slamming the door on Nasser—much as we sometimes feel like it—would help anybody but the Communists. We doubt cutting off aid completely would change his policies.

3. We will not let Nasser swallow up Saudi Arabia.

—We will continue to "support Saudi integrity." We have often restated that purposely vague assurance, but Faisal may want to pin us down. He would like to know whether we will send troops or aircraft. We cannot give that kind of assurance (a) because we do not want to give him a blank check for triggering a showdown with Nasser and (b) Vietnam makes us more wary than ever of involvement. The best way to answer him is to repeat our general assurance but to say that it is impossible to say exactly what our response would be. It is in his interest as well as ours that we retain maximum flexibility and not commit ourselves to jump in militarily when other tools might be as effective—and better both our interests.

4. We hope Faisal will play a constructive role in South Arabia and the Persian Gulf as the British retrench there.

—That area is the prime candidate in the Middle East for the kind of sub-regional cooperation we are pushing in Africa and the Far East. The British pull-back will leave a vacuum which Nasser is trying to fill. There is room for cooperation among the moderates—Saudi Arabia, Kuwait, Iran and even Pakistan and Afghanistan—to help financially and politically as the shaky new nation emerges in South Arabia.

—If you could capture Faisal's imagination on steps he might take to promote these developments, this could be the top accomplishment of the visit and a big step forward for our Mid-East policy.

I recommend you take a good look at the strategy and talking points papers in the smaller State Department briefing book (Tabs A

1 and 2).[2] If you have time to look at a few of the background papers (under Tab II in the larger book), I would start with the rundown of our security assurances (Tab C) since you may have to discuss this in some detail. Beyond that, it might be worth glancing over Tabs A (Saudi objectives in the Middle East), B (Yemen) and D (South Arabia and the Persian Gulf).

Walt

---

[2] None of the tabs is attached. Briefing material for Faisal's visit is ibid., King Faisal Visit, Briefing Book, 6/21–23/66; and National Archives and Records Administration, RG 59, S/S Visit Files: Lot 67 D 587, Visit of King Faisal of Saudi Arabia, June 21–23 1966—Volume I—Briefing Book.

---

273. Memorandum From the President's Special Assistant (Rostow) to President Johnson[1]

Washington, June 20, 1966.

Our goal with Faisal is to persuade him not to break with Nasser and split the Middle East. We also want him to feel you are his friend without thinking he has a blank check to pick a fight with Nasser. Suggested talking points:

1. You would like to outline your views on the Middle East and then hear his. You will be frank and hope he will.

—You assume Nasser is Faisal's most immediate concern. You have problems with him too. You are discouraged with trying to get closer to him, but you want to keep the door open.

—You share his concern over Communist penetration, and you know how Moscow exploits local nationalists like Nasser.

—Our goal is to keep Moscow from splitting the Middle East into radical and moderate camps. Slamming the door on Nasser would help only the Soviets. A Yemen settlement would thwart them.

—Economic and social progress is the best check on Communism. You are making our own reform programs the base for a worldwide attack on poverty, illiteracy and disease.

---

[1] Source: Johnson Library, National Security File, Country File, Saudi Arabia, King Faisal Trip to U.S., 6/21/66–7/1/66. Secret.

2. You would like to hear Faisal's views—on the widening Middle East split, Yemen mediation, and social and economic progress.

3. You would like to hear how Faisal plans to fill the gap the British will leave in South Arabia and the Persian Gulf. (I hope you can get Faisal excited about cooperating with his moderate neighbors, either through the World Bank, the UN, or an Arab Development Bank. You can cite how we push the Asian Development Bank, Mekong Valley development, the Ganges–Brahmaputra River projects.)

4. You want to reiterate our support for Saudi Arabia's integrity. If he asks exactly what we would do if Nasser attacked him, your best answer is that we do not think either of us should be committed in advance to any specific course. But we will not let Saudia Arabia get swallowed up.

For flavor, I am attaching a short summary by our Ambassador, Herman Eilts. You might also want to review State's fuller talking points.

Walt

Attachment[2]

KING FAISAL'S VISIT

The King is reserved and modest, but proud. A devout Muslim and conservative, he has much natural wisdom. He believes in evolutionary progress. He is sensitive with an occasional streak of stubbornness. He is pro-American and a great admirer of the President. He has long wanted to meet the President. Now, with the moment at hand, he is slightly apprehensive that he may be rebuffed or be unable adequately to convey his concerns. These are the growth of Communism in the Near East, Nasser (whom he equates with Communism), Yemen, and the security of Saudi Arabia. We share a considerable community of interest on all these points, but do not entirely see them as the King does.

In talks with him, it may be helpful to know that he reacts positively to warmth, candor and confidence. A good way to get him to unbend is to ask his views. He usually gives them frankly, even in dissent. Where he agrees, his word is his bond.

Somewhat greater flexibility on Yemen would be helpful on his part. The President may wish to ask him about the Kuwaiti mediation effort, and impress on him our interest in an honorable settlement for all. He has moved ahead on internal reform, but should be encouraged

---

[2] Confidential.

to do more. The subject is sensitive. A good approach would be for the President to tell him of our own efforts in areas of social reform, such as civil rights, etc., then casually ask him how his program is progressing. He, too, has his domestic obstacles, and sympathetic appreciation of them will show our continued interest and spur him on.

Above all, the King is a good friend. He would like to be reassured that his friendship is appreciated. Our ability to continue to influence him constructively in the months ahead, including in matters where we reap tangible benefits, will depend in part on whether we can make him feel that, despite certain differences of emphasis, our friendship for Saudi Arabia is real, that we appreciate his problems and that he can count on us to give appropriate help to try to solve them.

274.   Memorandum From the President's Special Assistant (Rostow) to President Johnson[1]

Washington, June 21, 1966, 4:45 p.m.

Secretary Rusk has briefed me on his discussion with King Faisal.[2] We jointly recommend that you raise the following points with him at 5:00 this afternoon:

1. Ask for his appraisal of the forces at work in the Arab world.

2. Suggest that we both have an interest in the return of Egyptian troops to Egypt; and that it is a common interest that we achieve a Yemen settlement.

3. Indicate your knowledge and support for Secretary Rusk's suggestion at lunch that we discreetly keep in closer touch about develop-

---

[1] Source: Johnson Library, National Security File, Country File, Saudi Arabia, King Faisal Trip to U.S., 6/21/66–7/1/66. Confidential.

[2] Rusk telephoned Rostow at 4:30 p.m. and said that Read had told him that the President wanted to know what to say to Faisal at 5 p.m. He said he told the King at lunch that the President would want to get Faisal's own analysis of what was going on in the Arab world. Rusk recommended that Johnson suggest that their two governments discreetly keep in closer touch on this as well as on major questions outside the Arab world. The Secretary agreed with Rostow's suggestion that the President ask for the King's ideas about working with the South Arab Federation. Rusk also thought that Johnson should emphasize U.S. interest in having a Yemen settlement which would return Egyptian troops to Egypt. (Record of Telephone Conversation Between Rusk and Rostow, June 21, 4:30 p.m.; National Archives and Records Administration, RG 59, S/S Files: Lot 72 D 192, Files of Secretary of State Dean Rusk, 1961–1969, Rusk Telcons)

ments in the Arab world—and, indeed, elsewhere where we have common interests.

4. Indicate your knowledge that he has been carrying out important economic and social development programs in Saudi Arabia; ask him to discuss these; and encourage him—perhaps with some talk of your own Great Society plans in the U.S.

5. Ask the King to discuss the future of the South Arabian Federation; the possibilities of constructive work in that region in collaboration with the World Bank and other international institutions.[3]

Walt

---

[3] A handwritten notation in the President's handwriting reads: "W—I followed this point by point—all 3 papers attached. L" Two of the papers referred to are printed as Document 273 and its attachment.

---

275. Memorandum of Conversation[1]

Washington, June 21, 1966, 5:05–6:25 p.m.

SUBJECT

President's Meeting with King Faisal

PARTICIPANTS

The President
King Faisal

Mr. Isa Sabbagh, Interpreter

Before going into the Cabinet Room the President and King Faisal had spent one hour and 20 minutes in a personal chat and an exchange of views of a general nature at first with increasing emphasis on social reforms in the United States of America and in Saudi Arabia.

The President opened the personal tete-a-tete by once again assuring His Majesty of a warm welcome as an honored guest, adding how much the President had been looking forward to this visit. The President

---

[1] Source: Johnson Library, National Security File, Country File, Saudi Arabia, Memos, Vol. I, 12/63–4/67. Secret; Exdis. Drafted by Sabbagh on June 22. The time of the meeting is from the President's Daily Diary. (Ibid.) The memorandum is Part I of II. Part II is Document 276.

emphasized how heads of states had their own problems, some of which were very similar in nature and he went on to enumerate what he subsequently crystallized as "my bill of rights". These, if the President has the longevity of life and the tenure of office and the good health, would assure every citizen of equality, of a decent home, of a decently paying job, of fresh air and water, adequate education to the highest levels possible, medical facilities from infancy to old age, and the beautification of the United States of America. At this point, he invited the King to enumerate what he had been doing for his own people, given his acknowledged wisdom and determination. The King described at length the increasing efforts exerted during the last 3 or 4 years in the field of education with the result that in Saudi Arabia a school is being built every 3 days or less. Here, the President expressed his appreciation of this "wonderful work" particularly since "I started my working career as a school teacher". As to the problems that Saudi Arabia faced and is still facing in this field, the greatest of these is the shortage of teachers who, of necessity, have had to be imported from neighboring Arab countries. Problem number two was the need to revamp the educational curriculum for elementary schools because the original education plans were drawn up with the assistance of non-Saudi experts, mostly Arabs from other parts of the world, particularly Egypt. At this point the King said, "we have discovered that some of the subjects suggested according to those old plans included matters which would fashion the tender young minds of our youth in a way prejudicial to the interests of our country. In view of these two problems, we have come to the decision that it would be unwise to our future generations to place these easily molded minds in the hands of strangers who do not share with us the genuine interests of our country". Turning to the field of medicine, the King mentioned that his Government was doing its utmost about providing hospitals and clinics even in the remote parts of the vast Kingdom of Saudi Arabia but that there too Saudi Arabia faced the problem of the inadequacy of doctors, nurses, and professional people in their field. Here also, Saudi Arabia has had to resort to the importation of doctors and specialists from neighboring Arab countries, because it would be impossible to import a large number of non-Arabic speaking doctors without providing each doctor with a translator between him and the patient. King Faisal admitted, however, that all that has been done is not, in his opinion, enough. He was also looking forward to the time when they could feel that they have achieved self-sufficiency in this regard. As to the pace of progress and development, King Faisal thought that the pace was consonant with the smooth evolutionary development of that country given its built-in peculiarities and checks. In fact, some well wishers who had re-visited the country recently after the passage of some ten years expressed their opinion that progress was moving at too fast a rate.

King Faisal said he did not think so but in any case there was no room for comparison between what the country now had and what it did have or, in fact, did not have ten years ago.

At this point President Johnson expressed his deep admiration for what King Faisal and his Government were trying to do for their own people because, to the President, social advancement and meaningful development were the only reply to the Communist ambitions of infiltrating and gaining control of a country. The President noted that he was very pleased that he and King Faisal shared the same views as to the Communist dangers to the area and the tactics the Soviets resort to.

The President told King Faisal "Even before you say it, Your Majesty, I would like you to know that we are aware of Nasser's tactics, ambitions, propaganda and designs". "I have my problems with the fellow." In elaborating, the President expressed his opinion that the U.S. considers it in the long run prudent to leave room for a dialogue with somebody like Nasser because once you slam the door in his face you might heave him into the lap of the other side and, as a consequence, you might have another Dominican Republic develop in that area. As His Majesty is aware, the President said, we had to go in with armed forces into the Dominican Republic to put a stop to the Communist takeover of that country and to make sure that free elections were carried out. On the question of the U.S. relations with the U.A.R. the President mentioned that we seek reasonable relations and maintenance of our limited influence with President Nasser. The President said we are actively reviewing the extent of our future assistance, taking into consideration various actions of Nasser including his attitude toward and relations with Saudi Arabia.

With respect to the area generally, the President admired King Faisal's restraint in the face of all the intrigues, accusations and propaganda campaigns levelled at him and his country. Coupled with this admiration the President urged the King to keep up this attitude of self-restraint because "we both want to see a peaceful settlement of the Yemeni problem". At this point the President referred with appreciation to the King's restraint in replying to questions posed by a BBC representative lately.

The President expressed his knowledge of and support for Secretary Rusk's suggestions at lunch that "we keep discreetly in closer touch about developments in the Arab world and indeed elsewhere where we have common interests". The President said that he felt sure he could benefit and learn a lot from such a wise man as King Faisal whose word "my people tell me" is his bond. The President would therefore welcome the views of His Majesty on the following points (the President said maybe the King would wish to take a little time to ponder these points, therefore he did not have to answer right away). The points were:

1. Appraisal of the forces at work in the Arab world.
2. The possibility of helping such areas as South Arabia and the Gulf in developing peacefully. The President wondered what His Majesty felt about the possibility of Saudi Arabia cooperating with moderate elements and governments in the area for the purpose of helping those two regions such as the establishment of an Arab development body.
3. The areas where redoubled efforts could be exerted for increasing development in Saudi Arabia.

As to the President's remarks about Faisal's wisdom and the President's ability to learn therefrom, Faisal replied that such a generous remark indicated modesty which in this case was synonymous with greatness. It staggered Faisal's imagination to think that such a person, one human being, could really find time, energy and dedication to the solution of tremendous problems internally, to the carrying out of such terrific advances in the fields of civil rights and social development as the President had crystallized in his "bill of rights" and at the same time to keep up the healthy American leadership of the Free World, because "whether you like it or not" you are the leader of the Free World. To Faisal it was a sign of God's blessings that he granted the United States of America such an intelligent, determined and dedicated President. Heaven forbid that His Majesty should seek to malign the memory of the late President Kennedy, whom he admired greatly, but looking back on those days His Majesty felt that during President Kennedy's latter period in office and because of President Kennedy's bigness of heart and goodness of nature, there were a few areas where, if unchecked, social reforms might have tended to slip into the abyss of increasing socialism which in itself would in the long run almost automatically develop into Communism. His Majesty noted that since President Johnson's tenure of office that tendency had been firmly checked.

The President wished to take the opportunity to reassure His Majesty of our previous expressions of help and support for the wise programs that he and his Government were carrying out. He wanted His Majesty to know that he, the President, appreciates what King Faisal and his Government were trying to do for their own people and that such efforts were bound to forestall any Communist ambitions in the direction of Saudi Arabia. The President wished to reiterate the assurances given by the U.S. Government to Faisal of our concern for the safety, integrity and well being of your country and yourself. "As long as I am in office" said President Johnson, "I will not permit your country to be gobbled up by the Communists. And now, after I have had the pleasure of meeting you and knowing you, and especially after this rewarding conversation, I would like you to know that I appreciate Your Majesty personally much more this evening than I did even this morning, and I would like you to know that I wouldn't permit you to be gobbled up either." The President emphasized that it was precisely because we took this kind of attitude towards our loyal friends that he related with sorrow, that since World War II America has sacrificed something like 170,000 casualties in our fight for freedom and liberty and the betterment of mankind and in standing up to the Communist encroachments. King Faisal reacted almost emotionally to this by saying "We deeply appreciate the sacrifices and the efforts expended by the U.S. in behalf of humanity."

Reverting to the subject of President Nasser, President Johnson said that he doubted very much if Nasser, in the absence of any provocation on the part of Saudi Arabia, either directly or by helping the royalists in the Yemen to commit any provocative act, "would dare attack Saudi Arabia".

The President said we have sold arms and equipment to Israel as we have sold similar material to Jordan and to Saudi Arabia, but it was not the policy of the U.S. to be the major supplier of arms to that area.

Since time was running fast the President suggested that King Faisal and he join "our colleagues" in the Cabinet Room where, if he thought possible, King Faisal would give his observations on the President's remarks.

---

276. Memorandum of Conversation[1]

Washington, June 21, 1966, 6:25–7:10 p.m.

SUBJECT

President's Meeting with King Faisal

PARTICIPANTS

King Faisal	The President
Prince Sultan	Mr. Walt W. Rostow
Dr. Rashad Pharaon	Ambassador Raymond A. Hare, NEA
Ambassador Ibrahim al-Sowayel	Ambassador Hermann F. Eilts
	Mr. George C. Moore, NEA:NE
	Mr. Howard Wriggins
	Mr. Isa Sabbagh (Interpreter)

---

[1] Source: Johnson Library, National Security File, Country File, Saudi Arabia, Memos, Vol. I, 12/63–4/67, Secret. Drafted by Moore on June 22. The time of the meeting is from the President's Daily Diary. (Ibid.) The memorandum is Part II of II.

(The President and the King rejoined the others in the Cabinet Room after over one hour's private session.)[2]

The President said they had had a delightful talk together. They spoke of what they both hope to do in the development field, of US interest in the integrity of Saudi Arabia, of events in Southeast Asia, of possibilities for use of the World Bank, of their mutual problems with Communism and their attempts to build up their own systems as bulwarks. He said he did not know when he had so enjoyed such a visit and that he and the King had established real rapport. He said the King had expressed his views during the first part of their talk and that he had spoken during the second part. The King now had some comments to make.

The King emphasized that he was fully aware of US good intentions, good will and willingness to support Saudi Arabia. He was so reassured of the US position that he felt he should apologize for having even thought there was a need to mention it.

The King's major question related to our joint concern over the danger Communism presented for the whole world and for the Near Eastern area, which in turn could have great ramifications for the rest of the world. Communism was like a germ which, if allowed to grow, ultimately destroyed the whole body. South East Asia was a good example. It was his personal view that if firm decisions had been taken there in 1954 the present sacrifices of the flower of American youth would not be necessary. He recalled that many people, even in the US, used to refer to Mao Tse-Tung as merely a reformer.

The President interjected that we still had deluded people, the Near East had no monopoly on these.

The King continued that where situations, such as Vietnam, develop as the result of views of such naive, misguided people, it was lamentable when firm measures were not taken sufficiently early. While he does not favor the principle of military intervention, the US position is clear. It must intervene in all areas to stop the growth of such problems in their infancy.

The President said that the 170,000 US casualties since World War II were proof of our interest in stopping such developments.

The King, after expressing deep appreciation for and sympathy with the US for such sacrifices in US lives, urged that we not allow such a development as Vietnam to be re-enacted in the Near East. The King referred to the President's remarks about the Saudis cooperating with others in the area to stem the tide of Communism and stated that

---

[2] See Document 275.

such was precisely his aim, whether on the Arab or Islamic level, to make people conscious of this danger.

The King, referring to the President's comments concerning US–UAR relations, asked that he not be considered as advocating that we not aid any needy people, Arab or otherwise. It was up to the US, on the basis of its expertise, to determine how far it wished to go with such aid. He was sure that the US was aware of the need to help countries which were still young, to enable them to resist the still-immature Communist danger and eradicate it. He emphasized that he was not referring to Saudi Arabia. The question of US assistance in various ways to Saudi Arabia is one strictly between the two of us. He found it lamentable to hear so many people saying, "If you want help from the US, the quickest way is to speak out against the US." This of course was not true, but was frequently said and influenced a great majority of the people.

The King referred to the President's remarks on Yemen concerning the avoidance of provocative acts such as helping the royalists. He wished strongly to reassure the President that since signature of the Jidda Agreement he had done nothing provocative. It was the other side which had continued provocative actions. (The President interjected to say that he had spoken of the climate for a settlement being enhanced by the King's continued restraint, not resuming arms shipments and such.) The King continued that he wished only to show that there were only two possible alternatives for the resumption of hostilities: 1) consistent acts from the other side could finally force the royalists to retaliate; or 2) the other side could finally take action on the pretext that they had been provoked. In these cases, what could Saudi Arabia do to establish the fact that it had not undertaken any provocative acts? Saudi Arabia will continue to exercise self-restraint, but developments might force it to take action. This was not to imply that he had anything else in mind, however, other than continued restraint. However, every day that passed with the Egyptians still in Yemen meant one further day of Communist gains there.

The King, referring to South Arabia, said the British had made a major mistake by failing to develop, during the years of their presence, a cadre of competent local personnel who could run the country. Now they had suddenly announced their intent to withdraw completely in two years, including the military base, which left the country with little capability for government. The King was most happy to see independence come to these Arabs, but he feared that chaotic conditions would result. He hoped that the US and the UK could prevent this chaos. All he asked was that the US act to keep external aggression from the area.

Concerning aid to South Arabia, Saudi Arabia was ready to help, just as it was helping the Trucial Shaikhdom of the Gulf, but it did not wish to interfere in local affairs or try to dominate them. The President's idea of an international aid entity of some type was a good one, but he feared that if it were an Arab Development Bank or some such body it would be dominated by the UAR, Syria or such countries for their own purposes.

Mr. Rostow suggested that to begin development in South Arabia and the Gulf, concentration should be placed on smaller, specific projects. The King agreed that local aid of limited scope was a sound approach.

The King agreed in principle with Mr. Rostow's view that, for US aid, the first requirement was that the Governments and the peoples in a given area should request our help. But the King said that as a result of the avalanche of propaganda from the UAR, Syria and similar sources, there were few people willing to ask the West for aid. They were afraid for their own lives. Current terrorism in South Arabia, instigated by the UAR from Yemen, resulted in this. The methods pursued by the UAR and Syria there were clearly Communist methods. Not that the people involved are convinced Communists—they are believers in nothing—but their actions serve only to enhance the spread of Communism.

The President noted the recent success of peoples in asserting their rights in the Dominican Republic, Indonesia, and Ghana, and then suggested, because of the late hour, that they continue their talks at dinner and on the following day.

---

277. Memorandum of Conversation[1]

Washington, June 22, 1966, 10 a.m.

SUBJECT

Secretary's Meeting with King Faisal

PARTICIPANTS

The Secretary
King Faisal

Mr. Isa Sabbagh, Interpreter

---

[1] Source: National Archives and Records Administration, RG 59, Central Files 1964–66, POL 7 SAUD. Secret. Drafted by Sabbagh and approved in S on July 14. The meeting was held at Blair House. The time and place of the meeting are from Rusk's Appointment Book. (Johnson Library) The memorandum is Part II of II.

Before leaving, Secretary Rusk asked His Majesty for a private audience which would take up only a few minutes. The interpreter was asked by the Secretary to remain.

The Secretary then told His Majesty that, as His Majesty was doubtless aware, our PL 480 Agreement with the U.A.R. would come to an end by the end of this month. It was, however, unfortunate that the decision the U.S. Government has come to with respect to that agreement coincided with His Majesty's visit to the United States. The decision is that the U.S. Government was not going to renew the PL 480 Agreement with regard to wheat for Egypt, but that instead we would be inviting the Egyptians if they so wished to buy what they want, like anybody else, according to the C.C.C. system (Commodity Credit Corporation).

The Secretary expressed his belief that the reaction in Cairo will be a violent one and that not only the U.S. but also King Faisal himself would in all likelihood be subjected to a fresh tirade of propaganda from Cairo. The Secretary wished His Majesty to know of this development straight from him (the Secretary) rather than via Cairo's propaganda.

The King said that he had been so hardened to the Cairo propaganda outbursts and attacks against him personally that he was not worried. "They could not possibly say worse things than they have already said." Faisal added, "As I said yesterday, as a person and a human being I do find it very difficult to actually suggest that people be deprived of food in any way, but I also added that it was up to the giver to determine in his own best interests what to give, to whom, how much and when." King Faisal expressed the opinion that, of course, this kind of human sentiment President Nasser would not understand nor would he believe it as having been expressed by Faisal. On the contrary, Nasser was most likely to accuse Faisal of all sorts of wicked designs which he, according to Nasser, would suggest to the U.S. to carry out.

[1 paragraph (8 lines of source text) not declassified]

278. Memorandum of Conversation[1]

Washington, June 22, 1966, 5:05–5:35 p.m.

SUBJECT

President's Second Meeting with King Faisal

PARTICIPANTS

King Faisal	The President
Prince Sultan	Mr. Walt W. Rostow
Dr. Rashad Pharaon	Ambassador Raymond A. Hare, NEA
Ambassador Ibrahim al-Sowayel	Ambassador Hermann F. Eilts
	Mr. Howard Wriggins
	Mr. George C. Moore, NEA:NE
	Mr. Isa Sabbagh (Interpreter)

The President first ascertained that the King approved the draft joint communiqué. Commenting that he had another meeting scheduled at 5:30, he asked if the King had any further matters to take up.

The King said that they had closed their meeting of the previous day while discussing cooperation between certain states in the area. He wished to affirm that this cooperation was possible if it were confined to states whose policies were consonant with those we all share. A disturbing element was that many people in those countries with whom we would wish to cooperate were filled with fear of propaganda and other activities of the states who wish to make trouble. However, these presently fearful states would be greatly encouraged if they clearly understood that the U.S. was willing to ward off threats against them, to assist them and give them guidance. Unfortunately, those who fish in troubled waters have spread the impression that the U.S. is not ready to oppose evil actions, but turns a blind eye to certain events, for example, those in Zanzibar and Yemen.

The King, continuing his comments on Yemen, said all the leaders on the republican side are Leftists, whether or not they have specific ties to Moscow or Peking. He recalled that in 1962, after the Yemen revolution, he had pleaded with his friends in the U.S. Government not to rush into recognition, but to give events time to clarify and show the real tendencies of the new government.

The King said he did not advocate that the U.S. use armed forces to interfere in the domestic affairs of other states but recommended

---

[1] Source: Johnson Library, National Security File, Country File, Saudi Arabia, Memos, Vol. I, 12/63–4/67. Secret. Drafted by Moore on June 24 and approved by Walt Rostow on July 11. The meeting was held in the Cabinet Room at the White House. The time and place of the meeting are from the President's Daily Diary. (Ibid.)

that a clear indication that the U.S. supported the endeavors of like-minded states would stiffen the spines of those people who were presently fearful.

Saying that he was loathe to bring up the subject, the King noted that those who opposed our principles continued to argue that U.S. assistance to Israel was proof of American opposition to all Arabs. This greatly hindered the actions of states which in fact would desire to cooperate with America. Even the King had undergone tremendous abuse in the area for his continuing with his visit to the U.S. in the face of the recent U.S. announcement of its arms sale to Israel. It was claimed that this proved that the King and the U.S. were conspiring against Arab interests. However, the King ignored these attacks since he knew they were intended only to prevent his coming.

The President responded that it was the price of leadership that not all the 120 nations with whom we have relations are friendly with us. He agreed that it was not easy for us to use our influence wisely in every part of the world. He assured the King that we would carefully consider his comments and admonitions, and added that we cannot encourage other countries too much without being ready to back up our encouragement with military force if necessary. We were not able to use our military power everywhere in the world, but the 170,000 U.S. casualties since the end of World War II were proof that we used our power to oppose aggression, both direct and indirect. Just as President Kennedy had assured the King, we would continue to support those leaders who shared with us the principles of freedom, of working for the betterment of their own people, and of peaceful settlement of disputes. He told the King that our concern for the integrity of his country was no less now than had been expressed to him by President Kennedy.

Concerning arms sales, the President said that we supplied certain countries when we did not want them to obtain arms from other sources (e.g. Jordan, Israel) and when we thought that, by helping them with their own defense, we could ultimately keep them from fighting.

Concerning our relations with the U.A.R., we hope to maintain some influence with Nasser, particularly with respect to what he does in Yemen.

In conclusion, the President said that it is not easy to use our influence wisely in every part of the world. As you say, we cannot use our military power everywhere—we should not. We do, however, work on certain principles: (1) oppose aggression, direct and indirect; (b) support those who work for their people; (c) try to encourage peaceful settlement of disputes. It is not always easy to decide how to apply these principles. But His Majesty can be assured his views will be taken into account—and we are his friend—because he stands for all three principles. He thought the King's visit had been most useful and he was greatly appreciative that the King had come so far to see us. The King responded with an expression of gratitude for all the warmth of the President's welcome and the meeting of minds which they had.

While saying goodbye on the way to the car, the King asked the President to visit Saudi Arabia, saying it would be the realization of a precious dream which he had. The President responded that he would most like to make such a visit when the pressures of his work allowed.

---

279. Circular Telegram From the Department of State to Certain Posts[1]

Washington, June 27, 1966, 5:07 p.m.

2550. 1. Following FYI represents Dept preliminary assessment Faisal visit:

a. Visit successful and US aims in inviting Faisal generally accomplished:

(1) Faisal and President established good personal rapport which will be asset in our future relations. Faisal's public statements revealed extraordinary impact President made on him (e.g. at press luncheon June 22 King said hours he had spent with President were among most precious of his life).

(2) We apparently successful in focusing Faisal's attention on importance vigorous pursuit his economic and social development programs. Subject was dealt with extensively in meetings with President. King devoted bulk his remarks at press luncheon to development efforts.

(3) USG welcomed King warmly and was successful in reassuring him of our continued friendship and concern for safety his country. In

---

[1] Source: National Archives and Records Administration, RG 59, Central Files 1964–66, POL 7 SAUD. Confidential. Drafted by Korn and Moore; cleared by Bruce Buttles (NEA/P), Symmes, James B. Freeman (P), Thomas J. Hirchfield (EUR/GER), Country Director for Italy, Austria, and Switzerland Wells Stabler, Robert E. Barbour (EUR/WE), Country Director for Northern African Affairs John F. Root, Judd, Country Director for Turkey John M. Howison, and Officer in Charge of Political Affairs in EUR's Office of Atlantic Political and Military Affairs Edward G. Boehm; and approved by Deputy Assistant Secretary of State for Near Eastern and South Asian Affairs William J. Handley. Sent to Amman, Beirut, Damascus, Cairo, Taiz, Aden, Kuwait, Baghdad, Tel Aviv, Khartoum, Tripoli, Tunis, Algiers, Rabat, Ankara, Jidda, Dhahran, Tehran, Paris (also for USRO), Rome, London, Bonn, CINCSTRIKE, USUN, and Mogadiscio.

effort avoid contributing to further polarization of Near East into Soviet and Western-supported blocs, we did not give any new security assurances. Cairo press reaction has been relatively moderate. Close reading of communiqué and US officials' public statements should make clear US does not seek chosen instrument in area.

b. Visit marred somewhat by events stemming from Faisal's extemporaneous press luncheon remarks June 22 that "Jews of the world aid Israel . . . In our situation we consider those who aid our enemy as our enemy." (Press did not find so quotable Faisal's further clarification that he opposed not to Jews but to Zionists.) Remarks were made in response several baited questions on Israel, the Jews and Arab boycott. While unfortunate, statement reflects Arab view and King could not retract or apologize without severe damage to his position in Near East. King not particularly concerned re cancellation Lindsay dinner and Gov Rockefeller's call[2] and is understood be planning remain New York as scheduled until June 30 departure. He has reportedly received hundreds telegrams from Americans apologizing for Mayor's and Governor's actions. End FYI.

2. Addresses may draw on following as appropriate in answering host govt, press or other queries re visit:

a. As reflected in final communiqué, visit afforded opportunity for King and President to become personally acquainted, discuss broad range of world issues and strengthen long-standing cordial relations between two countries.

b. Both President and King were much interested in discussing internal development efforts. We greatly encouraged by progress Saudi Arabia making and King's determination energetically pursue his development program.

c. Question of security guarantees exaggerated by press. USG for many years has had strong interest in security and territorial integrity Saudi Arabia, as expressed by President Kennedy in his Oct 25, 1962 letter to Faisal.[3] (If questioned whether timing of visit does not demonstrate that US taking sides in inter-Arab disputes, you should make clear that visit planned months ago when atmosphere in Near East quite different from present; timing of visit unrelated to area developments.)

d. Re Faisal remarks on Jews and US public reaction, Dept spokesmen stating it not appropriate comment on statements made by

---

[2] In response to the furor over the King's remarks on Jews and Israel during his June 22 press conference in Washington, New York Mayor John Lindsay announced on June 23 that the dinner scheduled in Faisal's honor that evening had been canceled. Later that day New York Governor Nelson Rockefeller canceled his scheduled call on the King.

[3] For text of President Kennedy's letter to Crown Prince Faisal, see *Foreign Relations, 1961–1963*, vol. XVIII, Document 88.

King while he guest of USG. Our differences with Arabs on Israel well known to all sides. It not necessary have identity of views on all issues in order entertain friendly relations. Mayor's dinner and Governor's call were scheduled on their initiatives; decisions to cancel were made by them. No other events on King's New York schedule have been cancelled.

Ball

---

280. Memorandum From the President's Special Assistant (Rostow) to President Johnson[1]

Washington, July 14, 1966.

You will be interested to know that King Faisal since his return to Saudi Arabia has told a number of people that he considered his visit here a "complete success." He has spoken glowingly both publicly and among his own advisers of his meeting with you and reiterated that his main reason for coming was to become personally acquainted. He deeply appreciated our hospitality and easily shrugged off his brush with Mayor Lindsay. Ambassador Eilts reports that the visit boosted the King's spirits and has decidedly enhanced his prestige at home.

One of the most interesting indications that you really got through to him was his explanation to the British Ambassador after his return of your views on civil rights, education and Vietnam. He even took the British to task gently for criticizing any aspect of your Vietnam policy. The King's eagerness and ability to expound at some length on your policies indicates that everything you said registered loud and clear.

The problem now—as always with these visits—is how to capitalize on the momentum we have generated. You have established a rapport with him that will be helpful for some time to come. But there will also be misunderstandings as we urge Faisal to give a little to get Nasser's troops out of Yemen. However, we are already moving ahead on two fronts:

1. We are renewing our efforts to persuade him to give a fair look at Nasser's latest offer on Yemen. We are not overly optimistic that

---

[1] Source: Johnson Library, National Security File, Country File, Saudi Arabia, Memos, Vol. I, 12/63–4/67. Secret.

anything new will come of this, but we do feel the King is in a specially receptive mood as a result of his talks with you and Secretary Rusk.

2. Ambassador Eilts has offered to pick up his discussions with the Saudi Government on how we might continue the exchange of views on Communist penetration in the Mid-East, and the King has jumped at this.[2] Our chief goal is, by working with his people, to bring him to a more realistic view of what Communism is.

Walt

---

[2] In telegram 66 from Jidda, July 7, Eilts reported that he had discussed with Faisal the desirability of closer cooperation in meeting the Communist threat, and had urged that discussions as to what the U.S. Government and the Saudi Arabian Government might do individually and jointly in that sphere be undertaken expeditiously. The King emphatically agreed and instructed Saqqaf to proceed as soon as possible with the talks. (National Archives and Records Administration, RG 59, Central Files 1964–66, POL 7 SAUD)

---

281. Circular Telegram From the Department of State to Certain Posts[1]

Washington, September 1, 1966, 1:30 p.m.

39172. 1. Negotiations between Saudi Arabia MinDef and US Department Defense for purchase by SAG of mobility modernization package designed provide Saudi Armed Forces with modern vehicle fleet concluded with signature of contract August 28 by Saudi DefMin Prince Sultan. US SecDef signature contract anticipated about September 2 at which time Embassy Jidda and SAG will issue joint announcement. FYI only: Implementation of mobility program will extend over approximately five years and will involve some training by US military of Saudi personnel. Cost of program about $120 million. End FYI.

---

[1] Source: National Archives and Records Administration, RG 59, Central Files 1964–66, DEF 19 US–SAUD. Confidential. Drafted by Korn; cleared by Thieberger (OSD/ISA/ILN), Edward A. Padelford (NEA/RA), NEA Public Affairs Adviser Daniel Brown, Symmes, Captain Castillo (DOD/ASA/PA), Quinn, Warren, and Director of the Office of News in the Bureau of Public Affairs Robert J. McCloskey; and approved by Davies. Sent to Amman, Baghdad, Beirut, Damascus, Taiz, Aden, Dhahran, Tel Aviv, Cairo, Kuwait, Tehran, Ankara, Paris, London, Jidda, CINCSTRIKE, and MED DIV ENGRS Livorno.

2. Department/DOD not planning any publicity re contract but will answer queries as follows:

a. Agreement is result of study by Saudi Min of Defense and Aviation and is designed provide Saudi armed forces with fleet of modern military vehicles (mainly trucks) and spare parts together with related workshops, maintenance facilities and other installations required for logistical support.

b. Transaction in line with long-standing US policy of confining sales to Near Eastern countries within limits essential for defense and internal security.

3. If queried re price and other terms contract, we will state that, in deference to friendly government, USG traditionally prefers not discuss details of such agreements.

4. Posts may answer queries along lines paras two and three above.

Rusk

---

282.   Telegram From the Department of State to the Embassy in Saudi Arabia[1]

Washington, December 5, 1966, 6:24 p.m.

96790. Ref: Jidda's 2074.[2] Subject: Mobility Modernization.

1. Realize difficulties faced by Sultan if, as probable, Mobility Modernization purchases include items from boycotted firms. How-

---

[1] Source: National Archives and Records Administration, RG 59, Central Files 1964–66, DEF 19–4 US–SAUD. Confidential. Drafted by Moore and Korn; cleared by Quinn, Sterner, Fredericks, Warren, Colonel Cochran of the Corps of Engineers, Assistant Legal Adviser for Near Eastern and South Asian Affairs Donald A. Wehmeyer, and Thieberger in substance; and approved by Brewer. Repeated to Dhahran, CINCSTRIKE, CHUSMTM Dhahran, and DIV ENGR MED Leghorn Italy.

[2] In telegram 2074 from Jidda, November 29, Eilts reported his conversation with Mansouri, a legal adviser to Prince Sultan who had played a key role in negotiating the Mobility Modernization package. Mansouri had been asked by Sultan to seek the Ambassador's assistance in helping the Saudi Arabian Government to avoid the political stigma arising from purchase of equipment from U.S. firms on the Arab boycott list. Eilts had responded that the U.S. Government too was sensitive to the boycott issue and could not condone or approve it. He stressed that the vehicles were being purchased by the Saudi Arabian Government from the U.S. Government and not directly from U.S. manufacturers. He also emphasized that if the Saudi Government attempted to exclude boycotted firms, delivery schedules would be retarded and prices would rise. (Ibid.) Documentation pertaining to the Arab boycott of Israel is ibid., FT 11–2 ISR–ARAB.

ever, Saudis must realize boycott issue also of sensitivity in US and recent decision on Ford, Coke, RCA could in fact trigger action in next session Congress seriously damaging to broad USG policies in Near East. In face this situation we particularly desire avoid any appearance acceptance boycott decisions which could arise from, for instance, removing Ford nameplates as suggested reftel. (In any event latter action would be only of marginal usefulness since Ford parts, clearly labeled, present in many US-procured military vehicles even though chassis may be product another firm.)

2. Believe your best approach under these circumstances continues lie in emphasizing Mobility Modernization equipment being procured from USG and thus is outside boycott framework. In this regard we note from Amman 1348[3] that Jordan obtained specific Boycott Committee exemption for continued import of Ford military trucks. Similarly Saudis may be able justify their purchases under provisions "public purchase sanctuary" for which there are precedents. (e.g., Various messages sent inter alia to Jidda in spring this year re problem Emb Taiz import Jeep showed Jordan, Syria, UAR and Saudi Arabia all allowed some importation of either Jeeps or Jeep spares for army use.)

3. Dept/DOD will do all possible eliminate publicity on names of suppliers but obviously USG does not have complete control over question publicity.

4. Dept Army has cabled in AMC 48720, Dec 2,[4] list potential suppliers Mobility Modernization package. Suggest if at all possible you avoid giving Mansouri specific names at this time when boycott taking such prominent place in Arab concerns.

Katzenbach

---

[3] Dated December 1. (Ibid.)
[4] Not found.

283.   National Intelligence Estimate[1]

NIE 36.6–66   Washington, December 8, 1966.

THE ROLE OF SAUDI ARABIA

The Problem

To estimate the outlook for Saudi Arabia during the next few years, particularly its role in the Arabian Peninsula.

Conclusions

A. Contention with the UAR dominates Saudi Arabia's foreign affairs. Yemen is currently the principal area of confrontation. Each will continue to support elements in Yemen opposed to the other, but both will be anxious to avoid a renewal of large-scale civil war or a military clash between themselves. Faisal looks to the US to protect him though he recognizes that the US commitment is only in case of unprovoked aggression. (Paras. 1–6)

B. Faisal believes that the UAR is determined to dominate Aden and South Arabia when the British leave in 1968; thus Faisal will continue to help anti-Nasser elements in that area. Faisal also fears that Nasser is aiming to replace UK influence with his own in the Persian Gulf. When the UK leaves, Faisal may try to take over its role as protecting power of Qatar and the Trucial Sheikhdoms, and might even try to annex them if that seemed to be the only way to forestall Nasser's aims. (Paras. 7–11)

C. The prospects are poor for real accommodation between Faisal and Nasser. Each will continue to work against the other, not only on the Arabian Peninsula but in the Arab and Muslim world generally. Though a meeting or pact between Islamic leaders is unlikely, Faisal will continue to promote the idea of Islamic solidarity as a means of countering Nasser's influence. Faisal will recurrently seek support from the US and the West. Nasser will look to the Soviets for help and, in addition, will both blame the US for encouraging Faisal and urge that the US curb him. (Paras. 12–17)

D. Faisal's domestic position is strong. He has the support of the nation's principal political forces and of the military. Mounting oil revenues will bring continued prosperity and economic advance. The

---

[1] Source: Johnson Library, National Security File, NIEs, NIE 36.6, Saudi Arabia. Secret; Controlled Dissem. According to a note on the cover sheet, the estimate was submitted by Helms, and concurred in by the U.S. Intelligence Board on December 8. Paragraph references are to the Discussion portion of the estimate, not here printed.

latter will be inhibited, however, by the shortage of skilled and educated Saudis. As more sectors of society are modernized, discontent with traditional Saudi rule will increase, but this is not likely to become a significant factor in the nation's political life for some time. (Paras. 18–30)

[Here follows the Discussion section of the estimate.]

284. Telegram From the Embassy in Saudi Arabia to the Department of State[1]

Jidda, January 10, 1967, 1314Z.

2684. Subj: USG–SAG Relations.

1. Toward end four-hour session with Dr. Rashad Pharaoun Jan 6 on various matters reported previous telegrams, Rashad made general observation that SAG regrets what it considers USG's apparent reluctance cooperate more closely with SAG on matters of mutual interest. If USG attitude were less standoffish, he professed believe SAG could and would be more responsive assisting in matters of specific interest to USG. When I asked him what he had in mind, he spoke generally of USG's reluctance support SAG in aid to Mali and other African countries; its tepid view Islamic solidarity; its apparent continued reliance on Nasser; its apparent disinterest in Syrian situation; its failure pressure HMG retain its responsibilities in Aden area; its failure recognize Commie threat in Near East in proportions Saudis see it; its policy in Yemen where USG shoring up decrepit, discredited, despotic and puppet government, etc. He added SAG has also had recent reports from Washington and Cairo that USG intends resume concessional food aid to UAR. For SAG, USG policy in NE all rather disheartening.

2. I told him could not agree that USG attitude toward SAG standoffish. USG has been cooperating closely with SAG on many matters of mutual concern and will continue do so. USG's interest in security of Saudi Arabia deep and sincere. I recalled had just reiterated to him USG assurances against unprovoked aggression. Earlier in week I had offered MinInt Prince Fahd six training places for police training in US. These and many other past actions attest to USG interest in and high regard for Saudi Arabia.

---

[1] Source: National Archives and Records Administration, RG 59, Central Files 1967–69, POL SAUD–US. Confidential.

3. As for Islamic solidarity, this by definiton hardly a subject where USG can be directly involved. I acknowledged we sometimes regret Islamic solidarity is yet another factor contributing to current polarization of Arab world and resultant tensions, but noted USG neither disapproves nor approves of concept. As he knew we have [been] accused by UAR and others of instigating Islamic solidarity but, as he also knew, this charge absolutely baseless.

4. As for additional FFF Food for UAR, I called his attention to recent Department press officer statement that UAR request still under study and no decision yet reached. However, two things ought be noted: first, contrary widely-held belief in Saudi circles prior termination PL–480 food to UAR, termination has not forced UAR withdraw its troops from Yemen. On contrary, it seems have strengthened UAR's resolve remain there. Second, termination of food aid to UAR had curtailed still more limited leverage which USG is able use with UAR on area problems, including those of Saudi Arabia. Any such development hardly in USG and SAG's long-term interests. Moreover, UAR had now been able obtain some wheat from USSR.

5. In some cases, as in aid to African states, direct cooperation scarcely in SAG's interest. USG, quite wrongly but as inescapable fact, is unfortunately associated in minds some emergent African states with old colonialist states of UK and France. This not so in case of SAG which in various Muslim areas of Africa appears to have especial appeal. Fact is our respective efforts in Africa and elsewhere complement each other and, as such, are in our mutual interest.

6. As for our Yemen policy, he well aware USG view as expressed personally by Secretary to King during latter's state visit in June that we believe highest priority ought to be given to arranging evacuation UAR troops so that Yemeni people can themselves decide. This had to be done by peaceful means since experience of past four years should have proved conclusively military victory not possible for either side. I also recalled King's only recently applauding to me our determination to stay in YAR, despite all difficulties, in order give Yemenis at least some counterpoise to complete reliance on USSR, ChiCom or UAR aid.

7. Somewhat tepidly Rashad accepted this, but he obviously far from convinced. He still felt USG should consider channeling some of its aid through SAG which he believed might achieve greater impact. I twitted him that SAG beginning learn what USG has been experiencing since World War II, namely it costs money and much money for any state to pursue an active foreign policy. He laughed and ruefully agreed.

8. *Comment:* My impression is that, largely as result its current security frustration, SAG is again in one of its feeling sorry for itself moods. Inevitably whenever in this state of mind, SAG seems to like to believe USG pursuing standoffish policy toward it. SAG also of

course feels we are putting intense pressure on it to continue policy of restraint in Yemen, but are not pushing UAR, Kuwait or anyone else commensurately. Report that new FFF program for UAR again contemplated has doubtless added to SAG's worries. We shall have to continue intensive hand holding operation and seize opportunities where we can feasibly cooperate with SAG if our urgings that SAG continue policy of restraint in Yemen are to be heeded.

Eilts

285. Telegram From the Department of State to the Embassy in Saudi Arabia[1]

Washington, January 16, 1967, 7:06 p.m.

119317. Jidda's 2684.[2]

1. We were surprised Pharaoun's complaints re insufficient USG cooperation with SAG and fully endorse your able responses. In future discussions US/Saudi relations with Pharaoun or other ranking Saudis you may also wish use following points.

2. US diplomacy in Middle East follows principle of developing best bilateral relations possible with each country. Area of mutuality of interests varies from state to state but our aim is work with each state to maximum extent possible in that framework. We have no chosen instrument in Middle East (including UAR and Saudi Arabia).

3. We and Saudis are fortunate to have broad range mutual interests. This includes major USG concern for area tranquility which will permit SAG maximum opportunity develop in atmosphere stability. Area conflict threatens this stability and thus is not in Saudi or US interest. For this reason we have continued strongly urge Saudis exercise restraint in Yemen. We feel any resumption open hostilities there, with potential for spreading to include SAG–UAR, is not in interest any of the parties. Our "pressure" in favor of restraint reflects no intent get Saudi support for strictly US policy, but arises from what has been our understanding of mutual Saudi and US interests. (FYI—We suspect Faisal very much

[1] Source: National Archives and Records Administration, RG 59, Central Files 1967–69, POL SAUD–US. Secret. Drafted by Moore, cleared by Brewer and Bennsky, and approved by Davies. Repeated to Cairo.
[2] Document 284.

aware restraint is in his interests, not only until his defense sites in Najran can be completed but also in longer range. End FYI.)

4. Your remarks on Islamic solidarity (para 3 reftel) were particularly apt. Suggest you continue where suitable indicate that, as non-Muslim, non-area state, we have not in past felt it appropriate comment on Islamic solidarity concepts. However, insofar as movement tends contribute to polarization and friction in Arab World, we question whether Saudi Arabia or any of countries involved really profit from it. What might be useful aim in tranquil times seems hardly have served buttress solidarity concept in current charged atmosphere among key Islamic states. We aware this may not be SAG view but would hope our Saudi friends would not expect us to be less than candid on points where we may differ.

5. We concerned over Russian and Chicom imperialism in Near East no less than are Saudis. However, to extent Communism may have any regional popular appeal, it can be countered successfully in longer term only by efforts to work constructively with peoples concerned to attain their legitimate desires for economic, social and political development. Regional differences clearly hold back such efforts. This is, for example, among worrisome aspects Yemen imbroglio. Such general considerations continue important in USG attitude toward Republican YARG. Our dealings with YARG are designed to keep western presence in Yemen and not vacate field to Communists, originally brought into Yemen under royalists and at particular behest then-Crown Prince Badr.

6. Pharaoun and other Saudis need only recall discussions they participated in last June in Washington to realize extent our concern with future of South Arabia. We have hoped that powers in area would express their pleasure at ending foreign control by themselves offering continued and constructive help to preserve political and economic viability of new nation. We understand SAG has already made such offer and hope that it will continue appropriate help to fledgling SA state.

7. Comments on Pharaoun's views re aid to Mali sent separate tel.

Rusk

286.   **Telegram From the Embassy in Saudi Arabia to the
Department of State**[1]

Jidda, February 20, 1967, 0625Z.

3373. Para 4c Cairo's 4649.[2]

1. From time to time King Faisal has said to me that he needed clear indication USG position in event Saudi Arabia attacked to enable him make adequate contingency arrangements. Prince Sultan has also occasionally stated that if USG unable or unwilling help SAG, Saudis will have to look elsewhere. In making such statements to me, neither King nor Sultan has ever specified turn to Soviets. However, I am told by UK Ambassador that in making similar statements to him, Sultan has once or twice spoken of turning to Soviets if necessary. Both UK Ambassador and I are inclined dismiss this kind of a statement as typical "Sultanism" without great deal of meaning. Sultan has occasionally spoken of UAR urgings Saudis could obtain Soviet arms more cheaply.

2. In recent call on me by Saudi Ambassador in Ankara, he claimed Soviet Ambassador to Turkey has in past two months or so called on him several times to indicate USSR would like to have better relations with SAG. Soviet Ambassador allegedly deplored Saudi anti-Soviet policies and fact that no diplomatic relations exist between two countries. Soviet Ambassador also told Saudi Ambassador that in present circumstance USSR will support UAR as needed. Understand similar approach has been made during past year by Soviet Ambassador in Paris to Saudi Ambassador there. I assume Saudi Ambassadors have reported this kind of nibble to Riyadh, but no suggestion to date Saudis are biting.

3. Faisal's deep concern with spread of Soviet influence in Near East and concomitant Islamic solidarity policy which he considers to be a barrier against Commie inroads have until now shaped his area policy. We see no present signs of any change in Faisal's strong anti-Soviet stand. As long as he remains on the throne, we believe chances are good that SAG will wish to keep Soviets at arm's length. However, while no Saudis have specifically so stated to us, we have no doubt that there are Saudis who believe that closer relations with Soviets may be desirable, perhaps as some sort of protective umbrella or as means obtaining cheaper arms. At such time as Faisal goes, we would certainly

---

[1] Source: National Archives and Records Administration, RG 59, Central Files 1967–69, POL 27 SAUD–UAR. Secret. Repeated to Cairo and Moscow.

[2] Dated February 16. (Ibid., DEF 17–1 US)

not exclude possibility that a successor regime might wish to explore possible advantage of closer relations with Soviets.

Eilts

---

287.   Paper Prepared in the Department of State[1]

Washington, April 6, 1967.

USG ASSURANCES AND ACTIONS VIS-À-VIS SAUDI ARABIA IN
LIGHT CURRENT SAUDI–UAR CONFRONTATION

Development of US Policy Assurances

The body of our assurances to Saudi Arabia has grown gradually. As early as 1943 the Saudis sought US backing in their rivalry with the Hashemites of Jordan and Iraq. Our first explicit statements of interest in the Saudi security were made in response to Saudi concern, in the late 1940s and early 1950s, relative to Israel. It was against this background that President Truman wrote King Abdul Aziz on October 31, 1950 that aggression against Saudi Arabia would be a matter of "immediate concern" to the US.[2]

When, in the late 1950s, the UAR became the main threat to Saudi security, the SAG again turned to us for reassurance. With the advent of the Kennedy administration and the onset of the Yemen war, our commitments were directed at stimulating the Saudis to attain specific goals. These were: a) to encourage the SAG along the path of internal reform and development; b) to secure Saudi disengagement from Yemen; and c) to deter UAR attack and prevent the Saudis from taking actions which might provoke the UAR. As an inducement for Saudi cooperation in settling the Yemen civil war, Ambassador Bunker was authorized to offer Faisal a pledge of US military support in the event of aggression.

The Bunker proposal was the high-water mark of our assurances to the Saudis. Because of the SAG's failure to sever its ties with the

---

[1] Source: Johnson Library, National Security File, Saunders Files, Saudi Arabia, 4/1/66–12/31/67. Secret. Drafted in NEA's Office of Saudi Arabia, Kuwait, Yemen, and Aden Affairs. The paper was apparently prepared for discussion at the IRG/NEA meeting on April 12.

[2] For text of President Truman's letter to King Saud, see *Foreign Relations*, 1950, vol. V, pp. 1190–1191.

Yemeni royalists and Nasser's refusal to withdraw his troops from Yemen, the Bunker offer of a military guarantee never went into effect. Our experience in the emplacement of a squadron of USAF fighters in Saudi Arabia during the second half of 1963 (Operation Hard Surface) brought home to us the difficulties involved in the stationing of an Amerian fighting force on Saudi soil. The restrictive rules of engagement placed upon Hard Surface in the interest of avoiding involvement in hostilities with the UAR left American pilots almost defenseless in certain situations and gave the Saudis the impression our planes were running away from the Egyptians.

The close of the Bunker effort witnessed an attempt to define our assurances more precisely, as fears grew that we might become drawn into the Yemen conflict by an overly-aggressive stance on the part of the Saudis. Faisal was informed repeatedly in 1964, 1965 and 1966 that we would support him in case of "unprovoked attack" but would not serve as a shield behind which the Saudis could stimulate hostilities in Yemen. It was also suggested to Faisal that if UAR attack were to occur or appear imminent he take the matter to the UN.

Nature of Our Assurances

With the exception of the abortive Bunker proposal, we have never given the Saudis a specific promise of military help against an attack. Our assurances have been conveyed by Presidents and Secretaries of State in private meetings with Saudi leaders, in written and oral messages, and in Departmental instructions and public statements (see attached listing).[3] They have ranged from very general statements of interest in Saudi Arabia's "well being" to fairly specific declarations of "full United States support for the maintenance of Saudi Arabia's integrity" (Kennedy letter October 25, 1962).[4] Some mention of our interest in or concern for Saudi security is contained in almost all the several dozen letters exchanged with the Saudi rulers by Presidents Truman, Eisenhower, Kennedy and Johnson.

Our assurances to the Saudis have never been submitted for Congressional consideration and cannot be construed to be a formal US defense commitment. They have been sufficiently vaguely worded to allow us to interpret our response according to the circumstances. In practical terms, however, these statements do constitute a commitment, though of a purposely ill-defined nature. Our contingency planning has stressed diplomatic action to forestall and arrest a UAR–Saudi conflict. US military intervention (except to evacuate American citizens)

---

[3] Attached but not printed.

[4] For text of President Kennedy's letter to Crown Prince Faisal, see *Foreign Relations*, 1961–1963, vol. XVIII, Document 88.

has been contemplated only in the most extreme circumstances when we might consider our fundamental interests directly threatened.

US Interests and Programs

Saudi Arabia is important to the United States as a source of oil for free world use, a site of sizeable American investments, a growing market for American merchandise and a transit area for US military aircraft and forces. US exports to the Kingdom amounted to $138.7 million in 1966, as opposed to imports from Saudi Arabia of $95 million. The Arabian American Oil Company (Aramco) alone has a fixed investment of more than one billion dollars in Saudi Arabia. Its operations contribute significantly to our balance of payments. Saudi Arabia and the other Persian Gulf oil producers furnish about 60 percent of our petroleum requirements for Vietnam and East Asia (80 percent in the case of aviation gas).

Since before World War II, the House of Saud has been one of our best friends in the Middle East. The Saudis have turned a deaf ear to repeated Soviet overtures for diplomatic and trade relations and have staunchly opposed Communist penetration of the Peninsula. A violent overthrow of the monarchy would, in all likelihood, destroy our position of primacy in Saudi Arabia and open the door to the establishment of Communist bloc presence and influence. A revolution would probably not deny us Saudi oil (any government would be dependent on oil revenues) but could jeopardize our investments and make the terms of access to oil less favorable.

Our interest in the security and stability of the Saudi monarchy has been given expression through a variety of USG programs:

a. *US Military Training Mission:* The 235-man USMTM was first established in 1951 pursuant to an agreement with the SAG. The MTM is supported by an approximately one million dollar yearly MAP grant which in addition finances training in the US for approximately 100 Saudi officers yearly. Until recently the MTM effort was located primarily in Dhahran, but now more officers are regularly quartered in Riyadh. With the Yemen war, the need to preserve a distinction between training advice and assistance in combat operations has become important. We have taken the position that teams of up to 5 MTM officers may visit the border areas for short stays, on prior approval of the Ambassador and Washington concurrence as to timing.

b. *Military Sales:* Our last MAP arms grant program for Saudi Arabia was completed in 1962. Since that time we have sought to respond to Saudi requests for legitimate defense needs through sales programs, assisted when necessary by MAP credit or credit guarantees. Current major military sales programs are the $121.5 million Hawk missile contract signed by the SAG with the Raytheon Company in

May 1966 and the $120 million Mobility Modernization Agreement signed by Secretary McNamara and Prince Sultan in August–September 1966. Some ten Raytheon American civilians are now in Jizan helping the Saudis to establish an operational Hawk missile site there.

c. *Corps of Engineers Construction:* The Army Corps of Engineers has undertaken on a reimbursable basis to contract for and supervise construction of military cantonments ($140 million) and a television network ($22 million). The Corps also supervises the Mobility Modernization Program.

d. *Efforts to Promote Economic Development:* We have underway a variety of programs in the civilian field (all on a reimbursable basis) to assist the Saudis in economic development. Chief among these are: a US Geological Survey mineral exploration and mapping project, our November 1965 agreement with the SAG to assist in the construction of a desalting-electric power plant at Jidda, assistance in agriculture, and the supplying of technical experts for specific projects.

Saudi-UAR Rivalry a Quasi-Permanent Factor

The Saudi–UAR conflict has been a major element on the Near Eastern scene for almost ten years, since the Iraqi revolution removed the Hashemites as serious rivals to the House of Saud. Hostility between the Saudis and the UAR has flared over Yemen and could intensify with the struggle for supremacy in South Arabia. A multitude of other factors, however, are equally or more important: the personal contest between Faisal and Nasser for leadership in the Arab and Muslim world, incompatibility between the UAR's radical Arab socialism and the conservative Saudi monarchy with its commitment to capitalism, and a fundamental historical rivalry between Egypt, the focus of present day Arab culture and civilization, and Saudi Arabia, the site of the Muslim holy places. Though we may expect periods of détente, *underlying differences between Riyadh and Cairo are likely to be with us as long as the regimes which now rule those two capitals remain in power.* Where the US stands between the two Near Eastern rivals will continue to be a major problem in our relations with each as well as with other Governments in the area.

The Saudis place considerable reliance on us and have sought to involve us more actively in their defense. The assurances and assistance we have given have permitted us to exercise some restraint on the SAG's actions in Yemen and encourage Faisal along the path of reform and development. While there may in the past have been some tendency within the SAG to over-estimate the extent of our commitment (and possibly a temptation to use our assurances to provoke a showdown with the UAR) the limited nature of our assurances has been made clear to Faisal. Our refusal of the Saudi Defense Minister's request, following the January 27 UAR bombing of Najran, for the dispatch of US Army Hawk SAM units caused some disillusionment within the SAG.[5] While this may be salutary to some extent, Saudi disenchantment limits our leverage with the SAG and has reportedly prompted the growth of a "go it alone" philosophy in SAG councils.

Our interest in Saudi Arabia's security has been made almost as clear in Cairo as in Riyadh and Jidda. There is evidence that the UAR is attentive to the signals we send out. While our statements of support for the SAG have not prevented the Egyptians from occasional bombing of Saudi villages in the Yemen border area, they have probably helped deter the UAR from larger-scale actions. Our open backing of the Saudis probably heightens Nasser's antagonism toward Faisal and strengthens his determination to overthrow the SAG by subversion. However, any indication of a lessening of US support for the SAG under present circumstances would probably encourage the UAR to step up its military and subversive activities against Saudi Arabia.

Courses of Action

Our long-term aim should be a Saudi Arabia friendly to the West but sufficiently strong internally and externally to stand by itself short of full-scale aggression by a larger power. Achievement of this goal may take a decade or more. During this developmental period protection of our economic and political interests in Saudi Arabia will require continuing US support for the SAG's security and integrity.

Our concern over the stability of the Saudi regime should not cause us to lose sight of the fact that US and Saudi interests are not invariably identical or of the dangers of undue US military involvement in Saudi defense. At the same time, the UAR should remain aware that we intend to fulfill our commitment to assist the Saudis, by military means if all others fail. This policy will require walking a very fine line between friendship and support of the SAG and over-identification with the Saudis which could be as dangerous to us as to themselves. It will necessitate a degree of fence-straddling which is bound to create occasional dissatisfaction in Riyadh without winning us any real favor in Cairo.

Recommended actions toward this goal are:

a. *Diplomatic action* to forestall or arrest a Saudi-UAR conflict. While direct recourse to the UN Security Council may not be advisable, we should encourage the SAG to communicate directly to the President of the Security Council the facts of any new UAR attack on Saudi territory, for prompt circulation to Security Council members.

---

[5] See the Yemen compilation for documentation on the U.S. response to the UAR bombing of Najran.

b. *Military training activities,* through USMTM and CONUS training of Saudi officers be maintained at about their current level over the next few years. A fundamental distinction should be made between USMTM's training and advisory role in standard training areas as opposed to areas of potential hostilities. Anything which might tend to promote a permanent or quasi-permanent USMTM presence in the sensitive Yemen border area should be avoided. Guidelines contained in State 166314 (attached)[6] for USMTM travel to the Yemen border area should be kept under review, although significant relaxation of border area travel restrictions is unlikely to be possible in the immediate future.

c. *SAG purchases of US military equipment* should continue to be consummated when legitimately required for the Saudi defense. MAP credit or credit guarantees should continue to be made available for certain items or programs. This relatively inexpensive form of assistance permits us to demonstrate our interest in Saudi Arabia's security and helps ward off pressure for more direct USG action.

d. *Saudi internal reforms and development programs* should be encouraged with particular emphasis on the implementation of Faisal's promise to establish local government councils.

e. *New USG assurances,* even the reiteration of past statements, should be avoided or at least clearly limited to cases of unprovoked attack.

f. *Token US military forces* should not be ordered to Saudi soil unless it is previously determined that such units will be backed by all necessary force in the event of hostilities. Our unsatisfactory experience with Operation Hard Surface (July 1963–January 1964) demonstrated that, without prior assurance of backing, the dispatch of token forces risks involving us in hostilities for which we are unprepared or, alternatively, raising doubts about the credibility of our deterrent.

g. Mindful of the pitfalls described in subparagraph f above, be prepared to recognize a long-range need to *strengthen our naval presence in the Red Sea–Arabian Sea area* to improve our diplomatic leverage and enhance our ability to make good, if necessary, on existing assurances to the Saudis. One possible course might be to augment COMIDEASTFOR from its current force level of two destroyers. A more numerous US Red Sea–Arabian Sea squadron would enable us to react rapidly to any SAG requests for help without the need to station vulnerable forces on Saudi soil. It is recommended that the IRG request DOD and the

---

[6] Attached but not printed; a copy of telegram 166314 to Jidda, March 31, is in the National Archives and Records Administration, RG 59, Central Files 1967–69, DEF 19–8 US–SAUD.

Department of the Navy to prepare plans on a contingency basis for such increases in US naval strength.

---

288.   Memorandum for the Record[1]

Washington, April 12, 1967.

SUBJECT

Near East South Asia IRG Meeting
Wednesday, 12 April 1967
U.S. Commitment to Saudi Arabia

1. The State[2] and Defense papers prepared for this meeting have previously been sent to the DD/I and ONE. What follows is the report of the IRG/NEA meeting chaired by Ambassador Battle.

2. Before turning to the agenda item, Ambassador Battle said that he was "IRG-minded," wishes to continue the active use of the IRG, desires to have the IRG participate in policy formulation when possible and always to be informed of what is going on.

[Here follows discussion of another subject.]

The USG Commitment to Saudi Arabia

5. The White House (Harold Saunders) thought the President's statement to Faysal during his last visit—"we will not let that fellow (Nasser) gobble you up"—was probably the best point of departure for examining our USG commitment to Saudi Arabia.[3]

6. In a lengthy discussion there gradually evolved a consensus that: (a) the USG commitment was to preserve the integrity of a regime in Saudi Arabia that was friendly to the U.S. and prepared to assist the U.S. in protecting its interests, (b) the USG was not committed to the Saud regime, to Faysal as an individual, to the Monarchy as such or to the protection of the geographical area of Saudi Arabia, (c) it would be unwise to define the specific types or acts of aggression which would lead the USG to the decision to act to protect the Saudi regime and (d) the viability of the Saudi regime, the internal political

---

[1] Source: Central Intelligence Agency, Job 80–R01580R, DCI Executive Registry Files, IRG. Secret. Drafted on April 17.

[2] Document 287.

[3] See Document 275.

and security situation and the impact of aggressive actions on the stability of the regime would always have to be considered, ad hoc, in evaluating a current threat.

7. We noted that the UAR air attacks on Nejran, Jizan and Khamish Mushayt combined with the psychological impact of the parachute drop near Yenbo and the weakness of King Saud's regime had led the USG to the decision to put Hard Surface into Saudi Arabia. At the same time, we took note of the improved internal security situation and the social-economic progress under Faysal as being related to our low-keyed reaction to more recent aggressive actions by the UAR, including air attacks and the terror bombings carried out by Yemeni trained by the UAR in the Yemen.

8. Initially, there was evident an inclination to limit our IRG examination to overt military threats; in the course of discussion I drew upon the history of President Kennedy's recognition that friendly governments are more often threatened by subversion, sabotage, propaganda, terror etc.—all of which led to the building of the massive house of cards known as the "counterinsurgency" programs and that the Chairman of the IRG was explicitly the inheritor of this residual "Special Group CI" responsibility. It seemed to me that the Chairman had a special responsibility, stemming from NSAM 341,[4] to examine the non-military threat to Saudi Arabia as well as the U.S. military commitment based largely on an overt UAR military threat. This comment led to questions and discussions about the nature of "insurgency" in the Peninsula; Hoopes (ISA/Defense) wondered whether we were able to detect foreign influence and distinguish foreign-influenced "insurgency" from genuinely nationalist pressures for change. Also, he wondered if there was any evidence that externally-influenced insurgency was growing in the area. I responded that in Saudi Arabia, as elsewhere in the area, one found a local variety of nationalism, a second with the Cairo coloration and a third with a Soviet overlay. Watching foreign influence move into genuine nationalist forces in the Peninsula and the Gulf was, I said, like watching a tide come in; everytime you looked the water was a few more feet up the beach while here and there one discerned deeper pools that had filled more rapidly—Aden for example. This produced a general discussion of our posture in a number of Middle East countries where "insurgency" problems were a factor, what we were able to do, where we fell short etc. The USG actions on Jordan after the Samu raid by the Israelis in November 1966 was reviewed as having some relevance to the problem of Saudi Arabia. Ambassador Battle expressed some surprise at the extent of the USG actions in

---

[4] See footnote 3, Document 271.

Jordan, including the crash program to help the security authorities and the measures aimed exclusively at the attitudes of the military. From Cairo, he had missed much of the traffic on all but the military assistance package.

9. Turning to the question of U.S. capabilities to respond, Ambassador Battle sought the views of the JCS and the State Arabian Peninsula Director, William Brewer. Brewer thought we should now reenforce COMIDEASTFORCE with two destroyers, keeping them active in the Red Sea as a deterrent. JCS, supported by the majority of the members, thought we should either do nothing right now or start planning to put a carrier force into the area. Ambassador Battle asked a number of highly relevant questions about the availability of forces, time factors etc. The JCS offered no specifics but thought that a carrier force was not available and that the USG would be hard-pressed to put much into the area. It was noted that CINCMEAFSA and JCS maintain a Middle East Plan and that the CCPC had done a study on a Saudi–UAR confrontation. Ambassador Battle asked to be briefed on these. The IRG finally agreed that at this time no decision to move U.S. Forces into the area should be sought.

10. There was some discussion about the courses of action open to the UAR and what UAR current intentions vis-à-vis Saudi Arabia seemed to be. I suggested that the most likely course of action would be an attack on the Hawk Battery in Jizan—most likely by a guerrilla attack such as that at Pleiku. We might be thinking about what we would do if, say, eight or ten of the Americans at Jizan were killed in such an attack.

11. There was also note taken of the general trend toward "mercenaries" in the area—ranging all the way from the British and French mercenaries in the Yemen to the employees of Air Work and Raytheon who were fairly exposed. Also, note was taken of the trend among the Turks, Iranians, Saudis, Jordanians, Paks and others to collaborate in military matters—outside of any arrangements with the USG and in particular in the pooling of arms procured from non-U.S. sources.

James H. Critchfield[5]
Chief, Near East and
South Asia Division

---

[5] Printed from a copy that indicates Critchfield signed the original.

289.   Telegram From the Department of State to the Embassy in Saudi Arabia[1]

Washington, June 2, 1967, 11:23 a.m.

206728. 1. During brief June 1 call on DepAsstSec Davies, Prince Muhammad ibn Faisal, son of Saudi King, made following points:

a. SAG had to support UAR in current crisis[2] and, like Hussein, Faisal might have to go to Cairo if situation deteriorated;

b. USG action on Aqaba problem should be clearly based on world-wide legal considerations rather than as support for Israel;

c. Any "action" USG might take should be clear, quick and effective; and

d. Saudis would have "to do everything we can" oppose such action.

2. Davies stressed USG acting in accordance basic policies support for integrity every state in region and support for principle free international traffic through international waterways such as Aqaba. Prince Muhammad felt our actions so far had appeared unduly onesided in favor Israel and suggested more stress be laid on world-wide US policy on international waterways.

3. *Comment:* Prince Muhammad's remarks add up to suggestion USG should act strongly against Nasser and accept adverse consequences such action at hands Arab countries, including Saudi Arabia, since these would by implication not be of gravest character. We question whether Saudis could, in extreme circumstances Prince Muhammad had in mind, in fact so circumscribe their response.

4. We recognize Arabs will equate USG position on international straits with USG support Israel but addressees should nevertheless make every effort draw distinction between two. Dept plans send circular cable near future summarizing US legal position which may be helpful this respect.

Rusk

---

[1] Source: National Archives and Records Administration, RG 59, Central Files 1967–69, POL 7 SAUD. Confidential. Drafted by Brewer on June 1, cleared by Wehmeyer, and approved by Davies. Repeated to Amman, Cairo, Beirut, Damascus, Kuwait, Baghdad, Sanaa, Aden, and Dhahran.

[2] Documentation on the Middle East crisis is in *Foreign Relations,* 1964–1968, volume XIX.

290. Telegram From the Department of State to the Embassy in Saudi Arabia[1]

Washington, June 8, 1967, 4:37 p.m.

209305. 1. Ambassador requested immediately deliver to King Faisal following personal message from President Johnson dated June 8:

"Your Majesty:

In the light of my own high regard for Your Majesty, as well as the long-standing close and cordial relations between our two governments, I want to assure that you are fully informed regarding the views and policies of my government at this delicate juncture in the history of the Near East.

The United States Government had been engaged for several weeks in the strenuous attempts to reduce tensions in the Near East when, despite our best efforts, hostilities broke out on June 5 on a broad front. We had been in close touch with the parties and had received no indication that such fighting was in prospect. It is not clear to us how it started.

In this situation, the policy of the United States must be to seek urgently for concerted action through the United Nations to bring about an end to the current hostilities. We are bending all our efforts to this end. Far from seeking to become involved in this new conflict, we are doing our best to stop it. In so doing, we will strive to steer an even-handed course. Our sole endeavor will be to seek the earliest feasible return to peaceful conditions so that the underlying problems of the region can be addressed in relative calm.

As the situation evolves, I realize that we may not always see eye to eye on every issue. I recognize the imperatives of your position, just as I hope you will recognize those that govern our own. We continue to support the integrity and independence of all states involved in the current hostilities. We are opposed to efforts to change frontiers or resolve problems by force of arms. But this is not favoritism for any single state in the region, it is simple realism. The purpose of the United States Government must remain the prevention and limitation of hostilities which otherwise might well expand outside the Near East. Such has been our settled policy under four Administrations of both political parties since the end of World War II.

---

[1] Source: National Archives and Records Administration, RG 59, Central Files 1967–69, POL SAUD–US. Secret; Immediate; Exdis. Drafted by Brewer on June 5, cleared by Battle and Bromley Smith, and approved by Secretary Rusk.

At the same time I want to assure Your Majesty that it will be my firm determination that events in the present crisis not be permitted to affect the long-standing interest of the United States Government in the closest possible relations with the Government of Saudi Arabia. I hope that Your Majesty will understand and appreciate the current efforts of the United States for peace within this unchanging context. It would be tragic if misunderstandings between us, or ill-conceived efforts on the part of others, were to weaken the enduring relationship between our two countries from which both have derived such benefit for so long.

In this connection, I want to give Your Majesty my own solemn assurances that the charges being circulated in the Near East alleging that the United States has given military support to operations against the Arab countries in this crisis is totally false. I deeply regret that some of our Arab friends have seen fit to break diplomatic relations with us, particularly in view of the groundless nature of the charges and because of the urgent need for us to remain in close communication with all sides in the present difficult situation. You will have seen that my Ambassador to the United Nations has publicly invited the UN to send investigators to the 6th Fleet to establish for themselves the baselessness of these accusations.

I must tell Your Majesty frankly that I have been disturbed at reports on June 7 of mob action against American citizens in Dhahran. My Ambassador, Mr. Eilts, in whom I have the fullest confidence, has reported to me the assurances given by you and your senior officials that adequate protection will be afforded for all citizens.[2] I welcome this consideration and assure you that it is not my desire to take any action which would focus attention on your problems.

In this difficult time, I take comfort from the continued maintenance of cordial relations between us and our two Governments. As a continuation of our friendly talks in Washington a year ago, I would of course consider most carefully any views which you might wish to send me on the current situation. Meanwhile, Ambassador Eilts has

---

[2] In telegram 5119 from Jidda, June 7, Eilts reported that he had seen Saqqaf at the Foreign Office to inform him of the attack that day on the U.S. Consulate General in Dhahran and to request immediate and adequate protection. Saqqaf expressed the Saudi Arabian Government's regrets at the incident and telephoned Minister of the Interior Prince Fahd, who said that the demonstrations had already been stopped and the ringleaders apprehended. Eilts told Saqqaf he had received instructions to begin evacuation of U.S. dependents and non-essential personnel and to advise private citizens to leave as soon as possible. Saqqaf had been deeply disturbed and reiterated his assurance that American citizens were in no danger. (Ibid., POL 23–8 SAUD) In telegram 5124 from Jidda, June 7, Eilts reported that Prince Mishal, Governor of Mecca, had called on him, saying that King Faisal and Prince Fahd had instructed him to express their deep regrets over the attack on the Consulate. (Ibid., POL 27 ARAB–ISR)

been instructed to remain in particularly close contact with your Government throughtout the present crisis. If God wills, the fighting will soon stop, now that the Security Council has acted, so that we may address the underlying problems of peace and development in a more normal atmosphere.

All best personal regards,

Sincerely, Lyndon B. Johnson"

2. In delivering foregoing, you should suggest that USG desires ensure privacy this message and any subsequent exchange. You may add orally that Dept has instructed you make clear continued interest highest levels USG in maintaining closest contacts with His Majesty and top level SAG officials throughout the present critical period.[3]

Rusk

---

[3] In telegram 5180 from Jidda, June 9, Eilts reported that he had asked Saqqaf to arrange an audience for him in Riyadh to deliver the President's letter to King Faisal. Saqqaf had advised that in the present "somewhat confused situation" it would be better if he sent the letter to the King by special messenger. He thought it likely that Faisal would come to Jidda before long and would want to see the Ambassador there. Eilts said he had deferred to Saqqaf's judgment, but asked that the King be informed that he was ready to see him in Riyadh or anywhere else at any time. (Ibid.)

---

291.   Telegram From the Embassy in Saudi Arabia to the Department of State[1]

Jidda, June 9, 1967, 1039Z.

5187. 1. In talk with Saqqaf this morning at his home, he was much relaxed. He opined that with today's cease fire acceptances, things should soon return to a type of normalcy. King's position in crisis has been very difficult. Faisal feels deeply about Palestine, but scarcely less so about Nasser and Syrians. King has been trying maintain balanced position. He has sided with Arabs, but avoided cutting his ties with US and UK. Saqqaf expressed appreciation for our cooperation.

---

[1] Source: National Archives and Records Administration, RG 59, Central Files 1967–69, POL 27 ARAB–ISR. Secret; Priority. Repeated to Algiers, Amman, Baghdad, Beirut, Dhahran, Kuwait, and London.

2. King received message from Nasser yesterday, written before cease fire, explaining UAR defeat in terms of Israeli surprise attack on Egyptian airfields. As result, most UAR aircraft destroyed. However, "battle" will go on. It important that Arab world united to carry on. Great changes will have to be made in Arab world and Arab leader chosen for this purpose. (Nasser did not specify changes or who leader would be.) Had suggested King Hassan go to US and Boumedienne to Soviet Union to explain Arab cause. Also agreed to holding of Arab summit. Similar Nasser letter apparently sent to all Arab chiefs of state.

3. Saqqaf thought there good chance Nasser is finished. Certainly his prestige as Arab leader down, hopefully for good. Arabs, even Egyptians, recognize he has been all talk. Also Soviet lack of support for Arabs in their hour of need has disillusioned Arabs with USSR. In contrast, Saqqaf believes Faisal's prestige has gone up. Faisal has shown himself to be strong but wise Arab leader. Various Arab countries have urgently asked send delegation consult with Faisal on situation. First, a delegation from Iraq, scheduled arrive Riyadh today.

4. Saqqaf also believes Nasser is at the moment completely rattled and incapable making consistent decisions. He claims that on day following UAR's break of diplomatic relations with US, Nasser advised Hussein to retain diplomatic relations with US. Day later he had sent message to Hussein saying no objection if Jordan accepted cease fire, but UAR would never do so. Next day UAR also accepted cease fire.

5. Saqqaf also said SAG is now sure that there was no US collusion with Israelis in current conflict. So are other Arab states. Even Egyptian leaders aware of this. However, as usual UAR had resorted to "big lie" propaganda techniques which unfortunately have effect on Arab populace.

6. Told him I glad to hear SAG does not believe wild UAR charges. However, despite my three earlier requests to him to curb Saudi radio or at least allow US denials also to be broadcast, Saudi English language radio still as vicious as ever. Saqqaf admitted had forgotten speak to MinInfo Hujailan about this. Undertook do so right away. (Hope he will remember this time.)

7. I then again told him that, in deference King's and his wishes I not evacuating official American dependents. On my urging, American community heads also agreed stand fast. It important, however, that those private Americans who wish go on home leave or for other reasons be allowed do so. Some had reported difficulty in obtaining Saudi exit visas. If American community feels trapped, then pressures get out certain increase. If SAG wishes American community remain here, it in SAG's interest facilitate normal exit visa procedures.

8. Also told him as evidence American community's confidence in SAG and USG willingness to cooperate, Dept has waived general

ban on Americans traveling to Middle East to allow certain specific employees needed by American firms working here to leave for Saudi Arabia. I ready recommend Dept continue be helpful in such specific instances, but could only do so if Amcits who wanted to leave be allowed to do so. Saqqaf was appreciative. Said he saw no reason why normal exit visa procedures should not be resumed. I intend follow up on this which is important element keeping American community calm.

Eilts

---

292.   Telegram From the Department of State to the Embassy in Saudi Arabia[1]

Washington, June 9, 1967, 1:38 p.m.

209632. For Ambassador from Secretary. FYI.

We are making a major effort through as many channels as possible to convince King Faisal of US hope maintain good relations with him and to prevent possible break in relations between us. Toward this end we have under consideration possibility of Mr. Eugene Black visiting Jidda to see King. He is old friend of the King and of many leading figures in the Middle East. Before we proceed we would like your recommendation with respect to utility such visit. We would not wish to embarrass King by requesting audience for senior American. However, if such visit possible we believe there could be real value in such meeting. Please give us your recommendation as soon as possible.[2] End FYI.

Rusk

---

[1] Source: National Archives and Records Administration, RG 59, Central Files 1967–69, POL SAUD–US. Secret; Immediate; Nodis. Drafted by Battle on June 7, cleared by McGeorge Bundy and Eugene Rostow, and approved by Rusk.

[2] In telegram 5205 from Jidda, June 9, Eilts responded that he was confident that the King did not intend to break relations. At that moment, however, Faisal was anxious to avoid being too publicly identified with the United States until the current Near East crisis calmed a bit, and the Ambassador argued that it was in the U.S. interest to respect his wish. Therefore, although he personally would be glad to see Black and was sure the King would hospitably receive him, Eilts saw no need for such a visit at that time and recommended that he not come. (Ibid.)

293. **Telegram From the Department of State to the Embassy in Saudi Arabia**[1]

Washington, June 10, 1967, 4:20 p.m.

210102. 1. SAG Amb Soweyal called on Asst Secy Battle 12:45 pm June 10 without instructions to urge USG publicly oppose Israeli military operations. Battle noted Syro-Israeli cease-fire just agreed and UNTSO reps in process fixing cease-fire line. We hoped it would be honored. We had done all we could to prevent fighting and charges of USG military involvement totally false. Public invitation had been extended UN send investigators to 6th Fleet to ascertain true facts for themselves.

2. Soweyal asked re press reports Nasser–Husayn telecon on subject alleged USG military involvement. Battle commented papers indicated there had been tape of conversation but refused be drawn out.

3. Soweyal than said he calling as friend to make clear time had come for USG to speak out in censure of Israeli military activities. We should not continue leave initiative to USSR on this issue. Soviets had urged Israeli withdrawal in Security Council but USG had not. Friendly Arab leadership might know our true stand but emotional Arab mobs did not. To support friendly leadership such as King Faysal, USG had to make its position clear on public record. Arabs were already contrasting Soviet position favorably with that of USG, despite Moscow failure give them fullest support. Leadership in friendly Arab countries could not control emotional mobs without public manifestation acceptable USG position. We should condemn Israeli action and call for withdrawal forces. Mention longer-term issues, such as need for peaceful settlement, should for moment be avoided to let present passions cool.

Battle assured Soweyal USG interest in integrity all NE countries, noting this position publicly reaffirmed in Security Council June 9. He promised give careful consideration Soweyal's views and report them immediately to his superiors. We had all been gratified with SAG private recognition allegations against USG were false, and would do all we could in months ahead to strengthen USG–SAG ties. We had had no part in the fighting and were using every possible means to get this fact across to Arab peoples.

Rusk

---

[1] Source: National Archives and Records Administration, RG 59, Central Files 1967–69, POL 27 ARAB–ISR. Confidential; Priority. Drafted by Brewer, cleared by Deputy Director of the Office of United Nations Political Affairs William H. Gleysteen and Davies, and approved by Battle. Repeated to Dhahran, Kuwait, and USUN.

294. Memorandum From the President's Special Assistant (Rostow) to President Johnson[1]

Washington, June 13, 1967.

SUBJECT

King Faisal's Reply[2] to Your Letter[3]

Faisal reiterates his desire to continue your close personal relationship and urges us to be even-handed in picking up the pieces of the Mid-East war. He has no doubt that the Israelis committed aggression and asks you to help make sure that they don't gain territorially.

I pass this on only because it is typical of the strong pressures we are getting from our Arab friends to say that our support for the territorial integrity of all the states in the area means pulling the Israelis back behind the 1949 Armistice lines and not forcing a peace settlement. Mac Bundy has seen, and we will have recommendations for you soon.

Walt

---

[1] Source: Johnson Library, National Security File, Country File, Middle East Cables, Vol. V. Secret. A handwritten "L" on the memorandum indicates that the President saw it.

[2] A copy of telegram 5272 from Jidda, June 12, which transmitted an English translation of King Faisal's reply to the President's letter of June 8 is attached to the memorandum. Telegram 5272 is filed in the National Archives and Records Administration, RG 59, Central Files 1967–69, POL SAUD–US.

[3] Document 290.

---

295. Telegram From the Embassy in Saudi Arabia to the Department of State[1]

Jidda, June 13, 1967, 1340Z.

5305. 1. Thus far SAG has stood up admirably to Arab pressures sever relations with US. We have had private (but official level) assurances that King does not intend do so. But we should not take Saudi

---

[1] Source: National Archives and Records Administration, RG 59, Central Files 1967–69, POL 17 US–SAUD. Confidential. Repeated to Dhahran, London, DOD, CHUSMTM Dhahran, CINCSTRIKE/MEAFSA, and Rabat.

position for granted. Much will depend on USG actions these next few weeks indicating continued US concern for Arab interests. In Saudi Arabia, as elsewhere in Arab world, our prestige and influence have suffered as result of recent hostilities and belief is widespread that stunning Israeli victory somehow attributable to US. It behooves us urgently to do what we can to arrest adverse trend and begin difficult climb try to regain broader Saudi confidence. For this purpose various US actions desirable, viz:

2. Continue strictly even-handed policy on conflicting Arab–Israel claims. While some rationalization of some Arab–Israel boundaries may be justified and ultimately necessary, emphasis should be on credibility USG assurances at highest levels re political independence and territorial integrity Arab states as well as Israel. Rightly or wrongly, some of our statements have been viewed as equivocation here and as unwillingness to speak up forcefully to criticize Israel. Anything we could do to show that even-handedness applies censuring Israel as well as Arabs, where this justified, will be helpful here.

3. Continue USG programs of support for SAG in military and other spheres. Specifically, continue Corps Engrs cooperation on TV, military cantonment and SAMP programs. Also willingness proceed with RAMP if Saudi wish. Especially helpful would be early release of long expected Sidewinders for F–86 aircraft. Equally important continue USMTM advisory effort. This is a somewhat delicate subject since at moment most USMTM activities in limbo. We should discreetly be there ready to continue help Saudi military as wanted, yet for the moment not seek to push ourselves on reluctant Saudi military recipients. We have [*less than 1 line of source text not declassified*] reports indicating many Saudi officers severely critical of US, along with others, for Arab debacle and we will doubtless face difficult job reestablishing rapport with them. It will take patience and understanding on part of all USMTM officers and men.[2] Desalination project should continue.

4. Urge American firms continue do business here as usual, facilitate return to Saudi Arabia of their absent employees, and proceed with existing programs. Most heads of American firms have expressed willingness do so. We have done utmost keep American citizens calm during crisis and ensure adequate protection for them. It has not been easy for American citizens. However, generally speaking, they have

---

[2] Telegram 5260 from Jidda, June 12, reported Prince Sultan's assurances that the men, women, and children of USMTM would be looked after like he would look after his own family, and that the Saudi Government would provide full compensation for all losses. Sultan had also said that the soldiers and civilians who had participated in the rioting and looting were now in jail and would be punished severely. (Ibid., POL 27 ARAB–ISR)

cooperated splendidly. Barring renewed breakdown Saudi security situation, we hope this may continue.

5. Early initiation of widely publicized program of relief for Jordan. King and SAG have focused on this point. Any such action on our part would be consistent with SAG's activities. Admittedly we will receive only minimal credit for any such program and many Saudis (and other Arabs) will argue it represents blood money. Still such program would show our concern for Jordan's welfare.

6. Continue to hammer away at denials of UAR and other Arab accusations of US collusion with Israel in recent conflict. Unfortunately as result years of radio Cairo "conditioning" many Arabs want to believe worst of us, but it is essential that we actively refute all charges. All such refutations should be given fullest and continuing publicity in Arabic using VOA and perhaps BBC assistance. We were slow in starting our denials last week, which made problem more difficult. Would also recommend that in addition to US invitation send UN observers to Sixth Fleet, a request to do so might carry some impact here. Job of disseminating our denials exptremely difficult. We are having great difficulty getting USIS material published these days, hence much will depend on outside broadcasts.

7. Avoid placing King Faisal in position these next few days or weeks where he required show excessive public identification with US. However, where possible, look for ways of showing that his past policy of friendship toward US pays off, not only for Saudi Arabia but for other Arabs. It is distinctly in our interest at present time to push Faisal and other Arab moderates' causes in Arab community.

8. Continuously and quietly appeal to Saudi self-interest, this must largely be done here, but occasional helpful support may be given from outside.

9. At appropriate time resume encouraging King on need for reform program. In current Saudi mood of frustration over Arab military defense, growing sentiment appears be developing among young Saudis that an accelerated political and social reform is needed. Ironically, it also painfully evident during recent crisis that only reliable elements loyal to SAG and willing protect Americans were not young, would-be Saudi reformers, Saudi military officers or potential Saudi progressives, but National Guards comprised of strictly tribal types. King and Saudi establishment doubtless keenly aware of this and likely be more reluctant than ever move ahead.

10. Seek to be actively responsive these next few weeks to any emergent Saudi requests for help, e.g., police training, educational advisors, etc. we should try in all such instances minimize our administrative red tape and show we ready to move without delay.

Eilts

296. Telegram From the Department of State to the Embassy in Saudi Arabia[1]

Washington, June 21, 1967, 8:36 p.m.

214082. Jidda 5496.[2]

1. In addition general guidance you have re current US posture in Near East crisis (e.g. State 212576),[3] you authorized make following points when you see King Faisal June 22:

a. The President deeply appreciates His Majesty's thoughtful letter of June 12 which was most timely in connection with continuing problems growing out of recent Arab–Israel hostilities to which he is devoting so much of his attention. Views expressed are being given careful consideration.

b. As indicated in President's June 19 address,[4] USG feels strongly situation cannot merely be permitted return to unsatisfactory state which prevailed before fighting began. We recognize that troops must be withdrawn but believe other steps must also be taken to assure that territorial integrity and political independence of all states of the Near East receive greater recognition than heretofore.

c. In this connection, you may wish to remind His Majesty that USG has at various times supported territorial integrity one or another Arab state against one of its Arab brethren. Our position on this question has been of longstanding and without discrimination as between Israel and the Arabs. His Majesty will recall in this connection special efforts we made in 1957 in connection resolution Suez crisis.

d. At the same time, Arabs should be under no misapprehension as to degree of influence which we able exercise over Israel. Fact of the matter is that all parties will have to approach current problems in spirit of some give and take to permit any significant progress on solving outstanding issues.

e. Highest levels USG deeply gratified by His Majesty's forthright statements to members diplomatic corps in Jidda June 19 as reported your 5467.[5] Faisal's obvious disbelief of totally false charges which have

---

[1] Source: National Archives and Records Administration, RG 59, Central Files 1967–69, POL 15–1 SAUD. Secret; Immediate. Drafted by Brewer, cleared by Davies and McGeorge Bundy, and approved by Katzenbach. Repeated to USUN.

[2] In telegram 5496 from Jidda, June 21, Eilts reported that he was seeing Faisal the next day and asked if there were any special instructions. (Ibid., POL 27 ARAB–ISR)

[3] Dated June 19. (Ibid.)

[4] For text of the President's speech, see *Public Papers of the Presidents of the United States: Lyndon B. Johnson, 1967,* Book I, pp. 630–634.

[5] Dated June 20. (National Archives and Records Administration, RG 59, Central Files 1967–69, POL 15–1 SAUD)

been directed against us, alleging USG complicity with Israel in recent fighting, is most heartening. His Majesty's courage and frankness in denouncing this canard should be most helpful in introducing greater note realism into assessment recent events.

f. We continue to be gratified at maintenance of cordial SAG–USG relations and hope that by keeping in close contact during coming difficult period it will be possible make real contribution to resolution some of present difficulties.

2. If conversation permits, you may wish raise Yemen problem in effort determine Faisal's current thinking. There have been indications Lebanese and possibly Tunisian contacts with view working out some compromise between Egyptians and Saudis but we unclear to what extent these may have factual basis. This connection, we endorse line you took with Iranian Ambassador (Jidda 5319),[6] counseling restraint on use force to expedite Egyptian withdrawal as long as it appears such action likely prompt brutal UAR military response on Saudi Arabia. Suggest you ask him how he sees Yemen problem affected by recent Arab–Israel developments.

3. Should South Arabia come up, you should also probe King's current views re outlook for peaceful transfer power there in light recent Egyptian military reverses in Sinai. For our part, we continue to be disturbed by deteriorating security situation. Recent British decision extend additional support to present government should be most helpful, but in our view the outlook still highly uncertain.

Katzenbach

---

[6] Dated June 14. (Ibid., POL 27 ARAB–ISR)

297. Telegram From the Embassy in Saudi Arabia to the Department of State[1]

Jidda, June 23, 1967, 1528Z.

5517. 1. I met with King Faisal for two hours last night. Also present were Crown Prince Khalid, Dr. Rashad Pharaon and Acting Deputy FonMin Masaud. Prior going in, Rashad sent word to me not to mention separate West Bank entity as he had previously suggested (Jidda's 5495).[2] I had not planned to do so but as talk developed, reason for Rashad's request obvious. King wished focus on present, not future. Faisal looked fit. For first hour or so he spoke vigorously; thereafter he largely rehashed previous comments. While essentially critical some potentially helpful procedural suggestions emerged.

2. After congratulating Faisal on his successful state visits to UK and Belgium, I spoke of President's deep appreciation for King's letter of June 12. I assured him that HM's views as expressed therein are being carefully studied by President who is devoting much of his time to Near East problem. I noted President's address of June 19 emphasized continued USG desire act evenhandedly in present Near East crisis. USG has no blueprint that it is seeking impose on area. As President's speech pointed out, USG trying to find some way in which parties themselves can constructively approach their own problems. Future of NE area largely for them to decide. Hopefully, this may lead to a permanent peace. USG would like to have views of both Arabs and Israelis how best to move in this direction. We particularly welcome Faisal's thoughts on future of area. We also most appreciative of strong stand he has taken to resist Arab pressures to break relations.

3. Before I could proceed with script sent State 214082,[3] Faisal did what for him is extraordinary. He broke into presentation. Said he wished President had accepted friendly advice set forth in his letter of June 12[4] on condemning "Israeli aggression." Not only is such condemnation justified, but forthright USG action along these lines would help America's friends in NE area. He complained that "policy planners" in USG do not seem to comprehend what he called "mob psychology" that prevails throughout Arab world. "You are dealing with irrational people," he stated. "This should always be borne in mind in developing tactics. Those of us who are trying to stand up for you are being let

---

[1] Source: National Archives and Records Administration, RG 59, Central Files 1967–69, POL 27 ARAB–ISR. Secret; Priority; Limdis. Repeated to USUN.

[2] Dated June 21. (Ibid.)

[3] Document 296.

[4] See footnote 2, Document 294.

down. Your actions at UN are intensifying pressures on me and other moderate Arab leaders." He expressed appreciation for UK FonSec Brown's statement of yesterday re war not leading to territorial aggrandizement. That kind of a statement helpful. Why cannot USG take similar helpful approach? USG speaks of evenhandedness and such no doubt its purpose. To the Arab public, i.e. those "crazy people" (to whom he kept referring), it comes through totally differently. USG putting him in bad spot. There is nothing in US public pronouncements to which he can point at Arab summit or elsewhere to show genuine USG concern for Arab interests. He pleaded for some statement which would be helpful to him and other moderate Arab leaders in resisting pressure of Arab extremists and Arab public. Soviets are rapidly gaining ground throughout area simply by stating "truth," namely that Israel started aggression. Like USG Soviets also seem to want some kind of durable peace, but their tactics calculated pander to Arab public opinion and to their advantage. In contrast, USG tactics working against USG and against interests its friends.

4. I told Faisal USG has made no judgment who started hostilities. We had no foreknowledge war would begin. Reports conflict on who started shooting. In any case, UAR actions in days preceding June 5 expelling UNEF, deploying massive forces to border, closing Gulf of Aqaba and bellicose radio Cairo statements equally responsible for outbreak of hostilities. I emphasized USG is seeking to avoid past recriminations and wants to look to future. This is only truly constructive way to proceed.

5. Here Faisal again broke in. He insisted there no question whatsoever that Israelis had moved first. Hence, whatever provocation may have existed, they deserve to be indicted for beginning hostilities. Apart from evidence of mass destruction UAR aircraft through surprise assualt, Faisal claimed Israeli Government spokesmen have publicly admitted that Israel preempted conflict. Radio KOL Israel has broadcast statements of Israeli officers boasting how they had moved first, SYG U Thant has stated Israelis started shooting, President de Gaulle has done so, etc. Why should USG try to obscure this. He not asking USG fabricate anything. He simply asking that USG take Israel's own public statements that they started shooting and censure party which first resorted to force.

6. He readily admitted that UAR actions prior to June 5 had been provocative and as such were a significant contributory cause. He suggested that in any statement, resolution or otherwise this UAR culpability also be cited along with "Israeli aggression." This would be consistent with US policy of even-handedness. "I am not trying to defend Nasser," he insisted, "all I ask is that USG give me something to work with in forthrightly condemning what USG must also know."

He rejected argument that inclusion of blanket condemnations will focus UN debate on past rather than on more important aspect of viable future arrangements. He pointed out course of current debate in UNGA is already focusing mainly on issue of who started shooting.

7. With some agitation, Faisal repeated that he unable go to Arab summit and defend USG position without something saleable to Arab public. He said he is trying to get the Arab summit postponed as long as possible in the hope that some helpful USG statement may yet develop. Without this he will be in intolerable position at such summit. What, he asked rhetorically, could he point to if an Arab summit were held today. "Nothing," he answered.

8. I insisted this not so. He had more arguments in his arsenal than he was admitting. Quite apart from Saudi self interest, there much he able point to as tangible evidence long standing USG concern for Arabs. For example, I reminded him of President's reference in June 19 speech that troops must be withdrawn and associating this with recognized rights of national life, political independence and territorial integrity of all states. To my astonishment, Faisal responded President had said nothing about troop withdrawal. After a brief "yes–no" debate, Rashad brought out both the English and Arabic texts of the President's speech. I was able point out to King President's pertinent statement. Faisal clearly puzzled and claimed it was news to him. (Khalid seemed to know about it.) I expressed surprise and recalled King had himself talked of the President's endorsement of withdrawal just a few days earlier at the Diplomatic Corps reception (Jidda's 5467).[5] I had wondered at the time how he had gotten his information so quickly just a few minutes after the speech had ended and before I had any text. Faisal grinned broadly and said, "I made it up. I had to have something to defend myself." He explained that immediately prior to going to that reception his radio monitors had given him President's five principles of peace. He had decided that he should interpret political independence and territorial integrity as withdrawal. We had good laugh over this one, but I took occasion emphasize to him that President had indeed spoken of withdrawal. Moreover, Faisal had found this point useful at diplomatic conclave. What was more, his personal interpretation of the President' remarks showed how much he and the President understood each other. Surely this mutual understanding should convince him as much as anything that I might say that the President is genuinely concerned with the interests of the Arabs and their future. He conceded this so. But he insisted his personal confidence in the President is of little help in dealing with Arab public reaction to USG

[5] Dated June 20. (National Archives and Records Administration, RG 59, Central Files 1967–69, POL 15–1 SAUD)

posture at UN. In any case, he added as an afterthought, what does statement mean withdraw 10 kilometers or so? Or does it mean that Arab troops should be withdrawn? In the absence of some indication as to what it means, he did not see how he could make much use of general reference to withdrawal.

9. I repeated that the President's withdrawal statement was linked to political independence and territorial integrity of all states of area. Ultimately all troops should withdraw from frontiers. Such is vital ingredient any durable peace. For this purpose Israel, just as much as the Arab states, must be taken into account. Arab states should be under no misapprehension re degree of influence which USG able to exercise over Israel. Notwithstanding, I wanted him to know in confidence that we have been in close touch with Israelis since crisis began. As result of these contacts, we believe that Israel is more interested in peaceful settlement than in territorial aggrandizement (SecState 212295[6] and 212330[7]). This seemed to be a further reason to think of some viable peace settlement. He listened with interest. He then stated that, in addition his earlier point of public condemnation Israeli aggression, some public USG endorsement of the principle that Israel should withdraw to the GAA frontiers is essential. He dismissed the contention that the USG unable pressure Israel to withdraw. "If you want to do so", he said "you can." I emphasized that, whether he believed it or not, our influence with Israel is limited. It can only be constructively exerted if Arabs, on their part, show some genuine interest in durable peace.

10. I asked that our talk get away from exclusive focus on past and that we discuss future. We anxious have his thoughts on that all-important aspect of problem. Faisal said he not able speak for all the Arabs. Speaking for Saudi Arabia alone, he wished USG to know that SAG will (a) never make peace with Israel, (b) never recognize Israel, (c) never accept new Israeli territorial aggrandizement by force of arms, but also (d) never attack Israel. As for any broader Arab interest in a future settlement, this will have to be discussed and decided at Arab summit. That was why he did not wish to talk about future. His immediate and pressing concern is present, i.e. creating an optimum atmosphere for that summit. The extremist Arab states will seek to use Arab summit to achieve their ends. They will attempt to whip up anti-American public sentiment for this purpose. Unless the USG takes a public posture, which will help the Arab moderates to resist these pressures, he could not predict what outcome might be. It might not

---

[6] Dated June 17. (Ibid., POL 27 ARAB–ISR)
[7] Dated June 19. (Ibid.)

be good for us or for him. Again, he asked rhetorically, what can I say at an Arab summit to defend your position and mine?

11. I responded that, in addition to withdrawal statement of President, Faisal might attack the "big lie" tactic which UAR, Syria and others have so blatantly used these past few weeks to conceal their own blunders. He wanted to know how? I reminded him that one recent UAR "big lie" against Saudi Arabia involved charge that American airbase exists at Dhahran. I had myself heard him tell UAR Ambassador to go to Dhahran and see for himself. Similarly, USG has invited UN or other impartial investigators to check logbooks, etc., of carriers, but no one has taken up invitation. They have not done so because UAR and others know their charges are utterly false. Why not take leaf from his own book by reminding Arab leaders who make such charges that they are free to accept USG invitation.

12. Additionally, Faisal able use numerous examples of USG support over the years for territorial integrity of all Arab states against other Arab states as well as Israel. As he aware, Saudi Arabia has benefited from this. So has UAR which might well recall USG efforts of 1956–57 in connection with resolution of Suez crisis. Faisal conceded these points of use, but insisted they not enough.

13. He recapitulated that what he and other Arab moderates need is (a) some public USG condemnation of "Israeli aggression" even if coupled with parallel condemnation of UAR (or other) contributory action, (b) some public USG endorsement that Israel should return to GAA frontiers. He did not want USG to assume the role of policeman in the area or anything of that sort. However, in making these two points, USG might further its aim of working for durable peace by adding to these provisos any conditions, proposals, or anything else" which it thinks might be helpful. All of these items could be concurrently discussed, if necessary, by a UN representative or any other acceptable mediator. However, to defend his own position of friendship to US he needs some public US recognition of above two fundamental aspects of the problem. Without such recognition, neither he nor other Arab moderates can be sure they able contain situation. He hoped USG would take his observations as an old friend who had many times fought US battle in Arab counsels, but now needs some "positive USG support" if he is to resist major onslaught of Soviets and Arab extremists on Western and moderate Arab positions. He could say that USG had too long disregarded his many warnings, but did not wish to cast blame. He simply looking to present out of which future must flow. He explained that as an Arab he could never accept Israel. However he was trying put himself in our shoes in search some mutually acceptable approach. He agreed our two governments should keep in close touch on this matter.

14. *Comment:* Faisal visibly agitated about USG posture. He feels we are deliberately seeking to avoid censuring Israel. He considers it both necessary and right that we do so, but has no objection coupling this with related censure of UAR deployment of troops, Syrian terrorism, etc. He also considers that some public USG endorsement of return to GAA frontiers necessary. As seen from here, his position is not unreasonable. His idea of linking such public pronouncements with recommended proposals for future settlement is intriguing. It deserves careful study. He and other Arab moderate leaders have a very real domestic public relations problem which should not be ignored. While Faisal certainly overstated his alleged lack of ammunition for use at an Arab summit (no doubt for our benefit) he could use sharper weapons. Our reading of Saudi public opinion indicates that US tactics at UNGA continue to be totally misunderstood here and have won US few supporters.

Eilts

---

298.   Memorandum for the Special Committee[1]

Washington, July 11, 1967.

SUBJECT

Exceptions to Interim Military Aid Policy in the Middle East[2]

On 30 June the President approved the following actions as described in the memo of 21 June from the Control Group to the Special Committee:

1. The $15 million sale of 4 C–130 aircraft to Saudi Arabia.

2. The $9.9 million program for weapons maintenance and repair in Saudi Arabia.[3]

---

[1] Source: Washington National Records Center, RG 330, OSD Files: FRC 72 A 2468, Saudi Arabia 400, 11 Jul. 1967. Secret. A stamped notation on the memorandum indicates the Secretary of Defense saw it on July 13.

[2] After the Six-Day War began, the U.S. Government stopped all aid shipments to countries that broke relations with the United States. For Middle Eastern countries that did not break relations, it let the arms pipeline continue to flow but blocked any new approvals.

[3] In a July 8 action memorandum for the NSC Special Committee, the Control Group recommended: (1) resumption of the $120 million Saudi Mobility Modernization program under the September 1965 sales agreement; (2) issuance of a Munitions Control export license for commercial sale of 10,000 pistols, holsters, and ammunition for the Saudi police; and (3) shipment of F–86 spares to Saudi Arabia under the $500,000 cash sale agreement of May 11, 1967. (Johnson Library, National Security File, Special Committee, Control Group Meetings, Minutes)

3. The negotiation and programming of the $14 million arms credit arranged between the President and King Hassan.

McGeorge Bundy

---

299. Telegram From the Department of State to the Embassy in Saudi Arabia[1]

Washington, August 4, 1967, 2232Z.

16312. Jidda 274 (Notal).[2]

1. Aramco representative here in brief talk with DeptOff August 4 characterized MinPet Yamani meeting New York area August 1 with Aramco parents[3] as "devoted oil, not politics". Yamani apparently did reiterate in plain terms his view that USG has lost much ground in Arab world which will take considerable time recover. However, most of discussion devoted oil problems[4] which representative promised go over with DeptOff on basis written record meeting when this received from New York.

2. Re Tapline, Aramco rep said line still closed despite activation IPC line for all exports except US, UK and GFR. Speculated one reason Saudi go-slow policy may be SAG desire make clear it "doing more" for Arab cause. Chief reason, however, is no doubt Yamani interest in what would amount to "bonus" for permitting resumption Tapline operations. Representative indicated Aramco parents had manifested no receptivity to Yamani discussion this point.

---

[1] Source: National Archives and Records Administration, RG 59, Central Files 1967–69, POL 27 ARAB–ISR. Secret; Noforn. Drafted by Brewer, cleared by Deputy Director of the Office of Fuels and Energy in the Bureau of Economic Affairs James E. Akins and David L. Gamon (NEA/ARN), and approved by Battle. Repeated to Dhahran and Beirut.

[2] Dated July 22. (Ibid.)

[3] Telegram 163 from Jidda, July 13, reported tentative plans for Yamani to meet with Aramco board members in the New York area July 24 or 25. (Ibid.)

[4] Most oil-producing nations in the Middle East, including Saudi Arabia, had embargoed oil shipments to the United States and the United Kingdom immediately following the Six-Day War. Telegram 163 stated that Aramco had informed Yamani that the estimated loss of revenue to the Saudi Arabian Government from continuation of the embargo on oil exports to the United States and the United Kingdom would be $9 million per month; from continued stoppage of the Tapline, $1.5 million per month. Aramco had also pointed out that even after the Saudi embargo was lifted, it might take some time before normal contracts could be resumed.

3. So far there seems have been no publicity Aramco/Yamani meeting which all parties continuing handle on most discreet basis.

Rusk

---

300.   Telegram From the Embassy in Saudi Arabia to the Department of State[1]

Jidda, August 27, 1967, 1230Z.

781. 1. I met with King Faisal for two hours Aug 26. Rashad Pharaon and Acting DepFonMin Mas'ud also present. Explained that following Essga and Khartoum meetings, I thought it might be useful have further exchange views on Middle East situation and where we go from here. In particular, with his departure next few days for Arab summit, I wanted be sure he understood fully USG position. I had earlier discussed this on number of occasions with Dr. Rashad, Saqqaf and Mas'ud and was confident they had conveyed substance our talks to H.M. Nevertheless some questions might remain and I would be happy attempt to answer them.

2. Drawing on SecState 14226[2] and 19843[3] I then recapitulated USG views. Recalled President's June 19 speech which had been drafted in knowledge Faisal's much appreciated letter of June 12. While USG has not attempted suggest specific details any settlement, five principles contained therein remain basic guidelines which USG believes essential for durable peace. Speech had noted Israeli troops must be withdrawn. Such withdrawal remains integral part principle of policy independence and territorial integrity to which both USG and SAG subscribe.

---

[1] Source: National Archives and Records Administration, RG 59, Central Files 1967–69, POL 27 ARAB–ISR. Secret.

[2] Telegram 14226 to Jidda, July 29, instructed Eilts to assure Faisal that the U.S. Government had in mind his comments regarding the need for it to adopt a public position to which Faisal could point at the Arab summit or elsewhere to show genuine U.S. concern for Arab interests. Nor had it ignored his procedural suggestions of June 23. As Faisal was aware, the United States had repeatedly stressed the need for Israeli withdrawal linked to the end of belligerency. However, withdrawal was hardly feasible when one party insisted it was still at war and refused to accept the right of the other party to exist as a state. The Department also instructed Eilts to assure Faisal that the U.S. Government fully recognized the current threat to Arab moderates from irresponsible Soviet actions and heedless radical Arab moves. (Ibid.)

[3] Dated August 12. (Ibid.)

I explained Faisal's procedural suggestions of June 23 had been carefully considered as are all of Faisal's views. It had not been possible follow these since (a) situation too fast-moving in Essga and (b) as I had earlier told him, USG does not believe simple public condemnation of Israel, UAR and others involved in recent conflict would really help achieve Israeli withdrawal. As Essga debates had shown, crux of issue is to find some mutually acceptable formula for durable peace. We had made clear during debates that, in our view, Israeli withdrawal should be linked with Arab renunciation of rights of belligerency. Notwithstanding their cynical public comments, even Soviets had in final days Essga joined US in espousing similar concept as evidenced by US–Soviet draft resolution which Soviets had unsuccessfully attempted sell to Arabs. My understanding UAR and Iraq had privately indicated agreement, but Algerian and Syrian adamance had aborted project. USG continues believe that such linkage formula offers only meaningful prospects proceed toward just and equitable peace. USG cannot dictate to Israel any more so than it can to Saudi Arabia or any ME state. We can use such influence as we have to help achieve a settlement and are ready to do so, but initiative must in first instance come from parties directly concerned and must be based on realism.

3. USG fully appreciates Arab no less than Israeli feelings. It does not want settlement that will humiliate Arab states or require them give up any legitimate rights or interests. However, Arabs can hardly claim rights of belligerency for themselves and object if Israel exercises same claims reciprocally. Abandonment Arab rights of belligerency would not necessarily entail formal recognition of Israel or formal peace treaty, although these obviously desirable in long run. I thought we ought to be clear, however, that renunciation of rights of belligerency should include inter alia rights of passage in both Straits of Tiran/Gulf of Aqaba and Suez Canal. Also implicit in any state of peace is some agreement on boundaries. Our support for US–Soviet draft resolution based on understanding it would be so interpreted (SecState 27525).[4] I said USG encouraged by apparent tone of realism at Khartoum and Baghdad meetings which we attributed to statesmanlike attitude of Arab moderate participants such as Saudi Arabia. With FonMins session now reconvened and Arab summit imminent, we hope Arab moderates will continue exercise constructive influence so that some means may be found to move ahead on resolving problem before respective positions rigidify still more.

4. Faisal listened attentively. After I had concluded, he immediately picked up reference to boundaries and wanted to know what

---

[4] Not found.

boundaries would need to be agreed upon. Were we talking of areas overrun by Israel? I reminded him that USG wants Israeli withdrawal, but said precise boundaries would obviously have to be agreed upon by parties directly involved. He nodded but did not pursue point.

5. He then said wished to make some general observations: He could not speak for all Arab leaders who will first have to meet at Khartoum and discuss situation. Speaking for himself, he saw two difficulties, first, Arabs have not yet shared fully and frankly with each other their views on how problem should be handled. His recent talks with King Hussein, PriMin Mahjoub and President Arif had once again showed this. They had identified problem, but had been chary on suggesting solutions. Second, quite apart from views of individual Arab leaders, they have to take into account fact that people in street, farmers and tribesmen in every Arab country unanimously regard Israel as threat that has to be eliminated. Referring to my comment that USG cannot dicate Israeli policy, he agreed but noted that all Arabs firmly believe USG is responsible for Israel's existence and development and can, if it wishes, exercise sufficient pressure to require Israel accept an equitable settlement. When I demurred, Faisal said did not want to rehash past history as immediate question is where do we go from here. Arab public sentiment about Israel limits scope of action for any Arab leader. For this reason, every Arab leader reluctant take initiative urge settlement based on renunciation of rights of belligerency and everything latter entails.

6. Given this domestic sensitivity which Arab leaders must take into account, Faisal felt Arab moderates are limited in what they can say or do. They, and particularly he, already under strong attack from Arab extremists for failing to react strongly enough to situation. Even many Saudis criticizing him on this score. In his view, therefore, question of solution should in first instance be decided by those Arab states who were directly involved in the conflict, specifically, UAR, Jordan, Lebanon and Syria. USG should work on them. If they agree, other Arab states will go along. I reminded him that USG has no relations with UAR and Syria, but recalled that UAR had privately acquiesced in US–Soviet draft resolution. This was hopeful sign. Lebanon had hardly been directly involved in conflict, but I knew USG also urging GOL use its influence for moderation. I did not see how anything but obstruction could be expected from present Syrian Govt. However, having often heard King's views on Baath govt in Syria, I hardly thought he would want to be guided by Syrian views. He laughed and agreed. This left Jordan with whom USG is discussing problem along similar lines.

7. Faisal noted that King Hussein badly wants some settlement. Hussein had told him of his talks with President and USG officials and

of his earlier desire that USG "mediate" between Jordan and Israel. He recalled Nasser had told Hussein UAR recognizes Jordan's need try to make some settlement and that USG could help him. Faisal said he cautioned Hussein latter should not go it alone. Nasser's advice might be sincere, but no one could be sure. He referred to his earlier statement that first Arab leader who moves toward bilateral settlement with Israel, even if arranged through UN, could find himself in serious domestic difficulties. Jordan and UAR, with widest possible Arab approval (which might leave out Syria and Algeria), should do it together or at least concurrently along parallel lines.

8. Continuing on subject of Jordan, Faisal said Rashad has passed on my message that US economic aid to GOJ is continuing. They very good and very necessary. However, Hussein also urgently needs military aid. I noted all arms sales and grants to Middle East area now under review. Both Congress and Executive Branch concerned over ME arms race. President had mentioned need for ME arms control and registration. USG has never been major arms supplier in ME. Current Congressional debate re arms question will affect what USG able do in future about matter of arms shipments and it not possible now give clear answer. I could assure Faisal, however, that USG aware of Jordan's problems and deeply interested in King Hussein (SecState 27534).[5] Faisal said hoped it might be explained to Congress that Hussein needs resupply of arms, perhaps for his very survival. If he does not get them from USG and soon, Faisal expressed concern that Hussein might turn to Soviets who have offered arms. I suggested King should exercise restraining influence on Hussein in this regard, at least until the picture somewhat clearer. I also suggested SAG should assist Hussein in this matter. Faisal claimed SAG doing so, but its capability provide military aid severely limited.

9. Speaking of forthcoming Arab summit, Faisal said USG knows his moderate views. He will do what he can at Khartoum Conference. He reiterated that USG posture does not make it any easier for Arab moderates. He hoped moderation will prevail at Khartoum, but could not be sure. Much will depend on how Israel acts. Its refusal extend deadline for returning West Bankers had been most unhelpful. I pointed out USG has publicly urged that deadline be extended. Faisal said "you must do more than urge, you must insist." I said was sure USG doing everything feasible, but Arab leaders should use their influence that returning East Bankers act as law abiding citizens. Otherwise, Israelis have no choice but take disciplinary measures similar to those which Faisal had himself taken against Yemeni saboteurs.

---

[5] Dated August 26. (National Archives and Records Administration, RG 59, Central Files 1967–69, POL 7 SUDAN)

10. I then mentioned briefly oil embargo and adverse effects its continuation will have on Arab states. Faisal responded SAG very aware of this, but Arab extremists are calling on Arab states make "sacrifices" in order recover overrun territories. Even Arif had spoken of need for sacrifices and cited Iraqi actions. I reminded Faisal that Iraq had long ago made mess of its oil industry, hence Iraqi comment on alleged oil sacrifices hardly germane to Arab–Israel conflict. Faisal agreed and said SAG still hopes be able lift embargo before long. He hoped USG would continue show patience with SAG on this score, including not canceling naval contracts. I said that on latter point US naval requirements are continuing and urgent and we could not wait indefinitely. Current ad hoc arrangements might soon freeze into long-term contracts, but I had heard no suggestion contracts being broken since earlier message I had passed on to him through Rashad (Jidda 5581[6] and State 216455).[7]

11. As I was leaving, I congratulated King on apparent agreement worked out by Mahjoub to move ahead on Yemen problem. I said all friends of Saudi Arabia pleased hear that progress might be made on this issue. Faisal quickly responded that, as I knew, he wants settlement Yemen problem. He cautioned that only general principles had been agreed upon, and he could not yet be sure what Nasser may have in mind in working out details. Saudi position unchanged, viz: (a) quick evacuation UAR military, (b) cessation Saudi aid, and (c) allowing Yemenis to decide their own future form of govt without any outside interference. He might know more of Nasser's intentions after Khartoum meetings.

12. *Comment:* Meeting was cordial and as always frank. On my arrival, King looked drawn and tired but as talk developed he became more animated. However, entire talk had listless quality about it. Faisal obviously very alive to domestic political sensitivity any Arab leader moving first to suggest settlement and is not disposed place himself in forefront any such effort. Same time I believe he will support it if Jordan and UAR indicate they want such settlement. I am confident he will in general use his influence for moderation. He has long wanted another Arab summit meeting, but is now slightly apprehensive about situation which has finally catalyzed it and about collective Arab pressures which he will most likely have to face there.

Eilts

---

[6] Dated June 28. (Ibid., PET 17 US–SAUD)

[7] Dated June 26. (Ibid.)

301. Telegram From the Embassy in Saudi Arabia to the
Department of State[1]

Jidda, September 7, 1967, 1392Z.

959. 1. In absence Saqqaf who is on leave in Beirut, Acting Deputy
Foreign Min Mas'ud asked me call today. He handed me letter from
King Faisal[2] in Taif to President Johnson. Translation prepared by
EmbOff follows (non-essential words omitted):

"His Excellency President Lyndon B. Johnson, President of the
United States of America.

Dear Mr. President:

In light decisions Arab summit conference held in Khartoum, Sudan, between August 29 and September 1, 1967, permit me, Mr. President, to explain my views to Your Excellency in all sincerity, since I
firmly desire preservation and strengthening of existing friendship
between our two countries, and since Your Excellency has encouraged
me to present my views on course of events whenever I find reason
to do so and assured me that Your Excellency would give them most
serious attention.

Arab summit conference issued wise and courageous decisions
which as whole indicate how well Kings and Presidents Arab states
and their representatives appreciate responsibility placed upon their
shoulders with regard their peoples and future their nation following
latter's injury at Zionist hands, in defiance decisions of UN and flouting
spiritual and humanitarian values proclaimed in its Charter.

In reviewing decisions of conference, two important decisions arrest our attention:

(1) Resumption flow of oil to all countries of world.
(2) Removal effects of aggression: that is, return to situation existing before June 5, 1967. This means it is possible for Arab states
study any proposal from which following four points are excluded:
Reconciliation with Israel, recognition of her, negotiation with her,
or any thing prejudicial to right Palestinian people to their homeland.

---

[1] Source: National Archives and Records Administration, RG 59, Central Files 1967–
69, POL 7 SUDAN. Secret; Priority; Exdis.
[2] A copy of Faisal's letter was transmitted to the President under cover of a September
9 memorandum from Rostow that reads: "Herewith a letter to you from King Faisal,
which reports that the oil will be moving; but is pretty stiff-backed on any relations with
Israel. Although it sounds like a stone wall, there is maneuver room for a formula which
would include:—an end to belligerence; and—a refugee settlement." (Johnson Library,
National Security File, Special Head of State Correspondence File, Saudi Arabia—
Presidential Correspondence)

Mr. President, it was not easy to arrive at this courageous and constructive step in conditions, of which Your Excellency can appreciate the gravity, where a wave of emotional agitation had taken possession of Arab peoples as result open Zionist aggression, after paralysis of UN in reacting to it and punishing its perpetrators, after the silence of the world's conscience in deterring it and doing justice to those who fell victim to it, all of which made leaders of Arab countries unable stand before violent popular current but were obliged conform to it in many of their actions.

Permit me to say, Mr. President, that decisions Arab summit conference were highly constructive. Door has been opened for Western camp to reconsider its hardened position, so as enable its friends among Arabs to persuade hot-headed Arab peoples that the West, and those who travel in its orbit, are not standing against them in their dispute with Israel, and in order give leaders Arab countries opportunity proceed to further constructive step toward producing just solution to problem. I can declare to Your Excellency that situation has now become propitious for arriving at prompt and rapid solution acceptable to Arabs, provided four points I set forth above are left aside. But should solution be delayed, pressures will return intensified and permeate the entire Arab world. Then solution would become impracticable and your friends would be unable control feeling of bitterness among Arab peoples toward position of Western camp concerning their cause. Other side would seize upon this as means of confusing thoughts and spreading anarchy.

I furthermore consider that it not in interest of United States of America to regard attitude of certain Arab countries toward it as reason stand against Arabs on issue which every Arab considers vital to himself.

Question of Yemen was discussed in Khartoum in ancillary meetings between myself and President Gamal Abdel Nasser. Together we arrived at agreement which we believe this time to be final, God willing.

In conclusion I send Your Excellency my sincere wishes for health and happiness and for our friends people of United States of America all progress and prosperity.

Your friend,

Faisal

1 Jumad al-Thuni 1387, corresponding to September 6, 1967."

2. Signed Arabic original will be pouched under cover airgram for White House records.[3]

Eilts

---

[3] President Johnson's reply, September 25, is scheduled for publication in *Foreign Relations*, 1964–1968, volume XIX.

Doc 447

302. Memorandum of Conversation[1]

Washington, October 4, 1967, 4:30 p.m.

SUBJECT

US Ban on Arms Shipments to Saudi Arabia; SAG Attitude on Chirep Issue

PARTICIPANTS

His Excellency Sayyid Omar Saqqaf, Deputy Foreign Minister of Saudi Arabia
His Excellency Ibrahim al-Sowayel, Ambassador of Saudi Arabia
The Secretary
Mr. William D. Brewer, Country Director, Arabian Peninsula States

During a meeting with the Secretary on October 4, the Saudi Deputy Foreign Minister raised the question of the current suspension of American arms shipments to Saudi Arabia. Saqqaf noted that each time there is a serious problem in the Near East, there seems to be an attempt to influence policy through arms procurement matters. The Saudis were coming to feel that there was nothing on which they could depend. Since June 5, all shipments had been stopped, even spares and training. This had caused deep feeling among the officers of the Saudi Army on whom the Government must depend.

The Secretary explained that two separate issues had happened to coincide in June which made the problem particularly difficult. Both with respect to the Export-Import Bank and AID legislation, there had been a major revolt in the Senate on the question of arms. A severe struggle was now under way in the Senate–House Conference Committee. This development plus the events of last June had simply made it impossible for us to move on this question. The Secretary said that he hoped the problem would be resolved soon, and added that he would himself do his best to this end. He informed Saqqaf that there had been an opportunity to settle the matter on the basis of limiting arms shipments in the area to Israel alone but that the Administration had rejected this approach. The Secretary hoped that we would soon be in a position to move forward on matters involving purchases and export licenses. Saqqaf assured the Secretary that Saudi policies remained the same. There had been no change in their support for Western positions. He indicated that there had been considerable pressure on Saudi Arabia from other Arabs to recognize Communist China or at least not to vote against Chicom admission to the UN. The Saudis had, however,

---

[1] Source: National Archives and Records Administration, RG 59, Central Files 1967–69, DEF 7 SAUD. Secret. Drafted by Brewer on October 10 and approved in S on October 19. The memorandum is part 2 of 3. The time of the meeting is taken from Rusk's Appointment Book. (Johnson Library)

resolutely refused to change their attitude. The Secretary expressed appreciation for this manifestation of continued Saudi support.

---

303. Memorandum From the President's Special Assistant (Rostow) to President Johnson[1]

Washington, October 10, 1967.

SUBJECT

King Faisal's Reaction to Your Letter[2]

Since you've now seen King Hussein's somewhat bitter letter, you will also want to be aware of King Faisal's testy reaction to your recent letter. Both reflect Arab feeling that we have let them down and are taking a pro-Israeli line by not pressing Israel to withdraw as we did in 1957. Ambassador Eilts reports that he had about as difficult a session with Faisal as he's ever had when he presented your letter.[3]

Faisal is sensitive about our intimating that the Arabs didn't go far enough at Khartoum. He feels we don't understand the risks Arab leaders are taking by any show of moderation toward Israel.

He, like Hussein, clearly sees Israel as the aggressor. He's no longer willing to admit that Arab provocation played a role in bringing on the June war.

Significantly, he says he'd be willing to end the "state of belligerency" provided Israel recognized such Arab rights as the refugees' right to go home. He, like Hussein, feels we're asking them to give up their hole card—ending the state of war—in return for Israeli troop withdrawal but not for settlement of *their* main long-term grievances. (This same theme creeps into Hussein's report that Nasser now links opening the Canal with a refugee settlement.)

---

[1] Source: Johnson Library, National Security File, Country File, Saudi Arabia, Cables, Vol. II, 4/67–1/69. Secret. A handwritten "L" on the memorandum indicates that the President saw it.

[2] See footnote 3, Document 301. In telegram 1356 from Jidda, October 5, Eilts described his 2-hour audience with King Faisal on October 4 to present the President's letter. (National Archives and Records Administration, RG 59, Central Files 1967–69, POL 27 ARAB–ISR)

[3] Eilts said this in telegram 1357 from Jidda, October 5, which commented on his session with Faisal. He noted that the King obviously felt that the United States was either unwilling or unable to understand the problems he and other moderate Arab leaders faced. (Ibid.)

At the root of Faisal's reaction are 20 years of frustration beginning with the UN resolution creating Israel, which he believes came about only as a result of US pressure. He was at the UN himself in 1948 and speaks from deep personal conviction. Ever since, with the exception of 1956–57, he believes we have leaned toward Israel. He just doesn't believe—no matter how many times we say it—that we can't influence Israel.

Jerusalem is his most sensitive spot. As guardian of Islam's holy places, he believes he has a special obligation. Our abstention on the Jerusalem resolutions in July hit him especially hard—as it did most Moslems.

Eilts did his best to calm Faisal, but he was clearly upset. He may relax a little when he has time to reflect.

Walt

---

304.   Telegram From the Department of State to the Embassy in Saudi Arabia[1]

Washington, October 24, 1967, 2337Z.

59213. Subject: US Military Supply Policy for Saudi Arabia. Ref: State 58793.[2] Re para 5 reftel, following is more detailed description of items which will be released for Saudi Arabia:

1. Saudi Mobility Program. Vehicles, construction material and other items in connection with SAMP will be released with exception armored personnel carriers, which will be held for time being.

2. Weapons Repair and Maintenance Program. Earlier authorization permitted completion of negotiations for and signing of RAMP Agreement. Implementation all aspects of program may now proceed.

3. Spare parts from commercial and military sources for F–86 and C–130 aircraft will now be released.

4. Release of TACAN (navigational) radar and related equipment is approved to UK for installation in Lightning aircraft.

5. Miscellaneous items from commercial and military sources, including: (a) 10,150 Colt revolvers and ammunition for Saudi police;

---

[1] Source: National Archives and Records Administration, RG 59, Central Files 1967–69, DEF 19–8 US–SAUD. Secret; Limdis. Drafted by Sterner, cleared by Quinn and Sober, and approved by Brewer. Also sent to London.

[2] Dated October 24. (Ibid., DEF 19–8 US–NEAR E)

(b) six cargo trailers; (c) 17 generator sets; (d) 40,000 rounds .50 caliber ammunition; (e) 120 radio sets of various models; (f) seven power supply units; and (g) miscellaneous repair parts. No heavy weapons or heavy weapon ammunition are being released at this time.[3]

For London. You may inform FonOff of US action on TACAN radar.

Katzenbach

---

[3] Telegram 2081 from Jidda, December 10, stated that although the partial lifting of the arms moratorium for Saudi Arabia had temporarily alleviated pressures on the United States, its initially helpful effect was beginning to wear off as the Saudis realized that those items on which they placed the greatest priority were still banned for them—specifically, long-sought Sidewinders; additional F–86 and T–33 aircraft; and 106 mm recoilless rifles. It noted that Saudi requests for these items antedated the June hostilities. Because these cases were looming increasingly large in U.S. relations with the Saudis, the Country Team urged that all possible efforts be made to break the aforementioned items loose from the moratorium list. (Ibid., DEF 19–8 US–SAUD)

---

305.   **Memorandum From the President's Special Assistant (Rostow) to President Johnson**[1]

Washington, December 7, 1967.

SUBJECT

    Letter to King Faisal

We've had reports that King Faisal feels we've been ignoring him in the swirl of negotiations that put the UN representative in the field.

He was in New York in 1948 when Israel became independent, and ever since he has deeply felt that we've taken Israel's side. Against that background, he can't understand our present position except as our digging in alongside Israel again.

The best we can hope for is to keep reassuring him that we have his concerns in mind and are trying to start an honest negotiation that will give Arab interests a fair hearing. The attached letter tells him we think the November 22 UN resolution[2] provides a good framework for a fair settlement.

---

[1] Source: Johnson Library, National Security File, Special Head of State Correspondence File, Saudi Arabia—Presidential Correspondence. Secret.

[2] For text of UN Security Council Resolution 242, see *American Foreign Policy: Current Documents, 1967*, pp. 616–617.

Secretary Rusk has instructed our ambassadors in all the Arab countries to take a similar line with each of the Arab foreign ministers before their meeting this weekend, but Faisal is worth a little extra personal attention. We will shortly be recommending to you a letter to Eshkol urging him also to give the UN representative full cooperation.

The attached is for your signature if you approve.[3]

Walt

---

[3] See Document 306.

---

306. Letter From President Johnson to King Faisal[1]

Washington, December 7, 1967.

Your Majesty:

Since the unhappy events of last June, I have tried to keep Your Majesty currently informed on the attitude of the United States toward developments in the difficult Near Eastern situation. In this spirit, I would like to share with you my views on the future now that the United Nations Security Council has unanimously adopted its resolution on this complex problem.

The extended debates in New York, both in July and for the past two months, have been difficult for us all. None of us has achieved everything desired. We have all had to adjust and modify our views to establish a workable consensus. Throughout the long effort, our own objective has been to work for a resolution with which both sides can in good conscience cooperate. The unanimous adoption of a resolution by the Security Council on November 22 makes clear that we have succeeded in this important initial step.

Passage of this resolution embodying an agreed set of principles—including withdrawal, an end to belligerency, and secure and recognized boundaries—and authorizing the Secretary General to designate a Special Representative to help the parties concerned work out solutions is most welcome. But it is only a first step.

---

[1] Source: Johnson Library, National Security File, Special Head of State Correspondence File, Saudi Arabia—Presidential Correspondence. No classification marking.

I recognize that neither our Arab nor Israeli friends are entirely happy with the outcome. We fully understand the concern of both sides on matters which so vitally affect both, and I know how deeply Your Majesty feels on such key issues as Jerusalem, troop withdrawal and a just solution to the refugee problem.

But all members of the Security Council have worked diligently to establish a framework for peace in which the legitimate concerns of all parties can be met. We believe that passage of the November 22 resolution has now set in motion a process which provides an excellent opportunity for us all to do what we can to help establish lasting conditions of peace in this long troubled region.

I recognize and appreciate the contribution to moderation and stability which the Saudi Government has made in recent weeks under your wise leadership. While Your Majesty's country is not one of the four states most intimately concerned, I have no doubt that Saudi Arabia will continue to take a constructive attitude toward the efforts, now in the hands of Ambassador Jarring, to work out a just and lasting settlement in full agreement with both sides.

You may be sure that we will continue to exert our diplomatic and political influence in support of this effort to secure a fair, equitable and dignified settlement so that all in the area can live in peace, security and tranquility. The unanimity of the Council's action gives us all a particular opportunity, which we should not let pass, to try to resolve outstanding problems on a basis mutually acceptable to both sides.

I value highly our continuing friendly exchanges on matters of key importance to both our governments. With understanding and good will, I believe that the many difficulties that still lie ahead can be surmounted and conditions of permanent tranquility established which will benefit all the peoples of the Near East.

All best personal regards,

Sincerely,

Lyndon B. Johnson

307. Memorandum From the Executive Secretary of the Department of State (Read) to the President's Special Assistant (Rostow)[1]

Washington, December 30, 1967.

SUBJECT

Letter to the President from King Faisal[2]

King Faisal's reply to the President's message of December 7[3] is enclosed. The Department does not recommend that a reply be sent at this time. While it is apparent that Faisal's views remain solidly aligned with the Arab camp, nevertheless it is worth noting the King's willingness not to interfere in any decisions in the Arab–Israel context taken by any of the Arab states directly concerned. He wished success to the Jarring mission.

Benjamin H. Read[4]

---

[1] Source: Johnson Library, National Security File, Special Head of State Correspondence File, Saudi Arabia—Presidential Correspondence. Secret; Exclusive Distribution.

[2] Attached to the memorandum is Faisal's December 26 letter in which the King stated that he was confident that the United States would not leave the aggressor to reap the fruits of his aggression and that the President would not approve an aggressor's use of his aggression as an illegitimate tool to accomplish ends inconsistent with justice. Faisal said that Saudi Arabia continued to attach great importance to three basic issues which were the key to a solution: 1) the question of Jerusalem; 2) withdrawal of Israeli forces from the Arab territories occupied in June 1967; and 3) providing a just solution to the problem of the refugees. The King expressed confidence that the President would devote close attention to this problem, as the United States was known throughout the free world for its support of right and justice.

[3] Document 306.

[4] Signed for Read in an unidentified hand.

308.   Memorandum From Secretary of State Rusk to President Johnson[1]

Washington, January 19, 1968.

SUBJECT

Release of Arms for Saudi Arabia

On the basis of recommendations of the IRG and the SIG, and in line with earlier approvals of selected arms shipments to Saudi Arabia, such as Hawk missiles, I have now authorized the release to that government of the arms listed below. These items are for purchase by the Saudi Government which, in fact, had already paid for those items so indicated before the June arms ban was imposed.

I believe that this action is in accord with our general position of continuing gradual relaxation of our arms restrictions affecting the moderate Arab states. It should be helpful in reassuring King Faisal as to our basic intentions as well as demonstrating that another Western-oriented Arab leader, in addition to King Hussain, continues to derive tangible benefit from a policy of close relations with the United States. I believe this demonstration will be particularly useful at a time when the Soviets are manifesting disturbing interest in Yemen and have indicated willingness to meet Jordan's arms needs.

The outstanding Saudi purchase requests which I have approved are the following:

—60 mortars and 150,000 rounds of ammunition for the National Guard (already paid for by SAG).

—100,000 rounds of mortar ammunition, 20 recoilless rifles with 20,000 rounds of ammunition and 40,000 rounds of .50 caliber ammunition—all for the Saudi Army and all already paid for by SAG.

—5 armored personnel carriers and 5 tank recovery vehicles for the Saudi Army under the SAMP Mobility Program (also already paid for by SAG).

—18 Howitzers which the Saudis paid for in March 1966.

—8 F–86 and 8 T–33 trainer aircraft for the fledgling Saudi Air Force.

—100 Sidewinder missiles with kits to fit them to the F–86's.

---

[1] Source: Johnson Library, National Security File, Saunders Files, Saudi Arabia, 1/1/68–1/20/69. Secret. A January 22 covering memorandum from Rostow to Johnson commented: "King Faisal has been helpful in urging Hussein not to turn to the Russians. Keeping our military supply line open to him should help assure him that we are a reliable source of supply and give us a stronger voice in encouraging him to move in constructively behind the British as they pull out of the Persian Gulf." A handwritten notation on the memorandum reads: "President read & put in outbox without comment, so I cleared telegram based on this memo."

In addition to the foregoing, I have approved normal action on more recent Saudi requests to purchase an additional 20,000 rounds of recoilless rifle ammunition and 10–20 American helicopters on which tentative assurances were given to the Saudi Government a year ago.[2]

Dean Rusk

---

[2] Telegram 102781 to Jidda, January 23, authorized the Ambassador to inform the Saudi Arabian Government at a high level that the U.S. Government had now relaxed its arms ban vis-à-vis Saudi Arabia with respect to items on order or under consideration prior to June 1967. (National Archives and Records Administration, RG 59, Central Files 1967–69, DEF 19–8 US–SAUD)

---

309.   Airgram From the Embassy in Saudi Arabia to the Department of State[1]

A–301   Jidda, February 11, 1968.

SUBJECT

　　　Annual U.S. Policy Assessment—Saudi Arabia

REF

　　　FAM Vol II, 212.3–5

[Here follows a table of contents]

Summary

U.S.-Saudi relations have been put to a severe test by the Arab–Israel hostilities in June, 1967, and the protracted Near East crisis still persisting. The U.S. and Saudi attitudes on the basic issues involved in the Palestine problem remain irreconcilable. However, patient exposition and explanation of our views, in exchanges at the chief of state level as well as through normal diplomatic channels, have helped to

---

[1] Source: National Archives and Records Administration, RG 59, Central Files 1967–69, POL 1 SAUD–US. Confidential. Drafted by Political Officer Robert W. Stookey; cleared by Deputy Chief of Mission Talcott W. Seelye, and in draft by Supervising Economic Officer C. Melvin Sonne, Jr., Public Affairs Officer George R. Thompson, Defense Attaché Lieutenant Colonel Robert F. Merino, Consul General Arthur B. Allen in Dhahran, and General J.S. Addington in CHUSMTM; and approved by Ambassador Eilts. Repeated to Aden, Amman, Ankara, Beirut, Dhahran, Kuwait, London, Paris, Rabat, Rawalpindi, Tehran, Tripoli, Tunis, CINCSTRIKE/CINCMEAFSA, COMIDEASTFOR, and USMTM.

minimize the effect of these differences. Our close cooperation with Saudi Arabia in a variety of fields—military, commercial, economic, cultural and security—has contributed substantially to the maintenance of stability and cordiality in our bilateral relations, and should be continued. However, we cannot take Saudi Arabia for granted should there be a renewal of Arab-Israeli conflict.

Developments in adjacent areas of the Arabian Peninsula have created new problems for Saudi policy. The USSR and other radical elements have replaced the UAR in support of the republican faction in Yemen; a left-wing regime has inherited control from the British in South Arabia. U.K. military withdrawal from the Persian Gulf states has become imminent. We should continue to encourage the Saudi leaders to deal with these questions in a statesmanlike manner, avoiding rash adventures of dubious outcome which might react against the security of the Kingdom and its regime.

I. Strengthening U.S.-Saudi Bilateral Relations

The validity of U.S. policies toward Saudi Arabia during past years was put to a critical test by the June 1967 Arab–Israel hostilities and the continuing Arab-Israeli confrontation. The structure of U.S.-Saudi relations has been severely rocked, but as a result of King Faisal's policy of friendship for the U.S. managed to withstand the strains. It is thus clear that we have generally been on the right track, and that the existing U.S. approach to relations with the country, suitably adapted to changing circumstances, provides a sound, proven base for the future insofar as broader considerations permit us to follow it.

The key limiting factor is, obviously, the tangle of issues related to Palestine, on which there is virtually no common ground between the U.S. and Saudi positions. The concept that history does not turn back to correct past injustices is utterly rejected by the Saudis, who can see no acceptable solution other than to return to 1947 and, instead of founding the state of Israel, make of Palestine an independent Arab state in which only the Jewish sabra community is accepted. Any proposal which seeks to deal with the problem in the shape in which it now confronts the world is, in Saudi eyes, an affront to right and justice. (A major factor in King Faisal's refusal to attend the Rabat Arab summit conference proposed for January 17 was his apprehension that he would be associated there with a position compromising Arab rights in Palestine as he sees them.) Saudi emotions on the subject are heightened by the presence in Jerusalem of sites sacred to Islam, particularly the al-Aksa Mosque. Sincerely, whether or not realistically, Faisal considers that his responsibilities as custodian of the Muslim holy places extend to those in Jerusalem, and the fact that these have passed beyond Arab control weighs heavily upon him. The Saudis are unshakably convinced that American policy-makers are obliged, out of concern for the votes of Jewish Americans, to pursue a policy of partiality toward Israel and against the Arabs.

While we cannot hope to persuade the Saudis to agree with our views on this issue, there is definite utility in explaining them fully, as we are doing, to the Saudi leadership, particularly as U.S. positions are frequently distorted, misrepresented or deliberately falsified in the region's information media. Patient exposition of our views, pointing out that they flow from general principles which the Saudis can accept (even though they draw different conclusions from them) helps to calm emotions and permit normal discussion and cooperation on other subjects where a meeting of minds is possible. The President's exchange of correspondence with the King on the problem has been helpful. While it has not brought the U.S. and Saudi positions into harmony, it indicates to the King that the U.S. at the highest level respects and values his views, and ensures that he is authoritatively informed of our own. It furthermore affords opportunity to encourage the King to persevere in the moderate orientation of his over-all policy and to exert his influence in this direction in inter-Arab councils. This dialogue at the chief of state level has enhanced the effectiveness of the Ambassador's frequent discussions with the King and his close advisors; it should continue as suitable opportunities present themselves, but not be overdone.

In the context of the June crisis both the U.S. and Saudi Arabia felt obliged to take measures damaging to our bilateral relations. The U.S. moratorium on arms shipment to the Near East was of particular concern to the Saudis, who had looked primarily to the U.S. as the source of equipment for their armed forces, and who had substantial quantities of matériel on order and paid for when hostilities broke out. Even though now totally lifted, the impact remains and the Saudis are looking to other sources as alternative military suppliers. The Saudis withstood pressure from the radical Arab states to sever diplomatic relations with the U.S. They felt forced, however, to demonstrate their solidarity with other Arabs by joining in the embargo on oil exports to the U.S. (and U.K.) until it was lifted by action of the Khartoum Summit Conference. While confronted with a considerable segment of public opinion aroused against the U.S., the Saudi leadership endeavored to limit the effect of the crisis on our joint activities. It was on urgent Saudi plea that we decided not to evacuate American dependents from the Kingdom. Whether this Saudi policy could have continued if the June conflict had been protracted is uncertain. We suspect some further retaliatory actions would have had to be taken against us.

During the ensuing six months, relations have evolved toward a situation approaching the normal. The Palestine problem, for which no solution is in sight, remains in the foreground, however, and retains its potential for setting off further crises. When these occur we should again try to minimize their harm to our bilateral relations by proceeding normally insofar as feasible with the various projects on which we are cooperating with Saudi Arabia. However, Saudi Arabia cannot be taken for granted and there is undoubtedly deep dissatisfaction with U.S. policies and the King's policy of friendship for the U.S. at grass roots, military, intelligentsia and perhaps even some Saudi "establishment" levels.

[Here follow sections II–VIII of the airgram.]

IX. Recommendations

1. That we continue to seek to strengthen U.S.–Saudi bilateral relations wherever possible, continuing the present high-level exchange of views, and reiterating where appropriate the expression of our interest in Saudi Arabia's security from unprovoked outside attack.

2. That we continue to urge the King and his advisors to seek a peaceful, negotiated settlement of the civil war in Yemen, and avoid actions tending to intensify or prolong it.

3. That we encourage the Saudi leadership to abstain from embarking on adventurous attempts to overthrow the present government of the People's Republic of Southern Yemen.

4. That we maintain discreet consultation with the Saudi Government concerning arrangements for the security of the Persian Gulf region upon withdrawal of the British, encouraging the Saudis to make a constructive contribution to a viable agreement among Gulf riparian states.

5. That we continue to be responsive to Saudi Government requests for military advice and for a reasonable amount of arms purchases for purposes of defense.

6. That we work to promote expansion of U.S. exports to Saudi Arabia, and continue to encourage the Saudis to manage their reserves in such a way as to ease the U.S. balance of payments deficit.

7. That we respond selectively to requests for assistance in improving the effectiveness of the Saudi internal security forces, without becoming too openly identified with them.

8. That we continue to take opportunity to stress to the King and his advisors the importance of moving more rapidly in social reform, and in satisfying popular aspirations to participation in Saudi Arabia's political affairs.

9. That we continue to schedule regular visits of U.S. Navy vessels to Saudi ports, as a visible indication of U.S. interest in the security of Saudi Arabia.

10. That we explore means whereby scholarship aid for study in the U.S. by a strictly limited number of Saudi students, where a specific U.S. interest would be served.

11. That we keep under review circumstances in which a visit to the U.S. by Prince Fahd bin Abdul Aziz, Second Deputy Prime Minister and Minister of Interior, might be arranged.

12. That we consider arranging for a visit to the U.S. by the Saudi Minister of Commerce and Industry, Shaikh Abid Shaikh.

Eilts[2]

---

[2] Initialed for Eilts in an unidentified hand.

---

310. Memorandum From the Director of Military Assistance of the Department of Defense (Heinz) to the Deputy Assistant Secretary of Defense for Near Eastern and South Asian Affairs (Schwartz)[1]

I–5794/68   Washington, April 29, 1968.

SUBJECT

   MAP for Saudi Arabia

Over the past three years Congress has questioned with increasing intensity the rationale for a grant program to Saudi Arabia. Basically the concern is not with providing training or a training mission to Saudi Arabia, but why Saudi Arabia should not pay the expenses when they are so rich in oil and can afford to spend large amounts to purchase military equipment as well as to aid Jordan.

Each year the grant program has become more difficult to defend. Insofar as student training is concerned, we have used the argument of having more control over the program and being able to select the students. This argument is getting weak, particularly since Saudi Arabia does purchase large amounts of other training.

Insofar as support of the USMTM is concerned, we have stated that Saudi Arabia does provide assistance-in-kind of about $1.4 million for the Mission. Congress wonders why they cannot pay it all, and I

---

[1] Source: Washington National Records Center, RG 330, OASD/ISA Files: 72 A 1498, 091.3 Saudi Arabia, 29 April 1968. Confidential. Copies were sent to Director for Operations Joseph J. Wolf in the Department of State's Office of Politico-Military Affairs and Deputy Director of Military Assistance James D. Dunlap in DOD.

find it difficult to justify, in view of Saudi Arabia's increasing expenditures and cash assets. The MAP costs of maintaining USMTM will be about $600 thousand in FY 69, and will probably decrease in the future as we reduce the size of the training mission.

As MAP is reduced, it will become more and more difficult to justify MAP funds of $600–$800 thousand annually for Saudi Arabia. Therefore I propose that we undertake to have Saudi Arabia pick up all of its student training on a sales basis, and to provide either a cash payment or contributed currency in the amount of MAP costs associated with the support.

The Ambassador probably would resist such an effort on the basis that it would disturb the current relationships we have with Saudi Arabia, and that it is hard to explain why the U.S. can't afford this amount. The trouble is that while the U.S. can, MAP can't. My opinion is that we will have to bite this bullet sooner or later, and the sooner we get started the better.

Saudi Arabia has freely picked up the tab for training missions in connection with sales contracts. We have a large Army Engineer group there in connection with the vehicle sales program. There are other trainers there supporting the Hawk program. In fact, each sales contract with Saudi Arabia carries with it costs for training.

If we start now we should be able, for FY 70, to arrange to have Saudi Arabia pick up all student training costs on a sales basis and to provide contributed currency to offset USMTM costs. I note that Ethiopia provides contributed currency to offset MAAG costs and I see no reason why Saudi Arabia cannot do the same. There should be a way of approaching this diplomatically without rocking the boat. Saudi Arabia has always contributed assistance-in-kind toward the Mission costs, and a new arrangement would require only that they also provide contributed currencies. We would then be in a position to justify USMTM before being forced to do something about it by Congressional action.

Request your reaction to this proposal.

Luther C. Heinz[2]
Vice Admiral, USN

---

[2] Printed from a copy that indicates Heinz signed the original.

311. **Memorandum From the President's Special Assistant (Rostow) to President Johnson**[1]

Washington, July 1, 1968.

SUBJECT

Your Meeting with Saudi Crown Prince—11:30 a.m. Tuesday, July 2

Your main reason in seeing Crown Prince Khalid is to reassure King Faisal of our continued friendship. Faisal is disillusioned by what he considers our support for Israel. He fears we have washed our hands of the Middle East.

The Crown Prince is less strong than Faisal. But he is intelligent and can talk substance if you get him going. I suggest the following leads:

1. You have the highest respect for King Faisal. You recall with pleasure his visit here. You continue to regard him as one of your best friends in the Middle East. How is he?

2. You know that the King is deeply concerned about Israel's continued occupation of Arab territory. You want him to know that we are doing everything we can to bring about a settlement that the Arabs as well as the Israelis would find honorable. This hasn't been easy, but a fair settlement remains our objective. Would he like to say anything about this?

3. You have just had a good talk with the Shah of Iran and would like to hear about the Shah's recent stopover in Saudi Arabia. You would be interested in anything the Crown Prince has to say about the future of Saudi Arabian relations in the Persian Gulf.

4. You would like to explain your purposes in South Vietnam and at the Paris talks. (The Saudis are interested because they see our steadfastness in Vietnam as a measure of how seriously we'd stick by the security assurances we have given Saudi Arabia over the years.)

5. You hope the Crown Prince has received all the medical help he wished. (He had a routine medical checkup at Bethesda last week.)

The Crown Prince had dinner at the White House with President Roosevelt in September 1943 when he was here with then Foreign Minister Faisal as an advisor.[2] One ice-breaker might be to ask him about that or to recall yourself a little bit about President Roosevelt at that time.

---

[1] Source: Johnson Library, National Security File, Saunders Files, Saudi Arabia, 1/1/68–1/20/69. Secret.

[2] For documentation on the 1943 visit to the United States of Prince Faisal and Prince Khalid, see *Foreign Relations*, 1943, vol. IV, pp. 840–852.

The Crown Prince speaks only Arabic. An interpreter, Luke Battle, and his Country Director, will be available.

W. W. Rostow[3]

---

[3] Printed from a copy that bears this typed signature.

---

312.   Memorandum of Conversation[1]

Washington, July 2, 1968, 12:03–12:24 p.m.

SUBJECT

Middle Eastern Developments

PARTICIPANTS

The President
Ambassador Angier Biddle Duke, Chief of Protocol
The Honorable Lucius D. Battle, Assistant Secretary for Near Eastern and South Asian Affairs
Mr. Harold Saunders, White House Staff
Mr. William D. Brewer, Country Director, Arabian Peninsula States

His Royal Highness Crown Prince Khalid Ibn Abdul Aziz
His Excellency Ibrahim al-Sowayel, Ambassador of Saudi Arabia

Interpreter—Camille Nowfel

The President welcomed Crown Prince Khalid, expressed pleasure that he was able to visit the US and asked how long he would be here. Prince Khalid explained that his final tests at the hospital would not be completed until Friday (July 5); so that his onward plans were still uncertain. He had talked the other day by telephone with King Faisal who had particularly asked that his respects be conveyed to the President. On his own behalf, he wanted to express appreciation for all the facilities extended, including the medical checkup at Bethesda. The President offered to arrange for any further help which His Highness might require.

---

[1] Source: National Archives and Records Administration, RG 59, Central Files 1967–69, POL 7 SAUD. Secret; Limdis. Drafted by Brewer, approved in S/S on July 11 and by Saunders at the White House the same day. The meeting was held at the White House, and the times are taken from the President's Daily Diary. (Johnson Library)

The Crown Prince then referred to his first visit to the White House 25 years ago, during President Roosevelt's Administration. The late President had been a great friend of his own father, the late King Abdul Aziz. There had been a meeting of the minds between these two leaders on the Middle East. Perhaps if both had lived longer the situation might have been different.

The President said the situation in the area was indeed difficult and he hoped His Highness would be having detailed discussions with Assistant Secretary Battle while here. Mr. Battle confirmed that he would be seeing the Prince separately. The President continued that he was very troubled regarding the Near Eastern situation and had spent a good deal of time going over it with Mr. Battle. He had a high regard for our Saudi friends. We would like to do things which would resolve problems. The difficulty was that what we wanted to do often could not be done because our friends would not be responsive to our suggestions.

Prince Khalid replied that King Faisal had the greatest appreciation and respect for the efforts the President had made in this difficult situation. The President remarked that some people believe that major actions are possible simply on the basis of an indication from the US Government. We had found, however, that even our strong indications to both sides had not been enough to bring our friends around. Prince Khalid said he hoped that the President would continue to do what he could to reach a solution. The President confirmed that USG actions would continue to be impartial and fair but one could not control one's friends. Right now he had a difficult problem even in controlling his own grandson. The President said he had strongly urged Premier Eshkol and Foreign Minister Eban not to move last June but they had not heeded this advice. He stressed to His Highness that we had been in no way involved, despite unfounded allegations which had misrepresented our position and our inability to convince Nasser at the time. We had tried to get an immediate ceasefire but the parties had not promptly agreed.

Noting that the Saudi Government appreciates the problems which the President has faced, Prince Khalid said it was still the Saudi hope that UN resolutions on the problem could be enforced so that the entire area would not be lost to the radicals, and ultimately to the communists. King Hussein right now was in a predicament involving pressures from his people, from Egypt, from Israel and from the communists. He hoped that the USG under the President's wise leadership would induce Israel to accept the UN resolutions, notably with respect to withdrawal and Jerusalem.

The President said that we had endeavored to be helpful. We continued to support the efforts of Ambassador Jarring to bring the two sides together but his success would require the cooperation of both sides. His Highness responded that it would be impossible for any Arab leader to arrange a face to face encounter with Israel. Nasser would like to see Hussein take this step but simply could not do so.

The Crown Prince concluded that he did not want to take too much of the President's time but would hope to continue his talks with Mr. Battle. The President asked the Crown Prince to convey his greetings to King Faisal, to assure him of America's continued high esteem for his leadership and to remind him that, while the USG is preoccupied with Viet Nam and other problems, the United States intends to stand by its commitments there as well as our assurances to Saudi Arabia and our other friends. The Crown Prince promised to do so and said that he wanted simply to sound one note of warning: Saudi Arabia feared being surrounded by "communists" from various quarters, north, south, east and west. The President expressed understanding of the Crown Prince's views and thanked him again for his call.

On the way back to his hotel, Prince Khalid commented to Ambassador Sowayel on the President's statement that the USG cannot impose its will on other nations by saying: "Perhaps, after all, this is true. Israel has a mind of its own, and it is conceivable that the USG is not able to sway her in any way." Ambassador Sowayel reportedly demurred.

---

313. Telegram From the Embassy in Saudi Arabia to the Department of State[1]

Jidda, July 20, 1968, 0958Z.

4811. Dept pass Cairo. Ball/Sisco Audience with King Faisal.

Summary

1. In two-hour audience with King Faisal, Ball emphasized importance USG attaches to settlement Middle East problem and reported on his talks in Israel, Jordan and Lebanon. Said he had impressed upon Israelis that their insistence on direct negotiation is an untenable position which will only lead to continued freezing of problem. Ex-

---

[1] Source: National Archives and Records Administration, RG 59, Central Files 1967–69, UN 7. Secret; Priority; Exdis. Repeated to Amman, Beirut, London, Tel Aviv, and USUN. A note on the telegram indicates that the Communications Office did not pass the telegram to Cairo.

pressed gratification that two questions GOI had asked Jarring to put to UAR might offer some scope for movement through indirect discussions. Ultimately some direct talks likely be necessary, but this is problem which need not be hurdled now. Israelis more anxious arrive at urgent settlement with Jordan than with UAR and, while in absence any negotiations GOI is not required formulate firm positions, he had gained personal impression that they sought only such border rectifications as necessary for security reasons. Jerusalem problem different and Israelis insist any settlement must be in context unified city which is capital of Israel. However, Eban had indicated awareness Israeli occupation their Islamic holy places intolerable to Muslims and expressed willingness "stretch imagination" to find some acceptable solution. Jarring mission continues offer best way to proceed, and presence FonMins in New York next month might also be helpful. USG will do utmost assist such efforts.

2. After expressing appreciation Ball's appointment and trip, Faisal gave long, cathartic monologue on background Arab–Israel question and dangers continued US support for Israel. King emphasized extent to which Arabs have moved to find settlement in context Israeli inflexibility. He took some credit for counseling moderation at Khartoum. He thought Hussein could not move before UAR does. Equating Israelis with Communists, he contended Soviets also support GOI and attributed all problems of area to them. His reaction to GOI's questions was that one already answered. While second could not be answered at this time, he was adamant on Israeli retention of Jerusalem reiterating that even if Jordan and UAR accept such arrangement, he would have to declare Jihad and would be supported in this by Muslims and Christians. He expressed deep concern Communist inroads into Middle East as result unsettled problem.

3. Ball said USG shares King's concern about Communist activities in area, but brought Faisal back to principal issue by reemphasizing need for indirect negotiations within the principles of UN resolution in order to break deadlock and move toward settlement. King expressed no objection such talks and affirmed his own interest in achieving settlement. Noted this would allow canal be reopened and relieve him of burden of financial subsidies. End Summary.

1. King Faisal received Ambassador Ball, Sisco and me in two-hour audience 10 p.m. July 19. Atherton and Stockey also attended. On Saudi side Prince Nawwaf (special advisor), Rashad Pharaon (Royal Counselor), and Omar Saggaf (Minister of State for Foreign Affairs) were present.

2. Ambassador Ball began discussion by saying when he accepted position Ambassador to UN, he told President Johnson he wished to visit Middle East because its problems are among the most important

the UN must deal with. President agreed and said Ball should visit Saudi Arabia and obtain Faisal's views and wisdom in order help US seek solution Middle East problems. Ball conveyed President's warm personal greetings. Faisal expressed thanks for the President's noble sentiments, which he said are fully reciprocated, and for sending Ball to confer with him. Faisal said he had welcomed news of Ball's appointment, because of what he had learned of his qualities and personality.

3. President Johnson, Ball continued, attaches great importance not only to ending Vietnam war, but to USG making a real contribution to permanent peace in Middle East. Ball was accordingly visiting Middle East with President's full approval. He had been to Israel, Lebanon and Jordan, and conferred with Israeli Prime Minister, Foreign Minister and other leaders, with King Hussein, and with Lebanese Government. He wished convey to King some of impressions gained from these consultations.

4. Israel Govt, Ball said, is in state some disagreement embracing wide range of opinion, and with no common position. He gained impression GOI will not attempt form common position until obliged to do so. It will be required to do so only when engaged in some negotiating process. Meanwhile, GOI has adhered to position it will accept no negotiating process except through direct bilateral discussions with Arab states. Since this principle inconsistent with decisions Khartoum Summit Conference, it relieves GOI of necessity come to grips with substance of problem. As his first task, therefore, Ball undertook impress upon Israelis that this position untenable. As result his discussions with Israeli reps in New York and later in Israel, he believed he had made progress in convincing GOI some form indirect negotiations with Arabs is necessary.

5. As an indication there has been some relaxation Israeli position, Ambassador Ball states, GOI recently gave two questions to Ambassador Jarring to give to UARG, requesting UAR reply. (Here King's interpreter read text GOI questions earlier provided to Saqqaf.) Significance this Israeli move, Ball said, not so much in content of questions as in indication GOI prepared enter into some process of indirect discussion with Arabs in order sharpen issues. This could be beginning of progress on problem otherwise completely frozen, Ball had not seen Jarring recently, and therefore unable say whether latter had transmitted questions to GUAR, or intends to do so. GOI's desire have reply these particular questions also gives UAR opportunity raise own questions, thus perhaps beginning process indirect discussions.

6. In Amman, Ball stated, he had told Hussein he had found GOI most anxious arrive at means living together with Jordan, its next door neighbor, and attached far less urgency to settlement with UAR. To extent GOI has any definite opinion, he told Hussein, it not interested

in increasing its territory at expense Jordan, but in arriving at secure borders. In his opinion, Ball said, Israel seeking some rectification June 4 boundaries, but on basis security considerations alone and without incorporating numerous Jordanians. Exactly what secure borders are can be worked out only through some form of negotiation.

7. In case Jerusalem, on other hand, there are other factors than security. Ambassador Ball said he had pressed GOI vigorously on Jerusalem question. Foreign Minister Eban had replied GOI cannot conceive of Jerusalem which not united. Furthermore, any solution must take account of fact Jerusalem is capital of Israel. At same time Eban said he well aware of fact no Muslim can tolerate situation in which Israel in control Muslim holy places. Within framework two principles mentioned, GOI will "stretch its imagination" to find some solution acceptable to Muslims. Ball emphasized he not seeking defend GOI position, but merely wished report it as he had heard it. He assumed it represented initial Israel negotiating position.

8. Ambassador Ball repeated US endeavoring find way of arriving at agreed solutions. Best instrument available for this purpose is Jarring mission. There will also be opportunity for progress when Foreign Ministers convene for opening UNGA in September, and he told King he had expressed hope to Saqqaf that Faisal would permit him attend UNGA.

9. Faisal thanked Ambassador Ball for describing his discussions, saying he wished preface his reply with a historical preamble. Ball was, King said, well aware of situation between Israel and Arabs before June war. No Arab could have conceived of discussions with Israel, direct or indirect. Since Israel was established, Arabs have never mobilized against Israel, whereas Israel has repeatedly concentrated forces and attacked Arab states. Before creation Israel Arab world lived in tranquility, without revolutions or disturbances, despite some difference of opinion. No one then could have predicted present state of indiscipline or present close relations with Communists.

10. While having no right or wish interfere in US affairs, and recognizing each country must follow own policy, but speaking as friend, without emotion but analyzing facts, Faisal contended support of Israel is not in interest US but on contrary great liability. US gives aid in form bonds, arms, etc., lavishly to Israel without getting anything in return, whereas US has genuine material interests in Arab world. Thirty or forty years ago, he said, no one would have believed US would participate in establishing intrusive state on land of a people, at the price of expelling and dispersing them. US, he acknowledged, not solely responsible for creation Israel. Communist countries worked for it also because it is in their interests and against those of US. Faisal recalled he was at UN when Soviet rep accused US of obstructing

formation of Israel. USSR had wanted precede US in recognizing Israel, but as UN located in US President Truman received news of formation Jewish state first.

11. After June war, Faisal went on, Arabs underwent unprecedented wave of hysteria which clearly evident at Khartoum Conference. Although having no more sympathy than other Arab states for Israel, Saudi Arabia sought moderate extreme proposals then being advanced, such as complete embargo oil exports, severance diplomatic relations, etc. Only Saudi Arabia stood against extreme ideas and was consequently accused of reaction, subservience to imperialism, etc. Following conference, Faisal sent President Johnson his views concerning its decisions. Unfortunately, his message had no effect on US position. Now more than one year has elapsed and nothing has happened. After much discussion November resolution was adopted which Faisal said he had thought no Arab could accept because close analysis shows it conflicts with Khartoum resolutions. Nevertheless, he said he had told the Arab states directly involved they are free to seek solution and assured them Saudi Arabia would not object, interpose obstructions, nor take opportunity to attack them. This, King said, was effort on part of Saudis to facilitate solution of problem.

12. Rejection of Security Council resolution, Faisal said, came from Israeli rather than the Arab side as he had expected. He attributed this to Communist influence on Israel. While Communists pretend be on Arab side, in reality they are with Israel and Israel is taking their advice. For example, whenever Arabs adopt moderate positions, Israeli demands increase. This can come only from Communists. It gives them chance spread own influence in Arab states on pretext of helping them. If problem settled, there no reason for Arab countries place themselves under Communist control or influence. Communists provide military assistance adapted for defense only, then claim Arabs inefficient and were unable use arms previously supplied them. They furthermore seek convince Arabs US presence in area is solely for defense of Israel. They seeking isolate Arab states such as Saudi Arabia which friendly to US. They are working in Syria, UAR, South Arabia, Yemen and wish to advance into Arabian Gulf. Saudi Arabia now stands almost alone, and is keenly aware of Communist danger. King Hussein had been on verge resorting to USSR for arms, since his country was defenseless and his government about to fall, but Saudi Arabia dissuaded him, and appealed to US to assist him. Now, Faisal said with note of bitterness, we can only wait and see what conditions Israel will dictate.

13. Adverting to GOI questions to UAR, Faisal asserted UAR had already replied to first by agreeing to Security Council resolution which provides for termination state of war. He dismissed second question as untimely and calculated only to cause difficulties. After basic princi-

ples of Security Council resolution have been fulfilled, Faisal said, terms can be worked out, and first of resolutions principles is withdrawal Israeli forces.

14. It inconceivable either Christians or Muslims can accept Jerusalem remain in hands of Jews, Faisal asserted. He recalled he had told me he would have to declare Jihad in defense holy places. He said even if Jordan and Egypt agree, we will not, and we will declare Jihad. We may die, but it will be with honor. He also recalled there is Security Council resolution on Jerusalem. Furthermore, freedom of navigation is assured by Security Council resolution. He could only conclude Israel intransigence is inspired by Russians.

15. Longer solution is delayed, King asserted, more Soviets will gain at expense of US. He deprecated significance East European states breakaway from USSR, since all are Communists. He requested Ball not to laugh if he asserted he fears communism even in US. He convinced race riots and other disturbances in US are fomented by Communists. He pointed to events in France one month ago and declared "If France goes all Europe goes." He said Communists have even been found in Saudi Arabia, where people strongly attached to faith. He asked us be alert to fact Zionism is a form of communism, and Jews applied Socialist doctrines as early as 1911. Saudis are not against Jews—"We have good friends among Jews"—but against Zionism. Faisal expressed conviction arrogance of Zionist policy will eventually turn entire world against it. In US, he pointed out, there are anti-Zionist Jews, who are not pro-Arab but simply conscious of real Jewish interests.

16. King expressed view intransigence not in Israeli interest. Arabs bound eventually to recover their rights. Jews are not more numerous or powerful than crusaders. Israel must realize Arabs now willing keep within own boundaries, which inconceivable formerly. Entire question, Faisal repeated, goes back to instigation by Communists.

17. Ball might reply, King said, as I had frequently told him, that US ability influence Israel limited, but if Israel does not take US advice, he said, US can withhold aid as it did with UAR, and this might be effective. Enormous US aid to Israel may even be significant element in US balance of payment difficulties. Tax-free concessions on aid to Israel are unique in world, and support for Israel had become object of auctioneering among candidates in elections. He would, Faisal said, not speak such words except as friend of US and as one who wants all Arabs to be US friends. Finally, Israel occupation of territory in 1967 runs counter to US guarantees to Arab states.

18. Ball thanked King for comprehensive statement his views of situation. Present difficulties, he said, are result of unnatural situation, and this is reason US is so anxious for settlement. Until then unrest

will spead and Communists will exploit it. Although Russians had role in bringing on June war, he continued, they appear interested in arriving at solution. With Suez closed they are finding it costly to supply Vietnam and are frustrated in extending their influence into Yemen, South Arabia and Indian Ocean. King commented Soviets already supplying Yemen and planting influence South Arabia. They are unloading aid shipments in Alexandria which transported overland to Egyptian Red Sea ports for shipment Yemen. Russians are trying convince world they want solution. But, King warned, one should never believe a Communist. Ball agreed Communists do not want permanent peace because they can exploit instability. He observed that he and King were in agreement on central point that so long as present situation exists, Communist influence will spread. Faisal expressed satisfaction Ball agreed with him; he had long tried convince, but no one listened. He hoped speedy measures would be taken to end Communist encroachment. Saudi Arabia stands alone, even US friends such as Iran and Turkey now have relations with USSR, which thus making inroads on US strongholds.

19. Ambassador Ball noted he was just beginning to approach problem. He believed, however, that we had reached point where we can achieve some movement on problem which has been on dead center one year and one month. He reiterated importance Israel questions to UAR not necessarily because of their substance, but because they can represent beginning of an exchange. Issues cannot be settled until requirements and positions on both sides are discussed and sharpened. US prepared play as vigorous role as it can to encourage such exchange, without however seeking replace Jarring mission or Security Council. He recognized Jerusalem question one of great sensitivity to Muslims, Christians and Jews. Faisal challenged idea there any place in Jerusalem holy to Jews. He dismissed Wailing Wall and Temple of Solomon as of no deep religious significance. Last thing in area sacred to Jews, he asserted, was rock on which Moses trod which UAR had allowed be shipped from Sinai to New York. Jews therefore can simply visit their holy place in New York. He again warned that unsatisfactory Jerusalem settlement would require him declare Jihad.

20. Ball noted US is pragmatic and believes only way to begin on existing dangerous, long-standing situation is to begin. Faisal saw no objection to beginning, and Ball expressed gratification, since US feels there has been some breakthrough and Israel has moved slightly away from rigid position which had heretofore been excuse for doing nothing. US, he said, will continue use all influence we have with parties to continue indirect discussion. He expressed personal feeling no final solution can be reached without some direct discussion, but this hurdle can be dealt with later. Final result must be some form of agreement

committing parties. Ball expressed confidence Jarring able negotiate agreement within framework principles Security Council resolution. US, he concluded, will take Faisal's views into careful account. Our diplomacy will not be idle during this period, and US will do all it can to bring end to present agonizing situation. He expressed his own and President Johnson's gratitude for this audience and opportunity to discuss with King problem of great concern to both countries. Faisal agreed support Jarring mission was best approach but insisted matter was urgent. Jarring had already been underway for six months without result. Jarring should be encouraged, but Israel also must be persuaded abandon its intransigence. Ambassador Ball reiterated hope UAR will take opportunity to ask questions of its own of GOI thus opening door to continuing exchange. "Open the door", Faisal agreed, "but quickly."

21. In connecton final reference to continued closure Suez Canal, Faisal indicated a settlement would enable Canal be reopened and relieve Saudi Arabia of onerous financial burden of subsidy payments to UAR.

Eilts

---

314. **Telegram From the Department of State to the Embassy in Saudi Arabia**[1]

Washington, August 29, 1968, 2224Z.

230121. Ref: Jidda 5140.[2] Subject: Saudi Armored Forces Planning.

1. As indicated Brewer letter of July 1 to Ambassador[3] believe it undesirable stimulate Saudi interest in purchasing new tanks. SAG

---

[1] Source: National Archives and Records Administration, RG 59, Central Files 1967–69, DEF 12–5 SAUD. Confidential. Drafted by Newton; cleared by Colonel Wix (DOD/NESA), E. Randall Backlund (AID/PPC/MAS), Colonel Bunte, and Lewis D. Junior (G/PM); and approved by John N. Gatch (NEA/ARP). Repeated to CINCSTRIKE.

[2] Telegram 5140 from Jidda, August 19, reported that, at the request of the Saudi Ministry of Defense and Aviation (MODA), USMTM was conducting a study of tanks for the future development and modernization of the Saudi armored forces, and that the Saudis were thinking in terms of eventually acquiring 300–350 new tanks. In order to make realistic recommendations, USMTM needed to know whether the U.S. Government in principle was willing to sell such U.S. tanks as the M–48A3, the M–60, the M–609A1, or the M–551 to Saudi Arabia. It stated that, in the Embassy view, the U.S. Government should, for purposes of current MODA planning, permit the Saudis to assume that in principle the United States was prepared to authorize the sale of U.S.-manufactured tanks to them. (Ibid.)

[3] Not found.

has already expended substantial funds on various types of military hardware and number of tanks quoted reftel appears to be considerably in excess of SAG's needs and of its maintenance and manpower capabilities.

2. It seems highly unlikely that tanks such as the M–60 and the XM–551 would be available for SAG purchase within time frame covered by study. Furthermore, we must consider possibility legal and policy restrictions overriding our general desire be responsive to Saudi requests. Thus we wish to avoid serious difficulties that would arise should planning exercise be taken by SAG as promise which we would later be unable fulfill. We, of course, also recognize our interest in maintaining US position as supplier military equipment to Saudis and would make every effort, upon specific request by SAG, to respond favorably within the limits noted above.

3. We have no objection to USMTM's providing MODA with comparative data as requested. However, would not appear that comparability study requires we give commitment as to availability two years hence. As previously stated by Ambassador to Prince Sultan, we are not in a position to make such commitment. Therefore Embassy should inform USMTM that possible legal and policy restrictions plus uncertainties of supply limit USG ability to do more at this time than provide comparability data without explicit or implied commitments.

4. Jidda 5140 repeated separately for info CINCSTRIKE.

Rusk

---

315.   **Telegram From the Embassy in Saudi Arabia to the Department of State**[1]

Jidda, September 12, 1968, 1545Z.

5325. Subj: US Naval Survey. Ref: Jidda 5186.[2]

1. US Naval Survey Team[3] (reftel), en route back to US after completing in-country portion of survey, briefed DATT Col Merino and myself today.

---

[1] Source: National Archives and Records Administration, RG 59, Central Files 1967–69, DEF 6–2 SAUD. Confidential. Repeated to London, Dhahran, CHUSMTM, COMIDEASTFOR, CNO, DOD, and DIA.

[2] Dated August 26. (Ibid.)

[3] Telegram 190428 to Jidda, June 25, noted that the U.S. Government had agreed to undertake a naval survey in response to the Saudi Government's expressed desire to plan for expansion of its Navy and related facilities, and transmitted terms of reference for the U.S. Naval Survey Team. (Ibid.)

2. Naval team's preliminary recommendations as outlined to US will include:

A. Operating base at Jidda.

B. Training and operating base at al Jabayl.

C. Headquarters ultimately located MODA Riyadh.

D. Requirement that acquisition any fleet unit be preceded by personnel, training, and base facilities.

E. Base maintenance and ship repair by contract personnel in order to free trained Navy units.

F. End strength in approximately 10 years to be 650 enlisted, 84 officers.

G. Anticipated end strength in 10 years of surface units in Red Sea: 3 torpedo boats, 1 gun goat (flagship), two coastal minesweepers. Same for Gulf.

H. Construction cost estimates based on stateside cost data, and area cost factors are not considered realistic. Costing data to be developed after arrival CONUS.

I. Next step in plan requires architect engineer study to accomplish preliminary engineering and develop detailed, reliable cost estimates.

J. Realistic phasing within capabilities of RSN to absorb new units and functions.

3. Team met with Gen Malik (Coast Guard Commander) and discussed role and mission of Coast Guard. Saudi Navy Mission, assumed by team and as understood result Aug 22 meeting with Sultan, compatible with Malik's view of Coast Guard mission. Malik indicated Coast Guard would cooperate with Navy but no joint usage of facilities.

4. Team returning CONUS via MAC Sept 13 and will be available in office Chief Naval Operations (OP–632) afternoon Sept 16. Team Chief Capt Morgan will contact Country Dir Arabian Penin Affs Brewer after arrival Pentagon. Amb Eilts may also wish briefing by Morgan. Suggest he or Brewer take opportunity request survey be completed soon as possible, since team gave Sultan estimate of 30 days total time required for survey including necessary stateside research.

5. We debated and then turned down idea of Morgan meeting with Prince Sultan before departing for CONUS. Courtesy of saying farewell outweighed in our judgment by Washington directive to team that survey recommendations must be cleared in DOD and State prior discussion with SAG and possibility of some misunderstanding of Morgan's remarks (especially re non-commitment of USG beyond survey) by Sultan or other Saudis at meeting. Saudi Naval officers asked that Emb notify Sultan of departure of team, and I plan write Sultan to inform him in-Country portion of survey now completed, Saudi cooperation excellent for which team and we grateful, and we shall do all possible expedite completion of survey.

Stoltzfus

316. Telegram From the Department of State to the Embassy in Saudi Arabia[1]

Washington, October 24, 1968, 1441Z.

260750. Jidda's 5646.[2] For the Ambassador from Under Secretary Rostow.

1. Appreciate your 5646 and your forthright and effective actions. We will try to have significant telegrams on US views on Near Eastern problems repeated to you so that you can continue to explain our positions and policies systematically to King Faisal, his ministers and to American oil company officials in area. We hope that appropriate and regular briefings of the King may help restore perspective which we fear has been impaired by coterie of counselors around him.

2. Jarring's mission is at critical phase this month. It is essential that both sides develop some confidence in professions by the other of willingness to move to an enduring settlement. We are seeking to encourage the exchange of substantive ideas on a solution. We are concerned of course to protect King Hussein at this delicate phase while pushing for a fair and dignified agreement between Jordan and Israel. At the same time we hope to maintain a dialogue with the UAR to encourage any inclination to move toward acceptable agreement. UAR October 20 gave Jarring written reply to Israeli proposals provided Jarring by Eban. Eban's willingness to give Jarring substantive negotiating positions represents major modification in Israeli insistence on direct negotiations, obtained in part by U.S. diplomacy. While we do not wish discuss substance GOI and UAR papers, we believe important thing is for process of substantive exchanges to begin in earnest and to mature. Understand Jarring has similar view.

---

[1] Source: National Archives and Records Administration, RG 59, Central Files 1967–69, POL 27 ARAB–ISR. Secret; Exdis. Drafted by Davies and Eugene Rostow on October 23; cleared by Atherton, Deputy Assistant Secretary of State for International Organization Affairs David H. Popper, Hart, and Brewer; and approved by Eugene Rostow. Repeated to Dhahran.

[2] In telegram 5646 from Jidda, October 16, Eilts reported to Under Secretary Rostow that top Aramco officials were "very disturbed" at what they considered an imbalance in the U.S. position toward the Arab–Israeli dispute, and were clearly worried about the ultimate consequences of U.S. policy on the major U.S. interest in the Arabian peninsula. They were especially fearful that gradual deterioration of U.S.–Saudi relationships and confidence would increase Saudi pressures on the company and in the long run perhaps even lead to nationalization, and were concerned about the security of the Aramco staff in the event of a new outbreak of hostilities that could lead to riots in Dhahran. (Ibid.)

3. Announcement of Phantom negotiations[3] made in light of considered U.S. assessment of trends and developments in the area including Soviet posture. It was in no way intended to set back process of conciliation on which Jarring is embarked. Regardless of when agreement concluded, delivery time obviously some time away. It is our hope that all concerned will push forward long before that time to agreement to establish just and lasting peace under November 22nd resolution.

Rusk

---

[3] On October 9 the White House issued a statement by President Johnson saying that he had signed the Foreign Assistance Act of 1968 and taken note of section 651 stating that it was the sense of the Congress that the President should take the necessary steps to negotiate an agreement with the Government of Israel providing for the sale by the United States of such number of supersonic planes as might be necessary to provide Israel with an adequate deterrent force capable of preventing future Arab aggression.

---

317. Telegram From the Department of State to the Embassy in Saudi Arabia[1]

Washington, October 28, 1968, 1647Z.

262448. 1. Following FYI and based on uncleared memcon, Noforn and subject to change on review:

2. Saudi Minstate for FonAffs Saqqaf called on Secretary Rusk October 25. Saudi Chargé Faki and Asst Sec Hart also present. Secretary began by remarking US now going through turbulent election period but elections would have no effect on US–Saudi relations. Saqqaf said he pleased to hear this but stressed that USG should not rely too much on Saudi Arabia. US and Saudi Arabia had had long history of close relations but US must take into consideration that these relations could be shaken by "something or other." To Secretary's comment that both sides would lose in that event, Saqqaf responded that if Saudi Arabia loses then whole ME area lost. Communism would spread throughout region. Regimes in radical Arab states are shaky and subject to commu-

---

[1] Source: National Archives and Records Administration, RG 59, Central Files 1967–69, POL SAUD–US. Secret; Limdis. Drafted by Brooks Wrampelmeier (NEA/ARP) on October 25, cleared by Brewer and Davies, and approved by Hart. Repeated to Amman, Beirut, Cairo, Kuwait, London, Tel Aviv, Dhahran, and USUN.

nist subversion. SAG cannot do much about this itself. However, Saqqaf asserted USG not doing much about it either. He expressed fear USG has lost interest in area.

3. Secretary noted US needed help from countries involved to do anything in region. Reviewing history of events surrounding June 1967 war, Secretary said Nasser had run headlong into USG commitment to maintenance of freedom of navigation through Straits of Tiran. Other Arab actions had been unhelpful to UN efforts arrange cease fire on first day of fighting and to Latin Americans' later unsuccessful attempt obtain Middle East resolution at extraordinary UNGA. Arabs had later regretted these actions when it was too late. Saqqaf said SAG doing its best to be helpful. Soviet trickery had led to developments which Secretary had just described. Secretary remarked that Syrians and UAR, as well as Soviets, bear great responsibility for what happened. Saqqaf rejoined that Israelis too bear great part of responsibility.

4. Secretary expressed hope that Jarring would successfully accomplish his mission. Saqqaf appeared dubious, remarking that perhaps after US elections Jarring's task might become easier. Secretary hoped UAR would enter into substantive discussions of ME settlement. USG has been pressing Israel to be flexible on direct negotiations question. Unless there is some movement on both sides Jarring can make no headway. Saqqaf insisted Israel will not withdraw but merely wants keep occupied territory. If Israel really intended to withdraw, it could put forth plan for discussion. Secretary replied that UAR must act to test Israeli intentions. If Nasser had not agitated Tiran issue, there would have been no problem of territorial changes. He emphasized that USG has no interest in change of even one inch of territory in area.

5. Secretary said USG doing its best to help Jarring get to heart of the matter. While some on Arab side skeptical of Israeli territorial motives, he felt this not crucial issue. Latter is Jerusalem. On this USG has its own view, disagreeing with both Israel and Jordan about city's status. Solution on other territorial aspects is possible. Saying he speaking privately, Secretary thought it possible that some generous arrangement concerning Holy Places could also be worked out. This would lessen area of Jerusalem in dispute. Saqqaf argued there really no sacred Jewish Holy Places in Jerusalem. City is Muslim and Christian. Hart reminded Saqqaf that Arabs in general had long regarded city as sacred to three religions.

6. Conversation terminated at this point due arrival of physician summoned by Secretary to examine Saqqaf, who had become increasingly unwell (septel).

7. *Comment:* Saqqaf obviously not at his best. Early termination of interview, which lasted less than half hour, prevented discussion of other matters. Tone of meeting was cordial throughout. Saqqaf did not

at any time refer to Phantoms but tenor of his opening remarks suggests he had been instructed by King to deliver firm warning that, although SAG continues desire maintain close and friendly relations with US, it might not be able to do so in face of US actions regarded by Arabs as hostile to their basic interests.

Rusk

318. Telegram From the Embassy in Saudi Arabia to the Department of State[1]

Jidda, December 8, 1968, 1545Z.

6239. Subj: Faisal–Scranton Talk.[2]

1. After long meeting with Saqqaf earlier in day in Jidda, Governor Scranton had two hour private meeting with King Faisal in Riyadh evening December 7. Governor informed that Faisal generally reiterated his known views. Subjects covered as follows:

2. Communism in Area. Faisal went round Arabian Peninsula outlining Soviet and ChiCom strength various states. Yemen is under Soviet influence. So is PRSY whose leadership leftist. (At Governor's request, Faisal agreed Saqqaf should prepare paper on PRSY for forwarding to Scranton.) Syria most leftist state in area. Iraq less influenced by Communists and situation there still salvageable, although King obviously dislikes leftist oriented Baath. In UAR communism also strong, but many Egyptians do not want it. Same applies to Algeria. Faisal expressed concern about Kuwait, which is now thinking of taking Soviet equipment. Despite ample funds, Kuwait not as stable as it ought to be. Spoke at some length about vulnerability of Trucial states to leftist subversion.

3. Saudi–Iran Relations. Faisal expressed his pleasure about recent meeting with Shah. Stated it his intention to cooperate fully with Shah to try to bring about a settlement of problems of Gulf.

---

[1] Source: National Archives and Records Administration, RG 59, Central Files 1967–69, POL 7 US/SCRANTON. Secret; Immediate; Limdis. Repeated to Tehran, Beirut, Cairo, Moscow, Kuwait, and London.

[2] Telegram 279191 to Jidda, November 28, transmitted a message from President-elect Nixon to King Faisal, stating that he was sending Governor William Scranton on a fact-finding tour of the Middle East and hoped that the King would be able to receive him and to give him a full and frank exposition of his views on the local situation and the region as a whole. (Ibid.)

4. Arab–Israel. Faisal repeated well known views. Israel is unique situation in history of mankind. Outsiders came in and expelled people already there. Faisal questioned whether it good that Israel exists in long run, at least not as a theological state. He could accept Jews in area if they did not seek impose theologic issue. He contended Israel is essentially a leftist, Communist state which is constant threat to area stability.

5. On what should be done to resolve problem, Faisal contended most important element is Israeli withdrawal to former boundary lines. On Sharm al-Shaikh, Sinai and Suez aspects, Faisal would go along with whatever UAR wants. Matter entirely up to Egyptians. Straits of Tiran should be open.[3] Tiran and Senafir Islands should be returned to him.

6. Arab refugees should be granted right to return. Of 1948 refugees, Faisal thought less than 5 percent would want to go back. Displaced persons of 1967 hostilities should also be allowed back. Most of them will do so.

7. Faisal was his customary strong self on Jerusalem. It is Holy City of Muslims. Jews have no right be there. Unless Israelis withdraw from it, Muslims will declare holy war to recover it. He willing to die for it.

8. Arab Leaders. Faisal was dispassionate in his comments on Arab leaders. Hussein had at times in past been vacillating, but should be supported. He was not bitter about Nasser, but wished keep him at arm's length.

9. Saudi–U.S. Relations. Faisal was clearly pleased with Mr. Nixon's election. Toward end of conversation he grasped Governor's hand and clutched it while expounding on U.S.–Saudi friendship, danger of Israel and Zionism and Communist threat to area.

10. Security. Faisal did not appear be concerned about security in Saudi Arabia. Felt he can control situation here, but was worried about what is happening around him. Large part of area already Communist-influenced and, unless Jordan is helped to recover from effects of June, 1967, hostilities, it too can fall.

11. *Comment:* Governor was struck by dispassionate nature Faisal's presentation. Faisal looked tired, but obviously welcomed opportunity make his views known to new administration through Governor Scranton. Saudis are very pleased about Governor's visit.

Eilts

---

[3] Documentation on Tiran and Senafir islands, which were occupied by Israel in June 1967, is scheduled for publication in *Foreign Relations, 1964–1968,* volumes XIX and XX.

Yemen

319. Memorandum From the Executive Secretary of the Department of State (Read) to the President's Special Assistant for National Security Affairs (Bundy)[1]

Washington, January 17, 1964.

SUBJECT

Letter of January 11 from Prince Faisal to President Johnson

Enclosed is a copy of a letter from Crown Prince Faisal[2] received in response to the President's letter of December 19, 1963.[3]

We are pleased with its emphasis on the importance of strengthening relations between the United States and Saudi Arabia and the desire for continued frank exchanges of views. Faisal agrees in this letter to extend the validity of the disengagement agreement in the Yemen for an additional two months or until March 4. Additionally, the Saudi Deputy Foreign Minister has stressed to Ambassador Hart that in this letter the Crown Prince tacitly shows himself amenable to an even further extension of the United Nations Yemen Observation Mission provided a plan can be developed which gives real hope for United Arab Republic troop withdrawals. This is an encouraging sign of a less rigid attitude on the part of Faisal toward easing the Yemen problem.

In view of Faisal's expressed desire for further correspondence with the President, the Department proposes to prepare at the appropriate future date a letter for the President's signature containing a general review of the current status of the relations between the United States and Saudi Arabia.[4]

Benjamin H. Read[5]

---

[1] Source: National Archives and Records Administration, RG 59, Central Files 1964–66, POL 15–1 US/JOHNSON. Secret. Drafted by Moore on January 15, cleared by Davies and Jernegan, and in substance by John C Dorrance (IO/UNP).

[2] For text of Faisal's letter, see Document 221.

[3] For text of the President's letter of December 19, 1963, to Crown Prince Faisal, see *Foreign Relations*, 1961–1963, vol. XVIII, Document 389.

[4] See Document 229.

[5] Don T. Christensen of S/S signed for Read.

320. Telegram From the Department of State to the Embassy in the United Arab Republic[1]

Washington, January 27, 1964, 7:48 p.m.

3430. Jidda's 755 to Dept;[2] Deptel 3306 to Cairo;[3] Cairo's 1649 to Dept.;[4] Jidda's 772 to Dept.[5]

While noting there are hopeful indications certain Arab League countries are promoting further UAR–Saudi contacts, we share Embassy Jidda's view that UAR–SAG relationship insufficiently improved to warrant our ignoring opportunity play catalytic role. We have repeatedly urged reconciliation and profferred our assistance in connection therewith. Also SAG no doubt reposes most confidence in USG middleman role. We inclined believe best prospect for inducing Faisal agree to détente lies in following Saqqaf's stategy.

Accordingly, unless you perceive strong objections, request you (1) make known to GUAR fact that Ambassador Hart has seen Saqqaf, who in reply to Ambassador's question stated SAG is now ready discuss matters in general with GUAR but without prescribed agenda and is ready to welcome anyone from GUAR to SA, (2) convey as much of material contained five numbered-paragraphs Jidda's 272 to Cairo[6] as you deem appropriate.

Ball

---

[1] Source: National Archives and Records Administration, RG 59, Central Files 1964–66, POL 7 UAR. Secret; Limdis. Drafted by Seelye, cleared by Davies, and approved by Jernegan. Repeated to Jidda, London, Taiz, and Dhahran.

[2] In telegram 755 from Jidda (sent as 272 to Cairo), January 20, Ambassador Hart reported that Deputy Foreign Minister Saqqaf had requested U.S. assistance through the U.S. Embassy in Cairo to make known to the highest level of the UAR Government that Saqqaf was ready to discuss matters in general with the UAR Government and was ready to welcome a UAR emissary to Saudi Arabia. Saqqaf asked that the U.S. Government make the following points: (1) after Faisal's recent visit to Cairo, the United Arab Republic should have no inhibitions about sending a top level emissary to Saudi Arabia; (2) the emissary should be "a truly important figure"; (3) both sides should start the talks with the concept that the Yemen problem could not be solved except by UAR–Saudi agreement; (4) there should be private talks between the UAR team and Saqqaf before and after each session with Faisal; and (5) several meetings would be required. (Ibid.)

[3] Dated January 21. (Ibid.)

[4] In telegram 1649 from Cairo, January 22, Badeau argued that the Embassy saw little profit in the proposal in telegram 755, noting a previous occasion when the United States had obtained UAR agreement for private bilateral talks with Saudi Arabia only to have the arrangement vetoed by Faisal. He recommended that the U.S. Government not involve itself in this question unless it received a direct request from Faisal. (Ibid.)

[5] Dated January 26. (Ibid., POL SAUD–UAR)

[6] See footnote 2 above.

321. Memorandum From Robert W. Komer of the National Security Council Staff to President Johnson[1]

Washington, January 31, 1964.

Yemen. This is merely to inform you that we have quietly and successfully redeployed our miniscule jet fighter force (8 planes) out of Saudi Arabia.[2] Defense has been panting to do so for months and you'll recall we finally agreed to leave them there till 31 January only to make sure Faysal extended the disengagement rather than reopening the Yemen war.

Your 19 January letter to Faysal[3] clinched his adherence, and he raised no objection at all when we told him we were withdrawing above "training" mission. His subsequent friendly letter to you[4] didn't even raise the question (we're preparing a suitable reply).

In fact, our best guess is that the Yemen flap is about over (there's been little fighting for months), and a UAR/Saudi reconciliation in the cards. I may be wrong but I think we can keep this messy little problem off your list of trouble spots.

R. W. Komer[5]

---

[1] Source: Johnson Library, National Security File, Country File, Yemen, Memos, Vol. I, 11/63–6/64. Secret.

[2] On June 13, 1963, President Kennedy approved the temporary deployment of an air unit (operation Hard Surface) composed of eight U.S. F–100D tactical fighter aircraft and one transport-type command support aircraft to Saudi Arabia in exchange for Saudi agreement to end all aid to the Royalist side in the Yemen civil war.

[3] Reference is to Johnson's letter of December 19, 1963; see *Foreign Relations, 1961–1963*, vol. XVIII, Document 389.

[4] For text of Faisal's January 11 letter, see Document 221.

[5] Printed from a copy that bears this typed signature.

322.   Memorandum of Conversation[1]

Washington, March 10, 1964.

SUBJECT

Yemen

PARTICIPANTS

Prince Abdul Rahman ibn Yahya, leading member of Hamid al-Din family
Mr. Ahmed Zabarah, ex-Yemeni Chargé d'Affaires
NE—Rodger P. Davies
NE—Talcott W. Seelye

The Prince covered familiar ground in presenting the royalist case to Mr. Davies, including the following:

1. The presence of an Imam in Yemen is essential to both the Zaidis and Shafeis. In the absence of an Imam as temporal-spiritual head of Yemen, the people are staying away from Friday prayers. (In response to a query, the Prince stated that while the Imam does not have to be drawn from the Hamid al-Din family, no other family qualified for the position has sufficient stature or the appropriate personality.)

2. The new Imamate, unlike its predecessors, is enlightened and seeks to introduce reform and modernization to Yemen. It would look to the United States for guidance and assistance.

3. The royalists cannot participate in a republican-led, UAR-supported coalition government, particularly while UAR troops remain in Yemen, since to do so would only reinforce the UAR position by enabling the UAR to claim to the world that it enjoys full Yemeni support, thus permitting the UAR to bring about a UAR–YAR federation.

4. Evidence of the UAR's determination to remain in Yemen, as well as its deceit, is exemplified by the following recent incident: In response to a request from the UN transmitted via Saudi Arabia the royalists "opened" an important road artery in Yemen in order to allow the UAR to "withdraw" some of its troops from outlying areas; however, instead of withdrawing troops, the UAR took advantage of the situation to attack the royalists.

Mr. Davies restated the USG position, including the following:

1. We seek similar objectives in Yemen, i.e. the withdrawal of foreign military forces, peace and security in Yemen, and Yemeni self-determination.

---

[1] Source: National Archives and Records Administration, RG 59, Central Files 1964–66, POL 27 YEMEN. Confidential. Drafted by Seelye on March 11.

2. The creation of a broader-based Yemeni regime offers the best hope for effecting a drawdown of UAR troops in Yemen sooner rather than later.

3. The failure to achieve a coalition-type regime in Yemen risks the danger that the UAR will be induced increasingly to take over running the YAR government machinery down to the provincial level and to add to its military forces in Yemen. (The Prince noted that the UAR is already "running things," notably security, and told of a British correspondent who was able to see Vice President al-Amri only in the company of two Egyptian officers.)

4. Our impression is that the UAR resists the proposal that the YAR be federated with the UAR. We understood that the UAR turned down earlier efforts by Sallal to bring about such a federation.

5. He reported his conversations in Yemen last October with Vice President al-Amri and UAR General Qadi and noted General Qadi's apparently genuine interest in helping develop Yemen.

6. He noted the recent suggestion that the UAR military force in Yemen be replaced by an Arab League force. (The Prince opposed this idea since he assumed such a force would be composed only of troops from pro-UAR countries. However, he would not oppose the dispatch of a "neutral" UN force.)

The Prince handed Mr. Davies the Arabic original, together with an English translation, of a letter from Imam Badr to President Johnson.[2] He expressed the hope that the letter would be transmitted to the President. Mr. Davies assured the Prince that he would see to it that the letter reached the White House.

---

[2] The Imam's letter to the President is ibid.

323.   Memorandum of Conversation[1]

Washington, March 17, 1964, 3:30 p.m.

SUBJECT

Yemen

PARTICIPANTS

The Secretary   The Lord Harlech, British Ambassador
NEA—John D. Jernegan   John E. Killick, Counselor, British Embassy
NE—Talcott W. Seelye

The Secretary expressed the view that the time had come to reassess
the situation in Yemen in the light of recently restored relations between
the UAR and Saudi Arabia.[2] He observed that the British have created the impression that they are actively supporting restoration of the
Imamate, inducing the YAR and the UAR to "go after" them in South
Arabia. He recalled that earlier in Cairo the USG had expressed support
for the British position in Aden. He wondered if the British believed
the UAR was seriously trying to evict them from their Aden position
or whether HMG felt itself committed to do something for the royalists.

The British Ambassador said that his government is endeavoring,
not wholly successfully, to discourage Aden-based operations in support of the Yemeni royalists and noted that the British mercenaries
fighting with the royalists are "a private enterprise." He denied further
that mercenaries are in the employ of either Faisal or the Aden shaikhs;
he contended that they are financed from private sources. He acknowledged that insofar as these operations were mounted from Aden, HMG
was placed in an embarrassing position. He called to the Secretary's
attention a recent report of YAR air attacks over Beihan on March 13
and a subsequent demand by the South Arabian Federation Supreme
Council for British retaliatory action. He said that London was at that
moment considering the matter.

The Ambassador commented that the British Government is "not
necessarily anxious" to restore the Imamate, believing that the Yemeni
consensus might favor such a development. He acknowledged awareness of the USG view that restoration of the Imamate appears impracticable. He stated that the British position remains flexible. Mr. Jernegan
emphasized that our position is also flexible and that we welcome any
regime which is viable. The Secretary alluded to the possible distinction

---

[1] Source: National Archives and Records Administration, RG 59, Central Files 1964–
66, POL 27 YEMEN. Secret. Drafted by Seelye on March 18.

[2] Saudi Arabia and the United Arab Republic resumed diplomatic relations, broken
on November 6, 1962, on March 3.

between what we might wish to encourage and what is realizable. He expressed the view that a formula other than restoration of the Imamate had a better chance of being acceptable to both Faisal and Nasser. He recalled that Faisal had indicated readiness to acknowledge any government in Yemen acceptable to the Yemenis.

The Secretary, recalling the YARG public statement of December 1962 affirming a desire to maintain good relations with the South Arabian Federation, wondered whether another such statement at this time would be useful. The Ambassador doubted that such a statement would be appropriate unless HMG were on the verge of recognizing the YARG. Unless the latter were the case, he felt it would be extremely difficult to get the Yemeni regime to make such a statement. Mr. Jernegan expressed our concern at the fact that neither side appears to be making a real effort to prevent serious trouble from erupting along the Yemen–Aden border. He questioned whether the British High Commissioner and other officials in Aden have been sufficiently energetic in endeavoring to restrain the gun-running and other activities in support of the royalists. The Secretary inquired as to whether the YAR had mounted land attacks across the border. The Ambassador said that there had been cross-border shelling. He noted that there had been long periods of quiescence along the border. The Secretary commented that UAR disengagement from Yemen would be facilitated if the UAR and YAR could be satisfied that HMG in Aden offered no threat. Mr. Jernegan said that the UAR is fed up with the Yemen problem and wants to find a graceful way out. The Ambassador noted that the Yemenis also are fed up with the Egyptians.

The Ambassador concluded by saying that he would be happy to report to his government the USG interest in damping down the border conflict and to suggest that HMG take stock of the Yemen situation in light of the UAR–SAG restoration of relations.

324.   Memorandum From Robert W. Komer of the National Security Council Staff to the President's Special Assistant for National Security Affairs (Bundy)[1]

Washington, March 30, 1964.

Mac—

You asked the other day what gestures we could make toward the Arabs. One smart move would be to show we aren't in sympathy with UK's foolish Sandys style Arab policy.

Most of us accept that Nasser's 22 February speech reference to Libyan bases[2] (which triggered current mess) was a reaction to Home's Ottawa remarks about Suez. Note also that UAR has nationalized two UK oil companies (pour encourager les autres?).

British covert support of Yemeni Royalists is breeding dangerous reactions too. Now Brits, in response to UAR/YAR border fiddling (which has killed only camels so far) have made retaliatory raid on a Yemeni fort.[3] This over-reaction will lead to much greater Arab pressure on UK, and us too unless we stand aloof.

Our man in Yemen urges (Taiz 549)[4] that we cease representing the UK in Sana'a, as a gesture of disengagement. Talbot and I quite agree (it's a small, low-key gesture that would get little if any publicity, but be read correctly in London, Cairo, and Sana'a).[5] But Rusk is so-so on this. If opportunity offers, put in a word. The Brits will lose us Wheelus if we're not careful.

RWK

---

[1] Source: Johnson Library, National Security File, Name File, Komer Memos, Vol. I. Secret.

[2] On February 22 UAR President Nasser made a speech declaring that no country could claim independence unless the foreign military bases on its territory were liquidated. The Libyan Government subsequently announced that it did not intend to renew the treaties whereby the United States and the United Kingdom maintained bases in Libya.

[3] British jets attacked a fort in the Harib area of Yemen on March 28 in reprisal for a March 27 attack from Yemen into South Arabian Federation territory.

[4] Telegram 549 from Taiz, March 29, urged that the United States cancel its British representation function in Yemen and argued that it would be more effective as a relatively disinterested party rather than in its present role, which was interpreted by many YARG officials as that of lawyer for the United Kingdom. (National Archives and Records Administration, RG 59, Central Files 1964–66, POL 32–1 ADEN–YEMEN)

[5] A handwritten notation on the memorandum reads: "RWK. I doubt that we should do this [at] this moment. McGB"

325. Telegram From the Department of State to the Mission to the United Nations[1]

Washington, April 1, 1964, 8:01 p.m.

2581. Subj: Security Council Meeting on Yemen–Aden Problem. Pending further clarification tactics British plan pursue in Security Council in countering Yemeni complaint[2] and, of course, subject to unforeseen developments in Council itself, following are our thoughts and general guidelines for your use in Council:

1. We inclined agree with British and your assessment that there will not be enough votes for serious condemnatory resolution directed against the U.K. We would expect therefore that the outcome of the Council meeting would be adjournment with no resolution or a relatively mild resolution deploring the situation and urging all parties concerned to refrain from further exacerbation of the situation and urging them to settle their differences.

We would hope to see the debate limited to the incidents per se but doubt that this can be done. If the debate expands to include a broad and vitriolic attack on the British position on Aden, we presume the British will respond by pointing to the fact that the UAR has failed to carry out its agreement to disengage and continued Egyptian military presence in Yemen has now given rise to the border incidents. While we would not want to initiate a debate which drags the UAR into the picture, if others have already done so we may wish to find some way of referring to the matter in our statement.

2. *Resolution.* The general parameters of an acceptable resolution seem to us to be as follows:

(1) Resolution should not be condemnatory nor fix blame. A paragraph which deplored the various violent incidents which had taken place without specific mention of one side or the other would seem appropriate. As an ultimate fallback, and providing the British are also prepared to accept, we could live with a resolution which deplored

---

[1] Source: National Archives and Records Administration, RG 59, Central Files 1964–66, POL 31–1 UK–YEMEN. Confidential. Drafted by Deputy Director of the Office of UN Political Affairs William G. Jones; cleared by Deputy Assistant Secretary of State for European Affairs William C. Burdett and Talbot; and approved by Assistant Secretary of State for International Organization Affairs Harlan Cleveland. Repeated to London, Taiz, and Cairo.

[2] In an April 1 letter to the President of the UN Security Council Yemen charged that the United Kingdom had committed more than 40 acts of aggression against it since September 1962, culminating in the air attack against Harib on March 28. A British letter of March 28 stated that the attack had been launched to protect the South Arabian Federation after a series of Yemeni air and ground attacks during the month of March. The Security Council convened on April 2 to consider the charges and countercharges.

the various incidents on both sides but in which specific mention was made of the British attack of March 27 which precipitated the Yemen complaint.

(2) We doubt the need or desirability at this juncture for injecting a UN presence or field operation of any sort into the situation and presume the U.K. would not want such presence at this time. Furthermore, we foresee a probable reluctance on the part of the SYG to become engaged in the tangled web of U.K.–Arab disputes. If the U.K. could accept, and if there is substantial pressure for involvement of the UN, we could agree to a general request to the SYG to exercise his influence as he deems appropriate with the parties concerned to restore peace and order on the Yemen–South Arabian frontier.

(3) In its operative paragraphs the resolution presumably would call on the parties to the conflict to cease violent action and attempt to settle their differences. We see some advantage to having the call made on all members of the UN to cooperate in avoiding actions which exacerbate tensions and lead to violence in the area. This broad language has the merit of embracing the UAR and USSR.

(4) We, of course, would not want to introduce a resolution ourselves and presume that this would be done by one or more non-permanent members of the Council, perhaps Brazil or Bolivia. Hopefully such a resolution would dissuade Morocco or others from introducing a strong and unacceptable condemnatory resolution which would have no chance of passing.

Rusk

326.   **Memorandum From the President's Special Assistant for National Security Affairs (Bundy) to President Johnson[1]**

Washington, April 9, 1964.

SUBJECT

Resolution on the British-Yemen Air Strike

The disputed resolution on the British-Yemen air strike has three parts. The first condemns reprisals in general as contrary to the Charter. The second deplores the British attack on the fort at Harib on March 28. The third deplores all other actions by any party which led up to the British attack.[2]

Stevenson argues that we must support the resolution because: (1) we have a consistent record of opposition to reprisals and strikes of this sort; (2) this particular strike was out of all proportion to the provocation, although the provocation was real; (3) the impact of abstention will be very severe in the Middle East and in the UN where we need support from many of those who will be most outraged—especially Africans, Arabs and Asians; (4) Stevenson has already spoken against the British action, with State Department approval,[3] and his own moral position (a matter of deep interest to him) will be affected.[4]

Rusk argues equally strongly the other way: (1) Rab Butler has fought a determined fight against the hard-liners in the British Cabinet to prevent a veto and to secure a British abstention;[5] (2) the provocation

---

[1] Source: Johnson Library, National Security File, Country File, Yemen, Memos, Vol. I, 11/63–6/64. No classification marking.

[2] The draft resolution, submitted to the Security Council by Morocco and the Ivory Coast on April 8, also called upon Yemen and the United Kingdom to exercise maximum restraint; and requested the Secretary-General to try to settle the outstanding issues in agreement with the two parties. (UN doc. S/5650)

[3] For text of Ambassador Stevenson's statement before the Security Council on April 6, see *American Foreign Policy: Current Documents, 1964*, pp. 713–714.

[4] In a 10:59 a.m. telephone conversation with Rusk on April 9, Stevenson declared that he could not abstain on a resolution that condemned reprisals and attacks and called for restraint; he argued that no one would respect the U.S. moral position any longer. The Secretary responded that it had been a considerable battle to keep the British from voting against the resolution; he noted that the British position in South Arabia was very important to us and that they needed U.S. help in this situation. If the United States voted for this resolution, it would undermine reasonable and moderate elements in London and make it difficult to get British help in other matters. Stevenson reiterated the moral importance of this. Rusk said that he felt strongly about it and would advise the President to abstain. (National Archives and Records Administration, RG 59, Rusk Files: Lot 72 D 192, Rusk Telcons)

[5] In a 10:02 a.m. telephone conversation with Rusk, the British Ambassador, Lord Harlech, said that Foreign Secretary Butler had gotten the Cabinet to agree not to veto the resolution. The Ambassador said he was very disturbed at the fact that having gotten the Cabinet to agree to abstain, the United States and France would not abstain with Britian. If the United States did not abstain, it would create a most deplorable situation in Britain. (Ibid.)

is more sustained and serious than Stevenson recognizes; (3) the U.S. itself may have to respond to provocations of a more serious but technically similar sort either in Cuba or in Vietnam; (4) We have other business pending with Sandys which makes this no time for a Suez-type reaction from hard-line British Tories.

My own reluctant but clear recommendation is as follows: (1) we should abstain; (2) we should go in very firmly to Home to say that this is a one-time act of loyalty which we could not repeat in parallel circumstances, because in our view the reaction, on which we were not consulted, was excessive and imprudent; (3) we should find a way of making it known that we have abstained in order to help prevent a veto, in order to support the wise Butler against the foolish Sandys, and because of an underlying feeling that these resolutions totally miss the real issues involved.

We should also seek to have the "good British" help us somewhat by explaining that their abstention indicates less of a sense of righteousness than a veto would have done, since they are in fact accepting passage of the motion.

McG. B.

---

327. Telephone Conversation Between President Johnson and Secretary of State Rusk[1]

Washington, April 9, 1964, 12:06 p.m.

Rusk: . . . in a lot of places here . . . he has not performed in Yemen, he is undermining us in the wheel of space, and he is pitching this arms race into the Near East.

Johnson: Well, this is not going to help us with him, is it?

Rusk: But I think it's important for Nasser to know that we're not . . . that he mustn't take us for granted on these things . . . I think an abstention on this is something of a warning to Nasser that we're coming close to the end of the trail on this business.

---

[1] Source: Johnson Library, Recordings and Transcripts, Recording of Telephone Conversation between President Johnson and Rusk, April 9, 1964, 12:06 p.m., Tape F64.23, Side A, PNO 6. No classification marking. This transcript was prepared in the Office of the Historian specifically for this volume. The first portion of the recording is inaudible.

Johnson: Don't you think they'll pound us like hell all over the United Nations and all over the papers of the country?

Rusk: Well, I think that there will be . . . will be . . . .

Johnson: Stevenson will be running around raising hell like he was about the Venezuela delegation, won't he?

Rusk: Oh, I think he will be . . . he will be personally unhappy for two or three days, but I don't think there's going to be any major press campaign picking this up.

Johnson: Have you already told him what to do?

Rusk: Yes sir. Well, I told him . . . we had an instruction for him several days ago not to have a resolution that condemned the British, and this does . . . it said it deplores this thing the other day, but to express a general regret about violence on that frontier. Well, the resolution went beyond the point where we felt we could in our total interest here support it, but as it now stands, he wanted . . . he is willing . . . he is ready to do what we talked about this morning, but he just wanted to be sure that you know it's a close balanced decision and that he had some concern about it.

Johnson: Well, you just tell them that I do know, but I knew it the last minute . . . didn't know anything about it beforehand . . . don't know anything else I got to do except go with my Secretary of State when he tells me he feels strongly about it, but I sure think they ought to talk to us ahead of time and we ought to know more about it before the last minute, don't you?

Rusk: Yes, I think that's right . . . I think that's right . . .

Johnson: All right. You tell him that, and I'll try to reach him too, if I can.

Rusk: Thank you.[2]

---

[2] On April 9, by a vote of 9 to 0 with 2 abstentions (U.K. and U.S.), the Security Council adopted the draft resolution as submitted on April 8. Resolution 5650 condemned reprisals, deplored the British attack on Harib, deplored all attacks and incidents that had occurred in that area, called upon Yemen and the United Kingdom to exercise maximum restraint, and requested the Secretary-General to use his good offices. (UN doc. S/5650) The text is printed in *American Foreign Policy: Current Documents, 1964,* pp. 715–716. Stevenson told the Council that his government did not consider the resolution equitable nor responsive to the realities and facts that had been reviewed in the Council's debate, and that, accordingly, it could not vote for the resolution as it would like to have done. (UN doc. S/PV. 1111, par. 7)

328. Memorandum for the Record[1]

Washington, April 10, 1964.

SUBJECT

Daily White House Staff Meeting, 10 April 1964

1. Mr. Bundy presided throughout the meeting.

2. *Yemen.* There was a crisis yesterday concerning US vote on the Yemen issue at the UN. Involved were the President, Bundy, Ball, Stevenson, and Rusk. The crisis was not anticipated in advance, either by the State Department or the White House. It involved our backing the British on a vote in the Security Council. The US and the British abstained, and nine others condemned the British. Stevenson called Ball, Rusk, and the President and tried to get a shift in the US position after we had already informed the British that we would go along with them. Bundy wanted a post-mortem by Sam Belk, to see why we got that close to a vote without recognizing the problem. Bundy said it should have been clear to a lot of people, including himself, that we were heading in such a direction. Komer, who is responsible for Yemen, was silent at first, but said yesterday afternoon, he asked State why they had not warned him. Bundy said another question was why the White House had not warned State. There were no hard feelings, but the whole affair made a bad impression on everyone, including the President.

[Here follows discussion of other subjects.]

WYS

---

[1] Source: National Defense University Library, Special Collections, Taylor Papers, Chairman's Staff Group, April 1964. Secret; Eyes Only.

329. Telegram From the Department of State to Secretary of State Rusk in Manila[1]

Washington, April 11, 1964, 2:55 p.m.

Tosec 11. President has received following message from British Prime Minister. Acting Secretary and White House concerting on possibly reply. Will endeavor advise you prior your meeting with Carrington.

"April 10, 1964.

I should like to thank you most warmly for your decision to abstain on the resolution in the Security Council on Thursday, despite the doubts of most of your own people. I am most grateful for this act of solidarity.

I should now like to build on this decision and see whether we cannot achieve a sense of common purpose and align our common policies more closely over the whole problem of the Yemen and Aden. Experience has shown that the general Western interest, as well as the particular British and American interest, are best served when British and American policies are in harmony. I should now like to do for the Middle East what we did for South-East Asia last February.

Our respective Secretaries of State are shortly to meet. I hope you will agree that they should use this occasion to reach a general understanding over these questions.

Alec Douglas-Home"

Ball

---

[1] Source: National Archives and Records Administration, RG 59, Central Files 1964–66, POL 31–1 UK–YEMEN/UN. Secret; Priority; Exdis. Drafted by Jeanne W. Davis (S/S); cleared by Special Assistant to the Under Secretary of State George S. Springsteen, Jr., and in substance by EUR Staff Assistant Jerome K. Holloway and Bromley Smith; and approved by Davis.

330. Message From President Johnson to Prime Minister Douglas Home[1]

Washington, April 12, 1964, 1603Z.

CAP 64114. 1. Many thanks for your note.[2] Our decision to abstain was indeed an act of solidarity, but I feel I must tell you quite frankly that I approved it reluctantly and only because as the matter finally came to me it seemed to me that you were entitled to expect that we would not oppose you directly. On the merits, in a future case, it would be hard for me to make the same decision again.[3] We may have to pay heavily for the abstention in a loss of authority and an awkward precedent that can be used against us.

2. I, of course, have no illusions about Nasser or the mischievous game he is playing. But I quite frankly doubt that at this point in time abrupt challenges to the Arabs are useful for our joint interests.

3. So I agree that this incident and its aftermath make it more than ever important that we concert our Near Eastern policies more closely. I hope that Rusk and Butler will be able to reach some solid conclusions when they meet during the CENTO session later this month. We both have such great interests to guard in that tortured part of the world that we cannot afford to pursue divergent policies.

---

[1] Source: Johnson Library, National Security File, Komer Files, Yemen, December 1963–March 1966. Secret; Nodis.

[2] See Document 329.

[3] In a 4 p.m. telephone conversation with Ball on April 10, Bundy said that the President wanted to send a message on the post mortem of the Yemen problem to the Prime Minister, making it clear that the United States did not want to get into the habit of getting caught in an abstention it really didn't believe in. (Johnson Library, National Security File, Papers of George W. Ball, Yemen, 4/9/64–2/23/66)

331. Memorandum From Robert W. Komer of the National Security Council Staff to the President's Special Assistant for National Security Affairs (Bundy)[1]

Washington, April 21, 1964.

Mac—

Rusk's talk with Butler on Yemen, Aden, and YAR policy is set for next Monday the 27th. *So lunch today may be the best time for LBJ to weigh in.*

There are signs the British themselves now see the Harib retaliation as involving excessive political cost. It got *all* the Arabs (not just Nasser) sore at them, and pointed the finger directly at Aden.

Let's also remember that trouble on Yemen/SAF border is largely result of UK clandestine ops in support of Yemeni royalists.

As for a tougher line toward Nasser, the overriding argument is that it will cost us more than we gain. The Aswan Dam episode and refusal of US military aid in 1955–56 is a case in point. They led directly to Soviet entry into the Arab world, and Nasser's seizure of the Suez Canal. We've spent some years digging out of that hole; why get into it again.

Sure Nasser is trying to oust us from US/UK bases in Libya and Aden, and opposes us on Israel. But the key point is that our support to him (which goes mostly into the bellies of the fellahin) constrains him from pushing too hard. He knows he has something to lose if he makes too many speeches about Libyan bases (one was bad enough).

We can't lick Nasser so long as he symbolizes Arab nationalism. So the best way to prolong our hold on our assets is to string him along, not give him a bloody nose. A flexible policy—using carrots as well as stick—best serves UK as well as US interests, and the Fonoff knows this.

Nor does succumbing to Sandysism buy us kudos in London. I'd argue that the British will be more amenable if we growl at them, than if we are apologetic about the Middle East. After all, our record is better than theirs.

RWK

---

[1] Source: Johnson Library, National Security File, Country File, United Kingdom, Meetings with Butler, 4/64. Secret.

332.   Circular Telegram From the Department of State to Certain Posts[1]

Washington, April 22, 1964, 7:59 p.m.

1971. Jidda's 981 (326 to Cairo).[2] Before Faisal comes to Cairo, Department believes Embassy Cairo might profitably make presentation along following lines to someone close to Nasser.

1. Present constellation of factors bearing on Yemen situation offers opportune and appropriate occasion to press toward normalization:

a. We presume Arab states wish preserve momentum of Arab détente, as symbolized by upcoming Faisal–Nasser meeting.

b. UNYOM[3] is up for renewal May 4.

c. Now that Spinelli[4] has been on job for over 4 months, his findings should be ready for examination by parties.

d. Harib raid and Security Council hearings thereon have had sobering effect. We have impression all parties would welcome acceptable formula to reduce tension along Yemen–SAF frontier.

2. USG has over-all interest in reduction Arabian Peninsula tensions, and specific interest in creating circumstances that will facilitate pursuance economic cooperation with UARG. UAR is in final stages concluding stabilization program and new standby agreement with IMF that will meet one of three prerequisites for US commodity loan. As emphasized from beginning, diversion of resources to Yemen opera-

---

[1] Source: National Archives and Records Administration, RG 59, Central Files 1964–66, POL 27 YEMEN. Confidential. Drafted by Symmes, Seelye, and Jones on April 21; cleared by Buffum, Sisco, Officer in Charge of Economic Affairs in the Office of Near Eastern Affairs Enoch S. Duncan, and Davies and by Officer in Charge of U.K. Affairs Thomas M. Judd in substance; and approved by Jernegan. Sent to Cairo, Jidda, London, Taiz, Dhahran, and USUN and repeated to Aden, CINCSTRIKE, and CINCMEAFSA for POLAD.

[2] In telegram 981 from Jidda, April 17, Ambassador Hart reported that he had told the UN Secretary-General's Special Representative for Yemen, Pier P. Spinelli, before the latter met with Crown Prince Faisal on April 14 that he hoped Faisal did not believe the U.S. Government could or would try to force Nasser to withdraw his troops from Yemen if Faisal made no helpful moves at the forthcoming Cairo meeting. Following the meeting Spinelli told Hart that Faisal was being very cagey regarding what he might be prepared to do in Cairo. The Ambassador reported that Spinelli's approach was to try to obtain withdrawal of the house of Hamid al-Din from Yemen with the simultaneous withdrawal of UAR troops and phasing in of UN troops. Hart commented that he saw no way to extract the members of the house of Hamid al-Din from Yemen. (Ibid., POL 27–14 YEMEN/UN)

[3] The UN Yemen Observation Mission (UNYOM) was established on July 4, 1963, following a June 11 Security Council Resolution requesting that the Secretary-General establish a mission to observe Saudi and UAR disengagement from the Yemen civil war. (UN doc. S/5326) For text, see *American Foreign Policy: Current Documents, 1963*, p. 607. UNYOM's mandate was renewed each 2 months thereafter with the mutual consent and financial support of the two parties involved, Saudi Arabia and the United Arab Republic.

[4] Spinelli was appointed Special Representative for Yemen on November 3, 1963.

tion has been obstacle to commodity loan type assistance. Earlier progress in reducing tensions over Yemen (e.g., restoration Saudi–UAR diplomatic relations) has encouraged us that problem of economic drain being reduced. It is important that progress continue, since difficult Congress believe US resources not being diverted to Yemen campaign when news full of alleged YAR violations of SAF air space, UAR–YAR propaganda campaign against British position in Aden, and indications continued high-level UAR expeditionary force.

3. We would hope that during next few weeks the parties concerned could explore following possibilities:

a. Complete SAG dissociation from Hamid al-Din family.

b. De facto pull-back of SAF and YAR troops from respective sides of frontier.

c. Extension UNYOM patrols to southern frontier.

d. Consolidation of YARG. We would appreciate UAR's views on advantages of according progressively increasing responsibilities to moderate republican elements, especially those in Political Bureau.

e. Encouragement of dialogue between these elements and northern tribes not irrevocably aligned with Hamid al-Din family.

f. Encouragement of YARG to normalize relations with Saudi Arabia, work for détente with UK, and freeze border dispute with SAF.

g. Immediate public and substantial withdrawal UAR troops to coincide with implementation of one or more of the above points.

4. Last week in separate conversations Talbot and NE officers impressed on Kamel importance of expeditious progress on disengagement, pull-back, and extenstion UN presence beyond May 4. By associating such progress with Nasser–Faisal meeting, UAR might hope to improve relations with SAG, reduce Yemen opposition capabilities, lay groundwork for negotiated solution to Yemen dispute, and begin to transfer some of onerous economic and military burden UARG has borne in Yemen for a year and a half.

5. Collapse of Imamate left vaccum that UAR is currently filling. However, Egyptians can read in historical record unlikelihood of any collapse of northern tribes' will to resist. UARG may find that, to normalize Yemen situation, it must make some unpleasant concessions such as those floated at Amran. Only early hope of dignified extrication from massive involvement 1500 miles from home seems to lie in melding moderate northern and southern Yemeni elements in viable YARG, under UAR and Saudi sponsorship.

6. If, as we suspect, UARG's main concern is to prevent restoration of Imamate and SARG's is to get Egyptians out of Yemen, grounds for negotiated settlement would appear to be taking shape.

7. In short, does UARG share our feeling that failure to make moderate concessions now could bring on costly consequences later? Or does it feel capable of maintaining heavy commitments in Yemen

indefinitely against Saudi and royalist opposition without damage to its wider national interests?

8. In any case, we believe UAR should immediately confirm to SYG that it favors extension UNYOM for at least two more months.

FYI: Department increasingly puzzled by UARG's lack of enthusiasm for broadened YARG or Spinelli initiatives. We would welcome addressees' estimates whether this attitude merely reflects indecision or whether UARG is playing for time in expectation of change in international circumstances (Labor victory in UK, trouble in Aden, etc.).[5]

Rusk

---

[5] In telegram 2514 from Cairo, April 27, Ambassador Badeau commented that the instructions in circular telegram 1971 impressed him as a shopping list of items already discussed in his many meetings with Nasser on Yemen, with the only substantive request being for UAR confirmation to the United Nations of its willingness to extend UNYOM. Badeau said he had arranged to meet with Nasser after his return from Yemen on a separate matter. When they met he proposed to inquire about Nasser's estimate of the Yemen situation based on his recent trip, which would give him an opportunity to raise most of the questions in the instructions in a more useful form than a formal presentation. (National Archives and Records Administration, RG 59, Central Files 1964–66, POL 27 YEMEN)

---

333. Memorandum From Robert W. Komer of the National Security Council Staff to the President's Special Assistant for National Security Affairs (Bundy)[1]

Washington, April 28, 1964.

Mac—

Butler's case to Rusk is "Nasser is our implacable enemy."[2] The UK recognizes this, and the US will too in time. The UK is the target now, but we'll be next. So, since Nasser has declared war on them, the British are going to fight back: (a) They'll match UAR/YAR subversion in South Arabia with a stepped up covert campaign in Yemen; (b) they

---

[1] Source: Johnson Library, National Security File, Country File, United Kingdom, Meetings with Butler, 4/64. Secret.

[2] For a memorandum of conversation recording Rusk's April 27 discussion with Foreign Secretary Butler, see Document 55.

want us to cut off aid to Nasser; (c) they plan to bring the case against the UAR to the SC, and want a promise of US support. (It was left vague whether UK wants us only to back demilitarization of a border zone, or to back a harsh condemnatory blast too.)

The Brits, in their frustration and concern over Aden, are grossly over-reacting. So far the UAR/YAR threat to Aden is more talk than anything else. With 40,000 troops in Yemen, Nasser still can't contol the place.

But the clinching argument against the UK proposals is that they can't win:

1. Regardless of the covert or overt pressure, we can't force Nasser out of Yemen. Since September 1962 he's repeatedly demonstrated that he'll send in whatever amount of force is necessary to hold on (it's 40,000 now). And instead of bowing to covert external pressure he'll up the ante with counter subversion (as he did with Saudis till we turned them off, and as he is now in countering *continued UK covert support of Royalists*).

2. We and UK couldn't win *in the UN either.* It would become a straight "colonial issue" on which we usually lose. The way to defend Aden is to keep it out of the UN.

3. True, we could *bleed* Nasser indefinitely in the Yemen (as UK has been doing in fact for months). But this is one of factors which make our disengagement policy fail. We keep Nasser in the Yemen by bleeding him.

Worse yet, we'd stand to lose far more than we could conceivably gain.

1. We wouldn't just be waging war with Nasser. *Except for the Saudis every Arab state would back the UAR.* In fact, we'd solidify the Arabs against us, largely because Nasser would again agitate US/UK support of Israel—the one surefire Arab cause.

2. When Nasser ups the ante the logical focus of his attack will be the bases in Aden *and Libya.* So instead of preserving our base rights we'd increase the ultimate pressure on them.

3. Butler says *they'd stay covert,* but this is impossible in the Middle East (we know). The whole affair will soon leak as Cairo trades legitimate charges of subversion with London.

4. The threat to Aden is far from immediate (it will take the UAR years to make Yemen a country). *But the threat of heightened Arab-Israeli tension is immediate.* This is the year of the Jordan Waters (and the US elections). There could hardly be a worse time to throw down the gauntlet to the Arabs, and have them react against our Israel policy.

5. Despite Butler's claim of a UAR/YAR/Soviet link, we see the UAR as wanting to limit the Soviet presence in Yemen (for its own

reasons). But the UK proposals could force the UAR to let the Soviets come in big. *Then* where's Aden?

In sum the Brits can't have thought through their proposals. They'd stand to gain us nothing but trouble. And this to bail out a *lame duck cabinet* whose policy might get reversed come October.

What to do? Unless we turn the UK off hard, I'm afraid we'll get whipsawed. Talbot proposes a gentlemen's agreement to pursue divergent lines for the moment. But I fear that their policy will inevitably rub off on us. Wheelus is, after all, another base like Aden. And if the Brits join the Israelis in sniping at our policy, the pressure may get out of hand. So the best defense may be a strong attack. And let's toss in counterproposals:

1. If the President is willing (the Brits are obviously trying to see if he's an easier mark than Kennedy here), let's tell Butler we flatly disagree, and LBJ wants to take the case to Home. This will raise the level from Rusk/Butler (Rusk's NEA people are in despair).

2. Diplomatic approach to Nasser suggesting UK will call off dogs in Yemen, if Nasser will lay off Aden.

3. Agree to back demilitarization of south Yemen border area, if and only if UK agrees in return not to raise hell in UN.

4. Make clear we don't want a fight with Nasser while Arab-Israeli issue hot.

5. Tell Brits we'll bite back if they start attacking our ME policy.

RWK

334. **Memorandum From the President's Special Assistant for National Security Affairs (Bundy) and Robert W. Komer of the National Security Council Staff to President Johnson[1]**

Washington, April 29, 1964.

SUBJECT

    Your Meeting with R.A. Butler

[Here follows discussion of another subject.]

The main topic Butler wants to take up is the Mideast (it's a commentary in itself on UK policy that when they say Mideast they mean Aden and Yemen). Butler's pitch to Rusk is that the British intend to fight fire with fire, and take the offensive against Nasser in the UN and in Yemen.

We're from Missouri on this one, and healthy skepticism is the order of the day. We simply doubt the British have thought through this matter. First, we don't see how going to war with Nasser (the British have already been needling him in Yemen covertly for months) will get him out of Yemen and relieve the threat to Aden. As he's already shown, he's much more likely to send more troops down there and raise more hell about getting UK colonialist bases off Arab soil. We can't win in the UN either, on a straight anti-colonial issue. Just as shooting up Harib, it will hurt more than it helps.

Worse yet, this is a game where Nasser is likely to up the ante. Jousting with him right now might well generate an across the board US/UK falling out with the Arabs, with repercussions on Libya as well as Aden, and even on our oil. This wouldn't be just a war with Nasser. All Arabs but the Saudis are highly suspicious of the US on Israel and the Jordan Waters, especially in an election year. They'd all back the UAR as a matter of Arab solidarity if we backed the UK against the UAR. But even if we don't join the UK, we'll suffer too, in Libya for example, from the Arab backlash against them. So we hope you'll go further than denying Butler's plea, and seek to persuade him our way.

For what it's worth, even the UK Foreign Office experts seem to join with ours in worrying over the bloody-mindedness of their ministers. This is just *not* the time to start a war with Nasser—especialy one which, like the Aswan Dam fiasco, we're not likely to win. And if

---

[1] Source: Johnson Library, National Security File, Meetings with the President, McGeorge Bundy, Vol. I. Secret.

Labor comes in next October, UK policy will probably become more like ours.

McG.B.

R.W. Komer[2]

---

[2] Printed from a copy that bears this typed signature.

---

335.   Telegram From the Department of State to the Embassy in Saudi Arabia[1]

Washington, May 7, 1964, 9:08 p.m.

706. We are somewhat concerned at possibility that as aftermath Nasser's speeches Yemen Faisal may be tempted jeopardize his détente with UAR by resuming aid to royalists or at very least by allowing Saudi Arabia be used as channel for possible future British aid to royalists. Accordingly, suggest at your discretion you make following points with Faisal at appropriate opportunity.

1. Since concern for security of Saudi Arabia was fundamental reason US became involved in advancing disengagement agreement Yemen, we particularly pleased that SAG renewed support for UNYOM[2] and continues to eschew sending aid to royalists. Full availability SAG resources for sustaining progress of development and reform program is doubtless best investment for security of country against subversive attacks.

2. In view increasing friction on Yemen's southern border and treatment of that conflict in much of Arabic press and radio as part of Arab liberation movement, security concerns Saudi Arabia would seem particularly served by continuing scrupulously avoid any implication involvement (i.e., assistance to royalists) which would doubtless be interpreted in Arab world in fashion detrimental to Saudi regime.

---

[1] Source: National Archives and Records Administration, RG 59, Central Files 1964–66, POL SAUD–UAR. Secret. Drafted by Moore; cleared by Judd and in substance by Campbell; and approved by Davies. Repeated to Cairo, London, Taiz, and Dhahran.

[2] In telegram 1020 from Jidda, May 2, Hart reported that Faisal had agreed to renewal of UNYOM for another 2 months. (Ibid., POL 27–14 YEMEN/UN)

3. We understand that recent governmental changes in Yemen may bring into office persons who command wider Yemeni support, including perhaps northern tribes. We hope Faisal will encourage royalists to keep open mind to possibilities of compromise with republicans.

4. Renewal SAG–UAR relations has opened way for more stable and fruitful development in area; would be shame if momentum this direction gained at time Amer, Sadat visit Riyadh were allowed lapse. We realize that events connected Nasser's trip Yemen may have discouraged Faisal from making contemplated journey Cairo. However, our own dealings with Nasser may have relevant parallel: while we frequently have not agreed with UAR policies and actions, we have found it of continued benefit to maintain dialogue with Nasser, leaving avenue open to explore areas of mutual interest.[3]

Rusk

---

[3] In telegram 1052 from Jidda, May 12, Hart wrote that he had concluded that it would be premature for him to make the suggested points to Faisal. When meeting with Acting Deputy Foreign Minister Mas'ud on May 9, however, the Ambassador had dwelt on the opportunities offered by the recent governmental changes in Yemen as suggested in paragraph 3. (Ibid., POL SAUD–UAR)

---

336.   Telegram From the Embassy in the United Arab Republic to the Department of State[1]

Cairo, May 8, 1964, midnight.

2631. Reference: Department Circular telegram 1990.[2]

I had intended devoting major part of upcoming interview with Nasser to situation in Yemen and Aden, with statement of US position as set forth in reference telegram. Shortly before appointment finally set Departmental instructions received concerning another topic whose importance seemed overriding. I therefore elected to deal extensively with second topic (which could only be presented to President)[3] and

---

[1] Source: National Archives and Records Administration, RG 59, Central Files 1964–66, POL 19 ADEN. Secret. Repeated to London and Taiz.

[2] Document 54.

[3] Telegram 2632 from Cairo, May 8, recording this portion of the Ambassador's conversation with Nasser is printed in *Foreign Relations, 1964–1968*, vol. XVIII, Document 52.

leave Yemen–Aden for discussion with FonMin Mahmoud Riad, who has followed question closely while Delegate to UN.

President Nasser received me 1930 May 7. After completing major presentation I stated that I had intended to discuss Yemen with him and set forth USA position, but now proposed to do this with FonMin Riad. President Nasser said that this would be a good move since Riad thoroughly conversant with matter and he was trying to make FonMin effective center for Ambassadorial representation. I noted that Riad would doubtless be busy during Khrushchev visit but that I needed to see him during coming week, the earlier the better. President Nasser responded that his FonMin "would not be very busy with Khrushchev" and indicated that he would see to it that Riad would be available. The President then briefly and on his own initiative made the following remarks on the Yemen–Aden situation.

1. Major purpose of President's Yemen trip was to set forward urgently needed reorganization of YAR Government. As he had told me many times in past, YAR Government has been "hopeless," beset with inexperience, inefficiency, personal rivalry, and tribal differences. Sallal has lost much support although he is a "good but sick man." When Nasser went to Yemen he requested Sallal to take with him Yemen expatriates in UAR such as Jaifi and Noman, who, while critical of Sallal, might provide a center of popular support. While in Yemen Nasser produced a new constitution and government structure in discussion with Yemenis, this including Vice Presidents who, while under Sallal, were in fact to be effective administrators of government. He also arranged for popular assembly and overhaul of Political Bureau. When organization completed on paper, Yemenis requested five days for study and reaction but Nasser said that with something of an impish smile, "I gave them only 24 hours and they accepted it." President admitted that paper structure of government is useless without competent operators but believed that some progress toward more stable and popular government has been made.

2. President's attack in Yemen on British position was generated by the fact that UAR has "completely reliable and convincing evidence" of British arms, money and military support to Yemeni dissidents flowing across Southern border. President said, "because of this our men are being killed and I cannot accept this, hence my attack on the British."

3. In general, the present UK Government under Lord Home seems to have reverted to the Eden outlook. Macmillan honestly tried to make a fresh start, letting bygones be bygones. Ever since Ottawa speech it has been clear to UAR that Home's Government has turned its back on conciliatory Macmillan policy and is now acting in Eden mood.

4. Butler's deliberate publicity of UK request for cut in American aid particularly irritated Nasser. He said that UK was publicly uttering

threats against UAR and "if they can threaten, we can threaten also." This, he said was natural extension of "harsh" policy to which he would continue strongly to react.

I pointed out to the President that it appeared to me unrealistic to expect that a government so near election as the Home Government could take any effective steps altering major UK policy. Nasser admitted this was true but emphasized again that when attacked he would respond in kind.

The President then requested that I review entire situation with the FonMin as suggested at opening of interviews.

Comment: It is interesting that Nasser chose to give me above details in light of my statement that I had not come to discuss Yemen–Aden and would make my presentation thereon to FonMin. I assume President's evoking topic partly due to extended discussions I have had with him on this throughout past year but more particularly to defensive mood wishing to register directly with me his alleged objectives. It is interesting that when mentioning UK request for curtailment US aid he did not ask what the American reaction had been or what we intended to do. It seemed to me that his obvious assumption was that request had been fruitless.

President Nasser was obviously under the weather, looking gray and drawn and perspiring frequently. He said that ever since his return from Yemen he had been ill and was still taking heavy doses of antibiotics. On May 1 when he delivered his fighting speech against Britain he had some fever and felt particularly sick.

Badeau

337.   Telegram From the Department of State to the Embassy in the United Kingdom[1]

Washington, May 15, 1964, 7:38 p.m.

7503. Taiz 643,[2] London's 5665[3] and USUN's 4126.[4] We continue attach great importance to early meeting between YARG and UK representatives under UN aegis re abatement Yemen–Aden border tensions. Accordingly, we pleased at report YAR Ambassador al-Aini seeking authority begin talks with Sir Patrick Dean at UN and at fact HMG has apparently not ruled out entirely possibility direct talks. On other hand, we are concerned at British Cabinet's apparent disinclination to authorize direct contact at this time and YARG's continuing to insist that UK must first agree recognize YARG.

For London: We recognize that HMG might have difficulty authorizing direct talks with YARG at this time in view recent area developments and domestic attacks on HMG position. Nevertheless, request you again approach Foreign Office urging British approval and, citing Taiz 643 (275 to London), stress fact Yemeni authorities continue to protest desire settle peacefully outstanding problems. Emphasize again that failure take advantage opportunity engage in direct dialogue, affording Yemenis opportunity appreciate UK desire abate tensions, will not only weaken ability new, more moderate Yemeni leadership resist UAR domination but force YARG into increasing reliance on UAR (and possibly USSR) in handling affairs affecting South Arabia.[5]

For Taiz: Following up Foreign Minister's earlier comments to you re YARG desire for "peaceful settlement" with British, you should stress fact that only practical first step in this direction is UN-sponsored YARK–UK meeting perhaps at UN. If YARG serious in this sentiment, it should waive all pre-conditions for talks. Immediate UK recognition of YARG totally unrealistic to expect, but could well flow eventually from understanding and rapport hopefully established through direct meetings. Latter present Yemenis with opportunity convince UK of

---

[1] Source: National Archives and Records Administration, RG 59, Central Files 1964–66, POL 32–1 ADEN–YEMEN. Secret; Priority. Drafted by Seelye, cleared by Judd and Campbell, and approved by Davies. Also sent to Taiz and Cairo and repeated to Jidda, Dhahran, USUN, and Aden.

[2] Dated May 12. (Ibid.)

[3] Dated May 14. (Ibid., UN 10–4)

[4] Dated May 14. (Ibid., POL 32–1 ADEN/YEMEN)

[5] In telegram 5686 from London, May 16, Ambassador Bruce reported that, although the Foreign Office was closed for a long weekend, he had conveyed the substance of telegram 7503 to the Arabian Department duty officer, who had noted that nothing less than a ministerial decision would suffice to authorize such direct talks. (Ibid.)

their desire for peaceful relations. Also would appreciate knowing what "specific steps" Foreign Minister has in mind (Taiz 643).[6]

For Cairo: Request you probe further stated UAR desire (as expressed by Riad to Beeley) for direct YARG–UK talks and indicate that if this in fact represents official UAR position, latter should urge Yemenis—as we are urging British—to agree to meet without setting pre-conditions. At same time you should stress that calling Security Council on Aden would hardly facilitate this. In addition, you should (1) express concern at reports we are receiving that UAR intensifying training of Adeni dissident guerillas and (2) call attention to HMG decision resume constitutional talks re Aden, apparently to include consultation with all Adeni political parties.[7]

Rusk

---

[6] Telegram 672 from Taiz, May 25, reported that Yemeni Foreign Minister Sirri stated that Yemeni representatives at the United Nations were authorized to meet with U.K. representatives, and that Yemen was willing to meet with the United Kingdom in New York or Cairo or "through friends." (Ibid.)

[7] In telegram 2747 from Cairo, May 18, Badeau reported that he had discussed the Department's telegram with Deputy Prime Minister for Foreign Affairs Mahmoud Fawzi, who responded that the problem was extremely complicated and that no single factor held the key to the solution. Fawzi said it was unreasonable to expect that training of dissident Adenis should cease without equal cessation of U.K. support for al-Badr, and called constitutional talks on Aden a "facade for inactivity." (Ibid.)

---

338.   Telegram From the Department of State to the Embassy in Yemen[1]

Washington, May 26, 1964, 4:23 p.m.

720. Embtel 674.[2] You should continue press YARG agree talk with UK under UN aegis. We have not given up hope UK will relent and

---

[1] Source: National Archives and Records Administration, RG 59, Central Files 1964–66, POL UK–YEMEN. Secret; Immediate. Drafted by Seelye; cleared by Davies, Judd, and Dorrance; and approved by Jernegan. Also sent to London and repeated to Cairo, Jidda, Aden, and USUN.

[2] Telegram 674 from Taiz, May 26, asked whether, in view of the reluctance of the United Kingdom to enter into direct talks with Yemen, the Embassy should continue to press the Yemeni Government for talks with the United Kingdom under the aegis of the United Nations. (Ibid.)

believe possible YARG approval will favorably influence UK. Meanwhile, we continuing press HMG both here and in London.[3] FYI. Fact that al-Aini and Dean held private, exploratory discussion New York prior al-Aini departure for Yemen should be closely held and not revealed by you. End FYI.

For London: You should inform Foreign Office al-Aini now in Yemen and that Embassy Taiz being instructed capitalize on his presence to press YARG agree to border talks. Unless you perceive objection, request you again express strong hope HMG will see way clear to agreeing series of meetings with Yemenis under UN aegis, noting that unilateral UK refusal—eliminating best immediate prospect for abatement Yemeni-Adeni tensions—would be extremely regrettable.[4]

Rusk

---

[3] Telegram 695 from Taiz, May 31, reported that Foreign Minister Sirri had stated definitely on May 30 in the presence of Ambassador al-Aini that Yemeni representatives were authorized to talk with the United Kingdom, but added that Yemen would not continue such talks unless British representatives were willing to discuss specifics. (Ibid.)

[4] In telegram 5906 from London, May 27, Bruce reported that he had conveyed the substance of the Department's telegram to the Head of the Arabian Department at the Foreign Office, Frank Brenchley, who expressed his personal view that if al-Aini returned to New York, the Arabian Department would be disposed to recommend to Butler that Dean have another talk with him. He assumed that Butler's reaction would depend in large part on whether Yemeni deeds were consonant with its oral protestations of friendship, and noted the great sensitivity of such talks; even Sandys did not know about Dean's first meeting with al-Aini. (Ibid.)

339. Telegram From the Department of State to the Embassy in the United Arab Republic[1]

Washington, June 25, 1964, 6:14 p.m.

6034. Jidda's 1167, rptd 361 to Cairo.[2] Department continues be concerned by UAR failure make even token withdrawal troops from Yemen in consonance its disengagement undertaking. This fact alone has complicated USG relations with SAG, hardened UK position vis-à-vis Yemen, jeopardized continuation existing level USG economic support for UAR and, currently, risks bringing about demise of UNYOM and all that connotes. Accordingly, we propose following three-pronged démarche to UAR over next few days: (1) Assistant Secretary Talbot call in Ambassador Kamel, (2) Chargé Boswell see Foreign Minister Riad, (3) First Secretary Horgan approach Presidency Advisor al-Kholi.

We believe prospective démarches should be made along following lines:

1. After period of one year, UNYOM has failed observe any net withdrawal of UAR troops, one of purposes for which it was designed. On contrary UAR troop level has increased since UNYOM arrived on scene. While we believe UNYOM has nevertheless served useful purpose, SAG—which has generally complied with terms of disengagement agreement—finding it increasingly difficult continue agree UNYOM's renewal in face continued UAR non-performance. Repeated USG assurances to SAG over past year that UAR would in reasonable time withdraw its troops from Yemen now fall on deaf ears. Fact is Faisal seriously considering discontinuing his monetary support for UNYOM owing lack of even token UAR troop withdrawals.

2. We believe dispensing with UNYOM in no one's interests, including UAR. For our part we shall endeavor urge SAG not cause UNYOM demise. But, speaking frankly, we question whether we will be

---

[1] Source: National Archives and Records Administration, RG 59, Central Files 1964–66, POL 27 UAR–YEMEN. Secret; Priority. Drafted by Seelye on June 24; cleared by Davies, Buffum, Cleveland, Quinn (DOD/ISA), and in substance by Colonel Robinson (G/PM) and Officer in Charge of Politico-Military Affairs in the Office of Near Eastern and South Asian Regional Affairs Colonel Donald W. Bunte; and approved by Jernegan. Also sent to Jidda and USUN and repeated to London, Taiz, Dhahran, CINCSTRIKE/CINCMEAFSA, CINCSTRIKE for POLAD, and Aden.

[2] In telegram 1167 from Jidda, June 24, Hart reported that Saqqaf had transmitted to him Faisal's intention to inform U Thant that although the Saudi Government had no objection to the continuance of the UNYOM presence, it saw no further reason why it should pay anything for it in view of UAR non-performance. (Ibid., POL 27–14 YEMEN/UN)

successful in this regard in light of current SAG frame of mind—unless circumstances change.

3. Collapse of UNYOM would risk opening up Pandora's box of problems, including (a) tossing Yemen problem into lap of Security Council where UAR nonperformance on disengagement would be openly aired and subject to attack; (b) inviting massive Saudi "re-engagement" on behalf of Yemeni royalists, further complicating UAR security problem in Yemen; (c) clouding and perhaps terminating incipient, friendly UAR–Saudi diplomatic relationship which, in turn, might lead to further drift in area away from "summit atmosphere"; (d) virtually eliminating prospect of damping down under UN auspices YAR–SAF border tensions; and (e) further setting back date when UAR enabled reduce its expensive Yemeni commitment.

4. In last few weeks USG has again heard reports of imminent UAR troop withdrawals from Yemen, including indication first step would be departure one UAR brigade. Nasser's June 18 speech also mentioned drawdown UAR troop complement in Yemen. Yet up to moment we have received no indications whatsoever that any reductions have occurred. If withdrawals about take place or in fact taking place, we urge UAR adduce proof for benefit UNYOM and thus indirectly for benefit Saudi Arabia. Would be pity if UAR failure act in time produces collapse UNYOM.

5. We wish remind UAR USG could not afford sit idly by and allow worsening situation in Yemen (which would no doubt flow from removal of UNYOM) threaten security and stability Faisal regime.

6. In conclusion USG strongly urges UAR make immediate token withdrawal UAR troops from Yemen in order avert possible demise of UNYOM, and in consonance with its disengagement undertaking.[3]

For Jidda: You may inform Saqqaf confidentially of fact we making three-pronged approach to UAR. At same time, know you will continue urge him not allow Saudi Arabia be cause of UNYOM's going down drain and impress upon him considerable advantages to SAG of its continuation regardless UAR failure perform on disengagement.[4]

---

[3] Telegram 6061 to Cairo, June 26, reported that the démarche outlined in telegram 6034 had been made by Deputy Assistant Secretary Jernegan to UAR Ambassador Kamel on June 26. Kamel had responded that anything that caused the demise of UNYOM would be a disaster, that the situation in Yemen was now in a "stage of relaxation" with the atmosphere ripe for gradual withdrawal, and that the United States should not permit Faisal to create suspicion when the situation was "moving forward." (Ibid.)

[4] In telegram 1189 from Jidda, June 28, Hart reported that he had talked to Saqqaf along these lines. (Ibid., POL 27 UAR–YEMEN) In telegram 1201 from Jidda, July 1, the Ambassador reported that on June 30 he had called on Saqqaf to congratulate him on obtaining Faisal's agreement to renewal of UNYOM. (Ibid., POL 27–14 YEMEN/UN)

For USUN: Believe you should outline for SYG our information about Faisal's thinking on question of UNYOM's extension, as reflected Jidda's 1167. Source should of course be protected. You might indicate this information does not seem to square with SYG's belief UNYOM extension will be easily arranged. (USUN 4593)[5]

For Cairo: Re your 3155,[6] you should respond to al-Kholi as you propose, e.g. UN best suited perform role of mediator and April 9 SC resolution requested SYG use his good offices settle outstanding issues re south Yemen, in agreement with parties concerned. FYI. We prefer avoid undertaking mediatory roles. End FYI.

Rusk

---

[5] Dated June 23. (Ibid.)
[6] Dated June 24. (Ibid., POL 27 YEMEN)

---

340.   Memorandum From Harold H. Saunders of the National Security Council Staff to the President's Special Assistant for National Security Affairs (Bundy)[1]

Washington, July 2, 1964.

McGB:

UNYOM will be renewed for another 2 months on 4 July. But Faisal agreed to pay his share of costs only on condition that the SYG report to the Security Council his intent to liquidate UNYOM by 4 September unless the UAR pulls out a substantial number of troops.

Stevenson is suggesting to U Thant today that he shouldn't tie his hands but might say he "may have to liquidate." *SYG's report will probably hit the press this weekend.*[2]

We made another pitch to the Egyptians both here and in Cairo, but so far response has been noncommittal. We've seen no signs at all

---

[1] Source: Johnson Library, National Security File, Country File, United Arab Republic, Cables & Memos, Vol. II, 6/64–12/64. Secret.
[2] An excerpt from the Secretary-General's report of July 2 (UN doc. S/5794) is printed in *American Foreign Policy: Current Documents, 1964*, pp. 726–727.

of troop withdrawals despite Nasser's 18 June statement that the Yemenis are "ready to fend for themselves."

Related subject. I've started the wheels turning in State and AID to develop a position by 15 July on the Salhia Project we talked about this morning. Undoubtedly they will start from our present impasse over Yemen in considering where next with Nasser.[3]

Hal

---

[3] A handwritten notation in the margin in Bundy's handwriting reads: "But the way they should look at it is this: What would be a good package, *with Salhia?*"

---

341. Telegram From the Department of State to the Embassy in Yemen[1]

Washington, July 7, 1964, 8:16 p.m.

10. In call on Assistant Secretary Talbot July 6 YAR Ambassador al-Aini reported following re his recent visits to Sana'a and Cairo:

1. YAR leaders immensely disappointed with Nasser's visit to Yemen. Although at first he had indicated understanding YAR viewpoint, just before returning to Cairo Nasser produced fait accompli of constitution prepared in Cairo. Instead of strengthening authority of Prime Minister, as YAR leaders had wished, UAR-imposed constitution accorded President "all authority."

2. Despite foregoing, Prime Minister Jaifi and other YAR leaders resolved to "do their best." Yemenis believe Nasser's "plan" for Yemen will fail in long run. For his part Nasser evidently still looking for dramatic change elsewhere to help him out of Yemen imbroglio. Egyptians in Yemen refer optimistically to UAR "gains" in Iraq.

3. In several meetings with UAR Foreign Minister Riad in Cairo al-Aini sought ascertain UAR intentions re Yemen and took exception to UAR use of Yemen as base for UAR attacks against "South Arabia."

---

[1] Source: National Archives and Records Administration, RG 59, Central Files 1964–66, POL 17 YEMEN–US. Secret. Drafted by Seelye; cleared by Davies and in draft by Campbell and Frazier Meade of EUR/BNA; and approved by Talbot. Also sent to London and USUN and repeated to Cairo, Jidda, Dhahran, Aden, and CINCSTRIKE/CINCMEAFSA.

Also urged UAR refrain from laying Aden problem before UNSC. He did not reveal nature Riad replies.

4. YAR leaders believe YAR–UK differences can only be resolved if UK recognizes YAR and allows "self-determination" for Aden complex. Once these achieved YAR prepared to make border settlement in accordance 1934 Treaty.[2] Without foregoing, deployment observers along SAF border, establishment DMZ, etc, impossible.

Ambassador asserted that in his private meeting with Sir Patrick Dean in New York before he left US he had stressed fact Aden liberal movement in existence long before Nasser became interested and UK policy vis-à-vis YAR only inducing UAR remain in Yemen.

In response Talbot question re prospect reconciliation divergent Yemeni factions, al-Aini said implicit UAR threats of reprisal made it difficult for Republican leaders keep in touch with northern tribes. Nasser had threatened that he could easily bring Badr back if Yemenis fail tow mark. Al-Aini acknowledged that Nasser's determination maintain pre-eminent UAR position in Yemen serves as deterrent to USSR penetration.

Talbot again urged YAR agree engage in preliminary discussions with UK without setting pre-conditions. Stated difficult for UK recognize YARG in absence evidence YARG acting independently of UAR. Talbot noted UAR had acquiesced in UNEF without recognition of Israel.

In response Talbot query re talk unity, al-Aini said he had urged Sallal in Cairo to take "no other steps" until YARG consultative council formed.

For USUN and London: Suggest you withhold contents paragraph four from your British colleagues until USUN has had opportunity discuss subject further with al-Aini during Harlan Clark visit to UN July 9–10.

Ball

---

[2] On February 11, 1934, the United Kingdom, India, and Yemen signed a Treaty of Friendship and Cooperation (the Treaty of Sanaa), whereby Yemen evacuated the areas it held in the Aden Protectorates and both sides, without renouncing any claims, agreed to accept the status quo as it had existed under the Anglo-Turkish border convention of 1914. For text, see *British and Foreign State Papers*, 1934, vol. 137, pp. 212–215.

342. Telegram From the Department of State to the Mission to the United Nations[1]

Washington, August 13, 1964, 9:20 p.m.

384. Asst Secy Cleveland briefed al-Ainy today on SYG's talks with Dept on Yemen problem (Deptel 785 to Cairo),[2] stressing that SYG prepared to set up UN presence in Yemen to succeed UNYOM if YARG wants it. US believes small UN presence could help (1) improve SAG–UAR relations, (2) find solutions YAR–UK–South Arabian Federation problems, and (3) find formula for reconciliation within Yemen. This would be in interests of YARG and peace of area generally.

In reply al-Ainy's questions, Cleveland said mission would be small, with somebody like Spinelli in charge and with only such assistants and communications staff as required. He explained such presence would be in traditional pattern for which there now many precedents. Might be funded either out of regular UN budget or by YARG. (Al-Ainy said YARG earlier had refused to pay for observers, but Cleveland noted new mission would be much less expensive.) In order to establish UN mission there no need for SC approval or big debate on Yemen question.

Al-Ainy noted this fine occasion for UN to help, but referred to need for overall solution. "We optimistic" for solution of UAR–SAG problem at Sept Arab summit meeting, he said. As for problem with UK, he recalled he told SYG and Asst Secy Talbot YARG would accept UN observers "and even demarcation of border according to 1934 treaty" if UK will recognize YARG and assure self-determination for people of South Arabia. (Deptel 55 to USUN, 10 to Taiz)[3] He represented this position as important concession by Yemen.

He continued however that SYG had told him UK will not recognize YARG unless latter recognizes SAF. He observed: "How can we recognize SAF? It isn't state. UK doesn't recognize it."

---

[1] Source: National Archives and Records Administration, RG 59, Central Files 1964–66, POL 27–14 YEMEN/UN. Confidential. Drafted by Campbell, cleared in draft by Moore and Buffum, and approved by Cleveland. Also sent to Taiz and repeated to Cairo, Jidda, and London.

[2] Telegram 785 to Cairo, August 10, reported that U Thant informed the Department on August 6 that Nasser told him during the Organization of African Unity (OAU) meeting that UNYOM's dissolution might make Saudi Arabia unhappy, but not the United Arab Republic. Nasser also said unequivocally that UAR troops would remain in Yemen; they could not pull out in face of the evidence of continued Saudi aid to the Royalists. The Secretary-General stated that he could envisage establishment of a UN presence to take UNYOM's place if the Yemeni Government requested it. (Ibid.) The meeting of the OAU Heads of State was held at Cairo, July 17–21, 1964.

[3] Document 341.

Cleveland said purpose of UN is to provide lubrication for solution and establishing UN presence should not be considered as part of substance of problem. As far as UN concerned, there no problem of recognition. As for second YARG condition—self-determination for South Arabia—YARG must negotiate this with UK. He then inquired about YARG–UK talks in NY. Al-Ainy said UK talked about observers, but YARG would only accept observers as part of overall solution. He added: since UK won't recognize YARG without our recognition of SAF, "I have no instructions to continue talks."

Cleveland said USG would not urge SYG to send observers if YARG doesn't want them, but concluded problem won't be settled by silence and this showed need for UN presence to help bring all sides together.

Al-Ainy said he would refer to YARG and also discuss with SYG.

Rusk

---

343.   **Telegram From the Department of State to the Embassy in the United Arab Republic**[1]

Washington, August 17, 1964, 5:07 p.m.

918. Cairo tel 562,[2] Jidda tel 127.[3] Continued UN Presence Yemen. It now appears that UNYOM may be at an end, having been all but written off by all parties, including SYG. Concur with Cairo view that Nasser–Faisal understanding is sine qua non of overall settlement. However, continued UN presence Yemen could be especially important catalyst for promoting internal settlement and easing southern border tensions, and could play limited impartial observer role on ad hoc basis. With such broad frame of reference, UN presence could also

---

[1] Source: National Archives and Records Administration, RG 59, Central Files 1964–66, POL 27–14 YEMEN/UN. Secret. Drafted by Moore, cleared by Buffum and Symmes, and approved by James P. Grant. Also sent to Taiz and repeated to London, Dhahran, USUN, and Jidda.

[2] Telegram 562 from Cairo, August 16, commented that the United States had expended a considerable amount of influence in Saudi Arabia to maintain in Yemen a UN organization that had now demonstrated it was incapable of preparing the way for a solution of the Yemen situation, and emphasized that the key issue in Yemen was the crisis of confidence between Faisal and Nasser. (Ibid.)

[3] In telegram 127 from Jidda, August 16, Hart reported that Faisal had told Spinelli that he had no objection to the continuation of UNYOM, but saw no reason to continue paying a share of the costs, since the United Arab Republic was determined to flout the agreement by retaining its troops in Yemen. (Ibid.)

serve as symbol of commitments undertaken by UAR and SAG in Bunker Agreement, which we consider remains broadly in effect even after departure formal UNYOM observation mission.

While USG willing acquiesce in demise UNYOM, we strongly believe that continuation UN representatives in country with political mandate would thus appear to be in interests all parties concerned.

For Cairo: You authorized approach UARG at appropriate level to urge UAR/YAR support for UN presence, using argumentation above and in ref Cairo tel.

For Taiz: In coordination with Spinelli you should urge YARG to request that SYG establish UN presence. (Understand from al-Aini that while he reported to Taiz gist his August 13 talk with Assistant Secretary Cleveland—Deptel 52 to Taiz[4]—he did not request authority ask SYG take action.)[5]

---

[4] Document 342; telegram 384 to USUN was also sent to Taiz as telegram 52.
[5] Printed from an unsigned copy.

---

344. Telegram From the Embassy in Saudi Arabia to the Department of State[1]

Jidda, August 19, 1964, 3 p.m.

135. Embtel 133.[2] Translation of Faysal's letter to President Johnson dated August 17.

---

[1] Source: National Archives and Records Administration, RG 59, Cental Files 1964–66, POL 27 YEMEN. Secret; Priority; Limdis. Also sent to Cairo, Dhahran, Taiz, and CINCSTRIKE/CINCMEAFSA for POLAD and repeated to USUN.
[2] In telegram 133 from Jidda, August 18, Hart reported that on August 17 he met with Crown Prince Faisal, who said that UAR planes had invaded Saudi air space twice in the last few days, and that he had received a report from inside Yemen that UAR troops were moving northward toward the Saudi border. Therefore, he had decided to send weapons and troops to defend the Yemen border, and considered the disengagement agreement as ended and would feel free to help the royalists after September 4. Faisal said it was essential to know where the United States stood if war broke out between Saudi Arabia and the United Arab Republic; if the United States could not help, he would seek help anywhere he could get it. Hart reminded the Crown Prince of the 1963 U.S. position on helping Saudi Arabia against unprovoked attack, but pointed out that the United States would consider aid to the royalists' provocation. The Ambassador urged Faisal to keep his troops in a defensive posture if he wanted U.S. help. (Ibid.)

Excellency:

I received with great appreciation Your Excellency's letter dated 15 June 1964.[3] I thank Your Excellency for informing me of the satisfaction expressed to you by your Secretary of State, Mr. Dean Rusk, following his meeting with our Permanent Deputy Foreign Minister in Washington June 15 concerning the results yielded by the visit to the Middle East of the USSR Prime Minister.

I considered that Mr. Khrushchev, in his statement to which Your Excellency referred, had not succeeded in finding accommodation but (rather) had spotlighted the basic conflict between the Communist concept of class unity and the Arab doctrine of national unity.

But I do not consider this statement important enough to outweigh the many advantages which his visit in this area won for the Soviet Union and the Communist system which is closely associated with it.

That statement troubled those who are sincere about Arab unity, which aims at strengthening the bond between all Arabs in all classes, yet for those who comprehend there is no truth in the Communist doctrines (they saw) it offers nothing new, since (they realize) these doctrines are basically aimed at the destruction of nationalist concept. The residual effect of this statement lay not in the fact it was made. It lay in the fact that it was published during his visit to an Arab country and in its hidden distant objective as shown when it attacked Kuwait. Were this the extent of its effect on thoughtful men, who comprehend Communist doctrines, the statement for the masses I believe would not have the effect which the visit itself had. Because the worker, and the peasant, has a limited culture; he is not affected by such a statement to the extent that he is affected by the spectacle of the Prime Minister of the Soviet Union being embraced and embracing his colleague, smiling for all to see. His host provided great propaganda for the Soviet Union and its leader as always supporting the people's desire for freedom and hurrying to offer every help to raise the standard of living, especially for the worker and the peasant.

In this regard I am happy to express to Your Excellency my deepest pleasure in the warm sentiments Your Excellency expressed about the program of reform which I am trying to achieve in the Kingdom of Saudi Arabia. I feel great confidence that Your Excellency will not spare any effort to offer assistance which will guarantee the achievement of well being for our country and which will provide the best evidence both of what links us and links the friendly peoples of our countries in strong friendship. I hope this sincere cooperation is increasingly strengthened with the passage of time.

---

[3] Document 229.

In connection with what Your Excellency indicated regarding the desire of the Republican leadership in Yemen to establish peaceful relations with the Saudi Arabian Kingdom, we have assured Your Excellency more than once that we sincerely desire friendly cooperation with any Yemeni Government deriving from the free will of the Yemeni people far from any foreign influence and following the withdrawal of the foreign troops from the soil of Yemen! We seek only stability and a cooperation with our neighbors which will enable us to implement the program of reforms we have charted for our country. This was why we signed the disengagement agreement—despite our certainty of the lack of sincerity of the other party regarding its implementation—and (why) we have renewed it six times for a total of one year. What induced us to sign it and to comply with its provisions was a desire:

1. To demonstrate our good intentions following the guarantee of the United States as expressed personally by Mr. Bunker, representing the late President Kennedy, that the honor and the dignity of the United States stood behind the implementation of this agreement. This guaranty was repeated every time the agreement was renewed.

2. To give the United Nations the opportunity to carry out its reponsibilities to establish peace and security in the area, fearing the spread of the flame of discord to other areas which would thereby help spread those extremist doctrines which you and I are trying to combat.

Now has happened what we expected from the beginning. Recently in an unmistakably clear fashion the President of the UAR informed Mr. Thant, Secretary General of the United Nations, that he will keep his army in the Yemen and he has no present intention to withdraw it. The Secretary General of the United Nations was confident of this before his meeting with the UAR President as he indicated in his report which he presented to the Security Council, No. S5794 dated 2 July 1964, regarding the operations of the UN observation mission in Yemen![4] He reported there was no benefit to be expected from continuing to renew the agreement as formerly done if something did not occur during the coming period of renewal which would represent compliance with its provisions. Mr. Spinelli, special representative of the Secretary General, also indicated this during his recent visit to me on August 15.

In recent days we have seen plainly what the UAR is harboring for our country, particularly before the meeting of the second Arab summit conference. We were shocked on August 13 and August 15 by violation of Saudi air space by Egyptian aircraft. Three aircraft circled

---

[4] An excerpt from the Secretary-General's July 2 report to the Security Council (UN doc. S/5794) is printed in *American Foreign Policy: Current Documents, 1964*, pp. 726–727.

repeatedly at low altitude over cities on our southern frontier. Therefore, we find ourselves obliged as of now to secure the defense of our country by various planned measures. I have explained the situation to Ambassador Hart in a more detailed fashion. He will forward it to Your Excellency.

I await with hope the day when stability will be realized in this region and when its reponsible leaders will be enabled to move their people toward progress and prosperity.

I am happy to convey to Your Excellency my best salutations and good wishes for yourself and for the success and the increasing happiness of the American people.

Signed Faysal.

Hart

---

345. Memorandum From the Executive Secretary of the Department of State (Read) to the President's Special Assistant for National Security Affairs (Bundy)[1]

Washington, August 22, 1964.

SUBJECT

> Letter from Crown Prince Faisal to the President on Renunciation of Disengagement Agreement

In the enclosed letter to the President[2] and in discussion with Ambassador Hart at the time of its presentation on August 17, Crown Prince Faisal of Saudi Arabia expressed his belief in a U.A.R.-sponsored plot to divide Saudi Arabia among Jordan, Iraq and Yemen. Referring to U.A.R. overflights of Saudi Arabia on August 13 and 15, he voiced his fear that a current U.A.R. military operation in Yemen would lead to an attack against Saudi territory. He stated that as a result he was sending troops and weapons to the Yemen border to defend his country and that he considered the disengagement agreement to be ended after September 4. He would then feel himself free to help the royalist dissidents in Yemen as he saw fit. However, he still intends to go to

---

[1] Source: Johnson Library, National Security File, Special Head of State Correspondence File, Saudi Arabia, King Faisal Correspondence, Vol. I. Secret.

[2] Document 344.

the Arab Summit Conference at Alexandria on September 5 where he will talk to Nasser concerning the Yemen if the latter raises the subject. He has not set a date for resumption of aid to the royalists.

We have no information concerning the highly improbable alleged Arab plot against Faisal. There are also no indications that Egyptian military activity in Yemen is directed against Saudi Arabia. The Egyptians, aware of continued Saudi assistance to the royalists, appear to have overflown Saudi territory only in connection with their present major offensive in Yemen, aimed at finally eliminating royalist opposition. Faisal may be seizing the overflights as an excuse to prop up the royalists in Yemen and thus strengthen his own position prior to discussions with Nasser. Of major concern is possible U.A.R. reaction to the movement of Saudi arms to the border. Should the Egyptians believe that this equipment is destined for the royalists, bombing raids on munition dumps across the frontier could occur in the pattern followed by the U.A.R. in late 1962.

Faisal asked specifically where we would stand in case of fighting between U.A.R. and Saudi troops. In restating our 1963 position of support for Faisal against unprovoked attack, Ambassador Hart noted that we would consider further aid to the royalists as a provocation. We intend to instruct him to repeat this stand to Faisal, to inform the Crown Prince of our intelligence estimates that no military threat to Saudi Arabia currently exists and to urge that Saudi Arabia not become reinvolved in the Yemen. We will press Cairo not to continue overflights and not to react unnecessarily against the movement of Saudi troops within their own territory. We will inform U Thant of Faisal's concern and ask if he has received an up-to-date assessment of the situation from the United Nations Yemen Observation Mission which could be passed to Faisal. We are considering the desirability of a subsequent United States Air Force fighter squadron training exercise in Saudi Arabia as a reassurance of our continued interest to Faisal, provided he clearly forswears provoking the situation by increased aid to the royalists.

Pending the results of the foregoing approaches, we do not recommend that the President reply to Faisal at this moment.

Benjamin H. Read[3]

---

[3] Deputy Executive Secretary Grant G. Hilliker signed for Read.

346. Telegram From the Department of State to the Embassy in Saudi Arabia[1]

Washington, August 22, 1964, 10:51 a.m.

104. Jidda tels 133, 134 and 143.[2] Faisal open reinvolvement Yemen clearly counter US interests of damping down struggle. It would seem equally counter Faisal's own interest of maintaining stability and forward thrust of development and reform program within Saudi Arabia.

Faisal understandably disturbed by UAR overflights which themselves provocative. At same time must be realized that UAR is aware of continued Saudi assistance to royalists and that overflights appear to have been observational, connected with major military operation in Yemen rather than hostilities directed against SAG. We have no indication that UAR proposing any military move against Saudi Arabia, either from Yemen in context current campaign or through tripartite deal. However UAR seems particularly intent in current operation on crushing royalists prior Arab Summit Two, with initial successes reported. Faisal strong reaction recent overflights indicates he may be seizing on them as pretext for final attempt bolster fading royalist cause and strengthen his own position before discussion with Nasser.

USG continues support integrity Saudi Arabia, but would consider resumption open aid to royalists, particularly at time present concentrated military operation, as provocatory. While we willing consider visible "re-statement" our concern for Saudi Arabia in form USAF squadron visit, such action would be difficult in face unprovoked SAG aid to royalists.

We gratified that Faisal does not appear intent on rushing aid to royalists. If this the case, major immediate concern becomes potential UAR reaction to movement Saudi arms and troops to border. If Egyptians interpret this as opening move to concentrate troops and establish munition dumps in preparation for massive assistance al-Badr, they may react with cross-border bomb attacks within military operational framework in pattern 1962–63. Thus urgent need exists dissuade UAR

---

[1] Source: National Archives and Records Administration, RG 59, Central Files 1964–66, POL 27 YEMEN. Secret; Priority. Drafted by Moore on August 21; cleared by Symmes, Campbell, and Stoddard (DOD/ISA); and approved by Grant. Also sent to Cairo, Taiz, and USUN and repeated to Amman, London, Baghdad, Dhahran, and CINCSTRIKE/CINCMEAFSA for Ramsey.

[2] Telegram 133 from Jidda, August 19; telegram 134 from Jidda, August 19; and telegram 143 from Jidda, August 20; none printed. (All ibid.)

from further overflights and from over-reacting to Saudi defensive move to frontiers.

Action Requested

For Jidda. You should re-emphasize to Faisal (or Saqqaf for Faisal) that our concern for and interest in Saudi Arabia remains same as it has in past, that in all sincerity we maintain our policy of support for SAG against unprovoked aggression. At same time, exacerbation by SAG of Yemen situation by provoking military confrontation with UAR, would make it difficult for us come to Saudi support. While expressing understanding for legitimate defensive posture, you should strongly urge Saudis avoid any appearance of becoming reinvolved in Yemen problem and suggest they may wish make very clear to UAR purpose, extent and limits their present mobilization on frontier in order avoid any mistaken hasty UAR reaction. Affirm that we have absolutely no indications that UAR troops Yemen intend transgress Saudi soil; nor do we have any report from any other source concerning alleged tripartite plot. (FYI. Department considering what further action may be desirable in light recommendations this subject contained your 146.)[3]

For Cairo. At highest possible level you should express our concern that UAR overflights Saudi Arabia serve needlessly to inflame UAR–Saudi relations and threaten confrontation which clearly would not be in UAR, Saudi or YAR interests in area. Urge strongly that UAR not react unnecessarily to Saudi frontier mobilization which SAG has fully assured us is entirely of defensive nature. You should stress our view that greater UAR–Saudi rapprochement, especially concerning Yemen, much to be desired; we hope this will be outcome Nasser–Faisal meeting in September.

For Taiz. In your discussions with YARG and UARG officials you should emphasize need for not allowing short range military requirements of present operation to obscure greater importance of avoiding actions which would arouse Saudi fears and be apt provoke sharp Saudi reaction to detriment possible easing of Yemen situation.

---

[3] In telegram 146 from Jidda, August 21, Hart recommended a warm Presidential letter to Faisal, and consultation with London on strengthening U.S.–U.K. cooperation in the Arabian peninsula. (Ibid.) In telegram 156 from Jidda, August 23, the Ambassador stated that it was in the U.S. interest for him to see Faisal with the message in telegram 104 and that he would talk it over with Saqqaf first. He noted that it now seemed clear that Faisal's action in reinforcing the south, although multiple in purpose, was weighted by his desire to show Nasser that he could react quickly and strongly. Hart did not think that Faisal would send forces over the frontier or renew aid to the royalists before the summit. (Ibid.) Telegram 106 to Jidda, August 24, advised Hart that he could delay the démarche at his discretion, and that a proposed draft letter was being sent by separate telegram. (Ibid.)

For USUN. You should inform UNSYG or Bunche of Faisal's concern that UAR military action against Saudi Arabia contemplated and of Saudi remilitarization border area (Jidda tel 133) and ask if he has up-to-date assessment of situation from UNYOM. You authorized tell him of our démarches in Cairo and Jidda, above.

Rusk

---

347.   Memorandum From Robert W. Komer of the National Security Council Staff to the President's Special Assistant for National Security Affairs (Bundy)[1]

Washington, August 24, 1964.

Mac—

I haven't bothered you to date, but we may have trouble over Yemen again: (1) UNYOM will probably breathe its last on 4 September, though we may be able to keep a UN presence there;[2] (2) UAR/YAR offensive to clean up north Yemen and present Faysal with a fait accompli at Alexandria summit seems to be going well; (3) Faysal and UK are very unhappy over this, in fact Saudis are sending supplies to their border area and threatening to resume aid to royalists; (4) our UAR friends made a few recon flights again over Saudi border.

So Faysal has again made emotional plea to LBJ[3]—since disengagement is a flop, he may have to start the war again. Will we protect him? He made same plea to UK.

Butler has neatly passed buck to us to note to Rusk. It's the old song—shouldn't US and UK at long last work together to put blocks to Nasser.

---

[1] Source: Johnson Library, National Security File, Country File, Yemen, Cables & Memos, Vol. II, 7/64–12/68. Secret.

[2] In response to an inquiry from the Secretary-General, Saudi Arabia responded on August 26 that it had carried out its responsibilities under the disengagement agreement, but the United Arab Republic had not. Saudi Arabia found itself unable to continue to share in UNYOM's expenses or to abide by the terms of the disengagement agreement after September 4, 1964. After receiving a U.A.R. reply that it had no objection to termination of UNYOM, the Secretary-General reported to the Security Council on September 2 that he intended to terminate UNYOM's activities as of September 4. An excerpt from the Secretary-General's report (UN doc. S/5927) is printed in *American Foreign Policy: Current Documents, 1964*, pp. 727–728.

[3] See Document 344.

Fortunately Rusk gave right answer to a sheepish Greenhill.[4] Talbot tells me Rusk sees no point in accommodating Brits till we see which HMG we're dealing with. We've also gone out to calm down Faysal, telling him again we back Saudi Arabia, but that if Saudis reopen Yemen war they do so at their own risk. Hart wants another LBJ letter, but State and I feel not just now, unless absolutely necessary.

The whole Yemen–Aden business may come to a boil at summit. Nasser will try to isolate Faysal and may bring off a compromise. But if he browbeats Faysal we'll probably get an open break, and a flareup again. We're urging Nasser to play it smart, but without great hopes.

We're doing our best to keep this one buried, but don't ask the impossible.

RWK

---

[4] A memorandum of conversation recording British Chargé d'Affaires Denis Greenhill's meeting with Secretary Rusk on August 21 is in the National Archives and Records Administration, RG 59, Central Files 1964–66, POL 27 YEMEN. See footnote 2, Document 349, for a brief summary of their conversation.

---

348. Telegram From the Department of State to the Embassy in Saudi Arabia[1]

Washington, August 28, 1964, 3:45 p.m.

117. Embtel 135.[2] Following Presidential message to be delivered to Viceroy:

"Your Royal Highness:

I fully appreciate the concerns expressed in your letter of August 17. Indeed I am glad that you wrote to me and expressed your views so candidly. This spirit of candor even where our views may differ has done much to insure a climate of genuine friendship and understanding between us.

---

[1] Source: National Archives and Records Administration, RG 59, Central Files 1964–66, POL 27 YEMEN. Secret; Immediate; Limdis. Drafted by Moore on August 27 with text from the White House; cleared by Symmes, L. Grant (M), and Komer; and approved by James P. Grant.

[2] Document 344.

You know that I particularly share your concern over the unauthorized aerial intrusions into your country about which you wrote. We are making urgent representations to the Government of the United Arab Republic. We shall keep the most careful watch on any futher such developments and will seek through appropriate methods to forestall their recurrence.

I also understand and sympathize with your feeling that you need to take further measures to defend Saudi Arabia against possible attack. Ambassador Hart has informed me in detail about this problem. At the same time, my concern that the Yemen dispute not again threaten to expand to Saudi Arabia leads me to hope that your responses will be measured so as to dampen rather than increase the flame of conflict.[3] I fully realize that our counsels of restraint are not always welcome, but I believe you will agree that they are honestly and sincerely meant. I would be failing in my duty as a friend if I did not express my strong belief that your own interests will be best served by your carefully refraining from reinvolvement in the strife in Yemen.

You, Your Royal Highness, are subject to singularly unique burdens. In addition to the responsibilities of leading your people on the road of social progress and economic reform, you have the added duty of maintaining the Holy Places of Islam. I well understand that this honor in serving a great world religion also has imposed on you obligations which are not shared by the leaders of other states. In the pursuit of peace which this responsibility demands, you may rest assured of the firm friendship and full support of the United States.

Let me repeat with all sincerity that our great concern for maintenance of the integrity of Saudi Arabia, expressed in word and deed over many years, remains as strong as always. We are determined to maintain and strengthen the spirit of cooperation which has linked us in friendship. As you continue to seek a stable and peaceful relationship with your neighbors, you may count on us.

May God grant to you and your people health, prosperity and peace.

Lyndon B. Johnson"

Rusk

---

[3] An August 26 memorandum from Komer to the President advised: "A warm but unmistakable word of caution from you, backed by a strong pitch from our Ambassador, will help keep Yemen damped down through the election." (Johnson Library, National Security File, Country File, Saudi Arabia, Memos, Vol. I, 12/63–4/67)

349. Telegram From the Department of State to the Embassy in the United Kingdom[1]

Washington, August 28, 1964, 3:58 p.m.

1454. Depcirtel 348.[2] Please deliver following message from Secretary to FonSec Butler:[3]

"Dear Rab:

We also are disturbed by the situation in Saudi Arabia and Yemen of which you wrote in your letter of August 20, and we are troubled by the renewed United Arab Republic overflights of Saudi Arabia. However, we do not anticipate that they are the automatic precursors of further Egyptian attacks, air or ground, on Saudi Arabia unless Faisal intervenes more actively in the Yemen. More recent intelligence has reassured us in holding this view. In any event, we are making urgent representations to the United Arab Republic to stop its overflights and to refrain from rashly reacting to Saudi defensive moves on the frontier. We are also impressing on both the importance for everyone that Faisal and Nasser reach an agreement on Yemen at their forthcoming meeting.

We continue prepared to support Faisal by whatever means seem appropriate in the face of unprovoked hostilities with the United Arab Republic. At the same time, we continue to feel very strongly, and are again so informing the Viceroy, that it is in his best interests not to resume open aid to the Yemeni royalists. We agree with you that he has become increasingly and dangerously isolated from the Arab states. We fear that his aiding the royalists tends to increase that isolation and encourages the threat to his regime from both within and from outside

---

[1] Source: National Archives and Records Administration, RG 59, Central Files 1964–66, POL 1 SAUD–UAR. Secret; Limdis. Drafted by Moore on August 27; cleared by Symmes, Grant, and Director of the Office of British Commonwealth and Northern European Affairs J. Harold Shullaw; and approved by Rusk. Repeated to Cairo, Jidda, Baghdad, Beirut, Damascus, Kuwait, Taiz, and Amman.

[2] Circular telegram 348, August 22, reported that British Chargé Greenhill called on Secretary Rusk August 21 to discuss an urgent letter from Foreign Secretary Butler concerning the threatened increase of friction between the United Arab Republic and Saudi Arabia in Yemen. Butler appealed for coordination of U.S. and U.K. policies and requested that the United States strongly urge Nasser to reach a political arrangement with Faisal at their Alexandria meeting. (Ibid.)

[3] In telegram 998 from London, August 29, Ambassador Bruce reported that after he delivered the Secretary's message to Butler, the Foreign Secretary had demurred at the suggestion that Faisal's resuming aid to the Yemeni royalists would be damaging to "all of our interests." He thought that such aid might prevent Nasser from triumphing in Yemen, which was all to the good, since having Yemen become "an Egyptian fief" was "not in any of our interests." Also, since recent developments made any coalition government in Yemen improbable in the near future, Butler did not see what agreement Faisal and Nasser were likely to work out in Alexandria. (Ibid.)

Saudi Arabia. A primary objective of the disengagement agreement, in our view, was to allow Faisal breathing space in order to face internal problems. To encourage him to increase his aid to the royalists, thereby inviting a return of these same problems, would appear dangerous for all of our interests in that area.

In the total framework of Anglo-American cooperation throughout the world our differences of view toward Yemen are a friction which it would be good if we could eliminate. As your Chargé stated when delivering your message, the basic problem seems to center around tactics in dealing with Nasser. This, I understand, is to be the subject of forthcoming working level discussions between our people, the outcome of which I have no wish to prejudge. I hope, however, that through our continued concentrated efforts we can more narrowly define those points wherein we differ in the Middle East so as better to focus our efforts on resolving them and on more closely coordinating our policies in that part of the world.

With warm personal regards,

Sincerely, Dean Rusk"

Rusk

---

350. **Memorandum From Robert W. Komer of the National Security Council Staff to the President's Special Assistant for National Security Affairs (Bundy)**[1]

Washington, August 31, 1964.

Mac—

We've had very strong reply by Faisal (Jidda 177)[2] to our counsels of restraint, backed by LBJ letter. In effect, Faisal says that disengagement is dead, UAR presence in Arabian Peninsula puts SA in "mortal danger," and SA will take all means necessary to prevent royalists from going under.

Hart thinks Faisal (who's still going to Arab Summit) hopes for some sort of solution but is braced for a showdown. Hart thinks we

---

[1] Source: Johnson Library, National Security File, Country File, Saudi Arabia, Memos, Vol. I, 12/63–4/67. Secret.

[2] Telegram 177 from Jidda, August 29, reported Hart's conversation with Faisal when he delivered President Johnson's letter. (National Archives and Records Administration, RG 59, Central Files 1964–66, POL 27 YEMEN)

should play it cool, not show panic or argue with Faisal any more. He and State both think Faisal as well as Nasser is engaging in pre-Summit brinkmanship.

For your amusement, Rusk took seriously Saudi request that US "oversee" Faisal's flight to UAR, commenting that Nasser is one leader who would stoop to assassination of competing leaders. NEA took great umbrage and did research job proving Nasser had never done so to our knowledge.

We can probably avoid too much Yemen trouble through Arab Summit (say till 8 September), but I'm starting to worry we'll have a minor flap after that. We'll do our best.

RWK

---

351. Memorandum From Robert W. Komer of the National Security Council Staff to the President's Special Assistant for National Security Affairs (Bundy)[1]

Washington, September 10, 1964.

Mac—

We may already be in early stages of a new *Yemen flare-up*. Reports indicate Faysal already started a massive resupply effort to stem royalist disaster as long ago as *24 August*. UAR probably knows about it. Thus, unless Faysal/Nasser talks now going on produce a quite unlikely accommodation, trouble is ahead.

Brits are actively abetting Faysal, giving him direct contrary advice to ours. Meanwhile, Rusk has been manfully fobbing off UK pressures, most recently Harlech coming in today.[2] I've been helping NEA feed him counter-arguments (see attached).[3]

My constant pitch to NEA is that overreacting now (with UK, Saudis *and* Nasser) is a lot wiser than trying to stem flood once it breaks. *If LBJ thought we ought to be brutal in telling UK not to commit*

---

[1] Source: Johnson Library, National Security File, Country File, United Arab Republic, Vol. II. Secret.

[2] A memorandum of conversation recording the Secretary's September 10 discussion of Nasser's activities in the Middle East with the British Ambassador, Lord Harlech, is in the National Archives and Records Administration, RG 59, Secretary's Memoranda of Conversation: Lot 65 D 330, Sept. 1964.

[3] Not attached.

us over Malaysia, same analogy holds good for ME. This could be done at Tuesday lunch, if events wait that long. I'll do a brief, but would you entertain moving earlier?[4]

RWK

---

[4] A handwritten notation in the margin reads: "Give me a call. McGB"

---

352. **Memorandum From the President's Special Assistant for National Security Affairs (Bundy) and Robert W. Komer of the National Security Council Staff to President Johnson**[1]

Washington, September 12, 1964.

You may be hearing from Rusk shortly about growing tension in the Middle East, particularly a new flare-up in the Yemen civil war. This is no Cyprus crisis, but could have still painful repercussions during our election campaign. If the Saudis resume aid to the Yemeni royalists, Nasser will no doubt resume bombing Saudi supply bases, in which case Faysal will scream for help. The British, who strongly disagree with our policy of pouring oil on troubled waters, have been at us hard to unleash Faysal, even at the expense of our relations with most other Arabs.

Though the Arab Summit seems at first glance to have been a dud, we also may have renewed muscle flexing toward Israel or a Jordan crisis. Either of these could bring new Israeli aid pleas just before the election, and new attacks on our Arab policy.

We assume that your own feeling about the Middle East is the same as your view on the Malaysia issue last week, i.e. we certainly don't want another war on our hands for at least two months. This word from you was very helpful in getting State to calm down the British. A few similar cautionary words about the Middle East on Tuesday would encourage State to weigh in with Arabs, Israelis and Englishmen as well. In our judgment, this would be a quite useful

---

[1] Source: Johnson Library, National Security File, Memos to the President, McGeorge Bundy, Vol. 6. Secret.

noise. I'll bring it up Tuesday & give you a chance to comment if you want.[2]

R. W. Komer
McG. B.

---

[2] The last sentence was handwritten by Bundy.

---

353. Circular Telegram From the Department of State to Certain Posts[1]

Washington, September 24, 1964, 6:40 p.m.

532. In call September 23 on Assistant Secretary Talbot, YARG Ambassador al-Aini made following points:

1. In light Nasser–Faisal September 14 communiqué, hope US will use its influence with both parties to promote a settlement in Yemen.[2]

2. Settlement envisaged by al-Aini personally would involve following:

a. Elimination of al-Badr; as necessary quid pro quo YARG would no doubt have to expel Sallal.

b. Conference of up to 300 representatives of various Yemeni elements to be held, preferably outside Yemen (Sudan or Kuwait for example) to preserve strictly neutral atmosphere; group to determine membership new Yemeni Government. SAG and UAR could divert some of their aircraft now used support military activities Yemen to transport the group.

c. UAR troops to withdraw from Yemen and Saudis to cease interference.

d. Joint Arab force from countries not involved in dispute might be required in Yemen for limited period of time.

---

[1] Source: National Archives and Records Administration, RG 59, Central Files 1964–66, POL 27 YEMEN. Secret. Drafted by Moore on September 23; cleared by Davies, Campbell, and Judd; and approved by Talbot. Sent to Cairo, Jidda, London, Taiz, USUN, and Aden.

[2] The joint communiqué of September 14 declared that the two countries intended to cooperate fully in solving existing differences between the various parties in Yemen and that steps would be taken to establish the necessary contacts with the interested parties in order to reach a peaceful solution to existing differences. Telegram 905 from Cairo, September 15, transmitted the text of the joint communiqué to the Department. (Ibid.)

e. UAR and SAG to devote fraction of their present expenditures on military operations to economic and developmental assistance for Yemen.

3. Emphasis must be on solution by Yemenis themselves, not imposed by outsiders. Any government not representing real will of Yemenis would not receive required long-term popular support.

4. Nasser–Faisal communiqué represents necessary start; but by its recognition that each side has followers in Yemen it shows possible intent of UAR and SAG to play with country, perhaps ultimately dividing it into spheres of influence in opposition to desires Yemeni people.

5. Concerning southern frontier, al-Aini repeated willingness as stated to UNSYG to establish DMZ, UN observers and even demarcation, provided these part of overall settlement in which British recognize YAR and concede rights of people in south freely to choose own government. (In response subsequent specific query from Department officer, al-Aini said recognition and provision for self-expression in southern Arabia were the only elements which YAR stood to gain from British since demarcation would mean giving up longstanding Yemeni claims to south; these items would have to be part of ultimate package settlement with British, although not necessarily first step.)

6. Foreign Minister Sirri has given al-Aini continued assurance that YARG doing all possible not exacerbate situation on border, although to some extent it is pushed unwillingly in this direction by Egyptians. Example of latter was UAR creation puppet National Front for Liberation Occupied South in violation of al-Aini–Mahmoud Riad agreement that UAR/YAR would deal with all nationalist groups in area. Al-Aini suggested UK–YAR solution to own problems would ease Egyptian anti-British interference in south.

In response, Talbot noted that Yemen problem had reached encouraging new stage with September 14 communiqué and now, for first time in two years, UAR and SAG talking directly with each other about situation. We hopeful for future and would keep in mind possibilities where we might be able to assist as situation develops.

Rusk

---

354. Editorial Note

On November 2, 1964, Yemeni republican and royalist representatives meeting at Erkowit, Sudan, concluded an agreement providing for a cease-fire in Yemen beginning November 8 and a national conference in Yemen beginning November 23. The conference, which was expected to agree upon a coalition government, was to be composed of 169 religious, military, and tribal leaders as well as the 18 delegates attending the Erkowit meeting. The agreement also called upon the United Arab Republic and Saudi Arabia for help in executing its decisions. Airgram A–322 from Cairo, November 7, transmitted the text of the cease-fire agreement to the Department. (National Archives and Records Administration, RG 59, Central Files 1964–66, POL 27 YEMEN)

---

355.   Circular Telegram From the Department of State to Certain Posts[1]

Washington, November 30, 1964, 7:57 p.m.

1056. In call November 30 on Assistant Secretary Talbot to discuss Yemen, British Minister Stewart stated HMG willing in principle recognize compromise Yemeni Government which might emerge from forthcoming conference but with number conditions to be sorted out before such recognition granted. Said HMG continued hold same criteria for recognition (i.e., general popular acceptance of government which exercising effective control bulk of country) however willing apply these leniently to situation to gain bargaining points. Stressing treaty obligation to obtain SAF approval before acting, Stewart read and left paper describing preliminary views Foreign Office on HMG pre-recognition desires as follows: (1) Substantial reduction UAR forces and firm prospect they will run down at least to a low level; (2) For purposes assuring acceptance SAF as a fact, would hope for statement from YAR at least equivalent to December 1962 assertion its respect for international agreements and calling upon Yemenis in adjacent territories to respect law and order (would be desirable for YAR make specific mention Treaty of Sanaa and HMG in acknowledging such statements would make clear it intended live in peace with Yemen); (3) Essential put stop to subversive and propaganda activities in SAF (required if HMG to persuade SAF acquiesce in recognition; HMG would make point directly to UARG but would welcome similar action by US); (4) Desirable obtain progress demilitarization, demarcation or observation proposals

---

[1] Source: National Archives and Records Administration, RG 59, Central Files 1964–66, POL 16 YEMEN. Secret. Drafted by Moore, cleared by Davies and Judd, and approved by Talbot. Sent to Cairo, Jidda, London, Taiz, and Aden.

put forward by HMG at UN in April (HMG prepared in return take all possible action insure that SAF rulers abstain from activity across border). Stewart emphasized HMG wanted continue discussions with US including US views on paper, and specifically desired parallel US approach in Cairo.

In response Talbot noted our understanding that many moderate Yemenis apparently strongly desire easing Yemen–SAF frictions and removal UAR troops. Indication to them now of British willingness recognize government provided certain criteria met could strengthen them in pressing get UAR out. He assumed that Saudi position on recognition would also play significant role for HMG. British, according Stewart, felt that informing Yemenis at this time of British position would lead YAR expect quick recognition after conference and result in unwillingness take conciliatory attitude toward manifold problems involved. Agreed that argument could be made both for and against informing Yemenis at this time and expressed hope Talbot could further discuss with Foreign Office during visit London next week.

Concerning any US approach in Cairo, Talbot noted problem was one of timing since Arabs still handling matter among selves and we deeply involved with UAR at moment on other matters. Stewart agreed, saying any contemplated approach would only be for consideration after results Yemeni conciliation conference known.

During discussion Talbot also mentioned Yemeni allegations inflammatory output Aden Radio. British Embassy subsequently informed Department that Foreign Office already investigating matter on basis previous démarches Washington and London.

Harriman

356. Memorandum of Conversation[1]

Sec Del/MC/51   New York, December 11, 1964, 3:30 p.m.

SECRETARY'S DELEGATION TO THE NINETEENTH SESSION
OF THE UNITED NATIONS GENERAL ASSEMBLY
New York, December 1964

SUBJECT

The Yemen Situation

PARTICIPANTS

U.S.	Saudi Arabia
The Secretary	Deputy Foreign Minister Omar al-Saqqaf
Mr. Walsh	UN Ambassador Jamil Baroody

The Secretary opened the discussion by asking the Minister for an assessment of the Yemen situation. In response, the Minister said that the meeting which had been planned between the royalist and republican factions in Yemen had been postponed because the UAR had withdrawn its concurrence to certain arrangements which had been agreed upon by Nasser and King Faisal. Whereas it had been agreed that representation at the meeting was to be on a 2/3 republican and 1/3 royalist basis, the UAR subsequently claimed that the republicans had refused to accept these proportions. As a result the meeting was postponed.

The Minister went on to say that he hoped that a solution could be found to the Yemen question but at the moment he was uncertain as to when or how this could be accomplished. He believed that a viable agreement would have to permit the Yemeni to have an Imam. He said that the King wanted Nasser to withdraw his troops from Yemen but he had not insisted that this occur prior to a meeting of the warring factions. Abrupt withdrawal would subject Nasser to increased domestic pressures from his army, as well as pressures from a variety of dissident Arab elements. The King contemplated phased reductions from the very high current level of over 50,000 troops. Some method of certification of these withdrawals would have to be agreed upon in addition to arrangements for joint Saudi–UAR policing of the cease fire in Yemen. Actually, he said, Saudi Arabia is less concerned about the UAR forces today than it was a year ago. His Government continues, however, to be seriously concerned about the dangers of anarchy and

---

[1] Source: National Archives and Records Administration, RG 59, Central Files 1964–66, POL 27 YEMEN. Confidential. Drafted by John P. Walsh on December 12. The memorandum is Part I of II.

Communist activity in Yemen. Today, virtually every facet of international communism, including the Russians, Chinese, Poles and Czechs, are at work in Yemen. About 900 Chinese are in the country.

The Minister said that the relative positions of King Faisal and Nasser had changed considerably in the past year. Faisal now has very broad support in Saudi Arabia and expatriate elements are returning to the country. In addition, his social and economic programs are showing signs of success. Furthermore, UAR propaganda attacks on King Faisal had largely ceased.

Nasser, on the other hand, is considerably weaker than he was a year ago. His economic situation is increasingly chaotic and there is growing opposition to him in the army. The King has no desire to destroy Nasser in part because of uncertainties about the nature of a successor regime.

Turning to the subject of U.S. aid to Nasser, the Minister said that at times it appeared that the U.S. was providing direct assistance to him to carry out policies in Yemen which the U.S. opposed. He recognized, however, that the U.S., as well as Saudi Arabia, was confronted by dilemmas in respect to this question. Saudi Arabia could not, for example, oppose aid given to help the people of the UAR. Yet this assistance freed other resources for utilization in Yemen. It is a difficult situation.

The Minister went on to express the opinion that the U.S. could be helpful in the present situation if it urged Nasser to come to an agreement with King Faisal in regard to the future of Yemen. The establishment of peace and stability in that country was clearly to the advantage of everyone but the Communists.

In response, the Secretary said that he was very pleased to note the progress that had been made by Saudi Arabia in the past year. Looking back upon the Bunker Mission, one had to admit that the disengagement objective had not been realized. After all, he said, there are more UAR troops in Yemen today than there were at that time. In another sense, however, there had been positive benefits. By means of Hard Surface and other means we had made perfectly clear to the UAR that we wished them to refrain from attacks on Saudi Arabia. Other internal Saudi Arabian factors had manifestly found expression in political stability and economic and social growth.

The Secretary stated that there are, of course, dilemmas in economic aid policy. We have employed economic aid, in part, as a means of maintaining a meaningful dialogue with the UAR Government. The situation today might have been worse if we had not been able to exercise certain restraint on U.A.R. policy decisions. The disengagement process in the Yemen has not been satisfactory and this has been a factor in our decision to halve the flow of certain types of economic assistance to the UAR. We continue, however, to advocate an accord that will bring peace and stability to Yemen and that will reduce some of the current difficulties that we have with the UAR.

In closing this segment of the conversation, the Secretary asked the Deputy Foreign Minister to convey to King Faisal the assurances of President Johnson that the United States firmly supports the independence, integrity and well-being of his country.

---

357. Telegram From the Embassy in Saudi Arabia to the Department of State[1]

Jidda, January 6, 1965, 1154Z.

504. Meeting with Faysal. Deptels 304[2] and 311.[3]

Proceeded Riyadh late January 1, having been notified I would have appointment with King following day. Faysal granted interview morning January 2 as soon as he was informed my arrival. I found him extremely cordial and forthcoming in course of meeting which lasted over two hours. I gave him personal regards President, Secretary, Undersecretaries and Asst Sec Talbot.

President Johnson's oral message obviously moved him deeply. For some minutes after hearing it Faysal groped for appropriate words to express appreciation and to reaffirm conviction importance of strengthening Saudi-American bonds. While much of ground covered was familar from previous conversations and will be summarized by airgram, of particular interest was prominence his concerns over Soviet infiltration Red Sea area. Faysal expressed conviction Russian and Chinese pressures on Nasir have played important role influencing against withdrawal UAR forces from Yemen. He also sees Anwar Sadat as having personal stake in twisting execution of Nasir–Faysal summit agreement of September 1964. This agreement, as distinct from published communiqué had been drawn up secretly and signed in dupli-

---

[1] Source: National Archives and Records Administration, RG 59, Central Files 1964–66, POL 15–1 SAUD. Secret. Repeated to Dhahran, London, Cairo, Aden, Amman, Baghdad, Beirut, Damascus, Taiz, and Tel Aviv.

[2] Document 236.

[3] Dated December 30, 1964. (National Archives and Records Administration, RG 59, Central Files 1964–66, POL UAR–US)

cate, Nasir and Faysal each retaining a copy. Without revealing text ("which preserves both our dignities") he made clear agreement provided that nature of Yemeni state would not be decided in advance but left for Yemenis to ultimately determine. National conference would be held while UAR troops still in Yemen (Royalists had objected but SAG had overcome their objections). By six to eight months after national conference UAR troops would be out. Plebiscite would determine new Yemen Government which would climax UAR withdrawal. Faysal stated he had proposed but Nasir had not yet formally agreed that interim government be named "state of Yemen" and headed by sovereignty council (Lijnat Ar-ra'Asa) of three or seven personages. State organs would include council of ministers composed of mixed Royalist-Republican representatives and consultative assembly (Majlis Ashshura) of 50 to 100 members whose membership component would be determined by decision of national conference. This interim government would conduct plebiscite.

King deprecated UAR maneuverings to select "rabble from streets" as true Yemeni representatives at national conference and to insist interim regime be called "republic," contrary to Nasir–Faysal agreement. He asserted recent resignations YAR ministers plus wave of arrests had fully exposed as lie UAR justification it was keeping troops in Yemen solely to help liberate Aden and Arab South. Faysal stated he has instructed his Ambassador to Cairo to inform UAR leaders he, Faysal, considered Alexandria agreement still binding and basis for any progress toward Yemen solution. He commented "Nasir told me at Alexandria he had then 49,000 men in Yemen" and that his intelligence sources report arrival of additional 7,000 troops since.

When he raised matter of US relations with Nasir, I replied that when I had discussed this with Secretary December 23, latter had smiled and told me I might relay to him that US–UAR relations were now worse than those of SAG–UAR. He grinned at this.

In commenting on my statement of Dept's position (Deptel 311) Faysal stated he had no desire see USG break off ties with UAR but maintained interests at stake in present situation were broader than those of either Saudi Arabia, UAR or Yemen due to Communist threat to area. He also dwelt on need for some Arab regime in south which would be completely independent of UAR or USSR and made clear his willingness to financially assist one whenever—as he had advised SAF officials as well as al Jifri and Asnaj—the various South Arab interests got together and settled their mutual differences. He expressed repugnance at recent UAR-inspired terrorist attacks in Aden, predicting they would not succeed in forcing pace of UK withdrawal.

Comment: In terms reminiscent of our mid-1963 exchanges, Faysal pressed for answer to question "When USG would act to force UAR withdrawal from Yemen?" Inconsistently and only half seriously he suggested that if USG used Sixth Fleet Nasir would get out at once. I replied this would play into Nasir's hands. His words were couched in much less emotional terms than on earlier occasions, reflecting perhaps his belief time is on his side in view Nasir's worsened relations with United States, UAR economic crisis and evolution of events within Yemen.

Hart

---

358.   Circular Telegram From the Department of State to Certain Posts[1]

Washington, January 13, 1965, 6:05 p.m.

1254. In call January 11 on Assistant Secretary Talbot YARG Ambassador al-Aini commented as follows:

1. Written resignation last month Nu'man, Iryani and others had been circulated as clear statement their opposition to UAR; it noted they had tried cooperate all possible ways but had been completely frustrated by Egyptians and that UAR forces were present Yemen only to support corrupt regime.

2. Al-Aini had just heard reports, which he unable evaluate, that Jaifi, Uthman and al-Ahmar had refused cooperate with new Government; that provinces Taiz and Hajja in revolt; and that some ex-Ministers now jailed.

3. He had written Sallal indicating general loss confidence in Yemen Government which now prevailed internationally and implying he ready resign if situation continues as at present. (Later commented to Department Officer he purposely vague on resignation, not wishing prejudice position his deputy, Jaghman, whom he had sent via Cairo on December 13 en route Yemen to ascertain facts of situation. Department Officer responded positively to al-Aini's hope that we would be willing transmit any messages from Jaghman.)

4. Al-Aini had approached Ambassadors Algeria, Tunisia, Kuwait, UAR (sic) in US to request their assistance for Yemenis in face UAR

---

[1] Source: National Archives and Records Administration, RG 59, Central Files 1964–66, POL 27 YEMEN. Secret. Drafted by Moore on January 12; cleared by Davies and Deputy Director of the Office of Northern African Affairs James J. Blake; and approved by Talbot. Sent to Algiers, Cairo, Jidda, Kuwait, London, Taiz, Tunis, and USUN.

takeover, noting that their countries willing interfere such areas as Congo and therefore should be ready help in this Arab problem. He said UAR Ambassador Kamel is "with us", understands problem and promised report to Nasser.

5. If appears useful, al-Aini will visit various Arab capitals to present Yemeni case for freedom from Egyptian control.

6. Suggested Nasser had full support USSR in preventing establishment any Yemeni Government which capable of running country and not being manipulated by UAR.

Talbot responded that we scarcely able act as arbiter in this Arab problem, but continued make clear to Cairo our concern with Yemen situation. Continuation of our aid program was one way we felt we could be generally helpful. Al-Aini agreed that little more we could do.

Rusk

---

359.   Telegram From the Department of State to the Embassy in the United Arab Republic[1]

Washington, February 4, 1965, 7:54 p.m.

4602. Taiz 304 (181 to Cairo).[2] Department disturbed at various reports in past weeks, culminating in Amer statement reported reftel, that UAR considers US has nefarious interests in continuation fighting Yemen and in supporting rigid position Faisal. UARG leadership may not fully believe this but may be setting stage for more open attack on US for alleged action Yemen. Thus insofar as possible believe we should make effort set record straight.

At your discretion, request you approach UARG at appropriately high level, note apparent trend UAR thinking, and review USG policy toward YARG, emphasizing our continuing efforts in Yemen, as well as in Saudi Arabia and UAR, since revolution have been aimed promoting

---

[1] Source: National Archives and Records Administration, RG 59, Central Files 1964–66, POL 27 YEMEN. Secret. Drafted by Moore, cleared by Jones, and approved by Davies. Repeated to Jidda, London, Taiz, and Aden.

[2] Telegram 304 from Taiz, February 1, reported that UAR Field Marshal Abdel Hakim Amer, who was in Sanaa attempting to resolve the political crisis, had told the Yemenis there was little chance that the postponed Haradh conference would come off because Faisal had imposed "impossible conditions." Amer said that Faisal had stiffened his position because of U.S. pressure and that the U.S. Government "likes war in Yemen." (Ibid.)

evolvement of an independent Yemen free of any foreign interference. This continues our goal.

In order protect Iryani as source information on closed meeting, you should avoid quoting Amer as exponent of UAR view.

Ball

---

360.   Special Memorandum Prepared in the Central Intelligence Agency[1]

No. 9–65   Washington, February 18, 1965.

NASSER'S PROBLEMS AND PROSPECTS IN YEMEN

Summary

1. Nasser is in a dilemma in the Yemen. The existing stalemate is a burden on his resources and an affront to his prestige. He would like to avoid outright annexation of the country. Yet he is unable to establish an indigenous government which is both independent enough to gain widespread support among Yemenis and docile enough to be a reliable ally in Nasser's scheme of things, in particular, as a base of operations for eliminating British influence from Aden and South Arabia.

2. Nasser is most unlikely to withdraw. Nor do we believe that he would accept any Yemeni regime that was much more than a puppet of Cairo. It is possible that he will launch a major campaign to smash the royalists, but he is unlikely to succeed in such an effort. In any event, we doubt that he could install and maintain a subservient Yemeni government. For some time at least, we look for continued statement, punctuated by desultory Egyptian-Saudi negotiations toward a settlement and by occasional outbursts of fighting. Given growing anti-Egyptian sentiment among virtually all Yemenis, the longer this goes on, the more unsatisfactory to Nasser the eventual conclusion of his Yemeni venture is likely to be.

1. The situation in Yemen over the past two years has been characterized by two factors—stalemate on the military front and increasing animosity toward the Egyptians on the part of a widening spectrum of Yemenis. Since September 1962, when the Egyptians first intervened

---

[1] Source: Johnson Library, National Security File, Country File, Yemen, Cables & Memos, Vol. II, 7/64–12/68. Secret; No Foreign Dissem. Prepared in the Office of National Estimates of the Central Intelligence Agency.

in Yemen with modest forces, their strength has grown to about 45,000 men—comprising 10 infantry brigades, plus armor, aircraft, and supporting units. The UAR military forces have remained largely on garrison duty in the principal towns of northern Yemen. While they have not shown much aggressiveness, they have probably lost about 5,000 dead and the attrition of equipment has been high. The financial burden is also heavy; it has probably exceeded normal peacetime costs by more than $60 million per year.

2. Nasser's original aim was to establish a Yemeni government which was republican in form and led by men willing to follow his policies of Arab nationalism and socialism. His efforts were frustrated by the unexpected durability of the royalists, backed by Saudi Arabian support. Failure to subdue the partisans of the Imam and bickering and factionalism among republican forces have led Nasser to increase his investment in men and material and to take an ever greater voice not only in the running of the war but in the control of the Yemeni Republican government.

3. Nasser has thus fallen into something very like the trap he has been seeking to avoid. He has plainly not desired outright annexation of the Yemen, or even a less complete union with Egypt such as the United Arab State which he formed in 1958 and which became moribund by 1960. On the other hand, he is unwilling to let the Yemeni republicans run their own affairs. This is in part because they have pretty clearly demonstrated their incompetence to do so in a fashion suitable to Cairo and in part because Nasser wants to retain sufficient control in Yemen to prosecute his campaign against the British position in Aden.

4. Yet Nasser's efforts to find a way out of the Yemen mess—which Prime Minister Ali Sabri has characterized as "Egypt's Vietnam"—have thus far been futile. Two efforts toward a negotiated solution have failed—the agreement negotiated by Ambassador Bunker in 1963 and direct talks between Nasser and Saudi Arabia's Faisal in the fall of 1964. The latter effort started well enough, as Faisal and Nasser each probably believed that the course of events would favor his own cause, and the preliminary conference at Erkwit in the Sudan seemed to show that royalists and republicans were able to compromise their respective difficulties with little trouble. But the Saudis subsequently refused to accept the designation "Republic" for the future state of Yemen, claiming that it would prejudice the outcome of the proposed talks; the republicans—some of whom had been excluded from the Erkwit talks—quarreled among themselves over the makeup of their delegation; and the Egyptians attempted to control its composition. The upshot was that the plenary conference did not convene and the cease-fire—which had been fairly widely observed—has broken down.

5. The shelving of the conference has been a severe blow to the Yemeni republicans. Their resentment at Egyptian domination of Yemeni affairs has been growing for a long time. A majority of republican leaders have withdrawn their cooperation from the present government, now virtually an Egyptian puppet. A mood of "Yemen for the Yemenis" is sweeping the country and is tending to increase contacts and perhaps even cooperation between republicans and royalists.

6. The Egyptians seem unable to visualize assisting a Yemeni regime which is not entirely dependent on them.[2] The recently appointed government of al-Amri is so obviously out of tune with the general sentiment in the country that several of its designated members have refused to serve. There is virtually no chance that it can be effective in governing or in prosecuting the struggle against the royalists. However, the continuation of this sort of regime probably appears preferable to Nasser than loss of face by admitting defeat or the risks of permitting the establishment of a government which insists on a substantial measure of freedom of action.

7. Nasser's use of Yemen as a position from which to mount paramilitary operations against the British position in Aden is, from his point of view, an additional reason not to give ground. Such a retreat in the campaign against the vestiges of the colonial position would be counter to his entire foreign policy outlook. Over the past year, the Egyptians have armed and paid dissident elements in Aden and the Federation to carry out terrorist actions. The republican leaders have a different view. Though they eventually want to see the British out of Aden, they would like to win their own war first. In response to Egyptian thrusts, the British have given clandestine support to the royalists, precisely to deprive the UAR of its point of vantage in Yemen.

8. Anti-Egyptian sentiment is widespread. Some republican worthies have retired to their tribal bases, and many have withdrawn their cooperation from the Sallal-al-Amri government. Nevertheless, they are inhibited from positive action to unseat it by a feeling of helplessness in the face of Egyptian military power. Some of them, moreover, remain opposed to the royal family and refuse any cooperation with it as an institution, although not with certain of its younger members. Nonetheless, a sharing of a common enmity towards the Egyptians will tend

---

[2] This is not only intransigence on Nasser's part; it is a reflection of a political characteristic of the Arab world, namely, that power is indivisible. A leader either has supreme power or he doesn't, and, if he shows in some specific instance that he doesn't, then doubts arise as to his power in general. Considerations of this sort lie behind the unwillingness of successive Iraqi governments to conclude arrangement with the Kurds for defining the degree of Kurdish separateness in Iraq. They also underlie the almost universal tendency toward authoritarian government—whether by King, president, or prime minister—in the Arab states. [Footnote in the source text.]

to bring royalist and republican closer together, and make the UAR's tack in Yemen more difficult.

Outlook

9. Nasser's several interests in Yemen and the extent of his commitment there make an outright withdrawal highly unlikely in the foreseeable future. Although his costs will continue to mount, and will contribute to grumbling and discontent within Egypt, there is little likelihood of a sudden and dramatic deterioration in the Egyptian position.

10. There are indications that the UAR may be preparing for another major offensive, perhaps aimed—as was a joint UAR–Yemeni effort in August 1964—at eliminating centers of royalist resistance and cutting royalist supply route to Saudi Arabia. Additional forces are arriving in Yemen, and the UAR command is employing such weapons as 6,600-pound bombs and chemical mines, apparently to terrorize the tribespeople. We would expect a major effort to have success in occupying territory and inflicting local defeats, but we do not think the Egyptians are able to penetrate the rugged mountain fastnesses to which the royalist tribes would retreat. Also, with many republican leaders disaffected, the Egyptians will have less tribal support to draw on than in the past. A heavy Egyptian offensive might lead to some bombing raids within Saudi Arabia. However, we do not believe that the UAR is likely to invade Saudi territory.

11. Over the next several months, the Egyptians and Saudis will probably continue their contacts in an effort to reach a settlement. Faisal will want to keep the talks going so as not to give Nasser an excuse for further attacks on him again. He also probably sees certain advantages for him in having the Egyptians expend resources in Yemen, and he appears to feel that time is on his side in the Yemeni question. Accordingly, Faisal will probably not be willing to compromise his basic objective: withdrawal of the bulk of Nasser's forces. He appears to view the establishment of a government chosen by and acceptable to a broad concensus of Yemenis as favoring this objective. For their part, the Egyptians want to keep the contact open, in the hope of finding some process or mechanism which can be manipulated to their advantage. Faisal and Nasser will probably attempt to get royalists and republicans together again, but the prospects for progress toward a solution in the coming six months or so are dim.

12. We do feel that the Egyptians will be forced to agree in time to a compromise settlement. The longer that time is, the less influence and the fewer supporters are they likely to have in whatever government emerges. The "third force" of anti-Egyptian republicans will almost certainly play a prominent role in any such settlement. There is a good chance that at least some of the Hamid-al-Din princes would

also be involved. The ultimate result could well be a regime which is neither republic nor monarchy, but which contains elements of both, as well as a strong tribal flavor.

13. Even so, hatred of the Egyptians may not prove sufficient cement to hold a compromise Yemeni regime together. There is on the horizon no single leader who has the ability to run the country. Nor has any one faction—royalist, republican, or independent—the capability of imposing its will on the others. Unless the Yemeni leaders succeed in subduing their personal, tribal, and political rivalries in the common interest, a measure of anarchy is a not unlikely prospect for Yemen, if and when the Egyptian hand is withdrawn.

For the Board of National Estimates:
Sherman Kent
Chairman

---

361.   Memorandum of Conversation[1]

Washington, February 24, 1965.

SUBJECT

    The Yemen Situation

PARTICIPANTS

    His Excellency Muhsin al-Aini, Ambassador of the Yemen Arab Republic
    NEA—Phillips Talbot
    NE—William D. Wolle

Ambassador al-Aini called at his request to discuss developments in Yemen. In summary, the Ambassador's remarks constituted a passionate indictment of the U.A.R.'s activities in Yemen and a request that the United States through diplomatic efforts encourage Saudi Arabia to support Zubairi's Party of God movement as an alternative to its policy of full backing for the royalists.

The Ambassador said that Zubairi and his people were continuing their efforts to build support for the Party of God. They were apparently having some success in gaining tribal support from both Y.A.R. and royalist sides. He did not know if Zubairi had had any contact with the Saudi Government so far.

---

[1] Source: National Archives and Records Administration, RG 59, Central Files 1964–66, POL YEMEN. Secret. Drafted by Wolle on February 26.

Mr. Talbot said it was the Department's impression that more U.A.R. troops are now in Yemen than ever before, and that the rather favorable atmosphere of last fall, when it seemed President Nasser and King Faisal were working toward settlement of the Yemeni problem, has unfortunately vanished. He said it seemed that the Arabs somehow ought to be able and willing to face the situation and seek a solution. Ambassador al-Aini said that his government had been promised that Jordan's King Hussein would contact Nasser in an effort to help clarify the situation and advance toward a solution, but he did not know whether Hussein had taken any steps as yet. Mr. Talbot said he had no information on this but that during his recent discussions with King Hussein in Amman on other matters, he gained the impression that the King would be anxious to help, if possible, on the Yemen problem.

Ambassador al-Aini said he was convinced that the Party of God movement gave the Saudi Government an alternative to continued support of the royalists. Why did the Saudis not take this opportunity and make contacts with the new movement? It was certainly more representative of the thinking and feelings of the Yemeni people than the Hamid al-Din family elements which were in the vanguard of the royalist camp. The Ambassador said he thought the U.A.R. would reconsider its policy in Yemen if it became clear that the Party of God movement had great support.

The U.S. Government, said the Ambassador, should not remain aloof from the problem but should help toward a solution. Mr. Talbot reminded him of the major American efforts of 1963–64 and of the Bunker missions. The Ambassador responded that Zubairi's movement was a new factor and that U.S. diplomatic assistance at this time could be effective. He then launched a bitter attack against U.A.R. activities in Yemen, describing the Egyptians as the "worst colonialists any country has experienced". He ascribed to the U.A.R. the objective of occupying and using Yemen for its own interests and said the U.A.R. would never willingly withdraw from his country. U.A.R. actions were savage and inhumane. Not content with bombing Yemeni villages by day, the U.A.R. was now conducting air raids at night against "thousands and thousands" of Yemenis. It had devastated huge sections of the Arhab district. Mr. Talbot asked if the Ambassador was aware of recent unconfirmed reports that the U.A.R. forces were using poison gas. The Ambassador responded that "everything is possible" and that the Egyptians would stop at nothing to carry out their designs. He claimed to have factual reports that U.A.R. forces had even burned persons alive in front of others. He declared that Nasser wished the Hamid al-Din family to remain at the helm of the royalist opposition so that he would have a popular pretext for his own designs in Yemen.

Mr. Talbot referred to the situation along Yemen's southern border, stating that an opportunity to establish greater peace in that area may have been missed, inasmuch as the new Labor Government in the United Kingdom might have seen fit to change somewhat the direction of British policy had it been met halfway by the Y.A.R. The Ambassador responded that the Egyptians are fomenting the difficulty in the south. He said the U.A.R. had organized the National Liberation Front to spearhead terrorism and that the Cairo press and radio are attacking all the old political groupings in the south which historically had been working for advancement of the peoples' interests. The U.A.R. is using violence indiscriminately in the south, he said, because it wants to replace the British as the occupying power.

The Ambassador concluded that Yemen must be aided for the sake of the entire Arabian Peninsula. It is, he said, the duty of Kuwait, Saudi Arabia, the United Kingdom and the United States to help out in this situation. It must be realized that the unified Yemeni people are facing "a tyrant" (the U.A.R.). Mr. Talbot assured the Ambassador that the Department watches the situation with sympathy and understanding. He said he wished to make it clear that he could not give any encouragement that the United States could entertain the idea of assisting the Party of God or any internal domestic group in Yemen. The U.S. continued to hope the situation would improve and that there would appear among the parties concerned the necessary concessions and willingness to change which might make a settlement possible.

362.   Telegram From the Department of State to the Embassy in Saudi Arabia[1]

Washington, March 2, 1965, 6:34 p.m.

426. Taiz tel 326,[2] Jidda tel 628[3] to Department.

Department concurs with Jidda in questioning utility US formally involving self as channel to Faisal for Zubairi group's views. (FYI. On February 24 al-Aini made strong pitch to Talbot for US support Party of God and was told we could not give encouragement to idea that we would support any internal domestic faction in Yemen.)[4]

Taiz is authorized at its discretion explain to Zubairi's emissary Faisal's attitude toward Yemen problem as we understand it (as recommended Jidda 628 to Department).

In keeping with non-involvement position, do not believe we should particularly encourage or discourage any attempt Zubairi send representative to Faisal. However, Jidda is authorized discuss Zubairi's opinions with Saqqaf on off-the-record basis in context general review Yemen scene if Ambassador considers appropriate.

Rusk

---

[1] Source: National Archives and Records Administration, RG 59, Central Files 1964–66, POL 27 YEMEN. Secret. Drafted by Moore and approved by Davies. Also sent to Taiz and repeated to Cairo, London, and Aden.

[2] Telegram 326 from Taiz, February 23, reported that the Embassy had been approached by a spokesman for the Zubairi group requesting that the U.S. Government pass to Faisal its declaration that it represented the most popular force in Yemen and deserved Faisal's support, and that Yemenis wanted neither a monarchy nor a UAR-dominated military dictatorship. (Ibid.)

[3] In telegram 628 from Jidda, February 26, Hart expressed doubt as to the utility of having the United States serve as a channel to Faisal for the Zubairi group views, noting that Faisal might well feel that the group would be useful in showing up the fragility of the Amri puppet regime but that they were no substitute for the royalists who alone constituted a palpable challenge to UAR domination of Yemen. (Ibid.)

[4] See Document 361.

363. Telegram From the Department of State to the Embassy in the United Arab Republic[1]

Washington, March 9, 1965, 1:32 p.m.

5335. Jidda tels 634 and 638 and Cairo 3059[2] to Department. Threatened UAR Attacks on Saudi Arabia.

Saudi avowed aid to royalists places US in extremely difficult position. If UAR attacks Saudi territory in strictly military context of Yemen campaign, any US move provide aircraft patrols similar "Hard Surface" opens us to charge giving air umbrella for SAG activities against regime which we recognize in Yemen. (Fact of Iranian assistance to royalists, presumably through Saudis, poses additional complication.) In absence extensive network ground observers, it would be difficult for us give credence any Saudi bona fides that aid not being supplied, if such should be offered as quid pro quo for US air cover. In any event, only really effective form in which we could come to Faisal's aid would be with US military strength, risking direct US–UAR clash. Saudi direct involvement in Yemen precludes present consideration such action. In these circumstances, must be made clear to Faisal that while we continue concerned with integrity Saudi Arabia, our commitment does not extend to providing defense against UAR attacks within framework Yemeni military campaign directed at armament dumps for royalists on Saudi territory. Despite fact Faisal claims he acting only in interest self-defense, we not ready give him this degree support in defending such an extended concept of defense. Obviously if UAR attacks expanded to other parts of country we would be required review our position.

At same time, agree with Jidda we should make clear in Cairo our continuing grave concern at any extension conflict in Yemen which would endanger Saudi integrity. Realize we have little leverage with Nasser, but in wake Haikal's threatening remarks on resumption attacks on Saudi Arabia it imperative we make certain UARG under no illusion about our continued concern for Saudis.

For Cairo: You should make following points at as high level in UARG as possible, perhaps Ali Sabri or Fawzi for passing to Nasser:

---

[1] Source: National Archives and Records Administration, RG 59, Central Files 1964–66, POL 27 YEMEN. Secret; Priority. Drafted by Moore on March 8; cleared by Davies in draft, and by Campbell, George L. Warren (G/PM), Quinn, Judd, Bunte, and Talbot; and approved by Ball. Also sent to Jidda and London and repeated to Taiz, Paris, USUN, CINCSTRIKE/CINCMEAFSA for Ramsey, and COMIDEASTFOR.

[2] Telegram 634 from Jidda, March 1; telegram 638 from Jidda, March 2; and telegram 3059 from Cairo, March 4. (All ibid.)

1. US was heartened by events following Nasser–Faisal conversations last September which seemed indicate Yemen on road to peaceful solution and to government acceptable to all Yemenis. Subsequent breakdown of ceasefire and apparent narrowing of YARG popular base have been discouraging.

2. Continued massive UAR troop presence Yemen is cause of concern by Faisal and has been steady source friction in US–UAR dealings since withdrawal undertakings made in connection Bunker Agreement.

3. US continues be greatly interested in support integrity and independence Saudi Arabia and views with concern continuation bloodshed Yemen, threatened increase armed action there and possible expansion of conflict to Saudi Arabia.

4. US would view with great seriousness any extension UAR military activities to Saudi airspace or territory as indicated by Haikal (Cairo tel 3002).[3] Such action would be further aggravation present US–UAR relations.

5. US urges UAR, and is similarly urging SAG, to resume discussions with Saudis for resumption of ceasefire in Yemen, perhaps strengthening joint patrols, and ultimate settlement by Yemenis themselves, as reportedly planned following Erkowit conference.[4]

For Jidda: Request you have full and frank discussion with Faisal in response his query for definition US attitude, making following points:

1. The oft-repeated US concern with Saudi integrity continues unabated; our friendship is of long standing and highly cherished by US.

2. As stated in past, US continues willing come to Saudi assistance against unprovoked attack. However, we frankly believe that continued Saudi material aid to Yemeni royalists can be considered provocative. With continuance such aid, US hard put to justify within world-wide framework any military reaction to assist SAG in face UAR attacks against purely military targets in Saudi territory near Yemen border. US can scarcely provide military umbrella for continuation Saudi support of a movement against the government in Yemen which we recognize. If UAR attacks should spread elsewhere in Saudi Arabia we naturally would review our position.

---

[3] Dated February 27. (Ibid., POL ARAB–ISR)

[4] In telegram 3439 from Cairo, April 1, Battle reported that on March 31 he had made the points in the Department's telegram to Deputy Prime Minister Fawzi, who said that the United Arab Republic had also been hopeful after the Nasser–Faisal meeting, but that Saudi Arabia had subsequently stepped up its supplies to the rebels. Fawzi assured the Ambassador that the United Arab Republic desired to settle the matter if it could be done honorably. (Ibid.)

3. As evidence US interest in Saudi defense, US made technical survey air defense requirements SAG and presented results to Saudis over one year ago, including recommendations for improving F–86's currently in Kingdom to enable SAG, pending procurement and delivery new air defense aircraft, develop some defense capability. US offers made at that time, and subsequently elaborated on, to supply interceptor aircraft and related ground environment systems, including training and follow-on spares, are still open for Saudi acceptance.

4. US was encouraged by Faisal–Nasser conversations last September and subsequent Erkowit conference but was disheartened by later breakdown ceasefire and current preparations on both sides for increased military operations Yemen. We are strongly re-emphasizing to Nasser our concern for integrity and independence of Saudi Arabia and our hope for resumption Nasser–Faisal negotiations for peaceful solution Yemen problem. Similarly, we wish emphasize to Faisal our hope he will resume contacts with Nasser—either directly or indirectly—for this purpose. Additionally, we should again warn Faisal about the inadvisability of reinvolving Saudi Arabia directly in support Yemen royalists, pointing out as one example the difficulty with which this faces us in aiding Saudi Arabia in case of attack.

5. If there were imminent or actual UAR attacks on Saudi Arabia, Faisal would probably wish to take matter to UN, giving him forum present his case to world opinion, and marshal such opinion against UAR aggression and in favor of talks between Faisal and Nasser. Hopefully, UN consideration would tend to inhibit further military action and renew pressure for negotiated settlement in Yemen, both of which we assume to be in Saudi interest.[5]

For London: You should inform HMG of above thinking and démarches and request British join us in urging restraint on Faisal. Clearer picture would be helpful of what, if any, commitments British have made to Saudis and of current British attitude and dealings with Yemeni royalists.[6]

---

[5] In telegram 680 from Jidda, March 16, Hart reported that he had delivered the instructions contained in the Department's telegram to the King orally on March 14. Faisal had thanked him for the statement of the U.S. Government position, but commented that it contained "nothing new." He insisted that following the Alexandria conference Saudi Arabia had done everything possible to facilitate UAR withdrawal of troops "without loss of dignity" and that the United Arab Republic and Yemen had broken the truce. Faisal stated that his country was obliged to support the royalists as long as UAR troops remained in Yemen. (Ibid.)

[6] Printed from an unsigned copy.

364. Telegram From the Department of State to the Embassy in Saudi Arabia[1]

Washington, March 20, 1965, 11:45 a.m.

466. In courtesy call on Secretary March 18, devoted entirely to Yemen, Saudi Ambassador Sowayel made following points:

1. Faisal extends regards to Secretary and appreciates US interest finding solution Yemen problem. Unfortunate that Nasser had not seen fit carry out agreements reached with Faisal last September and has now increased troops and begun insulting Saudis. Saudis ready consider any technique for solution we might suggest.

2. Frictions between Yemenis and Egyptians greatly increased. Royalists coming to Jidda preparing selves for new military action and are very confident, primarily because of growing popular genuine dissatisfaction with UAR presence.

3. Saudis certain Nasser in difficult situation in Yemen and are "only trying help him get out".

4. When he had asked Faisal if he should make representations against US PL–480 shipments UAR, Faisal had said no, that SAG would not want US stop sending food to Egyptians on Saudi behalf. (Secretary responded that honor and integrity US involved in completion present contract, but unless larger issues resolved it doubtful additional wheat would be sent UAR.)

5. In response to query, said most recent Arab League meeting devoted only to Germany, that Yemen not discussed.

Secretary responded as follows:

1. As Ambassador Hart recently informed King, we deeply committed to safety and security Saudi Arabia and encouraged at internal development progress King has made in last two years despite Yemen situation. Faisal can count on us to support safety and security Saudi Arabia. But with candor must be noted that situation on border poses great problem for us, particularly since we launching military strikes against North Vietnam because they sending aid South Vietnam rebels. Thus policy problem posed for us in Yemen is very great one. We desire keep close touch with SAG, develop our common ties and mutual search for solution in Yemen.

2. Our relations with UAR hanging by slender thread because of various problems, including Yemen and Congo. We have little influence in Cairo but we are in touch with Egyptians concerning these problems.

---

[1] Source: National Archives and Records Administration, RG 59, Central Files 1964–66, POL 27 YEMEN. Secret. Drafted by Moore on March 19, cleared by Staff Assistant Edward J. Streator (S), and approved by Davies. Repeated to Cairo, Taiz, and Dhahran.

3. Practically one-third USSR aid outside Communist Bloc going to Egypt. In this circumstance, we consider it particularly important for our Arab friends keep contact with UAR.

4. Unfortunate that search for inter-Arab cooperation has become confused with personal position of Nasser. There is much to be gained by Saudi Arabia and other countries from closer inter-Arab ties.

In response to Secretary's questions, Ambassador said that, to his knowledge, Saudis were not discussing Yemen problem with other Arab states except for brief indecisive talk with Bourguiba; and that current UAR anti-Saudi propaganda not particularly strong.

No further memcon is being prepared.

Rusk

---

365. Telegram From the Department of State to the Embassy in the United Arab Republic[1]

Washington, April 2, 1965, 8 p.m.

6051. Saudi-Yemen Border. We are gratified by indications (Cairo's 3439[2] and 3448[3]) UARG taking pains to avoid violation of Saudi territory. However, Jidda's 740 and 744[4] report two recent instances where UAR precautions broke down. Hope Embassy (perhaps Political Counselor to Al-Khouli) will have early opportunity insure UARG understands USG concerned over any violations SAG territory or airspace and USG commitment to support Saudi safety and security remains in effect. We trust reports of massive Egyptian troop movements in border area do not foreshadow increased border friction.

Rusk

---

[1] Source: National Archives and Records Administration, RG 59, Central Files 1964–66, POL 32–1 SAUD–YEMEN. Secret. Drafted by Jones and Moore, cleared by Davies, and approved by Jernegan. Repeated to Jidda and Taiz.

[2] In telegram 3439 from Cairo, April 1, Battle reported that in response to his expression of U.S. concern over any extension of UAR military activities to Saudi airspace or territory, Deputy Prime Minister Fawzi assured him that the United Arab Republic would exercise all restraint possible. (Ibid., POL 27 YEMEN)

[3] Dated April 1. (Ibid.)

[4] Both dated April 1. (Ibid., and POL 31–1 SAUD–UAR)

366. Memorandum From the Joint Chiefs of Staff to Secretary of Defense McNamara[1]

JCSM–295–65   Washington, April 21, 1965.

SUBJECT

 Possible Saudi Arabian–UAR Confrontation Arising Out of the Yemen Situation (U)

 1. The Deputy Assistant Secretary of Defense (ISA) requested by memorandum, I–21497/65, dated 3 March 1965,[2] subject as above, a review of the military options and alternatives open to the United States in the event the Saudi Arabian Government requests US assistance to complement the capabilities of its own armed forces to deter or contain possible UAR military action in or over Saudi Arabian territory.

 2. The development of US military plans for supporting the Saudi Arabian Government is complicated by the fact of US diplomatic recognition of the Yemen Arab Republic, a UAR-sponsored regime opposed by the United Kingdom and by the Saudis through their support of the Yemeni Royalists. The consequence of this aid to the Royalists is to provoke retaliation by or on behalf of the US-recognized Yemen Arab Republic. Therefore, US military planners face the paradox of supporting the Saudi Arabian Government against a Yemen Arab Republic also supported, at least diplomatically, by the United States. Similarly, any coordinated US–UK effort would be complicated by the fact that the United Kingdom and the United States recognize, diplomatically, different Yemeni factions. For these reasons, all feasible nonmilitary actions, including actions in the United Nations, should be undertaken prior to any US military action in the Arabian Peninsula.

 3. Consideration should also be given to the possibility of utilizing UK forces in the Arabian Peninsula before US forces are provided for assistance to Saudi Arabia. UK military forces presently in the area offer a significant capability and can conduct effective military operations in the Arabian Peninsula.

 4. It should be emphasized that token forces do not have a capability properly to defend themselves or friendly powers, or to engage and defeat a determined attack. Moreover, if such show of force fails to deter, then the United States must be prepared to conduct land, sea, and air operations on a scale large enough to achieve our political obligations; and our plans must cover these contingencies.

---

 [1] Source: Washington National Records Center, RG 330, OSD Files: FRC 70 A 1265, Saudi Arabia 381, 3 Mar. 65. Top Secret.
 [2] Not printed.

5. The military options available to the United States in support of Saudi Arabia range from increased military matériel and training assistance to the deployment and employment of sizable land, sea, and air forces. The courses of action in JCSM–188–63, dated 6 March 1963, subject: "Courses of Action in Saudi Arabia (U),"[3] were believed to be representative of an appropriate ascending order of possible US military force deployments to deter UAR aggressions. However, review with CINCSTRIKE/USCINCMEAFSA has resulted in some revisions and additions to the options previously furnished. For your information, a discussion of the composition, capability, closure time, effect on US readiness posture, and cost, where applicable, of the examples is included in the Appendices hereto.[4] It should be recognized that these examples are possible military alternatives, not recommended military actions. In addition, these options are not mutually exclusive; a combination of two or more alternatives may be the best course of action to produce the desired result. Moreover, the listing of only air and naval deployments is not meant to preclude consideration of the use of land forces as a show of force.

6. In the event that the situation in the Arabian Peninsula deteriorates, and any use of US military force is contemplated, the Joint Chiefs of Staff will provide further comments in light of the situation existing at the time.

For the Joint Chiefs of Staff:
L. J. Kirn
Rear Admiral, USN
Deputy Director, Joint Staff

---

[3] For text of JCSM–188–63, March 6, 1963, see *Foreign Relations, 1961–1963*, vol. XVIII, Document 177.

[4] Attached but not printed.

367.   Telegram From the Embassy in Saudi Arabia to the Department of State[1]

Jidda, April 21, 1965, 1827Z.

813. Conversation with Assistant Secretary Talbot with King Faysal, April 19.

Introductory Exchange.

Meeting attended by Crown Prince Khalid, Deputy FonMin Saqqaf, Royal Protocol official and interpreter, Abd al-Aziz Majid, and Ambassador Hart.

Mr. Talbot began by expressing appreciation that King had left proceedings Islamic conference Mecca to take time to receive him at Jidda. He brought warm greetings from President Johnson and Secretary Rusk and stated that strong US friendship for Saudi Arabia and interest in its integrity and independence remained unabated. Progress developing under Faysal's wise leadership was much admired by US and significance this effort, while retaining strong religious values guiding Saudi nation, was understood and appreciated. Talbot also referred to US global commitments, its efforts in Southeast Asia and its special interest in maintaining peace and stability in Middle East.

Faysal thanked Talbot for his greetings and comments. With regard to Vietnam, he remarked that as he had recently told Ambassador Hart situation there had deteriorated because initial US stand had not been sufficiently firm; once US took determined action Communist side immediately began to appeal for solution by peaceful means. Addressing himself to relation between Islam and progress Faysal emphasized Islam contained nothing which should slow up progress of any nation, in fact, greatest leaders Muslim world were those who had been devoted followers of prophet's teachings.

Conversation quickly turned to Yemen, Faysal referring to his 1962 talks with Talbot in Washington–New York,[2] when he had predicted that entry UAR troops into Yemen would create serious complications. Facts had borne this out and it was continued presence UAR forces in Yemen which constituted main problem. Had upheaval in Yemen been limited to Yemenis alone they would have settled matters in due course. SAG could not pretend to be indifferent to UAR intervention, which had proved to be directed against Saudi Arabia. Tracing history of

---

[1] Source: National Archives and Records Administration, RG 59, Central Files 1964–66, POL SAUD–US. Secret; Priority. Repeated to Tel Aviv for Talbot, Cairo, London, Taiz, Aden, Beirut, Baghdad, Damascus, Dhahran, Kuwait, and CINCSTRIKE/CINCMEAFSA.
[2] See *Foreign Relations, 1961–1963,* vol. XVIII, Document 58.

efforts to solve problem before and after Arab summit, Faysal said that once Yemen had been returned to Yemeni hands, SAG was ready respond to any request for help, no matter who Yemeni leaders then were. It was not in Saudi interest to have problems in Yemen. Solution now rested entirely in UAR hands. UAR and SAG should both get out of picture. Moment UAR desired solution it would be easy. It had only to leave Yemen. Nasir had made public statement that conversations between him and Faysal had no mention UAR military withdrawals.

Should Faysal publicize the secret agreement he had with Nasir? Meanwhile, UAR was publicly berating SAG and SAG was remaining silent. He had no intention of replying. However, this situation could not go on indefinitely. How long would UAR remain in Yemen? Faysal did not understand Nasir's ultimate aims for at Alexandria he had said he wanted some way out. Faysal had then paved way after return from Alexandria and had presented proposals which would have made it possible for UAR to withdraw from Yemen with dignity so as to avoid adverse reaction from people of UAR or other countries. Elements of these proposals were first of all, cease-fire, and secondly, mutual UAR–SAG efforts to bring together key people of Yemen to decide for themselves on their future. Observers had been sent. Faysal, right after Alexandria, had stopped all aid to Royalists as gesture of sincerity. Royalists abided by cease-fire for long time, but after Erkowit meeting UAR violated cease-fire so flagrantly Faysal ultimately felt obliged renew aid to Royalists. SAG had felt it useful in order to forestall complete stand-off by Republican–Royalist Yemenis at projected national conclave (Haradh) to suggest structure of a temporary govt ("state of Yemen"). Faysal then gave résumé its provisions, already known to Dept. Discussions over this SAG proposal had continued without success. Emissaries had come and gone and after Ramadhan Saudi Ambassador to UAR had returned to report to Faysal that UAR would accept Saudi proposal provided provisional govt were called "Republican" and Yemen in fact remained permanently republican. Faysal said this was form of dictation to Yemenis in advance of meeting for self-determination. Saudis could not accept this. Meanwhile, Marshal Amer had made speeches to same effect in Yemen and in UAR. Saudi Ambassador was finally instructed on return to Cairo to inform UAR Govt that such statements were contrary to Faysal–Nasir agreement. However, Ambassador had not yet been received. It was not fair to ask Saudi Arabia to accept a dictated solution.

Before responding on this matter, Talbot said he wished refer to Southeast Asia and to Faysal's remark that force should have been used sooner against Communists. US had helped Filipinos to get rid of Huks by policy of limited assistance and hoped to assist Vietnamese to solve their problem as Asians rather than by bringing in "white-faced Americans" to do job for them. However, South Vietnam had never lacked awareness of US sense of purpose. Talbot was glad Faysal believed North Vietnam was ready to have peaceful solution; up to now US aware only of North Vietnamese insistence on unacceptable conditions. To this Faysal responded that what he had meant to imply was that other side was now "crying all over the world" for peaceful solution. Talbot noted US did not yet rule out possibility of major confrontation with Red China. Faysal remarked that intervention of Red China in Vietnam would be understandable in its way, but why should some Arabs take similar position and intervene in un-neutral fashion against US in Vietnam, Cuba and other places?

Talbot said he would like to review recent developments in US relations with UAR. Particularly as concerned Yemen, including mention of his April 18 conversation at Cairo with President Nasir.[3] As Faysal already knew, US relations with Egypt had been narrowed by important differences to point where they were now very narrow indeed. Ambassador Hart, following his return from Washington, had reported to His Majesty elements of this situation as seen in Executive dept of US Govt and in Congress. Problems between UAR and US had almost nothing to do with internal situation of UAR. Here US had actively supported and encouraged development, indeed tried to get UAR to concentrate on domestic progress. Differences had arisen over relations with third countries in which US had interest and found Egyptians heavily involved. First of these third country situations was Yemen. US relations with Egypt had never been really satisfactory since start of Yemeni affair. Then came our deep concern over Egyptian assistance to Congo rebels. We also found ourselves questioning what was going on in South Arabian Federation and in Persian Gulf. During same period African students in Cairo set fire to US library and Nasir had made speech which US found unacceptable. We were now coming to end of chapter in sense that because of Yemen no new development loan had been made to UAR since 1963, and 3-year PL–480 program was running out at end of June. We also had problems over Jordan waters and UAR in connection with "an old and familiar subject." In this context Talbot had been instructed to go to Cairo and examine with Nasir and with others attitude of UAR toward US and to explain US position on various subjects. He had raised many subjects, including Yemen. He had told Nasir US had been greatly heartened last August when there appeared be approach to solution of this long, troublesome

---

[3] A report of Assistant Secretary Talbot's conversation with Nasser on April 18 was transmitted in telegram 3653 from Cairo, April 18. (National Archives and Records Administration, RG 59, Central Files 1964–66, ORG 7 NEA) A summary of Talbot's April 18 conversation with Nasser is printed in *Foreign Relations, 1964–1968*, vol. XVIII, Document 208.

and costly dispute. As His Majesty had mentioned, we ourselves—although not an immediate party—had made earnest efforts to help. Ambassador Bunker's work had, unfortunately, not been successful but we hoped parties directly concerned could find path to settlement. Meanwhile, our failure to give economic development loans to UAR, while never announced as policy, had been clearly understood in Cairo; however, we had kept food supply going. Subsequently we found our hopes for direct settlement had been premature. On earlier occasion Talbot had told His Majesty that US concern for security of Saudi Arabia would remain firm and indeed it had. Sometimes we heard rumors we favored keeping Nasir bogged down in Yemen because this helped Israel and because Israel favored this course. We do not know Israel's position on this matter or its activity, but as for ourselves, Talbot could assure His Majesty US position was that Yemen should be governed by Yemenis and we did not approve or condone presence large UAR forces in Yemen. In response to Talbot's questions Nasir had described events as he saw them and His Majesty would not be surprised to learn that there were differences with His Majesty's description. Nasir had admitted there were differences in interpretation of SAG–UAR agreement. Talbot had then asked Nasir what could be done to end this unfortunate situation. Referring to Cyprus, Talbot had said that US was urging interested parties to meet for substantive talks and hoped similar course could be followed on Yemen. Nasir had replied that he did not see much value at this stage in talks at ambassadorial level. Talbot had then asked whether he expected to meet Faysal again and, if so, whether in the near or distant future. Nasir had expressed strong view Yemen problem solvable only by direct Saudi–UAR agreement. Chance to meet Faysal might occur if Faysal attended Algiers Afro-Asian conference or next summit. Meantime since he had once sent Marshal Amer to talk with Sultan latter might undertake return visit and meet with Amer to discuss differences in interpretation of Nasir–Faysal agreement.

Talbot said Faysal would not be surprised to learn that Nasir spoke rather strongly of Saudi assistance to Royalists and termed it "breach of understanding." Nasir had also spoken without noticeable enthusiasm of situation in Yemen, where people were taking money both from Saudi Arabia and from UAR.

Faysal responded wryly: "We know our people there. They are the Royalists. If they can get something from the other side that is up to them." As for agreements, SAG and UAR had had two, each embodying exchange of notes, but there had been no result. As for sending Sultan to UAR, Faysal was agreeable to any recourse, even to going himself, but when Saudi Arabia was being insulted (in Cairo press) it would be interpreted as submission to blackmail. Nasir wanted to prove that writing one or two articles would force Saudis to come to him. Saudis could not accept that. Let UAR write hundreds of articles if it wished.

Talbot made clear he was not acting as another Ambassador Bunker. However, because Nasir knew he was coming to Saudi Arabia he was conveying Nasir's reflections. To this Faysal responded SAG was ready now and had always been ready to work to solve this problem but would not accept dictation. If Nasir found situation in Yemen good, then let it be. "We are at our ease." Talbot rejoined that he did not find Nasir "at ease." Economic conditions in the UAR made it in Nasir's interest to solve problem. Furthermore, Nasir very aware of US interest in Saudi Arabia's integrity and independence. Talbot had strongly affirmed there would be great trouble for UAR in its relations with US if Nasir brought trouble into Saudi Arabia. Faysal responded Nasir naturally wanted SAG to desist from helping Royalists so could dominate Yemen and threaten Saudi Arabia. Why should not both UAR and SAG stop interfering in Yemen, Nasir withdraw and Faysal stop aid?

Talbot commented US is frequently blamed by either side of controversy for favoring the other and cited India–Pakistan dispute over Kashmir. This seemed to be our lot and was not dissimilar to role in which leader of any country finds himself between domestic factions. To this Faysal replied, "We never suspected you were partial. Nasir is the one we are addressing. Why does he deviate from sound solution and seek some other course?" Yemen was different from Kashmir or Cyprus. Saudi Arabia did not have designs on Yemen nor did it desire even a preferential position in that country. What Saudi Arabia wanted was that both outside parties should quit; Nasir to quit and Faysal to quit.

Talbot rejoined that US shared Saudi desire that Yemenis govern themselves without outside interference. US had expended 160 thousand American casualties and hundreds of billions of dollars since World War II without seeking any territory or influence. Faysal again asked why Nasir stayed in Yemen. Talbot responded it was US belief that eventually Yemeni people would resolve their problems and have a Govt of Yemenis. This being case, we wondered whether it would be necessary to continue to give aid to Royalists. It was complicating factor as Ambassador Hart had already explained. Faysal asked how, if SAG stopped aid to Royalists, anyone could guarantee that Yemenis would be in position to resist UAR tanks and planes. Why not have both outside parties pull out? Talbot replied he did not disagree; in other places Arabs were having troubles with Arabs, Faysal knew Arabs better than we, and would perhaps be able to explain. Faysal responded that illogic comes from Arabs as well as from non-Arabs.

Talbot then reviewed food-grain program to UAR and said that question of unshipped balance originally promised FY 65 must be decided soon and probably would be. After that, there was larger question—partly political, partly economic and partly psychological—whether another food-grain program to UAR should be started. Faysal commented that in previous conversation he and Talbot had agreed needy people should be helped. However, if this permitted Nasir to divert money to cause trouble in the area, this disturbed him. Faysal said it was inconceivable he ask US to stop shipping food to the hungry, yet how was this problem to be avoided? Talbot and Faysal both agreed this constituted basic dilemma of the program.

[Here follows discussion of another subject.]

Hart

---

368.   Telegram From the Department of State to the Embassy in the United Kingdom[1]

Washington, April 30, 1965, 6:17 p.m.

6955. YARG Chargé Jaghman, acting on instructions from FonMin al-Aini, approached Dept April 30 with reference recent HMG note protesting overflights Harib area and giving notice possible turn to UN Security Council and armed action against interlopers (Deptels 6741 to London, 238 to Taiz).[2] Requested US try convince British of problems which such notes and possible airing of situation in UN posed for new moderate Nu'man government[3] during this critical time when it trying get feet on ground. Said Govt obviously needed respite in order get established before it would be able try get UAR stop such activity. Strongly hoped British could hold off "for at least two or three weeks" on any further actions or protests they might have. He referred to alleged sharp criticism YARG by British spokesman during UN Committee Twenty-Four discussion Aden earlier this week as further

---

[1] Source: National Archives and Records Administration, RG 59, Central Files 1964–66, POL 31–1 ADEN–YEMEN. Secret. Drafted by Moore, cleared by Judd and Campbell, and approved by Davies. Repeated to Taiz, USUN, and Aden.

[2] Telegram 238 to Taiz (6741 to London), April 23, transmitted the text of a British note protesting overflights of South Arabian Federation territory by MIG fighters from Yemen that the United Kingdom had asked the United States to deliver to the Yemen Arab Republic Government. (Ibid.)

[3] On April 20 Ahmad Numan, a pro-Western Yemeni moderate who advocated a program of internal reconciliation and eventual UAR withdrawal, formed a new Yemeni Government.

example type of thing which he hoped could be held in abeyance for time being to give moderate YARG breathing space.

Tone of approach was exceptionally rational, restrained and even pleading.

Dept discussing with British Embassy Washington, giving strong endorsement this request from new FonMin al-Aini who has made clear in number conversations with Dept over past months his firm desire end Egyptian interference his country, goal shared by USG and HMG. Request London make similar approach FonOff.

Rusk

---

369. **Telegram From the Embassy in Yemen to the Department of State**[1]

Taiz, April 30, 1965, 1200Z.

463. Following are main points made by Mohsin al Aini in my first call on him in his capacity as FonMin:

1. He expressed cordial friendship for US and urged that USG stand by Yemen's side and help it in this, its greatest hour of trial as well as of opportunity for peace and sound progress.

2. Numan govt represents what Yemen people hoped for when revolution of 1962 broke out, but were prevented from realizing by outsiders. It has backing of entire nation but lacks an army and is beset by many obstacles. He said UAR wants to discredit the group of leaders under Numan and is working hard to see that Khamir conference fails. Al Aini believes conference will succeed and lead to some changes in govt and particularly in powers of presidential council, where Sallal trying thwart Numan's policies.

3. YARG truly wants peace with SAG and UK and if they will adopt understanding attitude peace will come and UAR troops will withdraw. Yemen wants good relations with UAR but does not want to bow to Nasser's policy lines. Numan took brave step in dropping post of Minister of Occupied South and is under pressure from UAR to restore it. Numan trying take over radio and press against Sallal's

---

[1] Source: National Archives and Records Administration, RG 59, Central Files 1964–66, POL 15–1 YEMEN. Secret; Priority. Repeated to Cairo, Jidda, London, Bonn, Aden, and CINCSTRIKE/CINCMEAFSA for POLAD.

objections, in effort stop attacks on SAG and temper output on Arab South. He being accused of kowtowing to imperialism and must move cautiously. Faisal and British must be understanding and patient until he wins this battle. He cannot do so if they continue to help Hamid al-Dins, who do not have slightest chance of returning to power. We can help best by convincing British and especially Faisal of this fact. If as UAR hopes SAG brushes off Numan govt it will fall and all Yemen will decide UAR is right in saying Faisal does not want a Yemen at peace. Result would be a bigger war. (In response my question he said all Yemenis want to settle the Yemen question themselves and resent idea it can be worked out by Nasser and Faisal. It is rather for SAG and UAR to acknowledge fact of an all-Yemeni settlement once it occurs. Virtually all Yemeni tribes though not Hamid al-Dins will be represented at Khamir conference.)

4. Al Aini made no specific request for U.S. material aid, but implied one would be forthcoming after Khamir conference. He deplored growing Yemeni dependence on bloc and said there are many hundreds Yemeni students behind iron curtain who will constitute danger to stability when they return. Other hundreds should be accepted by universities in France, UK, West Germany and US. He hoped France would recognize YARG. He reaffirmed YARG would not recognize GDR (Embtel 461) and said I must know it was not Yemeni who organized anti-FRG affairs. Numan govt would submit written apology and make other amends but "not now".

5. In response my inquiry al Aini said in view of Numan's known pro-Western policies and charges circulated by his enemies that he is Western stooge, it would be better for me not to call on PriMin until after Khamir conference. I asked him convey Numan USG's best wishes for success and other points in Deptel 232,[2] which he acknowledged gratefully.

6. AID/Y Director John Benz accompanied me to Sanaa and had cordial and useful talks with Ministers of Public Works, Economy, Health and Finance.

Comment: While we are not yet sure UAR policy at least at highest levels, towards Numan govt is as anti-Numan as al Aini described it, there undoubtedly is campaign to pad Khamir conference with obstructionists and that Numan is facing many obstacles. I agree with FonMin's assessment of importance Faisal's attitude, and although it would be miracle if he could be brought to support Numan govt., it is to us equally great miracle that latter has come to power. (One indication

---

[2] Telegram 232 to Taiz, April 20, authorized the Embassy to inform Numan that the United States was pleased at current Yemeni moves to attain greater stability by establishing a broader-based government. (Ibid., POL 15 YEMEN)

that it truly has power is persistent report that UAR high command asked but was refused Numan govt's permission to bomb Royalists attempting to cut access routes to Khamir conference. Numan said he would rely on guarantees given by tribes.) We earnestly hope SAG and UKG will realize that the present opportunity is a golden one and that if lost is not likely ever to recur. I recommend US do its best in Riyadh and London to enlist the "understanding attitude" al Aini seeks.

Clark

---

370. **Telegram From the Department of State to the Embassy in Saudi Arabia**[1]

Washington, June 10, 1965, 6:32 p.m.

639. YARG Chargé Discussion with Talbot.

In call June 9 on Asst Secretary Talbot, Yemeni Chargé Geghman, who just returned from consultations Cairo with YARG FonMin al-Aini, made following points on behalf FonMin:

1. Present YARG, under Numan, is at critical juncture and vitally needs support friendly countries. Desperately hopes US will use its influence convince Faisal cooperate with Numan government as last hope for avoiding descent Yemen into utter chaos.

2. New YARG received full confidence representatives overwhelming number Yemenis at Khamr conference on basis that government would bring about expeditious withdrawal Egyptians. Nasser promised Numan during recent discussions Cairo that he would remove troops when Yemenis requested. (Geghman, in subsequent conversation Dept Officer, said tribal chiefs able force Egyptians withdrawal and took oath at Khamr they would do so if UAR did not act if and when requested by YARG.)

3. Faisal cooperation is key to settlement in Yemen. While Faisal's publicly stated plan for solution does not appear practical, YARG ready sit down to discussions with "Saudi brothers" at any time. Realize Faisal may have personal negative feelings toward Sallal; however, he

---

[1] Source: National Archives and Records Administration, RG 59, Central Files 1964–66, POL 27 YEMEN. Secret. Drafted by Moore, cleared by Davies and Director of the AID Office of Near Eastern Affairs James C. Flint, and approved by Talbot. Repeated to Taiz, Cairo, and London, and Aden.

should realize Sallal no longer chief spokesman for YARG but has "stepped down" to present position as head Republican Council.

4. Yemenis do not desire involvement in SAG–UAR problems but wish only seek improvement SAG–UAR relations.

5. YARG particularly grateful for US PL 480 wheat shipments. Food will continue be item critically important for stability in country for next six months; YARG hopes US will be able supply further shipments. (Talbot said would investigate.)

In response Talbot indicated our support for peaceful solution and government of Yemen by Yemenis. Said from our experience he doubted whether non-Arab power able appreciably help solve this Arab problem. Hoped various Arab leaders would have opportunity discuss matter in Algiers.

Geghman gave no specific reply when Talbot asked if YARG wished us transmit above points to SAG as direct message from Yemenis. (Assume his instructions not this precise.) However, suggest Jidda pass gist points 1–4 above to Saqqaf.[2]

Rusk

---

[2] The Numan cabinet resigned on July 1. On July 18 President Sallal asked former Prime Minister Hassan al-Amri to form a new government.

---

371.   Memorandum of Conversation[1]

Washington, August 2, 1965.

SUBJECT

UAR Sensitivities over Yemen

PARTICIPANTS

H.E. Mostafa Kamel, Ambassador of the U.A.R.
NE—H. Earle Russell, Jr.

Mr. Russell expressed our concern about provocative U.A.R. overflights over Jizan and the opinion expressed by the U.A.R. Consul in

---

[1] Source: National Archives and Records Administration, RG 59, Central Files 1964–66, POL 27 YEMEN. Secret. Drafted by Russell.

Taiz that the U.A.R. might broaden the Yemen war if the mission of Hassan Sabri al Kholi were unsuccessful or no progress toward a Faisal–Nasser meeting were made at the September Summit Conference at Rabat. We had the impression that al Kholi might have been disappointed with Faisal's reaction to his proposal for a Nasser–Faisal meeting. We thought, however, that Faisal did not wish to close the door to such a meeting but might find it difficult to comply with U.A.R. desires for fear of appearing to capitulate publicly to Nasser's threat of a confrontation. There might be some advantage to re-instituting the U.A.R.–S.A.G. border observation teams disbanded some months ago.

Speaking informally and personally, Ambassador Kamel said that Faisal's present policy in Yemen was an invitation to trouble in Saudi Arabia that inevitably would affect American oil companies and the U.S. Government. It would be unfortunate if by pulling down Faisal's house the U.A.R. caused the collapse of its own, but this was a necessary risk. There was hope and speculation in Egypt that the U.S. would use its good offices to convince Faisal of the desirability of working with the U.A.R. for a peaceful settlement in Yemen. A Nasser–Faisal meeting after such U.S. action would be useful. Kamel envisaged a U.S. effort similar to the one mounted in 1963. He stressed the desirability of a U.S. initiative to allay widespread suspicions among the U.A.R. military that the U.S. is seeking to undermine the regime in Egypt. Both the Odell case and the U.S. sales of arms to Saudi Arabia contributed to the conviction that the U.S. was backing Saudi Arabia against the U.A.R. in Yemen.

Ambassador Kamel suggested the desirability of a Battle–Nasser talk to 1) dispel suspicions arising from the Odell case and the Yemen situation; 2) convey to President Nasser the Secretary's hopes for a PL–480 agreement. A high level approach on these subjects both in Cairo and in Washington about a week before Nasser's visit to Moscow could have a restraining effect. A similar approach to Nasser through Tito might provide a useful means to reassure high level U.A.R. officials. In this connection, the Ambassador suggested the U.S. make a gesture by granting export licenses for hydraulic pumps ordered by the U.A.R. for use in the construction of the HA–300 fighter. This might provide Ambassador Battle with a useful pretext to call on Marshal Amer and explain the U.S. position in Yemen. While Ambassador Kamel appreciated the delicacy with which we had handled the deferral of a response to the U.A.R. request for these pumps, he felt that, while preferable to outright disapproval, even this might cause an adverse reaction given the sensitivity of the Egyptian army.

372. Information Memorandum From the Deputy Assistant Secretary of State for Near Eastern and South Asian Affairs (Handley) to Secretary of State Rusk[1]

Washington, August 6, 1965.

SUBJECT

Rising Tensions Between U.A.R. and Saudi Arabia over Yemen

Since Nasser's July 22 public offer of peace and threat of war with Saudi Arabia over Yemen,[2] *there have been a series of U.A.R. overflights of Saudi territory* in the Yemen border region, including bombing of a Saudi tent encampment near the latter town. *The Saudis have played down these occurrences both publicly and privately.* Faisal has given a temporizing response to Nasser's request for any early meeting but is expected momentarily to reply definitively.

We have informed both the U.A.R. and the Saudis of our hopes for an early solution to the problem and at the same time reiterated our continuing commitment to Saudi integrity. The Department's press spokesman, on August 4, gave a statement in similar vein in response to a question about the imminence of hostilities.[3] We have counseled the Saudis to cease their aid to the royalists in order to unencumber our commitment and have advised them to take the matter to the United Nations. *We have kept the U.N. Secretary General informed of the rising tensions.* We doubt that he will make any statement or otherwise take action, at least until he receives some word directly from the Saudis about the problem.

We judge Nasser does not want a confrontation with the Saudis but is seeking desperately for a way out of the Yemen impasse. A major problem is Faisal's conviction Nasser is bogged down to the extent he cannot do much against Saudi Arabia and his refusal to consider halting aid to the royalists. *Our efforts are concentrated on furthering a Nasser–Faisal rapprochement and avoiding a confrontation.* We have done some contingency planning, emphasizing diplomatic activities but also including the possibility of deployment of limited United States mili-

---

[1] Source: Department of State, NEA/ARP Files: Lot 69 D 547, Political Affairs & Rel., 1965, Saudi Arabia–UAR. Secret. Drafted by Moore and cleared by Davies, Russell, and Sisco.

[2] On July 22 Nasser made a bitterly anti-American speech that also offered renewed negotiations with Saudi Arabia over Yemen but warned of the danger of war if the negotiations failed. Extracts from Nasser's speech are printed in *American Foreign Policy: Current Documents, 1965*, pp. 619–620.

[3] On August 4 the Department of State spokesman reiterated U.S. support for the maintenance of Saudi Arabia's integrity. (Telegram 22 to Taiz, August 4; National Archives and Records Administration, RG 59, Central Files 1964–66, POL 27 YEMEN)

tary forces if necessary. If such deployment is required, it should be carefully considered to avoid the appearance of any provocation on our part.

373. Telegram From the Embassy in Yemen to the Department of State[1]

Taiz, August 10, 1965.

34. Ref: Embtel 31.[2] My two-hour interview with PriMin Hassan al Amri on August 9 was as trying as I had expected and doubtless was embarrassing to the half dozen educated aides who listened to him ranting and me rejecting his distorted statements. He has limited intelligence and is clearly incapable of balanced judgements. He indulged in such extremes as vilifying the United States one minute and shortly thereafter exclaiming "we Yemenis love the U.S. far more than the Saudis do". After repeating charges such as were included in the Beichman *Herald Tribune* article (Deptel 28),[3] he ended by quoting an Arab proverb that to complain to a friend is to show his love for him, and requesting a U.S. loan for development purposes. He urged me appeal to President Johnson to put a stop to Saudi machinations in Yemen.

The details are best left to a memcon, but I feel I succeeded in setting the record straight and injecting a much needed note of caution into current Y.A.R. and at least local U.A.R. deliberations. (The press and radio characterized our talk as a review of existing "friendly" YAR–US relations.) I was told that the captured American arms are being flown to Cairo as fast as they come in and that a plan is afoot

---

[1] Source: National Archives and Records Administration, RG 59, Central Files 1964–66, POL 15–1 YEMEN. Secret; Priority. Repeated to Cairo, Jidda, Aden, London, Amman, Baghdad, Beirut, Damascus, Kuwait, Tehran, USUN, and CINCSTRIKE/CINCMEAFSA for POLAD. No time of transmission appears on the telegram; it was received at 4:13 p.m.

[2] In telegram 31 from Taiz, August 8, Chargé d'Affaires Harlan B. Clark reported that Yemeni Foreign Minister Yaqub had told him on August 7 that after nearly 3 years of futile attempts to persuade the Saudi dynasty to stop committing aggression against the Yemen Arab Republic from bases in Najran and Jizan, Yemeni patience was now exhausted and that it appeared that the only way for Yemen to stop the aggression was to attack those bases. (Ibid.)

[3] Telegram 28 to Taiz, August 6, instructed the Embassy to make clear to Yemeni Prime Minister Hassan al-Amri U.S. displeasure with the attitude reflected in an August 6 *Herald Tribune* article quoting his statement that the "US encourages Saudi Arabia to war against us." (Ibid., POL 27 YEMEN)

to display them at the UN in connection with a YAR attempt to have Saudi Arabia condemned as an aggressor. I pointed out the damage such a move might do to the Republican cause, and urged peace talks as the only realistic course to pursue.

My talks with a number of other key persons including UAR Amb. Shukri and the top UAR military command showed that they were thinking in similar terms, but have not yet made up their minds as to what they should do next; Shukri said he would have some freshly captured arms for us to inspect in a day or two but acting UAR Commander General Kabir said the details would be given to Embassy Cairo. I urged them to let an Embassy officer here inspect some.

Shukri assured me that no military action would be taken against Saudi Arabia until all possibilities for peace had been exhausted in talks now proceeding. All UAR officials were calm, frank and cordial but made clear they would not indefinitely let Saudi Arabia keep on training and supplying the Royalists with a steadily rising number of US arms without taking action to protect their forces. Kabir asserted there are hundreds of thousands of Yemenis living in Saudi Arabia from which a steady flow of fresh recruits is being sent to fight the republic, with their wives and children being held hostage for their good behavior. (Emb Jidda please comment.) This, he asserted, was clearly aggression, and it was mainly US arms that were being employed. They seemed eager to have our help in stopping the war and reproachful we had not done more. Kabir said Royalists and Saudi spokesmen are broadcasting that the USG is fully behind them and this is having its effect on ignorant tribesmen. All Egyptians asserted their aim was to withdraw as soon as peace was achieved, leaving only a troop training contingent.

If al Amri were the only YAR critic of US policy re Saudi Arabia I would not be so concerned and would be tempted to blame the two suspected Communists (Shahari and Yahya Bahran) in the presidency for most of this anti-US campaign. From my talks in Sanaa over past three days with a variety of people including Arab diplomats, pro-Western Yemenis, UNTAB Amb Tinay and Yugoslav Chargé Grebovic, I gather that feeling is widespread in YAR circles that we are closing an eye to Saudi actions if not actually encouraging them. Unfortunately the press statement contained in Deptel 22[4] has strengthened this belief, since it does not single out Saudi Arabia as being involved in supplying

---

[4] Telegram 22 to Taiz, August 4, quoted the Department's press statement that the United States hoped that UAR–Saudi talks would lead to a situation where the Yemenis themselves would be able to decide their own national destiny free from any outside interference. The Department spokesman also reiterated U.S. support for Saudi Arabia's integrity and said that the United States would deplore any extension of hostilities in the area. (Ibid.)

Royalists and in YAR eyes seems to imply we will "protect" Saudi Arabia come what may. Much of my time was taken up setting statement in perspective, and Shukri told me YAR has seized upon the reference to Yemenis being left free to determine their own destiny as implying we think that republic should give way to something else since Saudi position is also that Yemenis should have right to "self-determination", meaning return of Imamate. This was a helpful tip and I made good use of it. I made a bold point of inviting Shukri, UAR Generals and all others to help me set record straight and in almost every case they gave lip service to idea. Grebovic said he would try but it would help him do so if USG made clear it would only protect Saudi Arabia so long as it did not permit its territory to be used to attack a friendly govt which nearly all countries of world recognize.

Grebovic contrasted Soviet and ChiCom policy in Yemen in a manner which is disturbing but should probably be treated with reserve. He said the Soviets were pledged to help republic and would continue to supply needed arms, but only wanted a peaceful, united Yemen which would cooperate in "co-existence". The ChiComs wanted to escalate the war as much as possible, on the other hand, and he had heard from Yemeni officials that ChiComs had offered as many well armed troops as needed, and would have 10,000 here in a month if requested. YAR had not requested them but its young military men were bitter, ill-informed and desperate, and anything could happen if the US "permitted" SA to continue its present policy. He urged us to pursue our "historic destiny" of ensuring a peaceful, progressive local order.

Comment follows.

Clark

374. Telegram From the Embassy in Saudi Arabia to the Department of State[1]

Jidda, August 11, 1965, 1531Z.

102. Acting Deputy Foreign Minister Mas'ud summoned me on one and one half hours' notice to meet with him and Minister of Defense Prince Sultan at Foreign Ministry August 11. After exchange courtesies, Sultan informed me of SAG decision purchase F–104G and associated package (subject separate telegram).[2] He reviewed close USG–SAG relationship and expressed desire it should continue. He pulled from his pocket sheaf of telegrams he had just received from Saudi border posts. Reading from telegrams he listed following aggressive UAR actions:

1. August 9, UAR tanks crossed Saudi border vicinity Jizan penetrating Saudi territory one-half kilometer vicinity villages Jalban, Twal, and Malwan. After reconnoitering, tanks withdrew behind border. (Unable locate on our maps villages named but presumed somewhere southeast Samitah.)

2. August 10, UAR observers suddenly pulled out of last remaining joint UAR–SAG observation post at Abs. (Department will recall Saqqaf stated to me August 1 (Embtel 64)[3] that Egyptians had withdrawn from all five observation posts.) According Sultan, Egyptians had earlier withdrawn from four posts and method of withdrawal throughout peremptory and "savage." Saudis had allegedly been forcibly escorted from posts to border and deprived of food and water.

3. UAR had bombed Saudi territory twice in vicinity Jizan some ten days ago, accounting for minimum damage (presume same bombings referred to in Embtels 66 and 72).[4]

4. UAR overflights of Jizan, Najran and, to some extent, Abha occurring almost daily. (SDI has received no reports overflights last few days.)

5. UAR "massing" troops in Yemen, including in such border towns as Harad, for purpose aggressive action against Saudi Arabia.

6. SAG has knowledge secret UAR plan bomb Taif and Al-Kharj, as well as Jizan, Najran and Abha. He claimed Al-Kharj listed as target

---

[1] Source: National Archives and Records Administration, RG 59, Central Files 1964–66, POL SAUD–UAR. Secret; Priority. Repeated to Aden, Cairo, Dhahran, London, Taiz, CHUSMTM, CINCSTRIKE/CINCMEAFSA, COMIDEASTFOR, and USUN.

[2] Not further identified.

[3] Telegram 64 from Jidda, August 1. (National Archives and Records Administration, RG 59, Central Files 1964–66, POL SAUD–UAR)

[4] Telegrams 66 and 72 from Jidda, August 2. (Ibid., POL 27 YEMEN and POL SAUD–UAR)

because of important military depot. (When I asked for sources this information, Sultan was evasive.)

Sultan said whereas Saudi military units along Yemeni border had earlier been instructed secretly not open fire on Egyptian ground forces (in order, he said, to avoid escalation), he had now instructed these border posts to fire immediately on any UAR–YAR units crossing border. In response my query, he said that previous Saudi instructions withhold fire had not applied to anti-aircraft units.

Sultan said he had asked to see me on King's instructions. View foregoing indicators re UAR intention attack Saudi Arabia, King had three requests to make of President Johnson and Secretary Rusk:

1. USG should be made aware of foregoing indicators.

2. SAG desires that USG dispatch destroyers to Saudi Arabia soonest to Jizan area for purpose deterring UAR.

3. SAG requests USG dispatch "unit" of fighter aircraft to Saudi Arabia as further deterrent to UAR attack.

My first response to Sultan was to indicate my personal impression that buildup of tensions over Yemen appeared to have subsided somewhat. I cited conciliatory nature recent UAR press commentary re Yemen developments (Cairo's tel 34 to Jidda)[5] and evidently beneficial effect USG public statement August 4. I then suggested that SAG immediately submit its bill of particulars to President Security Council. Sultan replied that while this move "under consideration" by King, SAG's experience with UN in connection with Yemen question indicated "Mafish Fa'edi" (it is of no benefit). He said Saudi Arabia relied on itself and on its friends. I reiterated advantages to Saudi Arabia of registering complaint with UN in order balance current YAR complaint before Secretary General and also as useful parallel action to relying on itself and its friends.

With regard to King's three points, I replied as follows:

1. I would immediately communicate to Washington information he had provided me.

2. I noted that an American destroyer is scheduled to call at Jidda on August 25. Sultan said this was too far off and SAG wanted several visits. In that case, I said, I would undertake to request that the visit of destroyer USS *Fox* be advanced, and that I would endeavor to ascertain possibility of subsequent early visits by other destroyers. Sultan asked to be informed immediately upon receipt USG reply to this possibility.

---

[5] Telegram 401 from Cairo (34 to Jidda), August 5. (Ibid.)

3. Re squadron US aircraft, I reminded Sultan of USG–SAG dialogue this subject over past two years and, in particular, Ambassador Hart's conversation with King in March.[6] USG position remains as before, i.e., difficult justify any USG military action to assist SAG in face UAR attacks against purely military targets in Saudi territory near Yemen border. While we have repeatedly informed SAG that we will come to its assistance against unprovoked attack, I said dispatch of USG military units to Saudi Arabia while latter allows its territory be used as base for Yemeni Royalists was, insofar as I aware, precluded. Possible exception this policy is if UAR attacks should spread elsewhere in Saudi Arabia (i.e., beyond purely military targets near Yemen border), at which time USG would review its position. I asked Sultan whether SAG had given serious thought to stopping its aid to Yemen Royalists. This triggered long lecture on how SAG had in fact stopped its aid for period of time only to find UAR had no intention fulfill its part of agreement, i.e., withdrawal UAR troops from Yemen. He claimed he could not understand, in view SAG's demonstrated cooperation with US re Bunker agreement, why Saudi Arabia should now be penalized for what he characterized as legitimate Saudi effort get UAR troops out of Yemen and return Yemen to Yemenis. Sultan said that if condition for dispatch air unit is cessation Saudi aid to Royalists, then Saudi Arabia did not wish air unit. He asked my forebearance if he were so bold as to criticize USG policy which forced staunch friends of US at times like this to seek military help wherever they could find it. I told Sultan that in any case I would forward King's request to Washington.

Comment: I regret Saqqaf's absence at this time since believe he might have talked Sultan and King out of requesting air unit—at least under circumstances in which Saudi Arabia continues actively support Yemen Royalists. Sultan obviously excitable and appears be exaggerating seriousness current threat. However, view his statement he speaking for King, am obliged convey as King's request plea that (1) destroyer visits Jidda and vicinity be stepped up and (2) air unit be dispatched immediately Saudi Arabia. I would be hesitant recommend dispatch air unit under any but most dire circumstances view problems we experienced in deployment Hard Surface 1963–64. Seems to me we should rather continue explore all possible alternative means for deterring possible UAR attack. Fact that up to now we have attached conditions to dispatch of air unit and fact Saudis now unprepared accept these conditions may be blessing in disguise. I do not take seriously Sultan's subtle threat re turning elsewhere for military support. Recommend we make effort cooperate re accelerating destroyer visits— including advancing visit USS *Fox* while politely demurring on air

---

[6] See footnote 5, Document 363.

unit, citing not only Saudi involvement Yemen but perhaps heavy USG military commitments elsewhere. This connection we might consider implementing current proposed plan deploy in training exercise reinforced rifle company supported by aircraft (tentatively scheduled for October 1). However, any decision proceed this exercise should be made soon in order permit advance planning.

Seelye

375. Telegram From the Department of State to the Embassy in Saudi Arabia[1]

Washington, August 12, 1965, 8:02 p.m.

68. Jidda tel 102.[2] Agree with Jidda's analysis that our efforts must be concentrated on means deterring UAR attack and bringing Faisal and Nasser to bargaining table. We are not considering dispatch air unit unless serious threat to Saudi Arabia's integrity develops. Believe there are strong parallels between situation now and that prevailing one year ago when UAR and Saudis were jockeying for military advantage prior to September meeting Alexandria.

For Jidda: In view known unreliability Sultan as channel for information and his past propensity for exaggerating dangers, it important you hear directly from King his analysis situation. In discussion with King you should take following line:

1. You have been given preliminary report by Sultan expressing King's concern. In view of situation you wished have benefit first-hand discussions with King on what occurring on border.

2. UAR tells us it desires talks with Faisal to reach peaceful solution Yemen problem. We encouraged by Cairo press report that SAG Ambassador Alireza met with Faisal August 11. We continue believe Faisal–Nasser meeting most desirous. What are King's views on prospects?

3. In response Sultan's request we can arrange early visit US destroyer to Jidda and speed up future proposed visits. (FYI: Navy has

---

[1] Source: National Archives and Records Administration, RG 59, Central Files 1964–66, POL 27 YEMEN. Secret; Immediate. Drafted by Moore; cleared by Davies, Bunte, General Sibley (J–5), Stoddart (DOD/ISA), Hart, Komer, and Warren; and approved by Handley. Also sent to Cairo and repeated to London, Taiz, Aden, CINCSTRIKE/CINCMEAFSA for POLAD, Dhahran, CHUSMTM, COMIDEASTFOR, CINCUSNAVEUR, and USUN.

[2] Document 374.

sent separate message to COMIDEASTFOR requesting program for stepped-up schedule visits, with Embassy to be consulted on suitability this schedule. You may inform King of exact date of visit if firm by time your conversation. Navy here estimates a destroyer, not the *Fox*, could be in Jidda in 55 hours. Destroyer cannot approach closer than two miles to Jizan because of the reefs and shoals. In any event call at Jizan probably unsuitable so long as Saudi aid to royalists continues. End FYI.)

4. FYI only: We seeking high level authorization proceed with planned visit early October reinforced rifle company involving 500 men with own air transport. You should not apprise Faisal of this possibility until instructed. End FYI.

5. Urge King make subject UAR overflights and penetration matter of record with UN. Should again be noted that Saudi case in UN as well as US ability aid Saudis seriously complicated by continued SAG assistance to royalists.

For Cairo: You should seek immediate appointment with appropriate UAR officials (perhaps Al-Khouli and/or FonMin Riad) for discussion on following lines:

1. Pass on Saudi report on occurrences Yemen border (points 1 through 5 of reftel).

2. Emphasize we doing utmost get Faisal agree to meet with Nasser but above forms UAR military pressure make this task virtually impossible.

3. As stated to Nasser by Assistant Secretary Talbot in April, UAR attack on Saudi Arabia could cause very great trouble in US–UAR relations. We strongly urge UAR halt any infringements Saudi territory or air space in order pave way for Nasser–Faisal meeting.[3]

Rusk

---

[3] Telegram 1001 to Cairo, August 13, informed the Embassy that the points in the Department's telegram had been made to Ambassador Kamel on August 13. (National Archives and Records Administration, RG 59, Central Files 1964–66, POL 27 YEMEN) Telegram 499 from Cairo, August 16, reported that Embassy senior political officer Richard B. Parker met with UAR presidential adviser Hassan Sabri al-Khouli on August 14 and passed on the Saudi report of border incidents contained in telegram 102 from Jidda. Parker also gave al-Khouli a paper containing points 2 and 3 of the Cairo section of the Department's telegram. Al-Khouli contended that the whole business of a UAR military threat was a concoction being spread with the help of the Beirut press and that if the threat were real and Faisal were really interested in negotiating, he would agree to a meeting with Nasser. Al-Khouli noted that so far, he had not done so. (Ibid.)

376. **Memorandum From Robert W. Komer of the National
Security Council Staff to President Johnson**[1]

Washington, August 13, 1965.

Saudi/UAR tension over Yemen is heating up. The worried Saudis
have asked us to send a fighter squadron to scare off the Egyptians,
who have increased minor crossborder activities from Yemen into Saudi
territory. They've also asked us to speed up a destroyer visit already
scheduled for Jidda on 25 August and to schedule a few more closer to
the Saudi-Yemeni border. Faisal has asked through his Defense Minister
that we bring this to your attention.

We're prepared to authorize the destroyer visit, but not any more
jet fighters like we sent to Saudi Arabia in 1963. We only sent the unit
after the Saudis agreed to stop clandestine arms supply, etc. to the
Yemeni royalists. Now the story is repeating itself. Fortunately, we've
told the Saudis repeatedly we couldn't send another air unit to deter
Nasser, if it would only serve as an umbrella for renewed secret aid
to the Yemeni royalists. Should the Egyptians unexpectedly launch a
full-scale attack on Saudi Arabia, however, that would change the name
of the game (and we'd reconsider). Meanwhile, we want to keep the
pressure on both Saudis and Egyptians to talk out a Yemen settlement themselves.

To protect your freedom of action on the above, I've said no air
deployment without Presidential OK. I've taken the same precaution
with another step State and Defense are considering—a long planned
exercise to stage a 500 man rifle team into Dhahran for a two week
exercise demonstration—as a quiet reminder to the UAR to lay off.
This isn't as risky, or as expensive as an air squadron, but I think State
and DOD ought to get your express approval before starting down
this Yemen road again.[2]

R.W. Komer

---

[1] Source: Johnson Library, National Security File, Memos to the President, McGeorge
Bundy, Vol. 13. No classification marking.

[2] A notation in the President's handwriting reads: "See me. L." Below this McBundy
handwritten wrote: "RWK—for action as indicated. McGB."

377.   Telegram From the Embassy in Saudi Arabia to the Department of State[1]

Jidda, August 15, 1965, 1033Z.

109. I opened audience with King morning August 14 in Taif with statement I had been instructed see him as follow-up my meeting with Prince Sultan August 11. I referred to three requests which Prince Sultan had made of USG on King's behalf.

Re first request, said I had transmitted urgently to Washington info re UAR aggressions and threats described to me by Sultan. Indicated I had also expressed in my message what Sultan had characterized as King's deep concern with developing situation.

I then asked King whether he considered situation as serious as it had appeared three days before. I noted Cairo press reports re meeting of Saudi Ambassador Mohammad Ali Reza with Nasir August 11 and of Ali Reza's subsequent return from talks with King.

King said degree of seriousness of situation at any one time difficult to gauge. Certainly threat exists, has existed and will continue to exist as long as Nasir's troops remain in Yemen. He assumed we had independent reports of UAR build-up in Yemen and could judge for ourselves extent of current threat. He commented that even in course of Saudi–UAR negotiations UAR planes flew over Saudi Arabia, tanks crossed into Saudi territory, and UAR threatened along border. What he had asked Sultan do in seeing me was to "make clear" to US nature of recent developments. I told King that largely on basis information SAG had provided we were again making representations in Cairo.

I said I knew that President and Secretary were very anxious that he continue his negotiations with Nasir. As he knew, in Viet Nam though faced with a very difficult situation, President continued to make himself available for negotiations with adversary. I urged that "thread of dialogue" with UAR, no matter how narrow, be maintained.

King affirmed without hesitation "we will continue to talk despite everything." (Mas'ud told me August 15 that King and Nasir would definitely meet before Arab summit conference.)

Re Sultan's second request, I said my government was arranging to dispatch destroyer to Saudi Arabia as soon possible. When date of arrival known, I would inform King through Mas'ud (did so August 15). Subsequent destroyer visits would also be accelerated. King seemed

---

[1] Source: National Archives and Records Administration, RG 59, Central Files 1964–66, POL SAUD–US. Secret. Repeated to Cairo, Taiz, CINCSTRIKE/CINCMEAFSA, USUN, Dhahran, London, CHUSMTM Dhahran, COMIDEASTFOR, and Aden.

pleased and implied he had proposed destroyer visits to Sultan "to deter the Egyptians." (No mention was made re visit to Jizan.)

Re third request—dispatch of air unit—I said unfortunately this was not possible at moment. Nevertheless, matter was under study and my government was following developments with care. As King knew, it was difficult for US justify US military measures in Saudi Arabia as long as SAG involved in Yemen imbroglio. On other hand, we had indicated several times our support for maintenance of Saudi Arabia's integrity. Important thing was to prevent escalation.

King said he assumed US would protect Saudi Arabia's integrity and fulfill spirit of friendship prevailing between our two countries. He said matter of dispatch of air unit decision for US to make in context foregoing. He did not desire place "unnecessary burdens" upon US. Re linkage our support to so-called Saudi involvement in Yemen, he wished state categorically that, unlike UAR, not single Saudi soldier fighting in Yemen.

Said I had one more matter to raise. My government held strongly to view that SAG should register formal complaint before UN re series of UAR aggressions. Absence of such complaint complicated Saudi case at UN and weakened USG ability support Saudis in possible UN debate. King replied that SAG had communicated much of this information privately to UNSYG in response latter's referral of Yemen complaint. However, he said SAG did not wish make public protests and noted fact SAG concealed from its own public information re UAR aggressions. (Latter is true: info re UAR aggressions kept out of local press and Prince Sultan has reprimanded officials in Jizan and Najran for relaying reports of UAR overflights, etc. to SDI pilots and others.) I said that, nevertheless, SAG should seriously consider registering formal complaint at least for procedural reasons, especially in UN debate in progress. King asked who SAG opponent in possible UN debate might be. I said I assumed UAR. He smiled, noting that current complaint before UN is YAR complaint (and no doubt was wishfully thinking that by then YAR delegate to UN would in effect be Saudi camp view current Taif reconciliation between Yemeni factions).

Comment: While it is clear Sultan acted on King's instructions when he summoned me August 11, also true King predictably showed himself less flappable than Sultan. However, relaxed way in which King received turn-down re dispatch air unit may be deceptive since Mas'ud told me August 15 that King disappointed with response. (I, therefore, agreed with Mas'ud's proposal that in his talk with King today Mas'ud emphasize "under study" aspect of my response. Mas'ud claimed UK had offered send unit. I made no comment. He said further that SAG prepared defray all costs of dispatch USG air unit.) King does not seem to question ultimate USG determination carry out its stated commitment re protecting Saudi integrity but does want US take every possible military measure nip UAR attack in bud. Sooner we can notify King of reinforced company exercise—assuming decision affirmative—the better. Also occurs to us that prompt dispatch US military mapping mission to undertake Persian Gulf median line survey would at this important juncture demonstrate helpful USG response to standing SAG request. Same time would add to over-all USG military presence in country.

King seemed sincere in his intention to keep negotiating door open with UAR, even though there was no suggestion he optimistic talks would lead to settlement Yemen question.

View similar request made of HMG by Sultan, have conveyed gist of foregoing to British Chargé Brown.

Seelye

---

378.   Memorandum From the Department of Defense Regional Director for Near East and South Asia (Strickland) to the Deputy Assistant Secretary of Defense for International Security Affairs (Solbert)[1]

I–36093/65   Washington, August 25, 1965.

SUBJECT

> Military Alternatives Available to US from Possible Saudi–UAR Confrontation over the Yemen

At Tab A[2] we have set out the military alternatives available to the US in the event of a Saudi-UAR confrontation over the Yemen. The alternatives set forth in Attachment A have been submitted by the JCS (Tab B).[3] These are not recommended military actions and have been labeled as possible military alternatives.

---

[1] Source: Washington National Records Center, RG 330, OASD/ISA Files: FRC 70 A 5127, 092. Yemen, 25 Aug. 65. Top Secret.

[2] Not printed.

[3] Document 366.

JCSM–295–65 (Tab B) notes that in the event the situation in the Arabian Peninsula deteriorates and any use of US military forces is contemplated, the JCS will provide further comments in the light of the situation existing at the time. In this connection, STRIKE's 788/65 (Tab C)[4] proposes under the guise of a combined training exercise with Saudi Arabia a show of force designed to initially position forces and initiate useful measures that would facilitate active operations if required.

In addition, there are STRIKE's contingency plans that can be considered in the event it is decided to come to a full-fledged exercise in shoring up Saudi integrity.

At the present time we are hopeful that the Nasser–Faisal dialogue goes well and some improvement in the situation is evident. We still have in the planning stage the idea of introducing an airborne rifle company into Saudi Arabia. This force (approximately 200 with 10–12 transport aircraft) would assist the Saudis in (a) tactical principles of employment of small units, (b) use of supporting weapons, (c) operation and care of vehicles and communications equipment, and (d) basic field military sanitation.

It is to be noted that the introduction of the airborne company may or may not be utilized. Our Embassies in Cairo and Taiz do not favor it at all (see Tab D).[5]

Other means of assisting the Saudis in the event the outcome of the Nasser–Faisal dialogue is good, and assuming the Saudis accept, are (a) in the buildup of Saudi air defense capability and (b) sales of US type equipment to the Saudi White Army.

The political courses of action available are set forth in Tab E.[4]

It is somewhat difficult to pin down the type of force required to enhance an effective military course of action without knowing what is required or the mission to be accomplished. If a high-level decision is made to undertake a US military course of action in Saudi Arabia, the JCS should be given specific guidance in order that the composition of the force can be determined to meet the stated mission.

Eugene L. Strickland
Brigadier General, USAF

---

[4] Not printed.
[5] Telegram 48 from Taiz, August 22.

379. Telegram From the Embassy in the United Arab Republic to the Department of State[1]

Cairo, August 25, 1965, 1112Z.

567. Believe Yemen agreement signed yesterday by Feisal and Nasser and reported to Dept in Embtel 562[2] is very promising development. While we do not yet know details of any secret side agreements, such as what if anything is to be done about Badr and Sallal, and 15 months' period required for implementation may give too much time for participants to come to blows over details, agreement clearly much more concrete than most expected. Elements which strike us as being particularly good about agreement are: (1) It is public and therefore harder for parties to back away from than was case with Alexandria agreement. (2) Egyptians have agreed to what we have understood was Saudi condition that determination future form of govt be left to Yemenis. (3) Definite time set for evacuation Egyptian troops, but evacuation spread out over period which will permit some efforts at ensuring stable transition period.

Egyptian willingness give on points which previously obstacles to settlement reflects what we believe is genuine determination get out of Yemen at almost all costs. We hope that Dept will be able inject note of optimism into any comments USG may make on settlement and that someone will be able to echo admirable remarks Senator Fulbright re Nasser's (and Feisal's) statesmanlike efforts settle problem.[3]

Battle

---

[1] Source: National Archives and Records Administration, RG 59, Central Files 1964–66, POL 27 YEMEN. Confidential; Priority. Repeated to Jidda, London, Taiz, and CINCSTRIKE.

[2] Telegram 562 from Cairo, August 24, transmitted the text of the agreement on Yemen reached by President Nasser and King Faisal that day in Jidda. (Ibid.) The Jidda Agreement called for: (1) a cease-fire; (2) a popular plebiscite to be held in Yemen no later than November 23, 1966; (3) UAR–Saudi cooperation in setting up an interim conference of Yemeni republicans and royalists to convene in Haradh (in Yemen) on November 23, 1965, to negotiate arrangements for a transitional government and the plebiscite; (4) withdrawal of UAR military forces within 10 months from November 23, 1965; and (5) Saudi agreement to stop immediately military assistance in any form to the royalists or use of Saudi territory for action against Yemen.

[3] On August 31 President Johnson sent King Faisal a letter expressing his pleasure upon learning of the agreement. (Johnson Library, National Security File, Special Head of State Correspondence File, Saudi Arabia, Presidential Correspondence)

380. Telegram From the Department of State to the Embassy in Yemen[1]

Washington, September 14, 1965, 8:39 p.m.

47. In call September 14 on Talbot and in subsequent conversation Department officer, YARG Ambassador al-Aini expressed considerable pessimism concerning motives Faisal and Nasser in Jidda agreement on Yemen. Al-Aini, who just returned from Cairo to resume duties in US and UN, said that before traveling Jidda Nasser in fact did not consult with YARG leaders on nature solution he contemplating. Similarly on his return, Yemenis forced rely on radio and press for information concerning agreement reached with Faisal.

Al-Aini greatly worried that some secret agreement reached whereby UAR and SAG would maintain their mutual influence in Yemen following withdrawal Egyptian forces.

Said that selection 50 participants for November Haradh Conference will be proof of Faisal and Nasser intent reach real solution. Truly Yemeni representatives will be able do so. He worried that participants will be only spokesmen for UAR or SAG, leading to deadlock. If latter develops, al-Aini speculates nationalists from both republican and royalist camps would make common cause.

Rusk

---

[1] Source: National Archives and Records Administration, RG 59, Central Files 1964–66, POL 27 YEMEN. Confidential. Drafted by Moore, cleared by Davies, and approved by Talbot. Repeated to Cairo, Jidda, and London.

381. Telegram From the Department of State to the Embassy in Jordan[1]

Washington, October 6, 1965, 6:06 p.m.

149. Re Taiz tels 97[2] and 98[3] to Dept. (Being repeated addressees.) Concur your response to Numan, pointing out continued US support for YARG, US policy non-interference, our support of Jidda agreement, and our serious concern if any country should take action to prejudice agreement or success of Haradh conference. While we intend continue our currently planned AID/Y activities in Republic,[4] believe decision any further US economic and technical assistance programs should be held in abeyance, pending formation transitional government which expected to evolve from Haradh conference. (US military assistance clearly out of question at this time.) In addition other considerations, we judge that starting new program, other than further deliveries under Title II aid, would open us to accusation taking sides prior to Yemeni Haradh conclave.

Realize, however, that whatever government develops after November 23 will be in immediate serious need of assistance, probably straight budgetary aid in addition to food and material help to rebuild country. As Taiz aware, expanded PL 480 program in north Yemen dependent on success present program. We believe for number reasons, however, that at same time area states should also be urged consider early, direct financial and material assistance to Yemen in order help

---

[1] Source: National Archives and Records Administration, RG 59, Central Files 1964–66, POL 27 YEMEN. Secret. Drafted by Moore on October 5; cleared by Israel, Lebanon, Yemen Desk Officer Harry F. Hemmerich (AID/NESA/NE), Robert W. Kent (EUR/GER), Symmes, and in substance by Grant V. McClanahan (A/FN); and approved by Davies. Also sent to Bonn, Beirut, Jidda, Kuwait, and Tripoli and repeated to Cairo, London, Taiz, Aden, and CINCSTRIKE/CINCMEAFSA for POLAD.

[2] In telegram 97 from Taiz, October 3, Clark reported that he had met with former Yemeni Prime Minister Numan, who delivered a strong appeal for U.S. military and financial aid to Yemen. Although he was suspicious of UAR motives, Numan also feared that if the Jidda agreement were implemented, the cards were stacked against the republic. The United Arab Republic had prevented Yemen from developing an independent, effective government and the country would be left without an army or treasury. Clark responded that the United States had recognized and supported Yemen by all appropriate means and that a cornerstone of U.S. policy was the principle of non-interference in internal Yemeni affairs. He noted that the U.S. Government welcomed the Jidda Agreement, and would be seriously concerned if any action were taken to prejudice the agreement or the success of the Haradh conference. (Ibid.)

[3] Telegram 98 from Taiz, October 3, transmitted Clark's comments on his conversation with Numan, including his advice that if the United States was to have any leverage with the current or future leaders of Yemen, further U.S. aid would be an important factor. (Ibid.)

[4] U.S. aid to Yemen in FY 1965 amounted to $4,520,000. (Airgram A–40 to Kuwait, June 23; ibid., AID (US) YEMEN)

new all-Yemen government attain stability. Moderate Arab states have obvious interest in success Jidda agreement and should be prepared support financially development moderate regime in Yemen. Additionally, public statements at present of interest and concern for Yemen and willingness deal with post-Haradh government would be encouraging gestures.

Unless reasons to contrary perceived, addressee posts are requested to discuss at appropriate level with host governments importance of above for future stability and development Yemen, and encourage them give urgent consideration to what assistance possible for them give Yemen.

On current situation you may say while that there is evidence of some behind scenes maneuvering, both Saudis and UAR appear to be moving forward with implementation of Jidda agreement. Joint Saudi–UAR ceasefire supervision teams reportedly now in operation, exchange of prisoners is being affected, and UAR forces reportedly beginning evacuation to Hodeida. We are optimistic re agreement's chances of success and hope all parties will cooperate in avoiding potentially disruptive actions. Where appropriate you may wish point out threat of Communist countries further solidifying their positions if Yemenis forced rely heavily on them for underpinning for new government. You should offer share with them on continuing basis our assessment of situation in Yemen as it develops.[5]

Ball

---

[5] In telegram 292 from Jidda, October 13, Seelye reported that he had discussed the contents of the Department's telegram with Mas'ud on October 12 and had emphasized that the U.S. Government hoped that the Saudi Arabian Government was planning to provide economic assistance to the new Yemeni Government, Mas'ud replied that the King had indicated that he was prepared to "do everything possible" in the area of economic and financial assistance to Yemen once an appropriate government was formed and stability returned. (Ibid.)

382.   Memorandum of Conversation[1]

Washington, October 19, 1965, 4:30 p.m.

SUBJECT

Yemen; US–UAR Relations

PARTICIPANTS

H.E. Omar Saqqaf, Deputy Foreign Minister of Saudi Arabia
H.E. Ibrahim al Sowayel, Ambassador of Saudi Arabia
The Secretary
NE—Harrison M. Symmes
NE—David Korn

1. Yemen

After an exchange of greetings, the Secretary said he would be interested in learning from Mr. Saqqaf how the Saudi–UAR agreement on Yemen is working out.

Mr. Saqqaf said the Saudis are fully behind the Jidda agreement and to date had encountered no difficulty in its implementation. Nasser was equally determined to make the agreement work, for he was anxious to be rid of the Yemen problem. This problem could be considered two-thirds solved. The Secretary said he had the impression that the Yemenis themselves might be causing some trouble. Mr. Saqqaf replied that the Yemenis were indeed "difficult" and, if left to themselves, would wreck everything. However, now that the Saudis and the UAR had reached agreement, he could assure that there would be no mix-up and that the Yemenis would take the right direction. Mr. Saqqaf indicated that the Saudis would be prepared to give assistance to a Yemeni coalition government following the Haradh conference.

The Secretary expressed pleasure over Saudi–UAR determination to make the Jidda agreement work and said the US would also be interested in helping the Yemenis if they get on the right path.

The Secretary asked whether the Jidda agreement had been reinforced by a private understanding between Faisal and Nasser. Mr. Saqqaf said that most of what was agreed on at Jidda was made public, although there had been a private understanding regarding the choosing of the royalist and republican delegations to the Haradh conference. Mr. Saqqaf said the Jidda agreement should not be looked upon as a

---

[1] Source: National Archives and Records Administration, RG 59, Central Files 1964–66, POL 27 YEMEN. Confidential. Drafted by David A. Korn (NEA) on October 21 and approved in S on November 12. The memorandum is part I of IV. Part III is Document 254. The time of the meeting is from Rusk's Daily Diary. (Johnson Library)

diplomatic victory for either side. However it did show that Nasser was a courageous man.

Mr. Saqqaf said the Jidda agreement had also been beneficial in shaking the socialist front in the Arab world. The Secretary said it was his impression that there was a mood of moderation in the Arab world now. Saqqaf agreed, stating that in Iraq there was no longer talk of socialism and the Syrians were fed up with socialist slogans. Iraq was now going the right way.

The Secretary asked how active the Chinese Communists were in Yemen. Mr. Saqqaf replied that they were not very active now and that in any case the Chinese were too poor to accomplish anything serious. They could do little more than spread propaganda. Mr. Saqqaf stated that Peiping is losing everywhere as the result of US policy. The world knows that the US is no longer a paper tiger. Mr. Saqqaf said that there is no profit in the US trying to "be nice".

Mr. Symmes remarked that he had noted considerable Chinese Communist activity in Yemen when visiting Yemen six weeks ago. Mr. Saqqaf acknowledged there are now 500 Chinese in Yemen and that a number of large projects are being considered for implementation by the Chinese. Mr. Symmes noted that the problem of Chinese Communist presence in Yemen could become critical.

2. US–UAR Relations

During discussion of the Saudi–UAR agreement on Yemen, the Secretary remarked that internal economic difficulties may have strengthened the UAR's desire to come to terms. The Secretary said the Yemen war had caused many strains in US–UAR relations.

Mr. Saqqaf asked if US–UAR relations had improved as a result of the Jidda agreement. The Secretary said we had hopes in this direction but time was required to repair our ties. The Secretary said there is no doubt that if the Jidda agreement is carried out it will make a significant impression on our relations with Cairo.

The Secretary asked if the return of the 50,000 Egyptian troops now in Yemen would cause Nasser trouble. Mr. Saqqaf said the soldiers would be brought back in small groups, discharged and put to work in light industry or handicrafts. Nasser had matters firmly in hand. Mr. Saqqaf said he had been pleased to learn of Mohieddine's appointment and anticipated that the UAR's economic situation would improve considerably as a result of this move. The Egyptian people had welcomed Mohieddine's appointment, he said.

383. Memorandum From the Assistant Secretary of State for Near Eastern and South Asian Affairs (Hare) to the Deputy Under Secretary of State for Political Affairs (Johnson)[1]

Washington, December 27, 1965.

SUBJECT

> Politico-Military Contingency Planning Pursuant to NSAM 277:[2] UAR–Saudi Arabian Hostilities over Yemen

1. Pursuant to Ambassador Thompson's memorandum of September 15,[3] there is enclosed a political-military contingency study on UAR–Saudi hostilities over Yemen. This study was prepared with the assistance of the Department of Defense (ISA, JCS, DIA and DOD Policy Planning) and CIA.

2. This study has been undertaken at a time when the situation in Yemen is in great flux. The Nasser–Faisal agreement of August 24 brought about a cease-fire in the three-year Yemeni civil war and led royalists and republicans to the conference table at Haradh beginning November 23. At the time the present draft was completed and agreed upon by committee participants the Haradh conference was still in session, but it had failed to make any significant progress toward the creation of an all-Yemeni provisional government. The Yemeni situation is so volatile that it is difficult to rule out any hypothesis, from the peaceful establishment of a royalist-republican interim government to full scale resumption of civil war, with UAR and Saudi participation. This uncertainty merely highlights the utility of contingency planning.

3. A central problem in any consideration of possible Saudi–UAR hostilities is to find a means of honoring our often reiterated verbal commitment (see Annex A of contingency paper)[4] to protect Saudi integrity while avoiding being drawn into a degree of direct military involvement which might redound to the disadvantage both of the US and the Saudi monarchy. One of the main potential dangers appears to be that of too precipitate US military action in the Saudi defense. For this reason we have stressed diplomatic action to forestall and arrest

---

[1] Source: Department of State, NEA/ARP Files: Lot 69 D 547, Arabian Peninsula Political Affairs & Rel., 1965, Yemen–UAR. Secret. Drafted by Korn on December 23 and cleared by Symmes and Officer in Charge of Politico-Military Affairs in the Office of Near Eastern and South Asian Regional Affairs Colonel Billy W. Byrd.

[2] Dated January 30, 1964 and entitled "Procedures for Anticipating Foreign Crises." (National Archives and Records Administration, RG 59, S/S–NSC Files: Lot 72 D 316, Master File of National Security Action Memoranda (NSAMs), 1961–1968, NSAM 277)

[3] Not found.

[4] Not printed.

a UAR–Saudi conflict and have foreseen direct US military intervention only in the most extreme circumstances.

4. While a paper covering the contingency of a coup in Saudi Arabia was done in 1964,[5] this is the first study of its kind on Saudi–UAR hostilities over Yemen. Owing to the volatile nature of the Yemeni situation, we believe it would be advisable to take a further look at this study within the next six months. A review during this period will enable us to take account both of developments in the rapidly changing Yemeni situation and comments by Embassies Jidda and Cairo.

Attachment

Contingency Planning Paper

UAR–SAUDI HOSTILITIES OVER YEMEN

I—Summary

While tension between the UAR and Saudi Arabia over Yemen has subsided as a result of an agreement between Nasser and Faisal in August of 1965, Yemen will probably remain a bone of contention between the two Arab countries for many years to come. The advent in Sanaa of a regime openly antagonistic to either Saudi Arabia or the UAR could spark renewed hostilities.

The United States has a long-standing and often-reiterated commitment to protect Saudi Arabia from foreign aggression. Behind this commitment lies our interest in the continued free flow of Saudi oil to Western Europe, the security of air transit facilities across the Peninsula, and the survival of a regime which is one of our best friends in the Middle East and a staunch foe of communism. We intend to remain true to this commitment. We must at the same time be cognizant of the danger of precipitate US military action in the Saudi defense which could ignite an explosion of Arab nationalist wrath against the Saudi monarchy and the United States as well. Consequently this paper stresses diplomatic action to forestall and arrest a UAR-Saudi conflict over Yemen and foresees direct US military intervention (except to evacuate American citizens) only in the most extreme contingency.

[Here follow the body of the paper and four annexes.]

---

[5] Not found.

384.   Telegram From the Department of State to the Embassy in Yemen[1]

Washington, December 30, 1965, 6:39 p.m.

132. Taiz tels 215,[2] 218.[3] Yemen Settlement.

1. Concur with Embassy's characterization Nu'man explanation Haradh Conference breakdown[4] as "oriental deviousness." Appears from here that basic reason for failure conferees reach agreement lay in continued individual and group jockeying on both sides for immediate power advantage, regardless of professed desires for peace and cessation foreign interference. Each side now blaming other (and Faisal and Nasser) for failure, wellsprings of which are decades-long Yemeni inability develop consensus support for central government rather than tribal diversity. More immediate contributory factors may of course include built-in ambiguities of Jidda Agreement and somewhat obscure role of certain SAG and UARG representatives, but we inclined believe these subordinate to foregoing.

2. Apparent continued efforts Faisal and Nasser press for solution offer hope for future. Anticipate, however, next two months until resumption Yemeni conference may see new strains in Cairo–Riyadh relationships, particularly if Faisal encourages some royalist military activity either in response any delay of UAR troop withdrawal or independently.

3. Pending further developments in Nasser–Faisal relationship re Yemen, do not believe it appropriate or useful for us try play more active role by, for example, exploring receptivity to neutral groups' supervision future conference as suggested by Nu'man. (YARG has easy access to Arab League and UN if it desires make use of it.) How-

---

[1] Source: National Archives and Records Administration, RG 59, Central Files 1964–66, POL 27 YEMEN. Secret. Drafted by Moore, cleared by Symmes, and approved by Davies. Also sent to Cairo and Jidda and repeated to London, CINCSTRIKE, and USUN.

[2] In telegram 215 from Taiz, December 29, Clark reported that Numan, now ranking member of the republican delegation to the Haradh conference, told him that the conference had not succeeded because Yemeni delegates on both sides were closely controlled by Nasser and Faisal respectively and were not permitted to reach a settlement. Numan argued that the only chance of an acceptable Yemen settlement would be for the Arab League or the United Nations to preside over the next session of the conference, and asked the United States to support his idea. Clark pointed out that in the eyes of the world the Yemenis themselves were to blame for failure to reach agreement, and argued that the Yemen complex of problems could only be solved by the parties directly involved. His report referred to the "oriental deviousness" of Numan's exposition and noted that Numan and several other YARG officials had left for Cairo by air that morning. (Ibid.)

[3] Dated December 29. (Ibid.)

[4] The Haradh conference adjourned on December 24 after failing to reach agreement on even the first steps toward a Yemen settlement.

ever, action addressees should use appropriate opportunities in discussion host government officials to indicate our continued desire peaceful settlement and to probe for information on next moves contemplated by UAR and Saudis.

Rusk

385. Memorandum of Conversation[1]

Washington, January 12, 1966.

SUBJECT

Yemeni Settlement

PARTICIPANTS

Muhsin al-Aini, Ambassador of Yemen
Assistant Secretary Raymond A. Hare, NEA
George C. Moore, NE

Ambassador al-Aini said that he was pessimistic about possibilities for a successful settlement in Yemen arising from the Jidda Agreement. Discussions at Haradh had proven that the only technique now suitable for an agreement would be for Faisal and Nasser to announce their exclusion of the Hamid al-Din royal family and of Sallal and his clique from political affairs in Yemen for a specific future period, perhaps five years; for the Saudis and UAR to cease their interference in Yemeni attempts to establish a future administration; and for the coming together of select Yemeni leaders—perhaps those who had participated at Haradh—without any prior "royalist" or "republican" labels in order to set up the framework of a future state. It was now clear that neither a purely republican nor purely royalist regime would be successful in ruling Yemen. It was also clear that the holding of a plebiscite in Yemen was a completely impractical concept.

In response to Mr. Hare's question concerning the extent of support of the foregoing view among influential Yemenis, Ambassador al-Aini indicated that a majority of the leaders and of the public, itself, held this opinion. He added that the basic problem at the Haradh Conference had arisen from attaching the designation republican or royalist to each

---

[1] Source: National Archives and Records Administration, RG 59, Central Files 1964–66, POL 27 YEMEN. Confidential. Drafted by Moore on January 17.

of the participants, thereby giving the individuals a certain personal feeling of responsibility for supporting one side or the other. He said that neither the republicans nor the royalists, but rather the tribes, were now the deciding factor in Yemen. If Faisal and Nasser were not realistic in their acceptance of this, they were liable to find the situation removed from their hands with the Yemenis seeking help from elsewhere. In response to Ambassador Hare's question of the meaning of "elsewhere", he mentioned the Chinese Communists and the Russians as possibilities. Answering a further question, Ambassador al-Aini said that Saudi and Egyptian help might perhaps be needed to set up the forthcoming conference, but only in its initial stages. The Yemenis themselves were most aware of who the real leaders of the country were. By and large they were satisfied with the representative character of the group assembled at Haradh. Subsequently he would anticipate establishment of a Presidential Council as the chief executive authority, possibly along the lines of the August Taif Agreement.

Ambassador Hare noted the present difficulty for a central government to operate in Yemen and said that it was clear the ultimate solution must be a Yemeni one, the result of efforts of a group working for the country as a whole and not just for its individual power interests. The need was for a consensus, although that was clearly a difficult thing to find in Yemen. Ambassador al-Aini expressed the hope that Jidda and Cairo were equally as well aware of the need for a Yemeni, not foreign-imposed, solution.

In a subsequent conversation with Mr. Moore, Ambassador al-Aini said that his reports on the Haradh Conference and his analysis of the prevailing opinion in Yemen had come from his father-in-law, Sinaan Abu Luhum, (a recent defector from the Republic who participated on the royalist side at the conference) who had recently telephoned him from Beirut. The Ambassador is considering going to Beirut himself in the near future for further consultation with various Yemenis assembled there.

386.   Telegram From the Department of State to the Embassy in the United Arab Republic[1]

Washington, January 20, 1966, 4:18 p.m.

4031. Embtel 1712,[2] Jidda tels 584,[3] 595.[4] Yemen.

1. In view indications of worsening Cairo–Riyadh relations, believe it appropriate you again discuss Yemen problem with top-level UAR.

2. Suggest you draw on following points:

a. US continues strongly desire peaceful solution to Yemen problem and development all-Yemen administration. Hopeful prospects for this, contained Jidda Agreement, have played significant role in improvement US–UAR relations.

b. We disturbed at reports cooling of atmosphere between Cairo and Riyadh, particularly in view importance good SAG–UAR relations not only re Yemen but for broader stable climate for development and progress in Near East.

c. Appears to us that problem may arise from lack detailed exchange views at highest SAG–UAR level, complicated by speculation at lower less informed levels. In this regard we understand SAG concerned that UAR troop withdrawals from Yemen not started. We hope initial failure Haradh Conference has not cooled UAR support for

---

[1] Source: National Archives and Records Administration, RG 59, Central Files 1964–66, POL 27 YEMEN. Secret. Drafted by Moore and Russell, cleared by Symmes and Davies, and approved by Hare. Repeated to Jidda, Taiz, and London.

[2] Telegram 1712 from Cairo, January 8, reported a meeting with senior adviser to Nasser, Hassan Sabri al-Khouli, to explore UAR attitudes toward Yemen. Al-Khouli described the basic problem as a four-sided interpretation of the Jidda Agreement and said that the solution lay in an agreed UAR–Saudi interpretation. He commented, however, that King Faisal was playing a "mysterious and evasive game" and said that all UAR efforts to arrange a high-level meeting or agreement on details of a settlement had been fruitless. (Ibid.)

[3] In telegram 584 from Jidda, January 16, Ambassador Eilts reported that following presentation of his credentials, he had a 40-minute conversation with King Faisal about Yemen. Faisal warned that unless UAR withdrawal took place to allow the Yemenis to work out their own destiny, there was a threat of communism taking over in Yemen. The King said that the United Arab Republic showed no signs of wishing to honor the Jidda Agreement and that no withdrawal was taking place. On the contrary, he had received reports of further UAR military deployment to Yemen. (Ibid., POL 17–1 US–SAUD)

[4] In telegram 595 from Jidda, January 18, Eilts reported that, at the King's suggestion, he met with Dr. Rashad Pharaon on January 17 to discuss the current situation in Yemen. Pharaon said that Nasser's most recent letter to Faisal, carried by Saudi Ambassador Ali Reza from Cairo to Jidda, reiterated his intent to implement the Jidda Agreement terms in letter and spirit. However, Ali Reza had also conveyed Nasser's oral message that he could not begin troop withdrawals until an interim government was formed. (Ibid., POL 27 YEMEN)

arrangements contained Jidda Agreement. At same time we recognize UAR and SAG may have honestly differing interpretations of troop withdrawal provision of Agreement. Would suggest that if UAR has timetable for troop withdrawals, informing SAG of details would greatly contribute to dissipating latter's concern.

d. We aware rumors and press speculation re pending development "Islamic Pact" of conservative forces arising from Faisal visit to Iran. We doubt likelihood creation such grouping and of course have played no role in matter.

e. Hope UAR will do utmost encourage Yemenis resume discussions as scheduled and assist where possible in enabling them reach successful conclusion.

f. Continued progress on Yemen helps us to defend aid to the UAR.[5]

Rusk

---

[5] Telegram 1855 from Cairo, January 21, reported that Parker met on January 20 with al-Khouli, who told him that if the United Arab Republic and Saudi Arabia cooperated, peace in Yemen was possible. He said that, in an effort to break the deadlock, Nasser had sent Faisal a personal letter proposing a new agreement including UAR withdrawal within the 10 months prescribed by the Jidda Agreement, i.e., by September 23; establishment of a transitional government to be composed of one-third royalists and two-thirds republicans to be called the "Transitional Government of the Yemen"; and banishment of the Hamid ad-Dins from Yemen until after the November 23 plebiscite. Al-Khouli argued that if Faisal really wanted a solution, he would have responded immediately to Nasser's proposals. (Ibid.)

---

387.   Memorandum From Secretary of State Rusk to President Johnson[1]

Washington, February 20, 1966.

SUBJECT

   Visit of Saudi Defense Minister, Prince Sultan ibn Abdul Aziz

I. Circumstances of the Visit:

   King Faisal has asked you to receive his brother who is carrying an urgent special message. We are unaware of the subject but believe

---

[1] Source: Johnson Library, National Security File, Komer Files, Saudi Arabia, 1965–March 1966. No classification marking.

it will reflect *Faisal's deep concern over the Yemen problem*. Prince Sultan is [*less than 1 line of source text not declassified*] well regarded by the King.

II. Faisal's Position on Yemen reflects the following:

1. Concern that *Egyptian troop withdrawals from Yemen have not yet started* and belief that Nasser does not intend to honor commitments to complete these withdrawals by the end of September 1966; (*We believe Nasser will withdraw* but not until the Saudis agree to an acceptable transitional regime.)

2. Belief that the *Soviets are financing Nasser's staying in Yemen* in order to establish a foothold in the Red Sea area, including submarine bases; (*We disagree,* believe *Saudi figures on numbers of Soviets and Chinese Communists in Yemen are highly inflated,* and consider unfounded Saudi claims of Soviet naval or military installations in the Red Sea region; *we are willing to share with the Saudis our detailed assessments* of the Communist threat.)

3. View that *U.S. PL 480 food deliveries to the UAR abet Nasser's remaining in Yemen;* (*We disagree: the threat of loss of our food aid is not sufficient to bring Nasser to accept humiliation in Yemen.*)

4. Expectation that *he will resume aid to the royalists if Egyptian troop withdrawals do not soon begin.* (We caution patience; *resumption of aid would result in renewed fighting, the Jidda Agreement contains obligations for both sides.*)

III.

Failure of Nasser and Faisal to agree on such vital arrangements as the form of the interim government in Yemen and the ratio in it between royalists and republicans make it unlikely a resumed Haradh conference could achieve results. *Faisal seems increasingly inflexible and his failure to respond to UAR overtures is a major factor blocking agreement.*

IV. Recommended points to make to the Prince:

1. The objective of all parties should be *an independent Yemen* in which the Yemenis are free to determine their own future without any outside intervention.

2. *The Jidda Agreement of August, 1965 provides the best basis* for achieving this objective. We believe it unlikely the current misunderstandings can be resolved without renewed *contact between King Faisal and President Nasser* of a serious, frank and flexible character. We urge that King Faisal seek this contact. *We are similarly urging President Nasser to be flexible.*

3. *Resumed fighting could well force the republicans into greater reliance on the Soviets and the UAR.*

4. *We continue highly to value the friendship of Saudi Arabia and reaffirm our support for Saudi territorial integrity.* As we have previously

informed the Saudi Arabian Government, we could not permit this commitment to be used as a shield for Saudi initiatives in the Yemen situation that would provoke UAR attacks on Saudi Arabia.

5. We most *appreciate Faisal's support for our position in Viet Nam* and his efforts at last fall's Arab Summit Conference in Casablanca to prevent condemnation of U.S. bombing of North Viet Nam.

6. You are *pleased at the cooperation between our two countries in the development field,* including the recently concluded agreement for assistance from our Department of Interior for construction of a *five million gallon per day water desalting plant at Jidda.*

Dean Rusk[2]

---

[2] Printed from a copy that indicates Rusk signed the original.

---

388. Memorandum of Conversation[1]

Washington, February 23, 1966, 12:40 p.m.

SUBJECT

  Yemen

PARTICIPANTS

  His Excellency Anwar al-Sadat, President of the U.A.R. National Assembly
  His Excellency Dr. Mostafa Kamel, Ambassador of the U.A.R.
  His Excellency Ahmad Hassan al-Feqi, Under Secretary of the U.A.R. Foreign
    Ministry

  The Secretary
  NEA—Raymond A. Hare, Assistant Secretary
  NE—Michael Sterner, Escort Officer

After welcoming Mr. Sadat and his colleagues, the Secretary asked how the meeting with President Johnson had gone.[2] Mr. Sadat expressed his entire satisfaction at his meeting with the President, and Ambassa-

---

[1] Source: National Archives and Records Administration, RG 59, Central Files 1964–66, POL 27 YEMEN. Secret. Drafted by Michael Sterner (NEA/NE) on February 24 and approved in S on March 3. The time of the meeting is taken from Rusk's Appointment Book. (Johnson Library)

[2] See *Foreign Relations,* 1964–1968, vol. XVIII, Document 274.

dor Hare also indicated that it had been both a friendly and productive discussion. Secretary Rusk commented on Mr. Sadat's personal familiarity with Yemen and asked for his assessment of the present situation there. Mr. Sadat replied that first he wanted to express his warm thanks for the Secretary's invitation and for the cordial reception he had received in the U.S.

As the Secretary knew last August Nasser went to Jidda and reached an agreement with King Faisal for a settlement in Yemen. The Secretary commented the U.S.G. had felt this was a very constructive episode in Arab affairs. Mr. Sadat said the main provisions of the agreement had been the holding of a conference to set up a provisional government, after which there was to be a plebiscite to approve this government. Thereafter, the U.A.R. would begin to withdraw its military forces from Yemen. The U.A.R. was in fact prepared to do this, but it could not leave the country before a workable provisional government had been set up. The Haradh Conference had failed to accomplish this task. Sadat personally had foreseen that the Haradh conference would fail unless the Egyptians and Saudis got together beforehand to agree on what the conference was to accomplish. The Saudis refused at that time and the conference had failed as expected. Again, the U.A.R. had asked the Saudis to sit down with them after the Haradh conference to discuss where the two sides went from there. This offer also was rejected by the Saudis. All told, there had been six offers by the U.A.R.G. for direct contacts with S.A.G., including an offer by Marshal Amer to go to Riyadh, all of which had been rejected by the Saudis.

The Secretary asked what exactly the point was on which the Haradh Conference had foundered. Mr. Sadat replied that on the surface it centered on the question of the title that should be given to the country while it was under the provisional government. The Saudis disliked the title "Republic" so the U.A.R. readily agreed to the term "state". Underneath, however, the dispute was really a question of whether the Hamid al-Din family was to participate in the future political life of the country. Because of the amount of blood and money the U.A.R. had expended in Yemen, the U.A.R. could not accept a restoration of the Hamid al-Din family in Yemen. This was also the way the vast majority of Yemenis felt about it. The U.A.R. thought it had an understanding with King Faisal on this subject but apparently not. It was clear at the Haradh Conference that King Faisal had not given clear orders to the Royalists that the Hamid al-Dins were to be exiled from future Yemeni political life. The Secretary said he had the impression that the Yemenis on both sides were somewhat resentful that the Saudis and Egyptians were making decisions about their country without consulting the Yemenis themselves. Sadat said this was indeed one problem, but not nearly as important a factor as the lack of U.A.R.-Saudi agreement as to how the Jidda agreement was to be carried out. The Secretary wondered whether, even if the U.A.R. and Saudis were in complete agreement, they could make it stick with the Yemenis. Sadat indicated his firm belief this was the lesser of the two problems. Once the Saudis and Egyptians had a meeting of minds, the Yemenis would have no choice but to fall into place.

The Secretary hoped the Saudi reply to Nasser's recent Yemeni proposals would be constructive. Ambassador Hare noted that the Saudi Ambassador in Cairo had been expected to get back to Cairo with a reply the very day that Mr. Sadat left the U.A.R. The Secretary commented that he had a feeling the personal equation was especially important in dealing with King Faisal. It seemed to him that the meeting in Jidda in August had been successful largely for this reason. Mr. Sadat agreed. He said the U.A.R. appreciated this and it was for this reason the U.A.R.G. had repeatedly tried to have direct contacts with the Saudis. It was difficult to know where to go in view of Saudi rejection of these offers. The rejections had been polite but rejections nonetheless.

Ambassador Kamel said he thought King Faisal's ultimate objective was to create a confrontation between the U.S. and U.A.R. Mr. Sadat added, that and to see the U.A.R. humiliated by a continuing costly involvement in Yemen as the only alternative to "total surrender", i.e., a restoration of the Hamid al-Din Imamate.

The meeting adjourned for lunch.

389. Memorandum of Conversation[1]

Washington, February 23, 1966, 3:33 p.m.

SUBJECT

Yemen; Communism in the Middle East

PARTICIPANTS

Prince Sultan ibn Abdul Aziz, Minister of Defense of Saudi Arabia
Ambassador Ibrahim al-Sowayel, Saudi Ambassador to the United States
The Secretary
Raymond A. Hare, Assistant Secretary for Near East and South Asian Affairs
Isa Sabbagh, USIA
George C. Moore, Officer-in-Charge, Arabian Peninsula Affairs

The Secretary welcomed the Prince and the Prince extended King Faisal's sincerest personal greetings.

Speaking on behalf of the King, the Prince said that the threat of Communism in the Near East was the biggest danger the Saudis now saw. They felt Islam was the strongest shield against Communism and endeavored to work on the basis of their religion against Communism just as we work against it as a doctrine. With full recognition of the broad intelligence gathering capabilities of the U.S., the Prince said the Saudis had strong indications that the Yemen problem and Nasser's activities there were part of the long range Communist blueprint for gaining strength in the area. Nasser's main aim seems to be to create chaotic situations and divert the constructive attitudes of countries like Saudi Arabia, which aim at building stability and economic progress.

Concerning Yemen, Nasser and Faisal undertook obligations to settle the problem in both the Bunker Agreement of 1963[2] and the Alexandria Agreement of 1964.[3] The Saudis worked hard to carry out these agreements in letter and spirit, but found Nasser unwilling. Joint Saudi–UAR observation groups in Yemen were set up under the Alexandria Agreement. They came to an end, however, when Nasser forcibly sent the Saudi participants back over the border.

In August 1965, the Prince continued, under internal economic pressure and probably after strong words from the U.S., Nasser entered

---

[1] Source: National Archives and Records Administration, RG 59, Central Files 1964–66, POL 27 YEMEN. Secret. Drafted by Moore on February 24 and approved in S on February 28. The time of the meeting is taken from Rusk's Appointment Book. (Johnson Library)

[2] For documentation on the April 1963 disengagement agreement negotiated by U.S. Ambassador Ellsworth Bunker, Presidential Special Emissary for mediation of the Yemen conflict, see *Foreign Relations, 1961–1963,* vol. XVIII, Documents 187–189, 193–196, 202–203, 205, and 209–211.

[3] See Document 353.

into the Jidda Agreement. Prior to his arrival at Jidda, Nasser had agreed with Faisal on the broad outlines of a settlement. As a result of the agreement, the Saudi ceased military and material assistance to the Yemeni royalists at the time of its signature on August 23. Subsequently, however, Nasser went to Moscow and developments took a different turn. Radio Sanaa violently attacked the agreement. The Yemeni Prime Minister travelled to various places ("including Russia and China"). Arms were brought into Yemen from various sources. (Three Soviet ships unloaded arms and equipment at Hodeida.) The Saudis reproached the UAR saying that these developments did not fit into the spirit of the agreement. The UAR responded that it was having trouble controlling the Yemeni republicans.

At the Harad Conference, said the Prince, the Saudis made all efforts to insure that the royalists would be responsive to opportunities to find a peaceful solution. Nasser failed to exert similar control over the republicans. When this was brought to his attention, Nasser suggested that the UAR and the Saudis again come together to work out a practical program for an agreement. Nasser responded by inviting Faisal to send his emissary to Cairo and at the same time forwarded to Faisal five suggested points: 1. the formation of a coalition provisional government; 2. this coalition government to be composed of 2/3 republicans and 1/3 royalists; 3. Yemen to be called, "State of Yemen"; 4. Egyptian troop withdrawal to be completed 10 months after the coalition government was formed; 5. the Hamid al-Din to be excluded from Yemen.

According to the Prince, Faisal became increasingly disturbed at the apparent Communist involvement indicated by the formation of "popular fronts" ("Tandhim al-Shaabi") in Yemen; the presence of some 400 Chinese and a similar number of Russians in Yemen; the report that the USSR was establishing a submarine base on UAR territory; and an alleged agreement between the Yemeni republicans and the USSR—concluded with UAR help—for the Soviets to establish a naval base south of Hodeida. As a result, Faisal's response to Nasser's five points was as follows: a 50–50 representation of royalists and republicans as previously agreed on; withdrawal of UAR troops should take place within 10 months from November 23, 1965, in accordance with the Jidda Agreement (although its completion within 10 months from mid-February, the current time, would probably not be unacceptable); and, after a provisional government had been formed and both Saudi Arabia and the UAR had completely disengaged from Yemen, it would be incumbent on Nasser and Faisal to enforce any decision of that government to exclude the Hamid al-Din or any other group.

The Prince was surprised to learn that Nasser had said yesterday that UAR troops would stay in Yemen until the British withdraw from

Aden in 1968. This appeared to indicate Nasser had no intention of carrying out the Jidda Agreement. The Saudis believed that this stemmed from Communist desires to continue the existence of chaos in Yemen.

The Secretary responded that we were most sensitive to any Communist moves to increase their control and would be particularly concerned with any such attempts to organize activity against Faisal. We believed it most important to have a close and systematic exchange of views on this subject with the Saudis. He requested Mr. Hare to work out the technique for implementing this on the basis most suitable to the Saudis (e.g., exchanges through our Embassy, or as desired). He said we had investigated and had found no confirmation of reports of Soviet submarine or naval bases in the area. He noted that Communist activity in other parts of the lower Red Sea also made it most important that we and the Saudis work closely together to improve our mutual understanding of what was going on, e.g., in South Arabian Federation, Somalia, etc.

Concerning Yemen, the Secretary said that he had today listened to UAR Vice President Anwar Sadat speak on the same subject. On the basis of the Prince's and Mr. Sadat's comments, he felt that the Jidda Agreement was not dead. He was inclined to discount Nasser's speech of yesterday (the U.S. very often was not spared such attacks) and believed that further exploration of the points of the Jidda Agreement could lead to a solution. King Faisal had made very substantial diplomatic gains in the Jidda Agreement; every effort should be made to preserve that agreement in the best interests of Saudi Arabia.

Turning to details, the Secretary gave his impression that Cairo still considers itself bound by a commitment to establish a provisional coalition government; that it expects to withdraw its troops from Yemen within ten months of the time such a government is established; that it is committed to support a plebiscite amongst the Yemenis to decide their own future; that Nasser has conceded the name, "State of Yemen," rather than "Republic of Yemen". The Secretary noted that it seemed indeed to be a fact that Nasser had had his problems with the Yemenis. He recalled that when speaking to the Yemeni Foreign Minister last fall, the latter had betrayed discontent with the UAR and Saudi Arabia having arranged an agreement without consulting the Yemenis. Despite troubles with the Yemenis, however, he believed that in the end Faisal and Nasser would have the final say concerning a settlement. The background elements at the time of the Jidda Agreement were much the same as they are today, which puts continued pressure on Nasser to carry out the agreement. Since that agreement was so much in Saudi Arabia's advantage, it would seem important for the Saudis to again attempt to make it work.

The Secretary commented on the great increase in stability and development in Saudi Arabia in the last three years, for which Faisal should be congratulated. He noted that implementation of the Jidda Agreement would contribute markedly to continuation of that stability, to the benefit of Saudi Arabia. He emphasized that we were not trying to intrude ourselves between the UAR and the Saudis, but hoped that they would explore every possibility for saving the valuable Jidda Agreement.

Mr. Hare said that he also had the same reaction after speaking to Mr. Sadat earlier in the day and had felt on reading the messages from Cairo and Jidda over the last few weeks that a certain spirit for agreement continued to exist on both sides. There was now only a cloud which needed to be pierced by quiet careful efforts from both parties.

The Prince said that his Government was fearful that the Yemen would explode, to the benefit of the Communists, if a settlement were not reached in the near future.

Mr. Hare asked if the Saudi reply to Nasser's five points had yet been delivered in Cairo. The Prince said that, to his information, Saudi Ambassador Alireza returned to Cairo the day before yesterday and presumably requested an appointment with Nasser. He guessed that, since Nasser's sharp personal attack yesterday on King Faisal, Ambassador Alireza might be instructed not to see the UAR President.

The Prince then asked if we had any doubt of Saudi sincerity in supporting the Jidda Agreement. The Secretary said he had implicit trust in King Faisal's word that they supported the agreement. The Prince continued that they were ready in letter and spirit to find a settlement in Yemen but this was the third time that they had been deceived and he hoped we would not blame them for what they might have to do. Mr. Rusk referred to his personal involvement in nearly every great Communist-Free World crisis since World War II and said that he had learned patience to be the most important virtue since the alternatives were so terrible.

After asking about the Prince's personal plans, the Secretary said he wished to discuss this matter in further detail with Mr. Hare and with the President and might be in touch with the Prince during the latter's stay in New York over the next two days. He assured the Prince that any suggestions we make are not merely maneuvers but are direct, honest views based on deep friendship.

At the close of the discussion, the Prince noted that he had received a telegram from King Faisal asking that we seriously consider Jordan's request for supply of aircraft to avoid Jordan's being pressured to acquire Soviet planes at the forthcoming March Arab Prime Ministers' Conference. The Secretary said we are much aware of the problem and are working hard to meet it.

The Prince expressed the hope that he could have some message from the President to take back with him to King Faisal.

---

390.   Memorandum of Telephone Conversation Between Secretary of State Rusk and the Assistant Secretary of State for Near Eastern and South Asian Affairs (Hare)[1]

Washington, February 24, 1966, 11:03 a.m.

TELEPHONE CALL TO AMB. HARE

Sec said he assumed H had been thinking about the best follow up for the Saudi-Egyptian business; Sec wondered whether he was too positive about the possibility of an agreement. H thought not, but Faisal has been needling Nasser. Sec wondered if he should see Sadat again. H said he had said he would, so he should. Sec said ok, and 5 pm Friday was agreed; Sec said he wanted to talk about reducing the arms race. H said they were working on a letter to Faisal for the Prince to take back tomorrow night. Sec wondered if we should be doing any dickering between the two while they are here; Sec thought it was better for them to deal straight with each other; H agreed. Sec said he needed to be in touch with the Prince in order to give the letter to take back.

---

[1] Source: National Archives and Records Administration, RG 59, Rusk Files: Lot 72 D 192, Box 929. No classification marking. Transcribed by Rusk's personal assistant, Carolyn J. Proctor.

391.   Memorandum of Conversation[1]

Washington, February 25, 1966, 5:05–6:39 p.m.

SUBJECT

Yemen

PARTICIPANTS

His Excellency Anwar al-Sadat, President of the U.A.R. National Assembly
His Excellency Dr. Mostafa Kamel, Ambassador of the U.A.R.
His Excellency Ahmad Hassan al-Feqi, Under Secretary of the U.A.R. Foreign Ministry

The Secretary
NEA—Raymond A. Hare, Assistant Secretary
NE—Michael Sterner, Escort Officer

The Secretary said that since seeing Sadat last, he had had a chance to talk to the Saudi Defense Minister, Prince Sultan, and get his views on the Yemen situation. After hearing both the U.A.R. and Saudi views, the Secretary felt there were no major obstacles to settlement. He would like to encourage the thought that with a little more work on the part of both of these great countries the gap between them could be narrowed.

Mr. Sadat hoped the Secretary's optimism would prove to be well founded. Since the Jidda agreement, the U.A.R.'s objective in Yemen was to evacuate its troops from the country completely. Now, in view of King Faisal's ambiguous attitude, the U.A.R. might be forced to change this objective. Faisal kept saying he wanted a settlement in Yemen, but his acts were beginning to point to another conclusion, and it was the acts that counted, not the words.

The Secretary hoped the Saudi reply, which should have been received in Cairo by then, would be constructive. Mr. Sadat said this raised another question. Suppose the latest Saudi response turned out to be more of the same—sugared words but no constructive action underneath—what should the U.A.R. do?

The Secretary said he had the impression from his recent conversations with both sides that the gap was not so great as might seem. It did not appear to be one which further discussion had no hope of bridging. The Secretary said he would like to make two comments, both against the background of our relations with the U.S.S.R. The fewer things that were said about the other side publicly with sharp

---

[1] Source: National Archives and Records Administration, RG 59, Central Files 1964–66, POL 27 YEMEN. Secret. Drafted by Sterner on February 28 and approved in S on March 28. The time of the meeting is taken from Rusk's Appointment Book. (Johnson Library)

edges on them the better. Secondly, he strongly urged that a decision not be made too quickly that further discussion was pointless. For one thing, the alternatives to discussion were not too pleasant. The Secretary felt diplomacy had a duty to be persistent.

Mr. Sadat agreed with the last statement. Before coming on this trip he had met with President Nasser on Yemen and they had agreed the U.A.R. would give Saudi Arabia another two months, from the date that they informed the U.S.G., before deciding on a "change of strategy" in Yemen.[2]

The Secretary said the U.S. would continue its friendly interest in a settlement but we didn't feel we could play a role that could substitute for direct contact between the U.A.R. and Saudi Arabia. Mr. Sadat said he knew this was U.S. policy, but he wished the U.S.G. would give further consideration to playing a helpful role. The U.A.R. saw the need to compromise but it could not abandon the field empty handed. The Saudis seemed now to want the complete extinction of the Yemeni Republic and the total discrediting of the U.A.R. for having supported it. This the U.A.R. would never accept. Aside from the blood and treasure the U.A.R. had expended in Yemen, there was the consideration that the Yemeni Republic had been recognized by the U.N. and most of the nations in the world.

The Secretary emphasized that internationally the U.S. had a great interest in seeing peace maintained between Saudi Arabia and the U.A.R. We also wanted to see a government in Yemen that was acceptable to the Yemenis themselves. The Secretary promised the U.S. would continue to follow the situation and if there were things the U.S. might do to help matters along, we would give them consideration.

---

[2] Ambassador Kamel later told Ambassador Hare that this statement was not intended to be an ultimatum. He said the intention of the Speaker was to say that the U.A.R.G. had decided to wait at least another two months before reviewing the situation to see whether a change of strategy was required. [Footnote in the source text.]

392. Telegram From the Department of State to the Embassy in Sudan[1]

Washington, March 8, 1966, 6:59 p.m.

305. Cairo tel 2267 to Dept (being rptd Khartoum).[2] Yemen.

1. Khouli's report (reftel) of Nasser response to Faisal message on Yemen gives hope real progress. Important we urge Faisal not lose opportunity presented or allow slackening in momentum.

2. *For Khartoum:*[3] Please deliver urgently following oral message from Secretary to Faisal:

a. Hassan Sabri al-Khouli has informed us of Nasser's March 5 response to King's recent message on Yemen. (Summarize gist of message as in reftel.)

b. As emphasized both to Prince Sultan and Anwar Sadat in recent visits Washington, we believe Jidda Agreement still affords best approach for peaceful solution Yemen conflict and hope way can be found move forward toward peace on that basis. We understand from UAR that present Nasser response supplied in spirit of advice given here to Sadat to keep dialogue going.

c. Nasser's present message appears open way by which King, through prompt statesmanlike act, can achieve immediate goal of bringing start to UAR troop evacuation Yemen which, once begun, could be carried through by end September. King's longer range goal of limiting Communist influence Yemen will be enhanced by bringing closer time when Yemen can be reunified and governed by all-Yemeni government giving Yemenis opportunity for realization legitimate desires develop in peace, dignity and freedom. Only under latter conditions can real halt to Communist penetration be expected.

d. Realize that questions ratio republican and royalist participation in transitional government and future of Hamid al-Din family not completely resolved but should be negotiable.

---

[1] Source: National Archives and Records Administration, RG 59, Central Files 1964–66, POL 27 YEMEN. Secret; Priority. Drafted by Moore; cleared by Symmes, Davies, Officer in Charge of Sudanese Affairs Robert W. Stookey, and Hare; and approved by Rusk. Also sent to Jidda and repeated to Taiz and Cairo.

[2] In telegram 2267 from Cairo, March 7, Battle reported that al-Khouli had informed him that Nasser met with Saudi Ambassador Ali Reza on March 5 to receive Faisal's long-delayed reply to his proposals for a new agreement on Yemen. The King asked for withdrawal by September 25 and an interim government with a 50/50 ratio of republicans and royalists, and said that he would consider banishing the Hamid al-Dins once withdrawal was complete. Nasser responded that the United Arab Republic was not prepared to withdraw its proposal for an all-Yemeni interim government with a 2-to-1 ratio of republicans to royalists. (Ibid.)

[3] Faisal was in Khartoum preceding the Arab Prime Ministers' Conference, March 14–17.

e. Present proposal contains possibility of solution with honor for both King and President Nasser. Doubt strongly that any settlement feasible in which honor and dignity do not accrue both sides.

f. Renewed expression my personal respects and deep friendship accompanies this urgent plea to Your Majesty that you give careful consideration to this further opportunity achieve peace in Yemen.[4]

3. *For Jidda:*

Request you pass foregoing to Saqqaf for his possible parallel transmission to King.

Rusk

---

[4] In telegram 636 from Khartoum, March 13, Ambassador William H. Weathersby reported that Faisal had expressed appreciation for the Secretary's message and his interest in a peaceful settlement in Yemen. Faisal told him that he had instructed Ali Reza to reply to Nasser that a 2-to-1 ratio of republicans to royalists was impossible; Nasser would have to live up to the Jidda Agreement for 50–50. Weathersby said he had emphasized the urgency of an immediate start in troop evacuation and repeated the Secretary's suggestion that the ratio of participation in the transitional government should be negotiable. The King replied that even if Nasser kept his troops in Yemen for 10 years, he could never accept a 2-to-1 ratio. Upon being urged again to keep the dialogue going, Faisal said that he had instructed Ali Reza to keep the door open and to respond to any initiative from Nasser. (National Archives and Records Administration, RG 59, Central Files 1964–66, POL 27 YEMEN)

393.   Telegram From the Department of State to the Embassy in the United Arab Republic[1]

Washington, March 15, 1966, 8:34 p.m.

5175. Your 2334.[2]

1. Concur with approach to Nasser on Yemen suggested reftel. You may say USG convinced Saudis sincerely want settlement and appears there are honest differences of opinion on interpretation and implementation Jidda Agreement, but these do not necessarily imply bad faith.

2. You should make clear, however, that detailed suggestion about ways out of impasse your personal views. USG wishes avoid becoming party to negotiations and does not espouse any particular formula for implementing Jidda Agreement.

3. Desirable you recall Kaissouni request for new PL–480 agreement and need for review within USG of developments in US–UAR relations before we decide whether or not to begin negotiations. This connection, you should indicate, in whatever way seems most appropriate, that among factors to be weighed will be UAR actions and attitudes vis-à-vis Yemen and South Arabia and tangible progress toward solution these problems.

Rusk

---

[1] Source: National Archives and Records Administration, RG 59, Central Files 1964–66, POL 27 YEMEN. Secret; Priority. Drafted by Russell, cleared by Atherton and Davies, and approved by Hare. Repeated to Jidda, London, Taiz, and Aden.

[2] In telegram 2334 from Cairo, March 14, Battle reported that he was disappointed but not greatly surprised by Faisal's negative response to Nasser's proposals as reported in telegram 636 from Khartoum. (See footnote 4, Document 392.) He had asked for an appointment with Nasser and planned to tell him that the United States was convinced that the Saudis sincerely wanted a settlement and that although it appeared that there were honest differences of opinion on interpretation and implementation of the Jidda Agreement, these did not necessarily imply bad faith. The Ambassador also planned to suggest that both sides ignore the republican and royalist designations and try to pick out a representative group of 20–30 men to run the country. (National Archives and Records Administration, RG 59, Central Files 1964–66, POL 27 YEMEN)

394.   Telegram From the Department of State to the Embassy in Saudi Arabia[1]

Washington, March 19, 1966, 3:11 p.m.

540. Yemen Settlement.

1. Question arises whether Faisal, confident in own strength, and perhaps misled by reports UARG internal difficulties, unduly rigid in pressing advantage in hope ultimately unseating Nasser or, at minimum, dealing lasting blow to Nasser's position outside Egypt. If so, appears great miscalculation strength UAR regime which could lead to prolonged instability Yemen and whole Peninsula, with ultimate serious effects for Saudi Government. Leave to your discretion how best convey this thought to King, but consider it essential he realize that durable Yemen settlement depends on freely consented compromise by both UAR and SAG.

2. Agree with your tel 794[2] that vague wording Jidda Agreement leaves room for honest difference interpretation Article 6 re timing UAR troop withdrawal. Doubt, however, that any party justified in citing individual article out of context. From practical point of view, UAR cannot accept public embarrassment of withdrawal without agreement on successor regime. Also, it questionable if leaving republican areas Yemen in vacuum would serve Western or Saudi interests.

3. Re points at issue, tentatively agreed list 100 acceptable Yemenis offers hopeful base for discussion transitional government, either by UAR–SAG reps or, as possible first step, by individual royalist and republican reps (e.g., Shami and Iryani). Concerning Hamid al-Din, it doubtful that Faisal could prevent them from future activity in Yemen in any event. (Spirit Jidda Agreement implies eventual halt Saudi financial aid, which has been prime tool for Saudi control royalists.)

4. In your next meeting with Faisal, suggest you reiterate our position along lines Secretary's message (Deptel 508),[3] urging focus on spirit Jidda Agreement as enunciated in preamble. Also might note Article 9 provides for direct Faisal–Nasser contact to avoid difficulties re implementation; we pleased learn SAG prepared send "high person-

[1] Source: National Archives and Records Administration, RG 59, Central Files 1964–66, POL 27 YEMEN. Secret. Drafted by Moore and Korn on March 18; cleared by Assistant Legal Adviser for Near Eastern and South Asian Affairs Donald A. Wehmeyer (paragraph 2), Symmes, and Davies; and approved by Hare. Repeated to Cairo, London, Taiz, Aden, and Dhahran.

[2] Dated March 13. (Ibid.)

[3] Repeated as telegram 305 to Khartoum, Document 392.

ality" to Cairo for this purpose (Embtel 814).[4] We recognize Saudis have been solely tried by Nasser but wonder if some further compromise would not pay dividends in getting UAR forces out of Yemen. In any event UAR failure honor any new Faisal–Nasser agreement would considerably strengthen Saudi position in eyes rest of world.

5. You should use this, or other early occasion and context which you deem appropriate, again to make clear to Faisal that our commitment to support Saudi integrity does not extend to providing military cover for SAG operations in support hostilities in Yemen or to any Saudi actions of provocative nature.[5]

Rusk

---

[4] Dated March 16. (National Archives and Records Administration, RG 59, Central Files 1964–66, POL 27 YEMEN)

[5] In telegram 844 from Jidda, March 22, Eilts reported that he shared the Department's view that at least some of Faisal's present rigidity was probably prompted by his belief that Nasser's regime was tottering. He said he would continue to impress on the King that the U.S. estimate of Nasser's internal position was different, and the dangers of basing Saudi policy on any such mistaken estimate. He would also stress that a durable settlement in Yemen depended on a compromise freely consented to by the United Arab Republic and Saudi Arabia. The Ambassador noted, however, that this was only one element in Faisal's hardened position. First, the King was deeply distrustful of Nasser. Second, he believed Nasser was seeking a pretext to avoid beginning any withdrawal from Yemen. Third, he believed that Nasser was willingly acting as a "commie agent" in the Middle East. And finally, he believed the Yemenis should have self-determination, rather than a Saudi–UAR imposed government. (Ibid.)

---

395. Telegram From the Embassy in the United Arab Republic to the Department of State[1]

Cairo, March 20, 1966, 0905Z.

2388. I have just returned from one hour of extremely cordial but very vigorous conversation with President Nasser. Before I could begin, he expressed extreme pleasure with Sadat visit saying Mr. Sadat had been well received and greatly impressed by everything and everybody he saw in the US. Meetings with Pres, Secretary and Congress as well as State govt officials had impressed him, had been productive and were encouraging.

---

[1] Source: National Archives and Records Administration, RG 59, Central Files 1964–66, POL UAR–US. Secret; Limdis. Repeated to Jidda, Taiz, Aden, and London.

I said that we too were pleased with the visit and presented him with the letter from the Pres[2] which he read carefully two or three times and obviously appreciated. I then stated that quiet discussions of problems represented best approach to dealing with difficulties between our two countries. I said that we had gone a long way toward solving some of our problems and that I hoped that through quiet conversation through usual diplomatic channels augmented by other visits we could keep issues on responsible level and make further progress without putting our differences in headlines. He assented.

I stated one of my roles as American rep was to foresee problems and hopefully to find a way of dealing with them before they became a threat to our bilateral relations, the success of which were most important to both countries. I said I wanted to lead off our discussion with two difficulties that might, given past experience and the magnitude of the problems, be issues in the future if we were not careful—Yemen and Aden. I stated that we were not a party to the Yemen dispute, but were good friends of both SA and Egypt and that while we could not mediate the complex issues between them we wanted to do what we could to preserve an atmosphere between the two that would be productive and helpful. I had been greatly encouraged by the obviously statesmanlike response to King Feisal concerning which al Khouly had informed me. The responsive tone represented an obvious effort, as had the Jidda agreement, to reach a solution to a difficult problem. The US has encouraged SA to be equally reponsive and I hoped that talks were continuing. Honest difficulties in interpreting the Jidda agreement could occur but this did not necessarily mean bad faith on either side. I said we were convinced that both sides wanted a settlement, at which point he interrupted vigorously and said, "do you really believe the Saudis want a solution?" I said we believed they did and that the interested parties must find a way to continue discussion and to rebuild confidence that had existed in the past.

The President then reviewed the Yemen problem over the past several years, adding little that was new. He then paused as though he was not sure where to go next and I mentioned, making it very clear that it was a personal suggestion, the thought that perhaps a transitional govt in the Yemen could be based on no formula of distribution between republicans and royalists but on the selection of individuals who might play a role but who were not identified completely with

---

[2] Telegram 5017 to Cairo, March 7, transmitted the text of a letter from President Johnson to President Nasser replying to the message from the latter delivered by President of the UAR National Assembly Anwar al-Sadat on February 23. The President's letter expressed the hope that continued UAR–Saudi talks would make it possible to reach a solution to the Yemen problem. (Ibid., POL 7 UAR) Johnson's February 23 conversation with Sadat is printed as Document 274 in *Foreign Relations, 1964–1968,* vol. XVIII.

either side. He said it was hard to tell a republican from a royalist in terms of what they stood for. That, I indicated, should make my suggestion more attractive. He said that it was impossible to look toward such a solution since all responsible people carried one or the other designation even though it really did not make much difference as far as their abilities or philosophies were concerned. We played around with the idea for a bit but it got nowhere.

The Pres then remarked that I had said we were not interested in the Yemen. I corrected him by saying we were not a direct party at interest and that one of my particular interests was the relationship of Yemen to US–UAR relations and beyond that to stability in the area. He said, "If shooting resumes, you will be a party at interest immediately." I nodded. "You must therefore follow this issue closely." I nodded again. "I have instructed my people to keep you completely informed on all aspects of the Yemen problem."

I expressed my gratitude and returned to my basic thesis, which was the need for continued talks. I asked whether the Haradh conf would resume. The reply was in the affirmative, but the Pres did not believe anything would come of it. I stated that as I understood the situation at present there was a possibility of talks at higher levels between the UAR and SA. The Pres stated that the UAR had suggested this some time ago and that King Feisal after first designating Prince Sultan to represent him had withdrawn from the idea. I stated that I had understood there was still a possibility of talks, not necessarily between King Feisal and Pres Nasser but at a senior level. He said no such suggestion was before him. I asked him 3 times whether I had understood him and said that I had hoped that the latest response from Saudi Arabia had included the suggestion for high level talks. Each time he denied this.

He then launched into a long discourse on his own situation. He said that King Feisal thought the economic drain was too great for the UAR to bear and that the UAR would eventually have to leave the Yemen. The UAR could stay for years as he had pointed out. I asked whether he meant at the present level of troop strength and he said, "No," that all military requirements could be met by reduction to about 50,000 or even fewer men. The current regrouping of troops is toward this eventuality if it becomes necessary.

To my surprise, the President stated that one of his main problems was the morale of the Egyptian army which would have great difficulty in accepting a defeat in the Yemen. "As you can realize, this would present real problems for me." He then said very emotionally, "I fear that a clash between the UAR and Saudi Arabia is inevitable." I said, "I do not accept that and I hope you will not. The stakes are too great to permit us to believe that there is no solution and I hope that the

Middle East and the world can count upon your patience and your wisdom to solve this difficult problem. We must not accept the inevitability of what will always be a defeat for mankind and I hope that you will continue your efforts as you have in the past to solve this problem." He replied that I could count upon him to continue to try but implied that he was discouraged.

He then said, "I understand the relationship of this problem to my relations with you and your country and I assure you we consider it carefully in that light."

After a pause we turned to Aden. I stated that we believed the British decision to grant independence to South Arabia and to close out its military installations there by 1968 provided an opportunity for constructive Arab action and was in fact exactly the development that he had sought. 1968 is close at hand and there are many problems that must be resolved in a short space of time. Political, social, and economic difficulties are many and it will take the constructive help of all concerned with peace and stability in the area to create a situation which will be helpful on the long term and offer a chance of stability. He had great influence in the area and a key factor is whether he wishes to play a constructive role which we very much hope that he will do.

I emphasized that there was great flexibility on the part of the British and on the part of all concerned with the future of Aden and South Arabia and that we must attempt to be constructive in working out solutions. The President mentioned immediately the UN resolutions but admitted very quickly that the difference between what the British had offered and the UN resolution was negligible. I said that we must try to look to realities and not form and that the opportunity that had been sought for the aspirations of the people of South Arabia could be found in the present framework.

Again I pointed to the flexibility on the part of the British in dealing with various groups in Aden and to the hope we all had for help from the UAR toward a constructive resolution of a difficult problem.

I was sure the Pres would realize that the alternative to the constructive approach I had outlined was that of a Yemen-like situation. At this point he reacted strongly, saying, "You cannot believe we would ever put troops in Aden!" I said I was not suggesting that he would but I would appreciate an interpretation of his recent speech in which he had appeared to tie his withdrawal from Yemen to the British position in Aden. There followed what he described as an explanation and which contained some elements of apology but which was in fact neither. He appeared to regret the speech as I suspect he does many of his speeches. He indicated he was talking to the British primarily and to a lesser extent to the Saudi Arabians that he had had inadequate time to prepare his notes for the speech. He assured me, however, that he did not connect the Aden situation with his own settlement of the Yemen problem. I asked whether I could assure my govt that he had not changed his position on Yemen to relate to the situation created by the planned British withdrawal. He most emphatically affirmed that I might do so.

I returned to the basic issue of Aden and to the situation created by the British decision and again asked for his constructive assistance. He stated that he did not know many of the issues in this problem in detail but that he would study them carefully in the light of what I had said and assured me he would attempt to be helpful and within the time framework that I had outlined to him. He said he would like me to have more conversations with FonMin Riad on Aden, going into more detail.

Comment: Several points struck me rather emphatically.

1. Pres Nasser still wishes a settlement of the Yemen problem but does not quite know where to go. If there is a "new element" in Saudi position (para 5 Jidda Embtel 814 to Dept)[3] he is unaware of it.

2. I believe there is still flexibility in Nasser's position provided Feisal forthcoming, but distrust is obviously great.

3. Nasser will make every effort keep us informed in hope we can be helpful.

4. This conversation was first in which he has admitted depth his concern about domestic problem military morale if defeat in Yemen obvious.

I dealt with both Yemen and Aden throughout conversation in terms their importance to US–UAR relations and at one stage referred to them in connection my continuing talks Kaissouni regarding aid which I hoped could be continued provided no new difficlties arose. I have no doubt he understood. I have been sending him messages to this effect via Eugene Black, John Badeau and others for some time, believing private expressions dangers to US–UAR relations by resumed Yemen hositilities were sometimes more effective than official expressions. In addition I have had own private talks with Kaissouni, Riad, Mustafa Abdul Aziz and Hassan Sabri al-Khouly.

It is interesting the President did not raise arms to Israel or the nuclear potential of Israel, particularly in view concern reportedly expressed in Arab PriMins meeting on these subjects.

Battle

---

[3] See footnote 4, Document 394.

396. Telegram From the Department of State to the Embassy in the United Arab Republic[1]

Washington, March 26, 1966, 3:25 p.m.

5397. Ref.: Jidda's 856 rpt info Cairo 218, London 236.[2]

1. Clear from reftel Nasser speech March 22[3] serious setback to Nasser–Faysal dialogue and progress toward peaceful settlement in Yemen. Such public statements can only impede settlement and therefore clearly inconsistent with description Nasser's attitude given earlier same day to Secretary by Amb. Kamel, who said Nasser sincerely wishes withdraw from Yemen. Therefore believe desirable you seek early meeting with Nasser to obtain clarification. On hopeful assumption Saudi-UAR differences still in fact relate to conditions of settlement and not intent, consider it important prevent possible misunderstanding and miscalculation on both sides from jeopardizing prospect solution Yemen problem. You should draw as appropriate on reftel and Deptel 5347[4] stressing:

(a) Faysal considers March 22 speech personal attack on him that belies UAR assurances to us that Nasser anxious extricate himself from Yemen in peace and with honor.

(b) Whatever motivation and intent of speech may have been, result is serious setback to progress toward peaceful settlement in Yemen. Present circumstances postpone possibility high level meeting we had hoped might break impasse and provide key to settlement.

(c) We appreciate pressures on Nasser, difficulties he faces and frustrations he feels but importance to all of peace in Yemen warrants exercise maximum patience, wisdom, hard work, sacrifice, and above

---

[1] Source: National Archives and Records Administration, RG 59, Central Files 1964–66, POL 27 YEMEN. Secret; Priority; Limdis. Drafted by Russell, cleared by Atherton, and approved by Davies. Repeated to Jidda and London.

[2] In telegram 856 from Jidda, March 24, Eilts reported that he met with the King on March 23, and once again urged an early Faisal–Nasser meeting as the best way to break the present impasse over Yemen. The Ambassador said he was aware of Nasser's March 22 speech attacking Saudi Arabia, but Nasser's speeches should be taken for what they were—emotional outbursts—and this should not be allowed to obstruct the search for a Yemen settlement. Faisal said Saudi Arabia had been trying for a long time, and noted that Nasser had said in his speech that he was prepared to stay in Yemen for 10 years. He said that in view of Nasser's speech, he was no longer willing to send a high-level person to Cairo, nor was he prepared to meet with Nasser. After much urging from Eilts, Faisal agreed that the U.S. Government might, if it wished, indicate to the United Arab Republic that he was willing to receive a high-ranking UAR official in Jidda and to designate a Saudi official of equal rank to discuss the Yemen problem with him. (Ibid.)

[3] In his speech on March 22 Nasser had threatened to attack "bases of aggression" in Saudi Arabia.

[4] Dated March 24. (Ibid.)

all quiet diplomacy. Peace with honor is two-way street, and alternatives clearly unacceptable.

(d) In light Faysal's reaction to March 22 speech and fact reply required to Faysal's message from Khartoum, next move clearly Nasser's. We believe situation offers opportunity for statesmanlike action.

(e) We believe indication by UAR of willingness send high level emissary to pay respects to King and discuss with Saudi official of equal rank such outstanding problems as exist might do much to mitigate unfortunate impression made by speech. Such meeting could provide way convey response to Faysal's latest proposals and conceivably pave way for eventual Nasser–Faysal meeting.

2. In manner you deem most appropriate, you should re-emphasize continuing U.S. interest in peaceful Yemen settlement leaving no doubt important bearing this issue on US–UAR bilateral relations and UAR hopes for new PL–480 agreement.

Rusk

---

397. Telegram From the Department of State to the Embassy in Saudi Arabia[1]

Washington, March 29, 1966, 4:42 p.m.

569. Ref Jidda's 877.[2]

1. Dept commends your handling Sultan request reftel. In addition points you made in which we concur, you may tell Sultan:

a. USG understands and sympathizes SAG concern its security and territorial integrity, which also of concern to us, and appreciates

---

[1] Source: National Archives and Records Administration, RG 59, Central Files 1964–66, POL SAUD–UAR. Secret; Priority; Limdis. Drafted by Korn; cleared by Atherton, Chief of the Near East Division in the INR Office of Research and Analysis for Near East and South Asia Harold W. Glidden, Quinn, Judd, Commander Cone of the Navy Department, Colonel Codding/Captain Zimmerman (JCS), and Meyers; and approved by Davies. Repeated to Cairo, Taiz, London, CINCSTRIKE, COMIDEASTFOR, and CHUSMTM Dhahran.

[2] In telegram 877 from Jidda, March 28, Ambassador Eilts reported that Sultan had told him that he had "reliable" information concerning UAR stockpiling of arms and ammunition in the Haradh–Abs area and a UAR troop buildup there. Sultan emphasized that his country wanted peace and did not want a resumption of fighting, but argued that, in order to be militarily prepared to defend itself in the event of a UAR attack, the Saudi Arabian Government urgently needed U.S. assistance. (Ibid., DEF 6 UAR)

Prince's informing us immediately reports he receiving re UAR military activities in Yemen border area.

b. Intelligence available USG indicates probable presence Harad–Abs area UAR commando and paratroop battalions mentioned para 2 reftel. We have nothing confirm presence other units reported by Saudis, and very much doubt UAR has ground to ground rockets in area. It possible there may have been some redeployment forces to northwestern coastal region following UAR withdrawal from eastern outposts but we doubtful this intended as prelude to offensive action against Saudi territory. It more likely that strengthening UAR forces Harad–Abs area, if true, prompted by fear possible royalist move from Jizan base to cut Sanaa–Hodeida road.

c. USG actions suggested by Sultan would merely complicate current delicate Saudi–UAR relations and might jeopardize possibility, however, slight, for Yemen settlement. USG will follow situation closely and remain in consultation with Sultan and SAG authorities. Hope Saudis will continue restrain Yemeni royalists from renewed military action, consequences of which could be serious under present circumstances.

2. FYI. Dept/DOD considering stepped up series naval visits to Saudi ports. End FYI.

3. Emb London should inform FonOff on strictly confidential basis Sultan request and US reply, expressing hope British will respond along similar lines should they be approached by Saudis.

Rusk

---

398. Telegram From the Embassy in the United Arab Republic to the Department of State[1]

Cairo, April 8, 1966, 1115Z.

2571. My April 7 conversation with President Nasser lasting just under one hour began with a discussion of my recent fishing trip to Red Sea. The President said he did not like fishing because he had to

---

[1] Source: National Archives and Records Administration, RG 59, Central Files 1964–66, POL 27 YEMEN. Secret; Limdis. Repeated to London, Aden, Taiz, and Jidda.

be patient all day every day and he found fishing an unnecessary drain on his patience. I said that regretfully I was there to ask for more patience with regard to a favorite topic of ours, Yemen.

I said that during recent months I had been convinced of President Nasser's basic desire for peace in the Yemen. I had repeatedly in reports to my government and in appearances before the Congress regarding the recent aid agreement drawn heavily on his efforts to reach a Yemen solution and praised his statesmanlike conduct, particularly in reaching the Jidda agreement. I was aware of the frustrations that the Yemen problem had caused him and of the continued requirement on him for wisdom and patience. I was now perplexed. The Department of State had asked me to reconcile my convictions of his basic purpose with his recent public statements, particularly the March 22 speech which had had unfortunate repercussions. For example, King Feisal had considered the speech an attack upon himself (Nasser nodded). On our side, we considered that the changes for a high level meeting between the UAR and Saudi Arabia were lessened by the speech. In effect what I hoped he would do was to write my report for me. How could I respond to my Dept's request for clarification of my own sympathetic view of his basic aim toward peace with what he had said publicly.

"The answer," he said, "is that we have given up. King Feisal believed when I entered into the Jidda agreement that it was a move from weakness but it was not. It was a move to avoid a clash between the United Arab Republic and Saudi Arabia. That clash now is before us." The avoidance of this clash was the basis for Nasser's efforts to reach the Jidda agreement which he now considered no longer existed. "The Jidda agreement is finished. There is no agreement. As I told you last time, we are consolidating our troops and will withdraw in large numbers, perhaps even up to half of them, but we can stay in Yemen for ten years. We are not weak. This does not cost us as much as Feisal thinks it does. It does not cost foreign currency. The present cost is 35 to 40 million pounds a year and with the steps I propose we can reduce that cost to something like 20 to 25 million." He stressed that this does not mean a resumption of hostilities by the UAR but that what happens depends on the Saudis.

I said that if he intended to withdraw, why could he not withdraw as part of his efforts to implement the Jidda agreement. Perhaps a concession toward implementing that agreement by him would bring concessions from the other side and this new situation might engender new possibilities of a solution. "This is impossible as the Jidda agreement is one piece," he said. "If I claim to implement that agreement by a withdrawal of troops, I am prevented from reentering Yemen if at a later date hostilities have been resumed and they need my assistance."

But if the other side resumes hostilities, this will be a new situation, I pointed out, and we must look upon the Yemen problem step by step. He repeated that the Jidda agreement is one piece and cannot be partially fulfilled unless the total understanding can be implemented.

I reaffirmed the need for patience and quiet diplomacy. He responded by stating that he could not do what the Saudis do—to talk one way and act another. Either there was a basic understanding and friendship between two countries or there was not. He could not pretend publicly what did not exist in fact and therefore must state what he felt to be the realities of the situation with respect to dealing with the problem. The Egyptian people have a deep interest in the Yemen and a right to know the situation.

I repeated that this problem could not be dealt with publicly. There must be a restrained quiet effort toward solution if there is a chance of improvement in the present outlook. He replied, "I have been restrained—there is much more I could say about the Saudis than I have said. They are spending money in Kuwait, Beirut, and other places against us. I know that but I have refrained from talking about it."

I pointed out that my country still hoped that a dialogue between the UAR and the Saudis could be resumed and in the light of the present situation the Saudis considered the next move up to Nasser. They believed that they had not had an answer to the Feisal communication from Khartoum. (The President shrugged indignantly.) I had reason to believe that an initiative by the UAR to send a high level rep to Jidda to pay respects to the King and to resume discussions at the level of the rep would be well received. The President replied most emphatically, "This is impossible." Later I brought up the matter again and the President said, "We will receive a rep from the Saudi Arabians but I will not initiate it and I cannot send anyone there at present." I then pointed out that my country wished to be helpful in this problem within the limits of its judgement that it could not mediate this complex intra-Arab problem but could only contribute to keeping a climate between the two countries which left hope for continued discussions. My own concern stemmed from my knowledge that the Yemen and its closely related problem of the Aden loomed large on the horizon as a problem between our two countries and this I sought to avoid as I had sought to avoid or remove any problems that might create difficulties between our two countries. I asked whether the President had any suggestions for me in this context and he said that he did not. He wishes us to be informed completely and thoroughly on his actions on the Yemen and will be happy to talk with me at any time since he knew of our interest in the Yemen.

During the conversation the President again mentioned the problem with the army. "If we bring it back, I can control it," he said, "but it will not be easy. I can make speeches and explain the situation and they will respond." (He seemed less than convinced on this point.)

I asked whether the President had had any further thoughts with respect to Aden since we last talked, indicating that this problem was closely related to the Yemen. He said that he had no suggestions. I repeated that we must look for constructive answers to the problem raised by the projected British withdrawal and wished to assure him again of the high degree of flexibility the British appeared to have on this matter. I urged that he look toward constructive action which would bring about stability and a government in Aden that reflected the will of the people—a goal he had long had.

As I rose to go he said there was one problem he wished to discuss with me. He had been informed this morning of my talk with Dr. Kaissouni on rice (see Embtel 2554),[2] and he considered our decision to exercise the option as a "threat." I said this was not the case and the exercise of the option stemmed, I was sure, from the general problem of food with which the US was faced around the world. He then said, "We have no rice. We cannot give you fifty thousand tons." He mentioned my discussion with Dr. Kaissouni about the Indian food problem and the copy of the President's message re India which I had given Kaissouni. He then stated, "India has its problems and we have ours."

The President referred to the US decision to exercise the option in a manner suggesting that he believed it stemmed from his recent public remarks on the subject of rice. I said I had accepted his assurances on many matters, and hoped he would accept mine on this one. The decision to exercise the option on rice had already been made before his speech and was not an outgrowth of those remarks. He indicated he would accept my assurances, but I do not believe he is convinced of the truth of my statement. I indicated that I was going into the facts of the rice situation in Egypt with Kaissouni and said that the understanding permitted the option to be met from rice from next season's crop.

With respect to American aid he said he did not even like to discuss this subject. He wished that relations between us did not involve aid but he had the problem of his people and the development of the country and while his job would be easier as President if he could ignore aid, he could not do so. You are giving us now only wheat and the economic assistance which we had hoped for and had been promised in the early days of President Johnson's administration has not been forthcoming. I referred to the importance of the wheat and

---

[2] Dated April 7. (Ibid., INCO–RICE UAR)

other various private credits which had been extended to the UAR and said that I hoped that the climate of our relations would continue to improve and that eventually other forms of aid might be introduced into the UAR. I only hoped that problems such as Aden and the Yemen would not cloud our relations in which there had been such marked improvement in recent months.

In the last moments of my conversation I urged the President to adhere to his basic goal which, as I understood it, was still peace and a UAR withdrawal from the Yemen and to find a way to bring this about. I asked whether the Harad conference would be resumed and whether we could look for progress in this context. He said that it would be resumed but would amount to nothing.

"I have a speech coming on May first," he said, "and I must continue to talk about the Yemen and I must discuss the Islamic pact." "But you must remember," I said, "that there is a great need to maintain flexibility in your position in order to respond to new situations that we hope will emerge and which will make resumption of talks between you and Saudi Arabia possible."

Comment: The conversation was at all times cordial, at times light and amusing, but in other moments very ominous. The President came very near to an explosion on the matter of rice and seemed very badly informed on the matter, referring to the fact that we were only going to pay 25 percent in dollars. I corrected this impression by saying this was entirely a pound transaction and diverted the conversation by saying I would talk further with Kaissouni about the matter.

I am very depressed about the chances of a Yemen settlement at this time and regretfully conclude that Nasser has decided at least for the present to remain there. This does not mean that he is not capable of changing his position quickly and completely for no apparent reason but such a shift seems a remote hope at present. Therefore we must decide the limits of our tolerance in the Yemen and must formulate a contingent policy based on the several possibilities that exist, ranging from stalemate to resumption of major hostilities. A separate telegram is being submitted regarding this matter.[3]

Battle

---

[3] Not further identified.

399.   Memorandum of Conversation[1]

Washington, April 12, 1966.

SUBJECT

Yemen

PARTICIPANTS

The Secretary
H.E. Mohsin A. al-Aini—Ambassador of the Yemen Arab Republic
NEA—Raymond A. Hare, Assistant Secretary
NE—Alfred L. Atherton, Jr.

The Secretary opened the conversation by enquiring when the Harad Conference would resume. Ambassador al-Aini said no date had yet been set but in any case no results were possible until Cairo and Riyadh had reached agreement on a Yemen settlement. At the Secretary's request, Ambassador al-Aini then reviewed the origins and principal issues of the Yemen conflict. Emphasizing that he was giving his own assessment and not reflecting the views of his government, the Ambassador made the following points:

(1) The 1962 revolution in Yemen had been unrelated to the Arab "cold war," but Saudi Arabia and the U.A.R. had made Yemen a cold war battlefield.

(2) Attempts by the Yemenis to solve their own problems had been frustrated by Saudi support for the royal Hamid al-Din family and by the U.A.R.'s refusal to withdraw its troops.

(3) Any attempt to return the Hamid al-Din family to power would prolong the Yemen conflict indefinitely, since it would not only be opposed by the Yemenis themselves but would threaten complete defeat for the U.A.R. and thus be totally unacceptable to Nasser.

(4) The Jidda Agreement had been unworkable from the beginning. A plebiscite in Yemen was difficult to envisage under the best of circumstances. If held one year after formation of a provisional government, as agreed at Jidda, a plebiscite would subject the country to a year of outside political pressures and maneuverings. An immediate plebiscite (which the Ambassador later defined as a plebiscite immediately after departure of the last U.A.R. troops) would be preferable, though still of doubtful feasibility. A solution better suited to Yemeni conditions would be an elected council of tribal representatives from which should be excluded members of the Hamid al-Din family on

---

[1] Source: National Archives and Records Administration, RG 59, Central Files 1964–66, POL 27 YEMEN. Confidential. Drafted by Atherton and approved in S on May 23.

the royalist side (the Ambassador subsequently said this meant eight to ten individuals at most) and members of the Sallal group on the republican side.

(5) There were some on both sides who benefited from the present situation, but the Yemeni people were the losers. While a solution now would be difficult to achieve, it would be much more difficult later—say five years from now.

(6) The Ambassador had discussed Yemen with Anwar Sadat during the latter's visit to the United States and had concluded that Cairo's new Yemen strategy was extremely dangerous. That strategy, as the Ambassador saw it, was to prepare for a long stay, while minimizing the cost to the U.A.R. by consolidating the Egyptian position in south Yemen where the U.A.R. had concentrated its efforts from the beginning. This would relieve the U.A.R. of responsibility for holding the difficult mountain areas but leave it in a position to launch air strikes against those areas whenever it felt this necessary. To relate his new strategy to future developments in Aden, as Nasser had done, was purely a pretext. It would not bring stability to Yemen or South Arabia; only the evacuation of U.A.R. troops and formation of a unified Yemeni government would do that.

(7) The "main and only solution" was to convince Saudi Arabia that it must guarantee the removal of the Hamid al-Din family from Yemeni political life. This would not be a defeat for Saudi Arabia, but a success for all concerned. Nasser and the Yemeni Republicans would then accept the "State (as opposed to the Republic) of Yemen" formulation, would agree to the exclusion of President Sallal and his followers, and U.A.R. troops would be withdrawn.

(8) If the U.A.R. were to withdraw before the threat of a return of the royal family had been eliminated, a number of Republicans would turn for support to the Russians and the Chinese, who now had a significant presence in Yemen.

(9) In summary, the essential elements of a Yemen settlement were: (a) elimination from Yemeni affairs of the Hamid al-Din family and of Sallal and his followers; (b) withdrawal of U.A.R. troops; (c) an end to Egyptian and Saudi interference in Yemen; (d) Yemeni neutrality with respect to inter-Arab differences. If these conditions were agreed upon, the United Nations could play a helpful role in guaranteeing that they were carried out. It was essential, however, that they constitute a single package. A piecemeal approach would not work.

The Secretary asked a number of specific questions about the Harad Conference of November–December, 1965, to which Ambassador al-Aini replied along the following lines:

(1) Harad failed primarily because the Saudis refused to permit the Conference to deal with the future of the Hamid al-Din family.

Having been assured by Nasser that exclusion of the royal family from a future Yemeni government had already been agreed upon, the Yemeni delegates discovered at Harad that this was not so and that the subject was not one they could settle at the Conference. The impression was conveyed to the Conference that King Faisal supported the Hamid al-Dins. This had the effect of strengthening Nasser's hand and dividing the conferees along pro-Hamid al-Din and pro-Sallal lines. In fact, however, there were no royalists outside the royal family itself. It was opposition to the U.A.R. presence in Yemen, not support for the Hamid al-Din, which united the "royalists."

(2) If it had not been for Saudi and U.A.R. pressures at Harad, and if there had been a firm guarantee that the royal family would have no future political role in Yemen, the delegates at Harad could have reached agreement on a "State of Yemen" solution. The Khamr Conference of May, 1965, had demonstrated that, if left to themselves, Yemenis could achieve an all-Yemen solution. The Government which emerged from that conference (with Ahmad Numan as Prime Minister and Ambassador al-Aini as Foreign Minister) had represented all elements of Yemeni opinion. It had not won Saudi support, however, and efforts to elicit the support of other Arab governments had failed. Finally, the Numan government had been actively opposed by Nasser, and this had led to its ultimate collapse. The Khamr Conference had nevertheless revealed the basic weakness of Nasser's position in Yemen at that time. It was thus the Yemenis themselves, not Faisal, who had obliged Nasser to conclude the Jidda Agreement. (The Secretary requested Ambassador al-Aini to send him copies of the Khamr Conference resolutions.)

The Secretary said it appeared from what Ambassador al-Aini had said that two basic questions were involved. The first was what would happen within Yemen. This was for the Yemenis themselves to decide, hopefully with a maximum degree of solidarity. The second related to the tensions between Saudi Arabia and the U.A.R. The latter problem, however, had become interwoven with the first. He wondered if the Yemenis could not find some way—perhaps through the United Nations—to show the world that they were prepared to agree among themselves. Perhaps this would have a good effect on Saudi Arabia and the U.A.R. He had a feeling that the problem was less one of Saudi emphasis on the Yemeni royal family than it was of simply making the voice of the Yemeni people heard in the world. Though he might be quite wrong, a Yemen settlement seemed just out of reach and might be achieved if the Yemenis could get together and make their voice heard. What role could the United Nations play?

Ambassador al-Aini replied that the U.N. could supervise the implementation of any agreement that might be reached. The previous

U.N. effort in connection with the Bunker Mission had not been fruitful because, largely due to Nasser's opposition, there had been no true agreement for the U.N. to supervise. If an agreement were now reached, there would be a role for the U.N. to play. The difficulty was that responsible Yemenis were too disillusioned and exhausted, too disappointed by the failure of the revolution, to seek a solution now on their own. They had come to feel that the matter was no longer in their hands. There were many like himself who were neither pro-U.A.R. nor pro-Saudi and who had nowhere to turn. In the Ambassador's opinion the United States, as a friend of all concerned, was in the best position to help.

The Secretary said that our influence was more limited than the Ambassador seemed to imply but we would give thoughtful consideration to this problem. He continued to believe, however, that the important thing was to make the voice of Yemeni solidarity heard in the world—perhaps through a new Harad Conference, which was after all a device that both Saudi Arabia and the U.A.R. had accepted. Wouldn't it be difficult for Saudi Arabia and the U.A.R. to reject a Government on which the Yemenis themselves had agreed?

Ambassador al-Aini thought it might be useful to seek support in other Arab capitals but outside of the Arab League framework. Earlier in the conversation he had noted that the Ruler of Kuwait was now in Cairo, reportedly to discuss Yemen, and that the Kuwaiti Foreign Minister had recently visited Saudi Arabia and had expressed hope that Kuwait might be able to play a useful role.

Turning to U.S.–Y.A.R.G. relations, Ambassador al-Aini praised the Taiz Municipal Water System, an A.I.D. project, and suggested similar projects in such places as Sanaa and Hodeida. Such projects were a demonstration of American support for the Yemeni people and unrelated to the republican-royalist conflict. The Ambassador also urged that the United States provide more scholarships for Yemeni students. Only about twelve Yemenis had been sent to the United States to study since the revolution, whereas hundreds had gone to the Eastern Bloc. The Secretary replied that we would look into both of these matters. Finally, Ambassador al-Aini urged that U.S. PL–480 wheat deliveries to Yemen continue.

400. Telegram From the Embassy in Saudi Arabia to the Department of State[1]

Jidda, May 2, 1966, 0808Z.

1040. King Faisal's comments on Yemen.

1. By prearrangement, Ambassador Hare[2] and I called on King April 30 in Riyadh. Meeting lasted more than two hours, was extremely cordial and informal. King warmly welcomed "long time friend" and after a while decided session should be considered "family" rather than official gathering and did rare thing invite us smoke. Also present were Prince Sultan (who made special flight from Jidda to be there), Saqqaf and Rashed Pharaon. After extending invitation to King visit US (septel)[3] Hare alluded to Sultan's able presentation of King's views to President, Secretaries Rusk and McNamara and others during MODA's recent visit to US. King and Sultan obviously pleased.

2. Most of meeting devoted to discussion of Yemen. Hare recalled his own previous connection with Yemen while Amb to Saudi Arabia. At his request, King then outlined background and status current Kuwaiti mediation effort. Noted Kuwaiti FonMin's recent visit to Saudi Arabia and UAR during which both sides had outlined their points of view. Kuwaitis have said they plan bring Khouli to Riyadh to discuss outstanding issues with Saudis, but SAG has heard nothing further about any dates for such visit. Kuwaiti FonMin also indicated his readiness join any such session to help parties minimize areas of disagreement. King said he agreeable such meeting, but was noncommittal on prospects for success.

3. This led King into lengthy review of development of Yemeni problem with emphasis on Nasser's failure comply with various agreements reached with him, despite lip service of willingness to do so. King specifically mentioned Bunker agreement, Alexandria conference and most recent Jidda agreement. Saudis, King insisted, have done all possible facilitate Nasser's withdrawal from Yemen with honor and dignity. Haradh conference aborted because of UAR failure tell YAR leaders of obligations assumed by Nasser in Jidda agreement. In contrast, Saudis have kept Yemeni royalists under control. Indeed Yemeni royalists were displeased with some aspects Jidda agreement, but King

---

[1] Source: National Archives and Records Administration, RG 59, Central Files 1964–66, POL 27 YEMEN. Secret. Repeated to Cairo for Ambassador Hare, London, and Taiz.

[2] Assistant Secretary Hare was on a trip to the Near East during which he visited several other capitals, including Amman, Beirut, Cairo, and Tel Aviv.

[3] Reference is to telegram 1038 from Jidda, May 2. (National Archives and Records Administration, RG 59, Central Files 1964–66, POL 7 SAUD)

had insisted they must accept it. Hare noted Secretary's strong view that Yemenis must ultimately decide their own form of govt. King said this also his view and referred to two major outstanding issues of composition interim govt and Hamid ad-Dins. Implication his comments was that Saudi positions on these two items intended allow Yemenis themselves to choose.

4. King's account was largely re-hash of what he and other senior Saudi officials have repeatedly related to us. Throughout session King kept reiterating unanswered question "Why" has Nasser apparently changed his position. He cited various reasons adduced by "some people" for this. One is that "outside" forces are pressing him to do so. (Pharaon here interjected account of Nasser's trip to Moscow few days after Jidda agreement. Thereafter Nasser had seemingly taken new tack.) Another is that Nasser afraid of reaction of UAR military to any withdrawal. Third is possible desire move into Aden vacuum when Brits leave. There even "some people" who argue USG wants Nasser remain in Yemen in order lessen prospects of Arab-Israeli clash. King noted all of foregoing conjecture and confessed he unable fathom reasons for Nasser's seeming change. He was deeply puzzled about it and its implications. He wondered if USG had any info which might throw light on Nasser's current position on Nasser's seeming turnabout on Yemen.

5. Hare disclaimed any special USG knowledge of what might be prompting Nasser's action. He asked King if His Majesty knew of anything internal in UAR which might have some bearing on Nasser position. King said he did not. King noted immediate aspect of problem watched by SAG is border situation where Egyptian military has regrouped. Sultan interjected account of recent intrusion several UAR tanks into Saudi territory about which he claimed he had not heretofore told King. Fortunately there had been no firing and Egyptians had subsequently apologized for incident and claimed tanks got lost. (This presumable same incident reported Embtel 1024.)[4] Sultan noted that if single Saudi or Egyptian soldier had panicked and started shooting situation could quickly have deteriorated.

6. Hare commended King's statesmanship in exercising patience and restraint in present admittedly difficult situation. Hare noted that our relations with UAR can hardly be described as satisfactory, but as with other difficult states we continue to try to keep dialogue going. King agreed on need for patience, but wondered how long forebearance can be continued. Sultan noted UAR has regularly been bombing certain Yemeni royalist villages last few weeks.

---

[4] Dated April 28. (Ibid., DEF 12–5 SAUD)

7. *Comment:* While nothing startlingly new came out of lengthy Yemen discussion, opportunity for King get things off his chest with senior American official from Washington was useful. Have subsequently been told by Saqqaf that King very satisfied with meeting. One point of passing interest, apropos of nothing, was comment by King in discussing Kuwaiti mediation effort that Kuwaitis quoted Nasser as telling them USG had told Sadat that Sultan had complained to Secretary about Soviet installations which UAR allegedly permitting be built on UAR territory. King's purpose relating this round robin exposition unclear, and he did not pursue point.

Eilts

401.   Telegram From the Department of State to the Embassy in Yemen[1]

Washington, May 5, 1966, 5 p.m.

247. Your 414[2] and 419.[3]

1. While major decisions re future Yemen rest with Saudis and UAR, Yemenis themselves continue have possibility wrecking attempts reach settlement. Inflammatory statements of type reported reftel are particularly destructive and seem represent to some degree Yemeni abdication responsibility.

2. Request at your discretion you discuss subject along following lines with appropriate high level Yemeni officials:

a. Continued USG policy is to work for cessation foreign interference Yemen and freedom Yemenis decide own future. Our recognition and support of Republic are manifestations this approach.

---

[1] Source: National Archives and Records Administration, RG 59, Central Files 1964–66, POL 27 YEMEN. Secret. Drafted by Moore, cleared by Symmes, and approved by Davies. Repeated to Cairo, Jidda, London, and CINCSTRIKE.

[2] Telegram 414 from Taiz, May 3, reported that the Yemeni news media had published statements by six top YARG leaders, including Prime Minister al-Amri, supporting Nasser's May Day speech. Al-Amri was quoted as saying that Nasser had expressed what was in the heart of every Yemeni, particularly regarding the aims of the revolution and the desire to regain the stolen parts of Yemen. (Ibid., POL 15–1 UAR) In his speech, Nasser had threatened to seize Najran and Jizan and return those provinces to Yemen.

[3] Dated May 5. (Ibid.)

b. Since termination Bunker Agreement we have tried avoid taking direct role in mediation efforts, but nonetheless have continued exert all feasible efforts encourage Saudis and UAR reach settlement and avoid hostilities.

c. Statements attributed YARG leaders in Yemeni news media May 2–3 inflame situation and make more difficult attempts by US and other friendly countries to ease Yemen problem. After three years fighting, Yemenis must share our hopes for return of peace and stability to country. We fail see that heightened UAR–Saudi tension furthers these goals.

d. We strongly urge YARG leaders contribute to our and others' efforts by avoiding such pronouncements.[4]

Rusk

---

[4] In telegram 429 from Taiz, May 9, Clark reported that he had met on May 8 with Foreign Minister Makki, to whom he had expressed his own great personal disappointment over developments and presented the Department's views regarding recent UAR and YAR statements. (Ibid., POL 27 YEMEN)

---

402.   Memorandum of Conversation[1]

Washington, June 22, 1966.

SUBJECT

Secretary Rusk's Meeting with King Faisal

PARTICIPANTS

King Faisal	The Secretary
Prince Sultan	Ambassador Raymond A. Hare, NEA
Dr. Rashad Pharaon	Ambassador Hermann F. Eilts
Ambassador Ibrahim al-Sowayel	Mr. George C. Moore, NEA:NE
	Mr. Isa Sabbagh (Interpreter)

The King opened the discussion with a general query about DeGaulle's visit to the U.S.S.R. The Secretary said we did not expect any surprises; that there had been some movement among the Eastern European countries for closer relations with Western Europe, but we

---

[1] Source: National Archives and Records Administration, RG 59, Central Files 1964–66, POL 7 SAUD. Secret. Drafted by Moore on June 24 and approved in S on July 14. The memorandum is Part I of II. For other memoranda of conversations recording King Faisal's meetings with President Johnson and Secretary Rusk during his June 21–23 visit to Washington, see Documents 274–278.

continued to treat signs that the Communist countries wanted a détente with considerable caution in the light of our past experience with them. The King expressed his view that no one could believe the promises of Leftists. He continued to endorse fully our firm positions in Vietnam and Berlin and hoped that we would be equally firm in not pulling out of the Near East.

The Secretary said we, as the only free world country capable of independent action, must take a global view of the Communist problem. We watch the situation in the Near East very closely. It is clear that the U.S.S.R. wants to build its policy around Nasser. Nasser goes along with this up to a point, but where his limits lie is not clear.

Concerning Yemen, the Secretary affirmed our hope that the U.A.R. would withdraw its troops. He noted, however, that with more troops in Egypt, the possibility existed for the U.A.R. to move toward the east, which would result in a full scale war; to the west, where we had our important base in Libya; or to the south, which would create a large problem with the Sudan and would not be welcome by the Africans. With these possibilities in mind he asked for the King's view concerning the strategic importance of the withdrawal of Egyptian troops from Yemen. He added that they had already spoken of the impact that these troops would have within Egypt itself, but that was Nasser's problem, not ours.

In response, the King suggested that consideration of Egyptian military movements to the east, west or south of the country was basically hypothetical. He did not think Nasser would have the interest or capability of taking such action. The practical realities were whether the Egyptians would or would not withdraw from Yemen. In his view, their staying in Yemen would have far more serious repercussions than would their return. (The Secretary interjected, "I agree".) The King continued that the presence of Egyptian troops in Yemen deprived the Yemenis of that domestic stability which is essential for improving their lot and would continue to pose a constant source of fear, particularly for the Gulf and South Arabian states. It would allow the Communists firmly to establish themselves among the Yemeni masses, not just in the government and army, and threaten development of another Vietnam. The King's fear was not particularly that he would be attacked, but concerned the long range penetration of the Communists which is abetted by the presence of U.A.R. troops in Yemen.

The King said he knew Nasser personally and was certain that he was not a believing Communist, particularly because he believes in nothing except his own personal domination. For this he would follow any ideological line necessary. He said this with pain since, when he spoke of Nasser, he spoke in a sense of a part of himself, for Nasser was an Arab, was counted among the Muslims, and was for a long time a good personal friend.

The King said he had recently received information that the U.A.R. had now returned 5,000 troops to Yemen, more than balancing earlier withdrawals.

The Secretary commented that maintaining troops in Yemen posed real problems for the U.A.R., not just economic ones, but other types. Among these were the growing opposition to the Egyptian presence among many Yemeni republicans, and the increasing dissatisfaction with and suspicion of U.A.R. activities by other Arab countries.

Responding to the Secretary's query about possibilities for the success of the Kuwait mediation effort,[2] the King said that he, just as the Secretary, had had hopes regarding the Jidda Agreement but that this was the third agreement on which Nasser had reneged. He attributed this to Nasser's fluctuating psychology which led him at times to be conciliatory (as when he went to Jidda) and a few days later to change to a mood of personal recalcitrance. With appropriate good will, a negotiated solution is always possible, but if that solution is to reflect solely Nasser's desires, then it is not possible. The King emphasized that the Kuwait proposals were clearly only Egyptian proposals, as shown by the timing of their presentation to him. He listed them as: 1) formation of a transitional government on a 50–50 basis; 2) that government to request withdrawal of U.A.R. troops (to be guaranteed by Nasser), withdrawal of the Hamid al-Din (to be guaranteed by Saudi Arabia); and a symbolic presence of up to 100 troops from each of several Arab countries to assist with the plebiscite. The King said he had problems with this, among them being that his agreement to this general proposal would displace the specific U.A.R.-Saudi accord reached in the Jidda Agreement, and instead would involve some type of projected accord between each country and the transitional government. The stipulation concerning the Hamid al-Din was difficult. As previously agreed, he would fully support requests by a transitional government, after withdrawal of Egyptian forces, for exclusion of any person or group. Additionally, the Hamid al-Din do not take orders from him and were not necessarily always amenable to his proposals.

---

[2] Telegram 3129 from Cairo, June 6, reported Ambassador Battle's discussion of Kuwaiti efforts to mediate the Yemen conflict with al-Khouli, who had just returned from Kuwait. The initial Kuwaiti proposal called for formation of a transitional Yemeni government (50 percent republican and 50 percent royalist) which would: set the date for a plebiscite in Yemen; ask Cairo to withdraw UAR troops from Yemen; ask Saudi Arabia to withdraw the Hamid al-Din family from Yemen; and ask the Arab League to send token forces to Yemen to help maintain order in collaboration with equal strength Saudi and UAR forces. (National Archives and Records Administration, RG 59, Central Files 1964–66, POL 27 YEMEN)

If the Hamid al-Din decided to remain, despite implementation of the Kuwait proposals, it was conceivable that the Saudis, as a party to those proposals, would have to send troops against the ex-royal family. The Jidda Agreement continued to be the basis for the Saudi position. In this they had agreed that the transitional government would be the sole authority in the country, absorbing both republicans and royalists. Basically the Kuwait—which should be considered Egyptian— proposals are all contained in the Jidda Agreement. The new suggestions are just a smokescreen. Concerning troop withdrawal, the Jidda Agreement had no ambiguities: Egyptian troops were to begin withdrawal on the date of the Haradh Conference and to complete it within 10 months.

The King sent for a copy of the letter containing the actual Saudi responses to the Kuwait proposal. These were: 1) adherence to the Jidda Agreement in letter and spirit; 2) adherence to the text of the Agreement, noting particularly that the first four articles discuss the desire for a solution in accordance with the desires of the Yemeni people and therefore provide for a transitional government, and that both the U.A.R. and Saudis are committed to assist this government; 3) the solution should involve (a) renewed Haradh Conference; (b) the name "state of Yemen"; (c) the government during the transitional period to be formed on a 50–50 royalist-republican basis (as was the clearly implied intent of the Jidda Agreement, reflected in the proposed proportion of representation at the Haradh Conference); (d) members of the transitional government to be appointed by the Haradh Conference; (e) both republicans and royalists to support the transitional government and not disturb the peace during the transitional period; (f) both the U.A.R. and Saudi Arabia agree to support implementation of the transitional government's decisions; (g) Egyptian troops to be withdrawn in a time period to be established, but not to exceed 5 to 6 months; (h) the Saudis to refrain from giving military aid to the royalists; (i) the transitional government to have the right to expel any person or group considered a threat to the people or whose presence would exert undue influence on the plebiscite; (j) symbolic forces of not more than 100 to be requested from Kuwait, Sudan, Libya, and Morocco to assist in supervision of the plebiscite.

The Secretary asked if the problem could be approached piecemeal with, for instance, the King and Nasser first agreeing to establish a transitional government on a 50–50 basis and then moving to the next step. He asked this because he had the impression that the Yemenis on both sides were becoming most restive with continued presence of the Egyptians and because he felt such a group, agreed to by Yemenis of both persuasions, would get very strong international support. He added that this query arose only from our interest, that he was not volunteering as a mediator.

The King said he had as yet not heard of any reaction from Cairo to the current proposals but believed that Nasser—as the probable author of the proposals—would doubtless agree to a 50–50 representation.

The Secretary said we continued to follow the situation with great interest, are keenly interested in peace in the area and believe withdrawal of Egyptian troops would contribute to this objective. We were at a relatively low point in our up-and-down relationship with Cairo, and our influence there was thus very limited.

403. Telegram From the Embassy in Saudi Arabia to the Department of State[1]

Jidda, July 7, 1966, 1230Z.

67. Jidda 36 (Notal).[2] Kuwaiti Mediation Effort.

1. In my first talk with King July 6 since his and my return to Jidda (Jidda 66),[3] I recalled our conversation in car en route JFK airport June 30 when King told me had just received details latest UAR proposal as conveyed by Kuwaitis. King's initial reaction had been UAR proposal represented retrograde step over what Kuwaitis had earlier led SAG to believe was Nasser's position (Jidda 1272),[4] but King had wished study matter further following his return to Saudi Arabia. I asked King if he had any further thoughts on subject and about status of Saudi reply. King answered SAG still studying latest UAR proposals. Dr. Pharaon currently drafting reply for his consideration. Observed he personally had not had much opportunity since his return to consider question further in view heavy accumulated backlog of work.

2. I recalled Secretary's observation to King that most important aspect Yemen problem is to get UAR troops out (Deptel 867).[5] In this

---

[1] Source: National Archives and Records Administration, RG 59, Central Files 1964–66, POL 27 YEMEN. Secret; Limdis. Repeated to Beirut, Cairo, Kuwait, London, and Taiz.

[2] Dated July 5. (Ibid.)

[3] Dated July 7. (Ibid., POL 7 SAUD)

[4] Dated June 13. (Ibid., POL 27 YEMEN)

[5] Telegram 867 to Jidda, June 24, summarized the Secretary's June 22 conversation with King Faisal. (Ibid., POL 7 SAUD)

context I stressed need keep dialogue going and expressed hope that King not overlook any practical opportunity achieve this aim even though some price might have to be paid for it. While caution clearly needed in dealing with Nasser, I urged that King earnestly consider further areas of "give" which would not jeopardize Saudi security. Where King felt he could not agree to UAR proposals as advanced by Kuwaitis, I further urged he offer constructive counter proposals. Seemed to me that area of disagreement was being reduced, even though slowly and painfully, and it important effort do so continue. In this context it also important that ways be sought give Nasser honorable way out.

3. King listened carefully. Re last point, claimed he had been seeking offer Nasser honorable way out of Yemen for last three years. Trouble is Nasser cannot be trusted. He recalled had agreed with Secretary's view on importance getting UAR troops out. He also recalled Secretary's observation that perhaps problem could be tackled piecemeal, first by setting up Yemeni interim govt on 50–50 basis and carrying on from there. Latter would have been consistent with earlier Kuwaiti proposal which Saudis believed Kuwaitis had first cleared with UAR. Latest UAR proposal, as conveyed by Kuwaitis, drops equal representation in interim govt and deliberately seeks weigh govt on republican side. King emphasized he not prepared give UAR diplomatic victory in Yemen when its massive military interventions had failed to achieve this.

4. King then dwelt on UAR insistence that he specifically agree to exclusion Hamid ad-Din. Reiterated he had no interest in Hamid ad-Din or anyone else in Yemen, but claimed sole purpose Nasser desire name Hamid ad-Dins is to achieve by political means what UAR has failed achieve militarily. King candidly admitted that Hamid ad-Din family, with all its shortcomings, is currently core of royalist cause. In King's view, the moment he specifically agrees to exclusion Hamid ad-Din, royalist cause will disintegrate and transform into tribal rabble. Nasser knows this which is sole reason, King insisted, that Nasser is so persistent about point. Moment King agrees to specific exclusion Hamid ad-Din, Nasser will leak word of it. Thereafter, he will jettison any guarantee he has given and keep in Yemen whatever number UAR troops remain there. This is constant Nasser tactic. I argued any such effort by Nasser to renege on solemn guarantee would mobilize world public opinion against him. King dismissed argument saying world public opinion, even if it could be mounted which he doubted, had never deterred Nasser from overt or covert activities against other states.

5. King continued his position remains that interim Yemeni Govt, if constituted on mutually agreeable basis, should be authorized ex-

clude any Yemenis whose continued presence is believed to be harmful to stability, but that he would not agree to specific exclusion Hamid ad-Din except after last UAR soldier out. Thereafter Yemeni people could decide in plebiscite or any other way type of govt they want for future and persons they want in it. If such Yemeni Govt wants financial help, SAG, along with other states, would be prepared consider such help.

6. I said I appreciated King's position, but cautioned against SAG appearing inflexible. If latest proposals not fully agreeable, I again urged that constructive counter proposals be offered. For example, would 2/5–3/5 ratio be so bad if Yemeni third force were charged to republican side. In any event, once UAR troops out, there likely be considerable realignment of political forces in Yemen on both sides with various what are now republican and royalist elements crisscrossing to form new groupings. I understood anti-Egyptianism rampant in Yemen which should offer some safeguard against UAR influence. As for Hamid ad-Din, could they perhaps be kept out during period of interim govt before plebiscite or perhaps they might be withdrawn after larger number UAR troops out than half but before all are out. I stressed I was advancing purely personal thoughts solely for illustrative purpose to identify possible further areas of "give" which might be explored in order to achieve principle aim getting UAR troops out. King, in his wisdom, Dr Pharaon and other Saudi officials intimately acquainted with Yemeni situation could doubtless devise other even better alternatives which would show SAG willingness compromise, yet prove viable. Important thing was that SAG–UAR dialogue carry on. King said SAG would do utmost, but noted "after three years of futile talks, UAR has tired US on Yemen just as USG efforts with North Vietnam to find peaceful solution have tired you." I seized on this to remind King that, despite all frustrations of Vietnam, President has made it clear USG continues search for peaceful solution and is doing so. I hoped King would do likewise in Yemeni situation. King merely responded "I will continue to do my best."

7. I shall also seek opportunity discuss matter with Dr Pharaon next few days. Deptel 1924 July 6[6] just received. I believe my remarks consistent with it.

Eilts

---

[6] Telegram 1924 to Jidda, July 6, endorsed the Ambassador's intention to further explore with the King specific areas of give in the Saudi position, and instructed him to encourage Faisal not to overlook any practical possibilities for achieving withdrawal of UAR troops from Yemen. (Ibid., POL 27 YEMEN)

404. Telegram From the Department of State to the Embassy in Yemen[1]

Washington, July 23, 1966, 10:44 a.m.

13996. Subject: Request for US Financial Aid. Ref: Taiz 79,[2] 80.[3]

1. While sympathizing with Yemeni efforts establish moderate government, believe it most important we avoid any impression of partisan involvement in factional Yemeni domestic politics. On this basis you should continue discourage requests for US assistance such as reported reftels.

2. If responsible YARG group subsequently requests UN role, we would be willing consider sympathetically what we could do to help in light of circumstances at time of request.

Rusk

---

[1] Source: National Archives and Records Administration, RG 59, Central Files 1964–66, POL 27 YEMEN. Secret. Drafted by Moore on July 22, cleared by Davies and Campbell, and approved by Hare. Repeated to Cairo, Jidda, London, Aden, Dhahran, and CINCSTRIKE.

[2] Telegram 79 from Taiz, July 18, reported that an approach had been made to Embassy AID Director Benz by a representative of a group of Yemeni republicans, who informed him that they were urgently considering the possibility of forming a new government against UAR wishes and wanted to know whether they could depend on friends like the U.S. Government and Saudi Arabia to help them financially. Benz replied that as AID director, he was unable to respond to this request but agreed to forward the request to Washington. (Ibid.)

[3] In telegram 80 from Taiz, July 18, Chargé d'Affaires Harlan B. Clark argued that unless Nasser and Faisal reached agreement, the proposed attempt to free Yemen of its financial dependence on the United Arab Republic would bring the United States into direct confrontation with Nasser, which might cause troubles elsewhere in the Near East. (Ibid.)

405.   Briefing Memorandum From the Assistant Secretary of State for Near Eastern and South Asian Affairs (Hare) to Secretary of State Rusk[1]

Washington, August 2, 1966.

SUBJECT

 Your Meeting with Yemeni Ambassador Muhsin al-Aini, August 3, 11:00 a.m.

Discussion:

Ambassador al-Aini will be accompanied by Mr. Held of NEA/ARP. A biographic sketch is attached.[2]

The Ambassador has just returned from consultation in Cairo with top officials of his government, having participated in the initial stages of a confrontation between Yemeni and UAR leaders over continued Egyptian domination of Yemen. He reports that formerly pro-UAR Prime Minister al-Amri and other top YARG figures are now prepared to stand up to the Egyptians and believes that the YARG is well on its way to limiting UAR control of his country. Ambassador al-Aini also foresees better US-Yemeni relations and has expressed the hope that the US would take steps to promote an improved atmosphere. Specific items the Ambassador may raise in this context are the YARG's request for famine relief and the proposed Sanaa water works project.

Probably unknown to Ambassador al-Aini, his assertions of Yemeni independence of Cairo have been reflected in clandestine approaches to our Embassy in Yemen by civilian and military officers of the YARG. These officials, who claim they speak for powerful but unnamed groups of Yemenis, have expressed disgust over high-handed YAR actions and stated that the formation of a new Yemeni government against UAR wishes is under consideration. They have asked for US and Saudi financial assistance sufficient to insure payment of Yemeni Army salaries (approximately $500,000 per month). We have instructed our Embassy to discourage such requests.[3] While we sympathize with Yemeni efforts to establish a moderate government, we believe it most important that we avoid giving any impression of partisan US involvement in Yemeni domestic politics.

---

[1] Source: National Archives and Records Administration, RG 59, NEA/ARP Files: Lot 69 D 257, Political Affairs & Rel., YEMEN 1966, POL YEMEN–UNITED STATES. Secret. Drafted by Korn; cleared by UAR Country Director Donald C. Bergus and Director of AID's Office of Near Eastern Affairs James C. Flint.

[2] Attached but not printed.

[3] See Document 404.

Following talks in Jidda and Cairo late last month, the Kuwaiti Foreign Minister announced that King Faisal and President Nasser have agreed to send representatives to Kuwait shortly for direct negotiations on Yemen. The UAR and the Saudis have reportedly accepted the principal elements of a six point Kuwaiti proposal but are apparently still in disagreement over the length of time to be alloted for withdrawal of UAR troops from Yemen and the point at which the Yemeni royal family should be banned from the country.

We have been trying since mid-January to arrange a program for distribution of food to all hungry Yemenis, both royalist and republican. The YARG has refused to accept a proposal for distribution of US-supplied food by the ICRC. We are at present attempting to arrange for distribution of food in all Yemen through the World Food Program (WFP) of the UN Food and Agriculture Organization. The YARG itself has requested help from this agency, but the WFP has not yet decided whether it can undertake an "all-Yemen" program.

Recommendation:

That you tell Ambassador al-Aini:

a. We sympathize with the YARG's desire to be master in its own house.

b. We are encouraged by the Kuwaiti Foreign Minister's apparent success in persuading the UAR and the Saudis to agree to send representatives to Kuwait for talks on Yemen. We are hopeful these talks will result in a settlement acceptable to all the parties involved.

If Ambassador al-Aini raises the Sanaa water project or the YARG request for famine relief, that you:

a. Suggest that he discuss the Sanaa water project with Mr. Macomber during their meeting scheduled for August 4. (Barring an increase in the AID allotment for Yemen, this project would require a sizeable diversion of funds from our very successful urban and rural development program. It is not currently under consideration by AID.)

b. Express hope that, for humanitarian reasons, arrangements can be made soon for food to be distributed to all hungry Yemenis, either through the WFP, if that agency is preferred by YARG and is willing to undertake the program, or through the ICRC, if the WFP cannot respond to YARG's request.[4]

---

[4] Rusk met with Ambassador al-Aini at 11:05 a.m. on August 3. (Johnson Library, Rusk Appointment Book)

406. Telegram From the Department of State to the Embassy in Kuwait[1]

Washington, August 5, 1966, 5:37 p.m.

22681. Kuwait's 79,[2] Cairo's 569,[3] Jidda's 67.[4]

1. *Begin FYI.* We gratified at energy and skill used by Kuwaiti negotiators in isolating issues and bringing SAG and UAR so close to agreement. While not surprised Hamid ad-Din issue remains unsettled, we concerned lest it has assumed proportions prevent settlement Yemen dispute for months if not years. We also concerned lest, with apparent interruption of Arab summitry, Kuwaiti mediation might be last chance to reach settlement for a long period to come.

2. We believe both Nasser and Faisal look upon Hamid ad-Din question as key to future of Yemen and basic to survival their own regimes. Nasser believes, not without reason, that Hamid ad-Din's remaining on Yemeni soil under any guise would make any UAR claims to "famous victory" in Yemen sound hollow. He is concerned lest anything other than reasonably plausible claim of victory raise discontent in UAR armed forces to intolerable level.

3. Faisal on other hand remains so deeply suspicious of UAR motives and distrustful of Nasser that he reluctant to compromise. King has however on several occasions indicated he not wedded to maintenance of monarchical principle in Yemen. His main interest in Hamid ad-Din appears to be tactical one of leverage he can exercise on Yemen situation through them. This attitude most recently reflected in King's July 6 talk with Ambassador Eilts (Jidda 67) when he expressed fear exiling Hamid ad-Din before completion UAR withdrawal would reduce royalist forces to tribal rabble and give Nasser sole mastery of situation.

4. Given above considerations, both Faisal and Nasser may prefer rock along with present Yemen situation, unpleasant though it may

---

[1] Source: National Archives and Records Administration, RG 59, Central Files 1964–66, POL 27 YEMEN. Secret; Priority; Limdis. Drafted by Bergus and Korn, cleared by Davies, and approved by Hare. Also sent to Jidda and Cairo and repeated to Taiz, Aden, and CINCSTRIKE/CINCMEAFSA.

[2] Dated August 2. (Ibid.)

[3] Telegram 569 from Cairo, August 3, reported that al-Khouli had confirmed that he would meet the Saudi representative, Dr. Rashad Pharaon, in Kuwait on August 15 to attempt to resolve their last disagreements on Yemen. Al-Khouli had indicated that the only significant remaining issue was disposition of the Hamid-ad-Din family. Both parties had agreed on the name of the provisional government (state of Yemen) and its composition (three-fifths republican and two-fifths royalist). (Ibid.)

[4] Document 403.

be, rather than make final sacrifice required for settlement. With accord apparently so close and consequences continuation conflict so dangerous to both sides, we strongly hope Saudis and UAR can be persuaded make necessary concessions while agreement still possible. *End FYI.*

5. *For Jidda:* You should approach Pharaon and reiterate keen USG interest in successful outcome August 15 meeting with Khouly. Suggest presentation along following lines: a) Forthcoming talks appear to be last remaining possibility within foreseeable future to bring about withdrawal of UAR forces from Peninsula. With agreement between two parties apparently so close, USG cannot believe Saudis would let pass opportunity to get UAR troops out of Yemen, particularly in view of serious threat they pose to future of Saudi Arabia. b) We recognize importance Hamid ad-Din issue for Saudis but wonder whether there not room for compromise even on this point. Would it not be possible for example that banning of Yemeni royal family might be arranged in stages, with exiling of Hamid ad-Din princes being echeloned to parallel withdrawal of UAR forces? (Similar suggestion was made to Ambassador Eilts by Kamal Adham during conversation March 12 (Jidda's 790).[5] Yemeni Ambassador al-Aini broached same possibility in talk with Department Officer August 3.) We have no idea what UAR reaction would be to such proposal and mention it only as illustration that legitimate possibilities for compromise exist. c) Even Yemeni republicans visibly tiring of UAR presence and are actively seeking means of asserting their independence. Once UAR has withdrawn we are confident SAG's ability establish influence and good relations with Yemeni Government. d) You may also wish reiterate points your excellent presentation to Faisal July 6.[6]

6. *For Cairo:* Chargé should approach Hassan Sabri al-Khouli or suitable other available GUAR official and state that all parties to Kuwaiti mediation effort have been kind enough to keep us informed of its progress. Seems to us that in current state of affairs in Arab world, Kuwaiti mediation may well be last opportunity to reach honorable settlement Yemen issue for a long time to come. We believe GUAR fully aware of wholesome effect freely negotiated and fully implemented Yemen settle-

---

[5] Dated March 12. (National Archives and Records Administration, RG 59, Central Files 1964–66, POL 27 YEMEN)

[6] In telegram 451 from Jidda, August 7, Eilts reported that he met with Faisal, Pharaon, and Saqqaf on August 6 and carried out the Department's instructions. The King responded that the Saudis had in the past shown great flexibility and been the only party that had genuinely sought to compromise. He stated that he would never agree to specifying removal of the Hamid ad-Din family by name; any exclusion would have to be in general terms of "undesirables." Second, he would not agree that the Hamid ad-Dins be excluded by any Yemen organ until the last UAR soldier was out of Yemen. Despite Eilts' urging that he reconsider the last point, Faisal continued to insist that these two points were non-negotiable. (Ibid.)

ment would have. We urge GUAR overlook no opportunity contribute to such a settlement at upcoming meeting in Kuwait.[7]

7. *For Kuwait:* You should inform Foreign Minister we making approaches Cairo and Jidda to urge both sides make every effort achieve settlement at forthcoming meeting. You should express our warmest appreciation to Kuwaitis for energy, tact, and skill with which they have pursued this difficult task. We hope for successful outcome August meetings, but would urge Kuwaitis to continue their efforts beyond this if required. A great deal is at stake, in terms of our mutual desire for a stable and prosperous Arabian peninsula.[8]

Rusk

---

[7] In telegram 683 from Cairo, August 8, Nes reported that he and Parker had met with al-Khouli that morning and spoken along the lines of paragraph 6 of the Department's telegram, noting that the United States was making a parallel approach to the Saudis in hopes that he and Pharaon would have maximum flexibility. (Ibid.)

[8] In telegram 99 from Kuwait, August 7, Cottam reported that he had met with Sayyid Bishara, Director of the Kuwaiti Foreign Office, who affirmed that Kuwait did not consider this the last and final round, although for tactical reasons it had said so. (Ibid.)

---

407.   Telegram From the Department of State to the Embassy in the United Arab Republic[1]

Washington, August 20, 1966, 2:54 p.m.

32315. Yemen Mediation.

1. In light Kuwaiti request,[2] Embassies Cairo and Jidda may indicate at appropriate level local foreign ministries continuing USG interest in solution Yemen problem and hope that governments will continue show forthcoming attitude as reflected in recently concluded meeting in Kuwait.[3]

---

[1] Source: National Archives and Records Administration, RG 59, Central Files 1964–66 POL 27 YEMEN. Confidential; Priority; Limdis. Drafted by Davies and approved by Hare. Also sent to Kuwait and Jidda and repeated to Beirut and Taiz.

[2] In telegram 137 from Kuwait, August 20, Cottam reported that Bishara had asked for U.S. support of Kuwait's proposal for a Yemen settlement. (Ibid.)

[3] In telegram 662 from Jidda, August 22, Seelye reported that he discussed Yemen with Mas'ud that day as instructed. (Ibid.) In telegram 1026 from Cairo, August 25, Nes reported that he discussed Yemen at length with el Fekki, expressing the hope that some progress had been made in the recent al-Khouri–Pharaon talks in Kuwait. El Fekki responded that the talks had gone well, but that subsequent Saudi secret contacts with royalist tribal leaders in Yemen indicated that King Faisal was not sincerely interested in a solution. (Ibid.)

2. Request Embassy Kuwait inform posts substance proposal as it emerged after Pharaon–Khouli discussions.[4]

Rusk

---

[4] In telegram 866 from Jidda, September 6, Eilts reported that following his return to Jidda, Saqqaf had informed him of the current status of the Kuwait mediation effort, which now called for: a) a transitional Yemeni government (3/5 republican, 2/5 royalist); b) UAR troop withdrawal within 9 months after a new Haradh conference convened October 1–15; and c) withdrawal of Hamid ad-Din and other "undesirables" when UAR troops were down to 3,000 i.e., a number equal to the proposed 3,000-man Arab peacekeeping force. Saqqaf also said that, on instructions from the King, Pharaon had insisted during the negotiations with al-Khouli that one-fifth of the republican three-fifths be "third force" republicans. The Kuwaitis had since told the Saudis that the United Arab Republic had demanded that the Hamid ad-Din be excluded when the half of the UAR forces had been withdrawn. (Ibid.)

---

408. Telegram From the Embassy in Yemen to the Department of State[1]

Taiz, September 4, 1966, 1300Z.

340. Ref: Cairo MRN 1116,[2] Kuwait 178.[3]

1. Reftels confirm our recent growing conviction that UAR playing double game in Yemen. Idea that Egyptians merely seeking honorable way out does not square with their activities here. Admittedly they appear be sincerely and patiently participating Kuwait mediation. But we note that only point among Kuwait proposals which actually reduces their power dominate Yemen or frustrate emergence representative leadership is one on which UAR balks, namely the withdrawal of its army. We can also not shake suspicion that UAR planning keep its forces in place here for day of "liberation" South Arabia 1968 in anticipation of new opportunities.

2. UAR with ease can manage arrange delays and postponements of the proposed Harad conference and the nine-month troop withdrawal specified in Kuwaiti proposals, just as UAR appears able create

---

[1] Source: National Archives and Records Administration, RG 59, Central Files 1964–66, POL 27 YEMEN. Secret; Noforn; Limdis. Repeated to Aden, Cairo, Jidda, Kuwait, and London.

[2] Dated August 30. (Ibid.)

[3] Dated August 28. (Ibid.)

circumstances to justify maintaining itself in effective control government Yemen. More important, it has tested its ability recently to do so and the angry but impotent and scattered government may be best evidence really of Egyptian sovereignty in Yemen.

3. Were there any hint that this smothering dominance of the Yemenis had begun be lifted during recent hopeful period of Kuwait mediation we might be inclined more relaxed view. But UAR controls, rumor mongering, incitements, military actions, pamphleteering, claims of British "overflights" and border intrusions" are increasing.

4. Part of the stepped up campaign is clandestine and open propaganda against US. Another leaflet (second seen by Embassy) has been circulated which links US (charging dollar subsidies) with anti-Sallalist Republican Council dissidents in Taiz. Radio Sanaa is constant purveyor claims to effect US is midst dark plots against republic. Newspapers are channels anti-Western diatribes. Al Khouli's assertion reported para 2 Kuwait's 178 is poppycock. "Hostile press" claim is evidence of government-controlled media UAR. We assume Kuwaitis as aware of this as Saudis.

5. UAR of course not pleased over presence US in Yemen. We are only mission observing UAR's blatant conduct affairs here Egypt has reason to worry about. While we can probably have little effect on UAR policy I believe time has come at least to register our displeasure at their propoganda and whispering campaign against US in Yemen. I suggest Department authorize Embassy Cairo to approach UARG at high level to protest unfounded and flagrant vilification of exemplary US conduct in Yemen.

6. Thus as Egyptian intervention in Yemen becomes even more devious and heavy handed, playing at negotiation through Kuwait mediation on one hand and on the other seeking undermine the group of reasonable men who are still determined gain sovereignty of their own country, we suspect UAR identifies us as prime obstacle to its having completely free hand in this region Arabian peninsula. We note that already a variety of anti-American activity led by Egyptians in Yemen has had its effect. In these efforts the UAR is aided and abetted by Soviets and Chinese. We are not quite quarantined from contact in the community but all Yemenis, particularly officials, are wary about relations with US. (Tribal personalities who disregard or do not feel this pressure are an exception to this general rule, but relations with these men have their limitations.)

7. Successful Kuwait mediation which guaranteed prompt exit UAR troops would be historic event of good omen here and would be crippling blow to what I believe are current Egyptian plans dominate Yemen, if necessary by force it is unable establish puppet government,

until such times Brits evacuate South Arabia when the whole area can be exploited.

Dinsmore

---

409.   Telegram From the Department of State to the Embassy in the United Arab Republic[1]

Washington, September 6, 1966, 5:07 p.m.

41545. 1. Department concerned at UAR tendency reported Taiz 340[2] make USG scapegoat for UAR's own problems in dealing with difficult Yemeni leadership. Accordingly Embassy Cairo should see either FonMin or Hassan Sabri al-Khouli at first convenient opportunity to make clear that gratuitous charges against US which are being floated in Yemen are not appreciated. Nor would we be inclined accept explanation that these activities are the result of initiatives undertaken by uninstructed or overzealous Egyptian satraps in Yemen. GUAR must accept responsibility for deeds of its military and diplomatic officials in YAR. These directly affect the broad spectrum of US–UAR relations. They run counter to assurances recently given by highest levels in USG and GUAR that we should work together to try to improve relations.

2. Embassy should point out that USG is one of few major Western powers to recognize YAR as sovereign and independent state. Our dealings with YAR have been on that basis. Our aid program, though small, has made real contribution to Yemeni development. We at a loss to understand how our goals for Yemen conflict with those of UAR. We remain desirous of a Yemen settlement based on honor and justice for all parties to dispute, including Yemenis.

Rusk

---

[1] Source: National Archives and Records Administration, RG 59, Central Files 1964–66, POL 27 YEMEN. Secret; Limdis. Drafted by Bergus, cleared by Moore, and approved by Davies. Repeated to Jidda, Kuwait, Aden, London, and Taiz.

[2] Document 408.

410. **Telegram From the Department of State to the Embassy in Yemen**[1]

Washington, September 27, 1966, 5:55 p.m.

55142. 1. In farewell call on NEA Assistant Secretary Hare September 26, YAR Ambassador al-Aini[2] gave lengthy account recent events Yemen[3] and his views future developments. Following is summary detailed pouched memcon.

2. Al-Amri and colleagues' trip to Cairo was last desperate measure to forestall outbreak fighting between tribes and Sallal supporters. Unhappy events which followed have one positive effect of showing whole world extent Egyptian control Yemen. Nasser no longer can legitimately claim he is supporting revolution in Yemen.

3. Concerning next steps of Yemeni "moderate" group, al-Aini said he had in past refrained from raising subject Yemen in UN in order avoid embarrassment to whole Arab cause arising from Nasser's suppression Yemenis. However, in last few days he had extensive discussions his Arab colleagues NY emphasizing Arabs themselves must now take action to settle problem. If this does not develop, it possible that moderate republicans would send delegation to UN Committee of 24 protesting Egyptian colonization Yemen and requesting UAR set date for withdrawal from Yemen just as British had set date in Aden.

4. In response query, said thought Egyptians wish remain Yemen but emphasized they could not do so in face growing consolidation Yemeni opposition. Added that Nasser does not know what he wants; return of troops to UAR in semblance of defeat would face him with possible Egyptian military revolt; staying in Yemen threatens Yemeni revolt.

5. Answering question on Russian interest Yemen, al-Aini said USSR seemed favor Nasser presence Yemen for pressure it put on British in Aden and had originally channeled all support to Yemen through UAR. Subsequently, at Yemeni request, Soviets made agree-

---

[1] Source: National Archives and Records Administration, RG 59, Central Files 1964–66, POL 17 YEMEN–US. Secret. Drafted by Moore, cleared by Gabriel J. Paolozzi (IO/UNP), and approved by Hare. Repeated to Cairo, Jidda, London, Aden, and USUN.

[2] Ambassador al-Aini resigned on September 21.

[3] On September 16 the UAR press announced the resignation of the Hassan al-Amri government, most of whose members were then in Cairo. On September 18 President Sallal announced formation of a new Yemeni cabinet composed almost exclusively of hard-line UAR supporters. Members of the al-Amri government were placed under house arrest in Cairo, and a purge of moderates in the Yemeni Government and Army began, culminating in the execution of former Minister of State for Tribal Affairs Muhammad al-Ruaini and four associates on October 25.

ments with Sallal for direct aid. However, few of these agreements fully implemented; Russians now seem to be shifting their support away from Sallal to more neutral stance vis à vis Yemeni Republican elements.

6. Sees little hope for success Kuwaiti mediation in view continued Nasser–Faisal distrust. Noted that Faisal unsuccessful in four-year attempt get UAR out by working through royalists. He now should trust Yemeni people (i.e., moderates) who equally desire ousting Egyptian troops. Moderates need only assurances that Hamid al-Din will not be forced on them by Saudis if they take action against Egyptians. If moderates thought for moment that Hamid al-Din controlled any important part of the country they would deal with them. However, royalists represent nothing but Saudis. Saudi support for Hamid al-Din continues give Nasser excuse stay in Yemen and limits extent anti-Egyptian activity by moderates. Expressed oft-repeated hope we could explain this to Faisal.

7. Shafai–Zaidi friction has little significance for present course of Yemen. Egyptians had tried use confessional differences as basis for split of country, but failed. With long history as single entity Yemen will continue stand as one country, be it all republican or all royalist.

8. Al-Aini expects leave US in week or so, traveling via Rome and Beirut, to accompany family as far as Asmara on their return to Yemen. Ambassador will determine in Asmara whether he also should return Yemen (which he desires) or possibly travel to other Arab capitals in service cause Yemeni moderates.

9. Al-Aini expressed particular gratitude to Secretary and Asst Sec Hare for continued sympathetic reception accorded him in Department during nearly four years in US.

Rusk

411. Telegram From the Department of State to the Embassy in Yemen[1]

Washington, September 30, 1966, 12:02 p.m.

57200. AP ticker carries Cairo dateline story quoting Al-Ahram that Yemen President Sallal has accused ousted cabinet ministers of collaborating with US agents to sabotage Yemeni revolution. Story also cites reports harassment US officials in Yemen[2] and distribution anti-American leaflets.

If queried re above Department spokesman will respond as follows: "The accusation of US activities against the Yemeni revolution is patently false. We are not involved in Yemeni internal affairs and have maintained normal diplomatic relations with the Republic since according it formal recognition in December 1962.[3]

While there have been incidents where local Yemeni authorities have delayed US officials in their travels, press reports of widespread anti-Americanism in Yemen are greatly distorted. We continue to discuss with the Yemen Government particular problems as they arise in a spirit of mutual respect."[4]

---

[1] Source: National Archives and Records Administration, RG 59, Central Files 1964–66, POL 15–1 YEMEN. Limited Official Use. Drafted by Ollison (NEA/P), cleared by McCloskey (P/ON) and Moore, and approved by Daniel Brown (NEA/P). Also sent to Cairo.

[2] On September 28 the Yemeni Government declared U.S. AID contract employee Michael Harriz, a U.S. citizen, persona non grata.

[3] Telegram 55933 to Cairo, September 28, instructed the Embassy to approach al-Khouli and state that Yemeni charges that Harriz was involved in disturbances in Taiz were patently untrue, as demonstrated by the fact that Harriz was in Sana'a at the time of the incident. Al-Khouli should be told that the United States had tried unsuccessfully to reach a responsible Yemeni official to discuss the Harriz case, and that it would be in their mutual interest if UAR authorities could persuade Yemeni officials to review the charges against Harriz with great care before ratifying the expulsion effort, which was bound to have a damaging effect on the overall U.S.-Yemeni relationship. (National Archives and Records Administration, RG 59, Central Files 1964–66, POL 27 YEMEN) Telegram 1671 from Cairo, September 29, reported that, since al-Khouli was absent from Cairo, an Embassy official had made the presentation at the Foreign Ministry that morning. (Ibid.)

[4] Printed from an unsigned copy.

412.   Memorandum of Conversation[1]

SecDel/MC/49   New York, October 7, 1966, 4–5 p.m.

SECRETARY'S DELEGATION TO THE TWENTY-FIRST SESSION
OF THE UNITED NATIONS GENERAL ASSEMBLY
New York, September–October 1966

SUBJECT

Yemen (Part III of IV)

PARTICIPANTS

U.S.
The Secretary
Mr. William L. Simmons, NEA

U.A.R.
H.E. Mahmoud Riad, Minister for Foreign Affairs
H.E. Dr. Mostafa Kamel, Ambassador to the United States
H.E. Mohamed Riad, Counsellor, Minister for Foreign Affairs, Cabinet Ministry of Foreign Affairs

The Secretary asked about prospects for success of the Kuwaiti mediation effort on Yemen. The Foreign Minister said that the sticking point related to the withdrawal of the royal family. The U.A.R. position is that the family should be withdrawn when half of the U.A.R. troops in Yemen are pulled out. The Saudi posture is that all troops must first be withdrawn. U.A.R. public opinion makes this completely unacceptable. The Saudis apparently fear that should the royal family leave Yemen, the U.A.R. would fail to complete its part of the agreement. This was unrealistic since the U.A.R. was asking only that the royal family leave Yemen and not asking for the family's exile to Africa or the Far East.

The Minister said that he had been informed by the Kuwaitis that the Saudis had accepted the proposed composition of the new YARG, i.e. three-fifths Republicans, two-fifths Royalists. The Foreign Minister said that troop withdrawal would begin at the moment the new government is established. He said that the points of dispute are trifling and if the Saudis were willing an agreement could be signed immediately.

---

[1] Source: National Archives and Records Administration, RG 59, Central Files 1964–66, POL 27 YEMEN. Secret. Drafted by Simmons on October 11 and approved in S on October 25.

413. Telegram From the Department of State to the Embassy in Yemen[1]

Washington, October 12, 1966, 6:54 p.m.

64728. 1. In call on Assistant Sec Hare October 11, Yemeni Foreign Minister Sallam made puerile impassioned plea for further US aid, particularly for paving Mocha–Sanaa road. Sallam stated Yemenis appreciated US recognition Republic, but felt US had done nothing further assist in developing Yemen, that major aid projects all given only to Imamate regime. Contrasted US lack willingness help with massive efforts Soviets and Chicoms.

2. Sallam blamed Saudis and British for present plight of Yemen. Emphasized that Yemenis welcomed UAR presence as first step toward larger unity Arab world.

3. Ambassador Hare stated (and reiterated number times during conversation) that US policy toward Yemen clear from beginning, never hidden or doubtful: we desired only situation where Yemen could develop at peace internally and externally and could control its own destiny. We in no way involved in trying manipulate internal affairs Yemen. Our activities open and above board. We not engaged in passing money, plotting or any of other allegations which currently being circulated in Cairo and Yemen. We desire nothing from Yemen except Yemeni self-determination. This being stressed to Foreign Minister not only to set record straight but also to give assurances that this has been and continues to be our policy. If YARG doubts this it will be unable understand our attitudes and future course our relations.

4. Ambassador Hare continued that in exercising our limited influence with UAR and Saudis concerning Yemen we had spoken only on above lines, urging the two larger powers to reach some accommodation which would allow Yemenis decide own future.

5. Concerning US assistance, Ambassador Hare emphasized our aid efforts before and since revolution had concentrated on helping Yemeni people, without reflection on what regime controlled country. Our current programs, involving smaller projects primarily in rural areas, specifically were designed this purpose. Was noted that approximately half of all US aid ever given Yemen had been supplied since revolution.

---

[1] Source: National Archives and Records Administration, RG 59, Central Files 1964–66, AID (US) 8 YEMEN. Secret. Drafted by Moore, cleared by Director of the AID Office of Near Eastern Affairs James C. Flint, and approved by Hare. Repeated to Cairo, London, Jidda, and Aden.

6. In subsequent call on AID Assistant Administrator Macomber, Sallam made similar but more restrained appeal for aid, concentrating on paving road. Macomber made no promises but indicated we were sympathetic toward helping Yemeni people within limitations our budget and as necessary stability and planning capability in Yemen evolve over coming years. Expected that our program would in near future continue emphasize rural self-help. Specifically commented that at present stage Yemen development there was some question whether paving road should have major priority.

Rusk

---

414.   Telegram From the Department of State to the Embassy in Saudi Arabia[1]

Washington, October 12, 1966, 10:30 p.m.

64986. (Following FYI Noforn, based on uncleared memcon, subject revision on review.) Following principal subjects discussed during Saudi Deputy Foreign Minister Saqqaf's call on Secretary October 11.

1. Yemen. Saqqaf convinced UAR does not want solve problem or leave Yemen at least before British departure from Aden in two years. (Secretary noted UAR still tells us they want solution and their attitude in Yemen not affected by developments in Aden.) Saqqaf believes Kuwait mediation efforts of no avail. Within Yemen, none of groups involved seems any longer satisfied with circumstances. Many Yemenis dying all parts of country from sickness and hunger. Fighting continuing in some areas where UAR is invading "royalist regions".

Secretary queried if, following Kuwaiti efforts, putting Yemen problem into UN would be helpful. Saqqaf demurred noting none of parties had mentioned subject in the UNGA speeches and little progress to be expected since Yemen Republic was UN member.

[Here follows discussion of other subjects.]

Rusk

---

[1] Source: National Archives and Records Administration, RG 59, Central Files 1964–66, POL 7 SAUD. Secret. Drafted by Moore; cleared by Officer in Charge of Somali Affairs Peter C. Walker, Director of the Office of Northern African Affairs John F. Root, Bergus, Atherton, Campbell, and Symmes; and approved by Hare. Repeated to Cairo, Taiz, London, Aden, and USUN.

**415.   Telegram From the Department of State to the Embassy in
the United Arab Republic[1]**

Washington, October 15, 1966, 12:49 p.m.

66851. Ref: Jidda's 1400[2] and Cairo 1972[3] (being repeated addressees).

For Cairo: Suggest you tell Fawzi we have reliable report several lives lost in Najran morning October 14 result bombing by aircraft and ask whether UARG has any information. If appropriate you should express hope UAR will exert greatest care avoid incidents which would counter Kuwait's mediation efforts and could exacerbate delicate situation Yemen.[4]

For Jidda: Line you have taken with Mas'ud just right. Believe we should maintain low key and urge restraint both sides until facts and UAR intentions clearer.

Rusk

---

[1] Source: National Archives and Records Administration, RG 59, Central Files 1964–66, POL 31–1 SAUD–UAR. Confidential; Immediate. Drafted by John T. Wheelock (NEA/UAR), cleared by Davies and Moore, and approved by Hare. Also sent to Jidda and repeated to Kuwait, London, Taiz, USUN, CHUSMTM, and CINCSTRIKE/CINCMEAFSA.

[2] In telegram 1400 from Jidda, October 14, Eilts reported that acting Deputy Foreign Minister Mas'ud informed him that four UAR aircraft had attacked Najran that morning killing three people, and that he had just delivered a strong oral protest to the UAR Ambassador. Eilts expressed shock at the bombing but also urged calm and restraint. (Ibid.)

[3] In telegram 1972 from Cairo, October 15, Battle requested guidance on the UAR attack on Najran for a previously scheduled meeting with Fawzi on October 17. (Ibid.)

[4] In telegram 2020 from Cairo, October 17, Battle reported that he discussed the Najran bombing with Fawzi that morning. (Ibid.) In telegram 2021 from Cairo, October 17, the Ambassador reported that 3 hours later he had been asked to return to receive the UAR response, which stated that UAR forces had noted unusual military activities and movements indicating Saudi aggressive intentions and endangering the security of UAR forces and had therefore taken preventive measures, such as day and night military explorations, which could result in the possibility of mistakes. (Ibid.)

416. Telegram From the Department of State to the Embassy in Saudi Arabia[1]

Washington, November 10, 1966, 6:06 p.m.

83055. Jidda 1762, Yemen.[2] Following points for use as you deem appropriate in discussion with King:

1. Assessment UAR intentions:

a. We frankly uncertain what Nasser's ultimate intentions in Yemen may be.

b. Believe, however, that domestic pressures coupled with rising Yemeni republican discontent UAR presence should incline Nasser to seek way to extricate UAR from its uncomfortable position. However, Nasser cannot, we think, make decision withdraw without concurrence military which cannot accept formula which gives other than impression success UAR arms. We speculate that minimum circumstances acceptable to military would be expulsion principal members Hamid al-Din and emergence of interim government capable of standing on own for at least some months after withdrawal. UAR attempts in last three months establish "strong" government by draconian measures signal all out effort obtain some form of stability. Regardless Nasser's ultimate intent, seems evident that a greater modicum of stability in Yemen is unquestionably a precondition if he is to decide to withdraw.

c. In these circumstances, resumption open hostility by royalists would not promote goal UAR withdrawal. Full-scale fighting for three years failed expel Egyptians. (Royalist threat "dump entire problem into Saudi lap" seems idle one; problem has been Saudi one for many months.) Expected UAR response to renewed fighting would be application more force, particularly increased air strikes and perhaps new augmentation ground troops, which presently down to about 40,000. Unleashing royalists would doubtless strengthen "hawk" mentality in UAR to point where concerted attack against Saudi Arabia could not be ruled out.

d. Present anarchic conditions Yemen work to weaken UAR position there. However, resumption more active SAG role, via royalists, could well coalesce many of presently divided Yemenis into front against Saudis which would negate internal forces currently working in SAG favor.

---

[1] Source: National Archives and Records Administration, RG 59, Central Files 1964–66, POL 27 YEMEN. Secret; Priority. Drafted by Moore and Davies, cleared by Judd and Bergus, and approved by Hare. Also sent to Cairo, Kuwait, and London and repeated to Amman, Taiz, Dhahran, and CINCSTRIKE.

[2] Dated November 7. (Ibid.)

e. We have no indications that UAR planning attack Saudi Arabia. However, Saudi connivance at resumption fighting by royalists could well serve as provocation for UAR retaliation. (UAR no doubt aware increased royalist pressure on SAG for resumed fighting and may resort to such isolated incidents as mid-October bombing Najran as warning of Saudi vulnerability of wide-scale fighting resumed Yemen.)

f. Just as we cautioned UAR re dangers mid-October Najran bombing we would caution Faisal against allowing royalists resume activity.

2. In our view, Kuwaiti mediation continues offer principal hope for settlement although we following with interest such other Arab lines of approach as those being pursued by al-Aini. Believe details current proposals and counter proposals relatively unimportant since, judging only from them, area of disagreement between Faisal and Nasser on modalities solution is very narrow. Vital missing ingredient is lack mutual trust between Faisal and Nasser. No third party can supply this, which is up to principals involved to work out in framework their common Arab concerns. However, Kuwaiti efforts provide required channel for the two to air their differences. We strongly advise King continue to operate through this channel. We currently urging Kuwaitis resume their efforts at early date.[3]

3. We are presently making similar démarche in Cairo concerning continuation mediation efforts.

4. *For Cairo.* Request you seek occasion make following points at appropriately high level UARG:

a. We are strongly urging Faisal follow policy restraint in Yemen and continue cooperate with Kuwaiti mediation efforts.

b. We realize broad range differences between Faisal and Nasser hinders Yemen settlement but believe it of extreme importance that both continue work to narrow their differences.

c. We urge UAR to avoid any actions which would exacerbate situation and to resume discussion, presumably through Kuwaitis, for settlement.[4]

5. *For Kuwait.* Request you inform appropriate level GOK of our foregoing démarches in Cairo and Riyadh, of our concern that more

---

[3] In telegram 295 from Dhahran, November 13, Ambassador Eilts reported that in a meeting with Faisal that day he referred to reports that hostilities might soon resume in Yemen and urged the King to restrain the royalists, outlining in some detail the assessment contained in telegram 83055. (Ibid.)

[4] In telegram 2662 from Cairo, November 15, Battle reported that he and Parker had reviewed the Yemen situation with al-Khouli that morning. Battle made the presentation outlined in telegram 83055, and al-Khouli presented the UAR perspective. Battle concluded pessimistically that he feared the United Arab Republic and Saudi Arabia might be drifting toward open, armed conflict in Yemen. (Ibid.)

extensive fighting may soon break out Yemen, and of our strong hope for early resumption Kuwaiti mediation efforts as Foreign Minister assured Secretary in New York he intended do.[5]

6. *For London.* Request you draw on foregoing and reftel for discussion current Yemen situation with HMG and suggest HMG may also wish similarly advise SAG against resumption hostilities Yemen.[6]

Rusk

---

[5] In telegram 449 from Kuwait, November 12, Cottam reported that he had conveyed the substance of the Department's telegram to Bishara, who assured him that the Government of Kuwait was actively continuing its attempts to mediate. (Ibid.)

[6] Telegram 88539 to Jidda, November 21, reported that the British Embassy had informed the Department that although the U.K. Government did not wish to see full-scale fighting resume in Yemen, it had decided not to approach Faisal on this subject. (Ibid.)

---

417. Telegram From the Department of State to the Embassy in Kuwait[1]

Washington, November 17, 1966, 1:12 p.m.

86358. Cairo 2662,[2] Jidda 1871,[3] Yemen.

1. Al-Khouly's analysis current status Kuwait mediation indicates basic sticking point is UAR concern that troop level at which Saudis willing oust Hamid al-Din is too low to insure security and order in Yemen.[4] To meet this concern might be useful if Kuwaitis would propose to SAG and UAR an increase in the planned number of troops to be requested from other Arab countries, e.g., two or three thousand

---

[1] Source: National Archives and Records Administration, RG 59, Central Files 1964–66, POL 27 YEMEN. Secret. Drafted by Moore, cleared by Bergus, and approved by Davies. Repeated to Cairo, Jidda, and Taiz.

[2] See footnote 4, Document 416.

[3] Dated November 16. (National Archives and Records Administration, RG 59, Central Files 1964–66, POL 27 YEMEN)

[4] Telegram 2662, November 15, also reported al-Khouli's statement that the only remaining issue to be settled was timing of the departure of the Hamid ad-Dins from Yemen. The United Arab Republic had proposed what he called a "reasonable compromise"—removal of the Hamid ad-Dins when evacuation of UAR troops was half completed. The Saudis rejected this and proposed their removal when UAR troop strength was down to 3,000. The United Arab Republic was unwilling to accept this, fearing that this was not enough to permit it to control the military situation. (Ibid.)

from each of three countries instead of the projected 1,000. This might or might not also involve a matching number of UAR troops as in first proposal.

2. We have no desire get directly involved in details of solution and are under no illusion that foregoing would be touchstone for settling problem. However, it might be useful gimmick to enable Kuwaitis keep door of negotiations open a bit longer, which seems to be desire of both sides.

3. Since Kuwaitis have in past asked for our ideas, request you discreetly suggest this possibility to them in your further discussions concerning their mediation effort.

Rusk

---

418.   **Telegram From the Department of State to the Embassy in Yemen**[1]

Washington, December 20, 1966, 4:40 p.m.

105650. Joint State/AID message. Ref Taiz 844 (TOAID 186).[2] Subject: FY 1967/68 Program and Staffing.

1. Washington agencies in full sympathy with problems faced by Embassy/AID/Y in maintaining US presence Yemen. However exceedingly tight budgetary situation coupled with continuing political instability in Yemen and UAR domination of YARG make it impossible to envisage increase in FY68 Yemen allotment. We were in fact fortunate hold country allotment at $2.4 million level in FY67. Yemen was only country in NESA area to escape cut from FY67 Congressional Presentation level.

2. While Sanaa watershed and Taiz Technical Institute surveys involve only relatively small amounts it would not be realistic authorize

---

[1] Source: National Archives and Records Administration, RG 59, Central Files 1964–66, AID (US) YEMEN. Confidential. Drafted by Korn, Flint, and Harry F. Hemmerich (AID/NESA/NE); cleared by Director of the AID Office of Development Planning for the Near East and South Asia Afred D. White; and approved by Brewer. The Embassy Branch Office in Sana'a, Yemen, was elevated to Embassy status effective December 15, 1966. The same day the Embassy in Taiz was redesignated American Embassy Branch Office.

[2] Telegram 844 from Taiz, December 1, complained that the reduced U.S. aid program for Yemen gave the Embassy no talking points with the Yemeni Government, since there was no possibility of dialogue other than the negative one of defending a dwindling program. (Ibid.)

either unless there appeared be some prospect of our being able effectively to initiate it in FY 1968. Near certainty of reduced world-wide availabilities next fiscal year unfortunately rules out such step. For same reason it impossible to consider dredging Mocha port or paving Mocha–Sanaa road as separate capital project. Because Yemen is not a general support country, see no reason broach with YARG general subject of Yemen aid level. To best of our knowledge this has not been done in past.

3. Realize this places burden on Embassy and AID/Y in their efforts maintain effective US presence, especially in face of large-scale Chicom and Soviet efforts. This situation places even greater premium than in past on imaginative use by Embassy and AID/Y of self-help funds. In this regard, two possibilities come to mind:

a. As stated in Farr-Hamer letter Nov 16,[3] we are prepared entertain proposal for pavement limited section Mocha–Sanaa road on self-help basis if this can be accomplished without sacrificing principles self-help program.

b. Embassy/AID/Y might consider self-help projects designed underscore US presence Sanaa area and foster better understanding on part Sallal and YARG that US program is most effectively serving interests both government and people Yemen by providing small, self-help projects which spread assistance to largest number of people.

4. Would appreciate Embassy/AID/Y comments on suggestions para 3 or other proposals which might broaden impact AID/Y program within limits current budget.

5. Embassy requested pass this message Taiz for AID.

Rusk

---

[3] Not found.

419. Information Memorandum From the Deputy Assistant Secretary of State for Near Eastern and South Asian Affairs (Davies) to Secretary of State Rusk[1]

Washington, January 4, 1967.

SUBJECT

U.A.R. Planes Overfly Saudi Border Area

1. Saudi authorities have informed us that U.A.R. planes overflew the province of Najran, on the Yemen border, on December 27 and January 1 but that earlier reports of bombings and strafings on these dates were incorrect. Taken together with a U.A.R. bombing sortie against a hamlet just inside the Yemen-Saudi border on December 26, these overflights are probably intended as a warning to Saudi Arabia against encouraging any renewed large-scale fighting by Yemeni royalists.

2. These incidents mark another phase in the war of nerves between Saudi Arabia and the U.A.R. By immediately publicizing an earlier series of explosions within Saudi Arabia, the U.A.R. press has sought to create an impression of growing popular dissidence and discontent with the rule of King Faisal. For their part, U.A.R. authorities are no doubt concerned over recent apparently successful Saudi efforts to bring Yemeni royalists and republican dissidents together into a single coalition, as well as by the threat of renewed royalist military action in the Sanaa region and indications of wavering loyalty on the part of a key tribal leader.

3. While not of a serious nature, the U.A.R. overflights are likely to strengthen rather than weaken the hand of those in Saudi Government councils who advocate a general renewal of organized hostilities in Yemen and a consequent showdown with the U.A.R. King Faisal has thus far resisted growing pressure in this direction from his advisors. It seems likely he will continue to move cautiously at least until work on air defenses in southern Saudi Arabia is completed, probably sometime this spring.

4. We are authorizing Ambassador Eilts to tell King Faisal that we have been impressed by his statesmanlike restraint and to urge him to continue to follow this policy. The Ambassador may confirm our earlier assurances with respect to *unprovoked* aggression against Saudi

---

[1] Source: National Archives and Records Administration, RG 59, Central Files 1967–69, POL 31–1 SAUD–UAR. Confidential. Drafted by Korn and Brewer. The initials "DR" on the memorandum indicate that the Secretary read it.

Arabia but at the same time is to stress our hope that the current psychological warfare between the U.A.R. and Saudi Arabia will not be a prelude to new outbreaks of tribal fighting in Yemen.[2]

---

[2] Telegram 111756 to Jidda, January 3, authorized Eilts, when meeting with Faisal, to express U.S. concern over recent reports of UAR bombings of the Najran frontier area, and to state that the Department was impressed by the King's statesmanlike restraint in face of this and other provocations, all of which appeared to be part of a propaganda war rather than a renewal of serious hostilities. Such restraint still remained in the U.S. view the best course. The Ambassador was also authorized to confirm earlier U.S. assurances regarding unprovoked aggression against Saudi territory. (Ibid., POL 15–1 SAUD)

---

420.   Telegram From the Department of State to the Embassy in Saudi Arabia[1]

Washington, January 20, 1967, 6:27 p.m.

122702. Jidda 2755 (Notal) SAG–UAR Tension.[2]

1. Agree SAG–UAR struggle has sharpened, with specific problems of Yemen and Islamic solidarity contributing to what has now become general Faisal–Nasser confrontation. Head-on military collision clearly not in our interest. Question arises, however, if such collision as imminent as has been true at other times in past, e.g., summer 1965. While Saudi and Egyptian troops are facing each other across north Yemen border, they have been in relatively static position for many months. We have seen no offensive troop deployments on either side

---

[1] Source: National Archives and Records Administration, RG 59, Central Files 1967–69, POL 27 SAUD–UAR. Secret; Limdis. Drafted by Moore and Brewer; cleared by Houghton, Officer in Charge of Economic Affairs in the Office of Near Eastern Affairs George M. Bennsky, and Country Director for Pakistan and Afghanistan James W. Spain; and approved by Davies. Also sent to Kuwait and Cairo and repeated to London, Beirut, Amman, Sanaa, and Rawalpindi.

[2] Telegram 2755 from Jidda, January 17, reported that recent indications were that Saudi–UAR confrontation was sharpening, and that as mutual Faisal–Nasser suspicion deepened, the few remaining threads of meaningful direct contact that might allow some dialog to be resumed on smaller matters were being severed. Eilts proposed that the U.S. Government continue to urge Kuwait to proceed with its mediation effort, but also take additional steps to ease present tensions, such as urging Faisal and Nasser to look for ways and means to bring about a Saudi–UAR détente as a prerequisite to resuming a meaningful dialog on outstanding problems such as Yemen. Alternatively, the United States might seek to have some mutually acceptable, uncommitted Arab chief of state, such as President Helou of Lebanon, use his good offices between Faisal and Nasser. (Ibid.)

which might foreshadow attack. Nasser has publicly threatened attack Saudi support bases for Yemeni royalists in Najran and Jizan, but such threat has been conditioned on Saudi resumption major aid to royalists. Current UAR policy seems blend propaganda and harassment which hard on Saudi nerves but unlikely escalate to military conflict. Meanwhile Faisal seems clearly recognize that continuing restraint of royalists is very much in his own self-interest. We do not discount existence royalist pressure on him but believe Saudi influence on royalists greater than vice versa and that SAG restraint likely continue be exercised at least until end pilgrimage season early April.

2. UAR emphasis on propaganda and support Yemeni subversion in Saudi Arabia may diminish in strength as non-Saudi subversive types rounded up, recently initiated SAG security precautions become more effective and absence significant popular Saudi support for anti-regime activities becomes clearer. (Jidda 2763[3] indicates such popular response to UAR efforts has not been forthcoming.) Just as Faisal has overestimated domestic impact on Nasser of lengthened UAR involvement in Yemen, so Nasser seems to underestimate extent popular acceptance Faisal within Saudi Arabia.

3. Foregoing is not to downgrade very real concern Dept shares with Embassy about present state Saudi-Egyptian relations, but does indicate that these relations have not yet deteriorated to point where area peace threatened. In this tense but not traumatic situation, and in absence any indication that either side ready for détente, we doubt there is at present any useful action which USG might take. In fact, US initiative at this time might make positions of parties more rigid, each believing our action was sign that other side weakening under existing pressure. Aside from question of whether Helou would be acceptable to both sides or willing undertake role (on which we have doubts), foregoing argument would seem apply any approaches at present by Lebanese. While Kuwait mediation dormant, it is an open channel available to parties whenever they choose to use it. Intervention this juncture either by USG or by Helou could result closing this channel. In event situation were to deteriorate to point where hostilities appear imminent, we would be willing consider high level US approach to both sides.

4. Both Embassies Jidda and Cairo should nevertheless continue make use suitable occasions to discuss SAG–UAR problems, importance for both of meaningful détente, and need exercise restraint on military activities Yemen in order avoid provoking direct Saudi-Egyptian hostilities.

---

[3] Dated January 17. (Ibid., POL 23–7 SAUD)

5. Possible encouragement for Pakistan effort (Dhahran 477 Notal)[4] is subject separate message.

6. *For Kuwait.* You should continue encourage GOK at highest appropriate level keep mediation effort active. DeptOff took this line with Kuwait Ambassador January 19 but latter indicated immediate outlook not promising.

Rusk

---

[4] Telegram 477 from Dhahran, January 19, reported that during a meeting with the Ambassador on January 18 Pharaon had expressed his personal view that the Kuwaiti mediation effort was "finished." He also informed Eilts that the Government of Pakistan had sent a letter to the Saudi Arabian Government indicating its willingness to help and suggesting a Faisal–Nasser meeting in Karachi. The Saudis had replied by sending Pakistan a statement of the Saudi position on the Yemen problem, to which there had so far been no response. (Ibid., POL 27 YEMEN)

---

421. Telegram From the Department of State to the Embassy in the United Arab Republic[1]

Washington, January 28, 1967, 6:44 p.m.

127476. Ref: State's 127384,[2] Jidda's 2926[3] and 2930.[4]

1. Acting Secretary made following points to UAR Ambassador Kamel this afternoon re UAR bombing of Najran.

a. SAG has informed us Najran bombed twice January 27 by UAR aircraft with loss at least eight lives, others wounded and property

---

[1] Source: National Archives and Records Administration, RG 59, Central Files 1967–69, POL 27 SAUD–UAR. Secret; Immediate. Drafted by Bennsky, Moore, and Korn; cleared by Davies, in substance by Director of the Office of UN Political Affairs Elizabeth Ann Brown, Quinn, and Judd; and approved by Katzenbach. Also sent to Jidda and repeated to London, Amman, Beirut, Kuwait, Sanaa, Dhahran, Taiz, USUN, CINCSTRIKE, and CHUSMTM Dhahran.

[2] Telegram 127384 to Cairo, January 28, informed the Embassy that the Under Secretary had called in UAR Ambassador Kamel to express U.S. concern over the UAR air attacks on Najran. (Ibid.)

[3] Dated January 28. (Ibid., E 11–3)

[4] In telegram 2930 from Jidda, January 28, Eilts proposed possible measures to signal U.S. concern at the Najran bombings while also demonstrating U.S. support for Saudi Arabia's integrity, such as a public statement, a strong U.S. démarche to Nasser, a symbolic military gesture, and an effort to get a leading international personality, possibly through UN channels, to mediate. (Ibid., POL 27 SAUD–UAR)

damaged. One of these raids reportedly witnessed by foreign journalists. We also have reports of third raid on January 28.

b. We have no evidence SAG has taken any actions which would have provoked such bombing raids. Our indications are Faisal has been making determined and successful efforts restrain Yemeni royalists from resuming hostilities in Yemen.

c. Such raids can only serve to harden positions and make solution in Yemen more difficult reach.

d. Acting Secretary expressed USG concern (1) over these raids in an area of world where we have strong interests and (2) that such incidents be avoided in this region where we desire see peace and stability maintained.

e. When these raids are reported by our press they will cause public reaction which, as Ambassador Kamel knows, will make more difficult our joint efforts improve US–UAR relations and reach agreement on various matters under discussion between us.

2. Kamel responded at length making following points:

a. He did not have facts this matter from his government.

b. Questioned fact foreign correspondents would be in out of way place such as Najran as raising doubts validity alleged bombing raids.

c. Gave detailed coverage Yemen problem from beginning, as seen from Egyptian viewpoint, concluding that Faisal out to humiliate and defeat Egyptians there rather than seeking mutually acceptable solution allowing their withdrawal. Made strong pitch USG should get active in Yemen matter via mediation or other means as he had been urging for some months.

d. Emphasized Najran was base for royalist infiltrators who were killing Egyptian "boys" and Egyptians could not give up right self-defense. If UAR bombed Najran there must have been provocation.

3. In response Acting Secretary stated we believe it true UAR planes had bombed Najran. He wanted emphasize strongly that this in no way helped situation of UAR or made solution Yemen problem easier. Faisal has been restraining resumption royalist activities including infiltration according to our information. Suggested correspondents could have been in Najran because of recent reports gas bombing by UAR in North Yemen near Saudi border.

4. Kamel said he would do his best express USG concern to his government and requested we restrain Saudi Arabia from provoking UAR.

5. Without specifically mentioning current top-level USG consideration UAR food request, presentations Acting Secretary (and Dep.

Asst. Sec. Davies afterwards) gave Kamel clear impression USG concern over bombing raids could at the least slow up the deliberations.

6. *For Cairo:* You requested take up Najran bombing raids with highest appropriate level UARG drawing on Acting Secretary's presentation paras 1 and 3 above for substance démarche.[5]

7. *For Jidda.* In response Saudi query re proposed US action (paragraph 2, Jidda telegram 2925)[6] request you speak to Saqqaf as follows:

a. Inform him of foregoing representation in Washington and of planned follow up in Cairo.

b. Should make clear to him that we deeply concerned over UAR action and that we indicating this concern in response press queries. (Unprovoked attack on Saudi territory should place SAG in powerful position vis-à-vis world press and public opinion. Presence foreign journalists in Najran strengthens Saudi case.)

c. Request he convey to King our renewed assurances of concern for Saudi integrity and indicate that various courses action in support Saudi Arabia are under active study by USG. We understand need for rapid action. At same time believe it of major importance that we avoid any precipitate step which could redound to ultimate disadvantage of both Saudi Arabia and US. King should be assured problem receiving urgent attention at highest levels USG and that we prepared consult continuously with SAG re most useful courses action.

8. FYI. Believe decision on issuance public statement should be deferred until receipt UAR reaction to our démarches. Concerning recommendation for dispatch infantry unit on "training mission," we need better assessment UAR intentions and motives before making decision. Our 1963–64 experience with Operation Hard Surface demonstrated problems involved in sending token force. If faced with determined UAR action, would probably be necessary either withdraw or strengthen such symbolic force. (May be appropriate allow USMTM advisers travel Najran but would prefer delay decision at least until Army Attaché Col. Broady returns from projected visit.) We studying possibilities of action within UN framework (initiated either by Saudis or others) or of prompting third party mediation as suggested by Jidda. End FYI.

---

[5] In telegram 4219 from Cairo, January 29, Battle reported that he had expressed U.S. concern over the bombing to Foreign Office Under Secretary el-Feki, following the Department's guidance, and had pointed out that there were newspaper reports from journalists who had witnessed the bombing. He noted that el-Feki, who was unable to give him an official response, made no real effort to deny the fact of the bombings. (Ibid.)

[6] Dated January 28. (Ibid.)

9. *For London:* Have informed British Embassy in general terms of representation to Ambassador Kamel. You may similarly keep Foreign Office informed.

Rusk

---

422. **Telegram From the Embassy in the United Arab Republic to the Department of State**[1]

Cairo, January 30, 1967, 1518Z.

4239. 1. I am deeply disturbed by increasing tensions between Egyptians and Saudis. While these tensions arise from many sources, current focus is, of course, Yemen. In Yemen problem there are various elements that can lead to rapid and dangerous escalation regardless of whether it is what anyone wishes or serves interest any party. Unfortunately this escalation may well involve us. I can well understand Amb Eilts' concern over situation and his belief we must reassure Feisal that we will back up often repeated words of assurance that we will come to his assistance in event of unprovoked aggression. It seems to me, however, that what is most needed by the Saudis, the Egyptians, the Yemenis and, most importantly, by the US, is time. Feisal needs time to provide excuses for not unleashing royalists and/or retaliating. Nasser needs time to keep from getting himself in greater mess than he already has stirred up. The Yemenis need time because they will be the greatest loser with the least influence on outcome of any participant. The US needs time because it does not want to risk instability, war, or direct and serious confrontation with Nasser in which US would be on side conservative regimes against Nasser and revolutionary countries, thereby increasing dangerous trend toward polarization which has been under way for some months. Time alone will solve nothing. It might, however, permit a loosening of positions already much too rigid and possibly the creation of a climate in which new elements can emerge.

2. Our choices for the moment are the following:

A. To rely on Kuwaiti or other efforts (Moroccan, Sudanese, Pakistan, etc.) with little hope of success.

---

[1] Source: National Archives and Records Administration, RG 59, Central Files 1967–69, POL 27 YEMEN. Secret; Priority. Repeated to CINCSTRIKE/CINCMEAFSA, Aden, Sanaa, USUN, Beirut, Amman, Kuwait, and Jidda.

B. Do nothing except continue our words of warning and concern to both UAR and Saudis.

C. Take such steps as necessary to reassure Saudis we will back up our commitment recognizing that such steps run risk escalation.

D. Take new initiative to resolve Yemen conflict or at minimum provide cooling off time for all countries involved.

3. Of the alternatives only the new initiative (para D) offers much hope in situation that is inherently dangerous and contains elements real risks for US. It is wiser for us to face fact we are already involved and to take relatively small risk of mediation than to permit drift which will bring us inevitably to point we will have to back up commitment to Saudis, presumably with US forces.

4. I understand reasons that have argued against direct US offer mediate Yemen since last Bunker mission. However, to offer to mediate now risks only loss prestige in effort preserve peace. I am quite willing see us risk minor loss of face to prevent or at least delay major confrontations which can be disastrous from our point of view.

5. Various ideas have been advanced in recent weeks re possible mediators from Arab or international world. I recommend we recognize that we are involved in outcome Yemen no matter what happens and try to make our involvement as helpful toward bringing solution as possible. I therefore urge that we make offer either of good offices or mediation in situation that is highly explosive. Suggest Amb. Bunker, long acquainted with Yemen problem and having great stature in area and world, be assigned task of mediation. It would at least give time for situation to sort itself out and avoid dangerous military escalation. Believe it especially important we take such a step before we find ourselves committing US forces in Arabian peninsula.[2]

Battle

---

[2] In a January 31 memorandum to Rostow, Howard Wriggins commented that although there was merit in Battle's proposal that the United States should undertake a new mediation effort, he agreed with Deputy Assistant Secretary Rodger Davies, who argued that the U.S. Government should attempt to reactivate the Kuwaiti mediation before involving itself directly. (Johnson Library, National Security File, Saunders Files, UAR–Saudi (Yemen issue), 4/1/66–1/20/69)

423.   **Telegram From the Department of State to the Embassy in Saudi Arabia**[1]

Washington, January 31, 1967, 7:35 p.m.

128727. Jidda tel 2930,[2] State 127476.[3]

1. Possible US responses to Saudi request for implementation our security assurances fall into broad fields of military and political. Separate message being sent indicating possible range our action in military field, which strongly limited by importance our avoiding direct involvement UAR/SAG hostilities.[4]

2. Action in political field required in first instance to prevent immediate outbreak hostilities and, subsequently, to bring Faisal–Nasser détente. (Anticipate that specific details Yemen solution would be outgrowth of latter rather than determining element.) As hours pass without renewal UAR bombing or immediate Saudi retaliation and with apparent continued SAG attempt keep diplomatic relations with UAR, certain amount of automatic cooling off is occurring. Prompt action by Kuwaitis could further ease immediate problem. Main aim at moment is to get Egyptians and Saudis talking again at any level as noted by Saqqaf (Jidda tel 2954).[5] Following are among possibilities for achieving this:

3. *Offer direct US mediation.* As suggested Cairo's 4239,[6] such offer might be best technique for immediate requirement of gaining time in order permit a relaxation of currently rigid positions. Ultimate success doubtful in view our lack sufficient leverage, particularly in Cairo. Faisal may also have some doubts about usefulness

---

[1] Source: National Archives and Records Administration, RG 59, Central Files 1967–69, POL 27 SAUD–UAR. Secret; Priority. Drafted by Moore and Campbell; cleared by Sisco, Buffum, Davies, Brown, L. Bruce Laingen (NEA/PAF), and Bennsky; and approved by Handley. Also sent to Cairo, Rawalpindi, Kuwait, Sanaa, and USUN and repeated to Amman, Beirut, and London.

[2] See footnote 4, Document 421.

[3] Document 421.

[4] Telegram 128587 to Jidda, January 31, a State–Defense message, authorized the U.S. Military Training Mission in Saudi Arabia to send a small number of technical experts to advise Saudi air defense units in the border area for a short period, but cautioned the Mission to exercise particular care that its role remained advisory and not operational. (National Archives and Records Administration, RG 59, Central Files 1967–69, POL 27 SAUD–UAR)

[5] Dated January 29. (Ibid.)

[6] Document 422.

direct mediation since he considers Bunker disengagement effort as failure.[7]

4. *New Third Party Effort.* If Kuwaitis are no more active or successful now than in last few months, may be useful for us encourage new mediator.[8] With Saqqaf's indication Pakistani effort would be acceptable (Jidda 2962),[9] Ayub may offer practical hope for bringing détente.

5. *Further possibility is to bring UN into problem.* (Note from Jidda 2963[10] that SAG also giving this active consideration. Baroody has seen UNSYG, but details this meeting not yet known.) Following factors enter into such consideration:

a. It is of importance that further increase in tensions and polarization of Arab world be avoided. Injection Saudi–UAR confrontation into UN framework could in fact sharpen polarization by focusing broad international attention on dispute in which US and USSR would predictably be taking opposite sides.

b. If, however, we become convinced Saudis must and will do something in retaliation Najran bombing which will complicate problem, more desirable alternative would be recourse to UN Security Council. Advantages of SC meeting are:

(1) It would provide cooling off period; and
(2) Saudis would probably have sympathetic response from most SC members and could reasonably expect 9 votes for satisfactory resolution even though USSR may veto.

Disadvantages:

(1) Meeting would result in bitter recriminations with further worsening SAG–UAR relations;
(2) UAR could probably make damaging counter charges against Saudi's continued support of group (Yemeni royalists) working to overthrow government accepted by UN;
(3) Saudis may not get as much in resolution—despite good case—as they might hope, e.g., condemnation of UAR. And in any event USSR might veto if UAR requested.

---

[7] In telegram 3034 from Jidda, February 1, Eilts stated that he agreed with Battle's proposal that the United States consider reintervening in the Saudi–UAR confrontation with a direct offer of U.S. mediation, either alone or in conjunction with the Kuwaitis. He commented that in view of the salability to Faisal of a renewed U.S. mediation effort, there might be distinct value in having a new mediator who could not be personally reproached with past failures, such as Governor Harriman. (National Archives and Records Administration, RG 59, Central Files 1967–69, POL 27 YEMEN)

[8] In telegram 4341 from Cairo, February 3, Battle stated his belief that the present Saudi-Egyptian imbroglio required more rapid action than they were likely to get out of the United Nations or the Kuwaitis and argued that if the United States wanted to seek a solution to the basic problem of Yemen, it was going to have to intervene actively. (Ibid.)

[9] Dated January 30. (Ibid.)

[10] Dated January 30. (Ibid., POL 27 SAUD–UAR)

6. Foregoing assumes Saudi charge will be limited to Najran bombing. It impossible to predict what would happen if Saudis leveled poison gas charges. That would depend on how provable their case is. If they raise charge without providing convincing proof, they may cast doubt on their general credibility, including Najran charges. We would prefer to suspend judgment on this until further info available on poison gas accusations.

7. Since there is no clear case in favor of going to SC, might be useful consider prompting different type UN action as suggested para 5 Jidda's 2930. Some interested party could ask SYG to step back into SAG–UAR problem with offer to continue his efforts which began in fall of 1962. On April 29, 1963 (S/5298) SYG reported he consulted regularly with SAG–UAR about "certain aspects of situation in Yemen of external origin with view to making my office available for such assistance as might be desired toward insuring against any developments which might threaten peace of area." As result SYG appointed Bunche to fact-finding mission, which eventually with Bunker's help ended in creation UNYOM. Although UNYOM terminated, SYG could revive his personal role and perhaps appoint a representative whose mission would be initially limited to easing current tension between UAR and Saudi Arabia and if successful to recommend additional steps for further mediation of basic SAG–UAR differences over Yemen. (In terminating UNYOM, SYG put himself at disposal of parties in search of peaceful solution.)

8. Whether USG or some other interested party requests SYG intervention could be decided later. It would be advisable, if possible, to obtain prior Saudi and UAR agreement before asking for SYG help. In any case SYG will insist on SAG and UAR concurrence at some point.

9. Posts are requested to comment urgently on foregoing possibilities.[11]

Rusk

---

[11] In telegram 773 from Kuwait, February 2, Cottam argued that Kuwaiti mediation still seemed to afford the most likely means of eventually resolving the underlying dispute. Any new direct U.S. mediation initiative would increase U.S. involvement, but probably with no greater chance of success than the present Kuwaiti effort. Of the various alternatives suggested in the Department's telegram, the Embassy believed reinvolvement of the UN Secretary General might be the most desirable. (Ibid., POL 27 YEMEN)

424. Memorandum From Harold H. Saunders of the National Security Council Staff to the President's Special Assistant (Rostow)[1]

Washington, February 3, 1967.

SUBJECT

Poison Gas in Yemen

Since your discussion in staff meeting this morning Peter Jessup has requested a full CIA rundown on the evidence of the UAR's use of poison gas. The intelligence community has already gone over the evidence we have with inconclusive results. The study Peter has requested will give us the latest judgment.[2]

Spurgeon Keeny is also in touch with the agency's scientific people and we will stay in touch with Dr. Hornig's staff. Spurgeon rightly feels that they can be useful in making sure the intelligence people make the most of the evidence we have.

State doesn't want us to get too far out in front on this, and I think they're right. The UN now has two formal requests—one from Yemen and one surprisingly from the UAR—to investigate Saudi charges.[3] The next step should be a UN investigation, which we'd support. (The convention on poison gas is a UN, not a Red Cross responsibility.)

Our public posture so far has been that we do not have conclusive independent evidence of our own and therefore can not pronounce ourselves on the merits of the case. However, we do deplore the use of poison gas anywhere. That may continue to be the best posture, but CIA's study will hopefully give us a better base for our behind-scenes maneuvers.

Hal

---

[1] Source: Johnson Library, National Security File, Country File, Yemen, Cables & Memos, Vol. II, 7/64–12/68. Secret.

[2] No CIA study has been found.

[3] In response to a Saudi suggestion that the United States analyze blood samples from alleged Yemen poison gas victims, telegram 123250 to Jidda, January 22, instructed the Embassy to state that it would be preferable if scientific tests to determine UAR use of poison gas in Yemen were performed by an international agency or in a country having no direct interest in the region. (National Archives and Records Administration, RG 59, Central Files 1967–69, POL 27–10 YEMEN)

425.   Telegram From the Department of State to the Embassy in Kuwait[1]

Washington, February 3, 1967, 10:55 a.m.

130616. Kuwait tel 763.[2] Please deliver following message from Secretary to FonMin Sabah:

"Dear Mr. Minister:

I recall with pleasure our most recent meeting in New York last September and the discussion we had at that time regarding our mutual concern for a peaceful solution to the problem in Yemen. Our interest in that problem has continued and we have followed closely and sympathetically your efforts to mediate the conflict within the Arab family. We have tried discreetly to supplement your efforts by encouraging each side to exercise moderation and to seek agreement.

We are now greatly disturbed over the effect which the recent aerial attacks on Najran may have on general peace and stability in the Near Eastern area, in addition to their discouraging impact on attempts to reach a settlement in Yemen. We have informed the Government of the United Arab Republic of our concern and have also discussed the matter with the Government of Saudi Arabia. We have urged both sides not to engage in further acts which would threaten the outbreak of hostilities between them.

Ambassador Cottam has informed me that you are still prepared to continue your mediation efforts between President Nasser and King Faisal. You have our wholehearted appreciation and support for these efforts and our assurances that we would welcome your recommendations as to how we could best assist your attempts to keep peace in the area.

Please accept, Mr. Minister, my warmest personal regards.

Sincerely, Dean Rusk"[3]

Rusk

---

[1] Source: National Archives and Records Administration, RG 59, Central Files 1967–69, POL 27 YEMEN. Secret; Priority; Limdis. Drafted by Moore on February 2, cleared by Davies and Bennsky, and approved by Rusk. Repeated to Jidda, Cairo, USUN, and London.

[2] In telegram 763 from Kuwait, January 31, Cottam reported that he and Brewer had made a strong appeal to Foreign Minister Sabah to take an immediate initiative to de-escalate the Saudi–UAR conflict, and had reiterated U.S. support for and appreciation of Kuwait's mediation efforts. (Ibid.)

[3] Telegram 836 from Kuwait, February 16, transmitted a summary of Foreign Minister Sabah's reply to the Secretary's letter, stating that Kuwait had been pressing mediation, but pointing out that the obstacle of Hamid ad-Din's withdrawal and its relation to the number of UAR troops remained and that neither the United Arab Republic nor Saudi Arabia would change its stand. (Ibid.)

426. Information Memorandum From the Deputy Assistant Secretary of State for Near Eastern and South Asian Affairs (Davies) to Secretary of State Rusk[1]

Washington, February 6, 1967.

SUBJECT

U.S. Military Involvement in Saudi–Yemen Border Area

1. U.A.R. air strikes on January 27 against the Saudi town of Najran, only a few miles from the Yemen border, have prompted the Saudi Government to invoke our long-standing assurances of support in case of unprovoked attack. We have sought to implement our commitment mainly by diplomatic means, e.g., the Under Secretary's representations on January 28 to the U.A.R. Ambassador and your letter of February 3 to the Kuwaiti Foreign Minister[2] encouraging continued mediation efforts. We have turned down a Saudi request for two U.S. Army-manned Hawk missile batteries to be stationed near Najran. The Saudis continue however to urge us to "do something" to protect them.

2. Saudi faith in our friendship would be seriously undermined if we were to be completely unresponsive to their requests for military assistance. We have accordingly authorized our 235-man Military Training Mission in Saudi Arabia to detail no more than three officers for short visits to the Yemen border area to advise on Saudi air defense arrangements. The officers, who are to visit Najran on February 8, have been instructed to maintain as low visibility as possible and to avoid any operational involvement. We have also approved in principle a Saudi request for purchase of Sidewinder air-to-air missiles for four Saudi Air Force F–86s, although delivery may be delayed for some time owing to unavailability of mounting devices. Our Defense Attaché in Jidda has just returned from a visit to Najran to survey the damage caused by the U.A.R. air strikes.

3. The Raytheon Company, which holds the Hawk missile contract with the Saudi Government, has agreed to a Saudi request, made directly to the Company and without our knowledge, to position its recently arrived first Hawk battery near Najran. Raytheon technicians would erect the battery, which could be in place by the middle or end of February, but would not fire the missiles. We are aware that placing the Hawks so near the border could result in their being fired into

---

[1] Source: National Archives and Records Administration, RG 59, Central Files 1967–69, POL 32–1 SAUD. Secret. Drafted by Korn and Moore. A copy was sent to the Under Secretary. The initials "DR" on the memorandum indicate that the Secretary read it.

[2] See Documents 421 and 425.

Yemeni airspace. Additionally, if Raytheon technicians at Najran should be inadvertently involved in hostilities it would add to U.A.R.–U.S. frictions. It could also pose legal problems for the individual Americans concerned. (We will be advising them of their legal position and of possible limitations on the extent of official U.S. protection which could be afforded them.) However, we have no legal control over the Hawk battery since it is now Saudi property. More importantly, we believe any official U.S. move to prevent Raytheon from complying with the Saudi request would result in loss of all Saudi credence in us and our oft-repeated assurances of support. On the other hand, continuation of the low-key type of support we are giving will come as no surprise to the Egyptians and, of itself, should not lead to a more serious confrontation with them than we are already in.

427.   Memorandum From W. Howard Wriggins of the National Security Council Staff to the President's Special Assistant (Rostow)[1]

Washington, February 17, 1967.

SUBJECT

Yemen Mediation

As you will have seen from the summary,[2] Luke Battle asks for authority to offer good offices to Faisal and Nasser. He is persuaded that: (a) the Kuwaiti mediation has run out of steam; (b) the UAR's tough action in Najran and a tough-talking speech by Faisal have put both in a position where they cannot by themselves make progress; (c) U Thant missed the boat last time and will not move with sufficient alacrity.

Therefore: Luke thinks he should take the opportunity given by Nasser's stopping our overflights[3] to discuss the full complex of Mid-

---

[1] Source: Johnson Library, National Security File, Name File, Wriggins Memos, 1967. Secret.

[2] Not attached.

[3] Telegram 4542 from Cairo, February 12, reported that the UAR Foreign Office had informed the Embassy that the UAR Government had decided to cancel its previous permission for U.S. aircraft to overfly the United Arab Republic carrying arms for Jordan. (National Archives and Records Administration, RG 59, Central Files 1967–69, DEF 17–1 US)

dle-Eastern questions and to offer a high-level good offices effort. Rodger Davies, Deputy Assistant Secretary, agrees and is shaping such a recommendation for Nick.

In my view unless some such step is taken, (a) polarization will sharpen, (b) our relations with the UAR will become increasingly more strained, and (c) the likelihood of our having to come to Faisal's help or lose our reputation for reliability will greatly increase. We are in the middle already, and the role of responsible statesmanship requires a U.S. initiative, rather than pretending we are on the sidelines.

Do you agree? I need to know in order to play a useful hand as the State Department shapes its position today and tomorrow.

---

428.   Telegram From the Department of State to the Embassy in the United Arab Republic[1]

Washington, February 18, 1967, 7:35 p.m.

140276. Ref Cairo 4649.[2]

1. Department agrees that continued deterioration Saudi–UAR relations makes it increasingly desirable for US direct offer of good offices or mediation, perhaps sooner rather than later. Whether this ultimately should take form of high level US statesman (probably Bunker) visiting both capitals, promotion of Saudi–UAR meetings in Europe (Jidda 3314),[3] or some other technique depends on further developments and recommendations addressees. Would appreciate receiving Amb Battle's proposed scenario for approach to Nasser offered para 8 reftel.

2. Final tour d'horizon with Nasser would, we believe, be useful in any event.

3. Although chances Kuwait mediation are fading, believe we should do all possible promote GOK efforts at least in interim until we decide act ourselves. Further GOK activity in any event not incompatible with US moves. Since Saqqaf visit Kuwait still scheduled for

---

[1] Source: National Archives and Records Administration, RG 59, Central Files 1967–69, POL 27 YEMEN. Secret; Priority. Drafted by Moore on February 17; cleared by Davies, Bergus, and Wriggins; and approved by Katzenbach. Also sent to Jidda and Kuwait and repeated to London, Beirut, Sanaa, and Amman.

[2] Dated February 16. (Ibid., DEF 17–1 US)

[3] Dated February 16. (Ibid., POL 27 YEMEN)

Feb 21, best hope lies in facilitating meeting at that time with al-Khouli or other appropriate UAR official. For that purpose request following action:

A. *For Jidda*—Recognize need for King's approval Saqqaf–Egyptian discussion and assume there no use pressing Cairo send al-Khouli until certain King would not oppose talks. Request you ascertain King's views soonest.[4]

B. *For Cairo*—Request you strongly urge UAR respond to Kuwait "direct question" (Kuwait tel 835)[5] that it in fact wants continuation GOK mediation. If it is clear by the time you make this approach that Faisal has no opposition Saqqaf–al-Khouli discussion, you should urge UAR take advantage Saqqaf presence Kuwait to initiate dialogue.

C. *For Kuwait*—If Faisal sanctions meeting, you should urge Kuwaitis invite al-Khouli meet with Saqqaf under GOK auspices.

Katzenbach

---

[4] In telegram 580 from Dhahran, February 20, Eilts reported that the King had responded that Saqqaf had not been instructed to discuss details of the Yemen problem and that any senior UAR officials would be welcome in Riyadh if the United Arab Republic wanted to send one for this purpose. In answer to the Ambassador's argument that such a meeting would be better in Kuwait or elsewhere, Faisal said he had not studied the matter and could give no answer at that time. (Ibid., POL 27 YEMEN)

[5] In telegram 835 from Kuwait, February 16, Cottam reported that Foreign Minister Sabah intended to call in the UAR Ambassador to pose a direct question through him to Nasser: i.e., does the United Arab Republic want Kuwait to continue mediation? (Ibid., POL 7 SAUD)

429.   Telegram From the Embassy in the United Arab Republic to the Department of State[1]

Cairo, March 28, 1967, 1206Z.

5738. Reference: Cairo 5030[2] and Jidda's 3391[3] and 3473.[4]

1. During President's dinner for Ould Daddah last evening Foreign Office Under Secretary El Feki asked me to call on him this morning which I have just done.

2. El Feki said President Nasser had been pondering most seriously suggestion of possible US mediation UAR–Saudi difficulties mentioned by Ambassador Battle during his farewell call on March 4. President now wished US to know that he would in principle accept Ambassador Raymond Hare in this role. If he could be made available, final decision on mediation would, of course, have to be reached in light his terms reference and parallel Saudi agreement.

3. I said I personally was greatly heartened by President's response to offer put forward by Ambassador Battle and knew that he would be also. I would report this development immediately and would recommend prompt and favorable USG consideration.

4. *Comment:* This is first break we have had in many months of deterioration US–UAR relations. I feel Ambassador Hare is logical and ideal choice and that assuming he is acceptable to Saudis will just by undertaking task greatly lower temperatures in area and give US–UAR relations much needed blood transfusion.

5. Would appreciate Department's reaction soonest and if possible prior Soviet Foreign Minister Gromyko's departure from Cairo April first.

Nes

---

[1] Source: National Archives and Records Administration, RG 59, Central Files 1967–69, POL 27 YEMEN. Secret; Priority; Exdis. Repeated to Jidda.

[2] In telegram 5030 from Cairo, March 4, Battle reported that during his farewell call on Nasser, he had raised the subject of Yemen and asked whether on his return to Washington he should urge the U.S. Government to join in one of several offers to mediate or to take the initiative on its own in that direction. Nasser responded that he had gone to Jidda and entered into the Jidda Agreement against the advice of his colleagues. He was not now hopeful of a solution in view of the other side's determination to view this as a sign of weakness, which it had not in fact reflected. Battle said that he took this to mean Nasser would not oppose U.S. efforts, but did not hold out much hope for their chance of success. Nasser agreed that this was his attitude. (Ibid., POL UAR–US) Printed in *Foreign Relations, 1964–1968*, vol. XVIII, Document 393.

[3] Dated February 20. (National Archives and Records Administration, RG 59, Central Files 1967–69, POL 27 YEMEN)

[4] Dated February 25. (Ibid.)

430. Telegram From the Department of State to the Embassy in Saudi Arabia[1]

Washington, March 29, 1967, 11:55, a.m.

164518. Cairo 5738;[2] Jidda 3967.[3]

1. Dept encouraged by UAR suggestion. We fully concur Ambassador Hare would make exceptionally effective choice, both from personal and professional standpoint. In our view, next step should be early discussion with King Faisal in effort secure his agreement in principle, following which detailed terms of reference could be worked out on ad referendum basis to both governments.

2. You are accordingly instructed seek immediate audience with His Majesty to raise this subject. You should inform him that Ambassador Battle, after consultation with Dept, took advantage his final meeting with Nasser before leaving Cairo to reiterate our hope that way could be found bring about peaceful resolution Yemen problem. On personal basis Ambassador Battle asked Nasser whether on his return to Washington to assume broader responsibilities for USG relations with Near East he should urge USG offer join in one of several offers mediate Yemen problem or take initiative on our own in that direction. Nasser response was noncommittal. However, our Cairo Embassy learned some days ago that Egyptians were continuing keep this suggestion under advisement and, on March 28, Deputy FonMin informed our Chargé that Nasser had reacted favorably Ambassador Battle's idea and now willing respond favorably to US initiative possibly through a US representative such as Ambassador Raymond Hare. Ambassador Hare well and favorably known His Majesty from long association with Saudi Arabia both in Dept and as USG Ambassador, and we would be willing propose him formally undertake this task. Accordingly Dept has instructed you immediately approach His Majesty in order discuss general idea with him, stressing Dept interest in constructive proposal and willingness be of whatever help we can in helping resolve this longstanding problem.

---

[1] Source: National Archives and Records Administration, RG 59, Central Files 1967–69, POL 27 YEMEN. Secret; Immediate; Exdis. Drafted by Brewer; cleared by Battle, Bergus, and Hare; and approved by Rusk. Repeated to Cairo.

[2] Document 429.

[3] In telegram 3967 from Jidda, March 29, Eilts stated that he believed Faisal could be persuaded to agree to resumption of U.S. mediation if Ambassador Hare were involved, but pointed out that the King would first want to know the terms of reference. (National Archives and Records Administration, RG 59, Central Files 1967–69, POL 27 YEMEN)

3. Assuming Faisal reacts favorably, you should tell him that we envisage next step would be preparation terms of reference which we would then refer both parties for their consideration and acceptance. Once this done, and nomination Ambassador Hare approved by both sides, new USG initiative assist parties in reaching settlement could formally get under way.

4. *For Cairo:* Inform FonOff soonest Dept most interested in UAR attitude on possible role for Ambassador Hare and we now urgently taking up with Saudi Government.

Rusk

---

431.   Telegram From the Embassy in Saudi Arabia to the Department of State[1]

Jidda, April 2, 1967, 1500Z.

4047. SecState 164518;[2] Jidda 4008.[3]

1. Met with King Faisal for about two hours late last night. Rashad Pharaon present throughout audience. At outset Saqqaf also there, but soon left and did not reappear. (He is ill.) King relaxed and in good form and spirits.

2. I first reviewed long-standing USG interest in encouraging peaceful solution to Yemen problem. Recalled that during first several months my mission here and in wake failure Haradh conference, we had done utmost keep direct SAG–UAR dialogue going to resolve divergent interpretations Jidda agreement. Subsequently, when direct dialogue aborted, we had actively encouraged Kuwaiti mediation effort. Although regrettable latter now also stalled, our interest in peaceful solution remains. I then carefully gave him substance para 2 State 164518. (In doing so, I thought it best gloss over delay between Ambassador Battle's original proposal and March 28 reply to avoid, if possible, King's taking similar time to reply.) I noted that in accepting in principle renewed US mediation, sole UAR stipulations were (a) Saudi concurrence in such mediation and (b) opportunity approve terms of reference.

---

[1] Source: National Archives and Records Administration, RG 59, Central Files 1967–69, POL 27 YEMEN. Secret; Priority; Exdis. Repeated to Cairo.

[2] Document 430.

[3] Dated March 30. (National Archives and Records Administration, RG 59, Central Files 1967–69, POL 27 YEMEN)

These perfectly understandable and, if His Majesty likewise agreeable in principle, such terms of reference as might be prepared would of course also be submitted to him for consideration and acceptance. Thereafter, and once nomination Ambassador Hare approved by both sides, new USG initiative to assist parties in reaching settlement could formally get underway.

3. Faisal listened carefully and with obvious interest. He then said wished speak very candidly and hoped USG would take his comments in spirit offered. From many previous talks with him on subject of Yemen, I certainly aware of background of problem and of details his position. He assumed USG fully briefed on these. They remain unchanged. All previous pertinent agreements had been broken by Nasser. He frankly doubtful Nasser any more sincere this time. More likely this another Nasser trick either to buy time or to obtain USG help. Nasser had cooperated with Bunker mission to keep PL–480 flowing. When assured of this, he lost interest. Similarly, immediately after Jidda agreement Nasser went to Moscow where, King charged, he used Jidda agreement to extract more Soviet aid and then jettisoned agreement. Also, time growing short before Brits leave Aden. There body of opinion in Saudi Arabia that believes USG is in "collusion" with Nasser and is not really concerned about getting UAR troops out of Yemen lest this aggravate Arab-Israeli problem. Similarly, there are reports that USG indifferent to possibility of Nasser-dominated South Arabia. In telling me this, King insisted did not wish to suggest he believes these charges, but they involve matters which have to be considered. He personally is convinced USG wishes SAG well and would do nothing deliberately hurt latter's interests. However, US unwillingness recognize Nasser threat inexplicable and worrisome.

4. USG, he recalled, had been first to attempt to mediate Yemen problem in form of Bunker mission. It subsequently disengaged contending Yemen entirely an Arab problem. SAG had initially placed complete reliance in US mediation effort. Solemn promise had been made to him from very chair I sitting on that all prestige President Kennedy and American people would be exerted get Nasser out of Yemen. Nothing had happened. Some Saudis contend USG did not really try. He does not share this view. USG had indeed tried, yet its efforts totally unavailing in getting Nasser out. Is renewed USG mediation effort likely be any more effective? Furthermore, while Amb Hare is esteemed personal friend, how could Nasser make Hare's designation a "condition" of any such mediation? Surely if Nasser really wants US mediation, it should be through USG rather than through any individual person. King could only speculate about Nasser's purpose in proposing specific individual. Faisal quickly added did not wish his comments be interpreted as a Saudi refusal, but he would obviously

have to know more about "basis" on which any USG mediation would operate before giving definitive reply.

5. I pointed out to King that Nasser had not made designation of Amb Hare a "condition" of USG mediation. While I did not know exactly what had prompted mention of Amb Hare, I wanted to suggest a more constructive reason for this than one he had adduced. To me, Nasser's mention of Hare as possible mediator highly heartening development. It suggested Nasser may be genuinely anxious try to resolve Yemen problem. Hare well and favorably known in UAR, in Saudi Arabia and elsewhere in Near East. Until his recent retirement he could properly be called Dean of American diplomats serving in Near East. We here in Jidda had in fact from time to time suggested Hare's name to Dept as possible mediator. If as King feared all of this no more than another Nasser trick, I thought Hare would surely be last person whom Nasser would want to bring into matter. Hare intimately acquainted with Yemen problem and with psychology of major protagonists. Prospects either party attempting pull wool over his eyes slim. If anyone able find way through maze of divergent viewpoints and recriminations, Hare ideally qualified to do so. Faisal acknowledged validity these points.

6. As for alleged USG–UAR "collusion" that he had mentioned, I hoped he would not take it amiss if I also spoke frankly and called charge utter nonsense. I confident Faisal too wise believe it. I recalled he and I had discussed identical charge prior King's trip to US last summer, and reminded him of Secretary Rusk's specific statement to him at Blair House that objective USG policy was get UAR troops out of Yemen so that Yemeni people might decide their own future. As far as I aware there no change in this policy. Faisal recalled conversation. As for indifference to future of South Arabia, without mentioning names, I said had also heard this claim here in past few days. I was authorized categorically deny any such charge and spoke to him along lines para 1 SecState 165551.[4] He seemed gratified. As for "basis" of US mediation, I reiterated purpose present talk was merely to ascertain if King also agreeable in principle to renewed US mediation. If so, appropriate terms of reference could be drafted and submitted to him, and to Nasser, for consideration and approval. I emphasized that US mediation offer made only after most careful study. It represents constructive effort continue search for peaceful settlement. As friend, I personally hoped he would give this offer very serious study it deserves.

---

[4] Telegram 16551 to Jidda, March 30, stated that the U.S. Government was concerned at the deteriorating security situation in Aden and supported British efforts to ensure an orderly transfer of power to the new state. (Ibid.)

7. Faisal responded that, in context my comments, he wished USG to know that he has "no objection in principle" to renewed USG mediation. However, he would not wish USG be under any misapprehension. It should be clearly understood from outset that any Saudi participation in renewed USG mediation subject to certain "qualifications." Specifically, (a) SAG not willing commit itself to any particular actions or restraints while mediation going on, but reserves right to act as its interests dictate; (b) aim of mediation should be that no vestige of UAR influence remain in Yemen and that Yemeni people have right decide their future; and (c) during period of mediation is in progress, no special USG aid to UAR should be offered or given. He reiterated his suspicion that primary purpose Nasser's agreement is to obtain renewed concessionary food aid. Once assured of this, Nasser will again lose interest. If these qualifications not acceptable, Faisal thought there little purpose in USG attempting mediate.

8. I asked him exactly what he meant by not being willing commit himself to any particular actions or restraints. I pointed out, for example, that unless Yemeni royalists continue be restrained from resuming hostilities, there little prospect for anyone's mediation. UAR could rightly be expected to hit back. Faisal claimed fighting already taking place in Yemen. UAR bombing of northern Yemeni villages going on daily, and Yemeni royalists must take steps defend themselves. I recalled various previous assurances he had given me that no Saudi arms going to Yemeni royalists and asked if this still represents Saudi policy. He told me that it did when we last discussed matter, but situation now changed. While he did not specifically admit that Saudi arms aid to royalists resumed, he said "if royalists ask us for arms, we will provide them." I urged him take another look at this. I recalled he had constantly assured me [he] wanted a peaceful solution and would leave no stone unturned to achieve this. While no one could say with any certainty whether renewed USG mediation will succeed, it offers sole present prospect continue search for a peaceful settlement. As such it is highly significant development. Many Saudi friends had urged that only USG could help break impassse. But if we are to try, it requires wholehearted cooperation of all. Alternative is war which no one can win and which in no one's interest. He again insisted that war is going on and that UAR air attacks on Yemeni royalists continuing. In this situation, if Yemeni royalists ask for arms, he insisted [he] has no honorable choice but to provide them.

9. Re any new US aid to UAR, said I doubted USG could make any such blanket commitment. However, drawing on SecState 165522,[5]

---

[5] Dated March 30. (Ibid.)

I noted UAR has withdrawn its long-standing request for food aid. Hence, question of food assistance to UAR no longer current matter in US–UAR relations. He made no comment.

10. Assured him I would at once convey his views to USG for study. In doing so, however, I had frankly to tell him that if Saudis encourage resumption of hostilities in Yemen by new arms aid to royalists or other means, it could well raise question in minds US officials whether SAG really wants a peaceful settlement and whether there any purpose to renewed US mediation. Faisal responded "You may assure them I want peaceful settlement, but that I will not be tricked by Nasser again. In my view, his main purpose is to gain time and to get renewed USG aid. Same time I have no objection in principle to renewed USG mediation, with Ambassador Hare as mediator, subject already mentioned qualifications. I shall want to see terms of reference."

11. King then rehearsed at some length his well-known theme re Communist encroachment into Middle East, Saudi Arabia only state standing against this, US interests here enormous, yet USG appears discount threat and doing little cope with it. Perhaps pertinent Saudi information sometimes exaggerated. However, even in lesser form, Communist threat very real. Who would have believed ten years ago there might be Saudi Communists. Now there are, all taught in UAR. Nasser himself may or may not be Communist, but he mainly responsible for furthering Communist objectives in Near East. Unless USG takes threat more seriously now, another Vietnam will ultimately ensue in this area. I assured King we take threat just as seriously as he does, but also believe vigorous programs of economic, social and political reform offer best way of grappling with this admittedly difficult problem. For this reason we applaud programs King has instituted and look forward to still more being done. It being close to midnight, we did not pursue subject.

12. *Comment:* Notwithstanding his "qualifications," Faisal's quick agreement in principle is encouraging. I had frankly thought he might ask for more time to think it over. His qualifications come as no surprise. They reflect areas in which he feels he has been burned in previous mediation attempts. They also reflect his utter lack of confidence in anything Nasser may say or do. As seen from here, most disturbing is his present unwillingness commit himself to continued restraint vis-à-vis Yemeni royalists. Even this may not be as ominous as it sounds. If we can get mediation moving ASAP with Amb Hare, and can obtain some indication of UAR willingness take tangible steps to defuse UAR–Saudi relations and to stop air attacks on northern Yemeni villages, I think there is still good chance that Faisal can be persuaded find quiet ways exercise needed restraint. Domestic and other pressures on him will be heavy and he (through us) will have

to produce, but I believe we should give it a try. We currently in process preparing some recommendations for possible inclusion in terms of reference.

13. In connection with foregoing, also recommend Dept now solicit HMG's early support as suggested by Saqqaf (Jidda 4008). I have of course said nothing to UK Amb about above approach. However, UAR Amb apparently informed by his govt. He pulled me aside at FonOff dinner for UN mission last evening to ask if King has accepted Hare as mediator. I could truthfully tell him had not yet seen King but hoped do so later that evening.[6]

Eilts

---

[6] In telegram 5937 from Cairo, April 3, Chargé d'Affaires David G. Nes commented on Faisal's conditions, stating that although condition A was acceptable, providing it was reciprocal, clearly B and C were not. He pointed out that it was unreasonable to expect the United Arab Republic, before entering mediation, to agree that it was going to lose out. In addition, condition C amounted to an attempt to interfere in U.S.–UAR bilateral relations. If Faisal were to impose such conditions, he suspected the Egyptians would prefer to forget the whole thing. On the other hand, when it got down to details, they would probably have conditions too. The problem was that the United States had to tell the Egyptians soon whether Faisal had accepted the offer and any delay or hedging would be seen as evidence that he had imposed conditions. Nes suggested the possibility of sending Hare to the region on an exploratory mission with no definite terms of reference to see whether could do something to resolve the crisis of confidence. (Ibid.)

---

432. Memorandum From Harold H. Saunders of the National Security Council Staff to the President's Special Assistant (Rostow)[1]

Washington, April 6, 1967.

WWR:

Secretary Rusk specifically asked that the attached cables[2] be cleared with you.

They put Ray Hare in business to try his hand at mediating the Saudi–UAR dispute over Yemen.

---

[1] Source: Johnson Library, National Security File, Country File, United Arab Republic, Vol. V, Memos. Secret.

[2] Not attached. Presumably reference is to telegrams 170451 to Jidda and Cairo, 170460 to Jidda, and 170459 to Cairo; see Document 433.

Both Faisal and Nasser have accepted Hare's mediation. Faisal threw out some tentative conditions, but the idea is to use the terms of reference to negotiate them out.

As far as we know, the Secretary simply wants you to know that we're formally launching this operation. No one expects you to dig into the details (look OK to us). He mentioned our mediation earlier to the President and did not ask for his clearance on these.

I'm glad to see us make this try, though I think the odds are against success. We have to keep trying to keep peace among the Arabs because a fight would either draw us in or force us to renege on our commitments. This may give them a face-saving way to back off from a confrontation, which they do seem to want to avoid. We're not excited about Hare since he's pretty passive, but the UAR picked him and he's persona grata in Riyadh.

Recommend you clear. A call to S/S will do the trick unless you have questions.[3]

Hal

---

[3] Saunders hand wrote the last sentence of this paragraph. Handwritten notations on the memorandum read: "OK. WR" and "S/S informed by phone April 7. BKS."

---

433. Telegram From the Department of State to the Embassy in Saudi Arabia[1]

Washington, April 7, 1967, 11:53 a.m.

170451. Yemen Mediation.

Following are proposed Terms of Reference which should be presented both UAR and SAG as soon as possible in accordance special instructions being sent separately:[2]

---

[1] Source: National Archives and Records Administration, RG 59, Central Files 1967–69, POL 27 YEMEN. Secret; Exdis. Drafted by Brewer on April 4; cleared by Hare, Bergus, Battle, and Walt Rostow; and approved by Secretary Rusk. Also sent to Cairo.

[2] Telegram 170460 to Jidda, April 7, transmitted talking points that the Ambassador was instructed to use when he saw Faisal to present the terms of reference transmitted in telegram 170451. Telegram 170459 to Cairo, April 7, instructed Nes to present the terms of reference to the UAR Government through the usual channels, i.e., el-Feki at the Foreign Office and al-Khouli at the Presidency, since there were protocol obstacles to a meeting between a Chargé and President Nasser. Nes could, however, note that the terms were being presented by Ambassador Eilts personally to the King and indicate that he was at Nasser's disposition if the latter wished. (Ibid.)

"TERMS OF REFERENCE

1. USG Undertakings:

—to name a Special Representative acceptable to both parties who shall seek to reduce current tensions between the UAR and Saudi Arabia.

—to prepare, on the basis of the Special Representative's discussions with interested parties, general guidelines for settlement of the dispute over Yemen. These guidelines would form the basis of subsequent detailed negotiations among the parties using USG continuing good offices as desired.

—to terminate its conciliation effort at such time as the Special Representative determines that one or the other of the parties is not observing its solemn undertakings as listed below.

2. UAR Undertakings:

—to cooperate with the Special Representative in carrying out the USG undertakings noted above.

—during the conciliation period, to refrain from aggressive acts or hostile propaganda against Saudi Arabia or Saudi Arabian forces which would prejudice the conciliation effort.

3. SAG Undertakings:

—to cooperate with the Special Representative in carrying out USG undertakings noted above.

—during the conciliation period, to refrain from aggressive acts or hostile propaganda against the UAR or UAR forces which would prejudice the conciliation effort."[3]

Katzenbach

---

[3] In telegram 6142 from Cairo, April 8, Nes reported that, in view of UAR sensibilities, he was deleting "aggressive" from the second paragraph of the respective UAR and Saudi undertakings as given in the Department's telegram. Telegram 171462 to Cairo and Jidda, April 8, instructed both addressees to drop the adjectives "aggressive" and "hostile" from the Terms of Reference. (Ibid.)

434.   Telegram From the Embassy in Saudi Arabia to the Department of State[1]

Jidda, April 12, 1967, 1152Z.

4220. State 170451[2] and 170460.[3] Yemen Mediation.

1. Two hour struggle session with King Faisal last night, at which Rashad Pharaon also present, produced somewhat inconclusive results. In summary: (a) Faisal still agrees in principle go ahead; (b) generally accepts terms of reference (TR), but was persuaded by Rashad seek some emendation; (c) generally accepted our interpretations of his qualifications re removing UAR influence from Yemen and possible USG aid to UAR and (d) utterly refused commit himself to stopping aid to Yemeni royalists during conciliation period. In order give flavor debate, and perhaps a fuller appreciation of King's views, following reports pertinent talk in some detail:

2. I first presented TR amended to delete word "aggressive" from paras 2 and 3 per State 171462.[4] These were read to him in Arabic translation prepared by EmbOff. In doing so I noted TR deliberately left general to give special representative maximum latitude in carrying out his functions. These same TR being simultaneously presented to President Nasser through FonMin Riad. I knew of no reaction as yet from UAR, but we hopeful both SAG and UAR will accept them. If they do, Amb Hare prepared promptly visit both countries to begin his consultations.

3. I then took up Faisal's various "qualifications":

A. In connection with essential acceptance of proposition that aggressive acts against each other should be suspended during conciliation, I stressed Saudis should agree suspend further support to royalists other than food. Added that Yemeni royalists should also continue to be restrained from resuming hostilities. On its part, UAR being asked cease bombings and support for harassment acts inside Saudi Arabia. This would at least insure standoff between principal antagonists and allow special representative see what he can from both sides should also tone down provocative propaganda. Noted that while we cannot vouch for Nasser's genuine interest in reaching settlement, we heartened by his acceptance US conciliation and his suggestion of Amb Hare as mediator; conversely, we convinced he prepared keep troops in

---

[1] Source: National Archives and Records Administration, RG 59, Central Files 1967–69, POL 27 YEMEN. Secret; Priority; Exdis. Repeated Priority to Cairo.

[2] Document 433.

[3] See footnote 2, Document 433.

[4] See footnote 3, Document 433.

Yemen as long as necessary. In such situation, resumption Yemeni royalist hostilities likely delay rather than accelerate any prospects UAR military withdrawal. More important, they expose Saudi Arabia to retaliation. TR drafted to be consistent with obligations which both parties have already undertaken in international instrument such as UN and Arab League Charters.

B. Re Faisal's qualification that all vestiges UAR influence in Yemen be removed, I said we interpreted this to mean withdrawal UAR military forces. In these terms, this consistent with Secretary's statement to King at Blair House and has always been USG aim. Neither we nor Saudis nor anyone else could hope to remove every vestige UAR influence in Yemen or anywhere else in ARP world. As largest Arab state, UAR bound to have influence in this part of the world.

C. On subject USG aid to UAR, I said was sure he not attempting place conditions on our bilateral relationships with UAR which we seeking improve if ways can be found to do so. Although food not a factor in current USG–UAR relationships, we could conceive situation where some USG help to UAR would be of benefit to us and SAF in moving toward an eventual Yemen settlement. However, assured Faisal USG has no intention undertaking any special programs with UAR that would prejudice conciliation effort.

D. As footnote, and having in mind question he had voiced during previous audience, I explained to him how Amb Hare's name had surfaced. Had earlier mentioned this to Rashad, but I wanted to be sure King got straight story from me.

4. After listening very carefully, Faisal commented as follows: Saudi policy has been and continues be seek peaceful settlement of Yemen problem. In this context King welcomes renewed USG conciliation effort. Qualifications he had set at previous meeting not intended obstruct this, but to reflect realistically his doubts about Nasser's intentions. They are based on his past experience with Nasser:

A. Taking these qualifications individually, he stated had no right or intention to tell USG what to do or what not to do in its bilateral relations with UAR. In spirit of frankness he had merely wished give us friendly advice. Once before Nasser had been cooperative up to point when he assured of USG food aid, then dropped any interest in Yemen settlement. As result, USG had found itself with food commitment which was in fact aiding, directly or indirectly, Nasser's foreign adventures. If any USG help is to be given to UAR once UAR military out of Yemen, he could have no objection. He fully satisfied with USG assurance no help would be given UAR which would prejudice conciliation effort.

B. He agreed reference to every vestige UAR influence in Yemen being removed should be viewed primarily as withdrawal all military forces. All other aspects of possible residual UAR influence could either be negotiated or be left to Yemenis to decide so long as they able make free decision. They unable do so when coerced by massive UAR military presence. SAG has no permanent interest in Yemen, and he perfectly willing take his chances in context friendly and peaceful competition in a free Yemen.

C. Faisal absolutely adamant in his unwillingness commit himself to any particular actions or restraints re Saudi aid to Yemeni royalists while mediation going on. While he was evasive on whether arms aid actually resumed, he reiterated would have to give arms aid if Yemeni royalists ask for it. Only condition on which he would again restrict his aid to Yemeni royalists and/or actively restrain them would be as part of agreement whereby UAR withdraws its military forces from Yemen. Fighting, he claimed, has never ceased in Yemen. Despite his efforts restrain Yemeni royalists during past year, UAR bombings of north Yemeni villages had continued without let-up. They still going on. He had first agreed Yemeni royalists should only defend themselves, but they have no defense against air and gas attacks. If they now retaliating more directly, this entirely up to them to decide and he not in position stop them. Insisted he is not actively encouraging Yemeni royalists, but could not accept equating his aid to royalists with what UAR is doing in Yemen. Although SAG recognizes Yemeni royalist govt, there are no Saudi soldiers in Yemen. This is in marked contrast massive UAR military presence. If because of Saudi aid to Yemeni royalists Nasser attacks Saudi Arabia, this makes no difference. He has already attacked Saudi Arabia when Saudi aid to Yemeni royalists still suspended. "We are not afraid of his attacks; all we can do is die defending our country." We rehashed this one again and again, but he would not budge.

D. He dismissed UAR propaganda as unimportant. In answer my suggestion mutual toning down of hostile propaganda would be a helpful indicator that both sides willing improve relations, he agreed. Insisted, however, that Saudi propaganda activities hardly comparable with those of UAR. Saudi public media had not deliberately attacked Nasser. Neither had he in his speeches which he hoped USG has noted have in tone been conciliatory and in marked contrast to Nasser's public utterances. Should Saudi Arabia, he wanted to know, be expected restrain its public media from stressing Islam as defense against godless communism? Or should Saudi public media be stopped from stating Saudi aversion to socialism? UAR has several times objected to articles critical of socialism. I said did not wish at this point get into details what respective parties ought to do to improve relations. This matter for special representative. However, I reminded him that SAG already has good relations with various countries that are in one way or another socialist. I had also read articles in Saudi press in which banner of Islam and anti-communism had clearly been waved as direct attacks on UAR. I doubted anyone would wish restrict constructive public media efforts. When they become instruments of attack on others, they breed distrust and ill will. In frankness I had to tell him Saudi public media sometimes also deserves share of blame. He agreed, but again insisted no comparison between what Saudis and UAR doing against each other in propaganda field. Added SAG willing stop direct attacks on UAR.

5. I then told him did not know whether USG would feel able carry on if other than food aid for Yemeni royalists is resumed, but nevertheless wanted to know more specifically his reaction to TR. He first said TR so general as to have little meaning. We could do without them: he did not wish at this time commit SAG to any "undertakings," but quickly added that this should not be construed as Saudi disinterest in proposed USG conciliation effort. "Let it proceed and we will see what happens." I pointed out both he and President Nasser had asked to see TR which, as result, now being presented to both. Speaking personally, I thought Faisal unwilling at this time accept broad undertakings of cooperating with special representative or refraining from prejudicial acts or hostile propaganda against UAR or UAR forces, there was little use in sending a special representative. There nothing in or inconsistent with SAG's undertakings elsewhere. USG not offering its good offices again because of any keen interest in involving ourselves in Yemen problem. We doing so solely and reluctantly in order help friends like Saudi Arabia and try to keep peace in area. I had always understood latter is also what King wants. TR, while general, are at least a further expression of willingness both sides again look for peaceful solution and offer broad parameters in which special representative might work. While I appreciated his point, I did not see how in these circumstances I could recommend to my govt that we go ahead. Moreover, if UAR accepts undertakings in TR and SAG is unwilling do so, I wanted to tell him as friend he will be in poor position posturally. Onus for continued impasse will then be largely on him. He thought about this for a moment. Then, with a great gesture of his hand, he said somewhat wearily, "All right, I accept the undertakings in their terms of reference."

6. At this point Rashad, who had sat by quietly during most of talk, intervened. (While King had not himself read TR and contented himself with hearing them, Rashad had been studying them closely.) Rashad argued inclusion of phrase "or UAR forces" in second sentence of SAG's undertakings is redundant. Moreover, it implies SAG has in past acted against UAR forces. He referred to King's earlier statement no Saudi troops in Yemen. He suggested this phrase be deleted. Faisal

agreed. I said did not think this would be possible. TR had been written identically not to suggest that both sides had done the same things, but to avoid implication USG attempting prejudge issue. TR presented to SAG and UAR should remain identical. King accepted this.

7. Returning to charge, Rashad then argued both texts be changed to read "During the conciliation period, to refrain from aggressive acts or hostile propaganda against Saudi Arabia (the UAR) which would prejudice the conciliation effort." (This reinserts "aggressive" and deletes "or UAR forces.") The UAR, he insisted, has carried on aggressive acts against Saudi Arabia such as recent bombings on Najran. This should not be obscured by bland reference to "acts." He thought his proposal placed into clearer focus obligations both SAG and UAR would undertake. I argued this a distinction without meaning. Our phraseology already encompassed that idea. Moreover, in terms his earlier concern about inference Saudi Arabia had acted against UAR forces, Rashad's proposed change could be inferred to suggest Saudi Arabia had in fact carried on past aggression against UAR. Finally, these TR already presented to UAR and Saudi nit-picking at this time hardly helpful in getting effort underway soon. Unfortunately, King agreed Rashad's proposed terminology preferable and would like it substituted for ours. I again pointed out to him that language Rashad proposed and that he now requesting could probably more easily be used against him in connection with his support for Yemeni royalists. He said wearily, "I suppose so, but they will do that anyway." He concluded that SAG will accept TR if aforementioned change is made and if UAR also accepts them as amended.

8. Session frank but cordial throughout. Comments by immediately following telegram.[5]

Eilts

---

[5] In telegram 4221 from Jidda, April 12, Eilts commented that the King's reaction to the terms of reference was disappointing, even if not entirely unexpected, and that most disturbing was Faisal's unwillingness to commit himself to stopping aid to the Yemen royalists during the conciliation period. (National Archives and Records Administration, RG 59, Central Files 1967–69, POL 27 YEMEN)

435. Telegram From the Embassy in the United Arab Republic to the Department of State[1]

Cairo, April 24, 1967, 1357Z.

6665. 1. In view possible effects yesterday's unleashing in Yemen of ex-King Saud[2] could have on our mediation effort, I asked for appointment and was received by Under Secretary El Feki this morning.

2. Referring to my meeting with Foreign Minister Riad on April 8 I said that more than two weeks had now passed and that I was naturally interested in UARG's reaction to our proposed terms of reference. I said that our Ambassador in Jidda had discussed these draft terms of reference with King Feisal on April 11 and that we would consult both parties again as soon as we heard from UARG. El Feki asked whether we had received Saudi reaction during our April 11 meeting and I said that we had but that in order to maintain strict impartiality it would not of course be possible to discuss King Feisal's views until those of Pres Nasser were also known.

3. As he had during informal corner conversation with me during the Danish Amb's reception of Apr 18, El Feki again indicated obliquely that UARG was aware in part at least of King Feisal's views.

4. In this connection I would appreciate learning what, if anything, Amb Kamel has been told in Washington. We have held on to this very tightly here.

5. Amb El Feki said he was sorry that he could only say our proposed terms of reference were still under consideration and assure me that he would get in touch immediately when he had something to say. I closed conversation on this subject by saying we wished to get to work as soon as possible. I asked whether he thought King Saud's Yemen trip would be harmful to our mediation effort. He said emphatically that it would not insofar as his govt was concerned. We left the matter there.

Nes

---

[1] Source: National Archives and Records Administration, RG 59, Central Files 1967–69, POL 27 YEMEN. Secret; Exdis. Repeated to Jidda.

[2] On April 23 former King Saud arrived in Sanaa from Cairo aboard a UAR plane with UAR Vice President Amer and was given full military honors before assembled ministers, diplomats, and high-ranking Yemeni Government officials. Radio Sanaa subsequently broadcast speeches by Yemeni President Sallal and Saud in which Sallal referred to Saud as the "legal king of the Saudi people"; while Saud announced that, on behalf of the Saudi people, he fully recognized the Yemen Arab Republic and President Sallal. (Telegrams 442 and 444 from Sanaa, April 23, ibid., POL 7 SAUD) Telegram 180743 to Sanaa, April 23, instructed the Chargé and other Embassy officers not to attend any official functions specifically honoring former King Saud. (Ibid.)

436. Telegram From the Department of State to the Embassy in the United Arab Republic[1]

Washington, April 25, 1967, 5:54 p.m.

181932. Ref: Cairo's 6665,[2] Jidda's 4389.[3] Yemen Mediation.

1. View unhelpful and dilatory nature el-Feki's response to Nes approach and unsettling effect of GUAR-sponsored trip of ex-King Saud to Yemen, we believe Chargé should seek earliest opportunity make following points to UAR Fonmin Riad:

a) Offer of USG to assist in mediatory role in UAR–SAG dispute over Yemen, made by Ambassador Battle in his farewell call on President Nasser, was based on a desire to help parties directly concerned avoid what could be an increasingly dangerous situation. We believed then as we believe now that USG could not hope to be of any assistance unless both Saudi Arabia and UAR voluntarily and wholeheartedly accepted our offer of assistance and were prepared to work with us.

b) We were therefore heartened by GUAR's preliminary and affirmative response to our offer. Matter has subsequently been followed with interest at high levels USG.

c) Identical terms of reference were delivered both to SAG and GUAR over two weeks ago. King Feisal immediately gave us his initial reaction to these terms of reference. Fonmin will understand why it would be inappropriate for us to discuss details of SAG response with GUAR at this time. Proper procedure is for USG to await substantive response of GUAR to terms of reference after which it can make another simultaneous approach to both capitals.

d) We are concerned at delay in GUAR response to US draft terms of reference. Document is brief, simple, contains no hidden meanings, and requires parties to assume no obligations beyond those already incumbent upon them through various multilateral undertakings such as UN and Arab League charters. We believe that 17 days which have

---

[1] Source: National Archives and Records Administration, RG 59, Central Files 1967–69, POL 27 YEMEN. Secret; Priority; Exdis. Drafted by Bergus, cleared by Brewer, and approved by Battle. Repeated to Jidda.

[2] Document 435.

[3] In telegram 4389 from Jidda, April 25, Eilts commented that the United Arab Republic action in taking Saud to Yemen was obviously a deliberate slap at Faisal. He noted that some Saudis might ask if, assuming the U.S. mediation effort was already formally underway, this kind of blatant UAR action would be regarded under U.S.-drafted terms of reference as reason for the mediator to terminate his effort. Nor was the long delay in the UAR response likely to be helpful in persuading Faisal that Nasser genuinely wanted U.S. mediation. (National Archives and Records Administration, RG 59, Central Files 1967–69, POL 27 YEMEN)

elapsed since April 8 have been ample for GUAR to prepare a position on terms of reference.

e) Our concern is heightened by recent surfacing of ex-King Saud in Yemen. Though it was Sallal rather than GUAR leaders who hailed Saud as "legal King of Saudi people," we do not wish to get into such legal niceties. Fact remains Saud was taken to Yemen in official GUAR airplane and in company of some of highest Egyptian officials. SAG has not complained to us about this behavior on part GUAR. Nor does USG propose insert itself into legal or political effects of this incident on UAR–SAG relations. We are, however, concerned at its effect on prospects for our own mediation proposal. Actions such as this make it more difficult for USG to be helpful.

f) USG has felt throughout that without some degree of cooperation and responsiveness from both parties, there would be little point in pressing mediation effort. We have no desire allow ourselves into situation in absence desire of both sides to work with us.

g) We would appreciate the GUAR's considered views on these matters.

2. FYI re para 4, Cairo's 6665. Ambassador Kamel has been informed by Cairo of US offer and UAR acceptance of US mediation. He has been told by us that terms of reference have been delivered both in Cairo and in Jidda. In response to his questions re Feisal's reaction he has been given line contained in State's 173904,[4] i.e. it would be inappropriate for USG to discuss SAG response until GUAR responds and USG can make simultaneous approach to both capitals. Kamel has accepted this as proper diplomatic procedure and has not pressed for details. End FYI.[5]

Katzenbach

---

[4] Dated April 12. (Ibid.)

[5] Telegram 182453 to Cairo, April 26, informed the Embassy that the Department was not impressed with el-Feki's explanation that the UAR response to the U.S. terms of reference was being held up pending a meeting of the Supreme Executive, noting that this small group was composed of individuals in daily contact with Nasser. It expressed concern lest the United Arab Republic have the impression it could keep the United States on a string while it acted as it saw fit in Yemen. (Ibid.)

437. Memorandum From Harold H. Saunders of the National Security Council Staff to the President's Special Assistant (Rostow)[1]

Washington, April 26, 1967.

Our Embassy office and AID Mission in Taiz were ransacked today by a Yemeni crowd. This followed the arrest of a Bureau of Public Roads official earlier in the day.[2]

We have lodged all the usual protests and have approached both the Egyptian and Yemeni governments to insist they guarantee the safety of our people there. Fortunately, no one has been hurt.

It will be a day or two before responsibility is clear enough for us to decide how we should play this—whether we should blame the Egyptians for it, pull out our road-building project, withdraw our Chargé, or close out entirely. No one is inclined toward the more radical steps at the moment, but our decision may depend on what happens next.

Hal

---

[1] Source: Johnson Library, National Security File, Country File, Yemen, Cables & Memos, Vol. II, 7/64–12/68. Confidential.

[2] Documentation on this incident is in the National Archives and Records Administration, RG 59, Central Files 1967–69, POL 23–8 YEMEN and POL US–YEMEN.

---

438. Telegram From the Embassy in the United Arab Republic to the Department of State[1]

Cairo, April 27, 1967, 1420Z.

6805. Ref: State 182453.[2]

1. Foreign Minister Riad received me this morning and as instructed I confronted him with Department's comments on current

---

[1] Source: National Archives and Records Administration, RG 59, Central Files 1967–69, POL 27 YEMEN. Secret; Priority; Exdis. Repeated to Jidda.

[2] See footnote 5, Document 436.

status our mediation effort as set forth paragraphs A through G State 181932.[3]

2. After introductory remarks to effect Washington found it difficult to understand long delay in receiving UARG reaction to our proposed terms of reference [garble] points verbatim adding to point F that we would back out of the exercise now if this is in fact the wish of the GUAR.

3. Foreign Minister Riad pondered my presentation for several minutes and then said that his government had appreciated very much our readiness to be helpful and to mediate their differences with Saudi Arabia.

4. It was fully realized that all sides must cooperate fully and frankly in such an endeavor and that the atmosphere must be propitious and optimistic.

5. Our proposed terms of reference had embraced obligations on all three parties which might require further clarification. His own personal feeling was that our draft was too short and too vague. In any event it required study and while no changes might be called for, some clarification might be sought. This study was now in process and must of necessity involve the top command of the UAR.

6. Riad said he would contact me immediately when views of Supreme Executive Committee were known. In this connection he mentioned in passing that President Nasser intended to take ten days rest from his official duties and this might involve further delay.

7. Referring to my reference to ex-King Saud under point E he smilingly said that at time when King Feisal was treating and referring to Badr as "King of Yemen" he could hardly complain about UAR references to Saud as King of Saudi Arabia. There did not seem to be much purpose in pursuing this subject.

8. *Comment:* It is quite evident that Foreign Minister Riad supports idea of our mediating Yemen embroglio and probably sees in it means of improving US–UAR relations in general. I find it difficult to predict exactly what decision of committee will be or when we will receive it but I strongly recommend we play this out to end as to withdraw our offer now would only magnify our problems which seem to be sufficiently difficult as they are.

Nes

---

[3] Document 436.

439.   Memorandum of Telephone Conversation Between Secretary of State Rusk and Director of Central Intelligence Helms[1]

Washington, April 27, 1967, 8:30 p.m.

TELEPHONE CALL TO MR. RICHARD HELMS

H. returned the call. Sec. asked if H. had been getting any reporting out of Yemen in the last few days. H. said yes—quite a bit. Sec. said the Yemeni have just put out a long statement expelling our AID Mission, etc. Sec. asked if H. knew anything about any of this, and if there was any possibility that any of our people are mixed up in this in any way. H. said these accusations have been going on for 48 hours—they have been interrogating these fellows with American witnesses. H's fellows are predicting a collapse of the Mission as they are making quite a case against them. H. said there was no espionage and nothing sinister going on—[1 line of source text not declassified]. They sacked the Embassy yesterday. H. said they feel it is quite clearly a political move against the United States. Sec. thanked him.

---

[1] Source: National Archives and Records Administration, RG 59, Rusk Files: Lot 72 D 192, Rusk Telephone Conversations, Box 928. No classification marking. Transcribed by Jane M. Rothe.

---

440.   Memorandum From the President's Special Assistant (Rostow) to President Johnson[1]

Washington, April 27, 1967, 10:45 p.m.

Mr. President:

I have been in touch with Luke Battle. Two Americans at the USAID mission in Yemen have been accused of blowing up the Capital. We are evacuating the AID mission, and only leaving a minimal staff. We have been in touch with the Yemen and U.A.R. ambassadors here. Since they have announced publicly, it's unlikely they will reverse their announced decision about our two men.

---

[1] Source: Johnson Library, National Security File, Memos to the President, Walt Rostow, Vol. 26. No classification marking. An "L" on the memorandum indicates that the President read it.

The background is that in both Cairo and Yemen, there have been some groups who have wanted to either keep the US connection, or get rid of it. The latter appear to have won.

We shall be announcing tomorrow that the charges are without foundation—which they are. Both State and I will follow closely.

WWR[2]

---

[2] Printed from a copy that indicates the original was initialed.

---

441. **Circular Telegram From the Department of State to Certain Posts**[1]

Washington, April 28, 1967, 6:07 p.m.

184507. 1. Following is background current crisis US–Yemen relations for addressee's information and use with diplomatic colleagues and host government officials as appropriate.

2. Mob violence April 26 against US Embassy Branch Office and AID compound Taiz apparently sparked by shooting and explosions of undetermined origin evening April 25. Yemeni and UAR security authorities entered AID "campsite" compound shortly thereafter and took into custody for questioning seven American AID employees including AID Director. Director and four others were subsequently released. Gradually became clear local UAR and Yemen authorities were alleging that two remaining personnel, Stephen Liapis and Harold Hartman, were responsible for a bazooka attack on ammunition dump Taiz in which a UAR soldier and a Yemeni were reportedly killed.

3. Mob shouting "No Americans after today" paraded through streets Taiz morning April 26. Crowd estimated at 3000 and carrying coffin gathered in front of compound and broke in, overturning vehicles and destroying furniture, plumbing and other official and personal effects. Although UAR military camera man was reportedly with mob,

---

[1] Source: National Archives and Records Administration, RG 59, Central Files 1967–69, POL US–YEMEN. Confidential. Drafted by Korn; cleared by NEA Staff Assistant Michael A.G. Michaud, Country Director for Ethiopia, Somali Republic, and Sudan Matthew J. Looram, Bergus, and Robert H. Flenner (EUR/SOV); and approved by Brewer. Sent to Addis Ababa, Amman, Asmara, Bonn, Baghdad, Beirut, Cairo, Damascus, Jidda, Kuwait, London, Moscow, Paris, Tehran, Tel Aviv, Rome, Aden, and Dhahran.

appears adequate Yemeni security contingent may not have been provided until after considerable destruction accomplished. Yemeni security forces were subsequently stationed in front of compound. Demonstration renewed April 27, but compound not subsequently attacked.

4. On learning of demonstration and arrests, Department summoned Yemeni Ambassador Washington to protest incident, request official apology, YARG agreement in principle make full repayment for damage, and ask immediate release detained American official personnel. Chargé Sanaa was instructed make parallel démarche. Representations were also made in Cairo and to UAR Ambassador Washington to request UARG assistance in securing release detained American personnel.

5. Despite initial hope more moderate elements might be willing to give us forthcoming response, we now forced conclude that Taiz riots and detentions AID personnel probably instigated by local UAR officials with support pro-UAR YARG elements, notably Minister Interior Ahnumi. Following facts point in this direction: (a) Equivocal initial response made by Vice Premier Juzaylan to Sanaa Chargé's first representation; (b) the ridiculous charges of "murder" and attempt to "blow up all of Taiz" brought against Liapis and Hartman, who are holders of U.S. official passports and considered by USG to have diplomatic status; (c) trumped-up Cairo press campaign including false report that USG gave YARG a "24-hour ultimatum"; (d) YARG unilateral termination US-Yemeni foreign assistance agreement. (We were first informed of this step by Sanaa radio broadcast, official notification having been given our Chargé subsequently.)

6. As a result YARG actions, USAID Mission Yemen being withdrawn. Arrangements being made immediately evacuate all dependents and all except key Embassy personnel. As retaliatory measure for restrictions placed on our personnel Taiz, Department has confined Yemeni Ambassador here to Washington area until further notice, subject to Department approval for travel outside Washington. Future US–Yemen relations still uncertain, but we are making it clear that we expect immediate release two detained Americans.

Rusk

442. Telegram From the Department of State to the Embassy in the United Arab Republic[1]

Washington, April 28, 1967, 7:16 p.m.

184712. Deliver following soonest to FonMin Riad from Secretary.

1. "Dear Mr. Minister: Over the last two days we have expressed to your Government through regular diplomatic channels our mounting concern at developments in Yemen. We have requested the United Arab Republic to use its influence with the Yemen Arab Republic to the end that American officials presently unjustly detained in Ta'izz be released and that they and those of their colleagues who are being withdrawn from Yemen be permitted to depart in dignity and safety. To these official communications I would like to add this note of personal concern.

2. I would not be frank if I did not make it clear that the events in Ta'izz and actions by Yemen government officials have significantly and adversely affected American public opinion. The fact that some United Arab Republic officials, particularly in the Ta'izz area, are participating in these events is public knowledge here. Tendentious and distorted accounts appearing in the Cairo press and over UAR radio are also widely known. All this can only prejudice and limit any efforts which either of us would hope to make to improve relations between our two countries. The improvement of these relations remains the goal of my Government as well as myself.

3. I have carefully examined the charges against certain of our American personnel in Ta'izz in the light of all the evidence at my disposal. I am convinced that these charges are absolutely without foundation. Nor have our representatives in Yemen delivered any "ultimatum" or threatened to withdraw United States recognition from the Yemen Arab Republic as press has reported.

4. We are in the midst of a very difficult and highly tense situation. I believe it in the interest of both our Governments that measures tending to calm matters down be taken as soon as possible. The constructive influence which you and your Government could exercise at this juncture is a very important element in the situation.

5. With personal regards. Sincerely yours, Dean Rusk."[2]

Rusk

---

[1] Source: National Archives and Records Administration, RG 59, Central Files 1967–69, POL US–YEMEN. Secret; Immediate. Drafted by Bergus, cleared by Brewer and Battle, and approved by Rusk. Repeated to Taiz and Sanaa.

[2] In telegram 6895 from Cairo, April 29, Nes reported that at noon that day he had delivered the Secretary's letter to Foreign Minister Riad, who said he had no comment. (Ibid.)

443. Telegram From the Embassy in the United Arab Republic to the Department of State[1]

Cairo, April 30, 1967, 1628Z.

6945. Ref: Cairo 6944.[2]

1. Following is text of unofficial translation of message from Field Marshal Amer addressed to Secretary:

2. I have received your message of April 29th 1967[3] on the developments related to the attack which took place in Taiz, Yemen Arab Republic which led to the present tense situation between the Government of the United States and the Government of the Yemen Arab Republic.

3. Notwithstanding the fact that the matter falls within the Yemen–U.S. relations, the U.A.R. Government has maintained a very close watch over its development. We have equally received your representatives and engaged with them in a frank and sincere discussion, with a view to avoiding any further deterioration in the situation.

4. I wish, however, to state some observations related to the April 25th attack and its consequent developments;

—On the night of April 25 bazooka shots were fired at an army ammunition depot in Taiz, resulting in the death of a Yemeni soldier and another from the United Arab Republic forces. Two other soldiers were gravely injured. This is no doubt a highly serious matter.

—The Yemeni authorities have carried out an investigation, which required the arrest of two United States citizens. They have been interrogated in the presence of the United States Consul in Taiz. The investigation has proceeded in accordance with the general norms and practice which insure its objectivity.

---

[1] Source: National Archives and Records Administration, RG 59, Central Files 1967–69, POL US–YEMEN. Secret; Limdis.

[2] In telegram 6944 from Cairo, April 30, Nes reported that he had met with Riad who gave him Field Marshal Amer's reply to the Secretary's message. Riad said Amer also wished to convey an oral message to the Secretary that a "quieter situation" would assist the United Arab Republic in its efforts with the Yemeni Government to stop the trial. If those efforts were successful, the next UAR step would be to obtain the release of the two Americans. Riad indicated that the "quieter situation" Amer was referring to involved lifting restrictions on the Yemeni Ambassador in Washington. Nes strongly recommended that this be done, noting that most of the Americans in Yemen had been evacuated and that equivalent restrictions were not yet placed on the U.S. Chargé in Sanaa. (Ibid.) On April 27 the Department had notified the Yemeni Ambassador that he and his staff were restricted to the Washington area until further notice. (Telegram 183980 to Sanaa, April 28; ibid., POL 17 YEMEN–US)

[3] See Document 442.

—I have been informed by the Yemeni Government that they have evidence which proves the implication of the two detained Americans.

—Despite the gravity of the events and the loss of lives, the Yemeni authorities, as well as U.A.R. authorities have maintained self-restraint.

—In the course of his meeting with the Deputy Prime Minister of the Yemen Arab Republic, the United States Chargé d'Affaires orally threatened that the United States would withdraw its recognition of the Yemeni Government if the latter does not respond to the United States protest within twenty-four hours. The attitude of the United States Chargé d'Affaires has undoubtedly left serious effects with the Yemeni Government and resulted in the deterioration of the situation.

—On our part, I instructed the commander of the U.A.R. forces in Yemen to provide their assistance with a view to insuring the safety of the United States citizens and to cooperate in securing the withdrawal of those American citizens who wish to depart.

—I wish to add that we shall exert our efforts to lessen tension in the present situation and to bring it to normalcy.[4]

Nes

---

[4] Telegram 185098 to Cairo, April 30, reported that the Department informed UAR Ambassador Kamel that the Department had received Amer's message and had particularly noted his expressed interest in lowering tension between their two governments. The U.S. Government was also interested in lowering tension and, as a result of the orderly progress in evacuation of Americans from Yemen, it had lifted restrictions on the Yemeni Ambassador in Washington. (Ibid., POL US–YEMEN)

---

444.   Telegram From the Department of State to the Embassy in the United Arab Republic[1]

Washington, May 4, 1967, 9:40 a.m.

187506. 1. After consultation with Nes, Brommell should approach Saleh Nasser and pass following message. We leave to discretion Nes and Brommel exact phrasing of message so that most effective presentation can be achieved.

---

[1] Source: Department of State, INR/IL Historical Files, Roger Channel Telegrams, Cairo. Secret; Flash; Roger Channel. Drafted by Bergus; cleared by Battle, Walter W. Harris, Jr. (NEA), and James R. Gardner (INR/DDC); and approved by William McAfee of INR/DDC.

2. Begin message: "Saleh Nasser's assurances that Liapis and Hartman would be released have been reported to Washington. These assurances well received as men are innocent and enjoy diplomatic immunity.[2] However there is another very serious problem.

3. USG officials have been denied access to AID buildings Ta'iz for more than one week. While denial access has been in name YARG authorities, inescapable fact is AID building under effective control of UAR military authorities. Our people in Yemen have clearly observed that guard detachment comprised of UAR military police commanded by UAR officer.

4. AID building in Yemen was considered by us as part of our diplomatic mission to that country and was treated as such. Consequently it contains archives and other US diplomatic papers. We frankly concerned that UAR authorities may seek to exploit this situation and attempt major penetration US interests.

5. We wish to make it clear that any attempt at penetration will raise serious doubt as to intentions and motives of UAR.

6. If the UAR believes it in its own interest to avoid such a situation, it should at once facilitate arrangements whereby the property and archives of the United States can be returned, uncompromised, to safekeeping by authorized representatives of the United States."

Rusk

---

[2] A May 10 memorandum from Rostow to Johnson informed the President that the UAR Foreign Minister promised that the two U.S. AID men in Yemen would be out of jail by May 15, and noted that the United States had evacuated all but a skeleton crew from Yemen. Rostow commented: "We don't think Nasser staged the incident in Yemen to get us out. However, once Egyptian mishandling on the scene created an opening, Cairo gave vent to its emotions and played it out for its full propaganda and intelligence advantage." (Johnson Library, National Security File, Country File, United Arab Republic, Vol. V) Rostow's memorandum is printed in *Foreign Relations, 1964–1968*, vol. XVIII, Document 417. The two Americans were released on May 17.

---

445.   Editorial Note

The President's Daily Brief for May 16, 1967, includes Item 6, "Egypt" which reads as follows:

[*1 paragraph (5 lines of source text) not declassified*] (Johnson Library, National Security File, NSC History, Middle East Crisis, Vol. 6, Appendix A)

446.   Memorandum From [*name deleted*] to the Chief of the Near East and South Asia Division in the Central Intelligence Agency Deputy Directorate of Operations (Critchfield)[1]

Washington, May 19, 1967.

SUBJECT

Suggestions for IRG Meeting on South Arabia[2]

1. The following suggestions are for your consideration in preparation for IRG meeting on South Arabia:

a. Most eyes in area are on our behavior toward the Egyptians. We will look foolish if we break relations with Yemen without going rather far down the list of what we can do to retaliate against Egypt. *As a minimum* we should use the vulnerability of our AID mission in Cairo under present agreements to insist on a clear statement of diplomatic immunity for its members or cut it back drastically—and preferably eliminate it.

[*1 paragraph (8½ lines of source text) not declassified*]

c. *If* we do not break relations with Yemen, we should argue for a radical shift in Embassy aims there. Until now the Embassy has run around looking for ways to help the Yemenis. We should cease all such activity and forget any public or cultural affairs activities too. We should maintain minimum contact with top Yemeni and Egyptian officials (the Chargé), protect American [*2½ lines of source text not declassified*]

d. In planning for South Arabia, we should prepare for the contingency of a split with an Arab socialist regime in Aden proper and the traditional rulers outside. This may call for [*1 line of source text not declassified*] perhaps diplomatic missions of some sort on each side too.

e. In such a chaotic and unruly world it may be far more important in protecting U.S. interests to have some collaborators [*less than 1 line of source text not declassified*] rather than to run around looking for "leverage" in AID or cultural programs.

2. The above points deal with the narrower elements of the problem, but might be worked into the discussion [*2 lines of source text not declassified*]

[*initials not declassified*]
[*title not declassified*]

---

[1] Source: Central Intelligence Agency, DDO/NE (Critchfield) Files: Job 80–00105A, Box 2, IRG/NEA Working File, Communist Presence, UAR/South Arabia. Secret.
[2] See Document 95.

447.   Telegram From the Department of State to the Mission to the European Office of the United Nations[1]

Washington, May 23, 1967, 9:06 p.m.

200653. For Tubby from Rostow. Ref: Geneva 3809,[2] 3821.[3]

1) When you seen Gallopin again you should stress seriousness our concern at use of poison gas by UAR against Yemen. We discussing this with ICRC in strictest confidence in hope they will take steps on their own to investigate gas use in part of world where for practical purposes they are only neutral, impartial observer. We hope ICRC will act fast to strengthen its representation in Middle East including Yemen.

2) Might be helpful to tell Gallopin you discussed subject with Freymond, who previously discussed subject on personal basis with me. Sieverts will bring additional info on gas types and use. Material for use with ICRC will be provided by telegram. Might be best to hold this material until Rochat returns and presents his findings.[4]

---

[1] Source: National Archives and Records Administration, RG 59, Central Files 1967–69, POL 27–10 YEMEN. Secret; Exdis. Drafted by Frank A. Sieverts (U), cleared by Battle, and approved by Rostow.

[2] In telegram 3809 from the U.S. Mission in Geneva, May 22, Ambassador Robert W. Tubby reported that, as instructed, he expressed to Jacques Freymond of the International Committee of the Red Cross (ICRC) U.S. concern at reports of repetitive use by the United Arab Republic of lethal chemical weapons in Yemen. Freymond had suggested that Tubby see ICRC Executive Director Roger Gallopin and that he personally urge a strong, formal ICRC protest to the UAR if the facts warranted. Tubby noted that it would be useful in this regard if he could be provided as soon as possible with U.S. Government information regarding the types of gas it believed the UAR had been using in Yemen. (Ibid.)

[3] In telegram 3821 from the U.S. Mission in Geneva, May 23, Tubby reported that he met that day with Gallopin who stated that it was unlikely that the ICRC would make a public statement in the absence of clear evidence of use of gas by the UAR. (Ibid.)

[4] Printed from an unsigned copy.

448.   Telegram From the Department of State to the Mission to the European Office of the United Nations[1]

Washington, May 25, 1967, 8:57 p.m.

202562. For Tubby and Sieverts. Ref: Geneva 3809.[2]

1. Information in paragraph 2 may be passed to selected ICRC officials on a non-attributable basis and cannot be further disseminated or used publicly.

2. Begin non-attributable information: Following are UAR gas attacks reportedly carried out in Yemen since January 1, 1967: (a) January 5 attack on Kitaf in which 155 people and many animals allegedly were killed and more than 40 people injured. (b) May 6 attack on Bait Maran in which 2 people killed and 15 injured. (c) May 11 attack on Gahr and Gadafa where 51 and 24 respectively were reported killed. (d) May 17 attack on Gadafa where 100 people hiding in cave allegedly were killed. (e) week of May 14–20 attacks at villages of Naugher, Queais, and Kor in the Arhab and Khaulan areas. International Red Cross official said total casualties in those three villages plus Gahr and Gadafa during week were 243. There is corroborative evidence that on at least one occasion a highly lethal nerve gas agent was present in the area attacked. Mustard and perhaps phosgene may also have been used. End classified non-attributable information.

3. Information this paragraph can be published. Following are examples of press and radio mention which has been made of UAR attacks: (a) UPI January 31 said correspondent John Lawton and other Western correspondents who visited site of the Kitaf attack believed there was little doubt gas had been used. Yemeni reports claimed 150 people were killed. (b) A Yemeni royalist radio broadcast heard February 12 claimed on February 8 UAR aircraft dropped gas bombs on Bani Salab village and killed 75 people and 40 sheep. (c) Reuters reported February 17 a Yemeni soldier alleged 19 people were injured and 32 killed during a UAR gas attack on royalist positions at Bayt Al-Suraym between Sanaa and Hodeidah February 6. (d) Spokesman for royalist forces in Yemen stated during broadcast from Jidda February 15 that on February 5 UAR aircraft used poison gas bombs for second time in Anis area. (e) Jidda press May 14 carried royalist report UAR planes made poison gas attack on May 11 on the Yemeni town of Hairan, northeast of Sanaa, leaving 75 dead. (f) Jidda paper al-Nadwa quoting royalist command reported May 18 that UAR planes attacked

---

[1] Source: National Archives and Records Administration, RG 59, Central Files 1967–69, POL 27–10 YEMEN. Secret; Priority; Exdis.

[2] See footnote 2, Document 447.

a village 30 kilometers from Sanaa on May 16. (g) According to Reuters, South Arabian Broadcasting Service announced May 20 that UAR bombers using high explosives and poison gas raided royalist villages of Bayt Ghadir, Bayt Jabas, and Nawfal 20 miles north of Sanaa on May 18 and killed 38 people. Begin FYI. In case you are asked about *New York Daily News* erroneous story May 20 reporting that US officials have evidence poison gas bombs dropped in an attack on Najran and Jizan "last weekend" bore markings indicating Russian origin, no evidence gas employed in Saudi Arabia. Story said scientists were seeking to determine whether "as suspected, the gas was a new kind of nerve gas," also stated "it has been established that phosgene gas was the lethal agent in the earlier attacks." The article said officials believed the gas used on Najran and Jizan was "a much more modern type of lethal agent and was being used for experimental purposes by Communist scientists." End FYI.

Rusk

---

449. Telegram From the Mission at the European Office of the United Nations to the Department of State[1]

Geneva, June 6, 1967, 0004Z.

4091. Ref: Geneva 4069,[2] State 206905.[3] From Sieverts. Subject: Poison Gas in Yemen.

1) Following is rough summary based on rapid oral description of ICRC delegates reports on use of toxic gas in Yemen, sent June 1 to four parties, obtained from ICRC in strictest confidence. Should be closely held and treated as Noforn. Summary repeated as provided, with no effort to smooth transitions or logic. Spelling in part phonetic and approximate. Begin summary:

2) Incident took place at Gahr in the Yemen, on May 10 or 11. ICRC team arrived four days later, having been delayed by the bombing

---

[1] Source: National Archives and Records Administration, RG 59, Central Files 1967–69, POL 27–10 YEMEN. Secret; Exdis. Repeated to London and USUN.

[2] Telegram 4069 from the U.S. Mission in Geneva, June 2, reported that an ICRC press release on the use of poison gas in Yemen, which, as expected, was a "bland statement," had been issued at noon that day. Reports, which were factual accounts of the ICRC findings but did not point to the guilty party, had been given to the UAR, Saudi, and Yemeni missions in Geneva and a copy sent to Jidda for transmittal to the Yemeni royalist authorities. (Ibid.)

[3] Dated June 2. (Ibid.)

attack on their convey. They interviewed four surviving victims and noted there were 75 dead. They examined the survivors and found objective symptoms of bronchitis, conjunctivitis, and facial edema. Their tympanum was intact, and there were no traumatic lesions. They exhumed one corpse from the common grave. The victim had died four days previously, and had been buried 12 hours. They noted a smell of garlic in the grave. There was edema all over the body. The lungs were soft and enlarged. There were no signs of traumatic lesions on this body or any other bodies, of a type which would have been caused by high explosive or pressure. Statements of the surviving victims are consistent with the objective finding that cause of death was pulmonary edema caused by inhalation of toxic gas.

3) This report of the delegates was brought to the attention of Dr. Lauppi in Bern, whose supplementary report was annexed to the report sent to the four parties. Report notes the finding of mucous in respiratory tract and lungs, indicating pulmonary and hemocoelic edema, and concludes there is no epidemic disease with these symptoms. Also notes absence of traumatic lesions and states that conclusion that toxic gas used is perfectly justified. Reviews types of gas that could have been employed: phosphoric esters (nervene gas), phosgene, mustard, chlorine, bromide, and a type of chloride. Considers mustard and lewisite most likely. Mustard consistent with garlic odor. Report concludes that evidence hard to evaluate since toxic material fades away quickly after bomb explodes. End summary.

4) Report does not point to guilty party, since ICRC unable acquire conclusive evidence. Statement and protest sent to UAR on bombing of ICRC convey does specifically identify UAR marked planes as source of attack.

5) Hamilton of NY Times attempting to piece gas report together on basis interview with Jamil Baroody, Saudi Ambassador to UN, who here past few days with Saudi King. Baroody advised Hamilton to get text from royalist Yemeni, suggesting he contact Abdul Raxman and Mr. Yassine at the Rome Hilton. Hamilton attempting to do this through NY Times man in Rome. I told him I unable assist him to obtain text. He reports Baroody plainly reluctant to be agent of delivering text to Times, since this would violate present spirit of Arab unity against Israel. When Hamilton noted Baroody's detailed comments this subject eight weeks ago in UN, Baroody quoted Arab proverb: "You join with your brother to fight your cousin. But you join with your cousin to fight your enemy."

Tubby

450.   Memorandum of Conversation[1]

Washington, June 7, 1967.

SUBJECT

US–YARG Break in Relations

PARTICIPANTS

His Excellency Abdulaziz al-Futaih, Ambassador of Yemen
Mr. Lucius D. Battle, Assistant Secretary for Near Eastern and South Asian
Affairs
Mr. William D. Brewer, Country Director, Arabian Peninsula States

Ambassador Battle said that he had asked Ambassador Futaih to call. He deeply regretted the purpose of this meeting. We had, however, been informed by our Chargé in Sanaa of the YARG's decision to break relations with the US.[2] This was a source of particular regret to us due to the baseless nature of the charges on which the YARG action was founded. Ambassador Battle noted that Ambassador Goldberg on June 6 had publicly invited the United Nations to send investigators to the Sixth Fleet to satisfy themselves that the charges that US aircraft had been involved in support of Israeli military operations were groundless. With a very minimum of effort, Ambassador Battle thought that the accuracy of these allegations could have been correctly established.

Ambassador Battle told Ambassador Futaih that we must now reciprocate the YARG action. Accordingly, we must request that all YARG diplomats accredited to the US be withdrawn from this country within 48 hours. Ambassador Battle assumed Ambassador Futaih, as his Government's accredited representative to the United Nations, would go to live in New York. Other members of the Embassy staff had until 3:00 PM on June 9 to leave the country, slightly more time than was being given to our representatives in the Yemen.

Ambassador Battle continued that he was deeply disturbed by reports just received that our installations in Taiz were on fire. He very

---

[1] Source: Department of State, NEA/ARP Files: Lot 69 D 350, POL YEMEN–US, YEMEN 1967. Confidential. Drafted by Brewer.

[2] Telegram 208565 to Sanaa, June 6, instructed the Embassy to take immediate steps to evacuate all personnel and to close both Sanaa and Taiz, and stated that the U.S. Government was asking the Italian Government to represent U.S. interests in Yemen. (National Archives and Records Administration, RG 59, Central Files 1967–69, POL 17 US–UAR) Telegram 210053 to Asmara, June 10, informed former Chargé d'Affaires Lee F. Dinsmore that the Italian Government had formally agreed to serve as the protecting power for U.S. interests in Yemen. (Ibid., POL 17 US–YEMEN) Telegram 210598 to Rome, June 13, instructed the Embassy to inform the Italian Foreign Ministry that the Somali Embassy in Washington had informed the Department that the Government of Yemen had asked Somalia to act as the protecting power for Yemeni interests in the United States. (Ibid., POL 17 YEMEN–US)

much hoped that the break in relations would be dignified and that full protection would be accorded our diplomats in Yemen as it would be to Ambassador Futaih and his staff here.

Ambassador Futaih said that he had received no word from his Government. There was nothing that he personally could do. He felt that the political and social system in the US made it easy for one group to manipulate public opinion. US policy then had to reflect this public opinion. He thought this had brought great trouble on the US and expressed hope that those responsible in this country would think increasingly of Near Eastern problems in their basic human terms.

Ambassador Battle said that we had recognized the YARG early on. We had extended considerable aid to the Yemen. The USG had extended much more aid to the Arab countries than to Israel, including over one billion dollars in assistance to the UAR alone. Ambassador Futaih commented that the USG had been held in much higher regard by the Arabs years ago, even before major aid programs had been instituted. Both Ambassadors expressed personal regret that their association had been so short.

---

451. Telegram From the Department of State to the Embassy in Saudi Arabia[1]

Washington, June 28, 1967, 5:32 p.m.

219929. Jidda 5498,[2] 5520,[3] 5538.[4]

1. Recent UAR military defeat in Sinai and accompanying area developments, including further Egyptian troop withdrawals from

---

[1] Source: National Archives and Records Administration, RG 59, Central Files 1967–69, POL 27 YEMEN. Secret; Limdis; Noforn. Drafted by Brewer on June 27; cleared by Under Secretary of State for Political Affairs Eugene Rostow, Davies, Bergus, Battle, and Deputy Director of the INR Office of Research and Analysis for Near East and South Asia Herbert J. Liebesny; and approved by Katzenbach.

[2] In telegram 5498 from Jidda, June 22, Eilts reported that Rashad Pharaon informed him that during the recent crisis several Arab states had urged Faisal to settle the Yemen problem. The Saudi response had been consistent; the King had indicated that if UAR troops were withdrawn from Yemen, Saudi aid to the royalists would also cease. The Saudis would expect a period of civil war, following which the Yemenis would decide their own government. In the absence of UAR troops in Yemen, Saudi Arabia would accept any government the Yemenis themselves chose. (Ibid.)

[3] Dated June 24. (Ibid.)

[4] Dated June 25. (Ibid.)

YAR, obviously have implications for Yemen problem. Jidda 5538 suggests these not lost on Royalists and their backers, who may well believe now is the time resume major fighting with maximum chance success in ejecting remainder Egyptian troops and causing downfall Sallal regime.

2. Royalist capabilities remain something of an enigma. They appear recently have scored some success in local fighting around Hajja, but whether they can interdict UAR communications and capture Sanaa would appear highly uncertain. Though reduced in numbers UAR Air Force in Yemen is still unchallenged. Ruthless gas bombings seem to have cowed populace in some areas, and such tribal leaders as al-Ahmar and Ruwayshan seem for moment to have swung toward YARG.

3. Particularly view radical successes South Arabia, UAR may well consider it should remain in Yemen at all costs in order (a) avoid additional loss of face which withdrawal now would mean; and (b) facilitate FLOSY's takeover in Aden. If UAR is so disposed, and we not in position to tell, new Royalist military effort could well backfire, prompting return more troops and increasing Egyptian military and subversive pressure on SAG.

4. Whether indigenous effort can force Egyptians out remains uncertain, but circumstances have now altered due Israeli triumph. Moreover, we have less to lose vis-à-vis UAR than formerly, should Yemen war intensify in coming months with active Saudi support.

5. Our reiterated counsels restraint on SAG in past were prompted by concern that UAR countermeasures, including occupation Saudi territory, would directly involve USG in view our commitments to Saudi regime. Now, however, even though UAR may still be able maintain itself in Yemen, Egyptian capability for offensive military action against Saudi Arabia would seem to be reduced. It would of course be error for us counsel SAG to "unleash" Royalists, since such palpable encouragement would increase our vulnerability to Saudi appeals were renewed fighting to backfire on Saudis. However, circumstances do suggest we might now be somewhat less emphatic and repetitive in recording our well-known reservations re increased Saudi support for Royalists. This would not substantively change our position but would be tactical modification.

6. Unless you perceive objection, you should be guided by foregoing in your future discussions Yemen problem with senior SAG officials. Suggest you point out, per State 214082,[5] that we continue believe any action which might prompt brutal UAR military response against Saudi Arabia might be ill advised. However, in absence normal means accu-

---

[5] Dated June 21. (Ibid., POL 15–1 SAUD)

rately assessing situation in either Yemen or Egypt, we no longer in position give Saudis as much meaningful counsel on this subject as formerly. In any case, decision re Royalist action obviously one entirely for SAG to take in light all circumstances.[6]

Rusk

---

[6] In telegram 5616 from Jidda, June 30, Eilts reported that he had mentioned to Prince Sultan that Yemen seemed to be quiet for the moment, to which Sultan had replied that things were not as peaceful there as it might seem and that he expected the center of attention would soon shift back to Yemen. Sultan also said that the Saudis were maintaining very strong restraints on the Yemeni royalists in spite of their eagerness to resume action. (Ibid., POL 27 YEMEN)

---

452. Editorial Note

On July 14, 1967, the 303 Committee, the interdepartmental committee which reviewed and authorized covert operations, discussed a [text not declassified] proposal for covert support on a trial basis of paramilitary operations by dissident groups in Yemen with the purpose of increasing Nasser's difficulties in Yemen and South Arabia. Deputy Under Secretary of State for Political Affairs Foy D. Kohler, representing the Department of State, stated that in view of the tenseness and uncertainty throughout the Middle East, he wanted to discuss the matter with Secretary Rusk. At a meeting with the President on July 18, Rusk stated his opposition to the proposal. Secretary of Defense McNamara expressed his agreement, and the President said it was agreed that nothing would be done. At an August 7 meeting of the 303 Committee, chairman Walt Rostow reported that the Yemen proposal had arisen at a "Tuesday lunch" with "higher authority," and that the Secretary of State was opposed. The 303 Committee did not approve the proposal. (Minutes of 303 Committee meetings, July 14 and August 7, 1967; National Security Council Intelligence Files, 303 Committee Files, Minutes—1967, and ibid., Yemen; memorandum from Helms to Rostow, July 15, 1967; ibid.; notes of meeting, July 18, 1967; Johnson Library, Tom Johnson's Notes of Meetings)

453.   Telegram From the Department of State to the Mission to the European Office of the United Nations[1]

Washington, July 22, 1967, 12:37 p.m.

11599. Ref: Geneva 145.[2]

1) ICRC concern over UAR gas use in Yemen fully justified by information available to us, including press reports. Gas attacks continued for two weeks after ICRC Delegation visit to Gahar (May 16), then stopped in June, during and after Sinai crisis. Attacks resumed July 2–3, with dozens of gas bombs dropped on several villages, including al Darb in area of Khaulan, with many victims killed or gravely affected by gas. Further attack occurred July 15 at Hajjah, with 150 reported dead.

2) As ICRC knows, we fully share their concern about this subject. Committee's public statement on gas use in Yemen, and delegation report sent to four parties, were significant actions in calling attention to subject, though these actions have not received the wide publicity they merit, due in part to fact that Middle East news coverage in past two months has been occupied by Sinai crisis. UAR may have been encouraged to resume gas attacks in July because of relative lack of public outcry.

3) We sympathize with ICRC request re gas masks, medicaments and related equipment. We see practical difficulties in mass distribution such materials, and wonder if this is what Committee has in mind. Effective use of masks, medicines, and equipment requires training or supervision of type not easy to arrange in conditions of this area. Many Yemeni illiterate and would require oral instructions in use of masks. Yemeni known to fear injections and would be hard to train to make proper use of medical kits.

4) Mass distribution might have significant propaganda effect and thus deter UAR from further attacks. If this is Committee's intention, limited or general appeal to societies or governments for masks, medicaments and equipment would seem more appropriate than private request to us. It goes without saying USG would be prepared respond positively.

5) As alternative to mass distribution, Committee might consider establishing small stock of needed items, to be stored with its own medi-

---

[1] Source: National Archives and Records Administration, RG 59, Central Files 1967–69, POL 27–10 YEMEN. Secret; Exdis. Drafted by Frank A. Sieverts (U) on July 21, cleared by Brewer and Senior Intelligence Officer Susan T. Tait (INR/RNA), and approved by Eugene Rostow.

[2] Telegram 145 from Geneva, July 12, reported that the ICRC was becoming increasingly concerned over unconfirmed reports that UAR planes had again carried out poison gas attacks on scattered villages in the royalist areas of Yemen. (Ibid.)

cal supplies, for its own use and for distribution to Yemenis in areas likely be affected. We would be willing quietly supply masks, medicines and equipment on this basis. However, most such equipment readily available commercially in Europe, so might be simpler for Committee to purchase items itself, financed from Committee's general funds to which we have made, and expect continue to make, substantial contributions. We understand West Germans may have 20,000 surplus masks in which Israel formerly interested. Committee might wish contact Bonn directly, suggesting Germans make available as whole or partial grant.

6) Particularly because inhumane gas campaign continuing, we believe additional actions needed focus world attention on this problem. We wonder whether ICRC has yet received replies from any of four recipients of its original report. If ICRC has no plans publish report, is Committee thinking of sending it to UN? In our view some such positive action would make significant contribution toward generating atmosphere in world public opinion which would render such outrages less likely in future.

7) We remain deeply concerned on this subject but desire stay in background because of sensitive intelligence and propaganda implications. Mission should discuss subject frankly and informally with Committee in this light and report fully.

Rusk

---

454. Telegram From the Embassy in Saudi Arabia to the Department of State[1]

Jidda, July 23, 1967, 0931Z.

281. State 10446.[2]

1. Appreciate rationale re Dept's conclusion that no positive action should be taken now to assist various anti-UAR Yemeni groups. I should point out, however, that pursuant SecState 219929[3] I have stopped actively urging Saudis not to assist Yemeni royalists or to

---

[1] Source: Department of State, INR/IL Historical Files, Roger Channel Telegrams, Jidda. Secret; Roger Channel; Special Handling.

[2] Telegram 10446 to Jidda, July 20, informed the Ambassador that after further examination of the possibility of assisting Yemeni groups, the Department had concluded that no positive action should be taken at that time. (Ibid.)

[3] Document 451.

continue restrain them. Instead, I have taken line with Rashad and others that Saudis aware of dangers and matter is one for them to decide. Saudis have quickly sensed our more relaxed line which, I suspect, is one reason we beginning hear rumors of Saudi help to Yemeni royalists and of permitting them try their luck.

2. I respectfully request Dept's reconsideration of one possible item of aid to Yemeni royalists, namely 20,000 (or as many as we can provide) gas masks. UAR continues indiscriminately use poison gas in Yemen. On our part we no longer seeking obscure this fact. Various items in US press including *US News and World Report* and Drummond's article in *Washington Post*, are publicizing it. Pursuant State 217282,[4] we here are also discreetly urging Yemeni royalists give wider, more effective publicity to these poison gas attacks. However, apart from more publicity, a real need exists for some gas mask protection. We could supply such masks though Saudis if we prefer not to be directly involved. Even if it became known, provision of such equipment could scarcely be labeled as offensive help to Yemeni royalists, but as essential defense need to meet blatant UAR use of gas against combatants and non-combatants alike in Yemen. It would also show Yemeni royalists that our concern with Yemen is an impartial one.

3. In this connection, I assume that with YAR withdrawal of recognition from USG our political commitments in Yemen have been wiped clean. We ought now try to establish contact with as wide spectrum of Yemeni political contacts as possible. We should seek develop at least some influence with all groupings, but at this time commit ourselves to none. By doing so, hopefully, we may at some future time be able to exert constructive influence for a broadly based Yemeni Govt. This will have to include Yemeni royalists who have shown remarkable staying power. It is unrealistic continue to ignore them. Apart from few personal contacts with Ahmad Shami, we have heretofore leaned over backwards to avoid contact with royalists to avoid embarrassing our relations with UAR and YAR. These considerations obviously no longer apply. Assume Dept has no objection to a discreet but overt effort on our part to broaden, our personal bases, our circle of Yemeni royalist contacts.[5]

4. [*less than 1 line of source text not declassified*] concurs.

Eilts

---

[4] Dated June 27. (National Archives and Records Administration, RG 59, Central Files 1967–69, POL 17 YEMEN–SAUD)

[5] Telegram 13532 to Jidda, July 27, informed the Embassy that the Department had no objection to a discreet effort to broaden its circle of Yemeni royalist contacts on a personal basis. Regarding the Ambassador's request for 20,000 gas masks for the royalists, the telegram stated that the United States should avoid direct involvement with any Yemeni faction at that stage. (Department of State, INR/IL Historical Files, Roger Channel Telegrams, Jidda)

455.   Telegram From the Department of State to the Embassy in France[1]

Washington, July 24, 1967, 2209Z.

12259. Rome 338,[2] Paris 1068 (Notal).[3]

1. FYI. While Dept has no desire get into numbers game with French or Italians re size UAR forces Yemen, our own best estimate is there still some 25,000 UAR troops there. End FYI.

2. Far from Egyptian withdrawal being "closer to route" as Quai-Off indicated Paris reftel, UAR seems determined remain. Egyptians have in fact recently reoccupied several outlying posts and have had renewed resort to gas bombing on several occasions so far this month. We have seen no evidence Egyptians have modified their decision remain in Yemen at least until after South Arabian independence proclaimed in January 1968.

3. Re French report suggesting Algerian troops for Yemen (para 2, Paris reftel), we of course unable confirm. As far as we aware, only Algerian combat until now outside Algeria is battalion posted along Suez Canal. However, UPI carried ticker item from Aden July 22 quoting "travellers from Republican areas of Yemen" that Algerian infantry and airmen are moving into Yemen. View greater role Algeria now seeking play in Near East, we cannot exclude this possibility and would appreciate any additional info addressees able develop. Repeat replies Aden.

Rusk

---

[1] Source: National Archives and Records Administration, RG 59, Central Files 1967–69, POL 27 YEMEN. Confidential. Drafted by Brewer, cleared by Rene A. Tron (AFN), and Country Director for France and Benelux Robert Anderson, and approved by Brewer. Repeated to Algiers, Jidda, London, Moscow, Rome, and Aden.

[2] Telegram 338 from Rome, July 15, reported that the Italian Embassy in Sanaa had informed the Italian Foreign Ministry that 20,000–21,000 troops had left Yemen during May and June. (Ibid.)

[3] Telegram 1068 from Paris, July 21, reported that the Quai d'Orsay estimated that fewer than 20,000 UAR troops were left in Yemen. (Ibid.)

456.   Telegram From the Department of State to the Embassy in Saudi Arabia[1]

Washington, August 2, 1967, 1524Z.

14947. Ref Jidda 383.[2]

(1) Re SAG interest in what USG had in mind in its public reference to support of international action to deal with gas problem[3] (para 4 reftel), you may inform Masud following response Dept spokesman to press question August 1 as to whether US trying to collect its own evidence on gas warfare situation: "No, I would not say that this is a case in which the United States is trying to lead the field. We have been concerned about the reports. We would like to see the countries most affected take some initiative and as I indicated before we would be prepared to support any appropriate international action."

(2) FYI. Understand British may shortly approach us on this problem (London 714).[4] We have no preconceived notions on this subject but character USG support would certainly take account of specific international action which might be proposed by state or states directly concerned. End FYI.

Rusk

---

[1] Source: National Archives and Records Administration, RG 59, Central Files 1967–69, POL 27–10 YEMEN. Secret; Limdis. Drafted by Brewer; cleared by Sieverts, Deputy Assistant Secretary for International Organization Affairs David H. Popper, and Daniel Brown (NEA/P); and approved by Battle. Repeated to Geneva, London, and USUN.

[2] Dated July 30. (Ibid.)

[3] On July 27 Robert J. McCloskey, Director of the State Department's Office of News, told a press conference that the United States continued to be deeply disturbed by the many reports regarding use of poison gas against civilians in Yemen, condemned such actions as inhumane and entirely contrary to the laws of nations, and would support international action to deal with this problem. (*American Foreign Policy: Current Documents, 1967*, pp. 630–631)

[4] Dated July 28. (National Archives and Records Administration, RG 59, Central Files 1967–69, POL 27–10 YEMEN)

457. Telegram From the Department of State to the Embassy in Saudi Arabia[1]

Washington, August 19, 1967, 1808Z.

24047. Ref: Jidda 631.[2]

1. Department understands Saudi hesitancy regarding initiatives on Yemen which it fears may merely be clever UAR attempt gain respectability by submission proposal which not only sterile but also cloaks Egyptian intention to maintain its course toward objective of subservient Yemen. Department finds this interpretation plausible but does not necessarily share it.

2. Saudi problem is complicated by encouragement from other Arab states. UAR proposals may appear to latter be sincere UAR offer to settle reasonably.

3. If you should find opportunity, believe expression following observations may be useful reminder at this point:

(a) Since other Arabs showing interest in expressing themselves on this Arab problem Saudis may find it useful to consider ways and means to invite other Arabs join in search for solution.

(b) In any event, we presume Saudis sense they must take reasonably positive stance in response UAR gesture lest they find themselves unfavorably isolated on problem in which they vitally concerned.

Rusk

---

[1] Source: National Archives and Records Administration, RG 59, Central Files 1967–69, POL 27 YEMEN. Secret. Drafted by Dinsmore, cleared by H. Eugene Bovis (NEA/UAR), and approved by Davies. Repeated to Amman, Beirut, Kuwait, London, Rabat, Tripoli, Tunis, Dhahran, and USUN.

[2] In telegram 631 from Jidda, August 17, Eilts reported that Deputy Foreign Minister Saqqaf had informed him that Saudi Arabia was under considerable Arab pressure to accept a UAR offer to revert to the Jidda Agreement. Saqqaf stated he had continued to make clear that the Jidda Agreement, which the United Arab Republic had scuttled, was no longer a valid basis for settlement of the Yemen problem. He said that his government was also unwilling to agree to establishment of a proposed three-man committee on the grounds that this would simply result in renewed Arab mediation and buy the United Arab Republic more time. (Ibid.)

458. Intelligence Note From the Director of the Bureau of Intelligence and Research (Hughes) to Secretary of State Rusk[1]

No. 713   Washington, September 1, 1967.

SUBJECT

Mediators for Yemen Face a Rough Road

The first tangible result of the Arab Summit meeting in Khartoum[2] is its authorization of a plan proposed by the Government of Sudan to end the Saudi-UAR confrontation over Yemen. This paper examines the latest mediation effort and its chances of success as one aspect of the summit meeting. The results with regard to the Arab-Israeli dispute are not yet clear enough to be analyzed and these aspects will be dealt with later.

The conference-approved device proposed by Sudan does little more than remove the Yemeni dispute from contention at the moment. Deliberately general, the summit-meeting resolution reflects an agreement in principle on the part of the UAR and Saudi Arabia, but neither protagonist has given significant ground on the issues in dispute or on the timing of the proposed disengagement. In sum, this new approach only transfers the task at which two earlier mediators had failed to a tripartite committee (Morocco, Iraq, and Sudan); Prime Minister Mahgoub serves as the "neutral" chairman. Although Mahgoub has stated that he wants to start from the viewpoint of the Yemenis themselves, both the Yemeni republicans and the royalists have denounced the plan before it has even gotten under way. And the committee has no magic formula for gaining access to the several dissident factions within Yemen.

The most optimistic development is a slightly softer attitude on the part of the UAR, to whom the cost of the Yemen occupation must now be doubly burdensome. Nasser no longer demands the exile of the former Yemeni ruling house, the Hamid al-Dins, as a condition precedent to his withdrawal. But there is no sign that he is willing to accept open and humiliating defeat. Furthermore, Nasser's "reasonableness" could be merely a tactical device to help create a facade of Arab unity and to secure moderate support against radical pressures

---

[1] Source: National Archives and Records Administration, RG 59, Central Files 1967–69, POL 27 YEMEN. Secret; No Foreign Dissem. Prepared by the Bureau of Intelligence and Research.

[2] The heads of state of 12 Arab nations (minus Syria) conferred in Khartoum, August 29–September 1.

from Algeria and Syria. Saudi King Faysal, who now feels that he has the upper hand, is in an even less generous mood than before.

Another factor also enters into the calculation. According to reports from Khartoum Saudi Arabia will contribute $140 million to a fund of $378 million designed to alleviate the economic difficulties of the UAR and Jordan. Kuwait ($154 million) and Libya ($84 million) are the other two contributors. It is not clear when and how these funds are to be made available and what proportion of the total for the UAR ($266 million) will come from Saudi Arabia. In any event, the fact that the UAR needs Saudi money strengthens Faysal's position and may give him a weapon to obtain concessions from the UAR.

Finally, Sudan's internal politics will affect the performance of the Committee. Sudanese President al-Azhari desired the original plan as part of an intricate maneuver to expel or neutralize the leftists and Nasserites in his government, and to carry it back to the former moderate coalition. But the leading role now has been seized by Mahgoub, whose backing includes the more radical nationalists. Political maneuverings within the Sudan may thus affect the committee's chances for success.

459. Information Memorandum From the Assistant Secretary of State for Near Eastern and South Asian Affairs (Battle) to Secretary of State Rusk[1]

Washington, October 13, 1967.

SUBJECT

New Cabinet in Yemen

President Sallal announced a reorganization of his government on October 13. Dropping the most thoroughly discredited stooges of the UAR from his Cabinet, he has chosen several well-known moderate and conservative personalities whose credentials should be acceptable to all but the most die-hard Royalist oppositionists to the Republic. Sallal himself has become Prime Minister and Foreign Minister, as well as President and Commander-in-Chief.

---

[1] Source: National Archives and Records Administration, RG 59, Central Files 1967–69, POL 15–1 YEMEN. Confidential. Drafted by Dinsmore and cleared by Brewer.

Of particular interest is the appointment of a person as Adviser for Presidential Affairs who maintained fairly close and cordial relations with the American Embassy in Yemen, and who is acceptable to Yemeni tribes.

Sallal quite obviously is trimming his sails as he heads into a precarious period when his Egyptian supporters finally leave Yemen. They have announced they will be out of the capital, Sanaa, by October 15 and completely out of Yemen by December 15. Meanwhile several members of the outgoing Cabinet, known for their loyalty to the UAR, are believed to have left Yemen for safe-haven in Egypt.

Hard-bitten Royalists will not be mollified by the announcement of a new government but will continue to insist upon and may cause the ouster of Sallal. Nevertheless, he is demonstrating an ability to gain the cooperation of a few of the country's most important tribal leaders and to maintain Army loyalty. Sallal is trying to ride out the storm which Egyptian withdrawal will set in motion. It is too early to determine whether he has more courage than good judgment in making this attempt.

---

460. Circular Telegram From the Department of State to Certain Posts[1]

Washington, November 7, 1967, 0018Z.

65492. Recent Yemen coup[2] represents move in more moderate direction and may improve possibility some YARG/Royalist compromise settlement. However, picture still far from clear and atmosphere civil war likely continue characterize situation for some period. In these circumstances, we are refraining from substantive public comment on Yemen developments, both (a) to prevent any embarrassment moderates which US welcome recent move might cause at this juncture Arab-American affairs; and (b) to avoid giving impression to new YARG that we would be receptive to renewal formal relations and provision

---

[1] Source: National Archives and Records Administration, RG 59, Central Files 1967–69, POL 23–9 YEMEN. Secret. Drafted by Brewer on November 6, cleared by Davies, and approved by Brewer. Sent to Aden, Amman, Beirut, Dhahran, Kuwait, London, Rome, Tehran, Tel Aviv, and USUN.

[2] On November 5 Sallal was removed from office by a military coup as Qadi Abd al-Rahman al-Iryani was named Chairman of the Presidency Council and former Yemeni Ambassador to the United States Muhsin al-Aini became Prime Minister.

specific help at early date. In our view, US attitude should be one of quiet encouragement to both sides to compose their differences in order stable and viable central government can be established which would merit broad international recognition. Addressees should be guided by foregoing and should in general avoid speculation re USG attitude towards new regime.

Rusk

461. Memorandum From John W. Foster and Harold H. Saunders of the National Security Council Staff to the President's Special Assistant (Rostow)[1]

Washington, November 13, 1967.

SUBJECT

The Situation in Yemen

Just a background word about Yemen since it provides a measure of Nasser's and Faisal's relative fortunes and of prospects for future Arab-Arab cohesiveness. Very simply, *Nasser continues his pull-out, and the Yemeni Republican coup improved chances of an internal political settlement.*

It's still too early to tell whether the Yemenis are gong to be able to work out their problems and whether the Saudis and Egyptians will buy their solution, but prospects have improved.

The *coup was led by moderates,* some of whom were under house arrest in Cairo until recently. The coup leaders have so far succeeded in keeping the Republicans united, and opposition to the coup has been weak.

Because the new government isn't pro-Nasser, it will deal more easily with those anti-Republican tribes which have been motivated primarily by anti-Egyptian rather than pro-Royalist sentiments. The coup leaders are already claiming some success in winning over these people, who contribute significantly to Royalist strength. One factor which could limit Republican ability to make progress with lukewarm

---

[1] Source: Johnson Library, National Security File, Saunders Files, Yemen, 4/1/66–1/20/69. Top Secret.

Royalists, however, is the natural reluctance of the coup leaders to share their power with their potential allies.

The hard-line Royalists, as far as we can tell, still think they can win the civil war and haven't yet shown any interest in negotiating. The cease-fire reported in the press this morning was a local deal around Sanaa, not a general arrangement involving all Royalists.

Both Egyptians and the Saudis are becoming less involved. Nasser is acting as if he has given up on controlling Yemen, although he clearly expects to have close relations. Over half the Egyptian troops have already been withdrawn, and plans still call for the remainder to leave by the end of the year. There's some chance that the Saudis—who never liked the Yemeni Royal family—might decide that they can live with the Republican moderates. We have one report that Faisal has already suspended his financial support of the Royalists, but the Saudis are keeping their own counsel for the moment. Faisal would face a tough decision in cutting off those who have carried on the fight these five long years.

The *coup may have been a temporary setback for the USSR* since the coup leaders are basically "conservative" Republicans. However, the new crew, while somewhat more moderate, is not so much so as not to turn for help wherever it can be found. There will be a vacuum to exploit, and I see no signs of anyone else hurrying to fill it.

We aren't rushing to pat the new fellows on the back. This time, we want to hold our blessings until we're sure how completely the government represents all Yemen and how acceptable it is to the Saudis and Iranians. We also want to avoid a situation where the Yemenis ask us to pick up the bill the UAR may no longer pay. With relations suspended and us still smarting from ill-treatment even before the war, we are generally inclined to sit back. This makes the Communist-watchers jittery, but given our aid resources I can't see our rushing in even if we thought it was wise before we are a lot surer of Saudi support for the new regime.

Hal
JWF

**462.   Telegram From the Department of State to the Embassy in
Saudi Arabia[1]**

Washington, November 22, 1967, 2104Z.

73272. 1. Yahya Jaghman, senior Yemeni UN delegate, lunched unofficially at own request with Dept Off in Washington November 21. Jaghman clearly had two objectives: (1) reestablish informal low key contact, and (2) seek USG assistance vis-à-vis SAG to cease assistance to Royalists. During extended discussion, DeptOff noted it our impression Saudis, as their part of bargain struck in Khartoum, no longer assisting Royalists. Royalist leaders who had fought Egyptians so long nevertheless represented clear power element in situation. Yemen had suffered enough and all factions should seek compromise, since they owe country opportunity settle down peacefully.

2. Jaghman said his understanding had been that Saudi policy one of opposition to foreign army in Yemen. Said he was under impression SAG opposed "occupiers" but not particularly concerned about Yemen's internal situation. Over past five years YARG had relayed messages to SAG saying "recognize us and your problems with Egyptians in Yemen will disappear". SAG had refused. Now that Egyptians going, what is holding Saudis back from making peaceful gesture of recognition? DeptOff noted that problem is one between two peninsula countries and ought be solved by them.

3. Jaghman called attention recent public statement made by FonMin Hassan Makki re Yemen "disturbances" and YARG's adherence to "positive neutrality and non-alignment". He read from personal letter from PriMin al-Aini which stated "situation serious and confused," that "communists and harakiyin" (which Jaghman defined as ANM) "influenced by Chinese" are playing devious game trading on situation as at an auction (muzayid) to escalate confusion. Jaghman professed see connection between al-Aini's concern and Makki's reiteration of YARG non-alignment. (Department notes that if al-Aini's letter genuine both Saudis and Aini have reservations over ANM activities. Also possible al-Aini's Baathi sentiments involved.)

4. Jaghman professed but did not stress YARG desire resume relations with USG "on same basis" as previously. DeptOff referred to difficulties YARG created for Embassy, reminded him that YARG, not USG, had broken relations, that US property had been burnt and wrecked, and that private American plane still held in Yemen. Said

[1] Source: National Archives and Records Administration, RG 59, Central Files 1967–69, POL 27 YEMEN. Confidential. Drafted by Dinsmore, cleared by Root, and approved by Brewer. Repeated to Kuwait, London, Aden, and USUN.

that YARG initiative to return plane and make amends for losses would be evidence of good will.

5. *Comment:* Jaghman's comments are further evidence YARG reluctance deal with Saudis on any basis other than Republic. We are reminded of Numan's claim to Embassy Taiz some 18 months ago that Faisal reportedly would not tolerate anything except monarchy in Yemen. Jaghman was unspecific on question resumption USG/YARG relations and we surmise USG intervention vis-à-vis Saudis was a more important objective. As indicated, we gave him no encouragement.

Rusk

---

463.   Telegram From the Department of State to the Embassy in Italy[1]

Washington, December 5, 1967, 2123Z.

79591. 1. Italian Counselor informed Department December 4 that their Chargé in Sanaa had met with former PriMin Hassan al-Amri, now member of Republican Council and Commander of Armed Forces, on November 30 (PriMin al-Aini in North Africa and FonMin Makki in Moscow). Al-Amri reportedly received Chargé cordially, expressed regret over action which led to departure US Embassy from Sanaa last June, condemned "dirty actions" against us by predecessor government (Sallal's). Al-Amri asked Chargé to convey on behalf of himself and Yemeni people Yemeni desire to resume diplomatic relations with US. Amri further stated he prepared release US mission aircraft immediately (septel).[2]

2. Amri expressed appreciation and gratitude to Italians for Ambassador Ortona's discussion with Assistant Secretary Battle (State 77503 pouched USUN).[3] He told Chargé that YARG willing give King Faisal full assurances of YARG's good intentions and of its determination to be good neighbor with Saudi Arabia. YARG would be grateful if US and Italy would use their good offices with SAG to that end. As for Soviet influence, Italians and US could assure Saudis that YARG would not allow any foreign state to interfere in its internal affairs.

---

[1] Source: National Archives and Records Administration, RG 59, Central Files 1967–69, POL 27 YEMEN. Confidential. Drafted by Dinsmore, cleared by Arthur R. Day (IO/UNP), and Rush W. Taylor, Jr. (EUR/AIS), and approved by Brewer. Repeated to Jidda, Aden, London, and USUN.

[2] Not further identified.

[3] Dated November 30. (Ibid., POL US–YEMEN)

YARG is presently obliged to accept Soviet help in order to protect its frontiers, but Yemen is prepared accept help from any side, "especially from US" and even from Saudis. Amri concluded by suggesting that best way to circumscribe Soviet relations with Yemen is for US to resume diplomatic relations.

3. DeptOff expressed appreciation for Italian role in foregoing. Noted we had offered meet with YARG representatives informally to discuss outstanding problems but had not yet seen any specific Yemeni response. We also watching situation as closely as possible and will be most interested note developments next few days including final withdrawal UAR troops. Italian Embassy's report (State 79142 pouched USUN)[4] seemed indicate that widespread civil war is about break out again. DeptOff repeated willingness of Department to engage in informal talks with Yemeni representatives and said we would be willing send DeptOffs to New York on these occasions to meet with Yemenis there in YARG UN delegation.

4. Re Saudis, DeptOff noted we had on occasion privately counseled moderation on SAG re Yemen and would always do what we could to facilitate settlement. However, we pointed to unique position Italians currently have for using their influence with SAG, since they represented both in Yemen and Saudi Arabia. DeptOff suggested GOI might consider passing al-Amri's remarks to Saudis through Italian Embassy Jidda. Italian Counselor said he would report this suggestion. He wondered whether USG would take further action with SAG should situation in Yemen worsen. We commented that Italians' own reports suggested situation deteriorating and indicated it would be preferable have clearer picture of events on the ground before considering any formal approach to SAG.

5. Counselor phoned later and told DeptOff that his Foreign Office had contacted PriMin al-Aini in Rabat regarding informal discussions with us. Al-Aini had stated he fully agreed regarding contacts in New York and would immediately instruct YARG delegation accordingly. Counselor later called to report that YARG del had on December 4 asked for appointment with Italian del New York on December 5 on means arranging contact with US officials.

6. *Comment:* Department plans move cautiously with these talks. Our main interest will be to show good intentions toward Yemen, while seeking YARG commitment on property claims which we shall make. With Yemen situation obviously in turmoil, Department not prepared at this time positive steps toward resumption diplomatic relations.

Rusk

---

[4] Telegram 79142 to the U.S. Mission at NATO, December 4. (Ibid., POL 27 YEMEN)

464.   Memorandum From Nathaniel Davis and Harold H. Saunders of the National Security Council Staff to the President's Special Assistant (Rostow)[1]

Washington, December 8, 1967.

At day's end, we want you to know what the Intelligence Community is doing on Soviet activity in Yemen. OCI this afternoon is putting the finishing touches on its memorandum on the subject. ONE is doing a more estimative memo which will be ready early in the week. INR is writing an all-sources memo to bring together a complete record of the intelligence.[2] Luke Battle has long been concerned about this situation and is watching it closely but still sees nothing more that we should be doing.

You will be interested in some of the preliminary observations which the authors of these papers have made:

—The Soviet airlift since November 17 looks dramatic but we ought to remember that this is the only way the Soviets can get to Yemen with the Suez Canal closed. Compared to the airlift to the UAR last summer, this one is relatively modest. While about 100 flights to Yemen are now scheduled compared with 300 to the UAR over the summer, we have to remember that the resupply to the UAR also included 2–3 dozen shiploads of equipment. The total so far moved to the Yemen amounts to the equivalent of about one shipload.

—The evidence clearly points toward the direct involvement of Soviet pilots in combat—although the Intelligence people are still not willing to say they are sure. Flights by Soviet pilots may have been a stop-gap measure pending the arrival and readiness of the Syrian pilots who have been flown in. (Soviet pilots also flew sorties in Yemen in 1963 during the Egyptian campaign, when the Egyptians were not yet combat effective.)

—The Soviets look to us as if they are out on a limb. However, we have not had people on the ground in Yemen for more than six months, and they may know more than we about the balance of forces there. However, they may simply have decided along with the Egyptians that they just could not let the Republicans down without trying to help.

—If the Yemen's Republicans lose, the Soviets have lost their stake. They may figure that this additional effort is at least worth a try. They

---

[1] Source: Johnson Library, National Security File, Saunders Files, Yemen, 4/1/66–1/20/69. Secret.

[2] None of these documents has been found.

may also calculate that the stakes vis-à-vis the United States are not very high, and their vigor in supporting an Arab friend will offset the "neo-colonialism" aspect of the matter.

—People do not appear to be thinking in terms of any Soviet commitment of ground forces. The shuttle flights are carrying personnel, but their nationality is not clear and they may be advisers, trainers, etc.

When the intelligence papers are all in early next week, we will sit down with Bob Ginsburgh and see if they provide any new insights. Meanwhile, today's developments on the ground do not take us much beyond where we were when we talked this morning.

Nathaniel Davis
Harold H. Saunders[3]

---

[3] Printed from a copy that bears these typed signatures.

---

465. Telegram From the Department of State to the Embassy in Saudi Arabia[1]

Washington, December 8, 1967, 2102Z.

82430. 1. In course your coming audience with King Faisal we hope you will be able discuss in some detail recent Yemen developments. You should express our growing concern at indications increasing Soviet involvement and make clear to him USG has no intention in present circumstances resuming relations with present YARG regime. Insofar as we have had contacts with Yemenis of various groups, we have taken line with them all that the Yemen problem cannot be settled from outside nor by force. Both Royalists and Republicans have their sympathizers and their tribal levies. No clear-cut military solution seems likely. Royalists should not expect turn clock back to unpopular Imamate nor should YARG insist on republican concept and refuse to negotiate with Royalist leaders who clearly command significant support in certain areas. Both sides should accordingly make renewed efforts to move their differences from military to political arena by finding some formula (e.g. State of Yemen concept; revitalized Arab

---

[1] Source: National Archives and Records Administration, RG 59, Central Files 1967–69, POL 27 YEMEN. Secret; Priority. Drafted by Brewer and approved by Davies.

Tripartite Committee) which would permit meaningful negotiations to get under way. We would hope all those with interests in seeing Yemen problem gradually de-escalated would see things in similar light.[2]

Rusk

---

[2] In telegram 419 from Dhahran, December 13, the Ambassador reported that he discussed the Department's concerns with Faisal that day and asked the King for his assessment of the situation. Faisal noted that if his earlier warnings had been heeded, the situation might be different now. He had only one suggestion. The U.S. Government should talk to the Soviets and try to make them understand that their intervention would only keep the parties apart and perpetuate the Yemeni civil war. (Ibid.)

---

466.   Action Memorandum From the Assistant Secretary of State for Near Eastern and South Asian Affairs (Battle) to Acting Secretary of State Katzenbach[1]

Washington, December 11, 1967.

SUBJECT

Yemen: Prime Minister's Letter to Secretary

In line with our willingness to meet informally with officials of the Yemen Arab Republic Government (YARG) to discuss outstanding problems, Ambassador Goldberg and NEA/ARP officers on December 8 met with Yahya Jaghman, YARG delegate to the United Nations, in the New York office of Italian Ambassador Vinci, who heads his country delegation to the UN. Ambassador Goldberg was present for an initial few moments with the conferees. The substance of the talks with Jaghman was reported in State 82442, which is attached at Tab A.[2]

---

[1] Source: National Archives and Records Administration, RG 59, Central Files 1967–69, POL 27 YEMEN. Confidential. Drafted by Dinsmore and Brewer and cleared by Davies.

[2] Telegram 82442 to Rome, December 9, described the December 8 meeting with Jaghman, who alleged that the Saudis were currently providing "massive" assistance to tribes supporting the royalists and indicated that the U.S. Government could, if it wished, limit Saudi support of the royalists. A Department officer noted that U.S. information about the situation in Yemen was not reassuring, especially concerning the use of Soviet pilots. He pointed out that the Yemeni Government's refusal to meet with the royalists offered the opposition no alternative but military action. (Ibid.)

During the meeting Jaghman delivered a letter dated November 30 addressed to the Secretary from YARG Prime Minister Muhsin al Aini. The letter, and a Yemeni translation thereof, is attached at Tab B.[3]

Al Aini was YARG Ambassador to Washington and to the UN until October 1966. During al Aini's incumbency in these positions the Secretary apparently developed respect and regard for him. Thus, al Aini writes as to a close acquaintance.

The Prime Minister, writing from outside his country (he has been on a trip to North African capitals) states his government's aim to establish peace, stability and unity in Yemen and asserts his surprise over what he alleges is a new "deluge of money, arms and supplies flooding the country." Al Aini declares that this effort cannot "force the monarchy anew upon Yemen" but that it will cause "war and strife." The Prime Minister asserts that the Yemeni civil war "is about to become a war among bigger powers" and refers to Viet Nam. He then asks the Secretary to "give the matter the consideration it deserves . . . for the sake of world peace."

We do not believe that a formal reply is necessary. The United States has no diplomatic relations with Yemen at present and the military situation within Yemen is highly confused, with Republicans and Royalists fighting fiercely for control of Sanaa. A reply at this time would be misinterpreted as implying USG support for the YARG at a time when it is receiving active military help from the Russians and Saudi support of the Royalists is continuing.

Nevertheless, in view of the Secretary's personal regard for al Aini, we believe it would be appropriate to convey a brief oral acknowledgment to Jaghman in New York. We would simply plan to acknowledge al Aini's letter on the Secretary's behalf, express the Secretary's continuing personal friendship for the Prime Minister and note our own view that compromise among contending Yemeni elements seems the only sure way of ending the country's five-year civil war. We would note confirmed reports of Soviet activity, deny Egyptian and Yemeni controlled press stories indicating that the United States is in any way involved, and express regret that Yemen continues to lend itself to false propaganda campaigns against this government.

Recommendation

That you approve an oral response along the foregoing lines.[4]

---

[3] Not attached.

[4] Katzenbach initialed the approval line on December 13. A handwritten notation reads: "Action taken 12/13/67. See outgoing telegram." Reference is presumably to telegram 84379 to Rome; Document 467.

467.   Telegram From the Department of State to the Embassy in
        Italy[1]

Washington, December 14, 1967, 0208Z.

84379. State 83247[2] and 82442[3] (Notal).

1. DeptOff telephoned YARG UN Delegate Jaghman December 13
to acknowledge on Secretary's behalf PriMin al-Aini's personal message
(reftel). DeptOff expressed Secretary's continuing personal friendship
for YARG Prime Minister and noted our own view that compromise
among contending Yemeni elements seems only way of ending country's five-year civil war.

2. Jaghman expressed appreciation for December 8 meeting with
DeptOffs (reftel) as well as for acknowledgment al-Aini's personal
message. Noting DeptOff's concern at status Yemen problem Jaghman
asked what specifically YARG should do, for example should effort be
made induce such moderate Royalists as FonMin Shami and tribal
leader Qasim Munassir come to Sanaa to collaborate with YARG.
DeptOff recalled existence Arab Tripartite Committee, and described
Sudanese PriMin Mahjub's recent public statement calling for renewed
action by it. On personal basis he thought it would be helpful if YARG
could give Mahjub initiative positive response.

3. DeptOff then said we increasingly concerned re stories coming
from Yemen indicating USG in some way involved on Royalist side.
DeptOff quoted chapter and verse from recent tickers, citing in particular statement by YARG Culture Minister Marwani December 10 in
Aden asserting "Yemeni authorities have seized documents proving
that American, Belgian and French mercenaries are directing the disorders and the attempt to attack Sanaa." Jaghman said he unaware these
reports which he admitted caused him concern. He volunteered attempt
do something about them, emphasizing YARG eager for USG do what
it could in advising "others" not to exacerbate problem. DeptOff said
we by no means confining our efforts to YARG alone but felt he should
know Yemeni tendentious propaganda of type we now seeing hardly
likely improve atmosphere. DeptOff noted these reports without foundation and recalled similar unfortunate propaganda by YARG last

---

[1] Source: National Archives and Records Administration, RG 59, Central Files 1967–
69, POL 27 YEMEN. Confidential. Drafted by Brewer on December 13; cleared by Country
Director for Italy, Austria, and Switzerland Wells Stabler; and approved by Battle. Repeated to Jidda, Aden, London, Moscow, USUN, Beirut, Amman, Kuwait, Paris, Rabat,
and Tripoli.

[2] Dated December 12. (Ibid.)

[3] See footnote 2, Document 466.

spring which had adversely affected our relations. Jaghman said he knew mercenaries were operating with Royalists including American named Conde. DeptOff replied Conde renounced US citizenship some years ago. As far as we aware only nine Americans in Yemen, eight of whom defenseless missionaries in Republican territory near Taiz. Ninth Bushrod Howard admittedly employed by Royalists but as far as we aware in non-combat role. In any case, would be unjustified for YARG spread propaganda condemning USG on basis putative private actions one American citizen.

4. Referring Tripartite Committee, Jaghman said al-Aini was in close touch with Mahjub and was worried re further deterioration in situation. DeptOff suggested it would be opportune for YARG manifest more concrete interest in Tripartite Committee's work than evidenced publicly hitherto. Jaghman expressed appreciation exchange views and indicated he would promptly contact PriMin.

Katzenbach

---

468.   **Telegram From the Department of State to the Embassy in Saudi Arabia**[1]

Washington, December 15, 1967, 0033Z.

84871. Reference: Dhahran 419.[2] For Ambassador.

1. FYI—In connection Faisal's suggestion that we talk to Soviets re Yemen problem, Deputy Under Secretary Kohler did raise this question with Ambassador Dobrynin here December 11. Kohler stated we had been surprised by extent and nature of Soviet involvement in the fighting going on in Yemen. Dobrynin commented that USSR for years had been supplying aid to YARG and that this was simply continuing in present more difficult situation for YARG. Dobrynin volunteered he confident Soviet policy of not using Soviet personnel had not changed. USSR had supplied planes and other military equipment, but he was confident Soviets not being used except as instructors. End FYI.

---

[1] Source: National Archives and Records Administration, RG 59, Central Files 1967–69, POL 27 YEMEN. Secret. Drafted by Brewer on December 14, cleared by Battle and James W. Pratt (EUR/SOV), and approved by Kohler. Repeated to Dhahran.

[2] See footnote 2, Document 465.

2. Without referring foregoing, you may pass to Faisal fact that USG has been in touch with USSR on Yemen question at high level. Situation under study and further contact will depend on developments.

Katzenbach

---

469. **Telegram From the Department of State to the Embassy in Saudi Arabia[1]**

Washington, December 20, 1967, 2301Z.

87479. Dhahran 419.[2]

1. Dept continuing watch Yemen situation closely, particularly evolution Soviet airlift of military assistance and any further indications combat involvement Soviet pilots. For present we planning restrict public comment to minimum level that may be required by new developments and resultant press interest here. Meanwhile, we will continue (without illusions) to give appropriate encouragement to efforts find political solution, including possible new activity by Arab Tripartite Committee.

2. As indicated State 84871,[3] we have already flagged our interest in problem to Soviets. To provide additional signal to them of area concern, we are inclined believe might be desirable for Saudis discuss problem frankly with Egyptians. Accordingly, unless you perceive objection, you should approach senior SAG officials along following line.

3. While tactics obviously for SAG decide, it has occurred to us might be useful if Saudis were to make known to Egyptians their concern over recent indications increasing Soviet involvement in Yemen. We would think Saudis could well point out that UAR/SAG Khartoum agreement implemented in good faith by both parties but neither presumably desired simply replacement past arrangements with weak Sanaa regime dependent on Soviets for support. Egyptians

---

[1] Source: National Archives and Records Administration, RG 59, Central Files 1967–69, POL 27 YEMEN. Secret. Drafted by Dinsmore and Brewer on December 19; cleared by Battle, Country Director for Iran Theodore L. Eliot, Jr., Country Director for United Arab Republic Affairs Richard B. Parker, and MacCracken; and approved by Under Secretary Rostow. Repeated to Moscow, Tehran, London, and Cairo.

[2] See footnote 2, Document 465.

[3] Document 468.

and Saudis are prepared let difficult Yemen problem seek its own level, provided there no interference from outside, and Saudis remain prepared accept any regime worked out among Yemenis themselves. However, Saudis would hope UAR would agree that establishment firm non-Arab position in strategic Yemen region hardly bodes well for future of independent Arab states themselves. Saudis might conclude by raising with Egyptians possibility that latter might use their influence with Soviets to exercise moderation in involving selves further in Yemeni inter-tribal morass. (FYI. We aware UAR influence on USSR likely be small. However, our thought is UAR might get point that future SAG financial help could not be counted upon if spirit Khartoum understanding violated by Egypt's Russian friends. Even if possible approach to Soviets not specifically raised, UAR still no doubt sufficiently aware implications Saudi concern that Egyptians might well be motivated to do what they could with Soviets in direction greater caution. End FYI.)[4]

4. *For Tehran:* We had hoped Iranians might be prevailed upon also flag their concern over Yemen developments to USSR. However, in light FonMin's negative attitude on this point (para six Tehran's 2552),[5] we leave to your discretion whether specific approach now warranted.

Rusk

---

[4] In telegram 2190 from Jidda, December 23, the Ambassador reported that he presented the Department's suggestion to Mas'ud that day, stressing that the U.S. Government was not suspending its efforts with the Soviets. Speaking personally, Mas'ud expressed his doubts about the U.S. proposal. He believed that recent Soviet activities in Yemen had been going on with UAR knowledge and approval, and doubted that Faisal would want to approach the UAR on this matter. Nevertheless, he undertook to convey the U.S. suggestion to the King immediately. (National Archives and Records Administration, RG 59, Central Files 1967–69, POL 27 YEMEN)

[5] Dated December 16. (Ibid.)

470.   Circular Telegram From the Department of State to Certain Posts[1]

Washington, January 4, 1968, 0030Z.

92898. 1. Addressees may find following useful in continuing keep appropriate host govt officials up to date re current situation in Yemen:

A. We have no evidence combat flights by Soviet pilots since early December. Yemeni ex-PriMin al Ayni reliably reported to have said Soviets stopped combat missions after Yemenis attempted press them for increased assistance. Soviet Ambassador said to have remarked: "Russians never flew planes in Vietnam and they are not going to get involved in the Yemen war."

B. Soviet Ambassador left Yemen after mid-December for consultations Moscow. He was followed by departure numbers Soviet economic aid technicians. Unclear whether several Soviet diplomats may remain in YARG capital but Russian Embassy seems to have moved to Hodaydah amid stories Republican annoyance USSR "pulling out." However, so far as we aware inputs of Soviet matériel are continuing.

C. Military situation around Sanaa little changed in recent weeks. While city itself in full YARG control it remains isolated by Royalists and dependent air supply for essential items. With Ramadan now over, further fighting seems likely with YARG seeking reopen surface communications while Royalists try tighten noose.

D. In part due continuing military stalemate, diplomatic efforts find some compromise solution have recently been reviewed. Each Soviet counselor, in recent talk with Italian Chargé in Sanaa, has indicated growing Russian recognition re desirability of political settlement. Arab Tripartite Committee on Yemen has renewed its efforts find settlement and is seeking arrange 15-man preparatory committee meeting Beirut January 12 to select Yemeni participants for a proposed national reconciliation conference (State 91905 Notal).[2] YARG issued public statement December 30 accepting Tripartite Committee good offices. Royalists publicly have expressed skepticism their side will receive

---

[1] Source: National Archives and Records Administration, RG 59, Central Files 1967–69, POL 27 YEMEN. Secret. Drafted by Dinsmore and Brewer on January 3; cleared by Vladimir Toumanoff (EUR/SOV), Chief of the South Asia Division in INR's Office of Research and Analysis for Near East and South Asia Thomas P. Thornton, and Director of INR's Office of Research and Analysis for Soviet Bloc Helmut Sonnenfeldt; and approved by Battle. Sent to Aden, Algiers, Amman, Beirut, Cairo, Jidda, Kuwait, London, Moscow, Rawalpindi, Tehran, Tel Aviv, Tripoli, and Tunis.

[2] Circular telegram 91905, January 2. (Ibid.)

adequate representation, but Saudis have welcomed Committee's new initiative while expressing concern re Soviet military intervention.

E. USG position has been limited to public confirmation December 13 early evidences Soviet activity together with continued diplomatic encouragement for an Arab political solution as envisioned under Khartoum agreement (State 84178 Notal).[3] We have made clear USG has not in past, nor is it now giving arms to Royalists, and that YARG claim Americans are serving as mercenaries with Royalists is ridiculous (State 84504).[4]

F. We continue believe that foreign military intervention in Yemen only likely to increase level of tension in region. As Under Secretary Rostow made clear to Italian Ambassador December 30 (State 91625),[5] we consider indigenous Arab political solution is most sensible approach. We continuing watch situation carefully and believe other friendly states should also do what they can encourage current efforts achieve indigenous political solution to Yemen problem without further intervention from outside.

Rusk

---

[3] Circular telegram 84178, December 13, 1967. (Ibid.)
[4] Circular telegram 84504, December 14, 1967. (Ibid.)
[5] Dated December 30, 1967. (Ibid.)

---

471. Circular Telegram From the Department of State to Certain Posts[1]

Washington, January 20, 1968, 1713Z.

102181. State 92898.[2] Yemen Situation.

1. Recent weeks appear have been characterized by sharp but inconclusive fighting. Air attacks and ground action by Republicans have held off but not stopped Royalists. Both sides employing tribes-

---

[1] Source: National Archives and Records Administration, RG 59, Central Files 1967–69, POL 27 YEMEN. Secret. Drafted by Dinsmore on January 10, cleared by Director of the INR Office of Research and Analysis for Near East and South Asia Granville S. Austin, and approved by Brewer. Sent to Ankara, Aden, Algiers, Amman, Beirut, Cairo, Jidda, Kuwait, London, Moscow, Rawalpindi, Tehran, Tel Aviv, Tripoli, and Tunis.
[2] Document 470.

men. Reports indicate skirmishes, attacks and battles as widely spread as Rada west of Dhamar, Maswar and Hajjah west of Sanaa, Maabar south of Sanaa and Khamr to north of it. While some of these locations as far as 80–100 miles from Sanaa, we also note reported shelling city itself. This connection, only Embassy believed still Sanaa is Chinese, others either moved to Hudayda or Taiz. Royalists claim two airports Sanaa now under their control. Republican air access Sanaa said be limited DC–3 type planes using small dirt strip northern suburbs city. Roads from Sanaa to Taiz and Hudayda apparently still cut. Second MIG aircraft reported downed by Royalists but confirmation lacking.

2. Soviets remain visibly less involved than early December. Syrian pilots as well as Yemenis reportedly flying combat missions. USSR undoubtedly backing YAR but *Pravda* has shown sensitivity over public references to its involvement by disclaiming reports re participation Soviet citizens in combat and by drawing attention instead to mercenaries in Royalists' employ. Notwithstanding radical Arab propaganda, according British observer with one Royalist group only handful 13 foreign mercenaries, mainly French, in important Eastern sector commanded by leading Hamid al-Din Prince Muhammad Hussain.

3. Arab Tripartite Committee's efforts organize Yemeni session Beirut to prepare for wider popular Yemeni conference, so far have failed. Republicans refused sit with Hamid al-Din representative and Royalists refused meet until Soviets and Syrians ceased aid to YAR. Tripartite Committee has now called for Nasser and Faisal intercede to try eliminate obstacles to a conference. On January 19 Tass commented that Tripartite Commission failed yield results "primarily because of uncamouflaged subversive activities Saudi Arabia."

4. Meanwhile YARG UN representative Jaghman has confirmed to Dept YARG willing allow American (or, presumably, third country national) pilot to remove US mission aircraft from Yemen. Jaghman indicated YARG might also be willing consider USG's claims against damage sustained US property in Yemen. Jaghman also sought unsuccessfully persuade us assign officer to Italian Embassy in Yemen. (FYI. Plans now underway remove plane and compensation claim will be submitted, but we avoiding any action (e.g. assignment USG personnel to Yemen) which might at this juncture be seen as favoring either side. End FYI.)

5. USG position regarding developments in Yemen has consistently been to encourage indigenous peaceful solution. Department made statement along these lines available to press January 16 reiterat-

ing no Americans in Yemen serving either side.[3] USG position has been made clear to King Faisal.[4]

6. *Comment:* Apparent failure Tripartite Committee's most recent effort bring Yemenis to conference table are disappointing and suggest that neither Republicans nor Royalists believe they likely be defeated. Outlook thus for further bloodshed, at least until military situation less inconclusive than at present.

Rusk

---

[3] For text of the Department's statement on January 16, see circular telegram 99676, January 17. (National Archives and Records Administration, RG 59, Central Files 1967–69, POL 27 YEMEN)

[4] Telegram 94464 to Jidda, January 6, instructed the Embassy to urge the Saudi Government to exert its influence to persuade the royalists to cooperate more fully with the present Arab conciliation effort. (Ibid.) In telegram 2315 from Jidda, January 7, Eilts reported that he had conveyed the Department's concerns to Mas'ud that day. (Ibid.)

---

472. **Circular Telegram From the Department of State to Certain Posts**[1]

Washington, February 24, 1968, 0051Z.

120053. State 102181.[2] Yemen SITREP.

1. Since reftel military situation in Yemen has been altered by YARG success February 6–7 in reopening Hudayda–Sanaa road. Since that time road has been used to transport reportedly large quantities of food, arms, ammunition and other supplies. Saudi and Royalist sources in Jidda confirm loss control strategic road.

2. Reports indicate that part of reason for Republican success may have been clumsy handling by Royalist prince of local sub-commanders in charge Royalist road blockade, resulting disaffection latter from duties. There is also speculation that Royalist tribesmen feared flow of financial subsidies to them might dry up should Royalists take capital

---

[1] Source: National Archives and Records Administration, RG 59, Central Files 1967–69, POL 27 YEMEN. Confidential. Drafted by Dinsmore and Brewer on February 23, cleared by Robert H. Flenner (EUR/SOV), and approved by Brewer. Sent to Ankara, Aden, Algiers, Amman, Beirut, Cairo, Jidda, Kuwait, London, Moscow, Rawalpindi, Tehran, Tel Aviv, Tripoli, Tunis, and CINCSTRIKE.

[2] Document 471.

and no longer need maximum support tribal levies. Whatever the combination of reasons, Royalist pressure on Sanaa has for the moment been relieved.

3. Meanwhile Republicans have embarked on new initiatives to discuss reestablishment of diplomatic relations with USG.[3] YARG leadership reportedly prepared talk about inclusion Royalists in a Republican government, excluding Hamid al Din (Imam's) family. They also continue express desire friendship with Saudi Arabia and with West. These actions suggest some YARG concern at becoming overly dependent on Soviets but neither Republican nor Royalist positions yet appear be flexible enough to encourage meaningful negotiations toward peaceful settlement.

4. New Italian Ambassador has arrived in Yemen and had initial contacts with top level YARG. He has also conveyed to Rome interest on part YARG leadership in resumption relations with West. GOI particularly interested this prospect to provide for greater Western presence in Yemen.

5. YARG has reiterated that plane formerly assigned US mission in Yemen may be removed. Tentative arrangements underway do so around end February, using British crew.

6. YAR and PRSY cooperated in military action in border region Bayhan/Baidha in mid-February to rout "infiltrators" and capture alleged arms cache of tribal elements said to be loyal exiled South Arabian sultans. According Sanaa and Aden radios coordinated action was success. President al-Shaabi in talk with our Chargé made it clear PRSY considers arms stockpiling was stimulated by Saudis and hinted at trouble PRSY might make for Saudis if latter were to encourage new anti-PRSY schemes.

7. According Saudi press King Faisal replied to Arab Tri-Partite Committee request for new Saudi-Egyptian effort to solve Yemen problem (following failure convene protagonists in Beirut) by stating Yemenis should choose provisional government from all contending factions. Reply added all others should abstain from military-political interference. Within this framework King reportedly willing assist any efforts toward settlement. According Saudi Deputy FonMin, Nasser's reply to Committee's request had signified UAR willingness work with SAG toward solution through Tri-Partite Committee. Meanwhile, indications are Saudis resuming arms aid to Royalists.

8. Soviet assistance to YARG continues but at lower level than December. Soviets seem to be interested in preserving the regime.

---

[3] Documentation on these initiatives is in the National Archives and Records Administration, RG 59, Central Files 1967–69, POL 17 US–YEMEN.

Comment: Situation on ground still unclear with further military action likely. Republican aircraft still active and Sanaa in less immediate danger from Royalists. As Hajj period in Saudi Arabia approaches (late February) there may be lull in military operations while both sides reassess and restock from outside. Remains be seen whether Royalists in near future able mount decisive offensive. Meanwhile, we continue question whether military solution feasible and will do what we can encourage efforts looking towards political settlement.

Rusk

---

473.   **Telegram From the Department of State to the Embassy in the United Kingdom**[1]

Washington, February 29, 1968, 1645Z.

122374. Jidda 2692.[2]

1. Dept has been giving considerable thought to implications for Yemen civil war represented by Faisal's decision resume arms shipments to Royalists (reftel). As in past, our main concern re Yemen situation is whether opportunity may be provided by prolonged fighting for expansion and consolidation Soviet presence. While our own info admittedly incomplete, we continue to believe neither Republicans nor Royalists likely achieve decisive victory for some time. We accordingly continue hope renewed efforts can be made, perhaps through Arab Tripartite Committee with Saudi and UAR support, to move this problem to the political arena. While past conciliation efforts have aborted, we gather there still flicker of interest in such solution in certain Arab quarters. In our view, these flickers should be fanned, as this development would be likely reduce opportunities for expanded Soviet and radical Arab (e.g., Syrian) presence in Yemen.

2. FYI. While admittedly highly sensitive, we would appreciate any info you can develop re HMG policy toward Yemen civil war, now

---

[1] Source: National Archives and Records Administration, RG 59, Central Files 1967–69, POL 27 YEMEN. Secret; Exdis. Drafted by Brewer, cleared by Battle in draft and by Irving G. Cheslaw (EUR/BMI), and approved by Davies. Repeated to Jidda, Tehran, Aden, Kuwait, and Dhahran.

[2] In telegram 2692 from Jidda, February 4, Eilts reported that the King had informed him that Communist interference in Yemen had nullified the Khartoum agreement and that he had therefore decided to resume arms aid to the royalists. (Ibid.)

that UK out of PRSY and withdrawing from Gulf. We aware British in past extended some support to Royalists but unclear whether any tangible help continuing. We inclined to view that early resolution Yemen conflict should be overriding goal, but British in past have apparently thought differently. End FYI.

3. Embassy accordingly instructed approach FonOff informally and casually. You should note it has been some time since we compared notes on Yemen developments and express concern at implications protracted fighting might have for consolidation Soviet position. You may draw on substance para 1 above and inquire how British view situation now that they no longer present in Southern Arabia. We particularly interested in current British position on Yemen problem and how best they think Communist presence there can be reduced.[3]

Rusk

---

[3] In telegram 6998 from London, March 6, Ambassador Bruce reported that he discussed the Yemen situation with Assistant Under Secretary of Foreign Affairs Brenchley on March 5 and with Head of the Foreign Office Aden/Yemen Department McCarthy on March 6. Brenchley expressed the opinion that no military solution in Yemen was possible and argued that the civil war there was of no concern to British or U.S. interests; every foreign power that intervened in Yemen got bogged down in a morass of inter-tribal rivalries. McCarthy stated that even if they tried hard, which seemed unlikely in view of their December experience, the Soviets could not succeed where the Egyptians with 70,000 troops had failed. (Ibid.)

---

474.   Telegram From the Embassy in Italy to the Department of State[1]

Rome, March 30, 1968, 1205Z.

5178. Summary. Following summarizes extended three hour session between YARG MinFin, ARP Country Director and EmbOff on civil war and future USG/YARG relations during which MinFin conveyed official message re restoration diplomatic ties and USG assistance vis-à-vis Saudis in resolving long-standing civil war.

1. YARG MinFin Ahmed Abdu Said arrived Rome for meeting with EmbOff in accordance arrangements earlier worked out here at

---

[1] Source: National Archives and Records Administration, RG 59, Central Files 1967–69, POL 27 YEMEN. Secret; Limdis. Repeated to Jidda, Aden, Kuwait, Tehran, London, and CINCSTRIKE.

YARG initiative. Already in London on other business, ARP Country Director Brewer participated in session at Italian FonMin March 29. Min Commerce Attar accompanied Said to Ministry but Said met alone with Brewer and EmbOff.

2. Burden Said's presentation, which he stressed specifically authorized by YARG Presidential Council, was two-fold: (a) USG should recognize YARG or at least take lesser step, such as assigning officer Italian Embassy Taiz, which would manifest USG interest in Yemen; and (b) USG should communicate to SAG YARG interest in mutual efforts to end civil war.

3. MinFin asserted top level YARG united in desiring progress on foregoing. Cos [sic] abd al-Wahhab, who MinFin claims supports cabinet, had heartily endorsed Said's mission, saying he himself prepared even "Go to Israel" if necessary end civil war. As MinFin described it, present republican leaders worried about radical threat from unnamed junior officers with either Baathist, ANM, or Communist sympathies, as well as concerned with growing radicalism in Aden. Faced with these pressures as well as royalist activities, YARG leadership fears radical influence in Yemen likely increase at their expense unless some YARG/SAG détente achieved. MinFin said continuation low level of fighting of last four weeks would ease situation but renewed heavy fighting would undercut YARG moderates and render almost impossible later peaceful solution.

4. As to message which YARG hopes we will convey SAG, MinFin said his government is inflexible on only one point—exclusion of Hamid al-Dins from Yemen. Leadership prepared consider compromises other points. When Brewer asked if this included "state of Yemen" formula and inclusion non-royal family royalists in cabinet, MinFin said all possibilities could be considered in context Saudi/Yemeni efforts end conflict. Problem was YARG did not know what Saudis desired, but feared worst.

5. MinFin then reviewed what he described as past efforts current regime improve contacts with SAG. Sallal had been dropped. In November–December YARG had been in contact with Saudis and elderly respected figure Mohammad al-Hijri (imamate ex-minister now on republican side) had "ticket bought" go Asmara in December as al-Amri rep to meet Saudi emissary. For reasons unclear YARG, Saudis had called off at last minute. YARG also had sent delegation Beirut meet tri-partite committee, though some officers had objected. YARG disappointed SAG "allowed" Hamid al-Din Prince head royalist delegation. YARG had also sent Attar to Kuwait to see if GOK could again be active but has heard nothing.

6. In reply, Brewer assured MinFin our basic friendly intentions Yemen people. We aware current leadership had been in Cairo jail

not in power Sanaa when YARG broke relations with US. However regrettable, this had produced factual situation we had to recognize. We nevertheless always willing meet informally with senior YARG reps, such as Said, to discuss outstanding problems. YARG efforts in connection evacuation aircraft had been appreciated in Washington. MinFin interposed that YARG also recognized compensation due for damages US official and personal property. Brewer welcomed this assurance but noted continuation civil war situation created serious problem for US in considering any formal steps improve ties. We had no wish become involved on either side in internal dispute but did desire do whatever we could advance a settlement.

7. Re YARG efforts mentioned para 5 above, Brewer asked whether present cabinet had sought through such means get word to SAG that Hamid al-Din issue is only item on which regime not prepared consider compromise. MinFin replied he thought not. Brewer noted our influence vis-à-vis SAG is limited and indicated message might have more impact coming directly from YARG. He was confident Arabs could find means contact other Arabs directly if they wished. Perhaps neutral Yemenis in Beirut could help. MinFin said Nu'man and Pasha reluctant but Kuwaiti was coming SAG April 6 on FAO business and cabinet might send message back through him.

8. Brewer stressed necessity YARG recognizing that Saudi control over Hamid al-Din limited and SAG did have legitimate security concerns re Yemen developments. In Saudi view, royalists still lawful government. If YARG seriously interested in compromise, it no good simply calling publicly for meeting with SAG, as Saudis would have to reject this. Republicans should be more flexible in seeking quietly get their views across. YARG might regard SAG as threat but opposite also true. Saudi villages had in past been bombed by planes based Yemen and Yemeni infiltrators had caused trouble. Though in no position speak for SAG with whom we had not recently discussed this question, Brewer speculated that chief Saudi concern was to see their country not menaced by foreign forces operating from Yemeni soil. Replacement Egyptian by Soviet help to YARG thus hardly an improvement.

9. MinFin sought play down Soviet involvement, asserting only Russians now Yemen were mechanics needed service aircraft. He agreed YARG should itself continue seek ways bridging gap with SAG but asked that YARG views be conveyed Saudis by his old friend Ambassador Eilts. Brewer replied conversation would be reported fully and we would of course do whatever we could help resolve current impasse. Extent to which Ambassador Eilts might be in position communicate these views, would, however, depend on circumstances. Saudis might well discount another message through Americans. If YARG

sincere, it should not expect others solve its problems but find way acting on its own behalf.

10. Said repeatedly pressed for assurance USG would at least agree assign officer to Italian Embassy Taiz. We gave him no encouragement, noting effective means contact already exist and possibility American official presence could be used by Yemeni extremists to set back prospects favorable evolution our relations. Said saw point but indicated he anxious take something concrete back to cabinet.

11. *Comment:* MinFin gave every evidence candor and friendliness throughout conversation. While no doubt disappointed not be able achieve more tangible results from single talk, we believe he does recognize USG wishes YARG moderates [well] and will so report. His pleas for continuation low level hostilities obviously self-interested but we feel this attitude stems more from concern at future republican moderates than out of alarm at royalist military capabilities and should thus not be taken as sign military weakness. His primary concern seemed to be for future Yemeni moderates like himself unless somehow a compromise with Saudis can be worked out. We believe MinFin grasped our primary message that further YARG efforts on own behalf to achieve compromise on civil war are needed before great progress on USG/YARG bilateral relations likely. We hope he will use this message prod his colleagues accordingly but believe, assuming Dept concurs, that Ambassador Eilts might be authorized pass substance foregoing to Saudis at level and in manner he deems appropriate. Should of course be stressed to Saudis that information arose in course one of our periodic informal discussions with YARG officials at their initiative on which we anxious Saudis be promptly and fully informed.

Ackley

475. Telegram From the Department of State to the Embassy in Saudi Arabia[1]

Washington, April 2, 1968, 0122Z.

140117. Rome 5178.[2]

1. Department concurs recommendation para 11 reftel that Ambassador Eilts be authorized convey to Saudis substance Brewer–Said meeting, in manner and at level he deems appropriate but without disclosing names or venue. Ambassador may wish stress meeting at Yemeni initiative another in series to discuss outstanding problems but that YARG emissary obviously instructed take advantage session to put forward official feeler re ending civil war.

2. While these Yemeni views not inconsistent with earlier similar expressions moderate YARG leaders, we are impressed by attitude compromise and particularly with what appears genuine desire republican moderates overcome rising threat from radical left. These YARG leaders seem regard any long continuation civil war as destined increase power to Yemeni radicals and cause loss control by present government. This connection, YARG's willingness permit return FLOSY leaders to Taiz bears witness to their reservations re PRSY developments.

3. Department continues want avoid direct USG role in Yemeni-Saudi question but desires keep SAG fully informed re periodic informal USG/YARG contacts. View indications Jidda 3408[3] [less than 1 line of source text not declassified] that Saudis ceasing aid to Royalists and have open mind about type government for Yemen, would appear that juxtaposition sentiments both sides provides opening for progress. We thus believe Saudis should be particularly interested this indication YARG views.

4. In Rome meeting YARG was encouraged seek communicate its views to SAG via Arab intermediary or directly but unclear what YARG may do. If Saudis have means communicating directly (as reported

---

[1] Source: National Archives and Records Administration, RG 59, Central Files 1967–69, POL 27 YEMEN. Secret; Limdis. Drafted by Dinsmore and Brewer on April 1 and approved by Davies. Repeated to Aden, Kuwait, London, Rome, Tehran, and CINCSTRIKE.

[2] Document 474.

[3] Telegram 3408 from Jidda, March 30, reported that, on the King's orders, Prince Sultan had informed royalist leaders that effective immediately all Saudi financial and material aid was being stopped until and unless royalist leaders united and showed that they could work together to find a solution to the Yemeni problem. (National Archives and Records Administration, RG 59, Central Files 1967–69, POL 27 YEMEN)

abortive Asmara meeting last December suggests), chance arrange new direct contact might be well worth taking.[4]

Katzenbach

---

[4] In telegram 3550 from Jidda, April 9, the Ambassador reported that he had briefed Mas'ud on the recent U.S.-Yemeni exchange as instructed. (Ibid.) In telegram 3608 from Jidda, April 14, Eilts reported that he had discussed Yemen with Saqqaf, who said that the King did not believe that the Yemeni expression of interest in better relations had any meaning as long as the republicans continued to demand the exclusion of the Hamid al-Dins. (Ibid.)

---

476. Telegram From the Department of State to the Embassy in Italy[1]

Washington, May 20, 1968, 2213Z.

167296. Jidda 4043.[2]

1. Recent reports make clear that question of position Hamid al-Din family members, at least during next stage Yemen's political evolution, continues be key consideration at this point in any attempt reconcile views of YARG and Royalist moderates.

2. Recent exchanges between YARG representatives and Italians, between Ahmad Numan and Embassy Beirut, between Saudi Prince Sultan and Yemeni Royalists, and among Royalists before, during, and after their conference at Saada, suggest there may be opportunity during this period of regrouping and reassessment for low key approaches with both sides designed stimulate greater mutual flexibility.

3. Accordingly, to supplement approach reported Rome 6033[3] and in interest trying move situation off dead center, Embassy should propose to FonOff that in our view it might prove useful if GOI were (a) to ask Ambassador Bernucci to encourage further thinking by al-Iryani or al-Amri of either some limited role for modest Hamid al-Din participation in government as Yemeni individuals or their possible accept-

---

[1] Source: National Archives and Records Administration, RG 59, Central Files 1967–69, POL 27 YEMEN. Confidential. Drafted by Dinsmore and Brewer, cleared by Rush W. Taylor, Jr. (EUR/AIS), and approved by Brewer. Repeated to Aden, Beirut, Jidda, and London.

[2] Dated May 18. (Ibid.)

[3] Dated May 19. (Ibid.)

ability in number diplomatic posts abroad; and (b) to suggest Ambassador Sabetta call Saudi attention to Iryani's recent comments (State 162566)[4] and raise question SAG giving further thought to desirability continuing to insist on support whole family on basis its former royal status.

4. Embassy may tell GOI that we would be prepared support any such Sabetta approach, along lines suggested para four State 161441,[5] if our two Ambassadors believed this useful.[6]

Rusk

---

[4] Telegram 162566 to Jidda, May 11, informed the Embassy that the Italian Ambassador in Taiz had been summoned on May 6 by Republican Council President al-Iryani, who stated that his government's aim was to resist Soviet penetration and noted that it was now fighting on three fronts—against the royalists, against the PRSY extremists, and against internal subversion. Al-Iryani called for "enlightened intervention by Faisal to prevent an irreparable situation in Yemen." (Ibid.)

[5] Paragraph 4 of telegram 161441 to Beirut, May 9, stated that if, as reported, there was a positive desire for compromise on the republican side, including the key question of the Hamid al-Dins, prospects for a negotiated political solution might be improved. (Ibid.)

[6] Telegram 6088 from Rome, May 22, reported that an Embassy officer had reviewed the Department's telegram with Vice Director General of Political Affairs Perrone in the Italian Foreign Ministry, who agreed that the recent conversations mentioned provided some basis for a new approach to the Yemenis and the Saudis. He said that the Italian Ambassador in Yemen would be asked to sound out Yemeni leaders along the lines of paragraph 3. Perrone stressed that any new joint approach to the Saudis should await the results of this step; if the YARG leaders remained adamant on participation of royal family members, he doubted the utility of any effort in Jidda. (Ibid.)

477.　Airgram From the Department of State to Certain Posts[1]

CA–8598　　　　　　　　　　　Washington, June 11, 1968, 9:28 a.m.

SUBJECT

　　Capsule View of Situation in Yemen

In the course of a discussion with an Italian Embassy Officer June 5, Department officers made the following observations on the situation in Yemen:

---

[1] Source: National Archives and Records Administration, RG 59, Central Files 1967–69, POL 27 YEMEN. Confidential. Drafted by Dinsmore, cleared by J. Stapleton Roy (EUR/SOV) and William B. Dozier (EUR/AIS), and approved by Brewer. Sent to Addis Ababa, Aden, Asmara, Beirut, Jidda, Kuwait, London, Mogadiscio, Moscow, Rome, and Tehran.

1. A military solution of the Yemen problem is not possible.

2. The solution must be a peaceful one.

3. The United States will not take sides.

4. Both Republican and Royalist elements must compromise.

5. If no solution of Yemeni political differences is forthcoming, the effects on the Western position are unlikely to be serious unless a continuation of the civil war should stimulate the Soviet Union markedly to increase its own position in the country.

6. We have the impression that the Soviets have been less active in Yemen during the last several months. They may have learned that the Yemen Arab Republic Government will hardly be able to establish its control throughout the country even with major foreign help, and that the YAR is not representative enough to control the turbulent population. Moreover, Eastern Europe may be claiming the USSR's attention, giving Yemen a low rating in the Soviet scale of priorities at the present time.

Rusk

---

478. Telegram From the Embassy in Saudi Arabia to the Department of State[1]

Jidda, July 21, 1968, 1330Z.

4831. 1. I paid call on King Faisal today to pay respects before departing on home leave. Told him while I knew his current view on Arab–Israel problem as he had outlined it during Ball–Sisco visit, I wondered if he might bring me up to date on his thinking on Yemen problem and his evaluation current Iraqi problem.

2. Yemen

Faisal recalled we had in past frequently discussed Yemen question. He expressed his regret that there has been no real change. He said in somewhat general terms that Yemeni republicans have sought to contact SAG to suggest Saudi "mediation" with Yemen royalists. He had sent reply that SAG is not a party to Yemen dispute and that republicans should work out solution directly with royalists. He dis-

---

[1] Source: National Archives and Records Administration, RG 59, Central Files 1967–69, POL SAUD. Confidential; Limdis.

missed what he called republican idea of accepting a few royalists in cabinet as insufficient. What is needed is a new conference between republicans and royalists to agree on principles of a settlement. In this context, while SAG has no desire impose Hamid ad-Dins on Yemenis, Hamid ad-Dins are Yemenis and should have same right to determine future of Yemen as do others.

3. I asked if he sensed any sign of movement between republicans and royalists to compose their differences. He said he did not. Republicans are divided between leftists and Amri–Iryani elements, which he called more moderate. Royalists also divided, but he contended their fissures not so severe. He did not know whether Tripartite Committee still extant. It has never been formally disbanded, yet seems quite moribund. Yemeni republicans are receiving considerable aid from Soviets, Chinese, UAR and Syrians. When I asked about alleged UAR aid to Yemen, he insisted UAR is still giving active help to republicans. Hence, Saudis are continuing to give royalists some aid. They are not giving as much as royalists would like, but it is keeping royalists going.

4. I indicated responses USG has been giving to occasional republican overtures to resume diplomatic relations. He said he thought this was wise and expressed hope that USG will use any such approaches to urge republicans work for national reconciliation conference. I said we had already spoken along these lines to republicans. He also thought US should give tangible support to royalists. I told him this was not in the cards, and that I doubted any US aid would be available even for a united Yemen.

[Here follows discussion of Iraq.]

Eilts

479. **Telegram From the Department of State to the Embassy in Saudi Arabia**[1]

Washington, October 3, 1968, 1509Z.

249230. For Ambassador.

1. Following guidance provided in connection your prospective call on King Faisal.

2. *Yemen.* When you last discussed this issue with Faisal (Jidda 4831),[2] he said he noted no sign of movement between Republicans and Royalists to compose their differences and commented, among other things, that Republicans were divided between leftists and more moderate Amri/Iryani group. Subsequent developments would appear have changed this picture. Recent "exile" 22 leftist officers to Algeria, reconstitution YARG cabinet and Amri/Iryani approach to Italians (State 245488[3] and 248204,[4] para 3) suggest situation may be somewhat improved. Saudi public statement Oct 2 on Yemen (Jidda 5504)[5] would appear reflect this trend. Current Amri trip Moscow hardly reassuring, but you may note confidentially we understand that what YARG regards as SAG failure react positively to recent Yemen developments may have played part in timing Amri trip. Dept would be interested King's current assessment situation, particularly whether Imam's return Yemen likely foreshadow further fighting or real effort get Yemeni peace dialogue going which King and we both favor. You may add USG policy on non-resumption relations with YARG remains firm and we continuing do what little we can encourage parties establish mean-

---

[1] Source: National Archives and Records Administration, RG 59, Central Files 1967–69, POL SAUD–US. Secret; Limdis. Drafted by Brewer on October 2; cleared by Deputy Director of the Office of UN Political Affairs William H. Gleysteen, Eliot, and Atherton; and approved by Davies. Repeated to Tehran and USUN.

[2] Document 478.

[3] Telegram 245488 to Jidda, September 26, reported that on September 22 Italian Ambassador to Yemen Bernucci met with Prime Minister al-Amri and YAR Republican Council Chairman Iryani, who told him that the Yemeni Government had now purged itself of extremists. They described this as a guarantee of its good intentions to work for improved relations with Saudi Arabia but warned that this was the "last act of moderation" that could be expected; if the Saudis did not respond, the present regime would be unable to resist for long Soviet pressure for the return of the extreme leftists to positions of influence. (National Archives and Records Administration, RG 59, Central Files 1967–69, POL 27 YEMEN)

[4] Telegram 248204 to Jidda, October 1, stated that it was unclear how the Yemeni desire for improved contacts with the Saudi Government had been communicated to the Saudis. (Ibid.)

[5] Dated October 2. (Ibid.)

ingful contacts. This connection, you may wish probe for any evidence continuing quiet SAG/YARG contacts.[6]

[Here follows discussion of Arab–Israel and Persian Gulf issues.]

Katzenbach

---

[6] In telegram 5721 from Jidda, October 23, Eilts reported that he had discussed Yemen with Rashad Pharaon, who acknowledged that some YAR emissaries had been in touch with the Saudis. He said that the King had reiterated his long-held position that the Saudi Arabian Government was not a party to the dispute and that the republicans should meet with the royalists to work out a settlement. (Ibid.)

---

480.   Telegram From the Mission to the United Nations to the Department of State[1]

New York, October 16, 1968, 0107Z.

7118. Yemen Problem.

1. During visit New York Oct 15, ARP Country Director Brewer had opportunity for informal exchange views on Yemen problem with new YARG FonMin Jaghman who accompanied by incoming YARG UN PermRep Mohammad Said Attar and outgoing PermRep Muhsin al-Ayni (whose future assignment not revealed). FonMin began by expressing hope YARG/USG relations might soon be normalized, stating this one of his real goals as FonMin. Brewer responded we continued recognize the republic as state; that we remained prepared do what we could assist parties work out some settlement to long-standing civil war; but that question resumption relations premature as long as civil war continued, since for USG act affirmatively would be form of intervention in Yemen's internal affairs.

2. Jaghman then expressed concern at what he said was recent USG action in notifying some ten Yemeni students here that their grants being terminated. Jaghman felt this unworthy pinprick by great nation. Brewer responded major factor was simply that Dept funds for purpose had been severely cut. Given this financial problem, it would have been exceedingly difficult justify renewal grants with state with which USG has no diplomatic relations. Jaghman argued some cuts under-

---

[1] Source: National Archives and Records Administration, RG 59, Central Files 1967–69, POL 27 YEMEN. Secret. Repeated to Aden, Rome, Jidda, and London.

standable but elimination program hard to accept. Brewer said would look into but frankly thought nothing could be done.

3. FonMin noted recent USG announcement re supersonics for Israel and said had asked Somalis, who represent Yemeni interests Washington, protest on YARG behalf. He felt our action would only make Israel more intransigent. Brewer took established line, noting coming negotiations would take time and that it could be argued USG move actually strengthened Israeli "doves" rather than contrary, providing reassurance on all-important security question.

4. After general discussion, FonMin took Brewer aside for further review Yemen problem. Jaghman said he had hoped as FonMin be able work out some compromise. He agreed with Brewer comment that all parties seemed recognize no military solution feasible. In response question, Jaghman agreed YARG might be willing consider acceptance one or two Hamid al-Din Princes as Ambassadors abroad and said SAG could be so informed. Brewer asked whether there some flexibility along lines "state of Yemen" concept. Jaghman said not, that regime had had trouble in August from leftists who had felt YARG had already gone too far, and that no compromise on "republic" was feasible. FonMin continued that "key is in Saudi hands", asserting SAG had sent Imam Badr back into Yemen to put pressure on YARG. Brewer queried this conclusion, opining Saudis also favor settlement. Jaghman said he thought they did but that questions Hamid al-Din (except as noted above) and status "republic" not negotiable. He agreed that this made further fighting most likely prospect but said YARG always willing come to understanding with SAG. Brewer encouraged FonMin seek develop direct contacts with Saudis in effort work out some compromise between two peninsular neighbors who must learn live together.

5. *Comment:* Opportunity frank exchange views with new YARG FonMin useful even though Jaghman revealed no significant give from past YARG positions. He planning return Yemen in about ten days.

Wiggins

Index

ISBN 0-16-049828-7

90000

9 780160 498282